MARGARET FULLER
An American Romantic Life

MARGARET FULLER

AN AMERICAN

ROMANTIC LIFE

The Public Years

CHARLES CAPPER

OXFORD

UNIVERSITY PRESS

2007

OXFORD

UNIVERSITY PRESS

Oxford University Press, Inc., publishes works that further
Oxford University's objective of excellence
in research, scholarship, and education.

Oxford   New York
Auckland   Cape Town   Dar es Salaam   Hong Kong   Karachi
Kuala Lumpur   Madrid   Melbourne   Mexico City   Nairobi
New Delhi   Shanghai   Taipei   Toronto

With offices in
Argentina   Austria   Brazil   Chile   Czech Republic   France   Greece
Guatemala   Hungary   Italy   Japan   Poland   Portugal   Singapore
South Korea   Switzerland   Thailand   Turkey   Ukraine   Vietnam

Published by Oxford University Press, Inc.
198 Madison Avenue, New York, New York 10016

www.oup.com

Oxford is a registered trademark of Oxford University Press

Library of Congress Cataloging-in-Publication Data
Capper, Charles.
Margaret Fuller : an American romantic life / Charles Capper.
p. cm.
Includes bibliographical references and index.
Contents: [2] The public years
ISBN 978-0-19-506313-4 (v. 2)
1. Fuller, Margaret, 1810–1850—Biography.
2. Authors, American—19th century—Biography.
3. Feminists—United States—Biography.
I. Title.
PS2506.C36   1992   818'.309—dc20   91-32599

1 3 5 7 9 8 6 4 2

Printed in the United States of America
on acid-free paper

For Emily

Contents

Preface

"Margaret had so many aspects to her soul that she might furnish material for a hundred biographers," Margaret Fuller's close friend James Freeman Clarke remarked to her early biographer Thomas Wentworth Higginson, "and all could not be said even then." Surely, this is right. Indeed, Fuller's friends compiled a long list of paradoxical psychological traits: sarcastic and reverent, serious and droll, self-regarding and self-sacrificing, alienated and engaged, full of broad good sense and of passionate temperament, and, perhaps most often cited, "masculine" and "feminine." "This alternation perplexes the biographer, as it did the observer," Ralph Waldo Emerson recalled. "We contradict on the second page what we affirm on the first."[1]

Yet every life, however multitudinous, has a distinctive shape. As in the first volume, my intention in this second one is to present a modern biography of a woman's thoughts and actions as they were embedded in the public and private discourses of her time. Although this is the first comprehensive biography of Fuller, her life and identity as an intellectual remains my principal focus. The term "intellectual" would not come into common usage until the end of her century, but she and her Romantic compatriots fully understood that was who she and they were. They were "thinkers" (to use Fuller's term) whose self-reflective ideas gave meaning to their lives, established their cultural authority, and mediated between their experiences and their expressions. I use the qualifier Romantic advisedly: to denote her embodiment of that movement's central proposition—that the life of the subjective mind contains infinite depths of meaning and value. I also seek the right tone to retain yet bridge the distance between Fuller's time and ours. However much Fuller's relentless quest for authenticity prefigured a "modern" sensibility in American intellectual life, as I believe it did, her Romantic language and transcendent spiritual hopes belong to a previous century and leave a gulf that only ironic empathy can fill.

The two volumes of this biography divide at 1840, a year that also marked the great divide in her life. Some changes were subtle. While her older female friends and followers and her Transcendentalist colleagues in and around Boston remained her social strongholds, they were joined by newer circles of admiring young women whom she tutored and befriended as well as by wealthy radical reform families to whose homes she often retreated. As her career as a writer took off, she drew closer than ever to her mother, with whom she shared houses but also the confidences she had sorely missed in her childhood. Boston's Unitarian Whig establishment continued to regard her as an arrogant outré bluestocking, but they counted for less as Boston itself became more ideologically outré in the 1840s and as Fuller emerged as a literary celebrity.

After she settled and resettled in Boston, Cambridge, New York, London, Paris, Rome, Florence, and elsewhere, Fuller's list of famous associates grew exponentially: Nathaniel Hawthorne, Horace Greeley, Lydia Maria Child, Evert A. Duyckinck, Edgar Allan Poe, Thomas Carlyle, George Sand, Adam Mickiewicz, Giuseppe Mazzini, Cristina Belgioioso, Robert and Elizabeth Browning, and countless lesser notables. More dramatically, within two years (1844–46), she published two books and over 250 articles. All of this adds enormously to the biographer's challenge of maintaining her social embeddedness along with an ongoing focus on the protagonist's "self," especially one as self-contested as Fuller's.

The biggest challenge, though, is a narrative one: to bridge the pre- and post-1840 halves of her life that my subtitles "private" and "public" broadly denote. For the first thirty years, Fuller's life could be described as outwardly provincial: growing up in a small university town, attending school for a few years, traveling but once briefly outside of New England, living under the family roof, followed by three years of private teaching and a modicum of anonymous magazine writing. Then, virtually overnight, Fuller became America's first female highbrow journal editor, first intellectual surveyor of the new West, author of the first philosophical American book on the woman question, first literary editor of a major metropolitan newspaper, first important foreign correspondent, and first famous American European revolutionist since Thomas Paine. How did she do it?

One answer is to say it was "fated," a term Fuller applied to herself with regularity in her last years. At moments both her rhetoric and her realities tempted me to suspend disbelief about the possibility. Certainly, Fuller's leap from the private and provincial to the public and cosmopolitan *would* seem to have sprung from something almost preternaturally congenital. Emerson captured the quotidian side of that "fate" exactly: "She excels other intellectual persons in this, that her sentiments are more blended with her life; so the expression of them has greater steadiness & greater character." Less sympathetically, Poe famously wrote: "Her acts are bookish, and her books are less thoughts than acts." A biographer, however, wants to know the changing sources, contours, and character of such (in Carlyle's phrase) a "predetermination" to live a life commensurate with "the universe."[2]

Twentieth-century biographers have confidently located these changes in a variety of liberating escapes. She got away from her Transcendentalist circle's contemplativeness, or her marital singleness, or America's innocence, its sexism, and its racism—all blocks to her "real" life happily removed. There is something to many of these claims, but like most ideological constructs, to borrow from Emerson, they skip no fact but one: life, which is lived in the flux of time, inward and outward. In my first volume I tried to show that, in fact, Fuller's "private" life contained the very ideas, tropes, and needs that necessarily overflowed into her imagined public life. Oscar Wilde says that Romantics begin at the climax, and Fuller's early years would seem to bear this out. Instead of beginning (as in a good German *Bildungsroman*) with the narrow world of innocence, her life begins with the intellectual equivalent of a very wide world: Latin grammar at six; most of the classical authors by ten; French, Italian, and Spanish works by twelve; and nearly the entire canon of Renaissance and early modern European literature by nineteen.

The question, though, remains: how did such a precociously cosmopolitan regimen produce a questing public intellectual, rather than, to rephrase Emerson's famous disparagement of imitative erudition, a cosmopolite "bookworm"? Two psychologically resonant intellectual ideologies helped. One was her scholarly Jeffersonian Republican father's Enlightenment-inspired regimen for her early education. "I love her if she . . . learns to read," Timothy Fuller, writing from his desk on the floor of the United States House of Representatives, instructed his wife to tell their daughter on the eve of her fourth birthday. "To excel in all things should be your constant aim," he exhorted Margaret six years later; "mediocrity is obscurity." John Stuart Mill would have recognized the type: an ambitious rationalist father's stingy parceling out his love and fantasies of fame in exchange for the child's precocious learning and unremitting study. One does not need to look much further to locate the psychological source for Fuller's (in Carlyle's phrase) "predetermination to *eat* this big universe as her oyster or her egg." Her father's classical Enlightenment reading list also kept her hungry and awake to the world: Virgil, Cicero, Horace, and myriad martial and virtue-conscious texts of the later Roman Republic and early empire. By her teens, she was devouring histories and memoirs of early modern European statesmen, men of action who eschewed, she admiringly noted, "Augustan niceties."[3]

This last phrase points to the second cultural ideology in Fuller's youthful cosmopolitan fantasies beyond that of her Addison-and-Steele-loving father. She was a daughter of a new and yet-to-be battle-tested *Romantic* cosmopolitanism. Contrary to the picture drawn by Henry Adams of the early Republic resolutely turning its back on Europe, Fuller, as an adolescent, had only to walk up Cambridge's main street to encounter this new transatlantic talk at every turn. Harvard's first returning band of German university–trained Ph.D.'s spoke its language. So did Cambridge's influx of European liberal political exiles escaping from failed revolutions on the Continent. And so, most earnestly, did a cohort of intellectually minded Harvard students who invited her to study in their Romantic extra curriculum, which they thought infinitely more relevant to their dawning individualistic age than the College's "Common Sense" textbooks. From this virtual college the equally ambitious and alienated Fuller took two transformative propositions that would guide her all her life: first, that the subjective life of the mind contained an infinite ocean of meaning and value—and, second, that heroic individuals might tap into that life to reenchant an otherwise alien and despiritualized modern world.

Was this vision any less bookishly cosmopolitan than her childhood Enlightenment regimen? To this question, one would have to respond, how *could* it have been? Barred as a girl from entering Boston-Cambridge's learned professions—even, as with her male friends, to revolt against them—she retreated to her prodigious studies and, after her father's unexpected death in 1835, to school-teaching. Yet, anxious to keep herself free of what she defensively called, in agreement with Coleridge, the "strong mental odor" of female teachers, she moved on several fronts to get beyond her suddenly shrunken world. She first turned herself into her circle's authority on Romanticism's most philosophical (and, in America, most suspect) literary source, German literature. She also determined to write for publication. And then she tried to leverage her deracinated Romantic cosmopolitanism into a transnational project. Her goal was to "teach" and "interpret" German Romantic authors as a "counterpoise" to her own nation's baleful utilitarianism. Unfortunately, after publishing several articles of a "Germanico" cast, she discovered that American periodicals were uninterested in touting Romantic writers, which most of her country's critics regarded as willful obscurantists or licentious infidels. She, in turn, stumbled over a confusion of purpose. If America's English-derived utilitarian culture was, as she argued, totally hostile to her inwardly turned Germans, to whom was she speaking? Indeed, reading her critically sophisticated but often condescending early essays, one could easily imagine Fuller becoming not a bookish dreamer, but a Germanized version of the self-described Wordsworthian "monarchist" Richard Henry Dana, Jr., who assured *his* oblivion by his refusal to publish or speak almost anything before his culturally crude countrymen.[4]

But Fuller did not become another Dana. There are many byways through this tale of why, which I explore in my first volume—from the impact of her father's un-Bostonian, high-toned Jeffersonianism and her bold embrace of scandalous German and French Romantics to her outsider status as a woman and her burning literary ambition. Three hinges connect the two halves of Fuller's life that I narrate in this second volume. One is self-recognition. I have not written a psychobiography. Yet whatever one calls the "unconscious," or that part of mental life resistant to the rational mind, Fuller and her Romantic colleagues would have readily assented to its existence even if their intuitions of such were not as dark as modern psychodynamic theorists might prefer. Moreover, Fuller left abundant psychological associations, often familial and sometimes sexual, that she recorded in an effort to understand the depressed condition into which she fell in the autumn of 1840.[5]

In fact, she had been subject to periodic bouts of depression ever since her father's death in 1835, an event that had suddenly forced her to give up hope of a European tour and with it her dreams of finding public recognition through Old World greatness and experience that would ground her cosmopolitan literary career. Then in the summer and fall of 1840, she tried what she would later recognize as a desperate and failed gambit. She transferred her yearning for "recognition," which her father's intrusive tutoring of her had stimulated but also frustrated, onto Emerson, thereby triggering probably the most fascinating psycho-philosophical debate over love and friendship in American literature. The experience produced seemingly endless confrontations and frustrating heartaches on Fuller's part, but she emerged from it with a new sense of her "feminine" identity and with her own peculiar Romantic seeking sensibility intact. Still fragile and fanciful, her new level of self-recognition would require shoring up at moments of crisis in the years ahead.

A second pivot in Fuller's turn toward outward experience and public life came through her engagement with the Transcendentalists. Despite an inward trajectory, the intellectual synergy of the Transcendentalists struck off cosmopolitan sparks. Fuller pressed her "demonic" Continental writers and artists on the somewhat wary Emerson and his colleagues: Dante, Goethe, Beethoven, George Sand, and the German Romantics. They pressed back, in turn, with English Platonists and Renaissance hermetics. The cerebral mix helped produce an important intellectual result: out of her confrontations with Emerson, and the post-Christian spiritual struggles of her colleagues, she formulated her own cosmology of humanity's fortunate fall into experience, struggle, and love. These were also the years of socialization in the Transcendental impulse: Brook Farm, Fourierist socialism, parlor mesmerism, and other "magnetic" perfectionist experiments that Fuller glossed with critical sympathy. In 1840, with the assistance of Emerson, she launched the *Dial*, which provided a forum for their young followers who were alienated from the Unitarian academic and literary institutions of their parents and shut out of the didactic and sentimental journals of the day. Her budding hope to stimulate much experiential writing superior to conventional "words—words—words" ultimately failed. But just trying to accomplish it with truant young poets whose spirit forbade them to "parse & spell" left a poignant legacy for America's future literary avant-garde.[6]

The third hinge of Fuller's private-public transition in the early 1840s was the nascent American discourse of women's rights. Fuller's female gender-consciousness had never been strong. She had sometimes lamented the vocational restrictions placed on her as a woman but also thought her mind more "masculine" than "feminine," a distinction that she believed set her apart from most women. She understood the need of female sentimentalist authors for a popular readership but found them no more deserving of literary respect than did Emerson and Hawthorne. Even so, inspired by her self-examinations, she peopled her early *Dial* sketches with "feminine" mythic archetypes. More seminally, two public efforts of Fuller radically altered her hopes for womanhood. Her "Conversations," conducted with women from Unitarian Boston's Transcendentalist and radical reform elite, forged her first female constituency. Out of these five years of meetings came her essay "The Great Lawsuit" and her book *Woman in the Nineteenth Century*, in which she articulated an original liberal Romantic vision of intellectual freedom and spiritual growth. Combining a Transcendentalist argument for women's self-reliance and a largely androgynous conception of gender, Fuller marked out a powerful feminist tradition whose influence would grow through the nineteenth century and periodically revive down to our own time.

In the background of Fuller's moves toward wider public experience lay a distinctive sense of American nationality. This is an even more underappreciated and misunderstood theme in Fuller scholarship than her Romantic Transcendentalism and feminism. In this most anxiously hypernationalistic era of United States history, Fuller's patriotism was always complex, often original, and sometimes problematic. From her adolescence, she had strongly identified with her country's republican polity. But her outrage over the proslavery annexation of Texas—her first political cause—made her doubt the efficacy of that ringbolt of freedom upon which she thought her country's only claim for national superiority anchored. Nor during her *Dial* years did she find anything in the United States to dissuade her from her long-held belief that its materialistic and utilitarian culture was woefully devoid of living spiritual resources. Nor, despite her call in her magazine for a new American critic-reader partnership to replace the ossified one promoted by dogmatic scholars and predictable reviewers, did her actual writings therein suggest any more hopeful views of American literature. She wrote pioneering essays on the reviled Goethe, little-known English Renaissance writers, and rarely performed European "modern" composers along with German Romantic–influenced dialogues and fables. But they had little in them that one might call national: almost none addressed national issues or even American authors. Like Thoreau, whose critique of the inadequacy of democracy without a moral imperative she foreshadowed, and Alexis de Tocqueville, whose darker views of his subject in his second volume of *Democracy in America* she much admired, she found her country's national democracy politically precarious and culturally thin.[7]

She was hardly satisfied with her high liberal stance. Her principal reason for taking her tour of the Great Lakes and prairies of the Middle West in the summer of 1843, in addition to its advancement of her career as a national author, was to discover a superior nation in the American future that she, like Emerson, thought somehow was taking shape beyond the region of their birth. After returning, she gave expression to her hope in her *Summer on the Lakes*, which joined the metaphors of the new West's wildly expressive and humanly cultivatable natural "garden" with the conceit of the boundlessness of a vast continent shaping national identity by beckoning ever beyond itself. Still, her book's pastoral tropes, however salutary as a counter to the East's cultural conventionality and conformity, perversely refuse to remain stable. Eastern female settlers try to "domesticate" the West by dragging untunable pianos to their new homes, western farmers escape from eastern artifice only to exploit the "still all new, boundless, limitless" land by destroying its beautiful trees for commercial harvesting, and white settlers expropriate Indians' *un*virgin land and nearly exterminate their culture. Western Nature was one thing, western human nature another.[8]

If the impulse toward a larger national life was a covert subtext of her life in New England, it emerged as almost the defining conceit of her move to New York to accept Horace Greeley's offer to assume the new position of literary editor of his *New-York Tribune*. Even her awkward erotic liaison with the German Jewish clothing merchant James Nathan that ended disastrously at least gave her an experience she would never have had in Boston. Above all, Fuller's "new era" in the "shallows" of New York was professional. She finally dispensed with her old dreams of literary "genius" and accepted her career as a critic employing the "slow pen," and welcomed the national influence she wielded. Furthermore, her nationalist associates were not only liberal Whigs like Greeley. She associated with the city's pro-Democratic literati, "Young America," who inveighed against (as Herman Melville, one of its rising stars, put it) "this Bostonian leaven of literary flunkeyism towards England" and logrolled writers whose works they deemed indigenously "democratic." At the same time, New York bolstered her Romantic cosmopolitanism. Greeley, who professed to admire the Transcendentalists' "un-American" depth of thought and trumpeted his paper as an anti-sensationalist penny newspaper, boasted to his readers that he had hired Fuller precisely because of her expertise in the great literature of Continental Europe. Her "Young America" circle was also not exactly a gang of cultural chauvinists. Their favored firm, Wiley and Putnam, reprinted many European classics in its new "Library of Choice Reading," which she frequently reviewed. Of Fuller's 150 literary articles and reviews for the *Tribune*, well over half were on European books and authors.[9]

Finally, Fuller advanced a new idea of an American literature. It would not be "merely . . . a collection of exquisite products" but rather "a means of mutual interpretation," a hermeneutic community in which "sincere," "refined," and self-reflexive works would be judged according to their different literary purposes and requirements. Fuller's idea was cosmopolitan in a national sense as well: the country's increasing importation of great Continental books would weaken the influence of imperialistic but culturally insular England while militating against any parochialism attendant on the nation's search for an American literary "genius" to express its boundless, diverse, and often mongrel life. In articulating her "higher standard," Fuller was never complacent. A new literature would come but only after the settlement of America's land, the fusion of its "races," and the creation of an experimental literary class devoted not to imitation but the imagination. Yet that fact did not keep her from appraising week after week the literary works that the United States was *already* producing—and with results that were amazingly prescient. In counterposing the hackneyed products of America's commercial print revolution *and* the imitative borrowings of popular middlebrow writers like Longfellow to the inwardly deep works of Emerson, Hawthorne, Melville, and Poe, she pointed to that cosmopolitan canon of the American Renaissance that would not be "discovered" until the early twentieth century. That she did not know that outcome only underlines her critical independence and courage.[10]

Where did Fuller think she would find that social "life" embodying the "idea" of America that she thought the nation's future depended? Just before leaving New

England she had come to find some hope in the abolitionist movement (if not its Garrisonian leaders) and Fourierist socialist theory (if not in practice). In New York, though, she probed a thick and variegated national political life. Thanks to her position at the *Tribune* and her connections with the city's circle of Christian and Fourierist socialists, she got her first taste of urban political battles with formidable opponents: the city's conservative penal and welfare administators, its pro-capital punishment ideologues, its racist nativists, its hectoring evangelicals, and its censoring publishers. Gotham city gave her a new language: that of "democracy," a term she now used for the first time honorifically as an ideological marker of her Romantic post-Christian values of "benevolence" and "mutual education." And in New York's mass of new immigrants, she found a social equivalent to the cosmopolitan nationalism she had envisioned for American literature. Foreshadowing arguments that would not become prominent until the twentieth century, she urged the birth of a new multiethnic nation, in which Anglo-Saxon natives, Continental immigrants, and subjugated nonwhite "races" contributed not their parochial prejudices, presumptions, and resentments but their most authentic and therefore most generous characteristics. "Let nothing be obliterated, but all regenerated," she wrote in one *Tribune* article hailing the appearance of a new German-language radical newspaper. And so, she argued, would America be regenerated.[11]

In Europe Fuller located this national future by returning to the European cultural yearnings and American revolutionary ideals of her youth. This is not the story usually told of Fuller's European years. At the beginning, she complained that she had come too late for her trip to alter much of her mind and character. By contrast, a legion of twentieth-century biographers have insisted that she arrived in Europe just in the nick of time, allowing her to find the wider experiences she had tragically missed in the United States. She came, in fact, well prepared to be provoked by and exploit what she encountered. As an established author critically acclaimed on both sides of the Atlantic, she achieved easy entry to literary and political circles of which she could only have dreamed a decade earlier. She was also welcomed, like Benjamin Franklin two-thirds of a century earlier, as an American cosmopolitan. Authors from the reactionary radical Thomas Carlyle to the social democratic George Sand feted her precisely because, as many noted, she appeared to be neither a Transcendentalist nor even much of an American, as they imagined those tribes to be. Even the two biggest new shocks she encountered—the social miseries of industrial England and the socialist stirrings of pre-1848 revolutionary France—she reconfigured as a pressing comparativist quandary. Would socialism, a cause with which she now identified as she never really had in the United States, come to democratic but undeveloped America or to economically and culturally advanced but politically reactionary Europe? The question would puzzle her to the end.

In Italy Fuller saw in the mirror of the Risorgimento's struggle for Italian unity and independence the greatest possibilities for a synthesis of her liberal nationality, cultural cosmopolitanism, and aspirations for "experience." Here her preparations ran deep. Since childhood she had filtered America's revolutionary idealism through her father's favorite classical authors of the late Roman Republic and early empire, and the same figures now inspired the militant youth of the Risorgimento. Goethe, Byron, Shelley, and other European Romantics had fired her imagination since her adolescence, as they had an entire generation of Anglophone readers, with an "Italophilia" that conjured the ancient nation as a trope for natural and artistic "genius" over against artificial and utilitarian "modern" culture. As with her adolescent Romanticism, however, neither modernity nor modern America were far from absent. First, she venerated the old but also the new Italy. Unlike her nineteenth-century expatriated compatriots, from William Wetmore Story, whom she befriended, to Henry James, who would later patronize her as an innocent precursor, she recognized, as did even Italian Moderates, the necessity of destroying the very historic institutions that had supported Italy's great culture. Second, although she privately entertained doubts, publicly she beamed confidence that the strivings of the Italian "people" would ensure a new era of Italian freedom and a cultural resurgence to follow. Third, to aid that movement, she exploited all the talents for democratic political journalism that she had honed in New York. As the only American correspondent in Italy, she provided her readers with gripping eyewitness reports of the revolutionary scene that was unfolding on the peninsula, as well as, by the spring of 1848, all over the Continent. After the initially liberal Pope Pius IX fled from Rome in the fall, she strongly, at times stridently, defended Mazzini's Radical Democratic Roman state from aspersions, largely gleaned from the English press, that it was little more than a ragtag gang of foreign thugs, assassins, and anarchists.

Probably what was most Romantic yet also most modern about Fuller in Italy was her willingness to put herself at risk in a turbulent moment in a society so different from her own, however much she liked to imagine otherwise. Forming close friendships with both middle-class Democrats and aristocratic Liberals, sardonically observing the wily conservativism of the Italian peasantry, struggling alternately with her Romantic empathy with an "alien" Catholic culture and her increasingly vitriolic anticlericalism, she regularly hazarded her own presuppositions. She also risked her life, most memorably when ensconced in her apartment in the Casa Dies in the Via Gregoriana, almost the lone foreigner still remaining, while cannonballs dropped all around her and soldiers she had befriended fell in droves before the invading French forces. Yet the risks had their benefits. Certainly, no one who had not done these things could have written her personally and politically searing dispatches. Even her riskiest personal act, her sexual liaison with Giovanni Angelo Ossoli, the sergeant and later captain in Rome's National Guard, with whom she conceived a son—a relationship often absurdly caricatured by biographers—gave Fuller the solid gains of heterosexual intimacy, domesticity, and motherhood she had long craved.

What significance can one assign to her dramatic death? It is easy to see the end of Fuller's life, as has been done for the last century and half, as somehow grimly fitting. It has often been imagined, even by some of her friends, that if she had returned it would have been to face disloyal friends, a hostile public, and a conservative politics relentlessly pursuing the proslavery agenda that she had frequently said made her want to stay in Europe permanently. In a burst of Hawthornesque fantasy, the intellectual historian Perry Miller even pictured the possibility of her refusal to leap from the ship as it sank within sight of the shore as a suicidal gesture of resistance to returning to America. Yet everything Fuller said or wrote suggests she was ready to face the likely "inquisition" about her marriage, and everything her friends said indicates that even the most nervous of them were willing and ready to stand by her. Politically, she had gotten about as much from European politics as she could have: the experience of revolutionary defeat did not destroy her faith in a coming social democratic era, as it did for most European radicals, who had to face a generation of political reaction. Meanwhile, as she wrote in the *Tribune*, her witnessing of American and English dismissal of "backward" Italian political capacities, which echoed racist justifications of slavery north and south, made her feel even more connected with abolitionists and their socialist allies (as from Europe she imagined them) than she had been in America. At the same time, her political experience in a nationalist struggle would have served her well in a decade when slavery became a political issue for the whole nation. The "thinking American" abroad only becomes more American, Fuller wrote in one dispatch, and it surely was true with Fuller. Even if she had found it economically or domestically too difficult to remain living in New York, where she probably intended to relocate, she could have gone back, if not to Italy, whose monarchical restorations would have largely precluded return for another decade, then to London or Paris, where friends and associates, including Carlyle, had offered to find her writing work. Most likely, had she survived, she would have become the transatlantic citizen that twentieth-century cosmopolitan liberals from Randolph Bourne to Susan Sontag would envision as the only ideal position for a civilized American. If Fuller's life then contained great possibilities, was her death unconsolably tragic? Certainly, Caroline Sturgis Tappan, Fuller's closest friend, who spurned the easy consolations of some of their friends, thought so. But Caroline only knew Fuller in life. We know her in the historical memory of her "extraordinary, generous seeking." If this is not the Romantic "infinite" that transcends the Fall and rewards boundless searching, it is probably as close to it as a modern is likely to come.[12]

Brookline, Mass.
July 2006

Acknowledgments

Margaret Fuller wrote a lot about the importance of "mutual interpretation" in criticism, but she did not say anything about mutual borrowing, although she and her colleagues did plenty of it. I know I have, and I take great pleasure in acknowledging the individuals and institutions that aided me most during the last decade and a half that I worked on this second volume of my Fuller biography.

Romanticism has often been stigmatized as an anti-institutional mindset, but institutions have been very important to my Romantic project. The Guggenheim Foundation, the National Humanities Center, the Institute for the Arts and Humanities at the University of North Carolina at Chapel Hill, and the Charles Warren Center at Harvard University generously provided me with fellowships to free up time for research and writing. Boston University's Humanities Foundation gave me a helpful grant to defray research and publication expenses. The libraries and archives without which I could never have brought Fuller alive in her time are numerous and widely scattered. For their many attentions and permission to quote from their collections, I especially wish to thank the staffs of Andover-Harvard Theological Library, the Boston Public Library, Brown University Library, Columbia University Libraries, Fruitlands Museum, the Harry Ransom Humanities Research Center at the University of Texas at Austin, Houghton Library of Harvard University, the Huntington Library, the Istituto per la Storia del Risorgimento Italiano of the Museo Centrale del Risorgimento in Rome, the Massachusetts Historical Society, the New York Public Library, the New Jersey Historical Society, the Schlesinger Library, Smith College Library, Stanford University Libraries, the State Archive of Rome, and the University of Virginia Library. The librarians at the interlibrary loan services at the University of North Carolina and at Boston University kindly put up with my endless requests for published material, doubtless wondering what kind of a project requires books on everything from art music in Germany and newspapers in New York to crime in Rieti and shipwrecks on Long Island.

Fuller's Transcendentalist circle would have been relieved to know that, besides organizations, individuals have provided me with another kind of nurturing soil. Without Robert Hudspeth's Herculean editing of Fuller's letters and willingness to answer every recondite question of mine, my biography might have taken yet another decade to write. Joel Myerson, whose scholarship, editorial ventures, and graduate training have helped ensure that American Transcendentalism has remained an academic enterprise for our generation, was an unfailing source of information and guidance in the literary world of antebellum America. Henry May, who steadily critiqued my chapters over many years, kept me focused on the moral implications and artistic craft of constructing a life of an American mind. I have also been exceedingly lucky in having a large circle of other colleagues who have read my manuscript in whole or in part, and their cogent comments have contributed significantly to my evolving conception of my biography. I particularly want to thank Jeremy Beecher, Ruth Bloch, Lawrence Buell, Andrew Delbanco, Alex de Grand, Robert Ferguson, Cristina Giorcelli, David Hall, David Hollinger, Daniel Howe, John Kasson, Barbara Packer, Robert Richardson, Dorothy Ross, Rosalind Rosenberg, and John Paul Russo. Colleagues in the history and American Studies departments of the University of North Carolina at Chapel Hill and Boston University proved loyal supporters and challenging questioners, helping me to situate but not sink Fuller within contemporary academic discourses. Members of the Margaret Fuller Society of the Modern Language Association, which has helped spur the current revival of interest in Fuller, provided me with a cadre of Fullerites with whom to exchange varying interpretations and useful research tips.

Others too many to name have made my work into a collective biography in several senses of the word. Susan Ferber, my editor at Oxford University Press, has given me shrewd advice about the editing of my manuscript and has expertly shepherded it through all the stages of its publication. Jessica Ryan deftly oversaw production in ways that ensured both the quality of the result and the calming of an author's anxiety over his suddenly absent manuscript. My copyeditor Martha Ramsey skillfully kept any transcendental sentences from spinning into the beyond. Jennifer Brown helped me with Italian documents, translating and clarifying mutilated handwritten texts that would have been scarcely readable in English. James Dutton proved vital in solving with ease innumerable computer glitches. Numerous scholars have sent me copies and transcripts of useful manuscripts they had turned up in their research, including Thomas Baker, Thomas Brown, Patricia Cohen, Phyllis Cole, Brad Dean, Helen Deese, Ezra Greenspan, Margaret Kellow, Lloyd Kramer, Giuseppe Monsagrati, Michael O'Brien, Nancy Stula, Donato Tamblé, Joan von Mehren, and Elizabeth Witherell. Finally, I have had a series of research assistants who have cheerfully gotten me books, chased down leads, and ferreted out information that I always seemed to need yesterday. For these labors I wish to thank Adam Tuchinsky, Eric Combest, Amy Kittlestrom, Vanessa Pool, Katherine Stebbins McCaffrey, and Aaron Lecklider.

Family was enormously important to Margaret Fuller, and I have learned from her to appreciate mine in new ways. Besides the memories of my father and mother, Nathan and Ellen Capper, and my father-in-law Paul Broner, whose personal gentleness and philosophical passion inspired me for some years, a remarkable genealogy of three generations of women has sustained me as I worked on my biography. My mother-in-law, Mildred Broner, was one of its biggest fans, and her appreciative reading and good cheer have hovered over its spirit. My wife Carole Capper's rigorous reading and expert writing advice, her patience with the Romantic sensibility that has infected our household, and the enduring love she has given me have been the deepest living source of this book and everything I write. I have dedicated this second volume to the future: my daughter Emily Capper, whose intellectual enthusiasm and aesthetic imagination I hope are personal bellwethers of a new cultural moment in a post-post-modern age.

MARGARET FULLER

An American Romantic Life

CHAPTER ONE

Transcendental Editor
(1840–1841)

I

"I did envy those who had kept within the protecting bound of a private life," Margaret Fuller confessed in her journal on the eve of launching the *Dial*. "But I will not," she said determinedly; "I will court severest trials." If she harbored any hope, however, that her status as America's first female editor of a major intellectual journal might have staved off criticisms for a while, she would have been disappointed. Three weeks after the *Dial*'s inaugural publication on July 1, 1840, the "*super*fine" literary dilettante William Pabodie repaid her for verbally "annihilating" him a couple of months earlier with a withering review of the issue in Providence's *Daily Journal*. Backhandedly conceding her "extraordinary" learning and "exquisite and satirical acerbity," which impressed "the superficial," he declared that she had "with all her application, no genuine love of knowledge, it seems to us, for its own sake, but for the eclat with which it is attended." As for her opinions, "in so far as they are her own," he sneered, "we regret to say we have no respect."[1]

While Pabodie attacked Fuller, hostile reviewers excoriated her magazine. Boston's official Unitarian journals, the *North American Review* and *Christian Examiner*, pointedly ignored it, but the city's Whig newspapers did not forbear. "Duck tracks in the mud convey more intelligible meaning," the *Daily Times* declared. The *Courier*'s reviewer, under the headline "Queer Book," confessed himself "petrified" and "confounded" by the journal's "stupendously stupid 'ejaculations.'" Non-New England newspapers were outraged. Entitling its review "The Licentiousness of Literature," the *Cincinnati Daily Chronicle* diagnosed the *Dial* as "sickly, fungous," a "wild raving, mixed up of German metaphysics and coarse infidelity,—the whole served up in a style turgid and affected." To the *Philadelphia Gazette* the Dialers were simply a new perfectionist sect gone insane: "These 'new lights' . . . Bedlamites . . . and fellow-zanies . . . are considerably madder than the Mormonites." Only New York's high-toned *Knickerbocker* managed to register a little modulation. After mocking some of the journal's more disembodied sentences, the reviewer predicted, "This school of Literary Euphuism cannot last." Such alternating ridicule and disgust would dog the *Dial* for its four-year existence.[2]

The magazine's first issues got considerably kinder treatment from New England's liberal and reform periodicals. In his *Boston Quarterly Review* the quondam Transcendentalist Jacksonian Orestes Brownson decried its foolish intentions to "*radicalize* in kid gloves and satin slippers" and its "unnecessarily offensive tone." Most, however, strained to find their worldviews expressed in the strange new magazine. The pro-Transcendentalist *Western Messenger* praised it for its profound thought. Although complaining about the *Dial*'s woeful disengagement from "the Great Reforms of the day," the radical abolitionist *Plain Speaker* gave it a ringing endorsement as a valuable "exponent of Literary Liberty." Even politically opposed liberal newspapers offered it hearty welcomes by their lights. The anti-Harvard Democratic *Boston Morning Post*, while put off by the journal's "dreamy, silly, Carlyle-imitating style," nonetheless heralded its freshness as a harbinger of "a true American literature." Horace Greeley's liberal Whig *New-York Tribune* worked the hardest to mimic the new magazine's voice. "The best periodical for earnest, large-souled inquirers yet published in the English language," the *Tribune* would soon announce, indeed, dropping the Transcendentalist qualifier, "The very best Magazine published in this country."[3]

A picture of those "large-souled inquirers" is harder to come by. Greater Boston naturally produced most of the *Dial*'s readers, although it had many in outlying Massachusetts towns, as well as in Providence, Philadelphia, and New York, where Transcendentalist notables like Fuller, Ralph Waldo Emerson, and Bronson Alcott had stirred up followings. Some issues also found their way to readers and bookstores in St. Louis, Cincinnati, and Louisville, where Fuller's liberal Unitarian minister friends preached; to England, where Emerson was beginning to gain readers and Alcott had a following; and even to some trend-conscious readers in literarily aspiring Richmond and Charleston. Anecdotal reports would suggest that the magazine's most enthusiastic aficionados were of a certain type: bookish, high-minded, restless Unitarian young people fascinated with New England's radical reform causes and enthralled by German, French, and English Romantic authors, above all Carlyle. Thomas Wentworth Higginson's crowd of Harvard students and their female friends, who fit that profile perfectly, read the new magazine, he recalled, with "religious awe." Yet its youthful, cosmopolitan air also appealed to young Boston Brahmins like James Russell Lowell and his circle, who were bored and irritated by their established elders' stuffy *North American Review*. Even Harvard's genteel cosmopolite Henry Wadsworth Longfellow, a mainstay of the *North American*, found the new magazine at least intriguing. "Have you ever read the *Dial*? the organ of the Transcendentalists?" he wrote his brother Stephen. "I am sure it would amuse you;—its affectation;—its beauty, its wisdom and folly, make a strange mixture."[4]

Longfellow was right: Fuller's and her colleagues' "Magazine for Literature, Philosophy, and Religion" *was* a strange journalistic mix. Intellectually serious yet stylistically unconventional, it flouted all the antebellum periodical genres: the staid, English-modeled quarterlies and theological reviews; the denominational religious newspapers; the didactically sentimental women's magazines; and the agitational reform journals. Indeed, programmatically, it hardly seemed an American magazine. The dual aesthetic touchstones articulated in its statement entitled "Editors to the Reader" could have been lifted from a European Romantic manifesto: "nature," because it "shames the record and stimulates to new attempts," and the "imagination," because it is "unpredictable; superseding, as every new thought does, all foregone thoughts, and making a new light on the whole world." The editors' sweeping cultural goals were also classically Romantic. "We do not wish to say pretty or curious things, or to reiterate a few propositions in varied forms," they declared, "but, if we can, to give expression to that spirit which lifts men to a higher platform, restores to them the religious sentiment . . . purges the inward eye, makes life less desultory, and, through raising man to the level of nature, takes away its melancholy from the landscape and reconciles the practical with the speculative powers." In short, they hoped to foment the same cultural "revolution" that for nearly two generations European Romantics had been conjuring: an overcoming of the age's enervating gods of mechanism and sentimentality through a reenchantment of human consciousness.[5]

Yet, if classically Romantic in program, the Dialers were liberally American in spirit: they wished, they said, to measure "no hours but those of sunshine." And why not? Never having known the terror and demoralization of a failed revolution, liberated from their "corpse-cold" Federalist-Unitarian heritage, and living in a time and place where, as Emerson put it, every man seemed to have a plan for "reform" in his waistcoat pocket, they were naturally hopeful. They also had two social circumstances to spur on their hopes. By assaulting Boston Unitarianism, they put themselves outside its elders' patronizing networks of learned professions. And like their European Romantic counterparts liberated from old systems of aristocratic patronage, they were keenly interested in what "the people" might provide as a substitute. What they meant by that term, though, was somewhat problematic. Most Transcendentalists disdained the populist rhetoric of that presidential-election year's Whig and Democratic parties. Like most European Romantics, they also felt anxious about the emerging literary marketplace, which seemed to threaten their vaunted values of individual creativity and imagination. Moreover, the "common" and "low" that the Dialers claimed to have "obeyed with great joy" in creating their journal were neither industrial workers nor rural peasants but déclassé souls of a very uncommon sort. Romantically marginal ("in lonely and obscure places, in solitude, in servitude") and trusting more in the private and universal "resources of man" than the public and partial "laws or the popular opinions," they were already starting to make "new demands" on politics, commerce, the professions, the schools, the arts, the household, indeed, even the "vast solitudes of prayer." They sounded very much like the Transcendentalists themselves. Whether the Dialers were holding up a mirror or a lamp, in pledging "not to multiply books, but to report life," they made one thing clear about their literary mission: the writings they expected to print were neither the vaporings of the

dying world of bookish gentlemen nor the chatterings of the coming one of entrepreneurial scribblers. Rather, they announced, theirs would come

> from the beautiful recesses of private thought; from the experience and hope of spirits
> which are withdrawing from all old forms, and seeking in all that is new somewhat
> to meet their inappeasable longings; from the secret confession of genius afraid to
> trust itself to aught but sympathy; from the conversation of fervid and mystical
> pietists; from tear-stained diaries of sorrow and passion; from the manuscripts of
> young poets; and from the records of youthful taste commenting on old works of
> art; we hope to draw thoughts and feelings, which being alive can impart life.

Never before had an American periodical enveloped itself in a mist so inwardly
turned yet democratically open-air.[6]

Actually, the Dialers' high-low "wild-bugle note" had a few muffled accents.
Certainly, it contained none of the "fierce" indictment of American culture that
Fuller had included in her scrapped introductory draft. Although she and her
assistant editors Emerson and George Ripley had all signed off on this final introduction, its buoyant formulations were, as discerning readers surmised, unmis-
takably Emerson's. It also elided two critical questions that she had raised in the
earlier version: what exactly was the *method* of the Dialers' "higher tone of criticism," and by what authority did they expect to wield it in the hyperindividualistic
culture they looked to with such hope? In her "Short Essay on Critics" following
the introduction, she offered some answers. In histories of American criticism,
her manifesto is almost invariably honored as a pioneering "romantic" brief for
subjective literary standards. That would not have been an innovation. For the last
couple of decades, American critics, following eighteenth-century British aestheti-
cians, had been downplaying neoclassical "judicial" policing and playing up
authors' intentions and readers' "common sense" associations as long as they remained empirical and moral. In fact, what was distinctive about her essay was not
its subjectivism but its unique appropriation of German Romantic-inspired inter-
subjective critical theory for an American protodemocratic cultural critique.[7]

Her starting point was the classic Enlightenment definition of the critic's vocation as neither that of an amateur "recluse" merely venting his personal impressions or a commercial "hack writer" devoid of "scientific" principles, but a thinker
exchanging evaluations within a "republic of letters" independent of state and
market. Intersubjectivity also defined her three critical categories. The "subjective" critics were merely dogmatists: "They love, they like, or they hate; the book
is detestable, immoral, absurd, or admirable, noble, of a most approved scope;—
these statements they make with authority, as those who bear the evangel of pure
taste and accurate judgment, and need be tried before no human synod. To them
it seems that their present position commands the universe." In sharp contrast were
the "apprehensive" critics. These were clearly not like current "reproductive"
Anglophone reviewers, who strained to render impressionistically the ideas and
feelings of the author. Rather, like Goethe, her beau ideal of this type, apprehensive critics deeply empathized with the *work* in order to illuminate its inner principle animating its parts and only then determined how successfully its forms

organically realized that principle. Lastly, the highest or "comprehensive" critics, after apprehending a work, placed it within the symbolic universe's organicist hierarchy of literary texts to establish its relative value. "We do not seek to degrade but to classify an object by stating what it is not," she explained. "We detach the part from the whole, lest in stand between us and the whole. When we have ascertained in what degree it manifests the whole we may safely restore it to its place, and love or admire there ever after." Such a classification also determined the scope of criticism: "The richer the work, the more severe would be its critic; the larger its scope, the more comprehensive must be his power of scrutiny." Finally, like the Romantic critics Friedrich and August Wilhelm Schlegel, she argued that the comprehensive critic practiced a polyglot and autonomous discipline:

> If he criticize the poem, he must want nothing of what constitutes the poet, except the power of creating and speaking in music. He must have as good an eye and as fine a sense. . . . He must be inspired by the philosopher's spirit of inquiry and need of generalization, but he must not be constrained by the hard cemented masonry of method to which philosophers are prone. And he must have the organic acuteness of the observer, with a love of ideal perfection, which forbids him to be content with mere beauty of details in the work or the comment upon the work.

Fuller's critic eschewed both dogmatic rules and sentimental impressions in favor of objective empathy, formal analysis, and comprehensive knowledge.[8]

Remarkably, after wielding this rigorous regimen of her "German benefactors," she completely ignored their usual claim that it was solely the property of an intellectual clerisy. Indeed, sounding like Emerson in his "American Scholar" rebuking "mincing and diluting" American intellectuals, she castigated elite journal critics for both their authoritative pretenses and pathetic ineffectuality. It was bad enough, she said, that they made their reviews either predictably partisan or vapidly consistent "at the expense of all salient thought, all genuine emotion of life," but, even worse, they spoke "intrenched behind the infallible 'We'" yet incongruously coaxed their readers. The result was inevitable: these blandly judicial middlebrow critics were rapidly losing their audience as scholars sneered at their superficiality while ordinary readers, trained by them to assent to their predictable judgments, increasingly preferred short digests of these conventional views gleaned from the daily newspaper. In place of this vitiated system of "languid" dictators and indifferent readers, Fuller proposed a new critic-reader partnership. "The use of criticism in periodical writing is to sift, not to stamp a work," she said. The critic should not be "an infallible adviser," but a critical helpmate to "earnest inquirers," giving reasons for their objections, stimulating their sympathies, and reminding them of the achievements of literatures beyond their own. Finally, she imagined this community of self-reflective readers would usher in a cultural revolution. Speaking now in the voice of an insurgent "We," she proclaimed:

> We do not want merely a polite response to what we thought before, but by the freshness of thought in other minds to have new thought awakened in our own. We do not want stores of information only, but to be roused to digest these into knowledge. . . .

> We would live with [critics], rather than be taught by them how to live; we would
> catch the contagion of their mental activity, rather than have them direct us how to
> regulate our own. In books, in reviews, in the senate, in the pulpit, we wish to meet
> thinking men, not schoolmasters or pleaders.

In offering her Romantic critical schema to a reconfigured democratic public, Fuller
presented an avant-garde counterpart to Emerson's imagining of the Transcendentalists (in her original words) "as thinkers to leaven this vast mass of actors."[9]

Fuller's "Short Essay" was the most complete statement of the responsibilities
of the critic made by an American to date, but there was one topic missing that
she had fretted about at length in her version of the introduction: the prospects of
American cultural production. Later in the issue, however, she made it a central
gambit in her review of the previous summer's Washington Allston exhibition at
Harding's Gallery. Privately, she had admired Allston's high European "standard."
The show itself had been spectacularly successful, drawing thousands of awed
Bostonians to view America's first retrospective devoted to a living artist. Yet
she bluntly declared that it was doubtful the country would anytime soon develop
an indigenously imaginative art, since that required not the superficial imitation
of European techniques but organic reproductions of the nation's spiritual life,
which then seemed rather barren. "There is no poetical ground-work ready for
the artist in our country and time," she wrote, anticipating in Romantic argot Henry
James's famous list of America's cultural blanks. "Good deeds appeal to the understanding. Our religion is that of the understanding. We have no old established
faith, no hereditary romance, no such stuff as Catholicism, Chivalry afforded. What
is most dignified in the Puritanic modes of thought is not favorable to beauty. The
habits of an industrial community are not propitious to delicacy of sentiment."
These deficiencies posed a particular difficulty, she said, for an artist who aimed
to represent not nature but "the Ideal": lacking a grounding in cultural life, "he is
in danger of being sentimental and picturesque, rather than spiritual and noble."
And that was precisely the problem with Allston's often mannered classical and
biblical paintings. Happily, though, his landscapes showed the opposite—an organic mingling of object and consciousness: "the painter is merged in his theme,
and these pictures affect us as parts of nature, so absorbed are we in contemplating them, so difficult is it to remember them as pictures."[10]

Fuller's cool appraisal of Unitarian Boston's internationally acclaimed hero
caused a local sensation. Certainly, Allston was not pleased. "People have a right
to their opinions," he wrote irritably to his conservative Romantic brother-in-law
Richard Henry Dana, Sr., "but they shouldn't be so absurd as expose their ignorance
in the form of criticism." Even Fuller's friend Sarah Clarke, who was Allston's
only student, told her brother James she was horrified by Fuller's "dogmatism."
There was something to this. Apart from mentioning drapery and coloration, then
regarded as two of Allston's strengths, Fuller stuck mainly to literary and thematic
interpretations of his paintings. Yet her Romantic dogmas contained no moralism
or chauvinism, the abiding sins of antebellum art critics, and unlike them, she was
painfully aware that her reliance on copied casts and small engravings severely

limited, despite her large art historical knowledge, her formal artistic understanding. Moreover, her "opinions" were mild compared with her antiformalist coeditor Emerson, who breezily told Sarah Clarke that Allston was no "Titanic genius" but "an inarticulate sound" (a brisk judgment, however, that he confined to his journal). Finally, there *was* something "audacious" (as James Clarke said) about giving Boston's overeulogized Great Artist the only serious criticism he ever received in America. There was also something prescient about suggesting that his legacy would be not his often-wooden historical paintings celebrated at the time but his later masterly landscapes. Indeed, in drawing attention to the latter's subjective reverie, she highlighted the use of mood by which nineteenth-century landscape artists evaded America's supposed lack of spiritual institutions. Whether there was a similar loophole for American literary production she did not say.[11]

II

After Fuller and her coeditors' aggressive sendoffs, disappointment quickly set in. Many supporters found the magazine was just the needed thing. "It is domestic, giving the every-day state of feeling and thought of the writers," Elizabeth Peabody assured George Ripley's wife Sophia Ripley. "There is no effort about it, and much strength behind." To the inner circle, however, it was *too* domestic. "How far it is from that eaglet motion I wanted," Fuller wrote glumly to Emerson. "I suffered in looking it over now." Indeed, *all* the editors, Sophia reported to their young contributor John Sullivan Dwight, "run it down unmercifully. It has not fire and flame enough for them." They did take some satisfaction in the "decided sensation" their magazine had caused. "I feared it would fall dead, but there is no dread of that now," Sophia's mild-mannered but increasingly radical husband excitedly wrote to Dwight. "People seem to look on with wonder, while the Philistines who dare show out are wrathy as fighting cocks." Even Fuller buoyed up a little after learning from Emerson about the praises for the magazine he had heard on a recent lecture tour. "I begin to be more interested in the Dial," she replied, "finding it brings meat and drink to sundry famishing men and women at a distance from these tables."[12]

Cheers and bravado, however, did not alter the fact that Fuller had to ensure that the journal served up those provisions. That was not easy. For academic heft, Ripley tried to bring on board James Marsh, the former University of Vermont president, but the Trinitarian Coleridgian preferred to stay as far away from the radical Transcendentalists as possible. Much more surprising, her Transcendentalist stable gave her trouble. Ripley himself, "fermenting and effervescing" over quitting the ministry to found a socialist community, contributed nothing after the third issue and soon thereafter resigned as coeditor. Even worse, her young ministerial friends, for whom the *Dial* was intended to be an outlet, were virtual no-shows. Frederic Henry Hedge, nervous about being associated with magazine's religious radicals, offered his sole prose contribution, "The Art of Life,—The Scholar's Calling," which pled, fittingly, for the intellectual's retirement from the strife of the age. Clarke sent in only a half-dozen "*crisis poems*" recycled from his pining youth. William Henry Channing did a little better, dressing up his theological quandaries in suitable Romantic clothes with his "Ernest the Seeker," but unfortunately the mercurial minister stopped his *Bildungsroman* after two numbers, while his hero was still wrestling with the seductions of Roman Catholicism and seemingly eons away from his Transcendentalist awakening.[13]

Fuller's biggest challenge, though, was keeping in harness not her faltering clerical infantry but her antinomian officer corps. Two opposites proved especially difficult. The most troublesome was Emerson's older colleague Bronson Alcott, whose fifty "Orphic Sayings" in the first issue had provoked by far the most hostile notices in the press. One reviewer retitled his series "Gastric Sayings" and rewrote it as a bathetic burlesque, with his portentous philosophical concepts replaced by foods, while the *Boston Morning Post* correspondent joked that his sayings "resembled a train of 15 railroad cars with one passenger." Although Alcott's Neoplatonic aphorisms were hardly meaningless, their vapidity and disconnectedness turned off even some Transcendentalists. This presented an awkward problem. Not only had Alcott originally been the most enthusiastic about producing a magazine and had even given it its name, but Emerson, while despising Alcott's "cold vague generalities," regarded this "majestic egotist" as his spiritual "conscience" and his contributions as essential to giving the *Dial* its distinctive profile. "You must show all kindness & countenance to this prophet of the Lord," he warned Fuller after learning of Alcott's growing discontent with the magazine. She did so but also tried to rein him in. She printed his name in full so that there would be no question about who produced these pieces of "spiritual chemistry." She cautiously hinted to him about his literary deficiencies. "The break of your spirit in the crag of the actual makes surf and foam but leaves no gem behind," she told him at one meeting. "Yet it is a great wave Mr. Alcott." She also postponed publishing his submissions, which earned her high praise from reviewers but grave disappointment from Alcott, who had been planning to publish boatloads of them in the *Dial*. When all else failed, she informed him that he had to "alter & expunge" his next sayings, causing him to irritably pull them from the "twilight Dial" and send them to his worshipful English followers' obviously superior *New Monthly Magazine*. Although the next year he was back with (Emerson assured her) a "more readable" set of his "Sayings," after she again pushed them aside to make room for other material, Alcott fired off an indignant letter "*To the Editor*," announcing his withdrawal from the magazine. "The Dial prefers a style of thought and diction, not mine; nor can I add to its popularity with its chosen readers," he coolly (and correctly) stated in his note, which Fuller duly printed.[14]

While Alcott was fretting over the *Dial*'s "epicurean" cast, the militant Transcendentalist minister Theodore Parker was worrying aloud about its otherworldliness. Too much like "a band of men & maidens, daintily arrayed in finery," he snarled to a friend. But it was not just the magazine's "young-mannish" pretenses that riled him, but also, as his metaphors suggest, the gender of the "Miss Dial" in charge. At least that is the most plausible explanation of why he so readily accepted as gospel the complaints of Alcott, whose judgments he ordinarily suspected. "To see one of vast gifts of intellect," Parker sighed in his journal after talking with Alcott, "great & diversified culture in elegant letters & the arts—of deep experience in the detail of life, one tried by suffering mind & body,—to see a woman giving way to petty jealousies, contemptible lust for power, & fall into freaks of passion[—]it is ludicrous first, & then it is melancholy." Yet, as newspaper attacks on the magazine kept up, the combative young minister warmed up, if not to Fuller, who would always fall short of his sentimental ideal of a "true woman," at any rate to her "daintily arrayed" band. "It is wonderful," he wrote in his journal, reversing his earlier gender tropes, "that 4 or 6 men called Transcendentalists should thus confuse the 26 states, & frighten all the females in petticoats & the females in boots." Mostly, though, he appreciated having an outlet, unlike the established Unitarian periodicals—in which he had to watch carefully what he said—to vent his ideas "without fear & without favor." His trenchant articles on theology and economic injustice would shortly make him Fuller's most popular contributor.[15]

With Parker alienated, Alcott sidelined, and Ripley soon out, that left Emerson as her sole collaborator. Although her friends Elizabeth Hoar, Sarah Clarke, and Jane Tuckerman assisted with transcribing and proofreading, Fuller made the final decisions about acceptances and rejections and did the scheduling and layout. Emerson alone helped her with soliciting manuscripts, critiquing submissions, and editing articles. He was also her most reliable "Dialese" contributor and strongest moral supporter. "I like your new Dial very well, & think the good Public ought to be humbly thankful to you," he wrote after the third issue, "as indeed it must & will ere long, if you will only hold your volatile regiment together, & not let your head ache." Most important, they shared, almost alone within their Transcendentalist circle, a commitment to making the magazine a vehicle of a radically new literature. That meant principally two things. One was keeping the magazine out of the hands of both crude social reformers indifferent to art and letters and pedantic "Scholars" afraid of confronting conventional tastes and prejudices. The other was implementing the Romantic "portfolio" program announced in "Editors to the Reader." If America's literature was to be vitalized, they both understood, it could not be accomplished through the "uncommonly smooth & elegant" but conventional verses of "pleasing sentiment" of society's "very select" (as Emerson wrote in one rejection letter to a young woman) but through the "ruder" but sincere expressions of the "unimitated & inimitable *voice of the individual*" and her "private experience." Occasionally, they found each other transgressing their expressive rules. Fuller told him "The 'eloquence' and 'wealth,' thus grouped, have rather l'air bourgeoise. . . . 'Dreadful melody' does not suit me. The dreadful has become vulgarized since its natal day," and so on down his "Thoughts on Modern Literature" manuscript. Chagrined that his piece "sounds like a sermon to you," he promised to change "the offending words," which he did.[16]

Yet, despite their programmatic cultural agreement, differences soon surfaced. One was over literary form. While she thought "universal" geniuses combined both mastery of form and revelation of spirit, Emerson often liked to imagine that artistic talent for artistic form was beside the point, if not corrupting, a view that he knew put him at odds with Fuller. "MF & FHH [Frederic Henry Hedge] must have talent in their associates & so they find that, they forgive many defects," he had written in his journal the previous fall, aligning Fuller with her most conservative Transcendentalist colleague. "They do not require simplicity. I require genius &, if I find that, I do not need talent: and talent without genius gives me no pleasure." He was right: although she certainly honored the "simplicity" of genius, she regarded great art and literature, as did her German Romantic teachers, as beautiful expressions of profound truths, whose forms and traditions, which her assistant liked to think of as "trumpery," were organic means of their manifestation. Practically, too, she thought, appreciation of the "talent" of formal execution expanded one's range of valuable authors. "My friend spoke it in blame, that I could prize talent as well as genius, but why not?" she asked in her journal after reading Emerson's passage about herself and Hedge in his journal, which Emerson had lent her. "The criticism of man should not disparage & displace, but appreciate & classify what one finds existent. . . . Cannot one see the merit of a stripling fluttering Muse like that of Moore without being blind to the stately muse of Dante?" In Fuller's view, Emerson's antiformalism even gave him a tin ear for many great authors as well. They especially argued about two such writers whose poems' musicality delighted Fuller: Lord Tennyson (too much "finish" rather than "rude truth") and particularly Percy Bysshe Shelley. After she sent Emerson her unpublished essay on "your demoniacal Shelley," she prodded him to read Shelley's famous peroration on poets as the "unacknowledged legislators of the world," which had just appeared in Mary Shelley's posthumous collection of her husband's poetry. He obligingly did but frankly said he had been underwhelmed. "All that was in his mind is long already the property of the whole forum and this Defence of Poetry looks stiff & academical." She was astonished:

> How can you, who so admire beautiful persons when you see them in life, fail to be interested in this picture of so beautiful [a] person. I do not look at Shelley's journals &c for me, but for him[.] He inspires tenderness. I do not care whether I knew the thought before or not. I am interested to know what *he* thought. But even from your point of view the Defence of Poetry seems to me excellent[.] It seems to me not "stiff" but dignified, and no otherwise "academical" than as showing a high degree of culture. If there are many statements as good I do not know them.

These were literary values she would hold all her life: a love of great canonical literature; an appreciation of multiple forms; a classificatory approach to establishing their worth; and a proclivity to find in "demoniacal" authors high cultural purpose—all ideals largely alien to the prophet of "genius" in "the near, the low, the common."[17]

Related differences over editorial practice also divided them. They emerged innocently enough the day after the first issue came out, when Emerson sent Fuller some suggestions about design. "In the next number pray let them print the word *Dial* in strong black letters that can be seen in the sunshine," he wrote. "It looks very cautious now, pale face, lily liver." He also urged her to make the smaller typeface for the poetry at least as large as the prose, especially when they had something, such as Henry David Thoreau's elegy "Sympathy," "good enough to

save a whole bad Number." Three weeks later, he moved on to ideological boldness, urging her to print Edward Palmer's "very good plain English" *Letter to those
who think*, a pamphlet advocating the abolition of money. "It is good enough and
yet I can easily guess that it is better for my Dial than for yours," he threw in,
adding, for good measure: "I hope our Dial will get to be a little *bad*. This first
number is not enough to scare the tenderest bantling of Conformity." Two weeks
after that, he waxed eloquent over the grand implications of his new suggestions.
Telling her he wished to see a less "purely literary" *Dial* than he had first imagined, he wrote expansively: "I wish we might make a Journal so broad & great in
its survey that it should lead the opinion of this generation on every great interest
& read the law on property, government, education, as well as on art, letters, &
religion. . . . So I wish we might court some of the good fanatics and publish chapters on every head in the whole Art of Living."[18]

How to interpret this seeming ideological divergence? Their different aesthetic
views were clearly not the issue: while Thoreau might fit Emerson's preference
for low "genius" over the high "talent," Palmer was neither one. Nor, on the other
hand, was politics the question: there is no reason to suppose that Fuller was any
more adverse than Emerson to a little social fanaticism in their journal. Although
she did not print Palmer's essay, she turned his pamphlet version of it over to
Ripley, who reviewed it from a point of view that Emerson would have endorsed
(change of hearts must precede change of institutions). Furthermore, who were
these "good fanatics"? Emerson never again suggested one—nor, for that matter,
when he became editor, did he publish any, except for Alcott's polished English
friend Charles Lane and the didactic Fourierist Albert Brisbane. Rather, what
Emerson really meant, his actions showed, was that the Transcendentalists themselves should write those radical pieces, filtering out, as he put it in his letter to
Fuller, the "partisan bigoted . . . whimsical" gall, "not universal & poetic." And
this was what Emerson, Parker, Lane, Elizabeth Peabody, and later Fuller herself
would do in the *Dial*. In fact, as her defense of both "talent" and "genius" would
suggest, in her mind their salient editorial difference was just the opposite of what
Emerson implied in recommending Palmer's pamphlet: *she* was the more latitudinarian. After relinquishing the editorship two years later, she would make the
point in protesting his rejection of a piece she had suggested:

> When I had care of the Dial, I put in what those connected with me liked, even when
> it did not well please myself, on this principle that I considered a magazine was
> meant to suit more than one class of minds. As I should like to have writings from
> you, Mr Ripley, Mr Parker &c so I should like to have writings recommended by
> each of you. I thought it less important that everything in it should be excellent,
> than that it should represent with some fidelity the state of mind among us as the
> name of Dial said was its intent. . . . You go on a different principle; you would
> have every thing in it good according to your taste, which is in my opinion, though
> admirable as far as it goes, far too narrow in its range.[19]

A glance at the contents of their two *Dials* shows she was right. Although
Emerson would add a pioneering department of non-Western "Ethnical Scriptures,"

as well as increase significantly the proportion of his own writings and the poetry of Thoreau and Ellery Channing, the range of authors in the magazine noticeably narrowed. In Fuller's *Dial*, seasoned Transcendentalists like herself, Parker, and Emerson shared the stage with literary novices like Dwight, James Russell Lowell, and Caroline Sturgis; female reformers such as Peabody and Sophia Ripley; and a medley of Unitarian, Trinitarian, Transcendentalist, Quaker, and even, occasionally, Calvinist seekers. If such a cacophony approached at times incoherence, it had one saving grace: it projected Transcendentalism as something more than either simply a circle of Unitarian renegades or, as it would largely be in Emerson's *Dial*, a literary vehicle for himself and his young literary protégés.

Yet Fuller's embrace of Shelley's legislating poets notwithstanding, Fuller's *Dial did* reflect an attenuation of her and her colleagues' original grandiose visions for the magazine. Without Hedge, Ripley, or, except for Parker, their younger ministerial colleagues on board, its Transcendentalist philosophy seemed, as some readers complained, hard to detect. With Fuller's sidelining of Alcott, even its distinctive radicalism appeared, as Emerson feared, a bit hazy. Nor did she rush to try to implement Emerson's grand cultural vision. Their dispute over his desire to have type that would "betray," as he put it, "a little large & glorious . . . consciousness" of their project and her desire to keep it, as she said in her reply, "neat and unpretending" is telling. Whether because of her high classical Romantic standards, her skepticism about their troops' talents, her doubts about America's immediate literary future, her own self-doubts, or simply the "common sense" that Emerson often credited her with—and her papers suggest all were in play—she lacked his extraordinary confidence in the efficacy of their magazine's central idea. That was the conceit that by intermingling the private, the "coarse," and the ideal, the *Dial* might actually, as Emerson put it, "read the law" to "this generation." Fuller's Romantic hopes were less "pretending." One was, as she told Emerson, to provide some semblance of a public voice to a motley movement. Another was what had motivated her in the beginning: to jolt America's provincial and philistine culture. The last was more "hodiurnal" (to borrow Emerson's word for his pieces): to make the *Dial*, as she characterized its function for her protégé Charles King Newcomb, into "the common ground of friendship, and the means of development to us all." In shuffling the "coarse" leavings of the "lonely and obscure," Fuller produced a Transcendental magazine for her time.[20]

III

Finding the right alchemy for transmuting these remnants into recognizable public works, though, proved almost as difficult as gathering into the fold her young ministers. Christopher Pearse Cranch, about to exchange the pulpit for art, contributed a dozen Transcendentalist-inspired philosophical verses, earning him credit with Emerson but hardly fulfilling the editors' call for wildly innovative poetry. Even further afield were submissions from young literary aspirants outside their circle. The two poetic sins the editors most lamented were sentimentality and imitation. Young poets needed to be "*objective*," use their "eyes," and concentrate, Emerson advised one rejected submitter, not on their sentiments but on the "fact" that comes to them as a "symbol or word," for only in this way could they express their "diviner Life" that lies "within or over this petty one which they now exercise." Fuller was blunter. She complained to Emerson that an art essay submitted that fall by William Wetmore Story, Chief Justice Joseph Story's son and recent Harvard Law School graduate, sounded virtually plagiarized from the painter William Page. Story's friend Lowell had better luck later with some sonnets, which she told Emerson had "the fault of seeming imitated from Tennyson, and, though they have some merit, it is not *poetical* merit." However, she added, "I do not wish to discourage these volunteers who are much wanted to vary the manoeuvres of the regular platoon," and so Lowell saw his "gay verses" in print several issues later. A note "To Contributors" that Fuller inserted at the beginning of the second year's series is telling. Explaining that many pieces "not without merit" had to be rejected but still hoping that the *Dial*'s "perfect freedom" would make it a vehicle for developing young writers, she promised that whenever any contribution met its standards of "individuality of character with vigor and accuracy of expression, it will be inserted." Evidently, few poems fit the bill, for only a handful ever made it into the magazine.[21]

The exceptions came from four of their "rude" young "portfolio" poets. Three were Fuller's friends Ellen Hooper, her younger sister Caroline Sturgis, and Caroline's friend William Ellery Channing. Publishing their verses had been one of Fuller and Emerson's prime reasons for starting the magazine, and seeing them come in gratified them. "It is the poetry not of parlours but of belief & plain dealing," Emerson beamed to Caroline Sturgis after getting her dozen poems for the second issue. "How can we help each other more than by being so proud & true as to speak never to expectation but from our private mind & from our utmost hope." Unfortunately, pride and privacy also marked their literary habits. Sturgis, terrified of public exposure, regularly refused to let Fuller print her poems. Channing was even more difficult. Coy and precious about his poems, he refused to revise them or allow Fuller or Emerson to do so, which annoyed his form-dismissing patron no end. "Is the poetic inspiration amber to embalm & enhance flies & spiders?" Emerson grumbled to Elizabeth Hoar. "Cannot the spirit parse & spell?"[22]

As Emerson's complaints would suggest, Fuller's stance toward Sturgis's "bold" and Channing's (in Thoreau's memorable phrase) "sublimo-slipshod" poetry was somewhat different. She, too, admired their "pretty blasphemies." "I have a verse of yours here, which is sublime," she told Sturgis. "It paints the situation with a firm grasp, on the reality no preaching, no O be loyal, or be lofty &c—it begins 'Bound in the prison of my own sad soul.'" On the other hand, although warning Sturgis about excessive carelessness and correcting some of her errors, Fuller clearly felt less anxious than Emerson, undoubtedly because her hopes for their "genius" had never been as high as his but probably also because she understood that if she was to get anything out of them, she had to leave them alone. "Till he needs the public, the public does not need him," she advised Emerson about the shy, introverted young Newcomb, whom Emerson was pestering for a contribution and Fuller was resisting criticizing for fear it would "chill" him. "The lonely lamp, the niche, the dark cathedral grove befit him best. Let him shroud himself in the symbols of his native ritual, till he can issue forth on the wings of song." Even then, the only song they got from him was his mistitled "Two Dolons" (there would never be another), his bizarre tale of a beautiful boy ritually murdered by a mysterious crazy man who worshipped mythological gods in the forest.[23]

Ironically, the young *Dial* contributor on whom Fuller was the toughest would turn out to be its most illustrious. Her rough treatment of the twenty-three-year-old Thoreau's submissions, whose "frequent aid" she had hoped to get, has often puzzled his biographers. Certainly, there was no animus involved. Although never intimate, they would always express cordial respect for each other. Thoreau may have even reminded Fuller of her brusque brother Richard, whom he would soon befriend. However, she did face an editorial dilemma. Parker hated Thoreau's "foolish essays," and the aesthete Sam Ward was equally disparaging of his "ethical verses." Emerson, however, regarded Thoreau as his chief literary protégé and a perfect counterweight to the *Dial*'s earnest "Morgue" of plodding religious and reform pieces that *he* despised. She satisfied neither side. After returning Thoreau's second submission, an essay on "the brave man" (later entitled "The Service"), a truculent counterpart to Emerson's "Self-Reliance," she penciled "good" and "bella" in the margins but also gave him solid reasons for rejecting it. "The essay is rich in thoughts, and I should be *pained* not to meet it again," she told him, but then added: "The thoughts seem to me so out of their natural order, that I cannot read it through without *pain.*— I never once feel myself in a stream of thought, but seem to hear the grating of tools on the mosaic." She conceded Emerson's point that the *Dial* had published inferior essays to his but countered that their more unassuming tone gave them, as she put it, "an air of quiet good-breeding which induces us to permit their presence. Yours is so rugged that it ought to be commanding." In this delicately pointed appraisal, she put her critical finger on precisely the two main difficulties Thoreau would always struggle with in his writing: finding the proper ironic voice to modulate his righteous stances and discovering a flexible structure to amalgamate his disparate elements. Indeed, her critique seems to have shaken him a bit; he resubmitted the article with revisions, but again she rejected it, and it remained unpublished in his lifetime.[24]

Over the next months, the cycle repeated itself, much to everyone's frustration. Thoreau submitted another essay and several poems, which Emerson again tried to cajole her to take, but which she again rejected. A month later Thoreau sent her his self-consciously sturdy poem "With frontier strength ye stand your ground," which she used to give him a thoroughgoing critical appraisal. After dismissing his efforts to pare his verse, which she thought still failed to give it needed "fusion and glow," she rattled off its faults: some images were crude, others were forced, still others were busy, and again, as with his essays, thoughts were detached, fragmented, and, in general, lacked fluency and therefore life. Addressing him as "the poet," she then drew him a shrewd portrait of his young poetic persona as sincerely "healthful, sane . . . ready, and noble" and (note the qualifier) "not wilfully pragmatic, cautious, ascetic or fantastical." But, she sternly added, before he could learn to "melt his verse," he would need to unfold his feelings and gain wider and deeper experience of other places and natures. "He will seek thought less and knowledge more," she wrote untranscendentally. And, oh yes, "Leave out 'And seems to *milk* the sky.' . . . The image is too low. Mr Emerson thought so too." He cut the image, but she still declined to publish the poem, as she did most of what he sent her. These repeated rejections disappointed Emerson. Yet his early *Dial* submissions did have a good deal of stiltedness, which Emerson would try to get him to eliminate. In any case, her tough critiques were apparently salutary, for almost immediately afterward, he began to examine seriously his formal writing problems. Yet his output remained minimal until Emerson took over the *Dial*, after which he published most of his mediocre poetry and his first sophisticated prose pieces. With Fuller's critical ballast and Emerson's mentoring gust, young Thoreau was ready to sail.[25]

How significant was Fuller's and later Emerson's *Dial?* Its yearly subscriptions of barely three hundred have always seemed unimpressive to scholars, but subscription numbers are by themselves a poor indicator of readership, especially in the antebellum era, when poor distribution ensured that single copies would often pass through many hands. Comparatively, the numbers were certainly respectable. Although smaller than those of the period's popular magazines, they were greater than those any other highbrow journal could boast, except barely the *North American Review*. Indeed, when one counts the *Dial*'s direct sales, which were nearly threefold its subscriptions, its longevity, which was twice that of most antebellum periodicals, and the thousands of readers of Greeley's numerous *New-York Tribune* reprints of its articles, the *Dial* was the most widely read intellectual journal in the country. Ultimately, the measure of the *Dial*'s significance is not numerical but historical. First, it produced for its hyperindividualistic coterie its "divine average." Nowhere else can one find its astonishing range of Christian and pagan spiritual quests; its anarchistic and uplifting social critiques; and, most literarily intriguing, its variously prophetic, mystical, and "lonely" tones. Second, while many of its writers had their say and promptly disappeared from history, it served a crucial apprenticing function for many others who would not. For older Transcendentalists like Emerson, Parker, and Fuller herself, it provided the only public forum they could have had for their radical critiques and literary experiments. And it gave their fervent young followers—both literary rebels like Channing and Thoreau and later cultural arbiters like John Sullivan Dwight and George William Curtis—their chance to publish and develop as writers.[26]

More important than what the *Dial* did for the Transcendentalists was what it did for American culture. In both content and style, it expressed, as did no other journal, the idealistic, anti-institutional, "come-outer" spirit of the era. "It provided," as the historian Henry Steele Commager aptly put it, "a place for religion without the Church, for education without the University, for law without the State, for culture without the Academy, for art without the Salon, for new views without organized Reform." As America's first and, until the next century, only avant-garde intellectual journal, it was also a seminal forerunner. Like the modernist "little magazines" of the early twentieth century, it eschewed academic affiliation, disregarded commercial demands, promoted experimental writing, offended middle-brow tastes, and critically engaged the major reform ideas of its time. While this idiosyncratically highbrow and countercultural mindset brought forth (as it would in many modernist magazines) a good deal of leaden, esoteric, and (as Emerson conceded about some of Channing's lines) "slightly ludicrous" writing, it also generated a decent body of novel, eloquent, and daring prose and poetry. And this in an era in which American magazines were forever proclaiming the need for a new national literature while busily stifling the originality needed to produce it. Without the *Dial*, the American avant-garde tradition would have lost a pioneering voice. And, without Fuller's labor and leadership, there would very likely have been no *Dial*.[27]

IV

While Fuller was straining to produce their sunshiny magazine, her personal life seemed to be moving toward an eclipse. Four days after the *Dial*'s first issue came out, she apologized to Emerson, who had complained about not hearing from her for several days: "I am very sorry to be inattentive, but I have felt entirely unlike writing. I have moods of sadness unknown I suppose to those of your temperament, when it seems a mockery and mummery to write of life and the affairs of my acquaintance." In letters to old friends, she was franker. Adding a copy of the *Dial*'s first issue in a package to Almira Barlow, she glumly wrote her, "I cannot make much use of a life which once seemed so full of promise and power." Indeed, when later that month Albert Tracy, the former congressman, whom her father had once hoped she would marry, called on her with his five-year-old son, she was so depressed that she could barely talk with them. "I was sick and, as I supposed, dying," she later explained.[28]

It is true she *had* been sick a lot since the beginning of the winter. But that had been true every winter since her father's death, and that summer her health was starting to improve a little. Other cares lessened. Her prelaunch jitters about her writing had largely disappeared. Family burdens were lightening. In October, she said goodbye to her economically precarious family: Arthur went intrepidly to a temporary teaching job in Westford, Richard grumpily to a Boston dry goods clerkship, Ellen nervously to a hoped-for teaching position in Louisville, and her mother for a year-long errand of mercy to settle Ellen and later Eugene's and William Henry's struggling families in New Orleans. Although Margaret shed a few tears over the family breaking up, she duly appreciated that, except for "pathetic" Lloyd, whom she had to try to "civiliz[e]," she was now free of hated domestic "drudgery." "This day I write you from my own hired house, and am full of the dignity of citizenship," she boasted to Emerson from her house, Willow Brook, in Jamaica Plain. "Really, it is almost happiness."[29]

However, there was one thing that summer that was far from "almost happiness." Although the previous fall she had claimed to put behind her her anguish over Sam Ward and Anna Barker's courtship, it was inflamed again. After recently rejecting Sam's marriage proposal because of her father's opposition to his plan to take up art instead of an "occupation with a view to profit," on August 6 Anna arrived in Cambridge, and three weeks later the couple announced their engagement. Suddenly their Transcendentalist friends were thrown into agitated waters, as they worried about the compromises that this "fall," as Emerson put it, would inevitably entail. None, though, worried more than Fuller, who had been infatuated with them both and had lavishly fantasized about Sam's great art career. "Ah! my friend," Emerson wrote plaintively to her on August 29, "*you* must be generous beyond even the strain of heroism to bear your part in this scene & resign without a sigh two Friends;—you whose heart unceasingly demands all, & is a sea that hates an ebb." The ominous "event" (as their friends spoke of it) finally occurred on the evening of October 3. Held at John and Eliza Farrar's Kirkland Street home in Cambridge, with the circle's recently returned western missionary, James Clarke, officiating, it had all the trappings of a regal Transcendentalist affair. "The wedding was serene & auspicious," Emerson contentedly informed Caroline Sturgis two days later. "The pair are so entirely detached from everything around them, that nothing which did not touch themselves could much affect the scene." He then offered this grand, if somewhat chilly, moral: "If we will only be careful not to intrude or chatter, the least occasion & the domestic hour will be grand & fated. We shall one day wonder that we have ever distinguished days or circumstances or persons." We do not know Fuller's immediate response to this cosmic-sounding wedding of the Transcendentalists' golden couple, but her letters afterward showed the stages of her "bereavement" (as Emerson called it), from vicarious sublimation ("the most moving event in my life") to eventual estrangement. "We are in different regions," she would tell Elizabeth Hoar a year and a half later, adding somewhat sourly, "I do not like to tell them what I am thinking and doing; they can tell one another what they think and do." Nor would Fuller ever quite lose her bitterness over Sam's trading art for banking, probably a condition of Anna's acceptance. "No!" Fuller would exclaim to Sturgis, who had asked her if she was sorry about Sam becoming a businessman. "I had all my sorrow out about Sam when he gave up being an artist. His life can never be wholly fit, nor ever fail to be full of acquisition." Although Fuller was here presumably referring to Sam's learning (and perhaps money), it could not have been lost on her that for this sophisticated yet (in her phrase) "sentimental" "petit maître" (who would tell Emerson after Ward's marriage "I like women, they are so finished"), his most prized acquisition was the beautiful Anna.[30]

So again, as the previous fall, when she had first learned of Sam and Anna's engagement, Fuller turned to introspection, although of a much more self-lacerating sort. Fuller biographers have generally omitted these sometimes-feverish self-inquisitions, either out of frustration with their obscurities or a desire to tell a more uplifting story. To be sure, their emotionalism is obvious, and their shifting tones and dense allusiveness make them hard to fathom. Yet they are also often revealing, frank, and sometimes penetrating. Certainly, they refute George Santayana's later charge that the "Genteel" Transcendentalists could never confess their unhappiness. Nor is Fuller's confessional mode, however self-pitying, sentimentally or narcissistically so. Instead, she shows a painful eagerness to use the Romantic therapeutic tools of her pre-Freudian world to make some sense of her emotional life.[31]

One major topic, not surprisingly, was love, although again unlike her previous fall's self-portrayals as a romantic failure but heroic "thinker," these ruminations struck a considerably more somber note. In her sly poem "A Dialogue," published in the *Dial*'s first issue, the speaker suggests the gloomy thought that the signal Romantic compensations, nature and knowledge, cannot make up for our frustrated romantic desires because they are symbolic expressions of them.

> DAHLIA.
> My cup already doth with light o'errun.
> Descend, fair sun;
> I am all crimsoned for the bridal hour,
> Come to thy flower.
>
> THE SUN.
> Ah, if I pause, my work will not be done,
> On I must run.
> The mountains wait.—I love thee, lustrous flower,
> But give to love no hour.

The poem's taut pathos is both obviously erotic (the "crimsoned" cup of the flower as it eagerly awaits its deflowering by the sun) and philosophical (the sun's light and receptive flowers often appear in the Neoplatonic writings she was reading as representations of consciousness and nature). In her journal several weeks after writing "A Dialogue," she exchanged irony for despair over her romantic frustrations. Recalling the poet Tasso, in Goethe's verse play *Torquato Tasso,* which she had translated, whose friends considered him insane or repellent because he offered his love and help "too officially to all," she analogized his plight with her self-fashioning as a steadfast virgin and bountiful confidante following her disillusionment with George Davis nine years earlier. Even that insight made her feel resentful. "If I wanted only ideal figures to think about, there are those in literature I like better than any of you living ones," she wrote bitterly, addressing her friends. "But I want far more; I want habitual intercourse, cheer, inspiration, tenderness; I want these for myself, I want to impart them to others." So, "what shall I do?" she asked and then answered: "I return to thee, my Father! From the husks that have been offered me, but I return as one meant not to leave thee!"[32]

This is a curious conclusion. Certainly, it leaves her far from the flowery cups "all crimsoned for the bridal hour." Yet it signals something important: that her frustrations over love and friendship had a strong spiritual dimension. "Perhaps I am spoiled and shall be nothing at all now that I have begun to deprecate will and practice and turn my thoughts to a wise submission," she had written in her journal several months earlier. "Surely I seem less rich and forcible, yet nobler & calmer for this change." By June, she was naming her new state. "I grow more and more what they call a mystic," she wrote in her journal. "Nothing interests me except listening for the *secret harmonies of nature*. I cannot bear *plan*, art, yet I see how godlike they are." This talk might bring to mind her first religious experience

professing a loss of "self," on Thanksgiving Day when she was twenty-one, following her break with Davis (which, probably seeing the connection herself, she
recounted in her journal that same month). Yet there were important differences.
Her descriptions of her new state sounded not, like those of that earlier Wordsworthian one, earnest, sublimated, and consoling, but eerie, ecstatic, and tortured.
Also, rather than experiencing merely an hour of being "taken up into God," these
new spiritual experiences preoccupied her, often turbulently, through the winter.
"She remained for some time," Emerson recalled, "in a sort of ecstatic solitude."[33]

Fortunately for a biographer, she was not in ecstatic silence. "Rivers of life flow,
seas surge between me and you," she wrote portentously on September 8 to Caroline
Sturgis, directly after learning of Anna's acceptance of Sam's marriage proposal. "I
cannot look back, nor remember how I passed them." More mysteriously, she added:
"I live, I am—*The carbuncle is found. And at present the mere sight of my talisman
is enough. The hour may come when I wish to charm with it, but not yet."* As the
wedding preparations approached their climax, so too did her mystical claims. "Of
the mighty changes in my spiritual life I do not wish to speak, yet surely you cannot
be ignorant of them," she excitedly told Caroline in her letter of the twenty-sixth,
announcing Sam and Anna's marriage day. "All has been revealed, all foreshown
yet I know it not. Experiment has given place to certainty, pride to obedience, thought
to love, and truth is lost in beauty 'I am no more below.'" Then, reassuring Caroline
that she had not risen so high as to have disappeared, she added, "I have no wish to
exclude any one, and of you I almost daily think with love. When we meet you may
probably perceive all in me. When we meet you will find me at home."[34]

Beautiful revelation and obedience, the obliteration of time and space, the effacing of empirical knowledge, the merging of the antinomies of "All" and "home"
—these would support her claim that she had entered into a new mystical state.
Moreover, her language, though literary, was psychologically revealing. Her key
symbol, the mysterious "carbuncle" in Novalis and other German Romantics, is a
glowing, rubylike alchemic stone revered by hermetic writers of the Renaissance
as a sign of a mysterious power that could engender deeply hidden yet, once un-
earthed, intensely energizing and revelatory knowledge. At the same time, the
magical stone also clearly had some bisexual significance for her, as suggested
by her multiple mentions in her journal a couple of years later that her own "emblematic" carbuncle signified her "male" inward "light" or "key" as well as "my
. . . love for Anna." Her literary associations were personally illuminating as well.
In a tale told in Novalis's novel *Heinrich von Ofterdingen*, from which she seems
to have derived much of her symbolism, a poor young man finds in the woods the
lost glittering, dark red, talismanic stone that a beautiful princess's mother had
given her to protect her from falling into another's power. In restoring it, he becomes her lover—something that Fuller's allusive language ("*The carbuncle is
found*," "my talisman," "I wish to charm with it") would suggest she wished on
some level might happen to her either as princess or lover. It was as if, in reaction
to Sam and Anna's impending marriage, she sought to transmute her disappointment over the disintegration of her platonically romantic circle into androgynous
fantasies of intellectual and sexual power.[35]

In this first phase of Fuller's mysterious plunge that September, though, any such mingling remained, like her carbuncle, still deeply buried. Meanwhile, her mystical ether passed through a daylight filter: not just that of love and spiritual transcendence, but friendship in the here and now. Tossing aside her self-fashioned identity of the one-way confidante who had "loved to give," she now declared in her journal she wanted to receive "more equal" friendships, if not of love, then of "recognition." What she meant by that coded word—which she used constantly, even obsessively, in her journals and letters that fall and winter—seems to have been something quite straightforward: the acknowledgment by her friends of the existential validity of her new emotional and spiritual state. Given her new desire for more intimate friendships—in a circle, moreover, whose very raison d'être was the seeking of new spiritual experiences—her new requirement made perfect sense. What she was asking for was the same empathetic affirmation she felt she had always given to others in their personal searches, but which she now demanded they apply to *her* new spiritual state. In short, she was proposing a test of the nature—and limits—of Transcendental friendship. The results were decidedly mixed. Anna Barker and Caroline Sturgis were sympathetic, but her closest new male friend, William Channing, was puzzled. What made her friendship trials so poignantly frustrating, though, was that her most skeptical friend was her chief assistant and Transcendental mentor.

V

Treatments of this vexed phase of Fuller's relationship with Emerson have been more judgmental than discerning. They have generally divided into two types, depending on which hero they are memorializing. In Emerson biographies, the tale usually represents the Concord sage as alternately bemused and mystified and his assaulting protégée as sentimental and hysterical. Some Fuller scholars, on the other hand, have narrated a different melodrama with Fuller as deprived victim and Emerson as cold Transcendental or (in its most extreme rendering) misogynist fish. The two friends' letters and journals, however, tell a much more interesting story than these victim-take-all narratives.[36]

To begin with, their four-year friendship had rendered solid benefits to each. To Fuller, Emerson had seemed an American culture hero as well as an encouraging critic, loyal patron, and solicitous host. Meanwhile, to Emerson, Fuller appeared as an exciting personality whose erudition, generosity, and magnetism, he knew well, none of his eccentric Transcendental friends and self-poised family members could match. They also shaped each other's recent intellectual interests. She stimulated his increasing respect for Goethe and his new fascination with European social Romantics like Bettina von Arnim and George Sand, and he clearly sparked her first moderate hopefulness about the possibilities of an American literature. Their colleagues noticed their intellectual closeness. Theodore Parker, after calculating that Emerson had imbibed less than a tenth of each of their comrades, asserted that their central figure had absorbed fully "1/2 of Miss Fuller." Whatever the exact mathematics, Emerson's conundrums then ensured a likely increase.

To understand these, one needs to put aside the well-worn Victorian stereotype of Emerson as the serenely aloof sage. To be sure, he resisted strong attachments. Partly he feared they intruded on the insights he gained by his deep communion with "the impersonal God," and partly he thought he was incapable of them. Yet he knew he had, as he confessed, "as large a hunger to love & to be loved as any other man can be." Nor was he exactly uncritical of his usual stance of psychic detachment, but, on the contrary, often berated himself over the "ludicrousness" of his "awkward & proud . . . churl's mask."[37]

One literary circumstance was also driving Emerson's double hex of self-criticism and romantic longing. He had decided to include in his forthcoming first collection of essays one on friendship, and he was feeling anxious. "I am intent some day to write out as I told you the whole chapter of friendship," he had informed Fuller in January, "but am perplexed lately with a droll experience of limitation as if our faculties set a limit on our affections." That last aside suggested his other concern: his growing fear that not only this essay but also *all* his lectures and writings suffered from his failure of heart. "I have not once transcended the coldest selfpossession," he wrote in his journal of his lectures that winter. "I said I will agitate others, being agitated myself," but instead of "extacy & eloquence" and "a new theatre," he was merely passing off, he said, "fine things, pretty things, wise things,—but no arrows, no axes, no nectar, no growling, no transpiercing, no loving, no enchantment." By that summer of 1840, his conflicted fires had reached a white heat. After finishing the transcription of his lecture "Love" for his book, he confessed: "I see well its inadequacies. I cold because I am hot,—cold at the surface only as a sort of guard and compensation for the fluid tenderness of the core,—have much more experience than I have written there, more than I will, more than I can write." Indeed, he ended his confession with a remarkable pledge to a new utopia of friendship "brave . . . because innocent & religiously abstinent from the connubial endearments, being a higher league on a purely spiritual basis. This nobody believes possible who is not good. The good know it is possible. Cows & bulls & peacocks think it nonsense." During the same weeks, he exclaimed in a letter to Thomas Carlyle's friend John Sterling, "I am a worshipper of Friendship, & cannot find any other good equal to it."[38]

Meanwhile, unbeknownst to Emerson, Fuller was getting ready to challenge that very claim. For months muffled sounds of her discontent with (as she characterized it to Caroline Sturgis) "that perpetual wall" that stood between them had been growing louder in her journal. Indeed, when one adds to these rumblings her previous winter's journal confession that she longed to "dare" express to him "the full utterancy of the heart of love," the obvious question suggests itself: was she in love with Emerson? Surely, there was *something* passionate about her feelings for him. As a longtime searcher for a male "Genius" whose cultural "victories" she would share, she certainly had it in her makeup to be enthralled with Emerson. She also had it in her to project onto him, however unconsciously, her ancient frustrated feelings for her father. After all, she had originally received her long-sought invitation to Emerson's house because Eliza Farrar, her maternal protector, had wanted her, after her father had died, to be "cared for spiritually" by Emerson while he drew her "within the potent circle of the enchantments of Criticism & the First Philosophy." Moreover, her portrayal some months later of her father in her "Autobiographical Romance" as intellectually stimulating but emotionally withholding would match almost exactly her complaints about Emerson that late summer and fall. Nor, for that matter, can one discount, given the possessive and occasionally, as in her "Dialogue" poem, sexual overtones of her journal entries inspired by her frustrations with Emerson, the likelihood that her feelings for him were, at least on some level, erotic. Finally, there were two manifest desires she clearly wanted him to satisfy: emotional intimacy and his "recognition" of what she now thought of as her deepest self.[39]

One further question remains, however. Since she had been expressing something of these last cravings since the beginning of the winter of 1839–40, why did she finally decide late that summer to demand from him some satisfaction of them? Certainly, she was in need of emotional reassurance during these weeks leading up to Sam and Anna's marriage. Their editorial collaboration probably also encouraged her to think she could draw Emerson out of his shell. Meanwhile, the *Dial*'s call to transmute "portfolio" papers into public works and its circle's discussions about establishing a new community must have suggested a hospitable atmosphere for trying new social experiments. In a remarkable sign of this, she actually inserted as the concluding lines of the first issue this Emerson exposé: "Did you never admire anything your friend did merely because he did it? Never!— you always had a better reason. Wise man, you never knew what it is to love." Finally, Emerson himself, wittingly and unwittingly, fed her hopes for him. One morsel he threw her in late July was an early draft of his essay "Friendship," which included several passages from letters he had written her on the subject. Even more sumptuous were his escalating demands for her store of secrets about Sam, Anna, and Caroline Sturgis. "I wish you would write me concerning your Friends. Are they not my friends?" he cooingly asked a month before the *Dial*'s first issue came out. A month after that, in response to yet another package of their letters she sent him, he pleaded, "I should like to have such an arrival every day; these are wings, perfumes, wine." Such begging for both friendship critiques and friendly secrets must have seemed to her a tantalizing encouragement to see, face to face, what was behind this coldly shining but now warmly gazing sun.[40]

Three days after the *Dial*'s first issue, she started planning. "I do myself great injustice with my friend," she announced in her journal.

> I am nobler than he can see. I often seem worldly, profane, and "wilful" when I am in reality intent in getting the highest view. In that way shall I never succeed to supersede that Ethical Man who can talk all his virtue and of whom I am weary. I am bent on being his only friend myself. There is enough of me, could I but reveal it. Enough of woman to sympathize with all feelings, enough of man to appreciate all thoughts. I could be a perfect friend, and it would make me a nobler person.

In this welter of high-minded motives for her perfectionist project of becoming Emerson's androgynous "only friend," she said not a word about its emotional dangers. In her next sentence, though, as if to reassure herself that she knew its limits, she immediately added: "I would never, to be sure, indulge towards him that need of devotion which lies at the depths of my being. He measures too much, he is too reasonable, I could not be my truest, childlike self. But I might be my truest manlike self, for the rest, il faut attendre till the angelic circle be reached." One month later, on the eve of Anna and Sam's wedding, she launched her somewhat incongruous campaign both to befriend and "supersede" the "Ethical Man" by being her "truest manlike self."[41]

On August 14, after she and Emerson visited with Anna, whom she had been seeing almost constantly since Anna's arrival, the two editors rode together to Jamaica Plain, where they briefly stopped before continuing on to Concord. Once inside Willow Brook, she began the assault. He afterward recounted it in his journal: "She taxed me, as often before, so now more explicitly with inhospitality of soul. She & C[aroline]. would gladly be my friends, yet our intercourse is not friendship, but literary gossip. I count & weigh but do not love.— They make no progress with me, but however often we have met, we still meet as strangers. They feel wronged in such relation, & do not wish to be catechised & criticised." In response he tried to defend himself: "I thought of my experience with several persons which resembled this: and confessed that I would not converse with the divinest person more than one week. M. insisted that it was no friendship which was so soon thus exhausted & that I ought to know how to be silent & companionable at the same moment. She would surprise me,—she would have me say & do what surprised myself. I confess to all this charge with humility unfeigned." Actually, he felt more than surprise and humility; he felt perplexed and more than a little wounded. "At the very time when I, slow and cold, had come fully to admire her genius, and was congratulating myself on the solid good understanding that subsisted between us," he self-pityingly recalled, she stigmatized their friendship as "commercial"! So, he revived the debate with himself over the relative psychic claims of friendship and solitude: "Yet would nothing be so grateful to me as to melt once for all these icy barriers, & unite with these lovers. But . . . such a one as I must do nothing to court their love which would lose my own. Unless that which I do to build up myself, endears me to them, our covenant would be injurious. Yet," he added wistfully, "how joyfully would I form permanent relations with the three or four wise & beautiful whom I hold so dear."[42]

For a while his tender hopes won out. The same day he recounted in his journal their confrontation on August 14, he wrote Fuller, toying with the idea of forming a little Transcendentalist "University" with nearby houses for their colleagues, who would serve as its faculty, and for the Wards, Ellery Channing, and others of their young friends and followers. "Now do you not wish to come here & join in such a work," he exclaimed. "What society shall we not have! What Sundays shall we not have! We shall sleep no more & we shall concert better houses, economies, & social modes than any we have seen." Although nothing came of it, the idea would continue to surface in his letters for another year. Meanwhile, on the twenty-second, at Emerson's urging, Fuller brought Anna and Caroline for a weekend visit at his Bush house. He afterward recalled their time there as "three golden days," and golden they must have been, for during them Emerson somehow got the definite impression from Anna that she would never marry, which spurred him to think their inner circle would establish something like the "ideal relations" that the Swedish mystic Emmanuel Swedenborg imagined in celestial marriages. Two days later, however, came Anna's "tremulous" confession to him, at the Phi Beta Kappa celebration at Cambridge's First Church, that she and Sam would marry after all. This "strange news" struck him, he confessed to Caroline Sturgis, "with a certain terror." Like many men in the wider Transcendentalist circle, he found the rich, beautiful, and gracious Anna more than a little titillating, but mainly he seems to have been terrified of losing his new dream of a Romantic nonconnubial ménage. "What shall I say to you of this my sudden dejection from the sunlit heights of my felicity to which I had been as suddenly uplifted," he plaintively told Fuller in his letter of the twenty-ninth that he had supposedly written to console *her.* "Was I not raised out of the society of mere mortals by being chosen the friend of the holiest nun [a play probably on both Anna's "celestial" virginity and her convent schooling] & began instantly to dream of pure confidences & 'prayers of preserved maids in bodies delicate,' when a flash of lightning shivers my castle in the air. . . . The fragment of confidence that a wife can give to an old friend is not worth picking up after this invitation to Elysian tables." In short, Emerson experienced a modified version of the romantic "terror" that had struck Fuller. Having assured himself of his induction into Fuller's circle of lovers, at least as a romantic voyeur, he suddenly had to face the fact that marriage—Anna and Sam's if not his—would soon bring down the curtain on his intoxicating dream of new nonmarital "Celestial" affinities.[43]

Happily for that dream, though, he was now getting reassurance of his transcendental charisma from yet another source—the twenty-one-year-old Caroline Sturgis. Part of her allure may have been that she reminded him of his exuberant "childbride" Ellen Tucker, whom he had never gotten over, or perhaps even more the Transcendentalist circle's current cult figure, the reputedly impulsive late German Romantic writer Bettina Brentano von Arnim. (Sturgis's *Dial* poem "Bettina!" would earn her the sobriquet the "American Bettina" to match Fuller's tag as the "American Corinne," after Mme. de Staël's vivaciously brilliant heroine.) Certainly, Emerson was eager to show that *he* would not be (as he had sneered to Fuller about von Arnim's hero Goethe the year before) "too discreet and cowardly" in meeting the "aims and affections" of one like Bettina. "If I count & weigh, I love also," he had told Caroline on August 16, explicitly answering Fuller's charge of two days before. Now that he had learned of Anna's betrothal, the day after he asked alluringly: "Are you not my dear sister and am I not your brother? . . . Can you not, my dear Caroline, sometimes sing me that sweet song." He particularly rejoiced that because (speaking presumably of his earthly wife) "I have no experience of the mode in which other perfect relations may coexist with this perfect relation," Caroline, he was sure, would "come to love your proper hero" with the "perfect trust" he needed. "Cannot the air be full of heat without ceasing to be full of light?" Caroline answered this request for both emotional heat and spiritual light in a way that could hardly have pleased her "proper hero" more: "You, my dearest brother, shall be my saint & purify me. . . . If my friend gives me thought more lofty & beautiful than my own, it seems that he must for the time, be my God." To this bit of Emersonian friendship philosophy, she gratuitously added an invidious comparison with Fuller's more extravagantly searching character: "Where we differ in nature from Margaret & others, is that we unfold from within, while they seek without, & having accumulated much treasure, look within for a treasure house that can contain it all."[44]

While Emerson and Sturgis were ecstatically finding in each other their romantic doppelgängers, Fuller received from Emerson no such equivalent invitation. Probably, his attraction to Caroline apart, he thought Fuller presented considerably greater dangers and difficulties than did the gamine Sturgis. In his consoling letter of August 29 to Fuller over Sam and Anna's marriage, he had referred to his *Dial* colleague as having a heart that "unceasingly demands all, & is a sea that hates an ebb." Although he was there being sympathetic, it was precisely those seemingly boundless and demanding qualities that had always worried him. But what most worried him now were her (in his phrase) new "mystical trances," which she began speaking to him about that very September, making him even warier. "She made many attempts to describe her frame of mind to me," he would later recall, "but did not inspire me with confidence that she had now come to any experiences that were profound or permanent. She was vexed at the want of sympathy on my part, and I again felt that this craving for sympathy did not prove the aspiration. There was a certain restlessness and fever, which I did not like should deceive a soul which was capable of greatness." His wariness would soon become apparent to Fuller.[45]

The first sign occurred on September 6, when he turned down her invitation to visit her at Willow Brook, pleading he had been recently seeing too many people. (He told Elizabeth Hoar, a little more truthfully, he had been getting too many "friendsick & lovesick" letters.) Then, a week later, he informed Fuller not to expect any letters from him for a while since he was only writing to Caroline, "with whom I have agreed that we are brother & sister by divine invisible parentage, and she has sent me golden epistles." Undoubtedly, too, Fuller's panic over Sam and Anna's wedding (now only a week off) was then adding further pressure on Fuller. For whatever combination of reasons, she raised the stakes when Emerson finally visited her on the twenty-third during a brief trip to Boston. Although he found her "undaunted" in her new mystical frame of mind, she was obviously not *too* elevated, because at some point in the conversation she directly charged him not just with not properly befriending her but also with not loving her. Three days later he wrote in his journal: "You would have me love you. What shall I love? Your body? The supposition disgusts you. What you have thought & said? Well, whilst you were thinking & saying them, but not now. I see no possibility of loving any thing but what now is, & is becoming; your courage, your enterprize, your budding affection, your opening thought, your prayer, I can love,—but what else?" The question set off a month-long outpouring of letters answering it.[46]

VI

To frame the problem of their relationship that way, of course—loving Fuller's "body" or her "becoming" virtues—was to leave it where it could never be resolved. Emerson's marriage, their monogamous beliefs, Emerson's discomfort with bodies, both his and others', obviously precluded the physical. In any case, in their letters they said nothing more about it. To twenty-first-century observers that move might seem a gross evasion of the clear erotic issue between them. However, it evidently did not seem so to *them*. Moreover, if they lacked, for better or worse, our contemporary clinical language for discussing the problem between them, they had their own equivalent discourse of Romantic friendship by which to illuminate it.[47]

In his letter to her after their meeting on September 23, Emerson framed a less offensively blunt but intellectually more provocative response than he had written in his journal. He frankly admitted that he had once considered breaking off their friendship because he thought her "nature & aims so eccentric" that they could only eventuate in a crisis that would be "painful to me to witness." Now, however, he could see "you have your own methods of equipoise & recovery, without event, without convulsion, and I understand now your language better, I hear my native tongue, though still I see not into you & have not arrived at your law." He was both mystified and troubled, however, by her most recent stances. Her demand for new levels of intimacy smacked of a desire for power and "exclusion in friendship." Furthermore, in her new mystical "theory," instead of something spiritual, he found "or fancy . . . a certain wilfulness and not pure acquiescence which seems to me the only authentic mode." But what made him "resolute . . . to fix one quarrel on you" was her claim in her last letter "that I am yours & yours shall be, let me dally how long soever in this or that other temporary relation." That was simply false: "I . . . constantly aver that you & I are not inhabitants of one thought of the Divine Mind, but of two thoughts, that we meet & treat like foreign states, one maritime, one inland, whose trade & laws are essentially unlike." And "thoughts," the Platonic Emerson emphasized, were the key to friendship: "Those who dwell in the same truth are friends; those who are exercised on different thoughts are not, & must puzzle each other." He made only one concession: that psychic movement or (as he termed it in his then unfinished essay "Self-Reliance") "Spontaneity" might overcome this "difference" in thoughts. "Nothing is more welcome nor to my recent speculation more familiar than the Protean energy by which the brute horns of Io become the crescent moon of Isis, and nature lifts itself through everlasting transition to the higher & the highest," he wrote, giving this transformative idea a gender twist, with one of Fuller's favorite goddesses thrown in for good measure. "Whosoever lives must rise & grow. Life like the nimble Tartar still overleaps the Chinese wall of distinctions that had made an eternal boundary in our geography." Moreover, he added, he could now see that her own character may well be of the sort that managed such mythical gender leaps: "I thought you a great court lady with a Louis Quatorze taste for diamonds & splendor, and I find you [at their Jamaica Plain meeting] with a 'Bible in your hand.' "[48]

Despite his eloquence, his protean idea of Platonic friendship, and his half-admiring and half-hopeful tone, this was still a distancing letter, certainly compared with the exultant ones he was writing to Caroline about *their* celestial relations. At least that was how Fuller took it then (she would later decide she liked his daring formulation about exchanging identities), and four days later she fired back an indignant reply. She defended herself against his oft-repeated charge that her passion for friendship masked a desire for selfish "power" or "exclusion," much less an intention "to violate the sanctity of relations," that is, marriage. "Could I lead the highest Angel captive by a look, that look I would not give, unless prompted by true love. I am no usurper. I ask only mine own inheritance." That point a little uncertainly cleared up, she turned to her main indictment of *him*. This past month, "when my soul, in its childish agony of prayer, stretched out its arms to you as a father," instead of providing her with the "highest office of friendship, by offering me the clue of the labyrinth of my own being," or even trusting her to figure out for herself what all her "crying for the moon" meant, he turned away from her. It was, she said, as if to say, "'I know not what this means; perhaps this will trouble me; the time will come when I shall hide my eyes from this mood.'" So, after indicting him as a failure both as a "father" and as a friend through his weak self-protectiveness, in a concluding kaleidoscopic verbal stream, she called for the reconstitution of their friendship, but on a new empathetic basis. Straining to fuse his theory of the affinity of opposites, her self-conception as a "manifold" character, and her recent "mighty changes in my spiritual life," she asked rhetorically:

> Did not you ask for a "foe" in your friend? Did not you ask for a "large formidable nature?" But a beautiful foe, I am not yet, to you. Shall I ever be? I know not. My life is now prayer. Through me sweetest harmonies are momently breathing. Shall they not make me beautiful,—Nay, beauty! Shall not all vehemence, all eccentricity, be purged by these streams of divine light? I have, in these hours, but one pain; the sense of the infinite exhausts and exalts; it cannot therefore possess me wholly; else, were I also one wave of gentlest force. Again I shall cease to melt and flow; again I shall seek and pierce and rend asunder. . . . I am now so at home. I know not how again to wander and grope, seeking my place in another Soul. I need to be recognized. After this, I shall be claimed, rather than claim, yet if I speak of facts, it must be as I see them.[49]

Here, then, for Fuller was the twofold psychological crux of their impasse. One part was her desire to "add" to her new spiritual assurance his "recognition" of her new spiritual character. To her this meant not a validation of her "thought," but, as she said, an empathetic response to the "facts . . . as I see them," or, in other words, her feelings. The other issue, directly following, was her claim that, once he gave her that recognition, she would be both "claimed" and therefore able to grow, not "in another," but into her own piercing and rending "Soul." In sum, what she seems to have wanted (to translate her Romantic idiom into a psychoanalytic one) was to transfer her blocked childhood need for loving acceptance onto him, "as a father," so that she might cease mourning for it. Once allowed this transference, she could become a self-reliant and loving adult woman, psychologically and spiritually "at home."[50]

This was a tall request even if he could have understood it. Yet he knew enough to graciously, even compassionately, but still emphatically, decline her proposal for "recognition." His reasoning was simple: he rejected the very concept that self-transformation could come from any such relational and therefore purely "external" emotional transaction. Thus, in his reply to what he aptly called (alluding to George Sand's newly published mystical novel of feminine heroic love, *Les Sept Cordes de la lyre*, which Fuller had recently urged him to read) "your seven chords of melody," he at first fully acknowledged her point. "You have a right to expect great activity great demonstration & large intellectual contributions from your friends, & tho' you do not say it you receive nothing. [You might] as well be related to mutes as to uncommunicating egoists." Nevertheless, he bluntly added: "It seems very just the irony with which you ask whether you may not be trusted, & promise such docility. Alas! We will all promise, but the prophet loiters. Strange disproportion betwixt our apprehension & our power to embody & affirm!" He then offered—in phrases that match in penetration, and exceed in pathos, any that he was writing in his similarly argued "Self-Reliance"—his solution to this "strange disproportion": his counterideal of the chartered libertine whose creative spiritual energy depended precisely on his forswearing social ties of any sort.

> Heaven walks among us ordinarily muffled in such triple or tenfold disguises that the wisest are deceived & no one suspects the days to be gods. . . . He must be divorced & childless & houseless & friendless a churl & a fool if he would accompany with the Cherubin & have the Alone to his friend. . . . As soon as we are more catholicly instructed we shall be helped by all vices & shall see what indispensable elements of character men of pride libertinism & violence conceal. I have no immediate thought of either burglary or arson, & am much more likely to keep a safe distance from all the instructive extremes of life & condition. Yet I would gladly dare to ask for wisdom & deserve it.[51]

His antinomian personal ideal thus emblazoned, where did that leave Fuller, who was obviously crying out for more than just "wisdom"? To *this* conundrum he gave, in a follow-up letter five days later, his only answer: she should set out on her own iconoclastic path to the Neoplatonic "Alone." Nor should the fact that she was a woman, he said, prevent her from taking this route. Indeed, as a woman, he assured her, she had her own counterpart to the wild energy that impelled heroic men along this way. Recalling such fierce examples as the "terrible women" of Islam and the female militants of the French Revolution, he told her: "[They] set me thinking on the *latent* and beneficent state of this wild element in woman. I suppose we are not content with brightest loveliness until we discern the deep sparkle of this energy which when perverted & outraged flashes up into a volcano jet, & outdares, outwits, & outworks man." Here, then, was where Emerson left *Fuller:* provoked, distanced, admired, and now, he hoped, inspired to go and become like *him*, or rather his ideal persona—the transgressive Transcendentalist "experimenter" that he was just then apotheosizing in his essays. Emerson's experimentally antinomian words spoke to an important side of Fuller's "manifold" character; if not, they could hardly have advanced as far as they did in their friendship. Neither the rootless experimenter nor the lofty ethicist, however, held out hope for answering the "more or less affection, of momentary moods" that he dismissively told her, in his letter of October 7, were "of no account," much less for his recognition of her as a spiritually transformed being.[52]

Yet, undaunted, she continued to press him. On October 16, three weeks following their first confrontation, fittingly, at Bush "in a cold room at abrupt & stolen moments" from talks with Alcott and the Ripleys about plans for a Transcendentalist community, they discussed their friendship, but again with bad results. They could have talked another day, Emerson wrote to her four days later, "yet what would another day have done to reconcile our wide sights?" By this time, his patience with their frustrating talks was beginning to wear thin. Instead of further "interpretation," he now frankly told her, the only way he could imagine they could ever advance their intimacy was through "an advancing private experience," and for that he could think of only two possibilities—"a strong passion" or a "great work." And neither, he said, would likely materialize for them: "The first will never come to such as I am; the second I do not absolutely despair of, especially in these days of Phalanx, though phalanx is not it." (He was alluding here to the "great work" of Fourierist socialist communities, to which some in their circle were beginning to become attracted.) Finally, two days later, in response to yet another of her pressing letters, he appealed to her, this time in almost brutally self-lacerating tones, to at least appreciate, if nothing else, the long "history" of his icy character. "This outside of wax covered an inside of stone" throughout his life, he insisted (directly contradicting his journal boast about his inward warmth only a month before). "Therefore, my friend, treat me always as a mute, not ungrateful though now incommunicable."[53]

This last appeal—either for them to keep on the lookout for a "great work" or for her to embrace him as a grateful mute—was evidently for Fuller the final straw. As soon as she received his letter, that same day, she dashed off a searing reply. The letter is lost, but others suggest it was a painful survey of the entire history of his emotional coldness toward her, concluding that their friendship either had to change or end. The letter alarmed Emerson, who wrote soberly to her on October 24: "I have your frank & noble & affecting letter, and yet I think I could wish it unwritten. I ought never to have suffered you to lead me into any conversation or writing on our relation, a topic from which with all persons my Genius ever sternly warns me away." He was here being disingenuous, as well as perhaps a little unfair, ironically, to himself. It had been his very Transcendental "Genius," both literary and personal, that had *encouraged* him to experiment with the limits of Romantic friendship in the first place. Still, one thing he clearly understood: whatever the results of that experiment for either his writing or his psychology, it now threatened to unravel the very friendship he now suddenly realized he badly needed. So, this time with feeling he never before had expressed to her, he pleaded with her to return to their old "native" ways, when "I was content & happy to meet on a human footing a woman of sense & sentiment with whom one could exchange reasonable words & go away assured that wherever she went there was light & force & honour. That is to be a solid good; it gives value to thought & the day; it redeems society from that foggy & misty aspect it wears so often seen from our retirements; it is the foundation of everlasting friendship." She, on the other hand, was now proposing to throw all that away, and that he could not accept.

> What will you? Why should you interfere? See you not that I cannot spare you? that you cannot be spared? that a vast & beautiful Power to whose counsels our will was never party, has thrown us into strict neighborhood for best & happiest ends? . . . Speak to me of every thing but myself & I will endeavor to make an intelligible reply. Allow me to serve you & you will do me a kindness; come & see me & you will recommend my house to me; let me visit you and I shall be cheered as ever by the spectacle of so much genius as you have always the gift to draw around you.
>   I see very dimly in writing on this topic. It will not prosper with me. Perhaps all my words are wrong. Do not expect it of me again for a very long time.[54]

She did not. Given the poignantly absolute nature of his appeal—that he could neither change nor stand to lose her—what alternative did she have? "His call bids me return," she wrote to Caroline on the twenty-second, the day she received his first plea to "treat me always as a mute": "I know not how, yet full of tender renunciation, know not how to refuse." Still, the fact that *he* refused—not only to be her loving facilitator into spiritual health but even, certainly by her lights, an affectionately articulate friend, was not easy for her to take. After reading on October 25 Emerson's final plea, she wrote that same day to her other psychologically intimate male friend in their circle, William Channing:

> [Waldo's letters] have singularly affected me. They are noble, wise, of most unfriendly friendliness. I don't know why it is, I always seem to myself to have gone so much further with a friend than I always have. . . . So here [he] asks me questions which I thought had been answered in the first days of our acquaintance, and coldly enumerates all the charming qualities which make it impossible for him to part with me! He scolds me though in the sweetest and solemnest way. . . . Why is it that the religion of my nature is so much hidden from my peers? why do they question me, who never question them? why persist to regard as a meteor an orb of assured hope? Can no soul know me wholly? shall I never know the deep delight of gratitude to any but the All-Knowing? I shall wait for [Waldo] very peaceably, in reverent love as ever; but I cannot see why he should not have the pleasure of knowing now a friend, who has been "so tender and true."[55]

If his recent letters had not given her enough reasons why he should not, her next discovery certainly did. On October 29 she set off with Caroline Sturgis for Newburyport, where they stayed for three days of constant downpours, in rented rooms at the Curson family's millhouse, a favorite getaway place of Caroline's. That first evening, in perhaps an inevitable gesture in a circle that regarded private papers as at once divine revelations, organically crafted works of art, and coterie newsletters, she read Emerson's letters to Caroline, which Caroline had brought with her. In substance, they mostly repeated what Emerson had written to her. However, two discernible differences hardly could have escaped her notice. One was their notably friendlier, even flirtatious, tone, and the other was the severity with which he sometimes critiqued Fuller's "superlative" and "occult" stances. On November 3, three days after Fuller returned to Willow Brook, Caroline visited her and the two read together all of Emerson's letters to both of them from that summer and fall. "They make a volume," Fuller wrote Channing several days later, "and passages are finer than any thing he has published."[56]

In fact, her feelings about this fevered three-way correspondence were hardly so cool. Throughout his letters to Sturgis she inserted in the margins little polemical comments. Next to the sentences in his October 18 letter deriding their innocent circle's daring to "name the great name of Virtue or pretend to translation & rapture" in light of the real "scarred martyrs" and "Seraphs of love & knowledge" of history, she wrote satirically, "How beautiful—more beautiful, pardon the repetition." Some markings simply underlined his shifting positions over the past two months. Along the side of his September 13 paean to the "Oracle in Woman" that defeats the questioning "little lawyer" in men to arrive at the "heights of Sentiment," Fuller pointedly drew wavy exclamatory rules. Other notations were simply scornful. By the side of the passage in his October 18 letter contrasting his "most intelligible . . . road to power" with Fuller's esoteric and amoral "dark lanterns" turned only toward a few, she jotted sarcastically: "Sometimes it has been said ay and by this writer that every high attainment was at first doubted and rejected. Do seers sneer?" Stung by his jabs at Caroline's recent sympathetic portrayal of Fuller's "superlative" religious rhetoric ("I have written you down in my books & in my heart for my sister because you are a user of the positive degree," he had closed his October 18 reply to Caroline), she jeered in a separate note:

> Waldo is still only a small and secluded part of Nature, secluded by a doubt, secluded by a sneer. I am ashamed of him for the letter he wrote about our meeting.— It is equally unworthy of him and of what he professes for you. . . . What is all this talk about the positive degree? Still this same dull distrust of life! When the sun paints the cloud, when the tree clusters its leaves, when the bird dwells more sweetly and fully on a note than is necessary just to let his mate know he is wanted, the comparative and superlative degree are used—The fact on which Waldo ever dwells in the world of thought, that whatever is excellent supersedes the whole world and commands us entirely for the moment, is expressed in the world of feeling by use of the superlative. Do we say dearest, wisest, virtuosest, best,—we make no vow, but express that the object is able to supersede all calculation[.]
>
> O these tedious, tedious attempts to learn the universe by thought alone. Love, Love, my Father, thou hast given me.—I thank thee for its pains.[57]

Here, then, she joined the philosophical issue: was Transcendental "friendship" created by "thought" or by "Love"? The question would linger for as long as they returned to the subject and would later bear on her social thought. Yet her derisive note suggests it would be a while before she became sufficiently detached from her and Emerson's clashing needs and temperaments to fully engage the problem intellectually. Her sour conclusion evidenced the point: "I cannot read these letters without a great renewal of my desire to teach this sage all he wants to make him the full-formed Angel. But that task is not for me. The gulf which separates us is too wide." After mixing up the intellectual and the personal, she offered a sardonic word of advice for the sage's putative "sister." "May thou be his friend, it would be a glorious office. But you are not so yet." After several weeks of restrained exchanges with him about *Dial* business, she managed a resigned but wistful note graced with a Christian trope: "What I want, the word I crave, I do not expect to hear from the lips of man. I do not wish to be, I do not wish to have, a *mediator*; yet I cannot help wishing, when I am with you, that some tonics of the longed-for music could be vibrating in the air around us. But I will not be impatient again; for, though I am but as I am, I like not to feel the eyes I have loved averted."[58]

VII

In the midst of trying to keep both her eyes and her contributors' *"objective,"* that November Fuller launched her second year's Transcendentalist Conversations with Boston women. As during the previous year, roughly twenty-five to thirty women gathered at 11 A.M. or noon usually either on Wednesday or Thursday, now at Elizabeth Peabody's West Street bookstore, for a couple of hours of talk. Fuller's topics also remained much the same. For the 1840–41 series, she repeated the previous winter's rubric of aesthetics and the arts, organizing the meetings around the categories of "poesy," poetry, and prose; the two sources of artistic creation, the "subjective" fancy and the "objective" imagination; and the requirements for different literary and artistic genres. As these would suggest, the guiding theorists were also the same. For some of the women, it was Samuel Coleridge, and for Fuller, Coleridge's German Romantic sources, particularly the Schlegel brothers and the post-Kantian philosopher Friedrich Wilhelm Joseph Schelling. Her methods were the same, too: discussions and a few lectures along with occasional papers by the women.[59]

She resumed the discussion of the previous year about the nature of "beauty." Closely following Friedrich Schlegel and Schelling, whose lecture on the subject, "Über das Verhältnis der bildenden Künste zu der Natur," she translated that year, she defined the concept as the aesthetic expression of "poesy," the universe's productive principle or creative power linking the finite with "the Infinite" and toward which we strove. Beauty was not ornamental "prettiness." She sympathized, she said in her opening lecture on November 4, "with the sensible people who were tired of hearing all the young ladies of Boston sighing like furnaces after being beautiful." At the same time, she insisted, poesy, or the "poetry of life," was scarcely, as these "sensible people" thought, "something aside,—a path that might or might not be trod,—it was the only path of the true soul." Was it also a path for realizing the "true soul" in society? In her lecture she continued to hew to her old position that in a utilitarian "prose" world, the aesthetic realm was compensatory. "We should only seek to live as harmoniously with the great laws as our social and other duties permitted," she said, "and solace ourselves with poetry and the fine arts." Yet the autonomy of the aesthetic sphere was a much-contested problem in German Romantic philosophy, which frequently led to ambiguities, and so, too, with Fuller. If beauty was supposed to integrate truth and goodness, aesthetic autonomy was hardly a stable referent. Furthermore, she was not speaking to a group of professional post-Kantian philosophers but women whose social position was an integral part of their intellectual problem: their "social duties," as she had put it the previous year in her first lecture, had excluded them from the sorts of institutions, discourses, and practices that nurtured "woman thinking." Also, quite apart from Fuller's view of reform crusades, most of the women were deeply engaged in them. From the start, Fuller's clear aesthetic pool mixed with murkier social waters.[60]

This mixing had already been noticeable at the end of the winter-spring 1840 series. She had assigned her "assistants" to write essays on the topic of "woman." During the discussions, according to Peabody's transcriptions, the participants had agreed on two things. One was Fuller's idea that women were not educated systematically enough. The other was a more psychological point: not just that men feared higher education would unsex women, but that women positively shrank from it, frivolously preferring fashion and gossip, because they feared the life of the mind. As one woman put it, they "feared to trust their own thoughts on the subject lest they should be wounded in heart." Disagreements had emerged, however, when Fuller turned the discussion from this self-culture line to the question of whether inherent differences between the sexes might account for this fear. Caroline Sturgis's sister Ellen Hooper, the group's skeptic, had argued that "women were instinctive—they had spontaneously what men have by study reflection & induction." Although Fuller privately thought women often showed greater spontaneity in the exercise of their faculties, put so sweepingly, Hooper's claim was hardly consistent with Fuller's notion of "woman thinking," and she rushed to counter it. At the beginning of the next Conversation, on "elevation of thought," she had said she had been happy to read that in their essays all the women "spoke of men & women as equally souls—none seemed to regard men as animals & women as plants. This caused a general laugh." Yet this sally also had a serious import of bolstering Fuller's critique of gender essentialism that surfaced at several meetings. "I see no attribute exclusively masculine, exclusively feminine," she had told the women. Drawing loosely on a Romanticized version of a faculty psychology of will, taste, and other intellectual "instincts," she had explained that "man & woman had each every faculty & element of mind—but that they were combined in different proportions." This was Fuller's first statement of her theory of proportional androgyny, which she would later develop in her "Great Lawsuit" essay, and the women had seemed, from Peabody's report, intrigued with it, asking whether there could be such a woman as Napoleon or a man as de Staël's Corinne. The correct answer, several said, citing instances from history and literature, was yes.[61]

In fact, Fuller's argument for intellectual androgyny had left wide room for contestation. Writing later in the evening she had affirmed her view that the "distinction of sex lies not in opposition but in distribution of attributes," but she had added: "Whether this dualism will always continue I know not but at present we cannot conceive of active happiness without it. To find oneself in another nature, likeness and unlikeness. Sun acting on the earth are conjugal,—sun and moon fraternal." (She even confessed feeling a certain aversion toward a man with a voice too soft or a gesture too pliant or a woman with a voice to sonorous or a gesture too large.) Yet it seemed obvious there were moments when it was legitimate for each sex to assume the traits of the other, and she bristled at the idea that a woman's concentration could not or should not be improved because of her sensitive "organization." "There can be no firm self-trust without it, and as the poet is by nature equally deficient in it why should it hurt woman as woman, more than poet as poet."[62]

At a subsequent meeting a couple of weeks later, similar uncertainty and certainty had reigned. Fuller had been troubled that she could not account for the fact that no woman had ever produced a "great work of art," which likewise bothered several of the women, who had suggested that their sex's preoccupation with their domestic responsibilities interfered. Fuller had thought it was more than that. "Women could be queens captains, learned, for all these are comparatively social," she had speculated, but artists of "Genius" operated on a transcendently "objective" plane, for which, she had implied, women had so far not shown an aptitude, a severe Romantic judgment that was probably colored by her own frustrations in that department. Her primary answer, though, had been liberal Romantic: forget explanations and excuses and simply explore one's inner powers and act bravely in accordance with them *wherever* they might lead. Thus, in answer to Ellen Hooper's further question, whether Fuller thought there was *any* mental quality that belonged exclusively to the masculine or feminine mind, Fuller

> said no—she did not—& therefore she wished to see if the others fully admitted this. Because if all admitted it, it would follow of course that we should hear no more of repressing or subduing faculties because they were not fit for women to cultivate. She desired whatever faculty we felt to be moving within us, that we should consider a principle of perfection & cultivate it accordingly—& not excuse ourselves from any duty on the ground that we had not the intellectual powers for it; that it was not for women to do, *on an intellectual ground.*

Nor had Fuller restricted her call for women's experimental self-exploration only to intellectual matters. "Margaret repelled the sentimentalism that took away woman's moral power of performing stern duty," Peabody reported her saying during an exchange about a favorite youthful republican historical parable of Fuller's—Brutus's assassination of Julius Caesar. After several women had asserted that a woman could have carried it out, she had said: "As we begin to calculate our condition & to make allowances for it, we sank into the depths of sentimentalism. . . . Nothing I hate to hear of so much as *woman's lot.* I wish I never could hear that word *lot.* Something must be wrong where there is a universal lamentation."[63]

Finally, adding further iron to her liberal Romantic feminism, she had stressed repeatedly at these meetings that no one should think that acting on that individual freedom was psychologically easy. Suffering, she had said, was the lot of all thinking women like all thinking men, and not just (answering Peabody's objection that Fuller seemed to make common women's everyday sufferings appear unimportant) "women of genius." Although the latter necessarily *did* suffer more because they aimed higher, she had replied, *all* women suffered precisely in proportion to the degree that they devoted themselves to their "higher faculties." How could it be otherwise? Even an obscure thinking woman would have to realize that conventional society did *not* want to reform or beautify or perfect itself, certainly if the cost was very high, and therefore she, like the thinking man, would always be alienated and often alone. Yet, she had gone on to say, this temporary suffering attendant upon self-conscious thought and feeling was essential to our conscious engagement with the world. "She did not love *pain*—nor should it ever be *coaxed*," Peabody quoted her. "Yet it must be acknowledged & accepted & allowed to act so as to be met by thought & feeling—Those who had not suffered had not *lived as yet*. The happiness that was worth any thing was not that which arose out of ignorance of evil—or of shuffling it aside or turning the back on it— but out of looking it in the face—accepting it—suffering it—yet feeling it was *finite* before the infinite Soul."[64]

This, then, was the agonized liberal Romantic conscience Fuller had recommended that previous winter and spring to her women: one that inwardly strove, outwardly suffered, and ultimately triumphed, if not in this world, then in "infinity." And, despite the evident qualms of some of them about where that heroic ideal left *them* as "ordinary" women—and, still more, *why* women so often fell short of it—they were clearly attracted to at least its uplifting aspects. Indicative was Sophia Ripley's paper for the class on "Woman," which Fuller published later that winter in the *Dial*, urging women, despite their inevitably "different positions" from those of men, not to be educated as "only half a being, and an appendage," but to be encouraged to cultivate their own individual opinions. ("Our path can never be another's and we must always walk alone.") "In our dear Margaret Fuller days we were taught to believe that character depended upon *being* rather than *doing*," Caroline Healey Dall would recall of those meetings a half century later, "and that success of any kind, in philanthropy as well as art, might be secured on very adventitious grounds." Fuller would have agreed that "being" had priority, although, even in her most rarefied Conversations, she made it clear that "doing" should never be too far behind.[65]

Meanwhile, that fall and winter of 1840–41 Fuller faced two very different challenges to doing her protean cultural feminism. One was her recent "mystical" submersions. At that first meeting on November 4, she confessed she now looked at things "less objectively" and more from her own subjective "law," and this made her a little nervous. "I told them the great changes in my mind," she wrote William Channing afterward, "and that I could not be sure they would be satisfied with me now, as they were when I was in deliberate possession of myself." She need not have worried. She had always shown in her Conversations (as Channing's sister Susan observed) "power undisputed in making people talk freely on abstract subjects," and it is unlikely she would have lost it while performing a little Transcendental soul-searching. If anything, her mystical searches strengthened her bond with the women. "Glowing," talking with "a new power," never seeming "so brilliant . . . or so heart-touching," raved numerous participants about that winter's series. Fuller felt the change too. "I think we shall have," she wrote Emerson, "a much more satisfactory communication than before." After she made her opening statement, she reported to Channing, "they all with glistening eyes seemed melted into one love.—Our relation is now perfectly true," adding, without irony, "and I do not think they will ever interrupt me."[66]

Fuller's other challenge was decidedly more interruptive. Just before her 11 A.M. Conversation on December 23, she received a letter from William Lloyd Garrison's formidable lieutenant Maria Weston Chapman, asking her to enlist her class to support the Massachusetts Antislavery Fair that had opened the previous day and to devote one of her meetings to the subject of antislavery. Fuller declined both requests, which earned her a memorable rebuke after her death from Chapman's close friend, Harriet Martineau. "While Margaret Fuller and her adult pupils sat 'gorgeously dressed,'" the Garrisonians' renowned transatlantic booster would years later sneer in her autobiography, "talking about Mars and Venus, Plato and Goethe, and fancying themselves the elect of the earth in intellect and refinement, the liberties of the republic were running out as fast as they could go, at a breach which another sort of elect persons were devoting themselves to repair." This notorious blast, as the former abolitionist Higginson would later take pains to point out in his biography of Fuller, was an astonishing smear of Fuller's women, many of whom were ardently antislavery. Several were activists and prominent supporters of Garrison's own largely Unitarian "Boston Clique," two of them, Lydia Maria Child and Louisa Gilman Loring, even close friends of both Martineau and Chapman. This large overlap between the two groups probably explains why Chapman, a maverick Unitarian and "aristocratic" radical, who had a keen nose for political hunting among Boston's high-toned, liberal women, had appealed to Fuller in the first place. What could have caused Martineau, who had once offered to be Fuller's mentor, to make (in Higginson's words) such an "extraordinary mistake"? One likely cause was Fuller's "immense letter" to her three years earlier, posthumously published in Fuller's *Memoirs*, severely criticizing the anti-Transcendentalist and (in Fuller's view) monomaniacally pro-abolitionist remarks in the signed copy of Martineau's *Society in America* that the British author had sent her. Mixing this remembered hurt with Martineau's ingrained utilitarian anti-Transcendentalism, bitter memories of Unitarian Boston's ostracism of her martyred Garrisonians, and hazy memories of gossip from Chapman about Fuller's rebuffing would have been more than sufficient to make Martineau paint Fuller's women, as she did others in her score-settling *Autobiography*, with an unflatteringly broad brush.[67]

What about Martineau's claim that *Fuller* was indifferent toward antislavery and contemptuous of the abolitionist movement? Both charges are distortions at best. In Fuller's belated reply to Chapman's requests, she expressed great sympathy for her comrades' goals, courage, and sympathy for enslaved African Americans. Moreover, she applauded the Garrisonians' recent splits from conservative abolitionists who had opposed their women's rights and anticlerical stances, which, she said, "have interested me more than those which had for their objects the enfranchisement of the African only." Why, then, did she rebuff Chapman? In her letter she explained that she would need at least a class to explain her attitude toward "such movements," which would interrupt the course. That was probably true, but behind that professorial excuse, one can also detect a distinct political discomfort. Although antislavery sentiments ran in her father's family, like most liberal Unitarians and many Transcendentalists then, she had long sympathized with William Ellery Channing's antislavery gradualism rather than the "immediatism" of the radical abolitionists. Like Channing, she also detested the rabid tone and martyr-minded profile of Garrison and many of his associates. But her most crucial reason for keeping Chapman at a distance was in her mind their very different approaches to the religion and woman questions. As far as she could tell, she frankly told Chapman, despite the Garrisonians' recent attacks on the church's complicity with slavery and their defense of women's leadership in the abolitionist movement, they had no philosophy, much less plan, for either reforming religious institutions or changing the "social position of woman" at large. And the proof of it, she said, was their failure to say anything coherent about either subject at the previous month's chaotic Chardon Street Convention, which abolitionists, Transcendentalists, and a hodgepodge of radical religious "come-outers" had called to explore common anticlerical perfectionist ground and at which Chapman had served as secretary. Chapman's sister Anne Weston, in her reply on Maria's behalf, conceded that very point. Observing that the only object of the Garrisonians was the abolition of slavery, she noted "the fact that the A. S. Reform is calculated to lead the minds of a community to still further reform is one that we have not disposition to deny—Great changes, religiously & socially must undoubtedly be produced." At the same time, she emphasized, "these results are collateral & not direct & must be modified by circumstances over which the Anti-Slavery community have no control."[68]

Here was the nub of the difference: insofar as Garrisonians thought that anticlerical religion and women's rights were ancillary and automatically grew in the wake of abolitionist activism, they could sidestep formulating any program for their realization apart from antislavery agitation. Fuller, on the other hand, wanted to encourage women's free intellectual development, which she knew her women would hardly get by making her Conversations into an adjunct of Garrisonian abolitionist activism. Like Emerson at this time, whose similar aloofness toward the abolitionist movement earned him like abuse from its militants, she, too, felt that she had, as he put it, "other slaves to free," and these *psychic* "slaves" to custom and authority were her special charge. Or, to put it more broadly, the difference between Fuller and her Garrisonian critics came down to her gendered version of the standard Transcendentalist critique of sectarian political agitation as a method of cultural reform. For Fuller that reform came not through sudden conversions to absolute moral truths—the perfectionist method of both evangelicals and abolitionists—but through introspection, self-criticism, and "conversation" directed at injecting a new rigor and creativity into women's intellectual culture. Prefeminist Romantic culture, in Fuller's mind, trumped prefeminist abolitionist politics.[69]

VIII

Getting warm sisterly support and successfully fending off a hostile ideological incursion, however, do not seem to have done much to heal Fuller's emotional

wounds attendant on "the great changes in my mind." For a while, she got some
consolation by turning from (as Emerson had styled himself to her) "the youngest
child of nature" to the person in their circle who truly fitted that description. To
be sure, Fuller's patronizing demands and Caroline Sturgis's "passive repulsion[s]"
had always made their friendship problematic. But ever since the previous winter, when Fuller had stopped (in her words) "exacting too much" demonstrable
affection from Caroline, she had started seeing in Caroline's Bettina-like quirks
paradoxically a certain "steadiness of nature" sometimes preferable to the relentless "earnestness of my life." Mostly, she came to appreciate Caroline's frankness. "With her," she would later tell Emerson, "I can talk of anything. She is like
me. She is able to look facts in the face. We enjoy the clearest, widest, most direct
communication." That would remain true for the rest of Fuller's life.[70]

It helped that Sturgis's alliance with Emerson was weakening. Despite Caroline's
summer assurance to him that the two of them were on the same Transcendental
wavelength, her expressions were beginning to suggest otherwise. "I am weary of
searching into things by thought, so little can be learnt by contemplation," she had
cried out in a letter to Fuller in July. "I want a home, I want to love One, but there
is no One—And oh! It seems as if I should die because I have not a child to love.
How the woman will revenge herself after all." By early October, Caroline started
questioning her self-poised "God." ("When will the better hour come dear brother?"
"Have you not faith in the intuitions of Love as well as of Truth?") Then, a week
and a half after Fuller had told her of the "mighty changes" in her spiritual life,
Caroline sent Emerson a spirited note, sympathetically portraying Fuller's "occult"
ideas, which "puzzled and disconcerted" him. In reply, he dashed off a "good scolding letter" to Caroline, as he afterward described it to Fuller, "for presuming to differ from me & siding with you & pretending to see your lights which I know to her
as to me must be stark naught." Caroline, however, held her ground. He was dumbfounded. He fully recognized Margaret's "wonderful . . . stream of eloquent speech,"
"native nobleness," and apparently now even "a certain progress out of her complex into a simpler life," he said. "But when you claim for her incompatible merits,
of wisdom of that world added to wisdom of this, the power of that which she is
renouncing added to the power for which she renounces, I am at a loss." Fuller was
overjoyed at this new turn in their triangle, especially coming from a friend who
had once looked askance at her "search after Eros." "Your recognition, my Caroline,
added to the happiness it could not deepen," she beamed in her October 18 letter.
"Rightly you say the past distrust was always forgiven by me as it is now by yourself. I knew it must come to an end and my truth at last be truly felt by one so true,
but I did not hope we should meet so soon after waiting so long." She got more than
just admiring "recognition" of her new spiritual self. A few days later Caroline sent
her a second letter that rhapsodized about her own spiritual musings. Fuller was ecstatic. "Love goes forth towards you as I read your truest words," she exulted. "I
would sound a trumpet note clear as light now that you are ready for the Genesis."[71]

Unfortunately, just as Fuller was readying Caroline for her spiritual genesis,
her own was beginning to darken. For several weeks, she remained in a high-
pitched state of spiritual euphoria. In a letter to William Channing, then preach-

ing in Cincinnati, she even maintained that she easily assimilated to her "calm consciousness of another life" her terrible headaches, which had flared up the day after she read Emerson's correspondence with her and Caroline. These brave claims mingled, however, with manic-depressive-sounding episodes. Eliza Farrar, on whose couch she had lain "totally helpless" with a migraine, reported that all afternoon Fuller had kept herself "in a strange, painful excitement, between laughing and crying, by perpetual brilliant sallies." The most revealing sign of that excitement, though, was her fervid October 22 letter to Caroline that she wrote after penning her painful ultimatum to Emerson about their friendship, which she filled with dramatic revelations of the effect of her month-long spiritual experiences on her feminine identity. No longer the quixotically "stern and fearless" aggressive "Amazon," she told Caroline, she had become "soft and of most delicate tenderness" and "secret" ethereality. Her most bizarre revelations were her biblically shrouded fantasies of sexuality and childbirth. "Like the holy Mother," she suddenly announced midstream, "I long to be virgin," a startling disclosure that she followed up by ventriloquizing the pregnant Mary: "I have no words, wait till he is of age, then hear *him*. / Oh Caroline, my soul swells with the future." She then plunged into a kaleidoscope of alternately ethereal and painful allusions to her future purification as a "lonely Vestal," culminating in a recollected night in Groton a month after her father had died (during the "first winter of my suffering health"), nursing an impoverished girl dying of tuberculosis, caused, "it was said," by the girl's recent botched self-induced abortion. Wildly mixing the sacred and profane, she claimed that as she had fixedly "*gazed* into" the "profaned" girl's face, it seemed to mirror the "star" that she afterward followed as she walked back early the next morning to her now dead father's silent room. There, she said, sitting in a chair close to his body, she "comprehended the meaning of an ascetic life." It was as if, having threatened Emerson only minutes before with a cessation of their platonically romantic friendship, she unleashed a crowd of feminine fears and fantasies to shore up her core sexual but "ascetic" identity.[72]

A swelling future of sexualized virginity yielding a divine son were fantastic oxymorons that could hardly have been of much help, however, for her conundrums of heterosexual love in the here and now. She seems to have recognized the fact. "Only one soul is there that can lead me up to womanhood and baptize me to gentlest May," she broke out at the very end of her letter to Caroline. "Is it not ready? I have strength to wait as a smooth bare tree forever, but ask no more my friends for leaves and flowers or a bird haunted bower." Moreover, by that winter, the "Winter spirits" that she had hoped would bring her, as did those in the defiled dying girl's sickroom, a "strange and mystic song" with which to "cradle my childhood" brought instead a mystic dirge. Her journal was gloomier yet. "I am weary of thinking," she wrote that January. "I suffer great fatigue from living. Oh God, take me! take me wholly! Thou knowest that I love none but Thee. . . . Father, I am weary! . . . No fellow-being will receive me." Indeed, a few days later, in mocking refutation of her October hopes of being raised that winter to "nun like dedication," while bitterly alluding to her recent breaking off of her correspondence with Channing (because she deemed him, too, insufficiently comprehending

of her), she ended with a tragic assertion. Her entire intellectual and spiritual liberation depended on her experience of "love," which, nevertheless, she seems to
have doubted she would ever have. "Though *I feel within me the genius of a God*
waiting only the full breath of love to call it into conscious existence, I will not
repine, I will not insist, will not prescribe to thee, Oh Friend who gave so much."
She did not let off her other male Transcendentalist friend so easily, however.
"Seeing thee, Sun, far and bright, though cold, I trust thou wilt enable me to wait
the fertilizing beam," she cried, echoing the allusions to Emerson in the sexually
charged metaphors of her "Dialogue" poem. Finally, in sharp contrast with her
ethereal November boast to Channing about not feeling her migraines, she made
them ring like physical symbols of an almost suicidal-sounding depression. "Daily
death, dred agony, privation, dry sterility . . . leaden anguish that I cannot keep
still beneath it," she wrote in her January journal while suffering one. "Sleep is all
the relief I have but every night I sleep many hours, the sweetest sleep, as an innocent captive condemned to the stake. In dreams the mind loves its dulness and
fliest to homes of healthful joy. Life is born out of death."[73]

What was the meaning of all this morbid talk, which exceeded any that she
had uttered five years earlier after her father's death? One clue, perhaps, lay in
her January 8 journal entry's linkage of "home" and "death." Earlier in the spring,
on the eve of her mystical plunge, she had drawn in her journal a somber lesson
connecting these two places. Recalling that while recently walking through Cambridge's Mount Auburn Cemetery, she had mused about the time when she had
lain (she supposed) dying of typhoid fever and her father had uncharacteristically
praised her unconditionally, after which she had recovered and three days later
he had suddenly died. She had then felt "disengaged from the body, hovering and
calm," she said, drawing this startling conclusion: "I believe that the mere death
of the body has no great importance except when it is in no sense accidental, i e
when the mind by operations native to it has gradually cast aside its covering and
is ready for a new one. . . . For what the mind wants to develop, it must have here
or elsewhere. A death from love would be perfectly natural. Reasons why there
are no good monuments I must write upon this subject." These are revealing
melancholic associations. In her coupling of love and death with her memories of
her recovery and her father's subsequent death, one is forcibly reminded of Freud's
argument in "Mourning and Melancholia" that the psychogenesis of depression
is often the failure to work through one's conflicted feelings toward a deceased
parent. Still traumatized by her guilt and anger toward her beloved but frustrating
father, feelings suddenly aggravated by her perceived romantic loss of Sam and
Anna and her failure to gain some equivalent "recognition" from Emerson, she
seemed to wish to share her father's fate. It was a melancholy conclusion, to be
sure, but one that appeared to promise the love and "home" she had never felt she
had gotten from him in life.[74]

For such an interpretation linking her unresolved feelings about her father's
death and her morose love cravings, one can find abundant evidence in her papers
that fall and winter. Six days after she had written her dithyrambic October 22
letter to Caroline about feeling like the "holy Mother" on the verge of receiving a

"wound" ending her earthly life—and one day before reading at Newburyport Emerson's critical letters about her to Caroline—she had written to Channing about the trauma of her frustrating relationship with her father. "I recall how deep the anguish, how deeper still the want, with which I walked alone in hours of childish passion, and called for a Father often saying the Word a hundred times till it was stifled by sobs." Compared to this, death might even have seemed sweet. Indeed, that January, with the final vanishing of her dream of rising through a virginal purification to a spiritual "home" where (as she had told Caroline) she would finally be "recognized with utmost joy," she seemed almost to live out, if unconsciously, that morbid paternal coupling of love and death. Thus, in one dream that month, she dreamt she lived in a castle surrounded by snow but warmed within by a fire that burned steadily while "domestic gods smiled benignly." This homey scene then suddenly transmogrified into a second one, she reported, in which "the patriarch" father Abraham, surrounded with angels, warmly greeted her. "In this vision my individuality passed wholly, it is the greatest refreshment I have had this dreadful month." Yet not all her deathly patriarchal dreams were so refreshing. A couple of weeks later, after being bled by a physician ("as the blood flowed from my arm, *I thought with joy there goes a part of my body*"), she had a series of terrifying mutilation dreams. In one, she even dreamt of some remarkably similar occurrences to ones she had had in her childhood nightmares following her tense tutoring sessions with her father. Then she had dreamed of stumbling through the cavernous dark while desperately grasping at twigs and rocks "that streamed blood on me." Here she wrote: "The light was darkness; my feet bled with the sharp stones I could not see to avoid; chills pierced my ardent heart; cold and foreign substances slid on either side from my seeking hands."[75]

So, it would seem that Fuller had subconsciously returned not just to her emotional frustrations with Emerson. Nor had she even just gone back to the "unsightly wound" (as she had alluded to it the year before) of her romantic disappointment with Sam and Anna. Rather, she seems to have regressed all the way to her self-punishing childhood nightmares engendered, she would soon claim in her "Autobiographical Romance," by her father's obsessively demanding nighttime tutoring that had both stimulated and terrified her. Love and death, paternal protection and physical pain, and finally, "*genius*" and the "full breath of love" from a "Friend": such ancient antinomies of self-acceptance and self-transcendence would have required a catharsis of classical proportions to resolve. After an autumn of frustrating hothouse confrontations and mystical experiences, her "protecting bound of a private life" could seem to have used a little protection from her sturdy public self.[76]

CHAPTER TWO

Romantic Recoveries
(1841–1842)

I

By winter's end, Fuller was inching toward some sort of public airing of her private woes. Over two days in mid-February 1841, she wrote a long letter to William Channing, with whom she had resumed correspondence, complaining that her "deep" friends who professed to love her expressed no warmth to match what she kindled in them. This was a familiar litany, but she abruptly interrupted it. "Once I was almost all intellect; now I am almost all feeling," she cried. "This cannot last long; I shall burn to ashes if all this smoulders here much longer. I must die if I do not burst forth in genius or heroism." Two days later she wrote angrily in her journal:

> *I wish I were a man*, and *then there would be* <u>one</u>. I weary in this playground of *boys*! proud and happy in their balls and marbles. Give me *poets, lawgivers,* <u>Men</u>.
> There are women *much less unworthy* to live *than you, Men!* The best are so un*ripe*, the *wisest, so ignoble*, the *truest so cold*!

This was all somewhat puzzling. True, she had gained new confidence in her Conversations' women. Granted, too, she was keenly disappointed with the "cold" Emerson and perhaps the "unripe" Channing who "should have been a knight . . . but alas!" was "but a preacher!" That she was finding women *"much less unworthy"* was understandable. But where did that leave *her*? Was her new wish to become herself a heroic "Man" any better a solution to her conundrum of female identity than her adolescent dream of discovering a great male poet or statesman around whom "asking aimless hearts might rally?" Most mystifying, how could her new *"mystical"* tendency bring her either love *or* "heroism"? That winter she tried to puzzle out answers in several fictional tales she published in the *Dial*.[1]

These are difficult stories. Densely esoteric and relentlessly allegorical, they have usually struck scholars as impossible to decipher much less digest. Recently, some women's literature scholars have compared them to popular antebellum female writers' sentimental floral sketches. But these tales of talking plants and nighttime spirits sprang from less wilted stalks. One was the eccentric hunchback physician Dr. William Eustis, who had told her about his recent imaginary "interviews" with a magnolia in Lake Pontchartrain and two yuccas in his Brookline garden. The other was hermetic vitalism and its darker ancient cousin metempsychosis, or the transmigration of souls into natural forms, as found in the writings of Neoplatonists like Plotinus and Proclus and Renaissance authors such as Paracelsus and Böhme, whom she been recently reading and whose phrases she sometimes repeats. She also clearly borrowed from Novalis's flower symbolism and, more generally, the German Romantics' *Kunstmärchen*, literary fairy stories or "wonder tales," in which liminal plants and animals think and speak. Finally, her tales' gendered themes, although also partly derived from Romantic figures like the "the mothers" in *Faust*, are heavily autobiographical. She claimed her mother's love of flowers had inspired her, as did obviously her recent fevered exchanges with Emerson and Sturgis over friendship. Most important, in their exemplary mother-figures and female archetypes, they resonate with Fuller's new "mystical" feminine self. In brief, they are gendered family romances narrated as Romantic internal quests.[2]

That was certainly true of the two flower tales that she wrote that winter and afterward published in the *Dial*. "Yuca Filamentosa" exploits the ancient esoteric dualisms of masculine/sun and feminine/moon found in much German Romantic writing to highlight the flowering of a "type of pure feminine beauty." The sun pours forth a harshly scrutinizing floodlight causing the yuccas to wither, as she had thought her father and Emerson had done to her, while the generative power of the maternal moon, a figure absent from her earlier sun-flower *Dial* "Dialogue" poem, pours down a "flood of gentleness" that makes them bloom. She thus hints at a second chance for her mother's love, which she had missed in childhood: "The flower brooded on her own heart; the moon never wearied of filling her urn, for those she could not love as children." She allegorizes spiritual withdrawal and reconnection with the once absent mother more elaborately in "The Magnolia of Lake Pontchartrain." The story tells of a once voluble orange tree that has become a beautifully fragrant but "lonely" and barren magnolia growing by the shore of the lake, which a traveler, who had once loved her, and who narrates the tale, later encountered as he rode by the lake. "The stars tell all their secrets to the flowers, and," he says in the opening sentence, in an often-quoted line, "if we only knew how to look around us, we should not need to look above." But this Romantic premise contains a gendered conceit: flowers are earthly, lowly, and therefore, the narrator says, "feminine." Their need for recognition also makes them tragic. After the magnolia discovers all her admired talk has earned her neither smiles from the "inaccessible sun" and the rebuking moon nor love from her fellow creatures, one day she ceases to speak and shrivels up. Rejected by "men," she suddenly finds herself before the "queen and guardian of flowers." So she is finally taken "home" by her new "Mother," the queen, who advises her to "'simplify'": "'Take a step inward, forget a voice, lose a power; no longer a bounteous sovereign, become a vestal priestess and bide thy time in the Magnolia.'" At the end,

the lonely magnolia arrives at a new psychological state: tempered, contemplative, and self-reliant—in short, where Fuller would have liked to have seen her
own movement from bountiful confidante and frustrated lover to self-poised
mystic. "'Nor shall I again detain a wanderer, luring him from afar,'" the Magnolia warns the hapless traveler; "'nor,'" she sternly adds—in the very words Fuller
had used about Emerson's "questioning"—"'shall I again subject myself to be
questioned by an alien spirit to tell the tale of my being in words that divide it
from itself.'"[3]

If Fuller's flower tales seem like German wonder tales of the "pure feminine,"
her darkly visionary "Leila" published in the *Dial* that spring would seem to have
stepped out of a nightmare of Carl Jung's anima. Indeed, Fuller rummages in a
potpourri of conceits from ancient metempsychosis and Renaissance alchemy to
Goethe's "*dämonisch*" directing nature and the Neoplatonic Orphic plot of the
soul's return to "the One." Yet from them she constructs a woman-centered Romantic myth. Whereas in the quest plot of canonical Romantic writings, the figure wedding "feminine" nature to human consciousness is almost invariably a
presumptively male narrator, Leila, like Isis in Apuleius's *Golden Ass*, is conjured
up by the narrator's "art magic" from the center of a lake in the form of a primordial, potent, and, above all, protean woman. Indeed, the demonic Leila, who drives
all men other than poets who gaze on her into "a kind of madness," takes an Orphic
roller coaster ride, flying through transmigratory descents from the "infinite" into
the soil and minerals of the earth, glowing like the blood-red carbuncle, Fuller's
symbol of hermaphroditic potency, until she crashes back to "human nature." In
an ending reminiscent of the final *Walpurgisnacht* in the second part of *Faust*,
Leila kneels in the dust as she prepares to descend deep into the temporal world,
while her earthly sibling-narrator, kneeling beside her, pledges to give up "necro-
mancy . . . for the talisman of humility," humanizing male and female alike.[4]

However gnarled and obscure, Fuller's tales deserve, if nothing else, a modicum of literary attention. Even more than Newcomb's creepy "Two Dolons" they
deserve the prize for the most experimentally Romantic prose to appear in the *Dial*.
They also represented her circle's most elaborate foray into the Western occult
and virtually its only one before Thoreau into narrative mythmaking. The myth
that most counted, of course, was her own: androgynous, vitalistic, and, in her
favorite self-description, "manifold." These tales were Fuller's first public performances of her new feminine self.[5]

Mainly, though, Fuller's wonder tales produced just wonderment. New York's
anti-*Dial Knickerbocker* sarcastically characterized her second *Dial* story as "a
sort of autobiography of a Magnolia tree" and even the pro-*Dial New-Yorker*, which
found her "Magnolia" "too fanciful to be profitable," said of "Leila," "we do not
like [it], simply because we do not understand it." The one slight exception was
Emerson, who was also then studying some of her tales' occult sources and seems
to have had at least an inkling of their latent psychology for her. After Caroline
Sturgis informed him of the authorship of "Magnolia," possibly alluding to the
similarities between the magnolia tree's complaints and Fuller's charges against
him, he wrote to assure Fuller, "Be it known unto you O woman of little faith, that

I can read affectionately." He added, a little more ironically, that its "fervid Southern eloquence . . . makes me wonder as often before how you fell into the Massachusetts." Still, its tragic tone disturbed him. While conceding the piece was written
"with greatly more than her usual spirit & elegance," he felt compelled to add, "I
. . . found beauty & wit in it and a certain Corinna's pathos which is sincerely sad
& yet discontents me a little; it ought not to be; it is a medicable grief though I
have not the balm for it." As for Leila's Isis-like tale of primordial "night, which
brings out stars, as sorrow brings out truths," Emerson did not record a response,
but one can imagine his reaction. Considerably more than "sincerely sad," this
"nightside" of nature (as Fuller's German Romantics called the irrational), which
symbolically mingled emotional suffering and intellectual transcendence, was
hardly an atmosphere that easily mixed with his sunnier Platonic climes. For Fuller,
however, this agonized consciousness was just the thing. "Man tells his aspiration in his God," she wrote in a *Dial* review later that fall; "but in his demon he
shows his depth of experience, and casts light into the cavern through which he
worked his course up to the cheerful day." What was needed was a tragedy with
a happy ending.[6]

Fuller wrote one other story that year that, although not fulfilling that goal, tore
away a few of her wonder tales' autobiographical veils. Composed at Emerson's
Bush house, probably that May or possibly in the fall, when she resumed her intimate sparring with him, it tells the story of a young child, her reading and fantasies, and, most of all, her relations to her doting but severe and overbearing
lawyer-father. Yearning for a mother who hardly appears, and obsessed with a
father whose harsh nighttime tutoring gives her nightmares of physical maiming
and dismemberment, the child soon retreats into a fantasy world of her mother's
garden and her father's books. Although her reveries turn out to be, as in Freud's
family romances, idealized versions of the real parents the child ostensibly rejects,
*un*like those in Freud's psychological narratives, *her* fantasies only lead to further self-alienation. Her beloved Roman and Renaissance books evoke a world of
masculine heroic action and worldly experience that, however enticing, remains
split off from the maternally nurturing feminine identification she craves. Finally,
after a visiting young Englishwoman inspires the child to imagine herself not as
a self-possessed girl but a young boy "intoxicat[ed]" over her, and then leaves
town, the bookishly Europeanized girl falls into a black depression, which makes
her perplexed father send her off to boarding school, much to her disgust.[7]

What should one make of such an autobiographical fantasy? Written in the first
person and conceived as a projected series of "autobiographical chapters," the tale
clearly drew on Fuller's memories of real experiences, from her father's tutoring
and her infatuation with her family's touring English friend Ellen Kilshaw to her
own childhood family romances. ("She really thought she was a princess, not her
own father's and mother's child," a friend once reported her telling her.) But to
use it, as do the editors of her *Memoirs* and most Fuller biographers, as a literal
rendering of her childhood is obviously wrong. It is filled with inaccuracies, in-
ventions, and embellishments, and its extensive meditations obviously reflect
preoccupations of hers at the time, especially with childrearing, friendship, and

the Western literary canon. Moreover, it blends two German Romantic genres: the Kunstmärchen of the child, such as Ludwick Tieck's *Der blonde Eckbert*, whose story of a tragic magical runaway that summer Fuller compared to her own "changling" plight, and the *Bildungsroman*, or narrative of a young person's apprenticeship to personal culture. Finally, its main point is the linkage of the child's alienation and her failed gender identifications with her father and mother, an idea that clearly comes out of Fuller's thinking over the past year about love and her problematic gender identity. And in the story that identity is certainly problematic. Rather than escaping into a world of magic, or launching herself on a young male *Bildungsroman* hero's journey of self-discovery in the wider world—or, as in Freud's idea, making out of her "family romance" of mistaken parental identifications an integrated independent ego—the child remains at the end as unhappily alienated as she had been in the beginning. Alienation is the story of the tale's failing, too. Stripped of any context or even other voices, it never moves outside of its heroine's recollected anguished longings. It is not surprising Fuller never wrote any subsequent chapters. Still, weak art sometimes produces useful lessons. "Give me rather the wild heath on the lonely hill-side, than such a rose tree from the daintily clipped garden," the narrator exclaims, after portraying her child-heroine's intoxication with "that thorough-bred *millefleur* beauty, the distilled result of ages of European culture!"—or as she puts it in the spirit of her *Dial*, "the fresh prairie, the untrodden forests." Romantic quests for love, feminine identity, and American literature were surely needed, but only if they were first rooted somewhere at home.[8]

II

After months of mystical exhilaration, depression, and fable writing, Fuller seems to have reached some sort of catharsis. In late February, a week following her long lament to Channing about being "almost all feeling," she confessed in her journal that her recent sightings of God's "inner network" were beginning to dim. Five weeks later, she reported to him that in January she lost "too much blood" (or passion) in one of her "nervous attacks" and had been "somewhat too ethereal and too pensive" ever since. "I begin to revive, though I have had too much fatigue lately and my head still aches and aches." Finally, on the night of August 2, after falling asleep, she experienced an "intimate communion far more full" than she had ever known before. She did not say what she experienced other than the bare facts that in the midst of dreaming of herself hovering between a "heavenly state" and death, at 2 A.M. she awoke and then sat up until dawn, when she realized "that some crisis in my life took place." Years later, she would tell Emerson, "angels certainly visited me." The following spring, she would broaden the timeframe for Elizabeth Hoar: that night culminated a "crisis in my constitution" beginning with the "era of illumination in my mental life" in the fall of 1840.[9]

What was that catharsis? In another letter to a friend, Fuller provided a slightly earthier clue. "During my last weeks of solitude I was very happy, and all that had troubled me became clearer. The angel was not weary of waiting for Gunhild, till she had unravelled her mesh of thought, and seeds of mercy, of purification, were planted in the breast." She alluded here to a medieval German legend she had recently read, in which a nun whose confessor had seduced and convinced her to run away with him returned to the convent to discover the sisters had not missed her because a guardian angel had taken her place, thus protecting her against any more "passion-stirred fancy, or curiosity." When one adds to this fanciful association of seduction, abandonment, and sisterly protection the facts of Emerson's platonic "seduction" and withdrawal followed by her fall-time yearnings for purification as a "lonely Vestal" and her morbid winter journal allusions to her father's emotional abandonment of her and immediate death, one could plausibly fill out the analysis suggested earlier. Triggered initially by her panic over losing her platonic love-objects Sam and Anna to marriage, and then Emerson to himself, circumstances that reawakened her mourning for her dead father and probably also her shunted-aside mother, her "crisis" appears to have been one of regression to a state of global mourning. Yet even delayed mourning can cure ego wounds, and so, it seems, with Fuller. Retrospectively purging herself of her father's demanding and withholding masculine imago, she appears to have arrived at, her *Dial* tales would imply, some form of the feminine self-"recognition" and self-acceptance that had heretofore eluded her.[10]

Whatever the psychogenesis, the psychological and physical results, she told family and friends, were abundantly clear. Shortly before her August 2 angelic visitations, she informed a "surprized" Harriet Martineau, to whom she had given dire reports of her condition that winter, that she had become almost all well again. The pressures from teaching and writing were still giving her some bad headaches, she told her brother Richard four months later, but, referring to the time just before her father's death, "I am far better than six years back and hope to keep so." By the following March, she was reporting to Elizabeth Hoar, her "insane" depression had passed, and along with it, the "keen pains and spasms" in her head that she had suffered again ever since her father's death. "I . . . never used to get well, but be always in a state of tension of nerves, while now I am not," she would insist. "Then I constantly looked forward to death." She also thought this recovery had made her a "more hopeful, more patient and above all more gentle and humble" person. "I am not yet so worthy to love as some others are, because my manifold nature is not yet harmonized enough to be faithful," she would say in a letter to another friend at this time. "Yet have I been true to the best light I had, and if I am so now much will be given." She had passed, she clearly hoped, at the age of thirty-one, into the beginning of mature womanhood.[11]

One hopeful sign of recovery was her bold decision that spring of 1841 to bring her two years' worth of women's Conversations on mythology into a larger public venue. Her plan promised to bring her badly needed money, but more than that. First, it seemed pedagogically sound. The men, she thought, who knew Latin and Greek from college, would elucidate the "historical part" of the myths, while she would provide interpretations of them drawn from classical and modern literature and art. It also spoke to recent interests in her Transcendentalist circle. For her female followers, the classes offered a chance to continue her popular mythological discussions at a level higher than that of (probably their main source) Alexander Pope's translation of the *Iliad* and the *Odyssey*. For the Transcendentalist men, her proposal gave an opportunity to explore some nonbiblical "scriptures" they had been citing in their theological battles with conservative Unitarians. So when Fuller's impresario Elizabeth Peabody canvassed for members at the end of the month, her expected small gathering of friends quickly mushroomed into a "veritable class." At the first session, at seven o'clock in the evening on Monday, March 1, an evenly balanced group of some thirty men and women crowded into the parlor of George and Sophia Ripley's house on Bedford Place, which would be the series' usual location. Fuller's profits swelled commensurately. In charging a hefty $2.50 per session, or $20 for a ticket to the ten-week series, twice the price of her regular meetings, she brought in nearly $600, putting her earnings close to the top of the American lecture scale.[12]

Along with strong interest and heavy purses, many of her attendees brought to the meetings sharp minds. The central women came from Fuller's faithful core, who were married to or close friends with the leading Transcendentalists: Peabody, Sturgis, Elizabeth Hoar, Lidian Emerson, Sophia Ripley, Sarah Shaw, and Anna Ward. She also attracted a cluster of more conventional Unitarian women eager to catch a whiff of the circle's "new views." The most conspicuous was Peabody's nineteen-year-old headstrong protégée, Caroline Healey. Hypersensitive over her Transcendental elders' snubs and painfully infatuated with Fuller, who did her best to ignore her, the indefatigable Caroline faithfully wrote up transcripts that, however eccentric and sometimes unreliable, provide the only substantial evidence of what transpired at the meetings. The men were also a formidable lot. All the principal older Transcendentalist leaders attended: Emerson, Alcott, Ripley, and Hedge, who came in from Bangor. Also present were Fuller's former soul mate James Clarke, who had recently settled back in Boston with his young wife and infant son, as well as, at the opposite Transcendental pole, the "insulated" Jones Very. A group of local schoolteachers made up the classes' backbench, but the most prominent "outsiders" were reform-minded relatives of Fuller's female followers: Sarah Shaw's husband Francis, Emelyn Story's husband William Wetmore, and William White, the brother of James Russell Lowell's fiancée Maria White. The only professional Greek scholar was Charles Stearns Wheeler, Very's promising successor as Harvard's Greek tutor. Curiously, the one Transcendentalist who knew the most about the subject declined to attend. "I should like to hear her bright sayings," Parker wrote in his journal after receiving his invitation, "but have not now the time." He added acidly, "To human arrogance—there is no bound." To Clarke, however, who was "struck quite dumb" by his refusal and begged him to reconsider ("Genius is plenty enough among us—but we need knowledge"), Parker pleaded his crushing schedule of theological writings. Besides, he said, he feared he would find it confusing to be studying biblical and Greek "myths" at the same time.[13]

Parker's usual cantankerousness toward Fuller notwithstanding, he did point to a genuine problem: How *could* a modern get the proper purchase on the ancient Greek myths? Through most of the Enlightenment, religious and secular authors alike had stigmatized them as pagan superstitions, fanciful stories, or, at best, crude anticipations of higher Christian notions. Nor did late eighteenth-century "scientific" theories of myths as primitive echoes of (in the euhemerist version) human heroes or (in fetishist theories) nature or planetary worship credit them with serious intellectual worth. The situation was only a little better in antebellum America. Although academic scholars applied methods of historical criticism imported from Germany to the study of Greek texts, Protestant moralism required the works' careful expurgation, and Christian beliefs ensured their treatment as archaic tales. In the following decade, Thomas Bulfinch in his popular *Age of Fable* would provide only a little gilding by celebrating the "extinct" myths as "charming fictions" helping us to understand "modern" Christian literature. Two generations earlier, however, the myth-yearning German Romantics, building on the philhellenism of Johann Gottfried Herder, Schiller, and Goethe, in treating myths as products of a superior mythic culture and religion, had given birth to the beginnings of a modern mythography, from which Fuller borrowed, as with their literary theories, heavily but also eclectically. The Greek myths, Fuller said in her opening lecture, were great religious narratives expressing both (as she put it) developing "national mind[s]" and "universal" ideas fusing the natural and the spiritual. Between the "classical" humanist line of Herder, who regarded the ancient Greek myths as humanity's highest cultural expressions, and the more progressivist vision of the early Romantics Friedrich Schlegel and Schelling, who called for a "new mythology" for "modern" times, Fuller, on this subject a classical Romantic, consistently followed Herder's view. Yet she also depended heavily for scholarship on the later German Romantic Friedrich Creuzer's four-volume *Symbolik und Mythologie der alten Völker* (1819), arguably the most important mythographic study of the nineteenth century, which had aroused heated controversy in Germany because it had weakened the Greek myths' privileged humanistic place by tracing them to Egyptian and Indian priestly sources. Furthermore, she borrowed three ideas from the early German Romantics. One was the "old [August Wilhelm] Schlegel idea" of using later artistic and literary appropriations of the myths to decode their meanings. Another was the notion, which she probably got from Schelling, that since myths constituted, as she said, "the history of the development of the Infinite in the Finite," the Greek gods were no mere historical or philosophical allegories but protean symbols fusing their meanings and their embodiments. Finally, vaguely echoing Schelling (and anticipating twentieth-century psychologizing of myths), she recycled her Conversations' metapsychology of the gods as representations of "human faculties" or cognitive powers.[14]

As in her first women's mythological Conversations, several Unitarian participants sometimes objected to Fuller's Romantic mythographic hermeneutics, not because they occluded revelation but because she seemed unwilling to concede that modern Christian culture represented great progress over the ancient Greeks' "barbarous age." This was an old fight for Fuller in liberal Unitarian circles. If by "progress," one meant social and ethical progress, then, of course, she said, modern society *had* obviously gained in benevolence, rationality, utility, and, above all, she wrote in her notes, for farmers and mechanics, in America the large majority, "much more dignity & independence." If, however, one meant intellectual progress, she flatly said in one class, following Schiller, the "age of Plato" *was* superior in one crucial respect: its poets and philosophers grasped altogether the "ideal," the "objective," and the artistic, something unimaginable in the present "age of Analysis," regardless of its laudable scientific advancements. If a Plato *were* to miraculously now appear, she told her rationalistic Unitarians, the "pride of knowledge" he would find would be a greater obstacle to enlightenment than superstition once was![15]

Her most articulate antagonists, however, were her Transcendentalist colleagues. With moderate progressivists like Hedge and Ripley, she was conciliatory, readily conceding Ripley's point that one could see in Europe a growing tendency to return to religious and poetic modes as well as the likelihood that the future would bring "something" in the "cycle of mind" beyond the aspiration of the Egyptian and the poetry of the Greek. The Transcendental fireworks, though, erupted in her interchanges, not with them, or even with Alcott, whose claims for an imminent "purer mythology" she dismissed almost derisively, but with her friendly antagonist Emerson. As in most areas, Emerson was his own man when it came to mythology. Neither a complacent progressivist like the Unitarians nor a wooden spiritualist like Alcott, nor a transcendental rationalist like Parker, who examined ancient myths for empirical refutation or confirmation of theological claims, he was a transcendental pragmatist. He looked to myths, as he looked to all human experience, not as a way station to the past or future but as momentary symbolic flashes in the present, linking "fact" and spiritual truth. So, from the first meeting he attended on March 8, he repeatedly argued, as he put it at one session, that the "secret" of each Greek myth could be easily found if we could only discover the living heroes from whom the myths ultimately derived, taking these "abstract ideas" and then "adjust[ing] them for ourselves." "If we knew the real meaning of the names of their Deities," he said, "the story would take to flight." To Fuller, this euhemerist theory seemed absurd. The myths were not persons but personified thoughts, and, as such, could just as easily have derived from a host of natural, social, and literary sources. What she most objected to, though, was Emerson's historical and hermeneutical innocence. "A fable [is] more than a mere word," she interjected. "It [is] a word of the purest kind rather, the passing of thought into form. [Emerson] made no allowance for time or space or climate. . . . The age of the Greeks [is] the age of Poetry; ours [is] the age of Analysis. *We* [cannot] create a Mythology." To this, Emerson responded, "Why not? We [have] still better material," citing historical heroes like Napoleon. Such hardly constituted a "mythos," she answered. "If they came, *we* should do nothing better than write memoirs of their hats, coats, and swords, as we had done already, without thinking of any lesson they might teach." Or, she added, we would go, like Carlyle, in his recent book *On Heroes*, to the opposite extreme and worship "mere men." Finally, their point-counterpoint reached its most sublimely parodic with this exchange recorded by Healey:

> R. W. E. thought every man had probably met his Jupiter, Juno, Minerva, Venus, or Ceres in society!

Margaret was sure she never had!
R. W. E. explained: "Not in the world, but each on his own platform."[16]

By this time, the transcript shows Fuller was plainly getting exasperated. "I [can]not see why we [are] not content to take the beautiful Greek mythi as they [are]," she exclaimed, "without troubling ourselves about those which might arise for us!" But after a futile-sounding attempt to refocus the class on the myths themselves by shifting to her schema of mythic "human faculties," she found herself enmeshed in yet another bit of "wandering," this time involving not progress or hermeneutics but morality. Initially, it was touched off by a reference to the Greek myths' lusty portrayal of the gods' violence, treachery, and sexual dalliances. She was especially sarcastic when one Unitarian innocent, Mrs. Jonathan Russell, the widow of the former minister to Sweden, who in response to Fuller's suggestion that Apollo's cruelties fitted his character, spoke indignantly about his destruction of the children of Niobe. Fuller, laughed aloud and said, "That is like being reminded of the 'poor mariner,' when I say that I like to hear the wind blow." Indeed, she added, riding high on her metaphorical hobbyhorse, "The Greeks ought to be respected for developing every human faculty into deity. [I think] lying, stealing, and so forth only excesses of a good faculty; and so did the Greeks."[17]

The one Transcendentalist who was not amused by Fuller's ethical aestheticizing was, once again, Emerson. This time the trigger was a discussion at the sixth meeting of Apuleius's tale in his *Golden Ass*, often appearing in Neoplatonic writings, of Cupid and Psyche. Why after Cupid had warned her not to look at him while he slept was Psyche so easily tricked by her wicked sisters into doing so, making him angrily leave her and beginning her trials to get him back? "Her temptations were strong," Healey reported Fuller explaining; "and if they had not come through her sisters, they must have come through her own soul. . . . Everything is produced by antagonism." After instancing the conflict in Hindu theology between Vishnu, the preserving god of innocence, and Brahma, the creative god who purified himself by wading through wickedness, she then added, extracting out of this German Romantic idea a little Christian theology, "There seems to be a need of sin, to work out salvation for human beings." At this point, Emerson suddenly broke in: "Faith should work out that salvation. It was man's privilege to resist the evil, to strive triumphantly; to recognize it—never! Good was always present to the soul,—was all the true soul took note of. It was a duty not to look!" At this, Fuller (with much "excitement," Peabody reported) gave a lengthy reply to Emerson's high ethical salvo, which Healey summarized as follows:

> [She] thought it the climax of sin to despair. She believed evil to be a good in the grand scheme of things. She would not recognize it as a blunder. She must consider its scope a noble one. In one word, she would not accept the world—for she felt within herself the power to reject it—did she not believe evil working in it for good! Man had gained more than he lost by his fall. The ninety-nine sheep in the parable were of less value than the "lost found," over which there was joy in heaven.

Fuller's Romanticized version of the ancient theological doctrine of the "Fortunate Fall" did not impress Emerson. "To imagine it possible to fall [is] to *begin* to fall," he declared. For Fuller that missed the point: not the ethics of evil but the psychology of sin; not immoral conduct but immoral imaginings, which, precisely *because* of their dangerous and painful character, were necessary to moral and intellectual growth. As she said at the next meeting, on the descending and searching Orpheus: "There is nothing worth knowing that has not some penalty attached to it. We pay it the more willingly in proportion as we grow wise. Depth, altitude, diffusion, are the three births of Time. It is this which makes the German cover the operations of the miner with a mystic veil. Bostonians laugh at the Germans because they think." Nor was it just the German Romantics for whom this circuitous plot was true. Goethe, she said, like the Neoplatonists, did not believe with Emerson "that all things were in our own souls, but that they existed in *the original souls*, . . . and we must go out to seek them." "The Seeker," she concluded, underlining the myth's modernity, "represents the Spirit of the Age." The Greek myths were another incarnation of her *Dial* tales' questing Romantic philosophy.[18]

According to Caroline Healey Dall, Fuller considered her meetings a failure. Peabody thought the problem was the large intellectual gap between her and her class: "Even in the point of erudition, which Margaret did not profess, on the subject, she proved the best informed of the party, while no one brought an idea, except herself." This was somewhat of an exaggeration. Charles Wheeler occasionally interjected useful etymological explanations in support of her arguments, and Hedge, Clarke, Sturgis, the Ripleys, and Peabody herself sometimes made interesting observations, while Emerson, if nothing else, served as a wonderful intellectual foil. But it seems to have been true that when it came to larger mythic interpretations, or even sustained literary exegeses, Fuller provided the overwhelming bulk. Yet, since similar gulfs were present in her highly successful women's Conversations, one wonders why she was not able to narrow the gaps here. Emerson thought the problem was the presence of men, who simply outtalked even the most talkative women. "Margaret spoke well,—she could not otherwise," he recalled. "But I remember that she seemed encumbered, or interrupted, by the headiness or incapacity of the men, whom she had not had the advantage of training, and who fancied, no doubt, that, on such a question, they, too, must assert and dogmatize." If one puts aside Emerson's little ironic digs at Fuller's dogmatism, this seems entirely plausible, considering that the Transcendentalist men were, after all, professional talkers, including of course Emerson. "The young people wished to know what possessed me to tease you with so much prose, & becloud the fine conversation," he told her after their first exchange at the second meeting. "I could only answer that it was not an acute fit of Monday evening, but was chronic & constitutional with me, & I asked them in my turn when they had heard me talk anything else? So I silenced them." Perhaps, too, there were sexual inhibitions in discussing all the debauchery and deflowering found in the myths. (At one point Fuller teasingly suggested that there were "too many clergymen" to discuss the fertile Diana of Ephesus, which elicited a probably awkward laugh.)[19]

The biggest obstacles, though, seem to have been two subtler ones. Fuller's hybrid "Conversations" genre of paid theater, intellectual revelation, casual bantering, and classroom didacticism seems to have been harder for her to bring off in these more formal meetings than it had been in her more sisterly women's Conversations. "The conversation last evening was 'well performed' still it seemed too much like a performance," Elizabeth Hoar complained to Emerson after the fourth meeting. (Caroline Sturgis registered her dissatisfaction by falling asleep on the arm of the sofa.) Most important was the quasireligious gulf between Fuller and most of her class, male *and* female, which Peabody thought went deeper than just Fuller's superior grasp of the German Romantic mythographic theories that underlay her interpretations. "They come,—myself among the number,—I confess,—to be entertained; but she has a higher purpose," to find "the spirit which giveth life." In searching for such a deeply felt literary religion in the Greek myths, Fuller seems to have been pretty much on her own.[20]

Yet her mythology meetings were not a historical failure. In counterposing her Romantic quest philosophy to (in Peabody's phrase) Emerson's "uncompromising idealism," she publicly aired for the first time her distinctive intellectual position within the Transcendentalist circle. Her mythological meetings also cleared a few cultural paths. Considering they took place in hyperevangelical antebellum America a decade and a half before Thomas Bulfinch's *Age of Fable* made the classic myths widely available to American readers, it is remarkable that they occurred at all. They were even on the cutting edge of American Transcendentalism. Within the next couple of years, Emerson and Thoreau would start publishing their "Ethnical Scriptures" series in the *Dial*, while Clarke, inspired by her classes, would begin his mythological research that thirty years later would culminate in his immensely popular *Ten Great Religions*, a pioneering book in American comparative religious studies. Of course, later Victorian philologists and anthropologists would undoubtedly have found the classes' mythic meanderings appallingly amateurish and dogmatic—although subsequent literary modernists, who were here as elsewhere closer to the Romantics, would say the same thing about the Victorians' positivist and pedantic glosses. In any case, she was after neither "science" nor scholarship but two cultural explorations: the metahistory of "modernity" and, in a venerable Plutarchian spirit, the stimulation of higher thought and character. The Hegelian educator William Torrey Harris, who would deplore Fuller's "Goethean" distortions of German thought, would exclaim in a lecture on her: "Her conversations on the Greeks and Romans showed a wonderful insight!" Her failed experiment presaged bigger cultural things than she could have guessed.[21]

III

With the publication of "Leila" in the *Dial*'s April 1841 issue, Fuller ended her first year of editorship. Until then, she had written very little for the magazine. "It is very difficult to me to resolve on publishing any of my writing," she had confessed at the end of the winter to Channing. "It never seems worth it, but the topmost bubble on my life; and the world, the Public alas!—give me to realize that there are *individuals* to whom I can speak." By that spring, though, as she came out of her depression, she accelerated her output, and by the fifth issue she was writing over a third of every number: essays, review articles, book notices, sketches, and some poetry, along with most of the last-minute filler required by each quarto number's 136 pages. Mostly, she contributed criticism informed by her formalist organicism and comparativist historicism that she distilled from Goethe, Schiller, and the Schlegels. That second year she also introduced two new forms. One was the literary dialogue, a standard genre in European Romantic criticism, rarely used by American critics but one she had experimented with both in her journal and, most recently, in her bookstore "Chats" in Brownson's *Boston Quarterly Review*. As a famous conversationalist, she obviously took to the genre, but she also liked it because it avoided what she so much disliked about essays in English and American quarterlies. "The regular build of an Essay (maugre the unpretending name) is dangerous," she had written in her *Dial* notebook projecting possible dialogues. "It tempts to round the piece into a whole by filling up the gaps between the thoughts with—words—words—words."[22]

Her two dialogues that year suggest Fuller also liked the genre because it kept open critical questions about which she felt ambivalent. Thus in "Dialogue. Poet. Critic" in the April issue, an overearnest critic confronts a hypersensitive poet over the classic Romantic problem of judging works presumed to be products of a divinely inspired individual imagination. "I must . . . verify the justice of my reasonings," pleads Critic. "I must examine, compare, sift, and winnow. . . . I cannot pass on till I know what I feel and why." This does not impress Poet, however, who abuses him for condemning works he could not understand because he could never create them. Two issues later, Fuller addressed the art-criticism dilemma more seriously, in "Festus," through the duo of Aglauron and Laurie, her heavier replacements for her old bookstore "Chats"' pedantic Professor Partridge and sentimental Reverend Nightshade. The text they argue about is the young English poet Philip James Bailey's two-year-old *Festus*, a labored but voguish product of the "Spasmodic School," whose theme "Evil the way to good" Fuller unsurprisingly liked. (The *North American*'s George Ticknor declared it simply "wicked.") But mainly she uses the Faustian poetic drama to explore the tensions between two modes of criticism she had put in opposition in her "Short Essay on Critics." The "apprehensive" Laurie advances two defenses of *Festus*. One is organicist: it successfully reproduces the crude thoughts of a tortured young man through a hero whose naiveté facilitates his openness to diverse worlds of experience essential to a *Bildungsroman*. The other is historicist: as a "subjective" and "*sincere*" book, it matches our inward-turned modern age. The judicial Wordsworthian Aglauron, however, rips into the poem's bombast, until Laurie finally concedes that perhaps he was too indulgent by ignoring formal performance, and Aglauron agrees that one can initially only judge a "poem of great opportunities" in Laurie's apprehensive way. Fuller's playlet also exposed a bit of autobiography. Aglauron's recording of Laurie's arguments in a notebook allowed the "apprehensive" critic to get over his writer's block, "for, maugre all my faith in the public mind, I do confess, I am more easily drawn out by the private one, whose relations with mine are so established." So, too, with Fuller, whose coterie magazine was starting to draw out her public voice—even if through the mouths of a couple of male dummies.[23]

In the same October number, Fuller also introduced her readers to art music. This was still an exotic form in America. Only that February the Boston Academy of Music had inaugurated the city's first regular concerts of secular orchestral music and the country's first series devoted to Beethoven's symphonic repertoire. These historic concerts generated tremendous excitement in (as one reviewer characterized them) their "small, but select" audiences, which Fuller followed up with her article "Lives of the Great Composers." A fifty-five-page collective biography of Bach, Handel, Haydn, Mozart, and Beethoven based on a series of recent German studies, it made almost the first elaborate American statement on behalf of the "modern" orchestral repertoire. First, she told her readers, echoing the famous declaration of the German Romantic E. T. A. Hoffmann, art music expressed the highest realms of human consciousness. Its simultaneously condensed, rapid, and delicate tones and rhythms, together with its purely abstract character allowed it to fuse the most instinctively affecting and the most deeply spiritual. Second, it was now "*the* living, growing art," thanks to the canon established by German critics during the last several decades. This list was not arbitrary or nationalistic but rooted in three fundamental principles of a "modern" aesthetic revolution: reliance on the "intuitive faculty," an "affirmative" attitude toward creative efforts, and "love of the work for its own sake." Finally, that revolution's polestar deserved all the accolades the German critics applied to him. Stern yet tender, painful yet soaring, intellectual yet prophetic—Beethoven, indeed, "seems to have chronicled all the sobs, the heart-heavings, and god-like Promethean thefts of the Earth-spirit." In articulating this now familiar claim for Beethoven's achievement as his tension-filled synthesis of (in the words of a recent musicologist) "structural control and expressive vehemence," she was again echoing her German Romantics, but in America, where his first performances produced mostly bafflement and consternation, just saying it was an avant-garde intervention. She also threw in a few domestic accents. She extolled Beethoven's "God-like" democratic demeanor radically unlike that of the politically deferential Goethe. And she was awestruck by Beethoven's stormy life of personal tragedies and public triumphs, the central fact of the modern artist-intellectual.[24]

Fuller's "half-effaced pencil" portrait was reprinted in the German émigré H. Theodor Hach's recently founded *Musical Magazine*, which published it with a selection of its usual English and German music criticism and where it undoubtedly found a receptive audience among Boston's small but growing numbers of art music aficionados. Of course, her quasi-religious take on the form squared with broader historical resonances, although obviously not those elitist ones that recent populist-minded scholars have detected in the Victorian era's "sacralization" of art music. For the Romantic Fuller, art music was neither a status marker nor a medium for controlling the rambunctious lower classes, but a unique conveyer of the transcendental spirit. And it was largely so too, if not for Emerson, who cheerfully claimed to be "tone-deaf," certainly for their younger, arts-minded colleagues John Sullivan Dwight, Christopher Cranch, George William Curtis, and Charles A. Dana, who found in her music reviews inspiration for their own belief in art music as the profoundest expression of religious and even social democratic aspirations.[25]

Yet her sketch barely skimmed the surface of her enthrallment with art music, especially Beethoven's. "Oh William, what majesty what depth, what tearful sweetness of the human heart, what triumphs of the Angel mind!" she exclaimed in her April 5 letter to Channing, after attending two nights earlier the Boston Academy's American debut of Beethoven's Fifth Symphony. "When I read his life I said I will never repine. When I heard this symphony I said I will triumph more and more above the deepening abysses." And when the abyss seemed close, her rapture over Beethoven's music grew stronger, she confessed, than the reverence she had even once felt for Plato, Goethe, Shakespeare, and all her other past genius-inspirers. "I think most of her friends will remember to have felt, at one time or another, some uneasiness, as if this athletic soul craved a larger atmosphere than it found," recalled Emerson, who had heard that tone from her more than he cared to. "She found no full expression of it but in music." Emerson was surely right. Even in the later music criticism of Dwight, who would build a half-century career echoing her religio-aesthetic line, one does not find the same Hoffmanesque "terror . . . pain . . . and endless striving" that Fuller gloried in almost as much as music's "triumphs."[26]

Although Fuller introduced art music and critical theory in the *Dial*, the bulk of her pieces were practical criticism. Here again she was largely on her own. Like most European Romantics, who preferred literary essays to formal critiques, the Transcendentalists wrote very little in this mode, leaving Fuller's thirty-five articles and reviews as almost the totality of the magazine's formal criticism. Yet her range was limited. She wrote almost nothing on Continental authors, her literary specialty, possibly because of the paucity of recent English translations, which she must have thought even her *Dial* readers needed. She had several manuscript essays on contemporary French novelists, but she held them back, perhaps because she felt their sensationalism made them a bad fit for a highbrow religious and philosophical journal. Even though her favorite German Romantic authors were becoming the rage in young Transcendentalist-influenced circles, she was determined not to publish anything old hat on them. "Read Carlyle and see what I have to say that he has not said," she wrote in her *Dial* notebook of a possible essay on Novalis, which never appeared.[27]

That left the Anglophone quarterlies' staple, English and American belles-lettres, to which to apply her cosmopolitan standards. She often compared the English Romantics to one or more of her lodestars Dante, Shakespeare, and Goethe. She also pushed against received Romantic Anglo-American opinion. The first collection of Alfred, Lord Tennyson, then little known in America, was something new under the sun, she told her readers. Not only in his rich musicality did it far surpass "stock poetry . . . deeply tainted with a sentimental egoism" but it did higher verse as well, which badly suffered from a surfeit of the "over-ethical or over-passionate." Her hostility to Romantic moralism even extended to the increasingly popular Thomas Carlyle, whom she had recently told Parker she had "outgrown," further shocking him with the accurate prediction that in the future the Scot's reputation would decline while Coleridge's fame would grow. In her review of Carlyle's recently published *On Heroes, Hero-Worship, and the He-*

roic in History, which she had knocked in her mythology class for its "vulgar" hero worship, she duly noted her generation's debt for his "truthful earnestness," his exposure of modern shams, and his sarcastic and picturesque wit, "rarely equalled in any age of English literature." But she upbraided him for his "endless repetition" and "hammering on a thought till every sense of the reader aches." She also decried what she detected was behind it: "an arrogant bitterness of tone which seems growing upon him (as alas! it is too apt to grow upon Reformers)" and which threatened to eclipse his earlier reputation as a self-poised Goethean humanist. A few months later Carlyle would complain to Emerson that the *Dial* badly needed a "stalwart Yankee *man*, with colour in the cheeks of him, and a coat on his back!" Perhaps he did not count a stalwart Yankee woman.[28]

Fuller's notices of American books also cut against popular "romantic" tastes. She tried to get around her deep doubts about America's literary prospects by proceeding along three tracks that she would roughly follow in the years ahead: ignoring popular sensationalist and sentimental authors, dismissing decorous middlebrow ones, and trying to discover a few "original" buds of "genius." Her second category seems to have given her no great difficulty. "Longfellow sent us his poems," she wrote Emerson. "If you have toleration for them, it would be well to have a short notice written by some one (*not* me)." Eventually she wrote a terse, one-sentence notice of his third volume of poetry, *Poems on Slavery*: "The thinnest of all Mr. Longfellow's thin books; spirited and polished like its forerunners; but the topic would warrant a deeper tone." James Russell Lowell, whom she had reluctantly published, presented a bit of a problem. Young, ambitious, petted by his young Brahmin friends, and desperate to launch his literary career, he had just published his first book of poetry, *A Year's Life*, and expectantly awaited the critics' verdict. Fuller tried to find *some* value in it: "Superficial, full of obvious cadences and obvious thoughts; but sweet, fluent, in a large style, and breathing the life of religious love." In sum, a bad first book from a promising "noble" youth.[29]

For potential young geniuses, she found only one. She had taken awhile to find him. Six years earlier in an old *Token* she had stumbled across the struggling Nathaniel Hawthorne's early anonymous story "The Gentle Boy," which she had assumed a woman had written because of its "grace and delicacy of feeling," a common characterization of his stories then. She corrected her mistake in her review of his enlarged edition of his first collection of stories, *Twice-Told Tales*. It was not sentiment, she said, that Hawthorne's stories showed but "what is rarest in this superficial, bustling community, a great reserve of thought and strength never yet at all brought forth." Yet that restraint was probably also the source of his biggest weakness: his characters were often more like phantoms than living figures. "But this would be otherwise, probably," she added, "were the genius fully roused to its work, and initiated into its own life, so as to paint with blood-warm colors. This frigidity and thinness of design usually bespeaks a want of the deeper experiences, for which no talent at observation, no sympathies, however ready and delicate, can compensate. We wait new missives from the same hand." Here with a few strokes, she fingered, as she had Thoreau's rhetorical difficulties, precisely the problems of remoteness and insubstantiality that would worry the budding Hawthorne about his fiction all of his life. Skepticism about American literature does not seem to have interfered with her prescient canonizing.[30]

Only in one writer she appraised in the *Dial* did she find these "deeper experiences." Her recognition was overdue. After five years of researching, outlining, and piling up notes, sometime before starting the *Dial*, she had decided to abandon her life of Goethe. She did not say exactly why, but one can guess at the reasons. One was publishing. Her deadline for doing it for Ripley's *Specimens of Foreign Standard Literature* series had run out, and the next year the series would end. Another was that her Conversations and magazine took up most of her time. Anna Jameson's "ungenerous" refusal to share her Goethe materials revealed, though, probably the main reason, which she herself had long worried about: to write the first major biography of the greatest writer of the modern era would have necessitated her going to Germany, which was financially out of the question. As for postponing it, she shuddered at the thought, she told Emerson, of "living so long in the shadow of one mind." That left only one option: to salvage her labors by publishing their fruits in the journal designed specifically for such rough operations.[31]

Much had happened to Goethe's reputation since he had died a decade earlier, when Fuller and her fellow young Germanico James Clarke had taken him up as their "master." Thanks partly to the growing interest in German literature that the Transcendentalists had provoked, the furiously anti-Goethe prejudices in American journals were softening a bit. But *why* the Weimar poet was deemed such a great writer remained for most Americans a mystery. On this point, even the Transcendentalists were confused. Clarke, their enterprising preacher, touted him, as Carlyle did, as a ceaseless actor and truth-teller. The more radical Ripley and Parker claimed him as a fellow liberal spiritualist, blanching, however, at his sexual conduct. Only Emerson—who had "contrived" to read, with Fuller's help, almost all of the fifty-five-volume German Goethe edition—had a tolerable sense of the range of his character: his "pagan" naturalism (which Emerson liked), his anti-idealism (which Emerson disliked), and his supposedly "velvet life" (which Emerson abhorred). ("The Puritan in me accepts no apology for bad morals in such as *he*," he confessed to Carlyle.) In two *Dial* essays Fuller raised the ongoing debate over Goethe to a new intellectual plane.[32]

She made her first push in the January 1841 *Dial* in response to Harvard professor Cornelius Felton's translation of *Die deutsche Literatur* (*History of German Literature*), a volume in Ripley's series by Wolfgang Menzel. A knowledgeable but unscrupulous critic and ferociously conservative Prussian nationalist, Menzel had included in his book a blistering attack on Goethe as a hedonistic courtier and indifferent patriot, which seemed to confirm everything his detractors, including pro-German ones like Longfellow, had been saying about him. Parker had opened the assault in the January 1841 *Dial* with a scorching critique of Menzel's survey, ridiculing everything from his narrowly political literary judgments to his predilection for personal invective. Fuller followed next with a rousing critical defense of Goethe. Menzel was a clever "Philistine," or a critic, she said, following Goethe, who attempted to comprehend genius only "by a rule beneath which he never lived." She also marshaled a couple of specific "apprehensive" arguments. One was historical. Goethe's much reviled cultivation of taste had supplied precisely what was needed to balance German writers' tendency to obscurity, extravagance, and pedantry. Her other was psychological. Goethe's personal "faults" that dogmatic moralists like Menzel were forever decrying had facilitated the poet's greatest artistic achievements. His skepticism ensured his universality of observation, and his lamented "subtlety, isolation, and distance" allowed him to turn life into art. As for Menzel's pitiful claims about Goethe's supposed debauchery, she answered contemptuously, "Here are sixty volumes, by himself and others, which contain sufficient evidence of a life of severe labor, steadfast forbearance, and an intellectual growth almost unparalleled."[33]

In the *Dial*'s July issue, she gave her readers a condensed forty-one-page treatise on the titanic German. She began her "Goethe" with a gambit, his move to the court of the young duke of Saxe-Weimar. "From this time forward he seems a listener to nature, but not himself the highest product of nature, a priest to the soul of nature." On the surface, this thesis would seem to have echoed Emerson, who in his previous year's *Dial* essay "Thoughts on Modern Literature" had called Goethe "the poet of the Actual, not of the ideal." The difference, however, was vast. To begin with, as in her Menzel article, she *defended* many of Goethe's worldly tendencies as reflections of his "Dämonische," or creative instinct, which gave him artistically exploitable experience. More important critically, Fuller engaged Goethe's works as literary texts, unlike both Emerson and Carlyle, who treated the poet mainly as a moral prophet. Indeed, although she praised *Faust* as containing "the great idea of his life . . . the progress of the soul through the various forms of existence," she picked out the compositions of his classical period, from *Iphigenie auf Tauris* through *Wilhelm Meister*, as the creative high point of his career. As for the relation between Goethe's life and works, she ridiculed all attempts to reduce Goethe's writings to moral messages. The hordes of critics who indignantly howled at Goethe's tragically ironic novel of sexual infidelity, *Die Wahlverwandtschaften* (*Elective Affinities*), were simply too dense to see that the entire tendency of this "surpassingly beautiful" book was severely moral. Perhaps, she sarcastically suggested, they would have been comforted if he had "larded his work here and there with ejaculations of horror and surprise," or, at least, had declared his sentiments in the "sixthly, seventhly, and eighthly style of the old-fashioned sermon." Instead of irrelevant moralism, she proposed two broadly aesthetic ways of understanding Goethe's writings. First, readers needed to grasp his fictive strategies for expressing his ironic moral sensibility. A character like Tasso, in *Torquato Tasso*, for example, she noted, drew deeply on Goethe's own suppressed Promethean self, although seemingly very unlike the self-poised poet. By contrast, the comparatively worldly figure of Wilhelm Meister served not as simply a vehicle for Goethe's point of view but as a window through which he was able to portray a broader fictive world. Second, at its deepest level, readers had to realize that that fictive world—which Emerson disparaged as artificial and amoral—gave them not a moral cognition at all but a spellbinding, almost mystical, sense of the inward reality of an astonishingly various outer world.[34]

Yet in the end, she, too, wanted something from Goethe she could not find. If Emerson wished Goethe had been more of an inspired prophet, Fuller wished he had been more of an inspired artist—or, as she wrote, an artist who would have "not stopped at humanity," as he had done at Weimar, "but regarded it as symbolical of the divine." Or, as she put it in Goethe's striving terms, in answer to his famous maxim—"'Care is taken that the trees grow not up into the heavens'"— "Ay, Goethe, but in proportion to their force of aspiration is their height!" Besides religion, she wanted from Goethe a deeply felt portrayal of love. Geniuses like Goethe, she said,

> *see* all that others *live*, and, if you feel a want of a faculty in them, it is hard to say they have it not, lest next moment they puzzle you by giving some indication of it. Yet they are not, nay *know* not, they only discern. The difference is that between sight and life, prescience and being, wisdom and love. Thus with Goethe. Naturally of a deep mind and shallow heart, he felt the sway of the affections enough to appreciate their working in other men, but never enough to receive their inmost regenerating influence.

In a word, she craved to see in Goethe a Romantic analogue of Christian agape, but through human consciousness and without Christian revelation. This was, of course, a spiritual version of a consciously self-transcendent will that he had learned to distrust in favor of nature's inner entelechy. Yet Dante, she claimed, had illuminated such an ideal, as well as, for our more anguished modern time, Novalis and Beethoven. These last were the "flame-like" figures who, ironically, she said, gave through their struggles, both high and low, more peace than Goethe's serene "self-collection," which, after all, was really a "collection of means for work" rather than a way of divining "the deepest truths of being." Still, she could not leave Goethe on that note. In her conclusion she extracts from his works one plausible Romantic religious element, which she says he most perfectly portrayed in his verse play *Iphigenie auf Tauris*, where the many-sided redeeming character of Iphigenie, like all his major female figures, embodied the highest principle in his writing—the beautiful contradictions of "virgin womanhood." "Where else is such a picture to be found? she asked.

> It was not the courtier, nor the man of the world, nor the connoisseur, nor the friend of Mephistopheles, nor Wilhelm the Master, nor Egmont the generous free liver, that saw Iphigenia in the world of spirits, but Goethe in his first-born glory, Goethe the poet, Goethe designed to be the keenest star in a new constellation. Let us enter into his higher tendency, thank him for such angels as Iphigenia, whose simple truth mocks at all his wise "Beschrankungen," and hope the hour when, girt about with many such, he may confess, contrary to his opinion, given in his latest days, that it *is* well worth while to live seventy years, if only to find that they are nothing in the sight of God.

So having begun by defending the worldly Goethe, she ended with a spiritual world now inhabited by the poet and enveloped in the "Eternal Feminine," Goethe's highest religious principle, where judgment came in angelic glimpses.[35]

"Goethe" was the high-water mark of Fuller's *Dial* criticism. The *New-Yorker* called it "luminous," and even the popular *Godey's Lady's Book* acclaimed it "beautifully written." Her Transcendentalist friends lavished unstinting praise on it. Emerson, who would liberally crib from it in his essay "Goethe" in *Represen-tative Men*, wrote to her two days after it came out: "I admired with all the world the Article on Goethe. I admired it first alone, and was very glad to learn I had so much company." Several years later, he would write, "Nowhere did Goethe find a braver, more intelligent, or more sympathetic reader." To be sure, as the distil-lation of a decade of intense thought and reading, her essay was overpacked. Nor would many modern critics likely find its fervid Romantic tones and striving re-ligious longings very congenial. Yet its intellectual empathy, aesthetic sensitiv-ity, and, above all, central question—Goethe as Romantic visionary or classical artist?—raised it far beyond the moralistic bugaboos in the Anglophone world that would make progress in understanding him, as one scholar has noted, "painfully slow" for the rest of the century.[36]

What was true of Fuller's "Goethe" was also true of some of her best literary pieces in the *Dial*: she infused into them a critical sophistication almost unique in antebellum criticism. Without attempting, like Coleridge, the German Romantics' principal English interpreter, a reconstruction of their concepts, she applied them with authority, relentlessness, and originality. That she tried to strike this "higher tone of criticism" in a country whose cultural character she distrusted, with an assistant whose literary standards she did not entirely share, and for a magazine that was, practically speaking, "a private and friendly service" for an unruly circle of half-talented and hesitant questing souls gave a certain heroic cast to her ef-forts. Her *Dial* criticism also showed some development in her writing. Emerson and Hedge thought she wrote some of her best pieces in the magazine, and other friends thought they demonstrated a notable new pungency, texture, and vocal strength. "You are gaining at length, it seems to me, the kind of free, simple, pointed, manly expression which you desire," Channing wrote to her after her second year as *Dial* editor, innocently invoking the gendered adjective she her-self often applied to her ideal critic. "And how close and comprehensive your observation is!" Ezra Pound would later deny, contra Whitman, that great readers are necessary for a great poet, but he said nothing about small audiences for a maturing critic.[37]

IV

While accelerating her *Dial* output that spring, she was also thinking about where to live. With her mother not scheduled to return until June and the children living elsewhere, she and her mother agreed that it hardly made financial sense to con-tinue to rent Willow Brook after the lease expired in April. Yet renting in the city was too expensive. One possibility was to join the new Brook Farm community in West Roxbury, which George and Sophia Ripley had formed at the end of March with a group of Transcendentalist-influenced writers, teachers, and ministers to teach and farm cooperatively. The idea had a logic. In the wake of the continuing economic depression and millennialist hopes inspired by decades of religious revivals, for the past year socialistic communities had proliferated, soon numbering over forty, mostly in the Northeast, with Fourierist Associationism's movement alone counting nearly one hundred thousand adherents. The Transcendentalists were also ideologically prepared. For the last several years, Emerson had been preaching that the age's commercial and materialist obsessions were impeding Americans' organic self-culture, and radical Transcendentalists like Ripley and Brownson had been denouncing their region's new factory "lords" for stripping laborers of their human dignity. Yet the troops hesitated. In the fall, the Ripleys met with Emerson, Alcott, and Fuller to discuss the "new social plans," but all three soon backed out. Emerson, who genuinely worried about all the inequalities around him, convinced himself that his "long trumpeted theory . . . that one man is a counterpoise to a city" required him to stay put in Concord. ("Shall I raise the siege of this hencoop & march baffled away to a pretended siege of Babylon?" he quizzically asked in his journal.) For several months, Fuller flirted with moving with her mother, who endorsed the idea, and with Channing, who had just resigned his ministry in Cincinnati. However, by summer's end, with Channing's plans still unsettled, and her brother Richard now talking about going to college in Cambridge, Fuller scotched the plan.[38]

As these practical maneuverings would suggest, Fuller's initial interest in the community was not especially ideological. She loved nature, but her uncongenial three years in Groton seem to have soured her on Massachusetts country communities. (The "savages of our New-England towns," she had reportedly said in one Conversation, recalling that experience, did not appear to have much interest in communing with nature.) She also had doubts about the leadership of the courageous but "heavy" preaching Ripley and his zealous but stilted wife Sophia. Nor, for that matter, did she have much confidence in the Transcendentalists' reform capacities. "We are not ripe to reconstruct society yet," she had told Channing in December after several talks with the Ripleys and Emerson. "Mr E. knows deepest what he wants, but not well how to get it. Mr R. has a better perception of means, less insight as to principles." In any case, although she felt sure that many persons would soon "somehow, somewhere, throw off a part, at least, of these terrible weights of the social contract," she knew *she* did not have the stuff, the needs, *or* the outlook of a social reformer. "Others have looked at society with far deeper consideration than I," she confessed to Channing the day after the Ripleys and their band of fifteen eager "colonists" moved into their farmhouse. "Also, I do not believe in Society. I feel that every man must struggle with these enormous ills in some way, in every age; in that of Moses, or Plato, or Angelo, as in our own. So it has not moved me much to see my time so corrupt, but it would if I were in a false position." She was not sanguine about the ultimate result either: "I do not know what their scheme will ripen to; at present it does not deeply engage my hopes. It is thus far only a little better way than others. I doubt if they will get free from all they deprecate in society."[39]

Not joining the "fledglings of Community" did not cut her off from them, however. That May she made the first of many visits over the next several years. Like their skeptical neighbors, she was also happy to do business with them, although the family cow she got Richard to sell them the first week does not seem to have done much for her reputation as a socialist. "Our transcendental heifer, belonging to Miss Margaret Fuller . . . is very fractious, I believe, and apt to kick over the milk pail," the Brook Farmer Hawthorne chuckled to Sophia Peabody, his fiancée and Fuller's Conversation assistant. "Thou knowest best, whether, in these traits of character, she resembles her mistress." Fuller's cleft-upper-lipped youngest brother Lloyd, whom she and her mother sent to the Farm for schooling, posed a more serious challenge for the community. Although apparently not yet showing the paranoia that would later make his family commit him to McLean Asylum, he does not seem to have had too firm a grasp on the community's principles. "I have a letter from Lloyd," Fuller wrote to Richard in late May, "stating that 'he did not like the Community as he expected, for he has to work when he does not wish to'!!" Evidently not mollified, he started writing in his journal denunciations of his fellow farmers, which he dropped in conspicuous places. "Lloyd Fuller, who has all the Fuller faults (entre nous . . .) without their merits," Sophia Ripley wrote stoically to Dwight, "serves to show us how a refractory member can be kept in check by the influence of the rest." Apparently, not very well, however, as that winter the members asked Margaret to remove him. "I do not know what to make of him, or what can be done with him," she wrote Richard worriedly after one visit with him. "He seemed very sweet, but every thing he said was so unreal." For someone who doubted the Brook Farmers' capacity to get free of "enormous ills," Fuller was not shy about sending them a hard case.[40]

Meanwhile, the new utopian spirit entered her home through her favorite brother, Richard. He was passing through a critical time. Rather than wanting to be her "man of business," he had just quit his hated wholesale dry-goods clerk job in Boston and was hoping to enter Harvard as an advanced sophomore. To cut expenses while preparing for his entrance examinations, that fall he moved into a bare room in a Concord farmer's house and in the spirit of his father (he thought) consumed little more than bread and water while studying fourteen hours a day. Margaret, hoping that Emerson's "pure and steadfast life" would rub off on him, also arranged to have him virtually adopted into the extended Emerson family circle. Elizabeth Hoar heard him recite his Homer and Virgil, Lidian Emerson cooked him meat pies, and for a small fee Thoreau took him on nature walks and tutored him in books and Indian lore. "I suppose even those who can live on board nails may sometimes wish to earn a little money," Fuller quipped to Emerson. The "great man" himself even gave his Transcendental blessing to Richard's desire to quit a commercial career in favor of some vocation, as Richard put it, "not only more elevated but better conformed to conscience." "He told me such feelings as mine were shared by many," including those "of the favored classes," he excitedly wrote Margaret. This was heady stuff for a headstrong and insecure eighteen-year-old mercantile dropout, which became clear when he started sending her militant Transcendentalist screeds cheering the "good scruff[s]" Emerson in his lectures "gave that starched, well dressed, dank bit of foppery & folly" nurtured by cities and "Mammon"-loving professions. By early December, he was reporting that "Mr Emerson (with true transcendentalism, which will not be clogged in mud of Earth, where many *grovel*) came to my abode . . . & took me to hear his lecture." He also airily told her that he did not care a fig "whether the institutions of man be worthy to stand, or not." She had warned Richard about Alcott's quixotic radicalism, but this kind of parodic Transcendentalism was even more worrisome, not only, of course, because it did not portend very well for the success of her "chief hope," but also because she evidently feared he was turning into a provincial crank. "You go to an extreme in your denunciation of cities and the social institutions," she replied.

> *These* are a growth also, and as well as the diseases which come upon them, under the control of the One spirit as much as the great tree on which the insects prey and in whose bark the busy bird has made many a wound. When we get the proper perspective of these things we shall find man however artificial still a part of Nature. . . . One may be gossiping and vulgar and idle in the country,—earnest, wise and noble in the city. Nature cannot be kept from us while there is a sky above with so much as one star to remind us of prayer in the silent night.

Two weeks later, she moved from defending cities to defending money. After mentioning she had just sent him some, she noted:

> So you see even your frugality does not enable you wholly to dispense with the circulating medium you so much dispise and whose use, when you have thought more deeply on these subjects, you will find to have been indispensable to the production of the arts, of literature and all that distinguishes civilized man. It is abused like all good things, but without it you would not have had your Horace and Virgil stimulated by whose society you read the woods and fields to more advantage than Stilman Lawrence, or Edward Rice.[41]

These last allusions to books and nature seem to have gotten his attention because he soon started backpedaling. By the time he started Harvard in the spring, he even confessed to Margaret the family wound that was probably behind much of his resentment and anxiety: his "hope, on coming here that I should be able to show that my father's blood circulated in at least one of his sons." He closed on a suitably chastened note: "I have discovered that mere love or admiration of the beautiful, without culture makes but a rude thinker after all." Margaret, of course, readily praised him for *that* insight but also pressed her advantage. She reminded him of their father's stellar record at Harvard and heroic life in politics, the importance of reading Transcendentalist philosophical texts critically, and the value of "self-reliance" *and* knowledge gained through "slow gradations of travel, study, speech, silence, bravery, and patience" as preached by "my Ancients." Judging by his increasing (as Margaret complacently put it) "attention to the importance of externals," her moderating inoculation of Richard with a little cosmopolitan classical virtue seems to have taken at least better than Brook Farm's attempt to inject Lloyd with a little "Oversoul."[42]

V

On April 6, 1841, the morning after the Beethoven Fifth Symphony concert at the Boston Academy, Fuller left Willow Brook, with *Dial* manuscripts in tow, for a year-

and-a-half vagabondage among the homes and vacation houses of her many friends. As she had been periodically doing since her adolescence, she stopped at the Farrars' Kirkland Street house in Cambridge, where she stayed for a month before leaving to spend a few days at Brook Farm and a couple of weeks at Emerson's Bush, and by early June, she was back at the Farrars. On July 30, she took her papers with her to Newport, where she and Caroline Sturgis lived in a farmhouse that William Ellery Channing's daughter Mary had arranged for them to rent. Beach scenes always delighted Fuller, but the picturesque "Paradise Farm," nestled in a lush sycamore grove along Sachuset beach, put her in an especially gay mood. While she and Caroline roamed the beach "in a somewhat savage dishabille," far from the "fashion-ables," the local farming people seemed wrapped in a Romantic-tale mist rather like what some Brook Farmers had probably imagined enveloped their fellow proletarians in West Roxbury. "This half fisherman, half farmer life seems very favorable to manliness," she wrote Willliam Channing. "I like to talk with fishermen, they are not boorish, nor limited, but keen-eyed and of a certain rude gentleness." Describing a young fisherman she had seen scrambling up a rock with his screaming and laughing little girl, who kept wanting to go farther, she noted, "When she found he did not wish it, she leaned against his shoulder, and he sat, feeling himself in the child like that exquisite Madonna, and looking out over the great sea." "Manly" yet feminine father figures were evidently becalming.[43]

Her working vacations continued through the summer. After two weeks at Paradise Farm, she and Caroline moved a mile and a half over to Fuller's spinster friend Mary Rotch's "Glen" in Newport proper, just down the road from the summer house of William Ellery Channing and his family, whom she saw daily. During the second week William Channing showed up for a happy reunion. On August 23, Fuller and Caroline were back in Cambridge, where Fuller stayed with the Farrars for most of the rest of September. At the end of the month, her vacation concluded with another brief visit to Brook Farm and a nine-day stay at Bush, followed by a two-week rendezvous with Caroline at her idyllic Artichoke River-front vacation house, "Curson's Mill," in Newburyport, bringing her, she reported to Richard, "tranquillity and rest, remote from care and excitement." To avoid giving her Transcendentalist brother the wrong idea about her cavorting in nature, she quickly added: "I should not like such a life constantly. There are few characters so vigorous and of such sustained self-impulse that they do not need frequent and unexpected difficulties to awaken and keep in exercise their powers."[44]

Fuller did have one probably expected difficulty that summer and fall on which to exercise her powers. The atmosphere for communing again with Emerson at Bush over the friendship question was promising. The month before she had visited in May, the Brook Farm rejecter had tried to introduce a little "noble" Associationism by inviting the Alcotts to live with him and Lidian and their maid and cook to join them for dinners. Although only the maid accepted his proposal of "Liberty, Equality, & a common table," he got Thoreau to move in to assist him in his garden and teach him his horticulture skills. In her letter to her brother Richard at the end of May when she was staying at Bush, Margaret enticingly depicted her twenty-four-year-old knotty *Dial* contributor Thoreau as a model school keeper, serious classical scholar, and "earnest thinker" who "yet intends being a farmer." "He has a great deal of practical sense, and as he has bodily strength to boot, he may look to be a successful and happy man." She also found him, however rough as a budding writer, a gallant guide in nature. "He has a boat which he made himself, and rows me out on the pond. Last night I went out quite late and staid til the moon was almost gone, heard the whip-poor-will for the first time this year. There was a sweet breeze full of appleblossom fragrance which made the pond swell almost into waves. I had great pleasure." Thoreau, for his part, would later speak admiringly of Fuller's "masculine" intellectuality, happily so different from the sentimentality and precious delicacy that he often lamented in women. Yet he seems to have preferred to respect her androgynous character at a distance. In a disguised sketch of their friendship that he would insert in his *Week on the Concord and Merrimack Rivers*, he wrote:

> I know a woman who possesses a restless and intelligent mind, interested in her own culture, and earnest to enjoy the highest possible advantages, and I meet her with pleasure *as* a natural person who not a little provokes me, and I suppose is stimulated in turn by myself. Yet our acquaintance *plainly* does not attain to that degree of confidence and sentiment which women, which all, in fact, covet. I am glad to help her, as I am helped by her; I like very well to know her with a sort of stranger's privilege.

Knowing Thoreau's niggardliness with his "confidence and sentiment," with men *or* women, she probably appreciated that "stranger's privilege."[45]

The confidence and sentiment that she hoped to get, though, was from Emerson. Since their tense confrontations the previous fall, anxious not to lose their intimacy, he had frequently urged her to visit for "as long or as short as you will." He had also tried to get her to make allowances for his self-confessed inexpressiveness. "My love reacts on me like the recoiling gun: it is pain," he had written her after her two-week May visit, thanking her profusely for a packet she had sent him of letters of herself, Caroline, and Sam. "I was going to add something concerning the capacity to love of this reputed icicle, but the words would tell nothing." Whether because of her depression's lifting or perhaps their constant "Dialling," she seems to have become more than willing to meet him halfway. Following a mix-up about the due date for him to deliver the second part of his poem "Woodnotes" for the upcoming July *Dial*, she apologized for her "very ill-natured, perverse, and unreasonable" reaction and wrote:

> I wanted this afternoon as soon as you were really out of the house to run after you and call as little children do kiss and be friends; that would not be decorous *really* for two Editors, but it shall be so in thought shall it not?
>
>   Your affectionate
>
>   MAGDALEN
>
>   I have changed my name for tonight because Cary says this is such a Magdalen letter.[46]

Another possible reason Fuller let up on Emerson was that she now had another male Transcendentalist with whom to explore the vagaries of Romantic friendship. When she and William Channing had started corresponding after becoming close during his visit to Boston the summer before, like Emerson, he had balked at "recognizing" her mystical experiences and "determined exaggeration." "If you saw me wholly, you would not, I think, feel as you do," she had replied in one letter; "for you would recognize the force that regulates my life and tempers the ardor with an eventual calmness. You would see, too, that the more I take my flight in poetical enthusiasm, the stronger the materials I bring back for my nest." That was probably at least half-true, but she had gotten closer to the social reality in responding to his sharper charge of "arrogance" that he had detected in her effusions. "The word 'arrogance' does not, indeed, appear to me to be just," she had answered in kind. "In an environment like mine, what may have seemed too lofty or ambitious in my character was absolutely needed to keep the heart from breaking and enthusiasm from extinction."[47]

Playing the card of Boston frigidity, which he knew well, evidently helped. So, too, did seeing how well she bore up in the midst of her emotional and vocational frustrations. "I saw how faithful she had kept to her high purposes," he would later recall thinking, "how patient, gentle, and thoughtful for others, how active in self-improvement and usefulness, how wisely dignified she had been,—I could not but bow to her in reverence." In fact, after he returned to Boston, his conservative Unitarian sister Susan, who had attributed his religious heresies to his association with the Transcendentalists, was disgusted by their closeness. "I see no great change of any kind, except the effect of the dangerous influence of Margaret Fuller, who is the only human being he says he ever had entire sympathy with," she huffed to her husband. "The extent of their intimacy would surprise you," she added glumly, speaking of Channing's patient (but to Susan "weak" wife) Julia, who had stayed in Boston during his two years in Cincinnati. "When J. asked me the other day, if I would bear it, in my own case, I had to evade the question." Channing, however, found Fuller's constant encouragement to trust the "divine" energy within himself highly salutary. "The very thought of her roused manliness to emulate [her] vigorous freedom," he later wrote, even effecting, he thought, his "new-birth to real self-hood." For her part, she found in Channing, whose pastoral talents were as great as his electrifying oratory, more openness than in any male friend she had ever had. "To you, dear William I was obliged to make myself known," she would write to him years later; "others loved me with a mixture of fancy and enthusiasm excited by my talent at embellishing subjects." She also found him, as many did, morally uplifting. "Your influence on me," she wrote him later that year, "in whatever shape it comes, has always been purifying, ennobling, and of late it has been so suggestive of thoughts on the greatest themes of the times that its influence, though pensive, has been most fruitful."[48]

As this last allusion to the great themes of the day would suggest, in her exchanges with the socialist minister about their friendship, they mixed in a good deal of socially aspiring talk. To skeptical modern readers, mixing friendship with social hopes might seem fantastic or self-deluding or both. Such utopian blending, however, was rife among many European Romantics. In raising that summer and fall the ideological stakes of the love-and-friendship question, Fuller was drawing on a deep well of ancient and Romantic conceits. Plato's ladder of love was one, although his rationalism, which was somewhat akin to Emerson's, put her off; his highest love was merely Beauty expressed in ideal "forms." More useful for Fuller were two great poets she had been avidly reading for the past year: Dante, who conceptualized love as a passionate facilitator of spiritual salvation, and Edmund Spenser, who synthesized Christian and courtly traditions into a bourgeois humanistic ideal making love the true goal of epic warfare and the final stage in a hero's education. Looming the largest, though, was the key post-Christian idea of many Romantics—that through mutual introspection and questing, one could experience a tension-filled merging with an unknown "other" on the cosmic ladder to the "infinite." In the philosopher Irving Singer's formula, "For medieval Christianity, God is love; for Romantic religion, love is God."[49]

Fuller also now had in her hands before going to Bush a native urtext. Emerson had even sent her a copy of his essay "Friendship" after it was published in his *Essays: The First Series* in late March. In it he argued that the foundation of true friendship was "great and sublime parts":

> Let it be an alliance of two large formidable natures, mutually beheld, mutually feared, before yet they recognize the deep identity which beneath these disparities unites them. . . . The higher the style we demand of friendship, of course the less easy to establish it with flesh and blood. We walk alone in the world. . . . I cannot afford to speak much with my friend. If he is great, he makes me so great that I cannot descend to converse. . . . The essence of friendship is entireness, a total magnanimity and trust. It must not surmise or provide for infirmity. It treats its object as a god, that it may deify both.

Here was Emerson's sublimely stoic—and deeply individualistic—Platonic-pragmatic philosophy of personal relations: without passion, without suffering, indeed, without much talk, and always with a constant nervousness that any adaptation of the self to the other threatens one's "spiritual astronomy." These ideas and even much of the language would have sounded familiar to Fuller, of course, as they had appeared in his journal entries and letters about his friendship with her and Sturgis that he had been sending them over the previous couple of years. In re-reading them now, though, she could see his full prescription for translating two "formidable" friends into a divine sphere. That summer and fall, Fuller used her rhetorical powers to show that it was deeply flawed.[50]

When she arrived at Bush on the morning of October 1, she was clearly ready to raise her old friendship quarrel to more elevated heights. Three months earlier, she had broached the subject with Channing in a letter criticizing Emerson's philosophy of friendship as "noble" but insufficient. "We are not merely one another's priests or gods" divinely inspiring us to "Right," she had said, but one another's "ministering angels," loving by faith in a friend's unseen perfection despite imperfections and obstructions. Now with Emerson himself, she was obviously nervous, symbolically marking the difference by communicating through letters sent between her red guest room and his study across the hall, with Waldo Jr. acting as Transcendental delivery boy. "I know you do not regard our foolish critiques, except in the true way to see whether you have got the best *form* of expression," she wrote with friendly irony her first night from the "sacred space" of his library. "I like to be in your library when you are out of it," she added. "When I come to yourself, I cannot receive you, and you cannot give yourself; it does not profit. But when I cannot find you the beauty and permanence of your life come to me." Her verbal tiptoeing abruptly stopped the following night. She had written earlier in the day to the Transcendentalist bad boy Ellery Channing, whom she had recently learned, to the "great shock" of their family, was about to marry her sister Ellen. The two had fallen in love in Cincinnati, where by happenstance they had each gone earlier in the year to find jobs. Despite this "blow," in her letter to Ellery, Fuller had welcomed him into the family but also included apparently (the letter is lost) some sort of cryptic allusions to herself in relation to his friend Sam Ward and himself as a mother figure, perhaps even in the Virgin Mary mold she liked to invoke. Emerson urged her not to send the letter, evidently contesting her fancies of maternal friendship but probably also knowing that the message was not likely to go down very well with their circle's ostentatious delinquent. So she substituted a toned-down version, but she also seized the opportunity to advance for Emerson her new Romantic friendship philosophy, which she evidently thought had grounded her appeal to Ellery. After defending in her letter to Emerson her conceit of "the mother and the child as seen in another nature" as perfectly natural, she moved to the central philosophical issue: loving the self as it appears or as friendship makes it. All "accidents of time"—even the loss of every grace, beauty, and wit—she said, should not matter at all to a loving friend.

> For it was none of these we loved, but the true self, that particular emanation from God which was made to correspond with that which we are, to teach it, to learn from it, to torture it, to enchant it, to deepen and at last to satisfy our wants. You go upon the idea that we must love the most beauteous, but this is not so. We love most that which by working most powerfully on our peculiar nature awakens most deeply and constantly in us the idea of beauty. . . . I seem to myself to say all when I say that the chivalric idea of love through disease, dungeons, and death, mutilation on the battle field, and the odious changes effected by the enchanter's hate answers my idea far better than the stoical appreciation of the object beloved for what it positively presents.[51]

Quite apart from her perfectionist argument and her chivalric examples, her new philosophical tone revealed something personal as well. By then she had worked through what she wanted and could get from Emerson. "Waldo has brought me your page," she wrote in her last letter that visit,

> and he looked so lovely as if he were the living word which should yet reveal to the world all that you do not feel ready to say. . . . Do not fancy that I complain or grieve. I understand matters now, and always want you to withdraw when you feel like it; indeed, there is nothing I wish more than to be able to live with you, without disturbing you. This is the main stream of my feeling. I am satisfied and also feel that our friendship will grow[.] But I am of a more lively and affectionate temper or rather more household and daily in my affection. . . . The genial flow of my desire may be checked for the moment, but it cannot long. I shall always burst out soon

and burn up all the rubbish between you and me, and I shall always find you there true to yourself and deeply rooted as ever.

My impatience is but the bubble on the stream; you know I want to be alone myself.—It is all right. As to the shadow I do not know myself what it is, but it rests on your aspect, and brings me near the second-sight as I look on you. Perhaps if we have Scotch trists enough I shall really see the tapestry of the coming time start into life, but, if I do, I shall not tell you, but with wise economy keep it for a poem which shall make ever sacred and illustrious the name of yours

Margaret.[52]

This was a gracious and generous and, in its way, sensible letter. Along with their other talks, it seems to have had its due effect on both parties. It is true, Emerson remained puzzled by (as he wrote in his journal) "these strange, cold-warm, attractive-repelling conversations with Margaret, whom I always admire, most revere when I nearest see, sometimes love, yet whom I freeze, & who freezes me to silence, when we seem to promise to come nearest." However, these latest talks at least helped him to see her complex character ("so proud & presumptuous yet so meek" and deeply "religious") in ways that made her more understandable. Certainly, he did not want to lose her as a friend. "I say to myself, it is surely very generous in such a rich & great minded woman to throw her steady light on me also, and to love me so well," he wrote her a few weeks later. "So now do not withdraw your rays; but still forgive all my incapacities; and it shall be counted to you for righteousness with all angels." Fuller's last letter was a prescient one as well. She would never get from Emerson either an acceptance of her Romantic friendship ideal or the "recognition" of her androgynous-heroic spiritual identity that she had once craved. But she could claim his friendship on both his truthful terms and her affectionate ones. She also would always retain a higher "second-sight" of how far the real Emerson remained from her ideal of the "living word." Finally, however much she remained enamored of him, her letter showed a new maturity. In giving up on the fruitless task of converting him to her Romantic ideology—as well as, on some level, a more romantic connection with her than was ever in the stars—she made it at least possible to start internalizing the stimulating rather than the frustrating part of their friendship. On that prospective conversational platform, both the stoic-Platonic and the striving Romantic could have agreed.[53]

The Fuller-Emerson argument that October at Bush concluded what was arguably the most intriguing private debate on the nature of love and friendship in American intellectual history, but it was not quite her last "living word" on the subject. Just as Emerson produced a text out of these debates, so did Fuller. She inserted it toward the end of her "Autobiographical Romance" written that year at Bush. After discussing the utilitarian and intimate ideals of friendship, she turned to her highest type, the fateful. "Born under the same star, and bound with us in a common destiny," she declares,

these are not mere acquaintances, mere friends, but, when we meet, are sharers of our very existence. There is no separation; the same thought is given at the same moment to both,—indeed, it is born of the meeting, and would not otherwise have been called into existence at all. These not only know themselves more, but *are* more for having met, and regions of their being, which would else have laid sealed in cold abstraction, burst into leaf and bloom and song.

Here she dispensed with the "chivalric" trappings and reformulated the ethical issue between herself and Emerson. That was not merely the divinization of friendship as a sign of spiritual transcendence, or the ineradicability of the individual personality, or even the fact of friendship's evanescent character, all stern Transcendentalist qualifiers that Fuller accepted just as much as Emerson. The distinction lay elsewhere in her statement: the momentary mingling of intimacy, thoughts, and, most important, "existence" that a fateful friendship created. For Emerson, deep friendship affirmed already existing individual nobility created by the self and residing in a sphere beyond human emotion and even personalities. For Fuller, the deepest friendship effected spiritual reality through *immersion* in the exigencies of human feelings and existence. Without a faith in that claim, it is hard to imagine her going as far as she would in the realm of experience that Emerson would later honor from a safe distance.[54]

VI

After her three weeks at Concord and Newburyport, Fuller returned to the Farrars'. Eliza Farrar, who knew something about Fuller's (as Farrar called them) "manifold difficulties," invited her to stay through the winter. Although the thought of the doting Mrs. Farrar and a cozy fire in Fuller's room "so that I can study and write to my heart's content" strongly appealed to her, at the beginning of November she instead went to board for the winter at her Uncle Henry and Aunt Mary Fuller's house on Avon Place in Boston. A cramped, cold room in a noisy house would not seem to have been a great idea, which her flu that January would appear to have confirmed. But to the surprise of her mother, who had long resented her in-laws' indifference to her after her husband's death, Margaret reported that her aunt and uncle looked after her "in every way." Also, the city was convenient for her Conversations and literature students. She could also practice what she preached to Richard. "I am . . . willing to bear the contact of society, with all its low views and rash blame," she wrote in her journal, "for I see how the purest ideal natures need it to temper them and keep them large and sure. I will never do as Waldo does, though I marvel not at him."[55]

Wintering in Boston also meant Fuller could conveniently see the January 1842 *Dial* through the press. She wrote over a third of it, but her major piece was "Bettine Brentano and Her Friend Günderode," a long essay review of *Die Günderode*, Bettina Brentano von Arnim's semifictionalized youthful correspondence with the canoness and poet Karoline von Günderode published the previous year. In her preface to its first volume, which she was then translating and Elizabeth Peabody would publish two months later, she explained her Romantic translation philosophy. She eschewed artificially reproducing stylistic peculiarities, as though language was merely dress and manners, and instead tried to produce linguistic accuracy and vernacular accessibility. "In translating I throw myself, as entirely as possible, into the mood of the writer," she explained, "and make use of such expressions as would come naturally, if reading the work aloud into English. The style thus formed is, at least, a transcript of the feelings excited by the original; and is a likeness, if a caricature." Notwithstanding her modesty, her protagonists' distinct voices come through quite well. Although she dropped the project due to lack of time, her young Cambridge neighbor next year, Minna Wesselhoeft, whose family had known Arnim in Germany, would complete them, using Fuller's translation unchanged, in her 1861 English version.[56]

In her article, Fuller used Arnim and Günderode's letters to add a couple of wrinkles to the friendship question. Although the previous year, she had sent with a package of *Dial*s a note to her fellow Goethean and democratic Arnim, thanking her for encouraging American youth to trust the "promptings of their own young hearts!" she disliked the sentimental Bettina cult among some Transcendentalists. She also blanched at Arnim's earlier "somewhat fantastic or even silly" spurious *Goethes Briefwechsel mit einem Kinde* ("more properly it should be named, 'A Child's Correspondence with Herself'"). In *Die Günderode*, however, she saw the portrayal of a genuine friendship. One requirement was equality, glaringly missing in Arnim's portrayal of the elderly, flirtatious, "Father Confessor" Goethe and herself as a fluttering girl trying "to entertain a lordly guest. . . . With Günderode there is no effort; each mind being of equal expense of keeping up the fires." Getting in a dig at a phrase in an old letter of Emerson's to her, she added, "They needed not 'descend to meet.'" The other aspect was *female* friendship. Fuller's portrait was not cultish: no cozy picture of "kindred spirits" as sentimentalized in nineteenth-century popular writing. The girls, she said, defied gender stereotypes altogether. Neither fancifully "heroic" like the comradeship of boys nor "foolish[ly] sentimentalist" like that of many girls, Bettina and Karoline's "feminine" friendship, she said, was a "poetic" bond secured by intimate affection, aesthetic appreciation, and, above all, intellectual inquiry. "They study no less than love one another," she wrote, soberly anticipating Olive Chancellor and young Verena Tarrant's self-conceptions in Henry James's *Bostonians*; "they cannot flatter, neither make weak exactions; the sentiment is too true to allow of sentimentality." Indeed, she said, contrary to common English and American swipes at German girls' pedantic intellectuality, their "transfusion" of high thinking into their "private lives" reminded one of the transcendental method of Goethe, Kant, Fichte, and Schelling without "cant and imitation"! She did not mention Günderode's suicide after the married Friedrich Creuzer rejected her, but she knew about it. "Gunderode is the ideal; Bettina, nature," she wrote William Channing just before starting her translation. "Gunderode throws herself in the river because the world is too narrow. Bettina lives, and follows out every freakish fancy, till the enchanting child degenerates into an eccentric and undignified old woman. There is a medium somewhere." Could she have been thinking of her own friendship with Caroline Sturgis, the "American Bettina"? In any case, the piece gave her readers an inkling of the rigorous feminine ideal she had been inculcating in her Conversations for the past couple of years. Both Boston's Democratic *Morning Post* and its Whig *Daily Advertiser* called it "beautiful."[57]

City living also made it easy for Fuller to take in Boston's increasingly lively cultural scene. Of course, this being Boston, that meant lots of lectures, including Emerson's popular reform-centered winter series, "The Times," at the Masonic Temple ("brilliant," she told her mother). But it also meant lots of opportunities to pursue her passion for spirit-lifting art music, her greatest compensation for the "fatigue and interruption" of boarding-house living. She heard the three-octave London tenor John Braham in Haydn's *Creation* and Handel's *Messiah*. She took in John Dwight's winter series of music lectures. Accompanied usually by Dwight or Caroline Sturgis, she faithfully attended the Academy of Music's concerts, including a second performance of Beethoven's Fifth Symphony and another of his Sixth, and those of the European instrumental soloists who performed in Boston that season. That winter she accompanied the Wards and a number of her other friends to a private recital, held at the rooms of the Boston piano maker Jonas Chickering, by the young German-born virtuoso Frederick William Rackemann, who performed on Chickering's acclaimed new cast-iron frame piano. "The very finest piano I *ever* heard," she told her mother.[58]

Yet Boston's cultural scene left her dissatisfied. Audiences were one problem. According to an "eye-witness" of Emerson's, at one of the Academy's Beethoven concerts at the Melodeon, Fuller's excited party of devotees were forced to endure incessant chatter by a young lady and her two male friends who sat behind them, oblivious to the nasty looks cast at them by those around them. After all was over, Margaret leaned across one seat, and catching the eye of this pretty and well-dressed girl, said, in her blandest, gentlest voice, "May I speak with you one moment?" "Certainly," said the young lady, with a fluttered, pleased look, bending forward. "I only wish to say," Margaret supposedly said, "that I trust, that, in the whole course of your life, you will not suffer so great a degree of annoyance as you have inflicted on a large party of lovers of music this evening." The eye-witness added, "This was said with the sweetest air, as if to a little child, and it was as good as a play to see the change of countenance which the young lady exhibited, who had no replication to make to so Christian a blessing." How "Christian" Fuller's "blessing" sounded to the young lady is debatable, but the story is a reminder that Fuller's new Romantic dispensation had a public ritual as well as a theology, mostly directed, as here, not at the poor, as modern-day critics of "highbrow" Victorian culture would have it, but the "well-dressed." "There are so few people who can hear music with their bodies even," later that winter she told a friend after coming back from a concert, "that you cannot be 'alone in the crowd' of a concert room, *and*, what is called a musical entertainment is usually in this country the best facsimile we have of purgatory. I mean the old fashioned purgatory where poor sinners, reft of grace but tuned to love, see through iron grates good angels playing all so happily on golden harps."[59]

Fuller vented her frustrations in her lengthy *Dial* article "Entertainments of the Past Winter." She had not gone cultural slumming. "The Dial affords no room for the encyclopedia of Entertaining Knowledge," she laughed. "We have not visited the Museum, have not seen 'Love in all shapes,' nor the Indians, real or supposed, nor the lady who advertises 'a hundred illusions in one evening,' not an offer to be slighted of a December afternoon." Yet, like her blasts at the "well-dressed," her bêtes noires were not the ignorant poor but philistines past and present. "What would the Puritan fathers say, if they could see our bill of fare in Boston for the winter?" she asked mischievously. "The concerts, the opera dancing, which have taken place of their hundred-headed sermons, how would they endure? How the endless disquisitions wherever a few can be gathered together, on every branch of learning, every folly of human speculation?" But she was not after the Puritans, nor, for that matter, their evangelical descendants, whom she ignored. Overwhelmingly, she aimed her critical guns at the "better part of the community"—the city's Unitarian cultural elite—who claimed to love art and poetry but were largely deaf to their aesthetic essence. That was neither the utilitarian nor the decorous but the "spirit that sings to sing, and models for the sake of drawing from the clay the elements of beauty." Happily, though, a recent "under-current" of young people was challenging these antiaesthetic New England views, but they lacked the ideas in the "appropriate language" necessary to justify art to the community: autonomous forms, spiritual purpose, "recreative" experience, and, not least, instruction from an empathetic but comprehensive critic capable of mediating between the artist and the public.[60]

After offering a job description for herself, she surveyed what she had seen and heard. On the perennial Boston "theater question," her report was grim. Thanks to the misguided desire to protect youths from the theater, Shakespearean drama was defunct in Boston, while "amusements of a lower order" flourished. However, the problem went much deeper than Boston's antitheater prejudices: the medium itself seemed to be dying. "The drama cannot live where man cannot walk in the freedom of a hero," and those days that had flourished in ancient Greece and Renaissance Europe had vanished in modern times. This was a common Romantic dogma, but one she thought especially true in America. Speaking of playwrights who vainly "pilfer and filter" history and romance for soliloquies crammed into lame plays with random contemporary allusions, she declared:

> Let them ask themselves, Do the men walk and talk before them so in their solitary hours? Did these forms advance from the green solitudes of the wood, or the dark corners of the chamber, and give themselves to the bard as delegates from the Muse of the age? Did you, as you walked the streets meet the demand for these beings from every restless, eager eye? Not so. Then let be the dead form of a traditional drama. Life is living, though this be dead. Wait the form that grows from the spirit of the time.

So, what might that be? That was difficult. Form had to follow spirit and, sadly, as she had said in her Allston review, Americans had, as yet, not much of a spiritual national culture. "If New England thinks, it is about money, social reform, and theology. If she has a way of speaking peculiarly her own, it is the lecture." The lecture, however, although perfectly natural in a "colony" still overrun by the productions of a parent country possessing a rich centuries-old culture, could hardly be sufficient to stimulate the American mind needing not just to know but to be touched inwardly. What America had of the less simply intellectual but more beautiful entertainments of music and dance were paltry. In composition, she said, Americans could only boast of two "folk" types. One was church music, especially psalmody, one of the few aesthetic aspects of America's spartan Protestant liturgies. Less popular but more creative was the African music and dance she said one could observe in the streets. "All symptoms of invention are confined to the African race, who, like the German literati, are relieved by their position from the cares of government," she wrote wryly. "Such of the African melodies as we have heard are beautiful." Boston's recent art music performances were a mix. With complimentary nods to European performers, she ran through oratorios, operas, and soloists she had heard that winter, balancing criticisms with frank acknowledgments of her lack of opportunities to hear the repertoire necessary to make comparative judgments. She saved her most extensive comments for two sets of exciting but problematic performances.[61]

One set was the recent concerts of Fanny Elssler, the Austrian ballet dancer whose sensual gymnastic turns in "maillot" (or skin-tight jerseys) in the reigning European Romantic ethereal style had produced an avalanche of rave reviews and shocked sensibilities. Even Emerson had to perform a few mental gymnastics to assimilate Elssler's performances. "The morals, as it is called, of this exhibition . . . lies wholly with the spectator," he wrote airily in his journal, yet he also worried that the concerts were "not the safest resort for college boys who . . . may not forget this graceful silvery swimmer when they have retreated again to their baccalaureate cells." In her article Fuller made such nervousness sound embarrassingly provincial: "Those who criticize the dancer as they would their neighbor should not witness the ballet." The rest of her critique was vintage high-low Fuller. On one hand, she was no mere Elssler worshipper. Although lauding her "naïve sportive" turns and alternately "coquettish" and "childlike" impersonations, Fuller found her lacking in the lofty *La Sylphide*, which demanded a more "refined and poetic" range of talents, such as those reportedly displayed, she said, by Europe's Romantic sylphlike prima ballerina, Marie Taglioni. Yet while leaving her American readers to yearn for Europe's greatest, she pivoted, Romantic-style, to praise not just "opera dancing" but also dance "performed" everywhere: "Everything tends in the civilized world to a reinstatement of the body in the rights of which it has been defrauded, as an object of care and the vehicle of expression. . . . The rope-dancer, the opera-dancer, the gymnast, Mr. Sheridan's boxing-school, and Du Crow, are only the comments on the books on physiology which they keep on their parlor tables and lend to their pale-faced, low statured friends." From "pale-faced, low statured" working men she swooped up into a Transcendental pirouette. Dance's highest claim was spiritual: an exhibition of "perfect discipline of limb and motion, till they are so pliant to the will that the body seems but thickened soul, and the subtlest emotion is seen at the fingers' ends."[62]

The other series she drew Romantic lessons from was the Academy of Music's concerts, especially of Beethoven's symphonies, which she praised unstintingly. She launched a furious attack, however, on the Academy managers' promiscuous programming of popular and serious music, a common practice in antebellum America. Although one historian has imagined it an expression of the "democratic" ethos of the era, Fuller deplored it, not on social but aesthetic grounds: the hodge-podge effaced both the artistic integrity and the spiritual resonances of great musical works. "Just as you have risen to a poetic feeling and are engaged in a pleasing flow of thought," she wrote, "you are jarred and let down by flat and unmeaning trifles, or by some even vulgar performance." Moreover, the problem arose not just from the American public's lack of aesthetic education compared to Europeans' but also from plain capitalist greed. And the losers were both artists and audiences. Mixing up "really beautiful music alternating with pieces intended only to catch the ear and prevent those of the hearers, who have not an earnest interest, from being tired" was a disaster for art.

> In this way the taste of the many will never be improved, for the performer goes down to them, instead of drawing them up to him. We think they should never do so, and the need of money is not an excuse. Compromise, always so degrading, is especially so with those beautiful arts which we expect to lift us above everything low and mercenary, and give us light by which to see the harmony destined to subsist between nature and the soul of man, when mutually purified, perfected and sustained.[63]

An organic popular culture, harmony between nature and the soul, professional leadership of performer and critic, and the integrity of the created work: this was not an easy prescription, but it was sincere and cogent and, if German Romantic in content, original in its application to the American scene. "It is a fine *manly* (that is the word that fits the thing) deliberate criticism on the men & the things before us, so flowing too & so readable," Emerson wrote her, "that I am glad & proud of my friend." The overture, if it did not turn into a dirge, would seem to suggest, like her "Günderode," many performances to come.[64]

VII

Whether those would appear in Fuller's *Dial*, though, had become a serious question. Trouble had begun brewing in the fall. The previous April, Jordan and Weeks, the magazine's publisher, had gone bankrupt, creating a legal headache for the journal's editors. Although their contract gave them the right to change publishers, by "book-selling usage" the firm retained ownership of the subscribers' list, for which the bankruptcy trustee, who happened to be the publisher William Jordan's brother, had demanded payment. Ripley, to whom the task of negotiating an agreement initially fell, had suggested they pay up, but Emerson, who would have had to foot the eighty-nine-dollar bill, refused. Instead, he and Fuller retained George Hillard, Charles Sumner's law partner, to renegotiate. Meanwhile, Emerson proposed that they end this "dull Chinese diplomacy" and simply call the wily Jordans' bluff: "We have nothing to lose by ending the Dial by Proclamation, as Victoria does her Parliament, for we shall interpose three mystic intercalary days and burst on the world in full dazzle to the relief doubtless of the gasping nations. But our Publishers, if they have any good name, have that to tarnish again by suffering us to do so. Write an advertisement & let Mr Hillard show it to these men on its way to the newspaper." She did, and the plan worked. Jordan handed over the list, and he and Weeks agreed to transfer the magazine and its name on the terms Fuller proposed. Meanwhile, on Emerson's advice, to avoid any such legal problems in the future, she had a contract drawn up making the *Dial* her "exclusive property." She also got a considerably friendlier (if no more efficient) publisher in their circle's loyal publicist Elizabeth Peabody.[65]

At first, the settlement seemed to coincide with a general good turn in the magazine's fortunes. To be sure, the city's conservative Whig and Unitarian publications kept up their relentless potshots. Both the *Boston Daily Advertiser* and the *Christian Examiner* confidently predicted the magazine's imminent demise, since, as the *Examiner* said, it was "too absurd and extravagant to last long" and was even now being ousted from "many a fashionable drawing-room and round many an aesthetic tea-table." However, they were in the minority. By that fall, as the shock of the magazine's newness wore off, the reviews, although fewer, were getting better. Even the high-toned *Knickerbocker* managed to mix some compliments with its ridicule, while *Hach's Musical Magazine* praised the journal's new coverage of the arts. The *Tribune* kept up its steady puffs, and the pro-Democratic *Boston Morning Post*, recognizing an antiestablishment journal when it saw one, complimented it, Transcendental-style, for displaying "Man's soul-nobility" in "letters of vivid light." Other good news came. On March 18, Emerson, having just returned from his lecture tour in New York, happily reported to Fuller that it was easy to see how "dear it plainly was" to many young people in the city. Then, wonder of wonders, Peabody gaily told Fuller that after printer's bills were paid, she hoped to be able finally to pay her annual *Dial* salary of $300, of which she had never seen a penny.[66]

Then the bombshell hit. The morning before Emerson reported on the *Dial*'s growing profile in New York, Peabody and James Clarke, who had gone over Jordan and Weeks's books, informed Fuller that, to Peabody's horror, the "rascally firm" had overstated subscription sales. Rather than the five to six hundred subscribers the editors had thought they had, there were really no more than three hundred, the rest being single sales. The consequences were grim. After deducting expenses, it was clear that not only would Fuller never receive any of her past yearly salary, but there was absolutely no chance that the *Dial* would ever be able to pay her for her services. Meanwhile, the workload remained unremitting. The previous summer, "crazy with work," she had written both her lengthy "Lives of the Great Composers" and "Festus" articles to fill nearly two-thirds of the *Dial*'s October issue. By that winter, the accumulated burdens of having to beg copy from unpaid, fickle writers had already begun taking a heavy toll on both her spirits and her health. "I am in a state of extreme fatigue," she had written her mother on Christmas Eve. "This is the last week of the Dial and as often happens, the '*copy*' did not hold out, and I have had to write in every gap of time." Despite her flu, her weekly Conversations, and her almost daily private literature lessons, she kept up this pace all winter, so much so that her brother Richard feared she was killing herself with overwork.[67]

In the end, though, what pushed Fuller over was her usual money problems, which were getting dire. She had "only 500$ in the world," she told Richard, and even that, which would have paid her bills for six months, she had pledged to secure money for a loan to the constantly indigent Eugene. So, after meeting with Peabody and Clarke, she immediately had Peabody draft a letter to Emerson outlining the results of their investigation. That afternoon she sent it, along with a frank account of why the new facts required her to resign immediately as the magazine's editor. First, she said, she had been "so unwell, and really exhausted" from illness and "severe labor I shall not recover fully for two or three months. Then if I must take up a similar course next winter and have this tie upon me for the summer I think I should sink under it entirely." Even then, she said, she would have been willing to struggle on if she could have gotten a salary sufficient to allow her to give up her teaching, but that was now clearly impossible: "I grieve to disappoint you after all the trouble you have taken. I am also sorry myself, for if I could have received a maintenance from this Dial, I could have done my duties to it well, which I never have all this time, and my time might have been given to my pen, while now for more than three months I have been able to write no line except letters. But it cannot be helped. It has been a sad business."[68]

This, of course, left only two alternatives: the *Dial* would be terminated with the April 1842 issue, or someone else had to become editor. In her March 17 letter to Emerson, she had suggested Parker or Emerson himself: "For him, or for you it would be much easier than for me, for you have quiet homes, and better health." Emerson's first response, which he dashed off immediately after getting her letter, was grateful and commiserating but noncommittal. "That you should be such a lavish spender of time labor & health for our poor Dial, with such a bankrupt's return, makes me very sorry. We are all your debtors & must always be. . . . Nobody is brave & faithful & self sufficing but you, so I think tonight." So he argued with himself. He still wanted the *Dial* both as an outlet for their young writers and for its cultural influence. He also knew that there was no one in their circle who shared their vision of publishing a magazine controlled by neither "the Humanity & Reform Men, [who] trample on letters & poetry," nor "the Scholars, [who] are dead & dry." The following day, he wrote her, "Perhaps I shall rue this day of accepting such an intruder on my peace and such a consumer of my time as a Dial." However, he concluded, "You have played martyr a little too long alone: let there be rotation in martyrdom!" So, "rather than have it stop or go into hands that know not Joseph," he would be the *Dial*'s new martyr-editor.[69]

"She put so much heart into it," Emerson would write in her *Memoirs* of her *Dial* editorship. "I remember, after she had been compelled by ill health to relinquish the journal into my hands, my grateful wonder at the facility with which she assumed the preparation of laborious articles, that might have daunted the most practiced scribes." Of course, after two years at the *Dial*'s helm, Fuller had become something of a "practiced scribe" herself. What that meant as a freelance writer in America she would soon find out.[70]

CHAPTER THREE

Liberal Awakenings
(1842–1843)

I

Fuller's resignation came as an unmixed relief. "[I] hav[e] given out from myself now every day and all the day for nearly six months," she sighed two weeks later to her Quaker friend Mary Rotch, but now the future looked bright. "By the time the trees are in full leaf, I doubt not I also shall feel fresh and ready once more." Meanwhile, she took her own advice to "concentrate my powers," which she thought two years of *Dial* burdens had denied her. On April 11, 1842, she moved out of her aunt and uncle's Avon Place house, and traveled to her Aunt Elizabeth Crane's farmhouse in Canton, where she luxuriated in "absolute retirement," completed her "Entertainments" article, and read Xenophon on Socrates and several plays of Euripides. "I have enjoyed the solitude and silence," she told Rotch. "It has been a thotful, tho' not a thinking time."[1]

Actually, she was giving a good deal of thought to a subject dear to the heart of every thinking Transcendentalist. Religion, she had come to feel, she told Rotch, was *the* topic that "*all* topics are in relation to." Not that since her freethinking adolescence it had ever been exactly unimportant to her, but even her year of biblical studies at Groton had done nothing to eradicate her doubts about the Christian revelation or about her capacity for religious faith of any sort. Her half-year "crisis" following her searing mystical "illumination" in the fall of 1840, however, witnessed religion for the first time cutting deeply into her inner life. Now, a year later, after she felt the "growths of the last year" had receded, she seems to have decided it was time to try again to settle on a personal theology. Like her self-mythologizing tales and friendship arguments, what she found would provide the private substrata for liberal public engagements for many years to come.[2]

She was not alone. The early 1840s ushered in a new phase of the country's "Second Great Awakening." All over the Northeast, new perfectionist sects, fueled by the same peculiar mix of millennialist rhetoric and economic depression galvanizing socialistic communities, were springing up or mushrooming. Sweden-borgian, Adventist, Mormon, Shaker, and other perfectionist churches were an-nouncing new angels, new revelations, and new "scriptures," as they gathered in thousands of roving converts who were eager to find ever stronger assurances of the "New Heaven and New Earth" their ministers prophesied. "The church here is open every night in the week," Sarah Clarke had reported to her brother James, then still in Louisville, referring to the sensational prophesying of the former Baptist farmer-preacher William Miller. "His view of things is that after next August, no more persons can be admitted to conversion, so he is very busy till then. After that time the institutions of the world are to crumble to pieces, and in August, 1843, the world will be destroyed."[3]

Sarah's drollness notwithstanding, the Transcendentalists were not mere on-lookers in this "come-outer" religious firestorm. That very fall of 1840, while Fuller had been immersed in her illuminations, Emerson, Ripley, Parker, and Channing had joined anticlerical abolitionists, communitarians, deists, evangelicals, and Transcendentalists in signing a call for the first of three "Conventions" at the Chardon Street Chapel to examine critically the claims of "the Sabbath, the Church, and the Ministry." Transcendentalists moved on other religious fronts. Parker delivered fiery, "spiritual" sermons from his pulpit, triggering Orthodox calls for his indictment for blasphemy and nearly unanimous ostracism by Boston's Uni-tarian ministers, while thousands of "common people" poured into his Boston lec-tures, delighted, Emerson said, to see his "beautiful fangs" in the "amphitheatre . . . worry and tear his victim." James Clarke began services for his new Church of the Disciples, soon drawing hundreds of more elite Unitarians to its mix of Christian Transcendentalism and egalitarian innovations, such as free pews and lay preaching. "It is high time," he had crowed to his sister, that the city's worldly Unitarian ministers "left off preaching about the moral beauty of steam ships and burial grounds, and preach on the question 'What shall I do to be saved.'" Even such an unlikley pair as the cautious liberal Elizabeth Peabody and the proto-Catholic Charles King Newcomb reported highly un-Unitarian "visions" of hu-man sin, "dark Chaos," and speaking Christ-figures. Of course, as those gestures suggest, coming out did not dictate what the Transcendentalists were coming *into*. The Jacksonian Transcendentalist Orestes Brownson, traumatized by the 1840 Whig presidential victory, was unique in starting to take actual steps leading him into the Roman Catholic Church, but theological differences were sprouting among all the Transcendentalists. At two Transcendental Club meetings during that fall of 1840, Frederic Henry Hedge had denounced come-outerism and vigorously defended the Unitarian Association as the flawed but historic liberal "organic" church, Ripley had urged a new socially radical but still Christian church, and Emerson and Fuller had argued for a "universal creed and church." Afterward, Parker had privately grumbled about both Hedge's standpattism and Emerson's pantheism. The meetings would be the Club's last gatherings.[4]

Where did Fuller see herself in this swirling Transcendentalist spiritual pool? Like Emerson, she had been more bemused than moved by the wildly anticlerical Chardon Street Convention meetings, observing that they were too socially and indeologically promiscuous to succeed (the high-toned Garrisonians looked "like bewildered sheep amid apes, and mastiffs, and wild boars"). Parker she found provocative but problematical. "I quite loved him," she wrote after hearing him deliver his courageous antisupernaturalist sermon on "Idolotry" to the moderate Purchase Street congregation, which was considering him as a replacement for Ripley. Yet, like her old friend Clarke, she thought there was something fundamentally unspiritual about Parker's relentless stripping of religious symbols to get to the ethical core of his God-dependent "Absolute Religion." "His outlook is wide," she would tell Mary Rotch after the Unitarians' Boston Association of Ministers met to berate him for his "deistical" pronouncements, but added "it will not deepen, unless his fount of inward knowledge shall deepen."[5]

The Transcendentalist minister whose theological twists and turns provoked her most positively was William Channing. It had been to him that she had registered in late October 1840 her memorable anti-Unitarian *cri de coeur* preferring evangelical "tears and groans" to "'*rational*'" ministers preaching to "that crowd of upturned faces with their look of unintelligent complacency." Urging him not to leave but to "ennoble" the ministry by seizing the "*thought* of today," she had told him: "None of us have it yet but you and I are nearer than others because not so ready to dogmatize as if we had got it, neither content to stop short with mere impressions and presumptuous hopes. I feel it is coming." After he resigned his Cincinnati pulpit in 1841 and returned to Boston, they had continued these theological discussions. His newest declarations shocked his family: that he no longer believed in either the divinity of Christ or his church but in Jesus as a "God-man" and the Christian Church as the "Divine Life" of "Humanity." On June 12, 1842, she heard him deliver a sermon in Boston on his new humanistic Christian religion and later talked with him about it. Shortly afterward she sent him a seventeen-page "Credo" responding to questions he had posed, a version of which he would later insert in her *Memoirs*, carefully censoring, at the urging of her devout Unitarian family, some of its more daring non-Christian formulations. Thirty years later, he would send the manuscript to Higginson for his biography of her, attaching a note calling it "most characteristic."[6]

It was definitely that. "There is a spirit uncontainable and uncontained," she began. "Within it all manifestation is contained, whether of good (accomplishment) or evil (obstruction). To itself its depths are unknown. By living it seeks to know itself, thus evolving plants, animals, men, suns, stars, angels, and, it is to be presumed an infinity of forms not yet visible in the horizon of this being who now writes." This mythic fragmentation from spiritual oneness into nature and knowledge, the key cosmological doctrine of the Western hermetic tradition, she would have found everywhere in her recent readings: in her favorite Plato, in Thomas Taylor's translations of the Neoplatonic Plotinus and Proclus, in Renaissance hermetics like Böhme, and in the works of early German Romantics, especially Schelling. Yet, apart from Emerson's *Nature* and Alcott's "Orphic Sayings," little of the theme appears in Transcendentalist writing. Moreover, unlike Alcott, who, like the Christian Gnostics, regarded this break from spiritual unity as a massive cosmological error that needed correction through an ascetic recourse to "pure spirit," Fuller found this "second development" a positive good. It demonstrated, she wrote in her Credo, the dynamic power of Spirit, unfolded the cosmic drama of overcoming impediments by faith, and facilitated man's widening and "ever evolving . . . consciousness of consciousness, and a soul of the soul." It was, in brief, as in her mythology classes the year before, the ancient doctrine of the Fortunate Fall in Romantic dress.[7]

The most controversial question for all Transcendentalists, of course, remained how their heterodox theologies comported with their inherited liberal Christianity. Although as a lay intellectual she had none of the professional stakes of her ministerial colleagues in the issue, in her Credo she, too, juxtaposed her theology to this tradition with which she had grown up. She staked out a position on her circle's radical flank. On the matter of the Gospels' genuineness, which her comrades had been publicly questioning for the past half-dozen years, her stance was pure Transcendentalism. If all that the Bible narrated really happened, she said, yet if men and women failed to interpret it "by the freedom of their own souls," it would be *religiously* untrue because it would be spiritually dead. But she went beyond this religious intuitionism, which Christian Transcendentalists like Clarke and Hedge completely accepted, to reduce Christianity's cognitive claim to nothing *but* an intuition, and not the deepest one at that. The literal truthfulness of the Gospels did not matter at all: if St. John had made up the entire narrative and offered it as a poem, "it would be just as real. You can see how wide the gulf that separates me from the Christian Church." Indeed, even the "type" of Jesus was dispensable.

> For myself, I believe in Christ because I can do without him; because the truth he announces I see elsewhere intimated; because it is foreshadowed in the very nature of my own being. . . . I am grateful here, as everywhere, where spirit bears fruit in fulness. It attests the justice of my desires; it kindles my faith; it rebukes my sloth; it enlightens my resolve. But so does the Apollo, and the beautiful infant, and the summer's earliest rose. It is only one modification of the same harmony. . . . There is nothing peculiar about it, but its form.

Nor was Jesus even that spirit's highest imaginable "form": "We want a life more complete and various than that of Christ. We have had the Messiah to reconcile and teach, let us have another to live out all the symbolical forms of human life with the calm beauty and physical fulness of a Greek god, with the consciousness of a Moses, with the holy love and purity of Jesus. Amen!" Apart from the "pagan" Thoreau, not even Parker, who stripped Christianity of its "transient" dogmas but retained Jesus' ethical core as a divinely superior ideal, pushed the circle's intuitionism so far beyond Christian dogma.[8]

Except for, of course, Thoreau's patron Emerson, whose different non-Christian religious views best illuminate the complexity of her theology. On the one hand, as the Club debates had brought out, none in their circle had a stronger belief in the sufficiency of the subjective source of religious truth and the transience and limitations of all religions. "I will not loathe sects, persuasions, systems, though I cannot abide in them one moment," she wrote provocatively in her Credo. "I see most men are still in need of them. To them their banners, their tents; let them be Platonists, Fire-worshippers, Christians; Oh Father of our souls, I seek thee. I seek thee in these forms; and in proportion as they reveal thee more, they lead me beyond themselves. I would learn from them all, looking to thee." On the other hand, this paean to seeking highlighted the very elements that made Fuller's natural supernaturalism so different from both Emerson's and that of his more moderate comrades. One was her theism. Despite her enthusiasm for Spinoza's pantheistic conception of a deity who acted immanently in "unconstrained nature," God remained comparatively "other" for her, a god to seek but never know. Unlike Emerson, for whom prayer to a personal deity was a disturbance, Fuller sprinkled her journals with "I-Thou" expressions, and not just of seeking, but of beseeching "a Power" that "at last" would order all things right. "There are so many, and such long, intervals," she wrote to a friend, "when we are kept from all we want, and must perish but for such thoughts." Her reason here pointed to a second distinctively un-Emersonian religious notion: human life was inherently tragic. "Man was made to mourn," she would tell Anna Ward a couple of years later, echoing repeated "pagan" declarations about man's "iron destiny" as a "mutilated" being scattered through her papers. Finally, the "forms" of seeking were manifold and revealing.[9]

Her Credo's formulation of "looking" in multiple "forms" had for some time been the pragmatic essence of all her strongest religious moves: in her Goethean yearning for "indefinite pilgrimages"; in her love of "exotic" spiritual plots and figures; and, most expectantly, in her Credo's millenarian eschatology of future "God-men" and "higher existences." It was as if only in multiplying, and not, as with Parker, erasing, different "transient" religious forms—or, as with Emerson, making them almost interchangeable spiritual symbols—could she find the spaces in which to express her Romantic need for spiritual plenitude. Nor did the fact that religious forms were for her symbolic and nonritualized (she had several years earlier stopped worshipping at churches in favor of Sunday "solitary reflection") make them any less powerful. These included Christian ones, which, like many European Romantics, she often drew on to symbolize divine mediation in the world. "I suppose few are so much believers in his history as myself," she wrote, affirming the "necessity" of every major event from Genesis down through Christ's virgin birth, resurrection, and ascension. Indeed, contrary to Parker, who had thundered in his notorious *Discourse of the Transient and Permanent in Christianity* that "the flesh creeps with horror" at the thought that God, in a fit of sadism or insanity, had commanded Abraham to sacrifice his son Isaac, she had "no trouble" at all accepting this (as Parker had called it) absurd "Oriental story" as "prefiguring a thought to be fully expressed by the death of Christ." Nor were these Christian tropes just a matter of "higher critical" rhetoric for her. "But I do not wish to do without him," she interjected after saying in her Credo that her inward faith allowed me to do without Jesus. "He is constantly aiding and answering me."[10]

Yet, as all her Christian Transcendentalist friends attested, whether supernatural admirers like Clarke or naturalist detractors like Parker, whatever aid Jesus provided her fell short of any recognizable Christian faith. She agreed.

"My tendency is, I presume, rather to a great natural than to a deep religious life," she wrote Channing that summer. "But though others may be more conscientious and delicate, few have so steady a faith in Divine Love." And Jesus would continue to fade. "I know many . . . seek in Jesus the guide and friend," she would write a friend five years later from Italy. "For me, it is my nature to wish to go straight to the Creative Spirit." To the end of her life, Fuller's faith was decidedly post-Christian: Christianity for her was a social ethic and even a deeply felt spiritual ideal, but, as a faith, one among several, and always surrounded by an oxymoronic aura of "Divine Love" and tragic "Fate." Indeed, just as she yearned for a "life more complete and various than that of Christ," she recognized—and accepted—how alien the Christian spirit of sorrow, renunciation, and salvation ultimately was to her basic Romantic character. "Is it my defect of spiritual experience, that while that weight of sagacity which is the iron to the dart of genius is needful to satisfy me, the undertone of another and deeper knowledge does not please, does not command me," she wrote Channing in another letter that June, critiquing his overbroad claims for Christianity's historical influence. "'Was ever sorrow like to his sorrow' is not for me, as I have been, as I am." Later that fall, while staying for a month with the Emersons, in recounting in her journal an "excellent talk" earlier in the day with her old theological guide Henry Hedge, she explained more fully her existential resistance to the Christian church and faith. After observing that both the conservative Transcendentalist Hedge and the radical Transcendentalist Channing embraced religions that emphasized "the Church & the Race," she wrote:

> I see that side, but care more for the other. What is done here at home in my heart is my religion. I said to H. I see not one step before me, and my only act is to live to day, and not hasten to conclusions. Let others choose their way, I feel that mine is to keep my equipoise as steadfastly as I may, to see, to think, a faithful sceptic, to reject nothing but accept nothing till it is affirmed in the due order of mine own nature. I belong nowhere. I have pledged myself to nothing. God and the soul and nature are all my creed, subdivisions are unimportant.—As to your Church, I do not deny the church, who can that holds communion on themes of permanent interest as I do with several minds. I have my church where I am by turns priest & lay man. I take these simpler modes, if the world prefers more complex, let it. I act for myself, but prescribe for none other.[11]

Fuller's faithful skepticism would always remain a puzzle to her religiously committed Transcendentalist friends. "The radical flaw [of her character was her want] of religion," Parker would write after her death. "She did not know, did not feel, did not trust the infinite God." Yet twenty years later, Channing would declare in a lecture, "She was the most devoutly religious person [I have] known." Both were right to some degree, although Channing, who talked with her more about religious questions than any other friend, would seem to have been far more so. "All my life is aspiration," she had written two years earlier in her journal on the eve of her psychoreligious "crisis." "Faith not works shall save us." And how do we know? "Ourselves are all we know of heaven," that same year she had told Emerson. Probably no antebellum intellectual expressed so insistently the Romantic longing for a post-Christian sacred sensibility that had been the hallmark, first in Germany and soon throughout Europe, of nineteenth-century intellectual religion. For Fuller, who wrote in the flyleaf of her Bible one of Novalis's "Hymns to the Night," the "deeper" religion that counted was always in the questing. If there was such a thing as a Romantic Transcendental seeker, Fuller was surely it.[12]

II

Fuller's peripatetic seeking that summer of 1842 also extended to more worldly concerns. For the past year she had been bouncing around among the Farrars, Brook Farm, her mother's family in Canton, and various homes of her friends until, in mid-June, landing in New Bedford to spend a week at her wealthy "Aunt" Mary Rotch's house. After riding around visiting Rotch's well-to-do Quaker and Unitarian friends in their mansions, she mused about the effects of their money. "How can one be sure of not sitting down in the midst of indulgence to pamper tastes alone," she wrote Channing, "and how easy to cheat one's self with the fancy that a little easy reading or writing is quite work. I am safer; I do not sleep on roses." Her narrow finances, however, did not inspire in her much affinity for her New England Whig friends' lower-class Democratic opponents. Arriving in Providence on the twenty-fifth to visit her old Coliseum Club colleagues, she found herself in a city in turmoil over the restrictive-suffrage Whig governor's declaration of martial law and jailing of the "People's Constitution" governor Thomas Dorr and many of his supporters. "A city full of grown-up people as wild, as mischief-seeking, as full of prejudice, careless slander, and exaggeration, as a herd of boys in the playground of the worst boarding-school," she reported schoolmarmishly to Channing. "What a change from the almost vestal quiet of 'Aunt Mary's' life, to all this open-windowed, open-eyed screaming of 'poltroon,' 'nefarious plan,' 'entire depravity,' &c. &c." Evidently Fuller could not work up much sympathy for a "democracy" fueled by Jacksonian populist rhetoric dedicated to establishing "universal" white manhood suffrage.[13]

Yet she acknowledged the value of the Dorrites' principle, and in her journal she reflected a little more judiciously on the concept of democracy, which had recently become the honored catchphrase of both political parties. It would terrible, she thought, if democratic movements caused people to jettison beautiful art and interesting ideas just because they seemed inconsistent with popular principles. Yet democracy was obviously a healthy outgrowth of the "genius of peaceful yet energetic Christianity" that had overturned oppressive and slothful societies. What was needed, then, was a new cultural renaissance to broaden and deepen the country's "great" but "brief" and "*unsated*" enlightened Revolution. "There is a blank in the public mind that requires to be filled up," she said, sounding like a Romantic Alexis de Tocqueville, whose half-friendly, aristocratic liberal critique *Democracy in America* she had admiringly read two years earlier.

> Would society burst forth so frequently into these superstitious ebullitions called
> *Revivals*, if the chords of genuine feeling were struck in the human heart,—if the
> pure tones of devotion were regularly and calmly, and sweetly elicited by the di-
> vine touch of art whether the poetical, the musical, or the graphical[?] They should,
> indeed, be as original and native, and as coincident with the genius of the new era,
> as were the political acts of the heroes of the revolution—the ends, the thoughts
> and expressions of a Hamilton, a Jefferson, or a Madison.

In short, despite her religious heterodoxy, after two years at the helm of the *Dial*,
she stuck to the same politically liberal, socially anxious, and culturally Romantic line with which she had begun.[14]

Still, she was restless and frustrated in her writing, so following her visits to
Providence and Brook Farm, that July she went with James Clarke and his wife,
Anna, to spend two weeks in the White Mountains in New Hampshire. While she
enjoyed renewing her intimacy with Clarke, this popular vacation spot of woods
and waterfalls did not alter her aggravated mood. After returning to Cambridge,
she wrote him that she hoped after their chats he would now "better know how to
pardon the probable . . . non-fulfilment" of her life's "earthly promise." The visit
even revived her old sense of misplacement in New England. "Merely gentle and
winning scenes are not enough for me," she wrote her pastoralist brother Richard. "I wish my lot had been cast amid the sources of the streams, where the voice
of the hidden torrent is heard by night, where the eagle soars, and the thunder
resounds in long peals from side to side, where the grasp of a more powerful
emotion has rent asunder the rocks, and the long purple shadows fall like a broad
wing upon the valley." After several weeks at the Farrars, she moved on to a seemingly unlikely place for satisfying this yearning.[15]

Since her frank exchange with Emerson the previous October over their phi-
losophies of love and friendship, she had continued to smooth rough patches in
their personal friendship. "It is to be hoped, my best one," she bluntly told him
that March—after he had written "You know best of all living how to flatter your
friend"—"that the experiences of life will yet correct your vocabulary, and, that
you will not always answer the burst of frank affection by the use of such a word
as "*flattery*." In fact, despite this residual twitch, he was becoming interested in
her Goethean and hermetic ideas about the "Daemoniacal" or "*instinctive*" in life
and literature. He also seems to have stopped expressing his skepticism about her.
"Waldo has done that, which I never expected him to do," she excitedly wrote
Caroline Sturgis after a visit with him a week following her knuckle rapping. "I
cannot tell how painful it has been to meet continually on so intimate a footing,—
to feel so great a mutual regard, and yet with no understanding, at least on my
part. . . . Now he has been so generous, and so given up, so his sceptical waiting,
that I feel we might meet at anytime, though there are such differences to reconcile." For a while, encouraged by Emerson, she even considered buying with her
mother a house and farm in Concord, although she dropped the idea as financially
unfeasible. Meanwhile, he urged her at least to come for a long stay and "establish your desk & inkhorn" at his house. So, "tired to death of dissipation" and

hoping for "inspiration" in a "congenial setting," she proposed just that. He immediately responded:

> Well, please to come, for this I have always desired that you will make my house in some way useful to your occasions & not a mere hotel for a sleighing or summering party. I admire the conditions of the treaty, that you shall put on sulkiness as a morning gown, & I shall put on sulkiness as a surtout, and speech shall be contraband & the exception not the rule. I say nothing, I think nothing in these days, & shall be glad of so fair a diplomatic veil for dulness.[16]

The arrangements graciously if a little ironically glossed, Fuller arrived on August 17. Actually, notwithstanding Emerson's usual monastic protestations, his extended circle continued to grow. Besides Thoreau, Elizabeth Hoar had been regularly staying at Bush, in her case to help Lidian after the recent birth of their second and third children, Ellen and Edith. Two new couples were also nearby. One was the newlyweds Nathaniel and Sophia Hawthorne, who had just moved into Emerson's recently deceased stepgrandfather Ezra Ripley's parsonage, the "Old Manse." Earlier in the month, Ellery Channing had left Ellen in Cincinnati and come to the Emersons' to stay while searching for a house in town they could rent. Unfortunately, Emerson's "isolated & sacred" kingdom had its communal snake. That was not just friendship, or even "love," but something carefully suppressed in his and Fuller's feverishly sublimated exchanges: marriage and sexual attraction. To be sure, she knew a lot about the literary Romantic ins and outs of the subject, as any devoted reader of Goethe and Sand would. And it had hovered unspoken in the background of everything she had said and heard about the "crisis" of Sam and Anna Ward. What she had never seen close up, however, was how it played itself out in actual, Romantic-minded, flesh-and-blood marriages.[17]

The first couple to lift its curtain for her was the Hawthornes. However one interprets Hawthorne's apparent later slander of her character and intellect in their son Julian's posthumous version of his father's journal after their deaths, their papers express wholly friendly feelings toward her that summer. Sophia, who proudly attended Fuller's Conversations, addressed her as "My Priestess!" in a sonnet, which she had enclosed the previous May in a warm note announcing her engagement to Hawthorne. Nathaniel's early comments on Fuller were more cautious and occasionally, as with his obstreperous Brook Farm cow joke, barbed. Yet even before her encouraging review of his *Twice-Told Tales*, which came out a few days before his wedding, his recorded expressions were graciously welcoming. "Margaret can now when she visits Mr Emerson, spend part of the time with us," he had told Sophia after they had decided to marry and move to Concord. While she was there, their friendliness seems to have increased. "We were delighted," Sophia wrote her mother, describing her springing from her husband's embrace when Fuller suddenly appeared in the hall. "'She came in so beautifully' as Mr Hawthorne truly said, & he looked full of a gleaming welcome. We put her into the easiest chair, for she was pale & weary, & disrobed her shawl & bonnet, & prevailed upon her to stay to tea. . . . She was like the moon, radiant & gentle." After that drop-in visit, Fuller described in her journal her and Hawthorne's musings as he walked her back to Bush: "We stopped some time to look at the moon[;] she was struggling with the clouds. He said he should be much more willing to die than two months ago, for he had some real possession in life, but still he never wished to leave this earth: it was beautiful enough. He expressed, as he always does, many fine perceptions. I like to hear the slightest thing he says." Two days later Hawthorne came across her on his way back from Emerson's, lying with a book near a path in the woods on the edge of Sleepy Hollow cemetery, which he afterward turned into a memorable pastoral journal entry. An old man passed by, smiling benevolently at Margaret reclining and Hawthorne sitting close by, as though he had thought they were a couple. They talked about autumn, about the pleasures of being lost in the woods, about the crows, whose voices Margaret had heard, about the view of mountains from a distance and from the summits, about the way early childhood experiences remained years later unconsciously shaping one's character, "and about other matters of high and low philosophy." The entry concluded with Emerson suddenly breaking in on them, a nice touch, by accident or design, illustrating their mutual interest in those twilight impulses of the heart that largely passed by the Concord philosopher and his upright Transcendentalist friends.[18]

Yet the truly dark and light dimensions of Hawthorne's heart and marriage were closed to Fuller (as they were to all but his most discerning readers). Although this is hardly surprising in view of the conventional reticence that would have stood between any single nineteenth-century woman and her middle-class married friends, with the Hawthornes, that barrier had a special firmness. Indeed, their ostentatious celebration of their marriage as an earthly heaven would make them perhaps the most famous literary couple in America to live out the Victorian quasi-religion of cloistered and mutually worshiping marital bliss. "We have soared into a region where we talk together in a language that can have no earthly echo," Nathaniel wrote to Sophia in one letter following her return from one of Fuller's Conversations, explaining his curious wish that "Miss Fuller might lose her tongue!—or my Dove her ears, and so be left wholly to her husband's golden silence." But what is more remarkable, in view of this perfumed exclusivity, is that Fuller found the Hawthornes' marriage—or at least what she imagined it to be—immensely attractive. In her response to Sophia's announcement of their impending wedding, she had described what it would be all about.

> It is a love given not chosen, and the growth not of wants and wishes, but of the demands of character. . . . I think there will be great happiness, for if ever I saw a man who combined delicate tenderness to understand the heart of woman, with quiet depth and manliness enough to satisfy her, it is Mr Hawthorne. How simple and rational, too, seems your plan of life. You will be separated only by your several pursuits and just enough daily to freshen the founts of thought and feeling; to one who cannot think of love merely in the heart, or even the common destiny of two souls, but as necessarily comprehending intellectual friendship, too, it seems the happiest lot imaginable that lies before you. . . . As far as bearing an intelligent heart I think I deserve to be esteemed a friend.[19]

As a picture of Fuller's emerging Romantic companionate marital ideal, this was a revealing snapshot. It also accurately captured that sexual ambiguity that lay at the bottom of Hawthorne's literary power and, probably, although one would not know it from Fuller's glowing account, psychological insecurity. As a portrait of the Hawthornes' marriage, however, it was somewhat fantastic. Certainly, it was fantastic in imagining that "character" overrode for Nathaniel and Sophia conventional "wants and wishes." More practically important, Fuller's happy caricature implied an authority on her part that once asserted, even with an "intelligent heart," was unlikely to be always met with an altogether hearty welcome. And sure enough, in a letter a few days after their Sleepy Hollow talk, Hawthorne flatly turned down her charitable suggestion to Sophia, made at Ellery's "earnest request," that they take in Ellery and Ellen as boarders at the Old Manse. Even angels would have interrupted Adam and Eve in their Eden, he graciously said, and besides, he wanted to protect Sophia, who was open to the proposal, from extra housekeeping work. More revealing, though, the burned-out former Brook Farmer also went on to pillory all nonconjugal living arrangements, wherein, he assured her, "four sensitive people" would inevitably find "but a trifle" would render "their whole common life diseased and intolerable." If she wanted to stretch the happy couple's conventional marital boundaries, she would have to try a different tack.[20]

The less angelic Channings posed a different sort of marital challenge to Fuller's unmarried Romantic ingenuity. Ellen would later prove heroically patient and resourceful in coping with her poor health and bad marriage. But like all Fuller's siblings, she could be stubborn and impetuous, and no more so, in the eyes of her friends and family, than in her insistence on establishing her Transcendental place in the sun by marrying the impecunious and irresponsible Ellery because she felt, as she said, a "holy" cause to develop his character. Then there was the motherless and now unemployed Ellery. Sporadically charming and clever, he was often moody and needy, as well as sometimes gripped, before and after marriage, by a perverse penchant for demanding special attentions from unmarried women in their circle. At first Fuller seems to have taken his Transcendentalist quirks in stride, even as he alternately complained about her "Germanity" and broadly hinted at his superior Transcendental ways. "I do not read," he had told her, after she sent him a gift of a volume of Shakespeare sonnets. "I am chiefly engaged with doing nothing. I own I have a large penchant for this species of occupation." After reading some of his poems, she felt impressed with his cheeky unworldliness, which she interpreted as a Transcendentalist commitment "really to live" sincerely, as though he were a slightly delinquent version of his friend Thoreau. As she saw more of his fits at Bush, however, she began to reevaluate. "It is terrifying," she reported to Caroline Sturgis, once a flame of his, "to see any one so sensitive, moody, and plastic to every change." A few months later, she would pithily describe him to Emerson as "a genius with a little wretched boy trotting by his side."[21]

These difficulties burst into view on the evening of September 9, when the stagecoach from Cincinnati arrived in a pouring rain and deposited at the Emersons' front door (in Margaret's words) "my poor little prodigal" Ellen yearning to see her husband. But he was not there. He had gone to Naushon Island, where Caroline had invited him to visit her. After he had told Margaret that it would be his "last chance" to see Caroline, she had thought it would be fine, as long he got back before Ellen returned. If Margaret had thought, however, as she seems to have, that Ellery's excursion would solidify both his new marriage and his old friendship, she had been a bit naïve. She might have guessed what would happen, since she knew from Caroline's letters that Caroline had been sorely disappointed over Ellery's marrying Ellen, whom she did not think "noble enough to be his wife," while Caroline remained, as Fuller had told her, "much in his mind." When Ellery failed to return on the day he had promised, Fuller recorded in her journal the enfolding pain and terror that gripped the Emerson household as she tried to keep Ellen from knowing where he had gone. "How people can ever bear the task of dissembling or concealing I can't think," she wrote in her journal, "one minute of it is so painful." The pain increased during a "wretched night" in bed with Ellen as Margaret tried to clarify her feelings about such nonmarital relationships.

> "I hope you will like Ellery so that he may enjoy being with you: he needs the stimulus of such minds. He values Cary's very much: he reads her letters a great deal: Do you know whether he has seen her?"—I believe, he has, said, I, & I *thought* "poor deluded innocent"—Then I thought over all these relations once more, but I still came to the same result that I always do. If I were Waldo's wife, or Ellery's wife, I should acquiesce in all these relations, since they needed them. I should expect the same feeling from my husband, & I should think it little in him not to have it. I felt I should never repent of advising Ellery to go whatever happened.[22]

Outwardly, there turned out to be no reason to repent. The next morning, right after Fuller fired off anxious letters to Caroline at Naushon and Clarke in Boston, urging them to find out "quietly" where Ellery was, he returned. Privately exculpating herself with the thought that her "great mistake" had been always to assume "that he & others will surely do as they intend," she described in her journal the closing scene that pitted Bush's freedom-loving men against the Transcendental but still family-minded women: "Mamma [Emerson's mother] & Lidian sympathized with me almost with tears, Waldo looked radiant, & H[enry]. T[horeau]. as if his tribe had won a victory. Well it was a pretty play, since it turned out no tragedy at last. Ellery told Ellen at once how it was, and she took it just as she ought."[23]

III

Presumably, taking it "just as she ought" meant they both saw matters as Fuller did: marriage should not be exclusive of other deep, if undefined, heterosexual ties. If so, the notion was only a temporary fix for the Channings' troubled marriage. For Fuller, though, it was the key, and she tried to insert it the furthest into the marital lock of their circle's most famous Concord couple.

In many ways, Lidian, who had been married to Emerson for seven years, was a perfect mate for Concord's poet-priest. Tall, witty, eloquent, and graceful, she had large eyes prominently set in a thin and "very . . . pale" face that accentuated her air of lofty abstraction, which she displayed even while entertaining family and friends. Yet they had their differences. A Swedenborgian, abolitionist, and animal rights vegetarian, Lidian was starting to cultivate an almost morbid identification with suffering in this world and resurrection in the next that mixed uneasily with her husband's sublimely naturalist and ethically self-reliant religion. "Lidian sometimes taxed me at home with an egotism more virulent than any against which I rail," Emerson had confided to Fuller a few months earlier. Still, even these thorns they usually cushioned by mutual respect and humor, sometimes a little acidic. He called her "Queenie" because of her grace, and, more ironically, because of her depth of feeling, "Asia." She wrote her own "Transcendental Bible," which he claimed greatly amused him: "Loathe and shun the sick. They are in bad taste, and may untune us for writing the poem floating through our mind."[24]

Two recent developments had given these differences a more acrid character. The worst was the death the previous January of their five-year-old "wonderful boy," Waldo Jr. "Shall I ever dare to love any thing again," Emerson had cried out in a letter to Fuller the next morning. "O my boy!" Fuller, along with Emerson's entire circle, mourned the loss of their heir apparent, "from whom I hoped more than any living being," she wrote William Channing, echoing what she had told Emerson about this "living word" who had carried their letters back and forth at Bush in the fall. When she first arrived for her visit, though, Lidian seemed to be the one in constant mourning, while Waldo appeared, Fuller thought, only "subdued." In fact, he remained deeply affected as he struggled to assimilate this latest family tragedy to his crystalline god of subjective "Truth." ("I will speak the Truth also in my secret heart, or *think the truth* against what is called God," he had written defiantly in his first entry in a new journal after Waldo's death.) Less catastrophic but also dangerous was Emerson's increasing openness about his ideas, undoubtedly stimulated by perfervid exchanges with Fuller and Sturgis (whose letters, in good Transcendentalist fashion, he showed to Lidian) on the philosophical problematic of marriage. In a remarkable passage at the height of these exchanges two autumns before, he had condemned as "frightful" the belief of Lidian's revered Swedenborg that marriages continued in the "celestial" world. "All loves, all friendships are momentary. *Do you love me*? means at last *Do you see the same truth I see*? If you do, we are happy together: but when presently one of us passes into the perception of new truth, we are divorced and the force of all nature cannot hold us to each other." In substance, of course, this was no different from what he had told Fuller in their debates over love and friendship, but the edgy tone and marital context marked a tense difference, which Fuller quickly perceived.[25]

Throughout her visit, these tensions kept surfacing. The first incident occurred when, after Fuller's first couple of days, she visited Lidian in her room, where she had been convalescing since Fuller's arrival, whereupon Lidian, who had been medicating herself with opium for facial swelling from a dental operation, burst into tears. With Fuller embarrassed and uncertain whether to stay or leave, Lidian then suggested that Emerson had been spending the evenings talking with Margaret. Suddenly, "a painful feeling flashed across me, such as I have not had, all has seemed so perfectly understood between us." She assured her that on both those evenings she had been with Ellery or Thoreau and Emerson had been writing in his study. Afterward she thought about whether she had been considerate enough, finally concluding not only that she had, but, given his personality, so had Emerson.

> I never keep him away from any such duties, any more than a book would.—He lives in his own way, & don't soothe the illness, or morbid feelings of a friend, because he would not wish any one to do it *for him*. It is useless to expect it; what does it signify whether he is with me or at his writing. L. knows perfectly well, that he has no regard for me or any one that would make him wish to be with me, a minute longer than I could fill up the time with thoughts.
>
>   As to my being more his companion that cannot be helped, his life is in the intellect not the affections. He has affection for me, but it is because I quicken his intellect.—I dismissed it all, as a mere sick moment of L.'s.[26]

"Sick moment" or not, the conversations continued, getting at once more philosophical and more personal. A week later, reporting on a "golden afternoon" on the way to the Concord hemlocks, talking of "Man and Woman, and Marriage" interspersed with Swedenborg's "celestial" marriages, French socialism's passions, and Dante's philosophy of love, Fuller wrote again in her journal:

> W. took his usual ground. Love is only phenomenal, a contrivance to nature, in her circular motion. Man, in proportion as he is completely unfolded is man and woman by turns. The soul knows nothing of marriage, in the sense of a permanent union between two personal existences. The Soul is married to each new thought as it enters into it. If his thought puts on the form of man or woman[,] if it last you seventy years, what then? There is but one love, that for the Soul of all Souls, let it put on what cunning disguises it will, still at last you find yourself lonely,—*the Soul*.
>
>   There seems to be no end to these conversations: they always leave us both where they found us, but we enjoy them, for we often get a good expression.

After this remarkable discourse on the "Soul" effacing not only the "contrivance" of love but gender as well, Emerson picked a more uncomfortably personal thread extending to marriage's stifling of "Soul": "Waldo said 'Ask any woman whether her aim in this union is to further the genius of her husband; and she will say yes, but her conduct will always be to claim a devotion day by day that will be injurious to him, if he yields.['] 'Those who hold their heads highest,' quote he, with a satirical side glance, 'would do no better, if they were tried.' I made no reply, for it is not worthwhile to, in such cases, by *words*."[27]

These Platonic exchanges of good expressions reached a culmination of sorts at dinner the next evening. Somehow Lidian had gotten the idea that the two had arranged to take another walk by themselves after supper, causing her again to burst into tears, after which the entire family looked at their plates and the "serene" Emerson stared at the ground. ("Waldo said not a word: he retained his sweetness of look, but never offered to do the least thing. I can never admire him enough at such times; he is so true to himself.") So Fuller took a stroll with Lidian instead, afterward thinking some more about their triangle. Things would never

be good between Waldo and Lidian, she thought, "because she has always a lurk-
ing hope that Waldo's character will alter, and that he will be capable of an intimate union." Things would also not get worse, though, "for he is sorely troubled
by imperfections in the tie, because he don't believe in any thing better.—/And
where he loved her first, he loves her always." As for herself and Emerson, although she was coming to appreciate their peculiar friendship, "I don't know that
I could have fortitude for it in a more intimate relation. Yet nothing could be nobler, nor more consoling than to be his wife, if one's mind were only thoroughly
made up to the truth." Finally, as for the truth of her and Lidian, "I have really
thought that she was happy to have me in the house solely for Waldo's sake, and
my own, and she is, I know, in the long account, but there are pains of every day
which I am apt to neglect for others as for myself."[28]

In fact, Fuller's real feelings about these contretemps, as her admiring aside
about the serene Emerson staring at the ground would suggest, were hardly so
balanced toward Lidian. Another conversation she had with her a couple weeks
made this apparent. After Lidian read to Fuller something she had written about
little Waldo, Fuller recounted, "She said the Angels look on what you do, perhaps with as much disdain as you and Waldo would on Mrs. Hemans." To this
Swedenborgian putdown of the pair's avant-garde elitism, Fuller stumbled out,
"but ever, ever we are striving to the more excellent. Forgive if we are narrow
and cold on the way." Then, evidently seeing an opening, Lidian read to her
Emerson's answer to a set of questions (now lost) that Fuller had posed to him
about his philosophy of marriage, causing Fuller this time to *defend* Emerson's
stoically Transcendental view of love.

> When she read me W's answer to my questions, & said when he would not answer
> so as to meet her wants, she thought Christ would if he were there. I told her yet
> just so did Christ answer *his* disciples again and again Feed my lambs & nothing
> more, no explanations, no going out of himself to meet their wants. Both she and
> Mamma were struck by this, but L. will not remember it. . . . Nothing makes me so
> anti-Christian, & so anti-marriage as these talks with L. She lays such undue stress
> on the office of Jesus, & the demands of the heart.[29]

Fuller's position between the Emersons, then, was complicated. She had at least
an inkling of how hurtful Waldo's bond with her was, rightly or wrongly, to the
depressed Lidian. Just before she left she promised herself she would "do more in
attending to her," which she did, and it seems to have helped. "She has such a
tenderness, such a reverence for you," Lidian would write three months later to
Waldo after Fuller made her a "very good" long call "—that I love very much to
speak of you with her." Yet the Emersons' marriage was troubled, and Fuller was
Emerson's closest female companion with charms for him that Lidian could neither replicate nor, despite her implied profession to the contrary, ignore. Furthermore, Fuller never was able to sympathize very much with Lidian's depression,
which seemed to her exaggerated. "I feel her child is far more to her imagination
than he ever was in reality," she wrote in her journal, echoing a view of others in
the Emerson household. And on the philosophical issue, there was no question: if

forced to choose between Lidian's somewhat morbid Christian spiritualism and Waldo's somewhat chilling spiritual stoicism, Fuller stood firmly with the latter.[30]

Fuller's five-week-plus visit to Bush had several fruits. One was her three philosophical poems that Emerson afterward titled "La Nuovissima Vita" after Dante's *La Vita Nuova*'s paean to love as an instrument of spiritual salvation. One meter-making argument is virtually a reply to Emerson: the "union of Two doth not exclude the All in one," as long as the "beloved object" does "not supply the needs of your poverty, / but call into action your riches." A second asserts transcendent love and not the transcendent self is the driving force energizing life:

> A force which knows both starting point & goal,
> A home in *heaven*, the union in the Soul.

Love is not merely "phenomenal"; rather it is the necessary means to develop ourselves, interact with our world, and find our way to heaven and thereby, in Romantic circuitous fashion, back "home." Emerson, too, got some good "expressions" from their visit. His interest piqued by her avant-garde Danteism, which predated by several years the Pre-Raphaelites' initiation of the English rage for the Italian poet, he tried to get her to translate Dante's *Vita Nuova* for him, and then after she declined, because she thought it technically too difficult, wrote his own "ruggedest" English prose translation, the first ever done. Meanwhile, he would mine their love conversations for his long poem "Intitial, Daemonic, and Celestial Love," whose scope for passionate love was notably greater than anything suggested in his earlier tepid essay "Love" written just before plunging into his friendship debates with Fuller. More seminal than a "good expression," Fuller took away from her visit a provocation to imagine a marital path diverging from both the Hawthornes' narcissistic nuptials and Emerson's sublimely evanescent coupling.[31]

The visit also provoked her to draw some conclusions about herself as an unmarried woman within her Concord Transcendentalists' circle. "I suppose the whole amount of the feeling is that women can't bear to be left out of the question," she wrote in her journal after thinking more about Lidian's dinner-table outburst.

> And they don't see the whole truth about one like me, if they did they would understand why the brow of Muse or Priestess must wear a shade of sadness. On my side I don't remember them enough. They have so much that I have not, I can't conceive of their wishing for what I have (*enjoying* is not the word: these I know are too generous for that). But when Waldo's wife, & the mother of that child that is gone thinks me the most privileged of women, & that E[lizabeth]. H[oar]. was happy because her love was snatched away for a life long separation, & thus she can know none but ideal love: it does seem a little too insulting at first blush.—And yet they are not altogether wrong.

Both a gainer and loser in the Transcendental love and marriage game, she realized, too, that her status as a struggling single woman also marked out a different life path for her than that of her Transcendentalist friends. To be sure, she remained proud of them. "I do not believe that a life has been ever lived which without effort so nearly approached that of the academic Grove," she wrote in her journal her last week. Yet she also knew that both her frustrated "*ambition*" and her craving for "deeper, wider, further, higher" experience put her outside their circle of delinquents and idealists. Recalling in her journal an earlier talk in her room with Ellery, who "rail[ed] at me as . . . disciplined, artificial . . . too ideal . . . & so on in the very tone of William's damning letter," she wrote: "A path has been appointed me. I have walked in it as steadily as I could. 'I am what I am.' That which I am not, teach me in the others. I will bear the pain of imperfection, but not of doubt. Waldo must not shake me in my worldliness, nor William in the fine motion that has given me what I have of life, nor this child of genius, make me lay aside the armour without which I had lain bleeding on the field long since."[32]

Finally, she knew she was approaching a last turning point with Emerson. "Waldo and I have good meetings, though we stop at all our old places," she wrote in her journal during her second week at Bush. "But my expectations are moderate now: it is his beautiful presence that I prize, far more than our intercourse." Along with their mutual relinquishment of sweeping claims on each other went a new mutual tolerance of their fundamental differences, including sexual-sounding ones. ("I said I never could meet him here," referring to his perpetually frustrated need to "press to the centre" to know nature's "whole secret," and her satisfaction "for the moment, full as if my existence were filled out.") Ultimately, their largest difference, as she saw it, was religious: "We agreed that my god was love, his truth. W. said that these statements alternate, of course, in every mind, the only difference was in which you were most at home, that he liked the pure mathematics of the thing." In fact, her closure went still deeper than a mutual tolerance of each other's differences; it also affected her "recognition" of *him*, which she described in a long letter she wrote from Bush to her very non-Emersonian Transcendentalist friend William Channing. She narrated an unsparing history of their friendship, beginning with their first exciting intimacy, when she was thrilled by his "spiritual purity" and "freedom and infinite graces of an intellect cultivated beyond any I had known," to the "questioning season," when "he absolutely distrusted me in every region of my life with which he was unacquainted." Nor was that all. "The same trait I detected in his relations with others. He had faith in the Universal, but not the Individual Man; he met men, not as a brother, but as a critic." Quoting liberally from the last two years of their correspondence, she summarized her new understanding of him.

> No one can feel his limitations, in fact, more than he, though he always speaks confidently from his present knowledge as all he has yet, and never qualifies or explains. He feels himself "shut up in a crystal cell," from which only "a great love or a great task could release me," and hardly expects either from what remains in this life. But I already see so well how these limitations have fitted him for his peculiar work, that I can no longer quarrel with them; while from his eyes looks out the angel that must sooner or later break every chain. Leave him in his cell affirming absolute truth; protesting against humanity, if so he appears to do; the calm observer of the courses of things.

At its deepest level, her coming to terms effected, she thought, her introjection of him as a salutary counter-self. "What did you mean by saying I had imbibed much of his way of thought?" she demanded of Channing, whose assertion she rightly took as at least partly a criticism. "I do indeed feel his life stealing gradually into mine. And it sometimes seems, as if the work of my own life would have been more simple, and my unfolding to a temporal activity, more rapid and easy, if we had never met. But when eternal growth is thought of I am conscious of having become far larger and deeper for his influence. . . . He stops me from doing and makes me *think*." She also added a prediction. The current "very noble" denouement of their social and intellectual wars had released her creative capacities: "You will see the change, if I am successful in producing anything."[33]

Her visit to Bush had brought to a virtual close her striving with Emerson, although for as long as they lived in the Boston-Concord axis, the balance would always require from her some effort to maintain. "I get, after a while, even *intoxicated* with your mind, and do not live enough in myself," she confided in a warm note a month afterward, explaining why she was glad she did not now live near him. "Now don't screw up your lip to an ungracious pettiness but hear the words of frank affection as they deserve 'mente cordis.' . . . You need not be terrified . . . nor look about for the keys of your cell. . . . I shall no more be so ruled by the affectionate expansions of my heart." For his part, more than just letting go his skepticism, he seems to have had some epiphany about her. "He apotheosized her," the startled Hawthorne reported to Sophia after talking with him following Emerson's return from his winter lecture tour, "as the greatest woman, I believe, of ancient or modern times, and the one figure in the world worth considering." But his most astonishing tribute—which he would later mine for his portrait of the ideal heroic woman in his essay "Manners"—was this deeply sympathetic one he wrote in his journal shortly after reading her "Vita Nuovissima":

> It is a great joy to find that we have underrated our friend. . . . She excels other intellectual persons in this, that her sentiments are more blended with her life; so the expression of them has greater steadiness & greater character. I have never known any example of such steady progress from stage to stage of thought & of character. . . . She rose before me at times into heroical & godlike regions, & I could remember no superior women, but thought of Ceres, Minerva, Proserpine, and the august ideal forms of the Foreworld. . . . She has great sincerity, force, & fluency as a writer, yet her powers of speech throw her writing into the shade. What method, what exquisite judgment, as well as energy, in the selection of her words, what character & wisdom they convey! You cannot predict her opinion. She sympathizes so fast with all forms of life, that she talks never narrowly or hostilely nor betrays, like all the rest, under a thin garb of new words, the old droning castiron opinions or notions of many years standing. . . . Meanwhile, all the pathos of sentiment and riches of literature & of invention and this march of character threatening to arrive presently at the shores & plunge into the sea of Buddhism & mystic trances, consists with a boundless fun & drollery, with light satire, & the most entertaining conversation in America.[34]

With her Romantic rapprochement with Emerson and her defense of her life of "prophetic" striving in a kinetic age requiring a bit more exertion than Plato's novitiates had needed, she concluded her days at Concord. Her last morning at

Bush was September 26. The previous one she had spent finishing reading the rest of Emerson's journals, after which she had had one last "best" talk about their favorite cultural themes of friendship, genius, and talent. Afterward she had chatted with Elizabeth Hoar, who asked her if he would not be sad when she was gone. "I told her, no, relieved rather,—for all the things he says in his Essays on these subjects are true of himself." The next morning Lidian and Mamma took her to Boston. "Farewell, dearest friend," she wrote, concluding her journal, "there has been dissonance between us, & may be again, for we do not fully meet, and to me you are too much & too little by turns, yet thanks be to the Parent of Souls, that gave us to be born into the same age and the same country and to meet with so much nobleness and sweetness as we do, & I think constantly with more and more." In fact, they did not. How could they? With Fuller's tribute to Emerson for stopping her from doing and making her "*think*" and his to her providing him with a model of heroic intellectual womanhood, they had achieved as close to mutual "recognition" as two great friendly foes were ever fated to do.[35]

IV

After spending the first week of October at Brook Farm, Fuller returned to Cambridge refreshed by her fall of communing. "I have plagues about me, but they don't touch me now," she assured Elizabeth Hoar, attributing the fact to her rare good health and "unaccustomed serenity." Helping with that, she and her mother that month acquired their first house since moving from Jamaica Plain, a new Queen Anne–style cottage at 8 Ellery Street in a recently developed section of the orchard she had rambled in during her family's flush time when they lived in the Dana Hill mansion a decade and a half earlier. She especially loved looking through their house's "sunshiny" window at the slowly flowing Charles, the distant Brighton and Brookline hills, and the glowing sunset over Mount Auburn, on which as a teenager she had gazed while studying the Italian Renaissance poets. Besides making her feel nostalgic, the place had next door the German homeopathic physician Robert Wesselhoeft, who obligingly examined her whenever she wanted, and his daughter Minna, who would later complete her *Günderode*. Even the bother of having to cram in, for part of the winter, Mary Rotch's niece Maria, Ellen, and the "very wretched, almost hopeless" Ellery, after he failed to find an affordable house in Concord, does not seem to have spoiled her equanimity. "Ay, surely, it is the enigma of my time that no genius shall bear both flower and fruit," she wrote Emerson, who was starting to feel the same thing about all their young Dialers; "may as well trouble myself for a thousand as one. So I am not troubled."[36]

True, she was troubled a little by one thing in her musings about her married state that she had not mentioned at Bush. "The darkest hue on my own lot," she wrote to her old would-be beau George Davis, "is that I have neither children, nor yet am the parent of beautiful works by which the thought of my life might be represented to another generation." Still, she now had her little family. Richard, who was also living in the house, was now eager to hear her advice about competing for prizes and grades at Harvard. In reversal of her father-centered youth, she

had also become very close with her mother. Going together to parties and concerts, mutually gossiping about friends, exchanging flowers, dress patterns, and
confidences gave them a mutually reassuring intimacy. "At *last*, she relies on me
and believes that I shall carry through what I undertake without killing myself,"
she told Hoar. "She has learnt not to be over anxious when I suffer, so I am not
obliged to repress my feelings when it is best to yield to them." Although she feared
"giving so many lessons makes more serious work impossible" (she sighed laconically to Clarke, "I shall never teach in heaven"), she also had substitute children of sorts in language-and-literature classes that she had been teaching for the
last couple of winters. She was especially solicitous of her protégées, on whom
she bestowed, along with her Italian poets and German Romantic authors, "little
confidential talks" on their private affairs. ("Do not waste these emotions," she
cautioned the fourteen-year-old Anna Loring, who had sent her a batch of her
letters. "I fear that the virginity of heart . . . may be endangered by too careless
excursions into the realms of fancy.") And she took pride in being able to support
herself and her family on what she earned. Charging $16 per student for weekly
hour-and-a-half lessons, she brought in roughly $160 a week to add to her yearly
income of $500 from her Conversations. "I . . . ask your congratulations," she
jubilantly wrote to Hoar at the end of January, announcing that her winter labors
had brought her enough money to pay all her first quarter's housekeeping bills.
"Otherwise I should have been in debt now, and I look on that proposition with a
horror worthy any old dutch burgomaster."[37]

Despite her bourgeois ethics, though, in Unitarian Boston-Cambridge where
she had now resettled she remained as controversial as ever. One old trait her
detractors would later tirelessly recall was her "personal satire." "I . . . have heard
her say terrible things to others, which brought the tears to my eyes," the worshiping but touchy Caroline Healey Dall later reported. Others, however, flatly
disagreed. "She was constantly overcoming this propensity," Ednah Dow Littlehale
Cheney would insist. "I attended her public Conversations constantly for the last
three years, and I never but once heard anything of the kind; and then, at the next
meeting, she made the most generous apology it was ever my good fortune to hear."
Emerson, who gave some credence to these charges in the *Memoirs*, nonetheless
dismissed the popular stereotype of Fuller as habitually sneering, scoffing, and
arrogant as a "superficial judgment"; what some heard as an arrogant tone, he
quipped, "was only the pastime & necessity of her talent." However that may be—
and it seems at least partly right—many of her close friends *loved* her forthright
dressing-down of hypocrites and phonies. "I have known her, by the severity of
her truth," one man contentedly told Emerson, "mow down a crop of evil, like the
angel of retribution, and could not sufficiently admire her courage."[38]

What people saw, of course, often reflected where they stood. She seems to
have had little or nothing to do with Boston-Cambridge's Calvinist, evangelical,
and, except as a sympathetic observer, Irish Catholic communities, or they with
her. Moreover, the Unitarian community was hardly a monolith. Boston's older
conservative Whig-Unitarians like Andrews Norton, George Ticknor, and their
friends seem to have despised her more than ever now that she was a public fig-

ure. Her friends would give various reasons for this: the memory of her father's Jeffersonian politics, her radical Transcendentalist associations, her biting criticism of their cultural icons like Allston and Longfellow. According to Sam Ward, who knew that crowd probably better than any in Fuller's circle, the main reason was their gender prejudices, which made them see her as a "typical blue-stocking," arrogant and pretentious. "By the bye—some lady in Providence, says, that there are three sorts of human creatures—Men, Women, and Fullers," Richard Henry Dana, Sr., fleered in a letter to his daughter. "'Capt. Fuller' is not generally liked in P, we know.—But with us in Boston, I don't know but that the Fullers outnumber the Women."[39]

Unitarian Conservatives, however, were not the only ones put off by Fuller. Some Garrisonian abolitionists continued to see nothing but arrogance in her aloofness from their movement. Some in James Russell Lowell's young Brahmin set perceived it also in her ethereal Transcendentalism, a feeling no doubt increased by her private dismissal of Lowell. "Had a long and unprofitable talk with James Lowell," she wrote in her journal after a party at the home of Convers Francis, the Harvard Divinity School professor, adding with Transcendental disdain: "He is very shallow and only sees principle externally." Even slightly antiestablishment Unitarian types found her formidable intellect made them nervous. The rising lawyer and politician Charles Sumner, then anxious to polish his image as a cultural sophisticate, who later recounted calling on her and her mother following a party at the college, described the visit as a purgatory:

> I was much frightened for everybody talked of her as a genius, etc. and a téte-à-téte (for I found Mrs. F[uller] out) was a horrible prospect. I nearly sank through the floor, as I found myself sitting by her trying some small talk. My fear increased when she began to catechise me on my reading. I told her I had been reading [John] Hoole's translation of Ariosto; she told me I was quite wrong—[William Stewart] Rose's was the best. I retired full of awe at a young lady who had not only read books in the original, but knew all about every translation. Next time I read Ariosto in the original.[40]

Yet Fuller was far from an outcast in Boston-Cambridge. As Dana's disgust with all the "Fullers" in Boston suggests, the city was changing, and in ways quite congenial to Fuller and her friends. When Sam Ward's younger sister Mary told her that her young New York friend Julia Ward (no relation), who was then guardedly taking in Fuller's Conversations and Emerson's lectures, had criticized Boston's "Coterie" culture, Fuller had to laugh: "Surely there never was a place where there was less of approximation to a harmony in views and tastes than here in Boston. It is a time of dissonance, of transition, of aspiration. No three persons think alike." Indeed, she added, alluding to all this radical reform ferment, "the preference, to be given to this over another place I should think would be that there is here a restless *almost* earnest spirit of inquiry as to What shall a man do to worthily fill the place assigned him in the universe." And these, Mary probably did not need to be told, were Transcendentalist compliments! In addition, within this ideological Boston kaleidoscope, personalities jostled, groups overlapped, and walls were permeable. Lowell's pro-Transcendentalist fiancée Maria White was a loyal member of Fuller's Conversations. While the tart-tongued wealthy Garrisonian Louisa Gilman Loring found Fuller's intellectual arrogance hard to take, Louisa's impressive lawyer-abolitionist husband Ellis liked Fuller a lot, and he and his wife put their cherished only child Anna under her tutelage. Then, too, Fuller was now a liberal literary star in the most liberal author-honoring city in America. Constantly going to lectures, concerts, soirees, and private dinners, she easily and often amiably socialized with the likes of the Bancrofts, Everetts, Howes, Greenoughs, and Francises and, of course, numerous Channings. Nor does she seem to have harbored any personal grudges except perhaps toward Holmes and Lowell, usually preferring, it would seem, to laugh off discomforts people had with her. "He seemed to be wonderfully struck by my having been a woman," she would later jokingly tell Caroline Sturgis after one visit with the Lowell set's "Byronic" Virginia classmate John Francis (or Frank) Heath, every time they met, "beginning 'On account of your sex'—'As a woman' &c." Even if nervous young intellectual males had some difficulty getting a fix on Fuller's "sex," they apparently at least thought they had to try, which she evidently enjoyed.[41]

One fact is indisputable: however controversial, she continued to enjoy a large circle of devoted friends. She suffered some losses. That fall Dr. William Ellery Channing died, provoking her to write a judicious tribute balancing his aesthetic blindness and "somewhat rigid and restricted" social manner against his admirably moderating antislavery wisdom and "true . . . respect" for woman. That fall, too, his nephew William Henry moved to Brooklyn to found a new Christian socialist church, but they kept up by letter, as did her moderate Transcendentalist friend Henry Hedge ("my first teacher"), who told her he wished he were back in Cambridge so they could learn Swedish together. Her old Cambridge neighborhood chums Eliza Farrar, Sarah Clarke, and Jane Tuckerman were nearby. Caroline Sturgis was constantly flitting about Ellery Street. Fuller's Conversations and private lessons brought her a couple of times a week into Boston, where she usually stayed overnight, often at James and Anna Clarke's Central Court house or the Wards' fashionable Louisburg Square apartment. Meanwhile, she seems to have lost none of her old tricks for gaining—or perhaps *seizing* might be a better term—intimacy. "By some secret," Ellery Channing, who rarely said anything nice about his friends, would write after her death, "she drew from most of those who surrounded her the cherished secret, which now runs like a vein of fire through all the meshes of each one's correspondence." Emerson would later testify that her innate talent for forcing intimacy and giving a "high & heroic" cast to the features of those she loved gave her more sway over others "than any person I have known." Indeed, her friendships were growing warmer. She happily noted that the Wards were now "more open to genial and inspiring themes." Her sometime-roommate at Bush, Elizabeth Hoar, who had earlier found Fuller's "restless," "Mephistophilic vein" difficult, now rejoiced, Hoar reported, in Margaret's newly "calm & affectionate" ways.[42]

Fuller also had a new line of defense in Boston liberal society in the West Roxbury Shaw and Russell families. Both Transcendentalists and Fourierists

George and Sarah Russell and Francis and Sarah Shaw were Boston's richest, most prominent, and most well-connected radical clan (Sarah Russell was Francis Shaw's sister, and Sarah Shaw was Caroline Sturgis's sister). Fuller was especially close to the Shaws, whose large house near Brook Farm she often stayed at when she visited the community. She loved to romp with their growing brood of "young uns," who included, besides the teenage Anna, later the wife of the *Harper's Weekly* editor George William Curtis, Anna's toddler siblings—the later charity worker Josephine and the future famous Union martyr Robert Gould. Accompanying Fuller to Boston galleries, operas, and concerts, the culture-loving Shaws, who liberally opened their purses to needy writers and reformers, also made sure she got gifts of money at opportune moments. Fuller gave in kind. "On reading over my letter I feel as if I assumed age and wisdom more than is natural to me," Fuller caught herself, after finishing one advice-filled note about Sarah needing to balance her parenting with some work and study of her own. "But you addressed me as Minerva and I easily took the pedestal." As with many other Boston-Cambridge women who received Fuller's "motherly" feminist homilies, Sarah was enthralled. "Of course I was nothing to her," she would later tell Higginson, "but that made no difference to her, generous soul that she was." She added, "I feel proud that I had the sense to love & venerate her as I did—I liked everything she *said*—every way she *looked*." Fuller's mien in Boston remained very much in the eye of the beholder.[43]

Fuller's "professional" circle remained, of course, as it had for the last decade, the Transcendentalists. By then the October *Dial* was out, their most cosmopolitan one yet. She was "*a little* vexed" at seeing all the typos in her review of Tennyson's *Poems* (which Emerson blamed on "the faithful Henry T.," to whom he had given the proofs), "having hoped my notice might meet the eye of the poet." But she liked the issue's variety, always a concern, singling out Parker's "almost courtly" polemical attack on the Unitarian Association, which Emerson hated ("unpoetic unspiritual & un Dialled") and his own Persian-influenced "Saadi," which she thought was one of his best poems. She did not mention her own lead contribution, "Romaic and Rhine Ballads," reviewing two new German scholarly collections of German folk legends and contemporary Greek songs. "Had we but as complete a collection as this!" she exclaimed, comparing the Greek songs to thin compilations on American Indians and nonexistent ones on poor Irish Americans at their wakes. To lift "this bustling, ambitious, superficial country" out of its provincial and materialistic torpor, she suggested that some German visit it to provide the "critical discernment" needed for the job. "Meanwhile, she urged Emerson not to give over the "Record of the Months" section while he was away on his lecture tour to anyone but her.[44]

She found maintaining her solidarity with increasingly radical utopian Transcendentalists a more difficult task. That October Emerson's "tedious archangel" had returned from his five-month stay in England, with three worshipful disciples from Alcott House in Ham, Surrey. After they were mobbed at a meeting for proselytizing their no-government views and Alcott got arrested for refusing to pay the poll tax, a gesture applauded by Garrison's *Liberator*, the following spring they purchased a ninety-acre plot in Harvard, near Concord, and shortly afterward established their "Fruitlands" "consociated family" of associated labor, Pythagorean vegetarianism, and spiritual love. "It is miserable," she wrote in her journal after reading Alcott's letters boasting about his success in England, "to see his boyish infatuation and his swelling vanity, already worse than ever." For a while Alcott's bankrolling English comrade Charles Lane impressed her, although, characteristically, not because of his views but because of his "lightning" brilliance in public debates. She likewise impressed him as a "rare woman" and "good German scholar" who "has caught the German spiritual or aesthetic philosophy but has not thereby wholly destroyed the *spirit life*." The radical Neoplatonist was right to be a little wary, as she found his "total abstinence experiment," including the refusal to exploit cows for their fertilizer, "puerile." She also questioned his socialist integrity after he retained the Fruitlands property following the community's collapse—after supposedly liberating the property from "human ownership"—and tried to peddle his English circle's one-thousand-volume "cabalistic collection" of hermetic texts, which had been entrusted to him with the understanding that he would make it available for scholarly research. ("A skilful piece of special pleading," she dryly noted, after getting his somewhat sarcastic response to her pointed questions to him.) As for his celibacy doctrine, to which he had disastrously tried to convert the Alcotts, she bluntly told him that, though she respected it, "it does not command my sympathy." "He wants living experience," she would write to another friend after visiting him, "and it is too late for many of the most precious things. There are but few who have lived a too intellectual life, but he is one of them."[45]

Fuller was beginning to look a little more favorably on the Fruitlanders' (to them) worldly rivals at Brook Farm, which she had been regularly visiting since its founding. Usually arriving by omnibus or, occasionally, aloft one of the Farm's horse-drawn farm wagons, she often stayed for several days, sometimes to check in on Lloyd, whom she had gotten temporarily readmitted to the community's school, but mostly to rest and write. She often stayed with the nearby Shaw and Russell families, who held mortgages to the farm, and sometimes dropped in on Parker, whose West Roxbury church many Brook Farmers attended, but she also had a couple of colorful boarders to host her. One was her old Cambridge chum the beautiful divorced Almira Barlow, Hawthorne's likely physical prototype (along with Fuller as an intellectual one) for Zenobia, the tragic heroine of his novel *Blithedale Romance*; Almira was highly grateful for Fuller's help trying to find her foreign language teaching and tutoring jobs. Her even more Hawthornesque frequent host was the frail and "monastic" young Charles King Newcomb, now practicing improvised Catholic rituals, complete with an altar and cross above which he hung Renaissance engravings of saints surrounding a picture of Fanny Elssler. As his "priestess," Fuller played her by now well-honed Romantic maternal role. She accompanied him on "religious" walks through the woods, took him to "divine" Boston Academy Beethoven concerts, called him her "sweet child" ("though I feel it is true Charles, what you said, that you are 'man within'"), and signed her letters, fittingly enough, "yours with the Madonna heart." Yet none of this "incense" stopped her from trying to keep him on a liberal Transcendentalist path. "I never do," she bluntly told him after he had asked her to pray for him. "Nature, in the commonest instincts is only present with me." Privately she doubted he would ever have strength to "rise above his doubts and fears" to accomplish anything publicly, and she would be right.[46]

Fuller's skepticism extended to other aspects of the Farm. Now in its second year, in exact reverse of the grimly ascetic Fruitlands, the community was still in its (in Emerson's phrase) "perpetual picnic" phase. A visitor could see young men and women, often Harvard students and their female friends, in the fields or in the house, donning blouselike black or blue tunics, or at daily lectures, dances, plays, charades, and tableaus. Partly inspired by the novels of George Sand and other French social Romantics, they craved to place themselves, Higginson recalled in his own case, "on more equal terms with that vast army of hand-workers who were ignorant of much that I knew, yet could do so much that I could not." Fuller had mixed feelings about this Transcendentalist May Day. Although she sometimes joined the masquerades and husking parties, she mostly kept to herself, studying, writing, or taking long walks in the surrounding two hundred acres of pinewoods. She also seems to have had a little trouble with the bad manners of the community's "Philistine" ideologues and bumptious young people, which were encouraged, she thought, by the general "want of conventional refinement" at the place. Although some of them found her occult "Leila" fascinating, to a number of others, she seemed to have had her own deficiencies. "When listening to her wonderful conversations," the "Amusement Group" leader Amelia Russell recalled, "and straining my mind to comprehend her meaning, I must own I have sometimes wished her English was rather plainer." Even George William Curtis, who greatly admired Fuller, would suggest delicately, "She knew so much more than all women and most of the men that she could not disguise her superiority." These tensions leap out of her journal account of a Conversation on "Education," the first of several she was asked to conduct during her October week's visit.

> I took my usual ground: The aim is perfection; patience the road. . . . The people showed a good deal of the *sans-culotte* tendency in their manners,—throwing themselves on the floor, yawning, and going out when they had heard enough. Yet, as the majority differ from me, to begin with,—that being the reason this subject was chosen,—they showed, on the whole, more respect and interest than I had expected. As I am accustomed to deference, however, and need it for the boldness and animation which my part requires, I did not speak with as much force as usual. Still, I should like to have to face all this; it would have the same good effects that the Athenian assemblies had on the minds obliged to encounter them.[47]

Fuller felt equally skeptical about the measures of her young Athenian delinquents' leaders. William Channing would later claim that her objections to Brook Farm's socialism were "preëminently . . . Transcendentalist": society was a living body that required not "forcing" but "Divine inspiration," and collective organizations of labor threatened "energy, heroism, and genius." Although this seems quite plausible, the reasons she gave that October to Sophia Ripley and several members who had gathered in Sophia's room to try to persuade her to join them

were more idiosyncratically Romantic. She told them that their hope to exclude
evil seemed to her chimerical, since, speaking in the lingo of her cosmology, "that
was a growth of nature, and one condition of the development of good." She also
said that while she thought the community to be "an *experiment* worth trying" as
an adjunct to the current "great wave of inspired thought" in American reform,
she could never have the kind of religious faith in the project that they seemed to
have. Finally, she voiced two practical objections. Although she agreed with them
about raising the "dignity of labor" by mixing tradesmen and scholars in both
schools and manual work, she balked at their current provision of equal payment
in time-shares for all labor. And she would not do physical labor!

> I said my position would be too uncertain here, as I could not work. Sophia said:—
> "They would all like to work for a person of genius. They would not like to have
> this service claimed from them, but would like to render it of their own accord."
> "Yes," I told her; "but where would be my repose, when they were always to be
> judging whether I was worth it or not. It would be the same position the clergyman
> is in, or the wandering beggar with his harp. Each day you must prove yourself
> anew. You are not in immediate relations with material things.

In laboring as a mind-worker, Fuller preferred to take her chances with the marketplace.[48]

Still, despite her misgivings, her visit ended cordially. On her last night she
gave a second deliberately provocative Conversation on "Impulse" to balance, she
said, the "great tendency there to advocate spontaneousness, at the expense of
reflection."

> It was a much better conversation than the one before. None yawned, for none came,
> this time, from mere curiosity. There were about thirty-five present, which is a large
> enough circle. Many engaged in the talk. I defended nature, as I always do;—the
> spirit ascending through, not superseding, nature. But in the scale of Sense, Intel-
> lect, Spirit, I advocated tonight the claims of Intellect, because those present were
> rather disposed to postpone them.

She concluded her journal with this aloofly friendly "good-by": "I have found
myself here in the amusing position of a conservative. Even so is it with
Mr. R[ipley]. There are too many young people in proportion to the others. I heard
myself saying, with a grave air, "Play out the play, gentles." Thus, from generation to generation, rises and falls the wave."[49]

The term "conservative," of course, is a relative thing. The question was, having for the past couple of years played the cultural provocateur for the intellectual
literati and their followers, when would she start doing it for her increasingly ideological generation?

V

"Margaret Fuller rusticates at Cambridge & does nothing," William Story sarcastically reported that March 1843 to a friend. In fact, Fuller was just then starting
to cultivate an ideological growth whose seed she had planted four years earlier.

1. Margaret Fuller, ca. early 1850s. Southworth and Hawes copy plate of daguerreotype by John Plumbe made in July 1846 for Plumbe's gallery of public figures one month before she sailed for England on assignment for the *New-York Tribune*. (Courtesy of Museum of Fine Arts, Boston)

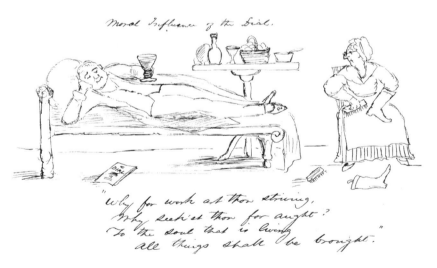

2. "Moral Influence of the Dial," cartoon by Christopher Pearse Cranch, ca. 1840. The caricature and lines taken from Caroline Sturgis's poem "Life" in the October 1840 issue of the *Dial* capture a popular image of the Transcendentalists and their younger followers in the early 1840s. The cartoon by the pro-Transcendentalist Cranch also displays a version of Romantic irony as the putative observer smiles down on his transcendent creations. (Courtesy of the Massachusetts Historical Society)

25. William Wetmore Story,
photograph, ca. 1849. (Courtesy
of the Harry Ransom Humanities
Research Center, University
of Texas at Austin)

26. Costanza Arconati Visconti,
oil portrait, ca. 1830s.
(Courtesy of the Museo del
Risorgimento, Milan)

27. Giovanni Angelo Ossoli,
daguerreotype, 1848, which
Fuller took with her to L'Aquila.
(Courtesy of the Houghton
Library, Harvard University)

28. Cristina Trivulzio
di Belgioioso, oil portrait
by Henri Lehmann, 1843.
(Courtesy of the Art
Renewal Center)

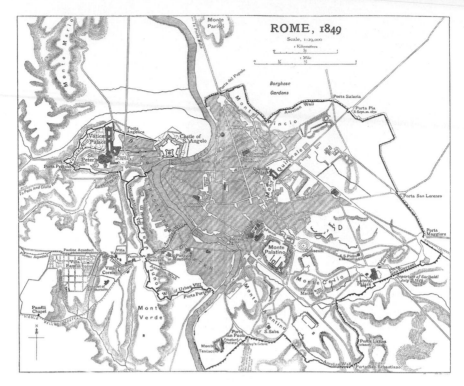

29. "Rome, 1849," Map III in George Macaulay Trevelyan, *Garibaldi's Defence of the Roman Republic, 1848–9* (London: Longmans, Green, 1907).

30. "Roman Republic Ringing a Liberty Bell," lithograph cartoon from *Il Don Pirlone*, ca. Feb.–Mar. 1849. The cartoon from the popular anticlerical Democratic humor journal depicts the Roman Republic, with the Roman wolf at her side, heralding the dawn of Italian unity by ringing a bell in the shape of the French Revolution's liberty cap, while Pope Pius IX and King Charles Albert are shown distressed by the sound. (Courtesy of the Anthony P. Campanella Collection of Giuseppe Garibaldi, Rare Books and Special Collections, Thomas Cooper Library, University of South Carolina)

31. "The Insurrection at Rome—Attack on the Pope's Palace" (lithograph from the *Illustrated London News*, Dec. 2, 1848, p. 337. "Nothing could be gentler than the disposition of the crowd," Fuller wrote in her *New-York Tribune* of the massive, threatening crowd outside the Quirinal on November 16, 1848. "I would lay my life that he could have shown himself without the slightest danger; nay, that the habitual respect for his presence would have prevailed, and hushed all the tumult"(December 2, 1848). (Courtesy of the Anthony P. Campanella Collection of Giuseppe Garibaldi, Rare Books and Special Collections, Thomas Cooper Library, University of South Carolina)

32. "First Attack of the French Troops at Rome, Near the Porta Cavellegiere," lithograph cartoon from the *Illustrated London News*, May 19, 1849, p. 321. The lithograph portrays the surprise attack in the morning of April 30, 1849, outside the Vatican walls, of the advance guard of 6,000 French soldiers led by General Nicolas Charles Victor Oudinot. (Courtesy of the Anthony P. Campanella Collection of Giuseppe Garibaldi, Rare Books and Special Collections, Thomas Cooper Library, University of South Carolina)

36. Margaret Fuller Ossoli, oil portrait by John Hicks, 1848. Although
Hicks probably painted this miniature of Fuller in Rome in the winter
or spring of 1848 before his departure to return to the United States, its
evident inspiration came from their time together in Venice in July 1847.
On a deeper level, it is politically iconographic. With Venice seen in the
background through the villa's window, Fuller appears as the pensive but
stoic and empathetic maternal presence for the Italian nation that many
of its compatriots would remember her as. (Courtesy of Constance Fuller
Threinen)

In inaugurating her women's Conversations, she had given two justifications for her meetings: negatively, women's exclusion from higher education and the learned professions, and positively, their need for a forum to discover for themselves the pursuits "best suited to us in our time and state of society." Yet for the next couple of years her cultural topics had had little to do with either gender or vocations. Even when they did, as in her meetings on "Woman" toward the end of the first series, she had tried to keep the discussions focused on women's *intellectual* capacities, which had been her key reason for rebuffing Maria Weston Chapman.[50]

If Fuller had hoped to keep them permanently so circumscribed, though, she would have had to swim against some strongly roiling gender tides. It had been exactly a half-century since the first ripples had appeared with the publication of Mary Wollstonecraft's book *A Vindication of the Rights of Woman,* which Fuller's Enlightenment-minded father had thought so valuable in rearing her. Inspired by the liberal hopes generated by the French Revolution, Wollstonecraft had delivered a rationalist assault on patriarchal prejudices and conventions suppressing women's rational understanding and moral functions. With the collapse of the French Revolution, however, this first small wave had so receded that even in England no edition of Wollstonecraft's book had been published since 1796. Meanwhile, in the early Republic, where radical Enlightenment currents had been weaker and Calvinism had a larger purchase on American religion, the current had been virtually buried by the revivals of evangelical Protestantism and its connected "cult of domesticity." Flourishing in an era when urbanization and industrialization were moving both men and production from farm households into offices, shops, and factories, this popular middle-class mindset fed on deep anxieties about the family and the proper roles of men and women. In countless sermons, lectures, books, and magazine articles, pundits propounded a galvanizing (if somewhat circular) message: because God's appointed sphere of the home nurtured religious piety and woman's true self-sacrificing nature, her education and activities had to conform to that feminized domain. Yet, like many seemingly unstoppable ideological waves, this one was encountering powerful countercurrents. The more sharply gender conservatives stigmatized man's selfish mart and forum as too immoral for women, the more many middle-class women began thinking they should enter these male arenas so as to ensure their moral character. Some gained entry as shapers of their children's moral and intellectual character and recipients of expanded education to fit them for that high civic role. Others rushed in as "benevolent" crusaders, distributing Bibles and tracts and teaching in the West to help swell the antebellum era's evangelical empire. Still others broke in more obstreperously as "moral reformers," combating urban sins like intemperance and brothel going. Meanwhile, emerging from the left field of this moralistic maelstrom, a zealous group of northeastern abolitionists raised a radical challenge to *any* limits placed on the exercise of women's altruistic impulse. "WHATSOEVER IT IS MORALLY RIGHT FOR A MAN TO DO, IT IS MORALLY RIGHT FOR A WOMAN TO DO," the South Carolina abolitionist Quaker Sarah Grimké proclaimed in her pioneering 1838 *Letters on the Equality of the Sexes*. Immediately, radical abolitionists around William Lloyd Garrison took up the slogan to justify women's

equal participation in the leadership of the American Antislavery Society, causing in 1840 their largely evangelical abolitionist opponents to walk out of the organization and touching off a nationwide debate over gender roles. As Sophia
Ripley noted the next year in her essay "Woman" in the *Dial*, "There have been
no topics for the last two years more generally talked of than women, and 'the
sphere of women.'"[51]

Yet for the moment, as Ripley also noted, the popular "separate spheres" conservatives were gaining the upper hand. The early 1840s brought an outpouring
of novels, tracts, gift books, articles, stories, and poetry summoning women to
assume their "true womanhood" of piety, submission, self-sacrifice, and domesticity. Arguably, the shrewdest was the widely read 1841 *Treatise of Domestic
Economy* by Sarah Grimké's antiabolitionist opponent, the influential educator
Catharine Beecher, who called for "professional" housewives, virtuous mothers,
and moral schoolmistresses whose cross-class self-sacrifice would help usher in
a national millennium of peace, prosperity, justice, and Christian love. Meanwhile,
the feminist abolitionists seemed to be deserting the gender field. While Sarah
Grimké (in an ironic bow to the power of domesticity) retired from antislavery
work to help her sister raise her children, the Garrisonians, preoccupied with a
new factional struggle against pro-electoral action "political abolitionists," virtually dropped the women's rights issue altogether. Then there was the limitation
of Grimké's message her conservative Quakerism imposed. Declaring she would
depend "solely on the Bible to designate the sphere of woman," she appealed to a
host of biblical "truths," including the fall of Adam and Eve, Christ's divinity,
and the dangers of "heathenism," which hardly resonated with Unitarians, liberal
Quakers, and Transcendentalists, who made up the majority of women's rights
abolitionists, especially in Boston. Resting women's rights solely on an ethic of
moral benevolence also weakened any claim on behalf of women's independent
self-interest. Finally, Grimké and the "ultraist" Garrisonians' reduction of the
gender question to moral equality and antislavery activism begged deeper gender
questions, as Fuller had perceived in rebuffing Chapman. What was the nature of
women's identity and psychology apart from their moral concerns? What was the
right sort of education and culture for women? How could the abolitionists' claims
of "benevolent womanhood" be reconciled with the notion of a gender-free moral
sphere? What were the causes of female subordination? What was the best means
of empowering women to act on their rights? What should the consequences of
equal rights be for the institution of the family or work? The women's rights abolitionists were not indifferent to these questions; privately they wrestled with them.
But publicly they were generally silent. With Enlightenment feminism dormant,
abolitionist feminism fading, and an antifeminist backlash growing, the gender
scene was ripe for a fresh intervention.[52]

Of course, to contemporary feminists, Fuller's initial interventions would seem
to have their own deficiencies, starting with her resistance to mixing social reform with self-culture. In that respect, Fuller was not so far from Catharine Beecher:
both sought to advance the intellectual autonomy of women without either calling for their political activity or challenging their social subordination, the only

difference being that Beecher advanced *her* domestic-millennialist call on evangelical grounds while Fuller did so on liberal Romantic ones. Yet Fuller felt some discursive pressures that both Beecher and Grimké did not.

One was the spreading contagion of socialism. Fuller and her Transcendentalist colleagues were increasingly making room on their bookshelves for, along with German theologians, philosophers, and poets, French radicals like Charles Fourier, George Sand, Pierre Leroux, and the Saint-Simonians, whose works bristled with demands for radically restructuring women's role in the family and society and heralded the coming of the "divine woman." Another was the ideological convergence of various radical perfectionist reform circles, a merger that two and a half years ago at the Chardon Street Bible Convention Fuller had thought was "so forced." Transcendentalists, Fourierists, and Garrisonian abolitionists, already linked together in Boston by their liberal religious backgrounds but now unmoored from their more moderate Unitarian, Whig, and antislavery communities, were starting to find in each other's ideas startling new compatibilities. Transcendentalists were coming out as socialists, abolitionists as Transcendentalists, and soon both, in the wake of the impending annexation of Texas, as militant antislavery politicos. And brooding behind all these shifts was the most loosely Romantic convergence of all: radical reformers were beginning to sacralize reform *itself*. The church principal, Emerson declared, was "falling from the Church nominal." However surely Fuller had begun with the idea of keeping reforming women's culture hermetically sealed off from social questions, those questions were seeping in from all sides.[53]

Meanwhile, something similar was occurring in her little corner of the Transcendentalist world. That spring, undoubtedly stimulated by their exchanges over love and friendship, Fuller and Emerson had started discussing the "state & duties of Woman" in the writings of Sand and Pierre Leroux. Although nothing is known about what they said, their simple posing of the question was provocative—although from Emerson's point of view, less than satisfactorily. "As always, it was historically considered," he grumbled in his journal, "it had a certain falseness so. For to me today, Woman is not a degraded person with duties forgotten, but a docile daughter of God with her face heavenward endeavouring to hear the divine word & to convey it to me." Although the antifeminism of this remark has often been exaggerated (docility toward God, the forgetting of duties toward man, and a special capacity to communicate divine revelations were hardly the stuff of conventional gender ideology), it is also true that his own gendered face could incline to the conventionally utilitarian as easily as the spiritually antinomian. And Fuller noticed it. A month later, he carelessly wrote her, speaking of the Wards' new baby, "though no son, yet a sacred event." "Why is not the advent of a daughter as 'sacred' a fact as that of a son?" she chided him. "I do believe O Waldo, most unteachable of men, that you are at heart a sinner on this point. I entreat you to seek light in prayer upon it." Considering that he wrote in his journal his "docile daughter of God" entry on the same day he penned his paean to "*Margaret*" rising before him into "heroical & godlike regions," she could hardly have gotten a better lesson on the gap between heroic talk and unheroic gender practice in even liberal American intellectuals.[54]

She was also feeling pressures to socialize gender issues in her recent West Street Conversations. Some of these continued to come from her assistants themselves. Despite her rebuff of Chapman, the meetings remained a magnet for radical-connected Boston women. Lydia Maria Child, who had contributed a Conversation essay to the *Dial*, moved to New York shortly after the end of the second year's series to become editor of the *National Anti-Slavery Standard*, but she left three colleagues: her close friend Louisa Loring; Ann Greene Phillips, the wife of Garrison's chief lieutenant, William Phillips; and Lowell's "transcendental" fiancée, Maria White. Fuller's Fourierist friends Sarah Shaw and Sarah's sisters-in-law Anna Blake Shaw and Sarah Russell also remained, as did proabolitionists like Lidian Emerson. And during the last two winters, as conservative Unitarians signed off, younger neophyte reformers were signing on. These included Fuller's future biographer Julia Ward (soon Howe), Ward's later suffragist colleague Ednah Dow Littlehale Cheney, and for "many" meetings during the winter of 1842–43, the recent Boston transplant and future women's rights movement founder Elizabeth Cady Stanton. Meanwhile, Fuller herself started blurring the line between cultural and social topics. In her winter 1840 series, she had first broached the woman question, but the shift became apparent during the third year. For her 1841–42 and 1842–43 series, she dropped most of her aesthetic subjects in favor of "Ethics" and "The Relations and Duties of Social Life," followed by reportedly "spirited" and "quite good" meetings on "the influences on Woman" and "the Family, the School, the Church, Society, and Literature." Even philosophical topics sometimes turned social corners, as in the winter 1842–43 series subject "How can constancy, or fixedness of purpose and perseverance in action be made to consist with a free development of character?"—which wandered into a discussion of the rival claims of marriage and individual spiritual growth.[55]

Besides all these private and public pressures nudging her over the bridge from women's culture to women's rights, Fuller had at disposal her Romantic language and concepts. First, there was her epistemology. Unlike Grimké's and Beecher's biblical truths and "common sense" reason, Fuller's two key Romantic methods—introspection and conversation—were always potentially destabilizing of all binding structural categories, including her own. Then there was her idea of "culture," which she thought of, as did other Romantics, as organic growth, or the *mingling* of thought and action, a conceptualization that put constant pressure (as it did for all Transcendentalists) on self-contained intellectual solutions. Finally, rejecting her cultural comrade Emerson's sublimely ironical acceptance of fated experience as a way to "truth," she had conjured her Credo's Romantic meta-narrative of humans' Fortunate Fall from divine oneness into struggle and love. These three Romantic concepts—introspection, the organic self, and faithful striving toward social love—gave her the intellectual foundations for a new "feminist" ideology.[56]

By the spring of 1843, her Conversations concluded, she started converting these circumstances, experiences, and ideas into a long essay on the woman question, which Emerson published as the lead article in the July 1843 issue of the *Dial*.

VI

To call "The Great Lawsuit. Man *versus* Men. Woman *versus* Women" a "women's rights" tract, as scholars have, would be partly right. That a woman has the same divine rights as a man is the liberal starting point of the essay and as robust a "rights" argument as can be made. Yet the label is also misleading. Published eight and five years, respectively, after the first important American works on the woman question, Child's *History of the Condition of Women* and Grimké's *Letters*, and eight years before the first women's rights convention's Declaration of Sentiments, it is neither a chronicle of women's achievements nor a political polemic, nor a movement declaration. On one level, it is a wide-ranging discussion of the intellectual origins, character, and shortcomings of the modern debate over women's nature and status. On another level, it is a philosophical text founded on a particular liberal Romantic ideology of inward and outward freedom. Indeed, its central argument is not one of *women's* rights but, as the subtitle plainly suggests, a transcendent *ideal* of manhood *and* womanhood measured against the opinions and actions of men *and* women. Finally, it is a highly self-conscious literary work, proceeding through dialogues, allusions, and metaphors, which both complicate and push it forward (and sometimes backward), and with a tone that often abruptly shifts to suit the metamorphosing persona of the narrator.[57]

Fuller highlights her Romantic religious perspective in her opening mythic pages on the divine incarnating itself in humanity. "Man" (in the generic sense), in her telling, had originally inherited an "angelic" ministry aimed at bringing his earthly kingship into conscious harmony with the "universe-spirit"'s "law" of "love." Eons of heroes, poets, priests, thinkers, and even obscure persons have left "unceasing revelations" of this human incarnation of the "All-Creating" living within and among us, a fact validated by all great secular and sacred literature in the Western canon, but most obviously in the prophetic Old and New Testament. "Sermons preached from the text, 'Be ye perfect,' are the only sermons of a pervasive and deep-searching influence," she declares, citing Matthew. To realize this perfectionist revelation, humanity has followed two methods: seeking ("Whatever the soul knows how to seek, it must find," quoting again from Matthew) and expressing: "As soon as the soul can say clearly, that a certain demonstration is wanted, it is at hand." Finally, to this syncretic quest, she adds a gendered dimension. Sometimes man has had to follow a circuitous course through the darkest depths of human experience to the "buried love" that produces redemption, as in the ancient Greek mystery cults' Orpheus, who descends to bring back his love Eurydice. Now, however, many are recognizing it is time for a Eurydice to call for an Orpheus. Since "man" and "woman" are organically linked through divine love, and since "the idea of man" has been brought out far more than that of woman, the conclusion is inescapable: if the sons of the age are to be led on (or back) to their divine birthright, the daughters, too, must have the chance to seek, search, and find.[58]

From these gendered heights of her Credo's Romantic religion, Fuller descends to unbury the modern sources of this potential new age of Eurydice. One is America's explosion of perfectionist reform movements, which evince a new craving for the "unceasing revelation" of "Love." Digging further down, she locates this craving's political sources in the French and American revolutions, whose egalitarian banners of a "fair chance" for *all* men have provoked many men to concede that *no* woman has such. Her liberal reading of these two events, though, is distinctively Protestant American. Unlike the French Revolution, which defined freedom as unobstructed liberty, giving way to license and bloodshed for both female and male citizens, the American Revolution promised to join this egalitarian outward liberty to moral laws of inward freedom and outward brotherhood. Sadly, however, America's version, too, is now mired, if not in blood, in covetous and self-indulgent sins. "I need not speak of what has been done towards the red man, the black man," she writes disdainfully. Indeed, so scornful is she of America's "pious words" that disguise these enormities that she pours scorn on the very perfectionist reform ferment she had invoked to support her claim that a new manifestation of "Love" was imminent:

> We sicken no less at the pomp than at the strife of words. We feel that never were lungs so puffed with the wind of declamation, on moral and religious subjects as now. We are tempted to implore these "word-heroes," these word Catos, word-Christs, to beware of cant above all things; to remember that hypocrisy is the most hopeless as well as the meanest of crimes. . . . We start up from the harangue to go into our closet and shut the door.[59]

She does not, of course. Rather, quoting Carlyle's friend John Sterling, she cries, "'Realize your cant, not cast it off.'" To do that, however, she reaches back to two American rhetorics that she liberally revises: her Puritan ancestors' jeremiad that the new world "incurs the utmost penalty, if it reject the sorrowful brother," and the nation's founding statement that "'All men are born free and equal.'" And *those* words are not just cant. Her reason is the abolitionist movement. Showing that she finally got the Garrisonians' point about its politically provocative power, which she had brushed aside two-and-a-half years earlier, she argues that not only are the abolitionists the first movement in American history to defend the rights of women but also they have transformed the entire discourse of womanhood by performing the words they declaim. To demonstrate this, she recounts an exchange, putatively overheard from her high perch, between an abolitionist and a conservative:

> "Is it not enough," cries the sorrowful trader, "that you have done all you could to break up the national Union, and thus destroy the prosperity of our country, but now you must be trying to break up family union, to take my wife away from the cradle, and the kitchen hearth, to vote at polls, and preach from a pulpit? Of course, if she does such things, she cannot attend to those of her own sphere. She is happy enough as she is. She has now more leisure than I have, every means of improvement, every indulgence."
>
> "Have you asked her whether she was satisfied with these indulgences?"
>
> "No, but I know she is. She is too amiable to wish what would make me unhappy, and too judicious to wish to step beyond the sphere of her sex. I will never consent to have our peace disturbed by any such discussions."
>
> "'Consent'—you? it is not consent from you that is in question, it is assent from your wife."

"Am I not the head of my house?"

"You are not the head of your wife. God has given her a mind of her own."

"I am the head and she the heart."

"God grant you play true to one another then. If the head represses no natural impulse of the heart, there can be no question as to your giving your consent. . . . But our doubt is whether the heart consents with the head, or only acquiesces in its decree; and it is to ascertain the truth on this point, that we propose some liberating measures."

In her little drama Fuller accomplishes two things. First, she exposes the ethical link between antiabolitionism and the reigning two-spheres gender philosophy: they both violate her Romantic liberal norms of individual conscience and organic wholeness, the first value by imposing restrictions without consent and the second by dichotomizing the masculine "head" and the feminine "heart." She also dramatically performs the fundamental contradiction in the conservative position, namely, the palpable dissonance between the claims of the bourgeois "trader" (whether slave- or mercantile) and the silenced voice of his supposed helpmate and "other half."[60]

Indeed, this conflict between lifeless rhetoric and gender reality, she argues, seizing back the rostrum, is at the heart of all the talk of the "numerous party" of separate-sphere advocates. They strive, she says derisively, "by lectures on some model-woman of bridal-like beauty and gentleness, by writing or lending little treatises, to mark out with due precision the limits of woman's sphere, and woman's mission, and to prevent other than the rightful shepherd from climbing the wall, or the flock from using any chance gap to run away." But the flock, she observes, is hardly protected. "Her circle, if the duller, is not the quieter. If kept from excitement, she is not from drudgery," she says, citing the grim realities of a host of marginalized working-class women, from prostitutes accompanying kings to the washerwoman who "stands at her tub and carries home her work at all seasons, and in all states of health." Nor is the flock staying put: the public roles women are *already* assuming, as writers, actresses, and preachers, show that the separate-spheres culture is breaking down. Ordinary women, too, constantly leave the home to attend balls, theaters, revival meetings, and other public events and to teach, do missionary work, and attend to other causes. In fact, this boundary breaching goes back to the Greeks: the women of Athens, shut out of the marketplace, made up for it by thronging the religious festivals. And the reasons are clear. Striking at the absurdity of a cult of domesticity in a capitalist society, she coolly notes that men themselves set the example: "Unless their own lives are domestic, those of the woman will not be." The most basic reason, though, is human life itself. "For human beings are not so constituted," she declares, "that they can live without expansion; and if they do not get it one way, must another, or perish."[61]

Finally, after exposing the separate-spheres ideology to the Romantic glare of reality, she advances her "liberating measures." First, a negative liberal one: "We would have every arbitrary barrier thrown down. We would have every path laid open to woman as freely as to man." Second, external freedom is not sufficient: since barriers are both subjective and objective, women's "inward and outward freedom" must be recognized. Third, just as the abolitionist argues for African Americans, because women are "souls" accountable only to "one master," that human freedom must be a "right" and not a concession and therefore not contravened even by well-intended restrictions. Finally, these are not just abstract propositions: this soulful tossing aside of "barriers" would supply precisely women's most basic need. "What woman needs is not as a woman to act or rule, but as a nature to grow, as an intellect to discern, as a soul to live freely, and unimpeded to unfold such powers as were given her when we left our common home." Or, as she puts the distinction between this primary psychic need and the secondary wants for money, notoriety, and authority that men have selfishly monopolized for themselves:

> It is for that which at once includes all these and precludes them; which would not be forbidden power, lest there be temptation to steal and misuse it; which would not have the mind perverted by flattery from a worthiness of esteem. It is for that which is the birthright of every being capable to receive it,—the freedom, the religious, the intelligent freedom of the universe, to use its means, to learn its secret as far as nature has enabled them, with God alone for their guide and their judge.

This, then, is her essay's high liberal argument that she extracts from the current debate over women's status: women need to be freed from imposed restrictions. At the same time, this negative liberty is but a necessary instrument to a higher freedom—the growth of the individual soul's self-consciousness, and therefore potential for organic growth and spiritual freedom. Hence, while women need material things for self-protection, their goal is spiritual freedom; material conditions are only important to facilitate that end. Fuller's gender stance, then, is thoroughly Romantic: it starts with the seeking "self" and organically expands outward into society in order ultimately to transcend it.[62]

Conceptually, Fuller's liberal "feminism" would thus seem, as organicist political theories often are, virtually seamless. Suddenly, though, she turns to consider "what obstructions impede this good era" and finds it in male prejudice. Turning herself back into a narrator, she dramatizes a recent conversation she claims to have had with a woman fittingly named Miranda, after the motherless daughter of the magical father Prospero in Shakespeare's *The Tempest* and (as she privately acknowledged) a thinly veiled self-portrait. "Her father was a man who cherished," Miranda avers, "no sentimental reverence for woman, but a firm belief in the equality of the sexes. . . . From the time she could speak and go alone, he addressed her not as a plaything, but as a living mind." Never indulgent, he called on her for clear judgment, courage, honor, and, most of all, the expectation that she would use the educational advantages he gave her to achieve great things. The result was wonderful. "A dignified sense of self-dependence was given as all her portion, and she found it a sure anchor." Of course, Fuller elides both her past misgivings about her Enlightenment father's rationalistic childrearing and her far from smooth assent to intellectual womanhood. But there is also a related conceptual gap within the text: it abolishes the gender problem! Indeed, so wonderful is her portrait that Fuller's moderate narrator steps in to cite Miranda's example to support her long-held suspicion that, as she puts it cavalierly, "the restraints upon the sex were insuperable only to those who think so, or who noisily strive to break them." On *that* Pollyannaish liberal claim, however, Miranda pours cold water. Yes, she says, men never got in her way, but that was because from childhood she had been encouraged to take a position of self-reliance, and that is rarely done for women, and herein lies the problem: "The difficulty is to get them to the point where they shall naturally develop self-respect, the question how it is to be done." At first she thought men would help, but then she saw that she was regarded as an exception, that men never wished to be women, that praises of women's intellect invariably were linked with her being a "'manly woman,'" or having a "'masculine mind.'" And that difference has been true throughout history: wherever a great woman has arisen in public or private life, men have invariably cheered her, but, Miranda shrewdly notes, "their encomiums indeed are always in some sense mortifying, they show too much surprise." Men appreciate someone like herself but rarely extend the same appreciation to other women not like herself.[63]

And the lesson takes: seemingly inspired by Miranda, Fuller again takes over from her putatively neutral narrator to give her own analysis of male prejudice. It is fairly tempered: nowhere does she paint the picture of grossly exploitative men that one can find either in Grimké's *Letters* or, ironically, Louisa McCord's anti-feminist screed "Enfranchisement of Women," which makes separate gender spheres seem a dire necessity for women to protect themselves from male brutality. Nor does Fuller view male prejudice as a monolith. Lovers, fathers, sons—who, after all, are "of woman born"—often *do* cherish women. Yet male prejudice is still palpable and ubiquitous. Even those lovers and fathers often mix sentimentally chivalric sentiments toward women with condescending dismissals of their capacity to reason and compete. What feeds these male prejudices? She mentions two social impulses: fathers' shortsighted desire to produce docile daughters who can attract protective husbands and, more culpable, men's selfish utilitarianism that make them see women as useful domestics or manners softeners. But at bottom the problem is men's self-image. Vain and hungry for power, they lack faith, she says, not just in women's moral character but also in their own. "No! man is not willingly ungenerous," she cries, citing historical and literary examples of strong men choosing strong women as their mates and weak men choosing weak women. "He wants faith and love, because he is not yet himself an elevated being." Nor are women innocent, citing examples from court favorites to shopkeepers' wives who, deprived of rights and self-knowledge, manipulate men sexually and emotionally and so confirm men's prejudice while destroying both sexes' self-reliance and happiness.[64]

So what is to be done to counteract this culture of mutually exploitative male prejudice and female dependency? In her essay, she fashions a cultural panorama of alternative models. Her sketches are neither wholly gendered nor inflated. She provides no celebratory catalogue, as in Child's and Sarah Josepha Hale's popular women's histories, of literary "women worthies," frankly conceding their "thread-bare celebrity." The great queens of early modern Europe's era of state formation get considerably stronger credits. She hands out her biggest prizes, though, to fictional and legendary female figures, which even if not reflecting social realities, she says, reveal past imaginings suggesting new possibilities in the present. Critically ransacking the Bible, classical and Eastern mythology, Greek drama, and English Renaissance literature, especially Dante, Spenser, and Shakespeare, with occasional bows to French, Spanish, and Italian late medieval and Renaissance writings, she finds a pantheon of male authors whose love for woman as a "'stair to heaven'" allowed them to portray complex, spiritually powerful women, both good and bad. She explores exemplary "signs of the times" more critically. Looking for the "living" word, she singles out abolitionism's female orators, such as Angelina Grimké and Abby Kelley, who demonstrate women's moral power when allowed to exercise it in the public square. She is lukewarm, however, about the two gender trends touted by liberal separate-spheres advocates. One is contemporary female authorship, which she notes but cites only European examples of, like Germaine de Staël and Harriet Martineau. She is even less enthusiastic about the era's ballyhooed gender improvement, women's education, which, she says, generally fails to stimulate critical inquiry. Just as male teachers pump in by rote bits of Greek and Latin, so female teachers in the women's seminaries, who are almost never "thinking women," do the same with their nonclassical curriculum. And, of course, she is blistering about the justification since the time of the American Revolution for these schools, namely, that they make girls into "better companions and mothers *of men!*" "The intellect, no more than the sense of hearing, is to be cultivated, that she may be a more valuable companion to man," she declares from her high Transcendental desk, "but because the Power who gave a power by its mere existence signifies that it must be brought out toward perfection." Still, she says, writing in her organicist Romantic mode, expanding women's education is good as a social stimulant, encouraging women to see that they are not "beings of affection and habit alone" but have an intellect that needs developing, as well as making it hard for society "to say just *where* they must stop."[65]

In her "signs" of everyday culture, she sees promise in two private gender performances: marriage and women's psychology. With marriage, her starting point is the modern "companionate" ideal of husband and wife sharing tasks and intimacy, but she gives it a couple of radical twists. First, she says, its spread does not mean women are free from constraints if they feel they *must* marry for economic support and a home. Second, she puts forward several different companionate models. Ranking them, she places at the bottom the utilitarian and narcissistic: the "household partnership" of complementary support and kindness with man the provider and woman the housekeeper, and the bond of "mutual idolatry" in which the infatuated couple shuts out the world to gaze in each other as reflecting mirrors. Much higher is the marriage of "intellectual companionship," such as that of Mary Wollstonecraft and William Godwin (whose choice of the "calumniated authoress . . . for his honored wife" she hails as another "sign of a new era"). The highest grade is "the religious" marriage, which includes the others but is also, she says, borrowing from Dante and later Renaissance Christian humanist authors, a "pilgrimage towards a common shrine." "The sexes should not only correspond to and appreciate one another, but prophesy to one another," she writes, applying to marriage the chiliastic friendship ideal she had advanced against Emerson's stoic Platonism, and "love in one another the future good which they aid one another to unfold." On marital alternatives, she is cautious. She blames George Sand's illicit affairs on her society's restrictions on women's roles and even daringly suggests that Shelley has a point when he argues that those limitations make marriage a false fetter. But she also says gestures of "wild impulse" such as Sand's are only harbingers of a new age and definitely not its parents. One nonmarital path she puts forward with panache is the road taken by society's despised "'old maids,'" or, as she more colorfully calls them, "mental and moral Ishmaelites," who "rove about" filling crucial social gaps by performing the role of the charity worker, domestic "drudge," or, echoing her own private self-descriptions, "intellectual interpreter of the varied life she sees." Ultimately, though, as with all her gender models, she touts single states, not as universally correct behavior, but as experiments of psychic self-sufficiency that, like Thoreau's economic experiment at Walden three years later, alter one's perspective and thereby liberate one's sense of possibilities. Indeed, toward the end of the essay, she argues that the "thought" of celibacy is applicable to marriage:

> Woman, self-centered, would never be absorbed by any relation; it would be only an experience to her as to man. It is a vulgar error that love, *a* love to woman is her whole existence; she also is born for Truth and Love in their universal energy. Would she but assume her inheritance, Mary would not be the only Virgin Mother. Not Manzoni alone would celebrate in his wife the virgin mind with the maternal wisdom and conjugal affections. The soul is ever young, ever virgin.

Virginity is a trope for the ever-youthful soul and Transcendental being itself.[66]

In a surprise move, the psychological gender performance she takes up is the very one that women's sphere proponents sentimentalized and moral-rights abolitionist feminists avoided—women's way of knowing. No other strand in her argument has proved so difficult and disconcerting for modern readers not attuned to Romantic idioms. "The especial genius of woman I believe to be," she writes, explaining cognitive "Femality" (a neologism she borrowed from a pair of recent articles in the Fourierist *New York Pathfinder*), "electrical in movement, intuitive in function, spiritual in tendency. [Woman] excels not so easily in classification or re-creation, as in an instinctive seizure of causes, and a simple breathing out of what she receives that has the singleness of life, rather than the selecting and energizing of art." Even on its face, that definition is hardly anti-intellectual, much less conventional. Certainly, it is radically different from the popular nineteenth-century notion that woman's special character derives from her passive and therefore pure absorption of common-sense values and divine wisdom. Rather, Fuller's "feminine" knowing yields roughly what the *Pathfinder*'s author claimed in his Romantic socialist articles: "internal" divine cognition, as opposed to "external" knowledge. In more Transcendentalist terms, it is reminiscent of what Friedrich Schiller would have recognized as a receptiveness to the mind's intuitive processing of the flow of sensuous experience, or for the German Romantics, who often explicitly labeled it as "feminine," *the* source not of external moral values mechanically internalized but of truths subjectively discovered and created. Both women and men, Fuller writes, need to be "as children of one spirit, perpetual learners of the word and doers thereof, not hearers only." Fuller's "feminine" requires not passivity but *activity* of both mind and body. Neither does she altogether mystify the sources of such a process. American middle-class women's susceptibility to spiritual phenomena is partly, she says, a product of social circumstances: their relative freedom from both European traditions and the competitive pressures faced by young men has given them more time and reason to read, muse, and develop an "inward life." Nor is she oblivious to the danger of this kind of "electrical" cognitive power in making women "easy victims of priestcraft, or self-delusion," or insanity. But the solution, she says, prefiguring, like her German Romantics, a modern psychoanalytical approach to the irrational, is not repression but sublimation and self-consciousness: the "magnetic" gifts need to be respected as in ancient muses and sibyls, while more ordinary women need to develop their intellect to serve as a "regulator" to maintain them in the proper psychological balance. "When the intellect and affections are in harmony, when intellectual consciousness is calm and deep," she writes, borrowing from the Romantic epistemological distinction between "objective" imagination and subjective fantasy, "inspiration will not be confounded by fancy."[67]

Finally, in her most radical move, she posits that the core of "femality" is androgynous. The notion of a bigender humanity and even divinity had been a strong undercurrent in hermetic thought from the Neoplatonists to Swedenborg, eventually flowing into early German as well as later French social Romanticism. Except for idiosyncratic pronouncements of divine androgyny among the Shakers and early Mormons, however, no American writer had ever exploited the idea, and certainly not, as German and French Romantics often did, as an argument for women's rights. First, she argues, "masculine" and "feminine" are merely signifiers for two human ways of knowing denoting fluid "faculties [that] have not been given pure to either" man or woman. Therefore, she says, anticipating Freud and Jung, there is "no wholly masculine man, no purely feminine woman," but only preponderances of masculine and feminine within each sex. Moreover, although in aggregate tending toward one or the other, in individuals, she asserts, gender characteristics are "perpetually passing into one another." Thus, in Greek and Roman mythology, "man partakes of the feminine in the Apollo, woman of the Masculine as Minerva," while in modern poetry, Shelley illustrates protean "feminine" man, and throughout history, one finds examples of famous men and women exchanging feminine and masculine roles and personalities. Indeed, she offers a colorful list of "gay . . . pranks" of nature, possibly taken from writings in German *Naturphilosophie*, such as people who read with the top of their head and see with the pit of their stomachs, declaring that "presently [nature] will make a female Newton, and a male Syren." For Fuller, gender like religion is neither a fixed category nor a meaningless social construct but a dynamic cognitive and relational sign of the constantly metamorphosing soul of the universe.[68]

Indeed, so dynamic is her androgynous idea of gender that it would seem to preclude any gender program for women. Yet she entertains at the end two gender prescriptions. One is that women concentrate on bringing out the stoic, self-dependent, rationalistic, or Minerva-like side of their sensibility that society has so discouraged. Likewise, she takes a similar pragmatic position on her second prescriptive call—that women "must leave off asking . . . and being influenced by men." Although again a temporary violation of the organic human "soul," such one-sidedness, she says, is required not only because of ordinary men's utilitarian conception of women but also because of women's psychology. Their spiritual personhood has been so repressed, they are so used to drawing their rule from without, that they are in danger of ceasing to be even living *parts,* much less wholes. "If any individual," she writes,

> live too much in relations, so that he becomes a stranger to the resources of his own nature, he falls, after a while, into distraction, or imbecility, from which he can only be cured by a time of isolation, which gives the renovating fountains time to rise up. With a society it is the same. . . . All tends to illustrate the thought of a wise co[n]temporary. Union is only possible to those who are units. To be fit for relations in time, souls, whether of man or woman, must be able to do without them in the spirit.

Combining, then, Miranda's insight that most men are unable to help women of varying strengths get to their "platform" with her "wise contemporary" Emerson's recent formulation that only individuals who are "absolutely isolated" can function with integrity and therefore, paradoxically, bring about a higher "Perfect" union, she advances her own radically individualistic feminist strategy. Women need to "retire within themselves, and explore the groundwork of being till they find their peculiar secret." Her Romantic conscience is clear. "It is love that has caused this," she writes earnestly, "love for many incarcerated souls, that might be freed could the idea of religious self-dependence be established in them, could the weakening habit of dependence on others be broken up."[69]

Given, then, her Romantic motive and rationale, why, though, does she think that *her* gendered "come-outerism" would ultimately produce the union of male and female that she had invoked at the beginning of her essay? She suggests three answers. First, "masculine" and "feminine" within individuals are dynamic tendencies potentially creative of one another: "Grant her then for a while the armor and the javelin. Let her put from her the press of other minds and meditate in virgin loneliness. The same idea shall reappear in due time as Muse, or Ceres, the all-kindly, patient Earth-Spirit." Second, the same process of free introspection that will adjust talents and functions between men and women to reflect their real desires will likewise present new complementary ground between the two sexes. "Ye cannot believe it, men," she cries,

> but the only reason why women ever assume what is more appropriate to you, is because you prevent them from finding out what is fit for themselves. Were they free, were they wise fully to develop the strength and beauty of woman, they would never wish to be men, or manlike. . . . It is with women as with the slave.

"Vor dem Sklaven, wenn er die Kette bricht,
Vor dem freien Menschen erzittert nicht."
    Tremble not before the free man, but before the slave who has chains to break.

Finally, consistent with her monistic claim that "one law rules" both men and women, she advances a vitalist reformulation of the Transcendentalist alchemy that Emerson had presented in *Nature* for producing one out of many but had recently begun to doubt. In Fuller's gendered application, withdrawal of nature's blocked feminine constituent liberates its "incarcerated" spirit to strive for a higher reunification with its masculine spiritual "other." Or, as she puts it, just as women's excessive devotion to men's wishes and opinions has diminished both partners and thereby encouraged a weak, utilitarian sense of self devoid of spiritual content, so the withdrawal of one of those partners to a devotion to the "central soul" would allow a new influx of spiritual energy. That energy would then infuse both halves of a partly splintered human soul, thereby allowing for new forms of "celestial" love to emerge. Three years earlier, she had privately conceded the inconceivability of presently imagining human happiness without a sexual "dualism." To that humanistic heterosexual vision of finding oneself "in another nature" she now added equal rights and a cosmic "sacred marriage" transforming the universe.[70]

    That last vision brought Fuller full circle: by converting the question of women's power from a problem of external *o*ppression into one of mutual *re*pression, she returned on a more comprehensive level to the cultural feminism that she had originally advanced in her first Conversations four years before. She also returned to a yet higher personal level as well. After describing her ideal "self-centered" woman, born not just for "*a* love" but for "Truth and Love in their universal energy," she concludes: "And will not she soon appear? The woman who shall vindicate their birthright for all women; who shall teach them what to claim, and how to use what they obtain? Shall not her name be for her era Victoria, for her country and her life Virginia? Yet predictions are rash; she herself must teach us to give her the fitting name." Fuller's return pushes her forward to something new rhetorically as well. That is a feminine version not only of Goethean "seeking" but also of the Emersonian pragmatic magic by which a prophetic persona is conjured up, whose self-reliant eloquence inspires others in theirs, and so becomes, by a circular kinetic psychodrama, the representative figure of one's era. Fuller's concluding prophecy was a question urgently awaiting an answer.[71]

VII

Despite its remarkable erudition and literary flair unique in the literature of women's rights until the twentieth century, "second wave" feminist critics in the 1960s and 1970s often found Fuller's "feminism" wanting. Their principal complaints were her skirting the question of political "power" and her failure to address working-class women's concerns. In her later book expansion of her essay, she would address these issues somewhat. But more to the historical point, both worries miss what cultural work her essay *did* do for feminist philosophy. First, it gave it a new Romantic plot: a woman's soul, permeated by the same energy that animates the universe, diversely growing through new revelations and experiences. Second, it offered a new gendered Romantic metaphysic: a self-conscious female identity defined by both its divine humanity and its dynamic androgyny. Third, the essay suggested a new Transcendentalist protofeminist method: gender change facilitated by individual introspection and cultural expression, gendered and nongendered. Fourth, and most culturally critical, the essay issued a new call to women's intellectual and spiritual self-reliance directed at both strategic and universal ends: as a way to counter male prejudice and female dependence, as a source of a new gender harmony, and as a distinctive appropriation of Western ideas about "masculine" and "feminine" going back to the ancients. Finally, her call was an intervention in a modern gender conversation. She offered a new American protofeminist ideology encompassed by neither the pathbreaking but one-sided rationalist-utilitarian Wollstonecraft tradition nor the galvanizing but intellectually parochial one of the moral rights abolitionists. The ideology's genealogy was also personal. In urging American women to take to heart her twin Romantic "laws" of humans' dynamic diversity and the individual's growth into transcendent selfhood, she discovered something of a public solution to a longtime private dilemma. That was nothing less than how to make her experience of a "masculine," European-centered, and comparatively isolated self-education yield a "feminine," national, and socially connected identity. Like countless liberal Romantics then stirring across the Atlantic, she had come to find in social emancipation personal liberation as well.[72]

Somewhat surprisingly, Fuller's hyperindividualistic inner circle was unanimously enthusiastic. Thoreau, their group's only elaborate reviser (who "will never like anything," Emerson told her), wrote to him and Lidian, "Miss F's is a noble piece, rich extempore writing, talking with pen in hand," worrying only about its lack of compression. ("In writing, conversation should be folded many times thick," he noted with Thoreauvian shrewdness.) Even her detractor Parker, although he could not abide her lavish tributes to "unlovely" goddesses like Isis and Minerva, told Emerson that her article was "the best piece that has seen the light in the *Dial*." Indeed, Emerson said, her essay was "felt by all to be a piece of life, so much better than a piece of grammar." Lest she take that as more flippant irony than Transcendental compliment, he went on to say: "I think the piece very proper & noble, and itself quite an important fact in the history of Woman: good for its wit, excellent for its character. . . . It will teach us to revise our habits of thinking on this head." Showing that his own habits could use some Fullerite revising, he added, "But does it not seem as if only in the poetic form could this right & wrong be pourtrayed?" No matter, he said, "you will yourself write to this theme, whatever you write; you cannot otherwise."[73]

One friend sounded a slightly sour note. "What do you think of the speech which Queen Margaret has made from the throne?" Sophia Hawthorne facetiously asked her mother. "It seems to me that if she were married truly, she would no longer be puzzled about the rights of woman. This is the revelation of woman's true destiny and place, which never can be imagined by those who do not experience the relation." After confessing that "it was always a shock to me to have women mount the rostrum," she added, in the soothing phrases of the era's official gender ideology: "Home, I think, is the great arena for women, and there, I am sure, she can wield a power which no king or conqueror can cope with." Perhaps reading Fuller's caustic critique of marital "mutual idolatry" hit a nerve! However, Fuller never read Sophia's note and possibly did not even know about her nasty censure. Even if she had, she could have found solace in the letter of the health reformer and later sex radical Mary Gove, who had recently escaped from her tyrannical husband, thanking Emerson profusely for printing Fuller's essay. Probably, though, the response that would have meant the most to her came from Horace Greeley's *New-York Tribune*. At the end of his preface to a lengthy extract of her essay, in which he copiously praised its "remarkable justness" and "brilliancy of expression," he concluded, matter-of-factly, "there is but one woman in America who could have written it."[74]

CHAPTER FOUR

Virgin Lands
(1843–1844)

I

On May 9, 1843, a week before delivering her "Great Lawsuit" manuscript, Fuller wrote Emerson, "I am trying to write as hard as these odious east winds will let me." Her geographical allusion was apt. She was trying to get *away* from the East, and the last thing she wanted, she said, was to drag around manuscripts and proof sheets with her. After toying with taking a trip to the West for nearly a year, she now had an incentive to go right away. "I . . . am constantly unwell, dull, head-aches putting me back in every thing I undertake," she complained to Sarah Clarke. "A change of air and scene I surely need." Mainly, though, she wanted to escape from writing for a while. "I am tired now of books and pens and thought no less," she wearily told her copy-begging editor, "and shall be glad when I take wing for an idle outdoors life, mere sight and emotion."[1]

In fact, her four-month excursion to the West and the Great Lakes would turn out to be more than a summer idyll. Although she was not taking off for the wild lands of the barely pioneer-invaded Far West, she was also not going to the half-urbanized Ohio Valley that her family and young ministerial friends had been traipsing to for the past decade for jobs and missions. She was headed for (in the day's mythic catchword) the "virgin" but rapidly settling upper Mississippi valley. Driven by hard times, cheap land, and the previous decade's removal of the last of the area's once numerous Indian tribes, this mass migration was forging America's now biggest and most kaleidoscopic frontier. Coming from farms and cities stretching from the Ohio Valley, New York, and New England to Germany, Ireland, and Scandinavia, its hordes of farmers, peasants, and tradesmen daily pouring into the "Old Northwest" were making up, in the words of one historian, "the largest and most rapid folk migration in modern times."[2]

Furthermore, books and thought had been preparing her for what she would see. For the past couple of years, her itinerant Concord friend had periodically preached to her that the West was the way into "America." "If I had a pocketfull of money," he confessed in one letter, "I think I should go down the Ohio & up & down the Mississippi . . . to cast out . . . the passion for Europe by the passion for America." For her part, Fuller, whose way into America had always lain through Europe, had been craving for months to see a landscape, in telling Romantic words, more "wild" and "sublime" than her New England one. Evidently also hoping to find some hints of folk culture that European Romantics celebrated, she read William Howitt's *Rural and Domestic Life of Germany* and borrowed from Long-fellow his copy of Clemens Brentano's pioneering collection of German folk songs, *Des Knaben Wunderhorn.* The new American edition of Carlyle's antimodernist *Past and Present,* however, which Emerson gave her as a going-away present, caught her up short. Notwithstanding her earlier grumbling over Providence's Dorrites, it perversely confirmed that she was headed in the right direction. "I cannot but sympathize with him about hero-worship; for I, too, have had my fits of rage at the pedantic and the worldly," she wrote Emerson, thanking him for the book. "Yet it is a good sign. Democracy is the way to the new aristocracy, as irreligion to religion. By and by, if there are great men, they will not be brilliant exceptions, redeemers, but favorable samples of their kind." In "going" West, Fuller was not prepared to look for the Enlightenment's "Western empire" or the Romantics' "primitive," or even, too much, a native equivalent of European clas-sical grandeur, to name the three great modern myths of the region. She was ready to encounter the romance of democratic America.[3]

For such a prospective journey, she had a supportive entourage. Besides the ever-wandering Caroline Sturgis, who joined up to go to Niagara, she had Sarah Clarke, who brought along her sketchbook, Sarah's brother James, whose letters from Louisville a decade earlier had given her her first look at the West, and, to remind her of the Boston they had left behind, Sarah and James's garrulous mother, Rebecca Hull Clarke. As the Clarkes were going to Chicago to see their brother William, Fuller could also look forward to a resident western host. And just be-fore going, Sarah Shaw gave her an unexpected "small fortune" in payment for some language lessons Fuller had recently given her.[4]

On the morning of May 25, they left Boston and traveled to New York, where they boarded the train to Albany. Most travelers found the recently introduced trains hot, crowded, and noisy, but hers seems to have enhanced her romantic mood. Lying on one of the car's couches, she sensed only the steady motion, the gently falling rain, the low talk of the passengers, the one lamp lighting "on some mysterious subject," which mingled with a dream, an occasional announcement "We are passing Genesee river," and imaginings of unseen places. "The whole night," she afterward wrote Hoar, "has to me the effect of phantasmagoria, as I look back."[5]

After a night in Albany and a couple more in Buffalo, they arrived at Niagara, where she got a less romantically promising look at her western prospects. The place was already a booming tourist spot, as well as at once "the ultimate in Ro-mantic landscapes" and an "icon of the American sublime," a combination she found deadly even before she got there. "Some ladies called on us, who extremely regretted they could not witness our emotions, on first seeing Niagara," she afterward related deadpan to Emerson of one encounter while stopping at Buffalo. "'Many,' they said, 'burst into tears; but with those of most sensibility, the hands become cold as ice, and they would not mind if buckets of cold water were thrown over them!'" Even at the Falls, she fretted. How could she keep out of her mind all the "very correct" borrowed images that *she* had gotten from "pictures and panoramas, &c"? How could she view the Falls through the needed "rainbows & other magical changes on the falling water" when the weather was cold and overcast? Still, "the sight of beauty, without the union of soul therewith," she decided, had its future reportorial value. "Carried away in memory, it hangs there in the lonely hall, as a picture, & may sometime do its message," she wrote in her journal. "I trust it may be so in my case, for I *saw* every object far more clearly than if I had been moved and filled with the presence, and my recollections are equally distinct and vivid." She would struggle with the rival claims of the real, the Romantic, and the picturesque for the rest of her trip.[6]

Following her week of viewing labors at Niagara, Fuller returned to Buffalo, where Caroline, deciding she had "known it all before" in books, gave up and returned to Boston. The way to Chicago does not sound as though the jaded Caroline missed much. The next day Fuller and the Clarkes set out in a heavy downpour on a steamboat on Lake Erie. After disembarking briefly at Cleveland to catch a "dreary, sullen" view overlooking the "grand" bluff, the party proceeded north in more cold rain past Detroit, up the St. Clair River, and then onto Lake Huron. On the fourth day, after rounding Michigan's northern tip, the boat stopped at the Manitou Islands to refuel, giving Fuller her first look at a "virgin" forest. Looking around, she discovered the oldest and grandest trees had all been torn up to feed the passing steamboats. Her most discouraging sights, though, for a would-be Romantic democrat, were the crowds of recently arrived settlers who gathered at the landings whenever the steamboat stopped. "I selected from the tobacco chewing, sharp, yet sensual looking crowd, (and it was, they said, the entire male population that was out to stare at the steamboats)," she wrote Emerson, "one man that looked more clean and intellectual than the rest, and was told he was a famous Land-Shark." She afterward wrote more glumly of her "lake voyage": "[It] left on my mind an impression of grandeur, of disconsolateness, of inevitable fate. The emigrants who accompanied us, the hordes of vulgar barbarians who crowd the landings, how unworthy they seem of these shores, of these sunsets, these moonlights. Can it be that from these a race shall spring who shall make amends to nature for the present violation of her majestic charms[?]"[7]

The "race," however, appeared a little more promising in Chicago, where they arrived in the early evening of June 10. With a population of a little over seventy-five hundred that would double every three years, but with its first railroad still five years away and its streets laid near a cluster of recent lairs of wild bears, the city had all the trappings of a large boomtown. Fuller found it a relief. "It does not seem half so unpleasant to see them really *at it*," she wrote Emerson, "as it did coming along to hear the talk of . . . what *they could get*." Seeing them "really *at it*" even made her think that the "dissipation of thought and feeling" in the West was preferable to that in the East; here "it is at least for *material* realities." Still, Chicagoans' *cultural* dissipation bothered her. The people seemed to have no goals *beyond* the material, and their manners were monotonously similar. Even the stony, endless shore of Lake Michigan, although much preferable to the city's dreary streets, seemed, without a consoling "sequestered walk," at once "public" and empty. "I do think it was well nigh the dullest fortnight I ever passed." So, missing her New England nooks, she stayed in her hotel room reading books about the region's Indians. Still, ever the earnest cosmopolitan, she berated herself: "It seems little not to feel more at home in any quarter of the globe."[8]

Fortunately for her *Wanderjahre* morale, on the morning of June 19, after James Clarke returned to Boston, she left hardworking but dull little Chicago and, with Sarah and Sarah's mother, bolted for a two-week journey through northern Illinois, where she got a chance to see real settlers and landscapes both more familiar and more exotic. After a day's coach ride straight west, they stopped at Geneva, an established settlement of mostly ex–New Englanders on the Fox River, where they stayed for a couple of nights. Leaving behind Rebecca Clarke, who had become too exhausted to continue, Fuller and Sarah rumbled on for several more days until, crossing the river at Dixon's ferry, they arrived at their midway point of Rock River Valley. They rode in a strong, white cotton–covered "*lumber waggon*" stuffed with all the necessary clothes, carpet bags, cooking utensils, and other provisions, leaving them, she reported to Emerson, "perfectly free to idle as much as we pleased, to gather every flower and to traverse every wood we fancied." They had as their guide James's younger brother William, who had been living in Chicago for nearly a decade, running with another brother a drug business. Fuller found him adventurous, witty, and knowledgeable. "He . . . knows every anecdote of the country whether of man or deer, drove admirably, with a coolness and self possession in all little difficulties that it is pleasant even to see," she wrote in her journal, concluding with judicious Romantic praise: "He knows his path as a man and follows it with the spirit of a boy[.] We do not see such people at the East, it requires a more varied life to unfold their faculties."[9]

Other things made this part of her trip more the "delightful pilgrimage" she had originally hoped to find in the West. Unlike the stark prairie of much of the rest of the state, the northern Rock River valley was covered with flowering vegetation, which made her think the expansive West could be more inspiring of Romantic contemplation than the tidier East. The land "gives a feeling of both luxury and repose that the sight of highly cultivated country never can," she wrote Mary Rotch. "There seems to be room enough, for labor to pause, and man to fold his arms and gaze." She liked roughing it, too: their daily camping out for meals, William's constant luck in supplying them with fresh fish from the rivers, and their wagon's steady rumbling through "all the jolts and wrenches incident to woodpaths, mudholes, and the fording of creeks." She even got along fine when they stopped for a night at a rough tavern settled in a thickly wooded grove near Papaw on the way to Rock River, where she slept on the supper table in the barroom, from which its drunken patrons got ejected late at night through a door without a lock. The owner told her to call him if they returned, "as he had 'con-quered them for us,' and would do so again," which seems to have reassured her.[10]

As the territory had almost no taverns or inns, they usually bedded down in private homes that William had arranged for them, which she much preferred anyway because she found that the settlers easily opened up: "Topics are before them and they take the hint." Although these homes included a park-like estate of an Irish earl, most were modest log cabins of ordinary settlers from the East. She was especially keen to see how they adapted to pioneer life—quite well, she generally thought. She found exceptions, waxing particularly sardonic in her journal about a "Master" from the East who answered their knock at his rugged prairie house, where they had sought shelter from a thunderstorm, in his bare feet, and, after some talk, "told us a story of the richest man in some place who used to go barefoot from taste!" She also found the missionary to the Unitarians, who made up a good proportion of Geneva, not up to her Transcendentalist standard but falling into the minister's "usual" error "of preaching *finely* & saying what he does not feel." But she also gave the "homespun" Unitarian preacher hearty praise for building his house and its furniture himself. Nor did her Transcendentalism blind her to the value of churchgoing, which struck her as sensible and poignant. "Let any one who think men don't ask for the church hear these people talk about it," she wrote in her journal, "as if it were the only indispensable thing." Most of all, she was moved by the settlers' generosity. "You feel so grateful, she wrote Mary Rotch, "for the hospitality of the log cabin, such gratitude as the hospitality of the rich, however generous, cannot inspire, for these wait on you with domestics and money, and give their superfluity only, but here the master gives you his bed, his horse, his lamp, his grain from the field, his all, in short, and you see that he enjoys doing so thoroughly, and takes no thought for the morrow."[11]

After a three-day stay at an absent wealthy Irishman's estate, Fuller and Sarah followed Black Hawk's original trail to Oregon, Illinois, where she saw her Uncle William Fuller, who had moved there to practice law. The natural beauty of the place amazed her, especially the tree- and flower-lined islands and the nearby three-hundred-foot-high, sharp-ridged bluffs along Rock River, running between the town and the double log cabin where they were staying on the opposite bank. On the morning of July 4, sitting on Eagle's Nest, the top of the area's tallest and most forested bluff, she experienced a patriotic epiphany, making her feel happier, she wrote, than she had ever felt about being born in America. She even indulged in a settlers' fantasy that would have pleased her Jeffersonian father. "I thought," she wrote Richard, "if we two could live and you have a farm which would not be a twentieth part of the labor of a N England farm, and would pay twenty times as much for the labor, and have our books and our pens, and a little boat on the river, how happy we might be for four or five years." That castle in the sky went nowhere, but she did demonstrate her own "go-ahead" eastern knack by reserving a two-acre plot and two-story building for her recently graduated brother Arthur in the "flourishing" eight-hundred-person village of Belvidere in Boon County, advising him to settle and convert the structure into an academy, which he did later that year.[12]

On July 9 she and Sarah were back in their hotel in Chicago. After a week of sickeningly hot hundred-plus temperatures, barking dogs, and sleepless nights, on the fifteenth Fuller and Rebecca Clarke escaped to Milwaukee to join Sarah, who had gone on ahead. The Wisconsin territory, which would become a state five years later, proved a bit of a letdown. Although she loved looking at "that vast mirror," Lake Michigan, her six-day trip at the end of the month exploring Wisconsin's interior and chain of lakes as far as Madison was by carriage driven by a young guide who safely kept to the roads. Then the area, while pleasant, was "not to compare" with her "Rock River Eden." The women also disappointed her. In Illinois she had been so eager to find in the western women's rough-and-ready ways evidence of their superiority to eastern women that she had even put her feminist principles in abeyance. "The men are all at work for money and to develop the resources of the soil, the women belong to the men," she wrote Emerson from Chicago. "They do not ape fashions, talk jargon or burn out life as a tallow candle for a tawdry show." She had gotten especially excited about a mother and her three daughters with whom she had stayed in the Rock River valley, who drove off with guns several gangs of "desperadoes" who were trying to lay claim to the property. The women in the Wisconsin interior, however, who seem to have been of a more genteel sort, told her a very different story. "All the Eastern women say," she wrote disappointedly to Emerson, "'oh it is well for the men, who enjoy their hunting and fishing, but for us, we have every thing to bear and no time or health to enjoy or learn.'" She was not sympathetic. She was glad to see that the foreign women, like those at the Swedish encampment off Pine Lakes, seemed to do fine, probably because, she speculated, they had been brought up to work outdoors and, as a consequence, had "better constitutions."[13]

By contrast, the Indians, whom she finally saw in significant numbers, really affected her. At the beginning in her journal, she could make them sound less moving than pathetic, especially the "poorer sort" from an encampment of a remnant of a once flourishing tribe in the region, whose painted young men she saw dancing before the stores and windows in Milwaukee to get whisky. She could also sound a little too clever, as with the "wild-eyed boy" "perfectly naked" except for a large gold bracelet. "We compared him," she wrote Sam Ward, "with the south Sea Island king who considered the cocked hat presented by the Europeans as a full court dress." Nor did she quickly expunge her visceral fastidiousness. "Their grave and graceful courtesy," she also wrote Ward of several other Indians, "near as they were, prevented even the dirt, though that was *as* great as I expected, from being offensive." But when she started seeing, along Black Hawk's trail, tomahawk tree marks, pottery, arrowheads, and burial mounds, she became deeply moved. "It is only five years since the poor Indians have been dispossessed of this region of sumptuous loveliness, such as can hardly be paralleled in the world," she wrote to Richard, speaking of the Sac and Fox tribes' cession of the last of their land to the United States. "No wonder," she indignantly said, alluding to Chief Black Hawk's final resistance a decade earlier, "they poured out their blood freely before they would go." By the time she got to Wisconsin, the terrible pathos of the plight of *living* Indians was beginning to sink in. "'I was,' said he, '*somewhat* moved by the melancholy of his look,'" she wrote Ward, reporting on a Wisconsin farmer whose log cabin they had stayed at, who had told her of recently seeing an Indian standing at the edge of the hill overlooking a beautiful section of the man's property on the shore of Nemahbin Lake, which had once been the site of one of the largest Indian villages in the region. "'When at last I did move,'" he had continued, she noted, "'he started, snorted out an angry *hui*, turned on his heel, and stalked away.'" The man's willful blindness would be another picture to hang in her hall for future use.[14]

On August 4, she and the Clarke women returned to Chicago, where the city sank her spirits as low as her first time there. In her letter she had boasted to Sam that her trip had made her "wonderfully the gainer in strength and spirits." She also brightened like a half-westerner when she found at their hotel a package from Emerson, containing the July *Dial*. "The letter from Fruitlands made me laugh till I cried," she told him; "it contrasted so whimsically with all I had been seeing and feeling in this region, where strong instincts and imperative necessities come upon you like the swoop of a hawk." After two more weeks in the city as "flat as Holland" and only "made for trade, and used as such," she abruptly changed her tune. "This is my last evening in Chicago, (*the place of onions*, is the interpretation of the Indian name, and I can attest there is some quality here fitted to draw tears and so can two or three infants that are screaming in the gallery at this instant)," she wrote with grim humor to Emerson. "I have just done packing[,] Sarah is quite unwell, and nobody comes in to claim my vacant hour." Then this shift:

> I shall scarce leave friends behind me though, perhaps, no foes. I have not reached forth the hand, neither has it been offered to me. I am silenced by these people, they are so all life and no thought, any thing that might fall from my lips would seem an impertinence I move about silently and look at them unnoticed.
>
> Truly there is no place for me to live, I mean as regards being with men. I like not the petty intellectualities, cant, and bloodless theory there at home, but this merely instinctive existence, to those who live it so "first rate" "off hand" and "go ahead," please me no better.

Going west to feel even more strongly she was a displaced person: this was not a happy conclusion. With William Channing she spoke, as usual, more drastically. After apologizing for not trying to make contacts for the *Present*, his new socialist magazine ("I have not been led to express one thought of my mind with warmth and freedom since I have been here"), she burst out with a lament that sounded more than just geographical:

> My friend, I am deeply homesick, yet where is that home?—If not on earth, why should we look to heaven. I would fain truly live wherever I must abide, but with full energy on my lot, whatever it is. He who alone knoweth will affirm that I have tried to work whole hearted, from an earnest faith. Yet my hand is often languid, and my heart is slow—I must be gone, I feel, but whither?—I know not, if I cannot make this plot of ground yield me corn and roses, famine must be my lot forever and ever surely.[15]

In fact, she did have a personal concern that was no doubt contributing to her gloomy feeling of displacement. Contrary to her laments, she *had* developed one new warm tie in the West. "I have become a friend to your brother William," she exulted to James Clarke just before returning to Chicago. "I do not know whether he is most engaging as a companion, or most to be loved as a man; he is so open and free and sprightly, yet large and noble in all his feelings." There also seems to have been some chemistry between them, although, as often with insecure young men onto whom she emotionally glommed, it evidently triggered some awkwardness, especially, it would seem, at their last meeting in Chicago, when she elicited from him some revelations concerning a past failed love affair, which startled him. "Afterwards, doubts arose in my mind whether there was not too much [illegible word], too little manly dignity in such unreserved revelations," he would later explain to her, "and especially whether you would respect one still who could make them so freely." So, for the rest of their meeting he became reserved, which deeply disappointed Fuller. "What she has, nobody wants," she shortly afterward wrote to Channing (modifying a line in Emerson's "Woodnotes"). The checkered memory of her "manly" symbol of western adventure would linger for many months.[16]

Happily, by this time she had gotten from James Clarke a gift of $50, which allowed her to take an "expedition" to the travel guides' celebrated Mackinac Island, which she had feared her depleted funds would not allow. She especially wanted to go there because several thousand Chippewa and Ottawa would soon be gathering at the island to receive their annual payments from United States government officials. Leaving behind Sarah, who was ill, Fuller traveled alone by steamboat, arriving at ten o'clock the night of August 19. Like virtually all middle-class antebellum women, she had never taken a trip by herself. So, while trudging along to the boarding house with a couple of sailors in the pitch-black darkness, in the midst of a cacophony of (as she would later describe them) "shrieking savages" reacting to the captain's release of some rockets from the boat, she had, not surprisingly, some "dismal" feelings. Finding all the rooms filled, she made do by sleeping in the parlor—"an arrangement that made me an early riser," she dryly noted in her journal, "yet not so early but that I had several visits while dressing." The next day, though, she got a room and was soon lapping up stories from some "half-wild" but amiable French Canadian traders boarding there and taking long walks with a little French Canadian girl and her American friend to hunt flowers and climb the steep, crumbling path of the giant arched rock. Most of the rest of her nine days on the island she spent observing the camping Indians, sometimes staring for hours from her window at their daily arriving families as they set up their tents among the by now nearly three thousand already swarming the shore. She also walked among them, trying to talk in improvised sign language, which she thought worked well enough. Once she approached some Indian women pounding corn for breakfast and began pounding, too.

> This pleased them mightily; they laughed gently, and in their mild, polite way, examined, though only with eyes and signs, my dress, and especially my little sunshade. This attracts a great deal of attention among them. A young man, with his

child in his arms, came up and signified his desire to look at it. He was charmed
with the opening and shutting of the two springs, and asked, What price? If he had
had the model of a canoe, I would have exchanged with him, for I fear not to be
able to get one.

After laboring but not trading, she climbed a tall bluff from which for several hours
she watched the doings of the families. "Certainly this encampment was wilder
and gayer than the other: young men jumping and running, and children playing,"
she noted in her journal, speaking of the one she had seen at Wisconsin's Silver
Lake, but added, referring to one Indian she had fixed on, "All looked degraded;
there is not one like my red-blanket Roman of Milwaukee." She still had not quite
come to terms with nonpicturesque Indians.[17]

Still, Indian encounters concluded her trip. On the morning of August 29, she
took a small steamer up to Sault Sainte Marie, which she had been longing to see.
After again arriving alone at night, the next morning she was out at the crack of
dawn to scout around a Chippewa burying ground and later to hire two canoe-men
"in pink calico shirts" to take her on a shoot down the rapids. She celebrated her
pleasurably dangerous spin by breakfasting with her boatmen on a white fish they
had caught while coming down the rapids. Later that afternoon, she returned to
Mackinac, where she tried to pack in as much time as she could with the now departing tribes. The next day she and the newly arrived Sarah went canoeing with
the tribal chief's sixteen-year-old son and a couple of friends, who (she thought)
had great fun showing off their paddling skills to two white women. Other encounters were considerably darker. Once, while visiting a family, Fuller found a child
with smallpox and took "tender care," Sarah would later recall, "not to let the mother
see that she shrank from the child." She spent her last hours with more Indians.[18]

By the middle of the first week in September, after a half-day stop at Detroit,
Fuller and the Clarkes were on board the steamboat *Wisconsin* heading home.
Leaving the Clarkes at Buffalo, Fuller went on by a separate train to Albany, and
then boarded the steamboat *Knickerbocker* ("the most splendid boat I ever saw")
and traveled down the Hudson to New York. She had not visited the city since her
Trenton Falls trip eight years earlier, but she soon got a quick immersion back
into familiar eastern reform culture. William Channing met her at the dock, and
on Sunday morning of the tenth, after breakfast at the City Hotel, where she was
staying, she went to his socialist Christian Union church on Crosby Street, where
she heard him deliver a sermon of "great power and beauty." Looking around at
the end of the service, "who should I see but Messsrs Alcott Lane, and Thoreau,"
she wrote to Sarah and James, the first two looking for handouts for Fruitlands
and the last for an editor to publish his writings. "The effect of this was queer
enough." She made other forays into this extended semi-Transcendentalist community. She rode to Staten Island, where she had a "delightful conversation" with
Emerson's lawyer brother William and his wife, with whom Thoreau was living
while tutoring their children. She attended another meeting of Channing's society, where he, Lane, and others discussed prospects for American socialism. She
breakfasted at the city's reformers' Grahamite Boardinghouse on Barclay Street

("excellent for one who can dispense with tea and coffee," she said, evidently excluding herself). She received two visits from the author of the "Femality" article she had praised in her "Great Lawsuit," the Swedenborgian socialist physician Dr. John W. Vethake, who "much pleased" her. In addition, she met another Swedenborgian socialist and Channing parishioner, the lecturer Henry James, Sr., whose sons William and Henry had both been born during the past year. "The dear noble woman!" James effused to his friend and hero Emerson, adding, in a heavy pun, that he hoped for "fuller conferences & sympathies." Finally, having finished her transregional transcendentalizing, on the nineteenth, in a thickening storm, she returned to Boston, and "immediately" went to Bush for a two-day visit. "Margaret came fresh from her Western journey," Emerson wrote to Caroline Sturgis, "& gave us anecdotes & also potions of divine scorn."[19]

Emerson did not indicate what those "drug[s] . . . in that sinister jar" were, but her comments to other friends suggest they must have included some happy ones at least about the West. "Surely I never had so clear an idea before of the capacity to bless of mere Earth, merely the beautiful Earth, when fresh from the original breath of the creative spirit," she told Mary Rotch. "In three or four years those vast flowery plains will be broken up for tillage, those shapely groves converted into logs and boards. I wished I could have kept on for two or three years while yet the first spell rested on the scene." Dropping the pastoral elegy for Rotch's niece Maria Rotch, then about to embark on a European tour, she drew the more expansive nationalist lesson that Emerson had delivered to her two years earlier: "To me Europe lost its interest as I looked upon these dawnings of a vast future." Although she had not found her western democratic "aristocracy," she had found in western nature and settlement a new prospective national self. She returned, too, knowing that through thunderstorms, flowery fields, and lonely excursions, she had finally performed her long-desired role of the adventurous traveler. She also returned, like a good cosmopolitan traveler, with new ambivalent feelings about home. Three weeks after writing Maria, she wrote to Henry James, who also was about to take off for Europe, that New England, "in these splendid October days, seems as good a place as any in the world." But she added pensively, "while traversing the ample fields of the West, it seemed a poor shady little nook."[20]

II

However poor or shady, though, it was not a *lazy* nook, as her copy-hungry editor reminded her. Could she not add three or four additional plays to the review of Carlyle's friend John Sterling's tragedy *Strafford* that Sterling had recently sent him? Then, too, he hoped she would not let lie unfinished her "autobiographic chapters once begun under this roof, as I gladly remember." She should not be "a Watcher in the heaven," he wrote. "The events & thoughts among which we play, look small & tangible when they arrive at our hands & understandings, but their pedigree has a million links & their parentage is old as Heaven & the First Cause." To his usual Transcendental encouragement to get on with her writing, Fuller replied with her usual teasing deflation: "Thy letter, o best Waldo, displays the wanted glorious inconsistency, beginning as a hymn in praise of indolence, and ending with demands of work." In fact, having written very little since "The Great Lawsuit," she was busy with a literary plan of her own. Belatedly answering Ellery Channing's taunt a year earlier that she write "not forever German people & things" ("Why not American, why not what is here under our noses"), she informed Emerson she had decided to write a book about her summer trip. "Don't expect any thing from the book about the West," she added nervously. "I can't bear to be thus disappointing you all the time. No lives of Goethe, no romances." She had her winter assignments.[21]

She also had her familiar winter duties and pleasures. She resumed her language and literature classes, although now, because she held them in Cambridge, to a reduced group of six or so, making up for the shortfall by doubling the time to two and a half hours and raising her charge from $16 to $25 per student for twenty-four lessons. "These terms, perhaps, are higher than is usual in Cambridge or the country any where," she wrote Abigail Francis, Convers Francis's wife, who sent their daughter to her. "But they are the lowest I have ever offered," she said of the bargain she was offering, "for I should much prefer a class at home to one in Boston." The numbers at her fifth year of morning Conversations, which she began on November 16, were also dwindling. "There is no persuading people to be interested in one always or long even," she resignedly told Emerson. Yet she enjoyed them, she said, because they gave her a chance to explore, along with "wide digressions" from war and Bonaparte to Goethe and Spinoza, new social and ethical themes that she had gotten interested in during her western trip. What these were she did not say, but under the rubric of "Education," the women discussed, "with much autobiographic illustration," "Culture, Ignorance, Vanity, Prudence, Patience," and—which she told Emerson she hoped would appeal to the perennially ill Lidian—"Health." Her winter pleasures also stayed close to the same as the previous year: lectures of Emerson's, parties at Elizabeth Peabody's, Boston Academy Beethoven concerts at the Concert House, and informal parties at the Wards' Louisburg Square apartment to hear again the pianist Frederick William Rackemann and, later that spring, the Norwegian virtuoso violinist Ole Bull.[22]

The single partial exception to these continued patterns was Brook Farm, now in its third year, which she was beginning to warm to. For one thing, she was apparently gaining a following among unhappily married women there. "If I were to write down all she and four other married women have confided to me, these last three days past, it would make a cento, on one subject, in five parts," she noted wryly in her journal during her late October visit. She also had new admirers among the community's single young women, who reportedly found in her, as they could not in the stiff Sophia Ripley, a Transcendental confidante and "*mother*." Of these, the most ardent was the young Englishwoman Georgiana Bruce, who "reverenced" her and to whom she lent money and counseled with anecdotes drawn from her own "ardent" life.[23]

Beyond new fans, Fuller was also getting her first strong whiff of the Brook Farmers' new Fourierism. Urged on by Albert Brisbane, its leading American exponent, and Channing, their ex-officio pastor, at the end of that year, they reorganized themselves into a "phalanx" dedicated to Fourier's theories for organizing work and social relations to make them harmoniously "attractive." Curiously, unlike some Transcendentalist visitors, who regretted what they perceived to be a loss of fun and merriment in the new dispensation, she *liked* the Brook Farmers' new serious atmosphere. To be sure, she continued resisting their socialist enthusiasm. After telling Channing that his prophecy at a lecture during her visit of a coming "revolution" unifying human consciousness would only come, if at all, very slowly, she asked: "Can we not wait very patiently, if sometimes sadly, steering the bark over the waste of waters and thus becoming ourselves that which we seek?" Contrasting his "tendency to pledges and plans" that were later modified to her ready embrace of experiences and "ideal passion" in private friendships, she added airily, "It is a constellation, not a phalanx to which I belong." Yet after attending on December 27 and 28 the Fourierists' first New England convention, where she read from Ellery Channing's poem "The Earth," and afterward their New Year's celebration at Brook Farm, she wrote in her journal: "The tone of the society is much sweeter than when I was here a year ago. There is a pervading spirit of mutual tolerance and gentleness, with great sincerity. There is no longer a passion for grotesque freaks of liberty, but a disposition, rather, to study and enjoy the liberty of law." Meanwhile, she read more socialist literature: Channing's *Present*, Pierre Leroux's *De l'humanité,* which called for a "communion" reconciling society and divinity, and *Association*, Brisbane's recently published study of Fourier's social science, which she borrowed from Brownson, momentarily a follower of Leroux.[24]

She also dabbled in Fourierism's latest social experiment that somewhat combined Channing's and her "different ways of steering" the socialist ship. Neither the parlor entertainment that she had encountered six years earlier in Providence nor the popular religious movement that spiritualism would later be, mesmerism had recently become a titillating adjunct of socialist reform. Brook Farmers and their fellow travelers especially, who (Margaret's mother reported) were "all agog on the subject," were starting to find in mesmerism's claim for a "magnetic" fluid running through the universe "scientific" support for their own hopes for the "third thought" of social love to which Channing had alluded in his talk in late October. On February 5 Fuller got her first buzz when she joined Sarah Clarke, James Clarke, and his wife Anna at James and Anna's Central Court house for an evening of "*Mesmeric* experiments," which they had recently started hosting, presided over by the young Fourierist Anna Q. T. Parsons. "Our new Ecstatica" (as Fuller called her) practiced a type of mesmeric clairvoyance called "Psychometry," or "reading," while hypnotized, the "energy" of writings and answering questions about the author put by attendees. For a month, Fuller had been trying to get Emerson to go, and one description she gave him of an earlier session where the mesmerized Parsons had read a letter of his must have at least piqued his interest. She happily reported it had revealed him as a person of "high" thought but "underdevelopment" that had reminded Parsons of a "circle with a dent in it"! ("'If he could sympathize with himself, he could with every one'—which is, in my opinion, a most refined expression of the truth, whether obtained by clairvoyance or any other means.") Meanwhile, Fuller had to reassure Sarah, who feared that Emerson's distrust of all this (as he called it) "peeping through the keyhole" would (Sarah said) "expose this delicate girl, whom I highly respect, to the scrutiny of one before whom she is to appear as a suspected person." Fuller brushed that cavil aside. "It is to be remembered that many of his friends have been obliged to approach Mr E. in that character," she said knowingly. "I myself occupied it opposite him for some years." In any case, she added gamely, "I do not like to have Mr E. deprived of the opportunity."[25]

On the evening of March 4 Emerson finally came, although the result must have confirmed his fear of social "peeping." This time the keyhole was a letter of Fuller's. In response to what sounds like rather hand-tipping questions, Parsons gave a remarkably Fuller-like analysis: the author was devoted to thought and art, suffered from "want of sphere of action," and had once felt "terrible . . . loathing and contempt" toward others but now, although still having "much to struggle with," had "high, very high hopes." Parsons followed up her psychological profiling with a little socialist editorializing: "As she grows older she grows younger. —I don't see how she can be contented with the present state of society." On a roll, Parsons turned to Emerson, provoking this virtual public rerun of the Fuller-Emerson friendship problem:

> (To R.W.E.) Have you ever had much intercourse with that person? You have had a great deal of influence upon him—(Is the person very susceptible of influence?) I should think not, but I have felt several times that you have had influence on the person. He may not be aware of it—You have sent him down deeper into his own Soul. (Is this influence reciprocal?) There are certain points in the character that have commanded your respect—I think he has influenced you not so much as you have him.
>
> Mr Emerson does not understand this person fully. He says he does not love him but I think he ought to.[26]

While such congenial revelations of herself and Emerson presumably appealed to Fuller, her interest in the new ideological mesmerism also inspired some serious reflections, which she inserted in the manuscript she was writing about her trip west. Her lengthy account of the "Seeress of Prevorst," which she took from *Die Seherin von Prevorst*, a late German Romantic text by the poet and seeress's physician Justinus Kerner that she had taken with her on her trip, was her considered response to her and Emerson's differences over these mesmeric experiments. In fact, her view of Friederike Hauffe's reported clairvoyant powers, while sympathetic, is cautious. She accepts their plausible therapeutic value for Hauffe but doubts their "prophetic" significance and suggests various psychological and cultural explanations for them. The same is true of her discussion's four-way debate among orthodox "Old Church," Wordsworthian "Good Sense," antiutopian "Self-Poise," and her stand-in "Free Hope," who, like some German Romantics, defends mesmeric investigations on the remarkably William Jamesian–sounding pragmatic ground that all scientific work must include some degree of belief or hope animating "hypotheses" that still must be tested empirically. (She even similarly defends a consideration of Fourier's theory of an "'aromal state'" surrounding the universe, which American Fourierists preferred to forget.) When Free Hope engages with Self-Poise, however, her stand-in for Emerson, she exposes her real stakes in the question. In response to her claim to Good Sense's appeal to be "completely natural"—that only by sharpening our faculties to apprehend the "infinite" can the miraculous in the ordinary be grasped—Self-Poise replies dismissively: "All this may be very true, but what is the use of all this straining. Far-sought is dear-bought." Only, he says, by rejecting the "manifold infatuations and illusions of this world of emotion," such as those exposed by mesmerism, in favor of a "clear intelligence" acted on in a spirit of "sublime prudence," can we discover the deepest truth, "that the ordinary contains the extraordinary." At that pure Emersonian prudence, Free-Hope fires back in defense of her new "infatuation." After repeating her usual criticisms of Emerson's theory as lacking room for "lyric inspirations and the mysterious whispers of life," she writes: "To me it seems that it is madder never to abandon oneself, than often to be infatuated; better to be wounded, a captive, and a slave, than always to walk in armor. As to magnetism, that is only a matter of fancy. You sometimes need just such a field in which to wander vagrant, and if it bear a higher name, yet it may be that, in last result, the trance of Pythagoras might be classed with the more infantine transports of the Seeress of Prevorst."[27]

Clothed in "science," Fuller's mesmerism added another wrinkle to her Romantic religion. "I would beat with the living heart of the world, and understand all the moods, even the fancies of fantasies, of nature," she has Free Hope conclude. "I dare to trust to the interpreting spirit to bring me out all right at last—to establish truth through error." For the Romantic quester, the earthy West had not changed her view that "far-bought" truth was potentially right-bought truth.[28]

III

Establishing truth through error also fairly well describes her personal life that winter and spring of 1844. She was anxious about producing her book. Renewed health problems also did not help. Having been "almost restored" by her western trip, within a month she had come down with the flu and even after recovering in December, for several months she was plagued with headaches "day and night," threatening to reverse her steadily brightening mood since her "crisis" depression and *Dial* resignation. "I suffer extremely now from a lack of vital energy," she wrote to Anna Ward the day after Christmas. Altogether, she confessed to another friend, "the tax on my mind is such, and I am so unwell, that I can scarcely keep up the spring of my spirits, and sometimes fear that I cannot go through the engagements of the winter."[29]

In March she experienced a further mental tax when William Clarke arrived in Boston and stayed until early June. Clearly, in her mind at least, their last awkward moment had not ended things. Evidently preparing for some sort of reengagement, she even got his sister Sarah to send her a package of his letters showing a "history of his feelings." It is easy to understand Fuller's continuing fascination with the thirty-one-year-old Clarke. Energetic, fond of his smoke and whiskey, and with a "system of notions" close to those of Carlyle and the Transcendentalists, he would seem to have been a reasonable facsimile of the rough but aspiring male "New Light" she had been hoping to find in the West. Ellen Sturgis Hooper later described him more romantically as a "mixture of sadness, simplicity, wild energy, softness and delicacy without the last finish of elegance and perfect taste" and "untamed at the core." Emphasizing the latter, she added that "perhaps his intimacy with Caroline would be legal evidence against him." His untamed youthfulness obviously appealed to Fuller. In a blank journal she gave him when he arrived, she wrote, "while more a man, may he be more the child"—a Romantic "hope" that sounds suspiciously like the maternal fantasies she had once unsuccessfully tried to impress on Sam Ward. And Clarke's feelings for Fuller? He admired her *Dial* articles and was deeply impressed with her psychological insight, but there also seems to have been more. Thirty years later, when he was laboriously tracing Fuller's 1844 journal with several passionate references to himself to make a copy, he wrote Caroline, "The memory of this dear friend and the perusal of her writings is one of my chief interests in life." Yet he clearly found her a little overwhelming personally, as well as a bit too radical in her gender views. "Although you recognize the facts of Femality & masculinity, so to speak," he wrote her after reading her "Great Lawsuit," "I think that you lose sight of the obvious functions which they indicate. Where out of yourself could you find another Miranda?" Add to that demurral his worry that her psychological probing made him show "too little manly dignity," his vague revelations of "many" past girlfriends, his annoying habit of spending more time with Caroline than Fuller, and one does not get a portrait of a very promising romantic relationship. In any case, he put an end to it. "Hope will linger long," he wrote in a poem for her in late May just before he returned. "But the time has come to sever what to join were wrong."[30]

Disappointed, sad, and, as usual, hypersensitive to rejection, she relapsed into painful introspection. In late April she wrote a clearly Clarke-inspired ballad lamenting that love had finally called her but, presumably referring to their ages, "all too late and all too soon," pensively adding, just before concluding that only the waters of death could still "this thirst":

> And if she had not had a heart,
> Only that great discerning mind,
> She might have acted well her part.

And that May, in another Clarke-provoked entry, while questioning whether "thou didst really love me," she wrote startlingly: "I cannot help wearying myself of this ugly cumbrous mass of flesh. I am such a shabby plant, of such coarse tissue. I hate not to be beautiful, when all around is so."[31]

One needs to be careful, however, in interpreting these painful musings. Emerson, who would read them while preparing her *Memoirs*, thought he knew what they meant. "The unlooked for trait in all these journals to me is the Woman, poor woman: they are all hysterical," he would write in his journal. "She is bewailing her virginity and languishing for a husband." There is much truth to this claim but there is also much missing. Besides lamenting Clarke, the third big romantic disappointment in her life, she may have also been feeling envious toward her sister Ellen and the recently married Jane Tuckerman King, Mary Mann, and Sophia Hawthorne, all of whom were pregnant and would give birth to their first children later that year. Furthermore, as had not been the case with her manic-depression episode of three years earlier following her much more complex friendship crisis over Sam and Anna, she thought her unhappiness would pass. "We . . . had a long & deep conversation happy in its candor," she wrote in her journal after talking with Sarah Shaw, whom she was visiting for a few days that May. "Truth, truth, thou art the great preservative. Let free air into the mind, & the pestilence cannot lurk in any corner." Her stoic truth-seeking potion, she decided, was even curative. "I prayed in very early years," she wrote in her journal at the end of the month, "give me truth: Cheat me on by no illusion. Oh the granting of this prayer is sometimes terrible to me. I walk over the burning ploughshares, and they *do* sear my feet. Yet nothing but truth will do." She did add, echoing her late April ballad: "With the intellect I always have always shall overcome, but that is not the half of the work. The life: the life Oh, my God! shall the life never be sweet?" Four days later, though, she recalled earlier at twilight looking out from her bedroom window at the rising moon, her favorite maternal image: "I felt stronger for the future; clearness seemed dawning on my mind. I could pray—O God make me more sincere and ground me more deeply in reality." Her God may have been "love," as she had told Emerson, but her lesser deity "truth" seemed to be sustaining her.[32]

Nor had she given up the consoling perspective on her single life that she had announced in her journal two years earlier at Bush. "Looking out on the wide view," she wrote in it while at the Shaws, after giving Sarah some friendly "counsels" about freeing up time from her domestic burdens for study, "I felt the blessings of my comparative freedom: I stand in no false relations: who else is so happy? Here are these fair unknowing children envying the depth of my mental life. They feel withdrawn by sweet duties from Reality. Spirit, I accept, teach me to prize & use whatsoever is given me." Even her "darkest hue" that she had alluded to in her letter to Davis a year and a half earlier about having parented neither children nor beautiful works, "by which the thought of my life might be represented to another generation," she managed to incorporate in a new sublimated impulse. The psychoanalyst Erik Erikson would famously call it "generativity," but she used a locution of her own time: becoming a "spiritual parent" for her society's future.[33]

She described with satisfaction to Channing the final gathering on April 25 of her Conversations, which she had designed to encourage women to combine, as she felt she had learned painfully to do, self-reflective learning and public aspiration: "We had a most animated meeting. On bidding me goodbye, they all and always show so much goodwill and love, that I feel I must really have become a friend to them. I was then loaded with beautiful gifts. . . . Then I went to take my repose on C's sofa, and we had a most sweet afternoon together." To Elizabeth Hoar she wrote simply the next day, "Our last meeting yesterday was beautiful; how noble has been my experience of such relations for six years now, and with so many, and so various minds! Life *is* worth living—is it not?" Finally, in contrast to her last couple of years' cries to "give me a son of mine own" and laments that boys had a much better chance in America than girls, she was starting to include in her generative hopes her own sex's future as well. Two days after her completion of her book and the birth of Ellen and Ellery's first child, whom they named Margaret Fuller, she wrote to Caroline, telling her, while she was walking in Mount Auburn Cemetery, her thoughts had turned pensive. After musing about the death of her last sibling, Edward, whom her parents had said would be "my child" but had died at one while Fuller watched over him at night, she wrote: "I thought much of the time when I, too, should drop this mask of flesh, and who would finish my work. I had a fancy the child was born that day, and hoped it would have been a boy. However my star may be for a girl, educated with more intelligence than I was. Girls are to have a better chance now I think." She obviously felt good knowing that, whatever her personal problems, her own "star" was contributing something important to that expanding firmament.[34]

IV

If Fuller did not go into an emotional tailspin that spring, it was probably also because she completed all her planned writings. In three essays she returned to the subject of the drama that a year and a half earlier she had cavalierly dismissed as moribund in postheroic "modern" times. In "The Two Herberts," published in Channing's *Present*, she presented a little closet drama of her own featuring the seventeenth-century poet George Herbert and his lesser known brother, the swashbuckling, intellectual statesman Edward, Lord Herbert of Cherbury, who debated the relative claims of the *vita attiva* and the *vita contemplativa*. In "The Modern Drama," which filled nearly a third of the *Dial*'s January issue, she divided the era's dramas into three categories: actors' plays such as *Metamora* and *Virginius*; intellectual dramas like Coleridge's *Remorse* and Shelley's *Cenci*, which investigated a philosophical problem; and, the closest to "true drama," historical plays. By these standards, none of the recent plays she concentrated on came off well. John Westland Marston's "refined" intellectual comedy *The Patrician's Daughter*, recently produced at Drury Lane, was all right because at least it flowed sufficiently to work on the stage. Longfellow's closet drama *The Spanish Student* failed because its elaborateness suggested a stage play but it had almost no movement or character development. Even the best of the lot, Sterling's *Strafford*, which Emerson had asked her to review, a sympathetic portrayal of Sir Thomas Wentworth, first earl of Strafford and chief advisor of Charles I, was a dramatic sketch rather than a drama, as shown in its unreflective minor villains. "We need to hear the excuses men make to themselves for their worthlessness," she observed, in one of her more memorable critical bon mots. (Emerson was so chagrined at her "censure so wide" that he wrote Sterling apologizing for the unexpected result.) As in her earlier survey of Boston "Entertainments," she blamed contemporary playwrights' incapacity to write much more than actors' vehicles and "dialogued monologues" on the culturally disunified age, whose best works were fragmentary and subjective, such as the oratorio, opera, historical novel, dance, and the highest, because the most subjective, music. Yet, "fresh from the prairies," she also gave this classic German Romantic historicism a new national twist. American playwrights might achieve something "entirely new, not yet to be predicted," but to do that they would have to create new plays and productions organically rooted in artists' original visions and audiences' real experiences. But, alas, she reported, that was not happening. Instead of "some drama, ready made to hand by the fortunes of Boon, or the defeats of Black Hawk," the storekeepers and laborers of republican America were treated to "Tamerlane and the like—Bombastes Furioso, and King Cambyses."[35]

In her subsequent mélange of musings on melancholy and the drama in her "Dialogue" in the April *Dial*, she let her old alter ego stand-ins Aglauron and Laurie express greater hope for the genre in America. Even the depressive Aglauron sees cultural potential in the surprising popularity of Shakespeare's plays. He excludes, of course, the exploitative and the genteel: yahooing absurd productions in saloons or mouthing banal platitudes in lecture halls. "Yet on reading Hamlet, his greatest work, we find there is not a pregnant sentence, scarce a word that men have not appreciated, have not used in myriad ways. Had we never read the play, we should find the whole of it from quotation and illustration familiar to us as air." Indeed, straining to find such a collective unconscious in antebellum America's Shakespeare cult, Fuller sounded more positive than Herman Melville would six years later in his nationalistic "Hawthorne and His Mosses," in which he would famously suggest that only an un-American "genius" like Hawthorne could reproduce the bard's subtlety. Significantly, perhaps, this would be the swan song of the European-minded Aglauron and Laurie and the *Dial*'s last issue.[36]

In Aglauron's nervous but hopeful spirit, Fuller also worked on her western travel book. Both emotions were understandable. Travel books registered second only to fiction as the antebellum era's most popular literary genre. In addition, with the last of the Indian tribes being driven across the Mississippi and a population on the move by ship and rail through supposedly "virgin" space, the West was the genre's most accessible but still exotic subject. Yet its worn formulas were not for her. Patriotic since her youth, she detested the malevolent travelogues of Frances Trollope, had bristled over Harriet Martineau "presumptuous" criticisms of America in her travel book, and dismissed as shallow the travel books of the friendlier Dickens, whose *American Notes,* published two years earlier, had portrayed the West as comically barbaric. She had nothing especially good to say about home-grown products either. She disparaged the "stereotype, second-hand" travel books of Washington Irving and Nathaniel P. Willis, who adapted the English "picturesque tour" to their narratives of America's framable natural wonders, and she much preferred dull exploration treatises or simple sketches, like Caroline Kirkland's quaintly realistic western books.[37]

Her models were of a very different sort. Her ideal was "intellectual narratives" that, like those of Goethe, combined narrative with "poetic" impressions and self-reflections. So she collected from friends poems and letters written to and by her while in the West, from which she planned to make, she said, along with "brief criticisms of books read there, a kind of letter box." She also liked travel books with some research behind them. Indeed, she became the first woman to be granted the privilege of working at Harvard College Library. "I can well remember," recalled Higginson, then a student at the Divinity School, "Miss Fuller sitting, day after day, under the covert gaze of the undergraduates who had never before looked upon a woman reading within those sacred precincts." She read most of the major eighteenth- and nineteenth-century European and American exploratory literature on the West. She read every book she could find in Harvard's small collection on American Indians. By the spring, she had settled into a writing routine befitting a Romantic travel writer. Except on her two teaching mornings, she usually wrote at her desk for about six hours straight, surrounded by freshly cut flowers and facing walls hung with engravings of Andrea del Sarto's *Madonna del Trono* and the Dionysian satyr Silenus, before taking a walk until dark.[38]

Meanwhile, she tried to get congenial publishing advice. On April 3 she went to New York where she stayed for a couple of weeks, taking time out to attend with William Channing a "great convention" of American Fourierists presided over by George Ripley, but mainly she interviewed editors and publishers. Both the *Dial*'s booster Greeley and the "smart set"'s Willis, now an influential coeditor of the *New York Weekly Mirror*, who had liked some of her writing that he had seen a decade earlier, promised her their "best support" in getting her book known and circulated in the city. Through April and early May, Emerson counseled her about getting a good contract. He rightly rejected Thoreau's advice that their circle publish and distribute the book themselves, taking all the risk (a bad plan that five years later would saddle Thoreau with a large debt and some seven hundred unsold copies of his *Week on the Concord and Merrimack Rivers*). Greeley gave her probably the canniest advice. She should take the offer she had gotten from the up-and-coming Boston house of Charles Little and James Brown, but get them to add "some eminent" New York firm to the title page, so it would also be "ostensibly" published there. Against Emerson's advice to go with his publisher James Munroe, who had offered more in potential royalties but only coverage for the cost of half the losses, she signed with Little and Brown, who gave her 10 percent royalties, no risk after production costs, and the co-imprint of New York's Charles S. Francis and Company on the title page. "I told [Brown]," her Concord literary factotum agreeably wrote her, "that it is your pleasure to make a somewhat less lucrative bargain with him for the sake of securing his best correspondence at South & West." It would be a national book.[39]

As her deadline loomed, she felt increasingly nervous and harried. All during May, proof sheets arrived from the printer, she joked to a friend, "like crabbed old guardians, coming to tea every night." She was also getting the same literary stage fright she had felt launching the *Dial* but now exacerbated by her awareness that this was her first original book, one aimed, moreover, at a comparatively popular audience. "The printing is begun, and all looks auspicious," she quipped to Emerson on the ninth, "except that I feel a little cold at the idea of walking forth alone to meet that staring sneering Pit critic, the Public at large, when I have always been accustomed to confront it from amid a group of 'liberally educated and respectable gentlemen.'" A week later, exhausted and still plagued by unending proof sheets, she exclaimed in her journal: "I begin to be so tired of my book! It will be through next Thursday, but I'm afraid I shall feel no better then, because dissatisfied with this last part. I ought to rewrite the Indian chapter, were there but time! It will, I fear, seem desultory and ineffectual, when my materials are so rich; *owre* rich, perhaps, for my mind does not act on them enough to fuse them." At just after one o'clock in the afternoon on May 23, her thirty-fourth birthday, she wrote the last line. "It was of heavenly beauty, but Oh, I am very, very sad," she wrote in her journal. "But the state of my mind is so deep. I think this must be an important era in my life." On June 4, Little and Brown published *Summer on the Lakes, in 1843*, shortly afterward bringing out a higher-priced issue that included seven etchings that Sarah Clarke had done on the trip.[40]

<h1 style="text-align:center">V</h1>

Over the years, Fuller's book has provoked a good deal of critical puzzlement. Recent scholars who like its comments about women and Indians express impatience with its interlaced musings, dialogues, tales, poems, book critiques, and other seeming digressions. Certainly, readers looking for a conventional travel book or even a straightforward narrative are likely to be frustrated. "I had no guidebook, kept no diary, do not know how many miles we travelled each day, nor how many in all," she nonchalantly writes. "What I got from the journey was the poetic impression of the country at large; it is all I have aimed to communicate." By "poetic impression," she means several things. One is the reader's impressions. "Read me, even as you would be read," she advises. Another is the impression she elicits through her multiple voices and personas. At times she is the colorful ironist wielding striking and sometimes startling images, intending to tell her tale, as she says in her poetic prologue, not "in dull words, with a poor reed / Breaking at each time of need," but in hinting flashes so her reader might "see the knights behind their shields, / Through dried grasses, blooming fields." At other times, she is the "apprehensive" critic spurning eastern judgments. "What! No distant mountains? what, no valleys?" she remembers thinking when she first spied the empty, sweeping prairie. Elsewhere, she is the Romantic perceiver approaching nature not as an outside observer but as her daughter looking into her mirrored and mirroring eyes. "Nature always refuses to be seen by being stared at," she writes, explaining how she came to see in the Great Lakes' "vast monotony" a beautiful "calmness." "But he who has gone to sleep in childish ease on her lap, or leaned an aching brow upon her breast, seeking there comfort with full trust as from a mother, will see all a mother's beauty in the look she bends upon him." In yet another guise the reverent daughter becomes the spunky traveler, undaunted by new challenges and ready for new adventures. Deflecting, parrying, and sublimating human and environmental threats, she seeks "to woo the mighty meaning of the scene, perhaps to foresee the law by which a new order, a new poetry is to be evoked from this chaos." Behind false appearances, she looks for a boundless West full of organic possibilities.[41]

Her first challenge is nature, whose spiritual accessibility she had anguished about at Niagara. What could be more ludicrous than this tourist spot? Rather than turn away disgusted, however, like a Transcendental frontier humorist, she has wicked fun with the scene's natural and human incongruities: the eagle chained to a stake for tourists to poke and tease, the "Recluse of Niagara" who chooses to be a "hermit of a showplace," and, of course, her nemesis, the philistine tourist. "Once, just as I had seated myself there, a man came to take his first look. He walked close up to the fall, and, after looking at it a moment, with an air as if thinking how he could best appropriate it to his own use, he spat into it." Yet unlike European travel writers, who made the spitting American into a stock character, she casts him aside and flashes different lights. One is on western nature's size. "I cannot sympathize with such an apprehension," she writes of the complaint that new buildings spoil the view of the falls. "The spectacle is capable to swallow up such objects; they are not seen in the great whole, more than an earthworm in a wide field." More often her flashing light is Romantic irony, deflating (as Thoreau would also do) the cosmic into the quotidian and reinflating it again. She gestures toward the "'guide to the falls,' who wears his title labeled on his hat; otherwise, indeed, one might as soon think of asking for a gentleman usher to point out the moon." But, she asks, twisting the absurdly commercial into the soaring sublime, "why should we wonder at such, either, when we have Commentaries on Shakespeare, and Harmonies of the Gospels?"[42]

Her hardest task at Niagara, though, had not been confronting the hackneyed and commercial but extracting spiritual meaning from the falls themselves. She begins with a startling gambit: an account of the strange effect of her first effort, which she had afterward jotted down in her journal:

> After awhile it so drew me into itself as to inspire an undefined dread, such as I never knew before, such as may be felt when death is about to usher us into a new existence. The perpetual trampling of the waters seized my senses. I felt that no other sound, however near, could be heard, and would start and look behind me for a foe. I realized the identity of that mood of nature in which these waters were poured down with such absorbing force, with that in which the Indian was shaped on the same soil. For continually upon my mind came, unsought and unwelcome, images, such as never haunted it before, of naked savages stealing behind me with uplifted tomahawks; again and again this illusion recurred, and even after I had thought it over, and tried to shake it off, I could not help starting and looking behind me.

Superficially, this nightmare of Indian-white violence sounds like a refrain from a popular captivity narrative. In fact, the scene (which a similar one in her old favorite Charles Brocken Brown's gothic thriller *Edgar Huntley* might have partly inspired) suggests the entire arc of her book. On one level, she trades the transcendent spiritual experience she did not have at the falls for a textbook Romantic sublime. She takes the reader up to the threshold of transcendent beauty, where the pleasure of spiritual transformation hints at the death of the self, and then suddenly draws back from the precipice. On another level, she reveals what will become increasingly manifest in her book: the American West cannot be freed from the memory of its former wronged inhabitants, which generate daymares within white minds, including, evidently, her own.[43]

She does not give up on her search for the spiritually transcendent, however. After awhile, she says, she left the falls and discovered for herself the fountain beyond Moss Islands, which she returned to watch many times. "In the little waterfall beyond," she writes, "nature seems, as she often does, to have made a study for some larger design. She delights in this,—a sketch within a sketch, a dream within a dream. Wherever we see it, the lines of the great waterfall, copied in the flowers that star its bordering mosses, we are delighted; for all the lineaments become fluent, and we mould the scene in congenial thought with its genius." Edgar Allan Poe would later admire this Romantic riff on the fountain's fluent and multiply mirroring microcosms, but her verbs are conditional. So, she tries again, reporting that, after several more failures, at nightfall, alone in the moonlight, without the "gaping tourists . . . eyeing with their glasses, or sketching on cards," she was finally able to see all "harmoniz[ing] with the natural grandeur of the scene." But her remembered Heraclitean sight of united "mutability and unchangeableness" only leads her to the conventionally deistical claim that she felt "a genuine admiration, and a humble adoration of the Being who was the architect of this and of all." Confessing her Romantic dead end, she writes wistfully, "Happy were the first discoverers of Niagara, those who could come unawares upon this view and upon that, whose feelings were entirely their own." From the "operatically sublime" to the "still small voice" of reverie (in the formulations of the art historian Barbara Novak), nature seems either threatening or irrecoverable.[44]

Fuller's tone changes dramatically, however, when she gets to the Great Lakes and northern Illinois in her second chapter, where she offers, in place of her uncertain water imagery, the controlling metaphor of the West as a "garden." Although since Virgil a bucolic place linking the wilderness and civilization has been a venerable trope in the pastoral tradition, in popular nineteenth-century books on the West it often served to disguise picturesquely the region's grimier or more banal versions of each. Fuller, however, uses the metaphor not picturesquely but expressively. In a characteristic passage, she invokes the conventional typing of northern Illinois as an "ornamental" garden but then shunts it aside. "The river flows sometimes through these parks and lawns," she writes, describing a view from a bank of Rock River,

> then betwixt high bluffs, whose grassy ridges are covered with fine trees, or broken with crumbling stone, that easily assume the forms of buttress, arch and clustered columns. Along the face of such crumbling rocks, swallows' nests are clustered, thick as cities, and eagles and deer do not disdain their summits. One morning, out in the boat along the base of these rocks, it was amusing, and affecting too, to see these swallows put their heads out to look at us. There was something very hospitable about it, as if man had never shown himself a tyrant among them.

In dispensing here with the "masterly mind of man" in favor of the "prodigal, but careless, motherly love of nature," she reverses gender values, not by "feminizing" nature (another nineteenth-century cliché) but by freeing it from artificial domination and "decorous" embalmment. The scene is alive with movement while the spectator lazily moves along with the flowing river, looking out on a view teeming with contrasting natural and artful metaphors: grassy ridges and arch columns, swallows' nests and thick cities, deer and eagles. Nature's expressiveness makes the West diverse and hospitable.[45]

Probably more appreciated by travel book readers than her representation of the West's nature was Fuller's depiction of its settlement. Yet here, too, she works hard to reveal promising aspects. She sometimes utters a remark that would warm the heart of a Boston Unitarian, as in her description of her Geneva Unitarian hosts as "points of light among the swarms of settlers, whose aims are sordid, whose habits thoughtless and slovenly." Mostly, though, she provides a compelling brief for the settlers. To many easterners, she says, western society seems vulgar and materialistic, but where, she asks, did these traits come from but the East? In her chapter "The Lakes," she ignores the tobacco-chewing "sharp, yet sensual looking" crowd she had spied on the landings and casts instead a cold eye exclusively on her acquisitive fellow steamboat travelers, almost all New Englanders, "talking not of what they should do, but of what they should get in the new scene." She found even more wearisome hearing their stale eastern doctrinal debates over the "Trinity and Unity . . . on these fresh waters." On western "freedom," however, she is cautious. She has no illusions, she says, that there is anything real about it, since it obviously reflects just the settlers' new entrepreneurial lives. "So soon as they have time, unless they grow better meanwhile, they will cavil and criticise, and judge other men by their own standard, and outrage the law of love every way, just as they do with us." On the other hand, she expresses nothing of the eastern fear that without more schools and churches the West would wallow in barbarism and licentiousness; her worry is Transcendentalist—not about the West's lack of strong institutions but its dearth of free minds. Meanwhile, it is at least refreshing to know, she notes, that the West's "clash of material interest" will temporarily silence vulgar and sterile theological squabbles.[46]

In an even more hopeful spirit, muting her worries about the region's destructive "mushroom growth," Fuller assimilates commercial development to nature. "I will not grieve that all the noble trees are gone already from this island to feed this caldron," she writes, passing over her initial grief over the loggers' deforestation of the Manitou islands. "[I] believe it will have Medea's virtue, and reproduce them in the form of new intellectual growths, since centuries cannot again adorn the land with such." Her description of the loggers' vocation even makes them sound like potential Transcendentalists: "I had thought of such a position, from its mixture of profound solitude with service to the great world, as possessing an ideal beauty." To further humanize western commerce, she manipulates organic metaphors. Buffalo and Chicago, she writes, are "two correspondent valves that open and shut all the time, as the life-blood rushes from east to west, and back again from west to east." She even finds possibilities for communitarian development in the West's wide-open spaces. "With a very little money," she exults, sounding like a real estate salesman, "a ducal estate may be purchased, and by a very little more, and moderate labor, a family be maintained upon it with raiment, food, and shelter." Indeed, the West's immensity of land seems a prophylactic against capitalism's ills, promising room "not only for those favored or cursed with the qualities best adapting for the strifes of competition, but for the delicate, the thoughtful, even the indolent or eccentric. She did not say, Fight or starve; nor even, Work or cease to exist." Ultimately, though, the West's enormous expanse is a symbol and guarantor of the country's potential cosmopolitan greatness. "Certainly I think I had never felt so happy that I was born in America," she writes, describing her July 4 morning spent meditating on the Oregon bluff's Eagle's Nest. "Wo to all country folks that never saw this spot, never swept an enraptured gaze over the prospect that stretched beneath. I do believe Rome and Florence are suburbs compared to this capital of nature's art." By identifying her epiphany with American nature, locating it in the lonely mind, and having it encompass Western civilization, she transmutes the event into a Transcendental patriotic conversion experience.[47]

Yet, these Romantic possibilities notwithstanding, Fuller is not oblivious to her western garden's many blights: stark poverty, untreated illness, unrelieved loneliness, gnawing disappointment, and, to her especially poignant, the sad plight of European families whose high culture and refined talents are now worthless in the utilititarian, go-getting West all make anecdotal appearances in her book. She pays the most attention, as she had in her journal and letters, to western women's status, which, she says, is *the* "great drawback" preventing the realization of an ideal West organically mixing thought and action. In fact, she is more sensitive to their constraints than she had shown in her letters: the decision to go west is invariably the men's and the women go reluctantly; the men get assistance in the field, the women rarely do in the home; the men enjoy outdoor sports, and the women do not; and the increased workload of farm and household often turns poor women into "slatterns." With upper-middle-class-aspiring women, on the other hand, she is tough. Obsessed with keeping up a show of refinement, they enmesh themselves in trivial household arrangements, but worst of all, they try to "help" their daughters to grow up in their genteel ways, which only ruin them:

> If the little girls grow up strong, resolute, able to exert their faculties, their mothers mourn over their want of fashionable delicacy. Are they gay, enterprising, ready to fly about in the various ways that teach them so much, these ladies lament that "they cannot go to school, where they might learn to be quiet." They lament the want of "education" for their daughters, as if the thousand needs which call out their young energies, and the language of nature around, yielded no education.[48]

To counter these maladaptations she makes some suggestions. She proposes the establishment of western schools for girls, although not with the object of eastern educators to "civilize" the barbaric West, but the opposite: to free the region of the "mania" of copying the East's irrelevant, and often Anglophile, standards. "Methods copied from the education of some English Lady Augusta," she notes acidly, "are as ill suited to the daughter of an Illinois Farmer, as satin shoes to climb the Indian mounds." Nor should organic education stop at the schools. She allows scope for feminine domestic touches in log cabins, veiling "every rudeness" and exploiting "every sylvan grace," but more often she highlights female settlers' "mixture of culture and rudeness," as with a couple of young ladies who were musicians and fluent French speakers but had learned to milk cows and kill the rattlesnakes that attacked their chickens. Finally, she says, western women's artistic culture also needs some hybrid rethinking. Instead of dragging to the West the piano, that icon of middle-class respectability—which cannot even be properly tuned there, she notes—she recommends "primitive" arts like guitar playing or social singing. "We cannot but think a fine Italian duet would be as much at home in the log cabin as one of Mrs. Gore's novels," she says, touting cosmopolitan singing over fashionable fiction. Clearly, she is not calling, as did Caroline Kirkland, for merely realistic adaptation to the West's roughness as a means of making it susceptible to middle-class eastern women, any more than she is summoning up the region, as did male writers from pulp authors to Francis Parkman, as a province of eastern masculine adventure and conquest. Rather, she is urging a western version of a national cultural "war" (as she predicts it will be) for Transcendental organic thinking and psychic self-reliance and against the "fatal spirit of imitation"—a war she had been advocating in print and in her *Conversations* for the past half decade.[49]

There is only one problem with her cultural call for a new western man and woman who would be "no thin Idealist, no course Realist": in making it she ironically sometimes leaves the West behind. Indeed, in places she unmoors her narrative entirely from her western experience to relate a fictional tale told to her by someone or plunge into an extensive book critique. Moreover, these digressions have one thing in common: they expose the secret psychologies of outsiders. This is true with her two most egregious digressions: her fictional story of the ill-wedded "Mariana," whose youth as a gifted, histrionic, and ostracized troublemaker at their boarding school draws on Fuller's adolescent experience at Miss Prescott's Seminary, and her forty-three-page critique of Kerner's *Die Seherin von Prevorst,* which takes up the last two-thirds of her penultimate chapter on Wisconsin. She herself hints at the problem when she notes, with some chagrin, the ludicrous contrast between this "very strange" book about illness and the irrational and the healthy, instinctive life she has been surveying. Her western experiences, she seems to be confessing, did not provide her with materials to illuminate the "inner" West she had aimed for, and for good reasons. She felt highly reticent about speaking about her hosts' private lives, without which she could hardly make marriage and madness very relevant to her narrative. As she could not speak the languages of most of the foreign settlers around the Lakes, she also could discover no traces of the Romantic folk cultures that she had initially hoped to encounter. It was as if, blocked from finding in the bustling new region the needed psychological and mythic "hints" of *that* ideal West, she gave up and, as she had done when frustrated with dull Chicago, curled up indoors with her books. After describing seeing Germans, Norwegians, Swedes, and other European national groups disembarking, she wondered aloud "how much of old legendary lore, of modern wonder, they have already planted amid the Wisconsin forests?"

I saw, in the newspaper, that the American Tract Society boasted of their agents' having exchanged, at a Western cabin door, tracts for the *Devil on Two Sticks,* and then burnt that more entertaining than edifying volume. No wonder, though, they study it there. Could one but have the gift of reading the dreams dreamed by men of such various birth, various history, various mind, it would afford much more extensive amusement than did the chambers of one Spanish city![50]

Yet she knows that this is whistling in the dark: hopeful glances at a mythic-minded multicultural West, nods to frontier magical tracts, clever swipes at evangelical missionaries, or wishes for clairvoyant gifts will not get her very far in exposing the West's mythic "blooming fields" behind its "dried grasses." She writes wistfully:

> Could I but have flown at night through such mental experiences, instead of being shut up in my little bedroom at the Milwaukie boarding house, this chapter would have been worth reading. . . . Had I been rich in money, I might have built a house, or set up a business, during my fortnight's stay in Milwaukee, matters move on there at so rapid a rate. But, being only rich in curiosity, I was obliged to walk the streets and pick up what I could in casual intercourse. When I left the street, indeed, and walked on the bluffs, or sat beside the lake in their shadow, my mind was rich in dreams congenial to the scene, some time to be realized, but not by me.

So Fuller remained, still clinging to her hope of a mythic West that might someday embody the "Real" and "Ideal," and still, in the end, as on Eagle's Nest, alone with nature, dreaming her national dreams.[51]

VI

With her last chapters on Mackinaw Island and Sault Sainte Marie, Fuller returns to what to her is by far the West's greatest blight: the plight of the Indian, whose dark imago she caught sight of at Niagara. The subject was obviously important, even if she were only writing about whites' mythic West. Since the Renaissance, writers had been conflating the "Indian," "Nature," and "America." With the completion the previous decade of the forced removals of eastern tribes beyond the Mississippi, the Indian was suddenly an object of moral and imaginative explication, a task taken up most famously by James Fenimore Cooper in his *Leather-Stocking Tales*. And, although further removal and expansion would within a couple of decades almost erase the topic in American literature, the controversy about its meaning was then still bubbling, heated by an ideology scholars have labeled "savagism." Actually, it would be more accurate to call it three savagisms, each with its objectified Other: the popular racist's bloodthirsty animal bent on killing whites; the Enlightenment's anachronism outside "civilization" based on private property, sociability, and Christian virtue; and the Romantic "Noble Savage," independent, eloquent, and stoic. All these variants of savagism had one thing in common, though—the belief that Indians were doomed to "vanish" and that this was a good thing, the only question being whether that would come through their extermination, forced removal, or "peaceful" movement beyond white settlement and eventual assimilation into white "civilization." In one form or another, "savagism" is also a label recent scholars have sometimes found handy to hang on Fuller's Indian ruminations. Yet that is a serious distortion.[52]

There is no question what Fuller thinks of the popular racist metanarrative. Indeed, her disgust seems to have built as she wrote. Telling Sam Ward of her kind Wisconsin host's story of once seeing a tall Indian gazing at the hill on the man's property that had formerly been an Indian village, she adds the scornful line "I scarcely see how they can forbear to shoot the white man where he stands." Furthermore, instead of quoting the man's halfhearted expression of sympathy, she darkens the irony still more by quoting him as saying (which perhaps he did, although it does not appear in her letter to Ward) "'They ought not to be permitted to drive away *our* game.' OUR game—just heavens!" More dispassionately, she explains, anticipating Herman Melville's "metaphysics of Indian-hating" in *The Confidence-Man*, the projective psychology at work: "This gentleman, though in other respects of most kindly and liberal heart, showed the aversion that the white man soon learns to feel for the Indian on whom he encroaches, the aversion of the injurer for him he has degraded." She is hardest on western women's aversion, perhaps because she was aware she had to work to rid herself of it:

> I have spoken of the hatred felt by the white man for the Indian: with the white women it seems to amount to disgust, to loathing. How could I endure the dirt, the peculiar smell of the Indians, and their dwellings, was a great marvel in the eyes of my lady acquaintance; indeed, I wonder why they did not quite give me up, as they certainly looked on me with great distaste for it. "Get you gone, you Indian dog," was the felt, if not the breathed expression towards the hapless owners of the soil. All their claims, all their sorrows quite forgot, in abhorrence of their dirt, their tawny skins, and the vices the whites have taught them.[53]

Despite these blistering denunciations, recent race-sensitive scholars have still claimed that *Summer on the Lakes* evinces either an Enlightenment "savagism" that dooms Indians to extinction or a "romantic" literary equivalent that "erases" them by making them into "Noble Savages." There is something to this. "With the Indians, hopeless—all their virtues . . . must be obliterated before they can be joined with civilized man," she had jotted down under the heading "Amalgamation of races" in her *Dial* notebook survey of American cultural prospects. "Let them go with the bears and wolves, noble wronged creatures that they are, it could not be otherwise." Even in her book, at one point she seems to assent to the idea of the inevitable obliteration of Indian culture. "Nature seems, like all else, to declare, that this race is fated to perish," perhaps because, she quotes the translation by a nearby "'gentleman'" of a Chippewa orator at Mackinaw, "'the white man looks to the future and paves the way for posterity.'" Yet, as this quotation suggests, she is using race, as did some (but increasingly fewer) white commentators, as largely interchangeable with mutable culture. Moreover, she is obviously uncomfortable with this secondhand progressivist conclusion, which in an article the following year she would decry as a "vulgar notion." In any case, she nowhere repeats it; indeed, she makes several nonracist Romantic moves that check it.[54]

One is her historicist idea of cultural change, which she took from Herder, and which she regularly trotted out in her arguments contesting linear Western progress. She repeatedly asserts that history moves in a tension-filled spiral, with gains and losses, advances, and returns at every step. "Man . . . is constantly breaking bounds, in proportion as the mental gets the better of the mere instinctive existence," she writes. "As yet, he loses in harmony of being what he gains in height and *extension*; the civilized man is a larger mind, but a more imperfect nature than the savage." Nor does her Romantic metahistory, as one scholar has claimed, blithely "make her Indians exhibit harmony of being only by sentimentalizing them"; on the contrary, she is acutely conscious of that danger. She brands Cooper's Uncas in his *Last of the Mohicans*, the American locus classicus of the "Noble Savage" trope of a dignified but dying race, a "masquerade figure" and "a white man's view of a savage hero, who would be far finer in his natural proportions." As for Fuller's "Romantic" savagism, she sees Indians as broadly "premodern," but just as the German Romantics thought of the Greeks—intuitive, objective, metaphorical-minded, and deeply admirable for the cultural achievements that sprang from these mindsets. She uses their almost Grecian "taste" in the arrangement of mounds (whose sophistication made many commentators deny their Indian origins), which she saw at a deserted Indian village off the Rock River, to refute the constant talk about Indian "dirt" and "brutality" that she heard during her trip. She also uses Indian nonmodernism to shine a critical light on the modern age's vaunted self-consciousness. After telling the story of an Indian who, upon receiving a medal for bravery from President Washington, replied that he had not known it was good when he did it but now knew that it was, she writes acerbically, "Were we, too, so good, as to need a medal to show us that we are!"[55]

Finally, in her last chapters she tries to get beyond speculative "Romantic racialism" by getting inside Indian culture through representing its lore and mythology. She was almost wholly dependent on variously untrustworthy and, if sometimes sympathetic, often racially prejudiced scholarship and compilations in books by George Catlin, Henry Rowe Schoolcraft, James Hall, Thomas L. McKenney, Daniel Drake, and other authors whose works she got from Harvard College's library. But she shows no interest in their religious and prescientific attempts to fit Indian origins and history into classical and biblical accounts of Creation. Her interest, like that of a modern anthropologist, is in Indian culture as an autonomous, organic, and perfectly legitimate belief system, using her authors' own data to dismiss "sentimental" or (as she also calls them) "white man's" interpretations. She is particularly hard on her chroniclers' insensitivity to the nuances of language in their translations and glosses. Even Schoolcraft, the dean of antebellum ethnologists, whose *Algic Researches* was the era's primary source of tribal tales, she derides for substituting for "the Spartan brevity and sinewy grasp of Indian speech" "the flimsy graces, common to the style of annuals and souvenirs."[56]

Trying to get around such "bad taste" without linguistic knowledge herself, she offers rereadings of scores of Indian myths, legends, animal tales, and nursery rhymes, often comparing them with ancient Greek and modern northern European oral texts. She treats with particular nuance and sympathy Indian religions, approvingly noting their animistic core yet also pointing out (unlike most of her compilers) their distinctive characteristics, especially their complex cosmic otherworldliness, many secondary powers, and stern (if less "refined") ethical codes in matters of truth and fidelity. Even rites that were shocking to many whites she interprets in ironically positive ways, as in her appraisal of the profound sympathy with which Indians speak of animals in their ceremonial sacrifices of them. And although she includes no extensive commentary on Indian society to match that on Indian lore and religion, she does address the much-debated question of the status of Indian women with something of the same sensitivity. After much back-and-forth, she concludes with most of her sources that they generally have less status in their society than do white women in theirs, but she puts in no good word for the "Christian civilization" that virtually all the authors invidiously contrasted with it. Indians' deference to female elders, for example, seems to her very similar to that of European and American middle-class cultures, which also give women the privilege of influence but no real power. Unusual in antebellum ethnography, too, is her attention to the everyday lives of women. She even shows a modern anthropologist's awareness of how her presence affects their behavior, as in her description of her encounter with a group of near-starving Pottawattamies on the bank of Silver Lake in whose lodges she and the Clarkes sought shelter from a sudden thunderstorm:

> They showed all the gentle courtesy which marks them towards the stranger, who stands in any need; though it was obvious that the visit, which inconvenienced them, could only have been caused by the most impertinent curiosity, they made us as comfortable as their extreme poverty permitted. They seemed to think we would not like to touch them: a sick girl in the lodge where I was, persisted in moving so as to give me the dry place; a woman with the sweet melancholy of the race, kept off the children and wet dogs from even the hem of my garment.[57]

In the end, she assigns the responsibility for any "decline" American Indians have experienced to whites. "All unprejudiced observers bear testimony that the Indians," she writes, "until broken from their old anchorage by intercourse with the whites, who offer them, instead, a religion of which they furnish neither interpretation nor example, were singularly virtuous, if virtue be allowed to consist in a man's acting up to his own ideas of right." It is whites, she says, who have systematically expropriated the Indians' lands, crushed their governments, and nearly destroyed their culture. Indeed, she even justifies reportedly horrific acts of Indian violence as being thoroughly consistent with the "Roman or Carthaginian part of heroic and patriotic self-defence. . . . Looked at by his own standard," she coolly observes, "he is virtuous when he most injures his enemy." Finally, she makes it clear that hypocritical whites must bear the total responsibility for the near impossibility of fairly integrating Indians into the nation. She runs down the list of offenders, from "the stern Presbyterian with his dogmas and task-work" and the college-bred urban philanthropists "with their niggard concessions and unfeeling stare" to the merchants who sell the Indians adulterated tobacco and poisonous rum and the priests who preach to them of "purity!"

> My savage friends, cries the old fat priest, you must, above all things, aim at *purity*.
> Oh, my heart swelled when I saw them in a Christian church. Better their own dog-feasts and bloody rites than such mockery of that other faith.

"The dog," said an Indian, "was once a spirit; he has fallen for his sin, and was given by the Great spirit, in this shape, to man, as his most intelligent companion. Therefore we sacrifice it in honor to our friends in this world,—to our protecting geniuses in another."

There was religion in that thought. The white man sacrifices his own brother, and to Mammon, yet he turns in loathing from the dog-feast.[58]

Having prepared her readers for contrition, she offers, however, no practical absolution. On miscegenation, she is uncertain, at one point seeming to defer to the claim of Catlin, whose writings she most respected, that "amalgamation" is not workable because people of "mixed blood . . . fade early, and are not generally of a fine race." Yet she is tentative about this, privately evincing a strong interest to know more about it and in her book wishing that America had more men like Alexander Henry, the late eighteenth-century trader and explorer who lived among the Chippewas, and combined the good qualities of both "races." Mongrelization, she says, is "the only true and profound means of civilization." As for government policy, she is deeply pessimistic. She dismisses as unfeasible Judge James Hall's plan in his and McKenney's *Indian Tribes of North America* to build on the removal of eastern tribes to the West, which McKenney had orchestrated in 1830 as head of the Office of Indian Affairs under President Jackson, to ensure their conversion to white "civilization" by legalizing their individual ownership of land. But she is also repelled by the idea: the only right way, she insists, would not be forcing Indian homesteaders to live under a "patriarchal" organization devised by a "white thinker" but simply leaving their leaders free to organize a government—an alternative, alas, that had been dashed by the "barbarous" removal of the Cherokee by Georgia and federal authorities six years earlier. Indeed, so suspicious is she of whites in their dealings with Indians that she says of the recent Chippewa petition to the state of Michigan for admission as citizens that if they were not admitted as "brothers, to the heart of the white man," what would be the point? "The white man, as yet, is a half-tamed pirate, and avails himself, as much as ever, of the maxim, 'Might makes right,'" she writes, turning savagism on its racial head. "All that civilization does for the generality, is to cover up this with a veil of subtle evasions and chicane, and here and there to rouse the individual mind to appeal to heaven against it." So, without any hope for "civilized justice," she offers only a modest liberal plea: create a national institute containing the excavated remains of Indian tribes, a picture gallery housing Catlin's and other collections, and the existing "scanty library" on the subject, headed by a historian, preferably an Indian. (The suggestion would be partly implemented three years later, minus Catlin's collection and the Indian head, with the founding of the Smithsonian Institution.) Her other plea is rhetorical. It may be that traders, missionaries, and government officials will only continue to ensure the Indians' "immediate degradation, and speedy death." But that is all the worse for whites. Citing the same biblical text that Lincoln would use in his Second Inaugural Address to draw a moral lesson from historically inevitable slavery, she writes: "The whole sermon may be preached from the text, 'Need be that offences must come, yet wo them by whom they come.'" Meanwhile, if nothing else, whites should "avoid all share in embittering, by insult or unfeeling prejudice, the captivity of Israel."[59]

In a buoyant Romantic counter-swoop, she follows up her sober jeremiad with a final lyrical chapter on her excursion to Sault Sainte Marie. Describing her sixty-mile-an-hour descent down the rapids with her pink-calico-shirted Indian canoe-ists gracefully maneuvering amid jagged rocks that come within inches of tearing a hole in the birch canoe, she exclaims, "I should like to have come down twenty times." She also crams in an account of some last liminal encounters: with her "half wild and wholly rude" but highly knowledgeable boardinghouse mates; with an Indian chambermaid who had left her dissolute husband and found happiness living "far freer than she would have been in civilized life"; with Illinois and Wisconsin farmers who regaled her with sportsman stories. "How pleasant it was," she exclaims, "to sit and hear rough men tell pieces out of their own common lives, in place of the frippery talk of some fine circle with its conventional sentiment, and timid, second-hand criticism." After another wild canoe ride with Sarah Clarke, with the Indian boys furiously paddling, to the loud laughter of the "two white women," to get out of the way of a steamboat they had purposely gotten in front of, Fuller leaves the island and ends where she began—with eastern tourists on the empty water. This time, though, she turns her former scorn into light satire of the eastern cultists and crazies on board: a shabbily dressed phrenologist examining heads bent with "half-conceited, half-sheepish expression," a bereaved lover seeking consolation in Joseph Butler's *Analogy of Religion* and the flirtations of pretty young women, knots of people talking theology, and others discussing the doctrines of Fourier. "It seemed pity they were not going to, rather than from, the rich and free country where it would be so much easier, than with us, to try the great experiment of voluntary association, and show, beyond a doubt, that 'an ounce of prevention is worth a pound of cure,' a maxim of the 'wisdom of nations,' which has proved of little practical efficacy as yet." There is some irony here, of course. The "practical efficacy" of communitarian socialism in the West is hardly something her book confirms. And the easterners, although a ship of fools, at least do not seem to have been as grim or greedy as those that so offended her on the steamboat going West. The easterners seem to be facing the right way. And so does Fuller: the East is still home.[60]

VII

As critics at the time noted, Fuller's *Summer on the Lakes* displays many of the virtues of her writing: expressiveness, forcefulness, sometimes eloquence, and often insight. On the other hand, ill-digested, elliptical, and fragmented, it can be an exasperating book. It shows the charm but also, as Higginson noted, "the way-wardness of a student and a talker," or perhaps, he speculates, of a neophyte author anxious to load her book in case she never got another chance. She herself feared her materials were too rich to "melt," and possibly so, but in any case she did not do so, even granting her Romantic strategy of moving from event to impression to reflection and back again. Or, to use her Romantic metaphor in her book, she does not follow the "dexterous weaver" who "lets not one color go, till he finds that which matches it in the pattern; he keeps on weaving, but chooses his shades." Too often, she fails to choose her shades, and the overall pattern disappears.[61]

Yet, whatever its formal virtues and shortcomings, historically, her book put the region on the national literary and intellectual map. Greeley, the West's self-styled patron, who no doubt appreciated her touting its socialistic promise, would hail it as "one of the clearest and most graphic delineations, ever given" of the Middle West's great unequal contest between "receding barbarism" and the "rapidly advancing, but rude, repulsive semi-civilization." Higginson, no western aficionado, thought it "almost the only book which makes that great region look attractive to any but the energetic and executive side of man's nature." Her book would also resonate in American literary history. Five years later Thoreau would follow it with his more poetic but also digressive and fractured *A Week on the Concord and Merrimack Rivers*, which would lay the groundwork for his masterpiece of Romantic inward and outward journeying, *Walden*. More broadly, her book is an insufficiently appreciated contribution to what Leo Marx in *The Machine in the Garden* has called the canonical American Renaissance authors' search for a "symbolic middle landscape" dialectically bridging the "wild" and the "civilized."[62]

Her small book also had several original accents. First, she narrated it through the personal voice of the lonely female seeker enacting what one critic has named a "poetics of adventure," or a first-person—and heretofore male—Romantic mode of travel writing in which the narrator enacts, records, and mythologizes her confrontations with the new and unknown. Second, unlike Hawthorne, who ignored the pioneer West except as a metaphor of the "frontier," and Thoreau, who largely absorbed it into Concord's "wild" self, Fuller made the region central to a capacious national vision. Third, unlike Whitman, who celebrated the West in absentia but whose appreciation of the Indian in it was minimal, she makes the figure crucial, both as a tragic victim and cultural influence, to the West's mythology and society. In short, *Summer on the Lakes* belongs on a short shelf of books that try to fill what Lewis Mumford would later call "the vast gap between the hope of the Romantic Movement and the reality of the pioneer period." She may not have found either her American "folk" or her democratic "aristocracy," but in succumbing to neither moral despair nor easy optimism about the expanding West, she opened up hidden possibilities for American democratic renewal. Finally, her book opened up two cultural fronts for *her*. She got her first chance to practice first-person literary journalism for a national audience. And, for a heretofore European-absorbed intellectual who had always felt frustrated in imagining an American audience, she discovered within her own nation a vast Romantic continent shaping national identity by beckoning ever beyond itself. "The Greeks worship[ed] a god of limits," she writes in her book, contrasting the "still all new, boundless, limitless" land of the northern Illinois prairies with the constricted cultural practices of most western women. Invoking the German Romantics' critique of their worshiped Greek culture, she declares: "I say, that what is limitless is alone divine." She had found Romantic America.[63]

And a part of America discovered her as well. Her friends were enthusiastic about her book. "If it is not popular it will be because people do not wish to be entertained or do not know how to be," Caroline Sturgis, who had read it in proof, told Emerson the day before it was published. Even less high-souled readers were impressed. Her book is "full of the best matter," Convers Francis wrote his Fuller-skeptic friend Parker. "I . . . think she has a noble soul, besides being our Mad. De Stael in intellect." Francis's sister Lydia Maria Child, then pursuing a successful journalistic career in New York, told Fuller that not only was her book full of "touches of beauty, and original piquant sayings," but also, she said, "I was struck, as I am in all you write, with the vigor and acuteness of intellect." She did have one concern for Fuller to ponder, however. "I might say your house is too full; there is too much furniture in your rooms," she told her frankly. "This is the result of a higher education than popular writers usually have; but it stands much in the way of extensive popularity." It was the judgment of her successful avant-garde intellectual friend that Fuller most fretted about, though. Happily, after hearing her disparage the book so much "that I feared it was bad," Emerson confided to Sam Ward, he was greatly relieved when four days after it was published he sat down to read it. "I am very well contented with it; for it has the indispensible merit of being interesting," he told Caroline. "Of course she will have thoughts & anecdotes & literature, but whether she could make a plain readable book,—was the question this book decides in the affirmative." Although he did worry about her failure "to weave a little web & weave her figures in, since she had so many strange figures from so distant places to combine in her piece," he had no doubt about its cultural significance: "[It] is an American, and not an English book, and has a fine superior tone which is the native voice of that extraordinary Margaret."[64]

Emerson's expectation that Fuller would find a national audience was somewhat fulfilled. After six months, sales totaled nearly seven hundred copies, exceeding a typical edition's sale, which usually ran no more than five hundred copies, and Thoreau's later first volume *A Week*, which sold less than half of that. Meanwhile, even non-New England literati talked up the book. Poe praised its "graphicality," while the New York critic Evert A. Duyckinck was impressed with its nationalism and its experimental qualities. "Miss Fuller's 'the Transcendentalists['] Book—A Summer on the Lakes is the only genuine American book I can think published this season," he noted in his diary. "Miss Fuller's . . . is . . . a book of travels with all the scaffolding struck away." Most helpful were the reviews. Although most missed entirely the book's novel formal aspects that concerned Emerson and impressed Duyckinck, that did not keep them from praising it unstintingly. And this was true not just of the *Dial*-friendly *New-York Tribune* and *Christian World* but also of the Democratic *Boston Morning Post*, the anti-Transcendentalist *Boston Courier*, the conservative Whig *Daily Advertiser*, and even the fashionable *Godey's Lady's Book*, all lauding its thoughtful yet entertaining quality and, importantly, its freedom from Transcendentalist jargon. Philadelphia's popular *Graham's Magazine* confidently predicted that it would deservedly extend Fuller's "reputation as an authoress" beyond the Transcendentalist "literary sect . . . whose excellencies and oddities are both distasteful to a

considerable portion of the 'reading public.'" Fuller's Transcendentalist friends
were dumbstruck. "It is a small thing that you learned and virtuous people like
it," Emerson wrote excitedly to a friend. "I tell you the 'Post [and the] Advertiser
praise it, and I expect a favorable leader from the 'Police Gazette.'" If American
writers needed, as Melville would later claim, to flash their deep truths while still
titillating popular readers, Fuller seems to have scored a bull's-eye.[65]

The quarterlies, however, were another matter. Probably *because* of her book's
combination of experimental Romantic style and popular subject matter, most
ignored it. Yet the two journal reviewers who did not overlook it boosted her reputation, too, albeit very differently. Caleb Stetson, the Medford Unitarian minister
and former occasional attendee of Transcendental Club meetings, writing for the
now largely anti-Transcendentalist *Christian Examiner*, seemed puzzled about
what to make of the book. Lauding the "extraordinary endowments of its author,"
he wrote, somewhat qualifiedly, "to a class of readers who can . . . appreciate her
philosophic and poetic insight, she has furnished a rare intellectual entertainment.
She has imparted a new and classic interest to the uncultivated regions of our
NorthWestern waters." He even applauded her "high degree" of subjectivity: "We
can never anticipate what she will say, from knowing her point of view and the
objects which surround her. She throws her own being into the outward world
and gives it a new character." The problem, the quarterly reviewer wrote, was
that Fuller was too intellectual! Her "reflective tendency," he said, like that of
Coleridge's, made for an "over-carefulness and severity in a mind unwilling to
trust to natural and simple impressions." This was further compounded by her
somewhat chilling style. "We find something cold, stately, almost *statuesque*, in
her language," Stetson complained. "It has not the warmth of life which her heart
would give it, if she would yield herself trustingly to its impulses with less of intellectual criticism." This was a classic Unitarian literary critique: sentimental
impressionism was good but difficult introspection was dangerous, especially, it
would seem, in the voice of a "cold, stately, almost *statuesque*" female persona.[66]

Fuller's "*statuesque*" Romantic stature was a considerably more upsetting
hobgoblin to her former editor, the freshly minted Roman Catholic convert Orestes
Brownson, who reviewed her book in his recently reincarnated and renamed
Brownson's Quarterly Review. "Her writings we do not like," he announced,
indeed, "We dislike them exceedingly." "Miss Fuller seems to us to be wholly
deficient in a pure, correct taste," this former roaring Jacksonian wrote, "and
especially in that tidiness we always look for in woman." And, he said, "we detest
her doctrines"; in fact, their combination of Germanic pantheism, Byronic skepticism, and Goethean aestheticism made her the most dangerous radical intellectual in Boston: "She is a heathen priestess, though of what god or goddess we will
not pretend to say. . . . We believe no person has appeared among us whose conversation and writings have done more to corrupt the minds and hearts of our
community." Then, astonishingly, he turned 180 degrees when he finally got to
the actual "book before us": "It is marked by flashes of a rare genius, by uncommon and versatile powers, by sentiments at times almost devout." Although Clarke's
Transcendentalist Unitarian *Christian World* chivalrously denounced Brownson's

review as "the most unmanly, vulgar, and abusive page of personalities we have
ever seen," it is hard to imagine a better vehicle for provoking interest in Boston's
"heathen priestess" and her work of "rare genius" than Brownson's dogmatic
outburst.[67]

All this attention naturally gratified Fuller. "It seems to be selling very well
[and] is much read," she exulted to her brother Arthur, adding, with half-relish, "I
shall be surprized if it is not assailed in some of the reviews." The local stir her
"underground" autobiographical tale kicked up also tickled her. "It is amusing to
see how elderly routine gentlemen, such as Dr Francis and Mr Farrar, are charmed
with the little story of Mariana," she told Channing. "They admire, at poetic distance, that powerful nature that would alarm them so in real life. . . . Nobody
dreams of its being like me; they all thought Miranda was, in the Great Lawsuit.
People seem to think that not more than one phase of character can be shown in
one life." Meanwhile, she eyed her market. "Newspapers from N. Orleans shew
that 'Summer on the Lakes' is advertised there," she wrote in her journal. "Am
glad it has penetrated there." She also tried to ensure that its penetration got a
helping hand. "Short notices by you, distributed at Phila New York and even Cincinnati would attract attention and buyers!!" she wrote to Channing a few days
after its publication. Still, she kept her professional priorities straight. "Outward
success in this way is very desirable to me," she confided to her socialist friend,
"not so much on account of present profit to be derived, as because it would give
me advantage in making future bargains, and open the way to ransom more time
for writing." It soon would, and much more besides.[68]

CHAPTER FIVE

Concords and Discords
(1844–1845)

I

With her book completed, at the beginning of June 1844, Fuller played catch-up with her personal life. She struggled to keep old emotional wounds firmly bandaged. "I shall never get through," she wrote in her journal after spending several days culling her papers of the last three years; "they interest me too much and excite too many thoughts as I go along." On June 4, the day *Summer on the Lakes* came off the presses, Caroline Sturgis arrived at Ellery Street and stayed for two weeks to talk and study. "The past *is* past," she wrote the day Caroline left, "only to be brought up for precept or poetic suggestion." After reading Sam Ward's old letter to her written while he was courting Anna, condescendingly dismissing the "'possibility of Platonic affection,'" she scribbled: "So writes the sentimental man of the world and he, once my Rafaello, would now write so too. I will seal up now and not read again ever perhaps." Sealing up her more recent memory of William Clarke was a little harder. "I have got beyond what gave me so much pain in the month of May," she wrote at the end of June, a month after he returned to Chicago. "It pains me to have close dealings with those who do not love, to whom my feelings are 'strange.' Kindness & esteem are very well[.] I am willing to receive & bestow them, but these, alone are not worth feelings such as mine, & I wish I may make no more mistakes, but keep chaste for mine own people." For the umpteenth time, she reminded herself, "feelings such as mine" required the proper objects.[1]

Yet, as also often before, the reminder did not entirely take. "O I need some help. No I need a full a godlike embrace from some sufficient love," she cried in her journal on Independence Day after returning empty-handed from the post office, which had closed for the holiday. "I know not why, but the wound of my heart has reopened yesterday & today. My head aches." Trying to recapture the "full music of soul" that she had felt the year before on Eagle's Rock, she worked on a cluster of "July Fourth" poems. What precisely the connection was between these esoteric poems and her reopened wounds is not clear. Their Egyptian sistrums, Rosicrucian knights, Virgin Marys, and other ancient, Christian, and Renaissance hermetic symbols of hidden powers certainly did not bespeak, as they would for some later Victorians, any sudden craving for an exotic religious system. "It is shallow of men to take such delight in their acts as if they could give permanence to the Mood," she wrote that week, speaking of the Brook Farmer Isaac Hecker's recent conversion to the Catholic Church. Nor do her poems echo any needy cries for a "godlike embrace"; echoing her *Dial* sketches, they speak of powerful fertility goddesses, female Titans, and androgynous demons. In "Raphael's Deposition from the Cross," her old self-referential "Leila" even appears as a transfiguring counter to the sorrowful Mary. Indeed, if there is anything new about her poems it is their fusion of symbolic estorica and strivings for wholeness within society. Thus in one she prophesies the overcoming of "tyrant stigma." And in her most mystical, her syncretic "Leila in the Arabian zone," illustrated by a sketch of Leila's six-pointed star surrounded by the hermaphroditic serpent Ouroboros swallowing its tale, the ancient Egyptian symbol of eternal return, which she would use as the frontispiece of her expanded "Great Lawsuit," she mixes gender, racial, and hermetic dyadic conjunctions:

> When the perfect two embrace,
> Male and female, black and white,
> Soul is justified in space,
> Dark made fruitful by the light,
> And centred in the diamond Sun
> Time, eternity, are one.[2]

On July 9, in an eternal return of her own, she began a three-week pilgrimage to her sometime "own people" in Concord. She found a couple of changes. One was a "detachment of Irish" from Cork, who had laid the railroad tracks for the new one-hour Charlestown-Fitchburg Railroad, which had replaced the old rumbling, four-hour omnibus, and who lived in a string of shanties in the Walden Woods. "What materials for romance are presented by these simple facts," she wrote in her journal, recounting Elizabeth Hoar's mother's anecdotes about their self-respect, devotion to their children's education, and, not least, gratitude for the sympathy of the Transcendentalists, who defended them against aspersions their nervous Yankee neighbors cast. "I mean to make some use of the residence of these people among us." What really got her attention, though, was the mini–baby boom among her friends. "This is the world of babies!" she exclaimed to Jane Tuckerman, speaking of Ellen and Ellery's six-week-old Greta, the Hawthornes' four-month-old Una, and the Emersons' second son, Edward Waldo, born the day after Fuller arrived. "The child is like a seraph," she wrote in her journal that first day, after Emerson put the three-year-old Edith "in her white nightgown and pretty bare feet" into her lap. Three days later she was enthralled watching Sophia nurse her namesake "little Greta" when the ill Ellen could not. The infant that she most marveled over, though, was Sophia's "beautiful" but ill-fated Una.

At the beginning of her second week there, she was already speaking with the tender possessiveness of a doting mother: "She has daily become attached to me; "she often kisses me in her way, or nestles her head in my bosom. But her prettiest and most marked way with me is to lean her forehead upon mine. As she does this she looks into my eyes, & I into hers. This act gives me singular pleasure: it is described in no initiation. . . . It indicates I think great purity of relation."[3]

One thing that did not change, however, was Fuller's scrutiny of the babies' parents for clues to her relations with *them*. She stayed for the first ten days as a guest of the Hawthornes at their rented Old Manse parsonage, then a week at her sister and brother-in-law's, and her last week and a half at Bush. Besides Sarah Clarke, who stayed with her at the beginning for three days, she had a couple of secondary cast members around. On her fifth day, at the crack of dawn, Thoreau showed up outside her window, calling in a hoarse voice, "Miss Fuller," to wake her up and whisk her away for a "very pleasant" two-hour boat ride on the Concord River. William Channing also popped in for a surprise visit. Mostly, though, she spent time with her hosts. With the Hawthornes, she had to contend with a few alterations. Some, as Sophia's shock over Fuller's "Great Lawsuit" would suggest, were ideological. Since Fuller's visit two summers earlier, the happy couple's distaste had been growing toward the Transcendentalists' increasingly radical ideas and associates. Sophia especially hated all their new dispensations, including not only women's rights but also the "immoral, irreligious" Fourier and their occasional socializing with African-American servants. Most of all, both Hawthornes felt a keener than ever self-protectiveness that fitted badly with the ardent sociability of the Brook Farmers and their Transcendentalist abettors, as Fuller once again discovered when the couple reacted with (in Sophia's words) "unfading horror" at Fuller's suggestion they temporarily take in another young Transcendentalist in need, the brooding and sickly Charles Newcomb. "You must not think I have any black design against your domestic peace," she assured Hawthorne. "Nor am I commissioned by the malice of some baffled lover to make you wretched!" This time Hawthorne graciously answered, saying he found it easier to say no to her than others "because you do not peep at matters through a narrow chink, but can take my view as perfectly as your own." In fact, neither this fuss nor Sophia's dyspeptic conservatism marred Fuller's days at the Hawthornes. "Margaret is magnificent," Sophia exclaimed to her mother after Fuller's third day there. Meanwhile, Fuller found Sophia's husband as magnificent as ever. "I love him much," she wrote in her journal after her boat ride with him on her last evening at Old Manse, "& love to be with him in this sweet tender homely scene. But I should like too, to be with him on the bold ocean shore." Looking back, she was no less enchanted. "I feel more like a sister to H. or rather more that he might be a brother to me than ever with any man before," she wrote from Bush. "Yet with him it is though sweet, not deep kindred, at least, not deep yet."[4]

The main reason it was never likely to be deeply "kindred" was less her unlikely Fulleresque oceanic fantasy than her growing skepticism about, if not marriage, certainly many marriages, yet another sensitive subject for Sophia. Just the previous fall Sophia had written an angry letter to her mother about her sister Elizabeth's invidious comparison of the Hawthornes' mutually idolatrous marriage with that of Sam and Anna Ward, which, Elizabeth had claimed, expressed the Emersonian ideal of preserving "*self-sufficing* worlds." To be sure, unlike Elizabeth, Fuller remained impressed with the Hawthornes' marriage. "She is . . . the child of a holy and equal marriage," Fuller wrote in her journal, after playing with Una. Yet, four days later, during a long talk in Sleepy Hollow, when the subject of marriage came up, she and Hawthorne evidently disagreed somewhat. Although someone later blotted out the passage, one can still make out the concluding phrase, "our intercourse could never be perfect," followed by this self-reflection: "At present, it skills not, I am able to take the superior views of life, and my place in it: but I know the deep yearnings of the heart & the bafflings of time will again be felt, & then I shall long for some dear hand to hold. But I shall never forget that my curse is nothing compared with that of those who have entered into those relations but not made them real: who only *seem* husbands, wives, & friends. H. was saying as much the other evening." Coming from the ostentatiously married Hawthorne, this surprising appreciation of singleness obviously pleased her.[5]

Five days later, however, she asked a new question that she had first raised with herself during her earlier visit to Concord: how much had she lost or gained *psychologically* by not having a strong marriage partner. The occasion was a boat ride with Hawthorne, after which she compared the marital virtues and vices of her arguably three strongest married male friends:

> Last night in the boat I could not help thinking each has something—more all. With Waldo how impossible to enjoy this still companionship, this mutual visionary life. With William [Channing] even: with whom I have for moments & hours been so happy could I ever depend on his being *at leisure*, to live thus; certainly for ages I could not. But then H[awthorne] has not the deep polished intellect of the one or the pure & passionate beauty of the other. He has his own powers: I seem to want them all: And through ages if not for ever promises & beckons the life of reception, of renunciation. Passing every 7 days from one region to the other. She grows weary of *packing her trunk* yet blesses thee. O rich God!

Did she want them or want their "powers"? That ambiguous ambition and her wish for "some dear hand to hold" hardly suggested an unqualified endorsement of her liminal life of "reception" and "renunciation."[6]

On July 19 she left the Hawthornes' still blissful-looking marital nest and went to her sister and brother-in-law's considerably more troubled one in their nearby rented four-room "Red Cottage." If anything, the birth of Greta had made the Channing household a "scene of distress" for the headstrong, frail mother and the moody, unemployed father. "Have never seen Ellery so disagreeable, churlish in so low a style as he was this evening," she wrote in her journal on her third day there. Fortunately, Ellery soon fled the scene to take a walking trip with Thoreau in the Catskills, Ellen left for Cambridge to visit their mother, and Margaret was left alone to keep house with Ellen's accommodating new African-American maid. "It is very pleasant," she reported to Caroline. "I write and muse and sleep much and study a little and go sit among the trees in Sleepy Hollow and the breeze flows around and the birds sing a few contented notes and the light streams in more and more gently and I feel cradled,—with me the rarest, happiest feelings." If she could not have a baby, she could at least feel like one.[7]

After a week at the deserted Red Cottage, Fuller moved over a short walk away through the Sleepy Hollow Cemetery to Bush, where her most important Concord "playmate" (as she called him) resided. As the Emersons also now had a new infant, they had around them even more than their usual colony of relatives, friends, and followers, who stopped by to see the growing family and its prophet who preached the virtues of being "alone with the Alone." Yet beginning the day of her arrival and every day thereafter, she and Emerson rendezvoused either at one of their three literary friends' houses or at Sleepy Hollow. During the first week, they danced around old feelings. "We talked of dreams & W. told the nature of his," she wrote after one very dark starlit night spent sitting on a rock in a nearby orchard. "He was a little eager & sentimental tonight, but I shall not forget the conscious subtle smile with which he looked up as he said, 'I seem so at times from sympathy, but I am not really so.'" Except perhaps for the irony, this was an old story; what was new was that now she translated their personal differences into a critique, not just of Emerson's theory of friendship, but of his increasingly ambiguous self-reliant philosophy. She also had as a textual aid his second volume of essays, which he was then anxiously making the last corrections on and read to her over the course of her first week there. Unlike the high prophetic idealism of *Nature* and the devil-may-care antinomianism of the *First Series*, in this *Second Series* he announced his chastened descent into "experience," which both impressed and disappointed her. "How beautiful, and full and grand. But oh, how cold," she wrote in her journal after he read to her on the third day his central essay "Life" (later entitled "Experience").

> Nothing but Truth in the Universe, no love, and no various realities.
> Yet how foolish with me to be grieved at him for showing towards me what exists toward all.
> Then we talked. He showed me a page from his journal which made me rather ashamed of ever exacting more. But lure me not again too near thee, fair Greek, I must keep steadily in mind what you really are.[8]

Actually, what most worried her about his new vision was not its coldness but its fatalism. "Waldo came in & talked his transcendental fatalism a little," she wrote after her sixth day at the Red Cottage. "Then went away, declaring he should not come again till he was less stupid. I had as lief he would sit here and not say a word, but it would be impossible to make him understand *that*." In fact, she had tried to make him understand something of that in two letters she had written from the Old Mouse and Red Cottage, letting him know the psychic losses for *him* of his new Transcendentalism. In the first, which she enclosed in a package containing her recent "rude" July Fourth poems, she added a comparison that parlayed her self-deprecating appraisal into a compressed survey of their different mental and literary characters:

You are intellect, I am life. My flowers and stones however shabby interest *me*, because they stand for a great deal to *me*, and would, I feel, have a hieroglyphical interest for those of like nature with me. Were I a Greek and an artist I would polish my marbles as you do, as it is, I shall be content whenever I am in a state of unimpeded energy and can sing at the top of my voice, I don't care what. Whatever is truly felt has some precious meaning. I derive a benefit from hearing your pieces as I should from walking in the portico of a temple, amid whose fair columns the air plays freely. From it I look out upon an azure sea. I accept the benignant influence. It will be eight years next week since I first came to stay in your house. How much of that influence have I there received! Disappointments have come but from a youthful ignorance in me which asked of you what was not in your nature to give. There will be little of this, if any, in future. Surely! These essays should be a sufficient protest against such *illusions*.[9]

This was a generous but pointed tribute to their respective idealist and Romantic positions, dwelling not, as two years earlier, on the half-personal, half-prophetic clash of his "truth" and her "love," but this time on the more quotidian one of "intellect" versus "life." A week later, the day after moving into Red Cottage, she had sent him a more pointed critique of his cool intellectualist stance. She took as her opening his declaration to her the previous day that he had declined to take a walk with her because he had been in a funk over his frustrations in trying to compose an upcoming address at the Court House, sponsored by the Concord Female Anti-Slavery Society. She offered him a diagnosis of this latest manifestation of the "dark aspect" of his "mental fortunes." One problem, she claimed, was his environment. Revising considerably downward her lofty journal claim two summers earlier that Transcendental Concord was America's "academic Grove," now she said he was being stifled by the placid town. "Heaven help thee, my Druid! if this blessed, brooding rainy day do not. It is a fine day for composition were it not in Concord. But I trow the fates which gave this place Concord took away the animating influences of Discord. Life here slumbers and steals on like the river. A very good place for a sage, but not for the lyrist or the orator." Reinforcing this creativity-checking local slumber, she went on, were his own dogmas. One was his self-sufficiency doctrine, which she recast as a hopeless male wish to give birth alone. He was like "Jove, under the masculine obligations of all-sufficingness, who rubs his forehead in vain to induce the Minerva-bearing headach!" Much worse, though, than his denial of the "feminine" or receptive side of the creative process was his new fatalism. She explored it in a poetic dialogue echoing the point and even the phrasing of her "Magnolia of Pontchartrain" three years earlier, which she inserted in her letter. The writer's female "Muse," evidently Fuller's persona, "breathes a soft kiss on his brow / And her lark-like song she sings," but suddenly she stops as she sees written above his "inmost" temple his credo of all opposites fatally dissolving into "One alone." The Muse then tells him (using the words she had privately written in her journal about him):

> Don't lure me here again with your sweet smile
> As the sweet herbs that on the mountain grow
> Allure the chamois to the path of toil

> And to the clefts beguile
> Through which he falls into the caves below
> Where in age-treasured snow buried!—
> He yields his breath,
> Quite unconvinced that life no better is than Death.[10]

There is no record of Emerson replying to this chilly exposé of her escape from his "all-sufficing" fatalism (which also included a gnomic parody remarkably prefiguring his poem "Brahma"), but one pointed riposte of his that she *did* record could be taken for an answer: "Waldo said my device should be a ship at sea in a gale. Motto 'Let all drive.'" Of course, there is much irony in her attempt to draw the line so starkly between his seemingly aloof individualist philosophy and her increasingly conflict-driven and quasi-democratic one. For one thing, she knew by now the practical pointlessness of these sorts of psycho-philosophical criticisms. A few days later, she wrote in her journal:

> I have just been in to see Waldo a few minutes. Sweet child.—Great Sage—Undeveloped Man!
>   I made some foolish critiques on his writings. What is the use? Let me get what I can from them & be thankful.

As for her explanation of his seeming paralysis, it was certainly an acute warning: a too-ready embrace of aloof individualism *and* fatalism *was* dangerous to Emerson as an "active soul." Yet, notwithstanding his skeptical lords of "experience" and "fate" that he had come to respect since Waldo Jr.'s death, he then was actually struggling to establish a new balance between them and his old moral idealism. Indeed, in so doing, he remained open, if not to Fuller's expansive Romanticism, then certainly to the exigencies of ethical life. She got a taste of this happy instability when she went to hear him finally deliver his "Address on the Emancipation of the Negroes in the West Indies." In it, astonishingly, with the same threatening clouds of proslavery Texas annexation looming that would soon also galvanize *her*, he jettisoned his longtime aloofness toward the antislavery movement, albeit with Transcendental caveats about merely denouncing rather than acting. "Waldo's oration," she wrote in her journal while at Bush later that night of August 1,

> O that was great heroic, calm, sweet, fair. All aspects melted and rendered into one, an archetypal face of the affair. So beautifully spoken too! Better than he ever spoke before: it was true happiness to hear him; tears came to my eyes. The old story of how the blacks received their emancipation: it seemed as if I had never heard before: he gave it such expression. How ashamed one felt to be sad, while possessing that degree of freedom which gave them such joy.
>   I felt excited to new life and a nobler emulation by Waldo this day. Yes: it is deeply tragic on the one side, my relation to him, but on the other, how noble how dear! If not an immortal relation, it makes me more immortal. Let me keep both sides duly balanced in my mind. Let me once know him & I shall not be disappointed.
>   But he is hard to know, the subtle Greek![11]

After four years of difficult and sometimes anguished confrontations, Fuller here finally recognized fully both results of Emerson's subtlety for her: frustration in their "immortal" friendship and inspiration for her "immortal" powers. She also responded to something new in his address. Rather than, as she said, merely reciting the old abolitionist story of the horrors of West Indian slavery, he had advanced two actually more radical propositions: black "anti-slave[s]" themselves had helped achieve their emancipation, and this fact, in turn, disproved the popular (and his own earlier private) notion of black racial inferiority. Indeed, in emphasizing African-American (and even violent) agency, he had left behind most abolitionists, who held the benevolent nonviolent (and predominantly white) "moral suasion" paradigm as their gospel. When she went to Bush to say goodbye two days later, Fuller displayed her complete sympathy with *that* bold turn even, or perhaps especially, in the face of the glum doubts of her hero's wife. "As usual," she afterward wrote wearily in her journal, "Lidian . . . manag[ed] to extract poison from the most healthful plants, says she has made herself sick by W's oration, choosing to think of the stories of Negro suffering instead of the high and deep thoughts which excused the anguish incident to the history of man." And so, after this Emersonian flourish, she bade a fitting farewell to the former mentor and frustrating "Undeveloped Man" who had given her her first taste of those "high and deep thoughts": "[I] took leave of Edith, the cherub, from whose head I cut a silken curl & inclosed it in a paper of verses her father gave me. Of the elder softened, half transfigured, of my Saadi so soft, so sweet to day! At parting I rose: he still sate with his eyes cast down. His hand I pressed to my heart: it was a gentle vow. He looked like the youngest child." She was ready to take the "youngest child"'s emancipationist core while leaving the husk of his "all-sufficingness" to slumbering Concord.[12]

II

On August 3, when Fuller arrived back at Ellery Street, the weather was drizzling, but the next morning gave way to "bright cool fragrant" days, a symbolically auspicious moment for her important decision. Probably in early April, when she had consulted Greeley about publishing options for *Summer on the Lakes*, he had asked her if she would be interested in moving to New York to become literary editor for his *New-York Tribune*. He would later credit the idea to his wife Mary, who had developed a "touching" attachment to Fuller as a confidante during Mary's frequent visits to Boston to attend Fuller's Conversations. Yet the proposition would have gone nowhere if Horace had not been prepared to like it. For four years, he had been writing puffs of the *Dial*, and, in his laudatory review of *Summer on the Lakes* had declared her "one of the most original as well as intellectual of American Women." On August 17, she wrote in her journal that she was "laying a plan." Two weeks later, she received Greeley's formal "proposal."[13]

What to do? To go would mean casting aside a lifetime of friends and family and her influential Conversations. Yet each was waning. The bloom had faded in her Transcendental friendships. Her "childish . . . pangs of surprize and disappointment," speaking clearly of William Clarke, had made her determined, she wrote Anna Ward, "to wean myself from such close habits of personal friendships."

Meanwhile, with Ellen married, Arthur still in Belvidere, and Richard that month moving to Greenfield, Massachusetts, to study law in George Davis's office, she was no longer her "children"'s indispensable materfamilias. With attendance at her Conversations dwindling, she was already contemplating stopping them. Fortuitously, that spring a second dispersal of her father's estate and the fall sale of the family's Cambridgeport house brought her a little over $600, a helpful cushion for any move. Finally, literary Gotham was hardly a foreign land to her. She had dealt before with New York's editors and critics, most originally Bostonians or New Englanders, as had recently other Transcendentalists. Greeley had encouraged both Thoreau and Ellery Channing to move to New York to try to break into its publishing scene, and, though both poets failed miserably and soon returned, William Channing and Lydia Maria Child had successful careers in the city. Curiously, her confirmed Concordian mentor, who had been periodically sending her and her friends positive reports of Transcendentalist fellow travelers he met while lecturing there, gave her the greatest encouragement. "For a national, for an imperial prosperity," he told her in one letter, "everything here seems irrevocably destined. . . . Me my cabin fits better, yet very likely from a certain poorness of spirit; but in my next transmigration, I think I should choose New York."[14]

Yet, for two weeks, she anguished. "O I do hate to have so many things to decide & while my headache demon too is seeming to vow I shall never do anything," she moaned after receiving Greeley's proposal. The rest of the week, "terrible headache[s]" and "much vertigo" kept her virtually prostrate. "Woke much depressed," she wrote in her journal. "I do not see clearly what course to take." So, after composing (she feared) "not the right" letter to Greeley, she tried to get away to think. The next morning, she joined Caroline Sturgis at one of their favorite resort spots, Nantasket Beach, near Cohasset on Boston's South Shore. Although she enjoyed, as usual, the ocean bathing with Caroline, she "had a miserable night," she wrote in her journal. "Kept dreaming (apropos to my bath of the morning) of slipping on the rocks, or great spiders running over me, and every time I woke, my head, which has never yet been set free, ached worse and worse." Finally, after dreaming of "slipping" and staying in bed all day, she returned on September 14 to find that her letter to Greeley had never been sent. The next day he showed up on her doorstep and got her to agree to go to New York "& at least try it." A week later, she wrote in her journal, "I now feel quite easy in doing it." Evidently to gain reassurance, though, she consulted her Concord advisors Emerson and Hawthorne, who, to her surprise, both told her the New York plan was "one of great promise" and that she should act on it.[15]

Even after deciding, she felt uneasy for reasons that went beyond concerns about leaving Boston. One was about her professional status. Some of her friends had serious doubts about her jumping into what Emerson called that "foaming foolishness of newspapers" that the "learned and virtuous" regarded as hopelessly partisan and sensationalist. She tried to reassure them—and herself. "If you remember Mr Greeley . . . such an arrangement may not seem to you seducing," she conceded to Mary Rotch's niece Maria a week after telling Greeley she would take the job, "but as a's not gold that glitters, so some things that do not glitter may be turned to gold." By "gold" she probably meant three things: her first reliable salary, a large national readership, and, extremely important to her, professional independence. "I am to *edit* the literary department," she emphasized to Maria, quickly repeating that she would be writing "the columns of *my department*." It was certainly a step up, especially, although she nowhere mentions the fact, for a woman who, like all women of her time, never had had the opportunity of stepping into *any* learned or influential profession.[16]

Yet she also faced several vocational quandaries her male Transcendentalist colleagues did not. One was becoming not, like Sarah Josepha Hale, the editor of a popular women's magazine, such as Hale's *Godey's Lady's Book*, but for virtually the first time in America, a female editorial staff member of a major metropolitan daily newspaper. Such a position was widely considered "proper only for the other sex" (as even Ann Stephens, the formidable New York assistant editor of *Graham's* magazine, had bristled after learning that she was rumored to be considering a newspaper editorial job). Mostly, she worried about a much more personal gender issue: casting off her mother and her female friends out of whose friendship she had painstakingly constructed her new avowed "feminine" identity. Clearly reflecting this fear, on September 23, the day after consulting with Emerson and Hawthorne, she dreamed that Caroline was "lost on the sea-shore & that I vainly attempted to go & save her. My feet seemed rooted to one spot: and my cloak of *red silk* kept falling off when I tried to go. At last the waves would wash up her dead body on the hard strand & then drew it back again. It was a terrible dream." She felt most anguished, though, about her mother. One perfectly rational concern, besides fearing to lose her, was how she could leave her facing old age without any family nearby. "I feel . . . that you do not sympathize entirely with my great desire to have a clear space round me for a time," Margaret gently explained to her in one letter. "It is very natural you should not; the purposes for which I would free my thoughts are not the same as those that act on your beneficent life." But there was obviously more, as suggested by an even more frightening dream she had the night after she had dreamed of Caroline drowning. "Had again that dream that makes me suffer so, of Mother's death and burial," she wrote the next morning in her journal. "I seemed left to think of it alone & the pathos almost overpowered me. I lay sobbing & could not waken." Suddenly having the matricidal nightmare she had repeatedly experienced in her childhood during the time her father was tutoring her to become his "heir" (as she later put it) would strongly suggest a wish to rid herself of her mother's imago as she prepared to take up a masculine role. To feel, even unconsciously, she had to bury her strongest female supports in order to take her rightful place in public life was a high price to pay indeed.[17]

Still, however agitating, psychological questions could hardly trump material interests and professional hopes. So, she got ready to go. With Margaret set to leave, her mother had decided to move to a smaller house on Prospect Street. "Farewell, dear river," Margaret wrote fondly in her journal on September 15, her last day at Ellery Street. "Farewell, my apple trees." After four days of negotiating with Greeley and dealing with the "dirt & manifold discomfort" of moving, she turned to parting visits. Having accumulated during her nearly thirty-five years in Boston-Cambridge "sixty or seventy persons" whom she considered her close friends, on top of a large extended family and many admiring followers, the task would seem daunting. "Poor little hand! Poor weary hand almost every body has kissed it now, though it holds no sceptre, neither Fortune's purse," she wrote in her journal on September 27, after a crushing day of goodbye meetings and parties, including one with her old Cambridge friends Elizabeth Cumming, Elizabeth's sister Belinda Randall, and Joseph Angier, who entertained her by singing their favorite trios, which made her nostalgic. ("It was indeed like old times.") For a more forward-looking send-off, in the evening, she rode out to West Roxbury with Frank Shaw, who confided his "excellent plans" for aiding socialist reform. After spending the night in Charles Newcomb's empty room, she said goodbye to him and her other Brook Farm friends. On the way back, she consulted Parker, who gave her, she gratefully noted, "much information that will be of use in my new concerns."[18]

Her last few days were full of little symbolic gestures. In Cambridge, to which she returned in the afternoon, she was loaded down with presents, including two that especially delighted her: an old, small crucifix from the Shaws and, to balance that, a sturdy writing desk from her pupil Sarah Hodges and Sarah's aunt Margaret Hodges Choate. In her thank-you note to Sarah, she let it stand as a synecdoche for her future post: "Its beauty and completeness will make it my companion, such as the good sword of the warrior was to him at an earlier day." Later in the day in Boston, the last persons she saw were Anna Loring and Dr. and Mrs. Peabody, "nodding adieux to the 'darling' as she addressed me, somewhat to my emotion." In the evening, she arrived at her aunt and aged grandmother's in Canton, where her mother had gone to visit. During her last night there, her mother wrote her blessing in Margaret's journal, expressing her "deep gratitude . . . for the love & tender care I have experienced at the hands of dear daughter Sarah" (as she still called her) and "praying god to . . . restore her again to me in his own time." Writing to her brother Richard the following week, speaking of her last moments with Anna Loring and the Peabodys, Margaret said, "They seemed like a frosty November afternoon, and a soft summer twilight when Night's glorious star begins to shine." With this seeming play on her favorite self-referential symbol of a nocturnal star rising from New England's soft but frosty twilight, she was ready to depart.[19]

III

Not scheduled to start at the *Tribune* until December, Fuller decided to take the trip up the Hudson River she had been craving since the beginning of summer. Leaving Canton on the morning of October 4, she traveled to New York, where she briefly saw the Greeleys at their "beautiful place" in upper Manhattan, and then continued on to Fishkill Landing, where she spent the next seven weeks. This resort village on the eastern shore of the Hudson sixty miles north of New York City seemed to her a writer's ideal retreat. She lived in a "well-ordered quiet" boardinghouse, she told Richard, with "nobody's humor, but my own, to consult." She had with her the ever-"wandering" Caroline who, contrary to their friends' predictions, turned out to be, Fuller reported, "friendly, sisterly, and enough of a companion." To spice things up, Ellery Channing, then writing for the *Tribune*, dropped by once, and for woodland walks she had the vacationing Christopher Pearse Cranch, who had recently moved to New York to further his landscape-painting career, and his new wife Elizabeth De Windt, the granddaughter of Fuller's father's revered John Adams. Most important, she had congenial scenery in glens, streams, waterfalls, and, especially pleasing, a couple of minutes from her door, the river. "This majesty, this calm splendor," she wrote, better than either Massachusetts's' "mere gentle and winning landscapes" or the West's "fallow flat fields," "could not but exhilarate the mind, and make it nobly free and plastic."[20]

It was good she felt that way, because she was there to convert her "Great Lawsuit" into a book on the woman question. Greeley may have suggested the idea when they had seen each other in New York in April or possibly in his subsequent letters to her in the summer. In any case, to judge by her repeated complaints of writer's block and headaches ever since beginning it in mid-August, it seems to have troubled her as much as deciding about his *Tribune* offer. "A week of more suffering than I have had for a long time," she wrote in her journal after her second week, "from Sunday to Sunday,—headache night and day! And not only there has been no respite, but it has been fixed in one spot—between the eyebrows!—what does that promise?—till it grew real torture." She duly noted the dark irony: "I think the black jailer laughs now, hoping that while I want to show that Woman can have the free, full action of intellect, he will prove in my own self that she has not physical force to bear it. . . . Yet, I will not be turned from the deeper convictions."[21]

What were those "deeper convictions"? Two that she mentioned in her journal were literary. The first concerned her literary identity, about which she had been puzzling since her adolescence. "In earlier years I aspired to wield the scepter or the lyre," she wrote, speaking of her youthful dream of becoming an intellectual statesman or a poetic "genius," who with "wise design and irresistible command [could] mould many to one purpose" by expressing the "harmonies of the universe." But alas, she said, "The gold lyre was not given to my hand, and I am but the prophecy of a poet." So she would be what she had essentially been for the past decade: a critic. "Let me use, then, the slow pen. . . . I assume no garland; I dare not even dedicate myself as a novice . . . but I will court excellence, so far as an humble heart and open eye can merit it, and, if I may gradually grow to some degree of worthiness in this mode of expression, I shall be grateful." Besides her literary vocation, her book also made her think hard about an immediate literary problem. Having written "The Great Lawsuit" as a philosophical essay for a small audience of like-minded intellectuals and highly literate readers, she was now preparing a more polemical work for a considerably more popular audience. How and to whom would she speak? She nowhere offered a formula for answering this question that had long vexed her, but her book would show the results of her thinking.[22]

Finally, she needed to be convinced about the intellectual propriety (as Emerson had challenged her) of even framing the woman question in an ideological way. In a long agitated entry, she debated the issue with herself. Why, she asked, did women even *need* political rights "to stimulate their energies, when they have all the life and art scarcely touched yet." But, she quickly added, she could see why: "for the comfort and independence of their lives they many [*sic*] need protection of property and a wider choice of lucrative professions." Then, too, besides material sustenance, there must be, she said, "a better state" for them than that of a sentimentalized ornament, a "battered utensil," or a "forlorn old maid," adding, in a packed rendering of the psychology of a new womanhood besieged: "I must resist the argument of the ages, and think the ballad of the matron with the child on one arm and the gun on the other. . . . 'Femininity raging,'—the lioness roused to defend her cubs,—More violent, *because* unusual, because incalculable to the subject is passion here!" In her most riveting passage, she vented simultaneously her Transcendentalist distaste for political polemics, feminist disgust over the popular antifeminist screeds she was reading, and a new readiness to face directly the country's emerging "woman question" wars:

> To those of us who hate emphasis and exaggeration, who believe that whatever is good of its kind is good, who shrink from love of excitement and love of sway, who, while ready for duties of many kinds, dislike pledges and bonds to any,—this talk about "Woman's Sphere," "Woman's Mission," and all such phrases as mark the present consciousness of an impending transition from old conventions to greater freedom, are most repulsive. And it demands some valor to lift one's head amidst the shower of public squibs, private sneers, anger, scorn, derision, called out by the demand that women should be put on a par with their brethren, legally and politically; that they should hold property not by permission but by right, and that they should take an active part in all great movements. But though, with Mignon [the enigmatic androgynous girl in Goethe's *Wilhem Meisters Lehrjahre*], we are prompted to characterize heaven as the place where
> "Sie fragen nicht nach Mann nie Weib [one asks for neither man nor woman]," yet it is plain we must face this agitation.[23]

To help her face it, she had brought with her a stack of books that show, whatever her intentions and purposes, she was not going to ignore her new work's intellectual footing. Two would have shored up her monist metaphysics: Taylor's Neoplatonist translations and Spinoza's "truly great . . . scientific" *Ethica*, whose pantheistic idea of God and nature as one substance had long appealed to her. Presumably for his humanist ethics and not his hierarchical social values, she had a new translation of Confucius's *Analects*. Undoubtedly chosen for examples of her Renaissance-derived ideas of love were Landor's *Pentameron* and Petrarch's Italian poems in praise of Laura. She also had with her collections and studies of Scandinavian myths, Catholic symbolism, Persian mythology, and other archetypal world literatures and religions, including Johann Adam Moehler's *Symbolik* and Emerson's copy of *The Desâtir or Sacred Writings of the Ancient Persian Prophets* (which she impishly told Emerson that she and Cary kept for their "*Sunday reading*"). She only took one contemporary work: *Le Nouveau monde industriel,*

Fourier's central industrial tract, whose ideas were undoubtedly behind her new discussions of women's economic concerns, although the recent talk at Brook Farm concerning a Fourierist restructuring of women's work may have also influenced her. "Institutions must be modified to give them a fair chance of establishing these characters," she wrote in her journal, criticizing the Unitarian author Catharine Sedgwick for considering only women's private and domestic education. "There will & must be action & reaction from character to institution & vice versa."[24]

Mostly, she did a lot of thinking about gender topics, both old and new. She did not anguish, as she had in her Conversations four years earlier, about whether women could become great artists or display the nervousness she had there about whether they could legitimately assume the characteristics of the other sex. As in her "Great Lawsuit," she took both as a matter of course. She did worry a lot about marriage and sexual relations. Possibly because of her recent disappointment with William Clarke, she felt she had gained considerable insight and equanimity about these matters. "How much better I understand the impulses of human nature now than two years ago!" she boasted in her journal just before coming to Fishkill. Indeed, after getting there, she penned the most hopeful appraisal of her single life that she had ever written:

> No one loves me. But I love a good deal, and see some way into their eventual beauty. I am growing better, and shall by and by be a worthy object of love, one that will not any where disappoint or need forbearance. Meanwhile I have no fetter on me, no engagement, and as I look on others almost every where, can I fail to feel this a great privilege. I have no way tied my hands or feet. And yet the varied calls on my sympathy have been such that I hope not to be made partial, cold or ignorant by this isolation. I have no child, and the woman in me has so craved this experience that it has seemed the want of it must paralyze me. But now that I look on these lovely children of a human birth what slow and neutralizing cares they bring with them to the mother. The children of the muse come quicker with less pain and disgust, [and] rest more lightly on the bosom.[25]

Getting a similar fix on the marriage question itself, however, flummoxed her a bit. Her elevated marital ideal remained intact. "How terrible must be the tragedy of a woman who awakes to find that she has given herself wholly to a person for whom she is not eternally fitted!" she exclaimed in her journal. "I cannot look on marriage as on the other experiments of life; it is one grand type that should be kept forever sacred." Moreover, although she considered alternative theories of marital love, such as Plato's ideal of lovers seeking their souls' other half and Emerson's of marriage as a symbolization of "divine perfection," she concluded that her Renaissance-Romantic ideal of "sacred" marriage as a "stairway to the heavens" still seemed the far more noble one. Yet she was also growing increasingly aware of the fair number of her friends' marriages that had either broken up, like those of Almira Barlow, Joseph Angier, Ellen Sturgis Hooper, and Jane Tuckerman King, or seemed problematical, like the Emersons' and Channings'. Although she drew no global conclusions, in an unpublished tale that she wrote sometime before leaving for Fishkill, she did toy with the legitimacy of the kind of free-love sentiments she had rejected in "The

Great Lawsuit." Unlike Mariana in her *Summer on the Lake*, in which the pathetic heroine dies following the unraveling of her marriage, in the tale within her dialogue "A Drive through the Country Near Boston," the dreamy and rebellious Emily revolts, as George Sand's heroines do, at the constraints imposed by, in Emily's case, two loveless marriages. The story ends inconclusively, with Emily embracing the doctrine of free love, the sentimental Laurie denouncing her as selfish, and the grave Aglauron calling her an ardent seeker of love and truth who will eventually find a higher "divine purpose." The conflict between sacred marriages and single seekers remained unresolved.[26]

Nor did she get much further with the related question of women's sexual identity. However one interprets her passionate feelings for Anna Ward and at times Caroline Sturgis, she seems to have ruled out lesbianism. "Read aloud two of Sappho's poems, fine, simple descriptions of love as a passion," she had written in her journal while beginning her revisions. "As a woman she is repulsive, as poet attractive." Yet she continued to question the fixity of gender identities. "How entirely dissimilar that boy-baby I saw yesterday, in every act and attitude from Una and Greta," she wrote in her journal soon after starting to write her manuscript. "And yet where lies this difference betwixt male and female? I cannot trace it, more than in the plant world farther than *function*. As the two Shephardias are the same, except that only one bears the fruit.—How all but infinite the mystery by which sex is stamped in the germ. By what modification of thought is this caused? Impossible to trace: here am I the child of masculine energy & Eugene of feminine loveliness, & so in many other families." Beyond the androgyny of her "Great Lawsuit"—that the sexes differed but individuals defied rigid gender categorizations—she could not go: the essential nature of sex remained a great mystery.[27]

Yet, in her own case, she could carry her androgynous heterosexual idealism to extravagant heights. In another entry in her journal, following her appraisal of her marital dilemma, she wrote: "My history presents much superficial, temporary tragedy. The Woman in me kneels and weeps in tender rapture; the Man in me rushes forth, but only to be baffled. Yet the time will come, when, from the union of this tragic king and queen, shall be born a radiant sovereign self." And, in a poem she wrote that same October at Fishkill, entitled "To the Face Seen in the Moon," she balloons her ideal into myth, as she imagines androgyny transmogrifying out of the narrator's original relationship to the "Mother":

> In thy soft Mother's smile so pensive bright,
> Thou seemest far and safe and chastely living
> Graceful and thoughtfull, loving, beauty giving,
> But, if I steadfast gaze upon thy face
> A human secret, like my own, I trace,
> For through the woman's smile looks the male eye.

In the second half of the poem, though, the poet learns from this maternal "Moon in Man" to count "life's pulses thus alone" while still looking forward to one day becoming the spiritual mother *and* legal wife of "my Apollo," from which union will spring

> The promised King
> Who with white sail unfurled
> Shall steer through the heaven
> Of soul—an unpolluted world.

Such a utopian mixture of heavenly androgyny and regal heterosexual mother-hood could hardly go further.[28]

She made more progress confronting two more worldly gender developments. The first came out of the debates over the threatened annexation of Texas that abolitionists and antislavery Whigs believed was intended for new slave territory and that on November 5 took on new urgency with the election of the proannexa-tionist James Polk to the presidency. And so, apparently, it seemed now to Fuller. The change was dramatic. In May when, in almost a replay of her confrontation with Chapman three years earlier, her Garrisonian friend Louisa Loring had told her that Loring's abolitionist colleagues "want something" from her about Texas, she had resisted, although this time half-apologetically. "I don't feel ready," she had written in her journal, blaming her preoccupation with her editing of *Sum-mer.* "I never can do well more than one thing at a time, and the least thing costs me so much thought and feeling; others have no idea of it." Now, six months later, she went beyond giving just testimony—as in the "Great Lawsuit," on the aboli-tionists' contribution to the new women's rights discourse—to talking as though she were not only ready to join the fray but to lead it! "Might not we women do something in regard to this Texas annexation project?" she asked in her journal, probably after hearing of the "monster rallies" opposing annexation that were held in Boston over the first three days in October. "I have never felt that I had any call to take part in public affairs before; but this is a great moral question, and we have an obvious right to express our convictions. I should like to convene meetings of the women everywhere and take our stand." She did not, but within days, she wrote pages for her new book that expressed her convictions.[29]

She went a bit further with the subject of lower-class women. This was not entirely a new phenomenon to her. She often surprised some of her stiffer Boston Unitarian friends by her banter with "simpl[e]" and "dignified" stagecoach driv-ers, fishermen, beggar women, Irish railroad workers, and other laboring types, although her words sometimes sound less than egalitarian. ("She is a fine girl though made coarse by her democracy," she had written in her journal after a "good talk" at Bush with the Emersons' apparently un-Romantic maid.) Over the past several years, she had also occasionally ruminated over democracy as a theory, sounding more hopeful about it than when four years earlier she had read Alexis de Tocqueville's second volume of *Democracy in America*, whose skeptical views of American culture she had wholeheartedly seconded. As with her antislavery views, changing times probably helped, especially Brook Farm's recent conver-sion to Fourierism and the growing rage there for Sand, Eugène Sue, and other socialistic French novelists of the urban underclasses. Even Emerson was start-ing to troll Boston's North End to hear the rough talk of the streets to give his prose, he said, more bite and salt. For her, though, the event that awakened her to the intersection of class and gender came at the end of October, when at nearby

Ossining, New York, she got a close look at rougher sorts of working-class women than Emerson ever saw or probably could even imagine.[30]

Mount Pleasant Female Prison, Sing Sing's female department at Ossining, was arguably the nation's most liberal penitentiary. Established five years earlier, it was also its first (and for the next thirty years only) reformatory women's prison, no small achievement when prison administrators generally assumed female criminals, for the most part prostitutes and petty thieves, to be incorrigible and therefore best warehoused in large pens bereft of the intrusive rehabilitative reforms in many antebellum male prisons. Mount Pleasant's transformation, though, had begun earlier in the year, when after a riot in the prison, a new liberal state Board of Inspectors had appointed Eliza Farnham, a Democratic partisan and Hicksite Quaker, as its new matron. Unlike the evangelical "lady visitors" who periodically descended to redeem the "fallen" and mostly working-class Irish Catholic and African-American female prisoners at Mount Pleasant, Farnham, inspired by phrenology and environmentalism, thought crime was largely a product of inherited propensities that could be stemmed by the enlightened interventions of prison officials. To nurture prisoners' higher sentiments, she introduced gardening, calisthenics, reading, journal keeping, lectures, and concerts, while swiftly isolating incorrigibles. Until forced out four years later by a new conservative board upset by the prison's seeming leniency and substitution of novels for Bible reading during sewing sessions, Farnham seems to have dampened conflict and reduced recidivism. Meanwhile, on recommendation from Fuller and Mary Greeley, Farnham had recently hired as her assistant the young Brook Farmer and Fuller devotee Georgiana Bruce. That summer Bruce and Farnham invited Fuller to visit the prison.[31]

By that time, Fuller had read some of the prisoners' journals that Bruce had sent her, which seemed, miraculously, to jibe perfectly with the themes Fuller was developing in her book! "I was greatly entertained and instructed by the Journals," she had written to Bruce, begging her to send more as well as copies of their letters to her. "If you really think me capable of writing a Lehrjahre for women, . . . nothing could aid me so much as the facts you are witnessing." Indeed, she had told Bruce, these papers were crucial. "For these women in their degradation express most powerfully the present wants of the sex at large. What blasphemies in them must fret and murmur in the perfumed boudoir, for a society beats with one great heart." Although she was speaking here in a Romantic humanitarian idiom, the papers also showed, as she implied here, a grittier point about these women's failings: they were but a heartbeat away from those of her own supposedly "pure" female middle-class. "I have read it with great interest," she wrote Bruce from Fishkill about a couple of the African-American inmates' autobiographies Bruce had sent her.

> The two characters are such as I have had least opportunity of knowing. Satir's idealizing of herself in the face of cruellest facts belongs to the fairest, most abused part of feminine Nature.
>
> Eliza's account of her strong instinctive development is excellent, as clear and racy as Gil Blas.—I suppose these women have spoken with more spirit and freedom than any whites would; have they not?

You say few of these women have any feeling about chastity. Do you know how they regard that part of the sex, who are reputed chaste? Do they see any reality in it; or look on it merely as a circumstance of condition, like the possession of fine clothes? You know novelists are fond of representing them as if they looked up to their more protected sisters as saints and angels![32]

These were good questions, but in her autobiography, Bruce reported she had "serious misgivings as to my getting at their real opinions, should these differ from the novelists." She also doubted they would give them to her. When she therefore got up the courage to ask, she was amazed, she recalled, when "one of the most intelligent, but most impulsive of the women" bluntly answered Fuller's question in the negative. Of *course*, this woman told her, "everybody in the world" knew that society regarded sexual promiscuity as wicked and so when anyone found out, they would feel disgraced and ashamed, "but if no one knew, you did not seem a bit different from anybody else." As to Fuller's implied question about whether the women looked up to "pure" women like Bruce, she said no again: they decidedly did *not* look up to them for being "what I called 'chaste,' but because they could see that we were refined, and sincere, and so unselfish and patient in our treatment of them. Nobody could ever know how you lived, if you did not choose they should, etc., etc." Bruce quickly broke off the topic in her autobiography ("It is best not to dwell on this subject"). The women's papers, then, refuted the two conventional middle-class notions of the sole causes of prostitution: the moral reformers' male seducer and the conservatives' "fallen woman." That these women's dismissal of the necessary sinfulness of nonchastity also violated Fuller's own moral code of the sacredness of marriage must have provoked her to a little personal questioning as well.[33]

In any case, impressed with—even perhaps, as her rhetoric suggests, a little envious of—these women's "clear and racy . . . spirit and freedom," as well as eager to learn more about their sexual views, on October 25 Fuller left Fishkill with Caroline and the following afternoon took the steamboat Washington Irving up to Ossining. Accompanying them was William Channing, who as a founding member of the New York Prison Association was to deliver a sermon to the male inmates the following day. After spending the night in a room at the women's prison, the next morning they went to the chapel to hear Channing's address, which she thought electrifying because of not only its "noble and pathetic eloquence" but, even more so, the reaction of his audience. "I never felt more content than when at the words 'Men and Bretheren,'" she afterward told Elizabeth Hoar, "all those faces were upturned like a sea swayed by a single wind and the Shell of brutality burst apart at the touch of love divinely human." Even a month later, she remained enthralled by what she thought she had seen of the power of "divinely human" love to penetrate social conventions. "They listened with earnest attention; many were moved to tears, some, I doubt not, to better life," she wrote to her brother Richard. "I never felt such sympathy with an audience, as I looked over that sea of faces marked with the traces of every ill, I felt that, at least, heavenly truth would not be kept out by self-complacency and a dependence on good appearances."[34]

It was the women, though, she had come to see, and in the afternoon, Farnham released a large group of them for Fuller to talk with. Although what she told them is not known, it apparently was sufficiently encouraging that several of them asked to see her alone ("as they could then say *all*, and they could not bear to before one another," she afterward wrote). She was pleased with the results. "These women, some black and all from the lowest haunts of vice," she reported to Richard, "showed a sensibility and a sense of propriety which would not have disgraced any place." Indeed, to Elizabeth Hoar, she described them as better than that.

> They were among the so called worst, but nothing could be more decorous than their conduct, and frank too. All passed much as in one of my Boston Classes. I told them I was writing about Woman and as my path had been a favoured one I wanted to ask some information of those who had been tempted to pollution and sorrow. They seemed to reply in the same spirit in which I asked. . . . It is very grati-fying to see the influence these few months of gentle and intelligent treatment have had on these women: indeed it is wonderful, and even should the State change its policy, affords the needed text for treatment of the subject.[35]

Wanting to put her two "Classes" in contact, she afterward got a few of her Conversation attendants to round up some books for them. In her letter to the prisoners, she said she wanted to encourage their taste for reading "which it gave me pleasure to hear that so many of you show" and those—clearly "the greater number"—whose "naturally good disposition" obscured by neglect in childhood could grow by getting "proper food for the mind and heart." But she also wanted them to know, "though on returning to the world you may have much to encoun-ter from the prejudices of the unthinking, yet there are many who will be glad to encourage you to begin a new career, and redeem the past by living lives of wise and innocent acts, useful to your fellow-creatures and fit for beings gifted with immortal souls." Whether the inmates took these redemptive injunctions and prom-ises in the spirit Fuller meant them is again unknown, but at any rate, she was determined, she told Hoar, to make them a return visit "and take some time for this." Meanwhile, she had a different "decorous" group of women besides her Con-versation assistants to think about as she revised her book.[36]

On the morning of October 28, Fuller returned by boat with Sturgis and Channing, who talked to them, as he paced back and forth on the deck, of the "wickedness of man" and his new "fermentation of thought." The next day she went mountain climbing and returned at night to think of nature's nearby predator and prey: "The hawks nestled near, as in the Beacon rocks, the mice turned their slender pipes beneath my pillow." The following day, she resumed work on her book. After two weeks of constant writing, during which she squeezed in a final section on the ongoing antislavery battle against Texas annexation, on November 15, ten days after Polk's election to the presidency, she finished "at last" her final draft. "I have been happy now in freedom from headach and all other interruption," she reported to Emerson two days later, "and have spun out my thread as long and many-coloured as was pleasing." Writing that same day to Channing, she was charac-teristically more radiant: "After taking a long walk early on one of the most noble exhilarating sort of mornings I sat down to write and did not put the last stroke till

near nine in the evening[.] Then I felt a delightful glow as if I had put a good deal
of my true life in it, as if, suppose I went away now, the measure of my foot-print
would be left on the earth."[37]

That confident "glow" continued to burn over the next couple of weeks, although it seems to have dimmed somewhat as she mulled over again her book's
likely reception. "The writing, though I have tried to make my meaning full and
clear," she nervously wrote to Channing, "requires, shall I say? too much culture
in the reader to be quickly or extensively diffused. I shall be satisfied if it moves
a mind here and there and through that others." Meanwhile, she made one sensible decision to facilitate that trickle-down Romantic goal: she decided to sell
her rights for only one edition. "I should hope," she explained to Channing, whom
she asked to contact Greeley about his publishing it, "to be able to make it constantly better while I live and should wish to retain full command of it, in case of
subsequent editions." With that forward-looking hope, soon after arriving in New
York with Caroline in late November, she signed a contract with Greeley and
McElrath. At the end of the year, *Woman in the Nineteenth Century* went into press
and on February 16, 1845, it was for sale.[38]

IV

How different was her book from "The Great Lawsuit: Man *versus* Men. Woman
versus Women"? In recent years, some scholars, struck by the new title, have
imagined that the book substitutes a woman-centered critique for Transcendentalist individualism. The problem with this claim is obvious: except for a few
slightly altered sentences, Fuller's essay appears virtually verbatim as part of her
book. Moreover, in her preface she makes a point of emphasizing the two works'
argumentative continuity. Apologizing for dropping the old title, she says she *liked*
its awkward subtitle for the very reason some did not: it forced them to stop and
think about what it denotes—namely, the conflict between the ideal and its manifestation in both genders. Indeed, after reinvoking the Romantic millennialist vision of Man's angelic destiny to make in "time" the "earth a part of heaven," she
restates its organicist bigendered terms: "By Man I mean both man and woman:
these are the two halves of one [divine] thought. I lay no especial stress on the
welfare of either. I believe that the development of the one cannot be effected
without that of the other." Yet it would also be wrong to suggest, as some have,
that Fuller's book is merely a more illustrated (or, less generously, inflated) version of her essay. For one thing, the new material in the book's second half triples
its size. For another, the added literary illustrations and theoretical discussions *do*
give the book in places a more scholarly air. Finally, reflecting her year and a half
of rising outrage over racial and gender bigotry, the bulk of the new material
polemically engages contemporary gender and reform talk. So Perry Miller had it
partially right when in two different books he came to two opposite conclusions
that her book is more "reasoned" *or* more "dithyrambic": it is both.[39]

In the book's largely philosophical first half, taken from her essay, the change
is sometimes only an added phrase or sentence darkening her portrayal of male

prejudice. To her essay's sly observation about men's encomiums of great women showing too much surprise, she adds, in a sardonic voice: "Can this be you? he cries to the transfigured Cinderella; well I should never have thought it, but I am very glad. We will tell every one that you have '*surpassed your sex*.'" Yet she also highlights male exploitation and misogyny that she had dismissed or under-played in her essay. Thus, in the middle of her putatively neutral opening section on the current debates over women's social place, she adds allusions, with which she claims to have firsthand familiarity, to "scores" of drunken husbands who under the cover of law cheat their wives out of their earnings and kidnap their children. Toward the end of this half, she even injects a gender-conflict dimension into her theory of woman's intuitive power. Now male prejudice appears as the principal threat to women's opportunity to contribute to humankind's "spiritual tendency." Most philosophers, she says, even great ones like Plato and Spinoza, ignore or sometimes even inveigh against intuitive ways of knowing *and* the women who use them, while many ordinary men are downright misogynist toward both. If such a man is married to such a woman, he will detest her for disregarding her sex's approved "self-restraining decorum . . . with all the bitterness of wounded self-love," taking "the whole prejudice of manhood upon himself," imprisoning and torturing her. Men do not just lack faith in expressive women; they now some-times hate them as well.[40]

Her second half is more boldly bifurcated. Some of the new material gives added support to the arguments of her essay. She adds a myriad of new illustrations of complex portrayals of women in the Western canon—including a new appendix that contains, along with extracts from Plato and Spinoza, excerpts from the Neoplatonist Apuleius on the goddess Isis, Scandinavian myths of the "World mother," and speeches of female characters in classical Greek plays. Taking off from Proclus's Neoplatonist teaching that every life contains the totality of all the animating powers although with one predominating, she spins out an elaborate typology of twelve "powers" encompassing various "spheres" occupied by fig-ures in classical mythology to develop her androgynous theory of gender psychol-ogy. Most important, she expands her essay's discussion of Goethe into a triptych of "three male minds" differently prophesying the "coming age." Swedenborg she passes over quickly, merely endorsing his spiritualized companionate idea of man and woman sharing an "angelic ministry." Her prophetic foils are Goethe and Fourier. Goethe's "profound suggestion" for making men "ready" for change is his version of the German concept of *Bildung*, or personal culture, which, as he uses it, is no hermetic process: the individual's many-sided development comes through encounters that produce progressively deeper experiences and higher levels of self-consciousness—in brief, the organicist self-culture ideal of her es-say and book. But in an original turn, she feminizes his *Bildung*, dissecting the complex ways in his *Bildungsromans, Wilhelm Meisters Lehrjahre* and *Wilhelm Meisters Wanderjahre,* his circle of brilliant women interact with the hero during his travels along his "upward path." Indeed, she imputes to Goethe a protofeminist intention: "He aims at a pure self-subsistence, and free development of any pow-ers with which they may be gifted by nature as much for them as for men. They are units, addressed as souls. Accordingly the meeting between man and woman, as represented by him, is equal and noble."[41]

Her former "master" does not get the last word, however. Noting that Goethe's idea of self-culture assumes free will, she writes, "Ay! but Goethe, bad institutions are prison walls and impure air that make him stupid, so that he does not will." To be sure, she is clear that Fourier's opposite error of assuming "outward" arrangements without regard to the "inward needs of man" is the more serious one intellectually, marking him as a superficial thinker. But she also says Fourier was right in thinking that women need, "especially at this juncture, a much greater range of occupation than they have, to rouse their latent powers." Despite her distaste for Fourier's social mathematics, she even undergirds her androgynous argument in "The Great Lawsuit" that males and females have varying proportions of the other sex's psychological characteristics by supporting his notion that one-third of women are as likely to have a taste for "masculine pursuits" as one-third of men are for "feminine" ones. She avoids, however, endorsing his elaborate plans to harmonize labor by dividing workers into "groups" and "series." ("If these attempts are made by unready men, they will fail.") And she completely shies away from Fourier's communal childrearing to free women for other vocational tasks. What she likes is the liberal Romantic Fourier. That means his pluralism. The majority of women in the future might still prefer to be homemakers, but "*all* need not be constrained to employments, for which *some* are unfit." That also means his ideal of furthering women's unfolding self-activity by giving them "the needed means of self help." To Fuller, as to the "New Liberals" of the later nineteenth century, the "negative" liberty of freedom from constraints and the "positive" freedom of social supports for individual growth reinforce each other.[42]

Mostly, though, the new material in the second half of her book concerns gender practices, which she rates for their potential for promoting or constraining that organic growth for women. She culls newspapers, magazines, and popular novels, Carlylean fashion, for "signs of the times." She dismisses out of hand the crowd of husband-pleasing tracts that, she says, "I have of late been—no: *not* reading, but sighing over." She pushes aside the "refined" Anna Jameson's character building as "sentimentalist," and her only praise for her would-be mentor Harriet Martineau is for the influence she shows a woman can exercise in a sick room! She endorses a few tougher-minded schemes. She wholeheartedly approves the rationalistic liberal home-schooling methods of her father's favorite Maria Edgeworth. She devotes considerable space to women's health reform, praising the "moderate and sane" ideas of Catharine Sedgwick for her recommendations for women's hygiene, including cold water in place of "quack medicine" and simplified dress instead of "artificial" corsets, exchanges that Fuller glosses as means of achieving spiritual wholeness. Her boldest new forays into gendered reform, though, are two considerably more controversial ones she added to the latter part of her book.[43]

The one that would provoke by far the most controversy was something not raised in her essay: reform of the unequal allotment of sexual power both inside and outside of marriage. Some suggestions for stemming this are practical. As

American women's rights advocates would soon do, she urges equalizing husbands and wives' rights of property and household decision-making. The issue
that most concerns her, though, is the dynamics of sexual power exposed in society by prostitution. Here she knowingly stepped into an ideological minefield.
Although in urbanizing America the practice was attracting the attention of reformers, many in "polite" society, as she notes, found its public airing highly distasteful. Nor was there exactly a consensus over what to do about it. Ironically,
both conservative pundits, in periodicals and in the pulpit, and penny-weekly
scribblers writing for young men in the cities' "sporting life" claimed that the
trade's flourishing proved that men had greater needs for sexual satisfaction and
that women who illicitly serviced them were an unredeemable breed apart. On
the other side, middle-class reformers, while agreeing that men must hew to the
same standard of chastity and monogamy that society rightly demanded of women,
were divided over the means. Evangelicals saw prostitution as an opportunity to
convert the fallen and redeem America through antiprostitution laws and public
exposures of its male customers, while religious liberals thought "fallen women"
could be raised to middle-class respectability by rational philanthropy and temperate moral exhortation. Not for a few years more would a tiny number of American radical sex reformers publicly argue that prostitution was no worse than (in
the words of Fuller's fan Mary Gove) the "legal licentiousness" of bourgeois
marriages on which women depended for economic survival. To this sexual discourse Fuller contributed her liberal companionate prescriptions.[44]

Her starting point is an abhorrence of prostitution, which ensures, as she puts
it, the "degradation of a large portion of women into the sold and polluted slaves
of men." Yet her generic rhetoric here is a bit misleading. For one thing, she attacks the practice on a host of realistic grounds: in Christian societies it is necessarily hypocritical and secretive, it makes its female practitioners into social
pariahs, it destroys intimacy in marriages, and it bleeds its male practitioners of
self-respect. In addition, she does not put the blame for the institution's flourishing, as did most conservatives, on irremediably "depraved women" or primarily,
as did many middle-class reformers, on their sensual lower-class customers. Instead, she places it squarely on the upper-middle classes, including, unlike most
sensationalist antiprostitute crusaders, who publicly exposed wealthy brothel-
goers, the women as well as the men. She daringly makes her case by encouraging her readers to look at the problem through the eyes of the convicted prostitutes
she interviewed at Mount Pleasant. When she asked these women "stamped by
society as among the most degraded of their sex" how they had wound up in prison,
they gave honest and perfectly understandable reasons: the "love of dress, love of
flattery, love of excitement. They had not dresses like the other ladies, so they
stole them; they could not pay for flattery by distinctions, and the dower of a
worldly marriage, so they paid by the profanation of their persons. In excitement,
more and more madly sought from day to day, they drowned the voice of conscience." Comparing these women's values to those of some fashionable women
whom she had recently observed cackling about their dresses and flirtations at a
party she had attended, she demands, "Now I ask you, my sisters, if the women at

the fashionable house be not answerable for those women being in the prison?" Prostitution is thus not, as most antiprostitution crusaders saw it, an exotic cancer on an otherwise healthy middle-class body but a "miasma" that freely flows into society's bloodstream through the veins of commodified courtship and marriage, which prostitutes, and not just their reformers and abettors, can help us understand.[45]

So what is the proper social purgative? Ideologically, she is not radical. She gives only a passing pitch for the increasingly expressed Fourierist idea that expanding women's employment would give working-class single women an alternative to prostituting themselves. And she implicitly rejects, as in her essay, the free-love option, which she seems to regard as exclusively a European practice, associated not, as for later free lovers, with integrity and equality but rather with "old regime"–style aristocratic duplicity and licentiousness. Instead, she advances a cultural remedy: get rid of the sexual double standard that presumes men's greater sexual needs and that therefore excuses their practice of illicit sex. But what to put in its place? This, she says, is a "hard" question, as the idea of women's "passionless" innocence has only disabled women as well as corrupted marriage:

> Men have, indeed, been, for more than a hundred years, rating women for countenancing vice. But at the same time, they have carefully hid from them its nature, so that the preference often shown by women for bad men, arises rather from a confused idea that they are bold and adventurous, acquainted with regions which women are forbidden to explore, and the curiosity that ensues, than a corrupt heart in the woman. As to marriage it has been inculcated on women for centuries that men have not only stronger passions than they, but of a sort that it would shameful for them to share or even understand. That, therefore, they must "confide in their husbands," i. e., submit implicitly to their will. That the least appearance of coldness or withdrawal, from whatever cause, in the wife is wicked, because liable to turn her husband's thoughts to illicit indulgence; for a man is so constituted that he must indulge his passions or die!

In short, to do away with prostitution what was needed was more than doing away with the double standard; what was needed was a transformation in heterosexual relations toward an enlightened center: men had to exercise sexual self-control, and women had to gain sexual knowledge and rights enabling them to negotiate sexual boundaries.[46]

One question remains: if society's asymmetrical double-standard is so entrenched, how to achieve this centrist solution? She suggests that equal property, earning, and child custody rights for married women would help by giving women more independence and therefore more influence within marriage, but she does not dwell on them, and she says nothing at all about the explosive issue of divorce, which would divide the women's rights movement a decade later. She is also not naïve about the difficulties of weakening the influence of the double standard in society. She holds out little hope that men can be shamed into adopting women's standard of purity, since men will stigmatize the effort, she says frankly, as merely reflecting women's "prudery, or ignorance, or perhaps, a feeblemindedness of nature which exempts from similar temptations." She gives a half-favorable nod to the reform physiologists who were then imploring young single

men to embrace celibacy through "external" remedies like exercise and cold water. After all, she says, echoing the era's extreme taboo against masturbation, which
would get her brother Lloyd put in a mental asylum, since early marriages usually come to disaster, what is the alternative? She is also sure, citing Milton and
promarriage Renaissance writers (as well as men she knows, she quickly adds!),
that a man is just as capable as a woman of seeking the "aid of the Spirit" to control sexual passion. Addressing women, she is more pointed. "Clear your souls
from the taint of vanity" and eschew narcissistic fantasies of sexual "conquests,"
which, she says sternly, "in nine cases out of ten," are the causes of unwanted
male attentions. Most important, she boldly urges married people to discuss honestly their sexual feelings. Only in that way, she says, can intimacy be promoted
and purity not seem to the man "an exotic that could only be preserved by the
greatest care." Finally, as for publicly exposing womanizers and brothel habitués
as moral reformers did, she is cautious, encouraging private ostracism. Indeed, in
her only mention of upper-middle-class males' seduction of lower-class young
women, her interest seems to be more in promoting discussion than punishing
wrongdoers. Praising Lydia Maria Child's recent public defense of the young New
York working-woman Amelia Norman, who was acquitted of charges of stabbing
her seducer, she writes that by such efforts as Child's, people at least may be provoked to challenge the entrenched double standard. "They begin to fear that the
perdition of a woman must involve that of a man. This is a crisis." Her prescription in a word: no sexual exploitation, no affairs, and no sexual "seeking" à la
Goethe and Sand, but heterosexual fairness and benevolent sisterhood.[47]

Besides sex and marriage, the other gendered wound she probes in the last part
of her book is antislavery. She still says nothing about women's suffrage, an idea
she had endorsed in her Fishkill journal, probably because it was not a public issue for most radical reformers, who were then indifferent or even hostile to electoral action. Instead, she advances a political version of the "moral suasion"
abolitionism that for the past decade had successfully attracted many women to
its cause. Building on both the invocation of abolitionist discourse in her "Great
Lawsuit" and the antiracist nationalism of her *Summer on the Lakes*, she implores
women to realize that they, too, have an ideological stake in the current fight over
annexation of Texas. Appealing to the memory of female British freedom fighters during the first-century resistance to Roman conquest, the memory of Puritan
radicals like Anne Hutchinson, and the "mothers of our own revolution," she asks
in wonderment, "have you nothing to do with this?" Annexation obviously threatens, as the abolitionists correctly say, to expand the "leprosy" of slavery, but for
her it menaces much more: the subversion of America's founding liberal ideals,
upon which, ultimately, along with Romantic religion, she places so much hope
in her book for gender change. Sounding like a Romantic Thomas Paine, she cries:

> Ah! If this should take place, who will dare again to feel the throb of heavenly hope,
> as to the destiny of this country? The noble thought that gave unity to all our knowl-
> edge, harmony to all our designs;—the thought that the progress of history had
> brought on the era, the tissue of prophecies pointed out the spot, where humanity

was, at last, to have a fair chance to know itself, and all men to be born free and equal for the eagle's flight, flutters as if about to leave the breast, which, deprived of it, will have no more a nation, no more a home on earth.[48]

Swiftly pivoting, she turns from her American exceptionalism to address her well-off women readers, urging them to take up a gender battle, which she had studiously avoided in "The Great Lawsuit." Telling them to refuse the "glittering baubles," big houses, and abundant servants that might come to them from the men who acquire these things by selling, directly or indirectly, their fellow creatures, their country's honor, and their immortal souls for the "money market and political power," she thunders: "Tell them that the heart of women demands nobleness and honor in man, and that, if they have not purity, have not mercy, they are no longer fathers, lovers, husbands, sons of yours." She then makes a cross-class gender appeal, reminding women, as would Harriet Beecher Stowe seven years later, although here more sternly than sentimentally, "if you have a power, it is a moral power. The films of interest are not so close around you as around the men. If you will but think, you cannot fail to wish to save the country from this disgrace. Let not slip the occasion, but do something to lift off the curse incurred by Eve." Finally, addressing those daughters who would plead feminine "modesty" as a justification for shunning the abolitionists' petition campaigns, she writes scornfully: "It will, not so much injure your modesty to have your name, by the unthinking, coupled with idle blame, as to have upon your soul the weight of not trying to save a whole race of women from the scorn that is put upon *their* modesty. Think of this well! I entreat, I conjure you, before it is too late."[49]

From her liberal jeremiad, she then jumps "to retrace, once more," she writes a little cheekily, "the scope of my design in points, as was done in old-fashioned sermons." Her task is rather daunting: to weld together her buoyant literary-philosophical first half, taken mostly from her essay, with her darker and much more polemical second half. So she climbs an even higher intellectual peak than she had in her essay. After explaining a little more fully her "masculine" and "feminine" "methods" of "growth" of, respectively, Energy, Power, and Intellect, and Harmony, Beauty, and Love, and their fluid incarnation in both sexes, she presents a new metahistory. Because "in the order of time," she says, Energy and Power come before Harmony and Beauty, man abused his advantage by installing himself over woman as her "temporal master instead of her spiritual sire." The result, she says, was a cosmic gender tragedy: shorn of his equal other half, his children raised by "hand-maids," man and woman bred a species unable to fulfill its "angelic" destiny.[50]

After this mythic prefigurement of the argument that feminist "reform Darwinists" and progressives would make at the end of the century for women's equal integration into industrial society, she then swoops up from the abyss, Romantic-style, to prophesy a possible future transcendence. This requires some fancy dialectical footwork. She liberally flips her nationalist jeremiad in a way her Puritan ancestors would have half-recognized. Precisely because the nation's founding liberal egalitarian ideals expose its gender failings, they also make it a uniquely hospitable place to rectify them. Leaping ahead temporally, she echoes Kant's liberal Enlightenment formulation—that man is on the precipice of modern adulthood but can only cross over if he dares to know ("*Sapere aude!* Have the courage to use your *own* understanding!"), which she translates into her gendered Romantic idiom: woman, "so encumbered by tradition," at the "present junction," needs "self-subsistence in its two forms of self-reliance and self-impulse." With her rhetoric and history adjusted to her book's central prescription, she finally converts the major challenges into historic opportunities. Do men's prejudices mean that "at present, women are the best helpers of one another"? Then so much the easier for society: "Let them think; let them act, till they know what they need," she writes, adding confidently, "We only ask of men to remove arbitrary barriers." As for conservative skeptics' demand to know "what use will she make of liberty, when she has so long been sustained and restrained?" she provides two liberal evolutionary answers. For generations women have inherited a reverence for decorums and limits, and this would "gradually establish such rules as are needed to guard, without impeding, life." In addition, emancipation will not be suddenly given, she says, but will necessarily follow a process of democratic deliberation, citing a recent newspaper debate over enlarging women's rights over property, in which both sides "learned visibly as they spoke. . . . And so the stream flows on; thought urging action, and action leading to the evolution of still better thought." Equal-rights gender politics, then, will enter organically into the public sphere.[51]

Suddenly, though, in the midst of her liberal imagining, she stops, as if realizing that in her cosmic optimism she is on the verge of losing her central trope of "woman." In a remarkable allusion to an idea that Emerson had posed to her during their recent discussions about "fate" and discord, she writes, virtually replicating his words: "An idea not unknown to ancient times has of late been revived, that, in the metamorphoses of life, the soul assumes the form, first of man, then of woman, and takes the chances, and reaps the benefits of either lot. Why then, say some, lay such emphasis on the rights or needs of woman? What she wins not, as woman, will come to her as man." From her point of view, this is a seductive argument. Indeed, it echoes both Emerson's ideal of the "chartered libertine" in "everlasting transition" from man to woman, which she had once admired in his promptings to her, and Proclus's scheme of overlapping "powers," which she had earlier introduced in support of woman's androgynous sensibility. However, dissolving the very category of "woman" necessary to critiquing women's subordinate place could not have been an appealing prospect for Fuller to contemplate. Equally important, such an all-consuming metaphysical vision she clearly understood as yet another rejection of her Romantic worldview of the "self" growing through turbulent confrontations in the world rather than through (as she thought Emerson would have it) the individual's activity of "mind." So to his starry androgyny of woman winning as "man," she replies vigorously: "That makes no difference. It is not woman, but the law of growth, that speaks in us, and demands the perfection of each being in its kind, apple as apple, woman as woman. Without adopting your theory I know that I, a daughter, live through the life of man;

but what concerns me now is, that my life be a beautiful, powerful, in a word, a complete life in its kind. Had I but one more moment to live, I must wish the same."[52]

Here Fuller reaches into her Transcendentalist bag and pulls out a very practical regulative argument: womanhood as a category in history *exists,* and women therefore must *assimilate* it to their freely active (hence transcendent) selves. Nor does this "wish" for women only serve their isolated "selves"; it is consistent with the conscious vitalism undergirding her book's humanistic metaphysics and is also, she says, an existential way of being in the world. "Suppose, at the end of your cycle, your great world year, all will be completed, whether I exert myself or not (and the supposition is *false,*) but suppose it true, am I to be indifferent about it? Not so! I must beat my own pulse true in the heart of the world; for *that* is virtue, excellence, health." Gender is binary but not hierarchical and androgynous but not sexless. Most important, female emancipation requires organic action, not contemplative fatalism.[53]

In the end, though, what ultimately fires her confidence that the liberation of women from artificial barriers and gender dependency will bring new gender equalities *and* unities are neither idealistic metahistories nor existential vitalism. Rather, her transcendent gender hopes are buoyed by two unadulterated Romantic acts of faith. One is the same gendered version of Emersonian self reliance as God-reliance that she had articulated in "The Great Lawsuit." As she explains here in a more psychological frame:

> I have urged on woman independence of man, not that I do not think the sexes mutually needed by one another, but because in woman this fact has led to an excessive devotion, which has cooled love, degraded marriage, and prevented either sex from being what it should be to itself or the other.
>
> I wish woman to live, *first,* for God's sake. Then she will not make an imperfect man her god, and thus sink to idolatry. Then she will not take what is not fit for her from a sense of weakness and poverty. Then, if she finds what she needs in man embodied, she will know how to love, and be worthy of being loved.
>
> By being more a soul, she will not be less woman, for nature is perfected through spirit.
>
> Now there is no woman, only an overgrown child.

The other act of faith flows from her new self-confidence, which she in turn offers to women. "But if you ask me what offices they may fill; I reply—any. I do not care what case you put," she declares, adding famously, with cavalier panache (alluding to a wish for herself she had once confided to her younger brothers at Groton), "let them be sea-captains, if you will. I do not doubt there are women well fitted for such an office."[54]

Hence, behind her mask of "woman," lay Fuller herself. In "The Great Lawsuit" she had asked if "the woman who shall vindicate their birthright for all women" would not soon appear. In *Woman in the Nineteenth Century*, she hinted at an answer. By dint of Romantic religion, Transcendental philosophy, gender androgyny, female mythology, and "sacred marriage," she had gotten beyond both her initial hilltop detachment from gender politics and her persona of the lone heroic

Miranda. In her book's conclusion, she returns to her hilltop, but this time in a voice
of neither detachment nor imprecation but of realistic hope for reconciliation:

> I stand in the sunny noon of life. Objects no longer glitter in the dews of morning,
> neither are yet softened by the shadows of evening. Every spot is seen, every chasm
> revealed. Climbing the dusty hill, some fair effigies that once stood for symbols of
> human destiny have been broken; those I still have with me, show defects in this
> broad light. Yet enough is left, even by experience, to point distinctly to the glories
> of that destiny; faint, but not to be mistaken streaks of the future day. I can say with
> the bard,
> "Though many have suffered shipwreck, still beat noble hearts."
> Always the soul says to us all: Cherish your best hopes as a faith, and abide by
> them in action. Such shall be the effectual fervent means to their fulfilment.

Hope, faith, and action: through these Romantic tropes, Fuller fashioned a liberating identity she had never before announced since her first tremulous dedication a decade earlier to German studies and the way of a "thinker"—a woman of
her own making in nineteenth-century America.[55]

V

Lofty and acerbic, crammed and elliptical, personal and political, highbrow and
popular, daring and reassuring—and filtered, like "The Great Lawsuit," through
interspersed dialogues, rapid tonal shifts, changing personas, and a fractured structure—Fuller's book invited and provoked readers' admiration, excitement, puzzlement, and outrage. Several of her friends had strong reactions to it. "Margaret's
book has made a breeze, I assure you," Mrs. Peabody wrote to her daughter Sophia
Hawthorne, zeroing in on what probably bothered more than a few Boston Unitarian readers: its "look of absolute irreligion" and, worse, its "too personal" and
indelicate formulations, especially horrendous, she said, "in a book designed for
the public." Sophia turned even paler and testier reading Fuller's "disagreeable"
book than she had with her article. "I did not like the tone of it—& did not agree
with her at all about the change in woman's outward circumstances." But what
most offended her was the new material about sex, marriage, and men. "I [do not]
believe in such a character of man as she gives. It is altogether too ignoble. . . . A
wife only can know how to speak with sufficient respect of man." Nor even a wife
publicly, apparently: "I think Margaret speaks of many things that should not be
spoken of." The book divided some of her radical friends as well. John Neal, her
old Whig utilitarian acquaintance, complained about its lack of political demands.
"You go for thought—I for action," he boomed. What a woman needed, he said,
was "the whip and spur," or "her *vote*," otherwise "all you and others are doing to
elevate women, is only fitted to make her feel more sensibly the long abuse of her
understanding, when she comes to her senses. You might as well educate slaves—
and still keep them in bondage." By contrast, Lydia Maria Child wrote to Louisa
Loring about "Margaret's book," which she had just read in proof, effusively praising it particularly for its new sexual politics: "I like it much. . . . It is a *bold* book,
I assure you. I should not have dared to have written some things in it, though it

would have been safer for me, being married. But they need to have been said and she is brave to do it. She bears a noble testimony to anti slavery principles in several places." For this courageous abolitionist who shrank back from saying anything publicly about the sexual hypocrisies she decried privately, getting women to "feel more sensibly" the abuse of their understanding was just the right thing.[56]

Several of Fuller's Transcendentalist friends, on the other hand, who had liked her article, worried about her book. Emerson did not leave a comment, but considering that he had already told her "only in the poetic form could this right & wrong be pourtrayed," he could hardly have been thrilled by all her new pages about prostitutes and Texas. Caroline Sturgis had a boatload of criticisms. "The style troubles me very much," she bluntly told her. "I cannot free myself from a feeling of great consciousness in all you write. There is a recurrence of comparisons, illustrations, & words, which is not pleasing." Taking Emerson's tack, she also wondered whether it was even legitimate to make the "poetic" gender question into a political or even an intellectual subject. "It is not a book to take to heart and that is what a book upon women should be," she wrote. Yet she took it partly back: "It makes me sad that it is necessary such an one should be written but since it is it cannot but do good to lift the veil as you have done—how hard a thing to do!" To this half-sensible and half-precious critique Fuller fired back her answer. On her book's illustrative overabundance, which she had somewhat lamely defended in her book as necessary to make her meaning "sufficiently clear," she conceded the point was "very true, mostly." But on publicly airing gender ills, she stood firm. It *was* too bad that she had to speak so harshly, but culpable men made it necessary: "They do feel their wounds probed, and healing promised by it." She obviously felt disappointed with her friends' dissatisfactions. "Many expressions of feeling from private sources come in," she told Richard a little sadly; "here as often before I have found the stranger more sympathizing and in my belief intelligent than some of my private friends."[57]

She *was* getting a lot of sympathy from "the stranger." "Margaret's book is going to *sell*," Greeley practically shouted at *Graham's* ex-editor Rufus Wilmot Griswold, cajoling him into writing a puff of it in his former magazine. "I tell you it has the real stuff in it." Evidently, Greeley was right. She had originally hoped to sell a thousand copies within a few years, but within a week of its publication, Greeley and McElrath sold the entire edition of fifteen hundred to booksellers, garnering her $85 for her share. "Not that my object was in any wise money," she hastened to add to her brother Eugene, then a newspaperman in New Orleans, "but I consider this the signet of success. If one can be heard that is enough!" Later in the year, she learned that the London publisher H. G. Clarke had paid her the rare honor of reversing the usual balance of trade in pirated books by having hers "beautifully issued" in its Library of Choice Reading. Ignoring being pirated, she was very glad women would be reading it there, she told Richard, "as our dear country folks look anxiously for verdicts, from the other side of the water." Meanwhile, booksellers on this side tried to stir her compatriots up. "The Great Book of the Age," screamed one advertisement. "The thousands who have perused this book speak of it as being the only one which has been written, in which WOMAN is portrayed in her real and true character." Grabbing the reader by the collar: "There are things plainly said in this book, which no female writer has dared before to touch."[58]

Fuller was pleased. "The opposition and the sympathy it excites are both great," she exulted to Sturgis. To Eugene she boasted that her book was "the theme of all the newspapers and many of the journals," adding, "abuse public and private is lavished upon its views, but respect expressed to me personally." This was partly true. She got lavish encomiums from her fellow liberal reformers. "It is from the pen of Margaret Fuller," Child wrote in a prepublication notice in the *Broadway Journal*, "a woman of more powerful intellect, comprehensive thought, and thorough education, than any other American authoress." But even newspapers unsympathetic to Fuller's politics honored her for writing (in the words of the *Charleston Mercury*) "the first work which has taken the liberal side in the question of 'Woman's Rights' since the days of Mary Wollstonecraft." Even her book's detractors called Fuller "no common woman," "a thinking, right-judging person," and a writer of unusual "strength of expression and depth of feeling." And, although she was right about the abuse of her views, the abusers ranged widely in their critiques and were well balanced by her defenders.[59]

Her conservative critics mostly fell into one of two camps. One was the staunchly patriarchal. In his three-part review in his and Poe's *Broadway Journal*, Charles F. Briggs, whose reputation for journalistic mordancy proved well deserved, assailed Fuller for inviting women to assume men's "natural" occupations and challenge their husbands' household decisions, and then told her basically what Sophia Hawthorne had told her mother: Fuller should shut up. "No unmarried woman has any right to say any thing on the subject." Orestes Brownson, fresh from his final conversion to Roman Catholicism, managed to outdo both Briggs and himself. After making an observation that he probably thought was a half-compliment— that the erudite Transcendentalist "chieftainess"'s book was no worse than any other prideful "Protestant" or Romantic revolt against divine authority—he targeted the terrible consequences of her self-culture philosophy for the sexual order. By encouraging women to explore their feelings and discover their needs, Brownson charged, she was inciting the very same "obscene" and "frightful" licentiousness practiced by her beloved ancient heathens. Nor was he above throwing in a little sexual scandal. "Miss Fuller . . . patronizes several renowned courtesans," he cried in a subsequent notice; "and the chief ground of her complaint against our *masculine* social order seems to be, that it imposes undue restraints on woman's nature, and does not permit her to follow her natural sentiments and affections."[60]

To more moderate pundits, on the other hand, Fuller's economic and sexual ideas were bad not because they threatened Augustinian orthodoxy or male authority but because they endangered the "two-spheres" gender order. By urging "perfect equality with man," the *Southern Quarterly Review* complained, Fuller denied the key point that women's "power" lay precisely in their "weakness." The *Ladies National Magazine* reviewer was more explicit. By urging women to enter the "yelling" fray of business and politics, the reviewer declared, Fuller was calling them to give up their "modesty," which inspired men to succeed and sustained women's "superior" moral influence. Marital mutuality and women's intellectual equality were fine—they were even to be celebrated—but Fuller's book was not just calling for those things but for an "overthrow" of the entire "Christian . . . social system." And this included the sexual order as well, since Fuller obviously favored easy divorces, if not, in fact, the reviewer strongly implied— and as one critic would later specifically charge Fuller's book with encouraging— the "loose" doctrine of "licentious France."[61]

If conservatives exaggerated Fuller's radicalism, friendly liberal reviewers, in underplaying it, often wound up almost equally off the mark. "Her notions do not seem *ultra* or extravagant," the Unitarian minister and future Episcopal bishop Frederic Dan Huntington happily wrote in the *Christian Examiner*. "She does not ask that woman may be thrust into man's sphere, but that she may have a right and honorable sphere of her own, whether as sister, daughter, mother, or 'old maid.'" Although well intended, this claim was almost the opposite of Fuller's point. She had denied that she was for "thrusting" a woman into "man's sphere," because a woman's entry into all social spheres should follow from her discovery of which ones suited her, which might include—indeed, in Fuller's view should include—work in conventionally "masculine" jobs. Likewise, all but the now ex-Shaker Charles Lane, writing in the radical antislavery *Herald of Freedom*, missed entirely Fuller's come-outer call for female self-"enfranchisement" and her Romantic assertion of humanity's "spiritual tendency" to elevate women. Most striking of all—and nearly mirror-opposite to her detractors—nearly all her defenders interpreted her call for the abolition of the sexual double standard as a conventional plea to subject men to women's passionless example. "If men are brutalized," cried William Channing, paraphrasing her argument in the *Tribune*, "women must redeem them, and raise them up to their own chaste ideal"—which was precisely what Fuller had said women should *not* be expected to do.[62]

In their literary evaluations, reviewers stood on firmer ground. To be sure, some revealed as much about themselves as her book. The dignified William Cullen Bryant worried about her "pretty strong and emphatic" style. The willfully misreading Briggs griped about the book's "want of distinctness," and the incorrigibly prolix Brownson grumbled about its diffusiveness. ("It has neither beginning, middle, nor end, and may be read backwards as well as forwards, and from the centre outwards each way.") Yet her book's tangled constructions and multitudinous allusions tried the patience of even some of her sympathetic reviewers. Many, including some hostile ones, singled out for praise two qualities of her book: its intellectual depth, especially remarkable, several noted, in a book on such a charged subject, and its freshness and forcefulness. Her "habit of thought that is morbid, inharmonious, without symmetry, and so, of course, unattractive" was often overridden, the sober Huntington wrote with some surprise, by her talent for wielding "the good Anglo-Saxon phrase so energetically." Probably the most balanced literary appraisal came from her newspaper colleague Child, who praised Fuller for having "more vigorous intellect and comprehensive thought, than any other among the writers of this country," male or female, but was more qualified about her writing. "Her style is vigorous and significant, abounding with eloquent passages, and affluent in illustration," she advised her readers, "but it is sometimes rough in construction, and its meaning is not always sufficiently clear." However, she quickly added, "this does not arise from affectation, or pedantic elaboration" but rather from her very "vigorous and comprehensive" intellect: "it is the defect of a mind that has too many thoughts for its words; an excess by no means common, either in men or women. She is a contralto voice in literature: deep, rich, and strong, rather than mellifluous and clear." William Channing probably put that "contralto voice"'s problem best: its simultaneous condensation of thoughts and fullness of allusions, many subtle and remote, sometimes obscured argument and method. "The candid and reflecting reader," however, he, too, promptly added, "will find it a rich mine, where every vein will repay the working." Learning to read Fuller, friendly reviewers agreed, was difficult but rewarding. She would soon have daily opportunities to renegotiate that intellectual journalist's high and low terrain.[63]

VI

Propelled by its ideas and Fuller's fame, *Woman in the Nineteenth Century* would enter and partly direct three swelling historical streams. One was the growing friendliness toward women's rights in the liberal northeastern press, heretofore indifferent or even hostile to the idea. "'WOMAN IN THE NINETEENTH CEN-TURY'—How must the heart of the gifted authoress of the great call to her sex . . . have swelled with indignation," a year later a writer in the *National Intelligencer* cried, "if her eye fell, as ours has just done, upon the following article in the New York Gazette." If the "gifted authoress" had read the Washington newspaper's blistering attack on the New York paper for denigrating women's political capacities and claiming their constitutional eligibility and special suitability for even secretary of war and president, she undoubtedly would have smiled in recognition. Fuller's book also reconfigured the intellectual movement that had provided her with her first public platform. Fuller's book remade two key Transcendentalist tropes—the intuitive imagination and "man thinking"— that Emerson, Parker, and Thoreau regularly identified with a "masculine" American intellectual culture into modes potentially exploitable by women. The book also altered the gender thinking of Emerson, Parker, James Clarke, and William Henry Channing, who in their later public embrace of "women's rights" would echo, if sometimes more moderately, many of Fuller's arguments in her book. A certain number of younger Transcendentalists would go further: Thomas Wentworth Higginson, Moncure Conway, Franklin Sanborn, and Caroline Dall would look back on the book and Fuller's life as major inspirations for their own careers as public intellectuals.[64]

The widest historical stream that Fuller's book altered was nineteenth-century American feminism. This is a story strangely missing from both Fuller biographies and feminist histories, which often assert or imply that her book floated somewhere far above the movement's turbulent waters. That was not the impression of Fuller's contemporaries. Her volume, Horace Greeley would write at the movement's radical high point two decades later, "is the ablest, bravest, broadest, assertion yet made of what are termed Woman's Rights." The claim was seconded by northeastern women's rights activists like Dall, Elizabeth Cady Stanton, Paulina Wright Davis, Julia Ward Howe, Ednah Dow Cheney, Elizabeth Oakes Smith, Anna Bracket, Mary Livermore, Frances Willard, and Lucinda Chandler, who would all look to Fuller's book as inspirations for their feminist lectures, writings, and careers. "To her," Davis would write, echoing, she claimed, a widely shared sentiment at the 1850 National Woman's Rights Convention at Worcester, Massachusetts, which Davis organized, "I . . . had hoped to confide the leadership of the movement." If Fuller's manifold interests and limited patience with organized activism would have probably led her to decline, the expectation was telling of her reputation in feminist circles. More important than her unlikely women's rights leadership was the intellectual credibility she lent to the movement. Citing its pioneering philosophical defense of women's rights, her Conversations' first organized effort to raise American women to the intellectual level of men, and her conversion of influential Transcendentalist men to pro-women's rights positions, Sara Underwood declared: "That the woman's movement of today is as successful as it is, is owing greatly to her steadfast loyalty to her sex." And Fuller's influence spread outward from these leaders. Livermore's lecture "What Shall We Do with Our Daughters?" which she delivered an estimated eight hundred times over twenty-five years throughout the country, took as its starting point the book's arguments, which she called still "far in advance of public acceptance." Likewise, Cheney, who reported that after Fuller's death she discovered clubs named after her all over the Middle and Far West, found people in the "most unexpected places, in Dubuque," asking her about Fuller.[65]

Nor in calling Fuller's book "the precursor of the Woman's Rights agitation of the last thirty-three years" (in Stanton's words) were these early feminists speaking in an intellectual vacuum; they were responding to real resonances between her outlook and theirs. First, there was the religious resonance: the book's liberal post-Christian perfectionism would broadly coincide, as the evangelically infused and Bible-centered abolitionists' rhetoric would not, with the almost uniformly liberal Protestant and freethinking views of most post–Civil War women's rights leaders. Second, there was the ideological tic. The book's central argument—that individual women had a right to autonomy not because the authority they would exercise was socially useful or uniquely benevolent but because they had universal rights as humans—was precisely the liberal principle whose espousal distinguished these feminists from their antebellum prefeminist predecessors. Third, while overlooking women's suffrage, her book's otherwise capacious application of those rights to women's education, employment, sexuality, and political discourse was also in harmony with the broad platform of the nineteenth-century's feminist movement. Fourth, there was Fuller's gender strategy: in her strong claim for the need for women's collective self-reliance, she prefigured the independent women's rights movement. And fifth, even the style of these early feminists, as displayed in their yearly conventions, mimicked the oratorical, testimonial, argumentative, and exuberant style of Fuller's book.[66]

Finally, there is the most intellectually important and underappreciated reso-nance of all: Fuller's Romantic idiom. Of course, like most nineteenth-century liberals, these early feminists intermixed a variety of warrants for their claims, from Enlightenment natural rights to utilitarian happiness and possessive individu-alist political economy. But especially in the feminist takeoff decade of the 1850s, during which a new edition of *Woman in the Nineteenth Century* sold in a few weeks in 1855 over three times as many copies as the first one had ten years ear-lier, the liberal Romantic strain vied, as never before or after, with these others. And to this strain Fuller contributed three critical concepts: individual self-devel-opment through studied introspection and boundless experience, social reform facilitated by organic spiritual conduits linking self and society, and transcendence through the infinitely contingent promise of the divinity's presence in the natural and historical world. Indeed, in various ways these concepts suffused several of the foundational feminist texts of the era. Stanton's "first 'set speech'" of 1848, a fiercely rationalist republican plea for woman's rights, concludes with *Woman in the Nineteenth Century*'s final embattled chiliastic poem: "Though rabble rout may rush between, . . . / So shalt thou see what few have seen, / The palace home of King and Queen." "'Give me Truth. Cheat me by no illusion,'" the later (and by then religiously liberal) Sarah Grimké quoted from Fuller's recently published *Memoirs* in Grimké's remarkably Romantic-minded letter to the 1852 Woman's Rights Convention. "If our movement will adopt this slogan as its watchword," Grimké said, "it will overcome all obstacles, outlive all opposition." Although ex-evangelical ultraists like Grimké and political feminists like Stanton were hardly Romantics, insofar as they used Romantic concepts and tropes to defend women's rights and progress, Fuller's book was unquestionably the principal reason.[67]

These accents continued to resonate. Even in the later nineteenth-century era of spiritualism, positivism, and social science, *Woman in the Nineteenth Century* would be reprinted in substantial (if diminished) runs once or more every decade until the end of the century, after which it would not be published again until the beginning of revived interest in Fuller seventy-five years later. Indeed, the aged Stanton's last suffrage movement presidential address in 1892, "The Solitude of the Self," rested her case for women's justice not on her age's Victorian pieties but on the lonely "individuality of each human soul"—a stoic harking back to the Romantic ethical core of Fuller's book. And even in these years, when younger feminist leaders often called for granting women the vote to counterbalance the votes of ignorant immigrants and workers, the feminist stream continued to bend in surprising Fullerlike ways. What, after all, were modernist feminist demands for men *and* women's "terrible honesty" in the 1920s, personal "liberation" in the 1960s, and, after that, the still salient integration of female "difference" and human "equality," if not a worldly return to the individualist and androgynous gender concerns that animated Fuller's restless Romantic seeking? It was a long swoop that the Romantic Fuller, who proclaimed "the soul is ever young, ever virgin," would have enjoyed.[68]

Meanwhile, in the space of six months, she had replicated her own foreshort-ened version of it. From the publication of her first original book and her discordant poems of the mourning Virgin Mary and resurrected androgynous demons to her final farewells to Emerson's Concord and her shocks of gender recognition at Sing Sing, she had packed into her second book more "lives" than most authors found in a lifetime of writing. Indeed, by that time, Fuller had been hard at work at her latest life, which, along with the book, had steadily loomed over her thoughts since the beginning of the summer.

CHAPTER SIX

New York Star
(1844–1846)

I

When *Woman in the Nineteenth Century* was published, Fuller had been in New York City for two and a half months. Arriving on November 28, 1844, she had sounded ready. "I feel refreshed for the melée and willing to take my share of the press of life," she had gamely announced to Sarah Shaw. When she first spied the Greeleys' house at Turtle Bay (now the site of the United Nations Headquarters) where she would be living, she might have also thought she could continue something of her "sacred" Fishkill living as well. Originally built as a summer residence for the president of New York's United States Bank, the rambling farmhouse sat on the edge of eight acres of woods overlooking a grassy ravine that sloped down to the East River opposite the southern tip of Blackwell's Island. True, "the Farm" had seen better days. The once picturesque grounds were overgrown with weeds, and the house, according to Lydia Maria Child, who sometimes visited her, was "dropping to pieces." Nearly four miles uptown from the settled bottom of Manhattan below Fourteenth Street, at night the place seemed "sepulchral" to Greeley, who had moved there from the gaslit downtown. Getting there was something of a trek. One had to ride for half an hour on the Harlem Railroad horse-drawn railcar on the "Great" or "Third Avenue," get off at Forty-ninth Street, and then trudge, at night holding a lantern, along the often-muddy Harlem Road to the narrow, zigzag quarter-mile footpath through the woods to the house.[1]

This frayed rusticity, however, does not seem to have fazed Fuller. "I have never been so well situated," she wrote her brother Eugene, telling friends she found the overrun pond, brook, and flower gardens "entirely charming." Most of all, a connoisseur of bodies of water, she loved to gaze at the river from the piazza, which was virtually on it, or from her nearby bedroom window, watching the ships' sails as they swept by appearing "to greet the house," a scene that in the moonlight seemed "truly transporting." Even the isolation did not bother her, since omnibuses and cars gave her constant access to the city, while the distance allowed her time and retirement. She did note a little disconcertingly that the house "is kept in a Castle Rackrent style," but for the moment that seemed unimportant compared with her free room and board and congenial-seeming landlords. "There is affection for me and desire to make me at home, and I do feel so, which could scarcely have been expected from such an arrangement."[2]

The arrangement she expected the most from, though, as she intimated to Sarah Shaw, was her new life in the press, which she began on December 1. Both the time and place were certainly propitious. The world's highest literacy rates, unprecedented population growth, and new technologies, from railroads and transatlantic steamers to steam-powered cylinder presses, had sparked the previous decade's "newspaper revolution." Nowhere was it more thoroughgoing than in New York, whose unrivaled population and strategic shipping position, which gave it a virtual monopoly on the distribution of national and international news, had produced America's first mass circulation dailies. Founded by canny, non-college-bred men, their papers slashed prices, created aggressive news departments, and directed armies of newsboys to hawk their one- or two-penny papers on streets throughout the city. They also invented a seductive new journalistic formula. Unlike the older subscription six-penny sheets filled with party propaganda and stodgy financial reports, they reported not just political and economic news but also human interest stories for an emergent urban middle class who were anxious to participate, even if only vicariously, in a "social sphere" that would make city life seem exciting and understandable. Yet, like most revolutions, this one alienated many. Although directed at families, including women, the papers' salacious police reports, reckless exposés, and antiblack demagoguery made many readers yearn for some modicum of rational argument, refinement, and uplift in their daily news. And that was precisely what Fuller's new boss eagerly sought to satisfy.[3]

To his enemies, and to many historians, Horace Greeley embodied an unpleasant mix of moral bombast, political maneuverings, and promiscuous reform nostrums that fittingly culminated, a month before he died, in his quixotic failed campaign for the presidency against Ulysses Grant. Yet whatever might be said about his life in politics, his newspaper career was unmatched in American history, and its long train of successes was just beginning when Fuller arrived in New York. A year her junior, Greeley in three years had already pushed the *Tribune* into a tie with New York's established *New York Sun* and *New York Herald* as the best-selling paper in the city, with subscriptions exceeding thirty thousand. Over the following decade, it would grow nearly tenfold, making it the most widely read periodical in the country. The secrets to its success were various, starting with the physical appearance of this Scotch-Irish, hardscrabble New Hampshire farmer's son, who seems as if he jumped out of casting in a Frank Capra film. Certainly, the paper fitted perfectly his self-fashioning as a morally idealistic and go-getting rustic people's "tribune": his hyperkinetic six-foot frame; his large pallid moon-face, soft white receding hair, and fringe of white throat beard; his rumpled duster, heavy work boots, baggy pants, and battered, pushed-back, low-brimmed hat; and his high-pitched and, when excited, squeaky voice. His elevated populist politics

helped, too: from his newspaper's democratic covering of working-class better-
ment and communitarian Fourierism (or "Associationism," as he preferred to call
it) to his relentlessly pushing his beloved Whig Party's program of national banks,
internal improvements, and protective tariffs.[4]

But more important than Greeley's image and ideology was the large journalistic niche he had carved out for it. Except for the genteel Bryant's liberal Democratic
Evening Post, New York's older papers promoted conservative Whiggery, while
the newer penny dailies mostly thumped for the Democratic Party, leaving the *Tribune* as the city's only cheap liberal Whig newspaper. It also served a specific readership. Unlike the sensationalist *Sun* and *Herald,* devoured by Bowery B'hoys and
Wall Street bankers, Greeley directed his *Tribune* at aspiring middle- and skilled
working-class readers. Nor was it only a New York paper; its *Weekly Tribune* edition
made it America's first national newspaper. In cities and small towns throughout
New England, New York, the Great Lakes, and the Ohio Valley, farmers, mechanics, and small merchants read the weekly aloud to their families, loaned it to neighbors, and organized "Tribune Clubs" to discuss its latest news and pronouncement
on national and international affairs. "The *Tribune* comes next to the Bible all through
the West," its roving reporter Bayard Taylor would soon brag to his boss, and considering the multiple times each copy was read and its articles reprinted in other
newspapers, Taylor's boast was almost an understatement.[5]

Beyond politics and constituencies, though, the key to the paper's success was
its uniquely high-toned penny press style. Like his competitors, Greeley offered a
new mix of politically engaged reporting: professional in its news-gathering but free
from (in his words) "gagged, mincing neutrality." Yet he also gave his "active and
substantial" middle-class readers (as he characterized them) not only a progressive
version of his competitors' papers but also a "virtuous and refined" one. He ban-
ished the prostitution notices but kept lottery, patent medicine, and theater ads. In
place of sensationalistic police reports, he published affecting stories exposing the
miseries of New York's poor, intended to stir up sympathy for the amelioration of
their plight. He also projected excitement. Shunning the cynical sensationalism of
the *Herald*'s James Gordon Bennett, he offered instead peppery and often caustic
editorials and debates that were unrivaled, even his enemies agreed, for both their
entertaining panache (as with his hilarious coverage of James Fenimore Cooper's
tedious libel suit against him) and their incisiveness and cogency. Already the nation's
premiere metropolitan newspaper, the *Tribune* was on its way to becoming the pre-
eminent site for robust middle-class public discourse.[6]

When Fuller joined Greeley's young paper, however, its glory days with Charles
Dana, Karl Marx, and other stellar contributors still lay ahead. One problem was
personnel. Greeley's assistant, Henry J. Raymond, the future editor of his great
rival the *New York Times*, who had covered books and cultural events, had earlier
quit. More serious was the paper's uncertain direction. Greeley always had to
struggle to keep his social idealism and partisan interests in sync. "The only thought
I have had worthy a true Scholar or Man is the 'Association' idea," he confessed
to a younger colleague; "and this would have stoned me to death, despite my practical training and inveterate industry, but for my usefulness to a party." Now,

though, he faced a major challenge to his strategy. For months his unceasing pro–Henry Clay editorials had nearly eclipsed everything else, only to leave him mortified by the Democrat James K. Polk's defeat of Clay, tipped, most humiliatingly, by New York's razor-thin Democratic margin. So to revitalize his paper, as well as, he hoped, his party, he had recently returned with redoubled energy to social crusading. And to replace Raymond, but more important, shore up his cultural front, he had hired Fuller, who, he boasted, in his prospectus published the week after the disastrous presidential election, was "already eminent in the higher walks of Literature" and one of America's best writers. "We are determined," he had declared, "to render this paper inferior to no other in the extent and character of its Literary matter." His literary editor was just as determined.[7]

II

"Nowhere is the contrast between circumstances & influence greater," Richard Henry Dana, Jr., would sniff five years later, after visiting Fuller's *Tribune* successor George Ripley in his dirty "little closet," than in the office of a leading newspaper editor in New York. The Brahmin literary lawyer, of course, was registering his condescension toward (and probably envy of) the cultural authority that America's newspaper revolution was already giving many journalists over that of ministers and his own guild, the country's traditional arbiters of public opinion. But even if not sharing Dana's nervousness, Fuller's more liberal Boston friends doubtless would have agreed with the substance of his contrast if they had followed her tracks on a typical day. When not staying at the Farm to "scribble" or proofread her articles, she usually arrived with the rest of the editorial staff in the late morning. Entering through the "dismal inky" front door on Spruce Street, she passed by the huge, ink-stained pressroom, where in the early morning a dozen blue-overalled, ink-smeared men and boys had worked furiously by flaring gaslights flickering against giant steam engines, before the jostling newsboys and newsgirls began streaming in for their papers at 5 A.M. As she climbed the dirty, narrow, winding stairs to the third floor, she could hear on the floor above early stirrings in the skylight-lit modern composing room, where another dozen aproned men, surrounded by rows of hooks with hanging proof sheets, were already laying out bright, copper-faced type on long tables. After opening the door to the third floor next to the sign "Editorial Rooms of the New York Tribune. H. Greeley" and walking past sofas, reference book cases, and metal speaking tubes through which the floors' staffs barked instructions to each other, she could see against the walls and windows a half-dozen simple pine tables occupied by reporters writing silently in their "*Tribune* uniform" of shirt-sleeves and mustaches. Conspicuous as the paper's lone female staffer, she finally got to her desk, cluttered with letters, clippings, manuscripts, and, on the floor, stacks of books from publishers.[8]

Finding her way to wielding the influence that Dana marveled at was somewhat trickier. She received no assistance other than very occasionally from Greeley, who wrote a few short notices of political and economic books, and briefly from her brother-in-law Ellery, who had joined the staff a couple of weeks before she arrived but got fired in the spring for being, in Greeley's estimation, unable "to make his own work." But the other side of that for Fuller was that she got the complete autonomy in her "literary department" she had badly wanted. When Greeley occasionally disagreed with her opinion, almost invariably on a political subject, he still published it, usually adding his own dissent next to it. She also received a decent starting salary: $10 per week, or two dollars more than what Raymond had initially gotten and twice what Ripley would begin at, as well as two-thirds of her egalitarian Fourierist editor's own pay. She attained maximum visibility as well, as Greeley placed virtually all her columns on the first page and afterward reprinted them in his *Weekly Tribune*.[9]

She also attracted attention with her signature of a large asterisk or "Star." To be sure, it sometimes caused confusion among readers not in the know. "Most heartily do I thank the writer for his bold and manly independence, and for the true courage that he has displayed in daring to speak as he has," wrote one inno-cent in response to her review of a theological book. Sometimes the knowledge that the Star was a woman created consternation. "Your philosophical (though female?) review . . . this morning," began one letter to the editor. One aggrieved author confusedly complained that her signature was obviously a ploy by Greeley to hide behind a woman and disguise the fact! For Fuller, though, writing under a gritty version of her old symbol for lonely femininity was clearly satisfying as well as journalistically meaningful. "It must be obvious that, as we always write under one signature, and any one who wishes may know to whom it belongs, we do not say anything by which we are not prepared to abide," she would answer one unhappily reviewed musician. "It must also be obvious that it cannot be for pleasure to excite angry or hostile feelings in the breasts of our companions in this bustling arena, and that, if we do what is calculated to produce such effects, it must be in the vindication of fixed rules of action." In short, "The 'Star' of the New York Tribune" (as the newspapers and magazines denominated her) was an apt sign of Fuller's persona as a professional critic. It also punctuated two impor-tant journalistic breakthroughs. One was in her column. In an era of longwinded gentlemanly quarterlies that hemmed and hawed and newspaper puffs and hatchet jobs, often stolen from other papers and sometimes libelous (especially when paid for by an author's or artist's rival), "the Star" signaled the first serious book re-view section in the country. The other innovation was in Greeley's paper. With her articles regularly stretching over four and sometimes five of the first page's seven columns, her "literary department" gave the *Tribune* a major makeover, beginning its transformation from a largely partisan newspaper into America's first mass-circulation periodical of ideas.[10]

However, she got off to a shaky start. She immediately came down with the flu and for over two weeks could only work "very moderately," which annoyed Greeley. But that was not all that bothered him. A tough editor, prone to legend-ary falsetto and profanity-spewing shouting at the slightest printers' errors, he found some of her first "higher" efforts somewhat disappointing. "They were al-ways fresh and vigorous," he recalled, but "not always clear," which he attrib-uted, with some plausibility, to her long immersion in foreign languages, especially

German. Like Emerson, he also could not get over, as he put it, "the contrast between the freedom and eloquence" of her talk and the "painful slowness and occasional awkwardness" of her writing. But it was its "painful slowness" that most
exasperated him. Even twenty years later, her workaholic editor and proud "hack-
horse of the daily press," who routinely put in sixteen-hour days, seven days a
week, was still complaining about it:

> A sufferer myself, and at times scarcely able to ride to and from the office, I yet did
> a day's work each day, regardless of nerves or moods; but she had no such capacity
> for incessant labor. If quantity only were considered, I could easily write ten col-
> umns to her one: indeed, she would only write at all when in the vein; and her head-
> aches and other infirmities often precluded all labor for days. Meantime, perhaps,
> the interest of the theme had evaporated, or the book to be reviewed had the bloom
> brushed from its cheek by some rival journal.[11]

But things soon got better, he recalled, after he recognized, no doubt grudg-
ingly, her inexperience with the daily harassment of newspaper deadlines. Her
increasing output probably also helped. By her second month, she was up to two
or three pieces every week, many short, but many three to six thousand or more
words. Eventually, she would write over 250 articles in a little over a year and a
half, an amount that would astonish Emerson, if not her editor. Greeley also thought
her journalistic style improved, which he took some credit for. "I think most of
her contributions to the Tribune, while she remained with us, were characterized,"
he wrote, listing the very traits he himself was known for, "by a directness, terse-
ness, and practicality, which are wanting in some of her earlier productions."
Meanwhile, he seems to have quickly come to appreciate the erudition, forcefulness, and, above all, fearlessness that her Boston friends had always admired in
her. "She never asked how this would sound," he recalled, "nor whether that would
do, nor what would be the effect of saying anything; but simply, 'Is it the truth? Is
it such as the public should know?' And if her judgment answered, 'Yes,' she
uttered it; no matter what turmoil it might excite, nor what odium it might draw
down on her own head." It is hard to imagine a better trait for a fellow tribune.[12]

And Fuller's view of her editor? Emerson, who sometimes saw him in New
York, had earlier warned her: "Greeley is a . . . mother of men, of sanguine temper & liberal mind, no scholar but such a one as journals & newspapers make,
who listens after all new thoughts & things but with the indispensable New York
condition that they can be made available; likes the thought but must keep the
power; What can I do with such an abettor?" Fuller seems to have known just what
to do with him. For one thing, she could appreciate, as Emerson could not, the
strength of character that lay behind his rough, go-getter exterior. "Mr. Greeley is
a man of genuine excellence, honorable, benevolent, of an uncorrupted position,
and, in his way, of even great abilities," she wrote Mary Rotch after her first month.
"In modes of life and manners he is the man of the people and of the *Amern* people,
but I find my way to get along with all that." Two months later, to her brother Eugene, she dropped the twinge of condescension in a succinct compliment Greeley
would have appreciated: "He is, in his habits a slattern and plebeian, and in his

heart a nobleman." By the summer she hit on his greatest value. "He teaches me many things," she told James Clarke, that her overawed or like-minded friends could not.[13]

The main thing she learned, of course, was what he had suggested: how to write more sharply in a confined space. She also learned how a great newspaperman coped with the vicissitudes of urban life. One occasion was in the early morning of February 5, when a massive fire, a regular scourge in antebellum New York, broke out and soon destroyed the *Tribune* building. Fortunately for Fuller, her *Woman in the Nineteenth Century* was in another building, but Greeley lost all his manuscripts and those of Greeley and McElrath publishers and had to come up with half the roughly $18,000 for losses not covered by insurance. "For a day I thought it must make a difference," she wrote to a friend, after their offices moved almost immediately into a new five-story building around the corner at Nassau and Spruce streets, across from City Hall Park and in the publishing district, "but it served only to increase my admiration for Mr. Greeley's smiling courage. He has a really strong character." Above all, she marveled at her irascible editor's seemingly bottomless fund for needy people and causes. "With the exception of my own mother," she noted to Clarke of this "mother of men," "I think him the most disinterestedly generous person I have ever known."[14]

In the beginning, Fuller, too, expressed uncertainty about her writing. "My associates think my pen does not make too fine a mark to be felt, and may be a vigorous and purifying element," she wrote cautiously at the end of December to Ward. Yet a week later, after getting some friendly criticism from her former editor James Clarke, probably about the sinewy syntax and digressive paragraphs that he used to complain to her about, she was not so sure. "What you say of my writing seems to be very true," she said, but she blamed it on her constant bodily pain and continual teaching, citing as examples of the "flow and obvious unity" she could achieve when she had time and felt well "Magnolia," "The Two Herberts," "The Great Composers," and the Mariana story in *Summer on the Lakes*. She also thought newspaper work might help her writing. "Now that I can choose my own times, and have a public of sufficient range or disposition and powers to interest me, also am in much better health[,] I hope my average writing will be better than it has been."[15]

She overlooked a few problems here. The articles she mentioned were not exactly newspaper material. Nor were her "times" exactly her own, which she discovered when she learned that her "European stock" would not arrive until the spring. Finally, however inspiring she found her large and diverse readership, it also created expectations of accessibility and relevance. It is true that Greeley knew what he was getting when he hired America's Transcendentalist critic. Indeed, he genuinely admired her *Dial*'s "un-American richness of culture and ripeness of thought," which was why he also tried to help get Thoreau and Ellery Channing published in New York. It was also why in his prospectus he had boasted to his readers that Fuller would give them the best "Literary matter" possible, "especially . . . interesting, instructive views of contemporary German and other Continental Literature." However, she knew—and undoubtedly she knew her editor

knew—that "un-American" was not wholly what most of his readers were looking for. "I doubt whether I shall put much outlandish matter into the paper," she
confided to Ward. "It is emphatically an American journal. Its readers want to
know about our affairs and our future. I shall illustrate from the past, and European life, but shall not dwell upon them." How truly bright her critical star would
shine would depend on how well she balanced these competing demands for
Europe's ripe experience and America's experiential future.[16]

Her maiden article in December addressed that very concern through a critique
of an author who had always most problematically raised for her those twin challenges of America and experience. Indeed, in picking Emerson's just published
Essays: Second Series to review, she chose the very work whose artistically subtle
but nonheroic ironies she had both admired and lamented during the previous
summer at Bush. Yet, in her article, she cast her gaze not through the hazy glass
of her "*illusion*"-shattering four-year-old Romantic friendship quarrel but through
a remarkably modern telescope on Emerson as America's first great democratic
public intellectual. That achievement had not been, she said—prospectively rejecting the future image of the Concord sage—a smooth or easy one. Not only did
Emerson's intellectually lazy—hence typically American!—listeners blanch at the
large mental demands that he made on them but so also did the middlebrow critics and partisans. They found unendurable, she said, his blithe disregard of "burrs
of opinion" and, worse yet, his constant recourse to a still "higher ground" from
which each side had an "infinite number of sides or bearings." But most tone-
deaf were the scholars, who foolishly overlooked the fact, as she succinctly put it,
"that Pindar's odes might be very well arranged for their own purpose, and yet
not bear translating into the methods of Mr. Locke." Yet numerous searching young
New Englanders, she testified, found inspiring Emerson's beautiful speech and
vision, including, she frankly said, warmly evoking her initial star-struck, Romantic
reaction to him, herself. "In the union of an even rustic plainness with lyric inspirations, religious dignity with philosophic calmness, keen sagacity in details with
boldness of view, we saw what brought to mind the early poets and legislators of
Greece—men who taught their fellows to plow and avoid moral evil, sing hymns
to the gods and watch the metamorphoses of nature."[17]

And the mature critic's view today? Plunging into the troubled waters of their
old argument, she came up with a fittingly ironic thesis: both his greatness and
his shortcomings lay in his unique protean intellectuality. On the negative side,
she said, summarizing her recent private Romantic critique of him, although a great
man of ideas, he did not belong to the realm of the world's greatest thinkers and
artists. "We miss what we expect in the work of the great poet, or the great philosopher, the liberal air of all the zones: the glow, uniform yet various in tint, which
is given to a body by free circulation of the heart's blood from the hour of birth."
Then, rolling out a clever, gender-accented Romantic aphorism that would be much
quoted, she added, "We doubt this friend raised himself too early to the perpendicular and did not lie along the ground long enough to hear the secret whispers
of our parent life. We could wish he might be thrown by conflicts on the lap of
mother earth, to see if he would not rise again with added powers." Nor was this

intellectual perpendicularity only a psychological problem; it was also an aesthetic failure, as he lacked a "fire" within to fuse his beautiful parts. "These essays, it has been justly said," she cuttingly observed, "tire like a string of mosaics or a house built of medals."[18]

After indicting him for not being an American Goethe or Beethoven, she then swung, Emersonlike, to the opposite pole: his modern, orphanlike intellectual sensibility also gave him his immense historical power. First of all, for America: his claims for individual culture countered precisely the nation's fixation on institution building and material results. "History will inscribe his name as a father of the country," she wrote, "for he is one who pleads her cause against herself." Second, for world culture: his devotion to "ideas" was not that of a disembodied Platonist but of an architect of a virtual religion, of which there came but a few in every age, "who worship the one God only, the God of Truth. They worship, not saints, nor creeds, nor churches, nor reliques, nor idols in any form. The mind is kept open to truth, and life only valued as a tendency toward it." Finally, his religion of "Truth" was powerful because (anticipating a critical insight of modern Emerson critics) it was not just flatly discursive but was expressed through a powerful kinetically metamorphosing language: "It is that by which he imprisons his hearer only to free him again as a 'liberating god' (to use his own words)." She concluded by urging her readers to ask themselves whether Emerson's books had given them a deeper sense of knowledge and beauty. If so, they "will lead to great and complete poems—somewhere." Bidding a cool-warm public farewell to America's greatest thinker, she invited her readers to join her in trying to awaken his more (she hoped) experiential literary offspring.[19]

III

Possibly because she was waiting for her "European stock," many of her first articles that winter, though, were on nonliterary subjects. One was the performing arts, to which she got, she exulted, "free entrance every where." Not every type got her attention. She probably did not give a thought to Gotham's bowery melodrama, blackface minstrelsy, and P. T. Barnum's nearby museum menageries and ballyhoo attractions, such as the dwarf "Tom Thumb," not to mention its famed tavern cockfights and bloody basement rat-and-terrier contests. She also did not review or probably even attend the city's popular musicals and burlesques on which her editor frowned because of their prowling prostitutes and antireform sentiments, such as expressed in the "dramatic satire" *Socialism* that soon hit the boards, in which an actor in "irresistible make-up" played the stumbling character "*Fourier Grisley*" to rousing applause. She did review a few productions of classic tragedies like Palmo's Opera House's production of *Antigone*, her favorite Greek drama, which she enjoyed but found uninspiring. She mainly concentrated on reviewing opera and art music, especially the "modern" repertoire she had been touting in Boston, from which she expected great things, and understandably so. Italian and French opera, long patronized by a mercantile elite free of Bostonians' antitheater prejudices, were attracting sophisticated immigrant audiences and

European singers of some renown. More important, although the New York Philharmonic Society had debuted only three years earlier, the city's many European-trained émigré players, particularly from Germany, were already giving it the edge it would always maintain.[20]

Yet her verdicts were mixed. Praising the "truly excellent" Philharmonic Society's performance of a Haydn symphony as "delicate, mellow, spiritual," she added, with a Boston bow, "it was such music as we hoped to find." As she heard more, however, her enthusiasm cooled. The New Orleans French Opera Company, America's leading French-singing troupe, she rated mediocre to poor. Her first New York Italian opera disappointed her even more. "All Donizetti and such like, poor flimsy melodies," she reported to her fellow arts aficionado Ward, "and performed in the common place Italian manner, vivacity gesticulation, bold clear sonorous singing, but no genius and no passion." Although she was captivated enough by the bel canto singing of New York's favorite mezzo soprano, Rosina Pico, in a production of Rossini's serious *Semiramide* to see it three times, in her review she mercilessly deprecated its "burlesque" direction and stilted acting. "Joy, grief, remorse, are all expressed by the same attitudes, the same gestures, with a serenity worthy the gods of Olympus," she wrote of one unhappy soprano. Even the German Society's concluding benefit performance of the demanding Fifth Symphony of her musical hero Beethoven got mediocre marks: "There was a want of fire and energy: the exquisite touches of grief and doubt were not so finely marked as to give due relief to the grand triumphal sweeps of sound." Worse yet, a listener had to endure her Romantic art music bugbear of mixing in popular ditties with works of genius. But she was most horrified by the fashionable audience's reaction to what George Templeton Strong, the city's chief musical connoisseur, called the "generally unintelligible" Beethoven. Reporting that a sizable section of the audience had walked out before the symphony began, she said she only wished more of their ill-bred chattering ilk had gone with them. "We need a musical police, to cry as they do abroad, 'To the door.'" "Fifty years hence," she predicted, people would be amazed they put up with such philistine programming and audiences. Even now "it is hard to believe we are in the midst of the *good* society of a Great Metropolis." Gotham's art music manners seemed worse than Boston's![21]

It was a different story with the philanthropic path that the city beckoned her to tread. This was not wholly new. Like her mother, whose "ideal sentiment" she admired, she had always been generous toward her down-at-luck friends. ("She helped whoever knew her," a Boston friend told Emerson.) She also always appreciated, as most of her Transcendentalist friends did not, the generosity of the Lawrences, the Phillipses, and others of Boston's rich Unitarian families she knew. Emerson, who had observed her sympathetic talk with servants and other lower-class Bostonians, insisted that her later philanthropic zeal, which surprised some of her old friends, was "as irresistible as her love of books," awaiting only an opportunity to express itself on a "grand" scale. Still, New York first gave her that chance. Poverty and crime were not only more plentiful there but also, thanks to the nearby Five Points slum and the penny press, which hyped the subject mercilessly, much harder to miss. Equally important, whereas Boston's Unitarian elite dominated its city's philanthropy, in New York, middle-class liberal reformers with whom Fuller closely associated, and not the city's old Knickerbocker families, led most of the efforts to ameliorate Gotham's urban ills.[22]

Stories abound about the hapless reformers, radical exiles, "fallen women," troubled maids, impoverished seamstresses, and lonely shopgirls whom she gave money to, found jobs for, or privately counseled, sometimes at some risk. One day while accompanying William Channing on one of his visits to the poor, she found a dressmaker's door ajar and went up the stairs, whereupon the woman shouted at her to stay away because the family had smallpox, but Fuller persisted, and the woman said tearfully, "You are the only one who is not afraid of us. How good you are!" Sometimes she displayed more than a little of the reforming philanthropist's presumption that she professed to detest. "I found her intoxicated and the scene that followed very sad," she wrote to an active reformer in the city, who had asked her to investigate a poor English woman. "I should say she was so much enslaved and her character so weakened by bad habit, that there is no hope of her doing any better, from her own resolves and that she ought to be separated from her children. I saw what her temper is, when excited, and it must be ruinous to them." But she was no Victorian lady bountiful. She knew the real lives of New York's lower classes were a closed book to her. "Loud shrieks just took me down into the little wood," she wrote in the summer to Georgiana Bruce, speaking of a shantytown of poor Irish and German squatters near the Greeleys' house, "there to see finely dressed, painted courtesans playing at being insulted by swearing men, whose lightest repartee was, 'God damn your soul!' Oh, these are woes cancerous, horrible, of which *we* know nothing."[23]

Female prisoners continued to interest her most. In the spring, she supported Bruce's campaign to secure a gubernatorial pardon, opposed by Greeley and most of the city's editors, for Honora Shepherd, a "notorious" forger incarcerated at Sing Sing. She afterwards counseled the girl at the Farm and raised a fund for Bruce to take her to Illinois to become a dressmaker. "I think she is *naturally artful*," Fuller reported to a friend of the spunky Shepherd, who had once escaped from prison in men's clothes, "in the sense of having a great deal of tact, but that it may all be turned to good." Also that spring, Fuller attended organizing meetings of the women's department of the New York Prison Association. Led by Abby Hopper Gibbons, who was the daughter of the Association's agent, Isaac Hopper, and supported by Caroline Kirkland, Catharine Sedgwick, and other prominent liberal Unitarian and Quaker women, the auxiliary organized the Home for Discharged Female Convicts (later the Isaac T. Hopper Home), the world's first halfway house giving temporary shelter, classes, and job placement to released female convicts.[24]

A contemporary reader might wonder about a self-aggrandizing impulse behind Fuller's infatuation with lower-class criminals. Yet, when Greeley, who thought of "fallen women" as victims of predatory men and unemployment but hardly as "sisters," afterward asked how they had seemed at one Prison Association women's meeting she had gone to, she coolly replied, to his astonishment,

"as women like myself, save that they are victims of wrong and misfortune."
"Women like myself," unjustly punished for making (as she said in her column
on the Hopper Home) "that first mistake": it is not hard to imagine that fueling
her "daring" compassion was less vainglorious or guilt-ridden "radical chic" than
her own sense of vulnerability as a potential female sexual transgressor herself.
Certainly, she was no uncritical fan of their "keepers." Despite puffs in her column of the Home, she privately expressed serious reservations about its rigid regimen of enforced isolation. She was especially hostile, like Gibbons and her liberal
friends, to the evangelical "asylum ladies" who would periodically descend upon
it. "It pained me to see the poor things so bowed down," she wrote to a friend
after visiting the Home, "much more so than they seem in their prisons; some *pious*
ladies were exhorting them, bible in hand." Also, although, as at Mount Pleasant,
she admired these poor women for making "no false pretensions" and not clinging to "shadows" when she chatted with them, she shrewdly guessed at what they
did *not* let her see and why. "They do not show the contamination and painful
images that must haunt their lonely hours," she told her friend; "they are pleased
and cheered, and show only the womanly and self-respecting side."[25]

In her columns, though, she initially skipped these nuances and misgivings and
concentrated on arousing sympathy for society's victims. She seems to have had
to strain a bit to adjust her Romantic idioms to newspaper prose. In her essay
"Christmas," one of several rambling, metaphor-packed civic sermons on the
winter holidays, she cried, after invidiously comparing meager American Protestant charity with the rich rituals of family giving in Catholic countries, "Were all
this right in the private sphere, the public would soon right itself." She showed
more ingenuity in using her old Romantic rhetoric for her new cause of prisoners.
In a piece pleading for contributions to the Home, she gave an inspired twist to
popular sentimentalist tropes she had always disdained. "These pleading eyes,"
she wrote, sounding like an urban reporter exposing her unthinking readers to the
dark, secret sorrows of their city, "these angels in stranger's form we meet or seem
to meet as we pass through the thoroughfares of this great city. We do not know
their names or homes. We cannot go to those still and sheltered homes and tell
them the tales that would be sure to awaken the heart to a deep and active interest
in this matter." Then, sounding like Harriet Beecher Stowe later manipulating her
sentimental readers' emotions in *Uncle Tom's Cabin*, she swerved: "But should
these words meet their eyes, we would say, Have you entertained your leisure hours
with the Mysteries of Paris or the pathetic story of Violet Woodville? . . . You
must have felt that yourselves are not better, only more protected children of God
than those. Do you want to link these fictions, which have made you weep, with
facts around you where your pity might be of use? Go to the Penitentiary at
Blackwell's Island." Best of all, send money to the Home![26]

Yet she also sharply critiqued New York's reformatory institutions in a series
of articles that winter. She had ample precedents. A commission to study the peculiarly "American democratic" character of prisons, asylums, and charities, as
she probably knew, had brought her favorite "democracy" theorist Tocqueville
to the United States fourteen years earlier. Lydia Maria Child had been writing a

little on them in her column. Her boss, of course, who fancied them potential Fourierist phalanxes, encouraged her to "make what use" of her series she thought best in the paper. Her most practical guidance, though, came from her old transplanted Transcendentalist Fourierist friend William Channing, a cofounder of the Prison Association, which backed the reformed Sing Sing administration. A seasoned urban minister to the poor, who knew New York's poorhouses, insane asylums, and prisons probably better than any clergyman in the city, he offered to escort her around to them, as well as to "Five Points," the notoriously impoverished and Irish-gang-infested section of lower Manhattan in the Sixth Ward. "It is a great pleasure to us to cooperate in these ways," she wrote Mary Rotch. "I do not expect to do much, practically for the suffering," she added, "but having such an organ or expression, any suggestions that are well-grounded may be of use."[27]

Indeed, encouraging suggestions were in the air. A couple of decades earlier, philanthropic reformers had started constructing massive private "benevolent" institutions where criminals, paupers, the insane, and the blind and deaf would be separated from families and communities that presumably had corrupted their morals or neglected their welfare and receive "moral treatment" aimed at inculcating self-discipline rather than punishment. Recently, other reformers had been pushing a more liberal agenda. The indefatigable Dorothea Dix was issuing blistering reports on the horrendous conditions at hundreds of northeastern public prisons and poorhouses. Dix's fellow Unitarians Samuel Gridley Howe and Charles Sumner were challenging prison administrators to adopt less evangelical and more rational methods of reforming deviants. And, on *their* left, perfectionist reformers, dispensing with older moralistic "common-sense" models of the human mind, were tapping into new social Romantic, humanitarian, and scientific ideas that emphasized predispositions and circumstances to explain crime and deviance. Rejecting prisoner isolation, lockstep labor, strict silence, constant surveillance, and sin-obsessed religious conversions, as well as, for the mentally ill, "heroic" regimens like bleeding, head shaving, and shaming, they called for treatments that would rehabilitate by gently stimulating rational and loving propensities. Thanks to Channing and his Prison Association, these voices were then getting a wide hearing in New York. Before beginning her "survey," Fuller tried to widen it a bit further.[28]

On Christmas day, at the behest of the Association, she returned to Sing Sing as one of its featured speakers. After being escorted into the chapel by the Association's executive committee, headed by Channing and Judge John W. Edmonds, the chairman of Sing Sing's Board of Inspectors, who had earlier addressed the male prisoners, Fuller sat down at a desk and gave the hundred or so assembled female inmates her gendered dose of the new humanitarian penal philosophy. She began by criticizing the standard line of most penologists, that once "fallen," women could not be rehabilitated. "It is not so!" she cried. "I know my sex better." Turning the purity-depravity cliché inside out, she declared that the inmates' past "wretched . . . conduct" and "license . . . and defying spirit" were probably caused not by depravity but by the conventional sentimental picture of womanhood. "They know that even the worst of men would like to see women pure as angels, and when they meet man's look of scorn, the desperate passion that rises is a perverted pride, which might have been their guardian angel." As for the women's crimes, she had no doubt that childhood neglect, bad associates, and bad habits had bred them—a standard liberal asylum line that she ratcheted up a little. After comparing them, probably much to their surprise, to liberal political prisoners in Europe, she said she could understand their feeling "that many without the prison walls were far worse than those within." As for the cure, after dismissing the superficial "agitation and excitement" of religious revivals, she gave three liberal "moral" prescriptions. One was self-culture. She urged that they read writings that provoked their feeling of their likeness to God, not just the Scriptures but also secular books (including Byron's!). Another was collective self-examination, dispassionately reflecting on their inner feelings and sharing with each other their secret faults. And they should beware the temptations after leaving their keepers, who were "friends to your better selves," when they were released. "How terrible will be the struggle when you leave this shelter!" she implored. "O, be sure that you are fitted to triumph over evil, before you again expose yourselves to it! And, instead of wasting your time and strength in vain wishes, use this opportunity to prepare yourselves for a better course of life, when you are set free." In brief, eschewing evangelical hectoring, but also ignoring their limited economic horizons, she offered these mostly African-American and Irish-Catholic inmates the Romantic self-culture and antimisogynist line of her *Woman in the Nineteenth Century* in the guise of the new liberal penal come-outerism. "Really beautiful," Matthew Arnold would exclaim to his mother after reading her claim that cultivating the spirit of prayer out of a deep desire for truth and goodness rather than agitation and excitement will make the women "daily learn how near He is to every one of us." "Nothing can be better than that."[29]

How much of it the women themselves took in, however, is impossible to say, although Rebecca Spring, who was in the audience, was impressed. "Margaret stood like an inspired person before these women," Spring recalled, "and spoke to them not as to criminals, but friends." At any rate, the experience gave Fuller some relevant facts as she started her visits to the city's "public *benevolent!* Institutions." She had begun them right after her Sing Sing visit but had to stop temporarily after her flu at the start of January. She visited roughly an establishment a week through early March, beginning with Bloomingdale Insane Asylum and continuing on through the notorious Tombs prison and finally ending with Blackwell's Island. This long, narrow, 120-acre strip of land just across from Turtle Bay housed the city's public complex of prisons and charity wards, including a "grim and unsanitary" women's penitentiary holding some seven hundred female inmates, whom she could see from her bedroom window and (mostly rightly) assumed to be prostitutes. "I have always felt great interest in these women, who are trampled in the mud to gratify the brute appetites of men," she wrote Mary Rotch, "and wished I might be brought, naturally, into contact with them. Now I am so." She did talk with some, and even read with a few, although her one recorded encounter suggests she had a tougher sell than she had had with liberal Sing Sing's inmates (several of whom Spring overheard to say "We are proud of

our keepers"). After someone pointed out to her a "hardened, sulky, and impen-
etrable" and apparently dying woman, Channing recalled, Fuller asked to see her.
"To her question, "Are you willing to die?" the woman answered, "Yes"; adding,
with her usual bitterness, "not on religious grounds, though." "That is well,—to
understand yourself," was Margaret's rejoinder. She then began to talk with her
about her health, and her few comforts, until the conversation deepened in interest. At length, as Margaret rose to go, she said: "Is there not anything I can do for
you?" The woman replied: "I should be glad if you will pray with me." At least
she seems to have gotten one "hardened" Blackwell inmate to respond to her
empathetic liberal therapy.[30]

In her February and March Fuller tried to apply something of the same magic
in her reports. The sole private institution she had visited was the thirty-eight-acre
Bloomingdale Insane Asylum on the Upper West Side (now the site of Columbia
University) directed by the liberal Quaker physician Pliny Earle, the country's
foremost "asylum doctor," who advocated holistic "moral treatment" as an alternative to the brutally "heroic" methods of physical constraints. Although he would
later write skeptically about inflated antebellum psychiatric claims of cures, Fuller
showed no hint of that skepticism. It was obvious to see, she wrote, that Earle's
"gentle care, intelligent sympathy, and a judicious attention to their physical welfare" were helping to "soothe" patients "into health, or, at least, into tranquility."
She did offer a Transcendentalist suggestion. Noting his patients' attention to both
his formidable lectures and their light amusements, she speculated that insanity
might be treated by both "concentration" to connect their morbid or manic "partial impressions" and deliberate "dissipation of thought" through contact with
nature. Her larger point, though, was psychological: both criminals and the insane, however ill, were not fundamentally different from us, because we all have
within us their propensities. "We are all mad, all criminal," she wrote, making the
point in reverse by describing a "lunatic ball," the asylum's Saint Valentine Day
dance that she had attended, in which an assortment of oddly charming inmates
had innocently mimicked the manners of high-society types. A half-century ago,
she declared, they "would have been chained in solitary cells, screaming out their
anguish till silenced by threats or blows," although again putting on this standard
prison reform narrative her own Romantic gloss. These new methods of emanci-
pating our wills and developing our individuality through this "miraculous power
of Love" when guided by divine faith and enlightened by "creative intelligence"
may one day be applied, she said, to transform the "government of families,
schools, and States." If, as some historians have claimed, antebellum institutional
reformers were obsessed with control and stigmatization, Fuller betrayed just the
opposite: a near utopian Romantic enthusiasm for the liberating possibilities of
the new moral treatments.[31]

Nor did her subsequent article "Our City Charities" demonstrate another historical claim often made—that antebellum reformers ignored government. That
these public institutions, unlike Bloomingdale, were for paupers made no difference: "Why should it be that the poor may still feel themselves men; paupers not?"

she demanded. Indeed, the main point of her article was to expose the shockingly different treatment inmates received at the private Bloomingdale and at the city's public institutions. The Bellevue Alms House had no meaningful work for its two thousand inmates, much less decent instruction. Its so-called Farm School, the Brook Farm sympathizer said, was "only a school upon a small farm, instead of one in which study is associated with labor." As for Blackwell's newer public insane asylum, it was obvious that its warehousing of children was responsible for their pathetic mechanical movements and grotesque behavior. Worst of all, the penitentiary, which should be treating "moral idiocy," was simply horrific. "Here are the twelve hundred, who receive the punishment due to the vices of so large a portion of the rest," she wrote, repeating the charge of social hypocrisy she had made in her speech at Mount Pleasant. "And under what circumstances! Never was punishment treated more simply as a social convenience, without regard to pure right, or a hope of reformation." As the problems were the failure of the city government, so the solutions, she said, were necessarily governmental. First, the administrators should be required to follow the basic principles of asylum management practiced at the "more righteous . . . Sing Sing and elsewhere": classification for appropriate aid, both intellectual and practical instruction, and a good sanitary system to promote self-respect and a healthy mind. Second, the state should keep policies and professionals from being discarded simply because of the "sport" and "delirium" of elections booting out government employees of the losing party. Finally, New York needed to provide more money. "There is wealth enough, intelligence, and good desire enough, and *surely, need enough*," she told her readers. "If she be not the best cared for city in the world, she threatens to surpass in corruption London and Paris." For Fuller evidently, professionalism, good government, and Romantic hopes were all part of the new liberal benevolence.[32]

IV

While sharpening her pen that winter, Fuller cast some weary glances back home. "Lloyd writes me, in answer to a letter which I wrote him at great inconvenience, for the sake of giving him pleasure," she snorted in a letter to Richard, "that he wishes, next time, I would write *at leisure*." Richard himself, who (Caroline Sturgis reported) missed Margaret's "companionship so much" while he was studying law with George Davis, peevishly complained that Margaret wrote to everyone but him. "You are mistaken," she corrected him. "I cannot. It is a physical impossibility. If you live to have sixty people or more write to you, and have a great deal of other script to do, you may see that I cannot. I feel sorry to have you take the view you do." As for his whining about having to look after their mother, she said, "You have felt as if my honor and the development of my powers, was really precious to you"; he should prove it, then, by taking "as far as possible my place in the family." Indeed, she added, she wanted a break from her whole private Boston life:

> I have now a position where if I can devote myself entirely to use its occasions, a noble career is before me yet. I want to be unimpeded by cares which I cannot, at this distance, attend to properly. I want that my friends should *wish* me now to act in my public career rather than towards them personally. I have given almost all my young energies to personal relations. I no longer feel inclined to this, and wish to share and impel the general stream of thought. I have nothing, at present, to communicate to any one, except what you may see indications of in print.

That last somewhat testy claim was neither wholly true nor altogether fair, but it underlined her point: she was determined to protect her "noble career" from distraction, if not contamination, from family sacrifices and Transcendental relationships.[33]

Fuller's brothers were not the only ones back home to feel uneasy about her New York career. "The Tribune office may be good treatment for some of his local distempers," Emerson quipped to Sam Ward about Ellery Channing, "but it seems a very poor use to put a wise man & a genius, to." Apparently forgetting his original encouragement of Fuller to throw herself into this "foaming foolishness of newspapers" (and perhaps bothered by her ambivalent review of his *Essays,* which had appeared the day before), he pointedly added "Is it any better with Margaret? The Muses have feet, to be sure, but it is an odd arrangement that selects them for the treadmill." Three months later, the third member of their romantic trio put her Transcendental fretting more personally. In her letter criticizing *Woman in the Nineteenth Century* as "not a book to take to heart," after somewhat condescendingly praising Fuller's recent critiques "for those who like introductions," Caroline Sturgis lodged a serious complaint about Fuller's anonymous mention of her in the Bloomingdale Asylum article. Considering Caroline's phobia about publicity and, possibly more significant, the mental illness that ran in her family, it had been, perhaps, a little indelicate of Fuller to refer to her anonymously as a sensitive friend who had been with her during Christmas at Sing Sing and had mused about how close our "manias" came to ranking us "among madmen." Certainly, Caroline thought so. "How could you put that . . . in the paper?" she demanded to know. "I begin to be afraid when I think how much has been told you. Is it quite fair to make your friends step before the public even in veils?" Even Fuller's new asylum cause came in for a little New England Transcendental twitting. "I see you are a great philanthropist," Caroline wrote teasingly the following day. "I suppose it is impossible to be anything else in N. York but Association will carry the day." Most gratuitously, noting she had recently seen Richard, she threw in "I find this difference between you & him,—that when he talks to me upon any subject he presents me with substantial food while you give me perfumes." Meanwhile, "are you not going to write me a more private letter sometime[?]" Fuller presumably never read Emerson's antinewspaper quip, but Caroline's criticisms of her negotiating the public-private divide riled her. Reminding Caroline that she had criticized *Woman in the Nineteenth Century* for not being personal *enough,* she asked, "Are you not inconsistent to reproach me for writing such outside things, and then fear that I will reproduce, even in veils, what I have known that is most interesting? Of what should I write then?" As for Caroline's catty comparison between the "substantial" Richard and herself, she wrote, "Perhaps a 'substantial' intercourse may take place between you, for he is really of your kind, the simple kind." Caroline did not answer her but gibed to Emerson: "Is not Margaret growing too good: I cannot write to her, I am so wicked." Except for a brief note asking for a contribution to a fund for Honora Shepherd, Fuller would not write to her again for nearly four months.[34]

The impish Caroline was an exception, however. Despite Fuller's commitment not to "fritter away my attention on incessant letter-writing," her friends wrote to *her* about the Boston scene "again and again." During late March and April she also "much" enjoyed seeing a lot of Anna Ward, who was staying at her grandmother's Beekman Street house. Meanwhile, she decorated her room with her parting mementos: in her alcove, Sarah Hodges's study-table and, just above it, the Shaws' "little crucifix," framed on each side by a drawing by Sam Ward and, appropriately for a militant critic, a picture of the Countess Emily Plater, whom Fuller had panegyrized in her book, with shorn hair and in battle gear. Yet, as her Plater portrait might have implied, her former spiritual hothouse felt far away. In her last letter to Caroline, recalling their Romantic nickname for Sam Ward, she wrote briskly, "The Raphael time is quite over—Let it go."[35]

As Fuller let go of Boston, she looked around to see what Gotham had to offer. Its swelling population of some 370,000, exclusive of Brooklyn, made it four times larger than Boston and half the size of Paris. Its risk-taking entrepreneurs and giant port, large rivers, and extensive canals and railroads efficiently linking it to the South, the West, and Europe also made it the still largely agricultural nation's unchallenged commercial and financial center. Most important socially, it was a city of startling contrasts. Physically, it boasted the nation's wealthiest neighborhoods and most fashionable boulevards around the corner from its most impoverished slums and dirtiest streets; its best water, from the new Croton reservoir, side by side, with the city's open sewers and leaking gas lines, its most foul-smelling air. The city's ideological contradictions were equally glaring. It contained the country's most ethnically diverse population and its strongest nativist movement, its most conservative Whigs and Democrats and its most liberal Whigs and Democrats, its most complacently old and nouveau riche upper classes and its largest hotbed of socialists, abolitionists, land reformers, trade unionists, and militant street gangs. Meanwhile, after eight years of depression, massive immigration and helter-skelter commercial development were producing mushrooming real estate prices, sprawling tenements, and massive political corruption and partisan factionalism. And with neither its old Knickerbocker merchants nor their rising entrepreneurial challengers much inclined to build the stabilizing philanthropic and cultural institutions Boston's city fathers had, these conflicts constantly simmered beneath the surface of the most competitive, cosmopolitan, unruly, and intractable city in the nation.[36]

She took to it. To be sure, she felt some privations. She missed her mother's "tender care" when she was ill, bemoaned New York's dirt and bad air, and complained about its high cost of living. Yet, as one might expect from her antipastoral ripostes about cities to Richard (*"these* are a growth also"), she came prepared to find in New York, as she had in the West—and as Frederick Law Olmsted, another transplanted New Englander, would find in designing Central Park—new organicist urban possibilities. Voicing none of Emerson's complaints about New York's "plaster-of-Paris" appearances making him feel all "surface in a world of surfaces," she wrote buoyantly to James Clarke: "I like to feel so fairly afloat in mid-stream, as I do here. All the signs of life appear to me at least superficially, and, as I have had a good deal of *the depths*, an abode of some length in *the shallows* may do me no harm. The sun comes full upon me." Even New York's darker shadows did not faze her. "I find I don't dislike wickedness and wretchedness more than pettiness and coldness," she told Sarah Shaw. Whitmanian more than Balzacian, she did not say exactly what *sort* of New York's "wickedness and wretchedness" she preferred. Still, apart from her shock over the "painted courtesans" in the woods, she never mentioned in her letters the usual Bostonian complaints about New York's brazen whoring, public drunkenness, and highest crime rate in the world. While even the doughty Child was sufficiently terrified by the "frightful" crime reports in the penny presses to scrupulously avoid going out past ten o'clock, Fuller often traipsed around the city (with an escort) well past midnight. Occasionally, she showed a flaneur's studied fascination with the city's grotesque spectacles. "A corpse has been disinterred grasping on one hand charred ledgers, in the other some gold," she wrote a friend after another fire in the city, "a clerk they suppose The Chevalier of the counting room, vowed to *duty* to the last moment of his life." Once she displayed a little urban aplomb herself in reacting to one of the city's anonymous surprises. One morning on her way to the *Tribune* office, a friend reported, she found herself riding on the omnibus with a lone passenger. "Margaret talked with him in a friendly manner and he finally asked her to marry him. 'I should not think you would want to marry one you know nothing about,' she said. He answered, 'I know you are a true woman. I like you. I am not afraid.'" How Fuller responded to *that* courageous reply is not recorded, but from her insouciant comments about the city, one can assume she handled it with grace.[37]

She did the same with her health. The condition for which she sought treatment was her increasingly painful kyphosis, or spinal curvature, which was probably the cause of her often-remarked-on trait of throwing her head forward, and perhaps some scoliosis, for which she inserted horsehair padding in her gowns to even out her shoulders. Her physician was Dr. Théodore Léger, an "animal magnetism" practitioner with a large clientele among artists and theater people in the city who treated a variety of functional disorders based on the mesmeric theory that a magnetic "fluid" or force that permeated the universe to which they were somehow attuned could be set in balance to effect healing. That was fine with Fuller, who mentioned nothing about the paranormal dimension that had excited her Boston Transcendentalist friends but said she simply wanted a "*cure*." (She may have gotten further encouragement from hearing that in a recent letter to Emerson raving about her miraculous restoration from the treatment, the formerly bedridden Harriet Martineau had recommended it to Fuller.) So that January she started going to Léger's "Mesmeric apartments" for an hour of treatment two mornings a week. Georgiana Bruce witnessed one in which the doctor slowly moved his hand up the spine to the base of the brain, "charging it with his vigor-

ous magnetism" as "he *willed* that power should flow from him to the patient."
After five months of this, Bruce claimed that it had not only straightened Fuller's
back but also caused her to grow three inches taller! This remarkable-sounding
restoration is highly doubtful, however, as both her friends' later reports on her
still noticeable spinal curve and her own testimony confirmed. In a friendly review of Léger's book *Animal Magnetism*, she said she could not vouch for his
reputed "decisive cures" but only his "power of transmitting vital energy" to soothe
and strengthen backs. "I have a very entertaining time with this," she reported to
Caroline Sturgis. "Nothing wonderful happens to me. I have no sleep, no trance,
but seem to receive daily accessions of strength from this *insouciant* robust Frenchman, and his local action on the distended bones is obvious." Probably as important as Léger's treatments, she also walked the four miles from the Greeleys' house
to his Broadway office and started regularly drinking a glass of wine, which she
thought good "medicine" for her headaches. "I . . . now seek physical remedies
for irritated nerves," she would write to Sam and Anna Ward after a year in New
York, "rather than struggle with them mentally, which I formally augmented the
ill by doing." To another friend, she wrote of her regimen, "[I] now obey Nature
as much as I can." "Nature," as she once told Richard, was also in the city.[38]

One thing there is no question about: despite her difficulties with the "harried"
pace of newspaper deadlines, the greatest charm of New York remained her job.
For the first time in her life, she told Richard, she did not have to worry "whether
the bread and beef can possibly be paid for." She also found the city a great learning experience. "It is so central," she told Sam Ward, "and affords a far more
various view of life than any I ever before was in." Most of all, she was pleased
with finally being able, as she exulted to a friend, to "speak effectually some right
words to a large circle." In her March summary of her professional situation to
her newspaper brother Eugene, she linked her success with these very newspaper
numbers that Emerson professed to disdain: "The public part . . . is entirely satisfactory. I do just as I please, and as much or little as I please, and the Editors express themselves perfectly satisfied, and others say that my pieces *tell* to a degree,
I could not expect. I think, too, I shall do better and better. I am truly interested in
this great field which opens before me and it is pleasant to be sure of a chance at
a half a hundred thousand readers." If Greeley still fretted about her work, either
he did not tell her or, in her enthusiasm for her new "great field," she did not think
it sufficiently important to note.[39]

V

Fuller's navigation of New York's lively "*shallows*" did not, however, entirely
efface her lifelong habit of plumbing social depths. It is true her prospects for
satisfying it seemed to her dim. "I can never, indeed, expect, in America, or in
this world, to form relations with nobler persons than I have already known," she
wrote a friend that winter. "Nor can I put my heart into these new ties as into the
old ones." As for New York's "'good society,'" she said disdainfully, "I am wholly
indifferent." In any case, "my present circle satisfies my wants": a few appealing

women, "yet more men," "good music, which answers to my social desires better than any other intercourse can," and several interesting children "in whom I always find more genuine sympathy than in their elders." The list is slight and the tone wistful, but it should not be taken as the last word. Because she virtually stopped writing home, the evidence of her goings and comings is skimpy. But putting together what there is, one finds that her New York social life was neither so bland nor so minimal as she led her Boston friends—and later biographers—to believe.[40]

To be sure, despite her professed tolerance for "wickedness and wretchedness," New York hardly made her into a gay "bohemian," a Parisian category that would not enter the popular discourse until the latter part of the next decade. Moreover, if she had nothing to do with the Knickerbocker or Episcopalian branches of "good society," she had *some* contact with its more cerebral Unitarian one. She enjoyed visits with Emerson's solicitous brother William and his wife on Staten Island. When Anna Ward was in town, Fuller went with her to the First Congregational (Unitarian) Church (later All Souls) led by the energetic young Reverend Henry W. Bellows. But, as in Boston, Fuller was happy to remain on the Unitarian margins. "With patience great mercies may be expected!" she wrote Mary Rotch, contemplating a visit from Orville Dewey, whose "very pretty moral sermons" (as the Knickerbocker diarist Philip Hone admiringly put it) at Dewey's fashionable Church of the Messiah she never attended, although she occasionally went to gatherings of writers and artists that he held at his house. Characteristically, she befriended not the prominent Stockbridge Sedgwicks, who attended Bellows's church, but their "*poor* branch (in money I mean)," who ran a school, which she puffed in her *Tribune* column, privately denouncing their wealthy relations' failure to help them ("as is the wont too often with such people"). Neither bohemian nor fashionable, she found like company elsewhere.[41]

One place was among the city's new generation of professional writers. Resembling neither the urbane circles once presided over by Washington Irving and James Fenimore Cooper nor Whitman's later convivial crew of Grub Street newspapermen and working "roughs" at Pfaff's, they were also unlike the staid male Unitarian ministers and academics and their radical Transcendentalist challengers who dominated Boston-Cambridge's intellectual life. They were instead hustling male and female editors and journalists, who jostled to secure their precarious careers in the dowdy but bustling rooms of the city's publishing and magazine houses, perfectly epitomizing the polyglot marketable maneuverings of New York's emerging metropolitan culture.[42]

Fittingly, she met most of these "Literati of New York City" (as Edgar Allan Poe would famously send them up) not in elegant drawing rooms, stuffy lecture halls, or smelly saloons but in the unpretentious parlors of Anne Charlotte Lynch. With wit, energy, and boundless tact, for nearly a half century, Lynch, as the wife of the Italian émigré scholar Vincenzo Botta, would oversee *the* salon that virtually every famous European writer coming through the city had to drop in on. Recently moved from Providence, where she had edited Fuller's old Coliseum crowd's anthology *The Rhode-Island Book* and sympathized with "all the ultra views," Lynch was just beginning her soirees. Every Saturday evening at 116 Waverly Place, across from Washington Square, upward of fifty artists, musicians, writers, and hangers-on crowded around the cookies, tea, and punch tables, for readings, music, dances, tableaus, and talk. "No entertainment except what they find in each other" was Lynch's crisp formula, and her list of famous attendees suggests how that could easily work. There Fuller saw, besides the city's high-minded liberal newspaper editors Bryant and her own boss, its foremost book editors Evert Duyckinck and George Palmer Putnam, as well as virtually all its diverse periodical editors. Mingling there with the fashionable Nathaniel P. Willis were Bryant's Fourierist Democratic son-in-law Parke Godwin; the *Democratic Review*'s enthusiastic John L. O'Sullivan; the blustery Whig magazine editors Charles Fenno Hoffman, Charles F. Briggs, and Rufus W. Griswold; and Lewis Gaylord Clark, the debonair editor of the influential *Knickerbocker* magazine, who kept alive the genteel tradition of Cooper and Irving. She also met these editors' rising stars: Greeley's reporter Bayard Taylor, Duyckinck's popular historian Joel T. Headley, and the recently arrived Poe. The city's (and nation's) leading women authors also regularly showed up: the sentimental poets Frances Osgood and Sara Jane Lippincott ("Grace Greenwood"), the health reformer and sex radical Mary Gove, the historical chronicler Elizabeth Ellet, the gift book editor and later women's rights lecturer Elizabeth Oakes Smith, and the esteemed female novel-ists Caroline Kirkland and Catharine Maria Sedgwick. The talk—gossipy, corny, and, among the men, faintly ribald or (as they liked to say) "Rabelaisian"—might have shocked members of the established Century Association, but insiders knew better. "To be invited to the reception of Miss Lynch was an evidence of distinc-tion, and one in itself," Elizabeth Oakes Smith would recall, "for she was strict in drawing the moral as well as the intellectual line." In short, it made a suitable venue for a transplanted Transcendentalist rebel.[43]

Reports about the impression she made there, however, as usual, are mixed. "In general society, she commanded respect rather than admiration," Oakes Smith later claimed. Some were "repelled," the New Yorker recalled, "by what seemed conceit, pedantry, and a harsh spirit of criticism" in Fuller's talk, while she "ap-peared to regard those around her as frivolous, superficial, and conventional." To these echoes of her Boston enemies' complaints, some women evidently added a little fashion-conscious Gothamite snobbery. New York women "have a pleased, elegant air," the always impeccably dressed Oakes Smith later explained to Emerson, which "plain Margaret Fuller," who "always looked care-worn even to haggard-ness," she said, "could never quite pardon." Not only women, though, were un-forgiving toward Fuller's unfeminine ways. "Miss Fuller is called a vigorous writer," Briggs wrote Lowell, defending himself from Maria Lowell's criticism of his attack on the "literary old maid," "but her vigor is that of hard dry soil, and not of a daisied meadow watered by bubbly brooklets." Others in Clark's "Rabelais-ian" Whig circle saw Fuller through the smoke of their regional rivalry with high-minded Transcendental Boston. "Miss Fuller's 'Woman in the Nineteenth Century' begins to make some talk," Hoffman hooted to Griswold just after her book came out. "There's a good story afloat about her and your friend Ralph Waldo. They were at the theater looking at Fanny Elssler for the first time—'Margaret, that is poetry!' contentedly observed this Carlislelist. 'No, Ralph that is religion!' rejoined his friend with mingled enthusiasm and rebuke."[44]

Of course, Briggs was whining, and Hoffman got the facts wrong. Fuller and Emerson attended different Elssler performances, no one called Emerson "Ralph," and Fuller hardly fawned over Elssler in her *Dial* review. Moreover, even scurrilous talk about the notorious Boston Transcendentalist bluestocking and now New York cultural arbiter created buzz. "All persons were curious to see her, and in full rooms her fine head and spiritual expression at once marked her out from the crowd," Oakes Smith recalled, adding, "I was surprised to find her height no greater; for her writings had always given me an impression of magnitude." A newspaper reporter covering a Valentine's party at Lynch's wrote of seeing her seated on the opposite side of the table from Osgood and Ellet, "her large gray eyes lamping inspiration and her thin quivering lip prophesying like a Pythoness." A New York editor even liked her "Pythoness"-like critical grip enough to appropriate it for his city's literary rivalry with Boston. "A PALPABLE HIT.—Miss Fuller thus snubs Boston," headlined the *Evening Mirror* that February, appreciatively quoting a suggestion by Fuller that a certain lecturer would be likely to find a more sophisticated and sympathetic audience in New York, "*where more various elements impeded too rapid spread of mental epidemics.*" Others praised her famous conversational talents, especially her calm but "swift" pace and her talent for extemporaneous concise and cogent yet eloquent formulations. Nor do observers seem to have found her talk always just oracular, despite her doting fans, of whom Greeley claimed she had many, even in New York. "There was no assumption of precedence, no exaction of deference, on her part," recalled Greeley (who had worried about this before she arrived); "for, though somewhat stately and reserved in the presence of strangers, no one 'thawed out' more completely, or was more unstarched and cordial in manner, when surrounded by friends." The most memorable portrait of Fuller's oxymoronic profile, though, came from her New York crowd's most famous member, who a few months later would put paint it for his "Literati of New York City" series in *Godey's Lady's Book*:

> She is of the medium height; nothing remarkable about the figure; a profusion of lustrous light hair; eyes a bluish gray, full of fire; capacious forehead; the mouth when in repose indicates profound sensibility, capacity for affection, for love—when moved by a slight smile, it becomes even beautiful in the intensity of this expression; but the upper lip, as if impelled by the action of involuntary muscles, habitually uplifts itself, conveying the impression of a sneer. Imagine, now, a person of this description looking you at one moment earnestly in the face, at the next seeming to look only within her own spirit or at the wall; moving nervously every now and then in her chair; speaking in a high key, but musically, deliberately, (not hurriedly or loudly,) with a delicious distinctness of enunciation—speaking . . . words . . . not by impulsion of breath, (as is usual,) but by drawing them out as long as possible, nearly closing her eyes the while—imagine all this, and we have both the woman and the authoress before us.

However much a characteristic "stroke-and-sting" job with Romantic graces, Poe's portrayal of the lip-curling and affectionate Fuller probably captured more than a little of what her admiring but often uncertain New York colleagues also saw and heard.[45]

To this admiration, rivalry, and prejudice Fuller seems to have reacted sensibly enough. She seems to have found the New Yorkers' literary tomfoolery tedious. (Oakes Smith recalled she looked like an "owl" when someone perpetrated one pun at a party.) Nor was she charmed by the garrulous careerism she heard. "Miss Lynch parties are not pleasant," she reported to Sturgis that March; "too much second hand literary gossip." Yet, she seems to have been happy to take in the good and ignore the bad. "He said . . . that he thought me capable of great affection," she would years later write Elizabeth Browning, picking out Poe's most complimentary stroke in his sketch. And she liked Lynch, probably because of her social charm but also, quite clearly, because of her literary connections. "At Miss Lynch's was introduced to me Headley," she gaily wrote Caroline in her last letter of the spring, listing also his Democratic comrade O'Sullivan and other "vivacious" and "pleasant" men who had caught her fancy, both famous and "unknown to fame!"[46]

As Briggs intimated to Lowell, her most "unstarched" relations, though, were with a more familiar crowd that she largely met through Child and Channing, whose careers were then partly converging with hers. Fed up with her Garrisonian comrades' sectarian bickering and eager to reclaim her literary reputation, Child had recently resigned from the editorship of the *National Anti-Slavery Standard* and taken up newspaper journalism. Not surprisingly, in her column Fuller praised Child's *Letters from New-York*, her popular Transcendentalist-tinged collection of urban reportage and reformist social criticism, for its attention to both the "inner" and "common life." Indeed, the politically no-nonsense Child and the culturally sophisticated Fuller, both keenly interested in New York's art music and humanitarian causes, particularly on behalf of female prisoners and "fallen women," forged a not intimate but fiercely loyal bond. "She is so entertaining, and her generous heart glows through all she says," Fuller enthused to Anna Loring. The tart-tongued Child loved Fuller's antislavery editorializing and sophisticated defenses of art music and had no patience for Fuller's enemies. "Briggs, though a man of considerable smartness, knows no more how to judge Margaret Fuller, than I do of Goethe's theory of colors, which I never read," she quipped to Francis Shaw. "His ideas of women are at least a century behind the age." She even tried to win over some of her skeptical Garrisonian friends, conceding that Fuller's "egotism" was a fault but blaming it on her father's tutoring pressures ("never *allowed* to forget *herself*"). "She is a great woman, and no mistake," she declared emphatically to Anna's mother Louisa. "I like her extremely."[47]

Fuller especially benefited from her renewed friendship with Channing. He gave her a taste of the family life she enjoyed by often having her over to his and Julia's house, where she lavished attentions and presents on their children. Most important, he widened her reform connections through his free-pew Society of Christian

Union. On Sundays, in his rented hall at the Apollo Rooms on Crosby Street, she heard probably more radical talk than she had ever heard in her life. On a typical morning, he would deliver his electrifying "conservative radical" antislavery and Fourierist "discourses," urging his "infidel" colleagues in "brotherhood and practical humanity" to see their desperate need for the "Spirit of Divine Love," followed by "loose and promiscuous" debates and speeches from a motley mix of merchants, professionals, mechanics, black and white shopkeepers, and domestics. Although in the fall Channing relocated to minister to the Brook Farmers, his circle remained intact, keeping her abreast of the abolitionists' and Fourierists' growing national movements. It also brought her closer to the Greeleys, the Cranches, the Godwins, and Henry James, Sr., who all attended the church, and it introduced her to William C. Russel, later acting president of Cornell University, and the Hicksite Quaker merchant and New York Prison Association cofounder Isaac T. Hopper, at whose house Child lived. Fuller became most friendly, though, with two wealthy and prominent Fourierist merchant families in the mold of the Shaws and the Russells: their fellow Brook Farm investor Richard Manning and his wife Mary and the liberal Quakers Marcus and Rebecca Spring, whom she had met the previous spring in New York at the national Fourierist convention. She often stayed at the Springs' spacious house in Brooklyn, and both families helped her financially. If not the "heart" ties she had known in Boston, her circle of philanthropic radicals gave her a solid community of aid and ideological provocation.[48]

Fuller's actual home, of course, remained at the Greeleys, which was turning out to be not quite the affectionate arrangement she had originally fancied. Partly their clashing life styles irritated her. Although she put up with Greeley's rustic preferences for "bare walls and rugged fare," she found it more difficult to finesse the issue of diet. Zealous Grahamites and homeopathists, the Greeleys did not stock meat, ground flour, or ordinary medicines. Worse, they bemoaned the fact that Fuller was "addicted" to strong tea and coffee, to which they attributed her habitual illness, which evidently did not go down well. One morning at breakfast after Greeley suggested that her "strong potations of the Chinese leaf the night before" had caused her excruciating headache, she bluntly told him that she "'declined being lectured on the food or beverage she saw fit to take.'" Henceforth, he and Mary avoided the subject, but he also admitted they could not forbear "looks and involuntary gestures." Then there was the rather more important matter of gender roles. Greeley would become a strong supporter of women's legal rights and employment opportunities as well as, he would assure Susan B. Anthony, "the vote and all other questions of woman's place in politics," but his political liberalism did not translate very well into his personal relations. Rather prudish as well as hypersensitive to social presumption, he was initially bothered, he confessed, by the sway Fuller seemed to exercise over so many women, discomfort that he vented in coarsely jocular-sounding ways. He took particular delight, he recalled, in exposing her "entirely inconsistent" exaction of conventional male courtesies: "Whenever she said or did anything implying the usual demand of Woman on the courtesy and protection of Manhood, I was apt, before complying, to look her in the face and exclaim with marked emphasis,—quoting from her "Woman in the

Nineteenth Century,"—LET THEM BE SEA-CAPTAINS IF THEY WILL! Of course, this was given and received as raillery, but it did not tend to ripen our intimacy or quicken my esteem into admiration." Nor should it have, since he himself conceded that behind his heavy "raillery" probably lay the "vulgar prejudice" that women who demanded to exercise male "functions" were frustrated with their single state. Indeed, sometimes he wanted to blurt out, he confessed, "noble and great as she was, a good husband and two or three bouncing babies would have emancipated her from a deal of cant and nonsense." While Greeley unstintingly gave Fuller valuable professional support, privately he sometimes seems to have stepped right out of her book.[49]

Then there was the Greeley family life. Mary Greeley had her share of life's tragedies. During their first ten years of marriage, she had two miscarriages, lost two children at birth, and saw two more die in infancy, each time leaving her on the verge of a nervous breakdown. She was also no intellectual naïf. A former schoolteacher, an avid reader of the *Dial*, and a knowledgeable devotee of most of her husband's nostrums, she had accepted Fuller's leading ideas and appreciated her counsel, which was probably why she had urged her husband to hire her. Yet she rather badly lacked the sublime self-reliance that Fuller preached in her book. Anecdotes abound about Mary's willful crotchets and eccentricities, of which she seems to have communicated to Fuller her full portion. One day, a mutual friend recalled, they all met on the street and, instead of saying hello, Mary touched Fuller's gloved hand with a little shudder and said, "Skin of a beast, skin of a beast!" Astonished, Fuller asked her what she wore, and when Mary answered silk and reached out her hand, Margaret touched it and shuddered, crying "Entrails of a worm!" Mostly, Mary's "deviltry" (in Fuller's word) made her extremely difficult to live with. She threw tantrums, wallowed in self-pitying hypochondria, fired servants, raged at her husband, and, although obsessive about cleanliness, left the house a mess. Greeley's workaholic habits did not help. He usually came home around midnight and left early in the morning, often escaping "Mother"'s storms by living downtown for weeks at a time at the Graham House on Barclay Street. As if this marital chaos were not enough, the Greeleys had a "beautiful" and precocious but unruly two-year-old named Arthur (nicknamed "Pickie"), who was prone to frightening bouts of screaming rage that his impatient and unhappy mother exacerbated by "whipp[ing] him often" and locking him in his bedroom, which led him to invent a Dutch substitute mother. "He evidently don't know the difference between his conceptions and absolute truth," Horace would write Fuller, which seems to have been fine with Pickie. "I don't live for *Truthness*," Horace would report him indignantly screaming at "you ugly creature" when Mary whipped him, "I like Fun."[50]

Somehow, Fuller salvaged the situation, at least for herself. She sympathetically heard out Mary's complaints about Horace and put up with her annoying attempts "to make me feel my faults," which seem to have kept Mary mollified. ("I have rarely known any one but you whose influence upon her was not irritating," Greeley confided to Fuller.) She spent hours with their son, sailing toy boats among the rocks on the East River, calming him down from his tantrums, swinging

him in a hammock slung on the back veranda. "He [is] very fond of me," she told
a friend, in the same satisfied tones she had used describing playing with Waldo
Jr. and Una Hawthorne. "He clings to my neck and says little assenting sounds to
the poetic remarks, and looks straight in my eyes; the look in a child's eyes at this
time is heavenly, so much dawning intelligence, yet so unsullied." Three things
seem to have helped thaw Horace out. One was just this skill of "Aunty Margaret"'s
with his doted-on Pickie, whom he was glad to remove from his wife's care. "She
had marvelous powers of personation and mimicry," he recalled of Fuller's playacting with Pickie and other children. "Had she condescended to appear before
the foot-lights, [she] would soon have been recognized as the first actress of the
Nineteenth Century." Another plus for Greeley was all the time and money she
spent on the poor, especially, he thought, in view of her inordinate appreciation
of "the material goods of life." "Had the gold of California been all her own," he
would later write, "she would have disbursed nine tenths of it in eager and well-
directed efforts to stay, or at least diminish, the flood of human misery." Most
important, perhaps, was the sympathy she evinced for the supremely "busy," harassed, and lonely Greeley himself, as comes vividly across in his later candid,
self-pitying letters to her about his "Castle Doleful," which showed a side to him
that he rarely, if ever, exposed to anyone else. Indeed, the attachment of all three
difficult Greeleys to her was probably largely what kept her from fleeing. Later
in the summer, after her sweet-tempered mother, who deplored Mary's "*almost
insane*" "follies" and "caprices" and her husband's "weak submission," which she
had observed when she visited, told Margaret she "could not conceive" of her being
content there, Fuller shrugged it off. "She could not fully see," she told a friend,
"how far the outward beauty of nature, and my confidence in the real goodness
and honor, which both my hosts have at bottom, outweigh with me the want of
order, comfort, and, far worse, mental harmony." In New York as in Massachusetts, beauty and goodness trumped comfort and harmony any day.[51]

VI

"That was a new era," Caroline Sturgis would years later say to Emerson. "The
persons she knew best were more vehement, adventurous, & various than her
friends here; less moral, less poetical, less beautiful than some she had known,
but she enjoyed their freedom from the puritanism that had annoyed her here."
That was all true, and no more so than of one friend she met at her first New Year's
Eve party at Anne Lynch's, whose freedom from "puritanism" she especially
enjoyed, at least at first. Her same age, James Nathan had emigrated fifteen years
earlier from Hamburg. Like many German Jews in New York, he had worked in
the clothing business as a wholesale broker before several years later becoming a
Wall Street banker and, the following decade, retiring and returning to Hamburg.
Although Fuller saw him almost constantly, for nearly a half century following
her death, because her family prevailed on her biographers to say nothing about
him, he disappeared from history. In the late 1890s, however, Nathan's grandson
sold her letters to an American publisher, who, to the horror of numerous Fuller

friends and descendants, printed an expurgated edition of them. From their originals and a few later surviving ones of his, one can get at least some sense—albeit
through a veil of intricate repression and sublimation that would have been grist
for a story of Henry James—of what she saw in him other than the narcotizing,
shadowy rogue that he appears in twentieth-century Fuller biographies.[52]

Clearly, one appeal was erotic. With a "strong" physique and a "rich persuasive" voice, he also displayed a "feminine" sensitivity that Fuller found extremely
attractive. "You have force," she told him, after their relationship heated up, confirming her longtime sense that "I should not be restless sad or weary with one
who combined force with tenderness and delicacy." She also seems to have looked
to him to make up for the past failings in that department of her intellectually
demanding father. "I don't know that any words from your mouth gave me more
pleasure, a strange kind of pleasure, than these, 'You must be a fool, little girl,'"
she would tell him in another later letter. "It seemed so whimsical that they should
be addressed to me who was called on for wisdom and dignity long before my
leading strings were off and so pleasant too." She underlined the point for him:
"As a child never finding repose on the bosom of love, I seek it now, childishly,
perhaps." Also attractive was Nathan's ethnicity. She had probably never personally known a Jew in Boston, where they were scarce, and even in New York the
German Jewish community around its secondhand shops in Chatham Street constituted only a small fraction of the city's immigrant population. Yet, long intrigued
with the figure of Moses the deliverer (a fascination that barely registered with
her New Testament–minded Unitarian and Transcendentalist friends), she was
something of an intellectual Semitiphile. Like alienated progressive WASP intellectuals in the early twentieth century, she fancied Jewish intellectuals as carriers
of modern cosmopolitanism, celebrating them in a later article for their vanguard
role in European literature and the "extreme radical party" in politics. The erotic,
ethnic, and exotic sometimes commingled. "I have long had a presentiment that I
should meet, nearly, one of your race, who would show me how the sun of to-day
shines upon the ancient Temple," she informed him in a come-hither letter after
their first meeting, "—but I did not expect so gentle and civilized an apparition
and with blue eyes!"[53]

How much the reality squared with her fantasies is hard to say. Certainly, Nathan
was no Heinrich Heine, Rahel Varnhagen, or one of the other emancipated German Jewish intellectuals she hailed in her article. However, he did have a few
cosmopolitan qualities that resembled theirs. He was a humanitarian liberal, acerbically condemning England's working-class poverty, its upper class's anti-Semitism
and callous complacency, and American officers' "*inhuman*" savage beatings of
sailors, which he observed while on shipboard. He was also a connoisseur of "advanced" culture. He sang and played lieder for Fuller on his guitar, followed the
New York art-music scene, bristled at the philistine "busy mart amid the falsehoods," longed to make it as a writer, and attended Channing's Christian socialist
church, espousing a belief in a coming pantheistic "new and greater religion," all
of which she naturally loved. "We will worship by impromptu symbols till the
religion is framed for all humanity," she wrote him, mentioning an upcoming

service at Channing's church. The most difficult question, of course, is determining, without his side of their New York correspondence, what he felt for Fuller. Rebecca Spring found him "selfish and self-seeking" and thought he hung around her because he found her useful, noting that she introduced him to Greeley, who kindly "took an interest in him as a decent and rather intelligent sort of a Jew." She also speculated that Fuller's extravagant talk, which "made men think better of themselves for a time, and for that they liked her for a time," appealed to his vanity. These are harsh judgments but also probably accurate, even if partial and not negating Nathan's charms for her.[54]

These quickly drove their friendship in a predictable direction. On their first day together, he told her of arriving in New York as a tearful and penniless immigrant on a landlord's doorstep. A few weeks later she was excitedly accepting "Mr. Nathan"'s offer to go together to a "New Panorama" of Jerusalem and suggesting that he take her to other "beautiful places which I do not yet know." By March, she was seeing or writing "My dear friend" almost every day. Meanwhile, she seems to have successfully kept their special friendship a secret, at least from her Boston-Cambridge family and friends (possibly another reason besides her "noble career" that slowed her letters to a trickle). Keeping it a secret in New York was harder. Child, the Springs, the Cranches, the Greeleys, and several of Nathan's business colleagues saw them together, and the Springs seem to have suspected it was romantic, as did, apparently, the Greeleys, from whom, after Fuller left New York, Fuller's mother got an idea of it. However, she wanted them to know as little as possible. "Have no confidant as to our relationship!" Fuller entreated Nathan. "I have had and shall have none. I wish to be alone with you in strict communion." The couple was especially careful about rendezvousing at the Farm, probably because of Mary's apparent jealousy of their friendship. They also tried to avoid, as Fuller said to Nathan after sending him away one night from the Springs' house, "living eyes that are over busy in taking note." So they went alone together to concerts and plays, picked each other up at friends' houses or Dr. Léger's apartments, or met at prearranged times and places on the way to or from their respective offices at the Tribune Building and at Cedar Street.[55]

Yet, despite these signs of something new, Fuller stuck to her well-honed Romantic friendship script, in which she instructed him. "Is it not by living such relations that we bring a new religion, establishing nobler freedom for all?" she asked, referring to famous egalitarian relationships she described in *Woman in the Nineteenth Century*, which he praised. As often with new friends, she tried to get him to reveal his personal history, which she claimed to divine. After he resisted explaining his allusion to a "'severe loss'" that made him "'heart-sick,'" telling her she may, probably, never know him wholly, she replied: "To know the natural music of the being, what it is, will be *or* may be needs not long acquaintance and this perhaps is known to her, better than to himself. Perhaps? *I* believe in the *Ahnungen* [premonitions] beyond any thing." He seems not exactly to have been a shirker in that department himself. "You have claimed me on the score of spiritual affinity," she told him in one letter. "You have claimed to read my thoughts, to count the pulses of my being; often to move them by your heart or will." Meanwhile, she gave him an accurate warning about her *Ahnungen*. "Trifles affect me to joy or pain but I can be absolutely frank," she told him. "You will see whether you find me fastidious and exacting. Our education and relations are so different and those of each as yet scarce known to the other, slight misunderstandings may arise."[56]

In April, two rather large ones did, forcing her to confront precisely how "exacting and fastidious" she *wanted* to be with Nathan. His answer the next day to her announcement of her "*Ahnungen*" triggered the first one. Suddenly informing her that he was planning to go abroad on a crowded itinerary that would take him from London to Hamburg and the Middle East, he dropped the mysterious revelation (he tore off part of his letter) about having a "krank" (sick) conscience yet having "only broken through the conventions of this world." Although feeling "startled" by the first news and left "in the dark" by the second, she nonetheless responded sympathetically. "*That* I know a generous and ardent nature may do," she wrote, adding the jumbled qualifiers "and unwisely, without deep injury anywhere, yet much outward difficulty may ensue," and concluding that she would not "seek to penetrate" his "veil of mystery" until he was ready to talk about it.[57]

Within a couple of days, she discovered what was probably behind his veiled confession. "Purely accidentally," she told him in an agitated note, she learned from a landlady in his neighborhood that he was involved with a young "English maiden." This time he gave her the (or a) whole story: the girl had been abused and he was trying to rescue her! What to make of such a claim? In fact, acting as both sexual predator and spiritual rescuer with prostitutes and other "loose" lower-class women, whether from duplicity or a confused morality, was common among both male moral reformers and young men in New York's "sporting life." And, even if this was not exactly Nathan's game, there is evidence that he had done *something* to feel guilty about with some young woman. Rebecca Spring would recall that an English girl named Louise whom he had "deserted" had followed him to the United States, a fact that would explain his later "painful" confession that he had initially not been "wholly disinterested" in his connections with the young woman. Rebecca would also later claim that Nathan's English friend Thomas Delf had brought Louise to Fuller and "Margaret was very good to her and tried to save her," which, besides jibing with Fuller's own "rescue" propensities, suggests some illicit behavior on the girl's part. In any case, it is clear that Nathan had been sexually involved with this Louise in England and she lived with him as a mistress for much if not all of the time he was in New York. Fuller not only initially bought his story, but she strained to assimilate it to her own confused mix of erotic desires and spiritual aspirations.[58]

To be sure, she felt queasy about it. When she first glanced at his letter as she was going out, she told him, she felt a "cold faintness" overcome her, as she hurriedly took off the flowers she had put on and gave them to a nearby blind girl. (The irony was not *quite* lost on her: "I almost envied her for being in her shut up state less subject to the sudden shocks of feeling.") Later that evening she carefully read his letter, but troubling questions "swam before her." Mixing her pronouns as she mixed her feelings, she explained: "I felt the falsity of the position in which you had placed yourself, that you had acted a fiction and though from honorable nay heroic motives, had entered the path of intrigue[.] I felt too, that he had, probably, been somewhat tempted by the romance of the position, and with a firmer determination to act always with simplicity, might have found some other way. He will tell me whether I was wrong in this." However, as if to release him from answering, after one more worried question about his reputation ("I do not see, my friend, how you can feel thus secure against this being generally known. . . . Do some of your male friends know where or how you live?"), she offered up a series of sympathetic rationalizations. She brushed off his suggestion that since she had once stopped going out with a certain lady with a disreputable public reputation, she might want to do the same with him. Indeed, she identified his misunderstood transgressions with her own! "I am myself exposed to misconstructions constantly from what I write," she said, probably referring to her sexual opinions and interactions with prostitutes. "Also there have been circumstances in *my* life, which if made known to the world, would[,] judged by conventional rules, subject me as probably to general blame, as these could you." In short: "You are noble. I have elected to abide by you." She closed with only one regret: "Oh, I wish nothing so grave had come up between us for judgment, thus early. My feeling with you was so delightful; it was a feeling of childhood. I was pervaded by the ardor, upborne by the strength of your nature gently drawn near to the realities of life. . . . Now this deeper strain has been awakened; it proves, indeed, an unison, but will the strings ever vibrate to the lighter airs again?"[59]

The answer was yes and no. The following week he gave her to keep at the Farm his Newfoundland dog, Josey, which she accepted lightheartedly, joking about his formidable bathing requirements. Yet once "this deeper strain" of new "realities of life" *had* popped out of the bottle, it started showing a life of its own. The next day, on April 9, in response to a "long and beautiful letter" from Nathan, Fuller wrote a self-confessed "incoherent" reply that, however characteristically metaphorical, sounds rather beckoning. While confessing she felt "timidity" as a result of the "many who have stretched forth their arms" having bungled their approaches to her, she said the situation now might be different: "The lark may never refuse her song if the true sun should dawn." She concluded even more provocatively: "I like to see the old fashioned Deutsche name written by your hand, and should like to hear it from your lips, but would rather myself not sign but come unannounced, and depart informally as if *at home*." She seemed to be saying two rather different things: their romance *was* a more serious one than any she had had before and therefore she wanted it to bring some different, if undefined, outcome—*and* that it still needed to stay in the safely exhilarating realm of Romantic conversation.[60]

Unfortunately, Nathan was evidently slow to grasp Fuller's suprasexual Romantic codes of love and friendship. Without his letters, of course, we will never know what was in his mind, although from his coded phrase to Fuller about his having with Louise "only broken through the conventions of this world," one might guess that his sexual ideas were, if traditional when it came to marriage, free-spirited, or perhaps vaguely free-love, when it came to affairs. Probably, too, he felt

some titillation over Fuller's loose statements about her own misconstrued transgressions and the lark not refusing her song "if the true sun should dawn." In any
case, we know he took some action during their meeting of April 11, although
what exactly—whether a pass, a proposition, or both—is unclear. But whatever it
was that he did after an "evil angel" made him "misread a word in my letter" (as
she put it), it was a first for her—and it shook her up. Indeed, her description in
her letter three days later, after another evidently unsatisfactory meeting, makes
his action sound like an assault:

> What passed yesterday seems not less sad to day. The last three days have effected
> as violent a change as the famous three days of Paris [the most turbulent days of the
> July 1830 French Revolution], and the sweet little garden, with which my mind
> had surrounded your image lies all desecrated and trampled by the hoofs of the
> demon who conducted this revolution, pelting with his cruel hail-stones me, poor
> child, just as I had laid aside the protections of reserve, and laid open my soul in a
> heavenly trust.

After a little more of this divining of a third-person "demon" on which to blame
his "act," she explained her reaction a little more literally: "When you approached
me so nearly, I was exceedingly agitated, partly because your personality has a
powerful magnetic effect on me, partly because I had always attached importance
to such an act, and it was asked of me so as to make me conscious, and suddenly,
partly because this seemed the moment to express all I had felt for you, but I could
not."[61]

Where did these two weeks of fallout from Nathan's two sexual bombshells
leave them? First, it left Fuller more shaken about his sexual character than she
had felt after her discovery of his "maiden." She tried to appreciate his "worldly
and *manly* way" of explaining his "act," she wrote him on April 14, but she could
not accept it. "It did not seem to me an act of "'providence,'" she told him the
next day, "but of some ill demon that had exposed [me] to what was to every
worldly and womanly feeling so insulting. Neither could I reconcile myself to your
having such thoughts, and just when you had induced me to trust you so absolutely. I know you could not help it, but why had fate drawn me so near you?"
Nor could she get out of her mind revived doubts about his character generally.
She insisted that she did not, as he had suggested, "'disdain'" him. (That would
have been, she said, rather generously, but perhaps not incorrectly, "to disdain
myself. Can I be deceived, then am I impure!") "Yet," she added, "forgive if I say
one part of your note, and some particulars of your past conduct seem not *severely*
true. Your own mind, strictly scanned, will let you know whether this is so. You
have said there is in yourself both a lower and a higher than I was aware of. Since
you said this I suppose I *have* seen that lower; it is, is it not? the man of the world,
as you said you see *"the dame"* in me. Yet shall we not both rise above it?"[62]

She certainly tried, but quite beyond their differently "manly" and "womanly"
worldly ways of thinking about his act and her worries about his "past conduct,"
there was one even greater obstacle to their rising above it: she was confused about
what she now wanted from him emotionally and apparently physically. In her April

14 letter, she had put the matter sensibly: she needed to feel reciprocally in love, which she did not, certainly not by her definition. "My friend! believe what I say, for I am self-conscious now. You have touched my heart, and it thrilled at the center, but that is all. My heart is a large kingdom." However, she was deceiving herself. A week later she told him what she really wanted: some sort of "experience of passionate life" that, she said, some friend (probably William Channing) had told her she needed to make her get beyond her "*unnatural*" way of thinking. Citing *Wilhelm Meister* as her model life narrative for their age, she said that was precisely what Goethe, or Festus, or, she supposed, Nathan had had.[63]

So, in one final gambit, Fuller both hedged and raised her bets. Her hedge was a reversion to an old move but in a higher metahistorical key: converting a sexual failure into a "pure high ministry [to] compensate for this loss which is to me unspeakable." Indeed, in an extraordinary letter on May 4, she made their receding relationship seem but the highest step yet in her heroic Romantic quest. "I hear you with awe assert the power over me and feel it to be true," she began humbly enough, but then suddenly announced: "There are . . . in every age *a few* in whose lot the meaning of that age is concentrated. I feel that I am one of those persons in my age and sex. I feel *chosen among women*. I have deep mystic feelings in myself and intimations from elsewhere." In case, though, he mistakenly thought that her heroic claim precluded a more literal or conventional future sexual coupling, she added insistently: "You will understand my song, but you will not translate it into language too human. I wish, I long to be human, but divinely human. Let the soul invest every act of its abode with somewhat of its own lightness and subtlety. Are you my guardian to domesticate me in the body, and attach it more firmly to the earth[?]" Finally, as if this oxymoronic claim of feminine heroism and bodily domestication were not enough, two and a half weeks later, on her birthday, she sent him her Fishkill poem, "To the Face Seen in the Moon," in which she imagines her androgynous "secret" of the "male eye" looking through the "woman's smile." It concludes with a vision of "an unpolluted world" where Tantalus "meets on his hard-won throne a Juno of his own."[64]

But, alas, Nathan was no Tantalus. Certainly, his Romantic professions notwithstanding, there was nothing in what is known of his character to suggest he was capable of responding to any of these poignant desires and grandiose myths. In any case, he seems to have decided that he had had enough. He protested that she was "too sensitive" to bear "fault-finding." As would come out later, he also chafed at the opposite—her superior moral and intellectual air. If that was not troublesome enough, he seems to have also felt some annoyance at her confusing gender rhetoric. "Mein liebster," she wrote to him later in the spring, after a couple of times calling him in her letters "mein liebste." "I will use the word again and correct my mistake. And yet was not that mistake an instinct, seeking the woman in you, when myself was in the melting mood." Perhaps so, but, as she guessed here, the "mistake" seems to have annoyed the "man" in him. But whether she did or not, their immediate relationship was doomed anyway when he decided to go abroad.[65]

Predictably, their evening meeting four days before his departure went badly. Nathan afterward reproached Fuller for trying to "alter" their "understanding," which probably meant he thought she tried to extract from him a stronger commitment without, of course, yielding to his earlier insistence on a "lower" relationship. Meanwhile, in her reading of the meeting that she sent to him the next day, she claimed *he* was the one who was backtracking "from ground to which you had led." ("You have approached me personally nearer than any other person, and have said to me words most unusual and close to which I have willingly listened.") She particularly took offense at his "talk of there being only one perfect relation"—which presumably referred to Nathan's expectation of a conventional marriage someday. "I want to cast soft light over these hours; why say to your moon that there might be a better light?" she asked. "She admits it, but when told that hers is *of no use even at present*, what can she do but veil in cloud the pallid beams?" In short, he wanted to keep his distance and she wanted to cling to the hope, if not of a "sacred marriage" some day herself, at least of continuing their nonmarital "spiritual affinity." Two days later, they had their final meeting at the Farm on the rocks overlooking the gently gliding water and in the "little paths of our dear wood," during which he sounded at least a little more promising. "I have not been able to write as I would," he told her, "but I *shall now* I shall answer in full, if you will write." The following day, on June 2, he left with his English maiden and his stationery for the letters he was to write to the *Tribune*, which Fuller had gotten Greeley to agree to publish, on his "stanch, heavily laden" packet ship bound for Portsmouth outside of London.[66]

Whether ultimately liberating or frustrating, Fuller's cosmic sexual scrutinizing filled in some important blanks in her history. Whether she chose to acknowledge it or not, not only had she *had* a passionate erotic experience, but also it had forced her to contemplate the "reality" of a mature heterosexual relationship, what she wanted out of it, and how it connected or not to her spiritual values and messianic hopes. Of course, none of these issues got resolved, nor was it conceivable that James Nathan could ever have helped her resolve them. Their parting gifts seem telling: she gave him a copy of a collection of poems of her heroically sublimating Shelley, along with a pen and pencil set to remind him to write! He gave her a much odder present, evoking a word that had appeared constantly in Fuller's letters—a white veil: a suggestion of their "love and purity," her bridal hopes, her virginity, or, perhaps, the thought that she *should* "veil in cloud the pallid beams"? Although puzzled, and, as it turned out, secretly thinking that it left open some sort of altered relationship, she for a while seems to have kept her promise that he extracted from her never to think "why you gave me that token." She eventually settled on the safest interpretation of love and purity: "I feel we were both within the pure white veil," she would later write to him. If not "severely" right, she was not entirely wrong either. At the very least, with Nathan's unintended help she had finally experienced a few of the impure experiences that her former "master" Goethe's hero Wilhelm Meister had made at way stations of *his* Romantic self-culture.[67]

VII

After Nathan's departure, Fuller resolutely worked once again at keeping any lingering wounds from festering. Following a week of "headach days," she took Dr. Léger's advice to suspend her treatments and try instead to "change the scene and air" and planned a few "excursions." She also tried to generate consoling memories. She took Josey to the couple's old riverside haunts, but the "very gay" Newfoundland proved as refractory as his master. "I cannot get him to go into the water at all," she reported in some frustration to Nathan; "last night I had to ask some boys to throw him in." More lugubriously, however, she arranged Nathan's letters with the white veil, her journal of their times together, and "some dead flowers that once bloomed sweetly in hours of sweet life." Nor was it a very good sign that after a couple of months, the first letter she got from him seems to have been largely prompted by his desire to get her to collect for him letters of introduction from her famous Boston literary friends. Yet she eagerly agreed to solicit his commendatory notes, including, awkwardly, from her Whig paper's recent butt of ridicule, George Bancroft, then President Polk's secretary of the navy. In response to Nathan's subsequent complaints about the burden of his "poor maiden," whom he had taken with him, she even offered to write to Harriet Martineau and Eliza Farrar's mother in England to see if they could scrounge up some friends and a job for her! (Although confessing that "there is somewhat" about the whole affair "that strikes me painfully," she told him she would say nothing about the "circumstances" and his initial "thoughts and possibilities which prevented your first action . . . from being wholly disinterested.") To be sure, over the ensuing months, during which she received only another note and a package of his "sweet" *Tribune* letters (whose faulty classical allusions she corrected), she sometimes faltered. "Why, why, must you leave me?" she wrote in one "heart-sick" letter, lamenting her lost chances for "so much natural joy and so many thoughts of childhood!" But by the beginning of the fall, despite his few "cold and scanty" letters without "the deep things of the spirit" and "*the promises*," she assured him that she was now feeling "much happier" about his absence. So "inexpressibly happy" did she feel, she wrote two weeks later, that "even for thee, I seldom feel regret."[68]

Whether regretful or not, as Nathan was no longer around to absorb her social time, she started going out (she told him) "a great deal." Also, probably feeling with him gone less self-conscious about her concealed liaison with him, she resumed writing to her old Boston friends. On July 10, in her first letter since their testy exchange in March, she contentedly wrote to Caroline Sturgis, cryptically alluding to a warm "flood" passing over her mind, uprooting old "landmarks" and planting new seeds that did not show outwardly. (Caroline caught the drift: "I have thought of writing but knew some new feeling had come to you, & was not sure that you would care to hear from me now.") She also dispensed what, under the circumstances, was somewhat ironic courtship advice to Richard, then trying to woo her former protégée the fifteen-year-old Anna Loring. He was certainly receptive enough: "Somehow, you seem to me the genius of *marriage* come down from heaven" to help save him from becoming a "victim" of the corrupt sexual connections she decried in her book. Unfortunately, actuated apparently by the "animal spirits" that he had worried about in himself, he soon bluntly demanded that Anna pledge herself to him before she left with her family for Europe. "Richard," Margaret wrote him anxiously, "I grieve to see how great the chance is of your making the miserable mistake that has wrecked so many of my best friends in marriage." She need not have worried, as his move (as she had predicted) scared Anna off, mortifying him but providing Margaret with yet another reminder of the dangers of unequal courtships and marriages.[69]

Mostly she used her extra social time that summer and fall to entertain visitors and travel. During the summer she saw a swarm of old Boston friends, including, besides Richard, George Calvert, Charles Newcomb, Anna Ward, Elizabeth Newcomb, James Clarke, and ("in serene beauty as ever") Emerson, in town to give a lecture nearby. She had her happiest visit with her mother, who arrived in mid-June and stayed through Independence Day, giving Fuller ample time to show her off to her New York friends. ("She is much taller than I, and larger and prettier and kinder," she guilelessly informed Nathan.) She especially appreciated having her "sweetness and elegance" around to help her soothe the domestic warriors at Turtle Bay. "While she stays," she sighed to Nathan, "I feel it almost like home."[70]

After a brief jaunt to Rockaway beach, on October 4 she scurried away to Boston, hoping "to keep in bodily motion all the time and not use my eyes for reading or writing." She deviated only slightly to visit a "Chinese Museum" exhibit that she would later use in her column to support China's historic view of Westerners as "barbarians" for their lack of the refinement that the Chinese prize so highly. Mainly, friends whisked her around her old haunts: the Shaws' house in Roxbury, Mary Rotch's in New Bedford, and the Cranes' in Canton, where she saw, much to her later gratitude, her sweet nonagenarian grandmother, who would die a month later. Contrary to Caroline Sturgis's prediction to Emerson that they would not want to see each other, she even had a "very good time" (Caroline said) with Caroline. Cultural bonds weathered less well. "I . . . did not enjoy being with Waldo as usual; our moods did not match," she tersely reported to Anna Ward about her visit with Emerson, who was working on his lecture on Plato. "He was with Plato, and I was with the instincts." During her last few days she visited the Brook Farmers. Despite seeing the "terrible weight of care" they were struggling with now that they were "real Fourierists," she continued to express respect for their earnestness, generosity, and socialism, about which she thought they were basically right but much too sanguine. "I have myself entire faith in the principle, as indicating movements inevitable in the coming age," she serenely wrote, "but I should begin prepared for fifty or a hundred years of failure." Overall, although fearing she had "worked too hard at human intercourse" to enjoy herself much, she enjoyed being for a change the "cheering" one for some of her weary friends in her old "nook."[71]

After she returned from her three weeks in Boston, she settled back at the Greeleys', but only for a couple of months more. In December, her patience having finally run out with their crazy "dissensions" and "grief," now increasingly "breaking out with violence," she moved downtown. Her first place was a "neat, orderly, still" boardinghouse on Warren Street in lower Manhattan at the edge of the financial district. "A most agreeable change in point of order and comfort," she wrote to Nathan, although she did not care for her mostly mercantile boarders, "men of business who seem like perfect machines," she sniffed to her professedly antibourgeois special friend. "No wonder they wearied you to death!" After she came down with another "very bad cold" right around New Year's, this time producing "abscesses or boils" inside her cheek and throat, she got her landlady's staff to bring her meals in her room. After recovering at the end of January, she moved into a more elegant boardinghouse at 4 Amity Place (now West Third Street), in the newly fashionable Greenwich Village.[72]

The move was certainly a cultural change from isolated Turtle Bay. Although the cluster of recently built four-story, red-brick Greek revival townhouses occupied by affluent merchants and professionals was a far cry from the immigrant and bohemian enclave it would become in its pre–World War I heyday, the neighborhood was starting to become attractive to aspiring young intellectuals and aesthetes. Although Herman Melville and his new wife were not yet living there, and the Jameses would not move back for a couple more years, Poe lived four blocks to the west on Amity. Also nearby were the Cranches and the architect Andrew Jackson Davis. Anne Lynch's salon was just across Washington Square, and the eminent critic Evert A. Duyckinck met his literary soirees at his house at 20 Clinton. The new University of the City of New York (later New York University) was drawing ambitious middle-class young men to its classical and "practical" curriculum. And the Astor Place Opera House, which at the end of the decade would be the site of the famous bloody riot between the feuding fans of the English actor Charles Macready and his American rival Edwin Forrest, was packing in audiences for America's most acclaimed theatrical and musical productions.[73]

Living downtown entailed some personal changes for Fuller as well. Now without free room and board and in the midst of a busy social scene, she worried about new expenses. "You have no idea," she groused in a letter that January to Mary Rotch, "how much, in this dirtiest of cities, it costs a poor scribe (what it costs the Pharasees Imagination shrinks from counting) who is far from all aid of unpaid affection in the line of sewing getting up clothes &c even to keep herself neat in the tightum line." She clearly got a kick out of playing the noted scribe around town, however. "I think she lives at disadvantage by keeping so entirely apart from the common stream of things," she opined to Rotch, speaking of Child's reluctance to attend evening parties because of all the time and money they took for white gloves, visiting cards, and carriage hires. "I shall never go out when busy, or to keep late hours, but to go sometimes is better and pleasanter for me. I find many entertaining acquaintances and some friends." And find them she did: at Lynch's Saturday night soirees, at parties at the Cranches', at overnight visits with the Springs, at tête-à-têtes with visiting Boston Transcendentalists and their hangers-on, such as that winter Charles Lane and later in the spring Sam Ward and then John Dwight, who delivered a series of lectures on music that she attended.

She also continued to branch out. She visited the Fourierist Godwins' "lovely place" at Hempstead Harbor on Long Island, where she hobnobbed with Fanny Godwin's father William Cullen Bryant and the novelist Caroline Kirkland and bathed in the surf. In early March she gave a successful party with the help of her landlady, who arranged things, she reported to Rotch, "as prettily and with as much interest as Mother."[74]

Her easy gadding about was interrupted by two social mishaps that shed a little darker light on her life downtown that winter. The first involved the now famous and infamous Poe. His strange amalgam of disruptive behavior, alcoholic morose-ness, literary ambition, and creative genius would make him a posthumous tragic hero to later nineteenth-century European avant-garde writers, but in prebohemian New York the combination could be deadly, keeping him in constant hot water, vocational as well as personal. As the new editor of the city's liveliest literary magazine, the *Broadway Journal*, and the author of the critically acclaimed *Tales* and *The Raven and Other Poems*, both published that year, he had suddenly be-come literary Manhattan's newest lion. Yet, beginning in the spring, he had started carrying on, despite his marriage to his consumptive "child-wife" Virginia, an odd flirtation with the impetuous Frances Osgood, conducted mainly in the pages of his magazine, where he printed their ethereally come-hither poems to each other. To cut to the chase of an opaquely Poesque story, after Osgood's rival, the also married writer Elizabeth Ellet, calumniated Osgood for writing compromising letters to Poe, in late January the now pregnant and frightened Osgood got Lynch and Fuller, as a self-constituted "committee," to traipse to Poe's house and de-mand that he relinquish Osgood's letters. Poe, however, having lost Osgood, Ellet, and only weeks before, after several furious public quarrels and binges, his *Broad-way Journal*, was in no mood to meet this further attack in rational terms. Instead, denouncing Fuller and Lynch as "Busy-bodies!" he told them to tell Mrs. Ellet that she had better come and "look after her *own* letters."[75]

Why did Fuller mix herself up in this "great war in *bluestockingdom*" (as Lynch sardonically called it)? No doubt sympathy for socially vulnerable female sexual transgressors had a lot to do with it, as did, perhaps, her recent dalliances with Nathan. She probably thought she and Lynch were protecting the reputation of a woman whose transgressions, whatever they were, were likely, if exposed, to extract a much greater social price from her, as Fuller often said they did with women, than from Poe. If she did think this, the messy result might have given her pause about trying to impose sexual rules on the righteously rambunctious literati. Although Osgood remained a friend of Poe, he found himself expelled from his lionizing salon for his (in Lynch's words) "very abominable" conduct and socially "bad odour." Yet, remarkably, if the thin-skinned Poe carried a grudge against Fuller, he seems to have suppressed it. Whether from distraction, toady-ing, or critical honesty—and with Poe all three were usually in play—later in the summer, in his New York "Literati" send-up, while getting in a dig at Lynch's hobbyhorse of duty "readily imposed upon by any artful person," he included his overall favorable sketch of Fuller with no such allusion. Fuller was also critically generous toward Poe. "He always seemed to me shrouded in an assumed character," she would tell Elizabeth Barrett Browning three years later, shortly after he died, in a letter decrying Rufus Griswold's scurrilously defamatory article on him in the *Tribune* and expressing regret she had not tried to befriend him. "Several women loved him, but it seemed more with passionate illusion which he amused himself by inducing than with sympathy; I think, he really had no friend." As for herself, she observed, "He seemed to feel that *I* was not prejudiced against him; he once said that he had faith in me, that he thought me not only incapable of baseness, but incapable of understanding it; that this was from him a strong expression of esteem, shows what his life had been." She was probably right about the "esteem," even if she seems to have missed, as he might have guessed, his probably intended cut.[76]

The social misfortune that brought *her* down, though, involved her still lamented-over special friend. It had now been nearly seven months since Nathan left, during which time she had gotten but two letters from him, the last informing her that he would be unable "to keep up a real correspondence" with her while traveling in Italy and the Middle East. Her bitter suspicions may be gleaned from her remarkable insertion, in a New Year's Day state-of-the-world editorial, of an allusion to "the good man" on whom she had seen a "spot of base indulgence, a fibre of brutality," about which she had "wept secretly in the corner for the ill we could not deny." In her letter of New Year's Eve, the anniversary of their meeting, sick from her infection, she angrily recalled his excuses in New York that he could not write because people at the office interrupted him or, she noted pointedly, "you had a person with you at home whom you did not wish to see you writing the letter." But her biggest grievance was not the memory of his paramour or his dilatory writing but his recent announcement that he had now decided not to travel to the Middle East that winter. This, she reminded him, had been his ostensible reason for hurrying away and, worse yet, now made it unlikely she would even see him, as she had hoped, in the spring. ("Write me of this as soon as possible!") She concluded by sounding a depressing tone that she had muffled through the fall: "I feel very lonely, sometimes very sad, and I still pine for you, my friend, and that home of soul where you used to receive me and strengthen me, and all the flowers that grew from frequent meeting." She would not hear from him again for another six months.[77]

Her renewed despondency over Nathan evidently lingered through most of the winter. Elizabeth Oakes Smith recalled a telling incident at a large party on the newly chic Valentine's Day theme at Anne Lynch's, which revealed a side of Fuller of "which, before, I had not dreamed." After "complimentary" valentines were read (including one by the blackballed Poe to Osgood), the party—during which Fuller, Osgood, "and other literary ladies, had attracted some attention"—finally ended. "As we were in the dressing-room preparing to go home," Oaks Smith remembered, "I heard Margaret sigh deeply. Surprised and moved, I said, 'Why?' —'Alone, as usual,' was her pathetic answer, followed by a few sweet, womanly remarks, touching as they were beautiful. Often, after, I found myself recalling her look and tone, with tears in my eyes; for before I had regarded her as a being cold, and abstracted, if not scornful." Privately, Fuller recorded in her journal her own dismal thoughts about her lonely state: "There comes a consciousness that I have no real hold on life,—no real, permanent connection with any soul. I seem a wandering Intelligence, driven from spot to spot, that I may learn all secrets, and fulfil a circle of knowledge. This thought envelopes me as a cold atmosphere. I do not see how I shall go through this destiny. I can, if it is mine; but I do not feel that I can."[78]

Yet, as usual, her sober stocktaking about her single life, although sadder than any she had ever expressed before, hardly seems to have paralyzed her social life. Among the outsized public figures she met that winter were the celebrated touring Norwegian violinist Ole Bull, the "stormy" Danish author and revolutionist Paul Harro Harring, and the antislavery editor Cassius Clay, who had recently escaped from proslavery mobs in his native Kentucky. "We have not had occasion to feel" such pride in sacrifice "for the cause of right," she wrote in a review of one of Clay's fiery Tabernacle lectures, "since, in childish years, we saw Lafayette welcomed by a grateful people." Indeed, after finally getting a letter from Nathan "full of soul and sweetness," she wrote him at the end of February a jaunty note from Amity Place "by my bright fire in the prettiest little room imaginable." After saying if they met no more their love would still "forever bloom . . . in memory," and explaining why she did not publish his last dispatch on the sights of ancient Rome (it was "too familiar" and hackneyed), she went on about her "outwardly gay and busy life," her "many new acquaintance," and her new friends "of heroic blood." "What you say of your new heroes I like to hear," Caroline Sturgis wrote to her at the end of the month, in reply to a similar accounting; "it makes the world wider and relations larger." Caroline was more right than she knew: although New York had immersed Fuller in urban culture, widened her class horizons, and given her new perspectives on mind and body, these "new heroes" added a cosmopolitan flavor notably lacking in both her more "vehement" and "adventurous" New York literary friends and her more "moral" and "poetical" New England ones. In the meantime, she generated a more intellectually cosmopolitan displacement in her *Tribune* writing, which she had started accelerating as soon as Nathan was out of sight.[79]

CHAPTER SEVEN

Young America's Critic

(1845–1846)

I

Picking up the pace of her writing was good news to Fuller's fretful editor, who had complained at the beginning of June 1845 that though he could not "bear to urge" her, he would have to cancel his scheduled business trip to the West unless she wrote more. "He is now quite content again," she reported to Nathan the following month. "I write often and at length." Writing more also seems to have made her reflect again on her journalism career. "This true life will never take form in art or literature," she wrote definitively in her July 10 letter to Caroline Sturgis. "I do not care, and never shall care any more." That last throwaway, however, sounded as though she did care at least a little.[1]

Nor did her gendered Romantic formula ("I believe I am the mother of a genius, more than a genius") suggest a very realistic blueprint for American newspaper book reviewing, where geniuses were in short supply. Nor did it help that a day or so after she reported Greeley's new contentment with her, she got a disconcerting letter from her admiring brother Richard, who implored her not to think she would never produce, as she had told her mother, anything more than miscellaneous articles; her style in *Woman in the Nineteenth Century* was almost "Shakespearian" and "nearly . . . perfect." Unfortunately, he added that he had recently been "pained" to hear Emerson say, apropos her book, "that you ought not to write, you *talked* so well." "Emerson is not your true friend," the former sage-worshipper angrily told her. "I know that thoroughly; & I rejoice you are away from him. His influence is bad, & he does not know you." Whether the thin-skinned Richard got right Emerson's ironic bon mot is not clear, but hearing it repeated could not have been pleasant. Nor could Emerson's continuing distaste for her "treadmill" journalism for a person of her "nobleness," if she had heard *that*, have made her feel any better.[2]

Fortunately, a week after getting Richard's letter she received a very different appraisal of her *Tribune* articles from James Clarke. "They seem to me to be better written than anything of yours I have read," he told her, singling out their "ease, grace, freedom and point," qualities he had missed in some of her earlier pieces for him and in the *Dial*. Most of all, he said, they will "do good. . . . I am extremely glad that you have such an excellent organ through which to speak to the public." Clarke's reassurance seems to have been what she needed to make her articulate more fully what she thought she was accomplishing at her newspaper. "I am pleased with your sympathy about The Tribune," she answered.

> I do not find much among my old friends. They think I ought to produce something excellent, while I am well content for the present to aid in the great work of mutual education in this way. I never regarded literature merely as a collection of exquisite products, but as a means of mutual interpretation. Feeling that many are reached and in some degree aided the thoughts of every day seem worth noting, though in a form that does not inspire me.[3]

This was a sensible statement of her ambition: nothing "excellent" but "great work" nonetheless. It was also a manifesto on the broad reach of "literature" that she thought her criticism engaged. In the *Dial* she had sometimes invoked the idea of untutored or naïve "sincere" literature, but she had reviewed very little in the category. Likewise, she had argued for a new reader-critic "pact" to replace the dogmatic and predictable criticism of most magazines and quarterlies, but she had never before articulated a hermeneutic ideal so broadly encompassing of literary production and reader responses. It would be wrong, however, to conclude that she had given up on separating out the strands of her hermeneutical web of "mutual interpretation." In numerous articles she clearly recognized works of "genius" whose organic fusion of form and content sprang from an original "imagination" that, in envisioning unseen forms reflecting the divine creative process of the universe, transcended their times and circumstances. Such geniuses also shared Fuller's literary stage with other authors who provided various lenses of interpretation: men "of healthy energy" who interpreted contemporary minds to each other; "scholars," who interpreted works of genius for the multitude; the "sincere," who provoked others to original expressions and so served as the foundation of the entire literary conversation. She would amend and complicate this schema, but it would always remain the basis of her most significant critical judgments at the *Tribune*. That she kept it in focus while writing week after week a steady stream of reviews for tens of thousands of readers all over the country marks one of the most remarkable achievements in American literary thought.

Fortunately, she had in New York a fitting literary culture for this kind of interpretive web. To be sure, New York would have a way to go to catch up with Boston, which was about to experience the founding of Ticknor and Fields publishers and the *Atlantic Monthly* and, soon thereafter, the emergence of Longfellow, Lowell, Holmes, Hawthorne, and Emerson as national literary icons. But in the 1840s, while Boston marked time, New York advanced. Exploiting the same geographical centrality, demographic density, and commercial hustle that had produced its newspaper revolution, the city was already foreshadowing some of the features that would make New York America's literary capital by the turn of the century. Not only did it house the country's largest publishing houses, Harper and Brothers and Wiley and Putnam, but also it boasted by far the country's richest and most diverse magazine scene. While Hawthorne and Longfellow complained that Boston had no literary magazine, New York had five: Lewis Gaylord Clark's urbanely conservative *Knickerbocker*; its popular counterpart the *New York Mirror*, edited by George Pope Morris, Nathaniel P. Willis, and Fuller's former principal Hiram Fuller; Briggs and Poe's *Broadway Journal*; and the country's two leading party-patronized periodicals, John L. O'Sullivan's pro-Democratic *United States Magazine and Democratic Review* and the Whigs' *American Review*. Furthermore, unlike comparatively sober Boston, New York bristled with colorful literary characters and exciting battles, which sometimes morphed into lawsuits and street assaults—a scene that got even wilder when, several months before Fuller's arrival, its most brilliant scrapper, Poe, had fortuitously appeared, soon to take over as the *Broadway Journal*'s sole editor.[4]

Fuller's allies in these famous "Wars of the Literati" were the "Young America" literary circle, whose leaders were the editors Evert Duycknick and O'Sullivan and included the critic William A. Jones, the playwright Cornelius Mathews, the Fourierist journalist Godwin, and the popular historian Joel Headley. Such a seemingly odd alliance between Democratic Party intellectuals and the literary editor of the country's premiere Whig newspaper has always puzzled scholars, yet it should not. In these years of radical ferment and intra-party dissension, many reformers were loosening or abandoning their connections with parties. In addition, although most of Fuller's family supported the Whigs, she herself had known little and cared less about their primary economic programs so important to Greeley. Even in pro-Whig Boston, her father's honored Jeffersonianism, her dislike of Unitarian Boston's staid complacency, and her association with the iconoclastic Transcendentalists had always kept her distant from official Whig culture.[5]

Most to the point, the Young Americans were her natural literary comrades. Quite apart from the fact that New York's prominent authors, exactly the opposite to the situation in Boston, were overwhelmingly Democrats, she could hardly have been expected to warm up to the conservative literary Whig *Knickerbocker* and *Mirror* crowd, who detested the Transcendentalists and gave Fuller the cold shoulder while Duyckinck, O'Sullivan, and their colleagues assiduously courted them. To be sure, the Young Americans, who were mostly Episcopalians, generally disdained the Transcendentalists' "pagan" religion" and "alleged mysticism." But they thought these minor New England ticks far outweighed by the New Englanders' "sincere" writings and admirable program for creating an "original" national literature. The Young America crowd's further appreciation of Continental literature, American regional inclusiveness, and, most significantly, professional critics as literary gatekeepers for America's print revolution were also all values that jibed with Fuller's. And they practiced what they preached. That year Duyckinck became the editor of two new series for the intellectually ambitious publishing house Wiley and Putnam. Skillfully marketed, inexpensively priced, and aimed at precisely the popular but discerning middle-class readership for which Greeley designed his newspaper, these "cheap" but "refined and cultivated" books occupied, in the words of their editor, the "middle ground" between scientific and theological tracts and "vapid" novels. As "classics," they also had a long afterlife. Duyckinck's Library of Choice Reading, the first from an American firm to pay foreign authors royalties, grew to be the most extensive series of contemporary European books yet to appear in America, and his Library of American Books became the first series of titles from serious native authors, including Hawthorne, Melville, and Poe.[6]

Fuller and Young America evidently recognized their literary and strategic comradeship. Duyckinck had praised her *Summer on the Lakes* as the "genuine American" article, Mathews sent her his books and manuscripts to defend from his legion of critics, and their hot-tongued South Carolina ally William Gilmore Simms begged her for back issues of the un-Southern *Dial* to "complete" his set. From her side, although Poe exaggerated when he called them her protégés, claiming Mathews shamelessly toadied her, she did promote their careers and boost their projects, particularly Duyckinck's two series, whose books she frequently reviewed, sometimes at his behest. ("Will you send me *Typee* and *Titmarsh's journey?*" she asked Greeley. "Mr Duyckinck wished me to look at them.") She especially valued the urbane, cosmopolitan Duyckinck, that "most Bostonian of New-Yorkers," whose appreciation of homegrown experimental writing and high critical criteria established a dual standard, she told him, "I can truly respect."[7]

Whether Fuller could truly respect everything in O'Sullivan and Duyckinck's "politico-literary" system (as Emerson pejoratively labeled it) is questionable. Their beliefs in Texas annexation, the Mexican War, and America's "Anglo-Saxon" duty to spread republican democracy on the continent were certainly not Fuller's. More important, they were never very clear about whether a "democratic" literature required a certain ideological point of view. The hotheaded Jones and Mathews often said so, while Duyckinck usually demurred. Then there was the related concern that had made Emerson decline to publish in the New Yorker's Library: the depth of these socially genteel and market-minded Young Americans' avant-garde commitment. A few years later he could have gotten some damning evidence when the "Rabelaisian" Duyckinck, writing in his influential *Literary World*, would sanctimoniously pan the books of their once great authorial hopes Hawthorne and Melville, criticizing the *Scarlet Letter*'s unhealthy gloominess and *Moby-Dick*'s iconoclastic religious musings and "transcendental" digressions. By that time, however, Fuller was dead. In the meantime, their "Young America" formed a congenial and useful army for advancing Fuller's literature of mutual interpretation.[8]

II

How Fuller's discursive theory worked in her practical criticism for the *Tribune* poses several problems. First, it contained multitudes: British and American belles lettres; Continental fiction, poetry, and drama; history, biography, autobiography, and travel; collections of criticism and treatises on foreign languages; music and art history and children's stories; religious and science books; and American quarterlies and European newspapers. She was also hardly free to write on what she pleased. Besides being restricted to new books, she had to produce copy fast and often had to treat important books cursorily or not at all. Yet some circumstances gave her opportunities for exposition. Duyckinck's two series furnished her with "choice" foreign classics and new American books from which to pick. Greeley's generous space allotments allowed her periodically to review, as she had done in literary magazines, several books around a single genre, tradition, or oeuvre. Finally, her original assumption that her readers would want light shed on their public affairs inevitably caused her to be preoccupied with the national identity and international status of American writing, questions that run like a bright thread through much of her criticism.

Fuller's educated readers had plenty of answers available to them. Since a quarter century earlier, following America's second war with England, the *Edinburgh Review* editor Sydney Smith had posed his notorious postcolonial question "In the four quarters of the globe, who reads an American book?" countless American journals, magazines, newspapers, novels, poetry, textbooks, and even spelling books had restated ad nauseam the sacred imperative of America's cultural nationality. But what that meant was much contested. In postrevolutionary America, writers had imagined it meant national subjects clothed in neoclassical or pre-Romantic European conventions. More recently, Romantic-influenced critics had urged that writers, lacking ancient folkways or aristocratic mores, needed to find some equivalent cultural basis for a distinct American literature. Still others debated a corollary question: did that literature require not just different subjects but also distinct forms, generic conventions, and critical standards? In the Jacksonian 1830s, the issue became political: how much did (or should) America's "democracy" determine the content and forms of a national literature? In the ideological 1840s, answers were exploding into fiery polemics. Young America firebrands tarred their Whig opponents as antidemocratic Anglophiles blind to America's social and geographic distinctiveness. Whig literary journals stigmatized Democratic nationalists as ignorant ideologues so naïve as to deny that foreign influences had always shaped national literatures. Off noisily to the side, America's self-declared philosophical critic Poe, while appreciating Young America's anti-England and anti–New England animus, scorned both sides for ignoring "universal" aesthetic standards.[9]

In that literary campaign Fuller articulated a distinct position. At the end of her tenure, she would summarize it in her survey "American Literature; Its Position in the Present Time, and Prospects for the Future." She might have subtitled her piece "A Cosmopolitan in Search of an American Literature," so great was her debt to German critics' vision of a "world literature" and so hard did she wrestle with the competing literary claims of cosmopolitanism and nationalism. She dismissed American literary boasts and hypersensitivity to foreign criticism as "national vanity" born of fears of inferiority, a mantra she regularly repeated in her reviews. She doubted America even had a literary identity. "It does not follow," she famously wrote, "because many books are written by persons born in America that there exists an American literature." *That* required, she said, in good Romantic parlance, a body of expressions growing out of an "original idea" animating the nation with "fresh currents" of life and thought. Writers who followed European methods and standards were still valuable, however, "if their books express life of mind and character in graceful forms," as "colonists and useful schoolmasters to our people" in America's long intellectual transition from the Old to the New World. At best, though, they merely refined tastes, and at worst, they damaged American literature when they encouraged servile imitation. The critical questions, she said, were, what foreign models were followed and, even more crucial, how to appropriate these.[10]

On the first question, she was aware of possible non-European exemplars. She upbraided William Prescott for missing in his *History of the Conquest of Mexico* a "great picture of Mexican life, with its heroisms, its terrible but deeply significant superstitions, its admirable civic refinement." Her reviews of non-European books, however, were very few. Publishers provided few, of course. Greeley himself had hired her to apply her expertise to European books. In addition, her growing friendliness to abolitionism and other reform movements seems to have modified her Romantic skepticism about Western cultural progress. "Our era," she declared in one review, had established "freer inquiry," "bolder experiment," and "nobler discovery," "on a firmer, broader basis." Mixing Enlightenment and Romantic enthusiasms, she cited the Christian church's rediscovery of brotherly love, modern philosophy's deconstruction of "vain dogmas," and the sciences' "new glimpses" into the "magnetic" processes of a spiritually harmonizing universe. Above all, Fuller was writing at a postcolonial moment in American history. For her as for all antebellum intellectuals, Europe was the country's literary Other that needed to be confronted, measured, evaded, or denied, but never ignored.[11]

Happily, European models were everywhere. "Copious infusions from all quarters," she wrote in a review of several new translations of classic Italian books, "mingle daily with the new thought which is to grow into American mind and develop American literature." The recent explosion of immigration was bringing a proliferation of foreign teachers, newspapers, and books, requiring in cities, she wrote expansively, "every person, of any pretensions to a liberal education" to acquire a knowledge of at least French, German, and Italian. She had only one caveat: the selection must be wide. "We have no narrowness in our view of the contents of such books," she wrote, sounding like a literary James Madison urging the multiplication of interest groups.

> We are not afraid of new standards and new examples. Only give enough of them, variety enough, and from well-intentioned, generous minds. America can choose what she wants, if she has sufficient range of choice. . . . Only give her what is good of its kind. Her hope is not in ignorance, but in knowledge. We are, indeed, very fond of range, and that if there is check, there should be counter-check.[12]

Of course, as with Madison, she also had in mind a little cosmopolitan filtering. She had often been accused, she said in her survey, of "undue attachment" to great Continental authors, but that was not so. What she loved in them, she explained, was what she had loved about Roman literature as a child: they embodied forms of both national *and* individual greatness. Furthermore, American readers

needed foreign books that would countercheck their nation's utilitarianism, parochialism, and slavish imitation of English literature. The literatures she picked out
for that were the same ones she had been working to diffuse among her Transcendentalist friends and highbrow readers for the past decade. The Italians, from
the profound Dante to the severe Vittorio Alfieri, she recommended for their "great
fiery" and "perfectly sincere" passions *and* intellect. "That truth which Rousseau
sought so painfully and vainly by self-brooding, subtle analysis," she wrote, "they
attained without an effort." The Germans, unsurprisingly, got her highest marks
for three qualities: their "indefatigable" cosmopolitan scholarship, their "searching, honest, and, in the highest sense, visionary . . . genius," and their wonderfully pictorial language, which put in the shade the "merely conventional, mere
phrases, the barren civilities and tactics of literature" of much English writing.
Even pedantic German texts, she said in one review—"judicious, dull, gentlemanly,
un-ideaed, well-informed, kind, cool" books, which she professed to "cordially
hate"—provided Americans with salutary cosmopolitan counterchecks. "The
Frenchman hastens with his showy generalizations. The Englishman cannot rise
above comparisons of all other experiences with his own. The German alone is
liberal enough to observe each growth by its own law and with reference to its
peculiar purposes."[13]

None of these possible influences, however, would provoke the growth of an
American national literature if readers did not know *how* to appropriate them. Fuller
was acutely conscious of the danger of being reduced to a state of unproductive
awe by the great achievements of Europe, which she had highlighted in her "Autobiographical Romance" as the central flaw of her bookish youth. In response to this
healthy "anxiety of influence," she gave two hermeneutical answers in her reviews.
One was pragmatic. Americans needed to appreciate the historical and cultural for-
eignness of classic European works and take them not as objects of imitation but as
provocations to the "aspiration" for a national literature. "The honey of Hymettus
need not spoil the taste of the American wild bee, but only teach him not to content
himself with the coarsest flowers when he might do better," she wrote in a review
defending the value of studying Latin metrical forms. The other answer she often
gave was cognitive. Recognize, she advised, in an article reviewing several recent
English editions of Dante, that great literary texts, whose spiritual characters are
expressed organically in their forms, require some organic self-culture in their readers. She severely mocked the "pedantic folly" of culture-aspiring readers, surrounded
with dictionaries, notes, and guides, anxiously searching to find "who Signor this
is, and who was the cousin of Signora that, and whether any deep papal or antipapal meaning was couched by Dante under the remark that such an one wore a
great coat." Rather than making the small chambers of their minds "look yet smaller
from being crowded with furniture from all parts of the world," she wrote, American readers needed to *enlarge* them by cultivating their own inward Dantesque spirits:
listen to human passions, go down into one's own psychic hell and writhe in the
"purgatories of speculation." Only cosmopolitan provocation and self-reflexive
assimilation could ensure that "foreign" influences helped rather than hindered the
emergence of a national literary culture.[14]

Despite these Italian and German lessons, probably because she thought these nations' belles lettres at low ebb, she reviewed few of their contemporary books. Instead, her "counter-checks" came almost exclusively from "showy" France and "utilitarian" England. Her reviews of recent French books and journals were her most deprovincializing. Although a handful of Fourierist and Young America reviewers appreciated the social democratic politics of many of them and middle-class English-speaking readers' found their urban sensationalism titillating, to most Anglo-American critics, French literature was awash in deplorable licentiousness and radicalism. She tried to dispel these prejudices culturally. Taking stories from New York's two French-language newspapers, the *Courrier des Etats-Unis* and the *Franco Americain*, she played up French theatricality, spontaneity, and perspicacity, which the English stupidly mistook for "heartlessness" and Americans, engrossed with money-making and politics, could not fathom at all. She especially panegyrized French newspapers for hiring eminent authors to write, as uncultivated English newspapermen and censored German writers could not, brilliantly "nimble" commentaries on public affairs. "Certainly it is with newspaper writing as with food; the English and Americans have good appetites, but do not and never will know so well how to cook as the French." There was one bit of French journalistic cooking, however, that did not please her. When during the summer the pro-Guizot government *Courrier des Etats-Unis* ridiculed Greeley for being "scandalized" by a reported "plot" by some beautiful Parisian court women, whom he had called brazen "courtesans," to embarrass the notoriously jealous visiting Queen Victoria by waging an "attack" on Prince Albert, she chivalrously struck back. Perhaps, she conceded, Greeley, who had read the story in a bad translation, had taken the distinguished journalist's "playful" joke a little too literally. Nonetheless, this "piece of raillery" *was* "very coarse in its substance." These cynical treatments of illicit liaisons sugarcoated the residual "Old Regime" "marriage of convention" and all its attendant evils of social hypocrisy, loveless marriages, and damaged children. Worst of all, they undercut marital reform.[15]

Fuller's boldest judgments, though, were those she made of the contemporary French novelists, dubbed in England and America the "modern Satanic school," whom she had been reading and writing about for a decade. She surveyed them most extensively in her "French Novelists of the Day" in the winter of 1845. Bucking popular trends, she was hardest on the best-sellers. Although appreciating Eugène Sue's socialist humanitarianism, his novels' incongruous mix of progressive hopefulness, sensationalist melodrama, and horrific flimflam made them hopelessly shallow. She gave only slightly higher marks to Alexandre Dumas, whose "vulgarly showy" plots were at least sometimes entertaining and even, as in his recent *Count of Monte-Cristo*, contained some pathos. On the other hand, Honoré de Balzac and George Sand, the French authors most excoriated by English and American critics, she judged by far France's best novelists. Anticipating Henry James's later appreciation, she praised Balzac's "unsurpassed" intellectual resourcefulness and uncanny psychological insight. She was bothered, though, more than James would be by Balzac's "passionless" scrutinizing, which after awhile, she said, became repulsive. That was not because of his refusal to moralize, which she thought appropriate, or even the "touch of the demon" that made him seem to enjoy the horrors he exposed. Rather, his dissections masked a cynicism that prevented him from ever portraying the heroic. "Balzac, with all his force and fulness of talent, never rises one moment into the region of genius. For genius is, in its nature, positive and creative, and cannot exist where there is no heart to believe in realities." As always for Fuller, portraying heroic ideals, while never occluding dark realities, was essential for the highest "genius."[16]

Fuller struggled the hardest to navigate between her aesthetic and social Romanticism with Balzac's contemporary. Sand's Byronic female characters and libertine reputation made her the bête noire of English and American critics, and even Fuller herself, despite her appreciation of Sand's independence and sincerity, had long doubted her strength of character and intellect. In her *Tribune* reviews she put Sand in a much more positive light. She was still tough on her as a writer. Despite Sand's inventiveness and strongly drawn characters, her early feminine protest novels were often tediously wailing, while her recent socialistic ones were artistically very crude. Yet her novels had none of "that subtle miasma" of prurience that infected so many popular French novels that readers gobbled up. Americans needed to put aside their squeamishness over her life and recognize her enormous influence in France and her great strength as a novelist: her rare capacity to understand and express how passion "at a *white* heat" molded character.[17]

Fuller's appreciation of Sand continued to grow. Later in the fall and again the following summer, in two reviews of Francis Shaw's new translation of *Consuelo*, she not only pronounced Sand France's "best living writer" but virtually declared her a cultural and gender comrade. She loved her treatment of the "aristocratic democrat" divided between high-culture enthusiasm and populist political zeal. More startling, she cast aside her worries about Sand's lack of "clean hands." *Consuelo* showed how Sand's sexual falls displayed an admirable "fearless, not shameless" sincerity, not just in refusing to hide them but also in exploiting them in her search for "Truth." Above all, unlike virtually all recent writers who had tackled intellectual heroines only to make them fail after rejecting "home duties," Sand made her readers see the full range of a woman's struggles with feminine ambition, "delicacy," and the "allurements of tenderness." "The shuttle is at work," Fuller intoned, in phrases she had used about herself, "and the threads are gradually added that shall bring out the pattern and prove what seems at present confusion is really the way and means to order and beauty."[18]

This last review of France's "best living writer" proved too much for the editor of the conservative Whig *Express*. Ever watchful of the *Tribune*'s ideological transgressions, he professed outrage over Fuller's panegyric of the scandalous author. Greeley was unfazed. "The *Express*, which never misses a case of horrible incest, abortion, or other revolting crime but gives it with the utmost pruriency of details," he sneered in his reply, offered "a grave reproof of *The Tribune* for commending (qualifiedly) George Sand's *Consuelo*—a book which is far purer in narrative, in sentiment and in tendency than the least impure number of the Express which has been issued these three years! O but this *is* a sanctimonious world!" In their tributes to aspiring French sincerity, the two different upright editors found common cosmopolitan ground.[19]

While qualifiedly recommending the French as salutary provocations for Americans, Fuller exercised greater caution toward many English authors. Their range was comparatively narrow, she explained in her "American Literature" survey. They had the "iron force of the Latins," she said, "but not the frankness and expansion." Yet because publishers mostly pirated and Americans mostly read English titles, they made up the largest share of the foreign books she reviewed. She also picked out older authors whose "English" character was transnational. Part of Shakespeare's power, for example, she said, came from his ability to "steep anew the dry husk of words in Spirit" and mix English forcefulness with the "rich coloring and more fluent life of the Catholic countries." Likewise, Milton produced poetry of the highest "poetic and reflective faculty" at the central point of convergence of the sacred and profane. He made as well profound investigations of the requirements of "conscience," thus exposing the libertarian springs that had once inspired America and now agitated Europe. For the Romantic poets she made especially strong cosmopolitan claims. She glowingly reviewed an American edition of Shelley, then known only to a few critics in the United States, most of whom detested his atheism and opaqueness. The former, she said, was a sad but understandable byproduct of his hatred of injustice and religious feeling for humanity, while the latter was simply not true of his poems: rather than mere abstractions, they expressed deep organic, if melancholic, thinking in lyrically dazzling forms. Happily, Shelley's star had been recently rising in Europe as a new liberalism was again on the rise. The recently republished works of minor Romantics also received their due for their non-English qualities: Coleridge's friend Charles Lamb (balanced yet affecting), the liberal critic William Hazlitt (too prejudiced but "richly observant"), and the recently deceased poet Thomas Hood (both comic *and* tender and therefore underrated in England). In a review of Wiley and Putnam's edition of Hood's writings, she urged Americans to contribute to a collection for his widow and children. "It would make us proud and happy to see our people do themselves that honor," she wrote, no doubt savoring the thought of Americans aiding a suffering English author.[20]

That during her entire year and a half at the *Tribune* she found no "genius" or even much "wit" to recommend to American readers she attributed to the increasing pressure on English authors "to sell themselves by inches" in "hack" writing, a force that was fast corrupting Dickens, she wrote before his major works had come out. Mainly, she limited herself to stringent appraisals of the broad middle, most of whom she found disappointing. In her mordant "Critics and Essayists," anticipating Dwight Macdonald's post–World War II assaults on modern "midcult," she rebuked a basketful of English critics for both dumbing down and gussying up their subjects through intellectual "shallowness," "unconscious . . . conventionalities," and "*over* refining." Mostly, she lambasted contemporary English critics for their parochialism. Except for a rare "honorable exception" like the German-influenced Coleridge, she wrote, they never seemed able to grasp that their dogmatic and impressionistic judgments "fail . . . of confirmation by the sense of the civilized world." Worst of all they often complacently talked about great Continental authors in a tone of "vulgar personal familiarity, a sort of *cuddling* way we may call it," or, like Leigh Hunt, in his book on Italian Renaissance poets, ludicrously enforce blame where they think "the moral well-being of the world calls for [their] guardian care." On the other hand, she praised "middle" English critics if they evidenced some scholarship, discernment, and ingenuity, as with Richard Monckton Milnes, Julius Hare, and Walter Savage Landor, who cultivated just that "deeper refinement" that Americans could use. Embedding their critiques in poetry, closet drama, or philosophical musings, these "gentle-men and scholars" *interpreted* rather than gilded or trivialized great works: although impressionistic, they were literary men of "talent" who told us what they knew, a rare commodity "in this age of book-making, got-up celebrities, and factitious action." They were middlemen for the discerning "multitude."[21]

While distinguishing between the genuine and the spurious among English middlebrow worthies of "talent," Fuller tried to do the same with books about or of the lower classes. The popular "Condition of England" books she treated with disdain for their patronizing tone, plots, and characterizations. "I have known more life lived in a day among factory girls, or in a village school," she wrote of the "paltry" novels of Catherine Gore, the "queen" of the "silver fork" school, "than informs these volumes, with all their great pretensions and affected vivacity." Fuller treated books by English workers themselves with much greater respect. In a remarkable review she wrote at the end of her first summer of two new poetry collections by the Scottish "weaver poet" William Thom and former factory hand John Critchley Prince, she applied to them her imaginative-talented-sincere prescription. After attributing these collections, as a phenomenon, to modern technology facilitating their publication and the "Spirit of the Age" touting aspirations for popular happiness, she predicted there would be even more of such works in the future when "there may still be many low and mean men, but *no lower classes*; for it will be understood that it is the glory of a man to labor, and that all kinds of Labor have their poetry." Yet on the *aesthetic* payoff of this marriage of "Labor" and "poetry," she was circumspect. England had not yet produced a genuine poet from the working class like Pierre-Jean de Béranger, nor did she favor conjuring up one by hailing every "sincere" poem produced by a worker. Prince's poems, she said, "are only easy expressions of the common mood of a healthy mind and tender heart, which needs to vent itself in words and metres." As for poetry of the higher imagination, although she decried excessive criticism of lesser poets, which stifled their creatively, discrimination remained essential. "Indiscriminate indulgence and a leveling of the beautiful with what is merely tolerable" would inevitably dull the appreciation of "excellent expression." Still, she knew, "the great efforts of art belong to artistic regions," such as Greece and Italy, "where the boys in the street draw sketches on the wall and torment melodies on rude flutes; shoals of sonneteers follow in the wake of the great poet." Indeed, that was exactly, she said, how Prince and Thom produced their poems: not by churning out the hackneyed wares of commercial culture but by informally reading them to their fellow factory workers who paid to hear them as they worked. And from there, she took a long leap into the future: these "simple, substantial" works might become the source of great literature produced by the "high constructive faculty, the Imagination" in some "golden age to which we are ever looking forward." But she gave no evidence of how or when. Meanwhile, she privately raised a subscription to send several hundred dollars to the struggling Thom.[22]

Although anticipating here something of John Ruskin's and William Morris's ideas about blending art and labor, Fuller saved her sharpest judgments on British books for post-Romantics, whom she regarded as at least potential "geniuses." She showed her continuing soft spot for intellectual but labored works like Henry Taylor's "noble" *Philip van Artevelde* and Philip James Bailey's "rich" *Festus*, but mostly she hailed what modern critics would consider the genuine article. In a review in the fall of 1845, she told her *Tribune* readers that Lord Tennyson was an ideal successor to Wordsworth as poet laureate (as he would become) because, befitting a new age, his poetry was marked less by ethics and more by "melody and voluntary finish." On the other hand, Carlyle, whose take-no-prisoners moralism was lifting his popularity to new heights, she found even more disappointing than she had in her review of his *Heroes* in the *Dial*. His *Oliver Cromwell's Letters and Speeches*, which delighted the heroic-minded Thoreau, was a disaster. First, Carlyle's rhetoric was not just shrill as before but now, if still entertaining, numbingly authoritarian. "Mr. Carlyle, indeed, is a most peremptory showman," she wrote, "and with each slide of his magic lantern informs us not only of what is necessary to enable us to understand it, but *how* we must look at it, under peril of being ranked as Imbeciles, Canting Sceptics, disgusting Rose-water Philanthropists and the like." Worse, though, beneath his colorful blustering, she detected a perverse will to revere not heroism but slavishness toward men of power. She was especially revolted by his glorification of the sanctimonious Cromwell's tyrannical brutality and crafty hypocrisy. "We think it rather too bad to rave at us in our time for canting, and then hold up the Prince of Canters for our reverence in his 'dimly seen nobleness,'" she wrote, speaking of Carlyle's gloating over Cromwell's slaughter of thousands of Irish Catholic peasants for refusing to obey Parliament's divinely ordained orders. "Dimly, indeed, despite the rhetoric and satire of Mr. Carlyle!"[23]

The post-Romantics in whom she invested her greatest hopes for import to America were two young intellectual poets whose interests uncannily resonated with her own. This did not exempt them from criticism, however. On the basis of Elizabeth Barrett's recent *Drama of Exile and Other Poems*, she put her at the top of her short list of female writers. Repeating her usual complaint about female authors' "morbid sentimentalism" about the "little things of life," she extolled her for having written philosophical poems that in their vigorous conceptions, spiritual depth, and classical erudition soared far above those of "any female writer the world has yet known." Yet Fuller also found much to disappoint her, singling out, besides diffuseness and overstrained expressions, this admirable invalid's "great book culture" that sometimes overwhelmed "actual life." "The lore is not always assimilated to the new form; the illustrations sometimes impede rather than help its course; and we are too much and too often reminded of other minds and other lives." Did it occur to Fuller that these were very close to the criticisms many had made of *her* books?[24]

With Robert Browning's prosodic experiments, Fuller gave her readers a taste of what an American critic could do with a putatively un-English author. Not only were his poems virtually unheard-of in America but also the few English who knew them, Hawthorne would later report, thought them inscrutably "queer." She made short shrift of that way of looking at Browning. In her first review, she singled out what virtually no critic had noticed—his realism—especially in his representations of elevated but still natural female characters. She also praised Browning's early difficult dramatic poem *Paracelsus*, which she lauded as il-lustrating—not surprisingly, in light of her own Paracelsian "Leila"—the mod-ern "self-conscious" intellectual's doomed quest for transcendent knowledge as against working within the limitations of human life and knowledge. Most of all, she applauded two innovative qualities about his poems that went largely unnoticed until the twentieth century: their "enchanting variety and an unob-trusive unity" and their tonal coloring, which allowed layers of ironies to soften his satires into subtle humor or raise them into powerful tragedies. But she also gave Browning, too, a little probably unconsciously self-referential writing advice. After defending the intellectual power of his recent narrative poem *Sordello*, whose Romantic philosophical obscurities had nearly destroyed his reputation, she noted that its multiple meanings twisted "their parasites over his main purpose." So she urged him to cut and condense. By contrast, in a subse-quent review, she singled out his recent shorter dramatic poems, now much admired by critics, as examples of how at his best, Browning *could* so compress. "If one tithe of what informs this little pamphlet were brought out into clear relief by the plastic power of a Shakespeare," she wrote "the world would stand trans-fixed before the sad revelation." Her hope for that kind of recognition would prove *too* avant-garde, as the bare beginning of Browning's vogue would wait for over a generation in both England and the United States. Apparently, nei-ther the once-conquering nation nor her cultural province was quite ready to act on Fuller's brand of literary cosmopolitanism.[25]

III

Notwithstanding Fuller's national and transnational appropriations of English books, England remained in her reviews America's lurid looking glass, seductive and dangerous but valuable for negatively defining its literature. "We use her lan-guage, and receive, in torrents, the influence of her thought," she wrote in "Ameri-can Literature,"

> yet it is, in many respects, uncongenial and injurious to our constitution. What suits Great Britain, with her insular position and consequent need to concentrate and intensify her life, her limited monarchy and spirit of trade, does not suit a mixed race continually enriched with new blood from other stocks the most unlike that of our first descent, with ample field and verge enough to range in and have every impulse free, and abundant opportunity to develop a genius wide and full as our

rivers, flowery, luxuriant, and impassioned as our vast prairies, rooted in strength as the rocks on which the Puritan fathers landed.[26]

This mythic vision of a regionally diverse but strongly national literary America has often proved challenging for commentators. Julia Ward Howe, Fuller's first biographer, would blanch at her statement's fervid nationalism. However, Fuller's cheers for non-English "stocks" (which also offended Howe), like her cosmopolitan annexations of foreign literatures, were hardly conventional nationalist moves. Other things complicated Fuller's literary "nationalism." For one, in her negative appropriations of "England," she betrayed her preoccupation with it. For another, national metaphors registered here, but so, too, did European Romantic tropes of expansion, diversity, and the pastoral. Finally, her vision was prospective. Not only did she doubt there was yet an American literature, but she also doubted there was even by her lights an American culture. "American facts!" she exclaimed in a review in the summer of George Palmer Putnam's strident defense of American culture against European aspersions.

> Why! What has been done that marks individuality? Among men there is Franklin! he is a fact, and an American fact. Niagara is another, in a different style. The way that newspapers and other periodicals is managed is American. A go-ahead, fearless adroitness is American; so is *not*, exclusively, the want of strict honor. But we look about in vain for traits as characteristic of what may be individually the character of the Nation, as we can find at a glance of Spain, England, France or Turkey. America is as yet an European babe:—some new ways and motions she has, consequent on a new position, but that soul that may shape her mature life scarce begins to know itself yet.

Meanwhile, Fuller detected a plethora of requirements necessary for that to happen: a more complete fusion of the country's "races," the exploration of the country's physical resources, allowing for "talent" to turn to "higher" literature, and, most important, a society capable of prizing moral and intellectual no less highly than political freedom. This is a sober picture and, in its mix of expansive freedom and specialized higher literature, a paradoxical one. Still, it marked a notable departure from the wail of despair about America's literary prospects that she had sounded while organizing the *Dial*. "That such a genius" was one day to appear, she wrote in her survey, "we are confident." In short, there were hurdles some day to be overcome, but the landscape was not forever condemned to be the cultural wasteland devoid of ancient fairylands and institutions that she had been, and as Hawthorne and Henry James later still would be, so worried about.[27]

Not everything, however, in her mind was likely to make American literature bloom. She ignored or dismissed the great mass of commercial polite novels, tales, poems, and essays published in mass-circulating magazines like *Godey's Lady's Book*. She passed over the enormously popular lugubrious poetry of Lydia Sigourney, the "American Mrs. Hemans" (except for an extended swipe at her "apologetic tone" about those "'peculiar'" or "'crazy'" souls who contemplate nature). With the smaller sentimental fry, she was beyond dismissive. "Flimsy beyond any texture that was ever spun or even dreamed of by the mind of man, in any other age and country," she declared of the bulk of ladies' magazine stories. "They are said to be 'written for the seamstresses,'" she harrumphed, "but we believe," she added, striking a characteristic note of highbrow humanitarianism, "that every way injured class could relish and digest better fare even at the end of long days of exhausting labor." She did exempt Child's magazine stories from her censure and gave honorable mention to Catharine Sedgwick's and Caroline Kirkland's regional novels of "skill and feeling," however "slight in their fabric, and familiar in their tone." In one review, she even showed a little Romantic mercy on *Evelyn: or a Heart Unmasked—A Tale of Domestic Life*, by the popular playwright and actress Anna Cora Mowatt, for its gentle animation of feeling, despite its being a "moral tale" with an absurdly improbable plot. Saying that Mowatt needed to learn how to lead the reader to accept the "most singular facts" by refracting them through the "minds of the agents," she suggested that the author read Godwin and Balzac! Finally, if she was more forgiving of sentimental "scribbling women" than Hawthorne would later famously be, she was less so with male sentimentalist scribblers, like the *Knickerbocker* group's drawing-room poets, whom she mostly ignored, or Nathaniel P. Willis, whose graceful poems and pencilings she said belonged "only the fashionable world" pining to imitate Europe.[28]

With official American literary culture, she was more appreciative but underwhelmed. In her survey she put America's most celebrated authors—William Cullen Bryant, Washington Irving, and James Fenimore—into her schoolmaster category of limited strengths and provincial borrowing. Bryant, the country's best poet, was an attenuated American Wordsworth, without much range or fertility of imagination but able to express the "language of his inmost nature" in "simple lovely garb." With Cooper, she had to swallow harder. Despite "the baldness of his plots, shallowness of thought, and poverty in the presentation of character," she said, he should at least get credit for redeeming America's forest scenery and the noble romance of the hunter-pioneer's life from the "corrosive acid of a semi-civilized invasion." The Boston Unitarian literati generally came off largely as Emerson had pictured them in the "American Scholar": passive and enervated. To be sure, in her survey she honored William Ellery Channing for his spiritual beauty and elevated devotion to truth, but she doubted his permanent importance, since his one great thought, the dignity of human nature, merely reflected the times. The quarterlies were so fearful of the tyranny of popular opinion that they often sank below the censored journals of Europe. The *North American Review* "ambles and jogs at an old gentlemanly pace along a beaten path that leads to no important goal."[29]

The Boston writers Fuller most raked over her Romantic coals, though, were Longfellow and Lowell. She was particularly severe with Lowell. She had given him a pass as a promising youth in her *Dial* notice of his first poetry collection, but when he stepped forth as a critic, she gave him none. In her review of his *Conversations on Some of the Old Poets*, after noting a few passages of humor and good sense that "agreeably relieve" his usual "high strain," she dismantled his book. His middlebrow tone failed utterly: he talked too fancily for an ignorant audience and too simply for a cultivated one. His critical opinions were mostly worthless. After taking issue with a couple of his readings, she simply stopped, declaring that even if newspaper space allowed it, any detailed examination would not be worthwhile, since "he does not profess to give the results of long acquaintance through varied moods" required for the best judgment. Indeed, he seemed to hew to the "affirmative" school of criticism out of formal ignorance. His point, on which he "labor[s] incessantly," that poetry was simply the natural expression of a spiritually elevated mind raised above the "lower necessities" of life might be abstractly correct, but it was formally naïve: "Metres themselves are actually *something* apart from the thought they are destined to convey. They are the music of that thought; its more or less perfect organization." Nor would this be the last word on the young poet by "the female ass of the Tribune" (as Lowell's friend Briggs sympathetically denominated her to him). "Lowell," she would announce in her survey a year later, "we must declare it, though to the grief of some friends, and the disgust of more, is absolutely wanting in the true spirit and tone of poesy." His newfound abolitionism even worsened his case: "His interest in the moral questions of the day has supplied the want of vitality in himself." In sum, she said, "his great facility at versification has enabled him to fill the ear with a copious stream of pleasant sound. But his verse is stereotyped; his thought sounds no depth, and posterity will not remember him."

As a final judgment on young Lowell, this was a little premature, betraying perhaps some competitive streak with him as a rising critic and possibly a residue of resentment of him and his young Brahmin circle for their disdain of her and her Transcendentalist friends. But she was right about posterity, although this verdict would have to await the twentieth-century to be confirmed. As for her judgment's timing, she may have thought it also right, before his poetic pretensions gave him an undeserved popularity. If that was her motive, she seems to have succeeded, as many in Boston thought she put a "blight" on his career, and neither his professional nor young male pride allowed him to forgive her for it. After reading her literary death sentence, he wrote angrily to a friend, "I leave time to settle my account with her."[30]

The issue of the overpraising of literary mediocrity also lay behind her notorious critical assault on Longfellow. The allegation that she had written it out of an "impulse in personal pique" is unlikely. For years, she had privately resented the acclaim his "prettinesses" got, while her "portfolio" poets' more genuine works were met with public indifference. Not that he would have cared. Celebrated as a poet not alienated and wild but well connected and decorous, Longfellow had already propelled himself ahead of Lydia Sigourney as the country's (and soon England's) most popular American bard. But after twice begging off reviewing his collections, citing the wide divergence between her views of poetry and that of "his school," she "reluctantly" (Greeley recalled) sat down to write a review of a new edition of a highly popular collection of Longfellow's poems.[31]

She raised the stakes with a virtual précis of her poetics. "Poetry is not a superhuman or supernatural gift," she wrote. Poetry is also diverse: apt imagery, metaphors, and cadences, she said, were present in all sorts of poetry, from that of "great bards" illuminating ideas and feelings buried in cultural consciousness to the "humblest minstrels" singing of nature down to the poetry of the "fireside" that merely kindled hearts. She required only two qualities: that the poetic vision be a "genuine" one—originating in actual observation—and that its expression be rooted in that vision. That was hard to do. Sounding a Romantic theme later developed by modernist critics of "mass culture," she said that as modern society's scramble for "rank and reputation" encouraged authors to gain attention by gimmicks and the superficial diffusion of knowledge, it also made their readers too aesthetically besotted to demand anything better. The result was a profusion of either sensational or sentimental writing: of "jingling rhymes, and dragging, stumbling rhythms" full of bombast, "or else an affected simplicity, sickly sentiment, or borrowed dignity" made insidious by the fact that the fake was often mixed together with a facsimile of the genuine. And that was exactly the case with Longfellow. His reputation depended not on the quality of his poems but "exaggerated praises" by publishers and hordes of "paid or undiscerning reviewers" who elevated his poems far beyond their worth, while a naïve public, little acquainted with foreign literature, liked his poems because they thought they got with them Old World sophistication. Finally, there was no inoculation against this danger because no one was providing an adequate formal critique of his poetry, including his detractors. Skewering at once Longfellow and Poe, who had been relentlessly hurling charges of plagiarism at him, Fuller wrote with devastating irony: "We have been surprised that any one should have been anxious to fasten special charges of this kind upon him, when we had supposed it so obvious that the greater part of his mental stores were derived from the works of others."[32]

To show that Longfellow had no style of his own growing out of his experiences and observations, either of nature or of the passions within, she hoisted him on his own metaphors. His "perpetual borrowing of imagery, this excessive, because superficial, culture" corrupted the basic elements of his poetry, as shown in his constantly artificial, inapt, and badly mixed images. Of the poet's flower invocations in his "Prelude" as he sought the woodlands while "musing upon many things," she laughed: "Musing upon many things—ay! and upon many books too or we should have nothing of Pentecost or bishop's caps with their golden rights. For ourselves, we have not the least idea what bishop's caps are;—are they flowers?—or what? Truly, the schoolmaster was abroad in the woodlands that day!" Concluding, she tried to be generous, pointing out a few of his affecting poems and noting his value as a "teacher to the people" of great works and his careful devotion to the craft of writing, but her final judgment was as damning as her one on Lowell. "Twenty years hence," critics would see him not as the giant that reviewers now took him for, but "as a writer of elegant, if not always accurate taste, of great imitative power, and occasional felicity . . . where his feelings are really stirred." As with Lowell, her prediction was only off by sixty years.[33]

Fuller's review caused a storm in literary America. It unsurprisingly aroused howls of protest in Boston. Longfellow himself, of course, was not pleased. "Miss Fuller makes a furious assault upon me in the New York Tribune," he scribbled in his journal. "It is what might be called 'a bilious attack.' She is a dreary woman." Even some Transcendentalist fellow travelers reacted nervously. "Her remarks on Longfellow," Sarah Helen Whitman wrote to a friend, "however just in the main were in manner & spirit most ungracious." A few years later, Emerson, who worried about her severe verdicts on Longfellow and Lowell, "two writers of such respectable ability," would urge Greeley to omit the reviews from her collected works. At the beginning of the next century, even her admiring biographer Higginson would lament her attack on the author who had established American authorship in the "literary courts of the civilized world." New Yorkers of all critical stripes, on the other hand, were impressed and pleased. "Did you see Margaret Fuller's notice of Longfellow in the Tribune?" the literary Whig Charles Fenno Hoffman excitedly asked his colleague Rufus Griswold, "an admirably done thing so far as pointing out his deficiencies." Duyckinck and other Young Americans were rapturous, although the Longfellow-obsessed Poe was even more enthusiastic. "The review did her infinite credit," he would write a few months later in his New York Literati sketch; "it was frank, candid, independent," noting as well its admirable balance (something not much noticeable in his own attacks on the poet). "In my opinion," he declared, presumably excepting his own, "it is one of the very few reviews of Longfellow's poems, ever published in America, of which the critics have not had abundant reason to be ashamed." Neither her boosters nor her detractors, however, got the cultural points of her demolition: to strike a blow against ersatz high culture to preserve readers' appreciation for the real article and to slow the ascendancy of an official literature that she thought could never deliver serious recognition in the literary *republics* of the "civilized world."[34]

IV

Alluding to her theory that the bad drove out the "excellent" by dulling the public's capacity for discerning the difference, Fuller wrote in her review, "Such works as Mr. Longfellow's we consider injurious only if allowed to usurp the place of better things." But what were those "better things"? If the country's older Romantics were fast fading, its sentimentalists mostly wan, and its leading literati not leading, who or what did she look to beneath America's "official" literary culture for the seeds of its later flowering she so confidently predicted? The broadest answer would have to be a Romantically informed literary "democracy." It is true that, given the right provocation, she remained as ready as ever to blast the country's popular culture. (In a review of a grammar book, she blamed the English language's "degradation" on, successively, "uncultivated" immigrants, slang-spewing businessmen, and unrefined housewives.) If one thinks, however, of a literary democrat not as a cheerleader of the given culture but as a critical encourager of avant-garde literary tastes and practices that she hoped would vitalize a potentially popular literature, then the label fit. Certainly, she knew in a modern capitalist democracy there was no alternative: without princes and nobles to patronize literature and the arts, she said in "American Literature," "here is only the public." She rested her cultural hopes on two current social "symptoms." One was society's current spirit of reform, although, she quickly added, before it could produce poets, it needed to "penetrate beneath the springs of action." The other was the widespread

felt need to be "even sternly sincere," not in the later attenuated Victorian sense
of honesty or frankness but in the Romantic meaning of integrity or authenticity.
"No man can be absolutely true to himself, eschewing cant, compromise, servile
imitation, and complaisance," she wrote in one review, "without becoming original, for there is in every creature a fountain of life which, if not choked back by
stones and other dead rubbish, will create a fresh atmosphere, and bring to life
fresh beauty. And it is the same with the nation as with the individual man." In
short, she assumed what she and Emerson had at the *Dial*: if individuals would
become, unlike Longfellow, authentic observers of life within and without, they
would collectively create a "fresh atmosphere" conducive to the birth of an original American literature.[35]

In her "American Literature" essay and several reviews, Fuller also demonstrated what Emerson did not: the democratic possibilities for that prescription in
the era's popular print culture. She approached it gingerly. She decried the "system of cheap publication" driven by new print technologies and the piracy of
English books, which so reduced royalties that only a handful could afford to
practice professional authorship and even those to write only what would immediately sell. She totally ignored lurid reform pamphlets, religious tracts, crime
novels, and other texts that literary historians have claimed "subverted" the middle-
class literature of sentimentality but that she no doubt would have considered
formulaic and (in a favorite word) "vulgar." In one impish article on Congress's
recent halving of the postal rate on letters, she tossed out enough skeptical barbs
at railroads, itinerant lecturers, and garrulous letter writers to have satisfied the
progress-skeptic Thoreau. Yet, unlike mid-twentieth-century critics of mass culture, she was hopeful about mitigating the tendency of the print revolution toward
superficiality and conformity. Like her Young America allies, she thought an international copyright law would raise authors' incomes and so make them more
willing to take unconventional risks in their writing. In her survey she also found
promise in her new profession as a venue for the "life of intellect." The new electric telegraph gave reporters more time to arrange and interpret the news, while
the need for brevity, rather than just encouraging the rushed and fragmentary, made
the newspaper a perfect repository for condensed essays, short stories, and even
lyric poetry. Most important, since one could not fully explain or revise, it encouraged sincerity and spontaneity in a new national "conversation." "Newspaper
writing is next door to conversation," she explained, "and should be conducted
on the same principles. It has this advantage: we address, not our neighbour, who
forces us to remember his limitations and prejudices, but the ideal presence of
human nature as we feel it ought to be and trust it will be. We address America
rather than Americans." Even Emerson would likely have been impressed with
that democratic Transcendentalist magic.[36]

Her primary medium for that, though, remained books, and in her American
literature survey and her *Tribune* reviews, she foraged for them in her two Romantic categories. One was the writings of "sincere" authors. Sometimes they
revealed, like ballads hawked in the streets, the latent aesthetic impulses in the
popular culture as a polished work never could, and sometimes they simply gave

an impression of a fact, refreshing when the fear of public opinion and the sprit of imitation made so much literature hackneyed or vapid. "It is thus that an American literature may grow up," she wrote in an early review of a young author's simple poetic "transcript" of his interests, "if men will write of what is rooted in their real lives, instead of copies from foreign models or ideals which rest only on the clouds above them." Contrasting the *Narrative of the Life of Frederick Douglass* with the "torrid energy and saccharine fulness" found in an Afro-European author like Dumas, she praised Douglass's memoir of "action and resistance" for precisely the opposite virtues: its controlled realism. ("Unspeakably affecting is the fact that he never saw his mother at all by day-light.") With Melville's first novel, *Typee*, she even took on something of her author's sardonic spirit. Applauding his "quick and arch manner," she cheekily invited ladies' sewing societies to read his jaundiced portrayal of Sandwich Island Protestant missionaries—which had enraged the evangelical press—before proceeding in their missionary fundraising. They would find his novel "the very book they wish to have read while assembled at their work," because the hero's ribald escapades with the "lovely" Fayaway—which aroused reviewers' ire almost as much as his send-up of missionaries—would remind them of Othello and Desdemona! Evidently, sincerity did not exclude irony.[37]

She found it considerably harder to discover American literary "geniuses" who authored self-reflexive works of "re-production" and illumination. The writers whom later modernist critics would canonize were barely visible on the horizon. Melville's *Typee* gave only a few hints, Thoreau would not publish his first book for another three years, Hawthorne had published none of his major novels, and Whitman was still grinding out sentimental tales and swaggering pro–Mexican War editorials for his *Brooklyn Daily Eagle* readers. One might think she would have found some such works among her Transcendentalist and new Young America colleagues who aspired to them, but contrary to Lowell and Poe, who complained she puffed them, she did not. She commended the Young Americans Headley, Simms, and Mathews for their exuberant vivacity, but she faulted them for their bombast. In her survey she applauded her ex-*Dial* Ellery Channing for dispensing with "customary" phrases and rhymes in order to tap into the inward flow of his mind, but her criticisms of his "frequently unfinished and obscure" poems and perverse diction were as blunt as Emerson's. On Emerson she registered in her survey a verdict as mixed as her first one in the *Tribune*. His poems, which thus far had appeared only in Transcendentalist journals, she rated high for their melody and subtle beauty but found them largely "philosophical" rather than affecting and with imagery that "wears a symbolical air." However, she rendered a generous judgment on him as a lecturer and essayist. Dispensing with her earlier caveats, she pronounced him a "profound thinker" who dealt with "causes rather than effects" yet illustrated them with a wealth of refined observations whose "melodic and subtle fragrance enchant those who stand stupefied before the thoughts themselves, because their utmost depths do not enable them to sound his shallows." Alone among her literary comrades, Emerson had prophetic power, which his lack of popularity could not hide.[38]

Of the remainder of the modernists' canon she wrote astutely. Of Poe she was a little skeptical, although not, like his legion of Whig critics, because of his dissolute behavior or supposedly cold stories. Although rightly praising him as a fellow opponent of the "system of mutual adulation and organized puff" (*his* puffs were neither usually mutual nor organized), she advised him to mix in with his valuable "severe criticism" a little "Affirmative" apprehension of writers' purposes and mingled virtues and vices, mischievously noting a few of his own poor word choices and "vulgar" images. As a poet and short story writer, however, she found Emerson's "jingle man" very impressive. The power of many of the poems in his collection *The Raven and Other Poems* derived, she happily observed in one review, from his expression not in "pronounced forms" but of a single mood through a harmonious "sweep of images, thronging and distant like a procession of moonlight clouds on the horizon." In her review of Poe's more acclaimed *Tales*, she mixed avant-garde solidarity with literary appreciation. Calling them a refreshing contrast to the "degenerated" junk in popular magazines, she argued that the power of his tales of terror, which Lowell complained lacked "household and fireside charm," lay in their organic form and subtle psychology: "They are the fruit of genuine observations and experience, combined with an invention, which is not 'making up,' as children call *their* way of contriving stories, but a penetration into the causes of things which leads to original and credible results. His narrative proceeds with vigor, his colors are applied with discrimination, and where the effects are fantastic they are not unmeaningly so." Her Romantic friendliness even led her to suggest that next time he try writing a higher "metaphysical novel," where he could explore his themes more thoroughly. Metamorphosing into a German metaphysical symbolist, however, was one Romantic trick this ambitious magazinist and agnostic mystic would (and probably could) *not* perform.[39]

At the beginning of the summer of 1846, shortly after composing her "American Literature" survey, she wrote an admiring review of another dark Romantic author whom she pronounced unhesitatingly "the best writer of the day." The following month she would expose her preference for "dark disclosures" of the hearts of intellectual types in her notice of her old youthful favorite, the nearly forgotten Charles Brockden Brown, whose recently reprinted gothic intellectual thrillers *Wieland* and *Ormond* she tried to revive. In her review of Hawthorne's *Mosses from an Old Manse*, she developed her point more boldly. Dispensing with her earlier misgivings about his bloodless characters, she singled out the very stories that modern critics have proclaimed as among his strongest—"The Birth Mark," "Rappaccini's Daughter," "The Artist of the Beautiful," "Young Goodman Brown," and, her favorite, "Roger Malvin's Burial." Fuller also grasped the central point about Hawthorne that Melville would make in his famous review of the writer's collection four years later: that his power derived not from gentle humor and quaint refinement, as appreciative critics like Longfellow fancied, but from his deep insight into the blackness of the human heart. In two ways she even went beyond Melville. First, she noted Hawthorne's fascination with the un-Melvillean theme of female psychology. Second, her characterization of Hawthorne's "delicate but fearless scrutiny" of the "familiar, yet pensive sense of the spiritual or demoniacal influences that haunt the palpable life and common walks of men" probably captured better than the thunderous Melville did the subtly uncanny tone in many of Hawthorne's stories. Third, in addressing his central vocational problem—his inability to gain a popular readership—she put forward not, as Melville would in his review of *Mosses*, the idea of a writer of "genius" writing simultaneously for two audiences, but a more hopeful diagnosis and remedy.[40]

The problem Hawthorne faced, Fuller wrote, was not the country's commercialism but its underdevelopment. "The immense extent of country over which the reading (still very small in proportion to the mere working) community is scattered, the rushing and pushing of our life at this electrical stage of development, leave no work a chance to be speedily and largely known that is not trumpeted and placarded." The answer, then, was not less but *more* "forced and artificial circulation." "Bad books will not be read if they are bought instead of good," she wrote—contradicting her fear of precisely that in her Longfellow review—"while the good have an abiding life in the log-cabin settlements and Red River steamboat landings, to which they would in no other way penetrate." And this was where a series like Duyckinck's that published *Mosses* came in: "Under the auspices of Wiley & Putnam, Hawthorne will have a chance to collect all his own public about him, and that be felt as a presence which before was only a rumor." Hawthorne undoubtedly appreciated the happy prediction even if it ran counter to his own fears that the popular genteel scribblers would drive darkly truth-telling authors like himself and Melville out of the market.[41]

"We love our country well," Fuller wrote in her fall 1845 essay on Renaissance Italian poets, even as she recited a litany of its failings to live up to its vaunted liberal ideals. Such "connected" criticism—invoking society's shared values to critique its practice—characterized much of her best criticism. More thoroughly and consistently than any antebellum critic, including after Fuller the two best, the slashing Poe and the uplifting Edwin Percy Whipple, she relentlessly projected a cosmopolitan national literary vision transcending both the boastful provincialisms of strident nationalists and the borrowed gentilities of their cosmopolite opponents. Something of this dialectic also drove her three leading critical methods: her conception of organic but autonomous aesthetic forms, her "apprehensive" interpretations and "comprehensive" standards of judgment, and her belief in literature's high moral and spiritual purpose. A similar double-sightedness animated the key cultural tensions of her criticism as well: her "prophetic" intimations and present-day sightings, her appreciation of both avant-garde authorship and democratic reception, and her canon of original American works from both Romantic children of light and of darkness, which was not formulated again until the work of the modern canonizers of the "American Renaissance" a century later. Finally, if Fuller, who left only sketches of her critical system, sometimes left her multiple categories more open and undeveloped than connected, that was not necessarily a bad or, perhaps, avoidable thing. What else, after all, *but* "multitudes" could contain such an emergent trope as "America," as Whitman would announce it nine years after tearing out a copy of Fuller's "American Literature" to save. Nor would any of her theories and criticisms have worked so

plausibly without her integrity, courage, sympathy, and high prospective pre-
science—unmatched in American criticism before the twentieth century.[42]

<h1 style="text-align:center">V</h1>

While Fuller was writing her literary criticism from the winter of 1845 to the summer of 1846, she was also producing social, cultural, and political criticism for
the *Tribune*. Although recent scholars have overlooked the former, which established her national and international reputation, they have rightly called attention
to the latter, even if they do not seem sure how to interpret it ideologically. Certainly, it was not negligible. Starting with her first winter's pieces on New York's
benevolent and reformatory institutions, such work eventually made up nearly a
third of her columns. This would seem a radical turnabout for a "born literary
woman" who, apart from "The Great Lawsuit," had never published a political
word in a periodical. Of course, she had done so in *Summer* and *Woman*. And she
liked the immediate impact some of her ideological pieces had. "The merit of such
things is for the day," she wrote Nathan her first summer, but, she happily noted,
they attracted "a good deal of attention."[43]

Fuller's biggest challenge was finding familiar Romantic forms and stances
appropriate to these subjects and to her newspaper. She seems to have found that
easy enough with the liberal religious and science books that came across her desk,
which she largely censured or praised according to how much dogmatic "cant" or
"poetic" discernment she found in them. "It is not as a seer of ghosts," she quipped
in a review of several new books on Swedenborgianism, "but as a seer of truths
that Swedenborg interests us." She also toed her Transcendentalist line in her reviews of health reform tracts, which aimed, she said, at treating not just physical
symptoms but also remote and inward influences. She likewise appraised books
on "animal magnetism" and "clairvoyance" much as she had Kerner's *Seeress of
Prevorst*, condemning alike credulous enthusiasts and rationalistic scientists who
dogmatically refused to investigate the "super-sensual element." She had no doubt
that once all these psycho-physical "facts," from metaphysics and chemistry to
phrenology and mesmerism, were sufficiently accumulated, they would presage
a new revolution in human consciousness.[44]

She also found social possibilities in art music. As during her first winter, she
wrote little formal criticism, but compared with the puffs and slashes of the city's
often bribed hack music reviewers, her notices were beams of critical light. Her
chief purpose, though, was a Romantic cultural one: to entice her readers, almost
exclusively attached to "sacred" or "entertaining" programming, as most Americans would be for at least another generation, to appreciate that only art music
could "animate, expand, and elevate our life," which was still mired in "dogmatic
theology" or a "coarse utilitarianism." As in Boston, she continued to address matters of musical production and reception, although with a greater practical sense.
As always, she remained a stickler for insulating art music's repertoire from the
pressures of the market. Impresarios should never "flatter" the public's musical

taste "for the sake of money or success." And, as she had said in her first music reviews, orchestras should cease their ridiculously promiscuous programming. Popular ditties and Italian arias, she said, were "well enough in their place," but inserting them, as was often done, in the middle of demanding compositions destroyed these works' aesthetic integrity and weakened listeners' ability to deeply experience them. She also berated audiences for not responding with sufficient appreciative applause. Even musical geniuses, she reminded her readers, "need the assurance of sympathy to fan into flame the coal of enthusiasm." In line with her increasing sensitivity to social conditions, she also suggested ways of making art music a more popular medium in America. Ticket prices needed to be as low as possible to bring in middle-class Americans of limited means   or (she added) excessive cheapness. For the working classes, she recommended the model of Liverpool's arts-conscious bankers and merchants, who financed concerts for the city's working classes. Indeed, for all her Romantic stringency, she was sure that if concerts were properly organized, with good translations, good programming, good playing, and, not least important in New York's stuffy halls, good air, ever-larger American audiences would embrace art music meant not only "to tickle the ear" but also to reach the "soul."[45]

Of a newer cast were her columns on public policy debates. The locale helped her. Unlike her "come-outer" Boston comrades, her Christian socialist, abolitionist, prison reform, and antipoverty New York colleagues had little problem with mixing it up in the grubby urban fray of institutional politics and partisan combat. And, of course, Greeley, the epitome of that type, could have used these pieces. He was just then embroiled in an intense newspaper war with his conservative Whig opponents over the propriety of his supposedly destructive association of their party with Fourierism, Land Reform, antislavery, anti–capital punishment, and other radical causes. Naturally, Fuller's efforts pleased him. "She is the most thoroughly learned woman on this continent, and of capacious intellect," he crowed to Schuyler Colfax, the later vice president, who had asked him who the "*" of the Tribune" was. "Look for a shining she is to give [the conservative Whigs] soon."[46]

That summer her "shinings" started appearing. Like the good republican patriot she was, she wrote off as a model for "endangered America" "bankrupt Europe" ("for surely nations are so who have not known how to secure peace, education, or even bodily sustenance for the people at large"). Like Greeley, she also eschewed the class resentments that New York's left-wing Democrats trafficked in. Most of all, she wholeheartedly endorsed Greeley's creed of responsible but committed journalism. She was proud to think that their paper's "first object" was to ascertain and report "the Truth," she wrote the following spring. If the facts were unclear, however, "it will always be most anxious to favor the weaker side with the means of utterance." Yet Fuller was no mouthpiece for Greeley's politics. Her first year she wrote respectfully, as in Boston, of socialist principles but skeptically about their relevance to America, where, as she put it, the absence of "authorized despotism" and "pervasive evils" naturally encouraged "private conservatism." She likewise steered clear of her editor's partisan Whiggery. After Andrew Jackson's death that summer, which provoked from Greeley a vitriolic anti-Jackson diatribe, she even found a good Transcendentalist word to say about Old Hickory: his "boldly sincere . . . straightforwardness may help others to a higher, wiser, larger independence of their own." On poverty, she also carved out her own distinct cultural niche. Largely ignoring material conditions, which Greeley, Child, and even Poe reported in their urban exposés, she expressed instead righteous fury at upper-class treatment of the poor. In her acrid "Prevalent Idea that Politeness is too great a Luxury to be given to the Poor," she recounted how a well-dressed woman had spoken rudely to a ragged and tearful boy who was holding an infant on a ferryboat. No one had the integrity to say to her, "'Your vulgarity is unendurable; leave the place or alter your manner.'" "Vulgarity" was the original sin: "For no one can suppose in such cases the offending party has really enjoyed the benefit of refined education and society." Its antidote was "feeling" and behavior: treating the lower classes with neither "vulgar abruptness" nor "condescending liveliness" but "with that genuine respect which a feeling of equality inspires." Charity workers should be, she said, quoting an "excellent" minister to the poor (probably Channing), "'horsewhipped'" for quizzing the poor about their habits in their homes.[47]

Her most inventive ideological recasting, beginning that summer, appeared in her treatments of the erupting controversy over European immigrants. With nearly 50 percent of its population foreign-born, about half of them Irish, another quarter German, and the rest mostly English, French, and Italian, New York had by far the greatest and fastest growing concentration of immigrants in the nation. It also had its fastest growing nativist movement. Just the previous year the publisher James Harper and the new anti-immigrant American Republican Party had captured the mayoralty and Common Council, before Democrats regained them in the 1845 elections. At first, she had sounded more like a cautious Whig than her liberal editor, who regularly denounced nativism and actively courted foreign voters. "Too many have come since for bread alone," she had written in her "New Year's Day" essay. "We cannot blame—we must not reject them, but let us teach them. . . . Yes! let us teach them, not rail at their inevitable ignorance and unenlightened action, but teach them and their children as our own."[48]

Fuller did not stay on her patronizing perch for long. She started attending meetings of European exiles and, more important, reading the city's Italian, French, Spanish, and especially German immigrant newspapers and translating excerpts from them for the *Tribune*. Within a month, in an article hailing the new weekly edition of the radical *Deutsche Schnellpost*, whose editor, Wilhelm Eichtal, she had gotten to know when he had occupied offices in the destroyed *Tribune* building, she offered an exuberant take on America's new immigrants. Ignoring the two main nineteenth-century antinativist programs—immigrants' wholesale assimilation into a republican-Protestant "American" culture or ethnic toleration as long as it bolstered the capitalist economy or the urban Democratic Party—she urged instead a new America.

> We do want that each nation needs to hear from those of her compatriots, able to
> guide and enlighten them. We do want that each nation should preserve what is

valuable in its parent stock. We want all the elements of the new people of the new world. We want the prudence, the honor, the practical skill of the English; the fun, the affectionateness, the generosity of the Irish; the vivacity, the grace, the quick intelligence of the French; the thorough honesty, the capacity for philosophic view, and deep enthusiasm of the German Biedermann; the shrewdness and romance of the Scotch; but we want none of their prejudices. We want the healthy seed to develop itself into a different plant, in the new climate. We have reason to hope a new and generous race, where the Italian meets the Dutch, the Swede the Jew. Let nothing be obliterated, but all regenerated.[49]

To appreciate the radicalism of Fuller's position, one needs to set aside presentist nervousness about all ethnic generalizations. She was clearly not a twentieth-century cultural "pluralist," suggesting, as Horace Kallen would in the 1920s (and many of his "multiculturalist" descendants later in the century), that the United States was a conglomeration of equally valid and separate ethnic cultural enclaves. Rather she was invoking a social cosmopolitan nationalism that served as a counterpart to her literary one. On the one hand, America's liberal national identity required that "all" immigrants become "regenerated": "We want all this new blood, but we want it purified, assimilated, or it will take all form of comeliness from the growing nation." On the other hand, America's "comeliness" was hardly something already achieved but, on the contrary, would require the regeneration of (as she said) *native* "souls . . . re-born here." Rather than needing to relinquish all of their distinctiveness to become "Americanized," these new arrivals, she argued, had cultural capital to contribute to that national regeneration, coming not only from northern and western Europe but also from the ongoing nationalist revolutionary movements in eastern and southern Europe. In an article later in the winter, reviewing a recent meeting she attended at Stuyvesant Institute celebrating the anniversary of the defeated Polish Revolution of 1830–31, Fuller even highlighted the potential *superior* aptness of European democratic nationalism for a new transnational America. After contrasting the "noisy" caucus oratory of the Democratic lawyer Theodore Sedgwick with the heartfelt speeches of the émigré Italian, Polish, and Swedish speakers, she praised an Italian speaker's "beautiful" Tuscan-accented argument for "Nationality" as humankind's necessary "Individualism" *and* "fellow-feeling" writ large. "May the same fervor of heart be turned to forward the good of the adopted land, for where there is genius, greatness and religion, blooms anew the true Italy, the garden of the world!" America as a "garden of the world" containing the "true Italy": a decade before Whitman sang of a "nation of nations" and three-quarters of a century before Randolph Bourne gave his modernist plea for a reconfigured "Trans-national America," Fuller sounded her Romantic call for a multiethnic liberal cosmopolitan patriotism.[50]

This patriotic vision did not necessarily fall on fertile soil, as Fuller discovered in two political encounters toward the end of her first year in New York. During the summer of 1845 she wrote two articles on the city's largest, poorest, and most disparaged of America's immigrant groups, just then numerically exploding in New York with the onset of Ireland's great potato famine. The charges against the Irish were endless. Evangelical Protestants reviled them as Catholic shock troops threatening to extend popery. African Americans feared them because they took away their laboring and service jobs. Whigs despised them for voting overwhelmingly Democratic. And abolitionists reviled them for their antiblack racial prejudices. (Dismissing Maria Weston Chapman's proposal to mobilize New York's Irish around a dual struggle against British imperialism and southern slavery, Child sniffed, "Voting and beating are all the *moral* agencies they have any idea of.") Since first seeing them the previous summer in Concord, however, Fuller had found them charming, especially in their love of conversation, which she likened to her own. A guest of the Greeleys would report that their old Irish cook had expressed astonishment to her that she had never seen Fuller. "Didn't you ever hear her talk?" the Irishwoman asked. "No," the woman answered again. "Well, I pity ye, for she did talk most beautiful!"[51]

Fuller's articles on the Irish were nothing if not sympathetic. In "The Irish Character," she dismissed nativist claims that the "race" was uniquely ignorant and politically pliant as calumnies, or, if sometimes true, an inevitable consequence of the discrimination they faced. By contrast, "their virtues are their own;—they are many, genuine, and deeply rooted," including, she listed, domestic fidelity, financial generosity, poetic eloquence, and, most of all, "indefatigable good humor, (for ages of wrong, which have driven them to so many acts of desperation, could never sour their blood at its source)." "They are at bottom," she declared, "one of the best nations of the world." Her second article was a response to subsequent letters she got from readers who inundated her with their bad experiences with the Irish as employees. "Just heaven," she cried, speaking of the common complaint from employers of Irish "ingratitude," as *they* were the ones who ought to be grateful for all the opportunities afforded *them* and not their servants, who were constantly preached to with "the cry 'all men born free and equal'" yet were still inured in poverty with only "crumbs" from their master's table. Even more ridiculous, she said, was the charge of Irish laborers' disloyalty because they often quit their jobs: how absurd for the most mobile people on earth to deny to the Irish this estimable way of getting acquainted with their new society! As for employers' complaint about their Irish employees lying to them, why would the Irish *not* be tempted to a little "prevarication" now and then when their urban businessman and housewife employers had nothing to do with them other than issuing instructions. Finally, on the Irish workers' supposedly terrible "Catholic Priesthood," she said priests were the only friends in authority these poor people had. Besides, as their parishioners came to be influenced by American democratic culture, they would inevitably demand that their priests serve their interests more than the Church and so gradually become, as then in Germany, indistinguishable from their Protestant colleagues. If Protestant employers wanted to develop their employees' character, they should integrate their domestic servants into their families. Such a "great patriotic work" of "mutual education," she said, invoking her journalistic motto, was really "mutual insurance."[52]

Not everyone was happy with her defense. The following week, the Irish-American activist John O'Connor wrote an ideologically baiting letter to the *Tribune*. Instead of refuting employers' claims about Irish domestics' ingratitude and lying, he

wrote, she admitted them, asking only they be treated lovingly, "which pre-
suppose the complete establishment of Association, or the advent of the New
Jerusalem." Indeed, he added, she seemed to think that Irish peasants should be
grateful that they lived in politically democratic America rather than still slaving
away as peasants on the estate of some English lord. "Unfortunately those poor
people," he wrote sarcastically, "know little about theories of the Rights of Man,
or, what is more deplorable, no doubt—of the Rights of Woman," or, he added
gratuitously, of the "transcendentalism" of his "*starry* friend." In reply, Fuller
ignored O'Connor's knowing barbs and insisted on her liberal democratic bona
fides. Her article's entire point, she said, was to demonstrate the *groundlessness*
of *all* objections to social improvement in the Irish on the grounds of their sup
posed ingratitude, which was inevitable, even in some cases commendable, in light
of the treatment they received. She knew that selfish employers, overrating the
benefits they conferred, often slander *all* laborers as ingrates. And this was because they were incapable of "doing as they would be done by—a rule transcendental in most men's eyes, and yet proposed by the head of the European and
American church as the only safe practical one for all men." In short, amelioration came not from group power but a categorical imperative of "mutual" rights
and recognition. Greeley could not have put the ethical core of his "Associationism" better.[53]

Fuller's exchange with O'Connor, though, revealed something else about her
politics besides its ethical idealism: however much Fuller detested American
Anglo-Saxon ethnocentrism, she remained convinced of America's sociopolitical
superiority. This became apparent several months later when she confronted a
representative of the better educated German Americans in the Lower East Side's
Kleindeutscheland, who were also often the object of nativist hostility, in their
case because of their often radical politics and easygoing love of Sunday public
drinking and entertainments. (A few years earlier a nativist gang had assaulted a
group of Germans who were serenading Fanny Elssler outside her hotel.) The figure was the young German émigré Hermann Kriege. A former member of Karl
Marx's communist circle and now a fierce supporter of the Land Reform movement and the editor of the new newspaper *Der Volks-Tribun*, Kriege would soon
be denounced by Marx's group for abandoning communism and the class struggle
for "slobbering" humanitarianism and free farms. To Fuller, however, Kriege's
hodgepodge of watered-down communism and Land Reform sounded dreadful.
In her review of the *Volks-Tribun*'s first issue, she indicated she had great respect
for its German craft worker readers and placed herself on the "'extreme left' of
the army of Progress," but she strongly objected to its class-war talk about "rich
oppressors" and their professional lackeys. "The spirit of defiance and haste exhibited by the *Volks-Tribun* is not the spirit for Young America," she declared,
invoking the decade's popular slogan, recently appropriated by Kriege's Land
Reform ally the western homestead advocate George Henry Evans for his newspaper. "She needs it not.—She only needs a deep intelligence of principles, a religious devotion to them in practice, and all things would be [hers]." She was
especially taken aback by Kriege's unwillingness to grant *anything* good about

America. "We cannot wonder, Germans," she wrote patronizingly, "if, having
thrown off so heavy and galling a harness, you fume and champ to find the bit
still in your mouths; yet let this impatience be transient, and prize more justly
and deeply the vast privileges you have already attained. Seek to extend them,
to complete and elevate their scope—but let it be with deep, earnest conviction
and well-considered acts, and not with heat and abuse." Fuller's idealistic tropes
of "transcendental" principles, "mutual" education, and national promise remained
the rock-solid ballasts of her liberal Romantic politics.[54]

VI

By the end of the summer of 1845, two ideological winds were weakening that
stability for Fuller. One was coming in from across the Atlantic. Notwithstanding
her upbraiding of Kriege for chomping at an imaginary class bit, she was becoming interested in the recent upsurge of socialist sentiment on the Continent. In
August, just a week after dismissing "bankrupt Europe," she translated a long essay
by the *Deutsche Schnellpost*'s Paris correspondent Heinrich Börnstein, a former
comrade of Marx, Friedrich Engels, and Arnold Ruge, whose circle two years later
would found the League of the Communists. With this translation of Börnstein's
cogent summary of the positions of Europe's various factions of "humanists,"
"socialists," and "communists," she very likely gave the first account in an American periodical of Marx and Engels's revolutionary program for extending the
French Revolution's ideal of "abstract" political equality into full economic and
social equality. More remarkable, in light of the antistrike views of her editor (who
dissociated the *Tribune*'s Fourierism from the German correspondent's formulations), she appended Börnstein's report on a recent strike of five thousand jour-
neyman carpenters in Paris. "The new era is not far off," she prophesied. "The
new era, when the laborer shall be thought worthy of his hire, and every man
entitled to express the wants that consume him, and ask relief from the cares that
now harass so many from the cradle to the grave." Although neither her sympathy
nor her translation meant Fuller much understood the specter of "communism"
haunting Germany and France, she at least felt its distant winds sufficiently to
pay homage to its expectant call.[55]

The other political storm on Fuller's horizon was that over Texas annexation.
Despite her recent tributes to abolitionism and her first winter's spate of anti-Texas
editorials, that summer she was still optimistically telling her readers that all the
country needed to stop the proslavery juggernaut were a "few men" of "eternal"
principles able to think and act in the spirit of the revolutionary founders. Indeed,
she publicly criticized the Garrisonians' come-outer rejection of cooperation with
all insufficiently antislavery parties and privately winced at their "tedious" mono-
mania and "rabid and exaggerated" tone, especially that of their leader. "We look
upon him with high respect," she wrote in her review of Douglass's autobiography, but unlike Douglass, who knew how to "allow for motives and influences,"
Garrison "has indulged in violent invective and denunciation till he has spoiled
the temper of his mind. Like a man who has been in the habit of screaming him-

self hoarse to make the deaf hear, he can no longer pitch his voice on a key agreeable to common ears." Humane rhetoric remained politically important.[56]

Yet, as the date approached for implementing the annexation bill that President Tyler had signed two days before leaving office, her pronouncements grew
increasingly alarmed. "The most shameful deed has been done that ever disgraced
a nation; because the most contrary to consciousness of right," she thundered in
her article "First of August, 1845," commemorating the anniversary of Britain's
abolition of slavery in the West Indies. "Other nations have done wickedly," she
explained with liberal cosmopolitan indignation. "But we have surpassed them
all in trampling under foot the principles that had been assumed as the basis of
our national existence and our willingness to forfeit our honor in the face of the
world." Meanwhile, Fuller's public criticisms of the Garrisonians ceased, as it
suddenly became obvious to her that more political pressure was needed to ward
off a national moral calamity than that afforded by just a "few men" of "eternal"
principles. "All is not yet lost," she declared. "There is here a faithful band determined to expiate the crimes that have been committed in the name of Liberty."
By the start of the year she was echoing the abolitionist line opposing compensation to slaveholders: "Nobody that needs a bribe shall be asked to further our
schemes for emancipation."[57]

Three days after President Polk on December 29 signed the congressional act
that made Texas a state, in her state-of-the-world editorial "1st January, 1846,"
she sketched an even grimmer picture of the moral miasma spreading throughout
the nation. "What a year it has been with us!" she exclaimed.

> Texas annexed, and more annexations in store; Slavery perpetuated, as the most
> striking new feature of these movements. Such are the fruits of American love of
> liberty! Mormons murdered and driven out, as an expression of American freedom
> of conscience. Cassius Clay's paper expelled from Kentucky; that is American free-
> dom of the press. And all these deeds defended on the true Russian grounds: "We
> (the stronger) know what you (the weaker) ought to do and be, and it *shall* be so."

Nor was it just a "lust of power" linking these illiberal acts; it was also greed:
"More money—more land! is all the watchword they know." With America's
founding pact virtually moribund, Europe looked not quite so "bankrupt." Indeed,
after barely mentioning any positive American markers—even abolitionism—but
finding "signs" of the future, filled with "providential meaning," in stirrings in
virtually every country in Europe, she highlighted as the single "trophy" of the
past year the spread of "Associative and Communist principles, both here and in
Europe." Noting their historical importance in reawakening the French Saint-
Simonian ferment of the early 1830s, she wrote: "Let the worldling deem as he
will about their practicability, he cannot deny [them] to be animated by faith in
God and a desire for the good of Man." And of the American nation in this coming democratic era?

> Altogether, it looks as if a great time was coming, and that time one of Democracy.
> Our country will play a ruling part. Her Eagle will lead the van, but whether to soar
> upward to the sun or to stoop for helpless prey, who now dares promise? At present

she has scarce achieved a Roman nobleness, a Roman liberty, and whether her Eagle is less like the Vulture and more like the Phoenix than was the fierce Roman bird, we dare not say. May the New Year give hopes of the latter, even if the bird need first to be purified by fire.

With this sober look at Janus-faced American "Democracy," she implied a curious corollary: if America *were* to "lead the van," it would seem to need a good deal of purifying "fire" from abroad.[58]

That winter and spring of 1846 Fuller fired off some social democratic missiles of her own. "We cannot recall one great genius at this day living," she declared, converting her old lament into a radical prophecy. "The time of prophets is over, and the era they prophesied must be at hand; in its conduct a larger proportion of the human race shall take part than ever before." A few months later, commenting on an exchange over political labels between the liberal monarchist *Courrier des Etats Unis* and the democratic *Franco-Americain*, she said it was right to make a further sharp distinction between liberal republicanism and democracy. While "republican" denoted a mere governmental "form" that could include, as in Europe and Latin America, the rule of a privileged aristocracy or single dictator, she explained, "democrat" embraced not just "equality before the law" but also the "'power of the people'" and their greatest possible "happiness."[59]

Did Fuller's new democratic self-identifications cause her to embrace radically new class stances? Yes and no. She continued writing Dickensian portraits of resilient washerwomen and struggling children rather than anything on factory workers and their low wages and tenement housing that Greeley regularly exposed. In "The Rich Man—An Ideal Sketch," which the anarchistic Skaneateles community afterward reprinted in their journal *Communitist*, she looked at capitalism through the lens of a liberal Romantic social gospel. Her ideal "merchant" would accept Jesus' belief in the moral superiority of the poor and powerless and also shun fancy clothes and "foreign manners" in favor of libraries and art galleries, solid nearby houses for workers, and cultural festivals happily mixing farmers and craftsmen with artists and statesmen "to the benefit of both." Her follow-up to this Brook Farm–like fantasy, "The Poor Man—an Ideal Sketch" was less utopian but more anachronistic. After defining the "poor" as ranging from the "hodman and washerwoman" through the "hard-working, poorly paid lawyer, clerk, schoolmaster or scribe," she recommended a thin gruel of stoicism ("he must accept his lot, while he is in it") and vague Transcendentalist advice to mingle inner resources with actual labor.[60]

Yet by that winter Fuller was clearly striving to come to terms with what seems to have finally struck her as a new industrializing America of wretched poverty and working-class subordination. In a review of a tract on the wages of New York seamstresses and Catharine Beecher's *Duty of American Women*, she endorsed Beecher's plan for recruiting single eastern women for the West as a practical application of her *Woman* book's message of female self-reliance, but she rapped Beecher for assuming that only single women needed extradomestic sources of support. The "vast majority" of *married* working-class women, Fuller noted, both in Europe and now increasingly in America, "do not, CANNOT" have a protected domestic sphere free of extrahousehold labor. "Accursed is he who does not long," she cried in "The Poor Man," speaking of the slum-dwelling poor, "to take out at least the physical Hell from this world!" Meanwhile, she hinted at more to come, announcing her growing belief—espoused, she said, by the majority of "thinkers" today—in a "thorough" and "radical reform" of our "present social system" of "mere calculating, money-making"—a system that was making the "social fabric totter to decay."[61]

More important than declarations, the liberal *tone* of her columns on the working classes was becoming more class sensitive. Unlike agents of the newly founded New York Association for Improving the Condition of the Poor, who monitored their clients' morals in order to cull the "deserving" from the mass of "undeserving," Fuller displayed great compassion toward the poor's misfortunes, little criticism of their moral failings, and deepening suspicion of middle-class meddling. "We who do not share" their plight, she wrote, "have no right" to tell them how they should live their lives. At the same time, like Parker in his "Sermon of Merchants," delivered in Boston that same winter, she evidenced a new readiness to indict the un-Christian selfish rich *as a class*. She spoke disdainfully of "rhetorical gentlemen and silken dames" who loved to talk "as if Woman need to be fitted for no other chance than that of growing like a cherished flower in the garden of domestic love" while caring nothing about the washerwomen, seamstresses, and prostitutes they jostled in the streets. Nor did she exclude her Unitarians from these class sins. Later that summer of 1846 she wrote a searing article condemning Dewey's chic Unitarian Church of the Messiah as well as the fashionable Grace Church and Broadway Trinity Church for their blatantly anti-Christian exclusion of the poor through high pew rentals. To judge by the heated letters to the editor the piece elicited, her arrow seems to have pricked at least a few rich liberal consciences.[62]

The social miseries she most grappled with that winter and spring, however, remained those of outsiders whose stigmas she could identify with and her liberal Romantic ideology could easily speak to, if now in new aggressive political accents. One group was her old cause of prisoners and asylum inmates. In a review in February 1846 of the annual reports of Earle's institution and other "Moral Treatment" prisons and asylums, she enthused about the reports' statistics showing a dramatic upward curve of "cures" and declining incidents of inmate infractions. Like most antebellum psychiatric reformers, she glided over the specific "causes" of crime and insanity, speculating only that probably early mistreatment and the "semi-mania" of materialistic and competitive modern life played large roles. She even came out as a former mentally disturbed person herself, alluding to her collapse following her father's death by recalling how a certain person's youthful "intellectual race" had pushed her to a "dangerous crisis" until she was saved by the prescriptions of "thoughtless culture" of another reform psychiatrist, Amariah Brigham. Mainly, she called attention to the new breath of "genuine philanthropy" in the air, demonstrating that transformations of "soul" were not just the creations of poets or private loves but also of institutions and humanitarian feeling. Most important, these reports reflected a new moral sophistication about deviants. "Harsh bigots" may sneer at this new Jesus-like sympathy for the prodigal son as "'sickly sentimentality,'" but it was hardly that. "Those who have understood and obeyed the laws are . . . not afraid that sin will seem less hateful or less noxious," she wrote, "because it may be traced back to hereditary taint, bad education or corrupting influences of a half-civilized state."[63]

Many, of course, were afraid of exactly that, as she found out several weeks later, when she addressed the question of capital punishment, then receiving as much attention as antislavery. Going beyond past middle-class objections to the cruelty and disorder of public executions, perfectionist reformers in the 1840s called for outright abolition. They were especially influential in New York city. The Prison Association and prominent writers and editors, mostly from liberal Unitarian and Quaker backgrounds, including Fuller's colleagues Greeley, Bryant, Child, Godwin, and O'Sullivan, denounced executions as a barbaric relic that usurped God's prerogative and made a mockery of rehabilitative prison reform. A phalanx of often evangelical politicians, editors, and ministers, however, defended them as the cornerstone of a just society. At their forefront was George B. Cheever, the hyperbolic editor of the *New York Evangelist* and pastor of the Church of the Puritans, who flailed the abolition advocates with the same righteous vigor he applied to liquor distillers and slave-dealers. Earlier in the year he had teamed up with Tayler Lewis, the conservative Dutch Reformed minister and New York University professor of Greek, to publish the era's most notable pro–capital punishment book. In their *Defence of Capital Punishment*, they argued (as did most antebellum capital punishment supporters) that executions for murder were right, not merely because they served as deterrents, but because they were inherently just, as was proven by prescriptions in the Old Testament, as well as the "common-sense" reality of human depravity, moral responsibility, and God's just requirement of exact retribution. The authors laced their chapters with broad epithets against capital-punishment abolitionists, calling them "shallow," "mawkish," "cowardly, skulking, unmanly" souls who espoused a position embraced by "infidels" and "ruffian incendiaries."[64]

Mainly she used their book as an object lesson in how not to carry on a public discussion of a moral question. They believed that punishment's purpose was to strike fear in depraved transgressors, whereas she believed it should promote repentance, altered character, and, if possible, future good behavior. While both positions, even if resting on opposite theological positions about God and human nature, might shed light on such a complex question as punishment, the authors of *Defence of Capital Punishment* were obviously incapable of doing so. They were special pleaders, acute in details and the application of precedents, rules, and some scholarship, but completely lacking in broad views, thorough reasoning, and, most of all, insight into motives either in the individual or society. Fuller's most damning charge, though, was that their book had a "diabolical spirit," in that it seemed *calculated* to suppress rational and sincere debate by awakening fears and prejudices. "How the studied introduction and coupling together the names of Paine and Parker?" she demanded. "*Does* the writer here sincerely express any conviction in his mind?" Worse yet, they seemed to be out of touch with their own thought processes. "Who can believe that such passages as the following stand for any thing in the mind of the writer?" she asked, citing such assertions as Cain fearing capital punishment and liberal criminologists panting to "dive down" into the "drivelings of depravity in malefactors." Indeed, this last claim showed not only how authoritarian but also how psychologically obtuse such supposed believers in the darkness of the human heart really were. "We can only wish for such a man that the vicissitudes of life may break through the crust of theological arrogance and Phariseeism and force him to 'dive down' into the depths of his own nature.— We should see afterward whether he would be so forward to throw stones at male-factors, so eager to hurry souls to what he regards as a final account."[65]

Fuller's assault on the weak intellect and bad faith of the most prominent champions of capital punishment triggered a further polemical round. Two days later, Lewis declared in Raymond's *Courier and Enquirer* that her article had so provoked him that he promised to write a future column on the entire question of "infidelity." As for the author herself, he would hold his fire. Instead, he said, he would stick to the high "chivalrous course" rather than follow the "heroic philanthropists" of the "Tribune school," who had the "meanness and cowardice to skulk behind a female, . . . who, however personal and abusive she might be, could not, especially on such questions as these, be treated as a proper and legitimate adversary." "Yet she should know," he added, that the proper discussion of the question so rashly ventured upon, requires something more than . . . doing up the slop literature of The Tribune, or writing unmeaning rhapsodies on the unutterable ideas of Ole Bull, or repeating the cant and drivel of the Harbinger about Dante and Beethoven, or praising the chaste 'creations' of that most chaste and 'spiritual' creature, George Sand." Fuller was elated that Lewis confirmed so well her point about his incapacity to engage in a rational discussion. "We are not aware that the Bible, or the welfare of human beings were subjects improper for the consideration of 'females,' whether '*fair*' or otherwise," she wrote archly in her reply in the *Tribune*. "We had also supposed that, in the field of literature, the meeting was not between man and woman, but between mind and mind." Meanwhile, she advised "heroic philanthropists" who hid behind the petticoats of an unassailable female to take warning from his "chivalrous" rhetoric. She concluded by playing with Lewis's portentous announcement:

> We wait with interest the future developments of T. L. as to the nature and precise limits of infidelity. The tax of reading will no longer be too much for our "patience" as the articles are not to exceed a column in length, and, if feminine incapacity prevent some readers from doing justice to the thoughts, we trust they will still be able to appreciate the dignity and temper with which they may be expressed, and to transfer a portion of the value received into "slop literature" addressed to the use of the common reader.

If Fuller worried that, in the words of the magazinist Ann Stephens, she could not "strike back without unsexing herself," she did not betray the feeling here.[66]

Although Fuller enjoyed a clear win, thanks to Lewis's "chivalric" dogmatism, coming up with practical solutions to the suffering of racial outsiders proved harder. Reviewing Commodore Charles Wilkes's volumes on the United States South Sea

Island exploring expedition, soon to be mined for evidence of the inherent inferiority of savage "races," she noted that even "good and generous" civilizers invariably failed because of their gross *ignorance* of the "cultivated man as he stands." "Would you speak to a man, first learn his language!" she exclaimed, echoing her favorite Herder. Yet in her review of Thomas McKenney's *Memoirs*, her Romantic multiculturalism became a casualty to her desperation to have something done "NOW, or never" for the trans-Mississippi tribes, making her hesitantly endorse McKenney's plan for an Indian territorial government and future assimilation, which she had rejected in *Summer on the Lakes* as the fantasy of a "white thinker." She did better with antiblack racism. Complicating matters was the fact that she, too, had doubts, shared privately by most abolitionists, about "amalgamation," or miscegenation. The previous summer she had found herself flummoxed when Greeley got a letter from a supposedly conscience-stricken Kentucky slaveholder asking if they knew someone willing to take in a female mulatto slave's child to be "educated as white." She herself, she told the Lorings in her query to them about the case, had once wished "to try a half-breed" Indian and white child to test conventional objections to such unions. "It would, I think, be an interesting task to one who feels or wishes to settle doubts as to the tendencies of African blood, of Amalgamation &c." Fuller's quixotically highhanded curiosity evidently went nowhere, but her commitment to racial justice for blacks was growing. "These are the most unanswerable arguments in favor of the *capacities* of the African race," she wrote, reviewing the Garrisonians' *Liberty Bell for 1845,* which had included contributions from African Americans. "Their *claims* need no argument." Indeed, in an assertion that would shock her biographer Julia Ward Howe, she had written in her Douglass review that if a genuine mixing of African and European characteristics ever took place, it would give to human "genius" a "balance and harmony beyond what has been seen heretofore in the history of the world."[67]

That spring Fuller tried to help the civil rights cause in her own city. As racial tensions between African Americans and the newly arriving Irish were reaching a boiling point, abolitionists and many liberals in both parties urged that the summer state constitutional convention drop property requirements for black males—a barrier that had effectively kept all but a handful from voting. Into this roiling debate Fuller flung her only fictional sketch in the *Tribune*: "What Fits a Man to be a Voter? Is it to be White Within, or White Without?" A parable in the form of her old literary dialogues, it casts Jesus and Mary as perfectionist abolitionists and satirizes both dogmatic racists and utilitarian moderates who debate planting traditionally honored white yet moldy English walnuts alongside supposedly "ugly" black butternuts that when cracked open turn out to be fresh and white. Her allegory's cleverness, however, was not matched by the election results. The constitutional amendment was handily defeated in the fall in a statewide referendum by a margin of nearly three to one, with her city voting overwhelmingly against it.[68]

The defeat might be seen as emblematic of the enormous gap between Fuller's editorial eloquence and any political results, but also between the liberal generosity of her views and the temper of her times and place. Certainly, no major literary intellectual of her era engaged so widely and felt so deeply about such a broad spectrum of social issues defining antebellum democracy. Naïve about the effect of moral exhortation on the selfish rich, she was nonetheless shrewd about what it took to touch the consciences of the wealthy and privileged. Silent about the structural conditions of poverty and largely ignorant of the everyday lives of most kinds of workers, she yet displayed in rhetorically effective ways enormous sympathy for the most marginalized and suffering among them. Originally slow to embrace radical abolitionism, she yet grasped the psychological power of white racism, which many even in that movement made secondary to other sources of American slavery and Western expansionism. Devoted to individual self-culture as a way of social transformation, she yet came to embrace institutions attuned to that ideal. Finding in the America's founding ideals its past moral strength, she saw in its "new stocks" of immigrants the basis of its future. Committed to the highest cultural sophistication and creativity in a "utilitarian" and evangelical time and place where she thought them woefully weak, she yet imagined possibilities for a genuine "sincere" and imaginative culture for the working classes. Trained to address an intellectual elite, she yet learned the rough but "mutual" ways of democratic public discourse.

A month after the defeat of New York's black suffrage referendum, Fuller and her abolitionist comrades had to face a much bigger antislavery defeat, bringing her growing political alienation of the past nine months to a culminating point. On May 12, the long-dangling diplomatic shoe finally dropped when Congress, ostensibly responding to Mexican cavalry attacks on American soldiers in a disputed region near the Rio Grande, overwhelmingly voted to support President Polk's request for a declaration of war against Mexico, triggering furious but futile opposition from both abolitionists and liberal Whigs. Fuller's antiwar arguments, though, were somewhat different from the norm. Neither a pacifist like the Garrisonians nor a fearful anti-"Jacobin" like the Whigs, the previous month, in her only public dissent from her editor, she no doubt had startled her Whig readers by qualifiedly defending Napoleon on precisely the grounds of his expansion of democratic forces on the Continent. Yet she had insisted there that *this* expansionist war was a "bad cause" because it flagrantly contradicted the essence of American nationhood—its declared commitment to freedom and equality. The precipitating cause of the war, she—like all abolitionists—had no doubt, was the expansion of slavery. But the war itself exposed a deeper illiberalism in America, she thought. In her July review of McKinney's memoirs, instancing again the mob murder of Joseph Smith and the expulsion of his followers (which she compared to the Egyptian persecution of the Israelites), she declared that the war was but the latest manifestation of that "intolerance and bigotry" that had been appearing for the past two years "in a thousand ways and on every side."[69]

One particularly illiberal aspect of the war most disturbed Fuller: its Anglo-Saxon racism. While Democratic war supporters like Whitman gloated that the fighting represented the advance guard of the irresistible army of Anglo-Saxon progress and "thoroughly chastised" a backward people, many antiwar Whigs denounced the war as a violent proslavery land grab that would lead to the conquest or absorption of an inferior race. Fuller, however, joined Lowell and a handful

of radical abolitionist writers in seeing this white racism as the war's defining characteristic. Thus, three weeks after Congress voted to declare war, in an otherwise
friendly review of *Recollections of Mexico* by Waddy Thompson, the former
ambassador to Mexico in the Whig Tyler administration—which Greeley had
earlier praised as statesmanlike and "generous"—she denounced Thompson's
racist characterizations of Mexicans, especially those of Indian descent, as under-
mining the very democratic ideals he professed. Worse yet, all of his remarks about
Mexican and California riches, the weakness of Mexico's Indian soldiery, and the
ease of taking lands from atrocious Mexican officials who preyed on their peoples
were "throughout," she wrote, "calculated to stimulate covetousness and dissipate scruples as to their 'annexation,'" and this despite his sincere claim "to have
no wish of the sort." And, if such racist constructions had poisoned so sophisticated a diplomat as Thompson before the war, she asked, what could be expected
of ordinary Americans during it?[70]

Already Fuller saw bad signs everywhere. A month later, she detected them in
a prowar French ditty sung in Louisiana that called for the "sons of America" to
arise and put down the "*feeble*" Mexicans ravaging American states. "Even in this
city," she wrote indignantly, "they were not ashamed to pen and sing verses calling on the citizen to fight in defense of 'liberty,' as if it were not the Mexicans
alone, the *feeble* Mexicans, that were fighting in defense of their rights, and we
for liberty to do our pleasure." In stark contrast with her affirmation in her fall
essay "Italy" that none of the "false deeds and low thoughts" of her country had
made her "despair of her yet fulfilling the great destiny whose promise rose, like
a star, only some half a century ago upon the hopes of the world," her conclusion
was bleak. "Our hopes as to National honor and goodness are almost wearied out,"
she confessed, "and we feel obliged to turn to the Individual and to the Future for
consolation." Ironically, what she had always doubted—a great future for American literature—now seemed possible, while what she had always touted—America's
moral superiority to Europe—now seemed highly questionable. In the most professedly democratic-minded but now most prowar northern city in America, such
possibilities as "mutual education," "genuine philanthropy," and the "tide of
Progress," fashioned out of Fuller's Romantic ethic of self-culture and social diversity, seemed remote indeed. Perhaps, she might have thought, if Paine's "Freedom"
had once fled Europe for America, as her father had liked to quote to her, the time
had come for Romantic-age cosmopolitan patriots to start looking for its asylum
back across the ocean.[71]

VII

The idea of going to Europe had been on Fuller's mind for some time. Originally,
she had told Greeley she planned to stay at the *Tribune* for no more than a year
and a half. "That is long enough for a mortal to look forward, and not too long,"
she had explained to Mary Rotch, "as I must look forward in order to get what I
want from Europe." For most of her first year, though, looking forward was all
her limited funds allowed her to do. But in early September, just before she left

for her Massachusetts vacation, her wealthy Quaker friends Marcus and Rebecca Spring made her a "proposition" for realizing her "long abandoned but secretly fervent desire to see Europe." If she would join them on a tour of Britain and the Continent they were planning to take, they would pay for a portion of her travel and lodging expenses in return for tutoring their son Eddie. "She cried for joy," Rebecca recalled. On February 12, 1846, Fuller finally got the word from Marcus that his partners had approved his leave and their trip was on.[72]

She did not say to Rotch exactly what she wanted from Europe, but three weeks after getting Marcus's letter, she revealed something of it to her anticipated travel companions of ten years before. "At every step I have missed the culture I sought in going," she wrote Sam and Anna Ward, speaking of that sadly scuttled plan, "for with me it [was] no scheme of pleasure but the means of needed development. It was what I wanted after my painful youth, and what I was ready to use and be nourished by. It would have given my genius wings and I should have been, not in idea indeed, but in achievement far superior to what I can be now." Now she did not expect seeing Europe would be very important to her: "My mind and character are too much formed. I shall not modify them much but only add to my stores of knowledge." Yet she did not underestimate the importance of *that*. "I feel that, if I persevere, there is nothing to hinder my having an important career even now," she wrote, "but," she added, repeating her professional point, as though to remind herself, "it must be in the capacity of a journalist, and for that I need this new field of observation." She would be wrong about her "mind and character" but more right than she knew about her career.[73]

She was right about one other thing: she still needed money. In addition to the Springs' contribution, which was probably worth about a $1,000, she had another thousand saved up, but a roundtrip steamer would take around $300, and expenses for a year could easily add up to $3,000. She initially counted on getting money from a second edition of her sold-out *Woman in the Nineteenth Century* and a column of "letters" to the *Tribune* from Europe that Greeley had suggested she write, but his business partner Thomas McElrath, a reputedly "close calculator," had made her no offer on either. "He acts towards me in a way that makes me think perhaps the boldness of my course does not suit his narrow mind," she wrote apprehensively to Richard ("entre nous, *strictly*"). Preferring anyway to take notes for a travel book rather than grind out columns for a pittance, she asked Sam for a $500 loan, assuring him of repayment from the writing she intended to do. Just before leaving, Greeley finally offered her an advance of $120 to write fifteen letters at $10 each, thus obviating, for the moment at least, any further begging.[74]

Meanwhile, as money troubles faded, others cropped up. That winter she had another bad viral infection that slowed her writing but hardly dampened her commitment to the paper. "I am more and more interested by the generous course of Mr G.," she wrote Nathan, "and am desirous to make my own position important and useful." More annoying was her brother-in-law's parody of her European yearning. Angry over his job failures and with Ellen about to give birth to their second child, Ellery decided it was time for *him* to go to Europe. In his letter informing Margaret of his plan, after suggesting that she would naturally sympathize with his urgency to see Europe's great works of art, he had the further gall to ask her to get Greeley, who had fired him, to make him "foreign correspondent to the Tribune!" and give him a "hundred dollars in advance!!" "I need hardly tell you what my feelings were on receiving this epistle," she gasped to Richard. "I had meant and hoped never to feel indignation and aversion towards Ellery, but the unnatural selfishness of a man who, having brought a woman into this situation of suffering peril and care, proposes to leave her without even knowing whether she lives or dies under it, is a little too much for my nerves." Warned by both Ellen and his former girlfriend Caroline Sturgis that he would sink into a funk if he did not go, she glumly asked her "poor frail" mother to move in with her sister to look after her. On March 3, the day she wrote to Sam and Anna her anguished letter about how she had sacrificed her original European trip to support her family, Ellery left for Rome; he stayed sixteen days and returned to Concord "full of distaste for all things foreign."[75]

Then there was Nathan, still gallivanting around Italy and the Middle East. In her last letter in late February, apprising him of all the exciting times she was having without him, she had casually mentioned her plan to go to Europe for a year and asked whether he would still be there so they could meet. Her insouciance, though, did not last forever. Later that spring, after not having heard from him for the entire four months he had been traveling, she wrote him that her recent visit to the Farm had renewed old memories of their times spent there together, making her feel a "desire for you that amounted to anguish." After getting back to Hamburg, he finally replied with a page of excuses for not writing, adding, a little disconcertedly, "Your coming to Europe is of the next interest to me and I am heartily glad of it, but how singular!" Despite his "but," he assured her that she would find in London a letter from him, "if not myself and then thanks to god! in all probability shall we meet either there or here." In the meantime, as he was now broke from his trip, could she correct his travel letters and talk to Greeley or some other "liberal journalist" about getting them published in an American newspaper? After receiving his letter detailing all their selling points, in the midst of a flurry of prevoyage tasks, she hurriedly wrote him that his publishing prospects were dim, adding, "I will hope to find a good letter if not yourself in London, early in Sptr." She obviously hoped for the latter.[76]

While putting up with Ellery's and Nathan's authorial demands, Fuller also dealt with two considerably more legitimate ones. The first stemmed from the publishing woes of the Danish author she had befriended in the winter. After two decades of getting expelled from almost every country in Europe for his revolutionary activities and writing over forty volumes of novels and plays, Paul Harro Harring had emigrated to Brazil and then New York, where he had signed a contract with Harpers Brothers to publish a new political novel. When the Methodist layman and former nativist Whig mayor James Harper, however, read Harring's manuscript of *Dolores: A Novel of South America*, filled with rambling critiques of capitalism, marriage, and organized religion, he refused to publish it on the ground that it was blasphemous. Easily outraged by mistreatment of authors, immigrants, and outré liberals—and here were all three!—Fuller swung into action, raising money for Harring's breach-of-contract suit, interceding in his quarrels with his attorneys, and attending his trial so she could testify on his behalf, although she was never called. In two long articles, she tried to turn him into a cause célèbre. In "Publishers and Authors," she tore into the Harpers' flimsy post facto legal justifications. How, she asked, could they *not* have expected something like Harring's book, since all they had needed to do was to read any of his previous books. Their religious indignation was even lamer coming from the publisher of Sue's almost identically heretical *Wandering Jew*. In her second review, she raised the stakes a couple of notches. First, the Harpers, who—she by now seems to have figured out—were probably trying to get out of publishing Harring's manuscript because they feared it would be a clunker, were money grubbing hypocrites. Here was an earnest and noble author driven from monarchical Europe for advocating Americans' own founding principles, who promised to rouse them from their current money- and land-besotted indifference to the rustlings of "oppressed" nations in Europe, yet "shut from the field." And by whom? "By those who bring forward so many sickly and miserable fictions, by those who can never have enough of the [high society] novels of James, Lady Blessington and Mrs. Gore." Second, the Harpers were acting worse than Old World governments, which merely censored passages, they suppressed entire books and destroyed careers. Third, that was true of "ninety-nine hundredths" of publishers, who likewise used maximum profit calculations to deny readers the chance to buy better books. So she suggested to the Harpers and their colleagues a code of ethics. Serve America's honor by paying royalties even without an international copyright. Give fair compensation for what *you* could never produce. Otherwise, if all "you" care about is profit, your name on the cover means nothing but that you think it will sell well. "One of the most eloquent and well-*put* articles I have ever yet seen in a newspaper," beamed the perennially publisher-aggrieved Poe.[77]

Unfortunately, neither righteous eloquence nor cosmopolitan patriotism won the day. "The offended Harpers have effectually prevented any chance of sale for it," Emerson reported from Boston, where he was trying to find a publisher for Harring, "& no paper dares mention the book." Then in late June Harring got his verdict: the jury split evenly, and the judge dismissed the case. Fuller still did not give up, however. Just before leaving, while trying to scrape together every penny for her trip, she loaned Harring $500, or half her savings, to help him publish his novel on his own, which he quickly squandered, apparently (he would claim) on a bad contract. When she later realized she would never get a penny from his book, she took the news, characteristically, with generous grace. "I would rather lose the money entirely than that anything should be added to the pressure on Harro," she would write three months later to William Russel from London, where she would see Harring. She wished her money had been "wiselier applied," she would tell the Springs. "Yet these are not the things one regrets. It does not do to calculate too closely with the affectionate human impulse; we must consent to make many mistakes or we would move too slow to help our brothers." Still, for an advocate of "mutual interpretation" and cosmopolitan liberalism, she could not have found the outcome very promising about her country's dedication to either.[78]

Her second publishing confrontation struck closer to home. Eager to get a little more money and visibility before leaving, earlier in the year she had started thinking about publishing "several volumes" of her numerous literary essays. After she pitched the idea to Duyckinck in early February, telling him "there is not one that has not excited a good deal of interest in this country and many of them have in England," he enthusiastically agreed to publish a selection in his Wiley and Putnam Library of American Books series. "Much pleased," she drew up a list of the pieces she wanted in her book, which included a balanced assortment of her criticism on English, Continental, and American literature and the arts, from her earliest articles in *American Monthly Magazine* to her latest ones in the *Tribune*. She also told him that she knew she would have to cut some, but exactly what and how much she does not seem to have made clear, an unfortunate error.[79]

On June 27, a day after the discharge of the jury in Harring's trial, she received a note from Wiley saying that she would have to cut her *Festus* review, as well as "all other matter of a controversial character or likely to offend the religious public." An evangelical Presbyterian, Wiley had already censored passages about Protestant missionaries in Melville's revised American edition of *Typee*, although had she known that it would have only added to her outrage. "Now you well know that I write nothing which might not offend the so-called religious public," she wrote in a blistering letter to Duyckinck, adding, with a Transcendentalist sneer: "I am too incapable of understanding their godless fears and unhappy skepticism to have much idea of what would offend them." Her second point was a more practical one: "There are probably sentences in every piece, perhaps on every page, which, when the books are once published, will lead to censure." Consequently, "I shall alter not a line or a word, on such accounts." Her third point was her shrewdest: most readers who would likely buy the book would miss precisely such essays as those on Bailey and Shelley that Wiley wanted to suppress. Finally, she rightly said, not only did she find such "temporizing" distasteful on principle, but she also objected to it as a "matter of policy," because it undermined her core strength as a writer: "The attractive force of my mind consists in its energy, clearness and I dare say it, its catholic liberality and fearless honor. Where I make an impression it must be by being most myself. I ought always to ignore vulgar prejudices, and I feel within myself a power which will sustain me in so doing and draw to me sufficient and always growing sympathy." She was right. And consistent with her claim, she threatened termination: if Wiley was not content to publish the articles "just as they stand" and "take the consequences you had better stop the transaction now." To that she added a threat: "If we do, however, I shall publish an account of this transaction for I wish in every way to expose the restrictions upon mental freedom which threaten to check the progress of genius or of a religious sentiment worthy of God and man in this country."[80]

Despite her tough talk, the practical outcome was mixed. On the question of altering her articles, she succeeded: apart from her revisions clarifying and sharpening her prose, Wiley printed everything exactly as she had written it. On the selection issue, however, her position quickly deteriorated. She had already agreed to drop her *Festus* and Shelley pieces but only, she said, because their lengthy

extracts made them too long. Meanwhile, Wiley kept demanding more cuts without, apparently, saying where, while she became frantic about how she could make
any kind of adequate representation. "Now I don't know how to arrange at all,"
she wrote desperately to Duyckinck. It is not entirely clear what happened at this
point. Fuller would later privately blame Wiley for the paucity of selections, but
she never explained exactly how her exclusion not only of important pieces—like
her Goethe article, which she had told Duyckinck she refused to cut—but of *all*
of her essays on Continental literature came about. In her preface she gave an
innocuous explanation: she had gotten to the end of the first volume and suddenly
discovered she had no room for all her materials. What likely happened was more
complicated and less innocent. By mid-July, with the proofs for the first volume
mostly finished, she was about to leave for Europe, and with Wiley continuing to
demand more cuts, she probably decided the "arrangement" of only English and
American criticism would at least add up to a coherent volume. She tried to make
amends in her preface. She favorably noted Bailey and Shelley and mentioned
her *Tribune* notices of Milnes, Landor, and Hare. And, perhaps feeling a little
guilty, after regretting not including her articles on the "great minds of Germany
and Italy," whose introduction had been "one great object of my life," she offered
an aggressive defense of the value for Americans of Continental authors. These
"great geniuses, the flower and fruit of a higher state of development," she had
hoped might set a "higher standard" for young American authors and readers. "By
being thus raised above their native sphere, they would become its instructors and
the faithful stewards of its best riches, not its tools and slaves." As with Harring,
it was another brave cosmopolitan gesture in a lost battle.[81]

Yet her two slim volumes of *Papers on Literature and Art* of a little over 340
pages were by no means made up of miscellaneous or "indifferent matter." The
first volume opened with her two *Dial* pieces on critical method, "Short Essay on
Critics" and "A Dialogue," and the rest were all on British literature of the Renaissance and Romantic eras, taken, except for her "Two Herberts" dialogue from
Channing's *Present* and her *Tribune* essay on Milton, from the *American Monthly
Magazine* or the *Dial*. These included her once-admired early essays "The Life of
Sir James Mackintosh" and "Modern British Poets," as well as, after her Goethe
essay, her two most ambitious *Dial* literary pieces, "The Modern Drama" and her
"Dialogue" on melancholy and American appropriations of Shakespeare. The
second volume had a similar unity and symmetry. Including articles on contemporary English and American writers taken from her *Tribune* column, it likewise
began with a theoretical statement, in this case her reviews of Prince and Thom,
retitled "Poets of the People," which highlighted her recent avant-garde populist
turn, reinforced by her notices of the Brownings and her articles on Swedenborgianism and Methodism at the end. Her only two articles on art, her *Dial*'s
"Great Composers" and Allston essay, at least gave an inkling of her artistic views.
In place of several of her best reviews of American books, such as those on
Emerson and Poe, she concluded with her "American Literature" survey, to which
she joined her reviews of Longfellow, Hawthorne, and Brown. In a last-minute
tribute to her Young America comrades, she added in an appendix a reprint of a

glowing report on Mathews's "Witchcraft" from the *Evening Post* on its opening Philadelphia performance. With the book barely finished at the printers on July 28, she had only to await the reviews at home and abroad.[82]

These last months before Fuller's departure for Europe were frenetic. Besides madly trying to extricate herself from the mess with her book while attempting to fulfill her promise to Greeley to "keep on writing for the Tribune up to the last," she frequently changed her living quarters. Wanting to cut expenses before her departure, on March 12, she reluctantly left her Amity Place rooms and returned to the Greeleys, where she stayed until the end of April, when they rented out their house. After that, she took lodgings with the Mannings in Brooklyn Heights, where she would remain until she left the city. Meanwhile, in these last few weeks, she continued to cram in tasks. "Continually unwell" and with constant headaches, she tried getting a little relief by bathing off Hempstead Harbor while visiting Fanny and Parke Godwin's "lovely place" there, but mostly she attended to pretravel business. Anxious that, as she told Richard, "there is always the possibility of never returning, when one goes so far and across an ocean," she wrote to her mother, siblings, and closest friends to make sure that she saw them either in New York or later in Boston. To create a more permanent memento for her family, she agreed to sit for a daguerreotype at the studio of John Plumbe, who had asked to take one for his gallery of celebrities. She collected letters of introduction from her literary friends, testifying to her standing as (in Bryant's note to the American consul in Florence) "a lady of extensive literary accomplishments" or (in Willis's to the consul's attorney in London) "one of our most distinguished authoresses, and a delightful person." Holding to her promise to Greeley to write up to the very end, during her last few days, she churned out a half-dozen reviews, which barely mollified him. "She knows them well and says what she knows very forcibly," he sighed to Rufus Griswold, speaking of wanting her to dash off an article on "Unitarian notables." "But it takes her a good while to say it, and she leaves for Europe on Wednesday."[83]

Before going, she left him with a final couple of tributes. She had become immensely proud of her paper. "If there are points on which we cannot sympathize with its objects or views," she wrote in her column, "we yet believe that, in sincerity and generosity of purpose, it has never been surpassed, perhaps never equalled, by any journal of France, Germany, England or America." To her adopted city, she gave an even more expansive salute. "Farewell to New-York City," she hurrahed in her "Farewell" article, "where twenty months have presented me with a richer and more varied exercise for thought and life than twenty years could in any other part of these United States." How could it not? The diversely teeming city freed individuals from "small cavils or scrutinies," exposed social evils for reform, and brought together the most advanced ideas of America and Europe—in short, the place to be for all "independent" persons. Certainly, its cosmopolitanism had been fruitful for her. Not only had she gotten many new views on these subjects, but she had encountered surprising encouragement in applying her "two great leadings" to the nation at large. One was her old Transcendentalist one of "promoting National Education by heightening and deepening the cultivation of individual minds," and the other was illuminating "the part . . . assigned to Woman in the next stage of human progress in this country." She had even found readers who appreciated her "aloofness" from the day's popular trends, sects, and parties in favor of the "free pursuit of Truth." Indeed, her column's "Truth" of cosmopolitan patriotism had now lured her to go to Europe. Her first goal was modest: to observe "with my own eyes . . . Life in the Old World, and to bring home some packages of seed for Life in the New." But from those seeds she could see her nation looming. Although she went to "behold the wonders of art, and the temples of old religion," she assured her readers, "I shall see no forms of beauty and majesty beyond what my Country is capable of producing in myriad variety, if she has but the soul to will it" and make the era's "catch-word of . . . a sense of DIVINE ORDER . . . no more a mere word or effigy, but a deeply rooted and pregnant Idea in her life." Leaving, it seems, was but another road to rooted American soulfulness.[84]

Not everyone was pleased with Fuller's New York farewell. If Fuller got so much from "this dirty city," her nemesis Briggs glowered six days later in a nasty parting shot in the Garrisonians' *National Anti-Slavery Standard*, now edited by Sidney Howard Gay and her old Boston detractor Maria Weston Chapman, "we cannot help thinking that Miss F. was never very thoughtful before coming to New-York." In the remainder Briggs leveled a relentless attack both on Fuller's aloofly engaged criticism and on her supposed love affair with the city. Fuller praised New York for encouraging independent persons to pursue their life projects: abolitionists have been threatened and assaulted for pursuing theirs. She touted independent thought: "Those who are elevated in a balloon by the aid of gas are of course quite conscious of soaring above the heads of their neighbors." She voiced an appreciation of European art: "To any one capable of relishing a work of art, or of tracing the spirit of the age in external forms, our own land furnishes as much food for thought as any other." Such a philistine distortion of Fuller's critical posture provoked howls from other reformers. "Her singular nobleness of character, her disinterested advocacy of unpopular truth, and her enlightened enthusiasm in the cause of human freedom and elevation," the Fourierist *Harbinger* declared, decrying the *Standard*'s ungentlemanly, spiteful screed, "should be sufficient to shield her from such aggression." That even some Garrisonians had privately expressed gratitude for Fuller's antislavery testimony in the *Tribune* should have also provided some protection. Apparently, though, for the *Standard* and its unlikely mouthpiece, being urbane, independent, and cosmopolitan precluded political awareness and American patriotism. Fuller's New York career had showed that claim wide of the mark. Europe would show it even more.[85]

"Tired and harried to death" and going on "no sleep or next to none," on the morning of July 28, she raced through the last of her book's proofs. Later in the afternoon the Greeleys and Pickie saw her off to the Fulton ferry to return to Brooklyn for some final packing. The next night Abby Hopper Gibbons and her husband James gave a going-away party for her at their home on West Fourteenth Street. "*Very* early" the next morning, she traveled on the Norwich and Worcester Railroad to Boston, where Richard met her laden with a "great deal of baggage" at the train depot. From there they went to her mother's rented house in their old family neighborhood of Cambridgeport, where she stayed through the following night entertaining a stream of well-wishing old friends, including, for an hour in the afternoon, Emerson. The following morning, August 1, while New York newsboys hawked the *Tribune* with her "Farewell," she and the Springs boarded the British Cunard steamer *Cambria,* departing on her maiden voyage from Boston Harbor to Liverpool. "I am glad Margaret Fuller has gone to Europe," Child wrote the next day to Frank Shaw, in a wistful letter confessing her unhappiness with her marriage and her dissatisfaction with the falseness of sexual relations in society. "I think it will refresh both mind and body. She is a woman of the most remarkable intellect I ever met with."[86]

CHAPTER EIGHT

Ambassador of the World
(1846–1847)

I

Although Child's prediction of refreshment for both Fuller's mind and body would turn out to be right in several ways, the voyage was not entirely one of them. While the weather was good, reducing the usual heaving around of passengers, the unremitting noise from the grinding of the *Cambria*'s paddles and the constant stink and heavy black smoke from its engine oil, typical of steamers of the era, ensured that, like most transatlantic passengers then, she was seasick most of the time. "I could hardly have borne another day," she afterward wrote her mother. She did appreciate, however, three features of the brand-new steamer. It was fast, getting to Liverpool in just ten and a half days, then a spectacular record for crossing the Atlantic. Unlike the coffin-like wooden compartments in which Emerson and his four fellow voyagers had slept during his first transatlantic trip fourteen years earlier, the *Cambria*'s sleeping rooms were ample and well ventilated, comfortably containing the ship's forty or so passengers.[1]

She found most of them "agreeable," apparently, even such high-toned travelers as Longfellow's wealthy debonair brother-in-law Thomas Gold Appleton, the originator of the phrase "Good Americans when they die go to Paris"; the English ambassador to the United States and his wife and daughter; and Lord Falkland, the just-ejected governor of Nova Scotia, and his wife Lady Falkland. In her first dispatch, though, she reminded her readers of her democratic travel tastes by mocking the English and the Americans "following their lead, as usual," for displaying such fascination with Lady Falkland's mother, the daughter of King William IV and his mistress, and her "left-handed alliance with one of the dullest families that ever sat upon a throne." She found much more to recommend in the captain, the line's commodore, Charles H. E. Judkins, "the Nigger Captain" (as the *Herald* styled him), who proudly regaled Fuller with his tale about having once placed several southerners in irons for trying to keep Frederick Douglass from leaving the steerage to deliver a speech to abolitionist sympathizers in the cabin. "If the Northern States had had the firmness, good sense and honor" to assume the same tone toward "insolent slaveholders," she added, the country would have been better off than it was.[2]

The passengers she most enjoyed, naturally, were the Springs, who had brought with them some congenial ideological baggage. Although good friends with the genteel Bryants, Sedgwicks, and Deweys, after leaving the orthodox Society of Friends and joining William Channing's Christian socialist church, they mainly socialized with the same liberal Quaker-and-Unitarian reform crowd that Fuller did. A rich cotton broker, Marcus had devoted much of his time and money to political abolitionism and moderate Fourierist socialism, later founding the arts-and-education-centered Raritan Bay Union in Perth Amboy. Like her gentle husband, Rebecca comfortably bridged social contradictions. Although she had no compunctions about having many servants and enjoying fine clothing and hotels, she was proud of her upright Quaker reform lineage (her father was Arnold Buffum, the first president of the New England Antislavery Society, and her cousin was Bloomingdale's Pliny Earle). Saucy and courageous, she would travel thirteen years later through raging mobs with her son Eddie to comfort and encourage John Brown in his Virginia cell. ("Then you will be our *Anti-Slavery Martyr!*" she would cheerfully answer Brown after he confessed to her that he had made many mistakes and deserved to die. "It is better to die for a great idea, than of a fever.") Rebecca and Margaret made a good team. With a "piquant" face and charming talk, Rebecca would win "rapture" from new acquaintances who were initially discomfited by Fuller's physical plainness and verbal pyrotechnics. Fuller would also include the Springs in her visits to literary notables and philanthropic institutions from which Marcus got ideas for his progressive ventures. Occasionally, Rebecca blanched at Fuller's "so severe" strictures on men and books, while Margaret regretted their lack of sympathy for her emotional conundrums. Yet they greatly appreciated her attentions to Eddie and felt enormous admiration and much affection toward her, and she felt deeply grateful for "that act of real valid friendship" that made it financially possible for her to go to Europe.[3]

Fuller had plenty of company in voyaging to the Old World. Although a minuscule percentage of Americans traveled to Europe, some ten thousand were annually crossing the Atlantic thirty years after the end of the Napoleonic Wars, which had made it safe, and eight years after the introduction of ocean steamship travel, which had made it reasonably comfortable. Their social makeup had also changed considerably from the previous century's handful of upper-class men traveling for trade, diplomacy, or Grand Tour finishing. Many were newly wealthy businessmen and their wives eager to get, like their English counterparts on Thomas Cook's Tours, a needed confirmation of their genteel standing. Others, particularly from Boston, were educated professionals traveling for the sake of the Romantic era's ubiquitous "self-culture," hoping to gain, as she had once hoped to do, "*intellectual capital*" to improve mind, morals, and taste. Still others were writers and artists like Fuller, looking for opportunities to practice their craft and improve their cultural status in Europe-minded America. "Can we never extract this maggot of Europe out of the brain of our countrymen?" Emerson asked exasperatedly in his journal. "Plato & Pythagoras may travel, for they carry the world with them and are always at home but our travelers are moths & danglers." Yet the next year he would follow Fuller to Europe for his second voyage, establishing his reputation as a cosmopolitan critic—a move replicated by numerous other Transcendentalists and reformers.[4]

Nor was Fuller alone in writing about her travels. For a decade, Murray's "infallible" English guidebooks and their American imitators had been informing readers about accommodations, must-see cultural shrines, historical background, and the proper behavior of travelers. Readers also had an array of transatlantic travel books from Irving's sentimental sketches and Cooper's political screeds to Willis's gossipy *Pencillings by the Way* and, most recently, Bayard Taylor's breathless *Views A-Foot*. A couple of decades later Mark Twain would famously send up the genre in *Innocents Abroad*. These books often played to antebellum Americans' national hopes and anxieties by projecting them on a bifurcated screen. From Irving to Taylor, Europe meant, above all, the old: old legends, castles, cathedrals, rituals, walls, schools, families—all, in a word, that made Europe a cultural Mecca. America, on the other hand, represented, for better or worse, the new, most spectacularly, everyone agreed, in its unique republican institutions. Any move beyond nostalgia and pride to a deeper dialectic of American "innocence" and European "experience" would have to await Henry James's international novels a generation later.[5]

Fuller, however, was already an exception. Partly this was because she created her own hybrid form. Travel narratives, as John Paul Russo has noted, are ideally a "hybrid, plastic, open genre" that can "absorb almost anything into itself and include a wide variety of authorial tones." These years of the "newspaper revolution" also brought forth a new hybrid type: the intellectual traveling journalist. Instead of picturesque travel "letter" writers, large papers like the *Tribune* and the *Herald* were starting to hire journalists as "foreign correspondents." Just that summer Greeley sent George William Curtis to Italy, and the following year he would send Curtis's Brook Farm comrade Charles Dana to France. Even so, Greeley especially appreciated Fuller's dispatches, which he kept in their usual front-page, first-column position, even during the Mexican War and the presidential election. He also gave her high compensation. "What we pay you by agreement ($10 per letter)," he told her, "is just twice what we pay for any other European Correspondence, but we are very well aware that the quality justifies this." By quality he meant all the literary and historical knowledge she packed into them, which was certainly true, but there would be other distinguishing features of her "Things and Thoughts" (as she called her series). First, no American travel writer mixed so thoroughly the personal, cultural, and political. Nor did any follow the three Romantic formulas for making travel writing "real" that she had recently articulated in a *Tribune* article on the genre: substitute "symptoms" directly observed for hackneyed "outward" details; apprehend the subjective sources of a people's institutions and manners; and write "intellectual" narratives intended to "grow" in the reader's mind. Above all, her "dispatches" transmitted a critical identification with *both* Old World culture and New World idealism that was unique in antebellum travel writing. Partly she brought its script with her, and partly it would be there for her to find.[6]

II

Arriving at Liverpool at noon on August 12, Fuller got her chance to see how much of this composite culture there was in England, where American "passionate pilgrims" (in James's condescendingly affectionate phrase for his precursors) loved to report feeling proud to "return." Her past anti-British swipes did not promise a lot. "Because she had done one good act, is she entitled to the angelic privilege of being the Champion of Freedom?" she had demanded in her article ostensibly honoring England's West Indies emancipation but, unlike most annual abolitionist tributes, listing also its imperialist behavior toward the Irish, Hindus, and Chinese. In politics so, too, in culture. "Greatly degenerate[d]," she had derisively characterized it around the same time, in a letter of travel advice to young Maria Rotch, then in London on her first Grand Tour; "as much encrusted in mere externals as any in the civilized world."[7]

A historian's bird's-eye view of early Victorian England would have given her much to both confirm and confound her dismissal. Its culture's keywords of mechanism, utilitarianism, and political economy were not exactly American Transcendentalists' lingua franca. Intellectual trends were also not encouraging. England's colleges continued to trail badly behind her vaunted German ones. Even English literary culture was somewhat stalled. All the major Romantics, except the fast declining Wordsworth, were dead, the Brontë sisters' first novels had not yet appeared, George Eliot's were over a decade away, and Dickens's greatest ones were still ahead of him. Yet advanced currents were easily detectable. In art, the just-published second volume of John Ruskin's *Modern Painters* extended the Romantic ethos into the Victorian era by recovering Gothic architecture and pre-Raphael painting and defending J. M. W. Turner's controversial luminously abstracted landscapes. There was also a new moral seriousness in religion and philosophy. The Anglican Oxford Movement had revived English spiritual traditions, Comtean agnostics were proclaiming a "religion of humanity," and sober young liberals were touting the increasingly revered Carlyle for putting forward ethical insights that their benevolent but mechanistic utilitarian fathers had missed. Meanwhile, the lingering economic depression in England's dirty and depressing industrial cities and the recent mass deaths and widespread starvation from the Potato Famine in Ireland had encouraged a new social gravitas. The old "silver fork" fashionable novelists suddenly seemed absurdly unfashionable. Mary Barton, Elizabeth Gaskell, and even the author of *Vivien Grey* turned to sober portrayals of the "Condition of England." The same earnest reform spirit was registering in politics. "Young England" Tories, eager to embarrass their Whig opponents, urged the moral imperative of factory acts regulating wages and hours imposed on workers by their "free trade" industrial masters. Robert Peel's Tory government, anxious to steal the liberal Anti-Corn League's thunder, had just gotten Parliament to abolish restrictions on imported grain, a key pillar of landed aristocratic rule. To their left, dissatisfied "Radicals," Protestant Dissenters, and conscience-struck liberal Whigs were calling for a new political economy that produced not just profits for mill owners and cheap bread and virtuous behavior among workers but also welfare programs, mechanics' institutes, artisans' cooperatives, and other humanitarian nostrums to mitigate operatives' suffering and uplift their minds. Further to *their* left, the Chartists were agitating for a "People's Charter" of working-class enfranchisement and democratic representation. In this supposedly "degenerated" land, such half-familiar winds of radical doubt, spiritual earnestness, and social hope could hardly not have warmed her at least a little.[8]

In her very first *Tribune* letter, she showed some appreciation of England's "mere externals." "There is not that rushing, tearing and swearing," she assured her readers, speaking of the bustling port city that Americans often compared to New York, "that snatching of baggage, that prodigality of shoe-leather and lungs that attend the course of the traveler in the United States." She could even see why solicitous English travelers in the United States became so quickly disgusted with its citizens' "bad manners, and careless habits." When consciousness of manners passed over into class consciousness, however, it got under her middle-class Romantic skin. "It amused me to hear the mechanical, measured way in which they talked of character," she would later jot in her journal, after an evening of friendly banter with some well-to-do English. "With all the abuses of America, we have one advantage that outweighs them all. Most persons reject the privilege, but it is, really, possible for one to grow." Nor did she forget—or let her American readers forget—their legitimate grievances with their country's ungenerous foreign judges like Mrs. Trollope. "Luckily I did not generalize quite as rapidly as travelers in America usually do," she laughed—recounting finding no bath at their hotels at Liverpool, Manchester, or Chester but having a maid tell her that she might get her a note to the infirmary—"and put in the note book—'*Mem:* None but the sick ever bathe in England.'"[9]

In Liverpool and Manchester she displayed more political ambivalence. In her dispatch recounting one night intrepidly trying to talk with mill girls as they strolled "bare-headed, with coarse, rude and reckless air through the streets" or sat in gin dives "drinking, too dull to carouse," she even sounded like something of a condescending Manchester liberal herself. Mostly, though, she found commonalities with the more democratic liberal hosts with whom she dined one night, Emerson's booster Alexander Ireland, the publisher of the *Manchester Examiner*, and William Hodgson, the political economist and principal of the Liverpool Mechanics' Institute. Like them, she stressed the benefits not of laissez-faire economics but of "self-help" philanthropy. While giving a passing bow to the Anti-Corn League's leaders, John Bright and Richard Cobden, she heaped praise on its grassroots printers and shopkeepers who pasted their self-printed pro–free-trade pamphlets on walls and doors, and the Mechanics Institutes' young artisans and clerks who were eager for classes in foreign languages, the fine arts, and the "higher branches." Suppressing any mention of her observation in her journal that at the Liverpool

Institute's new school for girls, women were "nominally, not really, at the head," she trumpeted it as a sign of "true civilization."[10]

She was especially thrilled to discover the influence of her American Transcendentalist liberals on these more prosaic English ones. "Some of the best minds in these especially practical regions," she wrote contentedly, looked to the *Dial* for their philosophical inspiration, although privately she gave a somewhat less pro-English spin on that fact. "How precious was the old Dial, with all its faults," she wrote afterward to Emerson, whose essays she reported these circles also eagerly read. "I felt this indeed after being in England. It had been manna in the wilderness to people there." True, she reacted defensively to the tweaking she got over the American bellicosity that had been expressed toward England over the "Oregon question." "'But you are mightily pleased, and illuminate for your victories in China and Ireland, do you not?'" she told her readers she had replied. Yet their answer seemed to her fair: on both sides of the Atlantic, hypocrites were many and the virtuous few. "To the new fraternity I think we belong," she afterward wrote Ireland, to whom she had given a copy of her *Papers on Art and Literature*, "whose glory is service, whose motto *Excelsior*."[11]

On August 18, she left English liberal humanitarianism and its grim industrial cities behind for a tour of the Lake District. After taking a train to Lancaster and then a canal-boat to the market-town of Kendel, she and the Springs arrived at Ambleside, where Harriet Martineau, who had recently built a house there, had arranged for them to rent one of the nearby stone cottages that dotted the region. Since their falling out a decade earlier over Martineau's anti-Transcendentalist slurs and (in Fuller's view) tendentiously harsh criticisms of the United States in *Society in America*, the two had resumed a friendly correspondence, no doubt helped by Martineau's declaration that Fuller's *Woman in the Nineteenth Century* was "Beautiful!" Yet old cultural differences intruded. Martineau became livid when she afterward heard that later in London Fuller had told Martineau's friends of her disappointment in Martineau's trumpeting her recent miraculous cure by mesmerism from years of chronic illnesses. Martineau seemed still so lacking in spiritual discernment, Fuller said, that no one could tell she had been mesmerized!—a remark that Martineau would chalk up to Fuller's usual "contemptuous benevolence which it was her wont to bestow on common-place people." But if the two found each other's respective Transcendental hauteur and spiritual obtuseness unchanged, neither seems to have shown it. Rebecca Spring remembered Martineau cheerfully calling on them every morning to tell them of her plans for them that day and Fuller saying none of her "unkind things" about her. In her column, too, instead of noting (as she did in her journal) Martineau's still "harried, excited, over-stimulated state of mind," Fuller reported only on her high reputation as an energetic and benevolent author. Evidently, for Fuller, unlike the gossipy Willis, discretion was an essential part of good foreign correspondence.[12]

Ambleside and its surroundings attracted numerous authors who lived or visited there, and thanks to Martineau, Fuller saw her share. The twenty-four-year-old Matthew Arnold, who with his brother Tom rowed her and the Springs in a small boat on Grasmere lake and talked to her about their deceased father Thomas

Arnold, the Regius professor of modern history, whose books Fuller had favorably reviewed, would afterward praise her "exquisite intelligence and fineness of apercu." Mainly, the Lake District and later Scotland allowed her opportunities to weave in for her knowing readers her memories of reading the regions' literary products. She got the aged Wordsworth, whom she and the Springs visited at his nearby Rydal Mount house, to stand before the portrait of his sister Dorothy and recite his famous poem about her to them. On their last day visiting Langdale, the scene of Wordsworth's "Excursion," she fondly recollected the great impression it had made on her in her "feverish" early twenties, to which she added, in Wordsworthian prose, a picturesque account of her ascent up Dungeon Gill Force, which the poet evoked in "The Idle Shepherd-Boys."[13]

After their "happy eight days" in Westmoreland, on August 27, they left Ambleside and traveled by coach through Keswick to Carlisle and, the next day, by train across the Scottish border to Edinburgh, along the way passing through Burns and Scott territory, which even triggered some surprising nostalgia for a childhood favorite she had long ago left behind. "Verily, these seem more like home than one's own nursery," she reported after seeing Branksome Hall, the setting of the border legends in Scott's *Lay of the Last Minstrel*, "whose toys and furniture could not in actual presence engage the thoughts like these pictures, made familiar as household words." She hastened to add that Burns, of course, was the "rarer man; precisely because he had most of common nature on a grand scale," a Romantic democratic judgment that reportedly "delighted" many of her readers. In "noble and stately" Edinburgh, she looked up from her hotel at Princes Street and saw a light in the window of Hume's house and was reminded of all the "active thinkers, fervent workers" of the Scottish Enlightenment "who had prepared for us some of their best gifts in these barren chambers." Unfortunately, they were dead, and the university and schools were on vacation, but she still saw "all the stock lions," whose old-fashioned virtues she fairly portrayed in her dispatch. Although Thomas De Quincey, the essayist and friend of Wordsworth and Coleridge, with whom she spent a long night talking in a "real Grand Conversatione," often dilated on now trite literary matters, his urbane talk was "subtle and forcible as the wind" and happily opposite to the current rapid "slang, Vivian-Greyish style" in literary conversation. "'Sixty years since' men had time to do things better and more gracefully than now." She noticed that the city had recently added to the monuments to Schiller, Goethe, and Beethoven, a newly erected statue of Scott, which had its back turned to the soon-to-arise railroad to London.[14]

On the morning of September 7, Fuller and the Springs left memorably noble but intellectually faded Edinburgh for ten days in the Scottish Highlands, where she experienced the contradictions of travel in modernizing Britain. Like many American travelers, she enjoyed whizzing along in the still common British stagecoaches. Although she was bothered more than she had been going to Niagara by the ubiquitous new railroads' loud noise, which precluded talking, reading, or even sleeping, making riding in them "the purgatory of dullness," she appreciated their speed, which allowed one to "fly . . . from one beautiful place to another"—a great boon, she said, without irony, to landscape artists. On the way to Loch Lomond, on the other hand, they had to step quickly to avoid hackneyed ground. They passed through Kinross, stopping for a look at the ruins of the castle where Queen Mary had been imprisoned, and then spent a day each at Perth and Crieff, paying perfunctory visits to the castles and parks of living nobility. The following day they traveled through the Trossachs to beautiful Loch Katrine, where they heard boatmen recite, "though not *con molte espressione*," the descriptive parts of Scott's poem "The Lady of the Lake," which they insisted to a doubtful Fuller were all true because they had been handed down so many generations. The next day, wisely avoiding "a hateful little steamer with a squeaking fiddle" playing "Rob Roy MacGregor O," they entered Rob Roy's country by walking the pass on foot for six miles from Loch Katrine to Inversaid, where they took a boat on Loch Lomond, rowed by "fine, athletic men," one of whom crooned sad Gaelic love songs. On the tenth, they arrived at the settlement of Rowardennan, where she encountered an instance of the kind of danger that could lurk in such intrepid exploring.[15]

Exhilarated by how much her newly gained health allowed her to do, she jumped at the chance to climb Ben Lomond, which towered over the town. Over three thousand feet at its summit and divided into congeries of smaller hills and countless crags and ravines, the Ben was one of the most treacherous climbs in Scotland. Indeed, at a dinner party at Ambleside, a "tedious" young woman had warned her of how easy it was for even shepherds to get lost in the Scottish mist, recounting the tragedy of a large party of men that had lost its way and got separated from a child, who had been found dead five days later. When she learned the next day that tourists had taken all the horses, she proposed to Marcus that they just walk. Almost everything happened that should not have. After relishing their afternoon of beautiful hills and views, at four o'clock they began their descent but could not find their path. Spring went to look for it but only managed to lose Fuller. What followed was a harrowing night for the lightly dressed Fuller of frantic searching, ripped clothes, freezing rain, tumbles into dark ravines, and periodic collapses from exhaustion, while the moon ascended through a black blanket of mist. Her emotions ran the gamut. When she saw the mist come on, "womanlike," she later said, she sat down and cried, fearing she would die or, if not, become a permanent invalid. She thought of what Emerson and William Channing would say of her if she died that night on the mountain. She recited Goethe's "Hymn to Immortality." Yet, realizing she *would* die "*if* I had not tried," she kept moving and rubbing her wrists to maintain circulation and stay awake, and when failing that, she clung to the heather on vertical crags so that she would wake up if she lost her grip. Meanwhile, back at the inn, upon learning that Fuller was lost, several men rushed up to Rebecca, shouting, "No woman can live on the mountain tonight. The cold mists were coming when we came down!" "No common woman," Rebecca replied, "but Margaret Fuller will not fold her hands and die." At daybreak, as Marcus combed the hills in the blinding mist with a search party of twenty shepherds, she scrambled on until, at about seven, two of them found her and carried her back to the inn.[16]

Except for losing most of her voice for a week of so, she did not suffer any permanent injuries. She also got a rousing welcome back when, later that night,

Marcus had the innkeeper organize a large dinner for all the shepherds, where they cheered the "man who saw her first!" and Rebecca, to more lusty cheers, recited with the men several of Burns's songs. Afterward they all streamed up to the parlor, where Fuller was resting, and shook her hand, which caused her afterward to write complacently in her *Tribune* letter, "this adventure created quite an intimate feeling between us and the people there." Her private reflections were conflicted. The next day in her journal, she dwelled on the "delightful emotions" she had felt among the alluring purple, heath-blossomed hills and sparkling lake and waterfall that she otherwise would not have seen! To Emerson, though, she described her dangerous "adventure" as a "hair-breadth escape with life." But whether a Romantic escapade or a brush with death, its graphic portrayal in her column startled many of her readers. "Have you read her adventures on Ben Lomond?" Rufus Griswold enviously wrote Frances Osgood—"such a blessed mishap for an authoress"; while Evert Duyckinck exclaimed to his brother George in Paris: "Miss Fuller's last letter is the most peculiar account of an ascent of Ben Lomond ever written." Whitman, whose omnivorous appetite for mythic self-dramatization was even greater than Fuller's, clipped her report for future reference.[17]

After leaving Rowardennan on the fifteenth by steamboat, "with its execrable fiddle, *à l'ordinaire*" screeching along the way, she and the Springs scurried back southward down the lochs and the Clyde and through the north and the Midlands, which her *Tribune* dispatches make sound like a forced march. After three days of more socializing with Edinburgh's notables, the "common" pilgrimage to Abbotsford, and a part of a day at Newcastle, where she was dropped by bucket down a coal mine ("a somewhat rare feat for a lady"), she raced through Warwick Castle, scanning its "superficial though commanding" Van Dyck portraits of a once "nobler" English aristocracy. She afterward cameoed Iverary's "Highland servant in full costume, stupid as the stones he trod on," and Warwick's "fat, pompous butler" mumbling out the subjects of the portraits on the walls. The following week at the duke of Devonshire's Chatsworth House, she noted in her letter, the "park and mock wilderness . . . did not interest me," "pretty Leamington and Stratford are hackneyed ground," and York's legendary cathedral looked "sorrowfully bare" since the Protestant despoliation of its Catholic statues and paintings three centuries earlier. Touring the British past was wearing thin.[18]

A contemporary subject, however, was beginning to stand out for her in bold relief. Up to then poverty had not registered much in her accounts. Although she had seen signs of it in Liverpool, Manchester, Edinburgh, and Perth, she had barely mentioned it in her dispatches. She had even avoided Ireland because she feared the horrors of the famine would interfere with her contemplation of the country's natural beauties! As she traveled through Britain's industrial heartlands, though, "frightful inequalities" eclipsed the picturesque. Her first real shock came in Glasgow, where she had stopped for a night before going on to Edinburgh, and where the crammed working classes' "stamp of squalid, stolid misery and degradation" appeared more appalling than any she had seen. "In the church yard I saw them leaning helplessly against the walls, and lying upon the graves," she wrote ruefully in her journal. "This seemed to [be] their only haven, and they had the air of having lost all faith in Providence too completely to have hopes of peace even there." As she had with New York's poor, she tried to imagine how they felt: "what must be the state of those who live so, when to be there for a quarter of an hour is insufferable and the memory a kind of shame?" At Sheffield, she watched its "sooty servitors" receiving their wages on Saturday night, "looking pallid and dull, as if they had spent on tempering the steel that vital force that should have tempered themselves to manhood." Yet, if the evils seemed even greater than in America, so did the remedies. She lauded Edinburgh's Chambers brothers, whose healthy workrooms, libraries, and evening classes marked a refreshing departure from the "vulgar and base" claims of American publishers that only sales and profits mattered. She was also impressed, in Edinburgh, by the clean infant schools and public baths organized by the educator James Simpson, whom she interviewed; she declared them models of institutions indispensable for any "progress in higher culture" for the working classes. "The manufacturing and commercial towns, burning focuses of grief and vice," she reminded her readers, "are also the centers of intellectual life, as in forcing beds the rarest flowers and fruits are developed by use of impure and repulsive materials." But if this "intellect and love" was not applied to these horrible ills, its working classes "*must* ere very long seek help by other means than words." There was an irony here: she had initially come to Europe with the intention of experiencing and selectively appropriating "the wonders of art, and the temples of old religion," but she wound up witnessing its social conditions with an ominous foreboding about industrial capitalism that she had never expressed in New York. The following day, October 1, she arrived in London.[19]

III

Four days before leaving the Midlands, Fuller had discovered a more personal reason for her hopes for England. "I find a surprizing number of persons who not only receive me warmly, but have a preconceived strong desire to know me," she wrote to her brother Richard. "This is founded mostly on their knowledge of 'Woman in the 19th &c.' Among these a number of intellectual and cultivated men." There was something else she liked: "I may add that from their habits of conversation so superior to those of Americans, I am able to come out a great deal more than I can at home, and they seem to be proportionately interested." Britons may have remained to her "encrusted in mere externals," but she also seems to have found many of them receptive enough to her talents. Her pleasure was probably accentuated by the mixed reception she had been getting in two matters of unfinished personal business.[20]

Because crucial letters are missing, the facts of the first are somewhat muddled, but the main lines are clear. On September 1, Fuller had written from Edinburgh to Nathan's English friend Thomas Delf, then working as an agent for Wiley and Putnam in London, to find out whether Nathan was, as he had promised, there or had sent a letter for her. On the assumption that he *was* there, she had urged Delf to suggest to him that he join her and the Springs on their tour of Scotland. A week later, in the morning just before leaving Edinburgh, she received from Delf a reply and an enclosure of Nathan's letter to her from Hamburg. She later told Nathan that the now lost letter made him seem "so changed and so much worse" that at first she thought it was a forgery. Actually, there was a more plausible reason that she tore it up and immediately came down with a monstrous headache: it contained the news that he was about to marry a young German woman. His wedding his "large, white, soft" bride gave Mary Greeley some perverse pleasure. "I think she rather enjoyed Mr Nathan's getting married to a person so unlike Margarett," Fuller's mother later speculated to her, "tho' she talks admiringly as ever of you." In a journal entry the next day, Fuller tried to sound philosophical about it:

> From 1st June, 1845, to 1st Sept., 1846, a mighty change has taken place, I ween. I understand more and more the character of the *tribes*. I shall write a sketch of it and turn the whole to account in a literary way, since the affections and ideal hopes are so unproductive. I care not. I am resolved to take such disappointments more lightly than I have. I ought not to regret having thought other of "humans" than they deserve.

Of course, minus the rare ethnic slur, she had made such resolutions before. Moreover, several remarks in her dispatch recounting her three days' travel to Rowardennan (such as a lugubrious retelling of stories of betrayed and jilted women in history and song) suggest that grim feelings dogged her. Still, she clearly tried to make the best of the situation. Immediately after arriving in London, she wrote to Delf asking to see him, a meeting that not only, the Transcendentalist fellow traveler told Nathan, "exalt[ed] her in my estimation more than anything I have hitherto read of her writings" but also made him wonder how their "friendship" stood now that Nathan was engaged. "Is she prepared for such a condition of affairs?" he asked. "I am stimulated to ask this perhaps impertinent question from the warmth with which she speaks of your friendship, which, by the way, may be too cold a name for her feeling; but of this I must not judge until I know her better, for perhaps I misinterpret her natural warmth of feeling." Delf was right to wonder. Certainly, if she expected to maintain her "friendship" with Nathan on some terms, the next turn of events quickly scuttled that.[21]

After waiting a month and a half to reply to Nathan's disturbing announcement (claiming to Delf she was too busy in London "to allow her mind a moment's repose to reply to it"), on October 25 she finally sat down to convey her "congratulations." But she also wrote, according to Nathan (this letter is also lost), in the "spirit of slight irritation and dissatisfaction" that much "grieved" him, "and perhaps the more for not finding for it right cause." The "cause," of course, seems clear: he had left her feeling that they had a special relationship that he now wanted to ignore. In short, he had led her on. He strenuously denied it. On the contrary, he said, nothing had changed: "at the beginning of our friendship my anxiety to be clearly understood has caused *you* much insult and *me* much pain," and so now, his admiration for her "capacious" mind and "womanly" heart and the "integrity, profundity, and holiness of your whole character" remained exactly as it was, "unshakable! by no event!" Furthermore, he had done nothing to alter that admirable "understanding" (conveniently ignoring his apparent pass at her) "until shortly before my departure"—namely, by giving her his gift of the white veil, to which she had evidently alluded in her letter. However, he reminded her, although that *might* have referred to some sort of pledge, it could just as well have referred to other things, and, in any case, he had given it to her on the condition that she was "never to give it that or *any* ordinary construction." Meanwhile, he had a few grievances of his own:

> The native mysticism of my being, perhaps, race, that suggested the idea of the gift, was ever alone enough of cause not to let me hope to dare join, so clear, broad, and disciplined an understanding as yours, for any length of time; had it even been possible for a moment to forget my entire deficiency and inferiority of education, the moral and social inequality etc etc but if you remember your own remark on the subject, *and which were very clearly made.*

After these obfuscating but perhaps partly sincere resentments (if one is interpreting him rightly) over her leading *him* on while foreclosing the possibility of marriage to him as a social and moral "inferior," he then got to the practical point. She had proposed in her letter, in "evident irritation and haste," that they return their letters to each other, "as though with what had happened, I had lost not only *all right upon, but even all your confidence to possess, them.*" Slow down, he said. In the first place, there was no express between Hamburg and London. In the second place, "even were there one, *my love and regard for you is and was too sincere, earnest and holy as to change with any new ties or external events so readily and to permit me to part with things so dear so suddenly.*" Third, she had conceded that she had asked for the letters not as a matter of right but only as (quoting her) "'most fitting for either party to have their part of the record.'" Therefore, he said, let her consider *his* moral case. Provocatively mixing marital allusions, he wrote, "Let me entreat you to let this spiritual offspring of our friendship that I take nearer to my heart even from a fear that the mother contemplates divorce, remain in the home they were born to and intended for, until *on our return to New York, we can talk the matter over more fully and fairly.*"[22]

Why *did* he not simply give back her letters, especially as, ever since his apparent pass, she had repeatedly asked him to (as she variously put it) "mutually exchange all her letters," "leave my letters," "let me burn them," "destroy them . . . as they are so intimately personal"? The suggestion often made that he kept them to sell or publish is possible, although there is no evidence he ever tried to do so. Probably, as he suggested, sentiment played some role, as did self-flattery and, perhaps, from his sarcastic rendering of their agreement about his "inferiority," resentment. In any case, whatever he said or inferred, none of it mattered to Fuller. When she got his letter, she evidently (the letter again is lost) exploded. Undoubtedly panicked that he would not give up "so intimately personal" letters that contained the most passionate expressions of erotic (if highly sublimated) feeling she had ever expressed to a man, and that one rejecting her, she now demanded them. Taking a leaf from his own earlier offensive, she also seems to have said to him what she had always suspected: he was a sexual liar and cheat. "*Mr. N. you know you have deceived me*," he quoted her, dropping all Christian names. "*Mr. N. how can you thus play with truth and appeal to god in heaven the while*," "how can you *talk of holiness and add sin to sin the while*." To all this "setting forth" of charges, "in all the subtle and attenuated shades of ideal procedure and with the stile of a philadelphia lawyer," compounded by reports about him that she had picked up from others—he told her, "'Keep cool.'" She was obviously too hostile toward him to receive his reasonable defenses, and meanwhile, she should know three things. First, he would *not* give up her letters until they met, and, if that never happened, they should each have them burned at death, a fair arrangement, since, as a married man, he, too, would have something to worry about, although, of course, he would never suggest, as she did with him, that she should! Second, *he* was the victim. "Miss F., you *have judged me, without a hearing, you have condemned and insulted me, trampled upon and wounded me*, nay! but for the consciousness of innocence, *would have destroyed me!*" Finally, although she obviously wished a "cessation of intercourse," "I might as well bid my heart to cease beating, as to cease feeling for you, a true and tender regard and friendship." After receiving Nathan's own bit of "Philadelphia" lawyering, she would never write or see him again, retaining only these last letters and probably destroying the rest. Fending off all entreaties and threats from her family, he would keep her letters until he died, by then having changed his name to the gentile one of James Gotendorf. If, as William Channing would suggest, probably referring to just this affair, such was her craving for love that, despite her usual keen psychological perceptiveness, "Margaret might be led away blindfold," with Nathan at least, she seems to have finally taken off the bandage.[23]

Her other bit of unfinished business was professional and ended more happily: she got her first major appraisals of her literary career. The first was Poe's knowing pencil portrait of her for the August issue of *Godey's Lady's Book*. Although it has usually been read selectively as a harsh attack, it in fact was a surprisingly balanced and often penetrating assessment. The one exception was, predictably, on the woman question, and even that was, considering his ostentatious sentimentality on the subject, surprisingly mild. Calling her *Woman in the Nineteenth Century* "a book which few women in the country could have written, and no woman in the country would have published, except Miss Fuller," he parlayed that half-compliment into a criticism of her "doctrine," presumably of gender androgyny, which he took to be sheer projection. ("She judges *woman* by the heart and intellect of Miss Fuller, but there are not more than one or two dozen Miss Fullers on the whole face of the earth.") At the same time, however, disavowing the "silly, condemnatory" attacks of his former coeditor Briggs, he declared her book, like all her writings, forcible, brilliant, "and to a certain degree scholar-like" (in her review of him she had given him the same qualified compliment). Much more important, though, certainly to him, the anti-Boston and publisher-hostile Poe completely aligned himself with her cultural stance, heaping lavish praise, as already noted, on her "Philippic" on the Harring case, as well as her demolition of his nemesis Longfellow. Mostly, though, consistent with his usual concern, he concentrated on the formal properties of her writing. To be sure, he gave her a few Poesque but also justified hits for her carelessness in grammar and diction, her "unjustifiable Carlyleisms," and her distended sentences. Yet, most notable, certainly for the fastidious critic, he offered a highly appreciative overall judgment of her writing. "I know no style which surpasses it," he declared. "It is singularly piquant, vivid, terse, bold, luminous—leaving details out of sight, it is everything that a style need be." Moreover, he rightfully located its source in two Romantic characteristics of hers. One was her "subjectiveness," which, he said, allowed her in *Summer on the Lakes* to paint a scene "less by its features than by its effects," producing "unrivaled" graphic descriptions by conveying "the true by the novel or unexpected." (Unsurprisingly, he cited as an example her gothic-touched recollected association of Niagara Falls with stealthily approaching Indians.) Then there was her personality: "Her acts are bookish, and her books are less thoughts than acts." Although this celebrated bon mot carried an obvious sting, in context it was more friendly than not, as was, at least by half, his concluding Romantic physiognomic portrait of her (quoted earlier).[24]

She did not have to wait long, however, for an unfriendly appraisal. It came from Poe's detractor Rufus Griswold, in his pioneering but crude anthology *Prose Writers of America,* which he expected would make "Young America" "rabid." He did pay her the compliment of including her with only four other female authors (the others were Catharine Sedgwick, Caroline Kirkland, Lydia Maria Child, and the sentimental short story writer Eliza Leslie). He also conceded that her writing style, while "sometimes pedantic and careless," was "generally excellent,— various, forcible, and picturesque." Otherwise, however, he denigrated her, with his signature "sulky magnificence of style," in an attack surpassed only by his violent assault on Cornelius Mathews. Her *Woman in the Nineteenth Century* was an "eloquent expression of her discontent of having been created female." Her "astonishing facility in the use of her intellectual furniture" accounted for the glibness of her prose. Most damning, the nationalist Whig scrapper said, as had the *Anti-Slavery Standard*, she was an anti-American elitist who "seems to think that books, like brown stout, are improved by the motion of a ship, and therefore generally eulogizes those which have been imported, and is very severe upon those of home production, excepting a few by personal friends." His assault naturally offended both her Whig and Democratic fans. "Greeley is angry at what I offer under the name of Margaret," he petulantly wrote the publisher James T. Fields, "which is very badly written though all true." But it was left to Duyckinck to explain in his new *Literary World* the critical weaknesses of Griswold's "shabby-genteel" attack. Relentlessly indulgent with almost every other American author, Griswold went out of his way to "*degrade*" Fuller as critic, willfully ignoring her critical discriminations just when, ironically, her reputation as an *American* author was taking off in Europe. "It is a little singular," Duyckinck wrote acerbically, "that while the critics of England and France are conferring distinguished honors upon Miss Fuller as a representative of American genius, the author of this big book on nationality should so pitifully deprecate her." A week later he issued a further warning: Fuller was a "species of antagonist of whom a man of moderate abilities should be particularly careful, in contests of the pen." Fuller may have left "Young America" behind, but her New York literary comrades kept their heavy guns at the ready.[25]

They were helped that September by the publication of her *Papers on Literature and Art*, which garnered her largest flood of reviews, although often along sharply divided lines. A majority of American reviewers praised her writing, especially, as usual, in contrast with that of her fuzzy Transcendentalist and bombastic Young America colleagues. Many singled out the candor and fearlessness with which she pursued her critiques, "thoughtless of consequences." Her old moderate Transcendentalist friend Henry Hedge, who had disliked her "extravagant" *Woman*, and had never thought (he confessed) she had much "perspicuity of style," was astonished by her new collection. "In the use of language—freedom, copiousness, richness, and precision of words—Miss Fuller has few superiors," he wrote in the *Christian Examiner*. "And besides this there is a fullness of meaning, and a kindness as well as boldness of utterance, which make us forget differences, or care not for them." Negative responses, on the other hand, were all over the map. Poe, who had boasted in his *Broadway Journal* about having her as a contributor, had loved her laudatory review of his *Raven* collection, and had lauded her own writing just the month before, became apoplectic when he saw himself unmentioned in her "American Literature" essay or in any other piece in her *Papers,* probably a casualty of Wiley's cuts. A "silly and conceited piece of Transcendentalism" by a "grossly dishonest," "ill-tempered and very inconsistent old maid," he fumed (an epithet he would soon up to "detestable old maid"). The two most hostile American reviewers registered typical opposite misreadings of what was so awful about Fuller's criticism. The self-described neoclassical critic for the *American Whig Review* declared it was, as Poe now claimed, her Goethean "eulogism" of authors. The popular *Graham's*, which had effusively praised her *Summer on the Lakes*, said, on the contrary, it was her dogmatic hypercriticism toward American books, complaining loudly, as did other American critics, especially of her "spiteful" treatment of Longfellow, Lowell, and Prescott. Only the *Democratic Review's* Sarah Helen Whitman noted Fuller's often nuanced and still hopeful critiques of American authors. As for Fuller's radical religious views that had so worried Wiley, except for a lone protest of her defense of Shelley's moral character, no reviewer said a word about them.[26]

Several, though, like Poe, spoke about her sex. Two did so positively, albeit from opposite ends of the cultural spectrum. "The learning, ability and taste displayed in these papers," crowed *Godey's Lady's Book*, "would suffice to make the literary fortune of a dozen male writers of our acquaintance, who are vainly striving to accomplish with painful labor what this extraordinary woman executes without any apparent effort." In rougher prose, Whitman, although grumbling about the title-page name ("why don't she print it Susan M. or Sarah M., instead of the S. Margaret—which is a sort of frippery way"), declared in his *Brooklyn Daily Eagle* that Fuller's sex was the *best* thing about the book. Denouncing the "common contemptuous . . . 'you-are-touching-on-our-field' manner" toward women who strove for attainments higher "than sentimental love stories, or weak rhyme," he yawped, "we therefore welcome Miss Fuller's papers, right heartily."

Most of those who raised the gender issue, however, used it against her. "The dogmatic tone" of her book, wrote the reviewer for the *Columbian Lady's and Gentleman's Magazine*, "would be in bad taste from one of the sterner sex, even did his literary standing justify it." "The Author's eulogy is unrelaxed and over-powering; she is the transcendental Boswell," the *American Whig* reviewer cried, adding contentedly, "which office, let us be happy to find it fallen where it be-longs, upon the gentler sex." For some, Fuller was still an unwelcome presence in the male public literary square.[27]

That fact, though, paled before the principal one: she had finally arrived in the international republic of letters that she had long honored. Several American re-viewers even signaled her future canonization by singling out her volumes, along with Hawthorne's *Mosses*, Melville's *Typee*, and Poe's *Tales*, as by far the best books of Wiley and Putnam's American series. Others noted her spreading influ-ence. "Miss Fuller's writings evince a rare talent," even one critical reviewer wrote, "and they will be read and admired by thousands who have not yet heard of her." But, as Duyckinck had suggested in rebutting Griswold, the strongest signals of her arrival came from her British reviews. Predictably, the stinging Tory *Black-wood's* magazine was condemnatory. Although acquitting her of the "flagrant absurdities" of her nationalist camp, the reviewer ridiculed her temerity in dis-paraging the magazine's hallowed Scott and Southey. "It is not to be supposed that this authoress" (to whom the critic also generously assigned the "more hon-orable title—Mrs Margaret Fuller") "is always so startling and original as in these passages. She sometimes attains, and keeps for a while, the level of commonplace." (The *Knickerbocker* cheerfully reprinted all of *Blackwood's* sarcasms.) Other British reviewers, however, while faulting her for occasionally lapsing into ob-scurity, offered considerable praise for her extensive reading and discriminating judgment, which "unquestionably" guaranteed her a "high position" as a critic in the best of that "higher class" of "speculative" critics. Most telling, the reviewer for the *Spectator*, England's journal of "magisterial seriousness," which had panned her *Woman in the Nineteenth Century* as a wooden imitation of Emerson, had nothing but praise for her this time. "We have seen enough," he wrote, of her aesthetic sensitivity, "full and discerning" mind, and "earnest, generous, and se-rene" criticism "to assure us that Margaret Fuller is worthy to hold her place among the highest order of female writers of our day." Although often decrying Ameri-cans' craven dependency on English verdicts, in this instance she had to have appreciated their usefulness.[28]

IV

Certainly, they were useful in London. She did squeeze in a couple of days for the "stock shows" at museums, galleries, gardens, and clubs, which she mined for cautiously progressive lessons for her compatriots. She was especially impressed with the free cost of the National Gallery, Hampton Court, and the British Mu-seum. She worried a little that all the noise the thick shoes of nursery maids and the boots of tradesmen made detracted from the "atmosphere of Art," but she was sure the "sight of such objects must be gradually doing them a great deal of good." Alert, as always, to the artistic avant-garde, she attended a private showing of the semiabstract paintings of Turner, which many critics ridiculed as collections of "strange blotches." These "hieroglyphics of pictures," she reported, which represented nature in its "elemental . . . transition state" and required prolonged viewing before their luminous dots and streaks metamorphosed into roofs and streams, were obviously beyond the utilitarian and sentimental "English mind." As Parliament was not in session, she said little about politics, but she did keep a steady eye on the "condition of England." In contrast to her praises of the progressive welfare experiments in Liverpool and Manchester, she turned in mixed reports on London's benevolent institutions. She recommended as a replicable model a public laundry where poor washerwomen could avoid exposing their children to dangerously damp, tiny tenement rooms (not to mention their customers' clothes to bad cooking smells!). However, the clean but bleak new "model-prison" at Pentonville lagged woefully behind the rehabilitative Sing Sing. Continuing to be amazed at England's horrific poverty, she now fervently prayed for a "peaceful revolution" that would destroy "nothing but the shocking inhumanity of exclusiveness" that prevents property from being used "for the benefit of all."[29]

Mainly, though, she immersed herself, as she had longed to do ten years before, in London's literary life. Her location was good. For three weeks she and the Springs stayed at the fashionable Morley's at Charing Cross on Trafalgar Square, before moving over to cheaper lodgings at number 17 "little narrow" Warwick Street and, in mid-November, to the even more economical but still nearby Grand Hotel. "In this enormously expensive country," she sighed to Richard, echoing many an antebellum traveler's lament, "people who are not very rich must be content, not merely with second but fourth or fifth best." Initially, she worried that, as in Edinburgh, many of the city's literati would be out of town, but after sending out all of her letters of introduction at once to "glean what few good people" she could, she received so many invitations that she hardly had time to dress "and none to sleep." The reason, she thought, remained the English edition of *Woman,* which had been "read and prized by many," but by that fall she could see it was also all the favorable notices of her *Papers,* even in, she was stunned to discover, the "high-handed 'Spectator.'" What a shame, she wrote Emerson, that Wiley had half-wrecked the volumes by his cuts! "It is a real misfortune," she moaned to Duyckinck, especially since her essays on Continental literature "and others of a radical stamp" would have made their mark right then.[30]

If by "radical" she meant Romantic or liberal, she need not have fretted, since she still met plenty of authors of both sorts, many of whom she had reviewed in America. She was disappointed to find Landor, Tennyson, Browning, and Barrett away, the latter two having just eloped to Italy, but she did see the "Faustian" Philip Bailey, as well as the working-class writers William Thom and Thomas Cooper. Inspired by their presence, or perhaps the "radical" times, she upgraded several. She found the "admirable" London production of John Westland Marston's socially conscious play *Patrician's Daughter,* which she had largely panned in the

Dial, a wonderful sign of the "new era in England." She also enjoyed meeting Richard Henry Horne, who impressed her more in person than one would have predicted from her *Tribune* review of him. Nor, despite her perennial eye for "intellectual and cultivated men," did she forget the ladies. She became acquainted with the Unitarian watercolorist Margaret Gillies, who had given up "many things highly valued by English women" while trying to shake off what Fuller thought were her paintings' sentimental artifices. She also dined with the salon leader Mary Berry and her celebrated dramatist friend Joanna Baillie, who knew William Ellery Channing, Eliza Rotch, and others of Fuller's Boston Unitarian friends. Fuller drew the right gender moral: readers should honor Baillie for refusing to sigh forever over "withered flowers of fond affection, and woman's heart born to be misunderstood" and grappling instead with "things which are good, intellectually, universally."[31]

Even more than in Liverpool and Manchester, she gravitated toward radical journalists. Despite her notice of Börnstein's analysis of Marx's and Engels's recent writings, she evidently had no contact with the Chartists for whom they wrote and from whom they drew some of their ideas about working-class behavior. On the other hand, she was disgusted with the moderate Reform Club's "stupidly comfortable" members for excluding women. (She laughed that she was at least glad to see all the apprentice male cooks crowding around their master chef, "as I hope to see that and washing transferred to their care in the progress of things, since they are 'the stronger sex.'") Overwhelmingly she associated with the largely Unitarian circle of left-liberal writers, artists, and activists who, like her Transcendentalist colleagues, had traded the attenuated supernaturalism of their sect for liberal post-Christianity and radical reform, albeit with an admixture of British utilitarianism. Many were contributors to the new *People's Journal* edited by John Saunders and William Howitt. The magazine's "prodigious" circulation (in its contributor Harriet Martineau's phrase) of nearly twenty thousand readers made it not only the progressive alternative to the working class-conscious Chartists' *Northern Star* but also, after *Punch*, the decade's most popular periodical. It also fitted well with Fuller's Romantic social liberalism. Dedicated "in the spirit of Thomas Carlyle" to the emancipation of labor, it opposed all "destructive" class enmity, dispensed crisp advice to workers on improving their domestic economy, displayed deep sympathy for their suffering, and attacked capitalists for shirking their philanthropic responsibilities. Along with articles advocating working-class suffrage, factory acts, producers' cooperatives, and mechanics' institutes, it also devoted large sections to stories about working-class life and, echoing Fuller's category, the "poetry of the people." Probably most catching Fuller's liberal cosmopolitan eye, it emblazoned on its covers a quotation from William Ellery Channing on the "grand doctrine" of self-culture, published American reform writers like Lydia Maria Child and Parke Godwin, and printed European socialist and "communist" authors whose radicalism exceeded anything advocated by Saunders and Howitt. Finally, their circle constituted the central feminist group in England, sharply critiquing the legal and political subordination of women and advocating the radical reform of marriage, including the right to divorce, with some even having extramarital partnerships themselves.[32]

Fuller easily found her way into this circle and its contributors. Alcott had known several of the group in London four years earlier and a number of them, like the Fourierist editor Hugh Doherty and the Swedenborgian James John Garth Wilkinson, were comrades of Godwin and Henry James, Sr., while others, like Marston and Thom, she had reviewed. Most important, on Hodgson's suggestion, before leaving Liverpool she had gotten from Martineau a letter of introduction to Saunders and Howitt. Through them she met Howitt's Quaker wife Mary, whose companionate "intellectual" marriage she had extolled in *Woman*; Dr. Thomas Southworth Smith, physician, secret lover of Gillies, and pioneering builder of healthy tenements for working people; and the circle's political doyen, the ex–Unitarian minister and Anti-Corn League orator William J. Fox. Of course, Fuller had a few Transcendentalist reservations. She asked Duyckinck to tell James that she liked Doherty and Wilkinson "exceedingly," but she privately thought Wilkinson's mind, though "sane" and "strong," was "in the last degree unpoetical," and certainly not one she could "go far with." In her dispatch she likewise judged Fox's "practical and homely" eloquence inferior to both William Channing's ex-tempore spiritual beauty and Parker's "fullness and sustained flow." Generally, though, she kept her criticisms private. Except for the also quasi-radical *Punch*, she told her readers, the *People's Journal* was a fairer "sign of the times than any other publication of England," and certainly more so than the "solemn" London *Times* "on which you all use your scissors so industrially." She even got into the circle's utilitarian spirit sufficiently to find the dressed skeleton of Jeremy Bentham —which he had left to Southworth Smith, an early advocate of dissection, who kept it in his library—not revolting, as she had feared, but an "agreeable sight" signifying Bentham's devotion to the "cause of science."[33]

And they liked *her*. Despite their own attraction to German Romantic literature and theology, a few seem to have found *her* Transcendental "fullness and sustained flow" a little hard to take. The Unitarian minister Goodwyn Barmby recalled seeing her at a large party corner the popular Fox, whose working-class constituents the following year would send him to Parliament. He seemed "fairly badgered, driven up a corner, talked to death. Miss Fuller had traveled far farther than he had from the common ruts of learning and literature," and her Neoplatonic talk (as Barmby characterized it) "came in a shining flow of words, and he appeared to be always retreating in vain, for as step by step he went back, on came the bright waters after him." By contrast, those of a more Romantic stripe, such as the Italian nationalism partisan William James Linton, warmed to her immediately. Indeed, even the no-nonsense Saunders, in a review of her works in the journal, characterized her alien intellectual identity in comradely terms: it was obvious that she belonged to the "school of transatlantic transcendentalism" only in the best senses of espousing sincere seeking after the highest truth and opposing the prevalent materialism of her country. Most important, he declared, she actually wrote intelligibly to ordinary readers and preached not the "duty" of absorption in "self-investigation, self-analysis, self-torture, self-watching, self-seeking" but the "primary Christian doctrine of self-negation"! After quoting copiously from her articles, including her series on Thom and Prince, he closed with a warm "transatlantic" welcome: "We congratulate America upon her production of such a mind as that of Margaret Fuller."[34]

Meanwhile, that fall her mind was receiving scrutiny from two formidable intellectuals of a very different sort from the uplifting utilitarian *People's Journal* crowd. The first one would not seem to have held out much promise. Once enthralled, like all her young Transcendentalist friends, by Carlyle's expressive early writings, his exposure of the humanistic depths of German literature, and his call for a new "natural supernatural" faith to replace the sham worlds of Christianity and utilitarianism, lately she had come to cringe at his increasingly mannered and overbearing writing. From his side, things did not look very promising, either. "Very high flights about Art, Self-sacrifice, Progress, etc., etc. . . . all of a very ghostly (not *ghastly*) character," he had yawned in a letter to Emerson after getting from him several *Dials* containing her articles. Carlyle's readiness to lump her with the rest of Emerson's wearisome ethereal friends comes through even more colorfully in a regularly quoted (if invariably mangled) anecdote. Although it later made the rounds among the New York literati, its original source was Henry James, Sr., who a couple of years earlier, shortly after meeting Fuller in New York after she returned from the West, had visited Carlyle in London. Who was this "'Margaret Fooler' (broad Scotch)" he had been hearing about, he had reported the Scotsman asking him. After giving a complimentary account, James had added: "When I last saw Margaret Fuller she told me she had got to this conclusion to accept the universe." "God, accept the universe, Margaret Fooler accept the universe! (with a loud guffaw) why perhaps upon the whole it is the best thing she could do—it is very kind of Margaret Fooler!" This legendary putdown of the self-aggrandizing Fuller has since gotten a couple of more positive spins from two equally tougher-than-thou Fuller watchers. One was Henry's son William, who used it to illustrate his religiously "healthy" rather than a sullenly "dull" metaphysical way of accepting reality or, as James also called it, the universe. The existential-minded Perry Miller would even turn the tables on Carlyle by suggesting that, in light of his puerile championing of might over right, the "honor" should go to Fuller![35]

Certainly, Carlyle was then having his share of difficulties with *his* universe. Raging at the "Phallus" and the "moneybag," as he piquantly called capitalism's twin fetishes, he was also growing deeply fearful of the radical "mobs" then menacing Europe, as well as blocked in writing a book intended to galvanize English society around the discipline of "Work." Domineering and sexually inhibited, if not impotent, he had also been quarreling with his intellectual and witty but increasingly morose wife, Jane Welsh, over his platonic pursuit of the charming Lady Harriet Baring. In the midst of these heated circumstances that summer, he received three successive letters from Emerson, raving about Fuller's credentials as a *Tribune* critic, an "exotic in New England," and a deep interpreter of Continental literature. "In short," he said, "she is our citizen of the world by quite special diploma." So, he directed, "you must not fail to give a good & faithful interview to this wise, sincere, accomplished & most entertaining of women. . . . We shall send you no other such." Emerson's hearty endorsement apparently worked, for

Carlyle "at once" went to see her at Warwick Street to invite her and the Springs to visit them on the evening of October 7 at their house at 5 Cheyne Row in Chelsea and a week later to a dinner party there. The two events seem to have been a study in (to borrow from James Freeman Clarke's later essay) "the two Carlyles." At the first one, they actually hit it off. "A strange *lilting* lean old-maid," Carlyle reported the next day to his brother John, "not nearly such a bore as I expected." Fuller was equally surprised, afterward writing Emerson, "I was delighted with him," especially his "very sweet humor, full of wit and pathos, without being overbearing or oppressive." She added that, in return for a witty riff on "fanatics" of the day that was "enough to kill one with laughing," she offered one of her own, which he fully appreciated. "Carlyle is worth a thousand of you for that," she wrote with a little sting, "he is not ashamed to laugh when he is amused." She resolved "to go out very often" to their house.[36]

At the party on the fourteenth, however, Carlyle's dark doppelgänger emerged. Jane may have felt a little tense residue from Fuller's first visit, when Fuller had "only *seen*" her ("for who can speak while her husband is there?"). If so, Jane's often jealous confidante, the novelist Geraldine Jewsbury, tried to increase it with some ostentatious anti-American Transcendentalism. "I loathe her heartily from your description. I have no patience with theoretical profligacy. . . . She must be, and cannot help but be, a hypocrite, if she be tempted to death to live a 'free and easy life,' and yet keeps herself strait-laced up in practice to keep in with Emerson & Co.!" But if Jane, who admired some of Fuller's writings, especially *Summer on the Lakes*, was touched by the sniping of England's would-be George Sand, it did not last, as both her and Fuller's later letters speak only warmly of each other's talents and charms. A greater difficulty may have been the guest list, which included, instead of the pro–women's rights John Stuart Mill, whose coolness toward Carlyle had made him "peremptorily" refuse an invitation, the clever intellectual popularizer George Henry Lewes, George Eliot's later consort, who was then starting in on Fuller's relinquished project of writing the first English Goethe biography. ("He must be as unfit," she sniffed, with her own Transcendentalist condescension, "as irreligion and sparkling shallowness can make him"). But the real problem was the "acrid" Carlyle, who fired off for his captive audience a blizzard of his crotchets, including rants against Tennyson, Burns, and Shakespeare for not having enough good sense (she recounted to Emerson) "to write straight on in prose, and such nonsense which though amusing eno' at first, he ran to death after a while." "The whole harangue," she wrote, "was one eloquent proclamation of the defects of his own mind." What proved "wearisome," though, was that he brooked no opposition. You simply "cannot interrupt him," she said, "so that you are a perfect prisoner when he has once got hold of you. To interrupt him is a physical impossibility; if you get a chance to remonstrate for a moment, he raises his voice and bears you down. True, he does you no injustice, and with his admirable penetration sees the disclaimer in your mind, so that you are not morally delinquent; but it is not pleasant to be unable to utter it." Still, the evening seems not to have been exactly a disaster. Rebecca Spring recalled that Fuller parried his jibes about her favorite Petrarch's Laura with "nice bright answers." Indeed,

Lewes remembered she more than held her own: when she spoke, they were "all silenced."[37]

In any case, she and Carlyle's mutual fascination continued. After he and Jane returned from their two-week trip, Fuller had them over for tea, where the dark Scotsman appeared grimmer than ever. "All Carlyle's talk, that evening," she reported to Emerson, "was a defence of mere force,—success the test of right;— if people would not behave well, put collars round their necks;—find a hero, and let them be his slaves, &c. It was very Titanic, and anti-celestial." But she seems to have been unfazed by it. Rebecca recalled it had been *she* who had gotten worked up when he loudly announced he had no pity on slaves if they consented to be such. (After Rebecca told him of the many slaves who had courageously run away, he frequently interjected, "I am glad to hear it! I am glad to hear it!") Indeed, even after this last less-than-"melodious" meeting, Fuller reported to Emerson feeling the "warmest friendship and admiration" toward Carlyle. Moreover, in her later sketch in the *Tribune*, she not only highlighted his still vital role as destroyer of English "shams and conventions" but she also veiled his unappetizing qualities in sharp but generous irony. Did he "not converse" but "only harangue"? Absolutely, but "this is not the least from unwillingness to allow freedom to others; on the contrary, no man would more enjoy a manly resistance to his thought, but it is the impulse of a mind accustomed to follow out its own impulse as the hawk its prey, and which knows not how to stop the chase." Was he "arrogant and overbearing"? Certainly, "but in his arrogance there is no littleness, no self love: it is the heroic arrogance of some old Scandinavian conqueror—it is his nature and the untamable impulse that has given him power to crush the dragons." She concluded with one of her finest character portraits and Romantic apologias:

> He seemed to me quite isolated, lonely as the desert, yet never was a man more fitted to prize a man, could he find one to match his mood. He finds them, but only in the past. He sings rather than talks. He pours upon you a kind of satirical, heroical, critical poem, with regular cadences, and generally catching up near the beginning some singular epithet, which serves as a *refrain* when his song is full, or with which as with a knitting needle he catches up the stitches if he has chanced now and then to let fall a row. For the higher kinds of poetry he has no sense, and his talk on that subject is delightfully and gorgeously absurd; he sometimes stops a minute to laugh at himself, then begins anew with fresh vigor—for all the spirits he is driving before him seem to him as Fata Morganas, ugly masks, in fact, if he can but make them turn about, but he laughs that they seem to others such dainty Ariels.

After more avian metaphors ("He puts out his chin sometimes till it looks like the beak of a . . . falcon"), she finished him off with one of her favorite Romantic defenses: "The Siegfried of England, great and powerful, if not quite invulnerable, and of a might rather to destroy evil than legislate for good. At all events, he seems to be what Destiny intended, and represents fully a certain side; so we make no remonstrance as to his being and proceeding for himself, though we sometimes must for us."[38]

Carlyle's final appraisals of her were equally generous. "A high-soaring, clear, enthusiast soul," he reported to Emerson, then getting ready to leave for Europe;

in whose speech there is much of all that one wants to find in speech. A sharp subtle intellect too; and less of that shoreless Asiatic dreaminess that I have sometime met with in her writings. We liked one another very well, I think. . . . But, on the whole, it could not be concealed, least of all from the sharp female intellect, that this Carlyle was a dreadfully heterodox, not to say a dreadfully savage fellow, at heart; believing no syllable of all that Gospel of Fraternity, Benevolence, and *new* Heaven-on-Earth, preached forth by all manner of "advanced" creatures from George Sand to Elihu Burritt, in these days, . . . a "*phosphorescence* from the dead body of a Christianity, that would not admit itself to be dead, and lie buried with all its unspeakable putrescences, as a venerable dead one ought!" To all which Margaret listened with much good nature; tho' of course with sad reflexions not a few.

Fuller's later *Tribune* portrait "*en beau*" pleased him even more. "She might have read the phenomena infinitely worse," he later remarked to Browning, "nay it is surprising she didn't." Hinting at the "phenomena" to Emerson, he would write half-sheepishly:

We have not a triumphant life here; very far indeed from that *ach Gott!*—as you shall see. But Margaret is an excellent soul: in real regard with both of us here. Since she went, I have been reading some of her Papers in a new Book we have got: greatly superior to all I knew before; in fact the undeniable utterance (now first undeniable to me) of a true heroic mind;—altogether unique, so far as I know, among the Writing Women of this generation; rare enough too, God knows, among the writing Men. She is very narrow, sometimes; but she is truly high: honour to Margaret, and more and more good-speed to her.[39]

Back home, after hearing Emerson read Carlyle's letters, Fuller's Transcendentalist friends positively glowed. Alcott, whom Carlyle had promptly chewed up and spat out when he had met him in London—and who evidently felt some vicarious vindication in her remarkable "reception and influence abroad"—waxed florid in his diary about the success of their "diplomatic" ambassador to "the best of the civilized world." Sarah Clarke thought the same, although she was surprised about one thing: "that he was disgusted by your philanthropic turn of mind—This seems whimsical that you should give offence in that way." Sarah missed the point, of course, about Fuller's increasingly radical politics, but also about Carlyle: the reactionary Romantic, who cared infinitely more about a "true heroic mind" than either literary trends or the "poisonous Cant" of reform, recognized a kindred spirit when he saw one.[40]

The other challenging character cut in a heroic mold whom Fuller met that October was someone of whom intellectuals from Carlyle to Nietzsche, who both admired him, could only dream they might be. The forty-one-year-old son of a University of Genoa professor of anatomy and an ardently republican mother, the Italian patriot and revolutionary Giuseppe Mazzini looked the part, with his large dark eyes, slight frame, finely chiseled features, and perennially black garb. His austere lifestyle and charismatic personality also helped. Although cursed with bouts of depression and a strong streak of self-righteousness that could make him difficult to work with, he displayed a severe seriousness, sensitive kindness, and lighthearted dreaminess that endeared him to the hundreds of Italian political refugees who had come to London after the failed risings of the 1820s and 1830s. These qualities also endeared him to a large and influential cross-section of English liberals and radicals who organized committees to raise funds through bazaars, balls, and concerts for his many relief programs for his refugees and his countless political schemes.[41]

Mazzini's own liberalism, however, was far from that of England's emerging Victorian age. Culturally, he was a Romantic, believing literature should promote social progress but exempting from the requirement geniuses like the despairing Byron and indifferent Goethe. Politically, he was a liberal democrat devoted to an independent and unified republican Italy to be achieved through a popular insurrection animated by three key ideas. First was the concept of political democracy encapsulated in his famous seminal phrase *"All for the people,—all by the people,"* balanced by his liberal caveat *"under the leading of the best and wisest."* Second was a social philosophy that rested not on French "Jacobin" rights, English interests, and German collectivism, which he thought bred "egoism," exploitation, and class dictatorship, respectively, but a secularized social gospel of individuals devoted to reciprocal "duties" to protect each other's divine dignity and capacities in an earthly kingdom of God. Third was the idea of a cosmopolitan nationalism in which national self-determination did not figure as an end in itself, and certainly not as a means of aggrandizement, but as a vehicle for the progress of humanity and liberty within and among nations. He also gave this hybrid idea, which to varying degrees many of the "Young Europe" nationalist movements of the period shared, an idiosyncratically Italian twist: while countries had different "missions," God had assigned to the peninsula the role of moral unifier of humankind. Meanwhile, as "Joseph Mazzini" in England, his identity remained poignantly anomalous. Having fled from the Piedmont government, which had sentenced him to death in absentia for his role in the 1834 Savoy uprising, he deeply appreciated the civic freedoms and the large circles of liberal admirers he enjoyed nowhere else in Europe. Yet he remained the consummate exile, propagandizing for Young Europe, supporting himself by writing on Continental literature and politics, despising both the bourgeois Whigs and the aristocratic Tories, and, while appreciative of the help and devotion of the *People's Journal* crowd, constantly fretting about their crude utilitarianism.[42]

Liberally Romantic, democratically cosmopolitan, and awkwardly ensconced in a Unitarian community whose intellectual women, who adored him, he preferred to its men: Mazzini was clearly tailor-made for Fuller. They also knew a bit about each other. While in New York, she had alluded to him in the *Tribune*, and she knew of his reputation among Italian exiles from his Young Europe coorganizer, Harro Harring, who had made him into a character in *Dolores.* He knew about her from Carlyle, who detested his populist fantasies but liked his call to "duties," as well as feeling great affection for him, and had given him some of her writings. Even so, Mazzini would later say he had thought she had initially felt a certain "distrust" of his cause, which may have been a spillover from her usual worry about European radicals: their animus toward America. If so, he gave her some reassurance. Shortly after their first meeting on October 24, which

Harring, then living in Soho, had arranged, Mazzini wrote her about his hotheaded comrade, still boiling about his "death" sentence from the "land of Washington." "You have no cause for fearing that Harro-Harring's sentiments could influence my opinion of the U.S.," he assured her, alluding presumably to his genuine admiration, despite his dislike of Americans' obsession with their "rights," for their idealism, especially that of the abolitionists and, of course, the Protestant and Young America groups that supported Young Italy. "Harro Harring is no fit judge. His opinions are all derived from personal impulses [and he is] held down, and led astray in all that he does, feels, or thinks, by a thirst for Fame, which is the most despicable thing I know of, whenever sought for not as a means, but, as an end. As we must, I hope, agree about many more important things, so we do entirely agree about Harro." She got further reassurance about Mazzini's sensitivity at her and the Springs' November 7 tea, where Mazzini's radical pronouncements had touched off an explosion of invectives from Carlyle at everyone's "'rose-water imbecilities.'" "We all felt distant from him," she reported on Carlyle to Emerson, while Mazzini (who just the month before had called Carlyle "a democrat by every instinctive tendency" even if he would deny it), after trying to answer him, "became very sad." Jane Carlyle, who was Mazzini's chief consoler in England, afterward said to Fuller, "These are but opinions to Carlyle; but to Mazzini, who has given his all, and helped bring his friends to the scaffold, in pursuit of such subjects, it is a matter of life and death." Mazzini's Cheyne Row confidante could hardly have come up with a more Fulleresque personal ground for admiring the Italian hero.[43]

If Fuller's "distrust" lingered at all, she dispelled it three days later, when she attended a fifth-anniversary dinner for his Italian Free School at 5 Greville Street, Hatton Garden. Established for poor Italian boys who had been finagled into leaving Italy to work in the streets of London as organ grinders and hawkers for often-abusive masters at starvation wages, the school put him in contact with both Italian workers and middle-class liberal sympathizers. Its Mazzinian curriculum certainly must have appealed to her: in addition to instruction in reading and writing, he and other teachers gave lessons in subjects like the "nature of duty," the social values of the Sermon on the Mount, and, to the outrage of neighborhood priests, the "ferocious hypocrisy of the Inquisition."[44]

So, asked to say a few words, following the awarding of student prizes and speeches by eminent English supporters and Italian exiles, the American Transcendentalist agreed, giving the audience a taste of *her* cosmopolitan liberalism. She began by touching on the comparative status of women in public life, suggesting, as she had been doing since coming abroad, that Europeans had a way to go to catch up with the United States, where women very commonly addressed public assemblies, she herself having often done so before "large numbers." (This caused even the nationalistic George Palmer Putnam, who was in the audience, and who evidently did not know about her speech at Sing Sing, to raise an eyebrow: "not a very accurate, though it might be a prophetic, remark.") She then segued into a plea for her favorite idea, which she thought the school exemplified: that countries needed an "international moral exchange." "We should accept from

each its own peculiar excellence," she said, replicating almost exactly the cosmopolitan line of her *Tribune* articles in New York, finding in the Germans "simplicity, unwearied industry, and extensive mental culture" and in the English, more
parsimoniously, "mechanical skill and a certain spirit of honour." She dwelt most
expansively, though, on the Italians.

> Italy, herself so fair, has bestowed on the rest of the world, beyond any other coun-
> try, save ancient Greece, those arts which, pourtraying the beautiful and the grace-
> ful, awaken the love of the beautiful and the good, and thus refine the human soul.
> To the poet and the artist, Italy must ever be most dear; nor can anyone, capable of
> thought on the subject, be indifferent to the emancipation of this fair land from
> present degradation.

According to the *People's Journal* reporter, who identified her as the author of
the "best book" on the woman question, the crowd of Italian and Polish exiles
and their English supporters, moved by her spontaneous fluency and Italian sympathies—and no doubt also her compatible Herderian sentiments—responded with
a prolonged burst of applause. Afterward, she stayed talking with them until 1:30
in the morning.[45]

Mazzini, who had reportedly nodded vigorously throughout her speech, was
deeply impressed. "The highpoint of the celebration was the speech of an American lady, an eminent writer, very well known here and in the United States," he
afterward excitedly wrote his mother, "who . . . made a very moving speech, in
which she said she would write about what she had seen, etc." Indeed, at the dinner following the addresses and distribution of prizes, he gave her another assignment: a "scheme" to smuggle him into Italy with an American passport as one of
their party, which she and the Springs agreed to do. Meanwhile, also helped him
by subsequently giving her American readers a poignant social Romantic tribute
to his school:

> Here these poor boys, picked up from the streets, are redeemed from bondage and
> gross ignorance by the most patient and constant devotion of time and effort. What
> love and sincerity this demands from minds capable of great thoughts, large plans
> and rapid progress, only their peers can comprehend, yet exceeding great shall be
> their reward; and as among the fishermen and poor people of Judea were picked up
> those who have become to modern Europe the leaven that leavens the whole mass,
> so may these poor Italian boys yet become more efficacious as missionaries to their
> people than would an Orphic poet at this period.

Her Romantic Orphism probably passed Mazzini by, but her poignant millen-
nialism undoubtedly did not.[46]

Her enthrallment was no mere afterglow of her tea and the dinner. "By far the
most beauteous person I have seen," she wrote a week later to Caroline Sturgis,
"one in whom holiness has purified, but nowhere dwarfed the man." In her *Tribune* letter afterward, she filled out that portrait intellectually. Mazzini, she said,
was that rara avis, an intellectual activist who measured all things by the "ideal
standard" yet had "no time to mourn over failure or imperfection; there is too much
to be done to obviate it." Second, he was a cosmopolitan liberal in a double sense:

he intuitively understood the divine doctrine that God is Love and Justice, and he transmitted its steady influence as an exile. "Thus Mazzini, excluded from publication in his native language, has acquired the mastery of both French and English, and through his expression in either shine the thoughts which animated his earlier effort, with mild and steady radiance." And American liberals could experience that glow as well if, instead of basking in the achievements of their revolution while remaining "indifferent to the idea they represent," they were to "look with anxious interest on the suffering nations who are preparing for a similar struggle." For "the human family is one," she said, sounding her cosmopolitan social Romantic battle cry, "'And beats with one great heart.'"[47]

V

After spending most of the day packing, the next morning Fuller and the Springs left for Paris, arriving there on November 13. Three days later, she started thinking more about her quickening immersion in Europe. Although she told Emerson she still thought England was a "mountain of shams," she liked its new liberal spirit "*very* much." Its promulgators liked her as well. "[Delf] thinks you have dazzled or awed the British coteries," Greeley cheerfully informed her, "and that they will insist on your remaining on their island." Delf was right. Just before she had left, the *People's Journal* and several other "excellent" periodicals had given her "fine" offers to write for them, which Carlyle hoped she would accept after she finished traveling on the Continent.[48]

To be sure, her old lament about not having come ten years earlier continued to haunt her. "Now my life must ever be a failure," she wrote that same day to Caroline Sturgis, "so much strength has been wasted on obstructions which only came because I was not in the soil most fitted to my nature." Yet, though her life was a failure, she now added cheerfully, "it is less so than with most others and the matter not worth thinking about. Heaven has room enough and good chances enough in store, no doubt, and I can live a great deal in the years that remain." Moreover, she had found more than literary opportunities in England. "I find how true for me was the lure that always drew me towards Europe," she exclaimed to Caroline. "It was no false instinct that said I might here find an atmosphere to develope me in ways *I* need." What was that "atmosphere"? Evidently, it went beyond just Europeans' "habits of conversation," which she mentioned in her September letter to Richard; it was also their characters. While she had not yet discovered anyone, she told Caroline, "so valuable" as Emerson, still, it was now clear how right she and Caroline had been in thinking that aristocratic Europe contained a greater range of men of individuality and depth. "I find myself much in my element in European Society," she explained that same day in a letter to Emerson. "It does not indeed come up to my ideal; but so many of the encumbrances are cleared away that used to weary me in America, that I can enjoy a freer play of faculty, and feel, if not like a bird in the air, at least as easy as a fish in water." In short, Europe's social density and variety gave her a "freer play of faculty" to "come out" as the many-sided "high-soaring, clear, enthusiast soul" that Carlyle called her.[49]

She soon discovered that France presented its own challenges. A major one for any American intellectual was its intellectuals' view of the United States. Their earlier myth of a nation of "noble" savages and homespun cosmopolitans like Benjamin Franklin had long ago faded and been replaced by a much more lurid image. Many French intellectuals, both on the right and left, had come to see Americans as woefully "bourgeois," denoting in French parlance conformists and philistines, as well as—except in the opinion of the aristocracy, who liked the South—hypocrites for their acceptance of slavery. If Fuller picked up any of this, however, she did not mention it. Indeed, in her first dispatch from Paris, she said nothing about anti-Americanism, which had instantly annoyed her in England, and signaled her readiness to engage the French. "I seem in wholly a different world," she wrote, in a chiaroscuro of her new disparate "atmosphere."

> Here in the region of wax lights, mirrors, bright wood fires, shrugs, vivacious ejaculations, wreathed smiles and adroit courtesies, it is hard to remember John Bull with his coal-smoke, hands in pockets, except when extended for ungracious demand of the perpetual half-crown or to pay for the all but perpetual mug of beer . . . [and] prone to the most solemn humbug, generally of the philanthropic or otherway moral kind. But he is always awkward beneath the mask, and can never impose upon anybody—but himself. Nature meant him to be noble, generous, sincere, and has furnished him with no faculties to make himself agreeable in any other way or mode of being. 'Tis not so with your Frenchman who can cheat you pleasantly, and move with grace in the devious and slippery path. You would be almost sorry to see him quite disinterested and straight-forward: so much agreeable talent and naughty wit would thus lie hid for want of use.[50]

On the ground, these graceful and "slippery" traits also attracted her. Like many American tourists, she was delighted with Parisian crowds' "fine shows." She did not care for the "files of men sauntering arm in arm" on the Champs Elysée with their "half-military, half-dandy" postures, but she loved the promenade of gay children, decorated coaches, and "passably pretty ladies, with excessively pretty bonnets," and, later on, the Mardi Gras crowds. French female attention to dress threw her only a bit. "We are *getting dressed*," she reported in her November 16 letter to Caroline, adding, in parentheses, "I do not wonder as I look around me here at the devotion of a French woman to her *mise* it is truly *deliceuse* as they call it with that absurd twinkle in their pretty eyes." She enjoyed, too, the pomp of that winter's presentation at court and ball afterward at the Tuilieries, where even "ugly" women and ordinary men overshadowed the American beauties present through artful dressing and graceful vivacity. "It was pleasant to my eye," she told her readers, sounding French herself, "which has always been so wearied in our country by the somber masses of men that overcloud our public assemblies, to see them now in so great variety of costume, color and decoration."[51]

Consonant with her aesthetic take on the French, the arts got much more of her attention in Paris than they had in London, and understandably so. However shocked American tourists professed to be by France's supposedly loose sexual mores (including the men who availed themselves of them), few quarreled with the proposition that Paris was the world's cultural capital, boasting not only Europe's

best music, theater, and art but also its greatest concentration of literary and artistic "genius." Yet the *Tribune*'s cosmopolitan reporter was not overwhelmed. After seeing for the first time the originals of her beloved Renaissance pictures, she
was anxious not to stereotype her reverence. "The American," she instructed her
readers, "must, if capable at all of mental approximation to the life therein embodied, be too deeply affected, too full of thoughts to be in haste to say anything,
and for me, I bide my time." On recent French art, she was not so reverent. Passing over American tourists' neoclassical favorites Poussin and Claude Lorrain,
she gave an Anglo-American Romantic rebuke to the fast-fading pre-Courbet Romantic art associated with Théodore Géricault and Eugène Delacroix. "The effort
of the French school in Art, as also its main tendency in Literature," she wrote,
citing its artists' portrayal of suffering with streams of blood and wickedness by
ghastly contortion, "seems to be to turn the mind inside out, in the coarsest accep-
tation of such a phrase." This was the opposite, she said, of Turner: for the more
subjective his paintings, the "more profound and enchanting." The music, too,
did not bowl her over, although she attributed that to her failure to get tickets to
the Conservatoire, where she would have heard, she was sure, the best music in
the world. Instead she heard opera, which, despite the excellent sets and costumes,
she found so mediocre that she rarely went. Even with Paris's superior Italian productions of Rossini, Meyerbeer, and other contemporary composers, she discovered "alas! nothing excellent, nothing admirable." Indeed, she dismissed Giulia Grisi,
the mannered soprano prima donna of the Théâtre des Italiens, who was despised
by Chopin's circle, with the same deadly dispatch she had New York singers: "Her
despair is that of a person in the toothache, or who has drawn a blank in a lottery."[52]

With French theater, on the other hand, she fell in love. "How different," she
exclaimed, from the "execrable music and more execrable acting" she had seen
in Drury Lane. "Not one touch of that stage strut and vulgar bombast of tone which
the English actor fancies indispensable to scenic illusion is tolerated here." Her
happiest discovery, though, was social: in Paris sophisticated theater was popular! "For the first time in my life," she wrote, "I . . . have found sufficient proof,
if I had needed any, that all men will prefer what is good to what is bad, if only a
fair opportunity for choice be allowed." She even touted the city's topical burlesques, a genre she had not deigned to mention in New York, finding hilarious
one spoof with Alexandre Dumas in person dressed as Monte Cristo in an Oriental juggler's costume tramping across the stage looking desperately for a theater
to stage his play. She saved her highest praises for the celebrated Jewish actress
Rachel, whom she saw in every role she played that season, especially admiring
her in her portrayal of the "darker passions" of impossible desire and desolate grief,
which gave Fuller, she said, her first sense of the power of French tragedy. "To
the noblest genius is joined the severest culture," she wrote Caroline Sturgis, ringing Fulleresque changes. She failed to meet her, however. Rachel's porter told
her she often got a hundred letters a day and usually threw them away unopened.
There was also one other troubling thing: "She has a really bad reputation as
woman." Amazingly, though, she told Caroline, this came not from her sexual
liaisons but her flamboyant manner of carrying them out: "A liberal Frenchman

says to me 'Me *Sand* has committed what are called errors, but we doubt not the nobleness of her soul, but it is said that the private life of *Mlle Rachel* has nothing in common with the apparition of the Artist.' Do not speak of this in America."[53]

Fuller was "assiduous daily" in sniffing out Paris's scientific and scholarly theaters as well. She marveled at the specimens at the Jardin des Plantes, she patronized the "amateur" discussions of suicide and the Crusades at the Athenée, and she regularly attended the lectures of the celebrated astronomer François Arago. The self-conscious worldliness of French academics, however, she found silly, while the ancient faces of artists and scientists that she saw at the Academy suggested that French academic life was running out of steam. But what galled her was its gross exclusion of women. When in January she went to the Sorbonne to hear the astronomer Urbain Jean LeVerrier lecture, only to be disdainfully turned away by the guard, who waved on Marcus Spring, she was shocked. After passing the time looking at antiquities at the nearby national museum, she returned to see the lecture rooms, "now that the talk, too good for female ears, was over," but to no avail.

> "You can go, Madame," said he "to the College of France; you can go to this and t'other place, but you cannot enter here." "What, sir," said I, "is it your institution alone that remains in a state of barbarism?" "Que voulez vous, Madame," he replied, and, as he spoke, his little dog began to bark at me "Que voulez vous, Madame, c'est la regle,"—"What would you have, Madame, IT IS THE RULE,"—a reply that makes me laugh even now, as I think how the satirical wits of former days might have used it against the bulwarks of learned dullness.[54]

She did have one half-successful experience of cutting-edge Parisian science that winter, when she went to have a bad tooth extracted and the dentist gave her nitrous oxide, whose discovery as a surgical anesthetic the American chemist Charles A. Jackson had just announced at the French Academy a few weeks earlier. Recounting inhaling the ether through the tube, she afterward described the event for her readers as a Romantic out-of-body experience.

> Even now the moment my mind was in that state seems to me a far longer period in time than my life on earth does as I look back on it. Suddenly I seemed to see the old dentist as I had for the moment before I inhaled the gas, amid his plants, in Faust-like, magical air, and he seemed to say *"C'est inuitile."* Again I started up, fancying that once more he had not dared to extract the tooth, but it was gone. What is worth noting is the mental translation I made of his words, which my ear must have caught, for my companion tells me he said *"C'est le moment,"* a phrase of just as many syllables, but conveying the opposite sense.

Unfortunately, her procedure left two unsavory residues: a bad taste in her mouth and a "neuralgic pain" in her head, which lasted until she went to hear her first performance of Mozart's *Don Giovanni*, when the pain, miraculously, disappeared! "Ah! if physicians only understood the influence of the mind over the body," she wrote, "instead of treating, as they often do, their patients like machines and according to precedent!" Romantic art still outdid new science.[55]

Her survey of French social and political institutions yielded mixed results. Compared with her notices of Britain's reforms, her comments were comparatively meager. Although she was moved by a "School for Idiots" just outside Paris that used music, poetry, drawing, and mathematics, and she also found admirable the private Parisian houses where poor women could leave their children while they were at work, France's welfare institutions seemed inferior to both England's and America's. "I see nothing that shows so enlightened a spirit as The Home," she wrote, after observing the cold formality of a Protestant refuge for formerly imprisoned prostitutes. The charities of the Catholic Church did not even rate a mention in her column.[56]

On the other hand, if Britain introduced her to the blights of industrial capitalism, France provoked her to attend to politics. Partly its political traditions awakened some congenial memories. "Yellow and faded age has made them," she wrote of seeing the manuscripts of her old hero Rousseau, which the librarian of the Chamber of Deputies privately showed her one afternoon, "yet at their touch I seemed to feel the fire of youth, immortally glowing, more and more expansive, with which his soul has pervaded this century." She also felt the fire of France's parliament's electric atmosphere, which she invidiously compared with America's duller republican one. "I should like," she told her readers, speaking of the hubbubs that exploded whenever a member droned on, "a corps of the same kind of sharp shooters in our legislative assemblies when honorable gentlemen are addressing their constituents and not the assembly, repeating in lengthy, windy, clumsy paragraphs what has been the truism of the newspaper press for months previous." Yet her observations of political leaders were mostly critical. She was disgusted with the historian-turned-politician François-Guillaume Guizot, the architect of King Louis-Philippe's "bourgeois" royalist policies and foreign minister and de facto head of government, who was widely admired by visiting Boston Whig notables. His "flimsy falsehoods" defending France's abandonment of détente with England and its new rapprochement with Austria were bad enough, but what provoked her ire was his blatant defense of the philosophy of expediency as the best policy. "This is the policy, said he, that has made France so prosperous," a formula she acerbically summed up in the "vulgate of our land" as:

> "O Lord, save me,
> My wife, child, and brother Sammy,
> Us four *and no more*."

After hearing Guizot's speeches, full of "shabbiness and falsehood," she yearned, she said, for the reactionary but blunt-speaking Prince Metternich, who seemed by comparison "noble and manly."[57]

French politics, of course, was more than its party chieftains, and she caught a glimmer of that as well. With a disenfranchised and increasingly restive middle-class, hungry and angry farmers in the countryside, and militant and often socialistic artisans in Paris and other cities, France was approaching a political combustion not detectable in reforming England. Like almost all observers, she thought all change would wait until the death of the king, although once it began, she pre-dicted, it would not stop at the political. "While Louis Philippe lives, the gases, compressed by his strong grasp, may not burst up to light; but the need of some radical measures of reform is not less strongly felt in France than elsewhere, and the time will come before long when such will be imperatively demanded." In her penultimate letter on Paris, she portrayed the time near at hand. "All signs of this are kept out of sight in Paris," she reported, speaking of the spreading hunger in the countryside. "A pamphlet, called 'The Voice of Famine,' stating facts, though in the tone of vulgar and exaggerated declamation, unhappily common to pro-ductions on the Radical side, was suppressed almost as soon as published, but the fact cannot be suppressed that the people in the Provinces have suffered most ter-ribly amid the vaunted prosperity of France." Furthermore, while the poverty she saw in Paris seemed less than what she had seen in British industrial cities like Glasgow and Sheffield, she was shocked at the despair she saw in the faces of the supposedly "lively" French in Lyons, where she stopped later that winter. After interviewing several of Lyon's female weavers, who told her that their long hours, financial anxiety, and physical exhaustion made reading, entertainment, or even proper nursing impossible, she read a physician's pamphlet advocating govern-ment-sponsored "*Crèches*" that provided, not just childcare, like those in Paris, but also wet nurses. "Here, again, how is one reminded of Fourier's observations and plans," she wrote, after recalling what she had heard of Manchester mothers dealing with the problem by feeding their children opium. France's rumbling politics seems to have provoked in her a new sense of urgency about the working classes that she had not felt in Britain.[58]

Most ideologically significant, in Paris she started thinking seriously about socialism as a political movement. With the overthrow of the Bourbons in 1830, Saint-Simonian leaders' call for a rule of the capable rather than the privileged and a female messiah to "rehabilitate the flesh" had swept through French intel-lectual circles, but in these waning years of Louis Philippe's reign, socialism re-appeared in much more radical forms. Responding to hard times and the growing disaffection toward a regime that served overwhelmingly the interests of France's tiny landed aristocracy and avaricious haute bourgeoisie, socialist critics appeared in the 1840s who combined liberal Christian and Romantic social ethics with tren-chant critiques of modern capitalist alienation and exploitation, and to increasing effect. While the English Chartists, whom Fuller had never mentioned, had found that deist messages appealed to many English workers, French socialists were discovering that urban artisans and professional classes were remarkably recep-tive to their different rhetoric of "spiritual" humanitarian socialism.[59]

The socialists with whom she initially spoke, though, were not the newer and tougher minded class-conscious followers of Pierre-Joseph Proudhon or the Jacobin socialists around Louis Blanc but the communitarian Fourierists whom Greeley had been pestering her to contact. That December, she met, at their headquarters at the rue de Tournon, Victor Considerant, the editor of their newspaper *Démo-cratie pacifique*," and his mother-in-law, Clarisse Vigoureux, a former associate of Fourier and one of the movement's financial backers. "They are full of hope and their propaganda has a real and increasing influence," she wrote on Christmas Eve in an upbeat account to their chief Transcendentalist booster, Channing, "as is proved by the taunts which every other party has in store, in turn for La Democratie Pacifique." To her readers she tried to explain the sources of this growing socialist influence. Partly, of course, she said, it reflected the ills of Europe's industrial cities, now exacerbated by economic depression, but equally important was the increasingly urgent need felt for a radical social ethics that had always been latent in Christianity: "some practical application of the precepts of Christ, in lieu of the mummeries of a worn-out ritual."[60]

And America? Before coming to Europe, socialism had seemed a far-off prospect. Ever since Brook Farm's conversion to Fourierism a couple of years earlier, she had repeatedly said that some sort would inevitably come but, given America's much greater democracy and comparatively weak class divisions, not for at least another half-century. After coming to France, however, where she witnessed not only the "starving times" in extremis but also a concentration of politically charged socialist talk she had never heard before, much of it resonating with millennialist strains in her Transcendentalist circle's social thought, she began to feel a new moral urgency about *America*'s class quandaries. "The more I see of the terrible ills which infest the body politic of Europe," she told her readers, recounting her "adieu to Paris," "the more indignation I feel at the selfishness or stupidity of those in my own country who oppose an examination of these subjects—such as is animated by the hope of prevention." So America might prevent through socialism the very ills that European socialists were hoping to cure. But, indignation aside, what were the odds? Or, to put the question comparatively, which was the more difficult political task—achieving a preventive social democracy in politically free but economically undeveloped America or a curative one in economically advanced but politically oppressed Europe? Sooner than she knew, she would face a case testing not just that question but also the more basic one of the chances for even liberal democratic change in Europe. Meanwhile, she met some notable intellectuals who encouraged her to think more about what those "precepts of Christ" might mean now.[61]

VI

Despite its political "lures," Paris proved to be more of a practical challenge for Fuller than London. Her apartments with the Springs at the Rougement, a new luxurious hotel on Boulevard Poissonnière, with thick flowered carpets and curtains, marble slabs, fireplace, French clock ("with Cupid, of course"), and the "inevitable large mirror," were so expensive that she initially worried that they would have to cut short their time there. Although Eddie's illness in mid-January required them to prolong their stay by more than a month, she still faced other problems. The almost uniformly overcast sky and damp air gave her constant colds. She also fretted about her time. "While we play, others work!" she announced one morning after reading a notice in an English paper reporting that Harriet Martineau had published her book on her Palestine travels. In fact, Fuller had fallen so far behind in her writing that she had had to compose all five of her dispatches about London from Paris. Nor, she thought, could she make it up like a London or Parisian journalist by late-night scribbling, since only mornings, she said transcendentally, awakened her best genius. "I can hardly tell you what a fever consumes me, from sense of the brevity of time and opportunity," she wrote Emerson. "Here I cannot sleep at night because I have been able to do so little in the day." She knew what the American Transcendentalist would say. "You will say, it is not so mightily worth knowing, after all, this picture and natural history of Europe. Very true; but I am so constituted that it pains me to come away, having touched only the glass over the picture."[62]

Her biggest obstacle in getting beneath it, though, was not time but rather the same disability that would soon afflict her book-taught multilingual Concord friend in Paris: even having read French literature since she was ten, her "very bad" spoken French. One effect of this was she was starting to feel lonely, especially in her charming Parisian crowds. In smaller settings, she found her handicap exasperating, because she was used to being so "eloquent and free in my own tongue," but most of all because it made social relations impossible. "French people I find slippery, as they do not know exactly what to make of me," she complained to Emerson in mid-January. "I see *them*, their brilliancy, grace, and variety, the thousand slight refinements of their speech and manner, but cannot meet them in their way." To *that* lament Emerson answered commonsensically, "It is too plain that you should conquer their speech first," to which he added with American pride: "They have translated modern civilization into conversation, and our queen of discourse cannot go by such a magazine until she has exhausted it." So she studied her French "hard" three hours every morning with her "master" Louis Nicauel, who charged her a hefty fee of twenty-five francs but also made her within a month not only reasonably fluent but also able, she thought, to infuse some of her natural spirit into her spoken French. Although Nicauel's remark to her that she spoke and gesticulated "like an Italian" was probably not meant as an unalloyed compliment, it was a good sign that she was probably right about her spirited French.[63]

She still lacked one thing important to her, however: "some friend, such as I do not find here," she plaintively wrote to Emerson, "to initiate me into various little secrets of the place and time. . . . My steps have not been fortunate in Paris, as they were in England." She did get some basic social help, though. The American consul general Robert Walsh and his wife Elizabeth befriended her, and Nicauel, who "knows all about Paris," got her "the entrée to almost any place I thought of." Her most important social facilitator was the English expatriate Mary Clarke, or Madame Mohl, as she would be known after marrying the distinguished French Orientalist Julius Mohl later that year. Having lived in Paris for twenty years, for a long time as a daily visitor at Madame Récamier's and as a host of one of the city's most brilliant salons, Clarke probably did know, as Fuller thought, "all the best people." Fuller also thought her "exquisitely witty, original, and no less generous and kind," a judgment Clarke confirmed by quickly introducing her into her circle. She also gave Fuller a laudatory letter to her close English friend Leonora Pertz, the wife of the director of the Berlin Academy, which gives a rare glimpse of how Fuller impressed a sophisticated European with her American and non-American traits. A "very distinguished" author, who had valiantly supported her widowed mother and younger siblings by her pen, Fuller was a "union of opposite qualities very rarely found," which Clarke listed, language barbs and all:

> She is a celebrity (in her own country) and not stuck up or egotistical. She is an American not always bothering about "our Free Country." She is enthusiastic and noble minded and yet has plain sense and discrimination of character which I reckon (I guess) is more rare than all. She says I guess and that's a pity. She has the American drawl and that is a greater but when you get over a little absence of the European graces you will find a grace in her total absence of pretension and in her noble simplicity of character.[64]

The Parisians Fuller most wanted to find were the city's leading authors and thinkers. Paris, she wrote in her dispatch, was the intellectual center of the modern world. It was that not just because of its many men and women of "genius" but also because of its national idea of literature as a "Chamber of Deputies" representing the people, as the "poor, limited Assembly politically so called" could hardly claim to do. She might have also mentioned two recent ideological turns. One was the emergence after the July 1830 Revolution of a new generation of social Romantics who had converted the values of feeling and wholeness from props of Catholic Bourbon monarchism into rationales for republicanism and social amelioration. The other was the movement of liberal Catholics led by Félicité-Robert de Lamennais, the defrocked Breton abbé whose *Paroles d'un croyant*, a lyrical call for a Gospel-grounded "new Christianity" and a government of mutual love and popular rule, had galvanized European progressives. Radical "utilitarian" London may have provided her with a social and professional circle, but in social Romantic Paris she found, as with its socialists, a congenial perfectionist site. "There is hardly any other," Emerson wrote her, "to whom I should think Paris had such values." She could not leave, he said, until she had opened all its "jeweled cabinets."[65]

To do so Fuller had several tools with her. She had her Transcendentalist passports: copies of her *Papers* and *Woman* and several volumes of Emerson she had been toting around. Mazzini had given her notes to deliver in Paris, instructing Giuseppe Lamberti, the national secretary of Young Italy in Paris, to provide her with the addresses of his closest French friends, Lamennais and George Sand. Others she ferreted out herself. She tried to find Balzac, but she discovered he frequented "the lowest cafés, . . . so that it was difficult to track him out." Mainly she concentrated on Paris's principal social Romantics. She caught up first with Pierre Leroux, Sand's intellectual guru and the editor of *Revue indépendante*, France's foremost radical journal, which he had cofounded with her five years earlier. It is not clear how much she got from him beyond what she had read in his *De l'humanité* a couple of years earlier, outlining his democratic "socialism" and pantheistic "religion of humanity" (terms he first popularized) in opposition to the authoritarianism of the Saint-Simonians and the materialism of the Fourierists. She and his circle did find, though, some practical uses for each other. His coeditor

Ferdinand François got their "assistant editor for English literature," the socialist feminist Pauline Roland, who was later imprisoned by Louis Napoleon, to translate Fuller's essay "American Literature" for the December 10 issue of the *Revue*, which made her first known to French readers (albeit, she laughed, with the French "delight at manufacturing names," under the byline "Miss Elisabeth Fuller"). This "interesting woman" solidified Fuller's Franco-American Romantic tie in other ways. She sent her articles by and about her comrades. She put her in touch with their friends, who were eager to talk with her about Emerson, whose writings were attracting the attention of liberal intellectuals, including the historians Edgar Quinet and Jules Michelet. And she and her coeditors asked her to be their American correspondent after returning to the United States, which Fuller thought would be "very pleasant and advantageous to me."[66]

Continuing her transatlantic networking, several weeks later she contacted at his Champs-Élysées house Sand's earlier inspiration, Lamennais. Fortuitously, she found him in his study with his friend Pierre-Jean de Béranger, whose wittily mordant antimonarchical verses she had appreciated better than Lamennais's writings, which had seemed to her merely an echo of the social Transcendentalism of her friends. Meeting him corrected that parochial assumption. "I see well what he has been and is to Europe," she afterward wrote in her dispatch. "He seems suffering and pale, but in his eyes is the light of the future," she said, playing on his newspaper's name, *L'Avenir*, and lavishly praising the paper for standing alone with his left liberal colleagues' *La Réforme* in condemning Austria's recent seizure of Kraków, Poland's only independent republic. She also ventured to strengthen further the Franco-American liberal bond by sending him a copy of her *Papers*, "as illustrative of the state of affairs in our country," saluting him on behalf of the many Americans who "delight to know you as a great apostle of the ideas which are to be our life."[67]

Visiting Sand allowed her to confront French social Romanticism on a more personal plane. In the *Tribune* she had been revising upward her assessment of the French author. However, gossip she picked up while waiting for Sand to get back from her house, Nohant, in Berry, shook her a little. "I find that all we had heard of her was true in the outline," she wrote in her account to Elizabeth Hoar (which Hoar circulated among their eager Transcendentalist friends); "I had supposed it might be exaggerated." But she also heard that Sand had recently subscribed a large sum of money for the relief of the poor people suffering in her province that winter and, although unlucky with a series of lovers, she now lived with Frédéric Chopin, "on the footing of combined means, independent friendship!" Fuller got a chance to corroberate these mixed reports after Sand returned to the city on February 7. She had to be persistent. At Nohant, Sand had gotten Fuller's letter but had put off answering it because she feared she would not be returning until the end of the following month. (Sand assured Mazzini that her "sullenness" in not answering his "excellent"-sounding American friend "is quite involuntary.") Not hearing from Sand, and unable to get Lamberti to accompany her, following the practice Fuller assured herself was common in Paris, she simply showed up a little nervously at Sand's "handsome modern" apartment at Number 5 Square d'Orléans. After an awkward beginning, when Sand's peasant-costumed goddaughter announced her as *"Madame Salere"* and, after returning, told her Sand said she did not know her, the author suddenly appeared. "I never shall forget her look at that moment," Fuller wrote, detailing Sand's high forehead, large dark eyes, and "strong and masculine" lower face, which, combined with her coiffed hair, elegant dark violet silk robe and black mantle, and simple "lady-like dignity," presented, she said, "an almost ludicrous contrast to the vulgar caricature idea of George Sand. . . . It made me very happy to see such a woman, so large and so developed a character, and everything that *is* good in it so *really* good. I loved, shall always love her." Sand's goodness and androgyny established, they chatted ("as if we had always known one another"), with Sand talking eloquently ("just like her writing") and Fuller presumably speaking in a reasonable facsimile of her "charmante" letter that Sand had told her she had so much liked. Despite drowning in proof sheets, Sand asked her to stay to talk, which they did for most of the rest of the day. ("It is better to throw things aside," she told Fuller, with Sand-like savoir-faire, "and seize the present moment.") A few days later, she saw Sand again, this time with her daughter, Solange, and several of Sand's colleagues, which suggested another parallel: "Her position there was of an intellectual woman and good friend,—the same as my own in the circle of my acquaintance as distinguished from my intimates."[68]

Despite all this mutual recognition, Fuller still struggled to come to terms with her ambivalences about Sand. She found two old concerns confirmed: Sand's careless churning out of popular books and, "as one sees in her writings, the want of an independent, interior life." Yet these highbrow Transcendentalist failings paled before Fuller's enjoyment of "so rich, so prolific, so ardent a genius. I liked the woman in her, too, very much; I never liked a woman better." Her feelings about Sand's sexual affairs, however, cut a little deeper. She dismissed the "fancy picture" drawn by some of her male admirers of a victimized ethereal being "all whose mistakes are the fault of the present state of society." The truth was more interesting: "She has that purity in her soul, for she knows well how to love and prize its beauty; but she herself is quite another sort of person." Why did she not love one man permanently? Obviously, no contemporary could command her complete interest—who could? "Also, there may have been something of the Bacchante in her life, and of the love of night and storm." In any case, she was "never coarse, never gross" and clearly had drawn "some rich drops from every kind of wine-press." This was a generous and insightful speculation, especially since Sand and her circle's passionately exalted sexual talk was not exactly something Fuller had known in America. Indeed, she saw these "impulses" of Sand, who liked to fancy herself devoted to the sacred institution of marriage shorn of inequalities and double standards, perhaps more honestly than Sand saw them herself. So the bold female French Romantic, who "holds her place in the literary and social world of France like a man, and seems full of energy and courage in it," had no real "faults." Ultimately, "she needs no defence, but only to be understood, for," in a Romantic formula Fuller liked to apply to herself, "she has bravely acted out her nature, and always with good intentions."[69]

Fuller had both her enthusiasm and her original uncertainty confirmed when a week later, on February 14, she went with Jane Wilhelmina Stirling, a Scottish prize pupil of Chopin with whom she had become friendly, to hear her lesson with the composer who had been Sand's frail special "friend" for the past decade. Fuller's *Tribune* account was wholly musical: she had been thrilled to hear him play because he was constantly ill and rarely performed but also because it rati- fied her recognition of his genius, which she had detected even in his badly played compositions in America. However, in her circular letter to Hoar and their Tran- scendentalist circle, she returned to the slightly more personal. "I liked his talk- ing scarcely less. Madame S. loved Liszt before him; she has thus been intimate with the two opposite sides of the musical world." In fact, Sand's intense but mostly platonic intimacy with Chopin was just then fast disintegrating under the weight of his violently expressed, but apparently largely baseless, suspicions about her sexual escapades, and Fuller got an inkling of that, too, which she tried to fairly summarize before finally throwing up her hands. "About all this, I do not know; you cannot know much about anything in France, except what you see with your two eyes," she sighed. "Lying is ingrained in '*la grande nation*,' as they so plainly show no less in literature than life." She got a somewhat different reaction, how- ever, from an unlikely source. "It was high time, dear friend," Emerson provoca- tively wrote, thanking her for her "excellent portrait" of Sand, "that you should run out of the coop of our bigoted societies full of fire damp & azote, and find some members of your own expansive fellowship. What you sought & found at home only in gleams & sparkles of red & yellow light,—in those older gardens is absorbed & assimilated into texture, form, hue, & savour of flower & fruit." Al- though Emerson meant all this symbolically, his pungent images must have made her stop and think, as she claimed his talk made her do, of what they symbolized.[70]

The day after hearing Chopin, Fuller encountered one more outsized social Romantic who fitted the category of "expansive fellowship" even better than Sand. The extraordinary range, rhythmical power, streams of tangible images, and sus- tained outbursts of passion of Adam Mickiewicz's "objective lyricism" consti- tuted some of the greatest poetry of the nineteenth century. When Fuller met him, however, Poland's "national poet" had over a decade earlier stopped writing po- etry and moved to Paris, where, along with Marx, Herzen, Heine, and other radi- cal exiles, he found just the kind of intellectual cosmopolitanism and, the city's government spies and regulations notwithstanding, comparative toleration that made an ideal home for plotting revolution. For him, as for them, though, this meant considerably more than political revolution, although for Mickiewicz's cause that was practically essential, since a free and independent Poland required the overthrow of the tsar of Russia and the emperor of Austria. Yet Mickiewicz's version of his generation's messianic dream of a revolutionary transformation of Europe was also far more than just strategic. His messianism was quite literal: he looked forward to a divinely sent messenger to spark it. In addition, unlike the ethics-minded Lamennais, whom he inspired, Mickiewicz expected the coming kingdom of God to entail, along with modern freedoms of speech and religion, Slavophile communalism and sacred rituals. Furthermore, his revolutionary "na- tionalism" was cosmopolitan, not only because, like Mazzini, whom he also influenced, he conceived of nationalist struggles as distinctive "missions" benefiting the world but also because he conceptualized them in peculiarly Christian Polish terms. While the other two of his trinity of God's "chosen" nations, the Jews and the French, promised to implement ethics and culture, respectively, Poland, the Christ among nations, through its unique national suffering, offered itself as a collective messiah to redeem mankind. Finally, in his poised, logical, but also sometimes frenzied lectures and speeches, he seemed to many of his contemporaries the most charismatic revolutionary in Europe. It is hard to imagine a better "guide" through the *Sturm und Drang* of revolutionary Romantic Europe than this handsome forty-eight-year-old "ecstatic" Pole with swept-back graying hair, Mongolian-looking broad face and cheekbones, and seductively heavy eyelids.[71]

Fuller seems early on to have had some premonition of this. "I did not meet him anywhere," she would tell Emerson shortly after she left Paris, yet "I heard a great deal of him which charmed me." One thing that charmed her was his lectures at the Collège de France, where for four years he had been the first professor of Slavic literature, until he was forced to resign in 1844 because of his attacks on the "official" church and his eulogies of Napoleon. In the collections of these lectures, which Quinet and Michelet had attended and which had first introduced Emerson to the French public, she read Mickiewicz's fulsome praise of her Concord friend's essays. Unlike Mazzini, he panegyrized Emerson's intuitionism, idealism, and heroic individualism, although he did worry that he overlooked the capacity of *collectivities* to intuit glimpses of the spiritual world. So, having failed to catch up with him, in early February she sent him Emerson's new first volume of poems, and he came to see her. "I found in him the man I had longed to see," she afterward told Emerson, "with the intellect and passions in due proportion for a full and healthy human being, with a soul constantly aspiring."[72]

Specific reports of their meetings are scant but telling. Rebecca Spring recalled that Mickiewicz, who sometimes dined with them, came often to see her, a remarkable fact, as he was just then embroiled in furious factional struggles within his circle that left little time for anything else. "He made a strong impression upon her," his son Władysław would recall, "and in turn, was astonished not so much at her masculine erudition as at the depth of her ideas and at the fact that they coincided with his own." This seems plausible. Certainly, the esoteric teachings of the messianic Towiański cult of Polish émigrés to which he had been in thrall for the past half-dozen years had some parallels in her thinking. As one Mickiewicz scholar has noted, Fuller's religious Credo's spiral pilgrimages through illuminist struggles and multiple spiritual realms beyond jibed very nicely with the messianic poet's similar metaphysical ideas, although the more extreme of these, such as actual metempsychosis, always wore in Fuller's writings a symbolical air. Alexander Chodzko, a fellow former student at the University of Wilno and an active member of Mickiewicz's circle (and later his successor as professor of Slavic literature at the Collège de France), left one account of meeting her and talking with Mickiewicz about her afterward. "The authoress of the most important book on the emancipation of women," Chodzko wrote on February 26 in his diary, is in her thirties, she is blond and has dark eyes. There is life in her eyes only, for her body is frail and worn out by the work of her spirit and by study. She knows Greek, Latin, and most European languages. She has presentiments and sees apparitions. She believes that in her next incarnation she will be a man and that the present is the era of the liberation of women. Her ideas on marriage and many of her notions about life and the destiny of mankind are quite identical with those of the Cause and seem to be taken therefrom. A friend of Emerson and co-editor of the *Dial*. She made a vow never to marry. She is certain that the man or woman charged with the realization of the new era has already come to earth and her aim in coming to Europe was to find this messenger of God. . . . Adam found that she had a full self taught knowledge of the Cause. He spoke to her in the presence of many other women and the impression he made upon her was so great that she fainted on the sofa. . . . Adam promised to recount to me later in detail his talks with Miss Fuller.[73]

It is difficult to tell where fact and fantasy separate in this account. Certainly, either Chodzko or Mickiewicz imagined or at least exaggerated some things, such as, probably, her fainting, and obviously her having had the Towiański impulse to come to Europe to find a "messenger of God." At the very least, however, Chodzko's report shows how she struck *them*, as well as how excited they were about her presence. Moreover, presentiments, apparitions, reincarnation, and, of course, the present age as the era of the liberation of women, a Saint-Simonian doctrine just then being intensively discussed in Mickiewicz's pro–women's rights circle, were old Fuller themes, even if she spoke about the first three only to her most intimate friends or through the veil of autobiographical fiction. These parallels received confirmation of a sort in a remarkable "address" Mickiewicz afterward gave or sent her:

Having gotten to the point of feeling it her innate right to take cognizance of her existence, aspiring to the right to acknowledge this existence, to manifest it in sighs, in words, in attempts at action, *called* upon to preserve her rights in her acts,

A spirit who has known the old world, who has sinned in the old world and who strives to make this old world known in her new world,

Her *point of support* is in the old world, her *sphere of activity* is in the new world; her *peace* in the world of the future.

She is called to feel, to speak, to act in these three worlds. The only woman to whom it has been given to touch what is decisive in the present world and to have a presentiment of the world of the future.

Your spirit is linked with the history of Poland, of France and is beginning to link itself with the history of America.

You belong to the second generation of spirits.

Your mission is to contribute to the deliverance of Polish, French and American womanhood.

You have acquired the right to know and the exigencies of virginity. For you the first step of your deliverance and of the deliverance of your sex (of a certain class) is to know, whether you are permitted to remain a virgin.

Thou shouldst bring to the new world fruit matured by centuries, exciting fruits. Thou shouldst manifest thy spirit by thy glances, by thy gestures, by thy action. . . .

Give of your spirit, and to those who are prepared to receive it, give it all with Thy brother A- - -[74]

To understand what this astonishing projection says about Fuller herself, though, would require, again, a look at her reply, but unfortunately, as with all of her letters to him, it has not survived. Nonetheless, the document does show several things about the evident extraordinary chemistry between them. Certainly, even if she did not faint, she must have spoken and acted in some manner that caused him to address her this way. On the other hand, he obviously ran with whatever she had said pretty far. It was as if, after hours of conversation, and probably a perusal of her *Woman in the Nineteenth Century* and her "American Literature" essay in *Revue indépendante*, Mickiewicz had ferreted out all of her favorite themes and, provoked by her own fervent talk and his familiar habits and intuitive powers, projected them onto an enormous screen of world-historical proportions. Some of these specific projections, particularly about Poland, of course, were at least partly, like Chodzko's, just that, although they, too, must have been reactions to *something* related she had said to him or he had read, such as her tribute to the heroic Polish warrior Emily Plater in her book. More important, his reference to the "second generation of saints," a Towiańskian doctrine anointing those with special knowledge of the coming of God's messenger, fitted with her own announcements in *Woman* of man's destiny to be seen as "an angel or messenger" heralding the fulfillment of the "new era of divine humanity." Indeed, even his claim that her inspiration lay in Europe while her field of action lay in America struck the very self-defining chord she had been sounding in her writing ever since she had arrived in New York.[75]

Finally, he managed, even if also in the strange light of Polish Romantic messianism, to strike several promising personal chords as well. For one, he seemed to offer her precisely what she had found her faltering Concord mentor reluctant to provide her with in America: acknowledgment of her "innate right to take cognizance of her existence" and act on it, even while gently mocking her way, so far, of doing this ("in sighs, in words, in attempts at action"). Most startling, he raised the very question of virginity, symbolically but also literally, that had been the bedrock of her sexual self-conception and that of "woman," or, as he more accurately put it, women "of a certain class." What, though, was she to do? "Thou shouldst bring to the new world fruit matured by centuries, exciting fruits": presumably he was speaking here of cultural and not sexual "fruits," although with Mickiewicz (again, like herself), it is sometimes hard to tell. In any case, she seems to have been ready to take his injunctions very seriously. "How much time had I wasted on others which I might have given to this real and important relation," she complained in her letter to Emerson exactly a month after her first meeting with the poet. "In France, among the many persons that brought me some good thing, it was only with Mickiewicz, that I felt any deep-founded mental connection." Having connected with the one European intellectual who directly addressed her deepest sexual yearnings—and outdid her in the department of Romantic messianism—she got ready, now reluctantly, to leave Paris for Italy.[76]

CHAPTER NINE

Risorgimento
(1847–1848)

I

"I hope, in Italy, I shall find myself more at home," Fuller had written Emerson from Paris, glossing her French teacher's tease that she spoke French like an Italian. While her Concord comrade had probably nodded at the joke, he must have wrinkled his brow a bit at her unlikely hope. Civically, the two countries were mirrored opposites: America was a new state without an old culture and Italy an old culture without a state at all. For a millennium and a half following the collapse of the Roman Empire, the peninsula had been merely a congeries of independent or semi-independent, often warring, and, since the fifteenth century, constantly invaded sovereign principalities. What dubious political unity these eight separate states could claim derived solely from the Habsburg Austrian Empire, which ruled Lombardy and Venetia in the northeast and reduced most of the others to satellites. Socially, too, Italy was a country of fragments, with hundreds of custom barriers, primitive railroads that did not cross state borders, gaping class differences, widespread illiteracy, and multiple dialects that prevented a majority of its people from understanding each other. It is no wonder that historians have argued that at the bottom of nineteenth-century Italy's struggle for nationhood lay a quixotically heroic assertion of sheer collective will.[1]

Yet, for ancient putative nations, appearances can be deceiving. Since Fuller's beloved Dante and Petrarch, Italian authors and artists had imaginatively kept alive multiple sites of Italian greatness: Rome, the seat of the West's greatest empires and church; Florence, Venice, and Genoa, its most powerful republican city-states; and Tuscany and Venetia, its leading centers of Renaissance learning and art. By the turn of the nineteenth century these long traditions had coalesced into a new dream of a "Risorgimento"—a term another old favorite of Fuller, the dramatist Vittorio Alfieri, had first coined to denote a future ethical and political Italian resurgence or, more connotatively religious, resurrection. Meanwhile, recent intellectual tides bolstered the dream. Beginning in the late 1830s, all-Italian scientific congresses had been meeting yearly to demonstrate Italy's unity and agitate for liberal legal and economic reforms to spur its development. The liberal turn in European Romanticism infused the Risorgimento with a new cosmopolitan spirit. Romantic conceptions of nationality seemed tailor-made for stateless but culture-conscious nations like Italy and Germany—especially the key idea traceable to Herder that nations were not just states, and never conquerors, but spontaneously generated cultures rooted in a common history and language that linked past and future and formed the organic substrata of humanity. Romantic movements in the arts suffused in Italy a common cultural language, most notably in literature, from Giacomo Leopardi's anguished poems and essays to Alessandro Manzoni's codifying refinements of Italian and realistic novels of the country's common people, but most popularly in opera. During Fuller's residence there, stirring productions of nationalistic Rossini and Donizetti works and, most politically pointed, Verdi's vernacular operas of historic heroism confronting monarchical artifice and foreign rule brought down wave after wave of ovations from zealously patriotic Italian audiences.[2]

If cultural memories and movements grounded the Risorgimento, post–French revolutionary developments politicized it. The Revolution itself had promulgated national self-determination as an integral element of its creed of liberty, equality, and fraternity, inspiring passionate nationalist hopes of oppressed central, eastern, and southern European peoples throughout the sprawling Austrian and Ottoman empires. In Italy, ironically, these sentiments got further stimulation from Napoleon's peninsular conquests, which aroused anti-French nationalist feelings while leaving a legacy of efficient bureaucracies, liberalized trade, and secular schools, to which a small but growing class of government officials and enterprising merchants yearned to return. Indeed, by then "Risorgimento" had come to denote specifically Italy's political struggle for unity and independence and the movements that fought for them in successive incarnations. By the early 1830s, the conspiratorial republican Carbonari of a decade earlier had given way to Mazzini's cosmopolitan democratic Giovine Italia, or Young Italy, which stirred up plots and spread propaganda to which urban artisans and idealistic intellectuals and professionals were especially susceptible. In the early 1840s, these republican "Democrats" were challenged in turn by a new generation of "Liberals." Reacting to the disastrous failures of the previous decades' peninsular uprisings, the horror felt by Italy's upper classes toward popular insurrections, and the contrasting successes of the peaceful Anti-Corn Law League in Britain and Louis-Phillippe's constitutional monarchy in France, these new "Moderates" called for making constitutionalist reforms the center of the Risorgimento. The Piedmontese priest Vincenzo Gioberti thrilled Italian readers with his claims, in his *Del primato morale e civile degli italiani*, for the divinely ordained "moral and civil primacy" of the Italian nation. Liberal aristocrats like Cesare Balbo, Massimo d'Azeglio, and Camillo Cavour published thoroughly researched books outlining an array of gradual nation-building reform measures like scientific congresses, industrialization policies, public education, and freedom of the press and association, arousing nationalist sentiments among Italy's liberal aristocracy and landed and commercial bourgeoisie. These Risorgimento parties differed, sometimes radically, not only in their programs and constituencies but also in their nationalist strategies and goals. While Balbo, D'Azeglio, and Cavour stigmatized Mazzini's idea of a "unitarian" republican government gained through popular revolts as puerile and dangerous, he scorned theirs of an Italian state under either Piedmont's King Charles Albert or, in Gioberti's "neo-Guelph" version, a constitutional patriotic pope, as politically insufficient and morally repellent. Their fortunes also fluctuated. When Fuller arrived, the Moderates, riding a wave of popular craving for reform, were in the ascendancy and Mazzini's followers largely marginalized. Yet the air was electric with optimism about impending progressive change that often blurred differences and raised the hopes of them all.[3]

Furthermore, like incipient nations, acquired homes abroad often have an imagined architecture, and this was especially true for Italy. European Romantic writers injected into their novels and poems countless references to Italy's classical and Renaissance art. Romantic critics projected the image of an ancient nation communicating lessons for a "modern" civilization weakened by excessive self-consciousness and mechanization, memorably epitomized by the fifth of Goethe's *Roman Elegies*, in which the poet gently taps out hexameter beats on the naked back of his Roman lover Faustina. Meanwhile, American writers refashioned these European conceits, mingling them sometimes with mythic memories of their forefathers' devotion to the ancient Roman ideals of patriotic "virtue" and pastoral civility and sometimes with fantasies of appropriating Italy's past but timeless glories to complete America's national identity. Like all complex imaginative recoveries, American Italophilia easily lent itself to commercialization and caricature, as in the mass of engravings and copies of Italian masters bought by travelers and ordered by those staying home in this prephotographic age. It also lent itself to evasion of current realities in Italy, in the easy assumption that while Italy's past was wholly glorious and happily consumable, its social and political present was hopeless and even repulsive. Italy's contemporary poverty, superstition, and subjugation proved decisively that it not only had no present but also—and what could be more un-American?—no future. Finally, none of the major American writers who were constructing imaginative Italophilia before Italy's unification—not the gentlemanly Cooper or Irving, not the Romantic Hawthorne, not the cosmopolite Longfellow or Lowell, not the genteelly realistic Charles Eliot Norton—grasped what every Risorgimento leader, from Cavour and Gioberti to Mazzini and Carlo Cattaneo, understood. That was: if Italy was to have a future, much of the country's feudal order underlying its admired culture required destruction or drastic reordering—and that was a good thing.[4]

Why did Fuller uniquely among American intellectuals readily accept such a realistic "modern" notion as part of her Italophilia? Her pioneering Italian studies and teaching undoubtedly partly explain it. At least as important, though, were two features of Fuller's Italophilia. One was its psychology: for Fuller, Italy's mythic past was not only not dead; as with William Faulkner's South, it was not even past. Evidence for this abounds: in her childhood love of Latin authors' "indomitable will," "self-command, and force of expression"; in her personal Romantic conceit of Italy as the "natural" source of "modern" culture; in her fervent proclamations of its distinctive mix of passion and intellect as "my language." Then there was the Risorgimento's cosmopolitan nationalist idiom, which chimed with, as the rhetoric of utilitarian reform England or class-conscious revolutionary France never quite did, the cosmopolitan liberalism that she had learned from her father and his cherished Founders. "Father is reading aloud the foreign news," the twenty-year-old Fuller had written excitedly to her best friend James Clarke, alluding to the destruction of the Bourbon dynasty during the recent French revolution of 1830, which had triggered the first wave of liberal nationalist revolutions in Italy and elsewhere in Europe. "There is a noble stir in the world; let us hope that soon the eye ear and heart shall talk busily to the mind and all that is morbid and stagnant pass away." Recently, she had used much the same liberal rhetoric in her blistering critiques of American racism and misogyny. And her recent solution for America's supposed cultural backwardness was almost eerily resonant: a morally renewed national covenant jump-starting a great cosmopolitan American culture. Here was a myth ready-made for merging with the Risorgimento's aspirations for a progressive cosmopolitan Italian nation. On the plausibility of those politico-cultural minglings would depend how much of a "home" Fuller would really find on Italy's shores.[5]

The actual road there proved a bit bumpy. For a time she was even facing backward. "Paris is the very focus of the intellectual activity of Europe," she wrote wistfully to Mary Rotch, thinking probably, too, about Mickiewicz's electrifying talk about her role in the coming age. "There I found every topic intensified, clarified, reduced to portable dimensions: there is the cream of all the milk." Weather did not help. On February 25, 1847, after leaving the damp city, she and the Springs traveled for thirty-six hours straight to Chalon and, the next day, to Avignon, but rather than getting rejuvenated in sunshiny southern France as she had hoped, she tramped through mounds of melting snow to get to the burial ground of Petrarch's beloved Laura. (Carlyle, no doubt, would have emitted a couple of guffaws.) The following day at Arles, she did a little better, at least in reviving childhood reveries, when she took in the ruins of its Roman ampitheater, where she imagined the "fierce excitement" of tens of thousands roaring down on fighting men and lions, and, even better, for a former bookish young Latinist, handwriting in stone. It "looked as grand and solid as I expected," she told her *Tribune* readers, "as if life in those days was thought worth the living." Disappointments, though, soon resumed. After a desultory stop at Marseilles, where only the crowds' "mixture of Oriental blood" interested her, and a "dull, tormented" sixteen-hour steamship ride that stretched into thirty hours, she finally arrived in the port city of Genoa, where cuttingly cold, New England spring–like winds ruined for her its beautiful waters and marble buildings. "I could not realize," she afterward sighed to her readers, "that I had actually touched those shores to which I had looked forward all my life."[6]

She received some social warming, however, when she visited Mazzini's family and friends. He had earlier written her from London that he had had to cancel their smuggling scheme because the risk of arrest was not worth it, although probably also because he thought the political scene in Europe was, he presciently told Lamberti, "tending rapidly toward crisis," requiring them to be "on guard." But he also had several other pressing things on his mind. One was Emersonian social philosophy, which he seems to have worried that she partly shared, possibly attributing to it her suspected initial "distrust" of their movement. Actually, his views on Emerson, if not as friendly as Mickiewicz's, were complicated. In his ongoing "Thoughts upon Democracy in Europe" series in the *People's Journal*, he singled out Carlyle and Emerson as the era's only eminent intellectual dissenters from the egoistic and materialistic delusions of utilitarian liberals and utopian socialists. Yet, in a letter she received just before leaving Paris, urging her to dispense with her Concord mentor's belief in "transforming the inward man" through contemplation, which she had evidently defended, he cried: "Contemplation! no; there are too many sufferings, too many gross iniquities, too many sacred causes in this world of ours, for us to indulge in contemplation. Life is a march and a battle. But it is to enable man to respect the 'small flower,' as you say, and to put away the necessity of those everlasting struggles for those who will come after us that these 'battles' must be fought."[7]

Mazzini did not specifically say what those "battles" were, although the looming Italian one was obviously one big one. Meanwhile, he laced his polemics with personal sweetness: "You do not know how much I esteem and love you." In other letters he gave her some practical assignments. He initially hoped to use her as a mail drop, which she seems to have agreed to, although after discovering that Italian authorities opened her letters to him, he evidently dropped the idea. He also tried to get her to help him "conquer," he conspiratorially told her, the *People's Journal* for the "People's International League," his new association dedicated to arousing worldwide sympathy and cooperation on behalf of oppressed nationalities. As a fellow partaker in "our spirit," he grandly told her, she would find great satisfaction in such a venture in "transforming, of spiritualizing, of elevating little by little" the magazine's "sterile benthamism," with the goal of turning England's "reactionary, materialist Democracy" into a "religious democracy." The time was now ripe for a gradual takeover, he wrote in a follow-up letter, because Saunders, who was now sole owner, was desperate for contributors. Such comradely talk evidently worked, since she promised to send him writing and try to get Emerson to do likewise, while dissembling a little to Mary Howitt when she turned down her request for a contribution to her and her husband's competing new *Howitt's Journal*. Mazzini would eventually drop the idea of grabbing Saunders's journal, but he remained more pleased than ever with her. "The confidence that you show me," he assured her, "makes me much better than you can believe." Continuing to appreciate her fame and presumptive influence in America, for the rest of the year, he would pester his mother and Lamberti about Fuller's whereabouts so he could write her. Most of her replies were lost or destroyed (a practice he often followed with his incoming mail as a precaution against government snooping). His provocations, however, would give her much to contemplate *and* do over the next three years, as he incited, shaped, and channeled the desire of America's leading foreign correspondent to act politically in Europe.[8]

In the meantime, Fuller got at least as much as she gave from his laudatory notes to friends in Genoa, Livorno, Pisa, and Turin, whom he instructed to show the visitors around and to bring her "wherever you will go." "An American, distinguished for her intelligence, famous in her country and in England, a close friend of Emerson," read a typical one; "and what's more important, a most rare woman in love and compassion active for everything that is beautiful, great, and holy; therefore, for our Italy." Most important, she got her first regular close contact with middle-class Italians, which almost no English or American travelers ever experienced. She right away found them "very attractive": "charming women, refined men, eloquent and courteous," and, most important, what was "so rare in an American face, the capacity for pure, exalting passion." She got all of this confirmed during her three-day stay in Genoa with Mazzini's widowed mother, Maria. In one affecting gesture, this ardent republican, who worshiped her son as Italy's messiah, showed her and the Springs his bedroom, where, sixteen years earlier, the Piedmontese authorities had seized him before banishing him to permanent exile and which she kept exactly as it had been, waiting for his return, which would never come. When he learned about all these "affectionate way[s]" of Fuller and Maria from their letters ("with expressions that one almost cannot repeat, so highly laudatory are they"), it made him, he told his mother, "very happy." "Put for a signature Benedetta [the Blessed Virgin]," Fuller urged her in one letter a couple of months later; "I will understand." (The Jansenist mother did.) In fact, looking for a little substitute maternal nurturing for her son, Maria told him that she wished Fuller would return to London so that she could take care of him! "Don't worry!" the ascetic revolutionary replied to his mother. "There are at least a half dozen young women, who contend with each other the privilege of surrounding me with loving care. The Lord knows if I feel grateful to them, but I cannot afford to grow soft in the midst of their attentions." Fuller got confirmation of that point well enough when she also met in Genoa some of his now married and prosperous old friends, who told her they loved him and hoped for Italy's freedom but only "secretly and in fear." "I can understand now," she remarked to the Springs, "why Mazzini has remained unmarried and homeless." She was beginning to learn about the costs of political commitment in old-regime Europe.[9]

On March 8, following her week in Genoa, Pisa, and Livorno, Fuller capped her uneven introduction to Italy with a festive trip to Naples. At Livorno, after running into John Wiley's partner, George Putnam, and his pregnant wife, Victorina, with whom they had dined in London, the two parties agreed to stay together for the rest of their southern excursion. If Fuller felt any lingering irritation over Wiley and his cavalier censorship—or Putnam with her over her dismissive review of his *American Facts*—it does not seem to have interfered with their fun. They had one common antebellum ocean travel mishap. Hours after boarding the *Tiger*, their highly recommended English boat, the wheelman, on a clear night on the Tyrrhenian Sea but apparently adamant as a tiger about his right of way, crashed the boat directly into a French iron mail steamer going full steam ahead in the opposite direction. She seems to have taken the scare coolly enough. Putnam recalled that immediately after learning that the crash had smashed the ship's wheel

and paddle-box, he had raced to the ladies' cabin, where he found her joking about
whether they should dress or jump overboard at once ("I'll throw you your things"),
which made the women laugh uproariously. In her dispatch she was a bit more
wry: "As a change on our part would have prevented an accident that narrowly
missed sending us all to the bottom, it hardly seemed worth while to persist for
the sake of convincing them of error."[10]

The following morning, after they boarded another boat headed down the coast,
her "natural" Italianate spirits took a marked upswing. On board she met the Countess Zaluska, a former lover of Mickiewcz, who naturally intrigued her, but it was
the country that finally got to her. "Here," she grandly announced to her readers
after getting to Naples, "I *have* at last found *my* Italy." From their seashore base
outside the city, she visited the nearby island of Capri, explored the Grotto of
Pozzuoli, where Saint Paul had once landed, ascended the erupting Mount Vesu-
vius, and visited Cumae and the port communes of Báia and Sorrento. She found
these ancient sites "familiar" yet expressive. "Nature" was too "prolific and exuberant," she wrote, taking the first of her many antitourist swipes in Italy, for the
"boots of English dandies [to] trample out" or the "raptures of sentimental tourists [to] daub or fade." Human nature, on the other hand, presented more of a problem. "The most I can say is that the divine aspect of Nature *can* make you forget
the situation of Man in this region, which was surely intended for him as a princely
child, angelic in virtue, genius and beauty, and not as a begging, vermin-haunted,
image-kissing Lazzarone." She quickly added that Naples was the capital of Italy's
most "priest-ridden," "misgoverned," and impoverished state, ruled by its most
ignorant and tyrannical monarch, the Bourbon King Ferdinand II, which may not
have made its notorious beggars in *her* Italy seem any more attractive but at least
made them sound understandable.[11]

On March 27 she, the Springs, and the Putnams arrived in Rome, where she
finally found her city. Actually, its political terrain was not much more promising
than that of the South. Parts of the Papal States rivaled Ferdinand's Kingdom of
the Two Sicilies in their poverty, the city confined its Jews in a ghetto and heavily
taxed them, as in the days of the Counter-Reformation, and its economy limped
along without railroads, which the previous pope, Gregory XVI, had banned.
Rome's cityscape, however, was another matter. With its two millennia of magnificent classical and baroque churches and palazzos, its "proletariat" of independent artisans still organized in medieval corporations, and its winding streets and
garden pathways, early nineteenth-century Rome, if not exactly Virgilian, retained
much of its grand pastoral appearance. "I am very happy here in Rome," she wrote
Richard after her second week; "the weather is now beautiful and all around as
magnificent as I expected."[12]

In her first dispatch, however, except for a passing mention of the Coliseum
and a few other sights, Fuller concentrated on her usual topics of art and politics.
She examined with a cool American Romantic eye the resident artists whose stu-
dios she had visited, including the German Catholic Nazarene Friedrich Overbeck,
whose paintings were "grave but dull," and the fashionable English sculptor
Lawrence Macdonald, who contrived to make his country's frigid notables ap-

pear to look "grave" and "resolute." She had warmer words for the works of her colleague Christopher Cranch and her new American friends Luther Terry, Thomas Hicks, and the sculptor Thomas Crawford, ranking Crawford above England's neoclassical star John Gibson. On Rome's historic art she was, as at the Louvre, restrained. Anxious to avoid the "ordinary cant of connoisseurship," she limited herself "as yet" to only a few low-key remarks, mostly hewing to the respectable but somewhat musty Romantic views of Italian art she had had in America. Despite Ruskin's defense in his *Modern Painters* of pre-Raphael art, she had nothing to say about it. She likewise ignored the city's ubiquitous baroque sculpture and architecture, although, unlike most nineteenth-century British and American tourists, she did not condemn their violence and theatricality. She gave restrained reactions even to her Renaissance favorites. She appreciated but did not get overexcited about Leonardo's drawings. Predictably, she saved her greatest praise for her old demigods Raphael and Michelangelo—however, less for Raphael, whose badly preserved frescoes depressed her, than Michelangelo, particularly his sculpture of her favorite national deliverer, Moses, in San Pietro in Vincoli. ("It is the only thing in Europe, so far, which has entirely outgone my hopes.") She did have one surprise: the "new and strange" paintings of Titian, whose boldly enigmatic nude figures almost invariably shocked American viewers. With his *Sacred and Profane Love* at the Palazzo Borghese, the learning came a little slowly. She thought it "absurdly called" (surprisingly missing Titian's Neoplatonic point in portraying rational love as the elegantly dressed, intelligently gazing-back woman and spiritual love as naked and sensually compelling but turning aside). Yet she was transfixed by it. "One of the figures has developed my powers of gazing to an extent unknown before." (Although she did not say which one, her use of the verb "gazing," a code word for Fuller meaning looking at the external, would suggest it was the sacred nude.) Finally, while thrilled to see even second-rate pictures and sculptures in the galleries of the Borghese, she retained intact her American Romantic nationality. In a line that could have come out of *Summer on the Lakes*, she wrote, "They are many and precious, yet there is not so much of high excellence as I had expected: they will not float the heart on a boundless sea of feeling, like the starry night on our Western Prairie." Her detractors who had worried that she went to Europe to forget her country did not know her well.[13]

Politics in Rome meant above all one person: Pius IX. Two months before Fuller had left New York, he had succeeded Gregory XVI, whose repressive edicts had shut down all dissenting publications, filled the jails with political prisoners, and driven hundreds of political figures into exile in France, exceeding by far the repressions in Piedmont, Tuscany, and even Austrian-ruled Lombardy. Consequently, political discontent and nationalist sentiment burned hotter in the Papal States than in any other part of Italy. Immediately after his accession, Pius seemed to set Rome on an almost opposite course by granting a general amnesty to political prisoners and exiles, loosening press censorship, relaxing restrictions on the Jews, and, three weeks after Fuller arrived, announcing his intention to create an unprecedented partly elected advisory council of laymen for the Papal States. For the first time in the history of the Church, a pope had appeared in the garb of not only a reformer but also God's avatar sent to drive out the Austrians and, to Moderates, realize Gioberti's "Neo-Guelph" dream of a constitutional papal confederacy for the entire peninsula. "The cult of Pio Nono was for some months the religion of Italy," the historian George Macaulay Trevelyan would write, "and of liberals and exiles all over the world." In Protestant America, too. "The portrait of the Pope hangs in all the windows of the shops," Charles Newcomb wrote Fuller from Boston that spring. "Pray, when you reach Rome ask the Pope to lend you a file of The Tribune," Greeley, whose paper the pontiff's predecessor had summarily banned from the Papal States, wrote her. "I don't know that he takes it directly, but judging from his policy and spirit, there can be little doubt that he ranks among its readers and disciples."[14]

In the light of this worldwide euphoria over the new "Democratic pope," Fuller's initial reports that spring were remarkably temperate. "It is easy to see," she assured her readers, he "has set his heart upon doing something solid for the benefit of Man," but at the same time, she noted, by American democratic standards, his reforms were highly limited. Privately, she portrayed him as a tragic figure, outwardly revered but isolated within his Church. "Imposing often, but oftener frivolous" (she wrote Mary Rotch), the pomps and shows of Holy Week (which had begun on Palm Sunday, the day after they arrived), "must I think be very oppressive to the present Pope, who seems truly a thoughtful noble minded man." More important, she told her readers, Austria's watchful suspicions and the machinations of the Gregorian party and other ultraconservative Church factions showed how hampered and inadequate were his political means to accomplish his ends. "The Italians do not feel it, but deliver themselves, with all the vivacity of their temperament, to perpetual hurras, vivas, rockets, and torch-light processions. I often think how grave and sad must the Pope feel, as he sits alone and hears all this noise of expectation."[15]

With less poignancy, she extended her skepticism to the current Liberal moment. After reporting on a massive torch-lit nighttime demonstration on April 22 of over fifty thousand Romans outside the pope's residence, expressing gratitude for his announced reforms, she followed with an ominous account of a subsequent open-air public dinner at the Baths of Titus. After the Liberal Moderate D'Azeglio, Manzoni's son-in-law and the future prime minister of Piedmont, panegyrized the medieval pope Gregory VII for defying the German emperor Henry IV, the Austrian ambassador, "with a modesty and candor truly admirable, that this passage was meant to allude to his emperor," got an order seizing the reporting paper and canceling the pope's fete day. "They tell me here, with a laugh, 'I fancy you have assisted at the first and last popular dinner.' Thus we may see that the liberty of Rome does not yet advance with seven-leagued boots." Ominous skepticism also showed up in her report on *Il contemporaneo*, a "progressive" newspaper that had been recently founded in the wake of the partial lifting of press restrictions in Rome but then had carefully adhered to a Moderate line. To be sure, she liked its advocacy, against the contemptible fears of "'timid retrogradists,'" of free trade, public education, scientific congresses, and an array of asylums, nurseries, and mutual aid societies—liberal Whiggish reforms she had been touting in her column for the last couple of years. A few days after the dinner, when the paper's editor, Luigi Masi, asked her to arrange an exchange with like-minded American papers, she sent copies to the *Tribune*, Bryant's *Evening Post*, and the Washington *National Intelligencer*. Yet *Contemporaneo*'s "'law of *opportunity*,'" which required always conforming (as she quoted it) "'with the will of our best of Princes, and the wants and expectations of the public,'" left her cold:

> It will easily be seen that it was not from the platform assumed by the *Contemporaneo* that Lycurgus legislated, and Socrates taught; that the Christian religion was propagated, neither its reform by Luther. The opportunity that the Martyrs found here in the Colosseum, from whose blood grew up this great tree of Papacy, was not of the kind waited for by these Moderate Progressists. Nevertheless, they may be good schoolmasters for Italy, and are not to be disdained in these piping times of peace.

Despite her final gracious Shakespearean bow, both her Transcendentalist caveat and her patronizing tone would seem to belie her entirely believing her throwaway.[16]

Meanwhile, in a letter she wrote on May 7 to William Channing, she made clear how much this political excitement, wherever it might lead, and her privileged access ("seldom permitted to a foreigner," she informed Emerson) were altering her sense of what Rome beyond its "magnificent shows and places" demanded of *her*. "All these things," she wrote—speaking of the art and "temples" she had initially given as her reasons for going to Europe—"are only to me an illuminated margin on the text of my inward life. Earlier, they would have been more. Art is not important to me now. I like only what little I find that is transcendentally good, and even with that feel very familiar and calm." Rather, she told her old Fourierist friend, politics was what now interested her, albeit not exactly that of his French comrades.

> I take interest in the state of the people, their manners, the state of the race in them. I see the future dawning; it is in important aspects Fourier's future. But I like no Fourierites; they are terribly wearisome here in Europe; the tide of things does not wash through them as violently as with us, and they have time to run in the treadmill of system. Still, they serve this great future which I shall not live to see. I must be born again.

But where? Perhaps, as her ambiguous "us" might suggest, she was waiting to see whether it would be in America or in Italy. Even without a rebirth, though, she would soon have plenty of opportunities for experiencing some real violent tides.[17]

II

By the time she wrote to Channing, Fuller's "terrible regrets" over leaving Paris had largely dissipated. The Roman spring had turned beautiful, she was feeling physically much better, and she had become at least fluent ("if incorrect") in her French, which was commonly spoken by upper-class Italians. "To know the common people, and to feel truly in Italy," she knew she had to speak Italian well, so she studied it "sedulously" with a "master." Unlike in her apartment in Paris, where she had griped about the nearby nighttime clamor, she was delighted by the loud talk and music drifting through her window "all night long" on the busy Corso, Rome's main thoroughfare, where she and the Springs lived. "Why was I not born here!" Rebecca remembered her bursting out. "Why did I ever live anywhere else!"[18]

Meanwhile, despite her derision of touring "herds," Fuller was happy to encounter kindred spirits among them. These evidently did not include many English, whose "good . . . society"—her ironic code phrase for patrician fashionables —she found largely inaccessible to an American, which seems to have been fine with her. Nor do some of them seem to have had a very friendly passing view of her. "A curious mode she had of lifting up her upper lip when she spoke, and the American *twang* in which her opinions were delivered," one Britisher who met her that spring recalled, "were to us the most repellent of her peculiarities." She was amused a "little" one day at the Miserere in the Sistine Chapel by running into her once unhelpful fellow Goethean Anna Jameson, who this time at least introduced her to the great poet's daughter-in-law, Ottilie von Pogwisch, who sat next to them. Mainly she sought out old congenial American connections. The day after she arrived, she left her card at the hotel of Evert Duyckinck's brother George, then traveling in Europe. She joined Christopher and Elizabeth Cranch, who had been living in Italy for the past two years, and the former Brook Farmer George William Curtis and his brother Burrill, who had arrived in Rome earlier in the winter, to make up little parties enlivened by Cranch's lieder singing. After they left Rome, they often asked about her in their notes to friends in Rome and wrote home appreciatively of "her wise and witty accounts of persons she has seen." Still, she lamented in her letter on April 15 to Richard, "I have not yet formed any friendship of the mind, such as I had in London and Paris."[19]

If so, it was not for lack of trying. One "companion" Fuller avidly pursued that spring was the twenty-four-year-old portrait and landscape painter Thomas Hicks, who for the last year and a half had been living in Rome, where he had a studio on the Via Margutta. "At first I was not intellectual enough for him," she later told Caroline Sturgis, by which she probably meant too personal for the sensitive, wound-up artist. "Dear Youth," she wrote him three weeks after she arrived, "I do not understand why you do not seek me more," adding, in her usual empathetic way when pursuing young male intimates, "you are the only one whom I have seen here in whose eye I recognized one of my own kindred. I want to know and to love you and to have you love me; you said you had not friendliness of nature but that is not true; you are precisely one to need the music, the recognition of kindred minds." Time was also running short. "Very soon I must go from here, do not let me go without giving me some of your life. I wish this for both our sakes, for mine, because I have so lately been severed from congenial companionship [Mickiewicz], that I am suffering for want of it, for yours because I feel as if I had something precious to leave in your charge." What that was she did not say, but Hicks apologized, albeit somewhat lugubriously: "I would like to tell you all about myself, you would then see that there is but little fire in the hut and that could you enter you would find but a few embers on the hearth of a lonely ambitious man." For someone supposedly trying to keep their relationship solely on an intellectual plane, this sounded more than a little come-hither, and he soon became her most intimate American male friend in Rome. As with other past artistic protégés, she also tried to aid his career, praising him in the *Tribune* as "a man of ideas, an original observer and with a poetic heart" and writing to Frank Shaw to make sure his paintings at the American Art-Union got seen, hinting that a little money to a young fellow Fourierist would be welcome. Meanwhile, her "brother" regularly brought his "sister" flowers for her room and hunted for artistic presents for her to send home, while he basked in the heroic-maternal presence that he would later try to inject into his portrait of her.[20]

If Hicks revived an old dance, another "youth" radically altered the steps. According to Emelyn Story's recounting, which she would later get from Fuller, she met the Marquess Giovanni Angelo Ossoli by accident on her sixth day in the city, on April 1, at St. Peter's. She and the Springs had gone to witness the papal ceremonies of Holy Week. Wanting to hear vespers in a side chapel, she had designated a time for them to meet again, but then she could not find them. So, after anxiously scrutinizing through her lorgnette the large throng leaving the church, she turned and saw a young gentleman, who asked if she was trying to find someone and if he could help her look. Here reports diverge a bit. In the version Story got from Fuller, after the two looked until everyone had left, as it was getting dark, he offered to find a carriage, and, after finding none, walked with her the entire distance from the Vatican to the Corso, talking in Fuller's rudimentary Italian. Then he departed, and she went up to her apartment and told the Springs of her adventure. Many years later, however, George Putnam recalled that she had quickly walked up to him and his wife on the arm of a young man, saying that she had lost the Springs. "She seemed quite bewildered—more alarmed, indeed, than when we were really in danger of being drowned in the Mediterranean," said Putnam, adding that she "certainly did not give her address to [Ossoli], but left him in the crowd" and walked back to her lodgings. Curiously, after returning to New York later in the summer, he gave Duyckinck yet another gloss, showing Putnam not exactly above embellishment, although her editor, who, like most of his New York colleagues, sometimes liked to put on "Rabelaisian" airs, probably added the final twist. "Within the precincts of the sanctuary it is said she received very singular suggestions from the young men of Rome," Duyckinck hohoed, "which may afford instructive notes to a future edition of Woman in the Nineteenth Century." Such a salacious remark from even a stalwart literary comrade would have given a hint of what she could expect should she choose to pursue too far, in Emelyn Story's delicate phrasing, "further knowledge & acquaintance."[21]

In the only extant daguerreotype of him, Ossoli appears tall, dark, and slender, with a soft but angular face showing seriousness and diffidence as he sits holding a spiral walking stick in front of him. Many thought him very handsome ("of Spanish rather than Italian aspect," reported one American), especially his "large, dark, melancholy eyes." William and Emelyn Story, who often saw him with Fuller in Rome over the next couple of years and knew him probably better than any of Fuller's American friends there, liked him "very much" as soon as they met him.

"He is much younger than Margaret," Emelyn later wrote to Maria Lowell, "being, as I should judge, about William's age (thirty), is good looking, quite handsome, as the Italians go, has a melancholy expression about the eyes—is tall and thin. In character he seems to be remarkably amiable and tender, not intellectual, simple, natural, and good."[22]

Ossoli was actually twenty-six, ten years younger than Fuller. He was born on January 17, 1821, the youngest of five surviving children, whose mother had died when he was six. Angelo (as his family called him) lived in an apartment on the second floor of the palazzo, at Via Santa Eufemia 188, of his sister Angela, a childless but maternal woman with whom he was very close, her husband, Marquess de Andreis, and Ossoli's invalid father, whom the young man was then nursing. (His other sister, Matilde, had set a non-Italian precedent for Angelo by marrying an Irishman in Limerick.) Although financially much declined, their family was still an old and noble one that over a couple of centuries had produced many important officials in the papal court. The tradition continued with Giovanni Angelo's father, Filippo, a highly respected regional administrator in the Papal States, his older brothers Alessandro and Ottavio, who were colonels in the pope's Noble Guard, and Giuseppe, later the would-be family patriarch, who was a head of one of the districts in Rome and a secretary for the pope's Privy Chamber. Why Giovanni Angelo did not follow suit is not clear: whether alienation from his brothers pushed him toward liberal sympathies, which he seems to have been inclined to before he met Fuller, or her influence pushed him toward them, which also seems likely, at least in the democratic Mazzinian form they eventually took. Either way, his sticking to his political beliefs despite his family background and education would indeed seem to bespeak (in Emelyn Story's words) "an uncommon degree of character." In any case, it made him the black sheep in the family, certainly to his brothers, who several times threatened to report him to the papal authorities.[23]

How much Fuller and Ossoli saw each other after their first encounter is unclear. According to Emelyn Story, Fuller told her that the following day, she saw him walking back and forth in front of her apartment, obviously wanting to see her but lacking the courage to stop and ring the bell. Fuller herself would later call their meeting "singular, fateful I may say." And so it certainly soon became, as Ossoli, just before she left at the end of the following month, offered her his hand in marriage! "I never dreamed I should take it," Fuller told her sister Ellen two years later. "I loved him and felt very unhappy to leave him, but the connexion seemed so every way unfit. I did not hesitate a moment." Yet suppressing the feelings he aroused was evidently not so easy. In a letter to Fuller three years later about her "good friend Giovanni," Marcus Spring recalled her demeanor as they had prepared to leave Rome the following month. "I saw . . . how you had left your heart there," he remembered, adding that he had even made two predictions to Rebecca, which he quoted to Fuller: "'that you would go back to Rome, & that you and Giovanni's attachment, which I saw was a growing one, would ripen into a marriage.'" All this, of course, was in retrospect. At the very least, however one sorts out precisely these remembered accounts, it seems clear enough that, even as she rejected his bold proposal, Fuller's feelings toward him were developing in a romantic fashion.[24]

She got provocative encouragement from letters she received that spring and summer from Mickiewicz in Paris. The first came several days after meeting Ossoli. Rebecca Spring later claimed that Fuller received a letter from Mickiewicz urging her to return to Paris to work with him on a joint literary project. But in a letter that Rebecca probably never saw, he pointedly expressed the opposite idea: he reminded her that he had not tried to detain her in Paris because he had thought she needed to be in Italy for her physical and mental health. He said he now wanted her to stay as long as possible. Yet the unhappily married Mickiewicz—even if not, as Rebecca Spring would claim, seriously contemplating a divorce so he could marry Fuller—was clearly taken with her, and more than just ideologically. "The idea of seeing you again is very sweet to me," he wrote in his letter. "I encountered in you a *true* person. I do not give you other praise. Such an encounter on life's journey consoles and fortifies. What happiness it will be when all women recognize the merit of sincerity and truth." Indeed, after reading this rather mixed message, Fuller told the Springs, Rebecca recalled, that she had to return right away to Paris. So, after a long late-night discussion on April 9, during which they tried to convince her to drop the idea, at breakfast the next morning, she handed them before going out with Eddie to the Villa Borghese a twenty-four-page confessional letter, her customary gesture in times of romantic crisis. In it she replayed her well-worn self-representation as the heroically sincere seeker destined from infancy "to walk by the inner light alone," even repeating, as here, phrases she had used in her letter to Sam Ward seven years earlier. After claiming further, perhaps half-truthfully, at least in her own mind, that she had "never sought love as a passion" and, more plausibly, did not even know if she had ever loved "at all in the sense of oneness," she got to the central question that the Springs evidently had posed to her during their discussion. "You ask me if I love M. I answer he affected me like music or the richest landscape, my heart beat with joy that he at once felt beauty in me also. When I was with him I was happy; and thus far the attraction is so strong that all the way from Paris I felt as if I had left my life behind, and if I followed my inclination I should return at this moment and leave Italy behind." Her conclusion was characteristically self-protective and portentous. After claiming, a little absurdly, that she had once loved Beethoven and Michelangelo, toward whom she now felt indifferent, she declared, "But when I loved either of these great Souls I abandoned myself wholly to it, I did not calculate, I shall do so in life if I love enough." Rebecca did not record her reaction to this remarkable confession and prediction, although she and Marcus must have felt added portentousness when, after returning, Fuller reported she had almost plunged into the villa's fountain into which Eddie had fallen when, rising to the surface, he had caught his stick and she had pulled him out. In any case, Fuller remained in Rome.[25]

Meanwhile, Mickiewicz continued prompting her to stop calculating and start abandoning herself. In Paris, he had made the point by picturing her as a historically new but dubiously virginal woman. Now, in the letter that provoked her, he made it less loftily and more fatherly, although just as insistently. "Your organism greatly needs" the physicality of Italy, he told her, so that her soul's great fund of strength and life would not, as it always had, dissipate in mental struggles before passing "into your body." She should, therefore, live in Italian nature, converse with Italian people, and hear Italian music. "You will have time to return to Mozart and Beethoven later. Now enjoy what surrounds you. Breathe the life in through all your pores." To make sure also that she understood that he meant by "body" something aesthetic as well as sensuous, responding to some remark she had made about all the beautiful women she had seen in southern Italy, he easily grasped the subtext and deftly turned it around.

> You are struck by the beautiful build of the women of the South. You will see models of this beauty in and near Rome. And the men in Italy are also beautiful! But what inner poverty! What childishness!
>
> I was in Italy in my youth and I stayed there a long time. No woman touched me. I preferred the paintings. The time is coming when inner beauty, inner spiritual life will become the first and essential quality of a woman. Without this quality woman will not exert even physical influence.
>
> Learn to appreciate yourself as a beauty, and after having admired the women of Rome, say, "and as for me, why I am beautiful!"

Physical experience and self-appreciation, Mickiewicz seemed to be saying, were the keys to changing her life. With advice like this, it is not surprising that she had wanted to drop everything and race to Paris![26]

In subsequent letters he raised the romantic stakes. "Do not leave lightly those who would like to remain near you," he cautioned. "This is in reference to that little Italian you met in the Church." What exactly was he suggesting here? Presumably, he saw romantic possibilities in Ossoli that she should not pass by. But it seems to have been more than that. In saying that he saw her as being in a similar state of mind to his when he had been her age and had lost the Countess Zaluska because he had been "too romantic and too exclusive," he probably also meant that she, too, needed to take these affairs more lightly. Indeed, he went further. After Fuller left Rome at the end of the next month, he urged on her some sort of free-love doctrine, and on the even grander platform of women's rights than he had raised for her in Paris. Upbraiding her again, this time for her last letter's melancholy and "romantic reveries which could exhaust your imagination," he told her:

> You have pleaded the liberty of woman in a masculine and frank style. Live and act, as you write. . . . I saw you, with all your knowledge and your imagination and all your literary reputation, living in bondage worse than that of a servant. You were obligated to everybody. You have persuaded yourself that all you need is to express your ideas and feelings in books. . . . Do not forget that even in your private life *as a woman* you have rights to maintain. Emerson says rightly: *give all for love*, but this *love* must not be that of the shepherds of Florian nor that of schoolboys and German ladies. The relationships which suit you are those which develop and free your spirit, responding to the legitimate needs of your organism and leaving you free at all times. You are the sole judge of these needs.

There is some irony here. It had been precisely her bookish but personal arguments with Emerson over the nature of love that had partly inspired him to write
the very poem that Mickiewicz quoted. Of course, the rights of Fuller's romantic
"organism"—much less her right to a love affair different from that of shepherds,
schoolboys, and German ladies—had certainly *not* been what her Concord friend
had had in mind. In any case, she would have months to ruminate on Mickiewicz's
provocative injunctions to liberate herself sexually. She would also have some
months to decide what *she* had in mind with "that little Italian."[27]

Whatever her uncertainties about these matters, Paris was behind her, and she
now felt "intoxicated" by Rome's "peculiar life." "Those last glorious nights in
which I wandered about amid the old walls and columns or sat by the fountains in
the Piazza del Popolo, or by the river," she afterward wrote to Caroline Sturgis,
"seem worth an age of pain both after and before only one hates pain in Italy." On
May 23, her thirty-seventh birthday, she wrote to Maria Rotch simply, "Italy ful-
fills my hopes; it could not do more, it has been the dream of my life." Later that
week, "again . . . suffer[ing] from parting," this time from Rome, she reluctantly
ended her two months in the city, left unhappy Ossoli, and joined the Springs for
their planned summer trip through northern Italy.[28]

III

Her first leg took her to Florence. To get there, Fuller and the Springs traveled by
carriage via the scenic Perugia route, which she afterward detailed in her *Tribune*
letter, mixing, as usual, historical and literary with political and personal observations. "Who can ever be alone for a moment in Italy?" she asked, describing
passing red poppy–filled vineyards as they climbed the hill to Assisi overlooking
the Umbrian plain. "Every stone has a voice," she answered, "every grain of dust
seems instinct with spirit from the Past, every step recalls some line, some legend
of long-neglected lore," making multiple allusions to Byron, Goethe, and other
Romantic authors who had exploited the scene for their real or fictional adventures. The art-filled churches inspired by Saint Francis and the ubiquitous posters
extolling Pius IX drew an ironic moral: "The old love which has made so rich this
aerial cradle of St. Francis glows warm as ever in the breasts of men; still, as ever,
they long for hero-worship, and shout aloud at the least appearance of an object."
She more generously extrapolated from the "very dignified and calm" female figures she spied peering into open Etruscan tombs on the way to Perugia to the
"noble" position women must have occupied. Finally, after hurrying through
Perugia's Etruscan art ("as if in a trance"), she arrived in Florence at the beginning of June.[29]

It did not immediately impress her. Although she liked her quiet apartment after
the boisterous Corso, what most Americans preferred about Florence—its familiar middle-class ambience—left her cold. "The natural character is ironed out here,
and done up in a French pattern," she noted in her dispatch; "yet there is no French
vivacity, nor Italian either." Indeed, the "busy and intellectual" Florentines, she
wrote to Caroline Sturgis, seemed just like Bostonians! Yet, as usual when mea-

suring Italy's social flaws, she blamed its regime, in this case Tuscany's tolerant but pliant Grand Duke Leopold II, who, she wrote sardonically in the *Tribune*, caught between the pope and the Austrians, "keeps imploring and commanding people to keep still, and they *are* still and glum as death." She did concede that, even if politically quiet compared with Rome, "within, Tuscany burns and flutters," thanks to the government's recent loosening of press restrictions. And, she agreed, for the fine arts, Florence was unsurpassed. It even revived her intellectual interest in art; she afterward wrote Caroline: "there I did really begin to study as well as gaze and feel." Nor was she bereft of quite a few "busy" and "intellectual" recently arrived Bostonians who were eager to shed a little of their middle-class busyness. George Curtis and his brother Burril organized parties with her and the Springs at which they related their adventures and sang Neapolitan songs. Expatriate artists like Joseph Mozier, a successful New York merchant turned sculptor, his much more celebrated sculpting colleagues Hiram Powers, in Italy for the past decade, and Horatio Greenough, who would spend most of his life in Europe, befriended her. As with her artist friends in Rome, their accomplishments did not overawe her, but she plugged them nonetheless, urging her compatriots to hurry up and order not just the minor popular portrait busts Crawford was producing but some "great work before the prime of his genius has been frittered away." Later that year, his American agent pasted her double-edged blurb on the front of a pamphlet extolling his work.[30]

After spending June socializing and visiting galleries, interrupted by a side trip to nearby Arezzo, so she could see the paintings in the house of the Renaissance art historian Giorgio Vasari and Piero della Francesca's frescoes at the church of San Francesco, on July 2 Fuller and the Springs left for Venice. Along the way, she stopped for "two full, rich days" at Bologna, where she got further evidence of Italy's respect for powerful women in the monuments, lecture halls, and archives of its celebrated female scholars and artists. "A woman should love Bologna," she told her readers, "for there has the spark of Woman been cherished with reverent care." After a stop at Ravenna and another at Padua, Italy's other great Renaissance university town, they arrived at "glorious" Venice. Unlike Rome and Florence, Venice was a city that most American travelers passed through but did not linger in. But to Fuller, despite being very ill her first week there, it seemed a "dream of *enchantment!*" Thanks to the Springs' largesse, they had a gondola and two gondoliers at their call to row them around the city's beautiful sites. Just as much as in Florence, it was Venice's art that most impressed her ("only to be really felt and known in its birth-place," she informed the still homebound Emerson). For the first time, she remarked on Italian architecture. She even praised the Bourbons and other aristocratic exiles for buying up and tastefully restoring the city's ancient houses. Yet artistic enchantment only went so far. After giving an exuberant account of a "fairy land"–like party that Caroline Ferdinande Louise de Bourbon, the duchess de Berri, gave for her son and his aunt, Marie Thérèse of Austria, Fuller added the sardonic republican hope that Europe's exiled royal families, "more rich in blood than brain, might come to enjoy a perpetual *villeggiatura* [vacation] in Italy. It did not seem to me a cruel wish. The show of greatness will satisfy every legitimate desire of such minds. A gentle punishment for the distributors of *lettres de cachet* and Spielberg dungeons to their fellow men."[31]

Besides her illness, Fuller experienced another aggravation. It is not clear precisely when or how the idea of separating materialized, but the Springs seem to have had it on their minds for a while. Back in early May, just around the time of their argument about Fuller returning to Paris, Rebecca had written to her cousin that Margaret intended to spend the next winter there and they wanted to spend it by themselves in Italy. "We have much that is pleasant together," explaining the last part, "but I do not think it desirable to travel all the time with her. She is one I should prefer to see occasionally, then she is very improving, but she is not one I should wish to live with constantly." She quickly added. "I would not on any account have you speak of this to any human being. We have never mentioned anything of the kind before. We see much to admire and love in her much of the time, and she has no idea of our feelings having in the least changed." For her part, Fuller had felt (in her words) "wicked irritation against them" for having kept her from returning to Paris, but apparently also for not understanding her desire to remake herself in Italy, arguably the best place in the world, Hawthorne would later suggest in the *Marble Faun*, for a free-spirited woman to imagine liberating herself from her past life. "I was very weary of the good friends who were with me, because they never knew what I was feeling, and always brought forward what I wanted to leave behind," she would later write to Caroline. "I wanted to forget myself in Italy, and, while with them, it was impossible." Meanwhile, just before leaving Florence, the Springs had received a letter from their cousin, with whom they had left Jeanie, their little girl, saying that as both she and Jeanie's nurse were going to get married, they needed to return home soon.[32]

Fuller faced a practical choice. She could go with them to Germany—for which purpose she had brought several glowing letters about her from her Cambridge neighbor, Dr. Robert Wesselhoeft, to, among other famous personages, Johann Peter Eckermann, Goethe's former secretary and the author of the first book she had translated. Or she could continue through northern Italy without them. She chose the latter. One reason was the decision she had made before leaving Rome to stay abroad another year; hence, she calculated, she had no reason to fly through Germany and Italy simply so the Springs could get home in time. But there was clearly also a more compelling reason: the lure of Rome, where she had decided to spend the winter rather than Paris. "I should always suffer the pain of Tantalus thinking of Rome, if I could not see it more thoroughly than I have as yet even begun to, for it was all *outside* the two months, just finding out where objects were," she explained in a letter to Richard. "I had only just begun to live with their life when I was obliged to leave." What exactly those living "objects" *were* she did not say, although her growing romantic attachment to "that little Italian" to whom Mickiewicz had urged her to return was probably the clinching reason for her to skip both her land of intellectual giants and her Parisian "cream of all the milk" and settle back in Rome.[33]

Yet, although feeling "it was high time" she and the Springs separated, she still fretted about the prospect. Without Marcus managing her practical affairs and, more important, paying her bills while she waited for remittances from home, she feared she might find herself in desperate financial straits. The Springs' insistence on leaving after only a week in Venice also rankled her. "Seemingly impatient to be delayed by the state of my health," they made her feel "some bitterness," she would tell Caroline in another letter, "at the indifference with which they left me, alone in a foreign land." They evidently felt badly, too. "The parting with Margaret was very painful as we stood on the deck of the Adriatic steamer and looked down upon her, weeping bitterly in the gondola," Rebecca recalled. "It was dreadful to leave her alone." However, Fuller seems to have put the best face on it. "Natural tears I shed at parting," she afterward wrote them, borrowing Miltonic cries, "but tried to dry them with the thought we had certainly done what was best under the circumstances." Nor evidently were there any hard feelings on the Springs' part, as the following year, they decided to name the child Rebecca was carrying Margaret (although it turned out to be a boy).[34]

Meanwhile, after recuperating, Fuller experienced her best week in Venice. The clerk at the Grand Canal hotel told her she could stay in the Springs' "delightful" two rooms, though she wondered, "How much *iced water* is to be charged on for all this gallantry I do not yet know." The American consul regularly checked in on her, and the Springs' devoted gondolier chauffeured her around with his black top over her so, he thought, "I shall so have a more retired ladylike air now I am alone." She also enjoyed the company of both Hicks and the Curtis brothers, who were visiting the city. "Margaret Fuller left yesterday morning," George Curtis wrote to Cranch on July 28. "She has never been so happy she says." And so she felt. In the gondola, at her window, "in the galleries and churches to see the great works of Venetian art," she afterward wrote to Richard of her nearly three weeks in the city, "I passed happier and more thoughtful hours than at all before in Europe."[35]

The rest of her trip continued alternating highs and lows. She quickly discovered she liked traveling by herself in Italy. As Mickiewicz advised, she now lived and spoke solely with Italians, which made her, if still not fluent, at least reasonably communicative in the language. In addition, on a whim, she could stop at places tourists and even literary travelers largely missed, inaugurating her love affair with small northern Italian cities and towns. On her way west to Milan, after seeing "really well" Venetia's "truly Italian" Vicenza and Verona and Lombardy's Mantua, she continued on to Lago di Garda, where she stayed for two days, enjoying yet another benefit of lonely but relaxing journeying. Apart from a jaunt by gondola to the island of San Lazaro to pay her Romantic respects to the Armenian convent where Byron had studied, she happily vegetated, sitting in her quiet room by her open window overlooking the lake, smelling the "sweet and pure" air, and hearing the waves break on the shore.[36]

To her mother back home, though, her situation seemed worrisome. "I was very sorry for the necessity of the Springs return," she replied to Margaret's euphoric account of her life on the lake. "I know it will occasion you loss and trouble for no lady can guide herself as well as a gentleman in travelling in this country, how much more difficult in Europe." Her mother turned out to be partly right. At Brescia, where Fuller stopped next to see Roman temple excavations and more

Raphaels and Titians, she became violently ill with a high fever and severe stomach pains, which she thought to be the cholera that had killed her father. Panicked that the fever was affecting her brain and with nowhere to get medicine, she left the next morning in a makeshift bed inside a carriage for a horrific-sounding ride to Milan. "I was afraid I should die on the road, and nobody know it but my courrier, a brutal wretch who robbed and injured me all he could under the mask of obsequiousness," she afterward told her mother, speaking of Dominico Albieri, the servant she had acquired from the Springs in Venice. "He wasted a good deal of money for me, before I could learn how to prevent it." Even after she fired him, he continued to stalk her. "If Dominico comes here, as he intended," she would write the Springs from Rome, "I think he will stab me some dark night in the street."[37]

After she limped, "very weak," into Milan on August 4, she began to flourish again, though she was still beset by "gastric troubles," which would plague her for the rest of her journey. She missed the art of Rome and Florence, and she found the "detestably harsh" Milanese dialect hard to understand. But she soon discovered Milan's great appeal: although militarily subjugated and elaborately monitored by a horde of Austrian spies, the city was the peninsula's urban heartland of anticlerical Liberals, middle-class republicans, and artisan and lower-middle-class Democrats, many with socialistic leanings. Her political contacts proliferated. She met Gaetano de Castillia, the honored Liberal and former prisoner in the Austrians' notorious Spielberg prison. She saw Pietro Maestri, the republican physician and statistician, and became acquainted with his circle of Mazzinians. She probably met some, at least, of those around the brilliant political theorist Carlo Cattaneo, whose advocacy of the link between science and republican citizenship and a federal Italian republic served as a modernizing liberal democratic alternative to Mazzini's Romantic "unitarian" vision. She formed many friendships with the city's militantly democratic university students, coming to "really love" the noble-born young lawyer and republican leader Anselmo Guerrieri-Gonzaga, who spoke no English but whose "brilliant and ardent, though not . . . great, mind"—which was probably a good description of many of them—caused her afterward to keep up a correspondence with him in French.[38]

Yet she did not ignore Milan's liberal literati. She interviewed the Milanese nationalist poets Giovanni Berchet and Tommaso Grossi, whom she apparently impressed as much as they did her. But her biggest literary catch was the "immortal" Manzoni, whose "very engaging, frank, expansive" manners and "habitual elevation of thoughts"—two key requirements of hers for Italian intellectuals— she loved, while he and his second wife reciprocated by asking her to return often. Typically, though, neither his renown nor her enthusiasm interfered with her cool literary judgment about him and his colleagues. While lauding his delicate satire and wide social sympathies, she frankly conceded in her dispatch that his standing was as high as it was partly because that of literary Italy was so low. "Where a whole country is so kept down, her best minds cannot take the lead in the progress of the age," she wrote, adding shrewdly, "they have too much to suffer, too much to explain." In any case, Manzoni spoke the accents of the past. "Young

Italy rejects Manzoni, though not irreverently; Young Italy prizes his works, but feels that the doctrine of 'Pray and wait' is not for her at this moment, that she needs a more fervent hope, a more active faith. She is right."[39]

Her most important Milanese connection, though, was the Marchioness Costanza Arconati Visconti, the sister-in-law of Manzoni's daughter, whose letter of introduction to his wife had facilitated Fuller's meeting with him. Fuller had first met Arconati in April in Rome, where Fuller had given her a letter of recommendation from Mary Clarke, who was an intimate friend of Arconati, as well as possibly one from Julia Ward Howe, whom Arconati had entertained three years earlier during Howe's honeymoon trip to Europe. Fuller had also seen Arconati in Florence, where she kept a house, afterward getting from her further letters to give to Arconati's aristocratic friends as she made her way through Bologna and Ravenna to Venice. It is not hard to see why Fuller was attracted to her. The Viennese-born wife of the Marquess Giuseppe Arconati Visconti of the famous Visconti dynasty, she counted among her close friends Fuller's admired female Romantic celebrities Bettina von Arnim and Rahel Varnhagen von Ense. Having lived for twenty years in exile with her husband in France and Belgium, where they had hosted parties at their castle near Brussels for distinguished Italian refugees, and belonging to one of the most prominent liberal families in Italy (her brother-in-law was Piedmont-Sardinia's minister to Paris), she was also a patriotic Moderate devoted to an independent Italy. In her description of her to Elizabeth Hoar, Fuller stressed the exotic *and* the familiar. "She is a specimen of the really highbred lady, such as I have not known, without any physical beauty, the grace and harmony of her manners produce all the impression of beauty," she wrote, adding, as though describing someone in her Conversations: "She has also, a mind strong clear, precise and much cultivated by intercourse with books and men." The books were important to Fuller. When they had first met, Fuller had urged Arconati to read Goethe's *Roman Elegies*, and Arconati translated into French several Milanese poems and read them back to her, winning her over to the dialect's charms. Their subsequent letters included many mutual literary recommendations, Arconati's in Italian and Fuller's mostly in English and German.[40]

Arconati was also strongly attracted to Fuller. When a few years later a friend of Fuller interviewed Arconati in Paris, she reported that she talked all the time about Fuller, "whom that lady seemed deeply to adore." She seems to have felt this adoration partly because of Fuller's reputation as a "distinguished" author, as well as her knack for establishing warm intimacy with those she targeted socially, but most of all because Fuller represented to her a kind of heroic figure. "I love you, and have the greatest admiration for you," Arconati wrote Fuller after she left Milan, as the epitome of "true merit and of veritable greatness" and a "spectacle of moral beauty [that] elevates the soul." Indeed, Arconati once expressed astonishment that she felt so close to Fuller, with whom she shared neither nationality nor religion, nor Fuller's "extraordinary superiority," an amazement shared by some of Arconati's friends, who thought Fuller had, Arconati laughingly said, "thrown a spell upon me." There was one difference that Fuller did not throw a spell over, however, and that was politics. Although a flexible and tolerant Liberal who befriended independent Democrats like the scholarly Giuseppe Montanelli, whom she arranged for Fuller to meet afterward in Florence, she could not abide the Mazzinians and other radical Democrats. She especially warned Fuller against Mickiewicz's influence, since, despite his genius and Arconati's own friendship with him, his ideas were too "exclusive" and unreal—as were, the thoroughly western European added, those of most Slavs. On the other hand, when it came to their friendship, Arconati assured her, politics meant nothing: "I cannot deceive myself as to the elevation and the energy of your soul, and your opinions cannot enter into it." Arconati's subsequent letters showed both sides well, expressing pride in seeing Fuller's opinion of Emerson quoted in the *Revue des deux Mondes*, while telling her what she should read of Arconati's political guru, Gioberti. "She seems to love me and to wish I should have whatever is hers," Fuller told Hoar. "I take great pleasure in her friendship."[41]

She also took pleasure socializing with the many prominent liberal marquesses and marchionesses and counts and countesses to whom Arconati introduced her. Such easy access to Italian aristocratic circles, liberal or conservative, was an even rarer occurrence for a non-Italian, and especially an American, than meeting middle-class Italians. Several had had her stay at their villas and palaces as she traveled through northern Italy, where they evidently talked freely with her about their personal lives. "It is rather pleasant to come a little on the traces of these famous histories," Fuller wrote to Caroline, after one conversation with several of them. "These ladies take pleasure in telling me of spheres so unlike mine and do it well." They actually revealed to her more than they knew, as Arconati showed her some of their personal letters. What Fuller got out of them is not known, but the results certainly satisfied Arconati. "You have penetrated the true character of Madame C," she would write after Fuller returned to Rome, "and explain it to me so that I understand it perfectly." Some of them also seem to have been impressed with Fuller, although the fact did not make her exactly complacent. "There is a Polish countess here, who likes me much," Fuller later wrote from Rome to a correspondent, speaking of Arconati's friend the "very handsome" Countess Radzivill. "She is a widow, very rich, one of the emancipated women, naturally vivacious, and with talent. This woman *envies me*; she says, 'How Happy you are; so free, so serene, so attractive, so self-possessed!' I say not a word, but I do not look on myself as particularly enviable." One can guess what she meant by that, but as the subject to which she immediately segued was her lack of money, one can assume that was undoubtedly at least one of the things.[42]

After her week in Milan, Fuller's immersion in northern Italian life continued apace. Following brief trips to Lago Maggiore, Turin, and Geneva, she hiked alone across the Great Saint Bernard pass through the Pennine Alps, where she savored being near "grand and simple" nature after all the excitement of Italian art and politics. In late August she traveled to Bellagio, where for two weeks she stayed at an inn on Lake Como with the Arconatis and their entourage of aristocratic friends. Floating on the lake, listening to the "stories of heroic sorrow" of the "fair and brilliant" Countess Radzivill, and receiving from a group of pretty Bellagio girls bouquets to "'the American Countess'"—who hoped, she happily quoted them, "'she would be as happy as she deserved'"—she luxuriated in a "peaceful external existence." So taken was she with the lake's beauty, for which even Goethe's accounts and Turner's pictures had not prepared her, she inserted in her dispatch a rare invidious comparison between an American and European landscape, along with a swipe at "persons who have pretended" they saw nothing there finer than their own lake country. ("I can only say that they must be exceedingly obtuse in organization—a defect not uncommon among Americans.") Her enthrallment with Bellagio also had a social dimension. "The life here on the lake is precisely what we once at Newbury imagined as being so pleasant," she told her old seaside sidekick Caroline Sturgis. "These people have charming villas and gardens on the lake, adorned with fine works of art; they go to see one another in boats; you can be all the time in a boat if you like." In another letter to a friend the same day, she reflected from her privileged lakeside perch on how much, despite all the cheating guides and drivers ("They think that is part of their duty towards a foreigner," she noted dryly), she had become enamored of Italians of all classes— and they of her. "I am everywhere well received, and high and low take pleasure in smoothing my path. I love much the Italians. The lower classes have the vices induced by long subjection to tyranny; but also a winning sweetness, a ready and discriminating love for the beautiful, and a delicacy in the sympathies, the absence of which always made me sick in our own country. Here, at least, one does not suffer from obtuseness or indifference."[43]

With her mutual temperamental sympathies with "high and low" Italians now established, by the first week in September she was back in Milan, where she discovered political affinities as well. Tensions had been rising between the reformist Pius IX and Austrian authorities in Lombardy and Venetia. On July 17, the anniversary of the pope's amnesty day, and twelve days after he had agreed to the formation of an armed Civic Guard, the Austrian government, growing ever more fearful that papal reforms would lead to nationalist revolutions throughout Italy, invaded the Papal States at Ferrara, just across the northern border from Lombardy. Instantly, Rome had seethed with protests, threats, and calls for a war against Austria, led by, most kept hoping, the now outraged pope, who, however, although pleased with his widespread popularity as Italy's national leader, still contented himself with only a strong protest. Meanwhile, the contagion had spread into Milan, Florence, and elsewhere in Lombardy and Tuscany. "All things seem to announce that some important change is inevitable here, but what?" On her return to Milan on September 8, the day of the great feast of the Madonna, she saw a large throng gathering to honor the new popular Italian archbishop sent by the pope. By the evening, crowds started shouting "Viva Pio Nono" and "Viva Italia," which provoked the police to respond with arrests and sword and bayonet charges, causing many injuries, while demonstrators hurled sticks and stones and a group of Milanese "youth" sang Rossini's chorus to Pius. In her dispatch, silently passing over the violence of the demonstrators, she blamed the bloodletting solely on the Lombardy authorities. "[Austria] could not sustain her police," she wrote, "who rushed upon a defenceless crowd that had no share in what excited their displeasure, except by sympathy, and, driving them like sheep, wounded them *in the backs*." Cheered by seeing her young radical Democrats in the midst of throngs of sympathizing citizens, she afterward wrote to Richard, "I left that city with great regret and hope to return."[44]

Encounters with mounting anti-Austrian nationalist sentiment also dominated her return visit to Florence. Following stops at Parma to see Correggio's and Parmigianino's "glorious" frescoes, and then on to Modena and once again her favorite Bologna, after crossing the crude roads through the central Apennines, she reached the city at the beginning of the last week in September. She had originally intended to stay only briefly, but, after coming down with nausea and fever even worse than at Brescia, she lingered for a couple of weeks at the apartment of Mozier and his wife Isabella, who fed her gruel while she gradually got better. Politics, though, remained uppermost in her mind. After reading for a week the new Mazzinian *Alba* and the Liberal constitutionalist *Patria*, she dropped her skeptical tone in May about the halting progress of liberty. "I have now seen what Italy contains most important of the great past," she wrote to Richard, blending, as usual, past and present, and adding what almost no foreigner would have then said, "I begin to hope for her also a great future." She had no doubts: "The signs have improved so much since I came. I am most fortunate to be here at this time. I feel most deeply interested." No laments about belatedness; she had arrived in the nick of time. "Italy," she wrote to Lizzy Hoar just before leaving Florence, sounding the other psychic leitmotiv in her letters that fall, "receives me as a long lost child."[45]

The final leg of her four-and-a-half-month journey had a fittingly bucolic feel. While chafing at the "sere and brown" landscape of the Italian summer that had aggravated her illnesses throughout her trip, she nonetheless continued to feel better as she traveled alone by carriage through the Tuscan countryside, periodically stopping to sample grapes hanging down from vines in "untouched" Siena. "The Italian sun has waked a luxuriant growth that covers my mind," she wrote in her journal. "The green may be all of weeds; I hardly care; weeds are beautiful in Italy." On October 10, she was back in Rome. Writing six days later to her mother, she added up what she had acquired of the Italian history, art, and especially language, in which, thanks to her "total abstinence from English," she was now fluent. But most of all she beamed over how traveling almost exclusively among Italians in places foreigners rarely went had made her feel, more than ever, the perfect fit between herself and them: "I made many and ardent friends, of all ranks, from the very highest to the lowest; the Italians sympathize with my character and understand my organization, as no other people ever did; they admire the ready eloquence of my nature, and highly prize my intelligent sympathy (such as they do not find often in foreigners) with their suffering in the past and hopes for the future." Two weeks later, she summed it all up in a letter to Sarah Shaw: "I have seen almost every important place in Italy and begin to know as well as to feel about this country, dream of my heart and realization of my mind." Now, though, that dream's realization resided in Rome, which she evidently divined. "To live here, alone and independent, to really draw in the spirit of Rome," she told her mother, "Oh! what joy!"[46]

IV

When Fuller arrived in the city, she found waiting for her a letter from Mickiewicz replying to her answer to his blunt entreaties to fulfill the "legitimate needs of your organism." Her letter is lost, but his scolding about her depressive and exhausting "romantic reveries" seems not to have gone down well. "You find my letter *harsh*," he answered. "Certainly there was nothing *harsh* in the sentiment that dictated it." She had evidently denied that she always felt blue, and to this he said, "I know that you often feel *gay* and always animated *internally*, especially when you meditate or when you dream and compose." But that was just his point: she needed to get this "inner life lodged and established in all your body." Gaiety only in the imagination and in solitude "cannot resist the first shock of reality" and so relapses into melancholy. This was a shrewd analysis of her manic-depressive tendencies, but what did he think was the solution? Essentially, the same one he had given her in Paris: she needed to believe in and manifest, in both her private and her public life, not only the "rights" of her body but also her historical mission as the incarnation of the age's new woman. "I tried to make you understand the purpose of your existence, to inspire many sentiments in you," he wrote. "Your mind still does not believe that a new epoch commences and that it has already begun. New for *woman* too." Yet she kept resisting. "You know it, but you don't believe it enough. You still live spiritually in the society of Shakespeare, Schiller, Byron. Literature is not the whole life," Poland's greatest poet told her. We do not know how she replied to that aphorism, but if her past reactions to Mickiewicz's messianic but sensible advice were any guide, she took it very seriously.[47]

In the meantime, she dealt with a few more everyday matters of life. The first was finding an affordable place to live. "Rome is not as cheap a place as Florence," she quipped to Richard, "but then I would not give a pin to live in Florence." She was lucky. After a couple of days, her banker found her an apartment that she rented for six months, again on the Corso but this time near the busy Piazza del Popolo and the beautiful Borghese Gardens. With its prime location, neatly furnished top-floor rooms ("more like England than Italy"), and fixed price for room and board, her new quarters gave her just the sense of permanence she wanted. She worried a little about the house's owner, a pretty widow who had become a marchioness after inveigling her marquess paramour into marrying her before his death, but Fuller's banker thought her landlady's questionable reputation would not present a problem. And she liked the woman's new lover, an Italian artist and officer in the new Civic Guard, who brought them the latest political news. "Of course," she assured her mother, "I seem to ignore all these circumstances; he appears here merely as a friend and a visitor, and if she observes strict good sense and propriety in her relations with me, all will go on well, but the ground is a little delicate." To ensure that her "most insinuating" *padrona* did not go "too far," she made it clear that she did not wish her company. "Thus I remain undisturbed."[48]

Determined to avoid the "restless impertinence of sightseeing," Fuller spent her first couple of weeks by herself. "After all the rush and excitement of the past year," she advised Emerson, "I live alone, eat alone, walk alone, and enjoy unspeakably the stillness." She read a passel of history and travel books. She spent afternoons in the Villa Borghese gardens, watching the races and listening to the music by the little lake. She meandered down to see the dances of the Trasteverini, the impoverished inhabitants of the Trastevere's maze of dark, winding alleys and passageways just across the Tiber; their "frank love-songs," costume dancing with tambourines, and "colours flying, drums beating" excited her. She was most excited, though, about mixing with the crowds during that month of feasts now tinged by the political ferment of Rome. "This morning I was out, with half Rome, to see the Civic Guard maneuvering in that great field near the tomb of Cecilia Metella, which is full of ruins," she wrote Emerson after her second week. "The effect was noble, as the band played the Bolognese march, and six thousand Romans passed in battle array amid these fragments of the great time." Her meandering seems to have been medicinal. "I have been getting better every hour since I came back to Rome," she assured Lizzie Hoar at the end of the month. To Richard that same day she wrote: "I am now truly happy here, really *in* Rome, so quiet and familiar," adding, for good measure, "Yes I *am* happy here."[49]

Her lonely vagabondage did not last forever, however. For one thing, she got news from home, some welcome, such as that of Eugene's newborn daughter "Margarette," and some, like Greeley's self-pitying accounts of his tantrum-throwing son and wife in their "Castle Doleful," that probably made her feel relieved to have escaped. Concurrently, her Transcendentalist friends traced her steps in her letters, which they eagerly circulated among themselves, while thousands of readers tracked her movements in her *Tribune* dispatches and their many newspaper reprints. On October 20, Emerson finally arrived in Liverpool, so now a colleague was nearby with whom she could swap letters about their European experiences.[50]

Meanwhile Rome's popularity as the Mecca for arts-minded foreigners, like Paris's standing a couple of decades later, ensured she soon had plenty of Americans around. That winter alone, she reported running into over a dozen she knew. Although the Curtis brothers and George Duyckinck had left by then, she had George Hillard, then collecting material for his popular *Six Months in Italy*, and, later in the winter, her old friend Henry Hedge. She continued to meet American painters and sculptors, who, while trying to gain reputations and perfect their craft, were establishing in Rome and Florence America's first colonies of expatriate artists. Besides Hicks, Crawford and his wife Louisa, Julia Ward Howe's sister, and Pearse and Lizzie Cranch, who had returned to Rome, the portrait and figure painter Luther Terry and the landscape painter and architect Jasper Francis Cropsey and his wife Maria regularly dropped by Fuller's "quiet little upper chamber" on the Corso. Rome also transformed her connections with them. "It is odd how people meet at last, being an American party," Fuller told Caroline. "I had not seen so many persons together connected with the old phase" when she had, speaking of her younger days, "walked rather sad and strange among them." To illustrate the change, she instanced Frank Heath, the Virginia born member of Lowell's set, then abroad to study philosophy and medicine in Germany, whom she would see a lot of over the next couple of years. In Boston he had always been "wonderfully struck" by her being a woman, she said to Caroline. Now, however, "every atom of his original composition" seemed different. "We made last night the tour of the Vatican by torch light."[51]

Of all these "passionate pilgrims" (in Henry James's graciously patronizing phrase), none, though, was more struck by this difference than the gay and witty William Wetmore and his pretty and sociable wife Emelyn Story, who would soon become Fuller's closest American friends in Italy. Having given up law, the Storys had arrived in Rome with their baby boy a couple of weeks after Fuller had returned; William had come to Rome to sculpt a commissioned monument of his recently deceased father, the United States Supreme Court justice Joseph Story. For James, the Storys epitomized his innocent "precursors." They found distasteful American philistinism and (in William's words) the "restraint and bondage of Boston" but not as much as later generations of artistic expatriates. Likewise, while they sympathized with the later Roman Republic, like most Americans, they remained skeptical about the moral character of common Italians. For Fuller, though, whose cosmopolitanism was considerably edgier, the Storys demonstrated what her encounters with Heath hinted at: the power of transatlantic "expatriation" to overcome inherited social prejudices. Having heard that they were arriving in October, Fuller immediately located a good apartment for them in "one of the very best places in Rome for the time of the Carnival," a task she would help them with again in late February, when they returned from Florence, afterward breakfasting with them and the Crawfords at Villa Negroni. Emelyn Story later recalled being astonished at the change in Fuller.

> To me she seemed so unlike what I had known in America that I continually said: how have I misjudged you—"You are not at all such a person as I took you to be in America." To this she replied, "I am not the same person but in many respects another. My life has new channels now & and how thankful I am that I have been able to come out into larger interests—but partly you did not know me at home in the true light." I had not known her much personally when in Boston but through her friends, who were mine also, I had learned to think of her as a person on intellectual stilts with a large share of arrogance & little sweetness of temper. How unlike to this was she now—so delicate, so simple, confiding & affectionate . . . & what to me a still greater surprise, was possessed with [so] broad a charity that she could cover with its mantle the faults and defects of those about her.

The Storys' old anti-Transcendentalist friend Lowell could not believe it. "I cannot help suspecting a flaw somewhere," he wrote in exasperation to William Story after receiving a glowing letter from Emelyn about their former bête noire. "There must be not a little of the desolate island where S.M.F. is considered agreeable." How different Fuller's personality actually was in Rome is hard to say. Not just the skeptical young Brahmin Storys but her close friends as well had been saying similar things for several years. Was it mistaken identity, a changed personality, new "channels," or the magic of Rome? The truth seems to have been, as she suggested to Emelyn, a bit of all four.[52]

Fuller returned in Rome to one social connection that virtually guaranteed she would not be alone. At their last meeting before she left, Ossoli had told her that she would come back to him, and, as Marcus Spring had sensed, he was right.

What happened next is not entirely clear. In the account that Emelyn Story got from Fuller, even though Ossoli continued to press his case, she continued to resist. "She still refused to look upon him as a Lover," that it was not fitting, that he should marry a younger woman, "that she would be his friend but not his wife." However, he contrived to be constantly with her, though in a "hopeless, desperate" way, until at some point she gave in. Because this skeletal rendition of their awkward courtship is generally consistent with other accounts Fuller later gave, it seems credible. But it leaves three important questions unanswered. Why did he persist? Why did she give in? What did she give in to?[53]

The pursuit of a somewhat frail, plain-looking American woman by a handsome soldier in the Civic Guard over ten years her junior would later astonish many. Rumors abounded. Emelyn Story declared the whispered story that Ossoli thought she was rich "utterly false," since Margaret freely communicated to him, as to all her friends, her lack of money. To others the connection gave ample fodder for mockery and disparagement. "What a strange story, is it not?" Frederick Gale wrote to his sister Anna, Fuller's former Greene Street School student, after meeting Fuller and Ossoli in Florence two years later. "Now that the scornful, man hating Margaret of 40, has got a husband, really no old maid need despair, while there is life in her body!" Some, however, were not at all surprised. A pronounced erotic component had often been a part of the attraction Fuller had held, especially for younger men and women, even in the rarefied and sublimated circles of Transcendental Boston. When several years later Emerson expressed surprise to Elizabeth Hoar at the homage made to her and even offers of marriage presented to her by distinguished men in Europe and Italy, Hoar answered: "There is nothing extraordinary in it. Had she been a man, any one of those fine girls of sixteen, who surrounded her here, would have married her: they were all in love with her, she understood them so well." Likewise, Rebecca Spring recalled, "Men fell in love with her wherever she went and wanted to marry her."[54]

This last claim was an exaggeration, obviously. (Emerson would claim that he had heard that both the married Mickiewicz and the very unmarried Mazzini had asked to marry her as well.) Still, it not only suggests the presence of something to exaggerate but also jibes with Fuller's own perception, which she expressed in letters to Caroline Sturgis, that European men responded to her in positive ways she had not experienced in America. Certainly, Ossoli was susceptible to Fuller's kind of charisma. Losing his mother at an early age, nursing his dying father, scorned by his older brothers, he seems to have been not just a black sheep but also something of a lost sheep in the family, one who may have yearned for a strong parent substitute and, above all, a maternal one. Not having a mother "has been a life-long want with him," Fuller would later observe. "He often shows me a little scar on his face, made by a jealous dog, when his mother was caressing him as an infant. He prizes that blemish much." Indeed, Angela, who had served as a surrogate mother for him since he was a child, and was sympathetic to their relationship, thought he was attracted to her for largely that reason. "If you had guided him, as was your duty, toward something certainly he would not have been forced to take that step which sealed his fate," she later angrily wrote "that Black heart"

Giuseppe. "Young, abandoned, deprived of everything, he found that help in his companion which he was supposed to hope for in you." Considering Ossoli's attachment to the maternal Angela, Fuller's habitual self-presentation with protégés as the maternal comforter, and her exotic appearance as a fiercely eloquent defender of Italy's Risorgimento—it would have been, perhaps, surprising if Ossoli had *not* felt that (in Story's version of Fuller's recollection) "he loved her & he must marry her or be miserable."[55]

With Fuller, too, a predisposition to say yes was not as outlandish as many of her friends would later think. Although she had since her early twenties fancied herself a fated "heroic" virgin, "obliged to live myself without the sanctuary of the central relations," over the last several years she had periodically expressed a deep yearning for exactly that, especially in the form of a child, even while accepting, or trying to accept, its unlikelihood. According to a number of her female friends in New York, her desire for "central relations" grew even stronger. She "never saw such a craving for affection as in Margaret," Child later reported to Mary Mann, saying one day that "she burst into tears when in *her* room, saying she feared she would die without being a mother." The craving does not seem to have abated in Europe. "I am tired of these literary friendships," Rebecca claimed Fuller had once said to her, "I long to be [a] wife & mother." Nor should one assume, as her enemies and even a few of her friends did, that in every respect but the "sensual" there was nothing about Ossoli that should have made Fuller respond positively to his particular overtures. Certainly, as many who met him later attested, he was no intellectual. His only formal education had come from an old priest, who had taught him nothing more, she would later freely admit, than "readin ritin and richmetic." Yet the claim that he was (as Hawthorne would supposedly have it from Mozier) "half an idiot" is not credible. As Emelyn Story noted, Ossoli's rudimentary schooling was standard fare for a young Italian nobleman headed for government or military service, while his smattering of French and Italian history probably made him at least somewhat conversant with the ancient Roman authors and heroes that fired the heroic patriotism of his classically educated peers.[56]

Furthermore, as Emelyn also noted, in his character he was hardly a cipher. Although it is undoubtedly true, as several have speculated, that Fuller influenced him politically, the fact that he joined the Radical-dominated Civic Guard sometime early in 1847 and rose to sergeant on November 15 would indicate, as suggested earlier, that his liberal proclivities at least somewhat preceded their deep involvement that fall. And, while she no doubt encouraged him toward the Democratic camp, once there he remained conspicuous, William Story later reported, for his "ardent adherence to Mazzini's views." Indeed, his earliest letters to Fuller show him hostile to the Liberal pro-Pius party as early as mid-1847, shortly after Radicals had publicly started to attack the pope but six months before their ascendancy. Even more revealing was his later conduct in battle. Story reported after visiting him at his post during the French siege of Rome that he had a reputation for showing great courage, zeal, and leadership, qualities also displayed in his military letters and reports. Nor did his disregard of the advantages of his family's ancient connections with the papal court and his staunch resistance to his "odious brothers" (as he called them in one letter) bespeak a weak character. That he appeared to many reserved and curt in his speech would not be surprising for someone who spoke no English in the midst of non-Italian speakers. The American sculptor Horatio Greenough, who later in Florence enjoyed talking with him, even gave him high Bostonian marks for his "singularly grave and dignified" demeanor and "self-poised and truthful" expressions—refreshing, he said, in an Italian! At the same time, even William Henry Hurlbert, the later New York newspaper editor, who admired Fuller and initially had been mystified as to why she married the "undeveloped and uninteresting Italian," recalled hearing him in Florence tell stories "remarkably well," sometimes even with a "quick and vivid fancy" and humor. He animatedly recounted, Hurlbert said, once battering down a library panel in his father's house to look in vain for a concealed treasure and later meeting the attorney who had rented the house, who appeared suddenly and unaccountably rich. If nothing else, having a sense of humor about his family's fallen status shows resilience he would need.[57]

But what of Fuller's specific feelings about him? Some have speculated that ideology played a part. Hurlbert crustily guessed at the time, "She probably married him as a representative of an imagined possibility in the Italian character which I have not yet been able to believe in." Certainly, as a fervent supporter of Italy's cause in exciting revolutionary times, she must have been reassured to have as a close companion an Italian nationalist who could be seen to embody its hopes and dreams. Perhaps these imagined possibilities of imminent revolutions of "the people" even suggested to her something of the "religious" union or, in her Romantic chivalric argot, "pilgrimage towards a common shrine," that she had held up to Emerson and that in *Woman in the Nineteenth Century* she had classified as the highest marital ideal. Yet she could hardly have thought this last was an ideological dream Ossoli was likely to grasp. She later conceded to her friends his lack of personal "enthusiasm" or interest in great ideas or even books, stressing instead motherhood and the sharing of "domestic wants in a most sincere and sweet companion" as the great fruits of her relationship with him. In that sense, he fulfilled her needs, not for the "sacred" marriage she had panegyrized in *Woman* but for the "household" marital ideal she had honored there. Yet what she got from him also clearly had something more than the conventional about it. Notwithstanding her maternalism toward him, she seems to have found in him also a kind of maternal love in masculine guise, like that (as she would later say) of little children or her mother or—as in his self-sacrifices for Rome, his father, and her— "the sacred love, the love passing that of women." Whether sacred, companionate, maternal, or heroic, it was evidently a love she felt she could not do without.[58]

Ultimately, we will probably never know what passed through Fuller's mind when she began a sexual liaison with Ossoli that fall, or even how much she calculated about it at all. We do know that Mickiewicz kept up, if not (as Rebecca Spring would claim) urgent advice to marry Ossoli, certainly prodding in that direction. "I regret to see that you do not profit enough from your stay in Rome," he wrote her in reply to a letter she had written him shortly after arriving in the city. "You will regret it one day." Her apparent hesitancy suggests one other relevant point: calculation, whether personal or ideological, only goes so far in matters of the heart, and apparently, too, for America's most Romantic public personality. She would grant as much herself two years later in her letter to her sister Ellen. "I acted upon a strong impulse," she would write. "I could not analyze at all what passed in my mind." She then added, in almost precisely the words she had used in claiming Sand "needs no defence" of *her* sexual affairs: "I neither rejoice nor grieve, for bad or for good I acted out my character."[59]

V

We can at least be sure about one thing: Fuller remained extraordinarily happy— happier, she thought, than she had ever been in her life. "Rome is so dear I do not know how I can ever be willing to live anywhere else," she exclaimed to her mother in her letter of mid-December. "Italy has been glorious to me," she exulted to Emerson four days later. "In Rome, I have known some blessed, quiet days, when I could yield myself to be soothed and instructed by the great thoughts and memories of the place." One dark cloud was her lack of money. All through northern Italy, as she depleted the $500 Marcus Spring had lent her, she had written increasingly anxious notes to friends and family about the whereabouts of remittances they had sent. Nor did she help herself by telling Greeley that the August 9 dispatch from Milan that it had "nearly killed" her to write would be her last. Fortunately, for her purse, that did not go down well with Greeley. "How you imbibed the mistaken notion that I wished you to write us only fifteen letters for the Tribune, I cannot imagine," he protested. "I do not deal in compliments, and shall not solicit contributions from you or others unless I desire to receive them." She resumed writing a week after getting back to Rome, causing her pleased editor to write her immediately that, "at discretion," she could draw money from the *Tribune* in advance if she needed to. By then, her financial picture seems to have started looking brighter. Her Uncle Abraham had recently died and, although she learned this inheritance would not be much, the promise of it, she told Rotch, came at a good time. That December, she finally received the $500 her mother had loaned her and another loan of roughly the same amount from Richard and Mary Manning. Most important, she realized she could make it in the city on a bare-bones budget of "at most" $450 for six months, or about half of what most of her American friends were spending. She mused to Rotch about the possibility of staying away for two more years, passing a winter in Paris and seeing Germany as she had Italy. "I trust heaven which has guided me thus far," she wrote Manning, thanking him for his loan, "will show me ways and means for the future."[60]

But it was not just the great weather, "great thoughts," and a little money that put her in such a great mood: it was Ossoli. She felt herself enveloped in a new glow. "I have not been so well since I was a child," she told her mother, "nor so happy ever as during the last six weeks." This childhood conceit ran like a leitmotiv in her letters. In a poem she wrote soon after arriving, describing her thrill at approaching the Campagna and seeing in the distance St. Peter's and imagining its glorious history "of ruined empire—shrine of art," she melded the city's past with her memories of reading its classical authors under her father's tutelage:

Love, memory, joy, all unrepressed
O'erflow this fountain in my breast;
And like a child returning home
I hail thee, Rome.

Her verse echoes the famous passage that she loved to quote from Byron's *Child Harold's Pilgrimage*: "Oh Rome! my country! city of the soul! / The orphans of the heart must turn to thee, / Lone mother." In one crucial sense the poet's lines were more apt than her own: she had always remembered her childhood as un-happily lonely, indeed, in her "Autobiographical Romance," virtually orphaned. "Many circumstances" combined to put her, she would confide cryptically to Caroline Sturgis the following month, "in a kind of passive, childlike wellbeing." Whether to Ossoli or to Rome, it seemed, she was returning to an old home newly remade.[61]

Above all, Fuller was finding herself "at home" in the city. "I am now truly happy here, really *in* Rome, so quiet and familiar," she wrote to Richard two weeks after arriving, "no longer, like the mob, a staring sight seeing stranger riding about finely dressed in a coach to see the Muses and the Sibyls." In a dispatch that fall, she offered that very distinction—between inwardly "seeing" Rome and outwardly "staring" or "gazing" at it—as the key to appreciating the city. As Rome was an archeological palimpsest, seeing meant mentally digging beneath its disconcerting present layers to get at its past spirit. "As one becomes familiar, ancient and modern Rome—at first so painfully and discordantly jumbled together, are drawn apart to the mental vision," she explained.

You see where objects and limits anciently were; the superstructures vanish, and you recognize the local habitation of so many thoughts. When this begins to happen it is that one feels truly at ease in Rome. Then the old Kings, the Consuls, and the Tribunes, the Emperors, drunk with blood and gold, the warriors of eagle sight and remorseless beak, return for us, and the toga'd procession finds room to sweep across the scene; the seven hills tower, the innumerable temples glitter, and the Via Sacra swarms with triumphal life once more.

Ah! How joyful to see once more *this* Rome, instead of the pitiful, peddling, Anglicised Rome first viewed in unutterable dismay from the coupe of the vettura; a Rome all full of taverns, lodging houses, cheating chambermaids, vilest vile *valets de place* and fleas![62]

As this last line suggests, however, her holistic Romantic eye still had to contend with a couple of motes. One was the effect this temporal mixture had on the Italians themselves. "Never was a people who have had more to corrupt them," she wrote, now showing Italy's "remorseless" past through a lurid light: "bloody tyranny, and incubus of priestcraft, the invasions, first of Goths, then of trampling emperors and kings, then of sight-seeing foreigners, everything to turn them from a sincere, hopeful, fruitful life." Fortunately, she told her readers, Italians evinced two ready defenses. To begin with, they were an "artist-people." Describing a recent elaborately orchestrated funeral for one of the Roman councilors, she declared, they "seize instantly the natural poetry of an occasion and with unanimous tact hasten to represent it." In addition, Italians now lived during an almost religious time of humanitarian reform: "Certainly there never was a people that showed a better heart than they do in this day of love, of purely moral influence." And her own hopeful inner eye colored what she saw. "I cannot look merely with a pictorial eye on the lounge of the Roman Dandy, the bold, Juno gait of the Roman Contadina," she wrote, "I love them, (Dandies and all?) I believe the natural expression of these fine forms will animate them yet."[63]

The second speck blurring her proper vision of Italians she had hinted at before: her growing alienation from her compatriots mobbing Rome. Distaste for English tourists in Italy was common among nineteenth-century American travelers, but Fuller's professed disaffection cut much deeper. First, she lumped in Americans with the English. "I go about in a coach with several people; but English and Americans are not at home here," she wrote in mid-November to a friend. "Since I have experienced the different atmosphere of the European mind, and been allied with it, nay, mingled in the bonds of love, I suffer more than ever from that which is peculiarly American or English." Indeed, this mingling "in the bonds of love" with the "European mind" (she of course said nothing of mingling with Ossoli) made her want to shut out from her hearing altogether the one element that Americans and the English shared. "I should like to cease hearing the language for a time," she frankly confessed. "Perhaps I should return to it; but at present I am in a state of unnatural divorce from what I was most allied to." How, then, could one—and just posting the problem differentiated Fuller from her complacent compatriots—hope to remain an American under *these* circumstances? In a sense, this had been her intellectual life problem since her early twenties, when she had dedicated herself to disseminating the great fruits of European literature. Now, however, her national "divorce" was immediate, physical, and hence suddenly "unnatural."[64]

At the end of November, in her prospective New Year's Day *Tribune* dispatch, Fuller tried to give an answer. To read this often reprinted piece as merely an example of Europeanist snobbery or of an elitist literary tradition of "antitourism" would be a mistake. For Fuller, the problem was not the seductions of European social class, as would be the case for many later Victorian upper-middle-class travelers, but the traps of American provincial culture and sensibility. She had introduced the subject in a dispatch she had written just before leaving Rome. There she had tossed a cluster of stinging barbs at her compatriots who looked, stared, and gazed but never *saw*: "vetturinoed from inn to inn, ciceroned from gallery to gallery," sticking wholly with each other, and so utterly failing to experience the cardinal psychological requirements of genuine travel—intimacy of feeling and abandonment of spirit. And why? Apart from simple laziness and linguistic ignorance, the principal reason, she wrote, was not some intrinsic American obtuseness but quite the opposite. "They retain too much of their English blood," and that from a people who, however admirable, as she had found them on their "island," for their "honor, truth, practical intelligence, persistent power," nonetheless, "as a tribe," were the "most unseeing of all possible animals." Just read their travel writers: most displayed the "vulgar familiarity of Mrs. Trollope without her vivacity, the cockneyism of Dickens without his graphic power and love of the odd corners of human nature." How could Americans, of all people, want to imitate them? Could they not see—giving a cosmopolitan twist to the American postcolonial wounds that Trollope and Dickens had pricked—that English condescension toward Italians was virtually identical to that which the English so often exhibited toward *them*? "I am indignant at the contempt they have presumed to express for the faults of our semi-barbarous state," she had exclaimed, in a fit of her own postcolonial indignation. "What is the vulgarity expressed in our tobacco chewing, and way of eating eggs, compared to that which elbows the Greek marbles, guide-book in hand—chatters and sneers through the Miserere of the Sistine Chapel, beneath the very glance of Michel Angelo's Sibyls,—praises St. Peter's as '*nice*,' talks of '*managing*' the Colosseum by moonlight,—and snatches '*bits*' for a '*sketch*' from the sublime silence of the Campagna." Having identified the two aggrieved nations of America and Italy, she implied a curious paradox: the problem with Americans in Italy was they were not American enough.[65]

In her long New Year's Day dispatch, she deepened this paradox by expanding its application to the broader problem of Americans, not just traveling in Europe, but thinking about their national identity in relation to Europe. As often in her ambitious critical pieces, she triangulated her categories. At one extreme was "the servile American": a bourgeois cosmopolite whose coarse appetite for fashionable clothes, good food, titled persons, and coffeehouse gossip exposed his Europhilia as "utterly shallow" status-seeking snobbery. Happily, such a type was historically doomed. Having "all the thoughtlessness and partiality of the exclusive class in Europe, without any of their refinement, or the chivalric feeling which still sparkles among them here and there," such "parasites of a bygone period," by cutting themselves adrift from America's fated "grand, independent existence," inevitably "must wither and drop away." She did not treat her second class, "the conceited American," with any more sympathy. On the contrary, she portrayed his thin-skinned patriotism ("instinctively bristling and proud of—he knows not what") as absurd:

> He does not see, not he, that the history of Humanity for many centuries is likely to have produced results it requires some training, some devotion, to appreciate and profit by. With his great clumsy hands only fitted to work on a steam-engine, he seizes the old Cremona violin, makes it shriek with anguish in his grasp, and then declares he thought it was all humbug before he came, and now he knows it; that the frogs in one of our swamps make much finer, for *they* are young and alive. To him the etiquettes of courts and camps, the ritual of the Church, seem simply silly— and no wonder, profoundly ignorant as he is of their origin and meaning. Just so the legends which are the subjects of pictures, the profound myths which are represented in the antique marbles, amaze and revolt him; as, indeed, such things need to be judged of by another standard from that of the Connecticut Blue-Laws. He criticizes severely pictures, feeling quite sure that his natural senses are better means

of judgment than the rules of connoisseurs—not feeling that to see such objects mental vision as well as fleshly eyes are needed, and that something is aimed at in Art beyond the imitation of the commonest forms of Nature.

Yet, after excoriating her fatuous American philistine on virtually every possible Romantic ground, she abruptly reversed herself, offering, as would Mark Twain in his double-edged satire of his "innocents abroad," a backhanded sanction to her "booby truant." "Add thought and culture to his independence," she declared, "and he will be a man of might: he is not a creature without hope, like the thick-skinned dandy of the class first specified." With a little experience and cultural cleaning up, he could even become her highest type, "the thinking American":

> Recognizing the immense advantage of being born to a new world and on a virgin soil, [he] yet does not wish one seed from the Past to be lost. He is anxious to gather and carry back with him all that will bear a new climate and new culture. Some will dwindle; others will attain a bloom and stature unknown before. He wishes to gather them clean, free from noxious insects. He wishes to give them a fair trial in his new world. And that he may know the conditions under which he may best place them in that new world, he does not neglect to study their history in this.

In the spirit of her transnational literary criticism, her ideal American mental traveler was eager to select and mix past European cultural seeds to grow a "grand, independent" culture. "The American in Europe," she wrote, summarizing her cosmopolitan patriotic paradox, "if a thinking mind, can only become more American." Her private heart may have been moving toward a "natural divorce" from America, but her public voice still kept the marriage intact.[66]

The union looked wobblier, however, when in the same omnibus dispatch Fuller turned from America's future cultural identity to its present political one. Not that she exactly saw Europe through rose-tinted glasses. Measured against the West's oldest universal ideal, Christianity, which projected a "genuine Democracy" wherein the rights of all men were holy and falsehood "in all its myriad disguises of cant, vanity, covetousness" was repelled, Europe was a mockery. England was inured in monstrous wealth, cruel poverty, and a conventional life guided by "low" practical aims. France, although full of talent, remained shallow and glossy despite its bloody revolutions. Poland and Italy were conquered nations. Russia was ruled by a brutal tsar over countless slaves. Austria's royalty represented nothing, and its people "are and have nothing!" America, though, was doing little better with *its* putatively universal dispensation. True, its Declaration of Independence's statement of the inborn rights of men, she declared, "if fully interpreted and acted upon, leaves nothing to be desired." Since coming to Europe, she had even become more appreciative of her country's liberal features, especially freedom of the press, governmental checks and balances, and an alert people living where talent has a free chance to rise. "It is much." Socially, however, what did she see? Certainly not a "new world, a new chance." Instead she saw a boundless lust of gain, the weakest vanity that bristles at every foolish taunt of the foreign press, and without any institutional antidote to capitalism's poverty and gaping inequalities in Europe, which were starting to come to America. She herself now believed that only "voluntary association" could allow her nation to progress, but, alas, only a "small minority" take seriously the challenges of modern capitalism. Then there was the most pressing of America's evils—"this horrible cancer of Slavery, and this wicked War" in Mexico "that has grown out of it." "How dare I speak of these things here?" an outraged American patriot might demand. The answer was obvious:

> I listen to the same arguments against the emancipation of Italy, that are used against the emancipation of blacks; the same arguments in favor of the spoliation of Poland as for the conquest of Mexico. I find the cause of tyranny and wrong everywhere the same—and lo! my Country the darkest offender, because with the least excuse, foresworn to the high calling with which she was called,—no champion of the rights of men, but a robber and a jailer; the scourge hid behind her banner, her eyes fixed, not on the stars, but on the possessions of other men.

Bringing her cosmopolitan liberal patriotism to a climax, she confessed that *Europe* had taught her a lesson she had not seen so clearly in America:

> How it pleases me here to think of the Abolitionists! I could never endure to be with them at home, they were so tedious, often so narrow, always so rabid and exaggerated in their tone.
>
> But, after all, they had a high motive, something eternal in their desire and life; and, if it was not the only thing worth thinking of it was really something worth living and dying for to free a great nation from such a horrible blot, such a threatening plague. God strengthen them and make them wise to achieve their purpose![67]

So was she politically an American or a European? Certainly her tribute to the abolitionists was not, as many scholars have claimed, a belated radical shift from and expiation of her previous indifference or hostility to them. Despite her private distaste for some Garrisonians' rhetoric, she had been beating the drum ever louder for their cause for the last several years. What Europe did for her was something more profoundly transnational. On the one hand, to find the Garrisonians heroic, she had to go to Europe, where she could see them filtered through the lens of an incipient revolution, however uncertain, that was absent in America, which had reviled its few earnest socialists and abolitionists. "I have found many among the youth of England, of France—of Italy also," she wrote, "full of high desire, but will they have courage and purity to fight the battle through in the sacred, the immortal band?" On the other hand, if for Fuller Europe offered the opportunity, America still provided the ideology. She symbolized that relationship exactly in her plea to her compatriots to raise money for a cannon to be called "AMERICA, the COLUMBO, or the WASHINGTON" and sent to the "the country of Columbus, of Amerigo, of Cabot" for use by the Roman Civic Guard. Cagily or naïvely, she suggested a Cabot as the man for the job, but a week later, after it possibly dawned her that a Cabot would be the last to enroll in her "small minority" supporting revolutions abroad, she wrote Frank Shaw, asking him to do the honors. In finding or inventing her "America" in Europe, she was acting like her thinking American—more American than most Americans. In an ultimate sense, then, she was seeing with both American and European eyes: to get Americans to see that the Risorgimento "is OURS, above all others," she merged revolutionary

Italy and her ideal liberal America, with both elevated to a world-historical plane that made each greater than either by itself. Whether her "America" and Europe's "Italy" genuinely mirrored each other or were merely dual projections remained to be tested.[68]

VI

Rumbling in the immediate background of these transnational ruminations was Italy's roiling politics. By then, Metternich's strategy for containing the inevitable revolutions (as he saw them) was in place: tightening repression at home, strengthening the empire's entente with Louis Philippe's government, warning Italy's monarchs that Austria's fall in Lombardy and Venetia would bring *their* instant falls, and preparing for military intervention at the first hint of insurrection on the peninsula. Meanwhile, emboldened by Pius's creation of the Civic Guard and announcement of a future lay advisory "Consulta di Stato," Liberals led by Balbo, D'Azeglio, and Gioberti intensified pressure on their monarchs to grant liberal constitutions. This, in turn, presented Democrats with a formidable problem. Although they joined the Moderates in demanding rules of law, free speech, public education, and welfare programs for the lower classes, their ultimate goal was to achieve a unified Italian republic based on universal suffrage, which to the aristocratic Liberals, just as much as to the pope, was politically utopian and socially dangerous. The Democrats' challenge, then, was considerably more difficult than either battling or helping the Liberals: to spark changes that, once begun, Moderates could not stop from going further.

Mazzini understood this situation, which was probably why on September 8 he boldly wrote the pontiff from London an extraordinary letter advising him what he needed to do to meet Europe's impending political crises. Their root, he bluntly told him, was religious: thanks to a despotic Catholicism and an anarchic Protestantism, faith was dead or dying. Nonetheless, the pope could stem this debacle, but only if he fulfilled three requirements: believe in the sacredness of "the People," lead the divine cause of unifying Italy, and renounce all expedient alliances with princes and surround himself instead with "those who best represent the national party"—that is, Mazzini's Young Italy. If he did, "we will cause to rise around you a nation over whose free and popular development, you, living, shall preside. We will found a Government unique in Europe, which shall destroy the absurd divorce between spiritual and temporal power, and in which you shall be chosen to represent the principle of which the men chosen by the Nation will make application." On the other hand, if he refused, he would be "abandoned by God and by men," swept aside by the inevitable historical march of the people. In short, the pope needed merely to dissolve his temporal power into a new spiritualized democratic state, which he would then (Mazzini was not very clear) constitutionally "preside" over or "represent." Historians would later disagree about Mazzini's intentions in writing this astonishing letter, although at the time he does seem to have genuinely hoped that Pius would seize the Risorgimento's leadership and thereby spare Italy bloodshed while opening the way for the country's Democratic movement. If Mazzini really did think that, however, on November 15, at the opening of the Council of State, the pontiff, who had read the letter sometime that fall, instantly scuttled that idea. "Greatly deceived," the pope told the councilors, is anyone who thinks he can exploit his purely advisory role to wring from him more concessions or, even worse, "sees in the Consulta thus set up, some Utopia of his own, and the seeds of an institution incompatible with the pontifical supremacy."[69]

In the midst of these maneuverings that fall, Fuller held to the latitudinarian course of her dispatches in the summer. She remained a staunch defender of Mazzini. His September letter to the pope, which she translated and inserted in her column, she declared "one of the milestones in the march of Thought." When Arconati expressed her extreme distaste for Mazzini's "presumptuous" tone toward the pontiff, Fuller dismissed it: "I do not wonder that you were annoyed at his manner of addressing the Pope; but to me it seems that he speaks as he should,—near God and beyond the tomb; not from power to power, but from soul to soul, without regard to temporal dignities. It must be admitted that the etiquette, Most Holy Father, &c., jars with this." In early October, in a postscript to her poem "A Daughter of Italy" in the *People's Journal*—enlisting her female icons of Mary, Isis, and Beatrice (with annotations!) to rouse women for Italy's cause—she inserted a stinging rebuke to the conservative London *Times* for its libelous sneer at the "'sanguinary schemes of Mazzini and his associates.'" "To couple this epithet, sanguinary, with the name of Mazzini," she laughed, "would be simply absurd, as to speak of the darkness of light, were the paragraph written by some Austrian hireling, but in a country where no tyranny veils truth, such an expression seems to bespeak a love of falsehood, or a vindictive spirit in the writer." She knew, of course, that even Mazzini's Moderate rivals could not understand, she said, "one so deeply penetrated as he with the truth that shall be a truism to the coming age . . . that liberty is an inborn right of man" and not a favor dispensed by princes. She also sounded a little sanguinary herself as she eagerly contemplated a war against the "Austrian vulture." "Italy may yet have need to recall all her true sons to her banner," she cried, "and it will then be seen if it is too sanguinary to be willing to give life, hope, joy, all for the sake of one's country."[70]

Yet, her steadfast Mazzinianism notwithstanding, as all the Risorgimento tendencies seemed to be moving together, she moved along with them. That December she treated generously even the "despotic" Catholic Church's rites, to which she had given short shrift in the spring. "It requires much acquaintance, much thought, much reference to books, for the child of Protestant Republican America to see where belong the legends illustrated by rite and picture, the sense of all the rich tapestry where it has a united and poetic meaning, where it is broken by some accident of history, " she lectured her Protestant republican readers. "For all these things, a senseless mass of juggleries to the uninformed eye, are really growths of the human spirit struggling to develop its life, and full of instruction for those who learn to understand them." Nor did she exclude herself from this need for Romantic empathy. Describing her visit several weeks earlier to a courtyard of the "Chapels of the Cemeteries" of Santo Spirito on a slope of the Janiculum hill, she painted a precisely observed portrait of herself struggling to enter the circle of a Catholic sensibility that often repelled American Protestant travelers: "It was a beautiful moment, and despite the wax saint, the ill-favored friar, the professional mendicants, and my own removal, wide as pole from pole, from the position of mind indicated by these forms, their spirit touched me and I prayed too." She even recounted climbing up the hill in her own imitation of Christ: "Going out, I took my road by the Cross, which marks the brow of the hill. Up the ascent still wound the crowd of devotees, and still the beggars beset them." Then the collective Mater Dolorosa promising the heavenly birth of a new Italy: "Amid that crowd how many lovely, warm hearted women! The women of Italy are intellectually in a low place, *but*—they are unaffected; you can see what Heaven meant them to be, and I believe they will be yet the mothers of a great and generous race." Above all, she appreciated the pope, on whom she rained considerably more encomiums than she had in the spring. After recounting one day meeting him walking on foot in the countryside with two young priests, during which her American companion surprised her by suddenly kneeling and receiving from the pope, who saw that he was ill, "a mark of interest with that expression of melting love," she wrote:

> He has shown undoubted wisdom, clear-sightedness, bravery and firmness, but it is above all, his generous human heart that gives him his power over this people. . . . What form the issues of his life may take is yet uncertain: in my belief they are such as he does not think of; but they cannot fail to be for good.—For my part, I shall always rejoice to have been here in this time. The working of his influence confirms all my theories, and it is a positive treasure to me to have seen him.[71]

That was on December 17, when Liberal victories seemed to be coming almost effortlessly. "Affairs look well here," Fuller informed her readers, recounting in a long list of these, including, most startling, the difficulties of Naples's ignorant and murderous Ferdinand II in repressing demonstrations. "The lazzaroni may be men yet!" she cried, a far cry from the contempt she had displayed during her visit in March toward the city's flotsam of beggars and lumpen proletariat. The most momentous event, though, occurred on December 23, when Austrian troops unexpectedly withdrew from the Papal States' Ferrara, raising enormous hopes that the pope would inspire, if not lead himself, a coming war of liberation. She did report one slight blemish. During the opening procession at the November 15 inauguration of the Council of State, papal officials, implementing a recent government proclamation, prevented her and her friends from holding up a banner with a "magnificent spread Eagle" they had brought to honor the event. But this was not the pope's fault; the ordinance was caused, "it is said," to keep "the Obscurantists," as Liberals and Democrats called the Jesuits, from provoking a disturbance if Neapolitan and Lombardo-Venetian flags were to appear draped in black. She even found excuses for Pius's address warning the Council. While conceding that it implied "he meant only to improve, not to *reform*" the papacy, he delivered it, "no doubt, more to reassure Czars, Emperors and Kings than from the promptings of the spirit."[72]

Within days, her broad-church line noticeably changed. One reason clearly was her receipt in late December of a long letter from Mazzini. He had just returned to London after two months in France, where he had soaked up the exciting news about prerevolutionary stirrings on the Continent and gotten buoyed by seeing Sand and Lamennais. In his letter he revisited the issue of Emerson, whom he expected to see soon—this time, though, more fairly than a year ago. "I admire him very much, of course," he assured her, "but feel fearful that he leads or will lead man too much to contemplation. His work, I think very greatly needed in America; but in our own old world we stand in need of one who will like Peter the Hermit, inflame us to the Holy Crusade and appeal to the *collective* influences and inspiring sources, more than to individual self improvement." In short, he said roughly what Saunders had in his *People's Journal* the previous year: although useful to counter America's materialism and conformity, American Transcendentalism had no application to Europe—and certainly not to the life-and-death battles against backward but entrenched tyrants in Europe in which Mazzini was trying to enroll her. Mainly, he wanted to make three vital political points. One was how important it was to him personally that she remain active in the cause. "I feel deeply grateful to the feeling which has dictated all that you have written," he told her, adding that though he had given up his "scheme for conquering [the *People's Journal*] to ourselves," as soon as the political scene in Italy got clarified, he wished to make her "*my* contributor." He also wished to explain his current political line on the pope. After the pontiff delivered his November 15 Allocution, Mazzini's September letter to him, which he had written "in a moment of [w or m]ild enthusiasm," no longer applied, as now all hopes for Pius had failed. Indeed, he wanted to disabuse her of any illusions *she* might still have about the pontiff. "Depend upon it," he promised her, speaking of an address supporting the pope that Greeley had delivered in November to a large pro-Italy rally at the Broadway Tabernacle, which her editor had asked her to circulate in Rome,

> your appeal would be utterly lost. Pius the IXth is evidently a good *man*: a charitable Christian, a zealous administrator of the *material* interests of his two millions of subjects; *un buon curato*: that is all. As a king he has neither genius nor energy: he fears the Jesuits and fears us. As a Pope he has been sent *to give the last blow to Papacy*; and it will be seen when he dies, "old bottles will not contain new wine." He is the Louis XVI of the Papal Rome.

Finally, he wanted her to understand the current underlying political dynamic: "Never mind what people say to you about me, or mind: they do not themselves know at what they are just now working. . . . There is no need of telling them this: it is not prudent now to do so. But let a few months pass: *things* will speak for me." All that she saw was the "mere surface-ebullition preceding the true creative crisis. Our two great enemies will save us finally: I mean Papacy and Austria; the first by obliging us to face, soon or late, the religious question; the second bound to compel us soon or late, to merge all petty local improvement questions into the great National one. Rely on them and upon God, whenever you are thinking of the fates of my country."[73]

She did. Indeed, just as he probably hoped, she started inserting versions of his analysis, sometimes even his exact formulations, into her letters and dispatches. At the same time, she deftly interwove accounts of the *"things"* that were now speaking for Mazzini. On December 24, the day after Austrian troops withdrew from Ferrara, Metternich did his part by signing an "alliance" reducing the two central duchies of Parma and Modena across the border from Lombardo-Venetia to near vassalage, thus giving the empire, as Fuller glumly noted in her dispatch of the thirtieth, direct control of all of northern Italy except Piedmont-Sardinia. More important were the pope's responses to a series of demonstrations that month organized by the recently organized Circolo Popolare, the association of Democratic clubs, to keep up popular pressure on him for further reform and a declaration of war on Austria. First, he let it be known he was deeply displeased by the Democratic-led demonstration of December 3 that had celebrated the recent victory of the liberal Protestant Swiss Diet over rebelling Catholic cantons, during which shouts of "Out with them" and "Death to the Jesuits," inspired by their expulsion from Switzerland, could be heard. Then, on the twenty-seventh, at a celebration of Pius's birthday, Angelo Brunetti, the popular wine dealer and chief organizer of the Democratic clubs, nicknamed Ciceruacchio (or Big Boy) for his large girth, presented a list of thirty-five anticlerical "demands," including the expulsion of the Jesuits, full civil rights for the Jews, and the secularization of many offices. Finally, on New Year's Day, in the wake of a planned demonstration at the Quirinal Palace, the pope's residence, ostensibly to express gratitude for setting up a partly reformed Council of Ministers but actually to display Democratic strength, the pope and his advisors resolved to draw the line. That morning, after thirty carabinieri ordered the demonstrators at their stepping-off place at the Piazza del Popolo to disperse, papal officials announced that the pope did not want to see them, Fuller reported, "in the most ungracious, irritating manner possible by saying, 'He is tired of these things: he is afraid of disturbance.'" Convinced that his Jesuitical advisors had libeled the demonstrators to frighten him, a great crowd, she wrote, rushed to the house of old Prince Corsini, the senator of Rome, to ask him to intercede, which he did, and the following afternoon, an ill and agitated pontiff appeared in his coach in the Corso before cheering throngs. Fuller captured the scene in a gripping report:

> Though rainy and of searching, miserable cold like that of a Scotch mist, we had all our windows thrown open and the red and yellow tapestries hung out. He passed through the principal parts of the city, the people throwing themselves on their knees and crying out "O Holy Father, don't desert us; don't forget us; don't listen to our enemies." The Pope wept often and replied, "Fear nothing my people, my heart is yours." At last seeing how ill he was, they begged him to go in, and he returned to the Quirinal, the present Tribune of the People, as far as rule in the heart is concerned, Ciceruacchio, following his carriage.[74]

In fact, this touching picture of an emotional pope, his ingenuous people, and their savvy leader tagging along behind belied her growing impatience with the cowardice and naiveté of Moderates of all stripes. That week she become especially angry with the Liberals in the Circolo Romano to whom she had given a few weeks earlier a copy of Greeley's Broadway Tabernacle rally address. "I read it and was proud of my country," she had beamed, praising in particular the parallel he had drawn between republican young America and ancient Italy "in the proud days of her unity." When the Club's newspaper printed it without comment, she put on a good face: "It is only the Roman Press that is so timid; the private expressions of pleasure have been very warm; the Italians say: 'The Americas are indeed our brothers.'" Privately, though, she told Arconati that all the papers' silence had "wounded" her. "Justice has not been entirely rendered to America in the old Europe," Arconati conceded, "and is still regarded a little '"du haut en bas.'" Even the "dignified" and "religious" people were getting on Fuller's political nerves. "There is something false as well as ludicrous," she wrote to Emerson on December 20, "in the spectacle of the people first driving their princes to do a little justice, and then *evviva*-ing them at such a rate."[75]

But it was not just the people's naiveté that bothered her. Whether because of Mazzini's promptings or the facts as she saw them, for the first time she started aiming sharp critical thrusts at the pope. Her turnaround was quick. In the same letter to Emerson disdaining the people's foolish "*evviva*-ing their princes," she specifically exempted the pope, whose "great heart" had initially given impulse to reform, from being one of them. By the end of the month, however, she seems to have discovered that she had been wrong about a few things. One was the November 15 suppression of national banners at the celebration of the inauguration of the Council of State. Although it is not clear how much she found out, she undoubtedly got the main point: rather than preventing a Jesuit provocation, as she had speculated, the scuttling had been an effort, insisted on by Russian, French, and Austrian ambassadors, to stop all the Italian states from marching together and turning the affair into a demonstration for a united Italy. She also evidently decided that she had been wrong in trying to excuse the pope's warning address that day to the councilors. In her dispatch in early January, she now put that speech in the context of other actions on his part that she had clearly known but had said nothing about and that, she said, were obviously not simply, as his Moderate supporters would have it, products of the machinations of the Jesuits and other reactionary Church functionaries. After excerpting a lengthy section of his December 17 Allocution, in which he had expressed his horror at the shocking calumny being circulated that he intended to introduce religious toleration and relinquish his temporal power, she brusquely cast him aside. Now blaming all the Italian journals' silence about Greeley's public address on Pius's fears of being labeled a Protestant pope, she declared: "If the heart, the instincts of this good MAN have been beyond his thinking powers, that only shows him the Providential agent to work out aims beyond his ken. A wave has been set in motion, which cannot stop till it casts up its freight upon the shore."[76]

Meanwhile, she learned something that helped more than Mazzini's message to provoke her to a new militancy. On New Year's Day, 1848, Risorgimento leaders in Milan launched their famous antismoking campaign, urging Milanese to boycott tobacco and lottery tickets, lucrative Austrian monopolies a tactic, Fuller happily learned, modeled on the Boston patriots' tea boycott. Like the American example, a mix of persuasion, intimidation, and imagination, it spread like an "electric spark" throughout the city and outlying towns and countryside. In response, Austrian soldiers and junior officers made a point of provocatively smoking cigars in public places. Soon rocks and pistols went off while the soldiers, many of them drunk, charged into the crowds with swords and bayonets drawn, pursuing some into their homes, and ultimately injuring sixty-four, five of whom died, including innocent bystanders, most of them from stab wounds to their throats and heads. The next day, virtually all of Milan, including both Radicals and Moderates like Arconati, who repeated to Fuller the rumor that the massacres had been provoked by senior officers (who would deny it), seethed with anger at the Austrian regime. Soldiers were harassed, police were assaulted, and officers were ostracized, causing further violent countermeasures, which the press in the reforming states of Piedmont, Tuscany, and the Papal Legations widely reported. Fuller, like all her Italian nationalist friends, followed these events with mounting excitement and high expectations. By then, she had learned something else: she was pregnant.[77]

CHAPTER TEN

Year of Revolutions

(1848)

I

If Fuller had looked forward to her pregnancy, one would not know it from her despairing letters after discovering it at the end of December. Several circumstances made her feel "very depressed" that late winter. One was the weather, which the week after she became pregnant perversely turned from unseasonably sunny, spring-like days to black skies and pouring rain, which would continue unabated for the next three months. "The atmosphere is dreadful," she wrote to Ellen, "far worse than that of Paris; it is impossible to walk in the thick mud. The air presses with such a weight as to destroy the appetite and everything I do eat hurts me." Worse, as she suggests here, was her terrible health, which almost nonstop during these same months kept her shut up in her dark apartment, with constant nausea, probably morning sickness, perpetual coughing and congestion, and "nervous headach, often of my worst kind." At one point, she felt desperate enough to try her hated "Greeley diet," giving up meat, wine, strong tea, and coffee, but apparently without much success. "I live on a little rice cooked with milk and such vegetables as Rome supplies," she wrote to Marcus Spring, "but even this light food hurts me." (Evidently, her complaints reached Duyckinck, who informed his *Literary World* readers that Fuller was seriously ill in Rome.) Needless to say, she could not work on her book, "the fruit of my travels," to which she had intended to devote her winter, instead saving what strength she had for her dispatches, which further depressed her. Even if they were "quite good enough" for the paltry money they earned her and valuable for the information they contained, they hardly added much, she thought, to her literary reputation. "I don't know when," she sighed to Spring, "I shall feel equal to writing any thing full or sustained."[1]

Beyond the bad weather, morning sickness, and writing paralysis was her "dread" of giving birth, something her letters in late October to Mary Rotch about taking off for Paris and Germany and in mid-December to her mother about being a joyful child in Rome clearly show she had not expected. "I thought I should not survive," she would later recall of those months, "but if I did and my child did, was I not cruel to bring another into this terrible world. I could not at that time get any other view." She said nothing in her letters about her plight, but it seeped in nonetheless. "I hope [Destiny] will not leave me long in the world, for I am tired of keeping myself up in the water without corks, and without strength to swim," she glumly wrote Emerson, then in London, at the end of the year. "Soon I must begin to exert myself, for there is this incubus of the future, and none to help me, if I am not prudent to face it." She did not say what this "incubus of the future" exactly was that made her so heavy, although, even if Emerson could not have guessed from the apparent word play, it sounded more ominous than just illness and fatigue. Her most revealing letter, though, was a lengthy emotional reply she wrote on January 11, 1848, to Caroline Sturgis. She was obviously relieved to hear from her after nearly a year of silence—"now I can hardly write for tears," she said—but there were clearly also other reasons for these.[2]

One was Caroline's startling news that after a decade of playing the "heroic" but tortured young single of the Transcendentalist set, she had just married William Aspinwall Tappan, the shy scion of New York's most prominent evangelical abolitionist family, whom Emerson, after confirming his liberal credentials, had introduced to her. This astonished Caroline's friends, but it flabbergasted her former soulmate in the trials of Transcendental singleness. "You have really cast your lot with another person," Fuller wrote, as if rubbing her eyes in disbelief, "live in a house I suppose; sleep and wake in unison with humanity; an island [of] flowers in the river of your life." Then, following this less than joyful reaction to the happy news of Caroline's marriage, she added a provocative musing that must have caused some puzzlement. "I cannot say anything about it from my present self," she said. "Yet permanent love for the same object does not seem to me impossible, though once I thought, I felt it and have ceased to feel. At any rate the union of two natures for a time is so great." But, even more than this rather tortuous account of Fuller's new appreciation of marriage—whether "permanent" or "for a time" was unclear—what must have gotten Caroline seriously thinking were the subsequent cryptic allusions and half-revelations with which Fuller studded her letter. "I have known some happy hours; but they all lead to sorrow, and not only the cups of wine but of milk seem drugged with poison for me," she wrote with obvious reference to some sort of calamity. "It does not seem to be my fault,—this destiny: I do not court these things, they come. I am a poor magnet with power to be wounded by the bodies I attract." Her conclusion about this new phase of her "destiny" was equally mysterious but more disturbing:

> With this year, I enter upon a sphere of my destiny so difficult, that I, at present, see no way out, except through the gate of death. It is useless to write of it; you are at a distance and cannot help me,—whether accident or angel will, I have no intimation. I have no reason to hope I shall not reap what I have sown, and do not. Yet how I shall endure it I cannot guess; it is all a dark, sad enigma. The beautiful forms of art charm no more, and a love, in which there is all fondness, but no help, flatters in vain. I am all alone; nobody around me sees any of this.[3]

This sad letter raises an obvious question: in her teasing self-revelations, what exactly was she revealing—and dissembling—*about*? Of course, her pregnancy, but what else? For a century and half, answers have run the gamut. In the later nineteenth century virtually all authors, many Fuller's friends, who were anxious to remove any taint of sexual impropriety from her reputation, knew for sure: she fell in love, married, became pregnant, and gave birth, in that order. In the iconoclastic 1920s, when Fuller's reputation was beginning to get resuscitated, self-consciously "modernist" critics, certain that Europe had finally emancipated Fuller from her New England "Puritan" mores, insisted just as assuredly that she did not marry. In the "second-wave" feminist 1970s, when Fuller was again getting significant attention, important scholars, eager to recover Fuller's suppressed feminism, have wholeheartedly agreed, although the liberation they charted was not from Puritanism but capitalistic patriarchy. Others have simply thrown up their hands. This is understandable: in the absence of hard evidence, such as a marriage certificate, which has never materialized, each of these positions has some plausibility. Yet one can say more.

It now seems almost certain that at *some* point Fuller did secretly marry. There were certainly important financial reasons for doing so: an illicit marriage and out-of-wedlock child would have seriously jeopardized Ossoli's inheritance claims and probably also Fuller's employment in America. Furthermore, the sometimes-stated counter-argument—that because Fuller was a Protestant, she and Ossoli would have had to receive a special papal dispensation, which her radical political views would have made impossible—is wrong. She was not publicly even very critical of Pius until later in the spring, after which she left Rome and did not resume her column until the end of the year. More important, Church canon law required that a Catholic and a heretic fulfill only two conditions: assurance they both had been baptized and their promise to raise their children as Catholics, the latter a largely unenforceable requirement. Keeping the marriage a secret was also doable: if a couple in good conscience requested it, priests could simply note the ceremony in the parish book and send the marriage certificate to the Archivio Segreto della Curia. Finally, there is strong contemporaneous evidence that they were married. Ossoli himself stated the marriage as a fact in later letters to his family and friends. Most crucial, in Fuller's later letters, including to her mother, sister, and closest friends, she numerous times explicitly said they had married. To think that she baldly lied to all of them would have been completely out of character, as well as, if exposed, an enormous embarrassment that would have damaged her relationship with many of them, with some probably irreparably.[4]

Nor does all the evidence for her marriage come from after the point at which she revealed it. Not only did she tell Emelyn Story and Lewis Cass about it while it was still a secret, but she had also given them documents confirming its occurrence. In several letters later that year and the next, Fuller and Ossoli specifically addressed each other as "Cara consorte" or "Cmo consorte," dear spouse or dearest spouse, or "tua moglie," your wife. Moreover, they were known in Rieti, where Fuller would later go to give birth, as husband and wife. On the envelopes of Ossoli's letters to her, he usually wrote "Mrs. M. Ossoli" or sometimes "M. Ossoli"

or "Marchioness M. Ossoli," while later letters they would get from their landlords and their child's physicians in Rieti were addressed to them as the Marchese
and Marchesa Ossoli as well as explicitly referring to them as husband and wife.
In addition, later in Florence, where they lived before leaving for the United States,
the couple was known to all their friends as a married couple. Indeed, for nearly
a year after their death, Ossoli's brothers, despite having disowned him, aggressively pursued a legal claim against Fuller's family on the patriarchal ground that
since the husband controlled his spouse's property, all that she and Ossoli had
possessed belonged to them (as Giuseppe excitedly put it in one note), "even that
of the wife!" Finally, the recently discovered record of their child's baptism specifically affirmed their marriage as a mixed couple ("the married Mr. Giovanni
Angelo of Marquis Ossoli from Rome and Mrs. Margaret Fuller heterodox from
America"). She would almost certainly not have lied on *that* document, since she
was then extremely anxious that it should "be legal," and with good reason. Not
only was it a valuable identification for crossing state borders in war-torn Italy
but, if exposed as falsified, it would have jeopardized both their legal custody of
their child and any claims of his on his parents' property should they die.[5]

Why, then, their secrecy about the marriage? Some biographers have claimed
it was because Ossoli's devout father would have been hurt that his youngest son
had married an American Protestant, but he died in February, yet they still kept
their marriage a secret. Fuller would later tell her mother and her family that she
had kept it from them because she did not want to cause her mother anxiety about
her childbirth, but, although that was probably a factor, even after she gave birth
she kept them in the dark. Clearly, her biggest reason for keeping her marriage
secret was the one she would later repeatedly claim: Ossoli's fear of losing his
share of his father's estate. Marrying a notorious American Protestant radical
Republican would have been precisely the sort of transgression, even if legal, that
his brother Giuseppe, their father's estate's administrator, would have gleefully
used to try to nullify Giovanni's claim in any contest over the will. He certainly
had the motive. Greedy, vindictive, and reactionary, he would later coldly tell their
sister Angela, at the very moment he was hiring a lawyer in Boston to finagle
Margaret's property for himself, that their brother's death had been his divine
punishment for his revolutionary activities. Moreover, given the papacy's overwhelming influence in the courts, Giuseppe would very likely have succeeded.
Nor would the pope's later temporary fall have helped, since civil legal proceedings were suspended during the months of Republican rule. What the couple evidently counted on was a secure government to provide Ossoli with not only a job
but also a fair adjudication of his claim. Finally, as a reinforcing factor, there was
Ossoli's feeling, which Fuller would report to Emelyn Story, that since he had to
hide his marriage from his family, nobody else in Rome should know about it.
Preventing them from knowing, however, would be no easy task, and as difficulties arose, the couple would sometimes waver.[6]

If they secretly married, when did they do so? In a letter Ossoli wrote in the
spring of 1850 to his sister in Ireland, he explicitly indicated he had been married
to "my wife" "for some time," which would eliminate the occasionally suggested

time of that winter and spring when they were living in Florence. In addition, the November 3, 1848, date of the child's baptism would have put it before then. That leaves two possibilities. One is one of the ten days of late August and early September, three months after Fuller left for the countryside to prepare to give birth. That was by far longest time that Ossoli visited Rieti, which ended with Fuller giving birth and Ossoli returning to Rome. Furthermore, in their first letters after Ossoli got back to Rome, they addressed each other for the first time as "consorte," or spouse, rather than "my dear" or "my love." The other date for which one can marshal a good circumstantial case is in early April 1848, which was around the time the couple were visiting towns and villas outside Rome, where a secret wedding would have been much safer than in the city. April would have been after Ossoli's father's death, "soon after" which, Emelyn Story said in her later narrative she worked up from what Fuller had told her, they married. By April, too, her pregnancy would not have shown too much, yet at the same time she would have been able to reassure herself, at least temporarily, that she would probably not miscarry. The April date also fits two possibly related dates: almost exactly when her mood turned from depressive to upbeat and before Ossoli's very first extant letter to her addressed to "Mrs. G. Ossoli." Finally, a year later, when Ossoli was away from Rome on military maneuvers, in a letter of April 3 he would urge her to mark the next day of the fourth as a special day that, though they were apart, she should celebrate by playing with "our darling" and giving him one more kiss for him. ("How very strange it is that we cannot spend this day together," she replied. "We must pray to be happier another year.") These are not ironclad proofs. Story's memory for specific names and dates in her later narrative is sometimes faulty, and the celebrated date may have referred to the first time they started seeing each other three days after they met. Nonetheless, it seems very likely they married during one of these two times, very possibly April 4, 1848.[7]

There is one thing that both these early April and late August-early September dates also have in common: they both occurred after she became pregnant. That would further explain why they took such pains for so long to conceal the existence of her husband and child from her family and friends. But there are additional facts that also fit, and some only, an out-of-wedlock birth scenario. One was the matter of timing. A frame of seven weeks between Fuller's arrival back in Rome and her impregnation was pretty short to resolve her strong doubts, proceed with a courtship, organize a wedding, ensure it was kept secret from Ossoli's large family and circle of friends, and get pregnant. An out-of-wedlock conception would also explain her later obstinate refusal, even after exposing her secret, to give her friends details, especially about the marriage's chronology, which they would anxiously seek in order to counter the rumors that were circulating about it in America, leaving some to conclude she had in fact not married until after the birth of the child. Then there were her later admissions, first to Arconati that "pecuniary reasons" were "only half the truth" for her past concealment, and to her sister Ellen that she could not then go into all the "matter of fact history" because Ossoli was "still a member of the Roman Catholic Church," which probably referred to the fact that she and Ossoli had committed fornication, a mortal sin in the eyes of the Church. Finally, such an out-of-wedlock scenario would explain certain peculiar formulations in Fuller's January 11 letter to Caroline. It would make, for example, her statement that she "cannot say anything" about marriage "from my present self," however misleading, literally true. It would also explain her confused but ominous references to expecting to "reap what I have sown" and feeling "no way out" of her unnamed calamity except for an "accident," presumably a miscarriage, or "through the gate of death." Even if she feared, as many antebellum women understandably did, possible death or serious complications attendant to childbirth (one historian conservatively estimates the odds at 1.3 percent and 10 percent, respectively), these anxious and despondent expressions of guilt and fear of retribution fit neither the happy expectations nor the legitimate physical worries of a married pregnant woman. They *do* fit very well, however, the feelings of an unmarried woman facing a childbirth she felt guilty about and whose consequences she feared much more than she welcomed.[8]

Then, too, there were several emotional reasons why Theodore Parker was probably right when he later speculated after reading Fuller's published letters that her union "was only a *continuation*, not a union . . . in the ecclesiastical or even the civil sense I think till near or perhaps after the birth of the child." One could have certainly been her initial doubts, which she would later confess to Channing, about her and Ossoli's suitability for a conventional marriage, which she never entirely lost. At the same time, as Lydia Maria Child, Rebecca Spring, and others of Fuller's female friends would later testify, during the previous couple of years, she had said she badly wanted a child. Indeed, in a later letter to Channing explaining why she had taken up with Ossoli (leaving open what that meant), she would write that, despite her not wanting a romantic love match and a conventional marriage at the time, "I . . . pined too much and my heart was too suffocated without a child of my own. I say I am not strong as we thought." And, at almost the same time, to her English friend Arthur Hugh Clough she would say outright, "But for the child I should have wished to remain as we were, and feared we should lose much my entering on the jog-trot of domestic life." So, uncertain whether to marry Ossoli, wanting a child but also knowing that because of her age she might not get pregnant and, given her increasing frailty, if pregnant, she might not deliver, she decided to postpone any decision until after being certain both things would occur. There was also a further plausible reason, not exclusive of these, and quite consistent with her personality, that she got pregnant without being married, which she would later imply to Ellen in saying that she "acted upon a strong impulse" and "could not analyze at all what passed in my mind": simply passion.[9]

Finally, it is also quite possible, as she would imply to Clough, that Fuller's evolving views about the institution of marriage influenced her marital decisions. There is something to Emerson's insistence, rebutting Channing's private speculation that her later radical principles would have kept her from marrying, that, like all reformers, though she might speculate, when it came to flouting "a vast public opinion, too vast to brave; an opinion of all nations & of all ages," she would not have transgressed it. Certainly, her panicked repulsion of Nathan's pass would suggest that something of that feeling might have inhibited her with Ossoli, at least for a while. However, Emerson's other claim—that her conviction as shown by her journal remark a few years earlier that marriage was "one grand type that should be kept forever sacred" would have stopped her cold—is much shakier. As with her prediction in "The Great Lawsuit" about married women becoming "virgins," Fuller hardly used these sorts of phrases literally. In any case, her position on marriage had evolved since then. Although Sand's "free-love" affairs made her nervous, that was because, she said, they were "lawless," like the sexual affairs of aristocratic "old regime" France, and ungrounded in some "higher aim." Indeed, in her unpublished tale "Aglauron and Laurie. A Drive through the Country near Boston" (which Emerson oddly cited against Channing's view), she has her stand-in Aglauron plead that the heroine's free-love doctrine was a perfectly understand able and even excusable step in her upward path to an independent soul. By that time, too, her skepticism about the *practice* of marriage had grown stronger than ever. "In the present arrangements of society," she lectured Richard in one letter that year, trying to discourage him from jumping into marriage by pointing to all her friends' awful marriages and bitter divorces—and there were many—"a choice of a companion for life acts as a Fate on the whole of life." On New Year's Day, by which time she knew she was pregnant, she sighed after learning that another of Richard's engagements had predictably been broken off: "God knows I have not myself been wise in life. But I wish you might be wiser and happy."[10]

If she *were* inclined to cross the line separating worldly doubt from illicit action, Fuller would have also had by that time some encouragement. Although circles of "free-love" radicals touting the moral superiority of nonmonogamous "spiritual marriages" over conventional ones would not emerge for a few more years yet, the recent American publication of books revealing Fourier's views about marriage as legalized prostitution and the virtues of the "butterfly" instinct gave the subject for the first time in the United States a public airing. Indeed, while Greeley dissociated himself from them in his scorching newspaper debate with his conservative rival Henry J. Raymond earlier in the year, privately, a few of her fellow-traveling Fourierist friends were starting to flirt with antimarital views, at least in talk. Nor did she exactly lack sexually transgressive models in Europe. Quite apart from Mickiewicz's encouragement to decide whether she would remain a virgin, once with explicit reference to Ossoli, she had before her eyes Sand and Princess Cristina Belgioioso, as well as several of Arconati's "emancipated" women friends, such as the Countess Radzivill, whom she admired and whose illicit liaisons she found ways of excusing. In fact, in several letters to friends two years later, she would seem to *apologize* for succumbing to "this corrupt social contract" and "the jog-trot" and "trifling business arrangements" of marriage, strongly implying that her marriage followed her discovery of her pregnancy. None of this conclusively proves that Fuller initially strayed from marital rules, but along with her guiltily depressive and frantic expressions that winter about having done something wrong or dangerous, it gives added circumstantial evidence that Fuller was not married when she became pregnant.[11]

Meanwhile, her secrecy about it created two "incubi of the future" pressing on her right then. One was just keeping the secret a secret, especially a problem as she was starting to show. Hedge, who saw a lot of her in Rome that winter, was stunned when he first saw her; she seemed so "much changed and subdued" and, most shocking, looked like a hunchback, which he attributed to her kyphosis but was undoubtedly also her stooping to hide her distended stomach. Then there was the emotional toll of dissimulation. Hedge recalled that when they had later said goodbye in early March, she threw her arms around his neck and burst into tears, making him think that she was struggling with "some pent-up secret." Even more wrenchingly frustrating than keeping up appearances in Rome, though, was keeping in the dark her far-flung circle of friends and family, from whom she desperately wanted solace. Beginning that winter, she started lashing out at the "long silences," especially from friends whose friendships, as she bitterly told Caroline, "I had paid for with so much heart's blood." This startled them a bit. "You could not have alluded to any of your old friends whom *I* know," her brother Eugene assured her, answering Fuller's fears that they had forgotten her. Richard answered that her immediate family did not write as often as they would have liked because they did not want to overburden her with heavy postage charges. (In Europe one then had to pay both ways for transatlantic letters, often $1.25 or more per letter.) Neither claim, however—nor the fact, which she knew well, that transatlantic letters usually took a month to a month and a half to get across the Atlantic, if they were not lost in transit, as many were—seemed to have mollified her. "I am tired of life and feel unable to face the future," she blurted out in her March 17 reply to Richard, after drearily listing all her physical illnesses and their paralysis of her writing.[12]

Almost as demoralizing as coping with her secret was her struggle to keep her perennially shaky finances from overwhelming her. She now owed the Springs, Sam Ward, and her mother over $1500, or three times what she made in an entire year writing for the *Tribune*. She cast around for moneymaking projects. She collected stories and anecdotes she had picked up in Europe for her second edition of *Woman in the Nineteenth Century*, and she thought about writing a book of cultural travel advice. But like her postponed book of "impressions" of her European travels, these promised only far-off returns. She tried to express her growing money anxieties to her family, but that only got her further entangled in her dissimulation. "Never forget how lonely my position is now," she admonished Richard a day after writing to Caroline, demanding to know the state of her debts, "and how desolate and suffering it might be made by a little neglect to write of these affairs." Concerned and a little flummoxed, Richard proposed that she return immediately and retire with him and their mother to a farm! She cautiously answered that she needed to put off considering any such plans until October. "There are circumstances and influences now at work in my life," she wrote mysteriously, speaking of course of her approximate due date, "not likely to find their issue till then." Although he undoubtedly missed another of her plays on her pregnancy here, in his next letter, he came up with a better idea. As an outright gift, he told her, he had paid $200 to Spring on her draft, and he promised to pay the rest off with her portion of the proceeds from the sale of land the family owned. He also said that in a couple of months they would send her an additional gift of $500.

"It is due to you as the bright ornament of our family, it is due for your cares and attentions in many years past." At that juncture, she probably appreciated the reassuring sentiment as much as the money.[13]

II

By the time Fuller received Richard's letter in early April, she was starting to recover her emotional bearings. She remained tense, especially over money. In the fall, she had brushed aside her Uncle Abraham's disappointing bequest to her, but when she discovered the details that spring, she became bitter. Although she thought she had an implied "contract" to receive some compensation for her sacrifices for her siblings, out of his estate of $80,000, each got only a little over $200 and her mother nothing, the rest going to his brothers and Harvard Divinity School. She became more aggravated when she got letters from friends (as Sarah Clarke wrote her in one) "tormented with an unholy curiosity" to know whether Abraham had given her a windfall so she could stay abroad longer. "I am rather sore at being continually congratulated about my uncle's legacy," she fumed in a letter in May to Mary Rotch. "My friends are under some mistake, I fancy. My uncle died as he had lived, hard-hearted against me." After detailing her clashes with him over releasing money from her father's estate for her younger siblings' "useless" education and defending her mother against his "rude tyranny," she stopped: "It makes me sad to think how easy it would have been for my uncle by a legacy of a few thousands to put an end to the embarrassments and cares of which I have, perhaps, had my share, without injury to others, for some to whom their legal fraction went were not in need." She ended on a sardonically pleased note. "If his ghost knows any of my plans have been aided at all through him," she laughed to Rotch, "it sighs at the thought."[14]

Her flippancy was telling: by that spring, she *was* feeling better psychologically. By late March, her nausea and other symptoms stopped, and, in perfect tandem, the three-month spate of downpours, mud, and overcast skies suddenly ended and daily sunny weather returned. "The Gods themselves walk on earth, here in the Italian Spring," she rejoiced in a letter that April to Jane Tuckerman King. Her jaunts that spring with Ossoli to resort towns on the Tyrrhenian seacoast and the Roman Castles just southeast of the city were also a tonic. "The sea breezes burnt my face, but revived my heart," she wrote in intoxicated prose in her April 1 dispatch after returning from seaside Ostia. "I felt the calm of thought, the sublime hopes of the Future, Nature, Man—so great, though so little—so dear, though incomplete." Now moving about again, she felt her Italianate identity unconsciously deepening. "I keep writing words wrong speaking and hearing constantly Italian," she apologized to Richard after writing a garbled sentence. Even her stalled writing plans looked brighter. "[I] have earned no money I have done nothing," she conceded to Richard, adding, however: "But when I *do* feel better, I will write again; no doubt things will look differently." Indeed, so much better did she feel, that in her letter to Jane she let drop allusions to her pregnancy. "But ah dearest," she wrote, the drama of my fate is very deep, and the ship plunges deeper as it rises higher. You would be amazed, I believe, could you know how different is my present phase of life, from that in which you knew me; but you would love me no less; for it is still the same planet that shews such different climes. I am very happy here; tranquil, and alone in Rome. I love Rome more every hour; but I do not like to write details, or really to let any one know any thing about it. I pretend to, perhaps, but in reality, I do not betray the secrets of my love.

As if her obfuscating "alone in Rome" and teasing "secrets of my love" that she only pretended to betray were not enough, she went further. "Whatever may be the future developments of my life, *you* will always love me, and prize my friendship," she declared—as if talking to herself as much as to Jane—and then followed with this tantalizing self-absolution: "Much has changed since we met; my character is not in what may be called the heroic phase, now. I have done, and may still do, things that may invoke censure; but in the foundation of character, in my aims, I am always the same:—and I believe you will always have confidence that I act as I ought and must."[15]

"Sublime hopes of the Future" was also not hyperbole. Three weeks and a day after abolitionists watched helplessly as their government triumphantly concluded its war of conquest against Mexico, aristocratic Europe experienced the greatest liberal political upsurge in its history. On February 24, following two days of virtually bloodless demonstrations, King Louis-Philippe abdicated his throne, and four days later, a provisional government proclaimed France once again a republic. The revolutionary contagion quickly spread. On March 13, after insurrections broke out that paralyzed Vienna, Metternich was forced to resign and flee the country. Over the next several weeks, the Austrian emperor and the Prussian king, in vain attempts to dampen the fires in their kingdoms, both granted the humiliating concessions of representative bodies, political liberties, and soon even universal suffrage. By the middle of May, insurrections and revolts had shaken Berlin, Prague, Kraków, Madrid, Budapest—indeed, cities in every major country on the Continent except Russia—creating the widest and most sustained burst of revolutionary activity in modern history and raising every Western liberal's hopes like nothing since the French Revolution. "The righteous Gods do yet live and reign!" even the idiosyncratic antidemocrat Carlyle exclaimed to Emerson on the day France declared itself a republic (before later thinking better of it). "It is long since I have felt such deep-seated, pious satisfaction at a public event."[16]

As their simultaneity would suggest, these eruptions, despite wide disparities in both their politics and degree of violence, had certain commonalities. One was the series of economic calamities to which Fuller had alluded in her dispatches, beginning with two massive crop failures in 1845 and 1846, followed by a severe financial crisis the next year and a near collapse of manufacturing that fall and winter, spiking unprecedented unemployment and starvation throughout Europe. A second common thread was "nationalism," a term first used in the early 1830s to denote the ideology behind the swelling national aspirations of the fragmented Germans and the subjugated peoples of the three great multinational Habsburg, Russian, and Ottoman empires. Historians have commonly discerned two versions of this idea: a French Enlightenment-inspired concept of voluntary association of free individuals and a German Romantic one of distinct social organisms expressing themselves in particular languages, histories, and sets of customs, although at this historical moment both types often overlapped. Yet a third similarity of these upsurges was their class origins: except in feudal eastern Europe, where nationalist aristocrats dominated the moderate parties, most were movements of the urban middle classes. A fourth common characteristic was the same fault line dividing Risorgimento politics. On one side, Liberals demanded the rule of law, the abolition of police regimes and confessional religious states, freedom of press and assembly, and an expanded franchise, but never so widely as to threaten property or give the poor a share in government. Democrats, on the other hand, while supporting the first set, also demanded universal suffrage, while some even, especially in the artisan neighborhoods of Paris and some cities in western Germany and northern Italy, where socialistic parties surfaced, urged the "rights" of workers *over* those of private property, including the right to organize and the creation of government work programs. Finally, as many 1848 leaders were intellectuals and writers, liberal social Romanticism infused this "Springtime of Peoples" with an intoxicating ethos of heroic impulses, spiritual forces, and messianic dreams that was never again expressed so fully in European politics until, perhaps, the 1960s.[17]

Although less politically and militarily important than those of France and Austria, the revolts in Fuller's Italian states were nonetheless central, and not just because they were rendering pieces of a crumbling empire now up for grabs. For one, they seemed to vindicate Mazzini's thesis that the fate of Italian national independence ultimately depended on the fate of revolution in Europe. Yet the Italian revolts were not faint copies. They started earlier and lasted longer, largely because of the unifying nationalist hatred of Austria, which helped suppress ideological divisions while constantly reigniting uprisings. Yet Italy's nationalism did not make its revolts any simpler or easier to effect. First, they faced the problem of, if not deep class conflict, as in France, class mobilization. Notwithstanding aristocratic leadership in Piedmont, peasant unrest in the south, and artisan agitation especially in the north, the bulk of the revolts' leaders and active participants were still largely drawn from the urban middle and professional classes, which in Italy, however, were proportionally smaller than in almost any other country in western Europe. Second, there was the difficulty of unifying Italy's disparate states. Not only did they often have, especially in Naples and Sicily, strong local interests and weak national concerns, but the vast differences in social conditions would likely have made a Sicilian peasant, language and weather apart, feel more at home in Hungary or Romania than in Lombardy or Tuscany. Third, there was the challenge of Austrian domination, which while often unifying Italians, also made them constantly subject to military intervention from both Austria and her allies and rivals. Fourth, nationalist enthusiasm still could not paper over the two pressing issues in every revolting Italian state: whether to accept embattled monarchs' proffered constitutions and reforms or fight on for a republic; and, closely intertwined with that, whether—and how—to make war on Austria. Finally, there was

the pope. In Italy, the Catholic Church ruled its own states and enormously influenced the others, thus making it a key power and rallying cry for the Risorgimento
as long as the pope was supportive, but posing an enormous obstacle if he were to
see it as threatening the papacy's temporal authority. The Church also helped prop
up the autocratic rulers of Catholic Europe, which gave them a vital stake in seeing that the pope preserved that authority as long as he continued to use it in their
favor. As with so much else in the preunified nation, the very thing that appealed
to Fuller—that Italy was not just Italy—also put it in a promising but precarious
position for revolutionary success.[18]

At the beginning of 1848, following Milan's successful antismoking campaign,
the possibilities were more evident than the precariousness. In neighboring Venice,
violent clashes broke out between protesters agitating for home rule and Habsburg
soldiers, which quickly spread throughout the Venetian provinces. On January
12, nine days after the bloody clashes at Milan, Sicilian peasants in Palermo rose
up against Ferdinand II's hated Neapolitan regime of the Kingdom of Two Sicilies,
immediately sparking uprisings on the Neapolitan mainland. Then, the following
week came news of the abdication of Louis-Philippe and the proclamation of a
French republic, arousing Italian republican hopes that new revolutionary France
would lend support to their struggle against the Austrian leviathan. Meanwhile,
out of fear of what the Sicilian revolt portended for their governments, the rulers
of Tuscany, Piedmont, and eventually Rome, to the outrage of the Austrian government, all followed Ferdinand II and nervously granted liberal constitutions.
But the truly galvanizing events for Italians everywhere were the revolts on March
12 and 13 in Vienna and the resignation and flight of Metternich, the empire's
architect, and Emperor Ferdinand's desperate promise of a constitution. After this
news reached Milan, on March 17, in exact tandem with the violent "Five Days"
insurrection in Berlin, the city began *its* "cinque giornate." Led by Cattaneo and
his colleagues and supported by the young Democratic students whom Fuller had
met the previous summer, the Milanese blocked off the streets from nearly a thousand police and some ten thousand garrisoned soldiers led by field-marshal Count
Joseph Radetsky. Volunteers from Rome and elsewhere poured into the city to
aid the insurgents, who, driven by sheer patriotic rage, waged a furious campaign
of street battles behind nearly seventeen hundred barricades. When the fighting
ended on the twenty-second, with nearly 200 of Austria's multinational force and
some 350 insurgents dead, Radetsky withdrew his troops from the city. The same
day Venice's newly organized Civic Guards, led by the determined republican
lawyer Daniele Manin, forced the capitulation of the two Austrian governors, thus
officially ending Austrian rule in Italy. "Milan, like Sicily," the historian Denis
Mack Smith writes, "had justified Mazzini's obstinate faith in popular initiative."
Yet the constitutional results satisfied Moderates just as much. From the most
backward and repressed sections of Italy in the south to the most developed and
liberal in the north, the first phase of the Risorgimento had begun.[19]

The second phase, however, turned on a tougher question than that of constitutions: whether and how to drive out from Lombardy entirely Radetsky's troops,
now ensconced in the Quadrilateral between his four fortresses. Certainly, no aid

was likely from liberal powers abroad. England, although hostile to Austria, had no interest in challenging the emperor's formidable forces, and republican France was preoccupied with conflicts over domestic policy. Within Italy itself, only one state was strong and dynamic enough to rise to that challenge: Piedmont-Sardinia— a nation of nearly five million partly bilingual people bordering on France and Switzerland, with an important maritime economy, and, with Cavour, D'Azeglio, Balbo, and others, containing the most sophisticated political class on the peninsula. Moreover, King Charles Albert, despite his past record of ultraconservative Catholicism and repression—which seventeen years before had brought Mazzini a death sentence—had been introducing legal and trade reforms, loosening press censorship, and, the month before, sanctioning a new constitution, partly to dampen radical ferment and partly to avoid losing his leadership of the Risorgimento to the pope. Meanwhile, he finally decided that the time to challenge his former ally had come. After wavering between wasting precious time during Milan's "Five Days" revolt out of fear that it would fail—or, worse, establish a Milanese republic—and worry that further delay would lose Lombardy to Tuscany or republicanism, on March 24, the king declared war on Austria, and the following day his army entered an already liberated Milan.[20]

III

Fuller reacted to these revolutionary upheavals with unbridled enthusiasm. "What great and stirring times are these of Paris," she wrote on March 8 to Chopin's student Jane Sterling, wishing only that she had been there *that* February as the year before. When Milan exploded ten days later, she wrote to Henry Colman, a politically moderate acquaintance studying in Europe, begging for a firsthand account of how things looked in revolutionary France. "We hear so very little," she said, "and it seems to me the French journals are afraid to publish the full truth, lest it should do mischief abroad." Art now dropped out almost entirely of both her dispatches and letters. "You do not speak of the paintings," her fellow aesthete Charles Newcomb wrote her later that spring in puzzlement. Instead of "deep old thoughts," she wanted to get where the action was. "I am nailed here by want of money, if by no other reason," she grumbled to Colman, saying nothing about her pregnancy.[21]

She was more expansive with her socialist friend William Channing. "I have been engrossed, stunned almost, by the public events that have succeeded one another with such rapidity and grandeur," she exclaimed in a letter to him on March 29. "It is a time such as I always dreamed of, and for long secretly hoped to see. I rejoice to be in Europe at this time, and shall return possessed of a great history." This is the first indication that her travel book had transmuted into a political history. In her excitement she seems to have wanted to rush in several directions at once. "Perhaps I shall be called to act," she excitedly wrote. "At present, I know not where to go, what to do. War is everywhere. I cannot leave Rome, and the men of Rome are marching out every day into Lombardy. The citadel of Milan is in the hands of my friends, Guerriere, &c., but there may be need to spill much blood yet in Italy. France and Germany are not in such a state that I can go there now. A glorious flame burns higher in the heart of the nations." She was right. A glorious flame *was* blazing higher, and as it did, it seemed to unfold before her a host of past dreams—from her adolescent Romantic one of an isolated, introspective intellectual suddenly "dilating" into a historical hero rallying "asking, aimless hearts" to her most recent cosmopolitan one of a new America renovated by the infusion of European lives and ideas. In that light even Rome looked a little backward. "As for the drum in these quarters, its rub a dub is even a little too constant," she told Colman, referring to the constant military maneuvers in Rome. "But I do assure you the men, woman and children of Italy show a noble spirit and one that should lead to a solid peace, a real growth."[22]

Although she never made it to Paris, Vienna, or Milan, that winter and spring two revolutionary heroes came to her. The first was the Princess Cristina Trivulzio di Belgioioso, who arrived to spend the winter in Rome. The "very celebrated" scion of one of the wealthiest and proudest families in Europe, she was a bit of an Italian Margaret Fuller with money, beauty, and privilege. Thin and frail from epileptic attacks—and probably also the opium she used to medicate them—with large black eyes, chiseled features, and diaphanous skin, which she accentuated by often dressing all in white, the charismatic princess had written tracts on Vico, the condition of women, and other Fulleresque subjects. Although then favoring a constitutional monarchy under Piedmont's King Charles Albert, because she thought Italians were unready for a republic, she had been a founder of Young Europe and was greatly admired by Mazzini. A Romantic socialist, after returning the previous year from exile in Paris, where she had befriended Mickiewicz and Sand (and was rumored to have slept with Sand's friends Balzac, Heine, and Liszt), she had organized on her estates Fourierist-like schools, industrial classes, and heated rooms in winter for the neighboring peasants. This time Fuller got no help from Arconati, who refused to introduce her. "We don't get along," Arconati explained, "but it will be easy for you to meet her. She has probably heard people speak of you and then she is in touch with Mazzini." Belgioioso was "a woman of superior intelligence who possesses the art of captivating," she added but cautioned her, "morally she has little value." Not surprisingly, these intriguing warnings did not stop Fuller from seeing the princess, who told her to come by her apartment any morning or early evening ("being of very early habits"), and she would be "always very happy to see you." Indeed, Fuller quickly formed a generous opinion of Belgioioso morally, even elevating her above Sand. "She is a woman of gallantry which Me Sand is not," Fuller wrote Richard after Belgioioso left for Naples, "though she also has had several lovers, no doubt. The public life of the Princess has been truly energetic and beneficent." In revolutionary Italy, even more than France, public gallantry excused sexual peccadilloes.[23]

The charismatic revolutionary to whom Fuller pined to talk was Mickiewicz, who arrived in Rome on February 6. "It was he I wanted to see, more than any other person, in going back to Paris," she exulted to Emerson, then still in London, "and I have him much better here." Her only regret was that she did not have a chance to measure in person the two heroes who had "been most to me in Europe" against her old Transcendentalist mentor. "Perhaps you would not have found common ground with them," she told Emerson in a subsequent letter, "but I should like to have had you see these personalities." Meanwhile, she publicized Mickiewicz and his Polish Legion, reporting on the massive crowds that furiously applauded his exhortations in French from his hotel balcony against the "barbarian of the North, the destroyers of liberty and civilization," and reprinting its liberal democratic Declaration of Faith, including a call, especially important in Catholic Poland, for equal rights for Jews. After he and his Legion got to Florence a couple of weeks later, he sent her letters of recommendation. "But choose among your acquaintances persons who have a bit of sacred fire!" he implored. "Probably you know few of them, for you have always lived with honest and well bred people (gentlemen). Now the persons I ask you to know generally have a bad reputation." One Mickiewicz biographer suggests he must have meant this as a joke or a trick to fool police spies, but the provocative Pole was probably deadly serious.[24]

Her dispatches' appraisals of the political scene that winter and spring were as enthusiastic as Belgioioso and Mickiewicz could have wished, but also cautious. She reported rumors of revolts on the peninsula but urged waiting for further confirmation and warned against provocations. Recounting on January 22 the recent "murder" of antismoking boycotters and the Austrians' subsequent attempts to provoke the Milanese to premature revolts in order to give an excuse for more repression, she praised the people for their self-discipline. She also kept her eye on the debates in the Paris Chamber of Deputies and Chamber of Peers. On January 27, the same day Tocqueville delivered his famous speech warning "the storm is brewing," she rightly marked as an ominous sign opposition members' "keenest satire" aimed at the king, although no more than Tocqueville or anyone else did she venture to predict his imminent dethronement.[25]

Provoked by Pius's political retreats, however, Fuller dispensed with caution that winter in her first major attacks on the Catholic Church. Two weeks after instructing her readers to trade their prejudices against its "senseless mass of juggleries" for an understanding of their "poetic meaning," she gave a chilling account of Cardinal Gabriele Ferretti, the papal secretary of state, officiating for a "quite worldly"–looking young noblewoman who was taking the veil, probably, Fuller guessed, because her family had found no suitable match. She conceded that monastic exclusion could be fitting, especially for the brokenhearted, but only if voluntary, rather than, as in this case, coerced by the Church or the family. "But where it is enforced or repented of no hell could be worse; nor can a more terrible responsibility be incurred by him who has persuaded a novice that the snares of the world are less dangerous than the demons of solitude." Mostly she directed her anticlerical ire at the Society of Jesus. Expelled by every constitutional government in Europe for its unstinting efforts to prop up the Continent's most reactionary powers and hated by Italians for its plotting with the reactionary Gregorian party and the thuggish Sanfedists, the Society was anathema to Liberals and Democrats alike. As with the monastic induction, the issue for Fuller was again not Catholic rites per se but Church power. In the same early January dispatch in which she upbraided some boorish Protestant Americans for their dumb remarks while impatiently waiting for the "sermon" during the pope's vespers at the Jesù, the

Society's principal church in Rome, she recounted lurid anecdotes about its political skullduggery. She excoriated their priests' recent attempt to sow popular
discord by plastering inflammatory handbills around the city to provoke anti-
Semitic outbreaks. And she exploded angrily at their transparent spread of a rumor that the Madonna del Popolo had cured a paralytic youth, who saw a vision
he interpreted as a severe criticism of the pope's recent reform measures. "Were
I a European," she exclaimed, "to no object should I lend myself with more ardor
than to the extirpation of this cancer." In fact, so dangerous did these "emissaries
of the power of darkness" seem to her that she aired a report that they were trying
to get a Jesuit-employed Italian consul for the United States. "This rumor seems
ridiculous; yet," she added, alluding to America's leading evangelical anti-Catholic
crusader, "it is true that Dr. Beecher's panic about the Catholic influence in the
United States is not quite unfounded, and that there is a considerable hope of establishing a new dominion there." She went on to warn against the American
administration appointing an Italian *or* a Catholic to a consulship. "The representative of the United States should be American; our national character and interests are peculiar and cannot be fitly represented by a foreigner," she wrote, as
though a Catholic could not be an American.[26]

This flirtation with American nativist anti-Catholicism, however, was an aber-
ration. Indeed, only once did Fuller let her hostility to the Church's worldly practices pass into an attack on Catholic ritual and belief. In early January she attended
the grand feast of the "Bambino," which venerated a small wooden statue of the
Christ child that purportedly had once, after being taken, returned on its own ac-
cord to Santa Maria in Aracoeli. What aroused her anger, though, was sitting next
to a struggling "orphan" (Ossoli) whose grandmother had left her vineyard to her
rich confessor, who occasionally had this child, his godson, to dinner. "Children,
so placed, are not quite such devotees to Catholicism as the new proselytes of
America!" she observed, swiping at the recent Transcendentalist Catholic converts. From there she launched into an ethical attack on the ritual. "Awake, indeed, Romans!" she cried, describing the parade of robed dignitaries holding aloft
the doll as the band played "'Sons of Rome awake!'" The true saving Christ is
"no wooden dingy effigy of by-gone superstitions but such as art has seen Him in
your better mood—a Child, living, full of life, prophetic of a boundless Future—
a Man acquainted with all sorrows that rend the heart of all, but only loving Man,
with sympathy and faith death cannot quench—*that* Christ lives or is sought; burn
your doll of wood." After urging her Romans to exchange their archaic religion
for her Romantic social gospel, she wondered, "How any one can remain a Catholic—I mean who has ever been aroused to think, and is not biased by the partiali-
ties of childish years—after seeing Catholicism here in Italy I cannot conceive."[27]

Her accelerated attacks against the Church got her predictable attention in the
United States. Her liberal friends liked them, of course. "I have been glad to hear
you speak so severely of the Roman Catholic Church," wrote, of all people, Charles
Newcomb, Brook Farm's Catholic-ritual devotee, telling her her attacks were a
fine rebuke of their Transcendentalist colleagues who had become so "infatuated"
with the Church's rituals that they, horrors, had actually converted to it! Catholic

readers were not so thrilled. "It is plain," wrote "Catholic Subscriber" in a letter to the *Tribune*, "this crusade [against the Jesuits] is indirectly a crusade on the Catholic Church, therefore as such your Catholic subscribers (who are by no means few) consider your foreign correspondent's letter a direct insult." Even Greeley, who assiduously courted Catholic voters and regularly denounced anti-Catholic nativism in his editorials, found her broadsides sufficiently disquieting that he initially considered censoring her line about not appointing a Catholic as ambassador to Rome before deciding against it. "Few of the people who cannot bear to hear what their neighbors think of them are wise enough to take the Tribune," he boldly told his readers. However, although noting that even the pope had "condemned and disbanded the Order," he strongly dissented from her objection to a Catholic ambassador and apologetically conceded that the "*" viewed the church through "ultra Protestant, though . . . liberal . . . spectacles." This was all true, although perhaps only a Catholic like Brownson would describe Fuller's Transcendentalist religion as "ultra Protestant." Furthermore, had she been back in New York, she undoubtedly would still have been fervently defending Irish-American Catholics from nativist slanders and admiring aspects of Catholic ritual and charity. The difference was that she was in Rome and her editor was in New York. Indeed, one might say, rather than looking through chauvinistic American anti-Catholic spectacles, she was seeing the Church through *European* liberal anticlerical eyes. Nor would she be the last European-minded American radical to let her hostility to a threatening authoritarian power abroad soften a bit her commitment to the civil liberties of its American supporters.[28]

How, though, did she think the Italian people's current political struggles could make them see her liberal "boundless Future"? In her dispatch of the previous November she had expressed doubts about whether they would have "courage and purity" to fight for their freedom, but now she was sure they would. First, she said, as Mazzini had said to her, events were propelling the people toward it: revolution in Sicily, revolts in Naples, constitutions from monarchs, the fall of Louis Philippe, and the uprisings in Vienna and Milan. "This week has been one of nobler, sweeter feeling of a better hope and faith than Rome in her greatest ever knew," she wrote in her dispatch on March 29—no small praise from a lifelong venerator of ancient Rome. More immediately transformative, she recognized, was the signal fact of nineteenth-century Italian political culture: its civic culture, as one historian has noted, was "lived in the piazza, as a place for meeting and endless talk in the shadow of power, and for public display of respectability asserted as *bella figura*." But the moment called for more than that: these "artistic" peoples' delighted in injecting new politics into old rituals. At the close of Carnival, she happily reported, they danced in the streets, clanking chairs, "emblem of the tyrannic power now vanquished by the people," to celebrate the recently announced revolutions in France and Austria. The next week they did the opposite: they postponed the picturesque feast of the *moccoletti* (tapers) to show their displeasure with the Jesuits. Weaving her strands of political narrative, eyewitness reporting, ideological critique, and outright bias, she described with gusto a cosmopolitan carvinalesque of immigrants, exiles, poets, and nuns burning Austrian arms in the

Piazzo del Popolo: "It was a transport of the people, who found no way to vent their joy, but the symbol, the poesy, natural to the Italian mind." They also burned up the historic selfishness and suspicions of each other that had been engendered by centuries of division and oppression. After writing of the people dancing in the streets and weeping with joy when they heard the news that the Milanese had pulled down the Habsburg double-headed eagle from the portal of the Palazzo di Venezia, she reported that young men rushed to enroll themselves to go to the frontier. Following the Radical Pietro Sterbini's announcement that those who did not wish to go might give money and to those who would go, the government would give bread and 15 baiocchi a day, a self-sacrificial pandemonium ensued. Men cried, 15 baiocchi a day was too much, they could live on a paul a day, princes answered by giving tens of thousands of dollars, and "the people," from peddlers to beautifully dressed women, by giving everything they had. "These are people whom the traveler accuses of being unable to rise above selfish considerations."[29]

And not just travelers were so blind: Americans at home and abroad had their own stereotype that Italians were a lazy, cowardly, ignorant, and superstitious people incapable of achieving a democratic polity. Its sources, she explained, were two, both sadly revealing America's limitations. One was social-political: Americans were tone-deaf to the Italy's current political idealism because the ideals of their own revolution had nearly evaporated in their stampede of money getting. The other was cultural: they aped, as in so much else, the English upper class (who were, indeed, now largely bored with Italophilia and certainly not interested in triggering a troublesome war with Austria). Worst of all, though, she said, was the awful influence of "the illiberal, bristling English . . . too often met here," who cast their "porcupine quills against everything like enthusiasm." To blunt them, she reverted to her well-honed genre of polemical drama. After recounting detachments marching, trailed by cheering crowds and weeping women ("for the habits of the Romans are so domestic, that it seemed a great thing to have their sons and lovers gone even for a few months"), she wrote:

> [They] laughed at all this. They have said that this people would not fight; when the Sicilians, men and women, did so nobly they said, "Oh! the Sicilians are quite unlike the Italians; you will see when the struggle comes to Lombardy, they cannot resist the Austrian force a moment." I said, "That force is only physical; do not you think a sentiment can sustain them?" They reply, "All stuff and poetry; it will fade the moment their blood flows."

And so on through the Lombards and the Romans, each successively cited as the "real" Italians who would prove their case as each in turn enthusiastically rushed to face suffering and death against the Austrians and their allies. "No, Messiurs, Soul is not quite nothing, if Matter be a clog upon its transports."[30]

Of course, she knew, as she also said, there were a few of "the more generous Saxon blood" who could appreciate the need for unclogging soulful transports. She only mentioned, however, her circle of liberal American intellectuals, artists, and expatriates, who had organized, she proudly reported, a George Washington birthday dinner at which Story had read a poem, and Hillard and Hedge, as well as Thomas Crawford, who would join the Roman Civic Guard after the pope's overthrow, had delivered tributes to the Risorgimento. Clearly, the bulk of her traveling compatriots needed encouragement, which was why, she said, Greeley's Broadway Tabernacle meeting in the fall had so much pleased her: by "instructing the Americans abroad!" Meanwhile, she would remain at her post instructing her readers back home on the proper ways of cosmopolitan patriotism in a revolutionary age.[31]

IV

Three weeks later, this popular front solidarity started suddenly getting complicated. Up to then events had made the Risorgimento seem unstoppable: constitutions in the three "reforming states" of Piedmont, Tuscany, and the Papal States, as well as even for a while in Naples; Milan and Venice's liberation, followed by the abandonment of Parma and Modena by their puppet rulers; and, on April 10, Charles Albert's defeat of Austrian forces at Goito. Then, however, came Pius's much-anticipated Allocution on the ongoing war in Austria. Despite the Piedmont king's bold attack on Austria, the pope retained enormous moral stature as the country's greatest Risorgimento leader, whom most Liberals and even many Radicals expected would lead a national war of liberation. The test quickly came. Following the massive prowar demonstrations described by Fuller, on April 22, against his wishes, Roman legions under papal colors crossed the Po to join the combined Italian forces under Charles Albert. The pope was caught on horns of an immense dilemma. On the one hand, a supposedly Church-sanctioned holy war against another Catholic power invited both an invasion by Austria and a schism in the German states. On the other hand, any attempt to pull back his forces now, as his ministers explicitly warned him, would likely foment a revolution. On April 29, before the "Secret Consistory," he delivered his answer. Urging the people to obey the dictates of their princes, he denounced all schemes to establish an independent Italian republic under his rule. More important, he dissociated the Church from the war, effectively denying sanction to the only military force within Italy capable of freeing Italy from Austrian rule and threatening his own Roman troops with being summarily shot as common outlaws.

Overnight, the myth of the liberal patriotic pope was shattered. After translations of the Allocution were posted around the city, angry crowds, some crying "down with the papacy," gathered in the squares and streets. Both of the two major *circoli*, or clubs, the Circolo Romano (Club of Rome), led by Prince Corsini and the philosopher Count Terenzio Mamiani, and the Circolo Popolare (Club of the People), led by Sterbini and Ciceruacchio, united in calling turbulent mass meetings. The Civic Guards, now the only military force in the city, swung mutinously to the side of the clubs. The pope's ministers, realizing they could do nothing, all resigned. Finally, on May 2, Mamiani, now the pope's new minister, created two ministries, one for lay foreign affairs and one for ecclesiastical matters, thus giving assurance to Liberals and Radicals that the war of liberation would continue and its soldiers defined as authorized combatants and assurance to the pope that he had no responsibility for it. The plan quickly proved unworkable: it was both a recipe for a stalemate over supplying the troops and a tacit concession that the pope was now effectively a constitutional sovereign, a status he refused to accept. For the moment, though, it staved off a revolution.

In her dispatch on May 7, Fuller took the measure of "this astounding performance." Essentially, she returned to her previous spring's skepticism about the pope but now, bolstered by recent events, turned it into a final judgment on both him and on the current dual-power regime. Applying Mazzini's hard antipapal line to the Allocution, she said the people had to understand that the pope's "final dereliction" was inevitable. For all of the pope's goodness and charisma, he was no great intellect, but even if he had been a genius, he could never satisfy the people's national aspirations while insisting on retaining his temporal power, which depended precisely on the autocratic regimes that guaranteed his throne. In addition, his entire political trajectory since the fall, which she reviewed in detail, had been propelling him toward this final disastrous decision. Finally, whatever his sympathies for reform, he would do little or nothing to suppress the most reactionary elements in the Church that constantly conspired against it. Characteristic was his stance toward the Jesuits. While ostensibly dissolving their order, he tolerated their secret presence, allowing them to do even greater mischief, as did no other Italian state, and "talked as if they were assailed as a *religious* body, when he could not fail, like everybody else, to be aware that they were dreaded and hated solely as agents of despotism." Then came the Allocution "lamenting over the war—dear to every Italian heart as the best and holiest cause in which for ages they had been called to embark their hopes—as if it was something offensive to the spirit of religion, and which he would fain see hushed up, and its motives smoothed out and ironed over." In short, out of naiveté. fear, and self-deception, he had made religion into a cloak to cover the political tyranny of the Church and the supporting monarchies he could not confront.[32]

The alternative was clear: not the just the clubs and the Civic Guard but the powerful force of "the people" behind both. Of course, she did not mean all the people, or, for that matter, even just the artisan, middle-class, and professional sectors that the Radical clubs were inciting. Rather, in Fuller's usage, it was the masses, whose sudden awakening she admiringly portrayed as almost that of a single character. Still, their disaffection from the beloved pope following his Allocation, as historians have noted, was a subtle process, and Fuller sensitively charted its vicissitudes: from a momentary stupefaction to indignation to grief but above all a practical dedication to keeping the news from leaving Rome to demoralize the provinces before the pope could be persuaded or superseded. Indeed, the people's "gentleness, clearness and good sense" was astounding. "Wonderfully has this people been developed within a year!" she cried. Meanwhile, the apostasy of the pope and the people's resolve to ignore him, she declared, "make a crisis." But that was good. First, she said, telescoping things a bit, with the pope's temporal power effectively ended, the papacy was now clearly dead. "The work began by Napoleon is finished," she declared more prophetically than empirically. "There will never more be really a Pope, but only the effigy or simulacrum of one." Second, the people's extraordinary self-discipline and the dereliction of the mad Louis Philippe and the blind Pius proved that republicanism would eventually spread all over Europe. "It seems as if," she wrote, spinning this confluence into myth, "Fate was at work to bewilder and cast down the dignitaries of the world and democratize Society at one blow." And that was true now in Rome: not even the Liberal Mamiani could prevent the inevitable collision that would soon arise between, as Fuller put it, "him who retains the name but not the place of Sovereign, and the Provisional Government which calls itself a ministry." Into that void, she hoped, would rush the self-declared sovereign people.[33]

There was only one problem: not every patriot could agree on who should lead the people and to what political end. Fuller discovered that quite personally that spring in a tense exchange with Arconati, who had been anxious about not hearing from her after offering to send her money. Even back in early January, while elated over the Milanese uprising, Arconati had nervously written Fuller about some rumors of recent "deplorable" violence in Genoa excited by Mazzini's letters and emissaries, who had stirred up plots "to assassinate the Jesuits & burn them in their houses." "What black and foolish calumnies are these on Mazzini!" Fuller had answered heatedly. "It is as much for his interest as his honor to let things take their course, at present," she had added, repeating what Mazzini had told her in his letter received in December. "To expect anything else, is to suppose him base. And on what act of his life dares any one found such an insinuation?" Arconati had backed down, conceding that it was "his partisans, the lowest of his party who do him harm."[34]

By April, this uncertain truce gave way to "partisans" on both sides. "It is no longer mere theory," Arconati shot back in reply to Fuller's appeal that she get to know Mazzini. "There is a wall that cannot be passed between Mazzini & all that surrounds me." After ridiculing his suspension of criticism of Charles Albert as long as he pursued the war against Austria as a ploy to keep from losing followers, she wrote with royal definitiveness, "We believe that Mazzini & his party are the ruin of Italy." In her reply Fuller responded, after a caustic gloss on *Arconati*'s hero, the "'Illustrious Gioberti,'" as a politically doomed, "self-trumpeted" celebrity, by stating her satisfaction over being on the other side of Arconati's wall. "Everything confirms me in my radicalism; and, without any desire to hasten matters, indeed with surprise to see them rush so like a torrent, I seem to see them all tending to realize my own hopes." In their last exchange that summer, they addressed the key political question behind all this personal thrusting: their difference over republicanism for Italy. "If I am opposed to an Italian republic, it is not from any aristocratic prejudice, far from me be such meanness," Arconati said, but because a republic would cause irremediable disunion in a country that barely even held together. "I am so convinced of this fatal result that I cannot be calm in assisting at this debate," she added heatedly. "We shall be again precipitated into the abyss, by the hand of those who pretend to be our liberators. But on that day I renounce all that has made my hope for twenty seven years, & my joy for some days." Treading on dangerous waters, Fuller backed off a bit. She, too, was being realistic, she insisted, if not for the present, certainly for the future: "I am no bigoted Republican, yet I think that form of government will eventually pervade the civilized world. Italy may not be ripe for it yet, but I doubt if she finds peace earlier." She concluded by tearing into recent anti-republican maneuvers of Charles Albert before ending with a friendly account of how she spent her days. Although they would remain mutually devoted as ever, the innocent, optimistic days of Risorgimento friendship were over.[35]

One aspect of Fuller's new "radicalism" that she did not mention to Arconati was her new political sympathy for socialism that spring. Why then? Perhaps the Parisian Romantic socialists she had met had influenced her more than she had said at the time. Possibly, her admired *La Réforme* writers' recent assumption of ministerial posts in France's provisional government impressed her, as certainly did the socialist-leaning radical young republicans she had befriended the previous summer in Milan, several of whom now served as ministers, she proudly noted in one dispatch discussing socialism, in its provisional government. Or perhaps just that spring's dramatic accumulation of democratic victories all over Europe fired her hopes for an ideology with which she had been sympathetic for the last several years but only in the abstract and with a string of qualifications, most important, its very far-off success. That was essentially the point of her March 29 dispatch. "It would appear that the political is being merged in the social struggle," she declared after reporting on the surprising downfall of Louis Philippe's "empire of sham." "It is well; whatever blood is to be shed, whatever altars cast down. Those tremendous problems MUST be solved, whatever be the cost! That cost cannot fail to break many a bank, many a heart in Europe, before the good can bud again out of a mighty corruption." In her April 19 dispatch, she even offered, in the first critical remark she had ever uttered about Mazzini, an elliptical but pointed socialist criticism of his politics. Mazzini saw further, certainly, than that "pompous verbose charlatan" Gioberti, who only caught the "echo" of the advancing democratic wave of thought without detecting the "wants of man at this epoch." However, without saying what those "wants" were, she added: "And yet Mazzini sees not all: he aims at political emancipation; but he sees not, perhaps would deny, the bearing of some events, which even now begin to work their way. Of this more anon, but not to-day nor in the small print of *The Tribune*. Suffice it to say, I allude to that of which the cry of Communism, the systems of Fourier, &c. are but forerunners."[36]

Here Fuller was saying nothing more than many European socialists said about Mazzini's socially naïve liberalism, or that the French democratic left was insisting on by demanding programs to relieve working-class misery. How socialism had a chance in comparatively backward Italy, however—where the national question was far from settled, the liberal aristocracy and commercial classes (as Arconati predicted) were sure to desert the movement if the Risorgimento did threaten to "break banks," and the peasantry, the overwhelming majority, remained generally indifferent to the nationalist struggle—she did not say. But then, in raising the specter of socialism, Fuller was not addressing either the French or Italians or, for that matter, Europeans, but Americans, a fact she made clear in her stern warning to her compatriots at the end of her March 29 dispatch. If they wished to avoid Europe's fate in resolving the labor question, where bloodshed, she thought, was inevitable and perhaps even welcome, they needed to start expanding their liberal political ideals into a full-fledged social democracy. "To you, people of America, it may perhaps be given to look on and learn in time for a preventive wisdom. You may learn," she wrote, now giving the French version of bougeois revolutionary ideals, "the real meaning of the words FRATERNITY, EQUALITY: wisdom. You may, despite the apes of the Past, who strive to tutor you, learn the needs of a true Democracy. You may in time learn to reverence, learn to guard, the true aristocracy of a nation, the only really noble—the LABORING CLASSES." Of course, as in her remarks from Paris on this subject, she again avoided the key historical question: whether America's chance for peaceful "preventative wisdom" depended on its more advanced democratic polity or its underdeveloped industrial capitalism, although presumably she still inclined to the more flattering former alternative. Regardless, though, she knew one thing: just as much as Europe's, America's future turned on the fate of socialism.[37]

Nor is it too far a stretch to suggest that she may have thought her own future turned on its fate as well. In her May 29 letter to Rotch, after saying "You must always love me whatever I do. [I] depend on that," she abruptly asked her: "And this thought puts me in mind to ask whether you are not aware that I am as great an Associationist as W. Channing himself, that is to say as firm a believer that the next form society will take in remedy of the dreadful ills that now consume it will be voluntary association in small communities. The present forms are become too unwieldly. But what I think on this subject I hope to have force and time to explain in print. Not in the Tribune." Why did imploring Rotch to "love me whatever I do," an obvious reference to her pregnancy, make her think of Associationist communities? And why her repeated rejection of her paper as a venue? Was she thinking about Fourierist ideas of communal childrearing, which might have appealed to her as a mother without easy means of support but not to her editor, whose belief in the sanctity of the conventional family, despite his own difficult one, surpassed even his faith in the protective tariff? In any case, that spring she did not elaborate in small *or* large print on what exactly these new socialist "forms" were that might fit with the largely middle-class democratic revolutions now sweeping Italy and Europe. Yet the cry of socialism would ring ever louder in her ears in the dark days ahead.[38]

Meanwhile, the timely question for an American critic in Europe was not socialism in either place but Americans' comparative democratic practice, which she addressed in the conclusion to her last full dispatch of May 7. Many Americans reading reports of these revolutions, which began coming in less than two weeks after the Senate ratified the Treaty of Guadalupe Hidalgo ending the war with Mexico and providing enormous territorial acquisitions in the Southwest, were also pondering this question, with most happily concluding that, of course, America had triggered them. Democrats were especially enthusiastic, seeing them as validation of their vision of their country's "Manifest Destiny" to spread American

republican institutions now not only on the American continent but also through-
out oppressed Europe as well. Indeed, in one of the great ironies of the era, many
Democrats, both mainstream and bellicose leaders, who had appropriated "Young
America" as a war cry during the Mexican War, saw in their cause an extension
and validation of America's supposed republican war of liberation against Mexico.
"The cry 'les États-Unis d'Europe' has already been raised by the French press—
may it be realized," George Duyckinck wrote excitedly from Paris to his brother
Evert that spring. "It is a proud thing now to be an American in Europe for our
country leads the world. May we set the world a good example by our treatment
of Mexico." In the eyes of Fuller's New York Young America colleagues, the
United States was not a future imperialist Austria but a benignly expanding democratic France! Fuller's take on these interconnections was less flattering. After
declaring her hope that the pope's "sad disappointment" would offer deep instruction on the dangers of princely government and the possibilities for a republican
European "commonwealth," she wrote: "Hoping this era, I remain at present
here.—Should my hopes be dashed to the ground, it will not change my faith, but
the struggle for its manifestation is to me of vital interest. My friends urge my
return; they talk of our country as the land of the Future. It is so, but that spirit
which made it all it is of value in my eyes, which gave all of hope with which I
can sympathize for that Future, is more alive here at present than in America."
Indeed, unknowingly standing Duyckinck's self-satisfied formulation on its head,
she said, rather than genuinely boosting national self-confidence, the recently
concluded Mexican War exposed an America that Europe totally shamed. "My
country," she declared,

> is at present spoiled by prosperity, stupid with the lust of gain, soiled by crime in
> its willing perpetuation of Slavery, shamed by an unjust war, noble sentiment much
> forgotten even by individuals, the aims of politicians selfish or petty, the litera-
> ture frivolous and venal. In Europe, amid the teachings of adversity a *nobler spirit*
> is struggling—a spirit which cheers deeds of brotherhood. This is what makes
> *my* America. I do not deeply distrust my country. She is not dead, but in my
> time she sleepeth, and the spirit of our fathers flames no more, but lies hid be-
> neath the ashes. It will not be so long; bodies cannot live when the soul gets too
> overgrown with gluttony and falsehood. But it is not the making a President out
> of the Mexican War that would make me wish to come back. Here things are before
> my eyes worth recording, and, if I cannot help this work, I would gladly be its
> historian.[39]

In one sense, she replicated here the democratic transnational line she had
sounded in New York, although now with added scorn provoked by the impending election to the presidency of the Mexican War hero and proslavery Whig
Zachary Taylor (whom Greeley, holding his nose, would eventually support). Her
line also echoed that of abolitionist supporters of the European revolutions, who
saw in their embodiment of American republican ideals not an occasion to celebrate America's "exceptionalist" superiority but an indictment of their country,
whose institution of slavery and imperialist war to extend it these movements threw
in high relief. But her new transnational sign-off signaled something more. As

she experienced a real revolution rather than a remembered one, Europe had become Fuller's America. As her last sentence suggested, in partial reversal of her idea of the "thinking American," while remaining an American in ideals, she herself was also becoming something of a European in practice as well. She sounded less and less like she would be coming home anytime soon.

V

There were also some specific reasons for that: her improving health, the "paradisiacal" weather, her mountain and seashore jaunts outside Rome, but most of all, the sheer magnitude of the political events on which she was reporting. Her tarrying surprised Emerson. "How much your letter made me wish to say, come live with me at Concord!" he had written her in the winter from Manchester after getting a couple of discouraged letters from her. (He had quickly added that "poor exhausted Lidian" unfortunately made that impossible right now!) The following month he expressed exasperation over Fuller's unaccountable lingering. "You are imprudent to stay there any longer," he told her. "Can you not safely take the first steamer to Marseilles, come to Paris, & go home with me." On May 19 she replied that she had too much to do and learn in Europe even to think about returning. "I am deeply interested in this public drama, and wish to see it *played out*. Methinks I have *my part* therein, either as actor or historian." Indeed, in response to his confession that his interest in Europe "already flags," making him want to return, she reproached *him* a little. "I cannot marvel at your readiness to close the book of European society," she wrote, but "why did you not try to be in Paris at the opening of the Assembly?" referring to the Constituent Assembly's inauguration on May 5, eight days before he arrived in Paris. "There were elements worth scanning." Ten days later reporting to Mary Rotch that she frequently got letters from Waldo, she observed: "He sees much, learns much always but loves not Europe. There is no danger of the idle intimations of other minds altering his course more than of the moving a star. He knows himself and his vocation." It was obviously not hers.[40]

The biggest reason, of course, why she was not going very far very soon was her pregnancy, about which rumors were already starting to circulate. "Yes, I am faithful and capable of sympathy, even when opinions do not agree," Arconati wrote in response to a puzzling plea of Fuller's. "But what is it? You make me uneasy. People have told me that you had a lover at Rome, one of the Roman Civic Guard. I would not believe it—but your mysterious words fill my heart with doubt." So that May Fuller decided to go into the country for a "confinement," albeit radically different from the strict rest at home that antebellum childrearing experts insisted on. To family and friends, she gave various reasons for her rustication: she could live there "very cheaply," the mountain air would strengthen her, she could more easily write her book. All these were undoubtedly true, but they omitted the essential fact that she wanted to give birth to her child away from the eyes of friends in Rome. To Greeley her explanations were flummoxing. The previous month, he had written her that he could not understand why she stayed in Italy "in such miserable health," especially as Europe was exploding, making it unsafe "for a lonely invalid, especially a woman," to travel. When he read in her last dispatch dated May 13, announcing that Europe's *"nobler spirit"* was keeping her from returning but also that that would be her last column, he became irritated. "I regret the resolution," he wrote her coolly after reading this, wondering why she would suddenly stop since she was staying anyway—and, reversing his earlier concern about her safety, politics in Europe were just then heating up![41]

Fuller did reveal her pregnancy to two friends. One was Hicks, who had returned to Rome to spend the winter and spring. By then they had become, they both reported, "very intimate." In May, fearing she would not survive the final months of her pregnancy, she gave him a box of her papers to take the following month, when he left for Paris and London on his way back to New York, and give to her mother, including a statement indicating her wishes about handling her affairs after her death and an account of her relationship with Ossoli. Telling Hicks in her attached May 17 letter to "say to those I leave behind that I was willing to die," she cried, "I have wished to be natural and true, but the world was not in harmony with me—nothing came right for me." The same week, she received an answer to the other friend to whom she had disclosed her condition and her despair. Writing from Milan, where he was staying with the Arconatis, Mickiewicz gave her, even for him, a startling mix of sensible advice, portentous encouragement, and rough admonishment. "I see little improvement in your moral state," he wrote bluntly, as if still berating her for her bookish inner life insufficiently rooted in her body! "You are frightened at a very natural, very common ailment," he told her,

> and you exaggerate it in an extravagant manner. It will depend on you more than you believe whether you suffer more or less. Have more faith in God and accept the cross with courage, if you do not have the courage to be happy about it. Once moral strength is established in you in such a manner as to dominate the physical, God will spare you physical suffering, or will diminish it. Do not forget that cowards are pushed into combat by canings and that the strong going thither by themselves have no need of such physical stimulation.

Childbirth as courageous combat: a heroic injunction that no doubt caused her to read his tough advice in its intended sympathetic spirit.[42]

On May 28, she and Ossoli left Rome for Tivoli and Subiaco, where they stayed for a couple of days before continuing northeast to L'Aquila, after which Ossoli returned to Rome. Appropriate distance was probably one reason they skipped nearby picturesque Tivoli in favor of rugged L'Aquila. Lying at the foot of Gran Sasso, the Apennines' highest peak, in the mountainous Abruzzi, L'Aquila was Italy's largest city just outside the Papal States, yet it looked and felt much farther from Rome than the trip of fifty miles—three torturous days by stagecoach—would suggest. Although it was the capital of Abruzzo, its mostly shepherd and farm families, ramshackle cottages, beautiful ancient churches, pine trees, and medieval piazza's fountain and town-hall clock, which chimed ninety-nine times a day, probably made it look something like the Italianized Bavarian town Frederick II had imagined when, six centuries earlier, he had merged ninety-nine villages to form it. She initially liked it. "Sated with the shows of Rome," she reported to friends that L'Aquila's "intoxicating beauty" of surrounding and still snow-topped mountains, luxuriant olive and almond groves, and colorfully flowered valleys and grain fields were just what she needed. "I have seen a thousand landscapes," she wrote one friend, "any one of which might employ the thoughts of the painter for years. Not without reason the people dream that at the death of a saint columns of light are seen to hover on these mountains." Mostly, she felt she "chose for the best" because the "pure" mountain air, together with her daily regimen of perambulations on donkey or on foot, quickly restored her health. That and her free time seem to have allowed her to make substantial progress on her book. "Even thus, I think it will take three months to write out what has passed in my head and before my eyes for two years," she added cautiously. "It is a thousand pities, I could not do it in Winter, but I could not and there is an end." That same day she wrote to Arconati, in another of her probably conscious, startling pregnancy puns, "It grows upon me."[43]

As for the people of this "very beautiful" land, she liked them also at first. She had already gotten an appealing picture of nearby peasants from seeing them at Subiaco and Tivoli, where they had seemed very industrious on their beautiful "rich inheritance," which had only increased her desire that they no longer be "deprived of its benefits by bad institutions." Also, instead of Jesuits exploiting the Church's rituals, L'Aquila was filled with Passionists and Capuchins, who appeared to her much better than the monks who lived near the cities. "It looks very peaceful to see their drape[d] forms pacing up the hills," she wrote Newcomb, "and they have a healthy red in the cheek, unlike the vicious sallowness of monks of Rome. They get some life from their gardens and flowers, I suppose." Even the churches had an anticlerical air: "There is sweet music in these churches, they are dresst with fresh flowers, and the mountain breeze sweeps through them so freely, they do not smell too strong of incense." Equally appealing were two other lacks: there were no foreigners and, just as important, no one around who might confuse *her* with them. "I love to see their patriarchial ways of guarding the sheep, and tilling the fields," she wrote Emerson.

> They are a simple race, remote from the corruptions of foreign travel, they do not ask for money, but smile upon and bless me as I pass for the Italians love me; they say, I am so *simpatica*. I never see any English or Americans, and now think wholly in Italian. Only the surgeon who bled me the other day was proud to speak a little French, which he had learnt at Tunis! The ignorance of this people is amazing. I am to them a divine visitant, and instructive Ceres telling them wonderful tales of foreign customs and even legends of their own saints. They are people whom I could love and live with.[44]

After a few more weeks, however, Fuller wrote a little differently about her mythical-sounding L'Aquila neighbors. She had with her Giuditta Bonanni, the sister of a soldier in the Civic Guard whom Ossoli knew, "a lively Italian woman" with a "good heart" to cook her meals and wash her clothes in the nearby stream, who also facilitated her mixing with the local peasant women. What they spoke about in her "chats" with them, though, is not so clear. She did get a disconcerting taste of their political innocence when the peasant women persistently asked her "if Pius IX. was not *un gran carbonaro!*—a reputation," she wrote her sister Ellen, "which he surely ought to have forfeited by this time." As to how they really regarded *her*, although it was probably true they smiled and blessed her as they passed, she also, she conceded, "disturbed" them. "'*E sempre sola soletta,*' they said, '*eh perche?*'" With Newcomb she was more direct. "The country people say 'Povera, sola, soletta,' poor one, alone, all alone! the saints keep her,' as I pass. They think me some stricken deer to stay so apart from the herd." "Stricken deer" (from Virgil's *Aeneid* on Dido) probably more commonly expressed their feeling than "divine visitant, and instructive Ceres."[45]

Then there was the question of her identity. Since Ossoli addressed the envelopes of his letters to "Mrs. M. Ossoli," one presumes she was appearing as a married woman who, though, for some reason, had chosen to bear her child in the country without her husband. This partial deception did not always go smoothly. One day after arriving, by happenstance she ran into two "outstanding personalities here," the elderly poet Ferdinando de Torres and his brother Bartolomeo, who said something "very indiscreet" to Fuller's servants apparently about her and Ossoli, which their connections in Rome may have informed them about. The remark "much perturbed" Ossoli, whether because he took it as a slight or as an indication of how easily rumors of their liaison could filter back to Rome, and he immediately wrote her, seemingly seriously, "If you do not tell me exactly what it is, I may come to you soon to know these Signori of Aquila." Fuller, though, was unperturbed. She conceded that running into them "was not too prudent," but since it had happened, they should forget about it. And she liked the marchesi's "great polish and culture," and they liked her, probably because, like her French-speaking physician, they enjoyed having an educated American in their small country town. They frequently invited her to their castles, where they showed her their original old masters, manuscripts of famous authors like her old favorite Tasso, and their family archives of the "most interesting documents" on European political affairs. "With comments on these," she wrote her sister Ellen, "and legendary lore enough to furnish Cooper or Walter Scott with a thousand romances, they enriched me."[46]

Fuller's spirits seem to have maintained something of their highs of the spring, although a month of being apart from Ossoli and unremitting headaches took a toll. "Today I received nothing," she wrote Ossoli on June 27, five days after her upbeat accounts to her friends, "now for two weeks I have not received any papers, nor have I heard from you in reply to my last letters. I know nothing about the things that I am interested in; I feel lonely, imprisoned, too unhappy. . . . Do not fail to come on Saturday; I will die if left so[.] It is very hot here; it does not rain and I do not like to go out anymore. As I suffered from a terrible headache, I had a bloodletting, I am weak and suffer in my chest, the rest is not bad." After it dawned on her to check the post office rather than the bookstore, she found his letters. On July 1, fulfilling his promise "to come to your arms," he arrived with more papers and a bottle of "excellent cologne" from Soave's, a favorite store of Fuller in the Piazza di Spagna, and stayed for several days, which made her "more relaxed" and apparently more stoic about her physical state. "The midwife says that we must have patience and suffer this, as it is not unusual at this time," she wrote Ossoli on the eighth after he returned. "According to these women, one must think that this condition is really a martyrdom." Meanwhile, he wrote her almost daily and sent her packages of letters, newspapers, and medicine. She also attended to *his* woes over family conflicts and juggling his guard duties with managing property for his uncle, which made *him* demand letters from her "every post day." "Do not be 'very sad,' do not become so thin," she wrote in her letter on the eighth. "We must hope that destiny will get tired of persecuting us."[47]

Yet she remained deeply anxious about her pregnancy. "Once I had resolution to face my difficulties myself, and try to give only what was pleasant to others," she wrote Emerson on the eleventh, without, of course, saying what her new problems were. "But now that my courage has fairly given way, and the fatigue of life is beyond my strength, I do not prize myself, or expect others to prize me." She even conceded something that must have startled him a little. "I thought you were unjust, because you did not lend full faith to my spiritual experiences," she said, speaking of her angelic "illuminations" eight years earlier, "but I see you were quite right." A "true elixir" should have made her forever courageous in facing death and deprivation, but hers had not. "There must have been too much earth,— too much taint of weakness and folly. . . . I know now those same things, but at the present they are words, not living spells."[48]

Exacerbating her gyrating moods was her epistolary dance with family and friends. She had them send their letters to Rome, always referring to her whereabouts not as a town but as "my lonely mountain home" or the "Mountains of Central Italy," a ruse she would keep up all summer. She was equally coy about when she would return, variously mentioning months, a year, "several years," or more. Determined to keep them in the dark but pining for their reassurance, she made her correspondence into an emotional roller coaster. Sometimes she could even sound provocatively cool. "I will not tell you where,—I know not that I shall ever tell where," she wrote breezily to Ellen, boldly comparing her behavior to the practice of "the great Goethe," who, she said, portrayed himself in his *Italian Journey* as "hid thus in Italy. . . . Why should not . . . I enjoy this fantastic luxury of *incognito*?" On the other hand, she returned to obsessing as she had in the winter about her friends forgetting her; they had not, but that did not stop her from doing it. So she wrote letters, lots of them, informing Arconati that she had at least a hundred correspondents, and adding, quite plausibly, "It seems every day as if I had just written to each." Yet, when they replied, she often seemed almost as sad as when she heard nothing from them. "There were letters from my family," she wrote Ossoli on July 13. "They made me cry very much begging for my return."

He could not understand. "This ought to make you glad, and not make you weep," he replied, "learning that they are well, and thinking that every day which passed brings you nearer to seeing them again." Despite Ossoli's sensible but unrealistic advice, her warring emotions would color her letters for the remainder of her pregnancy.[49]

At the end of July, Fuller abruptly decided to leave L'Aquila. Her stay there, she later told a friend, had had its charms, living "wholly among Italians, amid the snow peaks, in the exquisite valleys of the Abruzzi," the "thousand landscapes" of painterly beauty, and her acquaintances with the noblemen in their baronial hillside castles. To Ossoli, however, she afterward confessed, "I am glad I left, I was too bored there and too far from you." This was undoubtedly true, although the impetus for moving came from another source. L'Aquila was part of the Naples of the reactionary Bourbon Ferdinand II, and the "troops of these infants" (as she called them), whom he had been withdrawing from the war in Lombardy since his May 15 coup restoring his absolute rule, had been noisily invading her inn for meals. By mid-July, with Radetsky accelerating his Austrian counteroffensive southward and Ferdinand's Neapolitan soldiers continuing to filter into L'Aquila, the situation, she thought, was becoming perilous. "I do not know if I will be asked to flee from here and come to Rieti," she wrote Ossoli on July 13. "I ask every day but so far I hear nothing certain." After her brush with exposure by the indiscreet Torres brothers, which had probably unsettled her more than she had let on to Ossoli, she decided it was time to go. On the twenty-ninth, after Neapolitan soldiers started seizing and imprisoning people from nearby villages, she hurriedly left for Rieti in Lazio, just over the border of Umbria and safely within the Papal States.[50]

Moving twenty-five miles back west did not require many difficult physical adjustments. Although then (as now) comparatively depopulated and forlorn-looking, Rieti still had ancient Umbrian remains and houses from Roman-era times, which Fuller found intriguing. She also liked its geographical frame of sunlit mountains overlooking the twelve-square-mile plain with the Velino River rapidly snaking through the center of the town on its way north to Terni. While Rieti lacked L'Aquila's luxurious foliage, it had ample groves and vineyards, whose "most delicious" figs, olives, almonds, peaches, grapes, and salads made up most of her diet that summer, and all for a few pennies a day, making for the cheapest living she had found in Italy. Her brick-paved, upper-floor apartment had charms for her as well. Although sparsely furnished, it was spacious and separate from the family's rooms, with a chamber for Giuditta and a picturesque view of the plain, a ruined tower, and an old cypress-lined casino. She especially liked having off her bedroom a "rude," long wooden "*loggia*," or veranda, on which in the evening she could take walks in the moonlight and watch its reflection glistening below in the gentle-flowing, willow-hedged river, or from where during the morning she could see Giuditta washing their clothes on a large stone, leaving them "white as snow." "I never in my life had a room I liked as I do this," she exulted to Richard after her second week.[51]

The people in Rieti, however, proved more of a challenge for her. Probably because the town had fewer provincial elites than L'Aquila, she kept more to herself, which she liked for her work but which discontented the citified Giuditta, who wondered out loud, she wrote Richard, "I do not 'go mad writing.'" Yet, as in L'Aquila, she mixed in snatches with the local peasants, who seem to have been proud to have her in their town. Every Sunday, she wrote her mother, one contadina came in her colorfully embroidered silk holiday dress, bringing an immense basket of grapes and a pair of live chickens, "to be eaten by me for her sake, ('*per amore mio*'), and wanted no present, no reward; it was, as she said, 'for the honor and pleasure of her acquaintance.'" She did notice two less appealing qualities of the place. One was its ubiquitous dirt, coating animals and people alike, making her glad she had Giuditta to do her cooking, washing, and ironing. The other was the people themselves. The men seemed lazier than in other towns in central Italy, and more brutal in their treatment of their women. She reported repeatedly hearing "the cries of mothers and wives beaten at night by sons and husbands for their diversion after drinking," which women used in turn as "the excuse for falsehood, 'I *dare not* tell my husband, he would be ready to kill me.'" Pleasures and generosity mixed with violence and deception would sum up much of her experience in rustic Rieti.[52]

Meanwhile, Fuller faced two difficulties outside the town. One was aggravating confusions over money remittances. Richard's transfer never arrived because someone had forged her signature and cashed it, causing her bank to put a hold on his second one. Her dealings with Greeley were even more of a fiasco. Earlier in the spring, although financially squeezed, he had promised to send her a remittance for $600—$100 from what he owed her and $500 as a personal loan. By that summer, however, with no word from him, and having spent most of her money on presents for friends before leaving Rome, she wrote frantically to Richard that she would soon run out of money and be trapped in Rieti. In mid-August, after getting a letter from Greeley regretting her decision to end her column—but failing to mention the money—she exploded. "In an evil hour," she wrote Richard, she had trusted to Greeley for her summer expenses, but her life was becoming a nightmare of debts and privations. "*Now* I do not know what will become of me," she cried. "I shall not have the means to leave Italy, nor even to return to Rome, if indeed I could still have food and lodging here." Nor was that all. "Mr Greeley," she wrote, "shows no disposition to further my plans. Liberality on the part of the Tribune would have made my path easy," probably referring to not getting her an advance for a book. "I feel that if anyone in America had been interested to enable me here to live and learn on my own way, I could have made, at least, a rich intellectual compensation. But people rarely think one like me worth serving or saving."[53]

This was a bitterly sweeping blast (as an afterthought, she excluded the Springs, the Mannings, Eliza Farrar, and Richard and their mother from her indictment), venting probably, besides her anxiety about money and her impending childbirth, years of accumulated resentment over her impecunious state. Greeley, who kept hearing about her plight from her family and friends, was getting fairly annoyed himself. "I have to imagine a medley of bad luck and hallucination to account for this imbroglio," he wrote her at the end of July. Finally, after fruitless missions by Ossoli to bankers and the post office, in mid-September she got Greeley's letter explaining where he had sent the remittance. But that was not the end of it for Greeley. After "railing" to her friends and family about her complaints to them about his forgetting her, he wrote her a testy letter. "Well, just as I had forgotten *that*," he practically shouted, and his difficulty with raising a surprisingly large sum of money when he had no idea why she had even left Rome, "along came your notification that *you would write no more!*—and that amazed me. Once a month would have served me very well, but to have you break off utterly, just as Italy and Europe were in the throes of a great Revolution, and when I thought I had made an effort to oblige you, struck me as unkind. But let it pass now, and, if useful, we can talk about it over when we meet again." Two weeks later, she resumed her nearly seven-month-suspended column, and he resumed his gossipy and self-pitying letters to her about politics and family.[54]

Besides transatlantic misunderstandings over money, which would plague her all her years in Italy, Fuller suffered an immediate conundrum. Like the question of leaving L'Aquila, this one, too, came from the fortunes of war, now turning sharply in Austria's favor. On July 14, Radetsky's army, having crushed the papal troops in several cities in Venetia the month before, crossed the Po dividing Lombardy from the Papal States and reoccupied Ferrara, throwing both chambers, the pope's ministry, the Civic Guard, and the clubs into a tumult over how to respond. On the twenty-fifth, following brilliant soldiering by the eighty-two-year-old Radetsky at the Battle of Custoza, Charles Albert was soundly defeated, and on August 5, he signed the Salasco treaty, ending the war with Austria. "What times in Rome!" she exclaimed, the day after arriving in Rieti, to James C. Hooker, her banker at Maquay, Packenham. "If it were not too far," she said, seemingly unconcerned about exposure, "I would go there a few days, to see for myself." But with Austrian troops now massing in Romagna, she did not have to go that far to court danger. On August 8, a couple of days after Ossoli visited her in Rieti, an Austrian detachment invaded Bologna, whose enraged citizens managed to repel them. After the news reached Rome four days later, the ministry called for volunteers to defend the Papal States from the Austrian aggressor. Would Ossoli, now a sergeant in the Civic Guard, join them with Fuller's childbirth date so fast approaching?[55]

They agonized about it. "It seems very strange how everything is going against us," she wrote him on August 13. "The fact that Bologna has resisted is good, but that this would make it likely for you to leave at this moment!" But, anguishing over the suffering of her Milanese friends now back under Austrian rule and the danger to the Risorgimento if Rome failed to counter Austrian aggression, she quickly added: "Do what is right for your honor. I do not really think that the pope will decide to send the Civic Guard, but if it happens, and if it is necessary for your honor, leave and I will try to be strong." "All goes wrong," she wrote Richard. "But I do not quite despair yet. France may aid. If not Italy [w]ill be too hot or too cold to hold me." With each new political twist and turn, the couple went back and forth about whether Ossoli should leave for the front or come to her in

Rieti. "My state is the most deplorable that can be," he wrote her in a rare display of despair, heightened by his anxiety about quarrels with his "odious" brothers and worries about losing his property management job for his uncle. Remarkably, desperate herself about money and told by her doctor she was "close," following a "terrible night" of nosebleeds, she had the presence of mind to give him finally a little shrewd counsel: "My love, I feel a deep sympathy with your pains, but I am not able to give you perfectly wise advice. Only I think it is a very bad moment to enter the army other than for the reason of duty, of honor. The pope so cold, his minister irresolute, nothing will be well done nor successfully. As one hopes for the intervention of France and England, it is also uncertain if the war continues. If not, you leave Rome and the employment with your uncle for noth ing." He stayed put.[56]

Although the French did not intervene, the outcome supported her judgment that he should not go. The last week in August, the Austrians withdrew, and the pope suspended the departure of the troops. The crisis had been averted. On the twenty-second, she wrote breezily, if nervously: "To wait!! What a bore. But—if I were sure to do well, I would rather pass this ordeal before you coming, but when I think that it is possible for me to die alone without touching a dear hand, I prefer to wait. . . . It makes me unhappy that it is necessary to wait so many days before you come, so many so many. I am happy that now I have your little portrait, often I look at it." He immediately answered, "I shall be awaiting a message from you to come immediately to your arms." She wrote on the twenty-fifth: "I will wait for you on Sunday morning and again I will have your coffee ready; but no more now, because writing is truly difficult." Two days later, on Sunday, he arrived in Rieti. A week later, on September 5, with the help of a midwife, Fuller gave birth to a boy, whom they soon named Angelo Eugene Philip, after his father, Fuller's oldest brother, and Ossoli's father.[57]

VI

Angelo's birth did not dampen Fuller and Ossoli's consuming concern with the fast-moving Risorgimento. After returning on September 6, he resumed sending her newspapers, pamphlets, leaflets, and bulletins. He also relayed observations and café rumors sometimes with his own added democratic apercus. That day he reported on the sullenness detectable on the streets and among units of the Civic Guard toward the temporizing pope as he drove from his residence at the Quirinal to the Vatican. Yet in another, he advised her to take with a grain of salt the optimistic reports about political developments in the north in the Roman newspapers he sent her. Nor was he oblivious to the fact that not all "the people" were exactly Mazzinian Democrats. "All the way that he traversed in Trastevere was adorned as a fiesta, triumphal arches, and many shouts," he wrote in a subsequent letter of the pope's arrival there to assist at a mass. "How ignorant they are, poor people!" The following month he reported an even more depressing "sign of change." A mob, after a tussle with a group of Jews returning to the ghetto, whose walls Pius had ordered knocked down earlier that spring, launched an all-night assault on its inmates, severely wounding several and burning and plundering stores and houses until the rioters were finally quelled by a large contingent of Civic Guards and carabinieri. "Now to day it continues as last night, except that some Jews are seen, much disheartened," he wrote sympathetically, "their shops are all locked and it seems as if they were besieged." "This hatred between Jews and Romans must produce very bad effects some day if not now," Fuller coolly responded, as if the only overriding problem was the "effects" of mutual ethnic hatred on the Risorgimento. Ossoli knew better: Jews were the victims, and reactionaries orchestrated the attacks on them. Writing several days later, he excitedly reported that one of those arrested was "a man of the Gregorian party!" who had spent the whole night in Rione Monti enlisting "the lower people to go and make mischief in the Ghetto." "God knows what his intentions were," Ossoli said, but it was obvious, he added, as they found on him 500 scudi in gold, that he was in the pay of the Gregorians to make the riot a "bond of union" of their party. Ossoli was no mere naïve tail to Fuller's radical kite.[58]

Still, while politically attuned, they remained preoccupied with their newborn, who initially was not easy. "Dearest Husband," Fuller wrote Ossoli on September 7, "I feel much better than I hoped. The child is doing well too but he still cries a lot, and I hope he will be calmer when you come." Although the baby does seem to have been colicky, she actually had two bigger problems. One was her inability to produce much milk, which she attributed to a "nursing fever." The other was Giuditta, who seems to have been unable or unwilling to breastfeed Angelino, and Fuller's references to "perfidious" Giuditta and her "infamy" suggest it was the latter. In any case, Fuller peremptorily dismissed her. "She cannot do anything now," she wrote Ossoli the next day. "I [will] take one who can also breastfeed since my milk is not sufficient." The wet nurse she hired was a young woman from the town named Chiara, whom she liked but who after her own baby became ill had to stay home, leaving Fuller alone with Angelino, who refused her breast and cried all night. Now exhausted as well as ill, she could only dictate her letter to her landlord, which alarmed Ossoli, making him, he wrote her, "so sad that I cannot adequately express it." Within a few days, however, the nurse's baby became better, and so did Angelino, who, evidently now satisfied with his nurse's milk and his mother's body, started sleeping soundly through the night. Obviously still nervous about having no experience mothering and doing so in a tiny Italian peasant village four thousand miles away from family and friends, she nonetheless answered Ossoli in the tones of a mother decisively bonding to her baby:

> We must have courage but it is a great anxiety to be alone and so ignorant with a baby in these first days of his life. When he will be one month old I will have more rest; then he will be stronger for the changes which he will have to bear. Now he is well; he is beginning to sleep well and is very beautiful for his age and everybody, without knowing what name I intended to give him, called him Angelino because he is so nice. He has your mouth, hands, feet; I think his eyes will be turquoise. He is very naughty; understands well, is very obstinate to have his will.

The young father's courage grew vicariously in tandem with his wife's. "I rejoice . . . to hear that the dear baby is so lovely," he wrote, adding confidently, "as to his obstinacy we will not make much account of it, as it is the usual way of babies." And the next day: "I receive your dear letter, which tells me so much of our lovely baby, which makes me so happy that I am eager to give him a kiss, to be obliged to delay it gives me pain." Indeed, their love for Angelino and their struggles with childrearing seem to have bonded *them* more closely. In their letters one finds, along with Ossoli's expressive voice, invariably missing from descriptions of him, a mutual tenderness, compassion, and easygoing joking that suggest a loving and everyday intimacy that Fuller had never before experienced in a heterosexual relationship.[59]

What made her rearing of Angelino difficult, of course, was having to keep him a secret outside of Rieti. Contrary to the usual impression of her leaving him as easy, Fuller anguished about it. "How many nights I have passed entire in contriving every possible means by which, through resolution and energy on my part, I could avoid that one sacrifice," she confessed several months later to Caroline Sturgis. "It was impossible." In fact, she originally had hoped she could bring him with them. "He is so dear," she wrote Ossoli on September 19, "it makes him so happy to sleep on my breast; and I know very well that no one else can take care of him as well as I." Indeed, two days later she had an idea: Angelino's new nurse Chiara would love to go to Rome and keep him while she lived at her brother's place and looked for work as a dressmaker. However, Ossoli balked. "This matter ought to be treated with the greatest imaginable caution," he carefully answered, "since my thought would be, to keep the baby out of Rome, for the sake of greater secrecy, if we can find a good nurse who will take care of him like a mother." Yet she still resisted the conclusion. "I feel the truth in what you say that we must be very cautious in hiring a nurse," she answered. "I will wait about everything to take counsel with you. Only think that if the baby is out of Rome, you can not see him very often. On the other hand, without doubt the air of the country would be better for his health." In her next letter she tossed aside the qualifications. "He is always so nice, how would it ever be possible for me to leave him?" she asked him. "I wake up in the night, look at him, and I think ah, it is impossible to leave him," adding in the next, "he is still so pretty; he indeed has gestures as delicate as a ballerina's." Three days later, on October 1, Ossoli arrived, and they deliberated.[60]

They had common ground. She evidently agreed that keeping their marriage and child secret from his family in Rome required that Angelino remain in Rieti. As for the option of *her* staying in Rieti, she had already dismissed it. Besides her boredom with the place and her eagerness to return to politically exciting Rome, they badly missed and needed each other, which could hardly be satisfied, they both knew, by the short visits allowed by Ossoli's guard duties and work for his uncle. There were also health considerations. As she had intimated in her letter to Ossoli on September 19, she feared that remaining that winter would be dangerous to her health, and that was a plausible concern. Almost every winter for the past decade, she had fallen ill, and it would be hard to imagine how, especially right after childbirth, in a room with a brick floor, drafty windows, and no fireplace except in the distant kitchen, she could have escaped getting seriously ill. Finally, and most decisively for her, there was her writing. In addition to her *Tribune* column, which required her to be in Rome, the center of the roiling political scene, so too did her book, which she had come to see as vital to both her reputation and that of the Risorgimento, as well as a crucial source of desperately needed money for her family. That last point cannot be overstressed: over the next year whenever she reconsidered her decision to separate from Angelino, she dropped the idea as a financial impossibility. So, despite her growing delight and love toward Angelo, after a couple more weeks, she decided she would leave him, but not for too long. "I need to stay in Rome for at least one month and to be close to you," she wrote Ossoli in mid-October, "but I want to be free to come back here if I am too anxious and grieved about him," so he should try to rent an apartment for only a month and four months maximum. And it had to be cheap, because now "I must be very economical, for the child so beloved to us." Despite his "unwearied" efforts, Giovanni failed to locate a place both inexpensive and short-term, so she decided when she got to the city to take a hotel room temporarily while they looked together for one. "The child is indeed too good and beautiful today," she wrote, reminding him of their purpose. "I could die for him."[61]

Once the question of leaving Angelo was settled, however shakily, the next question was how they would get along in the meantime. Throughout that September and October, they had increasingly disquieting experiences that did not promise very comforting answers. They had begun at the time of Fuller's initial fever and nursing difficulties and soon escalated into a servant-and-landlord problem of an almost gothic character. At the time of her confrontation with Giuditta, the young woman had hotly disputed Fuller's charge and had threatened to take it up with Ossoli when she returned to Rome, which had outraged Fuller. She may have feared that Giuditta would broadcast their marriage and child in Rome. At least that seems suggested by her reaction to a servile letter Guiditta would write to her just before Fuller left Rieti, moaning about her family's illnesses and poverty and begging her to forgive her and "deign" to meet her and let her "carry the baby." "You know that because of the wicked Giuditta," Fuller darkly speculated to Ossoli, "it is possible that it could become very unpleasant for me to be in Rome this winter." Still, she at least thought they had one good thing going now that she had gotten rid of Giuditta: besides having Chiara, "the house where I live is very good for me, and I can have advice and help."[62]

She soon discovered her error about the Rietians, "the most ferocious and mercenary population of Italy," as she would later describe them to Caroline. "I did not know this when I went there," Fuller would write of her initial pastoral fantasies. "I expected to be solitary and quiet among poor people. But they looked on *the marchioness* as an ignorant *Inglese*, and they fancy all *Inglesi* have wealth untold. Me they were bent on plundering in every way." At the time, though, she tried to look on the best side. "Mr. Giovanni is good to me, but his sisters are detestable, meddling in everything and so stingy and self-centered," she wrote

Ossoli two weeks after firing Giuditta; "they want me to save money, so they can have it for themselves." Still, "I try to keep the peace with them; one can find bad people everywhere and these, if greedy and vulgar, at least are not as perfidious as Giuditta." But things got worse. "The family is more displeased with me than ever," she wrote Ossoli after he returned to Rome; they had discovered her buying wine elsewhere after *she* discovered them charging her 20 percent more than they did anyone else while boasting to her servants about their devotion to saving her money. "But Giovanni will be very happy anyway if you take a good gift for him," she wrote Ossoli, "and this is what I want and then to say goodbye to this house." In fact, Mr. Giovanni's wants were several, which Fuller learned two weeks later when she came upon him aggressively trying to "*corrupt*" Chiara, the prettiest young woman in Rieti. "[Chiara] told [Mr.] Giovanni that if he talks to her again she will come to me," she wrote frantically to Ossoli. "This I can tell only you, she has a great fear that her husband will find out. Also he told her that he has done so much for us and we have not given him anything." After calming down a "very angry" Chiara, Fuller convinced her not to leave her at least before she left Rieti. By the end of October, though, she sounded trapped in a household that was driving her crazy. "I dare not relax too much, because I find that if I don't continue, don't insist on spying on all these people, they will take advantage of me." (And probably with looks of great sincerity: William Clarke reported that when he went to interview the sisters after Fuller's death, they "wept much and spoke with much affection of her.") Her expected "peace" with Angelino was over.[63]

For the moment, though, she faced two pressing problems. One was getting Angelino vaccinated for smallpox, which since the summer had been spreading in Rieti, but the doctor, after promising to inject him with cowpox serum, for weeks kept saying he had not yet gotten it. "This Mogliani is detestable, untrustworthy like all the others," she wrote angrily to Ossoli on October 20. People were dying all around her, she added, while she was anxious to leave: "Who knows how long I will have to stay here for this, enough—I do not sleep at night and I cry all day; I am so disgusted, but you cannot help me, you are too far away." Mogliani finally suggested that she get the vaccine from a chemist in Rome whom he knew, and Fuller right away wrote Ossoli: "You do not have to say who you are or anything more than that you are asking him on behalf of Mogliani of Rieti not to delay." Meanwhile, although Ossoli warned her against ruining her health by staying in all the time rather than trusting in "God who has given him to us," she kept Angelino inside with her. "I dare not go out with the baby any longer," she wrote Ossoli on the twenty-eighth, "I thought I was safe taking him to the garden of the Bishop and [then] last week a child died there from small pox and it was mere chance that he didn't catch it. So I stay like a prisoner and I don't know for how long." The next day, she got a letter from Ossoli saying he had gotten the serum and was sending it "immediately" in a box with a bottle of cologne water.[64]

With Ossoli's arrival only days away, as important as getting Angelino inoculated was getting him baptized, a task that proved equally difficult. The first difficulty was recruiting a godfather. The ideal choice, she wrote Giovanni on October 7, was her friend Mickiewicz: "He knows about the existence of the baby[;] he is a devout Catholic, he is a distinguished man who could be a help to him in his future life, and I want him to have some friend in case something happens to us." But Mickiewicz at the end of June had left Milan for Paris to direct his Polish Legion and could not leave, so the following week she threw the ball back to Ossoli. "You have to find a *godfather*," she wrote. "Giovanni says that without the *legal agency* of some person the baptism will not be legal; and if it is not done while we are here the priest &c will make a great deal of trouble for us after our departure and probably they will in Rome. . . . I am very sorry, but it is necessary for you to speak to some friend." That, however, was evidently what Ossoli, presumably out of fear of exposure, did *not* want to do, so he then suggested Mr. Giovanni, although he himself worried whether it would be "prudent." "Do not think for a moment about Giovanni as godfather," Fuller shot back on the fifteenth, even before Chiara told her he had nearly raped her. "It would be, I think to trust too much in him; I do not think he is worth it. It is better for you to trust in someone your equal who as a gentleman will protect your secret." They then considered Ossoli's nephew Pietro, who was nearly his age and one of the only persons in his family other than his sister Angela with whom he got along, but he remained reluctant, mostly, it would seem, because he did not intend to tell Pietro that he and Margaret were the couple needing his proxy. "You must realize," she said, his nephew would finally hear about their marriage from someone whom Ossoli had apparently told or who had somehow found out about it. He apparently agreed, for he soon asked Pietro, who consented, and contacted a lawyer friend, who gave him the form of the "procura" or proxy dated November 4, authorizing "Mr. Gio. Angelo Marquis Ossoli to be able for me and in my name and stead raise at the baptismal font the infant born to Mrs. [blank space] married to Mr. [blank space]." "We can fill it up when I come to you," Ossoli assured her.[65]

While grappling with these two potential disasters, the Ossolis waited nervously. Although Chiara, as she had promised, did not quit after Mr. Giovanni's assaults, she did cut back her time for Angelino after her baby again became ill. With that burden, the now "very heavy" cranky Angelino, and another bout of severe headaches, Fuller became weighed down both physically and emotionally, with her only relief coming at night from walking on the veranda, holding him, and watching the river. "I could not sleep at all those months," she would later tell Caroline Tappan. "I do not know how I lived." But Chiara did agree to nurse and care for Angelino, which was a great relief. "Signora Rosati," she wrote Ossoli on October 8, "said so many good things of Chiara, she also said that her aunt is excellent and all the brothers are good. Mogliani says the same thing, this comforts me a little about the prospect of leaving my child." Meanwhile, the dominant mood of the couple's last letters was excited expectation. In the midst of running down bankers, gold dealers, apartments, apothecaries, and lawyers, Giovanni wrote Margaret, "I am always anxiously expecting tidings from you, (which I do not receive this morning,) that I may come to your arms, and give so many kisses to our dear love, as well as to you." She answered on October 28 with an appropriate tribute to their "dear love." "When he smiles in his sleep, how he makes my heart beat fast! He has grown much fatter and all white, he starts to play [and] dance," she added, evidently, like a good peasant mother, secure in the knowledge that fatness was a sign of health. "You will have much pleasure in seeing him again, he sends you many kisses. He bends his head toward me when I ask for a kiss." And for Giovanni himself: "I love you much more than during the first days because I have proof of how good and pure your heart is."[66]

As with much else in Rieti, the remaining time had a couple of snags. They had planned for Ossoli to come on Saturday, which was All Soul's Day, but his uncle would not let him off, to which Margaret responded caustically, "I am really sorry that your uncle is the only Italian who does not observe the holidays, just for our aggravation." Since Ossoli could not get a regular seat, he had to ride at night in "that cursed" small mail car (as she sympathetically called it). "I will prepare the trunks and all beforehand," she told him, so as to be free to be always with you." In the early evening, he took his bag and the large straw basket in which Fuller kept her books, stuffed it with Angelino's toys and clothes to give to Chiara, and rode in the cold air and pouring rain until arriving at Rieti the following morning, Sunday, November 5. Later that day Angelino was baptized in "the H[oly] M[other] Church." The couple then returned to Fuller's apartment to pick up their baggage and walk to the stagecoach that would take them to Rome, where their ingenuity in protecting themselves while fulfilling their political duties would undergo its biggest trial.[67]

CHAPTER ELEVEN

Foreign Correspondence
(1848–1849)

I

If the couple's journey was any premonition, they needed to be careful. They had planned to leave Rieti early the next morning of November 6, 1848, but decided instead to take a stagecoach hired by a marchioness's family, leaving a few hours later. While waiting they learned that their original coach, as it had crossed the bridge over the flooding Turano, had broken through the piling and plunged into the freezing river with all its passengers, severely injuring several. Two days later, after the rain abated, they set out again, this time with thirty passengers in two large stagecoaches pulled by all the route's horses, who gingerly trotted under the moonlight through the half-underwater road and marshes lining the Tiber until they reached the gate of Rome. "The scene was beautiful, and I enjoyed it highly," Fuller afterward perkily wrote her mother. "I have never yet felt afraid when really in the presence of danger," she added, generally accurately, "though sometimes in its apprehension."[1]

Meanwhile, back in Boston, her family and friends were beginning to feel afraid *for* her. No one had heard from her since her August 16 letter to Richard from the misleadingly identified "Mountains of Southern Italy." Their mother begged him for news of Margaret "to relieve my intense anxiety." "Where is she & when is she coming home?" a perplexed Eliza Farrar asked a couple of weeks after Fuller returned to Rome. More ominous, after getting back, she wrote letters like this one in late November to Sarah Shaw: "My private fortunes are dark and tangled. . . . I have thrown myself on God, and perhaps he will make my temporal state very tragical." Fuller's Italian life was beginning to look to her friends like a disconcerting mystery. Sarah Clarke impatiently asked her whether she intended to live there "always," teasing her in a subsequent letter that fall, "I do not know but we shall forget you if you stay away much longer." Many especially could not understand why, in view of her recent illness, she did not come back immediately. Even Greeley, while grateful for her "admirable" dispatches, was dumbfounded as to how she could remain "willfully absent" from her young country. "I cannot comprehend your long stay in such a region of the dead," he told her, adding if she did not return soon, "you will grow old yourself. I am sure one must grow wrinkled and rummyeyed by gazing at ruins—ruins." Explanations circulated. Lydia Maria Child speculated that Fuller was so much in love with Italy, "she will not return until she has expended her last dollar." Periodicals expressed opinions. "Miss Fuller's letters have of late grown quite rare in the Tribune," Duyckinck informed his *Literary World* readers in his "What is Talked About" column in early December, "—it is said, from the engagement of the writer upon a book at Rome."[2]

From one quarter, the talk was not so sympathetic. In late October Lowell published his *Fable for Critics*, a satirical survey of American authors, in which he finally made good on his promise "to settle my account with her" for wounding his professional career with her demolition of his writing. Initially, probably out of fear of angering Fuller's fans, many of whom were mutual friends, he had hesitated paying her back for her "ill-natured turn." "She is a very foolish, conceited woman, who has got together a great deal of information, but not enough *knowledge* to save her from being ill-tempered," he had told his fellow Fuller-disparager Briggs. "However, the temptation may be too strong for me." It evidently was. Although virtually all of his studied jocular send-ups were at least somewhat good-natured, his swipes at Fuller, while occasionally clever (such as her speaking "with an I-turn-the-crank-of-the-Universe air") were mostly mean or simply false, notably in his lines (following "She will take an old notion, and make it her own, / By saying it o'er in her Sibylline tone")

> There is one thing she owns in her own single right,
> It is native and genuine—namely, her spite;
> Though, when acting as censor, she privately blows
> A censer of vanity 'neath her own nose.[3]

Not surprisingly, Lowell's "series of jokes by a Wonderful Quiz" stirred up a critical hornet's nest, mostly unfavorable to Lowell. Partly, Fuller's critically acclaimed *Papers on Literature and Art* made them ill timed. In a telling turnabout, her detractor Griswold, in his new anthology *Female Poets of America,* confessed after rereading her books "some change of opinion in her favor," and now ranked her, for her wide literary culture and facile writing, among the first female authors in the world! Even conservative journals did not help Lowell much. In a rare convergence of opinion, Poe writing in the *Southern Literary Messenger* echoed the *North American Review*'s critic in wondering darkly why Lowell had gotten so worked up about the "Transcendental blue-stocking": "The reader is all the time aiming to think that so unsurpassable a—(*what* shall we call her?—we wish to be civil,) a transcendentalist as Miss Fuller, should, by *such* a criticism, have had the power to put a respectable poet in *such* a passion." From the ideological left, the Fourierist *Harbinger* put the point more chivalrously: "We regret that the poet should have been tempted into such retaliation upon a woman."[4]

Private Boston opinion was not any friendlier. "Miranda is too good," Fuller's envious former schoolmate Holmes predictably wrote to Lowell, adding with labored smugness, "I have heard of a peg to hang a thought on, but if I want a thought to hang a Peg on I shall know where to go in the future." Fuller's friends, however, howled at the caricature's unfairness but, even more, the irony of Lowell pummeling her for *her* spitefulness. Unlike Lowell, Elizabeth Peabody noted, mostly rightly, Fuller never answered all the attacks on her "with one particle of personal resentment." Several thought his lines were "too sharp" and juvenile. "I am sure it would be better for his reputation," Sarah Clarke later observed to Higginson, "if that 'Fable' with so many beautiful things in it had not been marred by the unmannerly attack upon a dear and valued friend of those persons he so charmingly praises." That was essentially William Story's opinion. Later that spring, when he and Emelyn had returned to Rome, in an otherwise appreciative letter about his *Fable*, he added, "There is but one thing I regretted, and that was that you drove your arrow so sharply through Miranda." That was too bad. "Because fate has really been unkind to her, and because she depends on her pen for her bread-and-water (and that is nearly all she has to eat), and because she is her own worst enemy, and because through her disappointment and disease, which embitter every one, she has struggled most stoutly and manfully, I could have wished you had let her pass scot-free." Although a bit patronizing (as if she *was* guilty of something), considering the two men's close friendship and Lowell's touchiness, it was no weak riposte.[5]

It certainly got to Lowell, who insisted to Story that he had penned his portrait "without any *malice*" and claimed "the parts about Miss Fuller as errors of the press." As for Story's tale of Fuller's woes, he professed he did not know she was poor but had assumed her Uncle Abraham had made her independent.

> I only knew that she was malicious, and it was not what she had written of me, but what I had heard of her saying, which seemed to demand the intervention of the satiric Nemesis. You may be sure I have felt more sorry about it than any one; only I always reflect *after* the thing is done. Nevertheless I imagine the general verdict was "Served her right," though it was also regretted that castigation was inflicted by my particular hand.

Most of this was disingenuous, as was obviously his nervy claim that his three pages of abuse, more than he had dished out to any other author including even Cooper, were a "misprint." Not much less so was his insistence that Fuller's public dismissal of his writing had not inspired his "satiric Nemesis." (Elsewhere he would claim he was defending not *his* honor but Longfellow's!) As for his expression of sorrow, his "Served her right" effectively canceled that. In any case, if he did regret his "misprint," he had the chance to correct it in later editions, but he never did. It is not known whether anyone else who knew Fuller in Italy besides the Storys read Lowell's assault, but if they had, they would have no doubt been struck by its ludicrous contrast with her life there.[6]

II

Both Child's and Duyckinck's speculations back home about why she was lingering in Rome were right as far as they went. She *was* making the "most vehement efforts" in writing her book. At the same time, the still sporadically sunny weather made her resolve, she told William Story, "*never* to make my hay when the sun shines: *i.e.,* to give no fine day to books and pen." That and her book were probably why she put off for nearly a month restarting her "too laborious" and "ill paid" dispatches. And, despite her "dark and tangled" private fortunes, she *was* in love with her life in Rome. "O Rome, *my* country bad as the winter damp is, and lazy as the climate makes me," she wrote to Emelyn Story shortly after arriving, "I would rather live here than any where else in the world." It certainly surpassed Florence, where the Storys had gone at the end of the previous winter, which she continued to dismiss, excepting the galleries and churches, as woefully un-Italian. "I do not like it, for the same reason you *do*," she wrote William, trying to lure them back to Rome, "because it seems like home. It seems a kind of Boston to me,—the same good and the same ill; I have had enough of both. But," she added, "I have so many dear friends in Boston, that I must always wish to go there sometimes." Go to Florence to experience Boston? America was sounding further off than ever.[7]

Then, too, Rome just then seemed especially delightful. Its political tumult had driven out almost all foreigners, including, happily, the English "Murray guide book mob," which had the added benefit of collapsing rents. She continued to disdain the resident artists' "dabbling and pretension" but reverenced more than ever the "relics of the past" ("we should do nothing but sit, and weep, and worship"). She fell in love all over again with the city's pastoral landscape of interwoven vineyards, gardens, and walks in the villas surrounded by "such ceaseless music of the fountains and from every high point the Campagna and Tiber so near." What she really loved was Rome's magical atmosphere, likening it in her first dispatch to a mist enveloping the everyday and transcendent alike: "The very dust magnetizes you, and thousand spells have been chaining you in every careless, every murmuring moment." Indeed, the city's past spells satisfied opposite moods. One was "Repose!"—"for whatever be the revolutions, tumults, panics, hopes of the present day, . . . the great Past enfolds us, and the emotions of the moment cannot here importantly disturb that impression." Yet equally enveloping was a mythic political hope very much on her mind in *that* moment. "Myriad lives still linger here," speaking of the city's burial grounds beneath the countryside's domes and temples, "awaiting one great summons."[8]

The quotidian parts also seem to have fallen back into place. Her new apartment at number 60 in the Piazza Barberini had figured as the narrator's dwelling in Hans Christian Andersen's *Improvisatoren*, but its main charms were quite real. The sunshine and soft breezes of "pure air" wafted in through its high windows and spacious room, which was both comfortable and elegant enough to double as a parlor. From its front window she could see across the street the Fontana del Tritone, Bernini's masterpiece with the merman Triton blowing a spindly column of water up into the air through a conch shell, and the art-filled Barberini Palace, as well as, a little further to the south, the pope's Quirinal Palace and Gardens. For all this she paid less than she had for her dark, cramped quarters the previous winter, allowing her, with a two-dollar-a-week food budget, she told Emelyn, to "screw . . . my expenses down to the lowest possible peg." Even her neighbors were an improvement. The childless owners, she told her mother, were "the dearest, delightful old couple" who tended flowers and caged birds on their balcony. Treating her and her neighbor, a Prussian sculptor, as their children, yet, unlike her former "cunning" *padrona* the marchioness, they remained too delicate and too busy to intrude. The tenants on the stories below at least sound colorful: "a frightful Russian princess with moustaches, and a footman who ties her bonnet for her; and a fat English lady, with a fine carriage, who gives all her money to the church, and has made for the house a terrace of flowers that would delight you." The only intruder she had to worry about was the priest living in the attic, who insisted on making Fuller's fire when her landlady was away and "pays himself for his trouble, by asking a great many questions."[9]

Less happily, most of her friends in the American colony were gone. "I am almost alone in Rome," she lamented to Emelyn, "there is hardly a person I know here." With Fuller, however, "alone" was a relative thing. She still had around both Heath and most of her artist friends, including the Crawfords, the Cropseys, and Charles Callahan Perkins, later an art critic and founder of the Museum of Fine Arts in Boston. The Italian friend she most often saw was Pietro Maestri, a former leader of Milan's defense committee, who was in Rome to organize the Mazzinians. And she had Ossoli. Although he was still living at his sister's house, listing himself in the directory as a "scapolo" (bachelor), he saw her daily, looking after her practical affairs and giving her the news he picked up in the cafés, evidently without revealing himself as her husband. "But to you I may tell," she wrote to William Story, who knew of their friendship, "that I always go with Ossoli, the most congenial companion I ever had for jaunts of this kind." These were mostly to the city's outskirts: to the Villa Albani with its collection of antiquities, to the Villa Ludovisi, the site of the ancient gardens of Sallust on the Via Veneto, and to the vineyards around the gates of the Porta Maggiore. "We go out in the morning, carrying the roast chestnuts from Rome, the bread and wine are found in some lonely little osteria; and so we dine; and reach Rome again, just in time to see it, from a little distance, gilded by the sunset."[10]

There remained one old problem: money, which, despite all her thriftiness, was becoming more pressing than ever. On this subject, her family was growing not only anxious for her but also a little impatient, especially Richard, her "manly" helper in the family, who got most of her urgent pleas for loans, although they were also starting to bother her mother. In a letter Margaret got that November, running down the list of her children's financial needs in their tenuous ventures and new careers, her mother drew a somber conclusion: "It is best for you to understand the actual poverty of your family, that you may not rely upon a false basis and become inextricably involved my precious child." Why did she not just come home? "Would that you were safe with us at this moment, I fear you will have a winter illness instead of joyfulness." Nor was that all. After repeating Greeley's whining to their friends about her staying abroad so long, she added, "13 yrs on Monday since your father was called away, did you think of him on that day? I need not ask."[11]

Her mother's heartstring-pulling clearly shook her, which was probably why on November 16, in her first letter to her in almost a year, Fuller came close to breaking her silence about her secret family. "Of other circumstances which complicate my position I cannot write," she said mysteriously. "Were you here, I would confide in you fully, and have more than once, in the silence of the night, recited to you those most strange and romantic chapters in the story of my sad life." As to returning, however, she said firmly, "of course, I wish to see America again; but in my own time, when I am ready, and not to weep over hopes destroyed and projects unfulfilled." Although she did not mention her book, she wrote with gusto about her renewed love for Rome, her friendships in her expatriate colony, and, most of all, her hopes for the Risorgimento. "Never feel any apprehensions for my safety from such causes," she assured her mother, after mentioning a bloody clash that day a couple of blocks from her apartment between the Civic Guard and the pope's Swiss Guard. "There are those who will protect me, if necessary, and, besides, I am on the conquering side. These events have, to me, the deepest interest. These days are what I always longed for,—were I only free from private care!"[12]

What her mother made of Margaret's case for her situation—especially her "strange and romantic" confessions in the night—one can only guess, but her family seems to have taken her report in its "conquering" spirit. "Margaret's letter carried much sadness & yet more thought here," Arthur wrote to Richard. "She has led an eventful life—however much trial." Her mother wrote Richard that she was pleased with Margaret's "hopeful letter," but added, "I cannot prevent, or avert the trials that beset her path dear child." Margaret also seems to have gotten somewhat of a lift from even confiding this much to her mother. "Should my hair then be white (don't be anxious, it is still brown and the admiration of the Italians), my soul will still be young, and richer than ever," she lightheartedly wrote in her first letter to Richard in a long time. Urging him to waste no time fretting about his professional perplexities, she added, to herself as much as to him: "I have wasted a great deal of my strength prematurely. Since, I have found that this life, if full of unexpected conflicts and strange agonies, also never ceases to open up new founts of joy and new great occasions for those who are fitted to use them."[13]

However much or little all this melancholy-tinged assurance calmed her family, it still did nothing to fix her financial crisis. "Is it not cruel that I cannot earn six hundred dollars a year, living here?" she asked in a rare self-pitying aside to her mother in her November letter. "Foreigners cannot live so, but I could, now that I speak the language fluently, and know the price of everything. Everybody loves, and wants to serve me, and I cannot earn this pitiful sum to learn and do what I want." A week later, in an otherwise upbeat letter to William Channing about her life in Rome, she wrote more bitterly:

I have these two terrible drawbacks, frequent failure of health and want of money but the first I should not mind, if it were not for the latter. Ah! my dear William, what a vast good would money be to me now, and I cannot get it. This is too hard, so many people have it to whom it is of no use, and to me it would give happiness, days and months of real life. I may complain to you, as you have none to give me; it is some relief to mourn.[14]

She soon had yet another reason to moan about money. In October she had learned that "Aunt" Mary Rotch, her wealthy New Bedford spinster friend, whose maternal attentions she had been lapping up over the last decade, had just died. "I cried so much that I became ill," she wrote Ossoli; "no one in the world was better and more affectionate to me than she was to me." She was therefore shocked to learn a couple of months later, in sadder shades of her Uncle Abraham's bequest manqué, that Rotch had left her nothing. Although she insisted to her mother that she knew she had no claim and had formed "no expectations," her earlier sour letter to Rotch about her hardhearted uncle's failure to leave her a few thousand dollars "to put an end" to her constant "embarrassments and cares" sounds suspiciously like a hint not to do likewise. In any case, she did not know what to think. "It seems to me strange she should not have left me at least a small legacy," she wrote in bewilderment to her mother. "I should have been very glad of money, but apart from that I am even pained that she should forget me. I cannot understand it." Nor is it easy to do so now. Certainly, Rotch's devotion to her companion, Mary Gifford, and, apparently, Rotch's lawyer, between whom she divided her estate of $150,000, was the major reason for cutting Fuller off, but it is also possible that, Fuller's perceptions notwithstanding, Rotch privately felt, as did other wealthy liberal Bostonians with whom Fuller had been friendly, some ambivalence about her. Emerson later specifically instanced Rotch as one of the "good sort of people" who regarded Fuller as "sneering, scoffing, critical, disdainful of humble people, & of all but the intellectual." Fuller knew none of this, of course, and tried to console herself with the thought that her "Aunt" had given nothing to any of her friends and relatives, but that fact, too, in light of Rotch's generosity in life, seemed "dreadful," as did, of course, the loss of the money. "[The] good of a little given to me would have been all but infinite," she would write to her mother later in the spring. "I presume the others feel the same. It seems quite unlike her and to me is as unaccountable as sad."[15]

It also seems ironic in light of Fuller's celebrated generosity, which reportedly reached its zenith in Italy. "Margaret's charities, according to her means were larger than those of any other whom I ever knew," Emelyn Story recalled, instancing Fuller's unsolicited loan of almost her last $50 to Hicks when she was about to leave for L'Aquila and without any assurance it would be repaid (which it was). Even Sarah Clarke, no uncritical friend of Fuller, who interviewed Isabella Mozier and Louisa Crawford two years later when Clarke was visiting Italy, would report to Elizabeth Hoar that they both spoke of Fuller "as if a mild saint & ministering angel," an impression that everyone Clarke talked to readily seconded. Recalling her mixed reputation in America ("she had enemies but many many warm friends"), Clarke wrote Anna Ward:

It was here with her as at home. She established true relations with all sorts of people, yet there were still some few who could neither stand nor understand her. To such she continued to be an offence and foolishness. It is unspeakably touching to me to hear her spoken of by the common people who had any thing to do with her as that good Madam Ossoli—that good Signora Margherita—tanta buona—knowing nothing of her genius they remember her goodness, and her kind interest in their affairs.[16]

So it was only justice when, later that winter, Fuller received news of a modest financial windfall from a genuine mother-substitute, Rotch's niece Eliza Farrar. Probably nudged by Fuller's comment in a recent letter about "some undertaking" requiring her to stay abroad for another year and a half (Farrar guessed a book), which she hoped she could "devise some means" to help her accomplish, Farrar had organized Fuller's "best and most loving friends" to provide her with $300 a year for life. "I feel unspeakably grateful," as well as "comfort and relief," she wrote that January to her mother, "for an act which will on my return, if I wish, after the efforts needed to pay a debt, enable me to live in the retirement and tranquility of the country." The sum she knew was small, but if she wanted additional funds, she could add to it income from her writing or occasional lessons. "It will not be always excitement, always care." There was only one drawback: she would not start getting the annuity until she returned to the United States. "I do not know why they put this condition," she wrote a little irritated, "and I wish they had not; the money would have been so precious in case of my wishing to remain a while longer." It should not have seemed such a mystery: they expected and wanted her home. However, they must have changed their minds, because in Farrar's reply to Fuller's letter expressing her gratitude, she included a draft for $100, telling her that she could get the same amount in four months, or in larger sums if she wanted it. Perhaps thinking herself that the money was comparatively small, she added at the very end: "I hear your Aunt Sarah is dead. I hope you are one of her heirs." She was not.[17]

III

One concern loomed even larger than money for her. "The position of a mother separated from her only child is too frightfully unnatural," she later said she constantly felt that winter. It had been a month since she had left Nino (as they now called him for his "house and pet name"). She especially worried about his being in the care of questionable Rietian peasants, worries that she and Ossoli had to suffer alone. On December 7, though, she finally took a step to change that. Since her tear-stained letter eleven months earlier mysteriously predicting she would "reap what I have sown," she had written nothing to Caroline, and she was nervous about doing so now. "It is of great importance that it should go straight and safe to Caroline," she implored Richard, enclosing her letter to her, adding that he should copy her address "exactly" into his next letter: "I have reasons for not wishing to send mine to the care of her father." Fuller's letter is now lost, but her later references to it show that she had requested a loan and some assurance that Angelo would be taken care of should she die. She would afterward call it a "sad cry from my lacerated affections," but it must have been something of a relief sharing the truth with her closest friend and a new mother herself.[18]

Seeking more immediate reassurance, on December 21 she traveled to Rieti. Unfortunately, her first discovery was that Doctor Mogliani had failed to vaccinate Nino with the smallpox serum that Ossoli had mailed him because, she suspected, she had not sent him enough money. "His family say that I am stingy," she wrote Giovanni angrily the next morning. "I suppose he thought it wasn't worth saving our child." Happily, the spots covering Nino's head and body turned out to be chicken pox, which left no visible marks. In addition, although the family continued to "plunder" and "disturb me greatly," she decided that he was thriving physically. Despite the chilly winds blowing into his room through gaping cracks in their "terrible" house, he had escaped getting a cold, which Margaret attributed to Chiara's keeping him swaddled in wool. She even decided this exposure his first few months would "surely" make him stronger. She worried a little about his psychology. "He has been a strangely precocious child," she later wrote Caroline, speculating that it was because of his "sympathy with me," which he had shown after she had left him, when he had reportedly cried uncontrollably and refused Chiara's breast while looking constantly at the door. His precocious "sympathy" evidently returned: "When I first took him in my arms he made no sound but leaned his head against my bosom, and staid so, he seemed to say how could you abandon me." On the other hand, she eagerly conjectured, he might be happy to be with these "more plebian, instinctive, joyous natures. I saw he was more serene, that he was not sensitive as with me, and slept a great deal more." Furthermore, although she confessed to Ossoli her anguish about leaving Nino, after getting a monstrous cold, she decided she could not stay any longer in the house. On the twenty-ninth she returned to her apartment with a blazing fire her landlady had readied and to Ossoli, who arrived after dinner, where they presumably talked of the "thousand things" she had learned about their "dear child."[19]

Over the winter, her personal life changed very little. She daily visited churches, villas, and galleries, happy to view its "transcendent" art, especially works and scenes, as one might expect from the label, trailing clouds of Romantic glory, many close by. She loved looking out her windows at the rooms of the Palazzo Barberini, where Leonardo's and Raphael's paintings hung, prized by Goethe. She visited the houses of Claude and Poussin, Keats's apartment, where he had died, in the nearby Piazza di Spagna, Raphael's casino next to the Villa Borghese, and the villa on the Corso where Goethe had lived while in Rome. "Ah, what human companionship here," she exclaimed in a letter to Richard, "how everything speaks!" Living companionship, however, was now fast dwindling. Although she remained glad to be rid of the tourists, she missed more than ever her circles of the previous winter. "I sit still in my corner," she wrote Emelyn Story a week after returning, "supposing Fate will, as usual, send me a little group of companions, sooner or later." But as none budged to come to the turbulent city, she kept her "lonely" vigil, which "seems my Rome this winter."[20]

Evidently taking seriously Sarah Clarke's tease in the fall (as Fuller put it) that "people in the U.S. are fast forgetting me," she kept open the lines of communication with them. With her younger siblings, this meant her usual big-sisterly caution and encouragement as needed, along with doses of sometimes incongruous progressive cheer. She described to Richard how "courageous youth" in Italy "dares a future of blood and exile to achieve privileges which are our (American) common birthright." Forgetting for the moment her vehement opposition to the Mexican War, she added that he should hurry up and start seizing the great opportunities its recent conquests now afforded! "I thought of the new prospects as to wealth opened to our country men by this acquisition of New Mexico and California the vast prospects of our country every way, and I thought how impossible it is that one like Richard, of so strong and generous nature shall, if he can but patiently persevere, be defrauded of a rich, manifold, powerful life." Ellen, who had recently given birth to her third child (as Fuller put it to Arthur) "by a man who ran away and left her to sustain alone her last time of trial," got her condolences, although here, as with Richard's potential loot, she did not let her social beliefs stand in the way of practical advice. "But since it is so, I hope she will, this time, have a son; that will please Dr. C."—Ellery's father Dr. Walter Channing. (She did, and he would grow up to be a physician like his grandfather, thus rejecting, like his brother Edward, the Harvard historian, his father's bohemian lifestyle tout court.) She did not forget the sad loser in the family, "poor Lloydie," whom the previous year her mother and brothers had temporarily committed to the insane asylum in Brattleboro, Vermont, after his outbursts started getting bizarre. (He had been accusing them of poisoning him—paranoid talk that her brothers, reflecting the anxious reform physiology of the period, privately blamed on his habit of masturbating.) Indeed, now that Lloyd had left Brattleboro, she even thought expanding America ought to provide a place for *him*. "Fain would I hope that some path may open to occupy his strong body and good will," she wrote Arthur expansively. "Can it be that our country, so rich in occasions, will offer none[?]." Family ambitions and national hopes would never die if she could help it, even while she was helping cosmopolitan revolutions across the Atlantic.[21]

For her Transcendentalist friends, she had an ideologically very different transatlantic message. In a jaunty letter that winter to Emerson, she conceded that her happiness in thinking only about the present was "superficial enough," but after her unspecified "demons" of the previous year, that seemed fine to her. "One don't want deep calling unto deep always," she wrote, tweaking a line from *Nature*, "the shallows with their gold and silver fishes may take their turn." And he should know these were not all Transcendental fish she had been swimming with. "I have made acquaintance this year mostly with thieves and prostitutes," she gaily informed him, probably alluding to her Rietians, "and must say my faith in the hopes of Lazarus are shaken. I did think bad people were more hopeful than good, but think now the chances are about equal." She wrote with edgier sangfroid in reply to James Clarke's plea to "let the good Pio Nono take care of his mad subjects as he can" and come home before their friends, bored with Alcott's "sufficiently misty" new series of conversations, replicated Brownson's conversion. (He "occupies his time in worshipping the bone of a saint, which he carries in his vest pocket.") "I find thee very inconsistent O Jamie," she laughed, to write me of Brownson Alcott and other rusty fusty intel. and spiritual-ities, and to tell me that the best the soul can do in some of your diggings is to put on the filthy popish rags which will scarce hold together on the worst of priests here, then ask me to come back. What come back for? Here is a great past and a *living* present. Here men live for something else beside money and systems, the voice of noble sentiment is understood, nor are they catiff in action. 'Tis a sphere much more natural to me than what the old puritans or the modern bankers have made. I would not have been born in this age other than an American for America is the land of promise but I was somewhat tired of so much promise.[22]

"I have written jestingly," she added in a postscript, "let not that deceive you, dear James, as to my feeling of the character of the paper I inclose," which was a copy of Mickiewicz's remarkable character analysis of her. "I look upon it with great reverence as one of the very few addresses to me to which I could respond." She did not say *how* she had responded to Mickiewicz's plea to her to decide whether "you are permitted to remain a virgin" on her way to delivering European and American womanhood from oppression. She did point out one tantalizing conflation of his of her cultural and personal selves that must have made Clarke ponder a bit: "What he says of my having sinned in the old world, still finding my sustaining point there and trying to make it known to the new is so deeply true, also of my being purely idealist. . . ." At this point the manuscript breaks off, leaving it unclear whether she explained to Clarke the connection among her "natural" self, her unexplained "sin," her transatlantic cultural mission, and her still "purely idealist" character. But whether she did or not, collectively the elements did seem to uncannily sum up the telos of her life in Europe.[23]

IV

The related element that would have most astonished the abolitionist Lowell, if not Clarke, was Fuller's continuing deep engagement in the changing fortunes of the Risorgimento. During the five and a half months she had been gestating in the Abruzzi and Apennine mountains, Europe had passed through momentous political developments. In the summer, France, the revolution's epicenter, had lurched to the right, with monarchists recapturing the provinces and middle-class republicans, hostile to socialistic programs of the democratic left, growing steadily nervous about an increasingly radical working class in Paris. Then came the famous "June Days," when government troops commanded by General Eugène Cavaignac violently put down a five-day uprising by Paris workers protesting the government's abolition of the National Workshops for the unemployed. Meanwhile, democratic and even liberal movements were withering elsewhere on the Continent. On the heels of Austria's successful campaigns in northern Italy and eastern Europe, conservatives and monarchists had begun regaining the upper hand both there and in Germany, and in August the imperial family returned triumphantly to Vienna. Only in Hungary and Romania did the Austrians continue to face serious resistance. By the end of that summer and continuing through the fall, the revolutionary tide was rapidly receding.

Everywhere, that is, but Italy, where the tide was moving in the opposite direction. To be sure, the Austrian army's recapture of Lombardy, following Custoza, and Charles Albert's flight from Milan had been staggering blows to the Risorgimento. But to Italian Democrats, the aftereffects of these military defeats produced one great result: they demonstrated the incapacity of liberal monarchist Moderates to lead the movement. Terrified by Paris's June Days, fearful of growing republican sentiments in their states, and worried about Piedmontese expansion almost as much as Austrian conquest, Italy's constitutional monarchies concentrated on preserving their rule at home. In Mazzini's phrase, the "war of the princes" ended, and the "war of the peoples" began. Almost everywhere in central and northern Italy, Democrats gained. Venetians successfully defended their city from Austrian assaults and reestablished the Republic of St. Mark. With widespread support from urban artisans, shopkeepers, and professionals, Democrats sparked large militant demonstrations in Livorno, Genoa, and Bologna. On October 12, Tuscany's Grand Duke Leopold II, bowing to pressure from Democrats, appointed to the prime minister's office Fuller's interviewee Giuseppe Montanelli, who called for a Costituente, or national constituent assembly, elected by manhood suffrage and bypassing the existing Italian governments.

In the meantime, two extraordinary events occurred that fall that drastically altered Rome's map in favor of the Democrats. In September, Pope Pius, desperate for firm leadership, had appointed as his new minister Count Pellegrino Rossi, a distinguished Italian exile, friend of Guizot, and, until the revolution, Louis Philippe's ambassador to the Holy See. A former professor of constitutional law at Paris and a moderate Liberal who had welcomed the Italian states' constitutional reforms, Rossi was no reactionary. But he *was* a staunch monarchist, who steadfastly opposed any plan to further weaken the pope's authority or enfranchise the lower classes, and a skeptical statesman with a deep appreciation of the geopolitical realities circumscribing Italian national aspirations. Probably most dangerous to himself, he often displayed a proud and sarcastic demeanor toward his legion of adversaries, both Gregorians, who loathed him for his religious liberalism, and Democrats, whose Club of the People he reviled. He was also considering expelling Rome's swelling influx of radical refugees, an increasingly important source of support for Roman Democrats. On November 15, a week after Fuller's arrival back in Rome, he drove to the opening of the Chamber of Deputies, where he was fatally stabbed in the neck by Ciceruacchio's eldest son, Luigi Brunetti, an act probably planned by Sterbini, the Club's president and now the Chamber's fiery leader of the Democratic opposition. The following day, at a chaotic rally of some ten thousand demonstrators, including much of the Civic Guard, organized by the clubs, in front of the Quirinal to demand Pius's agreement to support a patriotic war against Austria and a new Democratic ministry, Monsignor Palma, the pope's secretary, was shot and killed. A week later, to the shock of Romans and millions of Catholics all over the world, on the night of the twenty-fourth, Pius fled to Gaeta, a fortified Neapolitan border town in Ferdinand II's kingdom. With the assassination of Rossi and the flight of the pope, the Moderates' tenuous hold on power in Rome vanished.[24]

Its vanishing terrified moderate nationalists throughout Italy. "The folly, the perversity the impotence of my countrymen," Arconati cried in a letter to Fuller that January, was a "mortification." It was obvious, she said, "the Italians are unworthy of liberty, incapable of making use of it, & more disunited among themselves than ever," resigning her to the "cruel oppression" of Lombardy seemingly forever. She and her family could no longer bear even to see her dear friend Montanelli. "In the moment when politics cease to be a speculation," she explained, "one cannot exercise toleration with tranquility." She even hinted that Montanelli's fate might be in store for Fuller! "If you become Minister or President or Popess, I forewarn that I shall be obliged to break with you. Meantime I adopt this motto 'Hearts may agree, though heads differ.'" Fuller, catching the drift of the dark joke preceding the peace offering, responded with some alarm. All her life she had always tried "with all my force to march straight onwards" and respond to public events without heed of consequences, but Arconati should nonetheless know that she was emotionally "tender and weak" and suffered terribly from breaks in friendship. She was greatly relieved, therefore, she said, to be assured "that I am still dear to you as you to me," quickly adding, however, several qualifiers: "True, I have written, shall write, about the affairs of Italy, what you will much dislike, if ever you see it. I have done, may do, many things that would be very unpleasing to you; yet there *is* a congeniality, I dare to say, pure, and strong, and good, at the bottom of the heart, far, far deeper than these differences, that would always, on a real meeting, keep us friends. For me, I could never have but one feeling for you." She did not specify what those "very unpleasing" things were that she had done, but as she hinted here, they were personal as well as political and sometime she would have to inform Arconati of them.[25]

The collapse of the center that depressed Arconati and her friends electrified Fuller. In her November 23 letter to Sarah Shaw about her "dark and tangled" private fortunes, she wrote excitedly about her public ones: "It is a time such as I always dreamed of; and that fire burns in the hearts of men around me which can keep me warm." But she then asked, more seriously than she had in her breathless letter to William Channing back in March when Europe was exploding, about her own role in all this: "Have I something to do here? or am I only to cheer on the warriors, and after write the history of their deeds?" In other letters, she even expressed some uncertainty about where all of this radicalization in Italy was heading politically. She cheered the new ministry of Montanelli. She shed no tears over the departed Pius and his retinue. "I am living in a Rome without Pope or Cardinals," she wrote Emelyn Story five days later. "Some old persons weep the desecration. But Rome in general takes it very coolly." Yet she added this curiously antiprogressivist thought: "My fear is that Rome cannot hold together in her present form against innovation and that we are enjoying the last hours of her old solemn greatness." Against innovation? Many American and European literary travelers in the next couple of decades would have the same fear, which was why, unlike Fuller, they *shrank* from a radical Risorgimento. She might have said, in her favorite dialectical fashion, that in overturning Rome's social and political system, it would preserve on a higher plane Italy's "old solemn greatness." But if she felt so, she did not mention it here. Even in the midst of exciting political upheaval, Fuller's own Romantic Italophilia lay not far below the surface.[26]

V

On December 2 Fuller sent Greeley two lengthy dispatches interpreting the political events of the past six months. As always, she had scoured newspapers, especially the *Epoca* and *Contemporaneo*, now in the Democratic camp, but also *Il Don Pirlone*, an Italian *Punch* whose nasty cartoons of the pope and his monarchical allies she jokingly described for her readers. But much of her information was firsthand. Some of it she had gotten two summers before, when she had visited the principal scenes of battle in northern Italy, and some from observing military actions in and around Rieti and L'Aquila. But most came from café political gossip and speeches at meetings and rallies in Rome. Probably because this accumulation of facts, as well as her understanding of their "dramatic interest historically" and "infinite" importance "ideally," her dispatches became fiercer and more impassioned but also crisper, more focused, and more analytical. In her first one she had to explain her seven-and-a-half-month silence. She had retired into the country, she told her curious readers, to get some relief from the constant excitement of her last few years, and had returned because it turned cold and she wanted to meet "other eyes beside those, so bright and so shallow, of the Italian peasant." After this light allusion to her Rieti tormentors, she casually added, "Indeed, I left what was most precious that I could not take with me." Some of her readers must have scratched their heads, but like her coded asides in her letters during the summer and fall, it presumably satisfied her need for a safe public confessional.[27]

As Fuller portrayed them, the recent battles bolstered two points. One was the valor of the Italian people. "No one should dare," she wrote, "after the proofs of the Summer, to reiterate the taunt, so unfriendly frequent on foreign lips at the beginning of the contest, that the Italian can boast, shout, and fling garlands, but not *act*." By contrast, the supposed reform princes, who had first became reformers, she said, only because of popular pressure, by retreating in the face of the Austrian onslaught, had proved their total inadequacy as leaders of the Risorgimento. This was the Democratic line, but she added her own Romantic ideological twists in analyzing the failures of the two monarchs to whom Italians had looked for their deliverance. She was especially unforgiving of the war's leader, Charles Albert. As usual, she ignored class factors in his inhibitions, such as the forboding terror felt among his rich noble and commercial supporters after the Paris "June days" toward the peninsula's own republican shopkeepers and tradesmen. Her analysis of the antiheroics of the king, however, was pointed, comprehensive, and largely predictive of modern historical opinion. Dismissing the common republican accusation that he had secretly planned to subvert the war, she said his problem had been his selfish delusions. "He fought and planned," she wrote, "not for

Italy but the house of Savoy, which his Balbis and Giobertis had so long been prophesying was to reign supreme in the new great Era of Italy. These prophecies he more than half believed, because they chimed with his ambitious wishes; but he had not soul enough to realize them." She explained how these monarchical fantasies had shaped what later historians would call his "lost opportunities." He had trusted only disciplined troops and never the people, because he feared their republicanism; never good generals, because, as with Garibaldi, whose services he had rejected, he had feared they might act independently; worst of all, he had not trusted even his own generals if their judgments conflicted with his expansionist ambitions. Thus, because he had wanted to scare Lombardy and Venice into fusing with his kingdom during the "Five Days," he had delayed attacking Austrian troops until they had beefed up their numbers, recovered their spirits, and were burning to avenge their past defeat.[28]

But her most searing attacks were on the king's character. His supposed great courage on the battlefield was a useless class tick: "Charles Albert may possess, may have too much, of what this still aristocratic world calls 'the feelings of a gentlemen' to shun exposing himself to a chance shot now and then." His problem was his lack of "mental courage": "His decisive battle was made so by giving up the moment Fortune turned against him." As for the defense made then (and by some historians since) that in the Battle of Custoza, Radetsky's forces had been so strong that the king could have done nothing to defend Milan, she demanded to know, had a battle never been won against material odds? "Were the Austrians driven out of Milan because the Milanese had that advantage? The Austrian would again have suffered repulse from them, but for the baseness of this man, on whom they had been cajoled into relying: a baseness that deserves the pillory." And not just the pillory. Speaking of the howling mobs crying "Tradimento" (treachery) while he had tried to speak outside his palace balcony window as a bullet whizzed by him, her verdict was blistering: "Had the people slain him in their rage, he well deserved it at their hands." In refusing to give the proud king credit for the patriotism even she conceded he "more than half believed," she made even vengeance seem, not just understandable, but excusable.[29]

She did almost the same with the pope, whose "mental" failures over the past year and a half she depicted as even more egregious than the king's. After his spring Allocution denouncing the war against Austria, which had caused, as she had foreseen, the disintegration of the papal army in the north, she had portrayed him as a weak but still well-intended leader. Now, however, he seemed a pathetic pretender epitomized by his sententious self-justifications. "All the Popes, his predecessors, had meddled with, most frequently instigated, war," she cried; "now came one who must carry out, literally, the doctrines of the Prince of Peace, when the war was not for mercy, or the aggrandizement of individuals, but to redeem national, to redeem human, rights from the grasp of foreign oppression." But the people had also shown their own mental weakness by entering into a ridiculous dance with the pope by demanding a ministry to support the Roman forces fighting Austria but then naïvely accepting as its head the scholarly Liberal Count

Mamiani, "a man of rhetoric, merely," despite his prowar professions. The consequences of this charade were predictable. The pope, who might have been the liberator of suffering Europe, shut himself in his palace, surrounded by "selfish and insidious" reactionary advisers, who secretly wrote to foreign powers denying the acts he had sanctioned, while the Chamber of Deputies passed measures they could never get funded and legions formed that never received arms or uniforms. There was only one solution to this absurd stalemate, she said: a root-and-branch anticlerical revolution. The pope had to resign his temporal power, the cardinals had to be put under check, and the Jesuits and Austrian agents, as in France, had to be expelled outright.[30]

Her most remarkable move, to which she devoted much of her column, was her justification of the revolutionary violence of the assassination of Rossi on November 15. After coolly noting that had he lived to enter the Assembly, he would have found every member sitting on the opposition benches, she narrated in quick cuts the shocking denouement:

> His carriage approached, attended by a howling, hissing multitude. He smiled, affected unconcern, but must have felt relieved when his horses entered the courtyard gate of the *Cancelleria*. He did not know he was entering the place of his execution. The horses stopped; he alighted in the midst of a crowd; it jostled him as if for the purpose of insult; he turned abruptly and received as he did so the fatal blow. It was dealt by a resolute, perhaps experienced, hand; he fell and spoke no word more.[31]

Four features of this portrayal were striking. One was its genesis: despite its cinematographic immediacy, she had not actually witnessed the scene, although she had received accounts of it immediately afterward. Another was her silence about the perpetrators, though she must have picked up the rumors that Sterbini and Ciceracchio's Democratic Club and their allies among the Riduci, or the disreputable battalion of "returned men" from the Roman Legion, had something to do with it. Even more arresting was the complete absence of any condemnation of the act, even though Mazzini and most other Democrats had publicly censured it. The most curious aspect, though, is her silence about a crucial context: the legacy of political violence, perpetrated especially by Fideists and Gregorians but also some fanatical Democrats, particularly in the Romagna provinces. The result was not the calibrated chain of political acts and motives that she followed in analyzing Charles Albert's and Pius's moves but an impersonal, dreamlike narrative with all the trappings of a classical tragedy. Classical allusions permeated her comments on the event. "The sense of the people," she wrote, speaking of the complete silence of the crowd and guard afterward, "certainly was that it was an act of summary justice on an offender whom the laws could not reach, but they felt it to be indecent to shout or exult on the spot where he was breathing his last. Rome, so long supposed the Capital of Christendom, certainly took a very pagan view of this act, and the piece represented on the occasion at the theaters was 'The Death of Nero.'" Classical, too, was her report of crowds later running up and down singing (including under Rossi's widow's apartment, although Fuller did not mention that fact) "'Blessed the hand that rids the earth of a tyrant.'" Privately, she sounded more severely pagan yet. "The news of his death was received by the deputies with the same cold silence as by the people," she wrote to her mother the next day. "For me, I never thought to have heard of a violent death with satisfaction, but this act affected me as one of terrible justice." She did not recall her first published article defending Brutus, written almost exactly fourteen years to the day at the behest of her classically trained republican father, although in her dispatch she noted that the Brutus comparison was on the lips of many young educated Romans, who had suckled on their city's stern civic traditions of virtuous tyrannicide.[32]

Yet the political significance of the assassination, as she knew full well, was not in its classical trappings but in its modern political character and, specifically, in its effect on her two main dramatis personae, the pope and the people, whose confrontation the following day at the Quirinal she portrayed in lurid but also exculpating tones. She had viewed the massing crowd of citizens and politicians outside the pope's palace from the top of the Pincio hill between the Piazza del Popolo and the Villa Borghese. "Nothing could be gentler than the disposition of the crowd," she wrote, explaining that they had been merely hoping to use Rossi's death to convince the pope, whom they still loved and honored, to free himself from the clutches of the "retrograde party"—apparently either not hearing or not reporting the curdling revolutionary slogans shouted by some. She also stretched in placing the entire blame for the violence at the "gentle" demonstration at the Quirinal on a panicked guard who had fired into the crowd and on the pope. She conceded that Pius might have had some reason to panic when he saw the throng pressing against the windows, smelled the smoke from the burning of a palace door, heard shots fired by his alarmed Swiss Guards, and discovered his secretary and confessor, Monsignor Palma, shot dead. But all this amounted to "very little" bloodshed from which he had nothing to fear: "I would lay my life that he could have shown himself without the slightest danger; nay, that the habitual respect for his presence would have prevailed, and hushed all the tumult," which was probably true. "He did not think so, and to still it once more degraded himself and injured his people, by making promises he did not mean to keep," which was also true.[33]

His irretrievable fall came a week later, on November 24, with his flight from Rome for Gaeta, which she used to show the transformation of his faltering "mental courage" into out-and-out treachery. She recalled, largely truthfully, that until this moment, she had regarded him as more of a naïf than anything else. She even claimed she could still sympathize with his mental anguish facing the new Democratic-dominated government's commitment to pursuing war with Austria and ignoring his temporal authority, being surrounded by lying reactionary cardinals, and sincerely believing that the "Progress movement" in Europe had become a reincarnation of the worst excesses of the first French Revolution. His subsequent actions, however, were morally reprehensible and politically inexcusable. "To fly to Naples to throw himself in the arms of the bombarding monarch, blessing him and thanking his soldiery for preserving that part of Italy from anarchy—to protest that all his promises at Rome were null and void." "A strange plea, indeed, for the representative of St. Peter!" she sneered, naming Christian martyrs and popes who had faced torture and death rather than act against their convictions. Even worse was his appointment of princely nullities to govern in his place, who all ran away, and then his refusal to see any Roman delegation, including even that of the senator of Rome, whom he had sanctioned: "These are the acts of a fool or a foe." "No more of him!" she cried, adding, a bit rashly, that the moment of the anticlerical revolution had come: "His day is over." And Rome? With the pope refusing even to talk with them, the day of the Moderates was also obviously over.[34]

With the Moderates checked, the pope expunged from history, and the city peaceful but expectant in her telling, the question still remained: could the people rise above their historic divisions to achieve a government able to sustain itself and gain needed diplomatic recognition? Certainly, their reaction to the pope's flight boded well. "Rome remained quite cool and composed," she wrote, repeating her appraisal to Emelyn Story, but now with, instead of her expressed Italophilic fear then of the city losing its "old solemn greatness," a social democratic flourish: "In a few days all began to say, 'Well, who would have thought it?' The Pope, the Cardinals, the Princes are gone, and Rome is perfectly tranquil, and one does not miss anything, except that there are not so many rich carriages and liveries." Indeed, the pope's flight presaged some sort of social revolution of the poor throughout Europe. For a successful political revolution in Rome right then, however, she was uncertain: "It is one which requires radical measures, clear-sighted men." Elsewhere were leaders who had shown themselves during the summer. Mazzini, who had arrived in Milan on April 8, had cried like Cassandra against the treacheries of the pope and the king, Niccolo Tommaseo and Daniele Manin had courageously rallied the city to defend itself against a furious Austrian bombardment, and, most encouraging, Montanelli and his fellow ministers in Tuscany were becoming a focal point of a national democratic movement. But who would play their role in Rome, where leaders, since the pope's fall, were seemingly non-existent? (Privately, she was blunter, stigmatizing the demagogic prime minister Sterbini as a man of "little talent.")[35]

At the end of her first December 2 dispatch, she fantasized aloud about one possible source of help: a good American ambassador! Listing his qualifications, she said he should not be a party hack, but someone skilled in languages, with broad knowledge and views, principled commitments but understanding "variety in forms," and, above all, with a deep "appreciation of the great luxury of living in Rome." Who might meet all these Fulleresque requirements? "Another century, and I might ask to be made Ambassador myself," she answered, putting off radical gender change for a long time. "But woman's day has not come yet. They hold their clubs in Paris, but even George Sand will not act with women as they are. They say she pleads they are too mean, too treacherous. She should not abandon them for that, which is not nature but misfortune." After these gestures toward old constituencies and far-off futures, she dropped her ambassadorial fantasy for what she knew her real role to be:

> Of all this great drama I have much to write, but elsewhere, in a more full form, and where I can duly sketch the portraits of actors little known in America. The materials are over-rich. I have bought the right in them by much sympathetic suffering; yet, amid the blood and tears of Italy, 't is joy to see some glorious new births,— the Italians are getting cured of mean adulation and hasty boasts; they are learning to prize and seek realities. . . . Her leaders are learning that the time is past for trust in Princes and precedents—that there is no hope except in Truth and God; her lower people are learning to shout less and think more.[36]

What that history was that she was writing, we will never know. But in her dispatches that winter, we at least can see shards of the Romantic democratic arguments, narratives, and myths she was beginning to construct about her Risorgimento heroes' march through history on a new stage of "realities" and dreams.

VI

Meanwhile, Fuller could hardly sit still in her "corner" in the political present, which in Italy continued marching leftward. At the beginning of 1849, Democrats still controlled the city-state of Venice and, after Leopold II fled for Gaeta on February 8, the government of Tuscany. In Piedmont, they were gaining sufficiently to force Charles Albert to contemplate renewing the war with Austria. Still, at the forefront of this continuing Democratic resurgence was Rome. "This year cannot fail to be rich in events most important for Italy, Europe, the world," Fuller wrote excitedly on New Year's Day on the first page of a new journal. "Rome has at last become the focus of the Italian revolution and I am here." She was right. The pope's commission of notable aristocrats, as Fuller reported, had quit or fled, and on the day she had arrived in Rieti, Mamiani's "Giunta di Stato" announced the convocation of the Constituent Assembly, after which he resigned, and a new ministry prepared for elections the following month of January.[37]

In preparation for these, Fuller jotted notes on the change in public opinion since the pope's flight. She was especially pleased with the growth in anticlerical sentiment. "The power of the priests must be utterly overthrown before anything solid can be done for this people," she scribbled in her journal that January 1. "Everything tends to destroy their authority; only as it has long been founded on habit and not on illusion, an appeal to reason will not suffice." And habit was the rub. "How strange it seems," she wrote five days later, after viewing several papal palaces, "that the people has so long submitted to see a few men living in their superb edifices while they live in putrid cellars or smoky cabins. O it is frightful that they have been able to bear it so many thousand years." But in Rome even habits seemed to be changing fast. Trolling for anticlerical signs, she recorded a piquant description of the large crowd reacting on the night of January 5 to Pius's sweeping New Year's Day encyclical threatening to excommunicate everyone who voted for the "detestable" call for the Constituent Assembly or criticized the temporal authority of the papacy. "The silliest document possible, an astonishment in this age," she wrote. "The people received it with jeers, tore it at once from the walls and yesterday (Saturday), evening carried it in procession through the Corso round a candle's end," she exulted. "They ran along giggling and mumbling in imitation of priestly chants detachments occasionally digressing to throw copies into some privy. Such is the finale of St. Peterdom."[38]

A political finale required political action, but Fuller easily found that, too. The radical democratic oratory at meetings and rallies simply astounded her. "Things were said such as never before, rarely, echoed from the walls of modern Rome," she wrote in her journal on January 14, after observing a meeting at the Teatro Metastasio. The speakers ridiculed the excommunication, she reported, and out-did did each other in pushing forward "liberal measures," which they often justified by appealing to a Christian social gospel of spiritual freedom and amelioration of the lives of the poor. "What a vast stride for democracy made since then in this country," she exclaimed just before the voting for the Constituent Assembly. "How many men of straw have been put up and knocked down. May these deputies turn out representatives of realities." The elections of January 20 and 21 realized her hopes. Empowered by universal manhood suffrage, 250,000 voters cast ballots, shocking boycotting "retrogrades" who had predicted a poor turnout and bringing a crushing victory for the Democrats over Mamiami's Liberals. She captured the symbolism: fourteen months earlier, the princes of Rome had lent the Council of Deputies their coaches of state for their inauguration. "They rode in them and looked out of the window like Whittington and his cat. The present deputies walked on foot, ornamented only with the tri-colored scarf to the marching music of the Marseillaise. On February 9, 1849, the newly elected Assembly, after a passionate debate ranging over Italian history and modern political theory, proclaimed the Roman Republic in the form of a "pure Democracy," with Maestri, Masi, and others of Fuller's Democratic friends playing leading roles.[39]

She had her doubts and fears, which she expressed in her journal and letters. She worried about corrupt demagogues like Sterbini prominent at the time of Rossi's assassination, who would soon be marginalized. She fretted even more about zealots. "Treachery," she jotted in her journal on January 19. "The troops of the line fired on the dragoons crying Viva Pio. All will be dark indeed if disunion within as well as foes without." Most striking, even in these heady weeks, she privately expressed great reservations about the Italian peasantry, whose general indifference or hostility, outside of Romagna, to the Risorgimento she knew. "My poor Italian brothers, they bleed!" she cried out that January in a letter to Jane Tuckerman King. "I do not love them much,—the women not at all; they are too low for me; it will be centuries before they emerge from a merely animal life." Even the Trasteverini, whose colorful dances and love songs had enchanted her during her first autumn in Rome, sometimes grated on her. "I am now rid of all these women; they are so very unintellectual," she wrote to her sister Ellen at the end of the winter; "at first one likes the naiveté but people always tire, when it is impossible to draw them one single step beyond their habitual limits." These were minor chords, however, drowned out by a crescendo of enthusiasm for two things. One was the radicalized "people," as she called the students, professionals, tradesmen, craftsmen, and, occasionally, the Roman "poor." The other was "revolution," which she was sure would develop their capacities. Nor did she brook any ethnic prejudices against her revolutionary "people." "If you were here," she wrote Richard somewhat gratuitously, "I rather think you would be impassive, like the two most esteemed Americans I see[.] They do not believe in the sentimental nations. Hungarians, Poles, Italians are too demonstrative for them, too fiery, too impressible, they like better the loyal slow moving Germans, even the Russian with his dog's nose and gentlemanly servility please them better than my people." In Fuller's mind, the centuries needed for the peasantry and lumpen proletariat to emerge from their "animal life" neither refuted the immediate potential of a revolutionary people nor justified slandering the Italian national character.[40]

She certainly did not reveal any of this doubt and caution in her two *Tribune* dispatches of February 20. She excitedly described the concluding day of Carnival, dominated no longer by splendid coaches and the finery of dukes and princes but ubiquitous flowers, extemporaneous concerts, and extravagant costumes. She highlighted the astonishing "variety of tones" and "live satire" in the people's repeated taunts gaily parodying the "'respectable,'" while the red liberty caps, the brimless caps of the French Revolution, were reflected in the million swarms of lights of the slender miccoletti candles. "The Roman still plays amid his serious affairs," she wrote happily. She contrasted the duplicity and cowardice of the pope with the honesty and boldness of the people as they dismissed his absurd charges of "ingratitude" and grew in maturity after each of his provocations. Habitually respectful of his office and still venerating his memory as a reformer, most had even hoped he would come back to them, many superstitiously betting he would miraculously appear in the Quirinal one particular morning. Instead, when they had awoken to posted broadsides of his silly, vindictive, and bigoted threat of excommunication, they had responded with furious demonstrations, hurling the document into toilets (here she had them euphemistically "deposit" them in "places provided for lower uses.") The same point-counterpoint occurred after his "wicked advisers" had calculated that his selection of incompetents as ministers and his refusal to see Rome's emissaries would cause such confusion and consternation among the people that they would beg for his return. "Rome coolly said, 'If you desert me—if you will not hear from me—I must act for myself.'" But the best proof of the people's wisdom had been the ways they did this. They had turned out to vote in high numbers—higher proportionately than in elections in the United States—and had made good electoral choices. They also had refused to be bullied or provoked by the plotting "obscurantists" and reactionary priests into foolish acts of revenge: "A few words of brotherly admonition have been more powerful than all the spies, dungeons and scaffolds of Gregory." Downplaying the incident of the "little mutiny" of Civic Guards firing on the dragoons that she had nervously alluded to in her journal, she played up the people's response to some "zealous ignoramuses" who had shouted insults at carriages with servants in livery. "The Ministry published a grave admonition, that democracy meant liberty, not license, and that he who infringed upon an innocent freedom of action in others must be declared traitor to his country. Every act of the kind ceased instantly." Clever taunts of the upper classes and spontaneous political outrage were fine, but boorish class-conscious behavior was not.[41]

She omitted a few "realities." She was quite aware of the serious problem the government had in getting sufficient money in circulation because of the hording of solid coin and the lack of confidence in its paper currency. But whereas in her journal she had written that these financial difficulties "disgust[ed] this coarse people, selfish and ignorant," many saying, "'Che vantaggio apporta la repubblica'" (what advantage does a republic bring), in her dispatch she wrote poignantly: "The poor, always the chief sufferers from such a state of things, are wonderfully patient." In fact, the Republic was never able to solve its financial problems since, as the government refused to raise taxes even on the wealthy, it only had recourse to printing increasingly worthless currency, while the mass exodus of the nobility created enormous unemployment—class issues she never mentioned and perhaps did not even think about. Certainly, she was oversanguine in thinking that the currency problem would be solved once the new ruling Democratic party in Tuscany persuaded their government to join with Rome in creating a new Republic of Central Italy that would abolish petty trade restrictions and generate a flourishing trade. Because of increasing peasant opposition to the Tuscan Republican government's intrusive armies and taxes, its leaders were too busy just trying to survive to heed their Roman comrades' call for unification.[42]

But aside from class questions, which would largely remain the blind spot in Fuller's view of the Risorgimento, she was completely right about two more immediate things. By exhortation, appointments, and incorruptibility, the government *did* achieve, even while liberalizing the criminal code and abolishing capital punishment, an unprecedented degree of civic peace and order, particularly remarkable in a country where political violence was something of a cultural tradition. She was also right in claiming that popular confidence in the government was growing, among not only artisans and shopkeepers but also professionals, middling landowners, and Moderates, who accepted, as she suggested, the Republican leaders as the only possible effective government and feared that the hated corrupt and tyrannical cardinal-dominated regime would return if the pope returned. Yet another reason for the government's survival, though, which she did not say much about, was the Republic's bold yet not overbold reforms. Freedom of speech, press, and association, which Romans had never enjoyed under the popes was strictly enforced. Ameliorating measures, such as the abolition of salt and tobacco monopolies, the lowering of import duties to promote free trade, and social welfare experiments such as a state charity commission, slum clearance, free university tuition, and subsidies to the arts were moderately progressive. Anticlerical reforms were more radical. The pope's temporal power was abolished, the Inquisition done away with, clerical control of the university ended, and (in line with other European states) Church property nationalized, but his spiritual authority was constitutionally mandated and still widely respected, and the Church's civil rights were generally protected. Indeed, the government's most radical reform—the conversion of the Inquisition offices into tenement buildings and Church holdings into small farms and cheap apartments—was never implemented.[43]

Nor finally, notwithstanding that she somewhat exaggerated Charles Albert's freedom to act against Austria, was she wrong to think that the fundamental long-term political question was, indeed, whether democracy or liberal monarchy would lead and ultimately determine the character of a united independent Italy. For a while current events in Piedmont even seemed to confirm her answer. "The 'illustrious Gioberti' has fallen—fallen forever from his high scaffold of words," she exulted, piling up the delicious ironies of Charles Albert having recently appointed then dismissed him as prime minister for advocating sending troops to Tuscany to restore Leopold and check Austria, which she predicted, undoubtedly correctly, would have caused a civil war. She even rightly speculated that Charles Albert himself had probably planned the intervention and, once he met massive opposition to it among even Moderates, had made Gioberti a scapegoat. In small but sharp insights like these about the complex divisions plaguing the Risorgimento even at its new high-water mark, one can see the glimmerings of the history of the Italian revolutions she had begun composing after returning in the fall to Rome. "I expect to write the history," she told Richard in her February letter, "but because it is so much in my heart."[44]

More than fragments of her lost history, though, her dispatches that winter and spring were texts of their time. "Her recent political disquisitions have probably been as widely read as any of her writings," conceded a critic in the conservative *Southern Literary Messenger.* "No one can call in question the intellectual vigor they display, whatever antagonism of opinion they may excite." And antagonism they excited. "Miss Fuller's papers are the most heinous articles I ever read," one Virginia reader that winter wrote John Bigelow, the editor of the *New York Evening Post,* after the appearance of her dispatch lambasting Italian Moderates and American travelers and gloating over Rossi's dying one day after the pope had made him a Roman citizen, the title just bestowed on Mazzini. Both the respect and the antipathy were an indication of her dispatches' importance. Ever since the Parisian workers' uprising of the previous June, most American newspapers and politicians, after initially hailing the French and other European revolutions, had become increasingly skeptical and even, in the case of many Whigs, hostile to them, particularly their left wing in France, which was widely seen as a dangerous radical cabal bent on fomenting a bloody class war. If the *Tribune* was a rare exception, it was partly, of course, due to Greeley's social democratic sympathies and Dana's prodemocratic reporting, but it was also because of Fuller's correspondence from Rome. America's first war correspondent and the only American journalist then reporting from the city, she gave her readers in her dispatches, which were widely excerpted in newspapers around the country, the only eyewitness accounts they saw of what was going on politically in Italy. In doing so, she countered two powerful currents. One was the deep doubts that she repeatedly—and rightly—claimed many Americans shared with English but also Continental elites about the steadfastness, courage, and perspicacity of contemporary Italians as a race apart from "white" civilization. The other was the drum roll of libels on the

Roman Republic as a band of French-style "Reds," tyrants, and thugs—as was repeated constantly in the influential *London Times*—or as (in many American newspapers) "an ultra-democratic faction" with little popular support among the people of Rome. Against these slanders, she provided an authoritative and powerful voice on the Republic's behalf to the outside world.[45]

Her dispatches' authority also derived from their journalistic qualities. Even if they generally elided the conservative Italian peasantry and underplayed a bit the outbursts of violence in Republican Rome, they rested on a solid foundation of acute observation, wide reading in the Continent's newspapers, deep familiarity with European history and culture, and an intimacy with and curiosity about Italian actors on various sides of the political divides. As artifacts of journalism, they were also salient examples of the era's new foreign correspondence of searing political engagement, represented most famously by Dana, Börnstein, and later Marx, all commentators like Fuller on the revolutions of 1848–49 and all contributors to the *Tribune*. ("How happens it always that there gathers around the Tribune all of the Robespierres of the day?" New York's *Evening Express* churlishly demanded to know of the circle—a label she would have vehemently denied even while accepting the company.) Furthermore, if Fuller's dispatches lacked the social analysis of Dana's letters and the theoretical ballast and cool irony of Marx's, they injected into their democratic vitriol three agents of her own. One was her liberal Romantic plot: visionary and responsible leaders and passionate and gradually more aware followers heroically struggling among forces they did not control toward tragedies looming ahead and triumphs lying in the far distance. Another was her tension-filled cosmopolitan perspective: deeply committed to America's liberal democratic tradition but also increasingly doubtful about its fulfillment in the United States and progressively more hopeful about its social democratic evolution in Europe. Most distinctive was her voice: politically savvy, culturally alert, and electrically charged by a vibrant intellectual personality grappling with one of her deepest conundrums—her identity as an American cosmopolitan liberal—resounding off the screen of the greatest European political cataclysm of the nineteenth century.[46]

CHAPTER TWELVE

States of Siege
(1849)

I

One political problem Fuller did not try to gloss over that winter was the imminent threat of foreign intervention. "Could Italy be left alone!" she cried in her dispatch of March 20, 1849. She knew that was impossible. From virtually the day the pope fled, every major European power, Catholic and non-Catholic, felt he had to be reinstated with his temporal power, the only questions being by whom and how. Then there were the military actors. Even if Austria was for the moment mired in revived domestic unrest and Hungarian military successes, the Republic faced other equally strong threats. Although it was believed, Fuller reported in her February 20 dispatch, that the pope had not yet appealed for armed intervention from the Catholic powers (he secretly had), there was "little reason to hope he will be spared that crowning disgrace." Within the peninsula, the "bloody, angry, well-armed" Ferdinand II was poised to attack from the south. Meanwhile, Charles Albert's recommencement of Piedmont's war against Austria that very day was just posturing. He only undertook it because of popular clamor for it, and now that the "splendid lure" of becoming king of Italy "glitters no more," she predicted, one defeat on the battlefield would make him quit: "The rat will steal out and leave the lions in the trap." Certainly, he would do nothing to protect a republic he feared and hated.[1]

Finally, there was the Republic's supposed "natural ally." Although she had written more appreciatively of contemporary French literature than almost any other American critic, like most Americans of the early Republic, Fuller had long harbored suspicions of France as a nation prone to deception and tyranny. By contrast, Italian republicans generally, despite Napoleon's occupation, had long been, in the words of one Italian historian, "bewitched by France." Even Mazzini, who denigrated the French "Jacobin" tradition and believed only Italians could liberate Italy, thought that France would either leave Rome alone or possibly, he hoped, intervene to stop Austrian aggression. There was some basis for that. Four days after Pius's flight, General Cavaignac, the French Republic's defense minister, assured the National Assembly that his order for the embarkation of soldiers to "protect" the pope, which he would soon abort, included a clear warning against mixing in Roman politics or forcibly reinstating him to his throne. However, that December, a new player had suddenly entered the picture. In the Republic's first presidential election, Louis-Napoleon Bonaparte, the former emperor's nephew, exploiting the heterogeneous fears of peasants, monarchists, and even many workers, stunned all political parties by winning in a landslide. Historians continue to debate the question of the new president's position toward the Roman Republic at this time. Fuller, though, largely against prevailing opinion in Rome, began beating warning drums immediately after the election. "The Romans go on as if nothing were pending," she had written in her journal as early as January. "Yet it seems very probably that the French will soon be at Città Vecchia and with hostile intentions. Monstrous are the treacheries of our time." She kept up the warnings through the spring. Noting in her journal in mid-March that France had refused to receive Roman ambassadors in Paris, she wrote in her journal, "The French government will not be friendly to the Italian republics." As for the new president, she wrote in her March 20 dispatch, he obviously cared for nothing but self-interest. "The dereliction from principle of her Government seems certain," and except for the protests of "a few worthy men" of the Assembly's left-wing "Mountain," the nation "gives no sign of effective protest." It was a sober last thought.[2]

While dispatching sobriety about the Romans' diplomatic situation, she did not overlook one fact that bolstered the morale of every Republican in the city. On March 5, after nearly a year in Milan and Florence organizing his supporters and battling Moderates, Mazzini finally entered his world's putative moral center, which he had never seen. Although his long delay in entering Rome has sometimes provoked criticism, he hardly seems to have needed to be there to exercise enormous influence. On February 12, three days after the proclamation of the Roman Republic and two days before Mazzini entered Florence, the Republic's Executive Committee declared him a Roman citizen and ordered all laws released under Young Italy's motto "In the name of God and the people." On March 6, the day after arriving from Florence, he took his seat in the Assembly next to its president.[3]

To Fuller, his arrival was a godsend. She was no sectarian Mazzinian. In her reports, she ignored the differences among the Democrats, often putting in a good word for the cautious Manin, who had outraged Mazzini by agreeing to fuse Lombardy and the Veneto with Piedmont during the first war, and for Montanelli, whose plan for a confederated Italian republic Mazzini derided as too weak to ensure national cohesion. She also continued to think that Mazzini wrongly overlooked economic questions raised by socialists. On the other hand, there was no doubt in her mind that "Mazzini has stood alone in Italy," as she had written to Marcus Spring earlier in the winter, "far above" other men. "He has fought a great fight against folly, compromise, and treason; steadfast in his convictions, and of almost miraculous energy to sustain them, is he." In political philosophy, she was a complete Mazzinian. She panegyrized his liberal cosmopolitan formulation, in his first address to the Assembly, of a revolution to constitute, after a Rome of armed emperors and a Rome of proselytizing popes, a "third Rome" of the people that would conquer by the energy of example. Most important, she correctly understood that Mazzini was now Republican Rome's indispensable leader. "Now he is here," she fairly gasped in her journal, expressing the hope that he would check the corruption and incompetence of Sterbini and his colleagues. In her dispatch she battered away at the Moderates' stereotype of Mazzini as a sectarian mystagogue. Besides his steadfastness, which deeply moved her, she also applauded his tolerance—a term his enemies would have gagged on—citing his caveat in his address against disparaging former monarchists. She extolled the "simple conversational tone" he used in his speeches, a refreshing change, she said, from the "boyish rhetoric and academic swell common to Italian speakers in the present unfledged state." She especially celebrated the integrity of his intellect. "The speech of Mazzini is laden with mind," she told her American readers, "it goes straight to the mark by the shortest path and moves without effort from the irresistible impression of deep conviction and fidelity in the speaker." But, above all, he hewed to "the religion of his soul, of his *virtue*, in the modern and antique sense of that word," or, as she presumably meant, selfless devotion to res publica and mental toughness in the face of bad fortune.[4]

She did not mention to her readers one further aspect of Mazzini's character that was extremely important to her: his susceptibility to her kind of inspiration. She had spelled this out in a lavishly philosophical and personal letter she had written him just before he had left Florence for Rome. In sympathy and intelligence, the best and perhaps only friends of a "man of ideas and marked character," she said, must be women, adding modestly: "You have your mother; no doubt you have others, perhaps many; of that I know nothing; only I like to offer also my tribute of affection." This was familiar Fulleresque maternalist talk, but she intertwined it with two claims tailored to their shared intellectual sensibilities. First, they both envisioned Rome as a unique place for "exiles"—a city, as she put it, "to which all the orphans of the soul so naturally turn." Second, she had a Transcendental balm for the sadness she divined in his recent letter to the Roman Assembly. "You speak of 'few and late years,' but some full ones remain," she wrote, adding sensibly: "A century is not needed, nor ought the same man, in the same form of thought, to work too long on an age. He would mould and bend it too much to himself." Then, a metahistorical swoop upward: "Better for him to die and return incarnated to give the same truth aid on yet another side. Jesus of Nazareth died young; but had he not spoken and acted as much truth as the world could bear in his time?" In any case, "a frailty," she said, taking a line from her Romantic script, "seems the destiny of this earth. The excuse awaits us elsewhere; there must be one, for it is true, as said Goethe, that 'Care is taken that the trees grow not up into the heaven.'" She concluded with one wish for God's "appointed minister" that she could not fulfill. "For your sake I would wish at this moment to be an Italian and a man of action," she wrote. "But *though an American*, I am not even *a woman of action*; so the best I can do is to pray with the whole heart, Heaven bless dear Mazzini, cheer his heart and give him worthy helpers to carry out its holy purposes!"[5]

On the evening of March 8, three days after arriving in Rome, with posters all over Rome proclaiming "in giant letters, *Giuseppe Mazzini, cittadino Romano*," and mammoth crowds begging him to become president, he came to Fuller's apartment for a meeting, which she afterward described to Marcus Spring as a veritable revelation:

> I heard a ring; then somebody speaks my name; the voice struck me at once. He looks more divine than ever, after all his new, strange sufferings. He asked after all of you. He stayed two hours, and we talked, though rapidly, of everything. He hopes to come often, but the crisis is tremendous, and all will come on him; since, if any one can save Italy from her foes, inward and outward, it will be he. But he is very doubtful whether this be possible; his foes are too many, too strong, too subtle. Yet Heaven helps sometimes.

In fact, she now withdrew her denial of being a "*woman of action*," albeit conditionally: "Freely would I give my life to aid him, only bargaining for a quick death. I don't like slow torture." She even reconsidered the only American male friends she had ever thought of as potentially heroic. "What would I not give that my other two brothers, R.W.E. and W.H.C. could see him!" she declared. "All have in different ways the celestial fire, all have pure natures. They may have faults, but no base alloy. To me they form a triad. I know none other such." Still, she knew Mazzini was the far greater historical actor. Writing two weeks later to Caroline Tappan, who in her letter had asked her if she did not wish Italy had a great man, she replied, listing qualities she had never associated with Emerson and Channing: "Mazzini is a great man; in mind a great poetic statesman, in heart a lover, in action decisive and full of resource as Cesar. Dearly I love Mazzini, who loves me. He came in just as I had finished this first letter to you. His soft radiant look makes melancholy music in my soul; it consecrates my present life that like the Magdalen I may at the important hour shed all the consecrated ointment on his head."[6]

As this Christ allusion suggested, despite her recent dispatches' claims about the capacities of the Romans, Mazzini's doubts about the Republic's outcome clearly shook her. "Mazzini enters Rome for the first time as a Roman citizen," she wrote to her mother the same day she wrote Spring. "He enters to defend Italy, if any man can, against her foes. Can any?—I feel no confidence: they are so many. . . . I fear the entrance into Jerusalem may be followed by the sacrifice." The following day she wrote an even darker letter to her most chiliastic Transcendentalist friend, "the evil time's sole patriot" (as Emerson would aptly call him). While "the object of great love from the noble and humble" in Italy, she told Channing, "a kind of chastened libertine I rove, pensively, always, in deep sadness, often O God help me; is all my cry. Yet I have very little faith in the paternal love, I need; the government of the earth does seem so negligent." Nor did she seem to have had much faith in men: "I am tired of seeing men err and bleed. I am tired of thinking, tired of hoping. I take an interest in some plans, *our* socialism, for instance, for it has become mine, too, but the interest is shallow as the plans. They are needed, they are even good, but man will still blunder and weep, as he has done for so many thousand years." Old conflated doubts about divine providence and "paternal love" that had shadowed her star-crossed youth could evidently even make events of "great dramatic interest historically—of bearing infinitely important ideally" seem doubtful.[7]

II

None of these doubts, however, made it into Fuller's dispatches that spring. Instead, she seems to have thought that as the Republic's fate hurtled toward a turning point, her American readers needed some deprovincializing lessons. They even seeped into her first substantial report on Rome's contemporary American art scene. She doled out modest prizes to her friends Terry, Cropsey, Cranch, Story, Mozier, and Hicks, and only slightly bigger ones to the established Crawford, Greenough, and Powers. She conceded, a little cantankerously, that they would not be thrilled by her judgments. "My highest tribute is meager of superlatives in comparison with the hackneyed puffs with which artists submit to be besmirched. Submit, alas! often they court them, rather." She singled out the "crazy" panegyrics of Powers's sensationally popular *Greek Slave* as one example of how "drawing-room raptures and newspaper echoes" puff a small achievement out of all aesthetic recognition. She sympathized with American artists' plight in the unforgiving marketplace, but she urged in place of this hustling for puffs juried art shows based solely on artistic merit and patronage sufficient to sustain them in Italy. "Italy, compared with America," she said, "is not so very cheap, except for those who have iron constitutions to endure bad food, eaten in bad air, damp and dirty lodgings." For the benefit of potential benefactors, she inserted an itemized account of artists' typical expenses compiled for her by her Prussian artist neighbor. Noting that the Russian government gave $700, which was barely enough, she declared, "$1000 per annum should be placed at the disposal of every young artist leaving our country for Europe."[8]

Most of her cosmopolitan patriotic lessons, though, were political. England, as usual, was her anti-model, Its governing class's cynical "balance of power" foreign policy was hopeless. "She is guided by no great idea; her Parliamentary leaders sneer at sentimental policy, and the 'jargon' of ideas," mental ticks that squared perfectly with the Whig foreign minister Lord Palmerston's anti-Austrian but propapal Italian policy and England's imperialism in Ireland and India. But even worse were the faux aristocratic sensibilities of its travelers. "All their comfort was, 'It would not last a month,'" she recounted a group of English she ran into telling her. "'They hoped to see all those fellows shot yet.'—The English clergyman; more mild and legal, only hopes to see them (as the Ministry, Deputies, &c,) *hung*." Carlyle, she said, would be delighted with his countrymen, as they were eager to see a Cromwell for Italy and cared only for "order": "How dare they make a noise to disturb us yawning at billiards!" What was shocking, though, was professedly "democratic" American travelers' equivalents to these aristocratic ticks. "Receiving all his birthright from a triumph of Democracy, he was quite indifferent to this manifestation on this sacred spot," she wrote of one American impassively observing the ceremony of the reading of the Republic's Decree that had thrilled her. In Rome to study art, he was "insensible to this new life of that spirit from which all the forms he gazes at in galleries emanated. He 'did not see the *use* of these popular demonstrations.'" This "really thoughtful, intelligent" man had the temerity to observe that "'*the people*'" were just looking on and not taking any part—by which he meant, she said, a few beggars, errand boys, and "'only soldiers.'" "'Soldiers!' she answered. 'The Civic Guard; all the decent men in Rome.'" Her fatuous American traveler whose crude impressions and blunders made him "more ignorant for coming abroad" had become an intolerable political enemy.[9]

From her compatriots back home, she expected more. She knew, she said, that politically her country could not interfere, but at least individuals and private organizations could give them public support and raise money to buy weapons and uniforms, as they had done two decades earlier for Greek and Polish freedom fighters. "If there were a circle of persons inclined to trust such to me," she offered, trading in her proposed ambassadorship for something more realistic, "it would make me proud to have my country show a religious faith in the progress of ideas, and make some small sacrifice of its own great resources in aide of a sister cause, now." That was a poignant plea, although likely an ineffectual one, since, as she admitted, she needed a response "now."[10]

If Fuller's dispatches that spring had a more prickly air than usual, it might have also been because of her frustrations about her personal situation. She rejoined the Storys and their children, who had returned to Rome on March 2, for music at St. Peter's, rambles through the Villa Borghese, and walks by torchlight through the Vatican. But the Cranches, the Cropseys, the Crawfords, and her other friends had already left or would soon leave. "This is no time for an artist" or a "delicate" woman with "those two young children" to be here, she told Elizabeth Cranch, but she still missed them. Now hard at work on her book, she was also beginning to feel renewed resentment over relentless column deadlines. "Much writing hath made me mad of late," she crankily apologized to her readers. "Forgive if the 'style be not neat, terse, and sparkling,' if be naught of the 'thrilling,'" adding, gratuitously, "like all else that is published in America. Sometime I must try to do better." She stopped writing dispatches for over a month.[11]

As she was starting to think seriously about returning in a year or two, old anxieties about her financial situation also resurfaced. "Mrs. C[rawford] thinks herself very poor because she has only three thousand dollars a year and cannot keep a carriage," she wrote deadpan in mid-March to Ellen; "she comes here into my garret to tell me these distresses; how they must economize severely to have a thousand dollars in pocket when they leave Rome." She would be lucky, she said, if she even had a few hundred dollars to take a sailing ship. The money question was especially galling, as she started worrying again about people at home "fast forgetting me," worries now, probably, tinged with new nervousness about how they would react to her unlooked-for family. "I am now so neglected by my old friends," she glumly told Ellen, "that it quite takes away disposition on my side to write to them. Perhaps some letters are lost but I cannot know." In one week she wrote nearly a dozen long letters. Tellingly, in one to Anna Ward she recounted a dream about visiting her and Sam at their house in Lenox, in which they and their friends completely ignored her. "At last I suggested that I had been gone a long time," she wrote, "and you replied carelessly 'O yes, I think I have not seen you since Wednesday.'—You must not be indifferent when I *do* come," she laughed tensely.[12]

Her edginess increased in a tense exchange with her hapless brother Richard, who was growing weary of her mix of money laments and "advice" about careers and marriage. "I beg you to refrain from all expressions except of sympathy" if she did not want to estrange him altogether, he gruffly wrote, complaining of her rebuking him for saying—after several years of chastising him for his precipitous engagements—he would never get married and informing her he had just gotten married! Her reply was equally testy. He had *asked* her advice; if he read over her letters he would see that she had been "singularly guarded and tender" in her replies. After saying his sudden bulletin that he was married caused her "painful surprize"—especially, she said, since she always spoke freely of *her* life in Italy, adding quickly, "so far as I can"!—she noted sourly, "this news makes me even more indisposed to go back than I was before. I wish to see you all, but I feel sure now that in my family I can never find a tranquil abode. They have all their destinies to work out independent of me, and I must sustain myself alone as well as I can." Meanwhile, they should know how really bad things were with her. True, she had her history of the political struggle in Italy, but her poverty even spoiled that, as well as other opportunities "opened for me as they did for no other American": "I live in a chamber and thus cannot receive many persons whose society would be valuable to me. I cannot afford to dress or to ride, so that I can visit others very little. I cannot afford reference books, little journeys, many things that would be of great use. When I return, I shall not be able to buy engravings &c to illustrate what I have seen for classes." She closed by reminding him how she had always treated him with the sympathy of a sister, the goodwill of a parent, and the freedom of a friend. In his subsequent letters, he returned to his old posture of solicitousness and gratitude.[13]

Most unnerving was Caroline's seeming silence. It had now been three months since Fuller had revealed in her letter her marriage and motherhood, not an excessive time for a transatlantic exchange but nerve-racking nonetheless. On March 8, Fuller wrote her another note, this time, she hoped, in a soberer vein than that of that earlier letter of "lacerated affections": "Now I have learned more fortitude, I feel very calm but sternly towards fate." What "fate" she was referring to is hard to say, as someone has torn off the part presumably explaining it, although from her anguished remarks following about her having to leave Angelino in Rieti, that was clearly one aspect of it. In fact, however calm or stern she felt, she still gave Caroline, in sharp contrast with her cheeky January letter to James Clarke about their "rusty fusty" Boston colleagues, the most agonized appraisal about her living in Italy and returning to America that she had ever expressed. Taking off from a description of the "intoxicating beauty" of the flower-covered Abruzzi where she had lived the previous summer, she obsessively zigzagged:

> There is nothing like it in America. The old genius of Europe has mellowed all its marbles here. Earth is so full of it that one cannot have that feeling of holy virgin loveliness as in America. I cannot feel alive here, the spirits of dead men crowd me in the most apparently solitary places. I have no genius at all. I am all the time too full of sympathy. It would sometimes be so pleasant to be in America for a day. But I cannot want to go there yet . . . and here I have been so beloved, both by ghosts and fleshly men.

This is a curious confession: deeply involved in Italy's political present yet fearing its seductive past might suppress her "genius"—yet, despite her love of "holy virgin" America, seemingly not wanting to be there even for a day if it lost her the love of both "ghosts and fleshly men" that she had never experienced in her own country. Her American cosmopolitan persona could hardly have sounded more culturally dissonant.[14]

Fortunately, to allay a little this dissonance, a week later Richard's letter enclosing Caroline's reply arrived. "Your letter received yesterday," Fuller audibly sighed, "so full of sweetness and acquainting me so well with the facts of your life brought true consolation." The most important fact was the news that Caroline too had recently given birth, which probably encouraged her to vent all her anxiety about her most precariously placed "fleshly" loved one. She gave Caroline a brisk narrative of the "wicked" Rietians and the "many desperadoes" in Garibaldi's army, whose thousand-man Legion now stationed at Rieti she portrayed in considerably more lurid colors than she had in her dispatch's tribute to his great military skills. "Far worse" were the Neapolitan troops six miles off. "In case of conflict I should fear for the nurse of Angelino, the loveliest young women there." But what could she do? On the one hand, she could not move Nino to another place without "immense difficulty," but on the other, although she had intended to move back to Rieti, "now I do not know whether I can stay there or not." If she could not, she said, she definitely would at all risks remove him. Still, "every day is to me one of mental doubt and conflict; how it will end, I do not know. I try to hold myself ready every way body and mind for any necessity." As for keeping Nino a secret, which Caroline had questioned, she remained, if silent about the reasons, adamant about its necessity: "You say no secret can be kept in the civilized world and I suppose not long, but it is very important to me to keep this, for the present, if possible, and by and by to have the mode of disclosure at my option. For this, I have made the cruelest sacrifices; it will, indeed, be just like the rest, if they are made of none effect." What clearly consoled her, though, was Caroline's offer to adopt Nino: "I receive with profound gratitude your thought of taking him, if any thing should happen to us." If she lived, she could decide if she wanted him to be an Italian or American citizen; but if he were an orphan, he would have to live with Ossoli's sister, "a person of great elegance and sweetness but entirely limited in mind. I should not like that. I will think about it." She closed with brave Marian analogies:

Before he was born I did a great deal having the idea I might die and all my spirit remain incarnated in him, but now I think I shall live and carry him round myself as I ride on my ass into Egypt. We shant go so mildly as this yet.

You talk about your mangers, Carrie . . . ; we have no donkey and it costs a great deal to travel in diligences and steamers, and being a nobleman is a poor trade in a ruined despotism just turning into a Republic. I often think of Dickens's marchioness [Dick Swivelson's "small servant" in the *Old Curiosity Shop,* whom he promoted to a "marchioness" and taught to play cribbage] playing whist in the kitchen. So I play whist every where.

She added one postscript. Caroline could show her letters to her husband before burning them but must stick to Fuller's subterfuge: "No American here knows that I ever was in Rieti. They suppose I passed the summer at Subiaco."[15]

On March 26 Fuller left for Rieti, telling Richard her apartment lease was up, it was cheaper to live in the country, she needed mountain air, and, for good measure, she wanted to regain her appetite, all probably true, but purposely disingenuous. It had now been three months since her first brief visit after Angelino's birth, and her anxiety about his condition does not seem to have abated. His appearance bothered her a little. "He is very fat, but, strange enough, small," she wrote to Ossoli. "His hair does not grow, and he always wears those horrible black caps." Also, confirming her Romantic fancy that Nino and she uncannily affected each other through their mutual sympathy, they both came down with colds and aching teeth, putting her "in agony" that seems to have exceeded Nino's. A few days later, however, after tending to him all night, they both felt better. "Nino still has a cold; he coughs at night, but in the day he is very dear always laughing," she informed Giovanni. "He wanted your letter, but it was to put into his mouth."[16]

Still, Rieti remained Rieti, famous as a "hot-bed of homicide" and mountain blood feuds, of which she got a sample her third day at Chiara's house, when at dinner downstairs, Chiara's husband Pietro and his older brother Niccola, whom she had been assured were "good," got into a violent argument over some apparently long-running family dispute. Fuller, who was upstairs bathing, heard tables and chairs crashing and women screaming "aiuto" and rushed down to find the brothers fighting with knives and lumber, evidently trying to kill each other. "I spoke to Niccola," she reported to Ossoli the next morning, "he did not answer me but looked at me like a wild beast; the women held his arm so that he could not throw the knife[;] he grabbed them by their hair. Pietro who did not have a knife threw wood; a big piece just missed my head." Ossoli later related "with most reverent enthusiasm," an acquaintance recounted, that his wife, "with her calm, firm, well-known voice" in the midst of the chaos had miraculously calmed the crazed Niccola, who had then thrown the knife on the ground, grabbed and kissed her hand, and run across the room to embrace his brother. Probably this version was more telling about Ossoli's pride in his "well-known" wife than a fully accurate account of the incident. At least his story needs to be set alongside her more mundane but still scary account: "Immediately all the neighbors arrived; Niccola's master took away his knife but if our child had been down there he probably would have been killed." In any case, although evidently outwardly calm, she felt frightened enough for Nino that she told Ossoli that she wanted them to consider moving him to Rome. "If it is necessary for him, we will tell our secret," she wrote emphatically, "who knows if it will not be the best thing in the end? But it is necessary to think of everything, because our whole future lives depend upon the discretion of this moment." Ossoli answered that he, too, was "very much disquieted" by her report, but, although he did not outright veto the idea, he was clearly inclined against it, and they dropped it.[17]

The violence that most disquieted her in Rieti, though, came, as she had feared, from Garibaldi's soldiers. "Garibaldi has no control over these desperados of his band," she wrote anxiously to Ossoli. "It is said that on Sunday a friar, two citizens and 9 of their own were killed. Two bodies were found in the river. The presence of the regular group can prevent these excesses. But now I surely do not have courage to go out alone" or even "into the street." Whether these reports, similar to others constantly circulated by ultraconservative priests, were true or not is impossible to say. Even if true, it is doubtful they were chargeable to Garibaldi's soldiers, whom, despite their rough and often fearsome look, he successfully kept from committing any serious excesses. (In the anticlerical general's mind, though, those did not include seizing provisions from the churches and estates of wealthy prelates.) The more likely culprits would have been Republican zealots repaying killings and beatings from the priest-sponsored Sanfedists, which were common in the area around Rieti. In any case, she soon got a different picture of Garibaldi's men when, on April 16, she set off for Rome and stopped at a small inn to eat and rest. After she sat down, the proprietor suddenly rushed into the room, shouting, "We are quite lost, here is the Legion Garibaldi. These men always pillage and if we do not give all up to them without pay they will kill us." She looked out on the road and, seeing them, began to think that they might, if nothing else, take her carriage horses and leave her stranded. But instead of indulging her fears, she used her wits. After they boisterously burst into the dining room, she rose from her table and said to the owner, "Give these good men wine and bread on my account; for, after their ride, they must need refreshment." The noise immediately subsided, they bowed respectfully, and after eating and telling her about their journey, they gently escorted her down the steps of the inn, after which she drove off wondering, she later reported to Emelyn Story, how such men could have the reputation they had. Later that evening she arrived in Rome, bringing that early spring's arguments, adventures, and anxieties to an uncertain end.[18]

III

While Fuller was rising above her fears in Rieti, military and diplomatic developments were threatening to sink the Democrats' Risorgimento. The catalyst, of course, was the pope. On February 18, as Fuller predicted, to preserve the semblance of a Catholic united front, he officially asked Austria, France, Spain, and Naples to restore him to the Holy See, while fully expecting that only his favored powers, Austria and Naples, were ready to act. Then came the battle at Novara. Following three days of intense fighting, the Austrian army again defeated Charles

Albert's forces, abruptly ending his second declared war. Although she had thus been right in her March 20 dispatch that the "treacherous" king would quit after a single lost battle, she could hardly have taken much comfort in the fact. While she might have gloated over his ignominious abdication in favor of his son Victor Emmanuel II, Italy's future "liberator," she could not have failed to realize that, though Tuscany and Venice still remained shakily in the Democratic camp, none of the three republican states had an army capable of repelling a foreign invasion. Rome's encirclement, unseen in the winter of democratic expansion, suddenly loomed.

Certainly, the Republic's leaders perceived the danger. Six days after Novara, while Fuller was still in Rieti, a Triumvirate of Mazzini, Carlo Amellini, and Count Arelio Saffi were given unlimited powers to carry on the war against Austria and defend the Republic. Although Amellini and Saffi were both well-respected moderate Democrats, Mazzini was the Triumvirate's sine qua non and, in effect, temporary dictator. Preternaturally energetic, hopeful, and inspiring, he maintained Romans' confidence in the government through its darkest hours, rousing them to acts of courage and heroism, surprising the Republican leaders' bitterest enemies and often themselves. It was also this reputedly failed political dreamer and plotter, with no administrative experience, to whom they looked to expeditiously implement government policy and extricate them from the approaching disaster.

On March 31, eleven days after Fuller had prophesied Louis-Napoleon's "dereliction from principle," the French Assembly, fearful of an Austrian takeover of Italy after Novara, authorized an expedition to Civitavecchia, Rome's seaport, thus beginning, as Fuller denominated it, the "French comedy." To be sure, the authorization bill's moderate Republican sponsors insisted that its sole purposes were, like the earlier aborted one in November, to "protect" the Roman Republic from an Austrian attack and effect a mediation between the pope and his rebellious subjects. In fact, the more conservative Barrot ministry, which associated the Republic, as did most of the country's high bourgeois and aristocratic classes, with its own repressed radical worker's uprising in June, had a rather different objective. Theirs was to *restore* the pope under the original reform statute establishing lay advisory institutions and, in doing so, to win grateful Catholic voters for Louis-Napoleon's monarchist-backed party in the upcoming legislative elections and, more generally, the Catholic world's gratitude for "freeing" the pope from bloodthirsty radical Protestants and socialists, meanwhile blocking Austria and extending France's influence on the peninsula. This logic rested, of course, on two highly questionable assumptions noted during the Assembly debate by socialist and radical Republicans: first, that most Romans were Moderates eager to be delivered from their Republican oppressors, and second, that the pope would be happy to return as a liberal pontiff under the wing of the French. Without the first, the expedition would become an invasion, and without the second, it would defeat its "liberal" purpose. The government's tests began on April 24, when an expeditionary force of ten thousand soldiers under General Nicolas Oudinot, the son of Napoleon I's marshal, landed at Civitavecchia on the Tyrrhenian seacoast thirty-five miles northwest of Rome.[19]

The landing caught the Triumvirate by surprise. Mazzini and his colleagues, who still could not believe that republican France would attack a fellow republic, initially accepted Oudinot's spurious assurances that he solely intended to stop an Austro-Neapolitan invasion. The next day, however, after learning from a garrulous French emissary that the general's real object was to restore papal authority, and that he was prepared to use force if his army was blocked from entering the city, an outraged Roman Assembly voted to meet "force with force." Meanwhile, Fuller harbored a different uncertainty: whether the resistance would succeed. She had good reasons for worrying. The Roman army, although it had gotten some arms from abroad, was badly equipped, and ever since the French landing, morale in the city was low. Meanwhile, since Novara, political winds were blowing against republicans all over northern Italy, which Fuller duly noted in her journal. Not only were Piedmont's Democrats' clubs and newspapers shut down, its parliament suspended, and a "reactionary" ministry formed, she wrote on April 18, but also, even more disturbing, many Italians near Novara had acted "in the most infamous way *towards* Italians," a fact that the Moderate press tried to suppress. If that was not enough proof that Republicans and even Liberals were a minority in Italy, she said, the Florentines' growing disgust with the dour Guerrazzi and the Tuscan authorities' desperate attempts to cut a deal with Austria further proved it. Nor did she sound too confident about even the Romans. On the twenty-fifth, right after learning the French had landed, she went with the Storys to the Piazza del Popolo to listen to the stirring addresses of Mazzini, Belgioioso, and other government leaders and supporters speaking on the top of benches, but returned with little confidence in the people's capacities for resistance. On the twenty-eighth, the day Oudinot began marching his soldiers toward Rome, they attended another rally and heard more brave speeches, but looking down from her apartment on the Piazza Barberini, she grimly observed in her journal:

> The tragedy so begun is tending to a close. Rome is barricaded, the foe daily hourly expected. Will the Romans fight? . . . Outwardly they express great order. The chamber of deputies has warmly and unanimously voted to resist. At the review of the civic guard yesterday they gave great promise, yet somewhere I doubt them all. From my window I see now where they are bringing boards. I suppose to make a support for cannon and it seems to be such play for men and boys alike.[20]

The next day, April 29, Oudinot's soldiers took up headquarters at Castel di Guido just west of Rome. At that point, with Garibaldi's contingent, the Romans had a couple of thousand more men than the French, but the general, convinced (as he said) that "Italians do not fight," and assured by his clerical informers that grateful Romans were waiting to open the gates to his troops, felt so confident that he left behind siege guns and scaling ladders. However, when two of his columns moved out from Civitavecchia the following morning and approached the southwest and northeast sections of the Vatican walls, each encountered a hail of grapeshot and bullets from Roman cannons, artillery, and rifles. When Fuller and the Storys visited Ossoli at the Vatican three days later, soldiers told them that

they were "a little timid at first, but grew hotter and fiercer as the battle continued, and at last were full of courage and confidence, even to heroism." Following
this check of the French, Garibaldi's Legion launched two stunning attacks, first
on a thousand-man French infantry unit a mile south of the Vatican in open fields,
and then nearby on French regular troops between the Villa Pamfili and the Villa
Corsini. The battle ended six hours later, with the invaders retreating to Castel di
Guido, leaving 500 French killed and 365 captured. Indeed, they scrambled in
such disorder that Garibaldi's soldiers would very likely have routed them had
not Mazzini, fearing a rout would alienate the French Assembly's left-wing "Mountain," denied Garibaldi's request to attack. The following morning, after the cap-
tives were nursed, fed, and sent back to their camp to the cheers of forgiving Roman
crowds, Oudinot wrote a self-congratulatory report to the ministry, disguising his
defeated incursion as a successful "reconnaissance" and urgently demanding
speedy reinforcements.[21]

If Fuller was astonished at this unexpected victory, she did not record it. Not
that she had much time to do so. The morning of the attack on the thirtieth she
received a note from Princess Belgioioso, who cochaired the hastily organized
Committee for the Administration of Field Hospitals, informing her that she had
been named "Regolatrice" (or director) of Fate Bene Fratelli, a hospital on Tiber
Island across the bank from the Ghetto. "Go there at twelve if the alarm bell has
not rung before," the princess wrote her. "When you arrive there you will receive
all the women coming for the wounded and give them your directions so that you
are sure to have a certain number of them, night and day / May God help us." So,
after rushing to the Vatican garden following the battle to see that Ossoli was all
right, she went to the hospital, where she stayed through the night nursing the men.
With no more training than she had gotten watching her mother's celebrated family nursing, she joined the other women, principally of "high rank," who had been
recruited to superintend the military hospitals. It could not have been easy. Over
the coming weeks, both administrators and physicians would often object vocif-
erously to the interior department about (as one petition read) "the superiority and
tyranny displayed by the women" who ran the field hospitals, sometimes even
organizing boycotts and walkouts in protest. As Belgioioso had also enlisted scores
of prostitutes recently released from Roman jails to make up part of the staff of
six thousand women she had mobilized for the hospitals, some of which had formerly been convents, rumors spread that they were running illicit houses. As a
veteran of sex wars in the United States, Fuller probably found the claim, however ludicrous, not entirely surprising.[22]

Fuller and Belgioioso's first job was simply to get the hospitals, which the priests
in charge had left in disarray, running. "Night & day," Emelyn Story recalled,
they quietly and efficiently organized their staffs and parceled out work assignments, quickly bringing the hospitals to a state of "perfect regularity and discipline." Fuller also provided a good deal of care herself both at Fate Bene Fratelli
and at the Central Field Hospital at Santa Trinità dei Pellegrini. The conditions
were not ideal. The weather all summer was intensely hot, her health was shaky,
and the wounded were many. That first night she nursed some seventy soldiers,

both Romans and Frenchmen, many dying or very severely wounded, with arms or legs needing to be amputated, and groaning from embedded bullets. Although she effusively praised Belgioioso's valiant hospital work, Fuller said nothing of her own, so we do not have much of a picture of her nursing. However, Mazzini, Belgioioso, the Storys, and others later wrote feelingly of her stints, usually eight to ten hours with no breaks and often all night, and of the electric effect her efforts had on the soldiers. "Her heart & soul were in the cause for which these men had fought," one afterward wrote. "I have seen the eyes of the dying, as she moved among them, extended upon opposite beds, sweet in commendation of her unwearied tenderness. . . . And I have heard many of those who recovered speak, with all the passionateness & fervor of Italian natures, of her . . . sympathy & compassion, throughout their long illness." Emelyn Story was more graphic:

> I have walked through the wards with Margaret & seen how comforting was her presence to the poor suffering men. "How long will the Signora stay?" "When will the Signora come again?"—they eagerly asked. For each one's peculiar tastes she had a care; to one she carried books, to another she told the news of the day, & listened to another's oft repeated tale of wrongs, as the best sympathy she could give. They raised themselves up on their elbows, to get the last glimpse of her as she was going away.[23]

Meanwhile, Fuller coped with her own security. As the Piazza Barberini was deemed an "insecure abode," a couple of days after the initial attack, Fuller moved to the top floor of the Casa Dies in the Via Gregoriana. A quarter-mile northwest toward the Piazza di Spagna and nearer to the center of the city, it was protected by National Guard soldiers assigned by Mazzini and also housed the Storys, the Heaths, and the handful of other pro-Republican English and Americans who were remaining in Rome to raise money for the defense. Their landlords' hostility to the government annoyed Fuller, but they treated her and her other paying friends well, and the house's loggia would later serve as a perfect perch for viewing the pitched day-and-night battle below and around her.[24]

The safety she most worried about, though, was Ossoli's. The day after the battle, she went with the Storys to visit him and was shaken to see a large swath of blood that had streamed on the wall from a dying soldier close to where Ossoli had been firing. The visit also seems to have been frustrating. Ossoli looked "haggard, worn, & pale," Emelyn reported, and the camp was so busy that he and Fuller had only a few minutes to talk privately. "Please, do not fail to see me," she afterward wrote him, detailing her schedule at the hospital and begging him to come to her as soon as he could. "It is terrible to spend so many anxious hours without seeing you again. They say that the Neapolitans are not advancing, but all seems so uncertain." Anxious notes and hurried walks between the Casa Dies, the hospital, the Vatican gardens, and the post office would make up her daily routine in the weeks ahead. They seem to have melded in her mind into one, with her hospital work giving her solace, she would later claim, for the maternal protection she could not provide for her son and husband. "I was the Mater Dolorosa," she would say, expanding on the point to Ellen. "I felt all the wo of all the mothers who had nursed each" young man "bleeding to death or mutilated for life. . . . I felt the consolation too for those youths died worthily." Yet the consolation could not have come easily. "I well remember," Emelyn recalled, "how exhausted and weary she was,—how pale & agitated she returned to us after her day's and night's watching,—how eagerly she asked for news of Ossoli, & how seldom we had any to give her, for he was unable to send her a word for two or three days at a time."[25]

After a week, she resumed her dispatches, the first one, on May 6, with a dramatic flourish. "I write you from barricaded Rome," she began. "The Mother of Nations is now at bay against them all." France was of course the biggest culprit. "We must say France," because although most of the "honorable" left "has disowned the expedition," the Assembly had voted funds to sustain it and the general populace and the army had not uttered a peep against it. Nor should her readers be fooled by France's phony claims about checking Austria and Naples and forcing papal reforms, the first being merely a typical imperialist maneuver and the second a charade to cover its real objective of restoring the pope to temporal sovereignty against the democratically expressed wishes of the Roman electorate. As for the excuse that the French had been misled by Gaetan officials' propaganda about the readiness of Romans to support the pope if protected from the intimidating Republicans, as soon as France's soldiers arrived they could see, she wrote, that no one rose up to declare for the pope, indeed, "not a soul stirred." Yet they still attacked: "France, eager to destroy the last hope of Italian emancipation, France the alguacil [constable] of Austria, the soldiers of republican France, firing upon republican Rome!" So the Gallic hypocrites got what they deserved: confusion, demoralization, defeat, and, hopefully, divine vengeance. "If there be angel as well as demon powers that interfere in the affairs of men," she declared almost bloodthirstily, "those bullets could scarcely fail to be turned back against their own breasts."[26]

And Americans' stakes in all this? One was their Italophilia, which she exploited to the hilt but also reformulated in modern terms as a sacrificial lamb for the Risorgimento. "We all feel very sad, because the idea of bombs barbarously thrown in, and street-fight in Rome is peculiarly dreadful," she wrote poignantly, speaking of the remnants of her American colony. "Apart from all the blood and anguish inevitable at such times, the glories of Art may perish, and mankind be forever despoiled of the most beautiful inheritance." But that was a necessary tragedy that she was readily willing to accept. "I would defend Rome to the last moment," she coolly advised her readers. "She must not be false to the higher hope that has dawned upon her. She must not fall back into servility and corruption. And no one is willing." An even bigger stake for Americans was their country's liberal honor. Going beyond her call in February for private American contributions to support the Republic, she now urged official diplomatic recognition. After all, she said, the previous year Richard Rush, the ambassador to France, had immediately extended recognition to the new French Republic. But that act, which Rush had taken on his own without regard to the State Department's official policy of "de facto recognition" only of new governments that had proven capable of sustaining themselves, had occurred back the previous spring before the "June

Days" had made many Americans skeptical about the European revolutions. Other added factors explaining the difference were memories of French aid to American revolutionaries and ethnic prejudices toward Italians as unreliable. If, however, Fuller was aware of these things, she did not mention them, although even if she had, they would hardly have made any difference to her. The most important reason for recognition was not precedence but America's sense of itself: if it were not forthcoming, it would be to its everlasting shame, but if it were, she wrote, sounding her cosmopolitan patriotic battle cry, "all that is most truly American in America would have spoken to sustain the sickened hopes of European democracy." Fuller concluded her dispatch with a harrowing picture of Romans' anxiety as the French regrouped just outside the walls and the Austrians mustered their forces only a three-day march from the city. "But of this more when I write next," she said, in her cliffhanger. "Who knows what I may have to tell another week?"[27]

IV

As Fuller waited for a break in the stalemate, she attended to personal affairs entwined in the vicissitudes of revolution. One was the perennial one of money. The Republic's rampant inflation had so discounted her savings she was afraid to withdraw any of it. She also feared that the looting Piedmontese troops subduing the Genoese had stolen the note of exchange that Eugene had sent to a bank in the port city. However, the note turned out to be safe, and Heath gave her another one just before he left Rome that she could draw if she needed to.[28]

More troublesome than money worries was anxiety about Nino. "During all the siege of Rome," Fuller would afterward tell Caroline, "I could not see him, and though the Physician wrote reassuring letters I often seemed to hear him calling me amid the roar of the cannon, and he seemed to be crying." But it was not just that she could not see him; with mail and transportation between Rieti and Rome now frequently halted, for days at a time she heard nothing about him. "In the burning sun I went every day to wait in the crowd for letters about him," she would later tell her sister. "I imagined every thing; he was to be in danger of every enormity the Croats were then committing on the babies of Lombardy. The house would be burned over his head, but if he escaped, how were we to get the money to buy his bibs and primers. Then his father was to be killed in the fighting and I to die." When that May she finally heard from Nino's new physician, Luigi Bassini, she got some actual bad news. Chiara had told him if she did not get more money, she would abandon Nino. Somehow, Fuller managed to get some to Bassini to give her, and the doctor soon reported that "now she is satisfied and calm." Fuller next learned from him that the cowpox pus he had administered to Nino to ward off smallpox turned out to be too weak to be effective, and after that his fever, rash, diarrhea, and "coughing fits" kept him from trying again. Eventually, Nino got over his virus, leaving him with only a "convulsive cough" and a want of a "proclivity for nourishment and muscular vigor," for which as a "precaution" Bassini gave him cappuccino syrup. "To cheer you up," he wrote Fuller, "I will say that this morning when I was examining Angelino I made out a prescription and then I put it in his little hands; and he looked at it attentively, almost seeming to read it, and then from time to time he turned his eyes to me and smiled a smile a thousand times innocent: he was as dear as one of Raphael's little lambs." The doctor seemed to have known what a mother like Fuller would want to hear, but it is doubtful the report much allayed her fears.[29]

Certainly, an action she took that May suggests that it did not. Fearing after the first French assault that she might soon be killed, and knowing the Storys were about to leave for Switzerland and Germany, she asked Emelyn to come to her apartment. There she told her what among her old friends she had so far revealed only to Caroline: the young Republican soldier whom for six months she and William had known as her "most congenial companion" was her husband. She also revealed the undoubtedly more surprising fact of the existence of their child in Rieti, asking her, in the event of her death, to take him to her mother's and confide him to her and Carrie's care. It was also at that meeting that she showed Emelyn documents of her marriage and Angelino's birth, as well as a "book" chronicling the history of her relationship with Ossoli to give to Fuller's family. "If I live, it will be of no use, for my word will be all that they will ask," she said hopefully. Finally, she swore Emelyn to a "solemn pledge of secrecy," which she agreed to, although evidently only after Fuller persuaded her that protecting Ossoli's inheritance required it. Still, Emelyn remembered, she felt "tormented" about not being able to help her, although Fuller thought she and William had helped a lot just through their sympathy when she had no strength left to be much of a companion.[30]

The Heaths departed early that May, and the Storys followed on the twenty-fourth. "I remain alone in the house, under our flag," Fuller wrote to Richard, speaking of the stars and stripes the acting American consul James Freeman had placed on the balcony "to secure her, if possible from molestation" from the French and the papal authorities, to whom Freeman thought she had made herself "obnoxious." Although she was almost the only American left in the city, she managed to find several compatible replacements. One recent arrival at the Casa Dies was the English poet Arthur Hugh Clough, whose religious skepticism did not muffle the prorepublican sentiments that would infuse the ironies of *Amours de Voyage*, his epistolary poem about a self-doubting intellectual tourist during the French siege. Along with political militancy, they shared a keen interest in the contemporary literary scene. After he returned to England in the fall, he sent some of his poems and some by his friends Matthew Arnold and Thomas Burbidge, which "much pleased" her, and she evidently felt comfortable enough with him to write him frankly about her marriage while it was still a secret. "So generous, tender, and advanced in thought," she characterized him to Emelyn Story, using almost the exact adjectives he would adopt several years later describing her to his fiancée Blanch Smith.[31]

Fuller's most useful new supporters were diplomats. She did not much care for Nicholas Brown, the flirtatious married American consul, who had gotten recalled because of his ostentatious support for the Republic. She was much more drawn to the more politically cautious Lewis Cass, Jr., the new American chargé d'affaires who had arrived at the beginning of April with a background that could hardly have appealed less to Fuller. The son and namesake of the doughface Democrats' Michigan senator and recently defeated presidential candidate, he had had a reputation as a "dissipated" showoff as a young man growing up in Detroit. Fuller first met him the morning of the French attack on April 30, just after getting back from visiting Ossoli at the Vatican and before going on to the hospital. After learning that she was living alone at the Piazza Barberini, he had rushed to her apartment, offering to "do anything" to help her. "I liked you from the first time I saw you," he would later tell her. Their intimacy quickly grew, as hers with young men often did, as they exchanged disclosures, hers of her secret marriage and her fears about her or Ossoli being killed and his of his loneliness as a young bachelor. "I have told you more about my feelings than I ever said to another," he wrote her; in fact he felt more for her, than he had ever "before felt for any woman." She also evidently moved him politically. Convinced, like the English diplomats with whom he had spoken in London, that the Republic would not last a week, he had arrived thoroughly committed to the State Department's instruction that he withhold delivering his credentials to the Republican government. However, after only a few weeks, clearly influenced by Fuller as well as by what he himself saw, he started sending dispatches to the new secretary of state, John M. Clayton, testifying to the regime's efficiency and the populace's overwhelming opposition to the return of papal rule and determination to defend the Republic. By the middle of May he began sharing with her intelligence on the French and Roman governments' maneuvers. Indeed, Cass's sympathies with the Republic and Fuller's pro-Republican dispatches seem to have evoked hopes among its leaders that official American support might be forthcoming.[32]

If so, it was no doubt partly out of desperation. On May 4, four thousand fresh French troops joined Oudinot's forces. On the fifteenth, Ferdinand II put his final lock on southern Italy when his Neapolitan troops reoccupied Palermo, where a year and a half earlier the first spark of European revolution had burst forth. A week later, forty-nine hundred Spanish soldiers joined up with them to threaten a powerful assault from the south. Meanwhile, in the north, Italy was fast slipping into the hands of the Austrians. Following a valiant eight-day defense, republican Bologna surrendered, after which all resistance collapsed in the Romagna, as it soon did in all the Papal States, thus ending any slim chance of outside help for the Romans. Indeed, after the twenty-fifth, when two thousand Austrian soldiers marched into Florence and overthrew Tuscany's struggling republican government, virtually all of northern Italy outside of Piedmont and besieged Venice was effectively under Austrian control. As though that were not enough, the tsar sent three thousand Russian soldiers to help crush Austria's remaining internal troublemakers, leaving its army free to continue marching toward the city from the Marches and Tuscany. "An inland city cannot long sustain a siege when there is no hope of aid," Fuller later wrote of Rome's plight then, when four national armies menacingly encircled it.[33]

After waiting three weeks for the "decisive event" for Rome, Fuller strained to put the best face she could on Italy's bleak-looking situation. In her May 27 dispatch, she seized on Garibaldi's recent daring rout of Neapolitan troops across the frontier and Austria's "constantly increasing" troubles at home and in Hungary, but mainly she relied on ideological counters. One was her usual outrage at the Moderates. "The Florentines have humbled and disgraced themselves in vain," she wrote bitterly, speaking of their earlier recall of Leopold II from Gaeta, who preferred to wait for "his dear cousins of Austria" to "put everything in perfect order. . . . Now they crown their work by giving over [the triumvirs] Guerrazzi and [Antonio] Patracci to be tried by an Austrian Court Martial." A bigger chip was the political future: "Should the Russian intervention quell [the Austrian unrest] to-day, it is only to raise a storm far more terrible to-morrow." Indeed, tomorrow had already begun. "The struggle is now fairly, thoroughly commenced between the principle of Democracy and the old powers, no longer legitimate," she declared. "That struggle may last fifty years, and the earth be watered with the blood and tears of more than one generation, but the result is sure. All Europe, including Great Britain, where the most bitter resistance of all will be made, is to be under Republican Government in the next century." Her honored Jefferson, who had once waxed similarly complacent about a sanguinary future following the French Revolution, would have recognized a kindred spirit.[34]

Fuller mixed like realism, outrage, and prophecy in her exposition of Italy's future as foretold in its people's transformed political consciousness. She passed over peasant hostility to Lombard Republicans because of their taxes, confiscations, and impiety, which she must have gotten some comparable taste of in the Abruzzi, where, unlike elsewhere in pro-Republican Romagna, it was rife. Nonetheless, she accurately pinpointed the democratic dynamic in Rome and in other northern Italian cities over the previous two years: "When I first arrived in Italy, the vast majority of this people had no wish beyond limited monarchies, constitutional governments. They still respected the famous names of the nobility; they despised the priests, but were still fondly attached to the dogmas and ritual of the Roman Catholic Church." It required King Bomba (Ferdinand II, so named for his bombing of his own people during his "coup" the previous spring), the treacheries of Charles Albert and Pius IX, the pompous stupidity of Gioberti, the cowardice of Tuscany's Leopold II, the slaughters by the Austrians, the viciousness of Parma and Madena, "and finally the imbecile Louis Bonaparte, 'would-be Emperor of France,' to convince this people that no transition is possible between the old and the new. *The work is done;* the revolution in Italy is now radical, nor can it stop till Italy becomes independent and united as a republic."[35]

Most startling, though, was Fuller's searing anticlerical portrait of Italy's changing religious consciousness. "Protestant she already is," she declared, hyperbolically conflating anticlericalism with anti-Catholicism. The memory of the saints and martyrs and, of course, Mary as the "ideal of Woman" might continue to be revered, but Christ's message, suppressed in favor of the Church's exploitation of Madonna and saints for material gain, would gradually come into vogue, as already evidenced, she said, a little fantastically, by the new Italian translation of the New Testament. And that was not all. Exactly a week before, a mob had raided two churches and dragged out confessionals, symbols of Catholicism but also priestly rule, and piled them up in the Piazza del Popolo for a bonfire. Rather than expressing any discomfort over this revolutionary violence, she saw it all of a piece with the New Testament translation and the previous evening's production of Molière's *Tartuffe*. The incident horrified Moderates like Arconati and, as Fuller herself conceded, troubled the triumvirs, who quickly had it stopped and sharply criticized its perpetrators. Nonetheless, it, too, reflected Fuller's "realities" in Rome, even if seen through the eyes of a self-proclaimed "daughter of the Puritans"—for whom she had rarely had a kind word in America.[36]

In the remainder of her dispatch, Fuller returned with added intensity to the issue of American recognition. Again, she enlisted American Italophilia, although now in a more sober tone. "War near at hand seems to me even more dreadful than I had fancied it," she confessed, urging Americans who knew Rome through travel or even just guidebooks and histories to grieve for the terrible ruin it had visited on the city physically. "Rome is shorn of the locks which lent grace to her venerable brow," she wrote, speaking of the devastation of the gardens of the Villa Borghese and the trees of the Forum. "She looks desolate, profaned. I feel what I never expected to, as if I might by and by be willing to leave Rome." But what made American political nonrecognition shocking, though, was not just the destruction of the world's cultural patrimony but the policy's diminution of America's moral standing in the world. Even the "lowest people" constantly asked her why the Americans withheld recognition when they themselves had had a war to become free. What did the United States government want from Romans? It knew their republic had fulfilled the necessary practical conditions: the people's overwhelming vote for its constitution, their resistance to a foreign invasion, and their sustaining themselves at least so far. What was there to fear—that the papacy would avenge itself on the United States? The last thing the pope would want to do would be to alienate a country whose population was swelling with new Catholics. As for the practical American's question of how *did* she think the Romans could win "'without money, and against so potent a league of foes?'" she answered with a ringing statement of her American cosmopolitan liberal faith:

> I am not sure, but I hope, for I believe something in the heart of a people when fairly awakened. I have also a lurking confidence in what our fathers spoke of so constantly, a providential order of things, by which brute force and selfish enterprises are sometimes set at nought by aid which seems to descend from a higher sphere. Even old Pagans believed in that, you know, and I was born in America, Christianized by the Puritans—America, freed by eight years' patient suffering, poverty and struggle—America so cheered in dark days by one spark of sympathy from a foreign shore—America, first "recognized" by Lafayette. I saw him in traversing our country, then great, rich, and free. Millions of men who owed in part their happiness to what, no doubt, was once sneered at as romantic sympathy, threw garlands on his path. It is natural that I should have some faith.

In short, this was her and her country's great Puritan-laced national republican memory, with her own "old Pagan" doubts about providence suppressed. She closed with a compatible plea to send an ambassador, of course to help the Risorgimento, but also to affirm America's liberal cosmopolitan values of "the brotherhood of nations and of men—the equality of rights for all"—or "perish, like the old dominions, from the leprosy of selfishness.[37]

She faced an uphill battle. Ever since the "June Days" in Paris, conservative Whig papers and politicians had been condemning radical democratic violence in France and Italy and denouncing American Democrats for their sympathy with its perpetrators. American newspapers and political observers who had condemned the French invasion doubted that the government had much popular support or that Romans were capable of governing and defending themselves. Even conservative evangelicals were now joining Catholics in denouncing the anarchist, blood-thirsty "Jacobin" regime, making it unlikely that the United States government would extend recognition to the Roman Republic or any embattled revolutionary government. Did Fuller's dispatches make any difference? Government officials undoubtedly read them, although their reactions are unknown. They did seem to have had, though, one important effect. The following month, impressed by Cass's glowing reports about the Republic, in which he favorably cited Fuller and her American friends' steadfast support of it, President Zachary Taylor asked Secretary Clayton to change Cass's instructions from excluding recognition to leaving it to his discretion. Cass, however, would not get that directive until after the Republic's fall, so he stuck to his government's wait-and-see policy, which Fuller sardonically described as "*If they can do without us*, we will help them."[38]

If her dispatches did not affect policy, their strident anticlericalism and forthright defense of the pope's persecutors did shock and disgust many American Catholic readers. "The Romans and you have deprived me of the sight of the countenances of my late Rvds the Catholic Priesthood who have hitherto been my warm friends and supporters, but now are not," the antinativist Greeley wrote to Fuller after printing her column. "I am not sure that my very good friend Bp. Hughes will deem it is his duty to curse me at the Alter with 'bell book and candle.'" He was close to right about that. Three days later, John Joseph Hughes, the resourceful bishop of New York, wrote a blistering letter to the conservative Whig *Courier and Enquirer*, attacking both Fuller and Greeley for supporting the pathological radicals and thugs from the dregs of the Continent who had hijacked the Holy See. "They wield the stiletto," Hughes raged, in phrases that could have been taken from any reactionary European Catholic journal, sacrificing their "human victims . . . to propitiate the goddess of Young Liberty in Italy," most of them "strangers to Rome" expelled from other parts of Europe, who were imposing "a reign of terror over the Roman people." After alluding to the mob's burning of cardinals' carriages, which had seemed admirable to Fuller, he lit into the *Tribune*'s heretofore Catholic-friendly editor and correspondent for brazenly misinforming and, in Fuller's case he implied, lying to their readers. "This is the phalanx recognized by Mr. GREELEY as the Roman Republic!" he concluded. "Yet no ambassador from foreign countries has recognized such a Republic, except it be," he added sarcastically, "the female Plenipotentiary who furnishes *The Tribune* with diplomatic correspondence."[39]

The "female Plenipotentiary" was not there to defend herself, but others took up her cudgels. The bishop could expect, the Boston *Daily Evening Transcript* predicted, "a blow with a broomstick for this ungallant hit at Miss F." Meanwhile, two less gallant American liberals stood in for her politically. While conceding in his column reprinting Hughes's letter that the Roman Democrats' insistence that the pope relinquish all his temporal power was perhaps unreasonable, Greeley nonetheless endorsed Fuller's claim that the pope had now forsworn reform and become a tool of reactionary powers. As for Hughes's assertion that the Republican government ruled only through terror, Greeley was every bit as dismissive as she would have been. "Where is the evidence?" he demanded. "Despotism has its spies and emissaries there, and letter after letter from them appears in the London and Paris anti-Republican journals; but we cannot gather from them any specific statements which at all conflict with Margaret Fuller's express statement" in her May 27 dispatch. Fuller's most polemical defender, though, was none other than Lowell, who used his column in the *National Anti-Slavery Standard* to show that when the political chips were down, abolitionist principle trumped personal pique. As Fuller had, he blamed American indifference to the Romans' democratic struggle on the country's institution of slavery, which had "benumbed the heart" of his compatriots to plights of oppressed races in the world. He then honed in on the question of an American ambassadorship that Fuller had been agitating for. "It is a disgrace to America," he thundered—implying, unfairly, that the doughface Democrat's son was culpable—"that she is not represented at Rome by a man with brain enough and heart enough to sympathize with the struggle of a race in whom fifteen centuries of bad government have not extinguished the memory of a glorious past." That brought him to Hughes and Fuller:

> Bishop Hughes says sneeringly that the Roman Republic has been recognized only by the "female plenipotentiary of The Tribune." It is a pity that America could not be always as adequately represented. But Miss Fuller has not merely contented herself with the comparatively cheap sympathy of words, though even brave words are much if spoken at the right time. We learn from private letters that, the last American left in Rome, she was doing her duty in the hospitals as a nurse for the wounded, thus performing also her mission as a woman. Women have been sainted at Rome for less, and the Bishop is welcome to his sneer.

Had she read Lowell's fierce defense, Fuller probably would have ignored his characterization of her female "mission." Perhaps, she would have even revised her dismissal of his abolitionism as a shield to hide his lack of literary talent.[40]

What is most significant, though, is not speculative: neither Hughes nor Greeley nor Lowell was in Rome, and Fuller was, a great advantage in delivering compelling evidence. Speaking of a conservative French newspaper's "amusing" libel that the red flags flying from many Romans' houses displayed their bloodthirstiness, she dryly noted they were merely signals placed at the entrance of streets so coachmen could see that there was no barricade ahead. ("There is one on the house where I am, in which is no person but myself who thirst for peace, and the *padrone* who thirsts for money.") Greeley glommed onto her explanation for why the amount of crime was "almost nothing, what it was." "The Roman," he quoted her, "no longer pent in ignorance and crouching beneath espionage, no longer stabs in the dark. His energies have true vent; his better feelings are roused; he has thrown aside the stiletto." That was a slight exaggeration. That very month, a Roman mob murdered two Jesuit priests accused of aiding France or (in a less likely version) shooting at National Guard soldiers. Yet even antirepublican European observers agreed there was something remarkable about the near disappearance of serious political violence in a city with a besieged population long accustomed to violent crimes and political assassinations. Even if the triumvirs' effectiveness in stifling them contributed, her point was valid—the major political credit for Rome's "miraculous" law and order belonged to the democratic revolution that Hughes had pictured so luridly.[41]

V

In the immediate background of Fuller's May 27 dispatch, of course, was the French army, sullenly licking its wounds in Civitavecchia. The testing ground, though, was the upcoming elections to the new French Assembly: would they prove Fuller wrong about the French nation's culpability? She was not hopeful. "I do not dare to trust that people," she wrote. "The peasant is yet very ignorant. The suffering workman is frightened as he thinks of the punishments that ensued on the insurrections of May and June. The man of property is full of horror, at the brotherly scope of Socialism. The aristocrat dreams of the guillotine always when he hears speak of the people. The influence of the Jesuits is immense." Most of this was true, although at that point she did not know the election results that would tell, as she put it, "whether it be the will of the Nation to aid or strive to ruin a Government founded precisely on the same basis as their own." The answer was disastrous. The results did show one bright spot contradicting her analysis. The urban working class had been sufficiently militant to give the "*démoc-socs*," the coalition of democratic socialists and radical Republicans, the largest number of seats of any party. But the moderate Republicans who had molded the Second Republic were nearly wiped out. In their place, the "Party of Order," a coalition of three monarchist factions supported by the aristocracy, much of the upper bourgeoisie, and most of the peasantry, captured almost two-thirds of the seats, giving it a working majority and guaranteeing the Assembly's approval of Louis Napoleon's invasion of Rome.[42]

   In the meantime, while the elections were the leading player in this (as she called it) "second act of the French comedy," the recently arrived young diplomat Ferdinand de Lesseps, later the architect of the Suez Canal, arrived to play the role of an unwitting stooge. The ministry's real purposes for sending him had been twofold: to give Oudinot's reinforcements time to arrive, and to stall until the elections produced a conservative Assembly to nullify its predecessor's recent resolution demanding that Oudinot's expedition return to its original goals of protecting the Republic from invasion and encouraging conciliation with the pope. There was only one problem: Lesseps, whose instructions were ambiguous, seems to have taken these professions seriously. He also quickly saw that the Romans generally supported the Republican party of (as he described it in a report) sober tradesmen and educated youth, were adamant against the return of clerical rule, and were resolved to mount a furious resistance to another French attack. So the comic scenes began. Lesseps negotiated a truce, freeing Garibaldi to rout the Neapolitans camped among the Alban Hills fifty miles southeast of Rome, and urged Oudinot not to attack Rome. But the diplomat also pleaded with the Roman government to allow the French troops to enter the city to protect it from the Austrians then overrunning Romagna and the Marches. The triumvirs, however, now convinced, despite the truce, that the French government was determined to reinstall the pope in some temporal role, replied that they needed not military "aid" but diplomatic recognition and, if not that, at least neutrality, so they would not have to divert troops from defending the Republic against Austria. On May 20, Cass reported to Fuller that after a two-hour debate between Lesseps and a delegation of Roman deputies, the two sides remained deadlocked over a French occupation of Rome. Meanwhile, Oudinot, outraged that Lesseps had exceeded his instructions in negotiating a truce and anxious to enter Rome before the other advancing Catholic powers joined in, complained bitterly to the ministry about the diplomat's dangerous and time-wasting maneuvers. "Ah!" Fuller wrote, alluding to these assorted shenanigans and lies of Oudinot—which she probably learned of from Cass, who was serving as a go-between—such as the negotiated prisoner exchange, which the general had claimed had shown Rome's "readiness for *submission*": "the way of falsehood, the way of treachery, how dark—how full of pitfalls and traps!"[43]

After four more days of this, Lesseps got what he wanted. On May 31, he and a conciliatory Triumvirate signed a compromise agreement whereby the French, in order to protect Rome from Austria and Naples, were to take up positions just outside the city walls. Later in the day, however, Oudinot angrily refused to sign. By that time, Louis Napoleon, under pressure from his monarchist ministry and Assembly majority to rescue the pope now that Oudinot had received his reinforcements, and himself now deeply disturbed about the April 30 defeat's tarnishing his army's honor, had given the order to destroy the Roman Republic and (in Fuller's bitter words) "force back Pius IX. among his bleeding flock." By the end of the day, the diplomat and the general received their respective messages from the minister of foreign affairs: Lesseps was told he should return to France immediately and Oudinot was ordered to march on Rome without delay. The next day, while Lesseps left for Paris, Oudinot declared war on Rome.[44]

Oudinot promised Pietro Roselli, commander-in-chief of the Roman Republic, to "delay *the attack of the place*" until Monday morning of the fourth to give time for Frenchmen residing in Rome to leave. But in the spirit of his previous creative interpretations, he took "place" to mean only the city within the walls, thereby excluding Roman outposts. In the early morning of Sunday the third, two columns of French soldiers entered the grounds of the Villa Pamfili, attacking by surprise four hundred sleeping Roman soldiers guarding the San Pancrazio Gate at the Wall of Urban VIII, the city's westernmost wall on Janiculum hill, a mile and a half south of the Vatican. The French quickly captured the Pamfili and, even more important, the Villa Corsini, from which the Romans would have to dislodge them if they hoped to defend the city. Garibaldi certainly tried, launching successive sorties of soldiers, who repeatedly charged on foot through the villa's narrow gate, a "death triangle" opening up into a massive phalanx of French soldiers in the villa and spread out across the gardens, where the Italians were easily slaughtered. But mainly the forces were badly mismatched. Oudinot's troops, now augmented by fresh recruits, numbered about thirty-five thousand men, all supported by accurate artillery, powerful siege guns, and an expert corps of engineers. The Romans had fewer than half that number, poorly equipped and made up of a motley assemblage of national guardsmen, former papal guards, fierce-looking Trasteverines, foreign artists, university students, and patriots from battles in the north. After sixteen hours of furious fighting, with some five Frenchmen and nearly one thousand Italians killed, the French secured the Corsini, leaving them in control of the surrounding suburbs from the most commanding military position in the city, on the Janiculum, behind the highest section of its walls, affording a sweeping view of all of Rome.[45]

During these days, Fuller's feelings spun in different directions. "I miss you so much," she wrote five days before the attack to Emelyn Story. "At evening the house seems perfectly ghostly." On June 6, three days after the assault, she wrote her again. "Sunday, from our loggia, I witnessed a terrible, a real battle," she excitedly said, describing the sounds of "most majestic" cannon rolls, her sight of "the smoke of every discharge, the flash of the bayonets," and, with her spyglass, the "most obstinate valor" of both armies. After several more days of killing, however, she started feeling nervous. She wrote to Mazzini, complaining of his silence since the beginning of the battle. "Will you be *woman* and forgive?" he replied on June 9. "Could you spend a whole day near me you would wonder not at my being silent with those I love." He then launched into a detailed account of that day from seven in the morning to after midnight, deciding whether a "young poet and solider of promise" should have his leg amputated or be left to die, attending to the arrest of a Roman soldier, settling a violent disagreement between two generals over a tactical move, and so on. "Should the thing last long there is no human strength or will that can resist it," he added, leaving disturbingly unclear how long or with what result. "Keep this note for you: it *is* for you only. I do not like other people to know that I am working more than another man."[46]

Without getting much satisfaction from the man at the helm, the next day she wrote Emerson, obviously not expecting a response, but, perhaps for that reason, expressing the full range of her ambivalences about the war and worries about its outcome for both the warriors and herself. "I received your letter amid the round of cannonade and musketry," she began immediately. "The Italians fought like lions," but adding: "They make a stand for honor and their rights, with little ground for hope that they can resist, now they are betrayed by France." Describing her work at the hospital, she likewise balanced their terrible suffering and her "great pleasure" in witnessing the soldiers' nobility of spirit. "I carry them books, and flowers; they read, and we talk," and later at the Quirinal, then being used as a convalescent hospital directed by Belgioioso, "in those beautiful gardens, I walk with them,—one with his sling, another with his crutch. The gardener plays off all his waterworks for the defenders of the country, and gathers flowers for me, their friend." Then, suddenly, she swung into a strangely defensive apologia sua vita for her life in Italy:

> Should I never return,—and sometimes I despair of doing so, it seems so far off, so difficult, I am caught in such a net of ties here,—if ever you know of my life here, I think you will only wonder at the constancy with which I have sustained myself; the degree of profit to which, amid great difficulties, I have put the time, at least in the way of observation. Meanwhile, love me all you can; let me feel, that, amid the fearful agitations of the world, there are pure hands, with healthful, even pulse, stretched out toward me, if I claim their grasp.

If one recalls her past criticisms of Emerson's "healthful, even pulse," one wonders how confident she felt about the warmth of his "pure" hands, as distinct, it would seem, from her dirty ones. In any case, she does not sound too sure she would be there to grasp them. "I know not dear friend, whether I ever shall get home across that great ocean, but here in Rome I shall no longer wish to live," she wrote wearily, recounting the war's ravages of landscape and architecture, concluding, almost guiltily: "O, Rome, *my* country! could I imagine that the triumph of what I held dear was to heap such desolation on thy head!"[47]

In her dispatch that same day of June 10, she put her ambivalences about the war into a more sober key. "What shall I write in Rome of these sad but glorious days?" she asked. "Plain facts are best; for my feelings I could not find fit words." But after a suitably scornful account of France's diplomatic maneuvers, she turned back with a fury to the two things she had agitatedly mentioned in her letter to Emerson. One was the wounded soldiers in the hospitals, whose enthusiasm astounded her but whose defeat she was already starting to contemplate.

> All were only anxious to get out again and be at their posts. They seemed to feel that those who died so gloriously were fortunate; perhaps they were, for if Rome is obliged to yield, and how can she stand always unaided against the four powers? where shall these noble youths fly? They are the flower of Italian youth, especially among the Lombards are some of the finest young men I have ever seen. If Rome falls, if Venice falls, there is no spot on Italian earth where they can abide more, and certainly no Italian will wish to take refuge in France. Truly you said, Mr. Lesseps, "Violence and friendship are incompatible."

She marked with anguish the terrible devastation of hiding places for the French, mixing graphic details with historical associations: "Villa Borghese is finally laid waste, the villa of Raphael has perished, the trees are all cut down at Villa Albani, and the house, that most beautiful ornament of Rome, must, I suppose, go too. The stately marble forms are already driven from their place in that portico where Winkelmann sat and walked with such delight. Villa Salvaze is burnt, with all its fine frescoes, and that bank of the Tiber, shorn of its lovely plantations." The vicious calumnies on the Republic in the conservative European press naturally outraged her. The "solemn" London *Times*, which in England she had lukewarmly appreciated, disgusted her. Its pro-Austrian editorials and the sneering dispatches of its correspondent embedded with the French painted a horrific picture of the Republicans as a cabal of despicable and "degenerate" terrorists. But what most

provoked her about the Anglophone world's premiere journal was her fear that
American newspapers were swallowing its lies. "It is said to receive money from
Austria. I know not whether this be true, or whether it be merely subservient to
the aristocratical feeling of England, which is far more opposed to Republican
movements than is that of Russia; for in England fear embitters hate." And not
just in England:

> To think how bitter the English were on the Italians who succumbed, and see how
> they hate those who resist; and their cowardice here in Italy is ludicrous. It is they
> who run away at the least intimation of danger—it is they who invent all the "fe, fo,
> fum" stories about Italy,—it is they who write to the *Times* and elsewhere that they
> dare not for their lives stay in Rome, where I, a woman, walk everywhere alone,
> and all the little children do the same, with their nurses.

American revolutionaries' rabid disgust with English pride, which scorned inferior peoples who dared also, in Trevelyan's words, to aspire to freedom, was alive
and well in Rome.[48]

Meanwhile, two days later, Fuller's capacity for balancing "plain facts" and
political indignation confronted a series of successive events of enormous import
in France. On June 12 the Mountain's leader Alexandre-Auguste Ledru-Rollin
offered a resolution calling for the impeachment of Louis Napoleon on the grounds
that his order to assault the Roman Republic violated the French Constitution's
pledge that France would never use its armed forces against the liberty of any other
people. The Mountain, which represented the largest party in the Assembly, garnered 138 votes for the resolution against 388 opposed. Fuller's doubts about the
French working classes' readiness for resistance turned out justified. Although
they had given the *démoc-soc* coalition their votes the previous month, they were
in no mood, after the violent repression of the previous June, to take extreme
measures to oppose the will of the Assembly's majority, especially while a raging cholera epidemic was daily devouring hundreds in the city. For their part, the
Mountain's leaders, instead of retreating, acted foolishly. After bandying ambiguous slogans confusedly calling for a peaceful demonstration or an armed insurrection, the following day they led a large demonstration without arms facing an
army that easily crushed it. Having given the government the excuse to claim
falsely there had been an actual plan afoot to overthrow the government, many
démoc-soc leaders were arrested, their parties outlawed, and their presses shut
down, and they escaped into exile, not to return for over a decade.[49]

Instantly, the June 13 "*journée*" proved a disaster for many more than the leaders
of the French left. Their repression not only prepared the way for Louis Napoleon's
coup d'état two-and-a half years later, ensuring conservative political dominance
in Europe for another two generations, but also doomed any possibility that a new
left-wing French government would stop Oudinot's assault. Even Fuller was
shocked. "My journal, the Democratic is stopped," she wrote frantically to Cass,
speaking of *La Démocratie pacifique*, the newspaper of Victor Considerant, a
principal leader of the Mountain, which she relied on for news and radical opinion on the Continent, "its bureaux having been broken open, and Considerant under

arrest." (He was actually in hiding and would soon escape to Belgium.) "Have you not seen that the most liberal journals are all suspended? I was hoping to hear through you, some news from Paris." She then knew all hope for the Republic had vanished, although her conclusions were deeply ambivalent. "After the attempt at revolution in France failed," she later wrote to William Channing, "could I have influenced Mazzini, I should have prayed him to capitulate," even as she also knew, she said, "no honorable terms can be made with such a foe, and that the only way is *never* to yield." The question then became how much could she take of "the sound of the musketry, the sense that men were perishing in a hopeless contest"?[50]

The sound started up that day. Oudinot had sent an ultimatum to the triumvirs: unless they allowed his army to enter the city within twelve hours, he would bring up the breeching batteries and begin bombarding it, and he promptly did so in the morning. The war now raged on two fronts. One was on the small circle of points around the Villa Corsini, Garibaldi's headquarters at the Villa Savorelli, and other critical positions on the Janiculum. The other was near the city where the French concentrated their bombardment with the dual purpose of demoralizing the population and forcing a breach at points where barricades and brigades filled gaps in the enclosing walls. On June 16, Ossoli was commissioned a captain and ordered to take command of the Second Company of the First Mobile Battalion on the Pincio hill near the Piazzo del Popolo, from which Fuller had gazed down at the violent demonstration of November 16. This was a highly exposed position abutting the middle of the northern section of the ancient Aurelian Wall, which would be the center of the siege of the city for the rest of the war. It would also be a scene of extraordinary acts of bravery and heroism, as well as quarrels, desertions, and at least one retreat from "cowardice," which Ossoli usually dealt with, on his own or under orders, by either dismissal or arrest for trial.[51]

Fuller's initial reaction to the start of the bombardment gyrated between pride, horror, and foreboding. "The state of siege is very terrible," she wrote to Elizabeth Hoar on June 17 with stoic but half-faltering militancy:

> such continual alarms, then to hear the cannonade day and night and to know with every shot, some fellow man may be bleeding and dying. Sometimes I cannot sleep, sometimes I do again from sheer exhaustion. I did think, since this world was so full of ill, I was willing to see it all. I did not want to be cowardly and shut my eyes. Nor is this perpetual murder of men so bad as to see them indolently lying in the mud. The sad night is cheered by the sparklings of pure fire. Yet it *is* very sad, and oh, Rome, *my* Rome, every day more and more desecrated! One of the most gentle hallowed haunts, La Maria di Trastevere, is I hear almost ruined by the bombs of day before yesterday. Almost nightly I see burning some fair cascina. Adieu dear Lizzie, prize the thoughtful peace of Concord.

After two more days of round-the-clock bombardment and frenzied caring for the killed and wounded, she wrote an apparently frantic (now lost) letter to Mazzini about the rumor, which had even reached America, that Republican forces were about to blow up St. Peter's. "It is written that none will trust my heart, you too!" he replied angrily.

Can you believe for a single moment such nonsense . . . ? Have I proved a Vandal, or a man of 93? Is there a Frenchman here who has been molested? And whilst our best patriots and my best friends, Danielio and others, are dying under the musketry of those wretches outside the walls, am I not offering protection and this palace should he choose to come, to the only representative of France here, Degerando? My soul is full of grief and bitterness, and still, I have never for a moment yielded to reactionary feelings. Let people talk about St. Peters: it may be of some use, but depend upon a friendly word: no one has *seen* the mines; no one will see them, I repeat, whilst I am here.[52]

Presumably, the indignant denial gave her reassurance both about St. Peter's and, if she needed any, Mazzini, but it seems to have done nothing to assuage her now desperate dejection and foreboding. That same day she wrote to Ellen, mixing, as she was starting to do, dark tropes of war and her personal fate:

The world seems to go so strangely wrong! The bad side triumphs; the blood and tears of the generous flow in vain. I assist at the saddest scenes, and suffer for those whom I knew not before. Those whom I knew and loved,—who, if they had triumphed, would have opened for me an easier, broader, higher-mounting road,— are every day more and more involved in earthly ruin. Eternity is with us, but there is much darkness and bitterness in this portion of it. A baleful star rose on my birth, and its hostility, I fear, will never be disarmed while I walk below.[53]

While agonizing about her "baleful" fate and menacing future, as history, political and personal, unraveled before her eyes, the following day Fuller filed a dispatch filled with pure defiant outrage. Her judgment of Lesseps, whose mission many in Rome still hoped would be sustained by his government, was devastatingly succinct: either his conduct in dangling compromises before the Romans was "boyish and foolish" or it was "treacherous," since it gave the French precious time to rearm and, with the truce, move closer to Rome. She gave an even more searing summary of the pope's public disavowals of all his past liberal acts, exposing the folly of those who still apologized for him as a prisoner of the cardinals and the king of Naples or who actually believed that the French would install him as a constitutional monarch. "Could the French restore him, they must frankly avow themselves, abandon entirely and fully the position they took in February, 1848, and declare themselves the allies of Austria and Russia." She finished off the French with a denunciation of their heretofore unimaginable bombardment of Rome, almost fusing cultural and human carnage: "Ponte Malle, the scene of Raphael's fresco of a battle, in the Vatican, saw again a fierce struggle last Friday. More than fifty were brought wounded into Rome." Now, however, not American Italophilia, but sheer cosmopolitan rage fired her. "Yes! the French," she cried, "who pretend to be the advanced guard of civilization, are bombarding Rome. They dare take the risk of destroying the richest bequests made to man by the great Past. Nay, they seem to do it in an especially barbarous manner," she added bitterly, aiming especially at hospitals for the wounded, precious monuments, and the Capitol. Two days later, after learning that the French government had repudiated Lesseps and sustained Oudinot, she hastily inserted an addendum, reviewing with white fury every "shameless" French maneuver, down to that of the French foreign minister, Edouard Drouyn de Lhuys, who had assured the old Assembly he had given Lesseps no instructions beyond theirs to protect Rome against foreign intervention. Now de Lhuys had the gall to publish them, showing him insisting on countless restrictions, "which M. Lesseps, the 'Plenipotentiary,' dares not disown." "What are we to think of a great nation," she demanded, "whose leading men are such barefaced liars?"[54]

Mostly, she made an emotionally gripping eyewitness case for Rome's growing defiance wrought by the French bombardment. Before it, she had worried. "I am afraid it is too true," she had confessed in her letter to Hoar, speaking of all the northern Italians but also many Poles and even some French and Germans at her hospital, "that there were comparatively but few Romans," lending credence to the French and Austrian diplomats' slanders that Rome was controlled by a "faction" of "foreigners." She could have said, as many Italian republicans did, that it was ridiculous to think that a Milanese or a Florentine somehow had less national claim for defending Rome than a Frenchman or Austrian had for attacking it. Still, once the bombs started dropping, she was relieved. "It does me good that at least the Romans have done something," she wrote to Ossoli in a Mazzinian spirit, adding the un-Mazzinian qualifier "if only you can survive." In her dispatch she was more expansive. "Wounds and assaults only fire more and more the courage of her defenders," she wrote. "In proportion as there seems little aid to be hoped from man they seem to claim it from God." That was true—which was why it would take the French so long to enter the city—but for Fuller what was as notable as the result was, as she suggested here, the cultural and religious dynamics of the emboldened people in the streets. The night before, she reported, the crowds mixed militancy with the spectacles she always loved in Rome: in the piazza a "fine band" played Roman marches and, to add to the irony, the Marseillaise, while massive crowds shouted defiant slogans, and many danced to guitars. Most impressive to her was the courage of the poor, many now homeless, in extinguishing bombs. No longer one of the colorful but debased people she had lamented, one of the Trasteverines, "those noble images of the old Roman race," started it all, and soon others joined in: "Armed with pans of wet clay they ran wherever the bombs fell, to extinguish them. Women collect the balls from the hostile cannon and carry them to ours. As very little injury has come to life in this way, the people cry, 'Madonna protects us against the bombs; she wills not for Rome to be destroyed.'"[55]

The soldiers, though, always her first concern, she put in a more secular context. She devoted particular attention, as usual, to the Italian exiles from lost peninsular battles and, quoting an impassioned recent leaflet from the triumvirs, "'the flower of the Italian youth, and the noblest souls of age.'" "Many of these young men," she wrote, "students from Pisa, Pavia, Padua and the Roman University, lie wounded in the hospitals, for naturally they rushed first in the combat. One kissed an arm which was cut off; another preserves pieces of bone which are being painfully extracted from his wound, as reliques of the best days of his life." By contrast, she identified the wounded older exiles not with these Catholic sensibilities she observed but with classical associations out of "the heroic age" that she imagined. She concluded, as she had with Hoar, with a confession of both her suffering and her compensations as a reporter witnessing these acts of "true priests of a higher hope." "I would not, for much, have missed seeing it at all," she insisted, adding a higher hope for herself: "The memory will console amid the spectacles of meanness, selfishness and faithlessness which life may yet have in store for the pilgrim."[56]

VI

What life in Rome had in store that night was a fast approaching crisis. Later that day Casa Dies filled with crowds fleeing the Piazza di Gesù, where the rain of bullets and bombs fell thickest. The next night of June 21–22, at two in the morning, she was awakened by a "tremendous cannonade," which marked the beginning of the final, and most terrifying, stage of the fighting. Just then, in apparently the only major faltering of the Italian side in the war, several companies panicked and abandoned their post at a casino wedged between the walls, allowing the French to force a breach, enter the city, and entrench themselves. Meanwhile, their trenches around the city moved closer by the hour, protected batteries were crumbling, and on the Janiculum, fighting became fiercer than ever, as they kept trying and failing to dislodge the Romans from their remaining few villas. "The slaughter of the Romans became every day more fearful," Fuller wrote a week later of that night and morning bombing.

> Their defenses were knocked down by the heavy cannon of the French, and, entirely exposed in their valorous onsets, great numbers perished on the spot. Those who were brought into the Hospitals were generally grievously wounded, very commonly subjects for amputation. My heart bled daily more and more at these sights, and I could not feel much for myself, though now the balls and bombs began to fall round me also.[57]

By then, the war reached its critical point. Now, nine days after the crushing of the Mountain's coup, with the French for the first time within Rome's walls, Mazzini knew, as he would later concede, that a successful resistance was impossible. But believing it essential for the creation of a national myth that would facilitate the resumption of the Risorgimento led by Republicans that they go down fighting, he vetoed Garibaldi's proposal to flee with the army into the northern countryside and carry on the war from there. "I don't know whether I am witnessing the agony of a Great Town or a successful resistance," Mazzini scribbled the following day of June 28—somewhat disingenuously—in a note to Fuller giving her permission to enter the Quirinal gardens. "But one thing I know, that resist we must, that we *shall* resist to the last, and that my name will *never* be appended to a capitulation." It is not clear what Fuller thought of Mazzini's commitment to throw up barricades in the streets. On days just before and after the twenty-second, she had loudly expressed admiration for him standing "firm as a rock," presumably convinced, as she had said to Elizabeth Hoar at the start of the bombardment, that "this perpetual murder of men" is preferable to seeing them "indolently lying in the mud." She also expressed her own willingness to die in the cause if continued fighting would have required it. On the other hand, in her first postmortem dispatch, she would say that she knew by the twenty-second that "further resistance was idle" and that it had been "true policy" to avoid a street fight, in which the Italian, an unpracticed soldier, would have been no match for disciplined French troops. One thing we do know: the night of July 28, when Mazzini wrote her that he would "*never*" agree to surrender, was a "truly fearful" night, with bombs whizzing and bursting everywhere around her. "As many as 30," she afterward wrote, "fell upon or near the *Hotel de Russie*, where Mr. Cass has his temporary abode. The roof of the studio in the pavilion . . . was torn to pieces. I sat alone in my much-exposed apartment thinking 'if one strikes me, I only hope it will kill me at once, and that God will transport my soul to some sphere where Virtue and Love are not tyrannized over by egotism and brute force, as in this.'"[58]

That night of the twenty-ninth began what Oudinot was determined to make the final assault. Shortly after midnight, the French bombardment, Cass reported, "was very heavy, shells and grenades falling in every part of the city." The next afternoon Cass, to whom Fuller had been writing "heartsick, weary" letters, which she would later tell him to destroy, received a brief note from her, asking him to come to her apartment at Casa Dies. "I . . . found her," he later wrote in a detailed account of her doings that day,

> lying on the sofa, pale & trembling, evidently much exhausted. She informed me, that she had sent for me to place in my hands a packet of important papers, which she wished me to keep for the present, &, in the event of her death, to transmit it to her friends in the United States. She then stated that she was married to the Marquis Ossoli, who was in command of a battery on the Pincian Hill. That being the highest & most exposed position in Rome, & directly in the line of the bombs from the French Camp, it was not to be supposed, she said, that he would escape the dangers of another night such as the last, & therefore it was her intention to remain with him, & share his fate. At the Ave Maria, she added, he would come for her when they would proceed together to his post. The packet which she placed in my possession, contained, she said, the certificates of her marriage, & of the birth and baptism of her child. After a few words more, I took my departure, the hour she named having nearly arrived.[59]

The documents were probably mostly the same ones Fuller had confided to Emelyn Story the previous month, which Emelyn had given back to her just before she and William left for Florence and Switzerland. Did Fuller go? Evidently she did, although the sequence of events is unclear. Later that afternoon she wrote an emotional and somewhat incoherent note to Ossoli: "How hard it was for me, love, to miss you yesterday, and possibly also today, if you can come, I [will] go to Casa Dies, if possible inquire for me there, on the last floor, if I am still there or if I went to the hospital. God keep you[.] How much I have suffered in seeing the wounded, and I cannot know if any thing should happen to you—but I must hope." She also told him what she had done:

> In the event of the death of both of us I have left a paper with Angelino's birth certificate and a few words praying the Storys to take care of him. Should I by any chance die you can take back this paper from me, if you want, as from your wife. I

wanted Nino to go to America, but you will do as you wish. It was our duty to arrange this better, but let's hope that there will not be need for it.

In a postscript she added: "If you live and I die, be always very devoted to Nino.
If you ever love another woman, always think first of him, I beg you, beg you,
love." What is curious about Fuller's pleading here that Ossoli "be always devoted
to Nino" is that her decision to go to stay with Ossoli to "share his fate" increased
considerably the possibility that both of them would die, leaving Nino parentless.
Might she have changed her mind? That would seem to be ruled out by the remainder of Cass's account: "At the Porter's Lodge I met the Marquis Ossoli; and
a few minutes afterward I saw them walking toward the Pincian Hill." Then, however, Cass said something else happened that made the question moot: "Happily
the cannonading was not renewed that night, & at dawn of day she returned to her
apartment, with her husband by her side." She took with her a piece of a bomb
that had burst close to him.[60]

That was the early morning of July 1. By then they certainly knew the reason
why the bombardment had not continued. At midday, with the French bombing
and shelling the city with impunity and Garibaldi's new headquarters at the Villa
Spada surrounded, the general led his Legionnaires in one last hopeless charge
against the French position, in the front slashing his sword furiously yet somehow remaining unscathed. After four hundred more Italians were killed that day,
a truce was arranged. Meanwhile, the Assembly met to consider the devastating
facts and their impossible options. They could do nothing to defend Rome beyond the Tiber, Garibaldi reported, and if they tried street fighting on this side,
French cannons would destroy the city, so further resistance was impossible. Instead of surrender, however, he urged the government to quit Rome and join his
army of volunteers in the mountains. Because he had included the government in
the proposed flight, but probably also because the situation had gotten so desperate, this time Mazzini strenuously urged the adoption of Garibaldi's proposal. But
the majority opposed it, voting instead a resolution, "in the name of God and the
people," declaring that the Constituent Roman Assembly "ceases from a defense
which has become impracticable, and remains at its post." Mazzini and his fellow
triumvirs angrily resigned in protest, and three days later, on July 3, the day after
Garibaldi's four thousand volunteers galloped into the Abruzzi, the French entered Rome. Later that day Mazzini wrote Fuller:

> It is all over. I have struggled to the last against the weakness of the Assembly; and
> at last proposed that Assembly, Government, army and all should walk out of Rome
> and prolong their existence elsewhere; in vain. I have solemnly protested, and I will
> send you a copy of my protestation. But it is all over, for the present moment. I
> don't know what I shall do; I cannot think of it.[61]

That, of course, would quickly change. Meanwhile, the question that Fuller
had to think about remained the same tragic one she had often raised about the
defeated young soldier-refugees who had poured into Rome, but now applied to
Ossoli and herself: where on earth could they go?

CHAPTER THIRTEEN

Florence Exile
(1849–1850)

I

"Private hopes of mine are fallen with the hopes of Italy," Fuller wrote to Richard on July 8, 1849, five days after the French entered Rome. "I have played for a new stake and lost it." She did not say exactly what *were* these "private hopes," which Richard probably assumed meant her wish to stay in the city. Certainly, the political situation made leaving a compelling idea. At the end of that month, Oudinot resigned his civil powers to a commission of three cardinals, which began reconstructing, over empty French protests, absolute papal rule. "Rome is in a frightful state," Cass reported to Fuller later that winter. The economy was paralyzed, and the government was repressive "beyond all bounds. Fines, imprisonments & banishments are inflicted every day"; the authorities were "hunting out, with fiendish ferocity, every individual who is tainted with republicanism." Meanwhile, reactionary governments concluded the mopping up. Two weeks after Oudinot's resignation, Hungarian troops surrendered to Austrian and Russian armies, and several days afterward, the Austrians occupied a blockaded Venice, completing their reconquest of northern Italy. In Lombardy, Radetsky's forces unleashed a reign of imprisonment, torture, and execution, practices that were replicated in the Kingdom of Naples with added capriciousness and barbarity. Although Piedmont, as Italy's sole constitutional monarchy, became a magnet for republican refugees, Austrian pressure, government repression, and the rising influence of Liberals around Cavour, Victor Emmanuel II's brilliant new minister, ensured they would have no real political future there.[1]

Fuller's comrades took the cues. After the "Roman catastrophe," Mickiewicz escaped from Milan to Paris, where he took over the editorship of *Tribune des Peuples*, which—in a warm but sad letter—he asked Fuller to contribute to shortly before the French government shut it down. Belgioioso, who was hounded by the French to pay for all expenses incurred by the Republic's field hospitals, escaped

459

with Cass's help "by sleuth" to British Malta and afterward to Athens and Con-
stantinople, where she lived in virtual penury, before she regained some of her
seized Italian estates. Fuller, to whom Belgioioso had become close, tried to get
Greeley to give her a weekly column on European affairs, but since (he said) it
would be coming from a "stranger," he offered only half of Fuller's rate, and
nothing came of it. Considerably more awful, Ciceruacchio and his sons, for whom
Mazzini asked Fuller to try to get passports, wound up fleeing with Garibaldi's
army, only to be captured and shot by Austrian soldiers. Mazzini himself, after
nine days roaming the streets and daring the French to arrest him, was finally
persuaded by Fuller to go, taking with him a passport she had gotten Cass to issue
under the name George Moore and letter of introduction from Cass to the American consul in Genoa. "He had never flinched, never quailed," she wrote Channing,
describing the ashen and emaciated revolutionary who had daily sent his dearest
friends to die; "had protested in the last hour against surrender; sweet and calm,
but more full of fiery purpose than ever; in him I revered the hero, and owned
myself not of that mould."[2]

Even so, she remained in a dangerous situation. That she felt "sick of breathing the same air" with the cruel and false French to whom she had already made
herself "obnoxious" undoubtedly made it more so. She also worried about not being
able to leave the city. "From what I hear this morning, I fear we may be once more
shut up here," she wrote Cass on July 8, asking help in getting out. "I shall die, to
be again separated from what I most hold dear." Yet she worried, too, about her
wounded patients' situation. When two days later Oudinot ordered all foreigners
who had served the Republican government to depart from the city within twenty-
four hours, she agonized over leaving them. "But for my child," she told Cass, "I
would not go, till some men, now sick, know whether they live or die." A couple
of weeks later, she was still full of remorse for having to leave amputees under
her care to the beneficence of their enemies without a penny to leave behind for
their nursing. "Could I have sold my hair or blood from my arm, I would have
done it," she afterward wrote Elizabeth Hoar. "Had any of the rich Americans
remained in Rome, they would have given it to me; they helped nobly at first in
service of the hospital, when there was far less need; but they had all gone."[3]

Past heroism and present impotence was the theme of her last long dispatch on
the aftermath of the Republic's defeat, which she filed just before leaving. She
gave her readers a gripping snapshot of Garibaldi's departure on the second from
the piazza of St. John Lateran, appearing like a "hero of the middle ages," as he
rode ahead of his soon-to-die wife Anita, looked down the road through his spyglass and back at Rome, and then charged with his four thousand red-shirted volunteers through the gate. "Never have I seen a sight so beautiful, so romantic and
so sad." As usual, the class distinctions she cared about were not economic but
moral. "Gentlemen who perform their 'duties to society,'" she sneered, "by buying for themselves handsome clothes and furniture with the interest of their money,
speak of Garibaldi and his men as 'brigands' and 'vagabonds.' Such are they,
doubtless, in the same sense as Jesus, Eneas and Moses were. To me men who

can throw so lightly aside the ease of wealth, the joys of affection, for the sake of what they deem honor, in whatsoever form, are the 'respectable.'"[4]

Her real tragic heroes, though, were not Garibaldi's lower-class and young bourgeois recruits but the Roman people. Their first reactions epitomized republican virtue. Instead of the cheers and gratitude glibly predicted by European statesmen, the French confronted "icy silence" in restaurants, slammed shutters from "the ladies" they eagerly saluted, and howls and hisses from patriotic prostitutes, as the soldiers marched with advancing bayonets, showing how, even with all their numbers, they had still used bombs to "kill women and children in their beds." Yet the people were not angels. "In an evil hour," she wrote, "a foolish priest dared to break [the silence] by the cry of *Viva Pio Nono,* and the crowd jumped on him, severely wounding him with their knives and "one or two others were killed in the rush." French soldiers were missing daily, already over 250—some killed by the Trasteverines for daring to court their women. But that was the point: "In two days of French 'order' more acts of violence have been committed than in two months under the Triumvirate." Indeed, the most wrenching effect of the occupation, she said, was its reversal of the Romans' maturation, which the revolution had spurred:

> The men of Rome had begun, filled with new hopes, to develop unknown energy—
> they walked quick, their eyes sparkled, they delighted in duty, in responsibility; in
> a year of such life their effeminacy would have been vanquished—now, dejectedly,
> unemployed, they lounge along the streets, feeling that all the implements of labor,
> all the ensigns of hope, have been snatched from them. Their hands fall slack, their
> eyes rove aimless, the beggars begin to swarm again, and the black ravens who
> delight in the night of ignorance, the slumber of sloth, as the only sureties for their
> rule, emerge daily more and more frequent from their hiding places.[5]

With this final anticlerical flourish to her somber drum roll for the classical republican virtues of manly hope, energy, and duty metamorphosing into effeminate dejection, sloth, and ignorance, she brought down the curtain on the Roman Revolution. In her readers, though, who would have recognized these virtues as what they liked to think their revolution had wrought, she tried to arouse outrage and action. She rather weakly tried to stir up some by breathlessly reporting on Brown, with banner in one hand and sword in the other, driving out some French soldiers who had broken into the American consul's official residence, pretending to search for political fugitives. "Will America look as coldly on the insult to herself as she had on the struggle of this injured people?" she asked. (Evidently, Cass thought its government would, since he asked her not to mention his demand of "satisfaction for this insult" or even his name for fear the State Department would censure or recall him as it had Brown.) Her effective card was American guilt and shame. "I see you have meetings, where you speak of the Italians, the Hungarians," she wrote. "I pray you *do something*; let it not end in a mere cry of sentiment. . . . Do you owe no tithe to Heaven for the privileges it has showered on you, for whose achievements so many here suffer and perish daily? Deserve to retain them, by helping your fellow-men to acquire them." She left her readers with her liberal Romantic cosmopolitan battle cry: "Mankind is one / And beats with one great heart."[6]

On July 12, the same day Mazzini boarded his boat at Civitavecchia on his way eventually to London, Fuller and Ossoli left Rome for Rieti by carriage, carrying endorsed American passports that Cass had given them so they did not have to appear before French authorities. When they saw Angelino, they found their worst fear had materialized. "He is worn to a skeleton," Fuller wrote in panic to Cass. "He is so weak it seems to me he can scarcely ever revive to health." As just two weeks earlier Dr. Bassini had assured her that Nino's poor appetite and lack of "muscular vigor" were nothing to worry about, she was especially shocked, but she was floored, although she might have expected it, when she learned that the culprit was the "lovely and innocent" Chiara who had once threatened to abandon him. "For the sake of a few scudi," she reported to Cass, after her milk had started failing, she had given all hers to her own child and fed Nino only on wine and bread. "If he dies, I hope I shall, too," she wrote desperately, adding an ominous metaphor: "This last shipwreck of hopes would be more than I could bear." After a month of "incessant" nursing "day and night," however, Nino mostly recovered, "though still a skeleton, and requiring great care," although not much thanks to Chiara's replacement. This "fine healthy girl," Fuller told Cass, "(with a heart such as you may imagine, since she has two children already at the Foundling Hospital) is always trying not to give him milk, for fear of spoiling the shape of her bosom!" "The lower women of Italy," she ranted, had made her think of a woman's breast, not, as she had always liked to fancy, as "a home of angelic pity," but "almost a shrine for offerings to moloch."[7]

Although soured for the umpteenth time on Rieti, she still, as always, tried to make the best of it. "I seem to have arrived in a different world, since passing the mountains," she wrote Cass, describing the pretty vineyards and gleaming hillside summerhouses and convents facing the dirty streets where pigs and children wallowed, while "Madonna-veiled bare-legged women twirl the distaff at every door and window, happy to make five cents a day." Unable to find an apartment, they rented rooms at an inn, which gave her a good view of the provincial elite's "humours," including the local baronesses and countesses, "in the extreme of Italian undress," peeping through the blinds, or parading in their "mongrel French fashions," on foot, as they had no fancy carriages, down the narrow corso. She did assure Cass that she and Ossoli performed their "social duties" with discretion. They talked with the head priest of the monastery of St. Antonio, who made them take their "excellent coffee" outdoors, "for women must not enter, 'only' said he chuckling, 'Garibaldi obliged us to let his enter, and I have even seen them braiding their hair!'" She got more than coffee for her discreetness in her chats with the poet and professor Cavalier Angelo Maria Ricci. He was "one of the old fashioned literati of a class which will not long endure," but whom she liked to talk to because he had several "exquisite" Raphael and Claude paintings and shared his fund of knowledge of prelatic Italy, which she was eager to learn about. "The young Italy he of course abhors, but never dreams that I could have any sympathy with it."[8]

After a month of enjoying "these simple traits of a limited life," she and Ossoli confronted a dangerous one. Although Garibaldi had managed to elude the three national armies pursuing him, soldiers hunting for revolutionaries honeycombed central Italy. Once, an acquaintance reported, Fuller "undoubtedly" saved the lives of a family by getting them to pass over an insult from a drunken Spanish soldier. Then on August 8 Ossoli accidentally crossed into Neapolitan territory and was promptly arrested on suspicion of being one of Garibaldi's soldiers. "You can imagine in what torment I passed the night," she wrote Giovanni the next day. She immediately got the new Papal States delegate to write to the provincial governor, certifying that Ossoli's papers were in order. What saved him, though, ironically, were his detestable brothers. He fortuitously had on him a business letter directed to himself as the Marchese Ossoli, which the regimental chaplain recognized as the name of an officer in the Pope's Noble Guard, so the Neapolitan officers ordered him released and sent him back, with many apologies, in a carriage under an armed escort, into papal territory. Although Fuller mused to Cass that she could imagine that if they had money, they could be happy "living peaceably in one beautiful provincial town after another," they started thinking about leaving this one.[9]

Before they went, Fuller wrote one last dispatch, wading into the gathering controversy over postmortems on the Roman Revolution. She was still struggling to come to terms with her own role in its defense. "You say, you are glad I have had this great opportunity for carrying out my principles," she wrote Channing on August 28, sounding even more tormented than a month earlier. "Would that it were so! I found myself inferior in courage and fortitude to the occasion. I knew not how to bear the havoc and anguish incident to the struggle for these principles." Indeed, she remembered rejoicing that she had not been the one responsible for sending all the "beautiful young men" to their death or dismemberment. "I forget the great ideas," she confessed, "to sympathize with the poor mothers, who had nursed their precious forms, only to see them all lopped and gashed" like the trees of the Borghese. "You say, I sustained them; often they sustained my courage," she said. "One fair young man, who is made a cripple for life, clasped my hand as he saw me crying over the spasms I could not relieve, and faintly cried, 'Viva l'Italia. 'Think only, *cara bona donna*,' said a poor wounded soldier, 'that I can always wear my uniform on *festas*, just as it is now, with the holes where the balls went through, for a memory.' 'God is good; God knows,' they often said to me, when I had not a word to cheer them."[10]

As usual, none of these sad confessions appeared in her dispatch three days later, where her purpose was wholly political: to burnish the reputation of the Republic and its Democratic leaders, on which hung, she knew, their future influence. That was no small or easy task. Even her once admired liberal Tocqueville, who had become foreign minister on the day of the surprise French attack on the Janiculum hill and had privately denounced it a "flagrant disobedience" of the Assembly and the French Constitution, publicly defended it as necessary to preserve French pride and free Rome from the clutches of "the tyranny of Mazzini" and his "reign of terror." Toward these libelous exculpations of Tocqueville and the premiere Odilon Barrot she was contemptuous. They had put in power the tyrannical cardinals now carrying out mass arrests of innocent Republicans, and their government's impotent protests were "the object of contempt to all parties." The "hackneyed" slanders still appearing in the "now enslaved and hireling" conservative European press—and slavishly copied, she regretfully noted, in many American newspapers—she treated dismissively. The Romans welcomed their "protectors"?—the only instances were a few peasants, mostly drunk, egged on by "'potent, grave and reverend seigniors.'" Oudinot never risked destroying the monuments of Rome? "I see he feels far more sore under that accusation than that of betraying the Constitution," but his indignation was ludicrous. "I don't doubt he *was* checked in his operations during the siege by the fear," but nonetheless, it was only by luck that his bombs did not do more damage since they fell everywhere. The Republicans were terrorists? Priests were in danger, of course; the people thought them spies. But attacks on them were few. "Every one possible has now been raked up, as every old rag lost or mislaid in the occupation of huge monasteries as barracks has been put on the lists of robberies; and let any one compare the lists of murders and robberies with what has been said on that subject, and make his own inferences." After repeating the point she had made during the siege—that she had walked everywhere at all hours, in all quarters—she declared, "I never saw an act of violence," nor had she even been jostled in militant crowds. "I grant you, if I had cried *Viva Pio Nino!* Or *Viva Napoleon!* I might have angered them," but that never happened. As to robbery of citizens, even "my friends the bankers" had to confess that Garibaldi's "'brigands'" had sacked no houses and had not touched one strong box, even though the impoverished men badly needed help in retreat. "I hope all the alarmists will have the decency to confess how groundless all *that* talk was."[11]

How accurate was her picture of the Republic just before and after its fall? She omitted a few things. She overlooked some recent Church success in stirring up support, although that mostly occurred some time after her departure. She also said nothing about the assassination in mid-June of five priests by a rogue band of soldiers led by the fanatical anticlerical Colonel Zambianchi. However, that was a rare event, carried out, like almost all the anticlerical violence, while the city was under siege, and afterward government officials had denounced it and arrested and tried the assassins. Broadly speaking, Fuller's portrait of a city under attack, with most of its rich nobles gone but with little internal disorder and with both its bourgeois and working classes strongly opposed to the return of the pope and his cardinals to temporal power and committed to the defense of the Republic, was factual. In light of its crushing defeat, though, there remained the moral and practical question of whether all the war's slaughter and mutilation had been worth it. In her August 28 confession to Channing, she had implied it had not been, even admitting that for the soldiers' sake, she wished there had been a capitulation. In her dispatch, however, her answer was a resounding yes. The defeat and the resistance had radically altered the arc of history, and, as such, was a great democratic boon. "That intervention, the falsehood of France, the inertia of England, the entrance of Russia into Hungary," she insisted, ticking off all the seeming disasters of the Revolution—

all these steps tracked in blood, which cause so much anguish at the moment, Democracy ought in fact to bless. They insure her triumphs—there is no possible compromise between her and the Old. The Roman Moderates will not again welcome a foreign help that abandons them to exile. Hungary will not again believe it is of use to appeal to England, and declare she only wanted to maintain her old privileges; she will know that Radical Reform is the only one possible in these desperate days. Heroic Venice, the land of Garibaldi, the unyielding mildness of Mazzini, will be remembered as possessing the only wisdom. Next time all the Kings have to fly from their thrones, they will know that to return is to undertake an insoluble problem, and that Governments cannot be sustained by conscription of the whole youth of a country to oppress their own fathers and mothers. All the more for what has happened in these sad days, will entire Europe, at the end of this century, be under Republican form of Government, and then Republics will never again elect as President any member of families formerly reigning.[12]

She would be both wrong and right. On the one hand, revolution, as it usually does, bred not more revolution but reaction. In Rome, traumatized by the "red" Republicans, and secure in the knowledge that Austria guaranteed his temporal authority, after returning in the spring, the pope and his cardinals would reinstall the very same aggressive censorship, police spies, political jailings, clerical-controlled education, Jewish reconfinement, and revived Inquisition that had marked the reign of his reactionary predecessor. Furthermore, now distrustful of all the Catholic monarchs and emboldened by the Church's success in marshaling independent Catholic support in Europe during the siege, Pius IX soon resurrected the doctrine of "ultramontanism," or the Church's supremacy over all states, implemented through clerical parties and, most formidably, a reenergized Jesuit order. Indeed, within a few more years, his ultramontanism would mutate even further into militant "antimodernism," encompassing new dogmas, such as Immaculate Conception and Papal Infallibility, a deep suspicion of modern science, and a new crude anti-Semitism, which would define much of the Church's intellectual character into the early twentieth century. If she failed to account for the resiliency of the papacy or, even more crucial, its support in Italy's peasantry outside the Papal States, she also failed to appreciate the canniness of Cavour and the Piedmontese Moderates, who a decade later mostly won their country's independence under Victor Emmanuel II. On the other hand, Fuller's Democrats also had their day. Mazzini *would* be lionized by liberals all over Europe but especially in England and the United States, which made Moderates like Cavour and Gioberti more determined than ever to slander him as a coward, anarchist, or communist down to the end of his life. Moreover, a decade after Victor Emmanuel II's first victory, Pius IX would lose his temporal authority, and the peninsula would be politically unified, goals for which Mazzini had been laughed at but that now even many chastened European conservatives would realize were essential for a modern Italy. Indeed, his doctrine of a world of mutually supporting nonimperialist nations would become at various times the rallying cry of both liberals and radicals throughout the twentieth century. As for republicanism in Europe, it too would eventually triumph, as she predicted, although in places only temporarily, often with its social "democratic" character attenuated, and over the course not of a half but a century and a half—as well as following mass slaughters and totalitarian terrors the likes of which Fuller could never have imagined.

Yet history and politics were not, as usual, Fuller's only resource. Her second justification of violent revolution was considerably more Romantic, although its relevance for liberal resistance would not die with her prelapsarian age. "Meanwhile," she said at the end of her dispatch, mixing natural and political metaphors, "the Italian sun shines gloriously, and the earth teems plenteous more than ever to feed the crowd of invaders that wound her bosom, and prevent her own children from perishing the while. For me as I heard the tramp of a great force come to keep down every throb of generous, spontaneous life, I shuddered at the sense of what existence is under such conditions, and felt for the first time joy over the noble men that have perished. Farewell." Later that last day in August, the Ossolis left Rieti with Nino and traveled to Perugia, Umbria's provincial capital, still within the Papal States but fifty miles to the north.[13]

II

In this small medieval city of saints and flagellants, interlaced with rolling hills, streams, and "infinite" vistas, the Ossolis got their first relief from the scourges of war and sickness. Left alone by the pontifical authorities, in the mornings they visited Perugia's ornately decorated churches to see their abundant Umbrian art, whose understated "depth and tenderness" the natural surroundings helped her appreciate. In the afternoons they took hikes in the "perfect elixir" of mountain air, or just sat and read under the trees of the tenth-century basilica of San Pietro. After three weeks of this "generous and consoling" calm, in late September, they crossed the Tuscan border and traveled to Florence, where they had to start thinking about surviving.[14]

They had enough money to stay through the spring, but they had to scrape and scramble for it. As hard currency was scarce, she asked her banker in Rome to transfer all her money to Florence in gold. Giovanni tried to squeeze some "ready money" out of his family by offering to renounce his claims on an ancestral vineyard and houses, but his brothers, livid over his treachery and their humiliation (Giuseppe for a time had to hide in his cellar with Republican troops quartered upstairs), rejected that ploy. "It is odd how peculiarly things have turned against us," Margaret mused to Emelyn Story, updating the anecdote she had told in her dispatch a year and a half earlier about the "orphan" deprived of his inheritance. The Villa Santucci, the beautiful estate where Oudinot's troops were quartered, had once been the property of Ossoli's grandmother, who "in the religious weakness of her last hours" had given it to her confessor, Monsignor Santucci. "As he is Godfather to my husband there was reason to hope he might restore the unjust acquisition at his death; but he has had to fly and hide, his property has been ravaged by the war, and he will feel little love for a godson who served on the Republican side." The "black ravens" she had denounced in her dispatches had literally come home to roost.[15]

Fuller's biggest burden, though, was finally telling the truth about her secret family. She had long dreaded it, but she knew she had to do it sometime and had even expressed a desire to unburden herself. There was also no point in continuing the charade. Not only was the hope of a government position for Ossoli ended but also having a legitimate family in the open would have been preferable for his inheritance case before hostile papal authorities to having his brothers bring to light a hidden marriage between a former Republican officer and a radical American wife with a possibly out-of-wedlock child. Yet for weeks she procrastinated. She would later claim she had wanted to make sure Nino would live. (She implied in one letter that if he did not, she would have said nothing about him.) But even after he recovered she stalled. Three questions undoubtedly inhibited her: to whom to write, in what order, and, of course, what to say? Her mostly forced disclosures to Mickiewicz, Hicks, Caroline Tappan, Emelyn Story, and Cass were no guides, as she had pledged them to secrecy. Now she had to write to dozens, knowing they would write to dozens more, until virtually all of literary Boston and New York would know, guess at what she held back, and wonder why she had kept it all a secret.[16]

Although Fuller's disclosures were far from complete, they give the only window on her marriage we have. Most nineteenth-century commentators knew what it meant: in marrying and becoming a mother, Fuller shed her arrogance, eccentricity, and selfish devotion to self-culture, and so became a "true woman"—domestic, pious, and submissive. This conversion narrative was largely ideological fantasy. Her Goethean culture had been far from self-indulgently selfish, her religion would remain heterodox, and her social "arrogance" (if not her critical hauteur) had been evaporating for several years. If she did "come home humbler," it was not because of her marriage but, as she had advised Channing, the humbling tragedy of war and political defeat. As for "domestic," not in any submissive or privately sentimental sense but in being concerned with guiding the next generation, she had already shown that in parenting siblings, teaching students, and mentoring protégées. In that sense, the "second-wave" feminist scholars in the 1970s, in stressing her authoritativeness in her marriage and political interests outside of it, were infinitely closer to the mark. Yet, no more than with the question of Fuller's marrying or not, will it do to reduce her marriage to a matter of ideology or "power." At least she did not think of it that way. And, although it was, indeed, an ironic, if not bizarre, match for America's most self-consciously intellectual woman—and certainly not the egalitarian or "sacred" one she had often panegyrized—it nonetheless had, as she often said, an aura of intimate reality that was refreshing and new. It was another piece of her European experience.[17]

Fuller started in just before leaving Rieti with her two most simpatico friends in her two respective "countries." "Will you have patience with my democracy,— the revolutionary spirit" and Mazzinianism, now more fervent than ever? she asked Arconati. "Then, again," she wrote, as if it was all of the same package, "how will it affect you to know that I have united my destiny with that of an obscure young man,—younger than myself; a person of no intellectual culture, and in whom, in short, you will see no reason for my choosing; yet more, that this union is of long standing; that we have with us our child, of a year old, and that it is only lately I acquainted my family with the fact." None of these revelations, which Arconati probably half suspected, fazed the marchioness. "I wish I could give wings to my assurance that I see nothing in your change of state which need alter our relations," she told Fuller. "On the contrary, there will be one more bond between us, since we shall have in common our maternal affections." As for political differences, she knew before, she said, "that you are republican and radical, and," adding lightly, "as it is not Mazzini whom you have married, we shall not be more separated by the difference of *our politics* than we have been heretofore." To Fuller, who had feared the upright Arconati would not like her friends "running about in these blind alleys" or would have found her convoluted explanation of her secrecy "offensively strange," Arconati's generous letter was a great relief. After getting it, she even felt relaxed enough to mull over with her what to do with her appellation "Marchesa Ossoli." "It seems silly for a radical like me, to be carrying a title," she conceded, "and unsustained by fortune, is but a *souvenir* even for Ossoli," yet to drop it seemed to her like "disjoining" herself from him and giving up a right he might want to preserve for Nino. Her solution was a binational one: the time to drop it probably, she said, would be on becoming "an inhabitant of republican America," but meanwhile, in aristocratic Rome, she would use it, which she would also advise her family and friends to do.[18]

She was more emotionally revealing with her most intimate American male friend. "What shall I say to you of his father?" she asked Channing. "If earthly union be meant for the beginning of one permanent and full we ought not to be united, for the time was gone by when I could more than *prefer* any man. Yet I shall never regret the step which has given me the experience of a mother and satisfied domestic wants in a most sincere and sweet companion." In short, her age and perhaps new ideas precluded a romantic love match and a conventional marriage, but she was happy with a domestic partnership. But what did that mean? She explained: "The tie leaves me mentally free, as I wish him also to remain. I trust in the midst of a false world we may be able to sustain some degree of truth, though indeed children involve too deeply, in this corrupt social contract and truth is easier to those who have not them. I however pined too much and my heart was too suffocated without a child of my own. I say I am not strong as we thought." What, though, was she saying here? She seems to have caught herself up in a conundrum: her desire for a child had made her enter an undefined liaison with Ossoli, yet a child interfered with her idea of "free" and truthful union. What was the solution? In a subsequent letter to Channing, evidently in response to additional probing, she got to an answer by expanding on the deep emotional needs Ossoli satisfied for her. One was to be loved by a maternal or filial figure: "My love for Ossoli is most pure and tender, nor has any one, except little children or mother, ever loved me as genuinely as he does." At the same time, his love freed her from frustratingly seeking it by Romantic projection: "Others have loved me with a mixture of fancy and enthusiasm excited by my talent at embellishing subjects. He loves me from simple affinity; he loves to be with me, and serve and soothe me." Yet she was cognizant of the danger even such an unconventional "earthly union" posed to Ossoli's freedom and future need:

> Our relation covers only a part of my life, but I do not feel any way constrained or limited or that I have made any sacrifice. Younger I might, because I should have been exposed to love some other in a way that might give him pain, but I do not now feel apprehensive of that. There is more danger for him, as he is younger than I; if he should I shall do all that this false state of society permits to give him freedom he may need. I have thought a great deal about this; there are things I do not wish to put on paper. I daresay I shall tell them to you when we meet.

Presumably, what she resisted putting on paper was a full explanation of the kind of "free" marriage she seems to have come to embrace: one that potentially included separation, if not actually an affair, although her somewhat anxiously expressed liberalism on this point may have also reflected her knowledge that European men had affairs. In any case, however she saw her marriage working out, she clearly thought of it as *something* countercultural. Indeed, when one reads radical phrases like "this corrupt social contract" and "this false state of society," it is not surprising that Channing had told Emerson he believed she had never married.[19]

Fuller would make her marriage's unconventionality even clearer later in the winter to Clough. After speaking about the joys Nino gave her, she wrote:

> I like also much living with my husband. You said in your letter you thought I should at any rate be happier now because the position of an unmarried woman in our time is not desirable; to me on the contrary it had seemed that in a state of society where marriage brings so much trifling business arrangements and various soporifics the liberty of single life was most precious. . . . But for the child I should have wished to remain as we were, and feared we should lose much by entering on the jog-trot of domestic life. However, I do not find it so; we are of mutual solace and aid about the dish and spoon part, yet enjoy our free rambles as ever.

So, in a sense, she had not changed her position: in recent years she had often spoken of the advantages of the single life, even as she pined for a romantic, and presumably sexual, relationship and a child. On the other hand, everything had changed now that she *had* a husband and child, whose conception, she all but said here, had required that she marry. Meanwhile, even if fragile in the future, "simple affinity" and help in the "dish and spoon part" seem to have been more than enough for her.[20]

Unsurprisingly, she did not communicate any of these provocative marital thoughts to her family. She even delayed for several more weeks writing them. But her mother's lament in a letter that "I have not been present at the marriage of any child of mine yet" gave her "a great pang of remorse." She also did not want her mother to hear about her marriage from others. But what seems to have finally made her write was a letter she got from Greeley soon afterward. "Ah Margaret! the world grows dark with us," she read. "Rome has fallen; I mourn, for Pickie is dead!" After shedding "rivers of tears," she dashed off an effusively consoling tribute to the tantrum-throwing precocious boy who had adored "Aunty Margaret," in which she let it out—she could hardly have avoided it—that she, too, now had a little boy, who had recently been on death's doorstep. Six days later, just before leaving Rieti, she sent her mother a letter that, she later told Caroline, "half-killed me to write." "The first moment, it may cause you a pang to know that your eldest child might long ago have been addressed by another name than yours, and has a little son," she began, clearing her throat. "But, beloved mother, do not feel this long." Instead, she should realize that it had only been her great love for her that had made her hide the fact, which, of course, was hardly the "only" reason but still true enough. "I have abstained a hundred times, when your sympathy, your counsel, would have been most precious, from a wish not to harass you with anxiety. Even now I would abstain," she added, but the changed political situation now required "on account of the child, for us to live publicly and permanently together," presumably referring to Ossoli's legal claims. Of Ossoli, she gave a description roughly like what she had given Arconati and Channing. "He is not in any respect such a person as people in general would expect to find with me," she conceded, with his elementary education from an old priest, complete ignorance of books, and lack of her old Romantic requirement, "enthusiasm of character." But he had many compensating qualities extremely important to her:

> He has excellent practical sense; has been a judicious observer of all that passed before his eyes; has a nice sense of duty, which, in its unfailing, minute activity, may put most enthusiasts to shame; a very sweet temper, and great native refinement. His love for me has been unswerving and most tender. I have never suffered a pain that he could relieve. His devotion, when I am ill, is to be compared only with yours. His delicacy in trifles, his sweet domestic graces, remind me of [Ellen]. In him I have found a home, and one that interferes with no tie. Amid many ills and cares, we have had much joy together, in the sympathy with natural beauty,—with our child,—with all that is innocent and sweet.

After stressing Ossoli's practical, moral, and domestic virtues, she concluded with a toned-down version of her caveat to Channing about her uncertainty about their future together: "I do not know whether he will always love me so well, for I am the elder, and the difference will become, in a few years, more perceptible than now. But life is so uncertain, and it is so necessary to take good things with their limitations, that I have not thought it worth while to calculate too curiously." Her only concern was over *her* opinion. "However my other friends may feel," she wrote confidently, "I am sure that *you* will love him very much, and that he will love you no less."[21]

Her mother did not disappoint her. "I had thought that nothing could ever move the depths of my spirit," she began her reply. True, the long secrecy had been difficult to absorb, but after days of "tumult" and "calm reflection," she said, she felt "fervent thankfulness for it," completely accepting her daughter's explanation. ("I should have suffered tortures to have known that you were to become a mother and I so far from you.") As for her choice of a husband, she was equally trusting and grateful:

You are the only one who could judge of what could make you happy. I could have given no advice had I been consulted in so momentous a subject as a husband for my beloved daughter, knowing nothing of the person selected. If he continues to make you happy he will be very dear to me, for long have I felt in sickness great pain in the thought of putting off the body that I should leave you peculiarly lonely in delicate health and no mother to love and watch over you. Your letter on this point gives me true satisfaction—you have found a faithful tender bosom to rest your head upon, and God has given you a child—nothing gives joy in all circumstances to rich and poor like lovely children.[22]

If Arconati and Channing's responses were reassuring, her mother's was an enormous balm. "Dearest Mother," she immediately replied, "of all your endless acts and words of love, never was any so dear to me as your last letter so generous, so sweet, so holy! What on earth is as precious as a mother's love; and who has a mother like mine?" Then she let her mind wander all the way back to her childhood. "I was thinking of you and father, all that first October," she wrote (her mother had told her that she had received Margaret's letter on the anniversary of her father's death). "It is only since I had my own child that I have known how much I failed always to do what I might have for the happiness of you both. Only since I have seen so much of men and their trials, that I have learned to prize my father as he deserved. Only since I have had a heart daily and hourly testifying to me its love, that I have understood too late what it was for you to be deprived of it." She concluded with a warm recollection of a recent evening in their apartment in front of the fire that had recalled for her an ancient domestic scene: "The baby sits on his stool between us. He makes me think how I sat on mine, in the chaise, between you and father." And so, with a husband at once affectionate and "maternal," "domestic" and filial, dutiful and devoted, the resentful family romance with an overbearing father and an absent mother that she portrayed in her "Autobiographical Romance" would seem to have ended. Now a mother and a wife, she was saying, she could become what her parents were but also, which she did not say, what they were not.[23]

Margaret's siblings' reactions did not provoke any such deep psychological resonances. They were also a longer time in coming, which made her worry that her silence hurt them, especially Richard. In fact, they, too, turned out supportive, even if warily so, on the delicate issues of the marriage's date and the couple's age difference. "I know not your husband but am prepared to love him with all my heart," Arthur assured her. "All the particulars you choose to communicate I shall be most glad to hear. It is unpleasant not to know particulars in so interesting & near relation as that of a brother." In Richard's letter, which he waited until December 4 to write, he was typically blunter about one particular: "We were all greatly surprised" at the news of her marriage, "more particularly by the antedate of it." But he did not press her; indeed, remarkably, in view of his increasingly priggish Christian piety, he gave her a cautiously liberal endorsement: "For my part I came to the conclusion that it was *your act*, done at a great distance, and in circumstances not all under my ken: so I confided that it was all for the best. For my part, my experience of marriage, and my knowledge of your character, make me believe that it was needed by you, and must have developed new veins of experience in relief of your intellectual temperament." If there was a slight critical kick in that last sentence, Margaret overlooked it. "I was very glad, having become saddened and indeed surprized not to hear from you," she replied. "The way you speak of my marriage is such as I expected from you." As for the other "particular," the youthful age of their new brother-in-law—who was only a little over a year older than Arthur—Arthur wrote confidently to Eugene: "Margaret does not attract from *mere* personal beauty & doubtless her husband's regard will be lasting." Shortly, Ellen and Ellery, as their own marriage teetered, would honor their sister's by naming their next baby Giovanni Eugene.[24]

Fuller's most strategic newscasts were the ones she provided her friends, although many discovered the news from Channing, her family, or gossip. "Margaret Fuller is married to an Italian and has a baby," Anna Weston wrote excitedly to her sister Emma on October 21. Newspapers broadcasted the reports. "Miss Margaret Fuller, the bright particular star of the *Tribune*," the *Literary World*'s Geneva correspondent announced in the November 10 issue, "is married, and has been for nearly two years, to a Roman count. She is the happy mother of a thriving boy." Not to let his readers remain in dumb wonderment, he offered a "conjecture" about how the marriage had come about: "Doubtless her attainments which, in Italy, where female education is so much neglected, would naturally excite interest, and her intelligent sympathy with the people and their country— have won the affection of some titled *savant* or patriot." To Fuller's closest married friends, the Wards and the Shaws, she wrote directly, describing Ossoli to the Wards as she had to Arconati, Channing, and her mother: "entirely without what is commonly called culture" but with the simplicity, reality, and great tenderness and refinement that made her "a domestic place in this world."[25]

As most of their letters have disappeared, it is difficult to determine how they reacted to the startling news. Fuller at least was pleased with their initial responses. "Thus far my friends have received the news, that must have been an unpleasant surprize to them, in a way that à moi, does them great honor," she wrote Emelyn Story at the end of November. "None have shown littleness or displeasure at wanting my confidence while they were giving theirs. Many have expressed the warmest sympathy." In fact, a few of her American friends in Italy who got the news from others were a little rattled. "We were merely amazed at first," Rebecca Spring wrote her sister, "but now it seems all right and nice,—but isn't it queer she never told it before?" "I felt as if your friendship to me was, not dead, indeed, but sleeping," Margaret tactfully answered Rebecca. She felt bad about William Story, whom somewhat remarkably Emelyn, as promised, had kept in the dark but who had accidentally overheard the news that November at a *table d'hôte* in Venice. Margaret's marriage had "somewhat surprised me," he afterward told Emelyn, "tho perhaps it ought not to have done so, there was such a mystery attending her and O." that could only have been accounted for that way. Had Margaret been younger, too, "perhaps scandal might have imagined something else." Emelyn assured her, however, that though "a little hurt," his "second and prevailing thought" was only regret he had not known so he could have given her sympathy and gone to Rieti to check on her child. Fuller breathed a sigh of relief. She had often wanted to tell him, she wrote him, but she at least now felt liberated from "that painful burden of secret, which I hope never to bear again. Nature keeps so many secrets, that I had supposed the moral writers exaggerated about the dangers and plagues of keeping them, but they cannot exaggerate. All that can be said about mine is that I at least acted out with to me tragic thoroughness. The wonder," she said dryly, "a woman keeps a Secret."[26]

For some of Fuller's friends, however, her "tragic thoroughness" in acting out her secret marriage was less the problem than her exasperating vagueness about its details. "You say your friends appear to lay extraordinary stress upon your marriage," Sarah Clarke wrote her crisply. "It is not exactly that but we were placed in a most unpleasant position—because the world said injurious things of you which we were not authorized to deny—not one of us could say that we knew of your marriage beforehand, nor could we tell when it occurred or answer any question about it." She added, "To me it seemed that you were more afraid of being thought to have submitted to the ceremony of marriage than to have omitted it." Sarah was on to something here, but Margaret declined to take the bait. In her November 30 letter to Emelyn Story, she said Sarah's quizzing was understandable. "She was annoyed by things people said," she wrote, "and wanted to be able to answer them." Yet she was obviously worried, and in recounting what she had told Sarah, she laid out the line she expected her friends to take about these mysteries:

> I replied to her that I had communicated already all I intended to and should not go into detail as to the past that when unkind things were said about me, she should let them pass. You, dear E do the same. I am sure your affection for me will prompt you to add, that you feel confident whatever I have done has been in a good spirit and not contrary to *my* ideas of right; for the rest, you will not admit for me, as I do not for myself, the rights of the social inquisition of the U.S. to know all the details of my affairs. If my mother is content, if Ossoli and I are content, if our child when grown up is content, that is enough.[27]

Unfortunately, as she waited for further responses, it became clear it was *not* enough for many. She was especially nervous about Emerson and his Concord circle, toward whom she had sounded defensive from the start, especially about Ossoli. "Never blame him for ills I may have to undergo," she wrote Elizabeth Hoar. "All that he could he has done for me, all that he had has given." By early December, her defensiveness spilled over into a letter to Ellen. "I expect that to many of my friends Mr Emerson for one, he will be nothing," she wrote on the eleventh, notably reducing the proportion of her friends she now judged sympathetic, "and they will not understand that I should have life in common with him. But I do not think he will care; he has not the slightest tinge of self-love; he has throughout our intercourse been used to my having many such ties; he has no wish to be anything to persons with whom he does not feel spontaneously bound, and when I am occupied is happy in himself." Moreover, "*some* of my friends and my family" will appreciate his strength of character and, "should he continue to love me as he has done, to consider his companionship has been an inestimable blessing to me." In fact, he had already proven it,

> especially as I have been more sick, desponding and unreasonable in many ways than I ever was before and more so, I hope, than I ever shall be again. But at all times, he never had a thought except to sustain and cheer me; he is capable of the sacred love, the love passing that of women, he showed it to his father, to Rome, to me, now he loves his child in the same way. I think he will be an excellent father, though he could not speculate about it, or in fact about anything.

This was a persuasive tribute, although seemingly a little overemphatic in light of her more cautious statements to Channing and even her mother. Indeed, far from settling the issue, it still left open the question, still very much on the minds of some of her friends, of what *did* the future hold for a marriage nurtured by dreams of a failed revolution with a devoted lover for whom his wife's intellectual world was a closed book?[28]

For the moment, though, she worried about her friends' silences. "My love to dear Elizh," she concluded her letter to Ellen. "I wish she and Mr Emerson would write to me, but I suppose they don't know what to say[.] Tell them there is no need to say anything about these affairs if they don't want to." Then there was her editor, whose failure to answer her commiserating letter about Pickie, she wrote the next day to the Springs, "sadly disappointed" her. There was some basis to her worries. Perfunctorily answering his brother William's question that October, "Is it a suitable match?" Emerson evaded the question entirely. Greeley sent one more letter, including a note Pickie had written to "Aunty Margaret" before his death, by which time he could not have gotten hers to him about her new family, and, if he ever did send another, it has not survived.[29]

If they *were* withholding, they were in the minority. Most of her friends seemingly accepted her explanations. Some even showed a readiness to do battle in her defense. "I approve of Margaret's taste in having a private marriage all to herself," Lydia Maria Child wrote insouciantly to Ellis Gray Loring a week after Emerson wrote his brother, "and thus keeping a little of the *romance* of the tender sentiment." Sarah Clarke, in another letter to Fuller on the gossip about her marriage, assured her that Eliza Farrar, Margaret's childhood social mentor, and the doyen of intellectual Cambridge society, "continues your faithful friend—ever loyal." When Clarke asked Elizabeth Hoar later that winter if she had written her, Hoar answered, Clarke reported, no, but that did not matter as Fuller "could be sure about *me.*" Almira Barlow probably put the sentiment best to Emerson: "Her life, since she went abroad, is wholly unknown to me; but I have an unshaken trust that what Margaret did she can defend." As the "social inquisition in the U. S." got going, her trust would be a good thing.[30]

III

At the end of September, after a "delightful" ride in the first days of the vintage in the Tuscan countryside, the Ossolis arrived in Florence. "I feel better pleased than ever before," Fuller wrote Cass shortly after arriving. "Florence seems so cheerful and busy after ruined Rome. I feel as if I could forget the disasters of the day for awhile in looking on the treasures she inherits." She would still feel "homesick" for "Rome, *my* Country!" "*You* cannot dream what life was there during the glorious dream of hope," she wrote Curtis, who had grown skeptical of "Revolutionists" and was then living in their old apartment at the Casa Dies. "The artistic genius of the people displayed itself at every moment by some refined symbol, some glorious pageant; never in any place or time was every day life so poetical." And Florence? "Florence is a kind of Boston," she wrote to Sam and Anna Ward, giving a measured version of her well-worn putdown. "It has not the poetic greatness of the other Italian cities; it is a place to work and study in; simple life does not seem so great."[31]

It was then not entirely safe for revolutionists either, despite Tuscany's liberal legal codes under Leopold II, whose restoration meant more than just his return. The assembly had been abolished and even prerevolutionary press freedoms curtailed, while the Austrians, whose troops would occupy the country for the next five years, kept a careful eye on the grand duke to ensure he would not return Tuscany to its reforming days. They should not have been too surprised, then, when a few days after their arrival, the police, suspecting Ossoli was a Radical fleeing illegally from Rome, brought him in for interrogation about his American passport. Their pleas that Margaret was an American and the pontifical authorities in Perugia had not bothered them were to no avail. The "malevolen[t]" director, who Margaret guessed had been one of the officials chased away during the revolution, insisted that unless Ossoli obtained fresh papers from Tuscan authorities in Rome certifying his Roman citizenship, they would have to leave immediately. That would have been more than unfortunate, as they had no place to go that would not be even more dangerous, and they had just signed and given a deposit for a six-month lease on an apartment. They stalled for time while they rallied support. Horatio Greenough talked with his friend Andrea Corsini, the grand duke's minister of foreign affairs, who sent a brief of their case to the police. Cass wrote the American consul in Tuscany explaining the innocent circumstances of their leaving Rome. Finally, three weeks later, the police issued Ossoli a security card giving them permission to stay for two months, which they later extended to the summer. The Ossolis knew, though, they were still not entirely out of harm's way. "It is better for one not to write about these matters through the post," Fuller wrote William Story the day after they got their extension, after damning the cardinals. "I suppose letters are not opened here as the mean espionage is not likely to reach the same he[ight as] in Rome, but cannot feel sure, and we study to give no umbrage." For the rest of their stay, they would remain under surveillance.[32]

Despite this unpleasant start, Italy's "Boston" grew on her. Just being able to rest and relax, she wrote Emelyn Story, "has been balm to me after all the agitation and struggles I had undergone." They lived in a sixth-floor apartment in the "Casa Libri," a high modern building in the Piazza di Santa Maria Novella, whose tall windows opened on the "beautiful" piazza. As in the Barberini, she seems to have had tolerable or at least tractable inmates on which to use her reputed "decisive power" over quarreling Italians, reportedly once getting a hotheaded Rieti domestic and a young Jewish woman in the apartment above to apologize to each other after the former had tried to stab the latter for supposedly insulting her. After Rome's "heavy depressing atmosphere," she also rejoiced in Florence's "delightfully pure and animating" air, which helped Nino "grow better every day." She especially liked being only a few blocks to the west of the Duomo (Santa Maria del Fiore) at the city's center. They frequently attended many of the city's churches, where Giovanni worshiped, while Margaret appreciated the devotional power of the Church's rituals. "No one was there, only the altars lit up," she wrote Caroline, describing their walking through the Duomo after attending a Christmas eve midnight mass, "the priests who were singing could not be seen, by this faint light, the vast solemnity of the interior is really felt." By the spring, when she could enter the Uffizi without freezing, Florence's great art collections, which she had started exploring in the fall, finally seduced her. "I feel works of art more than I have ever yet," she informed Ward after viewing some of her favorite Raphael and Leonardo paintings. Even Tuscany's liberal middle classes, whose apathy depressed her, seemed to be waking up a little. In early March she happily reported to Cass a display of patriotic revulsion at some self-censorship at a performance of Bellini's *I Puritani*: "The singers use the word 'beata' in place of the original '*liberata*,' and the People hiss in Grand Duke's presence." It may have been true that in Rome, as she said to Cass, "every day is worth ten million Florences," but overall the Tuscan city sounds, if not exactly what she wanted, at least what she needed.[33]

"Tis but little I see of all this," Fuller added in her recounting of the disturbance at the Bellini opera, "living as quiet as possible, and associating only with a few friends." That was partly true, although like her claim in the spring about quietly sitting in her "obscure corner," it needs qualification. It is true she still missed her large circle of American friends in Rome. But George Curtis visited her in November, as did Cass the following March. Her massive correspondence (which caused her postage bill to zoom to $50) also belied her isolation. Indeed, sometimes she sounded as if she were running an intellectual Young Europe. "When you go to London do call on Mr. C.," she advised William Story, referring to Clough, Matthew Arnold, and their circle, some of whose poetry Clough had sent her. "Through him you will no doubt come in contact with young men really alive like the best of us in America." In a different mood, she doled out somewhat crass romantic advice to her young bachelor friends, telling Cass to avoid Rietian peasant girls whose papas were ever watchful, but to stick with married women, who seemed more accessible, for his "flirtations," and Curtis that he might want to contact a couple of "scandalous" Roman ladies whom Cass knew. "They might be worth knowing to one who has a curiosity to see that sort of thing," she yawned knowingly. "For my part, mine was easily satisfied[.] I found troubled water no deeper, because you could not count the pebbles at the bottom."[34]

Nor was her circle in Florence exactly negligible. Arconati lived there all winter, and almost daily they corresponded, or Arconati had Fuller over to her villa, or they went on drives or walks in the countryside, arguing good-naturedly about Belgioioso's wealth and Charles Albert's sincerity and sharing mutual concerns about their children's illnesses. Although fewer than in Rome, Fuller's American friends included a number of prominent artists and sculptors and their families. Powers and Greenough, along with Greenough's two artist-brothers, John and Richard, and their wives invited her to parties, plays, ballets, and operas, especially of Bellini and Rossini, whose melodramatic political themes she much enjoyed. The Moziers, who held weekly Saturday night parties for the American colony, kept her busy without making her worry that she had to reciprocate and "transgress the bounds of that rigid economy we must observe." Wealthy Bostonians, such as Frank Shaw's younger brother Quincy and William and Anna Aspinwall, also streamed in and out, as did such artistic British visitors as Catherine and Charles Christopher Black, later the curator of the South Kensington Museum in London, and two "very agreeable English ladies" at whose apartment she heard "some excellent (and German) music." Even old Transcendentalist associates occasionally popped up. "As I was coming past the Duomo the other day," she wrote Curtis of bumping into Charles Sumner's arts-loving younger brother and former Brook Farmer, then in Florence for his health, "I saw a pale, erect, narrow little figure, which made all my nerves tingle with old associations. This was explained by his accosting me and naming himself as Horace Sumner. Imagine Brook Farm walking the streets of Florence; every body turned to look at him[.] Ossoli who had not understood what he said thought he was some insane person and kept touching my arm for me to stop somewhere, while I was listening with a sort of pleasure to the echo of the old pastoral masquerade, or masquerade pastoral."[35]

As this droll reminiscence might suggest, the general impression one gets of Fuller's mood from her letters and others' about her that fall and winter is one of quiet satisfaction, which financial scrimping, political defeat, and the moderate politics of most Florentines, Italians, and Americans do not seem to have greatly affected. "There was a vein of intense enthusiasm threading with fire her talk about Rome," Curtis wrote to Story after visiting her that November, "which was fine & wonderful at the same time." Even observers initially skeptical of her seem to have soon come around to Curtis's view. At a large party at Mozier's house a couple of weeks after the one Curtis attended, Fuller's former pupil's brother, Frederick Gale, recorded in his journal that whereas her husband was young and handsome, she looked wrinkled and sad—"bent in body & in fact an old woman before her time." But he conceded that Italy's political misfortunes had probably contributed to this result. He also found her intriguing. "I heard nothing like that tone of scorn & contempt which I expected in her conversation. I talked a good deal with her & chiefly about the sad manner in which the progressive movements of the recent struggles have been managed." Two weeks later, after talking with her again, he wrote of her as a transformed woman.

> In eve to Mozier's—met a large party of Americans—had a fine supper in which cold turkey, duck, mayonnaise, champagne & whisky punch played a prominent part—and the transcendental ex-editress of the Dial devoted herself with unmistakable ardor to them all not even declining that vulgar, but comforting beverage—so unfashionable for Boston blues, *the whisky punch.* I danced two cotillions with her & found her none the worse for the liquor—but merry & agreeable.

In short: still formidable, charismatic, and surprisingly robust (certainly for a supposedly frail, prematurely old-looking forty-year-old woman with kyphosis) yet also more relaxed, more personable, more political, and, it would seem, with her comforting whisky and handsome young husband, more worldly than the American Margaret of old impressions and stale rumors.[36]

Naturally, individual relationships varied. The "vulgar" rich, as usual, raised her hackles, as she acutely felt the penury of her family. "Here has been a fat round-eyed old lady," she wrote acerbically to her mother, "who had taken seven thousand dollars, just for pocket money to buy pictures and engravings. I thought, now if you could just spare me fifty dollars of that to buy little common engravings to illustrate lessons on Italy, if I want to give some when I come home. But the round-eyed can get such a mass of things she can't use, while I have never had a dollar I could spare for what I could make so interesting to others as well as myself." Some old resentments were not forgotten. Speaking to her mother of Anna Breck Aspinwall, who arrived in the spring "rich in California gold" and "still pretty, simple and smiling in the way father used to like so much": "She enraged one or two persons here that are quite fond of me, by not echoing at all when they praise me. She was very civil, but I suppose thought I was just as odd and disagreeable as ever. . . . In fact," she conceded, "I was an odd and unpleasing girl to people in general." Yet, as this self-distancing concession might suggest, Fuller seems to have been as "civil" as needed. Louisa Greenough, for example, she initially sniffed at to Emelyn Story, as "a woman of the world" who "does not interest me," but soon decided was "sweet tempered and kindly," a fine complement to her fanciful husband, and a good companion for teas and lunches. "I like the Greenoughs much and they are very friendly," she wrote a few months later to the Springs, although, she added to Emelyn, speaking of Louisa, "not the Boston part of her." Louisa's sister-in-law Frances turned out even better. "I like her sense of what is humorous," she wrote Emelyn, "I like her loyalty. And for the ambiguously married Fuller, loyalty was a precious commodity.[37]

Indeed, the thing that that Fuller most appreciated about her Florence cirle of friends, notwithstanding their apparent initial shock, was their warm welcome of her and her newly revealed family. "I have been a little surprized," she wrote to Arconati, "at the even increased warmth with which the little American society of Florence has received me, with the unexpected accessories of husband and child, asking no questions, and seemingly content to find me so." Some even, rather than put off by her choice, as she had feared, extended their kindnesses to Ossoli individually. Arconati practically "adopted" him, Horatio Greenough enjoyed chatting with him about his soldiering and family, and, starting that November, the frail Horace Sumner, who sought out Margaret's sympathy and counsel, regularly came to their apartment to trade Italian and English lessons with him. "Ossoli is forming some taste for books," she reported with satisfaction to Emelyn Story, "which I never expected." She also found the welcome growing. "All true people seem to like Ossoli," she wrote the Springs later that February, "and he is particularly pleased with the Arconatis and Mr and Mrs Horatio Greenough. All speak Italian more or less; thus our position in point of society is very pleasant."[38]

What, though, did these associates think about their marriage? Mostly, it would seem, not too different from what she thought: despite its obvious intellectual limitations, it had ample emotional compensations. "Some 27 years, I should think," Curtis wrote William Story in his account of Ossoli whom he met during his November visit. "He is a dark-haired, quiet, modest man. He has no appearance of smartness. Does not seem, per esempio, as if he would ever learn to speak English. But he is very simple and affectionate & clings to Margaret with quite a touching confidence and affection." That same month, Emelyn sent Maria Lowell a more emphatic endorsement: "Ossoli is a devoted lover; he is all kindness and attention to her, and I think she has chosen the better part in marrying him, for his love must be most precious to her. Judging from what he was after a year's marriage, I should say he was more of a lover than before their marriage." Later recollections echo these views of Ossoli as a lover. "He cared not how trivial was the service if he might perform it for her," Emelyn would recall. "I remember to have seen him one morning . . . set off on an errand to get the handle of her parasol mended with as much genuine knightly zeal as if the charge had been a much weightier one. As he took it [he] said 'How sweet it is to do little things for you never attend to such yourself always leave them to me for my pleasure.'" More important, Emelyn repeated a string of anecdotes about his tender nursing of Margaret during her illnesses as he had his dying father and their mutual deep feeling for nature as evidence of their suitability. "It is abundantly evident," the American consul, William Kinney, later reported to Emerson, "that her young husband discharged all the obligations of his relation to her *con amore*. His admiration amounted to veneration, & her yearning to be loved seemed at least to be satisfied." Even the initially skeptical William Hurlbert, in Florence following his graduation from Harvard Divinity School, afterward recalled their domestic intimacy: "There, seated beside his wife, I was sure to find the Marchese, reading from some patriotic book, and dressed in the dark brown, red-corded coat of the Guardia Civica, which it was his melancholy pleasure to wear at home." He did note that Ossoli stayed as long as the conversation was in Italian, but if a number of English and American visitors came in, he would go to the Café d'Italia, "being very unwilling, as Madame Ossoli told me, to impose any seeming restraint, by his presence, upon her friends, with whom he was unable to converse. For the same reason, he rarely remained with her at the houses of her English or American friends, though he always accompanied her thither, and returned to escort her home." Evidently, the Ossolis' joint "society" was limited, although that seems not to have greatly bothered either of them.[39]

Fuller's most celebrated new friends presented special challenges. She had been on the Brownings' trail ever since she had arrived in London, but they had eloped to Italy the week before, and after that she had subsequently missed them in Pisa, Florence, and Rome. She pursued them armed with introductions from their American correspondents Mathews and Duyckinck, whose *Literary World* both Brownings admired, as well as from Carlyle. "I almost *must* see her, I do fear," the retiring Elizabeth had written her fiancé in a little alarm after noting Fuller's formidable credentials and reviews of their books, which Mathews had sent, stressing they were very positive about Robert's poems (he had said nothing about Fuller's mixed judgment of Elizabeth's). But, as exchanges of genial letters followed, Elizabeth's fear seems to have evaporated. In addition, the previous winter the Storys had met the Brownings in Florence—one of the first of a parade of literary Americans welcomed to the Casa Nigri over the decades—who no doubt raved about their American friend's talents and virtues. Finally, a few days after her arrival, Fuller went to see the soon-to-be-famous couple, visits she followed up with several more at their house just across the Arno, after which Elizabeth sent a friend this excited but measured account of her:

> The American authoress Miss Fuller . . . has taken us by surprise at Florence, . . . retiring from the Roman field with a husband & child above a year old!— Nobody had even suspected a word of this underplot, & her American friends stood in mute astonishment before this apparition of them here. The husband is a Roman marquis . . . appearing amiable & gentlemanly, & having fought well, they say, at the siege, but with no pretension to cope with his wife on any ground appertaining to the intellect. She talks, & he listens— I always wonder at that species of marriage; but people are so different in their matrimonial ideals, that it may answer sometimes.

Although prepared to judge Ossoli tolerantly, the Brownings seemed not to have had much to do with him, and Elizabeth predicted that the "Yankees" would not be able to do much with him either.[40]

Fuller, however, knew what to do with the Brownings: try to get beyond Robert's "vivacious" but "singularly external" manner and Elizabeth's pale but "intense" one. She confronted them six days after Elizabeth wrote about her to her friend. "It seemed to me when I was last at your house," she wrote Elizabeth, "as if a curtain fell down between us. A great sadness fell upon me, just as Mr Browning came in. . . . Did you share any such influence[?] I think probably it was confined to me, but have noted the day and hour in my diary, in case any interpretation should later be tendered." It is not known if she ever "tendered" any, but her reversion to Transcendentalist social scrutinizing seems to have brought down a little the protective shield the nineteenth-century's most tightly bonded literary couple habitually put up to visitors. Other things contributed. The Brownings were eager for gossip about America's literary celebrities, and Fuller readily obliged, sometimes, as with Poe, whom they had asked her about, in incisive detail. They also had a common bond in their babies, Nino and Robert, or (as the Brownings called him) Penini or Pen, whose cherubic and laughing behavior Fuller loved. ("It looks as if it was created fresh after a flood, and could not be the child of two people who had written books and such thoughtful sad books too.") The bond seems to have grown stronger after Elizabeth miscarried in late October. "I think babies seem amazed at one another," Margaret mused to Elizabeth shortly afterward, urging they put the two boys together in the Browning's nursery so they could "exchange a few looks." By the end of the winter, after more of this Romantic-inflected talk, Fuller enrolled Robert in her cosmopolitan golden circle: "He is like one of our best American men, I find nothing of the modern Englishman about him. Genuine Saxon!" She even finally felt "drawn out" by Elizabeth. "On Saturday I passed an entire day, very delightfully, with the Brownings," she wrote Emelyn Story. "I love and admire them both more, as I know them better; we meet more truly of late." That same day Elizabeth wrote to her sister: "While I was writing, in came Ma^{dme.} Ossoli—stayed dinner . . . stayed coffee . . . hours upon hours, the rain helping. I like her much."[41]

The one chink in their relationship for Elizabeth was political. A liberal but no democrat, two years earlier, after receiving a copy of *Woman in the Nineteenth Century*, she had snapped to Robert, "How I hate those 'Women of England' 'Women & their mission' & the rest—As if any possible good were to be done by such expositions of rights & wrongs." Her views of European politics were of a similar cast. Along with her more liberal husband, she sympathized with the oppressed Italians, but she doubted their intellectual capacities and later welcomed the coup of Louis Napoleon as a much-needed check of both Catholic monarchical reaction and France's grandiose "Reds." Naturally, she was shocked by Fuller's radicalism. "Ma^{dme.} Ossoli," she reported to a friend, was "one of the out & out Reds, & scorners of grades of society." Elizabeth's religion may have also fed her ideological doubts about Fuller. An ardent devotee of spiritualism as a kind of modern Christianity, Elizabeth was flummoxed that Fuller could be so venerating yet so patronizing about the Bible.[42]

Usually, though, Elizabeth dismissed their differences with gracious aplomb. "A very interesting person she is, far better than her writings," she would tell a friend on the eve of the Ossolis' departure, "truthful, spiritual in her habitual mode of mind, . . . not only exalted, but *exalteè* in her opinions, . . . and yet calm in manner." Indeed, she would later tell Sarah Clarke that she and Robert were astonished to read in her *Memoirs* that in America some regarded her as haughty or sarcastic; they "did not suspect her to be capable of those infirmities." Shortly after the Ossolis left, Elizabeth gave her sister a more complete, if still coy, account of her feelings about Fuller and her radical views. Saying that she disagreed with her perhaps on every serious point, she added:

> Yet there is a curious sympathy between us—she *drew* me, I felt, by her truthfulness & generosity, yes, & tenderness of character— I loved her, & could not bear to measure the depth of the gulf— Robert felt precisely so— She is a socialist by profession, & I had hints & glimpses of desecrating opinions connected with that doctrine, from which I shrank away in conversation— She said she "had thought much & made up her mind". . & discussion, where persuasion is out of the question on either side, is a cruel thing. Also, you know my favorite belief, that the heart is often wiser than the head—& her heart at least is wise. I like her *atmosphere* . . if you know what I mean by that.

"One of the very plainest yet most interesting women I ever saw!" she exclaimed. Presumably, she meant by that Fuller's social charisma, and that no one in Florence, whatever they thought of Ossoli's sociability or his wife's socialism, would have disputed.[43]

IV

If that winter Fuller appeared (as Catherine Black told her she did) "*so happy*," one reason certainly was her husband but at least as big a cause was her child. "My little baby flourishes in my care," she reported happily to Clough in February; "his laughing eyes, his stammered words and capricious caresses afford me the first unalloyed quiet joy I have ever known." Fair-skinned, with blue eyes and light hair, he seems to have inherited much more from his mother's side of the family than his father's. Physical descriptions of him vary. Curtis described him as "heavy and not handsome," and Frank Shaw's brother Quincy reported that he was "the image of his mother," but the wife of the captain with whom the Ossolis would later sail thought he was "very beautiful" and the "*whitest* child I ever saw, & very graceful." Margaret wrote the Wards that he was "a very fat baby, who looks like anything but an Italian." In any case, she treated his appearance lightly. "He grows every way; except hair, and people rather jeer at me, for having only a *bald* baby," she wrote Sam Ward, referencing the two biblical bears who, after some children mocked Elisha for his baldness, tore them apart. "I piously wish them the fate of the scoffers who did not prize that peculiarity in a Prophet."[44]

What sort of a mother was Fuller? After a nine-month absence interrupted by two long visits and several near calamities, she was clearly determined to bond with her child. "Just when our little one is unfolding," she wrote Emelyn Story, "just when he daily discovers some new trait, to have our acquaintance stopped to give him principally into the care of hirelings and turn my care to a new subject would be so painful." She could even sound possessive. "I thought I had loved the children of others as much as I could love a child," she told Sam and Anna Ward, "but find the thrill far more vital with my own." Yet he had a nursemaid for his feeding, and Giovanni, who doted on him, constantly played with him and looked after him. In addition, by January she stopped imagining his impending death or permanent disablement from his mistreatment in Rieti or from a nearby cholera outbreak. She did worry he would not do so well after he was weaned from his "great stout Roman mother in the flesh," but when she got down to feeding him herself in the spring she seems to have handled it well enough. "He takes it very kindly," she reported to Emelyn, "and after the first rage, has thought it great fun to sleep with me." Nor did she forget a light application of moderating Boston Unitarian morals. "[Nino] has been walking to day," she wrote in a long letter about him to Caroline that mid-December. "I have taken such pleasure in watching his little foolish legs. I am sorry to say he seems timid and yet a great bully. I hope these faults may be evoked up into respectable virtues by dint of steady maternal reasoning." Since she had succeeded so well on that score with her younger siblings, her hope would seem a reasonable one.[45]

She also leavened her Boston ethics with Romantic additives. She did not say much about Nino's sex, although she confided to her sister, who had also recently given birth to a boy, that she, too, shared the unfortunate "prejudice" that a boy "will conquer more ill, and effect more good, than is expected from girls." On the other hand, memories of her father's obsessive intellectual demands on her probably tempered any impulse she might have had to revive her lavish fantasies about bearing a hero or a Christ child. "I have no special visions about him," she told Sarah Shaw, and to Arconati, speaking of Arconati's son (who would become a decorated soldier in the Italian campaign of 1860–61), she wrote: "I do not believe mine will be a brilliant child, like Gian Martino." When Richard admonished her about the terrible responsibility of a parent to make sure their child "attains the second birth of the spirit," she said, yes, she felt a "solemn feeling" for Nino's growth, but "God and nature are there, furnishing a thousand masters to correct our erroneous . . . teachings." Besides, she said, she did not want to lose the simple innocent pleasure of watching his growth from day to day by thinking of his future. "Now he learns playing as we all shall when we enter a higher state. With him my intercourse thus far has been satisfactory and if I do not well for *him* he at least has taught *me* a great deal." By the spring, her Goethean maxims of growing with the child so he could "become what he is" seem to have paid dividends. "He is an intelligent little one," she wrote Emelyn contentedly, "but chiefly remarkable for his archness and gayety." Rather than regretting too much his aggressiveness, she clearly *liked* his saucy spirits. And she loved his playacting. "I was just up and Nino all naked on his sofa," she wrote Caroline of her Christmas morning after her and Giovanni's nighttime walk through the Duomo,

> when came some beautiful large toys that had been sent him a bird, a horse, a cat that could be moved to express different things. It almost made me cry to see the kind of fearful rapture with which he regarded them, legs and arms, extended, fingers and toes quivering, mouth made up to a little round O, eyes dilated; for a time he did not even wish to touch them, after he began he was different with all the three, loving the bird; very wild and shouting with the horse, with the cat pulling her face close to his, staring in her eyes, and then throwing her away. . . . It is sweet to see him when he gets used to them and plays by himself, whispering to them, seeming to contrive stories. You would laugh to know how much remorse I feel that I never gave children more toys in the course of my life. I regret all the money I ever spent on myself or in little presents for grown people, hardened sinners. I did not know what pure delight could be bestowed. I am sure if Jesus Christ had given, it would not have been little crosses.

Perhaps only someone who felt robbed of a playful childhood could have captured so graphically its exuberance, while turning a little her anticlerical knife.[46]

At her most deeply Romantic, she imagined Nino gave her a feeling of everyday spiritual wholeness. "What a difference it makes to come home to a child," she exclaimed to Emelyn Story, after describing a "glorious" walk along the banks of the Arno;

> how it fills up all the gaps of life, just in the way that is most consoling, most refreshing. I used to feel sad at that time; the day had not been nobly spent, I had not done my duty to myself and others; then I felt so lonely, now I never feel lonely, for even if my little boy dies, our souls will remain eternally united. Then I feel *infinite* hope for him, hope that he will serve God and man more loyally than I have and seeing how full he is of life, how much he can afford to throw away, I feel the inexhaustibleness of nature and console myself for my own incapacities.

She expanded for Cass on this Transcendental consolation she found with Nino: "I feel the tie between him and me so real, so deep-rooted, even death shall not part us. I shall not be alone in other worlds, whenever Eternity may call me." Yet to Caroline, she gave this conceit a somewhat more anxious twist: "This much I do hope, in life or death to be no more separated from Angelino." So intertwined with him in both realms, she would seem prepared for anything.[47]

Bonding with Nino did not keep her from her other major task that winter and spring. Hurlbert recalled that when he visited her in her apartment, he nearly always found her "surrounded by her books and papers" or "quite immersed in manuscripts and journals." When that December she read in a letter from Rebecca Spring, "it is better to give the world this living soul than a portion of my life in a printed book," she blanched a bit. "It is true," she answered; "and yet of my book," she said, "I could know whether it would be of some worth or not, of my child I must wait to see what his worth will be." In fact, she staked a lot on her book. "If I cannot make any thing out of my present materials my future is dark indeed," she wrote the Springs several weeks later. "I do not wish to throw away the studies and materials of 4 years, paid for by so many hours of bitter care as they have been already."[48]

Finding a publisher, however, was not easy. In August she had sent a proposal of a "partly finished work" to Carlyle, who had conveyed it to his own publisher Edward Chapman, the most literary partner of Chapman and Hall, which published Dickens, Emerson, the *Dial*, and many liberal Continental books, whom Carlyle assued her was "as much as any man I know, what passes to be the general voice of the Craft in London." To Chapman he wrote a Carlylean but still enticing endorsement:

> Miss Margaret Fuller is an American Lady, of ripe years, perhaps 40 and odd; deformed and lean in person, but full of ardent soul to the finger-ends; enthusiastic, resolute, eloquent; writes really strikingly and well, with a constant noble *fire* pervading all she says; style clear, brief and vivid; meaning high and true, tho' occasionally somewhat airy and vague. The Books that I have read of hers (which can be had at your Namesake's, I suppose) give me somewhat the notion of a *Spiritual Aurora Borealis*. She is a great ally of Emerson's, but deeper in German and Foreign things than he; and indeed a much more vehement and self-reliant, not to say dogmatic, autocratic and practically positive character.

Assuring Chapman her book would be profitable, he concluded: "She is, so far as I may note, *considerably* a higher-minded and cleverer woman than any of the Lady Lions yet on your Books; and if you and she could make any arrangement useful to both parties, I should be very glad indeed." Four days later, evidently proud of his efforts for "the heroic Margaret," he wrote Emerson, "She has a beautiful enthusiasm; and is perhaps in the right stage of insight for doing that piece of business well." Later that week, however, Chapman turned down her proposal. "Perhaps if the *Ms.* were actually *ready*," Carlyle afterward advised her, "and such as I expect it to be; and furthermore if this absurd 'decision of the judges' were *reversed* (as I consider it sure to be), this sagacious Book-Publisher might sing to a diff' tune." Meanwhile, he urged her to send him the finished manuscript, and he would push it again on Chapman or any other publisher she would like him to try. "I had foreseen from previous advices," she wrote Cass dejectedly, "or rather perhaps from a feeling of fate. It has been my fate that when I worked for others I could always succeed; when I tried to keep the least thing for myself, it was not permitted. Must this schooling be life-long?"[49]

The question of what kind of a book she was offering under the title "History of the late Italian Revolutions" is a difficult one. Elizabeth Browning would later guess that she had probably only collected the "raw material," but she did not indicate why she thought that, and Fuller's proposal to Carlyle clearly indicated that it was at least partly finished. She seems to have gotten little done on it during her summer in L'Aquila and Rieti, but she later told Caroline that during her subsequent winter in Rome, when she was determined to make "the most vehement efforts to redeem the time" while away from Nino, she wrote "at least two volumes." Continuing to work on it through the spring, she stopped during the siege and started in again in Florence, halting temporarily in December and January when her study became too cold to write in and the dining room with the stove had to be used for Nino and visitors. In February, the American *Home Journal* announced that "the Marchioness of Ossoli" had "nearly completed . . . an elaborate History of the late Revolutionary movement in Italy," expected to be published by the end of the season in both New York and London. This was probably an exaggeration, but she clearly had written at least a great deal of it.[50]

Determining its contents is even more difficult. Her own appraisals of it vary. The previous March, buoyed by the Republic's recent successes, she had written Richard, "This work, if I can accomplish it will be a worthy chapter in the history of the world" and, if sufficiently expressive, energetic, and attentive to details, of permanent literary value as well as "profitable to me pecuniarily." After the Republic's fall, she tried to lower expectations, especially, as usual, among her Transcendentalist friends. "Do not expect any thing very good of it," she wrote that December to Channing. "I suppose there are impressions worth the general hearing about as far as they are correct, and I am anxious to do historical justice to some facts and persons, but I am not aware that there will be *that* of advantage to a thinker. I do not know for I cannot read it over, but believe I have scarce expressed what lies deepest in my mind." Yet Elizabeth Browning thought it would probably have been her best book, recalling that she had told her "it was the only production to which she had given time & labour." Certainly its scope, according to the *Home Journal*, was broad, covering the "Social, Political, Religious and Esthetical condition of the country, notices of its most eminent persons, etc., etc." The sources she had been collecting also sound rich: Italian and French newspapers, state documents, official correspondence, pamphlets, broadsides, and gossip taken from Radicals and Liberals alike all over Italy. She even had contacts among some conservatives, as well as the experience of her extensive travels in northern Italy and, however star-crossed, of living among peasants in central Italy.[51]

About its arguments there are a few clues. It very likely would have had a strong dash of classic Whig liberalism. "He says James II was unable to get beyond this one idea," she wrote William Story of Thomas Babbington Macaulay's just-published "brilliant and fascinating" *History of England from the Accession of James II*. "'My father made concessions and was beheaded and therefore the only safe way for me to do is to make no concessions.' The Cardinals are just as stupid." Other readings she did after the fall of the Republic would have tilted her interpretations in a more radical direction. She read issues of the Geneva radical exiles' *Der Völkerbund* to find out "what the great disbanded are hoping and trying." She read with particular attention the liberal Republican Lamartine's new *Histoire de la révolution de 1848* and the democratic socialist Louis Blanc's *Révolution français: Histoire de dix ans, 1830–1840*, which would have given her alternative interpretations about what had gone wrong in recent French politics that had sealed the Roman Republic's fate. If it followed in the Romantic style of her dispatches, it must have included stirring set pieces, dramatic narratives, and piquant anecdotes with varying degrees of irony and tragedy. It undoubtedly also would have reflected her two recurrent themes: Italy as a cosmopolitan mirror of the ideals of America and a keen understanding, almost unique for an Anglo-American Italophile, that to enter modern history, Italy had to overthrow, at whatever cost, the feudal social and political structure that had sustained its once great culture. It certainly would have surpassed the only American account, Theodore Dwight's luridly anti-Catholic secondhand polemic *The Roman Republic of 1849*, published the following year, and perhaps might have been, as one Italian historian has conjectured, the cosmopolitan history of emerging modern Italy that no American in the nineteenth century would ever write.[52]

Then there is the question of her socialism. Elizabeth Browning was sure that if she had completed the book, it would have been "deeply coloured by those blood-colours of socialistic views, which would have drawn the wolves on her with a still more howling enmity both in England & America." Indeed, the coincidence of her embrace of socialism and her death has led some recent scholars to invoke it as the ideological telos of her life. Yet how "red" were her views really? The term itself then applied not to the handful of emerging communists but to socialists like those in the French "*démoc soc*" coalition, whose support of the workers' June 1848 uprising signaled their departure from their "utopian" predecessors and their embrace of political conflict and limited class struggle. In this European context, she was certainly a political radical. However much "tracked in blood," the 1848 revolutions' defeats, she had declared in her last dispatch from Rome, were "triumphs" that Democracy should "bless" as proving "there is no possible compromise between her and the Old." There is also another European context for her radicalism: whatever anguish she felt about the revolutions' attendant suffering and death, she put no stock, as did her American abolitionist and socialist friends, in "nonresistance" or pacifism. "What you say is deeply true about the peace way being the best," she wrote that December to her Quaker socialist friend Marcus Spring.

> [It] is true that while Moses slew the Egyptian, Christ stood to be spit upon and that Death to man could do no harm. You have the truth, you have the right, but could

you act it, Marcus in all circumstances? Stifled under the Roman priesthood would you not have thrown it off with all your force? Would you have waited unknown centuries hoping the moment when you could use another method? If so, you are a Christian; you know I never pretended to be except in dabs and sparkles here and there. Yet the agonies of that baptism of blood I feel oh how deeply in the golden June days of Rome. Consistent no way I felt I should have shrunk back. I could not have had it shed. Christ did not have to see his dear ones pass the dark river; he could go alone; however, in prophetic spirit no doubt, he foresaw the crusades.[53]

This is vintage European political Fuller: enthusiastic, militant, and prophetic, yet also frank, self-aware, and subtle (as in her use of Christ's life to justify both her shrinking back from and embrace of revolution). Most of all, her letter shows how much her socialism, halting and skeptical in America, had turned "red" in the flames of European revolutionary experiences. "I have become an enthusiastic Socialist," she boldly announced to Spring in her letter; "elsewhere is no comfort, no solution for the problems of the times." Like an entire generation of European intellectuals, she clearly saw 1848–49 as a turning point in history. Unlike many of them, she remained a political radical. Rather than defeat making her exchange the dream of socialism for the modern era's "antibourgeois" alternative of avant-garde art, she saw socialism as a logical *answer* to that defeat. At the same time, unlike her American communitarian compatriots, she saw socialism as deeply entangled with politics.[54]

Yet what, besides a new sense of political urgency, did socialism programmatically mean to her? Perhaps, if she had articulated an answer, it would have been close to what Blanc, probably her chief guide, said: state intervention to establish voluntary associations of production and welfare. Certainly, there was nothing revolutionary, much less proto-Marxist, about her socialism. There is no evidence that she would have accepted Marx's key argument that the bourgeoisie's support for mercilessly suppressing the Parisian workers during the June Days proved it an unredeemable class enemy of socialism and even democracy. Nor would her experiences have supported such a view. Italy had been principally a site not of a struggle of classes but of national liberation, one, moreover, mostly led by middle-class professionals and supported by the bourgeoisie, along with a skilled stratum of the working class that largely lacked an independent program of its own. And that reality had beamed through even in her most radical pronouncements: whenever she had denounced Moderates and Liberals, it had never been for their class interests per se but rather for their stupidities and betrayals of the national struggle. It is true she thought their betrayals flowed from their fear of democracy and democracy was the inevitable wave of the future and, in the inflammatory weeks before the final French assault, had even thrown out the possibility for her readers of a half-century bloody conflict between the principle of democracy and the old powers. But in her last dispatches she expressed the hope that even moderate Liberals would soon see the light of democracy (Moderates and Liberals alike "will know that Radical Reform is the only one possible in these desperate days"). And what was true of democracy was true of socialism. Indeed, contra Marx, for whom defeat was the crucible of even bloodier class warfare to come, she argued in her penultimate dispatch, just the reverse: reaction and repression were opening the eyes of many, not to just democratic nationalism but also to redressing the "frightful ills of Europe, by a peaceful though radical revolution instead of bloody conflict."

> The Kings may find their thrones rather crumbling than tumbling; the priests may see the consecration wafer turn into bread to sustain the perishing millions even in their astonished hand. God grant it. Here lie my hopes now. I believed before I came to Europe in what is called Socialism, as the inevitable sequence to the tendencies and wants of the era, but I did not think these vast changes in modes of government, education and daily life, would be effected as rapidly as I now think they will, because they must. The world can no longer stand without them.

To borrow a leaf from Leon Trotsky, the world faced democratic socialism or barbarism, though with democracy coming about in a nonviolent way that had somehow eluded Europe for the past two generations and socialism peacefully following in its wake, which Trotsky, needless to say, would have regarded as a bourgeois fantasy.[55]

Finally, if her class position was middle-class and her rhetoric universalist, her eyes remained overwhelmingly fixed, as always, on two countries, both refracted through optimistic liberal democratic lenses. In her last two dispatches of November 15 and January 6, she surveyed the evidence for that optimism: the growing contempt among the middle classes and Liberals for the lies of the French, repressions of the Cardinals, and the fearfulness of the moderate kings Leopold II in Tuscany and Victor Emmanuel in Piedmont. In only a few more years, she wrote, the defeated democratic-led nationalist revolution would break out again in Italy. Her prediction would be half right. By 1860 Italy would become mostly unified and independent, and ten years later, with the overthrow of the papal government in Rome, completely so, as well as free of theocratic rule. However, all of that would come out of violent battles orchestrated by Garibaldi but sanctioned by Charles Albert's son Emmanuel II, whose victorious monarchy would put off democracy, modernization, and elevation of the status of the country's overwhelming peasant majority—which Fuller, like most of her Risorgimento comrades, preferred to overlook—for another century. And America, her political urtext of contrast and projection? Here, too, she was optimistic. "Amid the pains and disappointments with which the past months have been overflowing, it is refreshing," she told her readers, after referencing several recent *Tribune* reports, "how cordially America sympathized" with the Italians. Forgetting her past denunciations of the United States for its despicable *lack* of sympathy, she wrote of an "America" that, she rejoiced, "did not hug herself in selfish content with her more prosperous fortune; she glowed at the hope of relief for the suffering nations of Europe; she deeply mourned its overthrow; she is indignant at the treachery that consummated it. I love my country for the spirit she has shown; it proves that the lust of gold, her peculiar temptation, has not yet cankered her noble heart."[56]

So it would appear that *America*, which she had thought only by historical luck had avoided the most "frightful ills" of industrial capitalism, now had the opportunity to progress peacefully toward a social democratic utopia. "Joy to those born in this day," she wrote in her last lines to her readers: "In America is open to them the easy chance of a noble, peaceful growth, in Europe of a combat grand in its motives, and in its extent beyond what the world ever before so much as dreamed." This was largely the conclusion her increasingly nationalist American socialist comrades were drawing from the failure of the 1848 revolutions. Of course, it would not turn out that way. As the battle over slavery flamed out that year with the Compromise of 1850 and the Fugitive Slave Law, burning hotter with each subsequent bill nationalizing slavery, the next decade and a half would bring not the [1]"easy chance" of "peaceful growth" but infinitely more violent rhetoric, bloody deeds, and mass slaughter than at any time in American history. Still, though she did not foresee this sharp turn toward America's liberal "grand combat" in its post-utopian decade, her European experience had certainly prepared her for it.[57]

V

"I am deeply homesick," Fuller had written Channing in a melancholy moment from Chicago three and a half years earlier, "yet where is that home?" Now she had two homes, which may not have exactly answered her Romantic question here of belonging in the world, but it did raise new problems and possibilities. Her first concern was keeping her family together. After Nino's birth, she had considered going to America and either Ossoli later joining them or her returning to Rome, but after the Republic collapsed, she decided against it. "It would not only be very strange and sad to me to be without his love and care for weeks and months," she confided to Channing, but he would badly miss Angelino, and she would feel very anxious to leave him exiled from Rome without a job, family, or friends. Her other option was to remain in Italy, at least for several more years, which she preferred. "I have lived in a much more full and true way than was possible in our country," she confessed to Sarah Shaw, "each day has been so rich in joys and pains, actions and sufferings, to say nothing of themes of observation." Several of her American friends in Italy thought she was right. "Her heart is now too much rooted in Rome, I think," Curtis wrote William Story, "ever to bear a long, never a life-long separation."[58]

Ultimately, where to live came down, as usual, to how to live. Magazine writing, which Carlyle had once proposed, was problematic. Although before she had left London, Thomas Delf had offered to secure her a regular periodical assignment so she could remain abroad, he never answered her follow-up letter. "He has been a great disappointment," she wrote angrily to the Springs, as she had let pass other publishing opportunities while waiting for him. American publishers were no help either. Mozier, who like all her Florence friends wanted her to stay, proposed she write a series of "Letters from Florence," but nothing came of it. Even though she still felt burned by Wiley's half-wrecking her *Papers on Literature and Art*, she asked Marcus Spring to try to interest him in publishing a second edition, but he did not bite. That left her Italian history, which she expected would be profitable. Her original idea had been to publish it England, but after learning in the fall that recent court decisions in England made it practically impossible for American authors to hold English copyrights, she decided it was just as well Chapman had rejected her proposal. That left getting from an American publisher a contract, which Wiley had offered her, but with no advance, which she thought predictable but still shocking and unacceptable. So it was clear: if she wanted decent terms and a reasonable opportunity to alter the manuscript and correct proofs, she had to be, as she told several friends, "on the spot."[59]

Yet she anguished about the decision all December. She stopped talking about money, probably because, as she also said, she figured that, besides publishing her book, she could earn a living from journalism assignments, teaching some classes, and bringing out an expanded edition of *Woman in the Nineteenth Century*. Her chief worry was how Ossoli would fare. "I feel he will feel very strange and lonely there," she wrote to William Story; "indeed I feel much more anxious about his happiness than my own." Two weeks after that, though, she wrote her mother that Ossoli was willing and even eager to go since, like all young Italians, he saw America as the land of liberty and he hoped a new revolution in a few years would allow him to return. "All this is dark; we can judge only for the present moment the decision will rest with me. I shall wait till the last moment, as I always do, that I may have all the reasons before me." Two days later, she wrote to her old Transcendentalist confessor Channing more pensively about their future in America:

> I trust we shall find means to make the voyage together and remain together. In our country he will have for resources, his walks and quiet communings with nature, which is always so great a part of his life; he will have the child, and I think my family, especially my mother, will love him very dearly and he will be learning the language with them. I suppose I must myself be engaged in the old unhealthy way, life will probably be a severe struggle. I hope I shall be able to live through it, and not neglect my child, nor Ossoli. He has suffered enough; it has plowed furrows in his life since first we met. He has done all he could and cannot blame himself. Our destiny is sad; we must brave it as we can. I hope we shall always feel mutual tenderness, and Ossoli has a simple child-like piety that will make it easier for him.

Finally, later that day, for her female soul mate Caroline, she settled on a formulation: "If we cannot place ourselves well there, it will be time to think where to go, when I have seen you all, and know whether Ossoli can learn English and to live with those of English blood." So it would be an experiment, which Ossoli seems to have accepted, telling his sister in Ireland "my wife" needed to return to the United States. A week later, on January 8, 1850, Margaret wrote Richard they were coming, probably in May or June, when their money would run out and the weather would allow for a safer voyage for Nino.[60]

Her decision made, the immediate future began looking a little brighter. She dwelled on the prospect of seeing her family, particularly her mother but also Eugene, whom she had not seen in ten years, and Arthur, whose wedding was to be in September, as well as her best friends in Boston, especially William Channing, Caroline Tappan, the Wards, and the Shaws. She encouragingly prepared her family to greet her new husband. "I may say of him, as you say of your wife," she wrote Richard that same day of the eighth, "it would be difficult to other than like him, so sweet is his disposition, so without an effort disinterested, so simply wise his daily conduct, so harmoniously his whole nature. Add that he is a perfectly unconscious character, and never dreams that he does well." She did concede that he had made little progress in his English studies (which Ossoli confirmed), and for a good while Richard may not be able to talk with him, "but you will like showing him some of your favorite haunts; he is so happy in nature, in sweet tranquil places."[61]

Where to live in America, though, remained a question. Her mother, who was living with Arthur in a leased house in Manchester, New Hampshire, where he was preaching, had encouraged her to move in with them, adding, "my income will go to support us till we can see what can be added." Margaret told Richard she very much liked the idea of living with their mother and near her most cherished friends in New England. On the other hand, she said, for Ossoli's sake, she might decide to live in or near New York City, where he would see Italians, often hear his native tongue, and generally "feel less exiled." They could also easily find a quiet and beautiful place with an easy access to Manhattan by steam and to Boston by rail. In either case, the time to decide was after she got to America, where she would consult with friends and see what employment openings there were for her. "I shall weigh all advantages at the time and choose as may then seems best," she told Richard, but the balance sounds like it was tipping toward New York.[62]

Notwithstanding all her past European-style criticism of America's materialism, conformity, and provincialism, as well as its complacency about slavery, she even began looking more kindly on her native country. She remained skeptical about its emerging mass culture. "I shrink as I think of the mass movements in our country," she wrote Emelyn Story in February, speaking of the "frightful" hysteria and "Phobia" she expected P. T. Barnum's orchestration of Jenny Lind's imminent American tour to touch off. "I am afraid I shall be trampled under foot, if I can't keep out of the way." But she was genuinely proud that her young Italian patriots, so different from British Tories and French socialists, saw her country as the "land of liberty." She also had criticisms of Europe. She had been particularly disappointed in not finding an American-style Romantic sisterhood among European women. Although it was true, she told the Wards, she had recruited "a large band of male friends" in Europe, she could only report three women (probably Arconati, Belgioioso, and Elizabeth Browning) with whom she had had any real intimacy. "My friends look very lovely to me in the distance, those who are round you now," she added, echoing Tocqueville's view of the social "superiority" of American women. "I do not find women in Europe to compare with those of America." And she found a few American cultural nuggets to appreciate. "Yes I shall like to go back and see our 'eighteen millions of bores,'" she laughed in a letter to Clough in February, cribbing a phrase from Carlyle's recent anti-democratic *Latter-day Pamphlets*, "with their rail-roads, electric telegraphs, mass movements and ridiculous dilettant phobias, but with ever successful rush and bang. I feel as if I should be the greatest bore of all when I get home, so few will care for the thoughts of my head or the feelings of my heart, but there will be some pairs of eyes to see, and a sense of fresh life unknown here." Such chipper self-deprecation colored her portrayals of her homecoming as well. Making light of her "vile" health, all "the more degrading as fate has annexed me so emphatically to the world of workies," she told Sam and Anna: "Prepare me an old, worn, easy chair beside your nursery fire. I am chiefly good now at crooning children to sleep with ballad stories. When childlike minded I will make you doze too." To her mother she wrote simply how excited she was about seeing her family and friends and being able to "pass together at least three or four years of our lives."[63]

"Three or four years": so America was to be, as she had implied to her mother in December, a temporary way station, even if in its details, as she had told her then, "all this is dark." Certainly, she could not have known at the time of an outbreak of a new revolution in Italy, on which both Ossoli and she banked to allow them to return under politically favorable circumstances. Nor, even less, could she have predicted their future financial circumstances and Ossoli's acclimatization in America, which would obviously also affect how long they would stay there. One thing, however, is clear: already in her mind she was contemplating becoming something other than the American she had always been. She was not thinking about becoming an expatriate like the Storys, who would be buried with their son in the same Protestant cemetery in Rome as Keats and Shelley, or, if she could have imagined them, the American writers, artists, and musicians who after World War I would never return. Her social, political, and cultural ties to the United States were too deep. If her likely status had a label, it would probably be something like what her cultural successor Randolph Bourne would announce sixty-six years later in his essay "Trans-national America" as the only true position for the "cultivated American": a "dual citizen" of both Europe and America.[64]

VI

One immediate social problem remained: while they were (she told Cass) "bend[ing] our eyes toward *America*," the talk about her there was beginning to rage. She got some unexpected strategic help in December, when Maria White, after receiving Emelyn Story's letter affirming that Margaret had "chosen the better part in marrying" Ossoli and that "family matters" had "solely" prevented them from announcing it at the time, made it into a chain letter. She sent a copy to the Shaws, who undoubtedly made sure it went the rounds among the Lorings and others in their Garrisonian circle who were less enamored of Margaret. Maria also sent a transcription to Sarah Clarke and her brother William, who sent copies to the Springs, Child, Channing, and Greeley, which seem to have buoyed them up. The Clarkes were thrilled that the wife of Fuller's chief detractor had taken this step. On New Year's Day, William Clarke wrote Margaret that Lowell had spoken to him of her "in a very kind manner," with none of the "little venom" in his *Fable*, "of which he is now heartily ashamed," an opinion William's sister Sarah shared. "I think James Lowell regretted that he had attacked you so rudely in his Fable for Critics," Sarah wrote her, "as he took the opportunity to defend you from the attacks of Bishop Hughes last summer." Child, who in the fall had breezily defended the "romance" of Margaret's secrecy to Louisa Loring, now wrote even more strenuously to Louisa's husband, Ellis: "I suppose you saw a copy of the letter which Mrs. Story wrote to J. R. Lowell about Margaret Fuller's marriage. I was very glad to see it; not on my own account, for I was perfectly satisfied to allow her to manage her own affairs in her own way, without remark of mine; but I was rejoiced to find that she had not imprudently put herself in the power of small minds, of both sexes." She repeated what had become a refrain among Fuller's friends and family: "The love and tenderness induced by these new relations I think will greatly soften and beautify Margaret's character."[65]

But if buoyed by the Lowells' action, her friends could hardly stop the "social inquisition of the U.S." "She *bought* the boy, I *know* she did!" Eliza Robbins, the "exceedingly disagreeable" elderly matron at Sing Sing gleefully cried to Child. As more of these nasty stories about Ossoli and the legitimacy of their marriage surfaced, Margaret started losing a little of the composure she had shown in the fall. "What you say of the meddling curiosity of people repels me," she wrote angrily in her December 17 letter to Caroline.

> It is so different here. When I made my appearance with a husband and a child of a year old nobody did the least thing to annoy me. All were most cordial, none asked or implied questions. Yet there were not a few that might justly have complained that when they were confiding to me all their affairs and doing much to serve me, I had observed absolute silence to them. Others might for more than one reason be displeased at the choice I made. All have acted in the kindest and most refined manner.

She gave as her number one exhibit Arconati, whom she described, swiping at Fuller's prudish detractors, as "an Italian lady . . . who might be qualified in the court Journal as one 'of the highest rank sustained by the most scrupulous decorum!!'" As the date of her return loomed closer, Margaret's exasperation increased. On February 5 she wrote a defensive but determined letter to the Springs about Ossoli and their future together in America, which they had quizzed her about. "I have expected that those who cared for me chiefly for my activity of intellect would not care for him," she freely conceded, "but that those in whom the moral nature predominates would gradually learn to love and admire him and see what a treasure his affection must be to me." She then listed once again all the strengths of Ossoli's character that she had previously communicated, adding now his steadfastness during the revolution: "His enthusiasm was quiet but unsleeping. He is very unlike most Italians, but very unlike most Americans too." But then again, in evident frustration, she waved away all defenses: "He is too truly the gentleman not to be respected by all persons of refinement; for the rest if my life is free and not too much troubled, if he can enjoy his domestic affections and fulfil his duties in his own way he will content. Can we find this much for ourselves in bustling America for the next three or four years? I know not but think we shall come and try." Finally, with the gossip continuing unabated, by the spring her annoyance over it reached a boiling point. Even the Lowells' chain letter now irritated her. "I had already heard from many quarters" of her letter and its "very happy effect," she wrote Emelyn Story on April 16, telling her she had felt gratified

that the Lowells "particularly should take pains to show it as they did. I am glad
to have people favorably impressed, because I feel lazy and weak, unlike the trouble
of friction or the pain of conquest, still," she added with escalating fury,

> I feel a good deal of contempt for those so easily disconcerted or reassured. I was
> not a child; I had lived in the midst of that blessed society in a way that entitled me
> to esteem and a favorable interpretation, where there was doubt about my motives
> or actions. Nor had I had foolish illusions or made mistakes in the objects of love.
> I pity those who are inclined to think ill, when they might as well have inclined the
> other way, however let them go; there are many in the world who stand the test,
> enough to keep us from shivering to death. I am on the whole fortunate in friends
> that I can truly esteem, where I know the kernel and substance of their being too
> well to be misled by seemings.[66]

Was she right? The surviving evidence suggests that she generally was. Certainly, most of her closest Transcendentalist friends and their associates continued to try loyally to do their best by her. The erudite Sarah Ripley even found a
historical precedent in the late marriage of their old cultural foremother Germaine
de Staël and her twenty-years-younger paramour John Rocca (by whom she also
had a male child out of wedlock). Yet, as Fuller herself suggested, there were obviously some who were in the rear ranks, if not missing in action. Until the spring,
Emerson let Elizabeth Hoar represent him to "Margarita Marchesa." Greeley, who
had heretofore steadily written to her, also remained silent, although Marcus Spring
told her he hoped her editor had answered her letter about Pickie (which he did
not) and blamed his silence on "business & politics & all manner of reforms." It
is hard to imagine that on some level Greeley, a vociferous public defender, against
his radical socialist comrades, not only of monogamy but also of "indissoluble"
marriage, did not have at least a few private misgivings or doubts about his ex–
assistant editor's conduct. The same might be said of Evert Duyckinck, who, for
all his "Rabelaisian" swagger, only the year before had cut off cold his close colleague William A. Jones for carrying on a flirtation with a young woman that
Jones's wife had thought largely innocent. And, of course, transcendentally upright or naïve colleagues like Elizabeth Peabody (who was sure George Eliot was
"a virgin still" even after her marriage to the younger George Lewes) must have
had more difficulty than even Emerson knowing what to say. Nor, if they remained
solidly faithful, did they all continue to take lightly the evidently accelerating
"meddling curiosity" and nasty talk. And Fuller knew it. "I know there must be a
cloud of false rumors and impressions at first," she wrote Channing, who had ap-
prised her of some, "but you will see when we meet that there was a sufficient reason for all I have done, and that if my life be not wholly right, (as it is so difficult to
keep a life true in a world of falsities,) it is not wholly wrong nor fruitless."[67]

Finally, that April, a group of her New York friends tried to stop her from
coming. Why they did so is difficult to say for certain. Their evident increasing
nervousness about "false rumors and impressions" might suggest they had panicked over the social awkwardness the sudden appearance of Margaret's impoverished and partly alien family would cause them. "The timorous said," Emerson

later recalled, not mentioning names but probably referring to some in this crowd, "What shall we do? how shall she be received, now that she brings a husband & child home?" Yet it is highly doubtful that it would have been the sentiment of all of them, and even less that it was their only sentiment. Rather, it seems reasonable to accept them at their word that they were genuinely worried about how she would be able to handle two things she, too, worried deeply about—contenting Ossoli and supporting her family. And none suggested she should stay away more than a couple of years. Still, whatever their precise combination of concerns, the New Yorkers, clearly more nervous about her return than her closer and less worldly Boston friends, felt strongly enough to act in concert. Spring rounded up Channing, Child, Hicks, the Godwins, and Greeley, who Spring thought would also be glad to publish her writings, and they all apparently endorsed his idea. For his lone Boston representative, Spring contacted Emerson, who immediately wrote Fuller, reversing his plea from Paris two years earlier for her to "take the first steamer from Marseilles . . . & go home with me." It was absurd for her to make the voyage just for her "proposed book," since he was certain he could easily find her a publisher either in Boston or in New York, and further that remaining in Italy for a while would strengthen her testimony and add to her reputation, "advantages which no bookseller can overlook for a moment." He added, with evident sincerity, the irony of his arguing the case for the "advantages of your absenteeism," as he had once urged her and several of her friends to a "neighborhood" alternative to the Brook Farm "community." "I, who had vainly imagined that one of these days, when tired of cities, our little Concord would draw you to itself, by the united claims of four families of your friends,—but surprise is the woof you love to weave into all your web." Although he said nothing of the "surprise" of her husband and child, he graciously concluded, "Well, we shall only postpone our claim a little more patiently. . . . You may stay in Italy, for now, but all the more we shall want you & must have you at last."[68]

The following week, the Springs made *their* plea. After telling her all about the touring Swedish writer Fredrika Bremer, who was staying with them (and who professed to be "much interested" in Fuller and her marriage), Rebecca blurted out: "I must now say my most important thing and stop. And that much as we should love to see you and strange as it may seem, we, as well as all your friends who have spoken to us about it, believe it will be undesirable for you to return at present." Indeed, she added, "It is because we love you that we say stay!" Three days later, Marcus threw in, after ticking off sundry other points, including the much lower cost of living in Italy, a congested ideological and professional appeal. John Sartain, the *Union Magazine*'s publisher and a fellow socialist, would be thrilled to get a column from her (which Caroline Kirkland, then its editor, confirmed), especially if she wrote about socialism. And then, "how much your residence in Italy must be worth to that noble & aspiring people, with all your enlightened & mature views of true republican freedom & how much good you will do your own country writing about it, & *to it*, somewhat as an 'outside barbarian' or from the standpoint of a foreigner, with all the advantage of intimate knowledge of our needs, which a foreigner cannot have."[69]

There may have been some manipulation and special pleading here. It is highly unlikely that Emerson seriously considered having her and Ossoli in Concord and may have even thought that, once in Europe, if she later returned, it would not likely have been permanently. Marcus did not say what were those "other things which might be named" necessitating her staying in Italy, and the sometimes unsympathetic Rebecca's strained exaggerations (such as that Margaret would "lose" her power to write "as well" because she would not be "so happy" in America) make one suspicious. Nor did any of them seem to have considered the political conditions that would have made it nearly impossible for the radical Ossolis to remain in Italy. Yet if this disingenuousness was at all the case, Margaret did not detect it. Indeed, she took no offense at all, but quite the opposite. "Your packet . . . contained the first word of encouragement," she answered the Springs on May 14, "the first glimpse of aid in case I wished to remain I ever received." Not only that, "I viewed the matter as you do for all the reasons you state." Indeed, she said, "I was most advantageously and happily placed here, if I could only have been sure of a narrow maintenance," adding other reasons: should she return, her "little band of fond and noble friends who sweetened my life here will probably be dispersed," and, "most of all," Angelino's health. "I have suffered terribly from anxiety that I must take him the long voyage just as his most dangerous teeth are coming."[70]

But it was too late: a few days before she got their encouraging letter, as she saw it, she had already booked passage for America. What was left to say? One thing was to remind her family and friends (and herself) of her two principal reasons for returning: the consoling sight of them and, most practically important, her book. To the Storys, who were then in Paris and had asked her to pass the next year with them there, she wrote in her April 16 letter to Emelyn condemning her vacillating associates, just before she booked her passage:

> How much I should have liked it, but I find it imperatively necessary to go to the U.S. if I want to have my arrangements made that free me from care. Will I be more fortunate in person? I do not know, I am ill adapted to push my claims and my pretensions, but at least it will not be such slow work passing from disappointment to disappointment as here where I wait upon the Post Office, and wait two or three months to know the result of any proposition. Enough! I trust it is not in the power of fate to make me feel bitterly towards any person, though there exist whose who by a very little stretch of good will and effort could have made me happy and ransomed for me so many precious hours for the worthier purposes of life. I go home prepared to expect everything that is painful and difficult.

In her May 14 letter to the Springs, she sounded, although no less ready to face "everything that is painful and difficult," more hopeful. "Let us hope Providence has ruled it for the best," she wrote after saying their plan came too late. "Having decided I feel tranquil, though I suffer much on leaving Italy.— Yet I long too to embrace my loved friends at home. Since my face was turned towards them I long much." Characteristically, in these final words to her friends, she tried to reassure *them* about the social battle ahead. "Say to my dearest William," she wrote, who had apparently also advised her to remain in Italy and send her book home for publication, "that in the hurry and fatigue of these days I have not time to write to him as I would but not to feel anxious about people's talk concerning me. It is not directed against the real Margaret, but a phantom." Meanwhile, they should know that "Americans here in Italy act towards me the same as foreigners—always with respect often with most loving kindness—I dare say it will be the same at home I think it will." Then, belying a little her confidence, not only in her friends resoluteness in dispelling the "phantom" but also in their own certainty about her, she immediately added, melding the two points into one:

> I have acted not inconsistently with myself. If I have practiced some reserve it was because I thought it wise and best. People when they see me will not generally be inclined to injure me, for they will see the expression of a heart bettered by experience—more humble and tender, more anxious to serve its kind than ever before. I think my path will somehow be made plain before me, though I cannot yet see distinctly how.[71]

If perhaps wishful thinking, this was still a plausible prediction. It was certainly a courageous one. Whether "Providence," which she had often professed to doubt, would have ruled in her favor was not yet clear.

CHAPTER FOURTEEN

Dark Passages

(1850)

I

By the time Fuller wrote to the Springs, much had already transpired. If in the winter her question was where and how to live, her immediate challenge that spring was how to get there. Her usual impecuniousness was probably the reason, after announcing at the beginning of the year she was coming to America, she put off for over three months doing anything about it. She had numerous rich friends, but she felt inhibited about asking them for more. "I want nothing of thee, dear Marcus, in the shape of dollars," she had told Spring after deciding to leave Italy. "What you have done for me I prize." But he sent her money as a gift anyway, for which she warmly thanked him, putting it away, though, for Angelino. "I cannot bear to spend a cent for fear he may come to want it," she said in justification. "I under-stand how the family men get so mean. I shall have to begin soon to pray against the danger." Meanwhile, though barely scraping by herself, her mother sent her some money. Richard did also, although he could not forebear remounting his old Transcendentalist high horse to perorate on the moral dangers of her yearning for "wealth or power" compared with his own contentment to be poor and humble. "You are very sublime and stern, my dear Richard, in your disownings of the lures and ambitions of this life," she responded with annoyed humor, "as well as amazed at the *worldliness* of your sister, who on her side was not a little surprised, to say nothing of other feelings, at such accusations, more than once repeated, too. At the risk of confirming this dark view of her character, she must observe, she has at times hoped much you would sometime have dollars enough to traverse land and waves and see some beauteous sights that will be to her memory a joy for-ever." She got no such lecture from Arconati, who without her asking lent her $200.[1]

Her biggest expense, of course, was transportation. The easiest and pleasantest way of going would have been to travel to Paris, where she could see the Storys,

498

then to go to a French port city and from there take a packet ship or steamboat to New York. But that would have cost nearly $400 for the two of them, which as of late February she did not have. Her alternative was to take at half the cost a merchantman from Livorno to New York, but that would have been less comfortable, as well as more dangerous, and would have taken much longer. Remembering her seasick suffering during her ten and a half days on the well-appointed *Cambria*, she shuddered at the thought of a likely two-month voyage on a spartan merchant ship. Perhaps, if the cost of the crossing had been the only factor, she might have been able to borrow enough to cover it, but she also worried about having funds to survive in America. On top of all her debts, by then over $1500, she had no publisher, no job, no students, and no prospects of getting anything from Ossoli's family property for the foreseeable future. She did have her three-hundred-dollar yearly annuity, but that was far from enough to support a family of three. Now that she was a mother, she wrote Sarah Shaw, she could really "feel poverty a great evil." In case she had any lingering fantasies about getting an inheritance, that winter she learned that that William Fuller, her other wealthy lawyer-uncle, had died and (as Arthur told her) "left us naught though dying rich," giving it all to his immediate kin, "who needed it not." The news should make her able, her mother pointedly wrote her, "to calculate your resources exactly."[2]

She tormented herself about her choice. For ten days over the turn of April, she had a "constant headache, and dangerous pressure on the brain" until she was bled, which left her feeling relieved but also exhausted and as undecided as ever. By that time, she had found two vessels soon to set sail: the packet ship *Argo,* leaving from Le Havre, and the Philadelphia merchantman *Elizabeth,* docked at Livorno. A few days after her bleeding, she went with the Moziers to inspect the latter and meet the captain. Satisfying herself that it was "an uncommonly good vessel for the merchant service, nearly new, and well kept," she picked out a room, suggested a few alterations she would like, and told the captain they would likely take it. But on April 12 she wrote Arconati, "I am suffering as never before from the horrors of indecision," describing friends, including the Greenoughs and Sumner and probably the Brownings, "daily" coming to her to try to talk her out of taking the *Elizabeth*, citing a hair-raising list of concerns:

> I cannot have an idea what a voyage of 60 or 70 days will be for me in point of fatigue and suffering, having the care of the baby without any female service or aid, or chance of medical advice if he should be ill; that the insecurity compared with packet ships or steamers is so great; that the cabin being on deck will be terribly exposed in case of a gale; that I cannot be secure of having good water to drink, far less to wash clothing, and therefore must buy an immense stock of baby-linen; that I cannot go without providing for us poultry, a goat for milk, oranges and lemons, soda hardbread, and a medicine chest, all things which in the passenger line are so much a matter of course if you want them, as in a Hotel of a city; that these things will cost as much as the difference of going round by France, while I shall suffer much more, and be exposed to greater risk.

She knew, she added, "volunteer counselors" were prone "to frighten and excite one all they can, and had generally disregarded them. But I feel a trembling

solicitude on account of the child, and feel harassed, doubtful, and almost sick."
Arconati begged off giving her any advice ("it is too important and I don't feel
competent"). A few days later, the *Elizabeth*'s captain, Seth Libby Hasty, and his
wife, Catherine, came up to Florence for several days, where they stayed with the
Moziers while Fuller showed them the sights. Spending time with the "frank &
gentlemanly" captain and his "excellent" wife finally convinced her that the voyage would be a socially happy as well as safe one and that she should take it. Hasty
seemed to her "among the best and most highminded of our American men." On
the sixteenth, she wrote to Emelyn Story that going to Paris would just be too
expensive and, again, that they would "very likely" take the *Elizabeth*, which was
highly spoken of. Within the next couple of days, Mozier wrote to Hasty that
Madame Ossoli wished to take passage with him and his wife to the United States.[3]

Rather, though, than ending her "torment," her decision only seems to have
triggered obsessive thoughts of dying in a shipwreck. These fears had considerable basis. Even on the new steam ships, ocean travel was dangerous in these mid-
century decades; numerous large vessels regularly sank, often taking the lives of
most or all of the passengers. Yet her incessantly morbid language would suggest
that other resonances were also in play. Ocean voyages had long frightened her.
"According to a calculation," she had written years earlier at the end of some notes
on an unrelated subject, "more than five hundred *British vessels alone* are wrecked
& sink to the bottom *annually*." Worries about Angelino also cast a pall over her
thinking. "For his sake indeed, I am become a miserable coward," she wrote
Channing that spring. "I fear heat and cold and moschetoes. I fear terribly the
voyage home, fear biting poverty. I hope Fate will not force me into being as brave
for him as I was for myself." These phrases suggest a couple of other things that
undoubtedly raised the specter of death in her mind. One, as she indicated, was
having come so close herself to it during the siege and another, though she does
not mention it here, must have been almost hourly seeing so much of it that she
was helpless to stem. Yet another she suggested by her telltale word "Fate."
Emerson was certainly right when he would later say there had always been something "a little pagan" about her taste for fateful talismans, omens, coincidences,
and anniversaries. "Fate is law," she had written in her journal years before, "and
the man that discovereth the law that rules him and follows it shall be firm when
other things shake. It is like the presiding star astrologers feigned. It shall lead
you to dangers and through them." But unlike her comparatively optimistic friend,
who liked to play with the trope, she had also always had a keen appreciation of
the many times in history and literature in which Fate did not lead one *through*
dangers, especially when tragic death by martyrdom seemed to be in the cards.
Repeatedly in her letters that spring, she spoke ominously of her "Fate" or "Destiny," almost invariably capitalized. "My life proceeds so regularly," she wrote
Channing, "far more so than the fates of a Greek tragedy, that I can but accept all
the pages as they turn." As she approached the time of the launch, her tone became more anxious. "One would think that so much fuss could not end in nothing," she wrote in her spring letter to Channing, "so Patience Cousin and shuffle

the cards, till Fate is ready to deal them out anew." Should the cards fall badly, she was already preparing a tragic Romantic narrative for dealing with it.[4]

As if on cue, beginning that early April, she started seeing stark omens. After letting slip the phrase "your last thoughts of me" in her letter to Arconati on April 6, she wrote: "I say, *last thoughts*. I am absurdly fearful about this voyage. Various little omens have combined to give me a dark feeling. Among others just now, we hear of the wreck of the ship Westmoreland, bearing Powers's Eve. Perhaps we shall live to laugh at these," quickly adding, ominously, "but in case of mishap, I should perish with my husband and child perhaps to be transferred to some happier state." With a subsequent series of signs, she did not mention laughing or a happier state. Ten days later, immediately after finishing her April 16 letter to Emelyn Story, telling her she was very likely taking the *Elizabeth* and asking her to retrieve a box of books, clothing, and engravings she had left in Paris with a friend of Madame Mohl, she read in a newspaper that the friend had just died. Nor was that the only "strange coincidence" that befell her, as she told Arconati five days later:

> It was an odd combination—I had intended if I went by way of France to take the packet ship "Argo" from Havre; I had just written to Mrs Story that I should *not* do so; and at the same time requested her to find *Miss Fitton*, who had my muff etc.: having closed the letter I took up *Galignani['s Messenger]*, and my eye fell on these words—Died 4th April at No 10 Rue ville l'eveque Miss Fitton—turning the leaf I read of the wreck of the "*Argo*" returning from America to France! There were also notices of the wreck of the "Royal Adelaide," a fine English steamer, and of the "John Skiddy" one of the fine American packets.

Her conclusion was contradictory. On the one hand, she was happily fatalistic: "Thus it seems safety is not to be found in the wisest calculation. I shall embark more composedly in my merchant ship." On the other hand, shunting aside Fate in favor of Providence, in which she often said she did not believe, she was darkly prayerful: "praying, indeed, fervently, that it may not be my lot to lose my babe at sea, either by unsolaced sickness, or amid the howling waves." Torn between Providence and Fate, she blurted out again her tragic wish: "Or that if I should, it may be brief anguish, and Ossoli he and I go together."[5]

She had two remaining tasks. One was scraping together some last-minute money. After getting letters from Eliza Farrar, who told her she had $100 for her, and her mother, who had placed another $100 at Barings for her, she hastily took out a bill of exchange of $336 for a hundred days at the bankers Fenzi and Hall drawn on Marcus Spring's account. "Should I arrive as I expect I shall meet it," she assured him. "Should I perish at sea I know you will not see it dishonored," as her mother or her brothers would raise it "I am sure if you show this letter." Her other task was harder—writing her farewell letters. They were not very happy. "I leave Italy with profound regret and with only a vague hope of returning," she wrote Cass bitterly on May 2. "I could have lived here always, full of bright visions, and expanding in my faculties, had destiny permitted." She finished with a half-ironic, half-heartfelt enumeration of some cosmopolitan patriotic tropes:

> I sail in the bark Elizabeth for New York. She is laden with marble and rags, a very
> appropriate companionship for wares of Italy. She carries Powers's statue of Calhoun.
> Adieu, remember that we look to you to keep up the dignity of our country; many
> important occasions are now likely to offer, for the American, (I wish I could write
> the *Columbian*) man to advocate, more, to *represent* the cause of Truth and Free-
> dom, in face of their foes, and remember me as their lover and your friend.

A week later, to William Story, her days seemed too hectic for much dwelling on
destinies or Truth and Freedom.

> We are upon the move and my head full of boxes, bundles, pots of jelly, and phials
> of medicine. I never thought much about a journey for myself, except to try and
> return all the things, books, especially, I had been borrowing, but about my child I
> feel anxious lest I should not take what is necessary for his health and comfort on
> this long voyage, where omissions are irreparable. The unpropitious weather, (for
> after our Siberian winter we have rain all the Spring rain from 4th April up to this
> 10th May,) delays as now from day to day, as our ship the "Elizabeth," look out for
> news of shipwreck; cannot finish taking in her cargo till come one or two good days.

Yet she was not much more confident about returning, at least very soon, than
she had been with Cass. "I leave Italy with most sad and unsatisfied heart, hoping
indeed, to return, but fearing that may not in my 'cross-biased [life]' be permitted
till strength of feeling and keenness of perception be less than during these by-
gone rich, if troubled years." She tried to be more positive in her last letter to her
mother four days later, although its overtones sounded, if anything, darkest of all—
so much so that her mother, when she got it six weeks later, found it "very sad"
and "painful" to read. "I will believe I shall be welcome with my treasures, my
husband and child," Margaret began, with an odd double future verb formation,
as though she was not sure but determined to make it happen. She followed that
with a roll call of goodbyes to family members, including even extended ones,
and a highly qualified hope, although speaking, as she invariably did to her pious
Unitarian mother, not of "Fate" but of God:

> For me, I long so very much to see you, should any thing hinder it on earth again
> (and I say it merely because there seems somewhat more of danger on sea than on
> land) think of your daughter as one who always wished at least to do her duty, and
> who always cherished you according as her mind opened to discover excellence.
>   Give dear love, too, to my brothers, first my eldest, and faithful friend, Eugene,
> God bless him. Love to my kind and good Aunts, my dear cousin Ellen, a sister's
> love to Ellen Channing,—
>   We sail in the "Elizabeth," Capt. Hasty, from Leghorn for New York; and I hope
> we may arrive by the end of June.
>   I hope we shall pass some time together yet in this world, but if God decrees
> otherwise,—here and hereafter, My dearest Mother, Your loving child,
>   MARGARET.[6]

Her final days in Florence were evidently more cheerful, although still marked
by some strange omens. Their farewell party seems to have gone fine. The
Greenoughs, the Moziers, and others of their circle were there, as were Robert

Browning and his invalid wife Elizabeth, whom he carried up the six flights of stairs to the Ossolis' apartment. Their last evening, however, the Ossolis spent at the Brownings', and there her talk, Elizabeth recalled, was full of "sad presentiment," apparently not always entirely conscious. "Do you know she gave a *bible* as a parting gift from her child to ours," Elizabeth wrote a friend right after her death, "writing in it '*In memory of* Angelo Eugene Ossoli' &c, . . . a strange prophetical expression!" Even the jokes sometimes seem to have had an ambiguous double edge. At one point, Elizabeth wrote her sister, "jestingly they told us it had been prophecied to the Marquis Ossoli, 'that the sea w$^{d.}$ be fatal to him & that he sh$^{d.}$ avoid traveling by it'—and then, SHE said, turning to me with that peculiar smile which lighted up her plain, thought-worn face, 'I accept as a good omen that our ship should be called the ELIZABETH.'" The following day the Ossolis traveled to Livorno. "She seemed in fine spirits and expressed great pleasure in the anticipation of seeing all her friends," Catherine Hasty recalled, "but spoke with particular delight of the prospect of meeting her dear mother." The next morning of May 17, they all went out on the Hastys' boat to the ship anchored two miles out. "As we went," she would later write Margaret's mother, "she playfully bade farewell to Italy [and] hoped she should again see its sunny shores. I saw no shade of sadness upon the brow of her husband." After inspecting their room and finding the excellent changes that she had asked for to make it more comfortable, she and Ossoli rejoined the captain and his wife on deck to view once more the Italian shore as the anchor was raised. With whatever mix of playfulness, cheer, anticipation, resolve, sadness, and foreboding Margaret felt, the Ossolis were now, as Mrs. Hasty happily put it, "*homeward bound.*"[7]

II

If Fuller *was* in fine spirits while embarking, one reason was undoubtedly that she had come to have confidence not just in her experienced captain but also in his ship. With a carrying capacity of 540 tons, it easily carried its full load of merchandise, valued at $200,000, of bulk hats, silk, olive oil, and other goods, as well as expensive paintings imported by William Aspinwall, Powers's statue of Calhoun for the city of Charleston, which Fuller had admired in his studio three years earlier, and 150 tons of Carrara marble. At the same time, for a sturdy merchant ship, the six-year-old *Elizabeth* was comparatively roomy and comfortable, with a covered cabin, cozy rooms, and an ample deck and sitting room for walking or relaxing.[8]

The human cargo was also reassuring. The other passengers were Horace Sumner, the captain's wife, Catherine, and Celesta Pardena, a "sweet" twenty-two-year-old Roman girl returning to New York, where she had earlier worked, whom the Ossolis had hired as a nursemaid for Angelino. Hasty's crew of seventeen also gave Fuller confidence. Mostly Britons led by a first and second mate, Henry P. Bangs and Charles W. Davis, they also included an American cook, a Swedish carpenter, and a British steward, all good at their jobs and highly solicitous, especially to Nino and Margaret. (Thoreau later reported "they used such expressions as 'fine lady' 'kind lady'" whenever they later spoke about her.) In fact, everyone seems to have gotten along quite well. Nino, now almost two and beginning to babble in English and Italian, scampered around the deck with his toys and played with the crew, especially the steward, who doted on him, with Celesta, to whom he quickly became attached, and with the twenty-six-year-old Catherine Hasty, who entertained him with her zither and treated him like a shared son. Catherine also liked Ossoli, who seemed to her a happy, warmhearted, handsome man with very beautiful hair, which he left uncut during the voyage, giving him ringlets "as long as my finger." For Fuller friendship and learning never being far apart, she gave the Hastys lessons in Italian while they did the same in English for Ossoli. "We studied in the morning," Catherine recalled, "walked or sat on deck in the afternoon and sang and played in the evening." All in all, Fuller's prediction of a sociable voyage seemed to have been borne out. "I thought during the voyage," she wrote after it began, "if safe, and my child well, to have as much respite from care and pain as sea sickness might permit."[9]

For the first week, she got the respite she wanted, although, as she predicted, she was not free of seasickness, which the second day struck both Ossolis and triggered one of her severe headaches. But their vomiting only lasted a few hours, and the next morning and for the rest of the trip she was free of her nauseating "enemy." The weather was also pleasant as the ship wended its way westward through the Ligurian Sea and into the Mediterranean. Two blows in quick succession, however, soon struck. The first hit Captain Hasty. Since leaving Livorno, he had complained of fever and head and backaches, and then on May 25, he showed the signs of a highly malignant confluent smallpox. Although both his wife and Margaret nursed him constantly, when in the evening of June 1 they finally got to Gilbraltar, where they could get him a physician, he started fading and the next morning died. As authorities feared the disease had spread to others, they immediately imposed a quarantine on the ship, preventing anyone from boarding it. About six in the evening the American consul's barge towed a boat with Hasty's body from the ship, and his crew buried him in the ocean. "You cannot think how beautiful the whole thing was," Fuller wrote the Springs the following day, describing the array of sadly reverent sailors, the line of flying ships' banners, the plunge of the decorated coffin into the sea. "Yes! it was beautiful but how dear a price we pay for the poems of the world." If she had known how high the price would be for losing their skilled, "highminded" captain, her portrait would no doubt have not been so beautiful.[10]

The officials' concern about spreading the smallpox was justifiable. Margaret kept up the devastated widow's spirits by telling her stories about her life and her friends. Catherine would later tell Elizabeth Hoar that she would have died "if it had not been for M. that she took her like a little child." As a preventative, the crew drenched the ship in sulfur. (Her letter from Gilbraltar to Marcus Spring smelled "so foul" and blurred from it that the Springs burned it after copying it.) Ossoli was safe because he had had the disease. The most likely victims, besides Catherine and the steward who served Hasty his food, were Margaret, who had also nursed Hasty, and Angelino, whom in the first days of the captain's illness

Margaret had carried twice into the sickroom after Hasty had asked to see him. "It is vain by prudence to seek to evade the stern assaults of Destiny," she wrote to Spring the day after the burial. "I submit." Two days after the *Elizabeth* resumed its voyage on June 8, Nino showed the first of the same symptoms that Hasty had had: pustules spread all over his body and face, which for five days was so swollen that it looked almost shapeless and he could not open his eyes. Margaret tended him day and night, reading and singing to him, which he loved, always keeping time, Catherine Hasty recalled, "with his little hands." But without medical help or medication, and fearing he would die, Margaret and Giovanni seemed to have been as stressed as during the siege. This took a toll emotionally. As Catherine later told it, once when Margaret wanted a book, and he did not understand though she told him repeatedly, she finally said impatiently, "Ossoli, if you don't understand now, it is of no use to tell you." He looked hurt, but after a moment's silence, he said, "I know I am stupid but I want you to have every thing *exactly as you wish*—& cannot unless I am sure what you want." At another point, they quarreled about something concerning Angelino's nursing. Putting his arm around her neck, he said, "I wish we could always think the same thing—& I never could differ from you, if it were not that baby's life depends on it." But if they exposed some apparently new tensions in their marriage, Ossoli seems to have smoothed them over. Even then, Catherine would profess, she "never saw two people happier or more devoted to each other & their child."[11]

After a week Angelino started noticeably improving. On the morning of the ninth day of his illness, a beaming Margaret burst into Catherine's cabin to tell her that he "*could see!*" After this, his recovery was rapid, giving his mother, Catherine recalled, joy "unbounded": "She would sit by his side *hours* and sing to him and before he could open both eyes he had toys and kept both parents occupied in arranging them. On the 14*th* day he was carried to the sitting-room and laid upon the sofa, and his mother thought him *quite* well. I am not aware that he suffered an hour's illness from that time, quite playful and sweet as ever and soon became strong." Despite her joy, after the captain's death and Angelino's near death, it must not have seemed certain to Margaret that God or Fate was on her side.

III

For a month after the *Elizabeth* sailed out of Gilbraltar, there was no sign of problems. As it sailed west, Angelino's smallpox marks almost completely faded, which pleased Margaret, who had been anxious about showing him to her mother badly scarred. Meanwhile, the weather remained so pleasant that one day on deck she told Catherine Hasty how much she would miss the beautiful vistas on the ocean, especially the "holy" moonlight nights. But because the trade winds that made the voyage quiet also made it slow, she cheered along with the other passengers when a strong southeast wind started blowing. After July 14, as the ship passed Bermuda, their progress became so rapid that the crew told the passengers they could expect to arrive in a few more days and could start packing. Margaret right away picked out the clothes she wanted Nino to wear when they disembarked. On the evening of the eighteenth, Bangs, the new captain, announced that he saw a New York pilot boat, putting all the passengers, Hasty recalled, "in perfect extacy, *so near home*," and fully expecting to be in New York the next evening.[12]

Bangs, however, who had only captained one or two ships in his life, spoke too soon. His pilot ship turned out to be a phantom. He was also not clear about exactly where they were. At 2:30 A.M., Friday the nineteenth, he and Davis, now the first mate, took soundings at twenty-one fathoms, and, deciding they were off the New Jersey shore, headed the ship northeast to avoid it, reckoning they would be just off the New York harbor the next morning. But they were completely mistaken. They had only taken their latitude, not their longitude. ("That was too difficult a calculation," Davis would later explain.) They then mistook the Fire Island lighthouse for a New Jersey one; rather than being off the Jersey shore, they were sixty miles further north. Even worse, they were going much faster than they realized, as the strong southerly winds they were riding started picking up speed, heading them rapidly straight for the south shore of Long Island. Finally, the winds quickly turned into an unseasonable storm, the worst, in fact, Long Islanders reportedly could remember, one that scattered wrecks of boats, huts, and even some houses in a hundred places for miles. During all this, Bangs remained in his room, if not asleep, coming out only once, Davis later reported, to "ask what the weather was." His placidity, however, got a jolt at ten minutes to four, when a loud dragging sound was heard. A few seconds later a tremendous thump sounded, bringing the passengers, whose cabin was tossing from side to side, streaming out onto the deck in their nightclothes. The ship had hit a sandbar off Fire Island beach, breaking a large hole in its side. At the same time, waves driven by furious winds were coming over both sides of the ship, causing shouts of "Cut away!" as sails and timber fell over the deck.[13]

Meanwhile, the captain's blunders were more than matched by the indifference and incompetence of those on shore less than three hundred yards away. Fire Island is the westernmost section of a thirty-two-mile island no more than a quarter-mile wide and separated from Long Island's South Shore, like a knife edge, by a very long and shallow bay four or five miles wide. Although attracting summer vacationers from nearby and the city, about fifty miles to the west, to dig for clams and oysters and swim in the waters, Fire Island was usually largely barren, with only a few temporary fishermen's bunks and three "low public houses" several miles to the east and the lighthouse four miles to the west. Most of those who populated the island seem to have been a sleazy bunch. The central figures were Smith Oakes and his wife, experienced thieves who had frequently been arrested or had their rooms searched by the police and whose place, which was the closest one to the island, Thoreau, who would later investigate with Channing, described as "a perfect pirate's house" of stolen goods and the debris of wrecks. Oakes, who would later boast of putting up the survivors for a night and readying a fire for the Ossolis, said he had been sound asleep until nine, when, after being told there was a vessel ashore, he had jumped up ("he jumped up again to show us," Thoreau wrote laconically in his notebook). But if he did jump up, it was probably not with too much concern about the welfare of the ship's passengers. That was certainly the case with the small crowd that began to gather about 7 A.M. "There were thieves of high & low degree whose deeds were described to me by themselves," Thoreau reported. "Some had heard that there were 3,000 dollars in jewels on the finger of the Marchioness. They stole from one another extensively—& whatever a guard placed over it, they rolled across the beach to their boats in the night."[14]

So for four hours that morning, from seven to eleven, while breaking into trunks that had washed ashore and making off with clothing and merchandise, although occasionally glimpsing the distressed passengers and crew, they did nothing at all to help them. To be sure, it would not have been easy. There was no system of paid rescuers, as on some American shores and all along England's coastline. The only rescuing devices were a mortar and a lifeboat, both at the lighthouse an hour and a half away. The boat required eight or ten men to carry it over the sand through roaring headwinds. Even the lighthouse mechanics, who reluctantly heeded the keeper Selah Strong's plea that they carry it, did not get it and the mortar onto the shore until after twelve o'clock, over eight hours after the *Elizabeth* was stranded and more than six hours after the wreck could easily have been seen. Their reported efforts do not make it sound as if it would have made any difference if they had gotten them there earlier. After the mortar to shoot out a rope to the ship failed to go off (or, as some later claimed, was never fired because the men had brought only one ball and wanted to save it as a last resort), the supposed rescuers refused to take the lifeboat out, insisting that it was too dangerous. Some just do not seem to have cared. "Oh, if we had known there were any such persons of *importance* on board," one of the wreckers afterward told Channing, after being advised of Fuller and her family's presence on the ship, "we should have tried our best." Whether from circumstances, indifference, incompetence, chicanery, or cowardice, the result was the same: when the tides were still low and everyone on board could probably have been saved, no aid was forthcoming from the shore.[15]

The *Elizabeth*'s passengers and crew did not know any of this, but they apparently surmised it because they soon stopped waving and shouting and concentrated on saving themselves. The rapidly shifting events and differing perspectives make the story complicated and at times murky, but the basic facts seem to have been these. Almost from the beginning, according to survivors, the passengers were amazingly calm. Nino cried loudly, but Margaret wrapped him up in some dry clothes and, holding him on her breast, sang him to sleep. Celesta let out a piercing shriek and cried uncontrollably for twenty minutes, but after the Ossolis calmed her down, she got on her knees and prayed for an hour, after which she remained quiet. Indeed, stoicism seems to have been the norm. Catherine Hasty recalled her meeting with Sumner in the cabin, clasping hands, and he saying: "We must die." "Let us die calmly, then." "I hope so Mrs. Hasty." The inward terror, however, can be imagined: sitting side by side for over two hours in the darkness, bracing themselves against furniture that Sumner had piled up, assuming they had been abandoned, as all the crew had scampered up into the forecastle, while enormous waves crashed down all around the cabin. Margaret, Davis reported, "sat in her white night dress, flat on the deck, with her back to the leewards on the upper or windowed side, & her feet toward the foremast." Eventually, the cabin walls started giving way, but just at that point Davis, with those of the crew whom he could persuade to climb down in the raging storm, arrived to help the passengers up to the forecastle, which was the least exposed to the storm and still holding strong.[16]

Making their way there was difficult. Rigging and rails had fallen across the midship, and the ship, which was parallel with the shore, was tipped up on its southern or windward side, making the slippery deck slope radically to leeward. Catherine Hasty, the first to try it, lost her grip on the railing when a giant wave crashed over her, sweeping her into the hatchway, saved only by Davis, who, ignoring her pleas to let her go ("your life is important to all on board," she remembered shouting at him), grabbed her long hair and pulled her up. Once the crew got everyone to the forecastle, things seem to have settled down. "There was no more confusion in that room than there is here in mother's parlour," Catherine Hasty later reported, which even if exaggerated was a remarkable statement to have made. As the waves washed over them, Ossoli encouraged people to pray, and he himself made a long prayer in Italian all kneeling, urging God's dispensation for Catherine, Margaret translated for her, "as a heretic." (He seems to have had no such anxiety about Margaret.) Meanwhile, the women asked Davis to return to their rooms to retrieve some things they had left. Margaret asked him to get her seal rings and breast pin and eyeglass with a gold handle, as well as two items of great importance to her. One was her portable desk inside her portmanteau, containing "what is most valuable to me if I live of any thing," by which Hasty understood she meant her manuscript history. The other was all her money, $70 in gold doubloons, which after she got it from Davis, who heroically risked his life retrieving these things, she put in a cotton handkerchief and tied around her waist. She said, optimistically, it would pay for their passage to New York.[17]

By ten o'clock, the situation looked grim. By then the ship's 150 tons of marble had broken through the hold. The winds had turned into a gale of nearly hurricane proportions, causing every wave to lift the forecastle roof and wash over the crew and passengers. An hour earlier one sailor who had jumped into the water could be seen making it to the shore, after which more followed, most of them successfully. But when, encouraged by their success, Sumner dived in, either he was hit by a piece of wood or some other object from the wrecked ship, or he was just overwhelmed by the waves. He sank and disappeared. So Davis, taking the initiative from the uncertain Bangs, proposed to the passengers an alternative plan. The carpenter and some of the crew would cut or tear off planks of wood from the ship on which each would lie, grasping tied-on rope handles and guided by a sailor, who would swim behind. Catherine Hasty again stepped forward to be the first, guided by Davis. After that about eight more of the crew tried, almost all, including Hasty and Davis, also making it to shore.

Before this, Fuller had made her controversial decision not to try for the shore. To some twentieth-century critics, it has seemed perverse, even, possibly suicidal, driven probably by depression over political defeat, or fear of facing the social ostracism awaiting her, or her European alienation from "America." These speculations and innuendos are not supported by the facts. While in the past she had sometimes expressed admiration for Greeks and Romans' great resolution and courage in committing suicide, as a practice she abhorred it as intensely selfish. "I can rarely think of any one so far unconnected with others," she had written in her journal several years earlier, "as to pardon his being able to inflict the amount of pain and horror caused in all concerned by an event which so far violates the natural order of things." Moreover, although her last letters had displayed a good deal of anxiety about her financial future, they had been anything but despairing. On the contrary, although much annoyed by the rumors about her marriage, she had dismissed them contemptuously, even cavalierly, and, like "everything that is painful and difficult" (as she had prospectively said in her letter to Emelyn Story about her future in America), was resolutely ready to deal with them. Likewise with politics: while she was deeply saddened by the fall of the Roman Republic, her last articles showed her leaving Italy firmly believing that the return of democratic revolutions in Europe was only a few years away.[18]

Yet the question remains: why did she not follow the example of Catherine Hasty and Davis, who, after all, like almost all the sailors, successfully made it to shore using a plank? In fact, over the four hours between when Davis and the others jumped onto planks and her final minutes on board, she made her decision not just once but three times in very different circumstances that were often changing, sometimes minute to minute. Before Davis and the others made it to shore, there was no guarantee of their success. Nor could Sumner's recent disastrous jump have seemed encouraging to her. While fourteen of the crew would eventually be successful swimming, many using planks, three were not. Davis's method was not a sure thing, and certainly not for all three Ossolis. There was also the fact that Davis went to shore not only to save Catherine Hasty but also to get the lifeboat launched. Indeed, not just Margaret and her family but Bangs, as well as four others—including the carpenter, cook, and steward—also stayed on board, partly to aid the Ossolis, to be sure, but undoubtedly also because they expected to be saved by the lifeboat. It probably seemed to her sensible to wait.

As the hours elapsed, however, that thought became increasingly less tenable. At eleven o'clock, Davis and Hasty, battered and bruised by floating plants and wood, landed on Fire Island's shore. An hour or so later, the lighthouse men finally showed up with the lifeboat. But they refused to man it, while most of the ship's sailors were then at the lighthouse, and the scavengers, who now numbered thirty or forty, were useless. "The men had not courage to launch the lifeboat," Davis afterward angrily told Thoreau. "They might have launched it without risk to their lives," he added, noting contemptuously that he had seen a whaleboat launched in as rough a sea. "If it had been the coast of England they could all have been saved. The men sat for an hour or two on the side of the boat doing nothing but now & then picking up a hat, (part of the cargo) that came ashore." By then it was nearly one o'clock. Bangs, notwithstanding his agreement with Davis to stay "to the last," decided he had had enough. But although he pleaded with Margaret to go with him, saying he would take Angelino and the remaining sailors would go with her and the others, she adamantly refused. She also refused to let him take Angelino alone; all would stay together. So he finally shouted, according to the cook, "I am a married man[.] I do not feel it right to throw away my life & can do nothing more on board," and then gave leave to the sailors remaining on board to save themselves. Davis would express contradictory sentiments about his captain's action, later telling Channing that he could hardly restrain from tearing the half-drowned man to pieces when they pulled him out of the water, upbraiding him "vehemently for breaking his pledge." Thoreau's quoted reaction of Davis to the question was more cautious: "Did the Captain do his duty?" "I should think he did what he could I don't know—He said that nobody would come ashore with him."[19]

Whatever one thinks about Bangs's deserting his post, the question remains: why *this* time did Fuller not go with him or allow Angelino to do so? Unfortunately, we have nothing from her about what was going through her mind. But we do have the testimony of some of the crew, who afterward told Bayard Taylor, the *Tribune*'s correspondent, what she said when Bangs urged her to trust herself on one of the planks and he would take Angelino: "She refused, saying that she had no wish to live without the child, and would not, at that hour, give the care of it to another." That other was, of course, Bangs, who she had good reason to think was considerably less trustworthy than Davis, who had taken Catherine Hasty and who was an exceptional sailor. Davis's exploit, Thoreau later judged, who knew something about surviving in nature, was "heroic—& proves great strength courage & skill." Indeed, Bangs's arrival on shore unconscious with his head half buried in the sand and seemingly dead would suggest that it had been at least plausible for her not to trust to him Angelino, who would have probably drowned.

On the other hand, three hours later, when she faced her third and last decision, the situation had become much more dangerous. The storm was in a brief lull, and the likelihood that the ship would not hold together through another flood was great. By then it should have also been clear that something had gone seriously wrong about the plan to launch the lifeboat. At that point, it is likely that less rational but understandable emotions were flooding over Fuller. One was simply fear of the water, which had probably been clouding her judgment from the beginning. It is not clear how well she could swim, but Caroline Tappan, her companion on many of her jaunts to New England rivers, lakes, and beaches, recalled that while she loved to frolic near or in their shallow ends, she became easily frightened when near any turbulent water, instinctively shrinking back to distant rocks and cliffs. Then there were special feelings. She had often associated bodies of water with the loss of her mother or some other maternal female friend. In her "Autobiographical Romance" nine years earlier, her narrative persona remembers, after a high-pressured tutoring session with her father, who she portrays as having usurped her mother's attention, dreaming of trees dripping with blood that became a pool rising closer and closer to her lips. In a later section of the "Romance," writing about her infatuation with a visiting Englishwoman, her narrator fantasizes about being the little Guy Mannering in Scott's novel, who vainly searches for his mother through long dark caves filling with water. Around the same time, while sleeping in a bed with Anna Ward, on the absent Sam's pillow, in their fashionable newlywed Louisburg Square apartment, she had a dream of being imprisoned in a ship at sea with waves dashing over her as the crew, to the indifference of her well-dressed friends, threatened to throw her in the ocean. While all these traumatic dreams came out of particular circumstances, their consistent association of water and drowning with traumas of feminine or maternal abandonment might have very well unconsciously resurfaced to give a further lurid and confusing coloration to her inhibitions about jumping into the ocean.[20]

What consciously and overwhelmingly inhibited her, of course, was Angelino. Ever since returning to Rieti, she had said repeatedly to friends, certainly out of love but perhaps also out of guilt, she would never allow him to be without her while endangered again. But she also wished to share his fate in life or death. Nor did she say this only to Bangs. "If he dies, I hope I shall, too," she had written Cass after arriving from occupied Rome in Rieti to find Angelino nearly starved to death. "I was too fatigued before," she had uncannily added, "and this last shipwreck of hopes would be more than I could bear." "I hope the cruel law of my life will at least not oblige me to be separated from him," she had written the following month to Caroline Tappan. To Emelyn Story, in her letter announcing she had decided to take the *Elizabeth*, speaking of the "selfish sympathy" she felt after reading Emelyn's remarks about the earlier death of Maria Lowell's first child, she had written: "I could not, I think, survive the loss of *my* child. I wonder daily how it can be done." That same spring before embarking to America, to Cass again, she extended her wish to the afterlife: "I feel the tie between him and me so real, so deep-rooted, even death shall not part us. I shall not be alone in other worlds, whenever Eternity may call me." It was as if, having at a great cost to her health and future reputation lost her gamble for political and family success in Italy, she saw Ossoli and Angelino as the last living remnants justifying those years, making any separation that risked her living and their dying intolerable.[21]

Yet not quite. When even she knew that the end was upon them and they had no alternative but to jump, she agreed to, as Channing, who interviewed several crew members, afterward put it, "*one* desperate effort for all." It was then two-thirty in the afternoon. Besides the Ossolis, Celesta, and an old sailor, those still on board were all the men whom Margaret most trusted after Davis: the American cook Joseph McGill, the Swedish carpenter and second mate John Helstrom, and the British steward George Bates. McGill later reported that he told them the ship was now rapidly breaking up at the stern, and this was their last chance to try to save themselves by boards and swimming. The rest transpired in fifteen minutes. A huge wave hit the forecastle a minute or two after they left it, and immediately afterward the foremast fell to leeward, casting up the deck on which they were standing as it went. Bates took Nino in his arms, apparently with Margaret's agreement, and either jumped or was swept overboard (accounts differ) and drowned with the child. At almost the same time, Celesta and Ossoli were thrown forward and, while they were hanging on to the bare mast, a subsequent wave washed them out to sea. After that, the cook and carpenter leaped into the ocean and swam to shore. Meanwhile, after the steward had taken Nino from her, but before the others were gone, Margaret had sat with her back braced against the fallen foremast, still in her white nightdress, her hair loose on her shoulders and her hands on her knees. McGill afterward reported that the last words she spoke were: "I see nothing but death before me—I shall never reach the shore." Almost immediately, an enormous wave came crashing over her and, as the cook recalled to Channing, she "was at once plunged into the sea & never rose," drowning, Helstrom told Thoreau, before her husband and child did ("*he was very sure of this*"). At three-thirty, just as one useless mortar ball and rope were finally fired from the shore, the *Elizabeth* broke up, twelve hours after hitting the Fire Island beech sandbar.[22]

IV

"FATAL WRECK—Dreadful loss of Life—S. Margaret Fuller Drowned," screamed the headline in the *Tribune*, announcing eight of the twenty-three on board the vessel lost. Within days newspapers from Maine to South Carolina picked up the story. But Fuller's paper naturally gave it the most coverage, for over a week featuring almost daily interviews with survivors and stories filed by Bayard Taylor, the paper's chief correspondent. Greeley weighed in with a stinging editorial, lambasting not only the "pirates" for their plundering but also the islanders for doing nothing to sound an alarm. "Our informant states," he wrote disgustedly, "that the people in the vicinity often exclaimed in his hearing that had they known that any such interest was taken in the lady on board as has since been manifested, the result would have been otherwise." The consummate Whig reformer, he demanded that the authorities not only "hunt up the robbers" and punish them but construct a life-saving system on the coast "by which it shall be for the *interest* of the rude population in such places to aid to the utmost the hapless strangers flung by the storm upon their sands." He got no reforms, but he later had the satisfaction of learning that several of the "rude population" were arrested, including the Oakses, for stealing property from the *Elizabeth*.[23]

Fuller's family and close friends expressed much more sorrow than outrage. "Poor dear Margaret & all her family are gone!" Marcus Spring the next morning scribbled a note to Rebecca, then at the North American Phalanx. "Oh! how can her poor mother and sister bear it!" Evidently, not easily. Margaret's mother, brothers Arthur, Richard, and Eugene, and sister Ellen had already been anxious about the delay caused by the quarantine, which many newspapers had reported. They had all been staying at Arthur's house in Manchester, as it was too costly to wait for Margaret's uncertain arrival in the city. ("We shall look constantly for you," her mother had written her in care of Spring after the *Elizabeth* left Gilbraltar.) After reading in a newspaper a telegram announcing the wreck, they immediately rushed to the Springs' house in Brooklyn. "Margaret's mother sat like a stone in our house," Rebecca recalled, "she shed no tears, she even smiled when we spoke to her, but she neither ate nor slept,—it was pitiful." Ellen too was so distraught for months that Ellery and her friends worried also about *her* sanity. "It seems to me I can hardly live here without Margaret," she wrote to Richard after returning home.[24]

Meanwhile, a squad of Margaret's friends descended on Fire Island. On the twenty-fourth, Spring, Greeley, Arthur, Eugene, and Charles Sumner, soon to be elected United States senator, who came down from Boston to look for his brother's remains, spent the day and part of the next looking for bodies among the ship's castoffs that littered the beach. Emerson, who at first thought he would go to make inquiries himself, had intelligently tapped the robustly ingenious Thoreau for the job, and he and Ellery Channing arrived the following day. They met William Channing, who had come in from the city. For three days, they conducted interviews with survivors and talked with many of the scavengers, trying to figure out what had happened and track down what was left of the Ossolis' things, which they discovered was not a lot, thanks to the energetic scavengers. "Almost every chest & box," Thoreau reported, "was broken open with thievish & dare devil curiosity by night & by day in spite of the guard." Nor was it easy to get what they found. Ludicrously (or pathetically), Thoreau later discovered at two houses that he went to in nearby Patchogue young men playing dominoes and wearing pilfered hats from the wreck that their mothers had already decorated for them with buttons and tassels from Margaret's dresses. Thoreau's most memorable material find was a button he ripped off Ossoli's coat. "Held up, it intercepts the light,—an actual button,—and yet the life it is connected with is less substantial to me, and interests me less, than my faintest dream," he later mused to a friend. "Our thoughts are the epochs in our lives: all else is but as a journal of the winds that blew while we were here." His sublimely indifferent Transcendentalist philosophy, however, did not keep him from his assiduous digging.[25]

Margaret's friends and family were most concerned about locating the Ossolis' bodies. At first there was some hope of finding them. Horace Sumner's body never turned up, but Celesta's had washed ashore naked less than an hour after the ship broke up. The next day Angelino's still warm naked body also washed up on the beach, and the following day a group of sailors carried it aloft in a chest donated by one of them to use as a coffin and buried it, as several of the hardened seamen wept, on the beach in a marked grave. The next day the Fuller family transported it home, eventually reburying it next to the bones of Margaret's father and her siblings Julia Adelaide and Edward Breck, who had died in infancy. However, neither of the Ossolis' bodies was ever found, although a couple of scholars have been tantalized by the claim of an ancient Arthur Dominy, then the nine-year-old son of Felix Dominy, who owned one of the public houses on the eastern end, that a Fire Island boatman had found the Ossolis' bodies sometime after the wreck. According to the boatman's story reported by Felix Dominy, who presumably learned it from his father, the man had tried to deliver them to Greeley, but the editor had refused to accept them because so much time had elapsed that he thought it was impossible to identify them, so the man had buried them on the Coney Island beach. There seems to have been something behind this. Four years after the shipwreck, Eugene, Richard, and Ellen were briefly excited about a letter from Felix Dominy telling them about a report of someone sometime discovering two bodies and making an "application" to Greeley about them, but after learning they were decayed beyond recognition, the siblings evidently never investigated further. Without documentation corroborating Arthur Dominy's half-century-old contradictory accounts, one must add this hearsay story to the list of legends that later grew up around Fuller's death.[26]

Besides the couple's bodies, Fuller's friends' other grail was her manuscript history of the Italian revolutions. Thoreau and Channing had two sets of facts to go on. Davis told Channing that he distinctly remembered putting the retrieved portable desk supposedly containing the manuscript inside a blue calico bag, which later in the afternoon he saw on the shore. "This proves it came & whole to the shore," Channing wrote. However, when they looked in it, the only thing they found was a package of her letters to and from Ossoli and some others from Mickiewicz and Mazzini. Channing concluded that either Margaret in the confusion of the moment had given Catherine Hasty the wrong impression of where it was "or else after the desk was open the papers mislaid—which seems inconceivable almost & may yet come to hand." They did not, however, and to Channing the whole business remained "a mystery." Assuming Hasty had been wrong about the desk, there was also the possibility that Fuller had put the manuscript in one of her trunks, of which, according to Davis, she and Ossoli had four or five plus a large case full of 30 or 40 books. Two of the chests turned up and were later carried to the Oakes's, where Thoreau saw them. One was a small, black ironbound trunk, in which Davis recalled she had put her gold watch, but it was empty, and the other was a large trunk that had rolled up on the beach, which held some clothes and letters that Mrs. Oakes had dried and spread out on a table, but no manuscript. A few futile tries were later made. When Thoreau was in Patchogue, where he assumed most of the pilferers came from, he advertised but got no responses. Some months later, Carlyle wrote Emerson that he thought it was in a sealed package Margaret had left in London with an obstinate woman who wanted to burn the parcel, but when he finally got it away from her, the manuscript was not there. And there the trail seems to have ended. The likelihood is probably what Greeley later guessed: either it washed away when the trunk (if it was there rather than in the desk) opened in the sea, as did several, or some of the scavengers, thinking it of no value, or wanting to get rid of it once the widespread anger at their actions spread, destroyed it. Whichever way the sheets likely scattered, it was a sad ending, as Greeley would write in his journal, for "pages so rich with experience and life," as well as, Hedge would lament, "a serious loss to the literature of the world."[27]

While Fuller's friends were digging for information at Fire Island, reports of her death were spreading by word of mouth through literary circles all over the Northeast and beyond. Henry James vividly remembered standing at the age of seven next to his father on a steamer from New York within a few miles of the shipwreck when Washington Irving told Henry Sr. that Fuller had drowned. Cass reported that in Rome the announcement of her death provoked Romans, both prominent and ordinary, to react "with a degree of sorrow, which is not often bestowed upon a foreigner, and, especially, one of a different faith." Her thousands of readers, though, read of the calamity in newspapers and magazines. What they learned was, somewhat surprisingly, in view of all the controversies during her lifetime and rumors afterward about her, almost universally positive. Liberal periodicals, of course, paid warm tribute to her. "America has produced no woman who in mental endowments and acquirements has surpassed Margaret Fuller," the *Tribune* affirmed in an unsigned article by Greeley, although even there he was still complaining about the "painful slowness and occasional awkwardness" of her writing. "Passages of rare beauty as well as signal elevation of sentiment may be gleaned from her works," he wrote judiciously, "but as a whole they must commend themselves mainly by their vigor of thought and by habitual fearlessness rather than freedom of utterance."[28]

Even periodicals that had severely criticized her in the past now paid generous tribute to her. "I am happy to notice," declared a writer in the *Southern Literary Messenger*, "that since her stormy exit, with scarce a single exception, the presses that were the loudest in her vituperation, are prompt to do her the most delicate and cordial justice to her memory." Perhaps inevitably, though, commentators disagreed about where her major contribution lay. Reform journals, including now friendly abolitionist ones, praised her women's rights writings and recent sacrifices in Italy, and literary ones generally asserted that her real achievement had been her criticism, while some stretched to accommodate contrary evidence. "Her natural vocation was that of a critic," the proslavery *Southern Literary Messenger*'s critic asserted, though conceding the influence and intellectual vigor of her dispatches. Politics "was not in accordance with her highest tastes, nor her peculiar gifts." Several periodicals, especially English and conservative journals, seemed anxious to dissociate her from her Transcendentalist colleagues. Although few went as far as the *Literary Messenger*'s author in saying that she had "scarcely a point in common" with "Reformers of that school," which he seems to have identified with Emerson and Brook Farm, most agreed she was a breed apart.[29]

Private reactions to her death ranged more widely. This was especially true in Boston, where she had been both a beloved and notorious figure for most of her life. There the whispered aspersions seem to have mainly come from conservative Unitarian types who had always disliked her, partly for her Transcendentalist associations but mainly for her image as an arrogant bluestocking who courted radical ideas and, perhaps worse, contemptuously dismissed Unitarian Boston's pretensions. "When the news of her death reached Boston," the liberal quondam Unitarian minister Octavius Frothingham would later recall, "one of Boston's eminent men in letters and public affairs quietly remarked: 'it is just as well so.'" Some of those who had felt her critical sting in her *Tribune* columns seem never to have forgiven her. "The general impression I have gathered of her," wrote William Prescott, whose history of Mexico Fuller had sharply criticized for its intellectual superficiality, "is that she was a woman of showy parts, with much whimsicality if not originality in her way of thinking & acting, and a singular degree of independence & self-reliance"—the last presumably the most damning. As with the calumnies of Mary Wollstonecraft a generation earlier, rumors about her sex life cast a lurid light on her reputation as a heterodox battler against patriarchal male presumption. Indeed, as the furor over the "Free Love System" burst out in the early 1850s, her supposedly taking the marriage vow "lightly," as the *New York Times*'s Henry Raymond would later put it in his debate with Greeley about socialism, would make her even more controversial in conservative circles than she had been in her lifetime.[30]

Some of the relief breathed after her death defies categorization. "Miss [Lydia] Greene says the country is thereby saved from much injury, which her example, & her writings would have produced among us," Mary Torrey wrote to Dorothea Dix. "I was not aware they could be so powerful." Much injury? Although unmentioned here, with the exploding antislavery movement in the wake of that year's Fugitive Slave Law threatening to upend the party system, conservative Whigs like Dix and her friends could hardly have been oblivious to the political fire Fuller could and would have brought back from Italy's comparable struggle for liberty to fan the flames at home. Even Fuller's final anguished dilemma on board the *Elizabeth* was grist for the deprecation mill. "I always thought there was a vein of impudence, if not folly," Henry I. Bowditch would write years later, of Fuller's "fate, in which she caused the death of the whole party by her unwise decision not to trust the seamen." That Bowditch made this gratuitously slanderous comment in a memorandum commemorating the "Martyr Soldiers" of the Civil War, including Margaret's brother Arthur, whose quick death after volunteering for a skirmish in the Battle of Antietam he likened to his sister's gesture, would suggest how long bad memories of Fuller lasted in some Boston and New York circles, conservative and liberal.[31]

Fuller's friends numbered many more and naturally felt much more deeply about her than her critics and enemies. Of course, their reactions to her death were as various as their individual personalities and friendships with her had been. Yet in their letters to each other, common themes emerged. They nearly all bristled with outrage (as Sarah Clarke would put it) at "those cruel charges" of "refined selfishness" in refusing to be separated from her husband and child. Caroline Tappan wrote Elizabeth Hoar that she had gotten enormous comfort on this score from the opinion of her father, one of antebellum mercantile Boston's greatest merchant mariners, that saving herself on a plank, much less her child, would have required more physical strength and fearlessness in the water than she had. Many friends wrote pages on the enormous influence she had had over them. "When I look back on our intercourse with Margaret," James Clarke wrote his sister Sarah, "it seems to me that my debt to her is very great, & I feel ashamed at ever having suffered my mind to dwell on any defects in her character." In a rare outburst of bitter emotion, Emerson wrote in his journal immediately after learning of her death: "Margaret dies on rocks of Fire Island Beach within sight of & within 40 rods of the shore. To the last her country proves inhospitable to her; brave, eloquent, subtle, accomplished, devoted, constant soul! If nature availed in America to give birth to many such as she, freedom & honour & letters & art too were safe in this new world." After more pages of remembrances, he added poignantly: "I have lost in her my audience. I hurry now to my work admonished that I have few days left."[32]

Emerson's reference to America's inhospitality to Fuller raises the question, much on her friends' minds, of how she would have fared in the United States, as well as the more general one of how they should look on her death. Acquaintances or fading friends like Sophia Hawthorne and her sister Mary Mann echoed the sentiments of a number of culturally conservative Bostonians. "I am really glad she died," Sophia wrote. "There was no other peace or rest to be found for her—especially if her husband was a person so wanting in force & availability." Mary concurred. "He was wholly unfit to be her husband in this country, alto' it might have answered in Italy. He would have been nothing here—he could do nothing, be nothing, come to nothing, & he would have dragged her down—for their only prospect of maintenance was by her pen—and it is supposed she was on the eve of another confinement." However, her friends did worry, if not about that meanly suggested unlikely possibility, as they had before she left Florence, about how trying this kind of malicious gossip would have been on her. "She was always so sensitive to coldness & unkindness even from strangers," Caroline Tappan noted to Elizabeth Hoar. Emerson, on the other hand, dismissed these "timorous" concerns with an Emersonian wave: "She had only to open her mouth, & a triumphant success awaited her. She would fast enough have disposed of the circumstances & the bystanders. For she had the impulse, & they wanted it. Here were already mothers waiting tediously for her coming, for the education of their daughters." Like many of Emerson's thoughts, however, this one would not be his last one about Fuller's death.[33]

Indeed, he and all her friends struggled to come to terms with its deeper tragedy or nontragedy. Most saw her future as grim quite beyond the gossip about her marriage, largely, it would seem, because they were so intent on consoling themselves. Some of Margaret's liberal Christian women friends, like Elizabeth Peabody and Anna Ward, emphasized the religious consolation that neither knew the other had died "till *all three* met to part no more—above—& beyond!" Most, however, spoke of what had most worried her—her financial difficulties. "In one point of view it was a happy release from life's troubles," Duyckinck wrote a friend, "for they were I believe entirely without resources except literary ones, and those of the higher class which our glorious country rather aid in the process of starvation than act as a bar against it." Her most Transcendentalist friends, though, elevated the meaning of her death quite beyond the financial or heavenly. A week after writing his anguished journal entries, Emerson wrote Carlyle, in a startling reversal of the bravura he had confidently attributed to her there, a sweeping self-consolation that converted, as did Lidian, grim prognostications into selfish-sounding good cheer: "She died in happy hour for herself. Her health was much exhausted. Her marriage would have taken her away from us all, & there was a subsistence yet to be secured, & diminished powers, & old age." Probably the most severely Transcendental judgment was that of the former Brook Farmer Almira Barlow that Fuller's death was "a fit & good conclusion to her life. Her life was romantic and exceptional," she told Emerson: "so let her death be; it sets the seal on her marriage, avoids all questions of Society, all of employment, poverty, & old age, and besides was undoubtedly predetermined when the world was created." Clarke put the religious case for "Margaret's Euthenasia" in probably its highest Romantic context. "Higher natures like hers," he wrote his sister Sarah, living for high aims, have a more evident Providence managing their destiny, & it was manifest that she was not to come back to struggle against poverty, misrepresentation, & perhaps alienated friendships and chilled affections. There seemed no position for her here, & her life was complete, so far as experience & development went. That she shd. have accomplished so little for the public in proportion to her genius & attainments is to us a loss—but her own aim was rather development than manifestation, & that first aim she perfectly fulfilled. Her life will seem to us now complete & round.

"Development" and "seem to us": the first a Fulleresque appraisal to be sure, even if the second remained as inwardly focused as Emerson's despair over losing his audience.[34]

But whether accurate, self-consoling, selfish, or Transcendental, these easy consolations were not seized on by all her friends. Caroline Tappan, who thought it was clear that Margaret had been happy with both Ossoli and their child, could not find any consolation in their death as a family. Indeed, with a sometimes nihilistic sensibility that resonated with Margaret's tragic one like that of none of their more Christian or Platonic friends, Caroline especially grieved that Angelino had died. "It would have been her life going on," she wrote to Elizabeth Hoar, "& it seemed but fair to her after her long struggle to assert her right to live. I wonder if all are to be so thrown away upon the sands." William Channing, who also knew what it was to struggle with doubts, even if he stifled them in his Christian socialistic enthusiasm, thought his dead friend had faced, rather than just a life of devastating struggle, at least as much future possibilities both as a mother and a politically engaged critic. "A great friend of new life was blossoming here," he wrote sadly after reading some of her letters to Mazzini and Mickiewicz, which he had picked up while Ellery Channing and her mother were sorting them after they returned home. Hedge, who thought there was "something poetically & even sublimely tragic" about Margaret's "awful" death in the shipwreck—"like a story out of a book" that he could not make "real"—nonetheless came down to the same sad reality that Channing had: her "life spilled at the very threshold of her joy." Ironically, the colleague who respected Fuller enormously even if she did not repay the favor, captured perhaps best the double-sided "tragic" meaning that she at least would likely have recognized as truer to her sense of her death than either Christian "Providence" or consoling disaster. Showing, as elsewhere, the insight into others that he sorely lacked about himself, Alcott wrote in his journal: "There was . . . a fate in her, and was in the struggle against this, that she wrought her greatest victories. I think her courage surpassed by no woman I have met. It made her life one of revolutions, and brought her to the tragic end." In short, hers was not an end of classical tragedy but of ironic Romantic pathos: not a character flaw but the same self-generated revolutionary hope that had fatefully cast her into turbulent waters, shunned by most of her contemporaries, governed the darker fates and absurd accidents of her end. It was a consoling myth with which Fuller, attuned to the fateful cast of her choices, would have recognized.[35]

Although eluding this deeper meaning, the subsequent decades would be kind to Fuller's public memory. Her *Memoirs*, edited by Clarke, Emerson, and Channing and published two years later, was crucial in that regard. While friends complained about Emerson's cool irony and Channing's vague etherealness, the public not only made it a best-seller but found in it appealing and heretofore unknown sides to her as a friend, mother, and self-sacrificing political liberal. Her first serious biographer, Thomas Wentworth Higginson, gave just the needed antidote thirty years later in his volume in Charles Dudley Warner's "American Men of Letters" series—a title she would have on some level rightly appreciated as a sign of her and American literature's arrival. With Higginson's characteristic cheerful charm, his biography brought to light the more practical, political, and literary aspects of Fuller that were largely eclipsed in the *Memoirs*. In the intervening years, Arthur Fuller, with crucial help from Greeley, brought out successive collections of her writings. Although bowdlerized by Arthur—whose squeamishness about anything that, like her writings on Sand, cast aspersions on her sexual uprightness often got the better of him—these volumes also became good sellers, keeping alive her intellectual presence through several editions to the end of the nineteenth century.[36]

Memory, of course, cannot substitute for life. Without indulging in the fruitless game of trying to imagine what Fuller might have accomplished had she lived, one can at least say that, historically speaking, powerful currents kept her image afloat in death as they would have in life—and here Channing's upbeat judgment was closer to the mark than his ordinarily more perceptive colleague Emerson's second downcast one. The political and tragically triumphant turn of antislavery and Civil War away from the moralistic perfectionism of the Garrisonian era would have made Fuller's recently acquired revolutionary experience more historically resonant in the United States than ever before in her lifetime. Certainly, her hard-won politically embattled Romantic liberalism fitted that turn better than the apolitical socialism of her Brook Farm colleagues and their demoralizing failed utopian experiments, or even the more individualistic resistant one of Emerson and Thoreau, which, however crucial to radical antislavery in the 1850s, could hardly yield insights about history that lay beyond the control of any individual. Indeed, her political socialistic voice would likely have mingled well with the *Tribune*'s socialist turn toward working-class cooperatives and political conflict in the 1850s, while her sense of historical tragedy might have carried her into the succeeding decades of liberal triumph and disillusionment after the war. Even the image of Fuller the idealistically driven and self-sacrificing heroine and healer in the siege of Rome would have countless parallels, most famously in Whitman, but also in the lives of untold numbers of American women during the Civil War, many taking heart from her example. The steady rise of feminism after the war also made a congenial climate for her reputation, as repeated tributes to her by virtually all of feminism's "First Wave" leaders would attest. "Margaret's reputation is now, I think, very much what she would have wished it to be," Sarah Clarke wrote Higginson at the beginning of the postwar Reconstruction era. "She will always stand among the first of her sex both in England and America who was both able and brave to speak a good word for the emancipation of women." Likewise, the maturation of America's national culture—with its ironies of growing national self-confidence and anxious cosmopolitanism, exemplified in its artistic institutions

and charted most brilliantly in the novels of Henry James—resonated with the paradoxes of her pioneering cosmopolitan literary patriotism. Sam Ward, Christopher
Cranch, and others of her more culturally sophisticated friends may have exaggerated when they later speculated, with the benefit of hindsight, that Fuller would have
had a much easier time had she lived into the later world of Victorian America, but
that she would have found many congenial currents seems uncontestable.[37]

However, there it ended. After the end of the nineteenth century, Fuller virtually disappeared from public memory, except as an also-ran in the "idyll" of Transcendentalism, whose movement, though sometimes nostalgically portrayed by
aged New Englanders, was mostly mocked by modernist critics, right and left,
for whom it represented an early "genteel" American Victorian dead end. This is
deeply ironic. If America had a modernist forerunner before the twentieth century, it was surely Margaret Fuller, who had managed to slip more completely
than any other intellectual of her generation the leash of proto-Victorian repressions and evasions that modernist authors revolted against. Certainly, her two
primary intellectual constructs of formalist-organicist criticism and rights-minded
androgyny suggest that. Variants of the first were bywords of mid-twentieth-
century literary theorists from Joel Springarn to the New Critics, and versions of
the second have been constantly recurring themes in feminism since the rise of
the "New Woman" after the turn of the twentieth century. Even the 1930s, when
American Transcendentalism's reputation was at its lowest ebb, would produce
the circle of New York Intellectuals, whose double commitment to highbrow avant-
garde literature and radical political critique uncannily mimicked Fuller's. Indeed,
as a rare parallel to Fuller's involvement in the Roman Revolution, this decade
also witnessed the Spanish Civil War, in which a generation of idealistic radicals
also found their fate as Americans wrapped up in a violent foreign internal conflict. As with so much else in American history, the 1960s marked a watershed,
too, in Fuller memory, when "Second-Wave" feminist scholars discovered her as
their ancient forerunner even while struggling to fit her into their era of iconoclastic populism. These are but partial resonances, though. Only the future will
reveal whether the Romantic Fuller of critical edge, spiritual transcendence, and
"extraordinary generous seeking" will fully appear in her own person on the historical horizon.

Abbreviations

The following abbreviations are used in the notes.

Sources

"AS40"   Joel Myerson, "Bronson Alcott's 'Scripture for 1840,'" *ESQ: A Journal of the American Renaissance*, 20 (4th Quarter 1974), 236–59.

BAL   *The Letters of Elizabeth Barrett Browning and Her Sister Arabella*, 2 vols., ed. Scott Lewis (Waco, Tex.: Wedgestone Press, 2002).

BC   *The Brownings' Correspondence*, ed. Philip Kelley and Ronald Hudson, 14 vols. to date (Winfield, Kan.: Wedgestone Press, 1984–).

BML   *The Letters of Elizabeth Barrett Browning to Mary Russell Mitford, 1836–1854*, ed. Meredith B. Raymond and Mary Rose Sullivan, 3 vols. (Waco, Tex.: Armstrong Library of Baylor University, 1983).

BOL   *Elizabeth Barrett Browning's Letters to Mrs. David Ogilvy, 1849–1861*, ed. Peter N. Heydon and Philip Kelley (New York: Browning Institute, 1973).

CA   James Freeman Clarke, *Autobiography, Diary and Correspondence*, ed. Edward Everett Hale (Boston: Houghton Mifflin, 1891).

CCC   *The Collected Letters of Thomas and Jane Welsh Carlyle*, Duke-Edinburgh Edition, ed. Charles Richard Sanders et al., 32 vols. to date (Durham, N.C.: Duke University Press, 1970–).

CF-1   Charles Capper, *Margaret Fuller: An American Romantic Life*, vol. I, *The Private Years* (New York: Oxford University Press, 1992).

"ChaL"   Francis D. Dedmond, "The Selected Letters of William Ellery Channing the Younger (Part One)," in *SAR*, 1989, 115–218; Francis D. Dedmond, "The Selected Letters of William Ellery Channing the Younger (Part Two)," in *SAR*, 1990, 159–241.

ChiL   *Lydia Maria Child: Selected Letters, 1817–1880*, ed. Milton Meltzer and Patricia G. Holland (Amherst: University of Massachusetts Press, 1982).

CL   *The Letters of James Freeman Clarke to Margaret Fuller*, ed. John Wesley Thomas (Hamburg: de Gruyter, 1957).

"CLS"   Sarah Clarke, "Letters of a Sister," proof sheets, Houghton Library, Harvard University.

CSmH   Huntington Library

CSt   Stanford University Libraries.

DM   Caroline W. Healey [Dall], *Margaret and Her Friends; or, Ten Conversations with Margaret Fuller upon the Mythology of the Greeks and Its Expression in Art* (1895; Boston: Roberts, 1897).

ECC   *The Correspondence of Emerson and Carlyle*, ed. Joseph Slater (New York: Columbia University Press, 1964).

ECW   *The Collected Works of Ralph Waldo Emerson*, ed. Alfred E. Ferguson et al., 6 vols. to date (Cambridge: Harvard University Press, 1971–).

EJMN   *The Journals and Miscellaneous Notebooks of Ralph Waldo Emerson*, ed. William H. Gilman et al., 16 vols. (Cambridge: Harvard University Press, 1960–82).

EL   *The Letters of Ralph Waldo Emerson*, vols. I–VI, ed. Ralph L. Rusk, vols. VII–X, ed. Eleanor M. Tilton, 10 vols. (New York: Columbia University Press, 1939; 1990–95).

ESL   *The Selected Letters of Lidian Jackson Emerson*, ed. Dolores Bird Carpenter (Columbia: University of Missouri Press, 1987).

EW   *The Complete Works of Ralph Waldo Emerson*, Centenary Edition, ed. Edward Waldo Emerson, 12 vols. (Boston: Houghton, Mifflin, 1903–4).

"FB"   Nancy Craig Simmons, "Margaret Fuller's Boston Conversations: The 1839–1840 Series," in *SAR*, 1994, 195–226.

FC   *Richard F. Fuller, Chaplain Fuller: Being a Life Sketch of a New England Clergyman and Army Chaplain* (Boston: Walker, Wise, 1863).

"FJ42–1"   Joel Myerson, "Margaret Fuller's 1842 Journal: At Concord with the Emersons," *Harvard Library Bulletin*, 21 (October 1979), 445–70.

"FJ42–2"   Robert D. Habich, "Margaret Fuller's Journal for October 1842," *Harvard Library Bulletin*, 33 (summer 1985), 280–91.

"FJ44–1"   Martha L. Berg and Alice de V. Perry, eds., "'The Impulses of Human Nature': Margaret Fuller's Journal from June through October 1844," *Proceedings of the Massachusetts Historical Society*, v. 102, 1990 (Boston, 1991), 38–126.

"FJ44–2"   "Fragments of Margaret Fuller's Journal," 1844–45, Fruitlands Museum, Harvard, Massachusetts.

FL   *The Letters of Margaret Fuller*, ed. Robert N. Hudspeth, 6 vols. (Ithaca: Cornell University Press, 1983–94).

FLL   *Love-Letters of Margaret Fuller*, 1845–1846, ed. Julia Ward Howe (New York, D. Appleton, 1903).

FMW   Fuller Manuscripts and Works, Houghton Library, Harvard University.

FP   Margaret Fuller Papers, Massachusetts Historical Society.

FPL   S. Margaret Fuller, *Papers on Literature and Art*, 2 vols. (New York: Wiley and Putnam, 1846).

FR   Richard F. Fuller, *Recollections of Richard F. Fuller* (Boston: privately printed, 1936).

"FS"   Margaret Fuller, "Scrapbook," 1838–44, Perry-Clarke Collection, Massachusetts Historical Society.

FSL   S. M. Fuller, *Summer on the Lakes, in 1843* (Boston: Charles C. Little and James Brown, 1844).

FW   S. Margaret Fuller, *Woman in the Nineteenth Century* (New York: Greeley and McElrath, 1845).

HO   Thomas Wentworth Higginson, *Margaret Fuller Ossoli* (Boston: Houghton Mifflin, 1884).

"HL-3"   Elizabeth Maxfield-Miller, "Elizabeth of Concord: Selected Letters of Elizabeth Sherman Hoar (1814–1878) to the Emersons, Family, and the Emerson Circle" (Part Three), in *SAR*, 1986, 113–98.

HW   *The Centenary Edition of the Works of Nathaniel Hawthorne*, ed. William Charvat et al., 23 vols. to date (Columbus: Ohio State University Press, 1962–).

LL   *The Letters of Henry Wadsworth Longfellow*, ed. Andrew Hilen, 6 vols. (Cambridge, Mass.: Harvard University Press, 1966–82).

LoL   *Letters of James Russell Lowell*, ed. Charles Eliot Norton, 2 vols. (New York: Harper, 1893).

LoNL   *New Letters of James Russell Lowell*, ed. M. A. De Wolfe Howe (New York: Harper, 1932).

MB   Boston Public Library, Department of Rare Books and Manuscripts.

MCR-S   Radcliffe Institute for Advanced Study, Schlesinger Library.

MH   Harvard University, Houghton Library.

MH-AH   Harvard Divinity School, Andover-Harvard Theological Library.

MHarF   Fruitlands Museums, Harvard, Massachusetts.

MHi   Massachusetts Historical Society.

MNS   Smith College Libraries.

MS   *Giuseppe Mazzini, Scritti editi ed inediti*, Edizione nazionale, 94 vols.
            (Imola: Galeati, 1906–43), supplements, Appendice, 8 vols. (1938–
            86), and Indice, 2 vols. (1973).

MWA   American Antiquarian Society.

NAW   *Notable American Women, 1607–1950: A Biographical Dictionary*,
            ed. Edward T. James, Janet Wilson James, and Paul S. Boyer, 3 vols.
            (Cambridge, Mass.: Harvard University Press, 1971).

NCC   Columbia University Libraries.

NIC   Cornell University Library.

NjHi   New Jersey Historical Society.

NN-B   New York Public Library, Berg Collection of English and American
            Literature.

NN-M   New York Public Library, Manuscripts and Archives Division.

NYDT   *New-York Daily Tribune.*

NYWT   *New-York Weekly Tribune.*

OC   Margaret Fuller Ossoli Collection, Boston Public Library.

OFC   Ossoli Family Collection, Archivio di Stato di Roma.

OM   *Memoirs of Margaret Fuller Ossoli*, ed. R. W. Emerson, J. F. Clarke,
            and W. H. Channing, 2 vols. (Boston: Phillips, Sampson, 1852).

OMW   Leopold Wellisz, *The Friendship of Margaret Fuller D'Ossoli and
            Adam Mickiewicz* (New York: Polish Book Importing, 1947).

"ON"   "Notebook Margaret Fuller Ossoli," [1851], in *The Journals and Mis-
            cellaneous Notebooks of Ralph Waldo Emerson*, vol. XI, 455–509,
            ed. A. W. Plumstead, William H. Gilman, and Ruth H. Bennett (Cam-
            bridge.: Harvard University Press, 1975).

"PFC"   Gary L. Collison, "A Critical Edition of the Correspondence of Theodore
            Parker and Convers Francis, 1836–1859" (Ph.D. dissertation, Penn-
            sylvania State University, 1979).

PGI   *Protocolo della Giovine Italia*, 6 vols. (Imola, 1916–22).

"PJ"   Carol Elizabeth Johnston, "The Journals of Theodore Parker: July–
            December 1840" (Ph.D. dissertation, University of South Carolina,
            1980).

PL   *Letters of Elizabeth Palmer Peabody: American Renaissance Woman*,
            ed. Bruce A. Ronda (Middletown, Conn.: Wesleyan University Press,
            1984).

PoLe   *The Letters of Edgar Allan Poe*, ed. John Ward Ostrum, 2 vols. (Cam-
            bridge: Harvard University Press, 1948).

PoLo   Dwight Thomas and David K. Jackson, *The Poe Log: A Documen-
            tary Life of Edgar Allan Poe, 1809–1849* (Boston: G. K. Hall, 1987).

RPB   Brown University Library.

SAR   *Studies in the American Renaissance*, ed. Joel Myerson (Boston: Twayne, 1977–82; Charlottesville: University Press of Virginia, 1983–96).

"SL"   Francis B. Dedmond, "The Letters of Caroline Sturgis to Margaret Fuller," in *SAR*, 1988, 201–51.

TC   *The Correspondence of Henry David Thoreau*, ed. Walter Harding and Carl Bode (New York, 1958).

TJ   *Henry D. Thoreau: Journal*, ed. John C. Broderick et al., 8 vols. to date (Princeton: Princeton University Press, 1981–), in *The Writings of Henry D. Thoreau*, ed. Elizabeth Hall Witherell et al. (Princeton: Princeton University Press, 1971–).

"TTE"   "Things and Thoughts in Europe."

TxU   University of Texas at Austin, Harry Ransom Humanities Research Center.

ViU   University of Virginia Library.

People

ABA   Amos Bronson Alcott

ABF   Arthur Buckminster Fuller

ABW   Anna Barker Ward

AHC   Arthur Hugh Clough

AL   Anna Loring

AM   Adam Mickiewicz

AOA   Angela Ossoli de Andreis

APB   Almira Penniman Barlow

CAV   Costanza Arconati Visconti

CB   Cristina Trivulzio di Belgioioso

CF   Convers Francis

CKN   Charles King Newcomb

CL   Charles Lane

CPC   Christopher Pearse Cranch

CS(T)   Caroline Sturgis (Tappan)

EAD   Edward A. Duyckinck

EAP   Edgar Allan Poe

EBB   Elizabeth Barrett Browning

EF   Eugene Fuller

EFC	Ellen Fuller Channing
EGL	Ellis Gray Loring
EH	Elizabeth Hoar
EPP	Elizabeth Palmer Peabody
ERF	Eliza Rotch Farrar
ES	Emelyn Story
FHH	Frederic Henry Hedge
FS	Francis Shaw
GAO	Giovanni Angelo Ossoli
GB	Georgiana Bruce
GM	Giuseppe Mazzini
GR	George Ripley
GWC	George William Curtis
HDT	Henry David Thoreau
HG	Horace Greeley
HM	Harriet Martineau
HWL	Henry Wadsworth Longfellow
JFC	James Freeman Clarke
JN	James Nathan
JRL	James Russell Lowell
JSD	John Sullivan Dwight
JTK	Jane Tuckerman King
JWC	Jane Welsh Carlyle
LC	Lewis Cass, Jr.
LF	Lloyd Fuller
LGL	Louisa Gilman Loring
LJE	Lidian Jackson Emerson
LMC	Lydia Maria Child
MCF	Margaret Crane Fuller
MF	Margaret Fuller
MR	Mary Rotch
MS	Marcus Spring
NH	Nathaniel Hawthorne
RB	Robert Browning
RBS	Rebecca Buffum Spring
RFF	Richard Frederick Fuller

RWE	Ralph Waldo Emerson
SC	Sarah Clarke
SGW	Samuel Gray Ward
SHW	Sarah Helen Whitman
SPH	Sophia Peabody Hawthorne
SR	Sophia Ripley
SSS	Sarah Sturgis Shaw
TC	Thomas Carlyle
TF	Timothy Fuller
TH	Thomas Hicks
TP	Theodore Parker
TWH	Thomas Wentworth Higginson
WEC2	William Ellery Channing II
WHC	William Henry Channing
WHCl	William H. Clarke
WHF	William Henry Fuller
WWS	William Wetmore Story

Notes

In these notes I have given full citations to all quoted material. I have also indicated some secondary works that have provided me with major sources of information or influenced my interpretations in substantial ways.

The copies of Fuller's letters and journal entries in the *Memoirs of Margaret Fuller Ossoli* present special problems. The censorship and rewriting of these fragments by the editors, especially her most effusively friendly ones, Channing and Clarke, have made them clearly corrupt sources. For this reason I have consistently used, in place of a Fuller *Memoirs* text (*OM*), an original Fuller manuscript, a Hudspeth edition (*FL*) letter, or, as a last resort, a copy in the Fuller Manuscripts and Works (FMW). Unfortunately, as some *Memoirs* texts survive in no other form, I have decided—as Hudspeth has—to use them. My main reason is that *not* to utilize these copies, which on the whole are more accurate than not, would be a more serious distortion of the historical record than to utilize them. In addition, by exploiting internal and external evidence, I have often been able to mitigate at least one of their weaknesses—their frequent lack of dates and (in the case of letters) identified recipients.

My editorial apparatus is as follows. In the text I have reproduced quotations as they appear in the sources cited, including their spelling and punctuation. Exceptions are slips of the pen, typographical errors, and obliterated but contextually obvious letters and punctuation marks, which I have silently corrected. I have also not reproduced editors' additions, authors' insertion marks, or (except occasionally and where I identify them as such) authors' cancellations. Unrecovered but likely words, punctuation marks, or letters occasionally required for clarity, and all other inserted material I have placed in brackets. In the notes I have placed within brackets and with an asterisk likely dates and recipients for *Memoirs* copies of letters and journal entries. I have also used brackets and an asterisk for date and recipient identifications that differ from those assigned in published editions. I have employed brackets without an asterisk for dates and recipients I have as-

530 Notes to Pages ix–xiii

signed for unpublished manuscripts. Brackets without an asterisk for published works are those used by the editors. Occasionally I have spliced together several sources for a single quoted passage. Where this is the case, I have cited all the sources in the note.

Preface

1. May 16, 1883, OC 197 ("so many aspects"); *OM*, I, 227 ("This alternation"). Although to maintain my narrative focus, I have kept my references to the many recent critical discussions of Fuller's writings meager, I have learned and profited from them, including those of Bell Chevigny, Phyllis Cole, Robert Hudspeth, Mary Kelley, Annette Kolodny, Joel Myerson, Larry Reynolds, David Robinson, Susan Belasco Smith, Jeffrey Steele, William Stowe, Joan von Mehren, Cristina Zwarg, and others. For Fuller scholarship since my first volume, see Joel Myerson, *Margaret Fuller: An Annotated Bibliography of Criticism, 1983–1995* (Westport, Conn., 1998); and David M. Robinson, "Emerson, Thoreau, Fuller and Transcendentalism," *American Literary Scholarship*, ed. Gary Scharnhorst and David Nordloh (Durham, N.C., 1988–present). Definitions of "the intellectual" abound, but I have found especially congruent with my eclectic definition here the perspectives found in Christopher Lasch, *The New Radicalism in America, 1889–1963: The Intellectual as a Social Type* (New York, 1965); Michael Walzer, *Interpretation and Social Criticism* (Cambridge, Mass., 1987); and Stefan Collini, *Absent Minds: Intellectuals in Britain* (New York, 2006). The classic work on authenticity and modernity in Western literature is Lionel Trilling, *Sincerity and Authenticity* (Cambridge, Mass., 1972). For ideas about the modern "self," see Jerrold Seigel, *The Idea of the Self: Thought and Experience in Western Europe since the Seventeenth Century* (Cambridge, England, 2005).

2. Mar. 23, 1843, *EJMN*, VIII, 368 ("excels other intellectual persons"); "The Literati in New York City," in *The Complete Works of Edgar Allan Poe*, ed. James A. Harrison, 17 vols. (New York, 1902), XV, 82 ("Her acts are bookish"); May 7, 1852, *CCC*, XXCII, 109 ("predetermination").

3. *ECW*, I, 56 ("bookworm"); Apr. 16, 1814, FMW, III, 7 ("learns to read"); Apr. 13, 1820, FMW, V, 6 ("mediocrity is obscurity"); May 7, 1852, *ECC*, 478 ("*eat* this big universe"); to Susan Prescott, Jan. 3, 1828, *FL*, I, 155 ("Augustan niceties").

4. To Anna Jameson, Dec. 22, 1837, *FL*, I, 318 ("'strong mental odor'"); to EPP, [1836]*, *FL*, VI, 274 ("teach"); to FHH, Mar. 6, 1835, *FL*, I, 226 ("Germanico").

5. Because my use of psychoanalytic theory is historical and mainly heuristic, I have found useful those dynamic psychological approaches that emphasize both relational and intrapsychic self-constructions, particularly the "ego psychology" of Erik Erikson, the "self-psychology" of Heinz Kohut, and the "object relations" theories of W. K. Winnicott. In integrating the related problem of gender identity, I have been influenced by Juliet Mitchell, Nancy Chodorow, Jessica Benjamin, and other psychoanalytic-informed feminist critics who subsequently built on and revised these schemas. See *CF-1*, 365 n8, 367 nn21, 28. For a suggestive discussion of psychoanalysis as a form of historical analysis, see Michael S. Roth, *Psycho-Analysis as History: Negation and Freedom in Freud* (1987; Ithaca, 1995). For a collection of cogent critiques of Freudian psychoanalysis that generally, however, in my view, assume a not always relevant positivist norm of science, see Frederick C. Crews, ed., *Unauthorized Freud: Doubters Confront a Legend* (New York, 1998).

6. MF, journal, [ca. Apr. 1840], FMW, box A ("words—words—words"); to EH, Sept. 12, 1840, *EL*, II, 331 ("parse & spell"). For the scholarship on Transcendentalism, see *CF-1*, 383–84 n37. Charles Capper and Conrad Edick Wright, eds., *Transient and Perma-*

nent: The Transcendentalist Movement and Its Contexts (Boston, 1999) is a collection of recent work in the field. I am aware that the term "avant-garde," especially in its stridently antibourgeois versions, is an anachronistic category when applied to American intellectual culture before the twentieth century. However, my point in using the term is simply to underline Fuller's and some of her other Transcendentalist colleagues' anticipation of later avant-garde movements, especially in their opposition to cultural gentility and their eagerness to eschew intellectual certainties and social securities in favor of experimentation and discovery. The literature on the avant-garde is large, but I have found particularly valuable, for conceptual clarity, Matei Calinescu, *Five Faces of Modernity: Modernism, Avant-Garde, Decadence, Kitsch, Postmodernism* (1977; Durham, N.C., 1987), and for historical understanding, Jerrold Seigel, *Bohemian Paris: Culture, Politics, and the Boundaries of Bourgeois Life, 1830–1930* (Baltimore, 1986). For a study emphasizing the continuities between European Romantics' and Victorian and modernist authors' outlooks, see Peter Gay, *The Bourgeois Experience: Victoria to Freud* (New York: 1984–98), vol. IV, *The Naked Heart* (1995), and vol. V, *Pleasure Wars* (1998).

7. The scholarship on nationalism is large, but of work since the topic's revival in the 1980s that has guided my thinking about Fuller's patriotic concepts, I have found especially useful Benedict Anderson, *Imagined Communities: Reflections on the Origin and Spread of Nationalism* (London, 1983; rev. ed. 1991); Yael Tamir, *Liberal Nationalism* (Princeton, 1993); David Miller, *On Nationality* (New York, 1995); Maurizio Viroli, *For Love of Country: An Essay on Patriotism and Nationalism* (New York, 1995). For the United States, see Rogers M. Smith, *Civic Ideals: Conflicting Visions of Citizenship in U.S. History* (New Haven, 1997); and Ronald Kersh, *Dreams of a More Perfect Union* (Ithaca, 2001).

8. *FSL*, 65 ("still all new").

9. "Hawthorne's Mosses," in *The Writings of Herman Melville: The Northwestern-Newberry Edition*, ed. Harrison Hayford, Hershel Parker, and G. Thomas Tanselle, vol. IX, *The Piazza Tales and Other Prose Pieces, 1839–1860*, ed. Harrison Hayford et al. (Evanston, Ill., 1987), 248 ("literary flunkeyism"); statement of HG in *OM*, II, 152 ("un-American").

10. To JFC, [Aug. 14, 1845], *FL*, VI, 359 ("mutual interpretation"). For the classic modernist "discoveries" of the "American Renaissance," see Lewis Mumford, *The Golden Day* (New York, 1926); and F. O. Matthiessen, *American Renaissance: Art and Expression in the Age of Emerson and Whitman* (New York, 1941). For an excellent collection of key essays on the theory of American literature against which Fuller's historical achievement can be measured, see Gordon Hutner, ed., *American Literature, American Culture* (New York, 1999). Like many scholars concerned with the emergence of the category of "culture" in modern capitalist society, I have been much influenced by Raymond Williams, *Culture and Society, 1780–1950* (1958; New York, 1983). Two influential studies of populist strains in antebellum culture that contrast with Fuller's avant-garde "democratic" stance are Lawrence W. Levine, *Highbrow/Lowbrow: The Emergence of Cultural Hierarchy in America* (Cambridge, Mass., 1988); and David S. Reynolds, *Beneath the American Renaissance: The Subversive Imagination in the Age of Emerson and Melville* (New York, 1988).

11. "Deutsche Schnellpost," *NYDT*, Jan. 25, 1845, p. 1 ("regenerated"). In thinking about Fuller's American ethnic cosmopolitanism, I have found particularly valuable David A. Hollinger, *Post-ethnic America*, 2nd ed. (1995; rev. ed., New York, 2005); Hollinger's "Amalgamation and Hypodescent: The Question of Ethnoracial Mixture in the History of the United States," in his *Cosmopolitanism and Solidarity: Studies in Ethnoracial, Religious, and Professional Affiliation in the United States* (Madison, 2006); and Anthony Appiah, *Cosmopolitanism: Ethics in a World of Strangers* (New York, 2006).

12. Perry Miller, ed., *Margaret Fuller: American Romantic* (Garden City, N.Y., 1963), xxviii (refusal to leap). The classic manifesto on the cosmopolitan American is Randolph Bourne, "Trans-national America," *Atlantic Monthly*, 118 (July 1916), 86–97, but the idea had a broad purchase on the thinking of numerous early twentieth-century liberal intellectuals. See David A. Hollinger, "Ethnic Diversity, Cosmopolitanism, and the Emergence of the American Liberal Intelligentsia," in Hollinger's *In the American Province: Studies in the History and Historiography of Ideas* (Bloomington, 1985), 56–73.

Chapter One

1. [Apr.] 17, 1840, FMW ("trials"); SHW, quoted in John Carl Miller, ed., *Poe's Helen Remembers* (Charlottesville, 1979), 227 ("*super*fine"); to RWE, May 31, 1840, *FL*, II, 135 ("annihilating"); "The Dial," *Providence Daily Journal*, 12 (July 27, 1840), 2 ("eclat").

2. "The Dial," *Boston Daily Times*, July 17, 1840, 2 ("Duck tracks"); *Boston Courier*, Oct. 6, 1840, 2 ("stupid 'ejaculations'"); *Cincinnati Daily Chronicle*, Aug. 5, 1840, 2 ("sickly"); *Philadelphia Gazette*, July 1840 ("Bedlamites"); *Knickerbocker Magazine*, 16 (Aug. 1840), 190 ("Literary Euphuism"). For a useful survey of periodical coverage of the *Dial*, see Joel Myerson, "The Contemporary Reception of the Boston *Dial*," *Resources for American Literary Study*, 3 (Autumn 1973), 203–20.

3. *Western Messenger*, 8 (Apr. 1841), 571 (profound thought); *Boston Quarterly Review*, 4 (Jan. 1841), 131–32 ("too . . . aerial"); *Plain Speaker*, January 30, 1841, quoted in Joel Myerson, *The New England Transcendentalists and the "Dial": A History of the Magazine and Its Contributors* (Rutherford, N.J., 1980), 62 ("Literary Liberty"); *Boston Morning Post*, July 14, 1840, 2 ("dreamy"); *NYDT*, Jan. 17, 1843, 1 ("best Magazine"); ibid., Apr. 2, 1842, 1 ("best periodical").

4. Edward Everett Hale, *James Russell Lowell and His Friends* (Boston, 1899), 61 (*North American Review*); Oct. 11, 1840, *LL*, II, 254 ("strange mixture"). My estimate of the geographical reach of the *Dial*'s readership is based on Myerson, "Contemporary Reception," contemporary reviews, and scattered comments in the letters of prominent literary figures at the time.

5. *Dial*, 1 (July 1840), 3, 3–4 ("shames the record"). No comprehensive analysis has yet been made of the social and cultural origins of the *Dial*, but much pertinent evidence may be found in the papers of its contributors and readers. Myerson, *New England Transcendentalists,* is the indispensable standard history. Although both *HO*, chaps. 9–10, and George Willis Cooke, *An Historical and Biographical Introduction to Accompany the "Dial,"* 2 vols. (Cleveland, 1902), exaggerate the *Dial*'s nationalism, they are still useful for the contemporary sources they catalogue. The most searching consideration of American Transcendentalist literary aesthetics remains F. O. Matthiessen, *American Renaissance: Art and Expression in the Age of Emerson and Whitman* (New York, 1941). For understanding the *Dial*-ers' literary ideals, Lawrence Buell, *Literary Transcendentalism: Style and Vision in the American Renaissance* (Ithaca, 1973), is essential. Helen Hennessy (Vendler), "*The Dial*: Its Poetry and Poetic Criticism," *New England Quarterly*, 31 (Mar. 1958), 66–87, provides a contrasting shrewd, if harsh, discussion of their poetics. For Romantic cultural programs, see works cited in note 7 below.

6. *Dial*, 1 (July 1840), 1, 2, 3, 4 ("no hours"). For post–French Revolutionary politics and English Romanticism, see M. H. Abrams, "English Romanticism: The Spirit of the Age," in Northrop Frye, ed., *Romanticism Reconsidered* (New York, 1963), 26–72. For varying discussions of Transcendentalist views of the antebellum "marketplace" of art and literature, see Michael T. Gilmore, *American Romanticism and the Marketplace* (Chicago,

1985); Lawrence Buell, *New England Literary Culture: From Revolution through Renaissance* (Cambridge, England, 1986), chap. 3; and Richard F. Teichgraeber III, *Sublime Thoughts/Penny Wisdom: Situating Emerson and Thoreau in the American Market* (Baltimore, 1995). In thinking about Fuller's idea of a literary public sphere in this chapter and in chapter 7, I have been especially influenced by Raymond Williams, *Culture and Society, 1780* (1958; New York, 1983); and Jürgen Habermas, *The Structural Transformation of the Public Sphere: An Inquiry into a Category of Bourgeois Society* (1962; Cambridge, Mass., 1989). For the problem of literary publics in German and English Romanticism, see Peter Uwe Hohendahl, ed., *A History of German Literary Criticism, 1730–1980* (Lincoln, Neb., 1988), 13–177; Jochen Schulte-Sasse et al., eds., *Theory as Practice: A Critical Anthology of Early German Romantic Writings* (Minneapolis, 1997); Patrick Parrinder, *Authors and Authority: English and American Criticism, 1750–1990* (New York, 1991), chap. 3; and Jon Klancher, "The Vocation of Criticism and the Crisis of the Republic," in *The Cambridge History of Literary Criticism*, ed. H. B. Nisbet and Claude Rawson, 8 vols. (Cambridge, England, 1989–), vol. V, *Romanticism*, chap. 14.

7. JFC, "Memoir of Ralph Waldo Emerson," *Proceedings of the Massachusetts Historical Society*, 2nd ser., vol. 2 (June 1885), 113–14 ("wild-bugle note"); to RWE, [Apr. 25], 1840, *FL*, II, 132 ("fierce"); Journal "1840," FMW, box 1 (indictment); "The Editors to the Reader," *Dial*, 1 (July 1840), 3 ("higher tone"). For the two versions of the *Dial*'s introduction, see *CF-1*, 347–48. On the shift in the 1820s and early 1830s from neoclassical judicial to more affirmative modes of criticism, see William Charvat, *The Origins of American Critical Thought, 1810–1835* (Philadelphia, 1936). A major reason why commentators misrepresent Fuller's critical position is they ignore the Romantic discourses from which she borrowed. Indispensable for understanding these is René Wellek, *History of Modern Criticism: 1750–1950*, vols. I–III (New Haven, 1955–65), which includes a useful brief appraisal of Fuller's practical criticism (III, 179–81). For more extensive recent treatments, see the contrasting studies of Ernst Behler, *German Romantic Literary Theory* (Cambridge, England, 1993); and Frederic C. Beiser, *The Romantic Imperative: The Concept of Early German Romanticism* (Cambridge, Mass., 2003). Also valuable are many of the essays in *Cambridge History of Literary Criticism*, vol. IV, *The Eighteenth Century*, esp. chaps. 23–25, 26–28, and vol. V, *Romanticism*. The philosophical basis of the German post-Kantians' and Romantics' wrestling with subjectivity and objectivity is discussed in Beiser's *German Idealism: The Struggle against Subjectivism, 1781–1801* (Cambridge, Mass., 2002). For a survey that demonstrates how uninformed English and American critics were about the principles of German Romantic literary criticism, see Hanna-Beate Schilling, "The Role of the Brothers Schlegel in American Literary Criticism as Found in Selected Periodicals, 1812–1833: A Critical Bibliography," *American Literature*, 43 (Jan. 1972), 563–79.

8. *Dial*, 1 (July 1840), 5, 6, 7, 7–8, 8 ("recluse").

9. "The American Scholar," *ECW*, I, 59 ("mincing"); *Dial*, 1 (July 1840), 8–9, 10, 11 ("living influence"); [Sept. 25, 1839], FMW, Box 1 ("as thinkers"). Differing appraisals of the Unitarian establishment's critical community that Fuller critiques may be found in Martin Green, *The Problem of Boston: Some Readings in Cultural History* (New York, 1966); Daniel Walker Howe, *The Unitarian Conscience: Harvard Moral Philosophy, 1805–1861* (Cambridge, Mass., 1970); and Lewis P. Simpson, *The Man of Letters in New England and the South: Essays on the History of the Literary Vocation in America* (Baton Rouge, 1973), 1–61.

10. To SHW, June 10, 1839, *FL*, II, 75 ("standard"); "A Record of Impressions Produced by the Exhibition of Mr. Allston's Pictures in the Summer of 1839," *Dial*, 1 (July

1840), 73, 74, 75, 82 ("no poetical ground-work"). For an example of Fuller's appreciation of the patriotic value of art, see her review "The Atheneum Exhibition of Painting
and Sculpture," *Dial*, 1 (Oct. 1840), 260–64.

11. Richard Henry Dana to William C. Bryant, [Sept. 23, 1840], Dana Family Papers,
MHi ("ignorance"); July 20, 1840, "CLS, n.p." ("dogmatism"); Aug. 20, 1838, "CLS, n.p."
("inarticulate sound"). Allston's reputation is appraised in Edgar P. Richardson, *Washington Allston: A Study of the Romantic Artist in America* (Chicago, 1948); and William
H. Gerdts and Theodore E. Stebbins, Jr., *"A Man of Genius": The Art of Washington Allston
(1779–1843)* (Boston, 1979). For Fuller's acknowledgment of her shaky understanding
of artistic "ways and means" because of her lack of opportunity to view original European
art works, see [to RWE]*, [ca. 1839]*, *FL*, VI, 129. Barbara Novak explores nineteenth-
century American landscape painters' formal strategies for achieving spiritual ends in
Nature and Culture: American Landscape and Painting 1825–1875 (1985; New York,
1995).

12. Quoted in Cooke, *Historical and Biographical Introduction*, I, 75–76 ("domestic"); July 5, 1840, *FL*, II, 146 ("eaglet motion"); quoted in Cooke, *Historical and Biographical Introduction*, I, 75 ("run it down"); Aug. 6, 1840, MB ("wrathy as fighting
cocks"); Nov. 7, 1840, *FL*, II, 181 ("meat and drink").

13. GR to James Marsh, Oct. 17, 1840, in *Coleridge's American Disciples: The Selected Correspondence of James Marsh*, ed. John J. Duffy (Amherst, Mass., 1973), 239–
41 (Marsh); JFC to Anna Huidekoper Clarke, Sept. 25, 1840, in *CA*, 133 ("fermenting");
to CPC, Oct. 1, 1841, *EL*, VII, 474 (Ripley resigned); "The Art of Life,—The Scholar's
Calling," *Dial*, 1 (Oct. 1840), 175–82 (Hedge's contribution); to JFC, July 26, 1840, *FL*,
VI, 325 (*"crisis poems"*).

14. ABA, "Diary for 1840," July 1840, 110, Alcott Papers, MH ("Gastric Sayings");
quoted in Mar. 23, 1842, *EJMN*, VIII, 211 ("one passenger"); to MF, May 8, 1840, *EL*, II,
294 ("cold vague generalities"); ABA, "Diary for 1840," Alcott Papers, MH ("no gem");
Sept. 23, "PJ," 96 ("alter"); ABA to J. Westland Marston, [Sept. 1840]*, in Sept. 1840,
"AS40," 251 ("twilight Dial"); Nov. ca. 14?, 1841, *EL*, II, 464 ("more readable"); "To the
Editor of the Dial," Dec. 6, 1841, *Dial*, 2 (Apr. 1842), 409 ("Dial prefers").

15. ABA to J. Westland Marston, [Sept. 1840]*, in Sept. 1840, "AS40," 250 ("epicurean"); to Convers Francis, Dec. 18, 1840, "PFC," 203 ("daintily arrayed"); [early] July
1840, "PJ," 1 ("Young-mannish" and "Miss Dial"); Sept. 7, 1840, ibid., 60–61 ("lust for
power"); Aug. 9, 1840, ibid., 33–34 ("females"); July 17, 1840, ibid., 17 ("without fear").
Parker later said he intended his short-lived *Massachusetts Quarterly Review* to be "'the
Dial' with a beard," which, Higginson remarked, "turned out to be the beard without 'the
Dial.'" *HO*, 161.

16. MF to RWE, Sept. 16, 1841, *FL*, II, 232 ("Dialese"); to MF, Jan. 12, 1841, *EL*, II,
376 ("volatile regiment"); Mar. 20, 1842, *EJMN*, VIII, 203 ("Scholars"); to Abby Dwight
Woodbridge, July 6, 1841, *EL*, VII, 461 (*"voice of the individual"*); to RWE, July 19, 1840,
FL, II, 152 ("my approbation!"); July 21, 1840, *EL*, II, 315–16 ("sermon").

17. Sept. 5, 1839, *EJMN*, VII, 236 ("MF & FHH"); Apr. 24, 1840, FMW, box A
("blame"); Oct. 19, 1842, *EJMN*, VII, 471 ("finish"); July 19, 1842, *EL*, III, 74 ("rude truth");
to MF, Mar. 3, 1840, *EL*, II, 259 ("your demoniacal Shelley"); Apr. 8, 1840, ibid., 275
("best"); May 29?, 1840, ibid., 299 ("stiff"); May 31, 1840, *FL*, II, 136 ("How can you");
"The American Scholar," *ECW*, I, 67 ("the near"). Others of Fuller's Transcendentalist friends
found it difficult to understand what she saw in Shelley. See her exchange with Clarke in
June 20, 1840, *CL*, 139–14; and to JFC, [ca. July 1840], *FL*, II, 144. Vivian C. Hopkins,

Spires of Form: A Study of Emerson's Aesthetic Theory (Cambridge, Mass., 1951), is useful on Emerson's literary aesthetics, but it needs to be supplemented by Matthiessen, *American Renaissance*, chaps. 1–4; Charles Feidelson, Jr., *Symbolism and American Literature* (Chicago, 1953), chap. 4; and Buell, *Literary Transcendentalism*, chap. 5.

18. July 2, 1840, *EL*, II, 311 ("strong black letters"); July 21, 1840, ibid., 316 ("little *bad*"); Aug. 4, 1840, *EL*, II, 322 ("different *Dial*").

19. July 2, 1840, *EL*, II, 311 ("partisan bigoted"); Nov. 12, 1843, *FL*, III, 160–61 ("different principle"). Fuller also expressed annoyance over Emerson's sending her submission to Thoreau and William Ellery Channing, who had vetoed it, thus seeming to take their word over hers (MF, Nov. 5, 1843, *EL*, III, 222; and to RWE, Nov. 12, 1843, *FL*, III, 160–61), but the broader issue for her remained that of inclusiveness. See, for example, her claim on this point in to RWE, Apr. 9, 1842, *FL*, III, 58. Indeed, Emerson's only specific suggestion to Fuller of an article by an "outsider" on a politically radical subject was one he proposed be written not by a "fanatic" but by his friend George Bradford, "the properist person to write on that topic, as he knows the facts, has a heart, & is a little of a Whig & altogether a gentleman" (July 27 and 28, 1840, *EL*, II, 318; to RWE, Nov. 7, 1840, *FL*, II, 182). Emerson even unsuccessfully tried to keep out of the magazine Parker's sensational article denouncing the Unitarian Hollis Street Council for ratifying the firing of the temperance minister John Pierpont, a topic that he bluntly told Parker was "most unpoetic unspiritual & un Dialled" (Sept. 8, 1842, *EL*, III, 86). When it came to *Dial* practice, Emerson was no ideological rough.

20. July 2, 1840, *EL*, II, 311 ("betray"); July 31, 1840, *EJMN*, VII, 388 ("hodiurnal"); June 23, 1842, *FL*, III, 70 ("means of development"); Sept. 25, 1839, FMW, box 1 (publish her writing).

21. To Eliza Thayer Clapp, Oct. 5, 1840, *EL*, VII, 415 (*"objective"*); Dec. 6, 1840, *FL*, II, 189 ("not *poetical* merit"); to JRL, Dec. 10, 1840, *EL*, II, 367 ("gay verses"); "To Contributors," *Dial*, 2 (July 1841), 136 ("not without merit"). *FL* (190 n5) identifies "these sonnets" that Fuller balked at as Ellery Channing's, but RWE-JRL, Dec. 10, 1840, *EL*, II, 367, makes clear that she was referring to Lowell's submitted verses.

22. To CS, July 21, 1840, *EL*, VII, 396 ("rude"); Sept. 12, 1840, *EL*, II, 331 ("parse & spell?").

23. May 25, 1840, *EJMN*, VII, 359 ("bold"); Nov. 15, 1851, *TJ*, III, 188 ("sublimoslipshod"); May 15, 1842, *EJMN*, VIII, 174 ("pretty blasphemies"); Aug. 30, 1842, *FL*, VI, 338 ("I have a verse of yours"); [ca. 1841]*, *OM*, I, 209 ("Till he needs the public"); Oct. 2, 1841, *FL*, II, 238 ("chill"); *Dial*, 3 (July 1842), 112–23 ("Two Dolons"). Emerson paid tribute to Fuller's superior handling of Newcomb in *OM*, I, 209.

24. July 5, 1840, *FL*, II, 146 ("frequent aid"); Aug. 10, 1840, "PJ," I, 35 ("foolish"); Nov. 6, 1839, *EJMN*, VII, 293 ("ethical verses"); to MF, Apr. 22, 1841, *EL*, II, 395 ("Morgue"); "Thoreau's 'The Service,'" in Kenneth Walter Cameron, *The Transcendentalists and Minerva*, 3 vols. (Hartford, 1958), III, 935, 956–57 ("brave man"); Dec. 1, [1840], *FL*, II, 185 (*"pained"*). *EJMN* editors claim that Ward's disparagement refers to Channing's "ethical verses," but Tilton convincingly demonstrates the reference is to Thoreau's (*EJMN*, VII, 293 n88; *EL*, VII, 360 n101). For another example of Transcendentalists' disparagement of Thoreau's early writings, see JFC, July 20, 1840, "CLS, n.p."

25. Oct. 18, 1841, *FL*, II, 242, 243 ("fusion and glow"); to MF, Nov. ca. 14? and ca. 15?, 1841, *EL*, II, 465 (disappointed Emerson). Thoreau later included a version of his "mountains" poem in his essay "A Walk to Wachusett," an account of the excursion he would take with Fuller's brother Richard, which Thoreau would eventually publish in the

Boston Miscellany of Literature and Fashion, 3 (Jan. 1843), 31–36. For appraisals of Thoreau's *Dial* writings, see Robert D. Richardson, Jr., *Henry David Thoreau: A Life of the Mind* (Berkeley, 1986), 74–76, 83–85, 111; and Charles R. Anderson, "Thoreau and *The Dial*: The Apprentice Years," in Charles Woodress, ed., *Essays Mostly on Periodical Publishing in America* (Durham, N.C., 1973), 92–120. Although he misinterprets Fuller's critical ideal as individualistic, Steven Fink, *Prophet in the Marketplace: Thoreau's Development as a Professional Writer* (Princeton, 1992), chaps. 1–2, is enlightening about Thoreau and the *Dial*.

26. Sept. 12, 1840, *EJMN*, VII, 395 ("lonely"). Horace Greeley estimated that the *Dial*'s total circulation averaged one to two thousand copies (Horace Greeley, *Recollections of a Busy Life* [New York, 1868], 170). For *Dial* sales figures, see also Joel Myerson, "A Union List of the *Dial* (1840–1844) and Some Information about Its Sales," *Papers of the Bibliographic Society of America*, 67 (1973), 325–28.

27. "The Significance of *The Dial*," in Henry Steele Commager, *The Search for a Usable Past, and Other Essays in Historiography* (New York, 1967), 156 ("without the Church"); May 25, 1840, *EJMN*, VII, 359 ("slightly ludicrous").

28. "The Editors to the Reader," *Dial*, 1 (July 1840), 4 ("sunshine"); July 5, 1840, *FL*, II, 145 ("sadness"); July 1840, ibid., 145 ("cannot make much use"); Sept. 26, 1843, *FL*, III, 150 ("dying").

29. [Ca. Nov. 1840], FMW, box A ("drudgery"); Nov. 1840, *FL*, II, 181 ("hired house").

30. Jacob Barker to Thomas W. Ward, September 12, 1840, Ward Papers, MHi ("view to profit"); to CS, Sept. 6, 1840, *EL*, VII, 404 ("fall"); *EL*, II, 327, 327–28 ("*you* must be generous"); *EL*, VII, 414 ("wedding"); Aug. 29, 1840, *EL*, II, 328 ("bereavement"); [Oct.] 3, [1844], "FJ44–1," 121 ("most moving event"); Mar. [8?], 1842, *FL*, III, 47 ("different regions"); December 30, 1849, *FL*, V, 307 ("No!"); July [5], 1844, "FJ44–1," 77 ("sentimental"); Sept. 4, 1842, "FJ42–1," 334 ("petit maître"); Sept. 4, 1842, *EJMN*, VII, 465 ("I like women"). How deeply the Barker-Ward marriage entered into the conflicted fantasy life of the Transcendentalists is shown by the ever-benevolent Elizabeth Peabody, who dreamed Anna had been captured, not by Ward, but by the financially needy John Sullivan Dwight! To JSD, Sept. 20, 1840, *PL*, 247. Eleanor M. Tilton, "The True Romance of Anna Hazard Barker and Samuel Gray Ward," in *SAR, 1987*, 53–72, is a useful chronology of the couple's courtship, although in my view Tilton's tart characterizations of the ultra-romantic Fuller, exculpations of the cool Emerson, and soft-focus portrait of the sensibly worldly Barker and Ward miss the complex pathos of that collective entanglement.

31. George Santayana, "The Genteel Tradition in American Philosophy," in *Winds of Doctrine* (London, 1913), 200 (could never confess). The Fuller *Memoirs* editors are probably the most forthcoming about her "mystical" crisis that year, although Channing is sympathetic and Emerson is cool. *OM*, I, 219–34, 308–11, and II, 9–12, 31–39; and *HO*, 96–102. For continuities between Romantic and psychoanalytic modes of psychological understanding, see Henri F. Ellenberger, *Discovery of the Unconscious: The History and Evolution of Dynamic Psychiatry* (New York, 1970).

32. *Dial*, 1 (July 1840), 134 ("Dialogue"); [Mar. 1840], FMW, box A ("too officiously to all"). Fuller used the name "Dahlia" for her signature in that July's *Boston Quarterly Review* book "Chat." For examples of her autobiographical use of the sun-flower image, see Jan. [24], 1841, OC, 91, and, in two literary versions, "The Magnolia of Lake Pontchartrain," *Dial*, 1 (Jan. 1841), 303; and "Yuca Filamentosa," ibid., 2 (Jan. 1842), 286–88.

33. [Ca. Jan. 1840], Margaret Fuller Ossoli Notebook, inserted between 148 and 149, Emerson Family Papers, MH ("wise submission"); OC, 119 ("mystic"); *OM*, I, 141 ("taken up"); ibid., 308 ("ecstatic solitude").

34. *FL*, II, 157–58 (*"carbuncle"*); ibid., 158–59 ("my spiritual life").

35. [Oct. 1842], "FJ42–2," 287 ("emblematic"); [June 27], 1844, "FJ44–1," 64 ("male").

36. In the pro-Emerson camp, the distortions of the Emerson-Fuller friendship began with Emerson's own account in the *Memoirs*, in which, carefully screening out his own involvement, he wears a half-true mask of surprise, puzzlement, and ironic detachment. (See, for example, *OM*, I, 287–89.) For examples of the Emerson-as-misogynist and Fuller-as-victim camp, see Joseph Jay Deiss, *The Roman Years of Margaret Fuller: A Biography* (New York, 1969), chap. 9; and Joyce Warren, *The American Narcissus: Individualism and Women in Nineteenth-Century American Fiction* (New Brunswick, 1984), chaps. 2–3. For equally caricatured pictures of Emerson as the wise and patient victim, see Carl F. Strauch, "Hatred's Swift Repulsions: Emerson, Margaret Fuller, and Others," *Studies in Romanticism* 7 (Winter 1968), 65–103; and Carlos Baker, *Emerson among the Eccentrics: A Group Portrait* (New York, 1996), chaps. 6, 11, 13, 16, 18. Recently the tide appears to be turning toward more balanced interpretations. For different versions, see Christina Zwarg, *Feminist Conversations: Fuller, Emerson, and the Play of Reading* (Ithaca, 1995); and Phyllis Cole, "Woman Questions: Emerson, Fuller, and New England Reform," in Charles Capper and Conrad Wright, eds., *Transient and Permanent: The Transcendentalist Movement and Its Contexts* (Boston, 1999), 408–46.

37. Dec. 6, 1839, "PFC," 153 ("1/2"); Nov. 14, 1839, *EJMN*, VII, 301 ("impersonal God"); ca. Summer 1841, quoted in *EJMN*, VIII, x ("hunger to love"); Nov. 14, 1839, *EJMN*, VII, 301 ("churl's mask"). For the opening act in the Fuller-Emerson drama, see *CF-1*, 323–30. The first Emerson biographer to comprehensively demolish the "aloof sage" stereotype is Robert D. Richardson, Jr., in his superb biography *Emerson: The Mind on Fire* (Berkeley, 1995), which emphasizes, as the subtitle aptly suggests, Emerson's intellectually passionate side.

38. Jan. 17?, 1840, *EL*, VII, 250 ("chapter of friendship"); Feb. 19, 1840, *EJMN*, VII, 338–39 ("little pleasure"); June 11, 1840, ibid., 368 ("I cold"); May 29, 1840, *EL*, VII, 384 ("worshipper of Friendship").

39. May 26, 1840, *FL*, VI, 322 ("perpetual wall"); MF, journal, [Jan. 22, 1840], Emerson Family Papers, MH ("heart of love"); to JFC, May 7, 1830, *FL*, VI, 167 ("Genius"); to SGW, *FL*, III, 89 ("victories"); Charles Emerson to Elizabeth Hoar, Mar. 6–[7], 1836, MH ("cared for spiritually"). For private expressions the previous winter of both Fuller's exclusivist love of and frustration with Emerson, see *CF-1*, 328–30.

40. *Dial*, 1 (July 1840), 136 ("Never!"); June 8, 1840, *EL*, II, 304 ("your Friends"); July 27, 1840, ibid., 318 ("such an arrival"). When Fuller first read in the printed *Dial* her outing neatly nestled at the end of a string of her verses headed by her Dahlia "Dialogue" love plaint, she seems to have had second thoughts. "Did you observe the absurdity of the last two pages," she wrote sheepishly to Emerson. "These are things they had to fill up blanks and which thinking twas pity such beautiful thoughts should be lost put in for climax. Admire the winding up, the concluding sentence!!" July 5, 1840, *FL*, II, 146. To get a sense of the changing atmosphere in Transcendental circles on the privacy question, one need only recall that Fuller herself, who only the year before had said she would feel "profaned" by printing her "personal" poems, now wrote in her journal that she felt "pleased with the thought of addressing" her friends in her esoterically personal poems. To JFC, Jan. 8, 1839, *FL*, II, 34; [ca. winter 1839–40], "FS," 172.

41. Folded sheet between pp. 176 and 177 in "Margaret Fuller Ossoli Notebook," RWE, journal, vol. III, Emerson Family Papers, MH ("his only friend");

42. Aug. 16, 1840, *EJMN*, VII, 509 ("She taxed me"); *OM*, I, 288 ("commercial"); Aug. 16, 1840, *EJMN*, VII, 509–10 ("icy barriers").

43. Aug. 16, 1840, *EL*, II, 323–24 ("University"); to CS, Aug. 28, 1840, *EL*, VII, 402 ("golden days"); to CS, Sept. 6, 1840, ibid., 404 ("ideal relations"); *EL*, II, 327–28 ("Celestial"). For a more detailed sketch of Emerson's idea for a Transcendentalist residential college in Concord, see To?, Aug. 16?, 1840, *EL*, VII, 398–400. His journal version, which he wrote in the entry immediately following his account of his conversation with Fuller on the fourteenth, may be found in *EJMN*, VII, 510. For an example of the giddiness Emerson could work himself into about Anna, see Oct. 7, 1839, *EJMN*, VII, 260; and to CS, Sept. 6, 1840, *EL*, VII, 404, and Oct. 5, 1840, ibid., 414.

44. "Bettina!" *Dial*, 2 (July 1841), 83 ("Bettina!"); George Willis Cooke, ed., *The Poets of Transcendentalism: An Anthology* (Boston, 1903), 316 ("American Bettina"); to MF, July? 31?, 1839?, *EL*, III, 210 ("discreet and cowardly"); *EL*, II, 325 ("I love also"); Aug. 28, 1840, *EL*, VII, 402 ("your brother?"); Sept. 6, 1840, ibid, 403–4 ("full of heat"); Sept. 11, 1840, Tappan Papers, MH ("be my God"). Tilton's volume VII of *EL* prints for the first time many of Emerson's letters to Sturgis as well corrects some dating and other errors that Rusk made in volume II. Although she includes lengthy excerpts from many of Sturgis's letters to Emerson, for the sake of completeness I have used the original manuscripts, which are in the Tappan Papers in MH.

45. *EL*, II, 328 ("demands all"); *OM*, I, 308–9 ("mystical trances").

46. Sept. 12, 1840, *EL*, 330 ("friendsick"); Sept. 13, 1840, ibid., 332 ("we are brother & sister"); to MF, Sept. 25, 1840, ibid., 337 ("undaunted"); *EJMN*, VII, 400 ("Your body?"). Despite the fact that this entry only shows *Emerson's* words, which he probably did not speak to Fuller, several scholars have suggested that the passage proves that Fuller declared her physical love for Emerson and he sensibly rejected her proposition without bothering to consider what she actually wrote about her feelings toward him. See, for example, Strauch, "Hatred's Swift Repulsions," 70.

47. Notwithstanding Emerson's famous call for a literature of the body in "American Scholar," in his journal in these years he frequently expresses displeasure with the state or appearance of his and others' bodies.

48. Sept. 25, 1840, *EL*, II, 336–37 ("your own methods"); *ECW*, II, 37 ("Spontaneity").

49. Sept. 29, 1840, *FL*, II, 159–60 ("no usurper"); to CS, Sept. 26, 1840, ibid., 158 ("mighty changes"); Sept. 29, 1840, ibid., 160 ("'foe' in your friend").

50. Even Bell Chevigny, who writes with great sympathy toward Fuller, asserts that Fuller's September 29 letter reveals "that her need for support on the eve of the Ward-Barker wedding has reduced her to passionate dependency." This is certainly partly true, but the letter also shows that she regarded such dependency, whether realistically or self-deludingly, as the way to independence—or, in psychoanalytic language, "regression in the service of the ego," in this case through invited transference. Emerson, of course, declined the invitation, causing, for better or worse, her extreme reactions discussed below. Bell Gale Chevigny, *The Woman and the Myth: Margaret Fuller's Life and Writings*, rev. ed. (1976; Boston, 1994), 124.

51. To MF, Oct. 7, 1840, *FL*, II, 344 ("external"); Oct. 1, 1840, *EL*, II, 340 ("seven chords"); Oct.?, ca. 2?, 1840?, ibid., 342, 342–43 ("you receive nothing").

52. Oct. 7, 1840, *EL*, II, 344–45 ("wild element"); Sept. 17, 1840, *EJMN*, VII, 395 ("experimenter"); to RWE, Sept. 29, 1840, *FL*, II, 159 ("manifold"); Oct. 7, 1840, *EL*, II, 344 ("of no account").

54. Oct. 20, 1840, *EL*, II, 349 ("cold room"); Oct.?, ca. 22?, 1840?, ibid., II, 351 ("a mute").

54. *EL*, II, 352, 353 ("wish it unwritten"). On Fuller's missing letter to Emerson, see, for example, to CS, Oct. 22, 1840, *FL*, II, 167.

55. *FL*, II, 167 ("His call"); ibid., 171 ("unfriendly friendliness").

56. [Ca. Nov. 1, 1840]*, *FL*, II, 178–79 (Curson millhouse visit); Oct. 18, 1840, *EL*, VII, 421, 422 ("superlative"); Nov. 8, [1840], ibid., 183 ("They make a volume"). For Fuller's movements that late October and early November, see *EL*, VII, 422–23 n184. My own account is largely consistent with Tilton's conclusions.

57. *EL*, VII, 422 ("scarred martyrs"); ibid., 422 n181 ("How beautiful"); ibid., 406 ("Oracle in Woman"); ibid., 421 ("most intelligible"); ibid., 421 n180 ("Do seers sneer?"); ibid., 422 ("Redeeming man"); ibid., 422 n182 ("Garrison"); ibid., 422 n184 ("positive degree"); [Nov. 3, 1840]*, *FL*, II, 170 ("secluded by a sneer"). This letter manuscript is misdated and possibly misidentified as a letter in ibid., 169. Cf. *EL*, VII, 422–23 n 184.

58. [Nov. 3, 1840]*, *FL*, II, 170 ("teach this sage"); [ca. late Nov., 1840]*, *FL*, VI, 144 ("*mediator*"). In her *Memoirs* Emerson cites this letter, which he identifies as having been written "to one of" her friends, to support his harsh verdict that Fuller's attempt to gain recognition "betray a pathetic alternation of feeling, between her aspiring for a perfect rest in the absolute Centre, and her necessity of a perfect sympathy with her friends." There is certainly something to this claim, although this particular letter does not demonstrate it but on the contrary shows her asking for "some tonics" of sympathy, as well as a realistic, if reluctant, willingness to adapt herself to his incapacity for displaying it. Emerson was surely right when he concluded about their quarrel over their friendship: "As I did not understand the discontent then,—of course, I cannot now. It was a war of temperaments, and could not be reconciled by words." *OM*, I, 288, 311.

59. For Fuller's earlier year's meetings, see "FB" and EPP, "Comments on Margaret Fuller's Conversations," [Fall-Winter 1839–40], Straker Collection, Antioch College. I have assigned dates of meetings on the basis of external evidence and the original manuscript used in "FB": EPP, "Journal of Margaret Fuller's Conversation Classes," EPP Papers, MWA.

60. [Ca. late Dec. 1839]*, "FB," 212, 213 ("the Infinite"); [ca. early Nov. 1840]*, *OM*, I, 342, 343 ("prettiness"); [ca. early Nov. 1840]*, *OM*, I, 341 ("compensation"). Fuller's translation of Schelling's lecture was its first one into English, although Coleridge had heavily paraphrased it in his *Literary Remains*, which she had read when it was published in 1836. Frederic Henry Hedge would later publish an abridged version of James Elliot Cabot's manuscript translation in Hedge's *Prose Writers of Germany* (Philadelphia, 1847), 510–20. Schulte-Sasse et al., *Theory as Practice* (180–94), include Friedrich Schlegel's seminal "Dialogue on Poesy" (1799). For a succinct discussion of the concept, see Beiser, *Romantic Imperative*, chap. 1.

61. [Ca. late Feb. 1840]*, "FB," 214 ("feared to trust"); [ca. early Mar. 1840]*, ibid., 215 ("intellectual differences"); [ca. mid-Mar. 1840]*, ibid., 217 ("women as plants"); Feb. 20, [1840], "FJ44–2" 39 ("no attribute"); [ca. late Feb. 1840]*, "FB," 214 ("different proportions").

62. Feb. 20, [1840], "FJ44–2," 37, 38, 39 ("distinction of sex").

63. [Ca. early Mar. 1840]*, "FB," 215, 215–16 ("objective" and "she did not"). Fuller would further explain her gendered distinction between "Genius" or the "self-conscious state of the faculties" and Minerva's realistic wisdom in "classifying and arranging upon it all that Genius creates—seeing the relations and proper values of things." *DM*, 78.

64. [Ca. mid-Mar.1840]*, "FB," 218 ("women of genius").

65. EPP, [ca. mid-Mar. 1840]*, "FB," 218 ("ordinary"); *Dial*, 1 (Jan. 1841), 362, 365, 366 ("walk alone"); "Concerning Women," newspaper column, Nov. 24, 1890, Caroline Wells Healey Dall Papers, MCR-S ("Margaret Fuller days"). Elizabeth Peabody's transcription of an extract from Sophia Ripley's paper "Woman" may be found in [ca. March 1840]*, "FB," 218–19.

66. EPP, report, [ca. Nov. 1840]*, *OM*, I, 340 ("less objectively"); Nov. 8, [1840], *FL*, II, 183 ("great changes"); Susan Channing Higginson to Susan Higginson Channing, [Feb.] 10, 1840, Higginson-Cabot-Channing Papers, MHi ("making people talk"); Julia Ward Howe, *Margaret Fuller* (Boston, 1883), 111 ("new power"); EPP, report, [Dec. 1840]*, *OM*, I, 340 ("so brilliant"); Nov. 7, 1840, *FL*, II, 182 ("satisfactory communication"); Nov. 8, [1840], *FL*, II, 183 ("glistening eyes"). The *OM* version of Peabody's report on Fuller's first conversation (Nov. 4, 1840) identifies this meeting as having been her "fifth," but this is clearly a slip, a misreading, or a misprint. Cf. *OM*, I, 340, and "FB," 223–24n4. For additional glowing reports on Fuller's new series that winter see, to MF, *EL*, II, 361; and statement of RWE, *OM*, I, 339.

67. *Harriet Martineau's Autobiography*, 3 vols. (London, 1877), II, 71 ("elect of the earth"); *HO*, 129 ("extraordinary mistake"); *Martineau's Autobiography*, III, 201 ("immense letter"). For Fuller's earlier falling out with Martineau over her letter on Martineau's book, see *CF-1*, 222–25. Sarah Clarke, who had seen a lot of Martineau when she had been in Boston and again when Clarke had visited her home at Ambleside, where she had spoken of Fuller "with the greatest respect," attributed Martineau's malice to her frequent "fevered and fitful" states of ill health and her capacity to believe and repeat the "wildest possible" gossip. SC to TWH, Apr. 18, 1977, Oc, 204. There was a kernel of truth to Martineau's characterization: Fuller's women were not quite all, as Higginson claims, "the very women who were fighting Miss Martineau's battles. Some were Garrisonians, but some were also moderately antislavery and a few even indifferent to the issue. *HO*, 128.

68. To Maria Weston Chapman, Dec. 26, 1840, *FL*, II, 197 ("late movements"); Jan. 1841, "Weston Papers," Anti-Slavery Collection, MB ("A. S. Reform"). For Fuller's earlier sympathy with Channing's antislavery position, see journal, [ca. Winter 1835–36]*, *OM*, I, 129–30. Examples of Fuller's private dislike of Garrisonian rhetoric may be found in CS, Feb. 7, [1839], *FL*, II, 48; and "TTE," [ca. late Nov. 1847]*, *NYDT*, Jan. 1, 1848, 1. For Unitarianism and antislavery, see Howe, *Unitarian Conscience*, 270–305; and Douglas C. Stange, *Patterns of Antislavery among American Unitarians, 1831–1860* (Rutherford, N.J., 1977). There exists no adequate study of the Transcendentalists and antislavery. For several decades views have run the gamut from versions of Stanley M. Elkins's line that the Transcendentalists and abolitionists were intellectual coconspirators to Aileen Kraditor's that they were radically at odds, the one similarity being the authors' hostility to the Transcendentalists. For much more sympathetic recent appraisals of individual Transcendentalists and the antislavery question, see Len Gougeon, *Virtue's Hero: Emerson, Antislavery, and Reform* (Athens, Ga., 1990); Richard F. Teichgraeber III, *Sublime Thoughts/Penny Wisdom: Situating Emerson and Thoreau in the American Market* (Baltimore, 1995), chaps. 3–6; Albert J. von Frank, "Mrs. Brackett's Verdict: Magic and Means in Transcendental Antislavery Work," in Capper and Wright, *Transient and Permanent*, 385–407; and Dean Grodzins, *American Heretic: Theodore Parker and Transcendentalism* (Chapel Hill, 2002), chap. 7.

69. Emerson's suspicion of abolitionist philosophy was even greater than Fuller's at this time. See Sept. 8, 1840, *EJMN*, VII, 393, and Oct. 24, 1841, *EJMN*, VIII, 119.

70. Oct. 24, 1840, *EL*, II, 352 ("youngest child"); [early 1840]*, *FL*, II,107 ("exacting too much"); quoted in *OM*, I, 206 ("talk of anything").

71. [July 10, 1841], "SL," 212 ("I am weary"); Sept. 22, 1840, Tappan Papers, MH ("better hour"); [Oct. 10, 1840], Tappan Papers, MH ("Have you not faith"); Sept. 26, 1840, *FL*, II, 158 ("mighty changes"); Oct. 18, 1840, *EL*, VII, 421 ("occult"); to CS, Oct. 18, 1840, *FL*, II, 163 ("puzzled and disconcerted"); Oct. 20, 1840, *EL*, II, 349 ("scolding letter"); Nov. 22?, 1840, ibid., VII, 431–32 ("at a loss"); to CS, [ca.

early 1840]*, *FL*, II, 105 ("search after Eros"); ibid., 163 ("Your recognition"); Oct. 22, 1840, ibid., 166–67 ("Love goes forth"). Sturgis's letter to which Emerson replied on October 18 is now lost, but its contents can be partly reconstructed from other letters that refer to it. Tilton quotes from a note initialed "C.T." (Caroline Tappan) and dated "Nov 1871" that further confirms the subject of Sturgis's missing letter (*EL*, VII, 421 n179).

72. To WHC, Nov. 8, [1840], *FL*, II, 184 ("calm consciousness"); *OM*, I, 229 ("totally helpless"); Oct. 22, 1840, *FL*, II, 168 ("stern and fearless"); to CS, Jan. 24, 1841, ibid., 199 ("images"); Oct. 22, 1840, ibid., 167–69 ("holy Mother"). Although Fuller implied that she had "comprehended" at the time this connection between her Groton experience and an ascetic life, it is likely she at least partly retrojected the link backward from this "crisis" year. Her Mariology, which had surfaced during her disappointment with Ward the previous fall, would surface again in a protofeminist context in her later writings on women.

73. To CS, Oct. 22, 1840, *FL*, II, 169 ("Only one soul"); *OM*, II, 38–39 ("take me!"); Oct. 22, 1840, *FL*, II, 168 ("nun like dedication"); Jan. [24], 1841, OC, 91 ("full breath of love"); January 5, 1841, OC, 132 ("Daily death"). For additional cryptic allusions to Fuller's libidinal conflicts intermixed with her religious meditations, see other entries on Jan. 5, 1841 (OC, 132).

74. [Mar. 1840], FMW, box A ("death from love"); "Mourning and Melancholia," in *Standard Edition of the Complete Psychological Works of Sigmund Freud*, ed. James Strachey, 24 vols. (London, 1953–74), XIV, 237–58.

75. Oct. 25 and 28, 1840, *FL*, II, 176 ("called for a Father"); to CS, September 26, 1840, ibid., 159 ("home"); Oct. 22, 1840, ibid., 168 ("recognized"); Jan. 5, 1841, OC, 132 ("domestic gods"); MF, journal, [ca. early Mar. 1834], FMW, box A ("sea of blood"); Jan. 24, 1841, OC, 91 ("feet bled").

76. [To GTD, ca. Oct. 1839]*, *FL*, VI, 134 ("unsightly wound").

Chapter Two

1. Feb. 19 and 25, 1841, *FL*, II, 202, 203 ("all feeling"); Feb. 21, 1841, OC, 95 ("*wish I were a man*"); to WHC, Feb. 25, 1841, *FL*, II, 203 ("knight"); to JFC, May 7, 1830, *FL*, VI, 168 ("asking aimless hearts"). Although in *FL*, VI, 330, the OC, 95, manuscript is taken from *HO*, 101–2, 111–12, and identified, following *HO*, as a fragment of a letter to Channing of Feb. 21, 1841, both the holograph and its contents show that it is part of this Feb. 19 and 25 letter.

2. To WHC[?], Oct. 19, 1840, FL, II, 165 ("interview"); to WHC, [Sept. 1?, 1844?], FL, III, 224 (mother's love of flowers). One of the few scholars to give serious attention to Fuller's fables is Jeffrey Steele, who presents a gynocentric mythic reading of them in his *Transfiguring America: Myth, Ideology, and Mourning in Margaret Fuller's Writing* (Columbia, Mo., 2001), chaps. 3–4. For the Western hermetic tradition, see D. P. Walker, *Spiritual and Demonic Magic from Ficino to Campanella* (London, 1958), and Frances A. Yates, *Giordano Bruno and the Hermetic Tradition* (Chicago, 1964). A classic discussion of the quest-romance is Harold Bloom, "The Internalization of Quest-Romance," in Harold Bloom, ed., *Romanticism and Consciousness: Essays in Criticism* (New York, 1970), 3–24.

3. Oct. 19, 1840, *FL*, II, 166 ("pure feminine beauty "); *Dial*, 2 (Jan. 1842), 286, 288 ("flood of gentleness"); *Dial*, 1 (Jan. 1841), 299, 300, 303, 304, 304–5; to WHC, Oct. 25,

1840, *FL*, II, 171 ("questioning"). Another source for Fuller's Magnolia tale may have been her mother's description of such a flower in a letter that winter from New Orleans. See MCF to RFF, Jan. 7, 1841, FMW, VIII, 95.

4. *Dial*, 1 (Apr. 1841), 462, 463, 464, 465, 466, 467 ("art magic"). Walker's *Spiritual and Demonic Magic* discusses numerous notions that parallel or resonate with ones in Fuller's fables. For German *Naturphilosophie*, see Robert J. Richards, *The Romantic Conception of Life: Science and Philosophy in the Age of Goethe* (Chicago, 2002), chap. 2 and pt. 2. For a cogent discussion of Neoplatonist plots of return in Romantic literature, see M. H. Abrams, *Natural Supernaturalism: Tradition and Revolution in Romantic Literature* (New York, 1971), chap. 3. For the gendered use of nature and the perceiving authorial eye in English Romantic writing, see Anne K. Mellor, *Romanticism and Gender* (New York, 1993), chap. 1.

5. "The Two Dolons. From the Ms. Symphony of Dolon. The First Dolon," *Dial*, 3 (July 1842), 112–23.

6. *Knickerbocker* 17 (Feb. 1841), 171 ("autobiography of a Magnolia tree"); *New-Yorker*, 10 (Jan. 23, 1841), 291 ("too fanciful"); *New-Yorker*, 11 (Apr. 10, 1841), 61 ("do not like"); Jan. 5, 1841, *EL*, II, 378 ("fell into the Massachusetts"); Jan. 13, 1841, ibid., VII, 443 ("balm"); quoted in *OM*, I, 219 ("night"); "Festus," *Dial*, 2 (Oct. 1841), 257 ("demon"). In Neoplatonic Orphism, night often figures as nature's primordial element, as does Isis, who in Apuleius's *Golden Ass* is called "Queen of the Night."

7. To MF, Nov. 5, 1843, *EL*, III, 222 (composed at Emerson's); *OM*, I, 33 ("intoxicat[ed]"). Clarke (ibid., 11) indicates that Fuller wrote her autobiographical tale in 1840, but both Emerson's later letter to her indicating she wrote it at Bush and its contents indicate it was written in 1841. Freud's classic discussion of "Family Romances" appears in the *Standard Edition*, IX, 235–41.

8. EPP, quoted in newspaper article on a conversation about Margaret Fuller at the Concord School of Philosophy, Aug. 25, 1883, MB ("She really thought"); to WHC, [July?, 1841?], *FL*, II, 215 ("changeling"); *OM*, I, 33, 39 ("foreign"). For a further discussion of the common use of this sketch as a literal rendering of her childhood, see *CF-1*, 363–64 n8.

9. Feb. 28, 1841, OC, 95 ("all calm"); [April 5, 1841], *FL*, II, 206 ("begin to revive"); [May 5, 1844], "FJ44–2," 6 ("intimate communion"); July 11, 1848, *FL*, V, 86 ("angels"); Mar. 20, 1842, *FL*, III, 55 ("era of illumination").

10. MF, "Romaic and Rhine Ballads," *Dial*, 3 (Oct. 1842), 147 ("passion-stirred fancy"); [ca. Spring 1842]*, *FL*, VI, 146 ("Gunhilde"); to CS, Oct. 22, 1840, *FL*, II, 167 ("lonely Vestal"). For a feminist psychoanalytic argument for the biographical centrality of Fuller's crisis of "mourning," see Jeffrey Steele, "Margaret Fuller's Rhetoric of Transformation," in Margaret Fuller, *Woman in the Nineteenth Century*, ed. Larry J. Reynolds (New York, 1998), 278–97. My understanding of the connections among family romances, mourning, and identity "crises" in Fuller's psychology here has been influenced by both postorthodox Freudian "ego" psychoanalytic theory and its recent feminist revisions. The classic work in the first category is Erik H. Erikson, *Identity: Youth and Crisis* (New York, 1968). For the second, I have found especially valuable Nancy Chodorow, *The Reproduction of Mothering: Psychoanalysis and the Sociology of Gender* (Berkeley, 1978); and Jessica Benjamin, *The Bonds of Love: Psychoanalysis, Feminism, and the Problem of Domination* (New York, 1988).

11. HM to MF, Aug. 9, 1841, FMW, XVI, 25 ("surprized"); to RFF, Dec. 1, 1841, *FL*, II, 254 ("far better"); Mar. 20, 1842, *FL*, III, 55 ("insane"); [ca. spring 1842]*, *FL*, VI, 146 ("worthy to love").

12. EPP, journal, *OM*, II, 348 ("historical part"); to CS, Feb. 26, 1841, *EL*, VII, 445 ("party"); to RWE, Feb. 20, 1841, *FL*, II, 203–4 (small gathering); to CS, Feb. 26, 1841, *EL*, VII, 445 ("veritable class"); Emerson's Account Book for 1840–1844, cited in *EL*, VII, 445–46 n19, CHD to TWH, May 29, 1908, FMW, box A, and *DM*, 9 (ticket prices).

13. June 16, 1839, *EJMN*, VII, 213 ("insulated"); Jan. 4, 1841, II, 23 ("bright sayings"); JFC to TP, Feb. 24, 1841, JFC Papers, MH ("struck dumb"); Feb. 25, [18]41, JFC Papers, MH ("myths"). For lists of class attendees, see JFC, "Notes on Grecian Mythology," [ca. spring 1841], Perry-Clarke Collection, MHi; and *DM*, 17–22. Healey's reports need to be used warily. She is often defensively prickly and, especially toward Emerson, outright hostile. In addition, trying to compensate for her lack of knowledge of speakers' assumptions and nuances, she wrote down "nothing but [their] very words," which undoubtedly accounts for the frustratingly summative and elliptical character of her record. (Journal, Mar. 22, 1841, in Joel Myerson, "Caroline Dall's Reminiscences of Margaret Fuller," *Harvard Library Bulletin,* 22 [Oct. 1974], 423). I have tried to reduce the transcripts' tendentiousness and obscurities by omitting Dall's gratuitously added complaints, cavils, and obvious distortions, especially in matters of tone, and by interpreting her speakers' recorded remarks in light of their larger views, about which Dall was often innocent.

14. *DM*, 40–41 ("national mind[s]"); Journal "1840," FMW, box 1 ("old Schlegel idea"); *DM*, 26 ("Infinite"). While there is no evidence that Fuller read Schelling's *Philosophie of Mythologie,* she was probably familiar with his *Philosophie der Kunst* lectures, in which he elaborated on his mythological ideas. Burton Feldman and Robert D. Richardson, Jr., *The Rise of Modern Mythology, 1700–1850* (Bloomington, Ind., 1971), is a useful introductory guide to early modern mythography. For German Romantic ideas of mythology, see Edward Allen Beach, *The Potencies of God(s): Schelling's Philosophy of Mythology* (Albany, 1994); and George S. Williamson, *The Longing for Myth in Germany: Religion and Aesthetic Culture from Romanticism to Nietzsche* (Chicago, 2004), chaps. 2–3. A helpful account of antebellum classical scholarship may be found in Caroline Winterer, *The Culture of Classicism: Ancient Greece and Rome in American Intellectual Life, 1780–1910* (Baltimore, 2002), chap. 3.

15. *DM*, 25, 29 ("progress"); journal, [ca. 1841], FMW, Works, I, 587 ("all but the majority"); *DM*, 29, 35, 45 ("age of Plato").

16. *DM*, 43, 44, 45, 47, 105 ("cycle of mind"). For a good discussion of Emerson's, Alcott's, and Parker's ideas about mythology, see Robert D. Richardson, Jr., *Myth and Literature in the American Renaissance* (Bloomington, Ind., 1978).

17. *DM*, 44, 63, 67, 102–3, 117 ("wandering").

18. "FB," 207 ("wild beast"); *DM*, 112–13 ("her temptations"); *OM*, I, 349 ("excitement"); *DM*, 113–14, 118, 124, 131, 142 ("evil to be a good"). An excellent discussion of Romantic appropriations of the Neoplatonic and Christian "Fortunate Fall" may be found in Abrams, *Natural Supernaturalism,* chaps. 3–5. Emerson himself sometimes appropriated the myth. See R. A. Yoder, *Emerson and the Orphic Poet in America* (Berkeley, 1978); and B. L. Packer, *Emerson's Fall: A New Interpretation of the Major Essays* (New York, 1982).

19. *OM*, I, 348 ("entirely failed"); ibid., 347–48 ("incapacity of the men"); Mar. 14, 1841, *EL*, II, 384 ("I silenced them"); *DM*, 117 ("too many clergymen").

20. Mar. 27, 1841, "HL-3," 120 ("'well performed'" and fell asleep); journal, Mar. 23, 1841, *OM*, I, 349 ("to be entertained"). The meetings' hybrid character was especially confusing to the young Healey, who at one point was told by her patron Peabody not to speak since the meetings were not intended for conversation "so free, as those held during the day." *DM*, 10, 11–12, 46; "DR," 423.

21. *OM*, I, 349 ("uncompromising idealism"); to MF, Dec. ? 1?, 1840, *EL*, II, 364 ("*tri-pod*"); to MF, Dec. 31, 1842, *EL*, III, 108 (Fuller liked); TP to Convers Francis, Feb. 22, 1858, in John Weiss, *Life and Correspondence of Theodore Parker*, 2 vols. (New York, 1864), I, 364 (Parker detested); Boston newspaper, Aug. 25, 1883, OC, 10 ("wonderful insight!"). Later that fall Harris wrote to Higginson, "I heartily wish we had satisfactory reports of her lectures on Greek and Latin mythology." Oct. 16, 1883, OC, 227. There is some evidence in Fuller's and Emerson's papers that Emerson's new interest in both Neoplatonic philosophy and non-Christian religious texts was partly attributable to Fuller's mythological and esoteric preoccupations at this time. See, for example, to CS, July 7, 1841, *EL*, 462–63.

22. Feb. 2, 1841, *FL*, II, 201 ("top-most bubble"); [ca. Apr. 1840], FMW, box A ("words—words—words").

23. *Dial*, 1 (Apr. 1841), 496 ("verify"); CF to TP, Mar. 22, 1842, "PFC," 242 ("wicked"); *Dial*, 2 (Oct. 1841), 235, 237, 260 ("*sincere*"). Nearly half of possible future articles Fuller listed in her *Dial* notebook she planned to cast as dialogues, a form she would frequently exploit in books and articles.

24. To CS, June 3, [1842], *FL*, VI, 333, and ibid., 334 n1 (Hoffmann); EPP, report, [ca. Nov. 1840]*, *OM*, I, 343 ("greatest of arts"); to WHC, [Dec. 8?, 1840], *FL*, II, 190–91 (*La sonnambula*); quoted in Thomas Broyles, *"Music of the Highest Class": Elitism and Populism in Antebellum Boston* (New Haven, 1992), 201 ("small, but select"); "Lives of the Great Composers, Haydn, Mozart, Handel, Bach, Beethoven," *Dial*, 2 (Oct. 1841), 149, 150, 150–51, 202, 203 ("*the* living, growing art"); William Kinderman, *Beethoven* (Berkeley, 1995), 147, 277–78 ("structural control"); *Dial*, 2 (Oct. 1841), 189, 197, 201, 202 ("democratic"). John Dwight's review of the Academy's preceding winter concerts had appeared in the *Dial*'s first issue (1 [July 1840], 124–34). Mark Evan Bonds, *Music as Thought: Listening to the Symphony in the Age of Beethoven* (Princeton, 2006) includes excellent discussions of German Romantic music theory. For a cogent brief appraisal, see Ronald Taylor, "Romantic Music," in Siegbert Prawer, ed., *The Romantic Period in Germany: Essays by Members of the London University Institute of Germanic Studies* (New York, 1970), 259–304. For Beethoven's critical reputation, see, for Europe, Robin Wallace, *Beethoven's Critics* (Cambridge, England, 1986); and for America, Anne Hui-Hua Chan, "Beethoven in the United States to 1865" (Ph.D. diss., University of North Carolina, 1976), and Ora Frishberg Saloman, *Beethoven's Symphonies and J. S. Dwight: The Birth of American Music Criticism* (Boston, 1995).

25. *Dial*, 2 (Oct. 1841), 149 ("half-effaced"). The idea of the nineteenth-century "cult" of art music as an upper-middle-class status marker and mechanism of social control has been pervasive in American cultural history scholarship over the last thirty years, but for a particularly influential example, see Lawrence W. Levine, *Highbrow/Lowbrow: The Emergence of Cultural Hierarchy in America* (Cambridge, Mass., 1988), chap. 2. Contrasting interpretations may be found in Mark N. Grant, *Maestros of the Pen: A History of Classical Music Criticism in America* (Boston, 1998), chaps. 1–4; Broyles, *"Music of the Highest Class,"* esp. the introduction and chaps. 8–9, 11; and Peter Gay, *The Bourgeois Experience: Victoria to Freud* (New York, 1984–98), vol. IV, *The Naked Heart* (New York, 1995), 11–35. Insofar as Fuller used her music reviews to police the social behavior of concertgoers, she almost uniformly directed her ire not at the lower but the boorish upper classes. See below and chaps. 6 and 7. For Emerson's musical puzzlement, see his journal rumination on the "mystic" that he *wanted* to hear when listening to music and the "ridiculous" that wandered into his mind (Dec. 6, 1840, *EJMN*, VII, 536).

26. *FL*, II, 206 ("Oh William"); Nov. 25, 1843, FMW, box A (past genius-consolers); *OM*, I, 232 ("some uneasiness"). For a bowdlerized version of this Fuller letter in which "Jesus" is replaced by "saint or martyr," see *OM*, I, 232–34.

27. Journal "1840," FMW, box 1 ("Read Carlyle"). In Fuller's *Dial* planning notebook, she had listed a couple of her recent essays on French writers, but they never appeared. *FL*, II, 184, 191; and Journal "1840," FMW, box 1.

28. *Dial*, 3 (Oct. 1842), 273 ("stock poetry"); TP, "Journal," I, 182, MH-AH ("outgrown"); *Dial*, 2 (July 1841), 131, 132 ("hammering on a thought"); Nov. 19, 1841, *ECC*, 312–13 ("stalwart Yankee *man*").

29. Apr. 9, 1842, *FL*, III, 58 ("*not* me"); *Dial*, 3 (Jan. 1843), 415 ("thinnest"); *Dial*, 2 (July 1841), 133–34 ("Superficial").

30. [Ca. 1836], *OM*, I, 168 ("grace and delicacy"); review of Nathaniel Hawthorne, *Grandfather's Chair*, *Dial*, 1 (Jan. 1841), 405 ("gifted author"); *Dial*, 3 (July 1842), 130–31 ("great reserve"). Hawthorne's future sister-in-law Elizabeth Peabody, to whom Fuller probably wrote this earlier letter about him, would later claim that she, too, had thought the author was a woman when she first read his stories. To Francis Henry Lee, [1885], *PL*, 419–20; and to Thomas Wentworth Higginson, [ca. 1880s], ibid., 451–52. For a case that Fuller's views influenced Hawthorne's writings, see Thomas R. Mitchell, *Hawthorne's Fuller Mystery* (Amherst, Mass., 1998).

31. To JFC, May 13, 1837, *FL*, VI, 294 (Ripley's deadline); to CS, Mar. 4, 1839, *FL*, II, 60 ("ungenerous"); June 3, 1839, ibid., 69 ("shadow of one mind").

32. Apr. 21, 1840, *ECC*, 269 ("contrived"); Nov. 20, 1834, ibid., 107 ("Puritan in me"). For Goethe's reputation in nineteenth-century America, see Henry A. Pochmann, *German Culture in America: Philosophical and Literary Influences, 1600–1900* (Madison, 1957); Maxine Grefe, *Apollo in the Wilderness: An Analysis of Critical Reception of Goethe in America, 1806–1840* (New York, 1988); and *CF-1*, 129–30, 253–54. For Goethe's reputation in Germany after his death, see Wellek, *History of Modern Criticism*, vol. III, chap. 6. Among the Transcendentalists, Thoreau probably came the closest to Fuller's appreciation of Goethe as a truth-telling artistic genius, although, not surprisingly, he worried more than she did about his lack of the savage and heroic virtues.

33. To George Washington Greene, May 28, 1840, *LL*, II, 230 (Longfellow); "German Literature," *Dial*, 1 (Jan. 1841), 315–39 (Parker on Menzel); "Menzel's View of Goethe," ibid., 340, 343, 345–46 ("Philistine").

34. *Dial*, 2 (July 1841), 21 ("listener to nature"); *Dial*, 1 (Oct. 1840), 154 ("poet of the Actual"); *Dial*, 2 (July 1841), 18, 21, 32, 33–34 ("Dämonische"). Emerson himself, very possibly as a consequence of reading Fuller's essay, later recognized the inadequacy of his ethically critical stance toward Goethe. See *EJMN*, VII, 410.

35. *Dial*, 2 (July 1841), 2, 20, 26, 29, 41 ("not stopped"). For a fine discussion of Goethe's religion that is remarkably consistent with Fuller's view, see Jaroslav Pelikan, *Faust the Theologian* (New Haven, 1995).

36. *New-Yorker*, 11 (July 10, 1841), 269 ("luminous"); *Godey's Lady's Book*, 23 (Sept. 1841), 141 ("beautifully written"); July 3, 1841, *EL*, II, 436 ("admired"); *OM*, I, 243 ("Nowhere"); Pochmann, *German Culture in America*, 337 ("painfully slow"). William Torrey Harris found Fuller's essay so advanced he had to read it a second time. William Torrey Harris to TWH, Oct. 16, 1883, OC, 227.

37. "The Editors to the Reader," *Dial*, 1 (July 1840), 3 ("higher tone"); *OM*, I, 322 (friendly service"); TWH, Notes, [188?], OC, 22 (best papers). July 7, 1842, quoted in

George Willis Cooke, *An Historical and Biographical Introduction to Accompany the "Dial,"* 2 vols. (Cleveland, 1902), I, 80 ("manly expression").

38. MCF to MF, Dec. 6, 1840, FMW, VIII, 201 (agreed not to renew); MCF to MF, Apr. 20, 1841, ibid., 206 (renting in the city); Carl Guarneri, *Utopian Alternative: Fourierism in Nineteenth-Century America* (Ithaca, 1991), 60 (one hundred thousand adherents); to William Emerson, Dec. 21, 1840, *EL*, II, 371 (inequalities); Oct. 26, 1840, *EJMN*, VII, 526 (shame); Oct. 17, 1840, ibid., 408 ("long trumpeted theory"); Oct. 17, 1840, ibid., 408 ("hencoop"); Oct. 17, 1840, ibid., 407 ("new social plans"); MCF to MF, Dec. 6, 1840, FMW, VIII, 201 (mother endorsed plan); to MCF, July 20, 1841, *FL*, 217 (scotched the plan). For the origins and development of Brook Farm, see Anne C. Rose, *Transcendentalism as a Social Movement, 1830–1850* (New Haven, 1981), chaps. 4–5; and Sterling F. Delano, *Brook Farm: The Dark Side of Utopia* (Cambridge, Mass., 2004).

39. Quoted in EPP, "Journal of Margaret Fuller's Conversation Classes," [ca. after Dec. 28, 1839–early Jan. 1840], EPP Papers, MWA ("savages"); JFC to WHC, Mar. 29, 1837, JFC Papers, MH ("heavy"); Oct. 28, 1840, *FL*, II, 174–75 (Ripleys); Dec. 13, [1840], ibid., 194 ("We are not ripe"); [ca. Nov. 1840]*, ibid., 180 ("these terrible weights"); Mar. 29, 1841, ibid., 205 ("Others have looked").

40. To RWE, May 10, 1841, *FL*, II, 209 ("fledglings of Community"); Apr. 13, 1841, *HW*, XV, 527 ("transcendental heifer"); to WHC, Oct. 28, 1840, *FL*, II, 175 ("pathetic"); May 25, 1841, ibid., 210 ("letter from Lloyd"); to CKN, [June 1841], ibid., 212 (Lloyd's measles); Georgiana Bruce Kirby, *Years of Experience: An Autobiographical Narrative* (New York, 1887), 95–96 (Lloyd's denunciations); SR to MF, Sept. 23, [1841], FMW, X (stay the winter); ABF to RFF, Jan. 30, 1842, FMW, XIII, 12 (asked to remove him); Jan. 6, [1842], ibid., 34 ("so unreal"). It is possible that Lloyd suffered from bipolar disorder or perhaps some form of paranoid schizphrenia, but because the diagnostic categories used by his family to describe his condition were hardly those of modern psychiatry, any such claim would be largely speculative. For Lloyd's behavior and psychology, see *CF-1*, 168.

41. To RFF, Apr. 6, 1841 *FL*, II, 207 ("man of business"); *FR*, 46–56 (Richard in Concord); to RFF, Nov. 17, 1841, ibid., 252 ("pure and steadfast life"); Sept. 16, 1841, *FL*, II, 231–32 ("board nails"); *FR*, 49 ("great man"); Jan. 1842, MH ("good scruff[s]"); December 12, 1841, FMW, XV, 25 ("stand, or not"); Jan. 6, [1842], *FL*, III, 34 (warned about Alcott); [Dec. 30?, 1841], *FL*, II, 263 ("You go to an extreme"); [Jan.? 15?, 1842?], *FL*, III, 40 ("circulating medium").

42. May 1, 1842, FMW, XV, 26 ("father's blood"); May 12, 1842, *FL*, III, 64 (praised him); Jan. 6, [1842], ibid., 34, and May 12, 1842, ibid., 64 (father); Aug. 11, 1842, ibid., 86 (philosophical texts); [ca. early 1840s]*, *FL*, VI, 108 ("my Ancients"); [May 7, 1844], FJ44–2, 13 ("importance of externals").

43. To CS, July 22, 1841, *FL*, II, 218 (Mary Channing's arrangement); to MCF, Aug. 5, 1841, ibid., 221 ("savage dishabille"); Aug. 6, 1841, ibid., 223, 224 ("half fisherman").

44. CS to MF, Aug. 28, 1841, "SL," 214–15 (back to Cambridge); CS to RWE, Oct. 16, 1841, Tappan Papers, MH (at Newburyport); Oct. 25, 1841, *FL*, II, 247 ("tranquillity and rest").

45. To William Emerson, Mar. 30, 1841, *EL*, II, 389 (Alcotts, cook, and maid); to MF, Apr. 22, 1841, ibid., 394 ("Liberty, Equality, & a common table"); May 25, 1841, *FL*, II, 210 ("intends being a farmer"); Nov. 13, 1851, *TJ*, IV, 184 ("masculine"); *A Week on the Concord and Merrimack Rivers*, ed. Carl F. Hovde, William L. Howarth, and Elizabeth Hall Witherell (Princeton, 1980), 279 ("I know a woman"). For examples of Thoreau's expressions of skepticism toward conventional women, see *HJ*, IV, 51, 183–84, 233–34, 311.

46. July 31, 1841, and Aug. 2, 1841, *EL*, II, 438 ("recoiling gun"); June 21, [1841], *FL*, II, 212–13 ("MAGDALEN")

47. Quoted in to WHC, [ca. Fall 1840–Winter 1841]*, *FL*, VI, 98 ("determined exaggeration"); ibid., 99 ("If you saw me wholly"); ibid., 99, 100 ("'The word 'arrogance'"). The biggest difficulty in elucidating Fuller's friendship with Channing is the spottiness of their correspondence. Not only did he destroy most of his own letters but he also censored and possibly destroyed some of hers. Probably knowing how much he had tiptoed, in his long section of *OM*, around the explosive subject of her liaison with Giovanni Angelo Ossoli in Italy, he later called his effort "cold gravy." Quoted in Octavius Brooks Frothingham, *Memoir of William Henry Channing* (Boston, 1886), 441.

48. *OM*, II, 37 ("bow to her"); Susan Channing Higginson to Susan Higginson Channing, Apr. 20, [1841], Higginson-Cabot-Channing Papers, MHi (association with the Transcendentalists); to Francis J. Higginson, Nov. 3, 1841, Higginson-Cabot-Channing Papers, MHi ("dangerous influence"); to MCF, July 20, 1841, *FL*, II, 217 (moving to Brook Farm); *OM*, II, 40, 114 ("roused manliness"); Dec. 17, 1849, *FL*, V, 300 ("To you"); [ca. Winter 1842]*, *FL*, VI, 95–96 ("Your influence on me").

49. Irving Singer, *The Nature of Love*, 3 vols. (Chicago, 1966–87), vol. II, *The Nature of Love: Courtly and Romantic* (Chicago, 1984), 294 ("love is God"). In addition to Singer's "philosophical history" of love, I have been instructed by Jean H. Hagstrum's literary historical studies, especially *Sex and Sensibility: Ideal and Erotic Love from Milton to Mozart* (Chicago, 1980); and *Esteem Enlivened by Desire: The Couple from Homer to Shakespeare* (Chicago, 1992). For placing Fuller's love and friendship theories in a nineteenth-century context, I have found helpful Gay, *The Bourgeois Experience*, vol. II, *The Tender Passion* (1986); and Stephen Kern, *The Culture of Love: Victorians to Moderns* (Cambridge, Mass., 1992). H. G. Schenk includes a useful brief overview of the subject of Romantic love and friendship in *The Mind of the European Romantics: An Essay in Cultural History* (London, 1966), chap. 16.

50. *ECW*, II, 123, 125, 126, 127 ("sublime parts").

51. To CPC, Oct. 1, 1841, *EL*, VII, 474 (arrived at Bush); [July? 1841?], *FL*, II, 214 ("ministering angels"); [Oct. 1, 1841]*, ibid., 233, 234 ("our foolish critiques"); to WEC2, [Oct. 3, 1841], ibid., 240 ("great shock"); to RWE, Sept. 8, 1841, ibid., 230 ("blow"); to WEC2, [Oct. 3, 1841], ibid., 239–40 (toned-down version); [Oct. 2, 1841]*, ibid., 234, 235 ("the true self").

52. [Oct. 1841?], *FL*, II, 235, 236 ("Waldo has brought me").

53. Oct. 12, 1841, *EJMN*, VIII, 109 ("attractive-repelling conversations"); Oct. 22, 1841, ibid., 131 ("so proud"); Nov. ca. 14?, 1841, *EL*, II, 464–65 ("I say to myself").

54. *OM*, I, 37 ("Born under the same star").

55. EF to MF, Oct. 9, [1841], FMW, XVII, 54 ("manifold difficulties"); to MCF, Aug. 31, 1841, *FL*, II, 229 ("study and write"); MCF to MF, [ca. Jan. 1842], FMW, VIII, 209 (mother's resentment); to MCF, Jan. 8, 1842, *FL*, III, 34 ("in every way"); MF, journal, Dec. 10, 1840, OC, 90 ("bear the contact of society").

56. *Günderode* (Boston, 1842), v–vi ("In translating"); *HO*, 192 (Higginson's opinion); Minna Wessselhoeft to ?, n.d., OC, 182, and *HO*, 193 (Wesselhoeft); *Correspondence of Fräulein Günderode and Bettine von Arnim* (Boston, 1861).

57. Nov. 2, 1840, *FL*, VI, 328 ("young hearts!"); Oct. 25 and 28, 1840, *FL*, II, 172 (disliked Bettina cult); to GB, [Dec.? 1844], *FL*, III, 250 ("'A Child's Correspondence with Herself'"); *Dial*, 2 (Jan. 1842), 316, 317, 319, 320, 322 ("Father Confessor"); [ca. Mar. 1841], *FL*, VI, 331 ("medium somewhere"); *Boston Semi-Weekly Advertiser*, Jan. 5, 1842, 2, and *Boston Morning Post*, Jan. 19, 1842, 1 ("beautiful"). For contrasting interpretations

of the nineteenth-century ritual of female friendship, see William R. Taylor and Christopher Lasch, "Two 'Kindred Spirits': Sorority and Family in New England, 1839–1846," *New England Quarterly*, 36 (1963), 25–41; and Carroll Smith-Rosenberg, "The Female World of Love and Ritual," in her *Disorderly Conduct: Visions of Gender in Victorian America* (New York, 1985), 53–76, 305–13.

58. Dec. 13 [1841], *FL*, II, 258 ("brilliant"); to MCF, Jan. 1, 1842, *FL*, III, 31 ("fatigue and interruption"); to MCF, Dec. 13, [1841], *FL*, II, 258, to MCF, [Dec. 24, 1841], ibid., 261, and to MCF, Feb. 5, [1842], *FL*, III, 44 (Braham); to JSD, [Feb. 10?, 1842], ibid., 45 (Dwight's lectures); to MCF, Jan. 1, 1842, *FL*, III, 32 ("finest piano").

59. Quoted in *OM*, I, 304–5 ("Margaret leaned across"); [ca. Winter 1841–42], FMW, box A ("purgatory").

60. *Dial*, 3 (July 1842), 46, 50, 52 ("Entertaining Knowledge").

61. *Dial*, 3 (July 1842), 46, 47, 48–49, 49–50, 52 ("The drama").

62. Oct. 16, 1841, *EJMN*, VIII, 110–11 ("not the safest resort"); *Dial*, 3 (July 1842), 64–65, 65, 66 ("opera dancing"). When it came to the morals of Elssler's art, even established types had to watch their social back. See, for example, Charles Sumner's account of the "scandal" he had created the previous year just for showing the dancer around the city. To Henry Russell Cleveland, Sept. 23, 1840, in *Selected Letters of Charles Sumner*, ed. Beverly Wilson Palmer, 2 vols. (Boston, 1990), I, 93–94; and to Francis Lieber, Sept. 1, 1840, quoted at 94 n4.

63. *Dial*, 3 (July 1842), 60 ("Just as you have risen"). For a claim for the proto-democratic character of antebellum America's aesthetically heterogeneous artistic performances, see Levine, *Higbrow/Lowbrow*, chaps. 1–2.

64. June 9, 1842, *EL*, III, 62 ("*manly*").

65. GR to RWE, Oct. 6, 1841, in *EL*, II, 457 n336 ("book-selling usage"); Nov. 9, 1841, ibid., 462 ("dull Chinese diplomacy"); to MF, Nov. 14?, 1841, ibid., 464 ("exclusive property").

66. *Christian Examiner*, 32 (July 1842), 398 ("too absurd"); *Boston Morning Post*, Jan. 14, 1842 ("Man's soul-liberty"); *EL*, II, 33 ("dear it plainly was"); EPP to RWE, [ca. Mar. 1842]*, cited in Cooke, *Historical and Biographical Introduction*, I, 85 ($300 salary).

67. EPP, quoted in Cooke, *Historical and Biographical Introduction*, I, 85 ("rascally firm"); to FHH, Mar. 23, 1842, *EL*, II, 36, to William Emerson, ibid., 38–39, and Cooke, *Historical and Biographical Introduction*, I, 85 (Peabody's report); *OM*, I, 323 ($200 yearly salary); to MCF, July 29, [1841], 219 ("crazy with work"); [Dec. 24, 1841], *FL*, II, 261 ("'*copy*'"); to RFF, Jan. 15, [1842], *FL*, III, 38 (lessons); RFF to MF, Jan. 9, 1842, MH (overwork).

68. To RFF, Nov. 5, [1841], *FL*, II, 249 ("only 500$"); [Mar. 17?, 1842], *FL*, III, 54 ("exhausted").

69. [Mar. 17?, 1842], *FL*, III, 54 ("much easier"); Mar. 18, 1842, *EL*, III, 33–34 ("all your debtors"); Mar. 20, 1842, *EJMN*, VIII, 203 ("Humanity & Reform Men"); Mar. 21, 1842, *EL*, III, 35 ("rotation in martyrdom!").

70. *OM*, I, 324 ("so much heart").

Chapter Three

1. Apr. 7, 1842, *FL*, III, 56, 57 ("given out"); to RWE, April 18, [1842], ibid., 60 (Aunt Elizabeth's); to MR, Apr. 7, 1842, ibid., 56 ("absolute retirement"); [ca. May] 1842, ibid., 62 ("thotful").

2. Apr. 7, 1842, *FL*, III, 57 ("*all* topics"); to MR, [ca. May], 1842, *FL*, III, 62 ("growths of the last year").

3. March 1840, "CLS," n.p. ("open every night"). There is no study of the theologically liberal religious awakenings in the Northeast that is comparable to the plethora of studies on its evangelical ones, but for a good beginning, see Leigh Eric Schmidt, *Restless Souls: The Making of American Spirituality* (New York, 2005), chap. 2.

4. [June 10, 1841], *PL*, 254 ("common people"); Sept. 1842, *EJMN*, VIII, 262 ("beautiful fangs"); Jan. 7, 1841, JFC Papers, MH ("high time"); EPP, "A Vision," *Pioneer*, 1 (Mar. 1843), 97–100, reprinted in EPP, *Last Evening with Allston, and Other Papers* (Boston, 1886), 62–72 ("visions"); JFC, "Notes & Reflections," [ca. 1840], Perry-Clarke Collection, MHi ("visible church"); EPP to JSD, Sept. 20, 1840, *PL*, 245–46 (debate); CPC to JSD, Sept. 12, 1840, quoted in F. DeWolfe Miller, "Christopher Pearse Cranch: New England Transcendentalist" (Ph.D. diss., University of Virginia, 1942), 126 ("universal creed"); Sept. 1, 1840, "PJ," 53 (grumbled). The best overall treatment of these theological shifts among Transcendentalists in the early 1840s remains William R. Hutchison, *The Transcendentalist Ministers: Church Reform in the New England Renaissance* (New Haven, 1959), chaps. 4–5.

5. To WHC, Dec. 13, [1840], *FL*, II, 194 ("bewildered sheep"); to WHC, [April 5, 1841], *FL*, II, 206 ("loved him"); quoted in John Weiss, *Life and Correspondence of Theodore Parker*, 2 vols. (New York, 1864), I, 93 ("deistical"); Feb. 5, 1843, *FL*, III, 120 ("His outlook is wide"). For Emerson's ironical report on these come-outer meetings, see his "Chardon Street and Bible Conventions," *Dial*, 3 (July 1842), 100–112. The best modern discussion of Parker's theological development may be found in Dean Grodzins, *American Heretic: Theodore Parker and Transcendentalism* (Chapel Hill, 2002).

6. Oct. 25, 1840, *FL*, II, 172 ("tears and groans"); [June 10, 1841], *PL*, 254 (shocked family); to WHC, June 17, [1842], *FL*, III, 67, and to RWE, June 23, 1842, ibid., 70 (hearing Channing); [to MR]*, [ca. June 1842]*, *OM*, II, 88 (accompanying letter); Oct. 16, 1883, OC, 189 ("most characteristic"). For William Channing's religious odyssey, see Octavius Brooks Frothingham, *Memoir of William Henry Channing* (Boston, 1886). *OM*, II, 88. Curiously, although Channing cut out more than half of the "Credo," some of the parts he left in were as heterodox as those he censored.

7. [Ca. June 1840], "A Credo," OC, 97, 98 ("spirit uncontainable"). A cogent discussion of Romantic writers' appropriations of Neoplatonic and Christian plots of the "circuitous return" and the "fortunate fall" is in M. H. Abrams, *Natural Supernaturalism: Tradition and Revolution in Romantic Literature* (New York, 1971), chaps. 3–5.

8. [Ca. June 1840], "A Credo," OC, 97, 98 ("just as real"). Although privately Parker intimated that at some future time Christianity would be superseded, he did not do so directly in his lectures. He would be shocked to read in a manuscript of Fuller's the many New Testament beliefs she blithely traced back to ancient Near Eastern religions. Even Alcott, although he was sure Christianity was *already* dead as a faith and dying as an institution, uniquely venerated the ethical Jesus as he thought the "pagan" (as he thought of them) Fuller and Emerson did not. She also disputed the claim of Channing, whose view of Jesus as a "man-god" was probably closest to hers, that Christianity was the dominant religious influence in the world. See to WHC, June 17, [1842], *FL*, III, 67.

9. [Ca. June 1840], "A Credo," OC, 97, 98 ("not loathe sects"); Aug. 6, 1844, "FJ44–1," 110, 111 ("unconstrained nature"); [ca. 1843]*, *FL*, VI, 149, 150 ("a Power"); Dec. 26, 1843, *FL*, III, 167 ("made to mourn"); to FHH, Feb. 1, 1835, *FL*, I, 224 ("iron destiny"). Emerson's views on religious forms were, as with most matters, complex. In general, though, he often suspected religious symbols in art and literature, whereas Fuller often luxuriated in them. See *OM*, I, 219–21, II, 31–34. For the Romantic idea of "plenitude,"

see Arthur O. Lovejoy, *The Great Chain of Being: A Study of the History of an Idea* (Cambridge, Mass., 1936), chap. 10.

10. [Ca. June 1840], "A Credo," OC, 97, 98 ("indefinite pilgrimages"); "A Discourse of the Transient and Permanent in Christianity; Preached at the Ordination of Mr. Charles C. Shackford, in the Hawes Place Church in Boston, May 19, 1841," in Joel Myerson, ed., *Transcendentalism: A Reader* (New York, 2000), 349 ("flesh creeps with horror"); [ca. June 1840], "A Credo," OC, 97, 98 ("He is constantly aiding").

11. *OM*, II, 94 ("My tendency"); to [?], Aug. [22?], 1847, *FL*, IV, 288 (go straight to the Creative Spirit"); June 17, [1842], *FL*, III, 67 ("Is it my defect"); Sept. 17, 1842, "FJ42–1," 336 ("faithful skeptic"). For an attempt of Fuller to square her Christian religious yearnings and her "pagan" Prometheanism, see her letter to Caroline Sturgis, enclosing Fuller's translation of Goethe's "Prometheus" (Apr. 17, [1838], *FL*, I, 330–32).

12. Journal, [ca. Dec. 1852], MH-AH ("She did not know"); "Margaret Fuller," newspaper clipping, Boston, May 23, 1870, ABA, [Autobiographical Collection], III, 138 (1868–71), Alcott Papers, MH ("devoutly religious"); [ca. Winter 1839–40], "FS," 173 ("aspiration"); 1840, *FL*, II, 111 ("Ourselves"); [ca. late July, 1850]*, *EJMN*, VIII, 259 (Novalis). For the Romantic and later nineteenth-century longing for a post-Christian sacred sphere, see D. G. Charlton, *Secular Religions in France, 1815–1870* (London, 1963), Frank M. Turner, *Between Science and Religion: The Reaction to Scientific Naturalism in Late Victorian England* (New Haven, 1974); and George S. Williamson, *The Longing for Myth in Germany: Religion and Aesthetic Culture from Romanticism to Nietzsche* (Chicago, 2004).

13. June [23?], 1842, *FL*, III, 69 ("sleep on roses"); July 1842, *FL*, III, 72, 74 ("city").

14. Journal "Mythology," [ca. Summer 1842], FMW, box 1 ("There is a blank").

15. July 31, 1842, *FL*, VI, 335 ("non-fulfilment"); Aug. 5, 1842, *FL*, III, 81 ("Merely gentle").

16. Mar. 10, 1842, *EL*, III, 28 ("flatter your friend"); Mar. [15?], 1842, *FL*, III, 52 ("correct your vocabulary"); Mar. 22, 1842, *FL*, VI, 331–32 ("Waldo"); to RWE, June 23, 1842, *FL*, III, 71 (buying a house); to MF, Apr. 2?, 1842, *EL*, III, 43 (long stay); July 19, 1842, ibid., 75 ("desk & inkhorn"); Aug. 10, 1842, *FL*, III, 83 ("tired to death"); Aug. 12, 1842, *EL*, III, 80 ("please to come").

17. May 8, 1842, *EJMN*, 51 ("isolated & sacred").

18. Julian Hawthorne, *Nathaniel Hawthorne and His Wife*, 2 vols., (Boston, 1884), I, 259–62 (apparent slander); "To a Priestess of the Temple / not made with hands," FMW, XVI, 29 ("My Priestess!"); quoted in SPH to MF, May 11, 1842, FMW, XVI, 30 ("time with us"); to Mrs. Elizabeth Palmer Peabody, Aug. 22, 1842, NN-B ("We were delighted"); Aug. 20, 1842, "FJ42–1," 325 ("We stopped"); Aug. 22, 1842, *HW*, VIII, 343 ("high and low philosophy"). The controversy over Julian Hawthorne's posthumous publication of his father's nasty journal excerpt about Fuller after her death as a "great humbug" and a fallen women and her husband as "half an idiot" was played out in newspapers at the time and has continued to this day. I find it quite plausible that Hawthorne's passages reflected some mix of conscious and unconcious misogyny, gullibility, and fictional sketching. See Sarah Clarke's shrewd guesses along these lines in SC to TWH, Mar. 12, 185, OC, 203. As for his comparatively strong Fulleresque female characters in his fiction, a great writer imaginatively sublimating his demons in his art is not a practice unique to Hawthorne. See Notebook, Apr. 3, 1858, *HW*, XIV, 155–57. For a recent interpretation that emphasizes Hawthorne's skepticism toward the gossip about Fuller

that he recorded in his journal in Florence, see Mitchell, *Hawthorne's Fuller Mystery*, chap. 2.

19. January 13, 1841, *HW*, XV, 511–12 ("lose her tongue!"); June 4, [1842], *FL*, III, 65–66 ("If ever mortal"). Hawthorne's marriage has received ample attention from his biographers, but I have found especially insightful T. Walter Herbert, *Dearest Beloved: The Hawthornes and the Making of the Middle-Class Family* (Berkeley, 1993); and Brenda Wineapple, *Hawthorne: A Life* (New York, 2003). An illuminating portrait of Sophia Hawthorne appears in Megan Marshall, *The Peabody Sisters: Three Women Who Ignited American Romanticism* (Boston, 2005). For religious motifs in nineteenth-century middle-class cults of courtship and marriage, see Karen Lystra, *Searching the Heart: Women, Men, and Romantic Love in Nineteenth-Century America* (New York, 1989); and Peter Gay, *The Bourgeois Experience: Victoria to Freud* (New York, 1984–98), vol. II, *The Tender Passion* (1986), 284–312.

20. Aug. 27, 1842, "FJ42–1," 328 ("earnest request"); Aug. 25, 1842, *HW*, XV, 647, 648 ("four sensitive people").

21. EFC to MF, Jan. 28, 1842, FMW, box 1 ("holy"); Mar. 20, 1842, "ChaL-1," 170–71 ("Germanity"); Feb. 26, 1842, ibid., 165 ("doing nothing"); Oct. 25, 1842, "FJ42–2," 286 ("really to live"); Aug. 30, 1842, *FL*, VI, 338 ("so changeable"); Mar. 23, 1843, *EJMN*, VIII, 374 ("little wretched boy"). Frederick T. McGill, Jr., *Channing of Concord: A Life of William Ellery Channing II* (New Brunswick, 1967) is a useful biography, but the best source for Ellery Channing is "ChaL." For varying appraisals of Ellen Fuller's character at this time, see Mary E. Channing to Kate Sedgwick, Sept. 21, 1841, Channing Family Papers, MHi; J. H. P. to WHC, Oct. 2, 1841, Channing Family Papers, MHi; and SPH to Mary Peabody Mann, [ca. late July–August 1850], NN-B.

22. Sept. 9, 1842, "FJ42–1," 335 ("poor little prodigal"); Sept. 2, 1842, ibid., 333 ("last chance"); CS to RWE, Oct. 16, 1841, Tappan Papers, MH, and to MF, Sept. 9, 1841, "SL," 218–19 (Sturgis disappointed); ibid., 219 ("noble enough"); Aug. 30, 1842, *FL*, VI, 338 ("much in his mind"); [Sept. 10, 1842]*, "FJ42–1," 335, 335–36 ("wretched night").

23. [Sept. 10, 1842]*, "FJ42–1," 336 ("pretty play").

24. To SSS, June 18, 1876, *ChiL*, 535 ("very . . . pale"); May 15, 1842, *EJMN*, VIII, 173 ("Constitutional"); Mar. 1, 1842, *EL*, III, 20 ("taxed me"); quoted in Ellen Tucker Emerson, *The Life of Lidian Jackson Emerson*, ed. Delores Bird Carpenter (Boston, 1980), 81, 82 ("Transcendental Bible"). Ellen Tucker's memoir contains valuable information about the Emerson marriage, but the best portrait of Lidian Emerson emerges in *ESL*.

25. Feb. 21, 1842, *EJMN*, VIII, 201 ("wonderful boy"); Jan. 28, 1842, *EL*, III, 8 ("dare to love"); Feb. 1842, *FL*, III, 42–43 ("more than any child"); to CS, Aug. 30, 1842, ibid., 337 ("subdued"); Feb. 4, 1842, *EJMN*, VIII, 199–200 (*think the truth*); Nov. 31, 1840, *EJMN*, VII, 532 ("frightful"). For a more wildly contradictory—and almost tragic—critique by Emerson of marriage as a permanent institution in this world, see Sept. 1841, *EJMN*, VIII, 95. Although I believe Richardson underplays somewhat the problematic state of Emerson's feelings about his relations with Lidian and Fuller's circle of young friends at this time, he is absolutely right when he argues that the evidence shows "that all was not well with their marriage now." Richardson, *Emerson*, 330.

26. To William Emerson, Aug. 22, 1842, *EL*, III, 82 (facial swelling); Sept. 2, 1842, "FJ42–1," 331 ("knows perfectly well").

27. Sept. 1, 1842, "FJ42–1," 330, 330–31 ("Man and Woman").

28. Sept. 2, 1842, "FJ42–1," 331, 331–32 ("not a word").

29. [Sept. 19, 1842]*, "FJ42–1," 337, 338 ("so anti-Christian"). For other philosophically radical but practically cautious critiques of marriage, including his own, that Emerson showed Fuller during her visit, see Sept. 1, 1842, *EJMN*, VII, 463, and Sept. 4, 1842, ibid., 467; and Sept. 9, 1842, "FJ42–1," 335.

30. Sept. 25, 1842, "FJ42–1," 340 ("attending to her"); Jan. 30, 1843, *ESL*, 118 ("She has such a tenderness"); "HL-3," 138n6 (Lidian's depression); Sept. 21, 1842, "FJ42–1," 339 ("her child").

31. Mar. 23, 1843, *EJMN*, VIII, 369 (admiringly titled); "La Nuovissima Vita," Sept. 1842, FMW, IX, 239 ("to Waldo"); to MF, Oct. 11, 1842, ibid., III, 91 (encouraged Fuller's *Vita nuova* translation); to RWE, Dec. [4?], 1842, *FL*, III, 103 (too technically difficult); to MF, July 11, 1843, *EL*, III, 183 ("ruggedest"); "Initial, Daemonic, and Celestial Love," in *Emerson: Essays and Poems* (New York, 1996), 1129–40. *ECW*, II, *Essays: First Series*, 97–127 ("Love"). Emerson's translation of the *Vita Nuova* has been published in *Dante's "Vita Nuova" Translated by Ralph Waldo Emerson*, ed. J. Chesley Matthews (Chapel Hill, 1960).

32. Sept. 2, 1842, "FJ42–1," 332 ("women can't bear"); Sept. 17, 1842, "FJ42–1," 336 ("true community life"); to GTD, Dec. 17, 1842, *FL*, III, 106 (*"ambition"*); "La Nuovissima Vita," Sept. 1842, FMW, IX "deeper, wider, further, higher"); Aug. 28, 1842, "FJ42–1," 329 ("A path has been appointed me").

33. Aug. 24, 1842, "FJ42–1," 326 ("expectations are moderate"); Aug. 19, 1842, ibid., 324 ("my god was love"); Aug. 25, 1842, *FL*, III, 91 ("first excitement"); Aug. 25, 1842, *FL*, VI, 336–37 ("What did you mean").

34. "FJ42–1," 340 ("Farewell"); Oct. 16, [1842], *FL*, III, 96 (*"intoxicated"*); Apr. 8, [1843], *HW*, VIII, 371 ("apotheosized her"); Mar. 23, 1843, *EJMN*, VIII, 368–69 ("underrated our friend"); *Essays: Second Series*, *ECW*, III, 88–89 ("Manners").

35. [Sept. 26, 1842]*, "FJ42–1," 340 ("I told her no").

36. To EH, Jan. 16, [1843], *FL*, III, 114 ("They don't touch me" and "unaccustomed serenity"); Oct. 31, 1842, "FJ42–2," 291, to CKN, Oct. 19, 1842, *FL*, III, 95, and to GTD, Dec. 17, 1842, ibid., 105 (Ellery Street house); [Sept.] 14, 1844, "FJ44–1," 117 ("little card house"); Oct. 16, [1842], *FL*, III, 97 (nostalgic); Minna Wesselhoeft [to TWH], n.d., OC, 182 (Wesselhoefts); Sarah Hodges to Esther Mack, Dec. 16, 1842, FMW, X, 155 (Maria Rotch); to EH, Jan. 16, [1843], *FL*, III, 114 ("very wretched"); Dec. 26, 1842, ibid., 110, 111 ("not troubled").

37. Dec. 17, 1842, *FL*, III., 105 ("The darkest hue"); Jan. 30, 1843, ibid., 118 ("At *last"*); to MCF, [Dec. 17?, 1841], *FL*, II, 260 ("serious work"); [Oct.] 25, 1842, "FJ42–2," 284 ("never teach in heaven"); to Anna Loring, Apr. 2, 1845, *FL*, IV, 66 ("confidential talks"); n.d., *FL*, VI, 148–49 ("do not waste"); Jan. 30, 1843, *FL*, III, 118 ("dutch burgomaster").

38. "Miss Littlehale's Notes on Margaret Fuller," Feb. 3, 1851, in ABA, Diary [1851], 265, 266, Alcott Papers, MH ("personal satire"); "ON," 500, 500–501 ("extreme candour & tenderness"); quoted in *OM*, I, 307 ("mow down").

39. SGW, *Ward Family Papers* (Boston, 1900), 103 ("typical blue-stocking"); to Ruth Charlotte Dana, Dec. 7, 1840, Dana Family Papers, MHi ("'Capt. Fuller'").

40. [June 18], 1844, "FJ44–1," 59 ("unprofitable talk"); Henry Arthur Bright, *Happy Country This America: The Travel Diary of Henry Arthur Bright*, ed. Anne Henry Ehrenpreis (Columbus, 1978), June 13, 1852, 155–56 ("much frightened").

41. [Apr. 9, 1842], *FL*, VI, 332 ("none such here"); LGL to Anna Loring, Feb. 8, 1852, Ellis Gray Loring Papers, MCR-S (hard to take); JRL to John Francis Heath, May 29, 1841, University of Virginia Library ("Byronic"); to CST, Mar. 8, 1849, *FL*, V, 199 ("wonder-

fully struck"). No study adequately captures the cultural diversity and ideological wildness of the city in the 1840s, although relevant discussions of establishment liberal Boston may be found in Martin Green, *The Problem of Boston: Some Readings in Cultural History* (New York, 1966); E. Digby Baltzell, *Puritan Boston and Quaker Philadelphia* (New York, 1979), chaps. 1, 3, 13–18; and Ronald Story, *The Forging of an Aristocracy: Harvard and the Boston Upper Class, 1800–1870* (Middletown, Conn., 1980).

42. Oct. 1842, *OM*, II, 69, 70 ("somewhat rigid"); [June 8, 1844], "FJ44–2," 28 ("my first teacher"); FHH to MF, Jan. 5 and 12, 1843, FMW, XVI, 31 (Swedish); Mar. [8?], 1842, *FL*, III, 47 ("inspiring themes"); to MS, June 5, 1851, "ChaL-2," 184, 185 ("secret magnetism"); *OM*, I, 298 ("more than any person"); [Mar. 27, 1841], "HL-3," 120 ("Mephistophilic vein").

43. To SSS, [ca. Mar. 1842]*, *FL*, VI, 117 ("young uns"); Sept. 1, 1844, *FL*, III, 226 ("On reading over my letter"); SSS to TWH, May 25, 1884, OC, 256 ("motherly"). The best sources for the Shaw, Russell, and Loring clans are their letters in EGL Family Papers, MCR-S; JRL Papers, MHi; *ChiL*; and *LoL*.

44. Oct. 16, [1842], *FL*, III, 97 ("*little* vexed"); to TP, Sept. 8, 1842, *EL*, III, 86 ("un Dialled"); to RWE, Oct. 16, [1842], *FL*, III, 97 ("almost courtly"); *Dial*, 3 (Oct. 1842), 179 ("superficial country").

45. 6, 1840, *EJMN*, VII, 539 ("tedious archangel"); [Aug. 27], 1842, "FJ42–1," 328 ("swelling vanity"); Sept. 1842, *EJMN*, VIII, 261 ("lightning"); Jan. 16, [1843], *FL*, III, 113 (admired Lane's debating); to William Oldham, Jan. 28–30, 1843, in Joel Myerson, "William Harry Harland's 'Bronson Alcott's English Friends,'" *Resources for American Literary Study*, 8 (Spring 1978), 42 ("rare woman"); to EH, Jan. 21, 1844, *FL*, III, 170 ("total abstinence experiment"); [June 27], 1844, "FJ44–1," 65 ("puerile"); to Charles Lane, [July 17, 1844], *FL*, III, 212 ("human ownership"); to William Emerson, Oct. 26, 1842, *EL*, III, 93 ("cabalistic collection"); to Charles Lane, [July], 25, 1844, "FJ44–1," 93–94 ("skilful piece"); to Charles Lane, [July 26, 1844], *FL*, III, 218 (sarcastic response); to Charles Lane, [July 17, 1844], ibid., 211 ("does not command my sympathy"); to GB, [ca. Nov. 15, 1845], *FL*, IV, 166 ("too intellectual life").

46. SR to MF, [ca. Winter 1841–42], FMW, XVII, 48 (Lloyd at Brook Farm); Louisa (Barlow) Jay, "Genealogical Notes on the Barlow Family," MH (Barlow at Brook Farm); APB to JSD, Jan. 6, 1843, MB (Barlow's admirer); APB to MF, Mar. 15, 1846, FMW, XI, 118 (Barlow's teaching job); statement of RWE, *OM*, I, 209 ("monastic"); CKN to CS, June 19, [1844], Tappan Papers, MH (altar and cross); to CKN, n.d., *FL*, VI, 113 ("priestess"); to RWE, Mar. 8, 1842, *FL*, III, 50 ("divine"); to CKN, n.d., *FL*, VI, 112 ("sweet child"); CKN to RWE, Mar. 27, 1852, Emerson Family Papers, MH ("Madonna heart"); to CKN, n.d., *FL*, VI, 113 ("incense"); to CKN, n.d., *FL*, VI, 114 ("I never do"); to RWE, July 5, 1840, *FL*, II, 147 ("rise above his doubts").

47. "Historic Notes of Life and Letters in New England," *EW*, X, 364 ("perpetual picnic"); *Cheerful Yesterdays* (Boston, 1899), 77 ("army of hand-workers"); to ?, 1843, *FL*, III, 111 ("Philistine"); *OM*, II, 74–75, 76 ("conventional refinement"); to MF, July 11, 1843, *EL*, III, 183 ("choice"); GWC to Daniel Ricketson, Apr. 23, 1856, quoted in Gordon Milne, *George William Curtis and the Genteel Tradition* (Bloomington, 1956), 228–29 ("her superiority").

48. *OM*, II, 80 ("preëminently . . . Transcendentalist"); ibid., 75–76 ("growth of nature").

49. *OM*, II, 76–77, 77–78 ("Impulse").

50. To J. F. Heath, Mar. 28, 1843, ViU ("does nothing"); to SR, Aug. 27, 1839, *FL*, II, 87 ("what pursuits").

51. *Essays of George Eliot*, ed. Thomas Pinney (London, 1963), 201 (*Vindication* edition); Sarah M. Grimké, *Letters on the Equality of the Sexes, and the Condition of Woman* (Boston, 1838), 122 ("MORALLY RIGHT"); *Dial*, 1 (Jan. 1841), 362 ("no topics"). For the fate of Wollstonecraft's feminist ideology in England at the end of the eighteenth century, see G. J. Barker-Benfield, *The Culture of Sensibility: Sex and Society in Eighteenth-Century Britain* (Chicago, 1992), chap. 7. A lively minority discourse about "women's rights" continued beyond the 1790s, but it was largely associated in England with Unitarians and liberal dissenters and in America largely died out by the 1820s. See the essays by Arianne Chernock and Rosemarie Zagarri in Barbara Taylor and Sarah Knott, eds., *Women, Gender, and Enlightenment* (New York, 2005). The best study of American thought about women in the revolutionary and postrevolutionary era remains Linda K. Kerber, *Women of the Republic: Intellect and Ideology in Revolutionary America* (Chapel Hill, 1980). Henry F. May, "After the Enlightenment," in his *The Divided Heart: Essays on Protestantism and the Enlightenment* (New York, 1991), 179–96, 210–13, cogently discusses the weakening of American Enlightenment traditions in the early nineteenth century.

The literature on the ambiguities of the ideology of domesticity is substantial. Important works are Nancy F. Cott, *The Bonds of Womanhood: "Woman's Sphere" in New England, 1785–1835* (New Haven, 1977); Ann Douglas, *The Feminization of American Culture* (New York, 1977), chaps. 2–7; Kerber, *Women of the Republic*; Carl Degler, *At Odds: Women and the Family in America from the Revolution to the Present* (New York, 1980); and Mary Kelley, *Private Woman, Public Stage: Literary Domesticity in Nineteenth-Century America* (New York, 1984). But see the caveats about domesticity rhetoric presented in Linda K. Kerber, "Separate Spheres, Female Worlds, Woman's Place: The Rhetoric of Women's History," *Journal of American History*, 75 (June 1988), 9–39. The best discussion of Sarah Grimké's women's rights ideas is in Gerda Lerner, ed., *The Feminist Thought of Sarah Grimké* (New York, 1998), 3–46. For treatments of the feminist abolitionists, see Blanch Glassman Hersh, *The Slavery of Sex: Feminist Abolitionists in America* (Urbana, 1978); Jean Fagin Yellin, *Women and Sisters: Antislavery Feminists in American Culture* (New Haven, 1989); Debra Gold Hansen, *Strained Sisterhood: Gender and Class in the Boston Female Anti-Slavery Society* (Amherst, Mass., 1993); and Karen Sánchez-Eppler, *Touching Liberty: Abolition, Feminism, and the Politics of the Body* (Berkeley, 1993).

52. Catharine E. Beecher, *A Treatise on Domestic Economy, for the Use of Young Ladies at Home, at School*, rev. ed. (1841; New York, 1846) (Beecher). Grimké, *Letters*, 4 ("solely on the Bible"). Good discussions of Beecher's reformist antifeminism may be found in Kathryn Kish Sklar, *Catharine Beecher: A Study in Domesticity* (New Haven, 1973). In her tract, Grimké included evidence on women's legal and economic disabilities, but she mainly emphasizes her argument about moral equality and her Quaker-cum-Enlightenment ideal of womanhood as sensible, ascetic, and benevolent. For abolitionist private views on women and the family, see Lawrence J. Friedman, *Gregarious Saints: Self and Community in American Abolitionism, 1830–1870* (Cambridge, England, 1982), chap. 5; and Chris Dixon, *Perfecting the Family: Antislavery Marriages in Nineteenth-Century America* (Amherst, 1997). I use the label "feminism" advisedly, since in the United States an organized women's rights movement did not get under way until later and the term itself did not come into general usage until after the turn of the twentieth century. I invoke it here as a heuristic label marking a broad ideological current identified with two claims: opposition to women's subordination and the assertion of their equal rights as individual humans. For useful discussions of this problem of labeling, see Nancy F. Cott,

The Grounding of Modern Feminism (New Haven, 1987), introduction and chap. 1; Karen Offen, "Defining Feminism: A Comparative Historical Approach," *Signs: Journal of Women in Culture and Society,* 14 (Autumn 1988), 119–57; and Ellen Carol DuBois, Nancy F. Cott, and Karen Offen, "Comment on Karen Offen's 'Defining Feminism: A Comparative Historical Approach,'" *Signs: Journal of Women in Culture and Society,* 14 (Autumn 1989).

53. To WHC, Dec. 13, [1840], *FL,* III, 194 ("so forced"). There yet remains to be written a comprehensive study of the amalgamating sacralization of various reform currents that suddenly got underway in the early 1840s, but for a happy remembrance of these shifts by one of its younger Transcendentalist participants, see Higginson, *Cheerful Yesterdays,* chap. 3. For useful discussions of aspects of this amalgamation mostly outside the Transcendentalist circles, see John L. Thomas, "Romantic Reform in America, 1815–1865," *American Quarterly,* 17 (Winter 1965), 656–81; Lewis Perry, *Radical Abolitionism: Anarchy and the Government of God in Antislavery Thought* (Ithaca, 1973); and Robert H. Abzug, *Cosmos Crumbling: American Reform and the Religious Imagination* (New York, 1994).

54. Mar. 23, 1843, *EJMN,* VIII, 372 ("duties of Woman"); Emerson, *OM,* I, 218, to RWE, May 9, 1843, *FL,* III, 124 (French socialists); *EJMN,* VIII, 372 ("docile daughter of God"); Apr. 29, [1843], *EL,* III, 170 ("though no son"); May 9, [1843], *FL,* III, 123 ("sinner"); Mar. 23, 1843, *EJMN,* VIII, 368–69 ("heroical & godlike). For an earlier and even more conventional version of Emerson's belief in women's distinctly private role, see Nov. 1841, *EJMN,* VIII, 149–50 ("Woman should not be expected to write or fight or build or compose scores, she does all by inspiring man to do all"). Emerson had, indeed, wished that his second child had been a boy that would be a "young poet that should come." See to William and Susan Haven Emerson, Nov. 22, 1841, *EL,* II, 466. Fuller herself sometimes dispassionately acknowledged the inevitability of society's preference for boys. See to Albert H. Tracy, Nov. 6, 1843, *FL,* III, 157; and to RWE, Jan. 28, 1844, ibid., 175.

55. James Russell Lowell to George Bailey Loring, Aug. 31, 1840, quoted in Hope Jillson Vernon, *The Poems of Maria Lowell with Unpublished Letters and a Biography* (Providence, 1936), 15 ("transcendental"); to CS, Oct. 18, [1840], *FL,* II, 164 (signing off); Elizabeth Cady Stanton, letter to the editor, *Woman's Journal,* Aug. 3, 1901 ("many"); Emerson, *OM,* I, 350 ("Ethics"); Peabody, *Reminiscences of Rev. Wm. Ellery Channing* (Boston, 1880), 402 ("Duties of Social Life"); Emerson, *OM,* I, 350 ("Woman"); [to WHC]*, Nov. 1842, *FL,* III, 99 ("spirited"); to EH, Jan. 16, [1843], ibid., 114, and to Mary Rotch, Feb. 5, 1843, ibid., 120 ("quite good"); to JFC, Sept. 9, 1842, *FL,* VI, 339 ("constancy"); to EH, Jan. 16, [1843], *FL,* III, 114 (rival claims). I am indebted to Phyllis Cole for calling my attention to Stanton's recollection.

56. For a classic discussion of the Romantic conception of "culture," see Raymond Williams, *Culture and Society, 1780–1950* (1958; New York, 1983).

57. "The Great Lawsuit. Man *versus* Men. Woman *versus* Women," *Dial,* 3 (July 1843), 1–47; Mrs. D. L. Child, *The History of the Condition of Women, in Various Ages,* 2 vols. (Boston, 1835).

58. "Great Lawsuit," 1, 2, 4, 5, 6, 7 ("Man").

59. "Great Lawsuit," 5, 8, 9 ("unceasing revelation").

60. "Great Lawsuit," 8, 9, 10, 11 ("utmost penalty").

61. "Great Lawsuit," 11, 12, 13 ("numerous party").

62. "Great Lawsuit," 14, 23 ("liberating measures"). In conceptualizing Fuller's liberal Romanticism, I have found especially useful George Kateb, *The Inner Ocean: Individualism and Democratic Culture* (Ithaca, 1992); Nancy L. Rosenblum's *Another Liberalism: Romanticism and the Reconstruction of Liberal Thought* (Cambridge, Mass., 1987);

and Gerald N. Izenberg, *Impossible Individuality: Romanticism, Revolution, and the Origins of Modern Selfhood, 1787–1802* (Princeton, 1992).

63. "Great Lawsuit," 14, 15, 16, 17 ("Her father"); to WHC, [June? 1844], *FL*, III, 199 (acknowledged). For Fuller's father's childrearing ideas and practices, see *CF-1*, chaps. 2–3. Despite Fuller's criticism of them, her image of her father as a protofeminist remained strong. See Frances M. White to TWH, 188–?, OC, 267.

64. "Great Lawsuit," 13, 16, 17, 18, 17–18, 19, 39 ("of woman born"); Louisa S. McCord, "Enfranchisement of Women," *Southern Quarterly Review* 5 (Apr. 1852), 322–41. For Grimké's stress on women's victimization, see *Letters*, 38–55.

65. "Great Lawsuit," 18, 26, 34, 35 ("thread-bare celebrity"). For an overview of women's history compendiums, see Gerda Lerner, *The Creation of Feminist Consciousness: From the Middle Ages to 1870* (New York, 1993), chap. 11.

66. "Great Lawsuit," 17, 28, 30, 32, 36, 37, 47 ("household partnership").

67. [John W. Vethake], "Femality," *Pathfinder*, 3 (Mar. 11, 1843), 35–36, and 4 (Mar. 18, 1843), 51–52 ("Femality"); "Great Lawsuit," 38, 39, 42, 43, 44 ("electrical"). A valuable set of documents on German Romantic ideas of philosophy and the "feminine" may be found in Jochen Schulte-Sasse , eds., *Theory as Practice: A Critical Anthology of Early German Romantic Writings* (Minneapolis, 1997), 359–462. For German Romantic psychological thought, see Oskar Walzel, *German Romanticism* (New York, 1932), 245–54; and Henri F. Ellenberger, *The Discovery of the Unconscious: The History and Evolution of Dynamic Psychiatry* (New York, 1970), chap. 4.

68. "Great Lawsuit," 42, 43, 44 ("not been given pure"). For the concept of androgyny as a model for sexual equality in early German Romantic writers, see Sara Friedrichsmeyer, *The Androgyne in Early German Romanticism* (New York, 1983). For androgynous and binary notions of gender and sexuality in the thought of the French Saint-Simonians, see Clair Goldberg Moses and Leslie Wahl Rabine, *Feminism, Socialism, and French Romanticism* (Bloomington, 1993). Classic Jungian and Freudian perspectives on bigender, bisexual, and androgynous proclivities in the human psyche may be found in Jean Strouse, *Women and Analysis: Dialogues on Psychoanalytic Views of Femininity* (1974; Boston, 1985), 195–238, 343–64.

69. "Great Lawsuit," 17, 19, 44, 46 ("leave off asking"); Nov. 26, 1842, *EJMN*, VIII, 251 ("absolutely isolated"); "Great Lawsuit," 44, 46 ("retire within themselves). A year and a half later, Emerson also inserted his "absolutely isolated" formulation that Fuller cited here, in his March 3, 1844, lecture "New England Reformers," *ECW*, III, 157.

70. "Great Lawsuit," 14, 23–24, 43; Feb. 20, [1840], "FJ44–2" ("dualism"). For a characteristic statement of Emerson's skepticism about actual social "Union" at this time, see his journal entry of Nov. 26, 1842 (also used in his lecture "New England Reformers"): "It is spiritual and must not be actualized. The Union is only perfect when all the Uniters are absolutely isolated" (*EJMN*, VIII, 251).

71. "Great Lawsuit," 47 ("soon appear?").

72. For a recent appraisal of the Western conversation about the relative claims of the "masculine" and "feminine" in political thought, see Norma Thompson, *The Ship of State: Statecraft and Politics from Ancient Greece to Democratic America* (New Haven, 2001).

73. To MF, July 11, 1843, *EL*, III, 183 ("never like anything"); July 8, 1843, *TC*, 124–25 ("with pen in hand"); TP to MF, [ca. spring 1843], FMW, XVI, 87 ("unlovely") ; Aug. 2, 1843, MH ("best piece"); July 11, 1843, *EL*, III, 183 ("piece of life").

74. [Ca. July 1843]*, quoted in Hawthorne, *Hawthorne and His Wife*, I, 257 ("Queen Margaret"); "Great Lawsuit," *Dial*, 4 (July 1843), 28 ("mutual idolatry"); Aug. 15, 1843, MH (Mary Gove's letter); quoted in George Willis Cooke, *An Historical and Biographi-*

cal Introduction to Accompany the "Dial," 2 vols. (Cleveland, 1902), I, 172 ("one woman in America").

Chapter 4

1. May 9, [1843], *FL*, III, 123 ("odious east winds"); May 8, [18]43, ibid. ("change of air"); May 9, [1843], ibid., 124 ("tired now of books").

2. Frank R. Kramer, *Voices in the Valley: Mythmaking and Folk Belief in the Shaping of the Middle West* (Madison, 1964), 67 ("folk migration").

3. Apr. 22, 1841, *EL*, II, 394–95 ("pocketfull of money"); to CKN, July 30, 1842, *FL*, III, 77, 78 ("wild" and "sublime"); to RWE, May 9, [1843], ibid., 124 (*Rural and Domestic Life*); to Henry Wadsworth Longfellow, May 3, 1843, ibid., 122 (*Des Knaben Wunderhorn*); June 1, 1843, ibid., 128 ("Democracy"). For the culture of the Middle West during these years, see Jon Gjerde, *The Minds of the West: Ethnocultural Evolution in the Rural Middle West, 1830–1917* (Chapel Hill, 1997).

4. To SSS, May 30, [18]43, *FL*, III, 127 ("small fortune");

5. To EH, May 30, [18]43, *FL*, III, 126 ("like lightning"). In my account of Fuller's western trip, because it is a retrospective literary text, I have generally avoided using her book *Summer on the Lakes* and instead largely relied on her letters and journal notes, which she wrote either at or near the time of her journey.

6. Christopher Mulvey, *Anglo-American Landscapes: A Study of Nineteenth-Century Anglo-American Travel Literature* (Cambridge, England, 1983), 187 ("ultimate in Romantic landscapes"); Elizabeth McKinsey, *Niagara Falls: Icon of the American Sublime* (Cambridge, Mass., 1985) ("icon"); June 1, 1843, *FL*, III, 129 ("'burst into tears'"); journal, ca. Summer 1843, FMW, box A ("very correct").

7. July 5, 1843, Tappan Papers, MH ("known it all before"); journal, ca. Summer 1843, FMW, box A ("dreary, sullen"); June 16, 1843, *FL*, III, 130 ("Land-Shark"); journal, ca. Summer 1843, FMW, box A ("a race shall spring").

8. June 16, 1843, *FL*, III, 129 ("really *at it*"); journal, ca. Summer 1843, FMW, box A ("dullest fortnight").

9. Journal, ca. Summer 1843, FMW, box A ("*lumber waggon*"); to RWE, Aug. 4, 1843, ibid., 137 ("perfectly free"); journal, ca. Summer 1843, FMW, box A ("knows every anecdote").

10. To RWE, Aug. 4, 1843, *FL*, III, 137 ("delightful pilgrimage"); Aug. 9, 1843, ibid., 140 ("luxury and repose"); to RWE, Aug. 4, 1843, ibid., 137 ("jolts and wrenches"); *FSL*, 41 ("'conquered them for us'").

11. To MR, Aug. 9, 1843, *FL*, III, 140 ("topics are before them"); journal, ca. Summer 1843, FMW, box A ("used to go barefoot" and "homespun"); Aug. 9, 1843, *FL*, III, 140 ("You feel so grateful").

12. *FSL*, 54–57 (patriotic epiphany); July 29, 1843, *FL*, III, 133 ("if we two could live"); to JFC, July 9, 1843, *FL*, VI, 343 ("leading men"); to JFC, July 9, 1843, ibid., 343–45, to JFC, July 16, 1843, ibid., 346, WHCl to MF, Aug. 2, 1843, FMW, X, 4, ABF to RFF, Nov. 1, 1843, FMW, XIII, 17, and ABF to RFF, May 29, 1844, FMW, II, 120 (Arthur's academy).

13. Aug. 17, 1843, *FL*, III, 144 ("that vast mirror"); to RWE, Aug. 4, 1843, ibid., 137 ("not to compare"); to SGW [and ABW]*, Aug. 3, 1843, ibid., 134 ("Rock River Edens"); June 16, 1843, ibid., 129, 130 ("They do not ape fashions"); Aug. 4, 1843, ibid., 138 ("Eastern women").

14. Journal, ca. summer 1843, FMW, box A (Indian sightings on the Michigan shore);

to SGW, Aug. 3, 1843, *FL*, III, 134, 135 ("poorer sort"); July 29, 1843, ibid., 132 ("only five years"); Aug. 3, 1843, *FL*, III, 135 ("an angry *hui*").

15. Aug. 3, 1843, *FL*, III, 136 ("wonderfully the gainer"); Aug. 4, 1843, ibid., 137 ("letter from Fruitlands"); to RWE, Aug. 17, 1843, ibid., 143, 144 ("*place of onions*"); Aug. 16, 1843, ibid., 142 ("where is that home?").

16. July 28, 1843, *FL*, VI, 348 ("become a friend"); Sept. 20, 1843, FMW, X, 5 ("doubts arose"); to WHC, Aug. 16, 1843, *FL*, III, 142 ("nobody wants").

17. July 10, 1843, *CL*, 143 (gift of fifty dollars); *FSL*, 170 ("shrieking savages"); journal, ca. summer 1843, FMW, box A ("while dressing"); *FSL*, 171, 237 ("half wild"); journal, Aug. 19, 1843, FMW, Works, V, 77–79, 79 ("this pleased them mightily").

18. *FSL*, 245 ("in pink calico shirts"); quoted in Ednah Dow Cheney to TWH, Nov. 12, 1883, OC, 195 ("shrank from the child").

19. To JFC and SC, Sept. 13, 1843, *FL*, VI, 350 ("most splendid boat"); Sept. 13, 1843, ibid., 350 ("queer enough"); William Emerson to RWE, [Sept.] 27, [1843], Emerson Papers, MHi ("delightful conversation"); *Dial*, 4 (July 1843), 42 ("'Femality'"); to JFC and SC, Sept. 13, 1843, *FL*, VI, 351 ("much pleased"); Oct. 3, 1843, MH ("dear noble woman!"); Sept. 29, 1843, *EL*, III, 207 ("divine scorn").

20. Sept. 13, 1843, *FL*, VI, 350 ("the West"); Sept. 20, 1843, *FL*, III, 147 ("vast future"); Oct. 13, 1843, ibid., 151 ("little nook").

21. Nov. 5, 1843, *EL*, III, 222 ("Watcher"); Nov. 12, 1843, *FL*, III, 159 ("glorious inconsistency"); Mar. 20, 1842, "ChaL," 171 ("Why not American"); Nov. 12, 1843, *FL*, III, 159–60 ("Don't expect any thing").

22. Dec. 5, 1843, *FL*, III, 163 ("These terms"); Nov. 12, 1843, ibid., 161 ("no persuading people"); *OM*, I, 350–51 ("Education"); Oct. [ca. 16], 1843, *FL*, III, 152 (Lidian); to Maria Rotch, Jan. 22, 1844, ibid., 172 (Rackemann).

23. July 11, 1843, *EL*, III, 183 (following); *OM*, II, 76 ("make a cento"); Georgiana Bruce Kirby, *Years of Experience: An Autobiographical Narrative* (New York, 1887), 173 ("*mother*"); to EFC, Apr. 1851, "ON," 492 ("reverenced"); [Feb.? 27?, 1844?], *FL*, VI, 352 ("ardent").

24. *Constitution of the Brook Farm Association, for Industry and Education, West Roxbury, Mass.* (Boston, 1844), 3–12 (reorganized into a phalanx); Oct. 27, 1843, *FL*, III, 154 ("Can we not wait"); to Mary Rotch, Jan. 21, 1844, ibid., 170 ("pledges and plans"); Oct. 27, 1843, ibid., 154 ("It is a constellation"); Dec. 31, 1843, OC, 135 ("The Earth"); [ca. early Jan. 1844]*, *OM*, II, 78 ("The tone"); to Orestes A. Brownson, Jan. 28, 1844, *FL*, III, 174 (borrowed *Association*). The best account of Channing's Fourierist career is in Octavius Brooks Frothingham, *Memoir of William Henry Channing* (Boston, 1886), chaps. 9–10.

25. To WHC, Oct. 27, 1843, *FL*, III, 154 ("different ways of steering"); to RFF, Nov. 19, 1844, FMW, VIII, 104 ("all agog"); to WHC, Oct. 27, 1843, *FL*, III, 154 ("third thought"); to RWE, Feb. 2, 1844, ibid., 180 ("*Mesmeric* experiments"); to RWE, [Feb.? 14?], 1844, ibid., 181, 181–82 ("our new Ecstatica"); Jan. 28, 1844, ibid., 178 ("underdevelopment"); to RWE, [Feb.? 14?], 1844, ibid., 181, 182 ("peeping"). This Romantic reformist phase of mesmerism has not received sufficient attention. Hawthorne draws a lurid portrait of it in *The Blithedale Romance*, in *Nathaniel Hawthorne: Novels*, Library of America Edition (New York, 1983), 635–36, 804–5. For a general treatment, see Robert C. Fuller, *Mesmerism and the American Cure of Souls* (Philadelphia, 1982). For the connections between mesmerism and the rise of dynamic psychology in Europe, see Henri F. Ellenberger, *The Discovery of the Unconscious: The History and Evolution of Dynamic Psychiatry* (New York, 1970), chaps. 2–3.

26. To MF, Feb. 16, 1844, *EL*, III, 240–41, and to SC, Mar. 1, 1844, *FL*, VII, 590 (putting off); "S. M. F. as read by Miss Parsons," ca. Mar. 1844, FMW, box A ("As she grows older").

27. *FSL*, 127, 130, 131 ("hypotheses").

28. *FSL*, 132 ("I would beat").

29. To RWE, Jan. 28, 1844, *FL*, III, 179 ("day and night"); Dec. 26, 1843, ibid., 164 ("lack of vital energy"); [ca. winter 1844]*, ibid., 167 ("cannot go through").

30. To MF, Nov. 12, 1843, FMW, X, 7 (*"ignore* it"); Susan Channing Higginson to Susan Higginson Channing, Oct. 2, [1840], Higginson-Cabot-Channing Papers, MHi ("system of notions"); Perry-Clarke Collection, MHi ("untamed"); "Verses, Given to W. C. With a Blank Book, March 1844," in MF, *Life Without and Life Within* (Boston, 1860), 386 ("more the child"); July 28, 1875, Tappan Papers, MH ("perusal of her writings"); Aug. 2, 1843, FMW, X, 4 ("facts of Femality & masculinity"); Sept. 20, 1843, FMW, X, 5 ("too little manly dignity"); "Lines on a Carnelian and Onyx found on the shores of Lake Superior," FMW, box A ("sever").

31. To AL, Apr. 2, 1845, *FL*, IV, 66 (sad); CST to EH, [ca. late July 1850], FMW, XVII, 59 (hypersensitive); Apr. 22, 1844, OC, 136 ("this thirst"); [May 31, 1844], "FJ44–2," 23, ("really love me"); May 1844, quoted in "ON," 498 ("mass of flesh").

32. "ON," 500 ("all hysterical"); May 1844, quoted in ibid., 486 ("Truth, truth"); May 31, 1844, "FJ44–2," 23, 24 ("Give me truth"); [June 4, 1844], ibid. ("ground me").

33. Journal, May 1844, "ON," 464 ("my comparative freedom"); Dec. 17, 1842, *FL*, III, 105 ("darkest hue"); Erik H. Erikson, *Identity: Youth and Crisis* (New York, 1968), 138 ("generativity"); *FW*, 85 ("spiritual parent").

34. Apr. 28, 1844, *FL*, III, 193 ("most animated meeting"); [Apr. 26, 1844]*, ibid., 185–86 ("worth living"); journal, Nov. 25, 1843, FMW, box A ("give me a son"); Nov. 6, 1843, *FL*, III, 157 (boys had a much better chance); to WHC[?], Dec. 3, 1840, *FL*, II, 187 ("my child"); May 25, [1844], *FL*, III, 197 ("finish my work").

35. "The Two Herberts," *Present*, 1 (Mar. 1, 1844), 25, 28, 34, 44 (relative claims); "The Modern Drama," *Dial*, 4 (Jan. 1844), 308, 309, 311, 312, 316, 318, 335, 340 ("dramatic sketch"); Jan. 31, 1844, *EL*, VII, 585 ("censure so wide").

36. "Dialogue," *Dial*, 4 (Apr. 1844), 458, 464, 468 ("Think you"): "Hawthorne and His Mosses," in *The Writings of Herman Melville: The Northwestern-Newberry Edition*, ed. Harrison Hayford, Hershel Parker, and G. Thomas Tanselle, vol. IX, *The Piazza Tales and Other Prose Pieces, 1839–1860*, ed. Harrison Hayford et al. (Evanston, Ill.: Northwestern University Press, 1987), 239–53. For popular appropriations of Shakespeare in antebellum America, see Lawrence W. Levine, *Highbrow/Lowbrow: The Emergence of Cultural Hierarchy in America* (Cambridge, Mass., 1988), chap. 1. Levine does not, however, discuss Romantic intellectuals like Fuller and Melville, whose complex literary democratic nationalism resists his dual categories of populist expression and elitist social control.

37. To RWE, Nov. 12, 1843, *FL*, III, 159 ("little plan"); to Harriet Martineau, [ca. Nov. 1837], *FL*, I, 307 ("presumptuous"); *FSL*, 32–33 ("stereotype"); "Books of Travel," *NYDT*, Dec. 18, 1845, 1 ("intellectual narratives"). For a survey of antebellum travel literature on the Mississippi Valley West, see Ralph Leslie Rusk, *The Literature of the Middle Western Frontier*, 2 vols. (New York, 1925), I, chap. 2. Recent accounts of the literary conventions of travel books on America at this time may be found in Mulvey, *Anglo-American Landscapes*, pt. 2; Sharon Rogers Brown, *American Travel Narratives as a Literary Genre from 1542 to 1832: The Art of a Perpetual Journey* (Lewiston, N.Y., 1993); Terry Caesar, *Forgiving the Boundaries: Home as Abroad in American Travel Writing*

(Athens, Ga., 1995), chaps. 1–2; and Beth L. Lueck, *American Writers and the Picturesque Tour: The Search for National Identity, 1790–1860* (New York, 1997).

38. *HO*, 194 ("Miss Fuller sitting"); Nov. 12, 1843, *FL*, III, 159 ("Letter box").

39. To JFC, Apr. 3, 1844, *FL*, VI, 353, and to ABW, Apr. 14, [1844], *FL*, III, 189; to ABF, Apr. 22, 1844, ibid., 191; to Little and Brown, June 3, [1844], ibid., 200; to MF, Apr. 11, 1844, *EL*, III, 246; and MCF and Barbara and Mary Channing, Apr. 21, 1844, Channing Family Papers, MHi (New York trip); *FL*, VI, 353, and RBS statement quoted in Katherine M. Zengerle, "She Told John Brown 'Twere Better to Die of a Big Idea Than of a Fever," *Los Angeles Record*, ca. 1905, NjHi (attended convention); Frothingham, *Memoir of Channing*, 207 ("great convention"); *EL*, III, 246–47, 247, 249–50 (Emerson's negotiations); to Little and Brown, June 3, [1844], *FL*, III, 200 ("best support"); HG to MF, Apr. 17, 1844, Emerson Family Papers, MH ("some eminent"); to MF, May 3, 1844, *EL*, 251 ("best correspondence").

40. To [?], [Summer] 1844, *FL*, III, 202 ("crabbed old guardians"); ibid., 196 ("walking forth alone"); [ca. mid-May 1844], quoted in *HO*, 195 ("tired of my book!"); to [?], [summer] 1844, *FL*, III, 202 ("among the graves"); [May], 23, [1844], "FJ44–2," 16 ("important era"); *FSL* (*Summer on the Lakes*).

41. *FSL*, 1, 26–27, 34, 35, 67, 256 ("no guidebook"). In recent years feminist-inspired literary scholars have reexamined *Summer on the Lakes* in a positive light. See Annette Kolodny, *The Land before Her: Fantasy and Experience of the American Frontiers, 1630–1860* (Chapel Hill, 1984), chap. 6; Stephen Adams, "'That Tidiness We Always Look for in Woman': Fuller's *Summer on the Lakes* and Romantic Aesthetics," in *SAR, 1987*, 247–64; Christina Zwarg, *Feminist Conversations: Fuller, Emerson, and the Play of Reading* (Ithaca, 1995), chap. 3; William W. Stowe, "Conventions and Voices in Margaret Fuller's Travel Writing," *American Literature*, 63 (June 1991), 242–62; and Susan Belasco Smith, "*Summer on the Lakes*: Margaret Fuller and the British," *Resources for American Literary Study*, 17 (1991), 191–207.

42. *FSL*, 7, 9, 9–10 ("hermit of a showplace").

43. *FSL*, 5 ("undefined dread"). In Fuller's original version of the Indian imagining, she emphasizes less the purely subjective character of her experience and plays up a little more the actual danger Indians posed. Journal, ca. summer 1843, FMW, box A. For additional early nineteenth-century writers' and artists' applications of the concept of the Romantic sublime to the representation of Niagara Falls, see Mulvey, *Anglo-American Landscapes*, chap. 11; and McKinsey, *Niagara Falls*, including in chap. 10, which discusses the theme in Fuller's *Summer*. For an astute discussion of a male literary tradition of scenes of attacking Indians as a "mood of nature" reflecting fears of women, see Nina Baym, "Putting Women in Their Place: *The Last of the Mohicans* and Other Indian Stories," in Baym's *Feminism and American Literary History* (New Brunswick, 1992), 19–35.

44. *FSL*, 7, 12–13 (little waterfall beyond"); Poe, "The Literati in New York City," in *The Complete Works of Edgar Allan Poe*, ed. James A. Harrison, 17 vols. (New York, 1902), XV, 76 (Poe would later admire); *FSL*, 12–13, 13 ("gaping tourists"); Barbara Novak, *Nature and Culture: American Landscape and Painting, 1825–1875*, rev. ed. (New York 1995), 28 ("operatically sublime").

45. *FSL*, 43, 44 ("river flows"). For Fuller's expressive language in *Summer*, see McKinsey, *Niagara Falls*, 217–18. The classic study of the myth of the "garden" in American thought is Leo Marx, *The Machine in the Garden: Technology and the Pastoral Ideal in America* (New York, 1964).

46. *FSL*, 37 ("points of light"); June 16, 1843, *FL*, III, 130 ("sensual looking"); *FSL*, 18, 19 ("habits of calculation").

47. *FSL*, 27, 28, 30, 53, 59, 60 ("mushroom growth").

48. *FSL*, 61, 62 ("great drawback").

49. *FSL*, 38, 58, 62, 63, 64, 103, 104 ("some English Lady Augusta"). For gender ideas and metaphors in American writings about the West, see Annette Kolodny's valuable studies *The Lay of the Land: Metaphor as Experience and History in American Life and Letters* (Chapel Hill, 1975), and *The Land before Her*.

50. *FSL*, 94, 125, 165, 165–66 ("very strange"). For Fuller's intentions in composing the Mariana tale, see to WHC, [June? 1844?], *FL*, III, 198. At the tale's end, Fuller inserts the suicidal ballad ("that great discerning mind") that she had written in her journal in late April, in the midst of her agitation about William Clarke, which she attributes here to Mariana. Apr. 22, 1844, OC, 136; *FSL*, 99–102.

51. *FSL*, 166 ("Could I but have flown").

52. The literature on white American ideas and images of Indians is ample. For a seminal study, see Roy Harvey Pearce, *Savages and Civilization: A Study of the History of the Indian and the American Mind* (1953; Berkeley, 1988). Robert F. Berkhofer, Jr., *The White Man's Indian: Images of the American Indian from Columbus to the Present* (New York, 1978) is a good overview. More recent contrasting interpretations may be found in Lee Clark Mitchell, *Witnesses to a Vanishing America: The Nineteenth-Century Response* (Princeton, 1981), chaps. 4–10; Brian W. Dippie, *The Vanishing American: White Attitudes and U.S. Indian Policy* (Berkeley, 1982); Philip J. Deloria, *Playing Indian* (New Haven, 1998); and Steven Conn, *History's Shadow: Native Americans and Historical Consciousness in the Nineteenth Century* (Chicago, 2004). In recent years discussions of "savagism" have often become subsumed under the problem of "otherness" in writings about colonized or subaltern groups. For two influential contrasting perspectives on that concept, see Edward Said, *Beginnings: Intention and Method* (New York, 1985); and Tzvetan Todorov, *The Conquest of America: The Question of the Other*, trans. Richard Howard (New York, 1985).

53. *FSL*, 115, 116 ("shoot the white man"); Herman Melville, *The Confidence-Man: His Masquerade* (1857), in *Herman Melville*, Library of America (New York, 1984), chap. 26 ("metaphysics of Indian-hating"); *FSL*, 183 ("white women").

54. Journal "1840," FMW, box 1 ("With the Indians, hopeless"); *FSL*, 199 ("fated to perish"); review of Henry R. Schoolcraft, *Oneata, or The Red Race of America*, *NYDT*, Feb. 12, 1845, 1 ("vulgar notion"). For claims made for Fuller's symbolic erasure of Indians in her text, see Lucy Maddox, *Removals: Nineteenth-Century American Literature and the Politics of Indian Affairs* (New York, 1991), 139–48; and Nicole Tonkovich, "Traveling in the West, Writing in the Library: Margaret Fuller's *Summer on the Lakes*," *Legacy*, 10 (1993), 79–102. Contrasting favorable treatments of Fuller's writings about Indians may be found in Zwarg, *Feminist Conversations*, chap. 3; and Charlene Avallone, "The Red Roots of White Feminism in Margaret Fuller's Writings," in Mary Anderson et al., eds., *Doing Feminism: Teaching and Research in the Academy* (East Lansing, Mich., 1997), 135–65. In his *Black Image in the White Mind: The Debate on Afro-American Character and Destiny, 1817–1914* (New York, 1971), chap. 4, George Fredrickson distinguishes between Herderian Romantic views of race, which Fuller generally follows in her book, and the sentimental racist versions predominant in antebellum America. For the variety of uses of "culture" for defining race in this period, see Bruce Dain, *A Hideous Monster of the Mind: American Race Theory in the Early Republic* (Cambridge, Mass., 2002).

55. *FSL*, 221 ("constantly breaking bounds"); Pearce, *Savagism and Civilization*, 148 ("sentimentalizing them"); *FSL*, 32 ("masquerade figure"); William Stanton, *The Leopard's*

Spots: Scientific Attitudes toward Race in America, 1815–59 (Chicago, 1960), 10–11 (mounds); *FSL*, 232 ("so good"). For an excellent study of Enlightenment and Romantic theories of the American "savage" or "primitive," see Anthony Pagden, *European Encounters with the New World: From Renaissance to Romanticism* (New Haven, 1993).

56. *FSL*, 31–32, 213 ("flimsy graces").

57. *FSL*, 119, 208, 213 ("white man's"). For a cogent discussion of the methods and motives of the antebellum scholars Fuller used, see Conn, *History's Shadow*.

58. *FSL*, 184–85, 208 ("All unprejudiced observers").

59. *FSL*, 182, 195, 195–96, 221, 232, 233, 235–36 ("mixed blood"). Thomas L. McKenney and James Hall, *The Indian Tribes of North America*, 3 vols. (Edinburgh, 1933–34), III, 219–345 (Hall's plan). The then deposed McKenney had opposed the use of force in removing the Indians. For McKenney's and other reformers' and politicians' positions on Indian removal, see Francis Paul Prucha, *The Great Father: The United States Government and the American Indians* (Lincoln, Neb., 1995), chaps. 7–11.

60. *FSL*, 237, 239, 245, 246, 248, 249, 250, 254–55 ("come down twenty times").

61. *HO*, 197 ("waywardness"); *FSL*, 63 ("dexterous weaver").

62. *OM*, II, 152 ("most graphic"); "Margaret Fuller Ossoli," in James Parton et al., *Eminent Women of the Age* (Hartford, 1868), 185 ("almost the only book"); Marx, *Machine in the Garden*, 71 ("symbolic middle landscape"). For a good appraisal of the literary strategies of the Transcendentalists, see Lawrence Buell, *Literary Transcendentalism: Style and Vision in the American Renaissance* (Ithaca, 1973), esp. chaps. 7–8. Valuable reconsiderations of "pastoral" themes in older and newer American studies scholarship may be found in Sacvan Bercovitch and Myra Jehlen, eds., *Ideology and Classic American Literature* (Cambridge, Mass., 1986), chaps. 2–4. For recent "ecological" and regional readings, respectively, see Lawrence Buell, *The Environmental Imagination: Thoreau, Nature Writing, and the Formation of American Culture* (Cambridge, Mass., 1995); and Nina Baym, "English Nature, New York Nature, and *Walden*'s New England Nature," in Charles Capper and Conrad Wright, eds., *Transient and Permanent: The Transcendentalist Movement and Its Contexts* (Boston, 1999), 168–89.

63. William C. Spengemann, *The Adventurous Muse: The Poetics of American Fiction, 1789–1900* (New Haven, 1977), 66 ("poetics of adventure"); Lewis Mumford, *The Golden Day: A Study in American Experience and Culture* (New York, 1926), 79 ("vast gap"); *FSL*, 65 ("god of limits"). For a discussion of the symbolic appropriation of the "West" by Hawthorne and other canonical authors of the American Renaissance, see Edwin Fussell, *Frontier: American Literature and the American West* (Princeton, 1965).

64. June 3, 1844, Tappan Papers, MH ("If it is not popular"); June 29, 1844, "PFC," 410–11 ("our Mad. De Stael"); to LMC, Mar. 13, 1844 (*Letters from New-York*); Aug. 23, 1844, *ChiL*, 410 ("too much furniture"); June 17, 1844, *EL*, VII, 602 ("feared it was bad"); June 9, 1844, ibid., 601 ("plain readable book"); June 17, 1844, ibid., 602 ("little web").

65. *HO*, 200 (typical first edition); "Literati," 75 ("*graphicality*"); July 16, 1844, Duyckinck Family Papers, NN-M ("only genuine American book"); *Graham's Magazine*, 26 (Sept. 1844), 144 ("reputation as an authoress"); [ca. summer 1844]*, quoted in Edward Waldo Emerson, *Emerson in Concord: A Memoir* (Boston, 1889), 161–62 ("I tell you"); "Hawthorne and His Mosses," 139–53 (Melville's claim).

66. "Notice of Recent Publications," *Christian Examiner*, 37 (Sept. 1844), 274, 275, 276 ("extraordinary endowments").

67. *Brownson's Quarterly Review* 6 (Oct. 1844), 546 ("heathen priestess"); *Christian World*, 2 (Oct. 12, 1844), 3 ("unmanly").

68. July 3, 1844, *FL*, III, 204 ("selling very well"); [June? 1844?], ibid., 198 ("It is amusing"); [Sept. 9, 1844], "FJ-1," 115–16 ("Newspapers from N. Orleans"); [June ? 1844], ibid., 198 ("buyers!!").

Chapter 5

1. [June 8, 1844], "FJ44–2," 28 ("never get through"); CS to RWE, June 3, 1844, Tappan Papers, MH (Caroline visited); [June] 18, [1844], "FJ44–1," 56 ("The past *is* past"); [July 5, 1844], ibid., 77 ("sentimental man of the world"); [June 27, 1844], ibid., 66 ("no more mistakes").

2. July 4, [1844], "FJ44–1," 71 ("godlike embrace"); July 2, [1844], "FJ44–1," 69 (Rosicrucians); [July 7, 1844], ibid., 79 ("It is shallow"); June 10, [1844], "FJ44–2," 31–34 and July 2, [1844], "FJ44–1," 69 ("Raphael's Descent from the Cross"); July 4, [1844], "FJ44–11," 74 ("Leila in the Arabian zone"). Fuller's "arcane" whimsies both fascinated and disturbed Emerson, to whom she sent several of these poems. Thoreau, wiser in these mythic ways than his patron, would later twit him for taking Fuller's occult symbolism too "gravely." To RWE, July 13, [1844], *FL*, III, 210; *OM*, I, 219; Dec. 12, 1851, *TJ*, IV, 202. Fuller's poetry deserves greater critical attention. The only significant discussion is Jeffrey Steele's suggestive "'Freeing the Prisoned Queen': The Development of Margaret Fuller's Poetry," in *SAR, 1992*, 137–75.

3. [July] 26, [1844], "FJ44–1," 100, 101 ("detachment of Irish"); July 22, 1844, *FL*, III, 217 ("world of babies!"); [July 9, 1844], "FJ44–1," 82 ("like a seraph"); [July] 12, 1844, ibid., 84 ("little Greta"); [July 18?, 1844], ibid., 89 ("attached to me").

4. [July 15, 1844], "FJ44–1," 85 ("Miss Fuller"); [Aug. 4], 1844, "FJ44–1," 111 (Channing popped in); SPH to Mrs. Elizabeth Palmer Peabody," Apr. 6, 1845, NN-B ("immoral, irreligious"); Rose Hawthorne Lathrop, *Memories of Hawthorne* (Boston, 1897), 188 ("unfading horror"); Jan. 16, 1843, *FL*, III, 115 ("black design"); NH to MF, Feb. 1, 1843, *HW*, XV, 670 ("can take my view"); SPH to Mrs. Elizabeth Palmer Peabody, June 26, 1844, NN-B ("Margaret is magnificent"); [July 18, 1844], "FJ44–1," 89 ("love him much"); [Aug.] 3, [1844], ibid., 108 ("like a sister"). For Sophia Hawthorne's growing disgust with the Transcendentalists' abolitionism, Fourierism, and protofeminism, see SPH to Mrs. Elizabeth Palmer Peabody, Sept. 3, 1843 and Apr. 6, 1845, NN-B; and SPH to Mary Peabody Mann, Apr. 6, [1845] and Jan. [16], 1848, ibid.

5. To Mrs. Elizabeth Palmer Peabody, Feb. 6, [1844], NN-B ("*self-sufficing* worlds"); [July 18?, 1844], "FJ44–1," 89 ("equal marriage"); [July 22, 1844], ibid., 92 ("our intercourse"). Somebody later deleted entries in "FJ44–1" that seem to refer to her encounters with Hawthorne and Emerson.

6. [July 27?, 1844], "FJ44–1," 105 ("want them all").

7. [July 9, 1844], "FJ44–1," 82 ("scene of distress"); [July] 12, [1844], ibid., 84 ("so disagreeable"); to JTK, July 22, 1844, *FL*, III, 217 (EFC visits Cambridge); July 25, 1844, *FL*, VI, 354 ("feel cradled").

8. To CS, July 25, 1844, *FL*, VI, 354 ("playmate"); to CS, July 20, 1844, *EL*, VII, 606 (read to her); [July] 14, [1844], "FJ44–1," 84 ("I am not really so"); [July], 11, [1844], ibid., 83 ("how cold").

9. [July 24?, 1844], "FJ44–1," 93 ("transcendental fatalism"); July 13, [1844], *FL*, III, 209 ("You are intellect").

10. Sept. 1842, *FL*, III, 93 ("academic Grove"); [July 20?, 1844], ibid., 213, 214, 215, 216 ("not in Concord"). For a virtually identical journal version of this poem, see [July] 25, [1844], "FJ44–1," 95–97. Of course, Concord had its social and political conflicts,

which Thoreau would later exploit in *Walden* in cosmic miniature. See Robert A. Gross, "'The Most Estimable Place in All the World': A Debate on Progress in Nineteenth-Century Concord," in *SAR, 1978*, 1–15; "Culture and Cultivation: Agriculture and Society in Thoreau's Concord," *Journal of American History*, 69 (June 1982), 42–61; and "The Celestial Village: Transcendentalism and Tourism in Concord," in Capper and Wright, *Transient and Permanent*, 251–81.

11. [July] 25, [1844], "FJ44–1," 94 ("'Let all drive'"); [July 27?, 1844], "FJ44–1," 105 ("Undeveloped Man!"); ibid., 107–8 ("Waldo's oration").

12. "An Address Delivered in the Court-House in Concord, Massachusetts, on 1st August, 1844, on the Anniversary of the Emancipation of the Negroes in the British West Indies," in *Emerson: Essays and Poems*, ed. Joel Porte, Harold Bloom, and Paul Kane (New York, 1996), 991 ("anti-slave[s]"); [Aug.], 3, [1844], "FJ44–1," 109 ("took leave").

13. [Aug.] 5, [1844], "FJ44–1," 110 ("bright cool fragrant"); [July 27?, 1844], ibid., 104 (Fuller wrote Greeley); statement of HG in *OM*, II, 153 (Mary Greeley's idea); Oct. 31, 1842, "FJ42–2," 291 ("touching"); *OM*, II, 152 ("graphic"); "Life in Illinois," *NYWT*, June 15, 1844, 1 ("most original"); [Aug.] 17, [1844], "FJ44–2," n.p. ("laying a plan"); [ca. Sept. 3, 1844], ibid. ("proposal"). In his autobiography Greeley says only that his wife "planned and partly negotiated" Fuller's coming to New York. Horace Greeley, *Recollections of a Busy Life* (New York, 1868), 176.

14. Apr. 2, 1845, *FL*, IV, 66 ("childish"); *FL*, III, 188 n2 (distribution of estate); ibid., 228 n 1 (Cambridgeport house); to LGL, June 22, 1845, *ChiL*, 223–24 (Child's career); to RWE, Mar. 8, 1842, *FL*, III, 52, to MF, Mar. 1, 1842, *EL*, III, 20, to MF, Mar. 10 and 12?, 1842, ibid., 29, to LJE, Mar. 19, 1842, ibid., 26, to CS, Apr.? 10?, 1842, ibid., 48 (Emerson's reports); Mar. 1, 1842, ibid., 20 ("I should choose New York").

15. [Ca. Sept. 1–3], "FJ44–2," n.p. ("O I do hate"); [Sept. 4, 1844], ibid., n.p. ("terrible headache[s]"); [Sept. 5, 1844], ibid., n.p. ("much vertigo"); [Sept.] 10, [1844], "FJ44–1," 115, 116 ("much depressed"); [Sept.] 12, [1844], ibid., 117 ("miserable night"); [Sept. 15, 1844], ibid., 118 ("try it"); [Sept. 22, 1844], ibid., 118 ("great promise"). Perry Miller's assertions that Fuller's Transcendentalist friends regarded her move to New York as "daring, not to say treasonable" and that Emerson looked on her acceptance of Greeley's offer "with cold disapproval" are misleading. Although Emerson would later have serious misgivings about her writing for a newspaper, at the time, and on the question of her moving to New York, he was encouraging. Miller, *The American Transcendentalists: Their Prose and Poetry* (Garden City, New York, 1957), 187. For additional encouragement that Fuller got from her Boston-Cambridge friends to take the job, see [Sept. 9, 1844], "FJ44–1," 115; [Sept. 22, 1844], ibid., 118; and [Sept. 30, 1844], ibid., 120.

16. To FHH, Apr. 12, 1838, *EL*, VII, 302–3 ("foaming foolishness"); [ca. summer 1844]*, quoted in Emerson, *Emerson in Concord*, 161 ("learned and virtuous"); Sept. 25, 1844, *FL*, III, 230 ("a's not gold"); Sept. 25, 1844, *FL*, III, 230 ("*my department*").

17. To George Graham, June 3, [1842], in Rufus W. Griswold, *Passages from the Correspondence and Other Papers of Rufus W. Griswold* (Cambridge, Mass., 1898), 112 ("proper only for the other sex"); [Sept. 25, 1844], "FJ44–1," 119 ("her dead body"); ca. early Jan. 1844]*, *FL*, VI, 104 ("you do not sympathize"); [Sept. 25, 1844], "FJ44–1," 119 ("Mother's death and burial"). Patricia Okker demonstrates that Hale was only the foremost among many antebellum female periodical editors, but most of them edited women's magazines, and none was an editor of a major intellectual journal or metropolitan daily. *Our Sister Editors: Sarah J. Hale and the Tradition of Nineteenth-Century American Women Editors* (Athens, Ga., 1995).

18. [Sept. 15, 1844], "FJ44–1," 118 ("Farewell, dear river"); [Sept. 26, 1844], ibid., 119

(parting visits); to CKN, July 8, [1844], *FL*, III, 206 ("seventy persons"); [Sept. 27, 1844], "FJ44–1," 119 ("Poor little hand!"). [Sept. 30, 1844], ibid., 120 ("much information").

19. To Sarah Hodges, Sept. 27, 1844, *FL*, III, 231 ("good sword"); quoted in [Oct. 4, 1844]*, "FJ44," 121–22 ("deep gratitude") to RFF, Oct. 15, 1844, *FL*, III, 234 ("Night's glorious star").

20. To RFF, Nov. 23, 1844, *FL*, III, 248 (start at the *Tribune*); to RFF, Oct. 15, 1844, ibid., 234, 235 ("beautiful place" and "nobody's humor"); CS to RWE, Aug. 9, 1844, Tappan Papers, MH ("wandering"); to CKN, Nov. 25, 1844, *FL*, III, 249 ("sisterly"); [Autumn 1844], ibid., 232 ("fallow flat fields").

21. [Aug.] 17, [1844], and Aug. [31], [1844], "FJ44–2," n.p. (starting her book); [Sept.] 6, [1844], ibid., 113, and [Sept.] 8, [1844], ibid., 114 (writer's block and headaches); [ca. mid-Oct. 1844]*, *OM*, II, 135 ("black jailer").

22. [Ca. Oct. 1844]*, *OM*, II, 138 ("the slow pen").

23. [Ca. Oct. 1844]*, *FL*, VI, 131 ("scarcely touched"); [ca. Oct. 1844]*, *OM*, II, 139–40 ("face this agitation").

24. [Aug. 4, 1844], "1844–1," 110–11 ("truly great"); [Oct. 19, 1844], "FJ44–1," 124, and *OM*, II, 137 (Fishkill reading); Nov. 17, 1844, *FL*, III, 243 ("*Sunday reading*"); [ca. fall 1844], Journal "1840," FMW, box 1 ("action & reaction"). For the growing sympathy for Fourierism in Fuller's Transcendentalist and abolitionist circles following Brook Farm's Fourierist conversion that year, see, for example, W. A. White, Sept. 19, 1843, *LoL*, II, 74–75; TP to CF, Mar. 18, 1844, "PFC," 350; CF to TP, June 26, 1844, ibid., 405; to MF, [ca. mid-Jan. 1845], "SL," 232; CS to RWE, Feb. 4, 1845, [ca. Aug. 5, 1845], Sept 1, 1845, and [Oct. 20, 1845], Tappan Papers, MH; and Jan. 29, 1845, and [Mar.? 5, 1845], "SL," 235, 242.

25. Sept. 12, 1844, "FJ44–1," 117 ("how much better"); [ca. Oct. 1844], OC, 120, and *OM*, II, 136 ("No one loves me). Although the *OM* printing of this entry adds some sentences that are missing in the mutilated original manuscript, it also deletes others (specifically touching on her craving for a child); my quotation, therefore, is an amalgam of both versions. This passage was misdated in *CF-1*, 288–89.

26. [Ca. Summer-Fall 1844]*, *OM*, II, 140, 141 ("sacred"); *FSL*, 81–103 (Mariana story); "Aglauron and Laurie. A Drive through the Country near Boston," FMW, box A ("divine purpose"). A generally accurate version of "Aglauron and Laurie" may be found in Margaret Fuller, *Woman in the Nineteenth Century, and Kindred Papers*, ed. Arthur B. Fuller (Boston, 1855), 183–216.

27. [Aug.] 6, [1844], "FJ44–1," 110 ("repulsive"); [Sept.] 8, [1844], ibid., 114–15 ("boy-baby").

28. [Ca. Oct. 1844], *OM*, II, 136 ("sovereign self"); [ca. Oct. 1844], "FS" ("To the Face Seen in the Moon"). Fuller's poem is partially quoted and misdated in *CF-1*, 287–88. Cf. to JN, May 23, [1845], *FL*, IV, 104–7; and "ON," 474.

29. [Ca. Spring 1844]*, quoted in *HO*, 122 ("don't feel ready"); [ca. Oct. 1844], *OM*, II, 141 ("Texas annexation project"); Louis Filler, *The Crusade against Slavery, 1830–1860* (New York, 1960), 178 ("monster rallies").

30. [July], 5, 1844, "FJ44–1," 76 ("dignified"); to WHC, Dec. 13, [1840], *FL*, II, 193 ("saint[s]"); Sept. 24, 1842, "FJ42–1," 339 ("fine girl").

31. Georgiana Bruce Kirby, *Years of Experience: An Autobiographical Narrative* (New York, 1887), 190 (Fuller's suggestion). For contrasting discussions of early antebellum female prisoners and urban charity workers, see Estelle B. Freedman, *Their Sisters' Keepers: Women's Prison Reform in America, 1830–1930* (Ann Arbor, 1981); Nicole Hahn Rafter, *Partial Justice: Women in State Prisons* (Boston, 1985); and Lucia Zedner, "Way-

ward Sisters: The Prison for Women," in Norval Morris and David J. Rothman, eds., *The Oxford History of the Prison: The Practice of Punishment in Western Society* (New York, 1995), 329–61. Useful details on the Fuller's connection with Farnham, Bruce, and Sing Sing may be found in Kirby's autobiography, chap. 10. For Farnham and Sing Sing, see W. David Lewis, *From Newgate to Dannemora: The Rise of the Penitentiary in New York* (New York, 1965); and Lewis's entry on Farnham in *NAW*, I, 598–600.

32. Aug. 15, 1844, *FL*, III, 221, 223 ("Lehrjahre for women"); Oct. 20, 1844, ibid., 236 ("feeling about chastity").

33. Kirby, *Years of Experience*, 218, 219 ("amazed"). Even forty years later, this still saucy woman remained sufficiently nervous about Fuller's sexual inquiries to change the words "feminine Nature" to "primitive nature" in Fuller's Oct. 20 letter as well as to claim that its second part (on Fuller's questions) was written by someone other than Fuller. Ibid., 211, 218.

34. Oct. [28], 1844*, *FL*, III, 237 ("'Men and Bretheren'"); Nov. 23, 1844, ibid., 247 ("never felt such sympathy").

35. To EH, Oct. [28]*, 1844, *FL*, III, 237 ("could then say *all*"); Nov. 23, 1844, ibid., 248 ("These women"); Oct. [28]*, 1844, ibid., 237 ("so called worst").

36. To the Women Inmates at Sing Sing, [Early Nov.? 1844], *FL*, III, 238 ("taste for reading"); Oct. [28]*, 1844, ibid., 237 ("take some time").

37. [Oct. 29, 1844], "FJ44–1," 125 ("wickedness of man") [Oct. 30, 1844*], ibid., 126 ("mice); to RWE, Nov. 17, 1844, *FL*, III, 243 ("at last"); Nov. 17, 1844, ibid., 241 ("my foot-print").

38. To EPP, Dec. 26, 1844, *FL*, III, 254, and Lydia Maria Child, review of Margaret Fuller, *Woman in the Nineteenth Century*, *Broadway Journal*, 1 (Feb. 15, 1845), 97 (in press); HG to Rufus W. Griswold, in Griswold, *Passages from the Correspondence*, 166 (for sale).

39. *FW*, v, vi ("two halves"); Perry Miller, *Transcendentalists: An Anthology* (Cambridge, Mass., 1950), 457 ("reasoned"); Miller, *American Transcendentalists*, 330 ("dithyrambic").

40. *FW*, 21, 22, 32, 90, 92 ("Can this be you?).

41. *FW*, 105, 109, 110, 114, 115, 172 ("three male minds").

42. *FW*, 105, 106, 110, 112, 160 ("Ay! but Goethe"). For the rise of social democratic liberalism, see James T. Kloppenberg, *Uncertain Victory: Social Democracy and Progressivism in European and American Thought, 1870–1920* (New York, 1986).

43. *FW*, 118, 143, 149, 150 ("sighing over").

44. *FW*, 159 ("polite"); *New York Weekly Herald*, Mar. 14, 1845, p. 86 ("legal licentiousness"). For an example of the growing private criticism of the institution of marriage among radical reformers in the late 1840s, see Lydia Maria Child's broad swipe against "legalized prostitution," in to LGL, Jan. 15, 1847, *ChiL*, 234–36. For the contentious discourse over sexuality in this period, see Helen Lefkowitz Horowitz, *Rereading Sex: Battles over Sexual Knowledge and Suppression in Nineteenth-Century America* (New York, 2002). Also illuminating on the New York sexual scene are Christine Stansell, *City of Women: Sex and Class in New York, 1789–1860* (New York, 1986), chap. 9; Timothy J. Gilfoyle, *City of Eros: New York City, Prostitution, and the Commercialization of Sex, 1790–1920* (New York, 1992); and Patricia Cline Cohen, *The Murder of Helen Jewett: The Life and Death of a Prostitute in Nineteenth-Century New York* (New York, 1998). For nineteenth-century American sex radicalism, see Hal D. Sears, *The Sex Radicals: Free Love in High Victorian America* (Lawrence, Kans., 1977); and John C. Spurlock, *Free Love: Marriage and Middle-Class Radicalism in America, 1825–1920* (New York, 1988).

45. *FW*, 118, 119, 132–33 ("degradation").

46. *FW*, 135, 136, 136–37 ("hard").

47. *FW*, 119–20, 123, 126, 127, 134, 135, 137, 138, 140, 201 ("prudery").

48. *FW*, 151–52, 152 ("nothing to do with this?").

49. *FW*, 152, 153 ("If you have a power").

50. *FW*, 154, 155, 156 ("old-fashioned sermons").

51. Immanuel Kant, "An Answer to the Question: What Is Enlightenment?" in James Schmidt, ed., *What Is Enlightenment? Eighteenth-Century Answers and Twentieth-Century Questions* (Berkeley, 1996), 58 ("*Sapere aude!*"); *FW*, 158, 159, 160–61 ("encumbered by tradition"). For later influential statements of the argument that women's economic marginalization caused the degeneration of the race or society, see Charlotte Perkins Gilman, *Women and Economics* (Boston, 1898); Thorstein Veblen, *The Theory of the Leisure Class* (New York, 1899); and Walter Lippmann, *Drift and Mastery* (New York, 1914).

52. *FW*, 162, 162–63 ("An idea not unknown"). For Fuller's accounts of Emerson's recent urgings on her of "his transcendental fatalism," see [July] 11 and [July 24?, 1844], "FJ44–1," 83, 93. For contrasting feminist comparisons of Fuller's and Emerson's gender thought that both deviate from and intersect with mine, see Christina Zwarg, *Feminist Conversations: Fuller, Emerson, and the Play of Reading* (Ithaca, 1995), esp. chaps. 5 and 8; and Phyllis Cole, "Woman Questions: Emerson, Fuller, and New England Reform," in Capper and Wright, *Transient and Permanent*, 408–46. If one strips Emerson's claim of its apparent androgyny and idealistic metaphysics, one could claim that it represents a move from the "modern" incommensurable "two-sex" model of sexual identity back to the premodern one of the species as "one-sex" or male. On this shift, see Ruth H. Bloch, "Untangling the Roots of Modern Sex Roles: A Survey of Four Centuries of Change," *Signs*, 4 (Winter 1978), 237–52; and Thomas Laquer, *Making Sex: Body and Gender from the Greeks to Freud* (Cambridge, Mass., 1990).

53. *FW*, 163 ("Suppose").

54. *FW*, 159, 161, 201 ("I have urged").

55. *Dial*, 4 (July 1843), 47 ("woman who shall vindicate"); *FW*, 163–64, 164 ("I stand").

56. Mrs. Elizabeth Palmer Peabody to SPH, [ca. early Mar. 1845*], quoted in Julian Hawthorne, *Nathaniel Hawthorne and His Wife: A Biography*, 2 vols. (Cambridge, Mass., 1884), I, 258 ("a breeze"); SPH to Mrs. Elizabeth Palmer Peabody, Mar. 6, 1845, quoted in ibid. ("disagreeable"); Feb. 28, 1845, FMW, XI, 117 ("You go for thought"); Feb. 8, 1845, *ChiL*, 219 ("*bold* book"). There is no record of Nathaniel's opinion of Fuller's book, although Sophia thought that her husband agreed with her about the immorality of Fourier's sexual views. They did write a now lost letter to Fuller about her book, which, given Fuller's cordial but evasive reply, probably muted Sophia's opinion of it. See to SPH and NH, May 22, [1845], *FL*, IV, 103.

57. July 11, 1843, *EL*, III, 183 ("poetic form"); Mar. 4, 1845, "SL," 239 ("troubles me"); *FW*, 154 ("my meaning"); Mar. 13, 1845, *FL*, IV, 58, 59 ("even in veils"); [ca. mid-Jan. 1845], "SL," 232 (Fourier-bitten); [Mar. 27, 1845], *FL*, IV, 64 ("stranger more sympathizing"). The rebellious but reticent Sturgis had the same problem with Fourier that she had with Fuller. "I am struggling through Fourier & wish he would not write for the public," she told Fuller. Jan. 29, 1845, SL, 237.

58. Jan. 15, 1845, in Griswold, *Passages from the Correspondence,* 163 ("going to *sell*"); to WHC, Nov. 17, 1844, *FL*, III, 242 (hoping to sell); HG to RFF, July 30, 1853, FMW, XVI, 88 (edition sold); to EF, Mar. 9, 1845, *FL*, IV, 56 ("signet of success"); *HO*, 203 (then rare); *NYDT*, Nov. 11, 1845, 2 ("beautifully issued"); [Nov.] 10, 1845, *FL*, IV, 166 ("country folks"); *New York Commercial Advertiser*, Mar. 7, 1845 ("Great Book").

59. Mar. 13, 1845, *FL*, IV, 59 ("opposition"); Mar. 9, 1845, ibid., 56 ("abuse"); *Charleston Mercury*, Mar. 11, 1845, 2 ("since the days of Mary Wollstonecraft"); review of *Woman in the Nineteenth Century*, *Broadway Journal*, 1 (Feb. 15, 1845), 97 ("pen of Margaret Fuller"); anon., review of *Woman in the Nineteenth Century*, *Ladies National Magazine* 7 (Apr. 1845), 143 ("no common woman"); Charles F. Briggs, review of *Woman in the Nineteenth Century* [First Notice], *Broadway Journal*, 1 (Mar. 1, 1845), 130 ("thinking, right-judging person"); *Charleston Mercury*, Mar. 11, 1845, 2 ("strength of expression").

60. Review of *Woman in the Nineteenth Century*, *Broadway Journal*, 1 (Mar. 22, 1845), 182–83, 183 ("no unmarried woman"); "Miss Fuller and Reformers," *Boston Quarterly Review*, 7 (Apr. 1845), 254 ("obscene"); "Transcendentalism, or the Latest Form of Infidelity," *Boston Quarterly Review*, 7 (July 1845), 312 ("renowned courtesans").

61. A.G.M., "The Condition of Woman," *Southern Quarterly Review*, 10 (July 1846), 172, 173 ("perfect equality"); anon., review of *Woman in the Nineteenth Century*, *Ladies National Magazine*, 7 (Apr. 1845), 143, 144 ("social system").

62. Review of *Woman in the Nineteenth Century*, *Christian Examiner*, 38 (May 1845), 416, 417 ("special pleading"); review of *Woman in the Nineteenth Century*, *Herald of Freedom*, 11 (Sept. 5, 1845), 1 ("chaste"); [WEC2], review of *Woman in the Nineteenth Century*, *NYDT*, Feb. 13, 1845, 1 ("women must redeem them").

63. Charles F. Briggs, Review of *Woman in the Nineteenth Century* [Second Notice], *Broadway Journal*, 1 (Mar. 8, 1845), 145 ("want of distinctness"); *New York Evening Post*, Feb. 18, 1845 ("pretty strong"); "Miss Fuller and Reformers," *Boston Quarterly Review*, 7 (Apr. 1845), 250 ("may be read backwards"); review of *Woman in the Nineteenth Century*, *Christian Examiner*, 38 (May 1845), 416 ("habit of thought"); review of *Woman in the Nineteenth Century*, *Broadway Journal*, 1 (Feb. 15, 1845), 97 ("contralto voice"); review of *Woman in the Nineteenth Century*, *NYDT*, Feb. 13, 1845, 1 ("repay the working").

64. Quoted in the *Boston Daily Advertiser*, July 6, 1846 ("'WOMAN IN THE NINETEENTH CENTURY'"). The connections between Transcendentalism and later nineteenth-century feminism are just beginning to receive attention. For a recent overview, see Tiffany K. Wayne, *Woman Thinking: Feminism and Transcendentalism in Nineteenth-Century America* (Lanham, Md., 2005). Some moderate Transcendentalists, such as Frederic Henry Hedge and Elizabeth Peabody, publicly opposed woman's suffrage or were lukewarm to hostile toward the feminist movement. In general, though, after the appearance of *Woman in the Nineteenth Century*, most prominent Transcendentalists readily embraced women's rights positions, often on grounds that echoed Fuller's stances, language, and presuppositions. For an early example of this trend, see James Freeman Clarke's report on the discussion of "'Woman's Sphere'" at his Church of the Disciples' "Social Meeting," in JFC, journal, Apr. 11, 1846, Perry-Clarke Collection, MHi; and for a late example, see Octavius Brooks Frothingham, *Transcendentalism in New* England: *A History* (New York, 1976), 176–83.

65. *Recollections of a Busy Life* (New York, 1868), 175 ("Woman's Rights"); Elizabeth Cady Stanton, Susan B. Anthony, and Matilda Joslyn Gage, eds., *History of Woman Suffrage*, I (New York, 1881), 217 ("leadership of the movement"); Sara A. Underwood, "Margaret Fuller—A Woman's Woman," [ca. 1882], Harriet Hanson Robinson Scrapbooks, vol. XLIII, Harriet Hanson Robinson Papers, MCR-S ("loyalty to her sex"); Mary A. Livermore, *The Story of My Life* (Hartford, 1899), 615 ("far in advance"). For links between Fuller's Romantic feminism and Stanton's women's rights thought, see Phyllis Cole, "The Ninteenth-Century Women's Rights Movement and the Canonization of Margaret Fuller, "*ESQ*," 44 (1st and 2nd Quarters 1998), 1–33; and idem, "Stanton, Fuller, and the Grammar of Roman-

ticism," *New England Quarterly*, 73 (Dec. 2000), 533–59. A discussion of the Romantic contours of the careers of 1850s feminist activist-intellectuals may be found in Susan Conrad, *Perish the Thought: Intellectual Women in Romantic America* (New York, 1978). Some evidence of Fuller's influence on early feminist figures may be found scattered throughout the first volume of Stanton's *History of Woman Suffrage*, but much more can be found in their published works and unpublished papers. For a guide to writings on Fuller by nineteenth-century feminists, see Joel Myerson's bibliographies: *Margaret Fuller: An Annotated Secondary Bibliography* (New York, 1977); "Supplement to *Margaret Fuller: An Annotated Secondary Bibliography*," in *SAR, 1984*, 331–85; and *Margaret Fuller: An Annotated Bibliography of Criticism, 1983–1995* (Westport, Conn., 1998).

66. Stanton et al., *History of Woman Suffrage*, I, 801–2 ("the precursor"). For valuable studies of the ideology of the nineteenth-century women's rights movement, see Ellen DuBois, *Feminism and Suffrage: The Emergence of an Independent Women's Movement in America, 1848–1869* (Ithaca, 1978); Sylvia D. Hoffert, *When Hens Crow: The Woman's Rights Movement in Antebellum America* (Bloomington, 1995); Jean V. Matthews, *Women's Struggle for Equality: The First Phase, 1828–1876* (Chicago, 1997); and Wiliam Leach, *True Love and Perfect Union: The Feminist Reform of Sex and Society* (New York, 1980). The best source for both the style and content of the early woman's rights meetings remains Stanton et al., *History of Woman Suffrage*, I.

67. ABF to EF, June 9, 1855, FMW, XIII, 150 (three times); "Address by ECS on Woman's Rights," in *The Selected Papers of Elizabeth Cady Stanton and Susan B. Anthony*, vol. I, ed. Ann D. Gordon (New Brunswick, 1997), 94, 115, 116 ("'rabble rout'"); Stanton et al., *History of Woman Suffrage*, I, 355 ("'Give me Truth'"). Fuller's poem in Stanton's address is unidentified in the volume.

68. *The Elizabeth Cady Stanton–Susan B. Anthony Reader: Correspondence, Writings, Speeches*, rev. ed., ed. Ellen Carol DuBois (1981; Boston, 1992), 247 ("individuality"); FW, 162 ("ever young"). For the printing history of *Woman in the Nineteenth Century*, see Joel Myerson, *Margaret Fuller: A Descriptive Bibliography* (Pittsburgh, 1978), 17–23, 49–54. Penetrating discussions of the early twentieth-century emergence of modernist American feminism appear in Nancy F. Cott, *The Grounding of Modern Feminism* (New Haven, 1987); Ann Douglas, *Terrible Honesty: Mongrel Manhattan in the 1920s* (New York, 1995); and Christine Stansell, *American Moderns: Bohemian New York and the Creation of a New Century* (New York, 2000). Three self-consciously modernist readers of Fuller's life—Katherine Anthony, Vernon Parrington, and Perry Miller—all portray her as a victim of "Victorian" repression. See Katharine Anthony, *Margaret Fuller: A Psychological Biography* (New York, 1920); Vernon Louis Parrington, *Main Currents in American Thought*, 3 vols. (New York, 1927–30), II, 426–34; and Perry Miller, ed., *Margaret Fuller: American Romantic* (Garden City, N.Y., 1963). The line between "Victorian" and "modernist" contexts should not be overdrawn, of course. For counter-examples of lingering "Victorian" tributes to Fuller as a "womanly woman" even into the twentieth century, see Kenyon West, letter to the editor, *Outlook*, 10 (June 4, 1910), 271; and Lavinia Egan, "Margaret Fuller—Feminist and Literateur," *Equal Rights*, 1 (Sept. 22, 1923), 256.

Chapter Six

1. Nov. 20, 1844, *FL*, III, 245 ("I feel refreshed"); to CKN, Nov. 25, 1844, ibid., 249 ("sacred"); to AL, Feb. 6, 1845, *ChiL*, 217 ("dropping to pieces"); Mary Greeley, cited in "Margaret Fuller Memorial Tablet," *New York Times*, July 20, 1901 (lantern); Horace Greeley, *Recollections of a Busy Life* (New York, 1868), 176–77 ("sepulchral").

2. Mar. 9, 1845, *FL*, IV, 56 ("well situated"); to [?], [Dec. 1844], *FL*, III, 250 ("entirely charming"); to EF, Mar. 9, 1845, *FL*, IV, 56 ("Castle Rackrent style").

3. Frank Luther Mott, *American Journalism: A History of Newspapers in the United States through 250 Years, 1690 to 1940* (New York, 1941), chaps. 12–19, remains the best survey of the newspaper "revolution" of the 1830s and 1840s. I have found persuasive Michael Schudson, *Discovering the News: A Social History of American Newspapers* (New York, 1978), especially chap. 1, which places the revolution's genesis within antebellum America's emergent "democratic market society." For a counterview that argues for the "artisan" and "republican" class-consciousness of the penny presses, see Dan Schiller, *Objectivity and the News: The Public and the Rise of Commercial Journalism* (Philadelphia, 1981).

4. James Parton, *Life of Horace Greeley* (New York, 1855), is still useful for its colorful oral testimony. Although it emphasizes mostly Greeley's political career, Glyndon G. Van Deusen, *Horace Greeley: Nineteenth-Century Crusader* (Philadelphia, 1953), remains the best scholarly biography. William Harlan Hale, *Horace Greeley: Voice of the People* (New York, 1950), is helpful for the journalistic background. For an appraisal of Greeley as a Whig "modernizer," see Daniel Walker Howe, *The Political Culture of the American Whigs* (Chicago, 1979), 184–97.

5. Remarkably, Greeley's *Tribune* is often skirted in recent scholarship on print culture, probably in part because it fits awkwardly with the "elite" and "popular" categories that recent social historians have offered to explain the "penny press" revolution. Useful overviews may be found in Mott, *American Journalism*, chap. 15; and Richard Kluger, *The Paper: The Life and Death of the "New York Herald Tribune"* (New York, 1986), chaps. 1–3. For the politics of Greeley's paper, see Adam-Max Tuchinsky's recent "Horace Greeley's Lost Book: *The New-York Tribune* and the Origins of Social Democratic Liberalism in America" (Ph.D. diss., University of North Carolina at Chapel Hill, 2001).

6. *NYDT*, May 3, 1841 ("active and substantial").

7. To Harvey Hubbard, Aug. 26, 1843, HG Papers, NN-M ("stoned me to death"); "Prospectus for the Year 1845," *NYDT*, Nov. 16, 1844 ("inferior to no other").

8. [Sept.] 26, 1849, *Journal of Richard Henry Dana, Jr.*, I, 390, 391 ("contrast"); to HG, [ca. 1845–46], *FL*, VI, 108 ("scribble").

9. To SGW, Dec. 29, 1844, *FL*, III, 256 (Channing's assistance); to RFF, Mar. 2, 1845, *FL*, IV, 54 (fired Channing); to William Emerson, Dec. 3, 1844, *EL*, III, 268 ("make his own work"); Ann W. Weston to Caroline and Debra Weston, [Jan.] 24 and 27, 1845, Weston Papers, MB (ten dollars per week).

10. To MR, Jan. 15, 1845, *FL*, IV, 46 ("Star"); *NYDT*, July 3, 1845, p. 1 ("manly independence"); ibid., May 4, 1846, p. 1 ("though female?"); "What Is Infidelity and Who Are the Infidels?" *Courier and Enquirer*, Mar. 7, 1846, 1 (hide behind a woman); "A few Words in Reply to Mr. U. C. Hill," *NYDT*, May 16, 1846, supp., 1 ("under one signature"); *Graham's Magazine*, 29 (Sept. 1846), 156 ("the 'Star' of the New York Tribune"). Characteristic of antebellum newspaper reviewing was Henry J. Raymond's bald order of a notice to Evert A. Duyckinck a few years later: "I want it laudatory & *readable*—& of course will pay for it." Nov. 14, 1856, Duyckinck Family Papers, NN-M. For book publishers' use of newspaper reviews to promote their books, see William Charvat, "James T. Fields and the Beginnings of Book Promotion," in *The Profession of Authorship in America, 1800–1870: The Papers of William Charvat*, ed. Matthew J. Bruccoli (Columbus, Ohio, 1968), chap. 10.

11. To RFF, Jan. 9, 1845, *FL*, IV, 42, and to MCF, Jan. 12, 1845, ibid., 44 (influ-

enza); to MR, Jan. 15, 1845, ibid., 46 ("very moderately"); *OM*, II, 154 ("not always clearly"); Greeley, *Recollections*, 177–78 ("no such capacity").

12. *OM*, II, 155, 157–58, 158 ("She never asked").

13. Mar. 1, 1842, *EL*, III, 19 ("mother of men"); Jan. 15, 1845, *FL*, IV, 46 ("of the *Amrn* people"); Mar. 9, 1845, ibid., 56 ("slattern and plebeian"); [Aug. 14, 1845], *FL*, VI, 360 ("teaches me many things").

14. To [?], [ca. Feb. 9, 1845], *FL*, IV, 48 ("For a day").

15. Dec. 29, 1844, *FL*, III, 256 ("not make too fine"); Jan. 9, 1845, *FL*, VI, 357 ("What you say").

16. To WHC, [Dec. 31, 1844], *FL*, III, 257 ("European stock"); statement of HG, *OM*, II, 152 ("un-American"); Dec. 26, 1844, *FL*, III, 256 ("outlandish matter").

17. To RWE, July 13, [1844], *FL*, III, 209 ("*illusion*"); "Emerson's Essays," *NYDT*, Dec. 7, 1844, 1 ("methods of Mr. Locke"). For differing modern interpretations of Emerson as an "organic" public intellectual, see Mary Kupiec Cayton, *Emerson's Emergence: Self and Society in the Transformation of New England, 1800–1845* (Chapel Hill, 1989); Richard F. Teichgraeber III, *Sublime Thoughts/Penny Wisdom: Situating Emerson and Thoreau in the American Market* (Baltimore, 1995); Christopher Newfield, *The Emerson Effect: Individualism and Submission in America* (Chicago, 1996); and Peter S. Field, *Ralph Waldo Emerson: The Making of a Democratic Intellectual* (Lanham, Md., 2002).

18. "Emerson's Essays," Dec. 7, 1844, *NYDT*, 1 ("the perpendicular").

19. "Emerson's Essays," Dec. 7, 1844, *NYDT*, 1 ("a father of the country"). For Emerson as "essentially a philosopher of language and literature" (33), see Richard Poirier, *The Renewal of Language: Emersonian Reflections* (New York, 1987).

20. To EF, Mar. 9, 1845, *FL*, IV, 57 ("free entrance"); Joseph N. Ireland, *Records of the New York Stage from 1750 to 1860*, 2 vols. (New York, 1866), II, 542 ("*Fourier Grisley*"); "Palmo's.—The Antigone," *NYDT*, Apr. 16, 1845, 2 (*Antigone*); "Music in New-York," ibid., Jan. 18, 1845, 2 ("modern"). For New York's theater productions while Fuller was there, see C. D. Odell, *Annals of the New York Stage*, 15 vols. (New York, 1931), V, chaps. 3–6. Vera Brodsky Lawrence's sprawling but shrewdly glossed compendium *Strong on Music: The New York Music Scene in the Days of George Templeton Strong, 1836–1850*, vol. I, *Resonances, 1836–1850* (New York, 1988) is useful for antebellum New York's musical culture. For comparisons of the Boston and New York music and opera scenes, see John Dizikes, *Opera in America: A Cultural History* (New Haven, 1993), chaps. 7, 11–17.

21. "Music in New-York," *NYDT*, Jan. 18, 1845, 2 ("It was such music"); to EH, July 6, 1845, *FL*, IV, 129 (poor); Dec. 29, 1844, *FL*, III, 256 ("All Donizetti"); to AL, [Feb. 16?, 1845], *FL*, IV, 49 (captivated), "Italian Opera on Friday Night," *NYDT*, Jan. 13, 1845, 2 ("serenity"); "Concert by the German Society," ibid., Mar. 10, 1845, p. 2 ("want of fire").

22. RFF, "Memorial of Mrs. Margaret Fuller," *OM*, I, 376 ("ideal sentiment"); ibid., 302 ("She helped" and "grand").

23. Quoted in RBS, "Journal Abroad," Spring Papers, NjHi, 2 ("not afraid of us"); to William C. Russel, Feb. 4, [1846], *FL*, VI, 363 ("bad habit"); [July 27?, 1845], *FL*, IV, 143–44 ("Loud shrieks").

24. *NYDT*, Apr. 23, 1845, p. 3 ("notorious"); to JN, [Apr.? 25?, 1845], *FL*, 89 ("*naturally artful*"); *Life of Abby Hopper Gibbons Told Chiefly through Her Correspondence*, ed. Sarah Hopper Emerson, 2 vols. (New York, 1897), I, 132–33, 149–51, and Margaret Hope Bacon, *Abby Hopper Gibbons: Prison Reformer and Social Activist* (Albany, 2000), chap. 4 (Gibbons and her colleagues).

25. Quoted in Greeley, *Recollections*, 180 ("women like myself"); "Asylum for Dis-

charged Female Convicts," *NYDT*, June 19, 1845, 1 ("that first mistake"); to LGL, Jan. 15, 1847, *ChiL*, 234 ("asylum ladies"); to JN, June 24, 1845, *FL*, IV, 121 ("poor things"). For an influential portrayal of later American radicals' self-aggrandizing motives in identifying with lower and marginal classes, see Christopher Lasch, *The New Radicalism in America: The Emergence of the Intellectual as a Social Type, 1889–1963* (New York, 1965). A more positive counterview may be found in Christine Stansell, *American Moderns: Bohemian New York and the Creation of a New Century* (New York, 2000).

26. "Christmas," *NYDT*, Dec. 21, 1844, 1 ("private sphere"); "Asylum for Discharged Female Convicts," ibid., June 19, 1845, 1 ("link these fictions").

27. To MR, Jan. 15, 1845, *FL*, IV, 45–46, 46 ("make use"); *Letters from New York, Second Series* (New York, 1845), 258–72 (Child's articles); Jan. 15, 1845, *FL*, IV, 46 ("great pleasure").

28. For a useful overview of antebellum institutional reform, see Steven Mintz, *Moralists and Modernizers: America's Pre–Civil War Reformers* (Baltimore, 1995), chap. 4. The historiography of nineteenth-century prisons and insane asylums is controversial. For varying treatments, see Gerald N. Grob, *Mental Institutions in America: Social Policy to 1875* (New York, 1973); David J. Rothman, *The Discovery of the Asylum: Social Order and Disorder in the New Republic* (Boston, 1971); Norman Dain, *Concepts of Insanity in the United States, 1789–1865* (New Brunswick, 1964); Andrew Scull, *Social Order/Mental Disorder: Anglo-American Psychiatry in Historical Perspective* (Berkeley, 1989); Adam Jay Hirsch, *The Rise of the Penitentiary: Prisons and Punishment in Early America* (New Haven, 1992). and Lynn Gamwell and Nancy Tomes, *Madness in America: Cultural and Medical Perceptions* (Binghamton, N.Y., 1995). W. David Lewis, *From Newgate to Dannemora: The Rise of the Penitentiary in New York* (New York, 1965), is valuable for the New York prison reform scene.

29. MF, manuscript, ca. late December, FMW, box A, and MF, notes, *OM*, II, 145, 146, 147, 148 ("It is not so!"); to Mary Penrose Arnold, [July 12, 1853], *Letters of Matthew Arnold*, ed. Cecil Y. Lang, 6 vols. (Charlottesville, 1996–2001), I, 267 ("Really beautiful").

30. RBS, "Journal Abroad," 2, Spring Papers, NjHi, ("inspired person"); Frothingham, *Memoir of William Henry Channing*, 192 (Five Points); Luc Sante, *Low Life: Lures and Snares of Old New York* (New York, 1991), 245 ("grim and unsanitary"); *OM*, II, 150 (seven hundred inmates); Jan. 15, *FL*, IV, 46 ("great interest in these women"); quoted in RBS, "Journal Abroad," NjHi, 2 ("proud of our keepers"); WHC, *OM*, II, 149 ("willing to die?").

31. "St. Valentine's Day—Bloomingdale Asylum for the Insane," *NYDT*, Feb. 22, 1845, 1 ("gentle care"). For Earle, see *Memoirs of Pliny Earle, M.D.*, ed. F. B. Sanborn (Boston, 1898). The classic treatment of the coercive and stigmatizing ideology of late eighteenth- and early nineteenth-century prisons and insane asylums is Michel Foucault, *Discipline and Punish: The Birth of the Prison*, trans. Alan Sheridan (New York, 1977), a view followed in Mary Ann Jimenez, *Changing Faces of Madness: Early American Attitudes and Treatment of the Insane* (Hanover, N.H., 1987). For a recent case study suggesting the limitations of Foucault's perspective applied to the "moral treatment" approaches that influenced Earle and others of his generation, see Ann Goldberg, *Sex, Religion, and the Making of Modern Madness: The Eberbach Asylum and German Society, 1815–1849* (New York, 1999).

32. *OM*, II, 149 (Channing's opinion); "Our City Charities," *NYDT*, Mar. 19, 1845, 1 ("public charity"); to CS, Mar. 13, 1845, *FL*, IV, 60 ("pauper insane"); "The North American Review," *NYDT*, Jan. 13, 1845, 1 ("moral idiocy"); "Our City Charities," ibid., Mar. 19, 1845, 1 ("twelve hundred").

33. Jan. 9, 1845, *FL*, IV, 41 ("Lloyd writes me"); Mar. 4, 1845, "SL," 239 ("misses your companionship"); Feb. 4, 1845, FMW, XVII, 17 (peevishly complained); Mar. 2, 1845, *FL*, IV, 53, 54 ("You are mistaken").

34. Dec. 2, 1844, *EL*, VII, 618 ("Muses have feet"); Mar. 4, 1845, "SL," 239 ("not a book"); "St. Valentine's Day—Bloomingdale Asylum for the Insane," *NYDT*, Feb. 22, 1845, 1 ("manias"); Mar. 4, 1845, "SL," 239 ("How could you"); [Mar. 5?, 1845], ibid., 242 ("great philanthropist"); Mar. 4, 1845, ibid., 239 ("not going to write me"); Mar. 13, 1845, *FL*, IV, 59 ("Are you not inconsistent"); Feb. 4, 1845, Tappan Papers, MH ("too good"); Apr. 17, 1845, *FL*, IV, 80–81 (Shepherd).

35. Mar. 4, 1845, "SL," 240 (depressed); to RFF, Jan. 9, 1845, *FL*, IV, 41 ("not fritter away"); to CS, Apr. 17, 1845, ibid., 81 ("much"); to SSS, July 1, 1845, ibid., 127 ("little crucifix"); Mar. 13, 1845, ibid., 59 ("Let it go").

36. For surveys of antebellum New York that emphasize politics and society, respectively, see Edward K. Spann, *The New Metropolis: New York City, 1840–1857* (New York, 1981); and Edwin G. Burrows and Mike Wallace, *Gotham: A History of New York City to 1898* (New York, 1999), chaps. 27–48. For New York art and culture, see Dell Upton, "Inventing the Metropolis: Civilization and Urbanity in Antebellum New York," in Catherine Hoover Voorsanger and John K. Howat, eds., *Art and the Empire City: New York, 1825–1861* (New Haven, 2000), 3–46. Frederic Cople Jaher provides an interurban comparison in *The Urban Establishment: Upper Strata in Boston, New York, Charleston, Chicago, and Los Angeles* (Urbana, 1982). For antebellum New York City radicalism, see Sean Wilentz's excellent *Chants Democratic: New York City and the Rise of the American Working Class, 1788–1850* (New York, 1984), chaps. 8–10.

37. To MCF, Jan. 12, 1845, *FL*, IV, 43 ("tender care"); [Dec. 30?, 1841], *FL*, II, 263 ("*these* are a growth also"); Mar. 20, 1842, *EJMN*, VIII, 204 ("plaster-of-Paris"); Mar. 20, 1842, *EJMN*, VIII, 204 ("world of surfaces"); [Aug. 14, 1845], *FL*, VI, 359 ("*in the shallows*"); Feb. 25, 1845, *FL*, IV, 51 ("I don't dislike wickedness"); to EGL, Sept. 28, [1841], *ChiL*, 147 ("frightful"); to JN, July 22, 1845, *FL*, IV, 136 ("A corpse"); RBS, "Journal Abroad," NjHi, ("marry him").

38. To MR, Jan. 15, 1845, *FL*, IV, 45 ("most unusually good"); GWC to Daniel Ricketson, Apr. 23, 1856, MH (throwing her head forward); to [MS], [ca. Jan. 1845]*, *FL*, VI, 355 ("*cure*"); HM to RWE, July 2, 1845, quoted in *EL*, VIII, 41 n140 (Martineau's restoration); Georgiana Bruce Kirby, *Years of Experience: An Autobiographical Narrative* (New York, 1887), 213–14, 114 ("he *willed* that power" and three inches taller); GWC to Daniel Ricketson, Apr. 23, 1856, MH, and FHH, quoted in Joel Myerson, "Caroline Dall's Reminiscences of Margaret Fuller," *Harvard Library Bulletin*, 22 (Oct. 1974), 427 (noticeable spinal curvature); review of Léger, *Animal Magnetism*, *NYDT*, May 30, 1846, supp., 1 ("power of transmitting"); Mar. 13, 1845, *FL*, IV, 59 ("Nothing wonderful"); ibid., and Kirby, *Years of Experience*, 214 (walked the four miles); to MR, Jan. 15, 1845, *FL*, IV, 45 (wine); Mar. 3, 1846, ibid., 192 ("I have grown wise"); [1845], ibid., 39 ("obey Nature").

39. To CS, Mar. 13, 1845, *FL*, IV, 59 ("harried"); Jan. 9, 1845, ibid., 42 ("bread and beef"); Dec. 29, 1844, *FL*, III, 256 ("so central"); [ca. Winter 1844–45]*, *FL*, IV, 40 ("large circle"); to JN, Sept. 13, 1845, ibid., 159 (Eugene's newspaper career); Mar. 9, 1845, ibid., 56 ("half a hundred thousand readers").

40. To RFF, Mar. 2, 1845, *FL*, IV, 54 ("noble career"); [ca. early 1845]*, ibid., 40, 40–41 ("I can never"). Higginson's editor Charles Dudley Warner noted this deficiency in Higginson's biography. "I know how cramped you are for space, but it seems to me that readers will be dissatisfied that there is so little of the New York period," he wrote to Higginson after reading his manuscript. "You know your own perspective of course, but

on your just theory of her delight in 'action' this specimen of it seems to lack." Feb. 15, 1884, OC, 263.

41. To MR, Jan. 6, 1846, *FL*, IV, 182 ("With patience"); *The Diary of Philip Hone, 1828–1851*, 2 vols., ed. Allan Nevins (New York, 1927), I, 398 ("very pretty moral sermons"); to AL, Dec. 3, 1845, *FL*, IV, 170 ("*poor* branch"); "School of the Misses Sedgwick," Aug. 25, 1845, *NYDT*, 1 (puff).

42. For studies of the New York literati, see chapter 7, notes 5, 6.

43. "The Literati in New York City," in *The Complete Works of Edgar Allan Poe*, ed. James A. Harrison, 17 vols. (New York, 1902), XV, 1–137 ("Literati"); Mary E. W. Sherwood, *An Epistle to Posterity* (New York, 1897), 128 ("all the ultra views"). Anne C. Lynch to Sarah Helen Whitman, Jan. 20, 1846, quoted in *PoLo*, 620 ("no entertainment"); *Selections from the Autobiography of Elizabeth Oakes Smith*, ed. Mary Alice Wyman (Lewiston, Me., 1924), 88 ("evidence of distinction"). For a spicy picture of a typical Lynch party, see George G. Foster, "New-York in Slices. Slice XXVI . . . The Literary Soirees," *NYDT*, Sept. 27, 1848, 1.

44. *OM*, II, 165, 166 ("respect," "repelled," and "want of feminine graces"); *Autobiography of Elizabeth Oakes Smith*, 144 ("pleased, elegant air"); Mar. 16, 1845, William Page and Page Family Papers, Archives of American Art, Smithsonian Institution, Washington, D.C. ("literary old maid"); Feb. 19, 1845, quoted in Homer F. Barnes, *Charles Fenno Hoffman* (New York, 1930), 256 ("good story afloat"). For lively accounts of New York Whigs' "local jealousy" toward their established Boston counterparts, see EAD to George L. Duyckinck, May 19, 1845; and Edwin Percy Whipple to EAD, Oct. 12, 1848, both in Duyckinck Family Papers, NN-M. Scholars commonly mangle this much-quoted apocryphal Elssler concert anecdote by reversing the lines of the two protagonists, thus putting Emerson at the butt-end of the joke and exactly reversing the two Transcendentalists' intellectual positions—a mistake the more knowing Hoffman did not make. See, for example, Martin Green, *The Problem of Boston: Some Readings in Cultural History* (New York, 1966), 110; Ivor Forbes Guest, *Fanny Elssler* (London, 1970), 145–46; Lawrence W. Levine, *Highbrow/Lowbrow: The Emergence of Cultural Hierarchy in America* (Cambridge, Mass., 1988), 109; and Peter Gay, *The Bourgeois Experience: Victoria to Freud* (New York, 1984–98), vol. IV, *The Naked Heart* (New York, 1995), 24.

45. *OM*, II, 166 ("curious to see her"); George G. Foster, "New-York in Slices. Slice XXVI . . . The Literary Soirees," *NYDT*, Sept. 27, 1848, 1 ("Pythoness"); *New York Evening Mirror*, Feb. 24, 1845, 2 ("A PALPABLE HIT"); James T. Congdon, *Reminiscences of a Journalist* (Boston, 1880), 120 ("swift"); Greeley, *Recollections*, 179 ("no assumption of precedence"); "Literati," 82–83 ("the *personal* woman"); Kenneth Silverman, *Edgar A. Poe: Mournful and Never-Ending Remembrance* (New York, 1991), 286 ("stroke-and-sting"). Poe may have borrowed the trick of Fuller looking within and looking at the wall from Johann Gottlieb Fichte's famous suggestion to his students of how to practice the transcendental method.

46. *Autobiography of Elizabeth Oakes Smith*, 91 ("owl"); Dec. 6, [1849], *FL*, VI, 289 ("capable of great affection"); Mar. 13, 1845, *FL*, IV, 59–60 ("literary gossip"); Apr. 17, 1845, ibid., 81 ("interest in Miss Lynch"); Mar. 13, 1845, ibid., 60 ("intimate with Fanny Kemble"); Apr. 17, 1845, ibid., 81 ("unknown to fame!"); to JN, Dec. 31, 1845, ibid., 178 ("vivacious").

47. "Mrs. Child's Letters," *NYDT*, May 10, 1845, 1 ("inner life"); Apr. 2, 1845, *FL*, IV, 66 ("so entertaining"); [Oct. 1846], *ChiL*, 231 ("Briggs"); to LGL, Feb. 8, 1845, ibid., 219 ("great woman").

48. Frothingham, *Memoir of William Henry Channing*, 192 (family life); "Unitarian Churches—Seats," *NYDT*, Dec. 2, 1845, 1 (Society); WHC to Wendell Phillips, May 23, 1844, MH ("conservative radical"); to Edward Cranch, Dec. 17, 1843, Cranch Family Papers, MHi ("discourses"); WHC to JFC, June 3, 1852, MH ("Spirit of Divine Love"); Frothingham, *Memoir of William Henry Channing*, 203 ("loose and promiscuous").

49. Statement of HG in *OM*, II, 153 ("bare walls"); 153 ("addicted"); MF quoted in 153–54 ("declined being lectured"); Feb. 8, 1855, Park Benjamin Collection, NNC ("the vote"); statement of HG in *OM*, II, 156 ("look her in the face"); Greeley, *Recollections*, 178 ("bouncing babies").

50. RWE to LJE, Mar. 1, 1842, *EL*, III, 20 (boarded at Brook Farm); Greeley, *Recollections*, 176 (accepted her ideas); HG quoted in Beman Brockway, *Fifty Years in Journalism* (Watertown, N.Y., 1891), 157 ("Entrails of a worm!"); to CS, Aug. 22, 1847, *FL*, IV, 291 ("deviltry"); HG to MF, Sept. 29, 1847, FMW, X, 48 ("Mother"); MCF to MF, Oct. 8, 1849, FMW, VIII, 222 ("beautiful"); HG to MF, July 29, 1847, FMW, X, 46 ("whipp[ing] him often"); to MF, Nov. 19, 1848, ibid., 54 ("don't know the difference"); HG to MF, Apr. 4, 1848, ibid., 50 ("I like Fun").

51. To JN, July 2, 1845, *FL*, IV, 136 ("feel my faults"); HG to MF, Jan. 27, 1848, FMW, X, 49 ("not irritating"); to JN, July 22 and July 27, 1845, *FL*, IV, 138 ("like being in a cradle"); HG to MF, July 23, 1849, FMW, X, 57 "Aunty Margaret"); Greeley, *Recollections*, 179, 180 ("marvelous powers"); *OM*, II, 157 ("gold of California"); to MF, Jan. 29, 1849, FMW, X, 55 ("Castle Doleful"); MCF to MF, May 27, FMW, VIII, 217 ("*almost* insane"); MCF to MF, Feb. 21, 1848, ibid., 218 ("follies"); to JN, [July] 22, 1845, *FL*, IV, 137 ("could not conceive").

52. Aug. 1, 1850, quoted in *EL*, VIII, 256 n95 ("new era"). Probably the most succinct (and partly true) characterization of the Fuller-Nathan relationship is Bell Chevigny's: "It would be difficult to say which of the effects Nathan had on Fuller was stronger: the awakening of her sensuality or the putting to sleep of her mind." Bell Gale Chevigny, *The Woman and the Myth: Margaret Fuller's Life and Letters*, rev. ed. (1976; Boston, 1994), 137. Except for three letters in FMW, Nathan's letters have disappeared, probably destroyed by Fuller. William Channing tried to get Fuller's from Nathan but failed. For her family's anxious efforts to retrieve them (including a threatened lawsuit), see FMW, X, 108–21. There is no suggestion that anti-Semitism was factor, although a half century later, Fuller's niece would express some. The family's overriding concern was clearly their desire to cleanse the record of any hint, however faint, of sexual propriety in Fuller's life. Higginson tried to dig up some evidence explaining Fuller's "Jewish" allusions in New York but apparently with no success. See JFC-TWH, Sept, 1883, OC, 198. For a characteristically indignant reaction to the publication of the Fuller-Nathan letters, see Caroline Healey Dall, "Margaret Fuller's Letters," *Springfield Daily Republican*, Dec. 10, 1903, 7.

53. To JN, Sept. 29, 1845, *FL*, IV, 162 ("strong"); Sept. 29, 1845, ibid., 162 ("rich persuasive tones"); [May 15?, 1845], ibid., 100 ("You have force"); July 22, 1845, ibid., 137 ("'a fool, little girl'"); "The Modern Jews," *NYDT*, Apr. 21, 1845, 1 ("extreme radical party"); [Feb. 7?, 1845], *FL*, IV, 47 ("blue eyes!"). For the antebellum German-Jewish community, see Avraham Barkai, *Branching Out: German-Jewish Immigration to the United States, 1820–1914* (New York, 1994), chaps. 1–4. While Fuller's Transcendentalist friends generally regarded Judaism as a primitive faith, they all vigorously denounced anti-Semitism, although Theodore Parker occasionally traded in negative Jewish ethnic stereotypes. See, for example, Dean Grodzins, *American Heretic: Theodore Parker and*

Transcendentalism (Chapel Hill, 2002), 31–32, 391–92. In contrast with Fuller's friends, her niece Edith Fuller would later play the anti-Semitic card in expressing her indignation over Nathan's grandson's selling of Fuller's letters: "Nothing could prevent a Jew from selling what he had if he got a high enough price for it." "Edith Fuller's interview with Mrs. Caroline Healey Dall," Apr. 27, 1910, FMW, box A.

54. "Wayside Notes Abroad . . . . No. I," *NYDT*, Aug. 8, 1845, 1 (*"inhuman"*); to JN, [May 31, 1845], *FL*, IV, 112 ("amid the falsehoods"); Caroline Healey Dall to Thomas Wentworth Higginson, May 29, 1908, FMW, box A ("atheist"); to JN, May 23, [1845], *FL*, IV, 104 ("new and greater religion"); to Caroline Healey Dall, June 19, 1904, in Dall, "Mrs Dall and Some Idealists," *Springfield Sunday Republican*, Mar. 19, 1905 ("selfish and self-seeking").

55. *NYDT*, Feb. 3, 1845, quoted in *FL*, IV, 48 n1 ("New Panorama"); [ca. Feb. 7, 1845], ibid., 47 ("beautiful places"); Feb. 22, [1845], ibid., 50 ("My dear friend"); MCF to MF, May 27, 1847, FMW, VIII, 217 (learn of it); to JN, Sept. 13, 1845, ibid., 159 ("have no confidant"); MCF to MF, Oct. 3, 1848, FMW, VIII, 219 (Mary Greeley's jealousy); to JN, Mar. 14, [1845], ibid., 62 ("living eyes"). The only allusion to Nathan in Fuller's surviving letters is a cryptic reference to Mary Rotch about being "now connected with a person who is anxious I should not overtask" her strength after her illness. Jan. 15, 1845, ibid., 46. For evidence of Fuller's mother's awareness of some sort of romantic connection between her and Nathan, see MCF to MF, Feb. 21, 1848, FMW, VIII, 218.

56. *WN*, 73 ("wedded love"); Mar. 14, [1845], *FL*, IV, 62 ("'severe loss'"); Mar. 31, [1845], ibid., 65 ("the *Ahnungen*"); May 30, 1845, ibid., 110 ("read my thoughts"); Mar. 14, [1845], ibid., 62 ("misunderstandings"). While already feeling "a strong attraction" to Nathan, Fuller wrote to Anna Loring, speaking of her "childish" disappointment over William Clarke: "I have tried to wean myself from such close habits of personal relations, and have, in some measure, succeeded." When it comes to analyzing Fuller's reports on her romantic feelings, the distrinctions among insight, prudence, self-aggrandizement, and self-deception are sometimes hard to draw. To JN, Apr. 14, [1845], *FL*, IV, 74; to AL, Apr. 2, 1845, ibid., 66.

57. JN quoted in to JN, Apr. 2, [1845], *FL*, IV, 67 (*"krank"* and "conventions"); to JN, Apr. 14, [1845], ibid., 74 ("startled").

58. To JN, Apr. 2, [1845], *FL*, IV, 67 ("in the dark"); to JN, Apr. 6, 1845, ibid., 69 ("Purely accidentally"); to JN, [ca. Feb. 28, 1846], ibid., 191 ("English maiden"); to Caroline Healey Dall, June 19, 1904, in Dall, "Mrs Dall and Some Idealists" ("deserted"). For Fuller's interest in Louise's welfare, see to JN, Aug. 12, 1845, *FL*, IV, 146–47. For a discussion of the contradictions and hypocrisies of both male moral reformers and devotees of New York's sporting life scene, see Helen Lefkowitz Horowitz, *Rereading Sex: Battles over Sexual Knowledge and Suppression in Nineteenth-Century America* (New York, 2002), pt. 2.

59. Apr. 6, 1845, *FL*, IV, 68, 69, 70 ("cold faintness").

60. Apr. 8, [1845], *FL*, IV, 71 (Josey); to JN, Apr. 9, [1845], ibid., 72, 73 ("beautiful letter").

61. Apr. 14, [1845], *FL*, IV, 73, 75 ("the demon").

62. *FL*, IV, 75 ("worldly and *manly* way"); [Apr. 15, 1845], ibid., 77, 77–78 ("It did not seem to me").

63. *FL*, IV, 75, 76 ("My heart is a large kingdom"); Apr. 27, [1845], ibid., 91 ("experience of passionate life").

64. [Apr.? 24? 1845], *FL*, IV, 87 ("pure high ministry"); ibid., 95, 95–96 (*"chosen among women"*); quoted in May 23, [1845], ibid., 105, 106, 107 ("To the Face Seen in the Moon").

65. May 9, 1845, *FL*, IV, 98 ("too childish"); [July] 22, 1845, *FL*, IV, 136 ("too sensitive"); JN to MF, Nov. 6, 1846, FMW, X, 113 (superior air); May 26, [1845], ibid., 107 ("Mein liebster"); to JN, [May] 7, [1845], ibid., 96 ("mein liebste"); May 23, [1845], ibid., 104 ("liebste").

66. JN to MF, Nov. 6, 1846, FMW, X ("understanding"); May 30, 1845, *FL*, IV, 111 ("words most unusual"); to JN, Sept. 30, 1845, ibid., 163 ("our dear wood"); quoted in to JN, Dec. 3, 1845, ibid., 178 ("I *shall now*"); JN, "Wayside Notes Abroad No. 3," *NYDT*, Sept. 10, 1845, 1 ("heavily laden").

67. To JN, Sept. 29, 1845, *FL*, IV, 162 ("love and purity").

68. To RFF, [June 13?, 1845], *FL*, IV, 119 ("headach days"); to JN, June 12, 1845, ibid., 118 ("scene and air"); June 5, 1845, ibid., 114 ("throw him in" and "dead flowers"); [July] 22, 1845, ibid., 139 ("poor maiden"); Aug. 12, 1845, ibid., 146, 147 ("strikes me painfully"); Aug. 31, 1845, ibid., 154 ("Why, why"); Sept. 5, 1845, ibid., 154 ("cold and scanty"); Sept. 13, 1845, ibid., 159 ("much happier"); Sept. 29, 1845, ibid., 162 ("Even for thee").

69. To JN, June 24, 1845, *FL*, IV, 120 ("great deal"); July 10, 1845, ibid., 132 ("flood"); July 21, 1845, "SL," 243 ("some new feeling"); July 6, 1845, FMW, XVII, 18 ("genius of *marriage*"); [Mar. 7, 1846], *FL*, IV, 194 ("miserable mistake"); to RFF, Dec. 27, 1845, ibid., IV, 176 (scare her off); RFF to MF, Feb. 16, 1846, FMW, XV, 30 (broke things off).

70. To JN, Aug. 12, 1845, *FL*, IV, 148 ("in serene beauty"); [July] 22, 1845, ibid., 137 ("much taller"); June 24, 1845, ibid., 120 ("almost like home").

71. To JN, Sept. 5, 1845, *FL*, IV, 157 ("keep in bodily motion"); "The Celestial Empire," *NYDT*, Nov. 13, 1845, 2 ("barbarians"); Sept. 29, 1845, Tappan Papers, MH (not want to see each other); to RWE, [Oct. 20, 1845], Tappan Papers, MH ("very good time"); Nov. 16, 1845, *FL*, IV, 167 ("moods did not match"); ca. Dec. 1845, quoted in Kirby, *Years of Experience*, 186 ("real Fourierists"); to ABW, Nov. 16, 1845, *FL*, IV, 167 ("worked too hard"); Oct. 26, 1845, ibid., 165 ("cheering").

72. To JN, [July] 22, 1845, *FL*, IV, 137 ("dissensions"); to JN, June 24, 1845, ibid., 120 ("violence"); to MR, Jan. 9, 1846, ibid., 181, 182 ("neat, orderly, still"); Dec. 31, 1845, ibid., 178 ("most agreeable change"); to MR, Jan. 9, 1846, ibid., 181, 182 ("very bad cold").

73. Useful essays on the Village may be found in Ride Beard and Leslie Cohen Berlowitz, eds., *Greenwich Village: Culture and Counterculture* (New Brunswick, 1993).

74. Jan. 9, 1846, *FL*, IV, 181 ("*tightum*"); to RFF, July 14, 1846, ibid., 217 ("lovely place"); to MR, Mar. 9, 1846, ibid., 197 ("as Mother"); to MR, Jan. 9, 1846, ibid., 181 ("ruby wine").

75. Elizabeth F. Ellet to Frances Sargent Osgood, July 8, 1846, quoted in Joy Bayless, *Rufus Wilmot Griswold: Poe's Literary Executor* (Nashville, 1943), 141 ("forgery"); to EBB, Dec. 6, [1849], *FL*, V, 289 (often saw); SHW to John H. Ingram, Feb. 11, 1874, in *Poe's Helen Remembers*, ed. John Carl Miller (Charlottesville, 1979), 20 ("committee"); EAP quoted, ibid., 21 ("Busy-bodies!"). I say "may have bought" Ellet's view, because Poe later implied that Ellet "instigated" Fuller and Ellet to "call & villify me—without even *their* being aware of the influence she has exercised." To SHW, [Nov.] 24, [1848], *PoLe*, II, 407. Poe's tangled trials and tribulations with Osgood, Ellet, and the Lynch set are recounted in Sidney P. Moss, *Poe's Literary Battles: The Critic in the Context of His Literary Milieu* (Durham, N.C., 1963), 207–21; and Kenneth Silverman's insightful *Edgar A. Poe*, 278–93.

76. Anne C. Lynch to Sarah Helen Whitman, Jan. 31, 1848, *PoLo*, 719 ("*bluestockingdom*" and "no moral sense"); Anne C. Lynch to Sarah Helen Whitman, Feb. 21, 1848,

ibid., 726 ("bad odour"); "Literati," 117, 117–18 ("readily imposed upon"); Dec. 6, [1849], *FL*, V, 289 ("assumed character").

77. Quoted in to JN, Dec. 31, ibid., 177 ("real correspondence"); "1st January, 1846," *NYDT*, Jan. 1, 1846, 1 ("spot of base indulgence"); to SGW and ABA, Mar. 3, 1846, *FL*, IV, 192 (sick); *FL*, IV, 177 ("you had a person").

78. Ann C. Lynch to Sarah Helen Whitman, Jan. 16, 1847, *PoLo*, 625 ("complimen-tary"); quoted in *OM*, II, 166–67 ("'Alone, as usual'"); [ca. Feb. 1846]*; ibid., 167–68 ("wandering Intelligence").

79. To GB, [ca. Nov. 15, 1845], *FL*, IV, 167 ("all nature and genius"); to JN, [ca. Feb. 28, 1846], ibid., 190 ("stormy"); "Cassius M. Clay," *NYDT*, Jan. 14, 1846, 1 ("saw Lafayette"); [ca. Feb. 28, 1846], *FL*, IV, 189, 190 ("outwardly gay"); [Feb. 22?, 1846], "SL," 249 ("your new heroes").

Chapter Seven

1. To JN, June 24, 1845, *FL*, IV, 120 ("bear to urge"); July 22, 1845, ibid., 138 ("quite content"); July 10, 1845, ibid., 132 ("I do not care").

2. July 19, 1845, FMW, XVII, 15 ("ought not to write"); July 31, 1846, *ECC*, 407 ("nobleness").

3. July 26, 1845, *CL*, 145 ("better written"); [Aug. 14, 1845], *FL*, VI, 359 ("mutual interpretation").

4. For the New York and London publishing world within which Fuller operated, see Ezra Greenspan, *George Palmer Putnam: Representative American Publisher* (Univer-sity Park, Pa., 2000). For New York publishing, see John Tebbel, *A History of Book Pub-lishing*, vol. I, *The Creation of an Industry* (New York, 1972), 262–365. William Charvat, *Literary Publishing in America, 1790–1850* (1959; Amherst, Mass., 1993), treats national trends. Comparisons with Boston are suggested in Lawrence Buell, *New England Liter-ary Culture: From Revolution through Renaissance* (Cambridge, England, 1986), chaps. 2–3. For a valuable analysis of antebellum New York literary culture in the context of the city's institutional development, see Thomas Bender, *New York Intellect: A History of Intellectual Life in New York City, from 1750 to the Beginnings of Our Own Time* (New York, 1987), chap. 4.

5. The best treatment of antebellum New York's literary battles remains Perry Miller's baroque but brilliant *Raven and the Whale*. More pedestrian but still sporadically useful is John Paul Pritchard, *Literary Wise Men of Gotham: Criticism in New York, 1815–1860* (Baton Rouge, 1963).

6. EAD, Diary, July 16, 1844, Duyckinck Family Papers, NN-M ("alleged mysticism"); "Wiley and Putnam's Library of Choice Reading," Mar. 1, 1845, ibid. ("middle ground"). For an appraisal of overlapping circles of New York's Democratic political intellectuals, see Edward K. Spann, *Ideals and Politics: New York Intellectuals and Liberal Democ-racy* (Albany, 1972). Although written in a breathless partisan spirit, Edward L. Widmer, *Young America: The Flowering of Democracy in New York City* (New York, 1999), ex-plores literary Young America's cultural politics. A better account of its critical ideals and practices may be found in John Stafford, *The Literary Criticism of "Young America": A Study in the Relationship of Politics and Literature, 1837–1850* (Berkeley, 1952); and Kermit Vanderbilt, *American Literature and the Academy: The Roots, Growth, and Ma-turity of a Profession* (Philadelphia, 1986), chap. 5.

7. Diary, July 16, 1844, Duyckinck Family Papers, NN-M ("genuine American"); EAD

to Wiley and Putnam, Jan. 27, 1845, ibid. and to EAD, [ca. Feb. 5, 1846], *FL*, IV, 184–85 (pitched books); to HG, [March] 20, [1846], ibid., 200 ("Will you send me"); to Fredrick W. Thomas, Feb. 14, 1849, *PoLe*, II, 427 (protégés); to George W. Eveleth, Jan. 4, 1848, ibid., 355 (toadied); to MF, [July 1846], in *Letters of William Gilmore Simms*, ed. Mary C. Simms Oliphant et al., 6 vols. (Columbia, S.C., 1952–82), II, 173 ("complete"); Edwin P. Whipple to EAD, Oct. 12, 1848, Duyckinck Family Papers, NN-M ("most Bostonian"); Feb. 2, 1846, *FL*, IV, 184 ("truly respect"). It had even pleased her that Duyckinck had written for the Episcopalian *"Orthodox" New York Review*. See MF journal, [ca. Spring 1837], FMW, Works, V, 689–91.

8. To MF, Feb. 12, 1843, *EL*, III, 146–47 ("politico-literary").

9. Three historical anthologies from three different American critical eras give helpful introductions to the national question in literary thought: Philip Rahv, ed., *Literature in America: An Anthology of Literary Criticism* (New York, 1957); Richard Ruland, ed., *The Native Muse: Theories of American Literature* (New York, 1972); and Gordon Hutner, ed., *American Literature, American Culture* (New York, 1999). Benjamin T. Spencer, *The Quest for Nationality: An American Literary Campaign* (Syracuse, N.Y., 1957) remains a still useful study. For contrasting interpretations, see Larzer Ziff, *The Declaration of Cultural Independence in America* (New York, 1981); and David Simpson, *The Politics of English, 1776–1850* (New York, 1986).

10. *FPL*, II, 122, 122–23, 123 ("national vanity").

11. *FPL*, II, 123, 127 ("Mexican life"); review of Anton Schindler, *The Life of Beethoven*, *NYDT*, Feb. 7, 1845, 1 ("Our era"). Lawrence Buell cogently evaluates the self-consciously "postcolonial" mindset of authors and critics in the period in his essay "American Literary Emergence as a Postcolonial Phenomenon," in Hutner, *American Literature, American Culture*, 592–612.

12. "Italy," *NYDT*, Nov. 13, 1845, 1 ("Copious infusions"); "Study of the German Language," ibid., Dec. 11, 1845, 1 ("any pretensions"); "Italy," ibid., Nov. 13, 1845, 1 ("no narrowness").

13. "Italy," *NYDT*, Nov. 15, 1845, 1 ("cautious, calculating" and "That truth"); "Study of the German Language," ibid., Dec. 11, 1845, 1 ("will refresh you"); review of Frederick Von Raumer, *America and the American People*, ibid., Dec. 4, 1845, 1 ("cordially hate"); "Translations from the German," ibid., Mar. 14, 1845, 1 ("well-intentioned mediocrity").

14. Harold Bloom, *The Anxiety of Influence: A Theory of Poetry* (New York, 1973) ("anxiety"); review of Charles Anthon, *A System of Latin Versification*, *NYDT*, May 12, 1845, 1 ("honey of Hymettus"); "Italy," ibid., Nov. 18, 1845, 1 ("pains-taking friends").

15. "French Gayety," *NYDT*, July 9, 1845, 1 ("heartlessness"); "Courrier des Etats-Unis," ibid., June 7, 1845, 1 ("good appetites"); ibid., July 26, 1845, 2 ("plot" and "courtesans"); "Courrier des Etats-Unis—Our Protegee, Queen Victoria," ibid., Aug. 4, 1845, 1 ("piece of raillery"). On the continuing censure of contemporary French fiction, see Howard Mumford Jones, "American Comment on George Sand, 1837–1848," *American Literature*, 3 (Jan. 1932), 389–407; and Henry Blumenthal, *American and French Culture, 1800–1900: Interchanges in Art, Science, Literature, and Society* (Baton Rouge, 1975), chap. 6. Slightly contrasting views of the Fourierist *Harbinger*'s coverage of the French social Romantic novelists are presented in George Joyaux, "George Sand, Eugene Sue and *The Harbinger*," *French Review* (Dec. 1953), 122–31; and Sterling F. Delano, *"The Harbinger" and New England Transcendentalism: A Portrait of Associationism in America* (Rutherford, N.J., 1983), 107–10.

16. To Thomas Tracy, May 6, 1847, in *Letters of Whittier*, II, 89 ("modern Satanic school"); Sept. 19, 1844, "FJ44–1," 117 ("low"); Sept. 8, 1844, "FJ44–1," 114, (*Wandering Jew*); "French Novelists of the Day," *NYDT*, Feb. 1, 1845, 1 ("not tragedies"); review of Alexandre Dumas, *Count of Monte-Cristo*, ibid., July 21, 1846 ("vulgarly showy"); "French Novelists of the Day," ibid., Feb. 1, 1845, 1 ("unsurpassed"). For Fuller's earlier studies of French Romantic authors, see *CF-1*, 259–62. For James on Balzac, see Henry James, *French Poets and Novelists* (London, 1878), 119–48.

17. "French Novelists of the Day," *NYDT*, Feb. 1, 1845, 1 ("cloak of hypocrisy").

18. Review of George Sand, *Consuelo*, *NYDT*, June 14, 1846, 1 ("best living French writer"); "Jenny Lind . . . The Consuelo of George Sand," ibid., Sept. 19, 1845, 2 ("aristocratic democrat"); "French Novelists of the Day," ibid., Feb. 1, 1845, 1 ("clean hands"); review of George Sand, *Consuelo*, ibid., June 14, 1846, 1 ("fearless, not shameless"). For Fuller's earlier sharp criticism of Sand as a thinker, see "FJ44–1," July 2, 1844, 70.

19. *NYDT*, Sept. 20, 1845, 2 ("sanctimonious world!").

20. *FPL*, II, 123 ("not the frankness and expansion"); "Study of the German Language," *NYDT*, Dec. 11, 1845, 1 ("great minds"); review of *The Prose Works of John Milton*, *NYDT*, Oct. 7, 1845, 1 ("poetic and reflective faculty"); review of *The Poetical Works of Percy Bysshe Shelley*, ibid., Dec. 27, 1845, 1 ("web of his imagination"); "Hazlitt's Table-Talk," ibid., Apr. 30, 1845, 1 ("richly observant"); "Thomas Hood," ibid., Aug. 9, 1845 ("make us proud").

21. "Thomas Hood," *NYDT*, Aug. 9, 1845, 1 ("wit"); "Thomas Hood," ibid., July 18, 1845, 1 ("sell themselves"); Dwight Macdonald, "Masscult and Midcult," in Macdonald's *Against the American Grain* (New York, 1962), 3–75 (assaults on the "midcult"); "Critics and Essayists," *NYDT*, June 10, 1846, supp., 1 (mordant essay); review of Anna Jameson's *Memoirs and Essays*, ibid., July 24, 1846, 1 ("shallowness"); review of Anna Jameson, *The Heroines of Shakespeare*, ibid., June 30, 1846, 1 ("*over* refining"); review of J. R. Lowell, *Conversations on Some of the Old Poets*, ibid., Jan. 21, 1845, 1 ("honorable exception"); review of Leigh Hunt, *The Indicator*, ibid., July 11, 1845, 1 ("*cuddling*"); review of Leigh Hunt, *Italian Poets*, ibid., Feb. 18, 1846 ("guardian care"); "English Writers Little Known Here. Milnes . . . . Landor . . . . Julius Hare," ibid., Mar. 4, 1845, 1 ("deeper refinement"); "Writers Little Known Among Us. Milnes . . . . Landor . . . . Julius Hare," ibid., Mar. 28, 1845 ("age of book-making"). Occasionally, Fuller's Romantic aesthetic critique could shade into a social putdown, as in her riff on "Cockneyism" in her review of Leigh Hunt's *Indicator* (*NYDT*, July 11, 1845, 1).

22. "Story Books for the Hot Weather," *NYDT*, June 20, 1845, 1 ("I have known more life"); "Prince's Poems," ibid., Aug. 13, 1845, 1 ("Spirit of the Age"); "Thom's Poems," ibid., Aug 22, 1845, 1 ("indiscriminate indulgence"); *Whistle-Binkie; A Collection of Songs for the Social Circle*, vol. I (Glasgow, 1890), 66 (subscription).

23. Review of Philip James Bailey, *Festus*, *NYDT*, Sept. 8, 1845, 1 ("rich" and "finish"); review of Thomas Carlyle, *Oliver Cromwell's Letters and Speeches*, ibid., Dec. 19, 1845, 1 ("peremptory showman").

24. "Miss Barrett's Poems," *NYDT*, Jan. 4, 1845, 1 ("little things"); review of *The Complete Works of Mrs. Hemans*, ibid., Dec. 10, 1844, 1 ("affections").

25. To William D. Ticknor, Jan. 3, 1856, *HW*, XVII, 425 ("queer"); "Browning's Poems," *NYDT*, Apr. 1, 1846, 1 ("loves and lures of life"); "Browning's Poems," ibid., July 10, 1846, 1 ("If one tithe"). For Browning's reputation in the United States, see Louise Greer, *Browning and America* (Chapel Hill, 1952).

26. *FPL*, II, 123–24 ("uncongenial and injurious").

27. Julia Ward Howe, *Margaret Fuller* (Boston, 1883), 159–61 (blanched); George

Palmer Putnam, *American Facts* (London, 1845) (Putnam's book); "American Facts," *NYDT*, May 25, 1845, 1 ("American facts!"); *FPL*, II, 124, 125 ("That day will not rise"). Fuller's fellow democratic "nationalist" also found Putnam's argument shallow. See [Evert A. Duyckinck], "Notices of New Books," *United States Magazine and Democratic Review*, 16 (May 1845), 507–9.

28. *FPL*, II, 130, 131 ("Flimsy beyond any texture"); review of Lydia H. Sigourney, *Scenes in My Native Land*, *NYDT*, Jan. 28, 1845 ("apologetic tone"); review of Anna Cora Mowatt, *Evelyn*, ibid., July 7, 1845, 1 ("minds of the agents"); "Story Books for Hot Weather," ibid., June 20, 1845, 1 ("only the fashionable world").

29. *FPL*, II, 127, 128, 129, 131, 138, 139 ("simple lovely garb").

30. Review of James Russell Lowell, *Conversations on Some of the Old Poets*, *NYDT*, Jan. 24, 1845, 1 ("he does not profess"); Jan. 17, 1845, PoLo, 488 ("female ass"); *FPL*, II, 132 ("posterity will not remember him"); to Charles F. Briggs, Friday Morning, Dec. 1848, *LoL*, I, 48 ("the American"); EPP quoted in "Margaret Fuller," Boston newspaper, August [25], 1883, OC, 10 ("blight"); to Edmond Morris Davis, Sept. 26, 1846, quoted in Leon Howard, *Victorian Knight-Errant: A Study of the Early Literary Career of James Russell Lowell* (Berkeley, 1952), 233 ("settle my account"). Despite Lowell's respect for his wife's literary knowledge, his letters display some insecurity about intellectual women. See, for example, to G. B. Loring, December 2, 1839, *LoL*, I, 51, and to TWH, Dec. 9, 1858, ibid., 287, where he urges Higginson in his recent article on women to add the word "perhaps" to his phrase the "natural equality of the sexes" because the assertion had not yet been "*demonstrated.*"

31. "Chat in Boston Bookstores.—No. I," *Boston Quarterly Review*, 3 (Jan. 1840), 128 ("prettinesses"); statement of HG, in *OM*, II, 158 ("reluctantly").

32. Review of Henry Wadsworth Longfellow, *Poems*, 3rd. ed., *NYDT*, Dec. 10, 1845, 1 ("not a superhuman or supernatural gift").

33. Review of Henry Wadsworth Longfellow, *Poems*, 3rd. ed., *NYDT*, Dec. 10, 1845, 1 ("exaggerated praises").

34. Journal, Dec. 9, 1845, quoted in *LL*, III, 93n3 ("furious assault"); SHW to Ida Russell, [ca. Jan. 1846], RPB ("most ungracious"); to HG, Aug. 5, 1850, *EL*, IV, 225–26 ("such respectable ability"); *Henry Wadsworth Longfellow* (Boston, 1902), 262 ("literary courts"); Dec. 29, 1845, Rufus W. Griswold, *Passages from the Correspondence and Other Papers of Rufus W. Griswold* (Cambridge, Mass., 1898), 203 ("Did you see"); "The Literati in New York City," in *The Complete Works of Edgar Allan Poe*, ed. James A. Harrison, 17 vols. (New York, 1902), XV, 73, 73–74 ("infinite credit").

35. Review of Edward Hazen, *Grammatical Reader*, and *The Illustrated Botany*, ed. John B. Newman, *NYDT*, June 26, 1846, 2 ("degradation"); *FPL*, II, 124, 125 126 ("only the public"). For an influential discussion of this terminological distinction, see Lionel Trilling, *Sincerity and Authenticity* (Cambridge, Mass., 1972).

36. "Cheap Postage Bill," *NYDT*, Feb. 24, 1845, 2 ("mere gazettes and circulars"); *FPL*, II, 139, 140 ("life of intellect"). In establishing my literary categories for Fuller's criticism, I have found useful David Reynolds's discussion of "subversive" and sensationalist antebellum writings in his *Beneath the American Renaissance*.

37. Review of Charles C. Green, *The Nubian Slave*, *NYDT*, June 24, 1845, 1 ("aesthetic impulses"); "Mr. Hosmer's Poem," ibid., Dec. 11, 1844, 1 ("an American literature may grow up"); review of *Narrative of the Life of Frederick Douglass*, ibid., June 14, 1845, 1 ("action and resistance"); George L. Duyckinck to EAD, Apr. 14, 1846, Duyckinck Family Papers, NN-M (enraged the religious press); "Wiley & Putnam's Library," ibid., Apr. 4, 1846, 1 ("sewing societies").

38. "Cranch's Poems," NYDT, Dec. 12, 1844, 1 ("customary"); *FPL*, II, 128, 132, 133 ("unfinished and obscure").

39. Review of Edgar Allan Poe, *The Raven and Other Poems*, *NYDT*, Nov. 26, 1845, 1 ("tomahawk"); review of Edgar Allan Poe, *Tales*, ibid., July 11, 1845, 1 ("refreshment"); "Edgar Allan Poe," *Graham's Magazine* (Feb. 1845), 54 ("fireside charm"); review of Edgar Allan Poe, *Tales*, *NYDT*, July 11, 1845, 1 ("not 'making up'").

40. *FPL*, II, 142 ("best writer"); review of Charles Brockden Brown, *Wieland; or, the Transformation* and *Ormond; or, the Secret Witness*, *NYDT*, July 21, 1846, 1 ("darkest disclosures"); review of Nathaniel Hawthorne, *Mosses from an Old Manse*, ibid., June 22, 1846, 1 ("fearless scrutiny"); "Hawthorne's Mosses," in *The Writings of Herman Melville: The Northwestern-Newberry Edition*, ed. Harrison Hayford, Hershel Parker, and G. Thomas Tanselle, vol. IX, *The Piazza Tales and Other Prose Pieces, 1839–1860,* (Evanston, Ill., 1987), 239–53 (two audiences).

41. Review of Nathaniel Hawthorne, *Mosses from an Old Manse*, *NYDT*, June 22, 1846, 1 ("forced and artificial circulation").

42. "Italy," *NYDT*, Nov. 13, 1845, 1 ("love our country well"); Paul Zweig, *Walt Whitman: The Making of the Poet* (New York, 1984), 154 (tearing out). I borrow the term "connected criticism" from Michael Walzer. See his *Interpretation and Social Criticism* (Cambridge, Mass., 1987) and *The Company of Critics: Social Criticism in the Twentieth Century* (New York, 1988). The uneven quality of Poe's practical criticism has often been noted. See René Wellek, *History of Modern Criticism: 1750–1950* (New Haven, 1955–65) III, 152–63; Robert D. Jacobs, *Poe: Journalist and Critic* (Baton Rouge, 1969); and Henry James, quoted in Eric W. Carlson, ed., *The Recognition of Edgar Allan Poe* (Ann Arbor, 1970), 66.

43. To JN, [July] 2, 1845, *FL*, IV, 138 ("merit of such things"). Almost all the recent anthologies of Fuller's writings downplay her literary criticism. See Jeffrey Steele, ed., *The Essential Margaret Fuller* (New Brunswick, 1992); Mary Kelley, ed., *The Portable Margaret Fuller* (New York, 1994); Catherine C. Mitchell, ed., *Margaret Fuller's New York Journalism: A Biographical Essay and Key Writings* (Knoxville, 1995); and John Carlos Rowe, *Ralph Waldo Emerson and Margaret Fuller: Selected Works* (Boston, 2003). A notable exception is Judith Mattson Bean and Joel Myerson, eds., *Margaret Fuller, Critic: Writings from the "New-York Tribune," 1844–1846* (New York, 2000).

44. "Methods of Religious Life," *NYWT*, May 23, 1846, 6 ("cant"); review of Theodore Parker, *The Excellence of Goodness*, *NYDT*, Feb. 26, 1845, 1 ("poetic"); "Swedenborgianism," ibid., June 25, 1845, 1 ("seer of ghosts"); "The Water Cure," ibid., June 27, 1845, 1 (holistically treating); review of J. Stanley Grimes, *Etherology or the Philosophy of Mesmerism and Phrenology*, ibid., Feb. 17, 1845, 1 ("super-sensual element"); "Clairvoyance," ibid., July 23, 1845, 1 ("facts").

45. "Ole Bull," *NYDT*, Nov. 28, 1845, 1 ("coarse utilitarianism"); "Philharmonic Concert," Jan. 20, 1846, ibid., 1 ("in their place"); "Philharmonic Concert," *NYDT*, Jan. 20, 1846 ("flatter"); "Ole Bull," ibid., Dec. 20, 1844, 2 ("assurance of sympathy"); "The Grand Festival Concert at Castle Gardens," ibid., May 22, 1846, 2 (ticket prices); "Music," ibid., Jan. 31, 1846, 1 (Liverpool's bankers); "German Opera at Palmo's Opera House," ibid., Dec. 11, 1845, 1 ("tickle the ear"). For art music criticism in antebellum New York, in addition to Vera Brodsky Lawrence, *Strong on Music: The New York Music Scene in the Days of George Templeton Strong, 1836–1850*, vol. I, *Resonances, 1836–1850* (New York, 1988), see Michael N. Grant, *Maestros of the Pen: A History of Classical Music Criticism in America* (Boston, 1998), chap 1. For the glacial pace in the United States of an appreciation of the German "modern" art music, see Katherine K. Preston, "Art Music from

1800 to 1860," in David Nichols, ed., *The Cambridge History of American Music* (Cambridge, England, 1998), 186–213.

46. Quoted in *NYWT*, Aug. 30, 1845, 3 ("intermingling"); Feb. 28, 1846, HG Papers, NN-M ("Look for a shining"). Valuable for understanding the larger partisan context of the *Tribune*'s newspaper battles are Sean Wilentz, *Chants Democratic: New York City and the Rise of the American Working Class, 1788–1850* (New York, 1984), chap. 9; idem, *The Rise of Democracy: Jefferson to Lincoln* (New York, 2005); and Michael F. Holt, *The Rise and Fall of the American Whig Party: Jacksonian Politics and the Onset of the Civil War* (New York, 1999), chap. 8.

47. Review of Caroline Norton, *The Child of the Islands* and John Critchley Prince, *Hours with the Muses*, *NYDT*, July 26, 1845, 1 ("bankrupt Europe"); "A Few Words in Reply to Mr. U. C. Hill," May 15, 1846, supp., ibid., 1 ("first object"); "French Novelists of the Day," ibid., Feb. 1, 1845, 1 ("pervasive ills"); "Fourth of July," ibid., July 4, 1845, 2 ("straightforwardness"); ibid., May 31, 1845, 2 ("Politeness"). For antebellum New York newspapers' treatment of the lower classes, see Hans Bergmann, *God in the Street: New York Writing from the Penny Press to Melville* (Philadelphia, 1995). Lydia Maria Child, *Letters from New-York*, ed. Bruce Mills (Athens, Ga., 1998) is an accessible introduction to Child's New York journalism.

48. "New Year's Day," Dec. 28, 1844, *NYDT*, Jan. 1, 1845, 1 ("Too many"). Despite its dated assimilationist viewpoint, Robert Ernst, *Immigrant Life in New York City, 1825–1863* (New York, 1949), remains a useful overview.

49. "Deutsche Schnellpost," *NYDT*, Jan. 25, 1845, 1 ("each nation"). For the New York German press, see Carl Wittke, *The German-Language Press in America* (Lexington, 1957); Henry Geitz, ed., *The German-American Press* (Madison, 1992); and Elliott Shore, Ken Fones-Wolf, and James P. Danky, eds., *The German-American Press: The Shaping of a Left Political Culture, 1850–1940* (Urbana, 1992).

50. "Deutsche Schnellpost," *NYDT*, Jan. 25, 1845, 1 ("all this new blood"); "Anniversary of the Polish Revolution," ibid., Dec. 1, 1845, 2 ("same fervor of heart"). Although I wrote the phrase "cosmopolitan patriotism" before I read his book, Jonathan Hansen aptly uses it in his *Lost Promise of Patriotism: Debating Identity, 1890–1920* (Chicago, 2003) to discuss a later generation of progressive intellectuals whose Americanist notions Fuller anticipated. For the concepts of pluralism, nationality, and cosmopolitanism, see the works cited in the preface, notes 7, 11, 12.

51. To Maria Weston Chapman, Apr. 26, [1842], *ChiL*, 170 ("voting and beating"); quoted in Caroline Healey Dall, journal, Aug. 21, 1895, in Joel Myerson, "Caroline Dall's Reminiscences of Margaret Fuller," *Harvard Library Bulletin*, 22 (Oct. 1974), 421 ("talk most beautiful!"). For remarkable examples of anti–Irish Catholic prejudice even in Fuller's Unitarian (but not Transcendentalist) circles, see the constant complaints about the lying, lazy ways of Irish servants caused by their Catholicism in the letters of Mrs. Elizabeth Palmer Peabody and her daughters Sophia Hawthorne and, less virulently, Mary Mann in NN-B.

52. "The Irish Character," *NYDT*, June 28, 1845, 2 ("one of the [b]est nations of the world"); "The Irish Character," ibid., July 15, 1845, 1 ("lower class of Irish").

53. "Irish Character," *NYDT*, July 22, 1845, 1 ("less cautious than kind"); "The Irish Character," ibid., July 24, 1845, 1 ("a rule transcendental").

54. John Dizikes, *Opera in America: A Cultural History* (New Haven, 1993), 232, 233 (nativist mob); "Der Volks-Tribun," *NYDT*, Jan. 17, 1846, 1 ("cannot wonder, Germans"); [Karl Marx and Friedrich Engels], "Circular Against Kriege," in *Karl Marx, Frederick Engels: Collected Works*, 50 vols. (New York, 1975–2004), VI, 46 ("slobbering").

55. "The Social Movement in Europe," *NYDT*, Aug. 5, 1845, 1 ("Communism"); ibid., Aug. 6, 1845, 1 (dissociated).

56. "Fourth of July," *NYDT*, July 4, 1845, 2 ("few men"); "TTE," [n.d.], ibid., Jan. 1, 1848, 1 ("tedious"); review of *Narrative of the Life of Frederick Douglass*, ibid., June 10, 1845, 1 ("screaming").

57. "First of August, 1845," *NYDT*, Aug. 1, 1845, 1 ("most shameful deed"); "Cassius M. Clay," ibid., Jan. 14, 1846, 1 ("needs a bribe"). For her puff that month of the entire Anglo-American abolitionist movement, see "*The Liberty Bell*, for 1846," *NYDT*, Jan. 9, 1846, 1.

58. "1ˢᵗ January, 1846," *NYDT*, 1 ("What a year").

59. "1ˢᵗ January, 1846," *NYDT*, 1 ("time of prophets is over"); "Le-Franco-Americain," ibid., May 23, 1846, 2 ("title of Democrat").

60. "The Rich Man—An Ideal Sketch," *NYDT*, Feb. 6, 1846, 1 ("instruction of the past") *Communitist*, 2 (Feb. 19, 1846), 105–6 (reprinted); "The Rich Man—An Ideal Sketch," *NYDT*, Feb. 6, 1846, 1 ("benefit of both"); "The Poor Man—An Ideal Sketch," ibid., Mar. 25, 1846, 1 ("hod-man").

61. "The Wrongs of American Women. The Duty of American Women," *NYDT*, Sept. 30, 1845, 1 ("do not, CANNOT"); "The Poor Man—An Ideal Sketch," ibid., Mar. 25, 1846, 1 ("the physical Hell"). Fuller's only two articles on middle-class women's subjects were brief and somewhat whimsical. See "'Mistress of herself, though china fall,'" *NYDT*, Apr. 15, 1846, 4; and "'Glumdalclitches,'" ibid., July 5, 1846, 6.

62. Review of Anna Jameson, *Memoirs and Essays Illustrative of Art, Literature, and Social Morals*, *NYDT*, July 24, 1846, 1 ("rhetorical gentlemen"); "The Consecration of Grace Church," ibid., Mar. 11, 1845, 1 (searing article). For an excellent discussion of ideological shifts in antebellum middle-class reform attitudes toward poverty and the urban poor, see Paul Boyer, *Urban Masses and Moral Order in America, 1820–1920* (Cambridge, Mass., 1978), chaps. 5–6.

63. To Pliny Earle, [Sept.] 24, [1845], *FL*, IV, 161 (visited Bloomingdale); review of Pliny Earle, *Twenty-Fifth Annual Report of the Bloomingdale Asylum for the Insane, NYDT*, Feb. 11, 1846, 1 ("Moral Treatment"); "Prison Discipline," ibid., Feb. 25, 1846, 1 ("intellectual race"); review of Pliny Earle, *Twenty-Fifth Annual Report of the Bloomingdale Asylum for the Insane*, ibid., Feb. 11, 1846, 1 ("causes"); "Prison Discipline," ibid., Feb. 25, 1846, 1 ("Harsh bigots"). For Fuller's first readings at Groton of Brigham and her comments on his theory, see her journal, [ca. Mar. 1834], FMW, box A.

64. George B. Cheever and Tayler Lewis, *A Defence of Capital Punishment* (New York, 1846). The best brief exegesis of the intellectual arguments of early American proponents and opponents of capital punishment remains David Brion Davis, "The Movement to Abolish Capital Punishment in America, 1787–1861," in Davis's *From Homicide to Slavery: Studies in American Culture* (1957; New York, 1986), chap. 2. For discussions of the antebellum debate in the context of middle-class reform culture, see Louis P. Masur, *Rites of Execution* (New York, 1989), chaps. 6–7; and Stuart Banner, *The Death Penalty: An American History* (Cambridge, Mass., 2002), chap. 5. Valuable details on the debate in New York may be found in Philip English Mackey, *Hanging in the Balance: The Anti–Capital Punishment Movement in New York State, 1776–1861* (New York, 1982), chaps. 3–8.

65. "Darkness Visible," *NYDT*, Mar. 4, 1846, 1 ("diabolical spirit").

66. "What Is Infidelity and Who Are the Infidels?" *Courier and Enquirer*, Mar. 7, 1846, 1 ("skulk behind a female"); "Darkness Visible," *NYDT*, Mar. 10, 1846 ("consideration of 'females'"); Ann S. Stephens to George Graham, June 3, [1842], in Griswold, *Passages from the Correspondence*, 112 ("cannot strike back").

67. Stanton, *Leopard's Spots*, 92–99 (Wilkes's expedition); "United States Exploring Expedition," *NYDT*, June 28, 1845, 1 ("learn his language!"); review of Thomas L. McKenney, *Memoirs, Offical and Personal*, ibid., July 8, 1846, 1 ("NOW, or never"); Aug. 22, 1845, *FL*, IV, 150, 153 ("interesting task"); "Lyceum of New-Bedford, Mass.," *NYDT*, Dec. 9, 1845, 1 (Emerson and Sumner); *"The Liberty Bell for 1845,"* ibid., Jan. 7, 1845, 2 (*"capacities* of the African race"); review of *Narrative of the Life of Frederick Douglass*, ibid., June 10, 1845, 1 ("balance and harmony"). Although Fuller said nothing about the enslaved mother's wishes, she did at least indicate to the Lorings that the slaveholder claimed he could provide proof that he was not the father of the girl. Fears of "amalgamation" in the racial politics of New York in the 1840s are explored in Leslie M. Harris, *In the Shadow of Slavery: African Americans in New York City, 1626–1863* (Chicago, 2003), chaps. 8–9.

68. "What Fits a Man to be a Voter? Is it to be White Within, or White Without?" *NYDT*, Mar. 31, 1846, 1 ("ugly"). For an account of the battle over the pro–black suffrage amendment, see Phyllis F. Field, *The Politics of Race in New York: The Struggle for Black Suffrage in the Civil War Era* (Ithaca, 1982), chap. 2.

69. HG, review of Joel T. Headley, *Napoleon and His Marshals*, *NYDT*, May 1, 1846, 1, MF, review of Joel T. Headley, *Napoleon and His Marshals*, ibid., May 4, 1846, 1, and MF, review of Joel T. Headley, *Napoleon and His Marshals*, ibid., June 18, 1846, 1 (Napoleon and "bad cause"); review of Thomas L. McKenney, *Memoirs, Official and Personal*, ibid., July 8, 1846, 1 ("intolerance and bigotry"). For pro-European revolutionary sentiments among soon-to-emerge "Young America" Democratic Party expansionists, see Merle Curti, "Young America," *American Historical Review*, 32 (Oct. 1926), 34–55. For antiwar views, see John H. Schroeder, *Mr. Polk's War: American Opposition and Dissent, 1846–1848* (Madison, 1973).

70. Walt Whitman, *The Gathering of the Forces*, 2 vols. (New York, 1920), I, 240 ("thoroughly chastised"); *NYDT*, May 16, 1845, 2 ("generous"); review of Waddy Thompson, *Recollections of Mexico*, ibid., June 2, 1846, 1 ("Observe"). The emphasis on racist rationales and causes of Texas annexation and the Mexican War has become a feature of much American historiography of the last two decades. See Reginald Horsman, *Race and Manifest Destiny: The Origins of American Racial Anglo-Saxonism* (Cambridge, Mass., 1981), chaps. 11–13; and Thomas R. Hietala, *Manifest Design: Anxious Aggrandizement in Late Jacksonian America* (Ithaca, 1985), chaps. 2, 5.

71. Review of Thomas L. McKenney, *Memoirs, Official and Personal*, *NYDT*, July 8, 1846, 1 (*"feeble* Mexicans").

72. Jan. 15, 1845, *FL*, IV, 46 ("what I want from Europe"); to MS and RBS, Dec. 9, 1847, ibid., 311 ("long abandoned"); to JN, Sept. 13, 1845, ibid., 159 ("proposition"); "Journal Abroad," NjHi, 6 ("cried for joy"); to RFF, [ca. Feb. 13, 1846], ibid., 187 (word from Marcus).

73. Mar. 3, 1846, *FL*, IV, 192, 193 ("At every step").

74. To SGW and ABW, Mar. 3, 1846, *FL*, IV, 193 (thousand dollars); to RFF, Dec. 3, 1845, ibid., 169 (second edition); to JN, Dec. 31, 1845, ibid., 178–79 (Greeley's "letters" suggestion); HG to J. B. Wilcox, May 17, 1844, HG Papers, NN-M (McElrath); James Parton, quoted in J. C. Derby, *Fifty Years among Authors, Books and Publishers* (New York) 153 ("close calculator"); [ca. Feb. 13, 1846], *FL*, IV, 187 ("boldness of my course"); *NYDT*, Nov. 11, 1845, 2 (sold out); Mar. 3, 1846, *FL*, IV, 193 (borrow from Sam); HG to MF, July 29, 1847, FMW, X, 46 ($120 advance).

75. Mar. 3, 1846, *FL*, IV, 192 ("physical remedies"); Dec. 31, 1845, ibid., 178 ("more and more interested"); to RFF, [ca. Feb. 13, 1846], ibid., 186 ("too much for my nerves");

RFF to MF, Feb. 16, 1846, FMW, XV, 30, and to MF, [Feb. 22?, 1846], "SL," 249 (best if he went); to CS, [Mar.] 9, [1846], *FL*, IV, 195 ("poor frail"); ibid., 216 n3 ("all things foreign").

76. [Ca. Feb. 28, 1846], *FL*, IV, 189–91 (last letter); Apr. 25, 1846, ibid., 204 ("amounted to anguish"); June 5–6, 1846, FMW, X, 111 ("how singular!"); July 14, 1846, *FL*, IV, 219 ("if not yourself").

77. *Dolores: A Novel of South America* (New York and Montevideo, 1846); "Publishers and Authors. *Dolores* by Harro Harring," ibid., Feb. 3, 1846, 1 ("oppressed"); review of Harro Harring, *Dolores: A Novel of South America*, ibid., Apr. 25, 1846, 1 ("sickly and miserable fictions"); "Publishers and Authors. *Dolores* by Harro Harring," *NYDT*, Feb. 3, 1846, 1 ("ninety-nine hundredths"); "Literati," 74 ("well-*put*"). For Harring's life and career in Europe, see the admiring biography by Alexander Everett that Fuller referenced in her review: "Harro Harring: A Biographical Sketch," *United States Magazine and Democratic Review*, 15 (Oct., Nov., Dec. 1844), 337–47; 462–75, 561–79.

78. To William Emerson, Mar. 7, 1847, *EL*, III, 382 ("The offended Harpers"); *New York Herald*, June 27, 1846, 1 (dismissed the case); *OM*, I, 302, and "Conversation on Margaret Fuller at the Concord School of Philosophy," newspaper article, Aug. 25, 1883, OC (five hundred dollars); Harro Harring to MF, [Oct. 22, 1846], FMW, X, 2 (bad contract); Oct. 30, 1846, *FL*, VI, 369 ("rather lose the money"); Dec. 12, 1849, *FL*, V, 296 ("wiselier spent").

79. Jan. 9, 1846, *FL*, IV, 181 ("several volumes"); to EAD, Feb. 2, 1846, ibid., 182–83 (pitching the idea); [ca. Feb. 5, 1846], ibid., 184 ("good deal of interest"); to RFF, [ca. Feb. 13, 1846], ibid., 188 ("Much pleased"); [ca. Feb.-May, 1846], FMW, box A (list).

80. To EAD, [ca. Feb. 5, 1846], *FL*, IV, 184, and to EAD, June 28, [1846], ibid., 212 (cuts); quoted in to EAD, June 28, [1846], ibid., 212 ("controversial character"); Hershel Parker, *Herman Melville: A Biography*, 2 vols. (Baltimore, 1996–2000), I, 416, 417, 461, and Andrew Delbanco, *Melville: His World and Work* (New York, 2005), 81n, 85, 89–90 (censored *Typee* passages); to EAD, June 28, [1846], *FL*, IV, 212, 213 ("so-called religious public").

81. To EAD, July 14, [1846], *FL*, IV, 219 ("how to arrange"); to EAD, Oct. 30, 1846, ibid., 234 (blamed, "obliged," and "arrangement"); to John Wiley, July 7, 1846, ibid., 216 ("make more haste"); *FPL*, I, vii ("object of my life"). Greeley would later say that Fuller's *Tribune* articles were "badly cut down and cut out" simply for want of room, without explaining why, although he probably at least partly knew, since she was consulting him about the volume. See to EAD, July 21?, 1846, *FL*, IV, 222; and HG to RFF, Dec. 11, 1853, FMW, X, 62.

82. To EAD, June 28, [1846], *FL*, IV, 213 ("indifferent matter"); EAD to George L. Duyckinck, July 28, [1846], Duyckinck Family Papers, NN-M (finished at printers).

83. To JN, [ca. Feb. 28, 1846], *FL*, IV, 191 ("up to the last"); to SGW and ABW, Mar. 3, 1846, ibid., 193, and to MR, Mar. 9, 1846, ibid., 196 (left Amity Place); to RFF, July 14, 1846, ibid., 217 ("Continuingly unwell"); [ca. Mar. 10, 1846], ibid., 198 ("never returning"); to RFF, July 4, 1846, ibid., 214 (daguerreotype); to James Ombrosi, July 8, 1846, in *Letters of William Cullen Bryant*, ed. William Cullen Bryant II and Thomas G. Voss, 6 vols. (New York, 1975–92), II, 436 ("lady of extensive literary accomplishments"); N. P. Willis to Richard S. Willis, 1846, FMW, XVI, 51 ("distinguished authoresses"); July 22, 1846, in Griswold, *Passages from the Correspondence*, 204 ("a good while").

84. "A Few Words in Reply to Mr. U. C. Hill," *NYDT*, May 15, 1846, supp., 1 ("never equaled"); "Farewell," ibid., Aug. 1, 1846, 2 ("twenty months").

85. *National Anti-Slavery Standard*, 322 (Aug. 6, 1846), 28 ("this dirty city"); *Har-*

binger, Aug. 22, 1846, 176 ("shield her"). For one abolitionist's appreciative notice of Fuller's antislavery articles, see Anne Warren Weston to Caroline and Debora Weston, [Jan.], 24–26, [1845], Weston Papers, MB.

86. To RFF, July 28, [1846], *FL*, IV, 224 ("Tired and harried"); Horace Greeley, *Recollections of a Busy Life* (New York, 1868), 162 (Greeleys saw off); to RFF, July 28, [1846], *FL*, IV, 224 ("*Very* early" and "baggage"); *EL*, VIII, 87 (Emerson); Aug. 2, 1846, *ChiL*, 229 ("refresh both mind and body."

Chapter Eight

1. Harvey Levenstein, *Seductive Journey: American Tourists in France from Jefferson to the Jazz Age* (Chicago, 1998), 16 (seasick passengers); Aug. 16, 1846, *FL*, IV, 225 ("I could hardly have borne"); *EJMN*, IV, 111 (Emerson's trip).

2. To MCF, Aug. 16, 1846, *FL*, IV, 225 ("agreeable"); "TTE," Aug. 23, 1846, *NYDT*, Sept. 24, 1846, 2 ("following their lead, as usual").

3. *FL*, VI, 353, and RBS statement quoted in Katherine M. Zengerle, "She Told John Brown 'Twere Better to Die of a Big Idea than of a Fever," *Los Angeles Record*, 1905, Spring Papers, NjHi (first met); "A Book of Remembrance," 121, Spring Papers, CSt, ("better to die"); Lillie Buffum Chace Wyman, *American Chivalry* (Boston, 1913), 51 ("piquant"); Goodwyn Barmby to Moncure D. Conway, June 17, 1870, in *Autobiography, Memories and Experiences of Moncure Daniel Conway*, 2 vols. (Boston, 1904), II, 395 ("rapture"); RBS, "Auld Acquaintance," Spring Papers, 82 CSt ("so severe"); to MS and RBS, Dec. 9, 1847, *FL*, IV, 311 ("real valid friendship").

4. To Joseph Story, July 13, 1837, in *Selected Letters of Charles Sumner*, ed. Beverly Wilson Palmer, 2 vols. (Boston, 1990), I, 27 ("*intellectual capital*"); May 10, 1840, *EJMN*, VII, 493 ("maggot of Europe"). For a valuable introduction to travel and travel writing in the West, see Paul Fussell, ed., *The Norton Book of Travel* (New York, 1987). For an overview of American travelers in Europe in this period, see Foster Rhea Dulles, *Americans Abroad: Two Centuries of European Travel* (Ann Arbor, 1964), chaps. 3–7. The most insightful books on American ideas about Europe remain Philip Rahv, ed., *Discovery of Europe: The Story of American Experience in the Old World* (New York, 1947); and Cushing Strout, *The American Image of the Old World* (New York, 1963). Evidence for the extensive travel of American liberal reformers in these years may be found in their papers and biographies.

5. For American travel writing, see Willard Thorp, "Pilgrim's Return," in Robert E. Spiller et al., *Literary History of the United States*, 3rd ed. rev. (1947; New York, 1963); and Ernest Earnest, *Expatriates and Patriots: American Artists, Scholars, and Writers in Europe* (Durham, N.C., 1968). More recent useful studies include William W. Stowe, *Going Abroad: European Travel in Nineteenth-Century American Culture* (Princeton, 1994); Terry Caesar, *Forgiving the Boundaries: Home as Found in American Travel Writing* (Athens, Ga., 1995); Mary Suzanne Schriber, *Writing Home: American Women Abroad, 1830–1920* (Charlottesville, 1997); and Larzer Ziff, *Return Passages: Great American Travel Writing, 1780–1910* (New Haven, 2000). Earnest, Stowe, and Schriber include discussions of Fuller's travel writing.

6. "The Unbroken Charm: Margaret Fuller, G. S. Hillard, and the American Tradition of Travel Writing on Italy," in Charles Capper and Cristina Giorcelli, eds., *Margaret Fuller: Transatlantic Crossings in a Revolutionary Age* (Madison, forthcoming) ("open genre"); "Prospectus for 1846," *NYDT*, June 19, 1846, 1 ("Foreign Correspondents"); HG to MF, June 27, 1848, FMW, X, 52 ("What we pay you"); "Books of Travel," *NYDT*, Dec. 18,

1845, 1 ("symptoms"); Larry J. Reynolds and Susan Belasco Smith, eds., *"These Sad but Glorious Days": Dispatches from Europe, 1846–1850* (New Haven, 1991) ("dispatches").

7. "First of August, 1845," *NYDT*, Aug. 1, 1845, 1 ("one good act"); to Maria Rotch, Jan. 22, 1844, *FL*, III, 171 ("degenerate[d]").

8. Elie Halévy, *History of the English People*, vol. IV (London, 1851; 1913), 103–50, gives a vivid portrait of social and political life in 1846. Like all students of the era, I have also found still very useful G. M. Young, *Victorian England: Portrait of an Age* (Oxford, 1936), and Asa Briggs, *The Age of Improvement, 1783–1867* (New York, 1959). For seminal studies of Victorian intellectual culture, see Walter E. Houghton, *The Victorian Frame of Mind, 1830–1970* (New Haven, 1957); and Raymond Williams, *Culture and Society, 1780–1950* (1958; New York, 1983), pt. 1. More recent assessments may be found in T. W. Heyck, *The Transformation of Intellectual Life in Victorian England* (New York, 1982); and Philip Davis, *The Victorians, 1830–1880* (Oxford, England, 2002), vol. VIII of the *Oxford English Literary History*, ed. Jonathan Bate.

9. "TTE," Aug. 23, 1846, *NYDT*, Sept. 24, 1846, 2 ("rushing, tearing and swearing"); journal, [ca. Aug. 16, 1846]*, in *HO*, 223 ("bad manners"); journal, [Aug. 23, 1846]*, in *HO*, 224 ("talked of character"); "TTE," Aug. 23, 1846, *NYDT*, Sept. 24, 1846, 2 ("'None but the sick'").

10. "TTE," Aug. 23, 1846, *NYDT*, Sept. 24, 1846, 2 ("bare-headed"); [Aug. 17, 1846]*, in *HO*, 221 ("woman nominally").

11. "TTE," Aug. 23, 1846, *NYDT*, Sept. 24, 1846, 2 ("best minds"); June 20, 1847, *FL*, IV, 276 ("the old Dial"); "TTE," Aug. 23, 1846, *NYDT*, Sept. 24, 1846, 2 ("'But you are mightily pleased'"); Oct. 6, 1846, *FL*, IV, 231 ("*Excelsior*").

12. Sept. 29, [1845], in *Harriet Martineau's Letters to Fanny Wedgwood*, ed. Elisabeth Sanders Arbuckle (Stanford, 1983), 85 ("Beautiful!"); RBS quoted in F. B. Sanborn, *Recollections of Seventy Years*, 2 vols. (Boston, 1909), II, 408 (calling every morning); *Harriet Martineau's Autobiography*, 3 vols. (London, 1877), II, 252, 253 ("contemptuous benevolence"); journal, [Aug. 18, 1846]*, *HO*, 222 ("harried"); "TTE," Aug. 27, 1846, *NYDT*, Sept. 29, 1846 (benevolent author).

13. RBS, "Journal Abroad," 8, NjHi (Arnold); to AHC Mar. 21, 1853, in *The Letters of Matthew Arnold*, ed. Cecil Y. Lang, 6 vols., II, 258 ("exquisite intelligence"); RBS quoted in Sanborn, *Recollections of Seventy Years*, II, 408–9 (Wordsworth recited); "TTE," Sept. 20, 1846, *NYDT*, Oct. 24, 1846, 1 ("feverish"); journal, [Aug. 27, 1846]*, in *HO*, 225 ("happy eight days");

14. "TTE," Sept. 20, 1846, *NYDT*, Oct. 24, 1846, 1 ("more like home"); MCF to MF, Feb. 7, 1847, FMW, VIII, 216 ("delighted"); Journal, FMW, box A ("We like to look up"); "TTE," Sept. 22, 1846, *NYDT*, Nov. 5, 1846, 1 ("stock lions"); to RWE, Nov. 16, 1846, *FL*, IV, 246 ("Grand Conversatione"); "TTE," Sept. 22, 1846, *NYDT*, Nov. 5, 1846, 1 ("Vivian-Greyish style").

15. "TTE," Sept. 30, 1846, *NYDT*, Nov. 13, 1846, 1 ("purgatory").

16. Journal, [Aug. 26, 1846]*, in *HO*, 225 ("tedious"); "TTE," Sept. 30, 1846, *NYDT*, Nov. 13, 1846 ("exquisitely dressed"); RBS, "Journal Abroad," NjHi, 11 ("womanlike"); "TTE," Sept. 30, 1846, *NYDT*, Nov. 13, 1846, 1 ("visionary shapes"); to RFF, Sept. 27, 1846, *FL*, IV, 228 ("*if* I had not tried"); RBS, "Journal Abroad," NjHi, 11 ("No common woman"); "TTE," Sept. 30, 1846, *NYDT*, Nov. 13, 1846 ("Yankee method").

17. RBS, "Journal Abroad," NjHi, 12 ("saw her first!"); "TTE," Sept. 30, 1846, *NYDT*, Nov. 13, 1846, 1 ("intimate feeling"); [Sept. 13, 1846]*, in *HO*, 228 ("delightful emotions"); Nov. 16, 1846, *FL*, IV, 246 ("hair-breadth escape"); Nov. 13, 1846, Rufus W. Griswold, *Passages from the Correspondence and Other Papers of Rufus W. Griswold*

(Cambridge, Mass., 1898), 213 ("blessed mishap"); Nov. 16, *FL*, IV, 1846, Duyckinck Family Papers, NN-M ("most peculiar account").

18. Journal, [Sept. 15, 1846]*, in *HO*, 228 ("execrable fiddle"); "TTE," Sept. 22, 1846, *NYDT*, Nov. 5, 1846, 1 ("beautiful and stately"); to RFF, Sept. 27, 1846, *FL*, IV, 228 ("feat for a lady"); "TTE," 1846, *NYDT*, Jan. 5, 1847, 1 ("real representative"); journal, [Sept. 16, 1846*], in *HO*, 228 ("pompous butler"); "TTE," 1846, *NYDT*, Jan. 5, 1847, 1 ("mock wilderness").

19. Journal, [ca. 1847], FMW, box A (avoided Ireland); "TTE," Sept. 30, 1846, *NYDT*, Nov. 13, 1846, 1 ("frightful inequalities"); journal, [ca. 1847], FMW, box A ("In the church yard"); "TTE," 1846, *NYDT*, Jan. 5, 1847, 1 ("sooty servitors"); "TTE," Sept. 22, 1846, ibid., Nov. 5, 1846, 1 ("vulgar and base"); "TTE," Nov. 1846, ibid., Dec. 23, 1846, 1 ("impure air").

20. Sept. 27, 1846, *FL*, IV, 228 ("desire to know me").

21. Sept. 1, 1846, *FL*, IV, 226 (urged Delf); JN to MF, Nov. 27, 1846, FMW, X, 115 ("so changed"); RBS to Caroline Healey Dall, June 19, 1904, in Dall, "Mrs Dall and Some Idealists," *Springfield Sunday Republican*, Mar. 19, 1905 ("large, white, soft"); Feb. 21, 1848, FMW, VIII, 218 ("I think she rather enjoyed"); [ca. Sept. 8, 1846]*, in *FLL*, 187 ("mighty change"); "TTE," Sept. 30, 1846, *NYDT*, Nov. 13, 1846, 1 (lugubrious retelling); to Thomas Delf, [Oct. 2?, 1846], *FL*, IV, 230 (arrange a meeting); Oct. 9, 1846, in *FLL*, 188, 189 ("Is she prepared"). Some scholars' tentative speculation that Fuller's Ben Lomond climb was a "suicidal gesture" rebounding from Nathan's letter is unlikely. It rests on the claim in Beatrice Borchardt's fictionalized biography of Rebecca Spring that Rebecca remembered the morning of their departure from Edinburgh a depressed Fuller staying out on the top of a coach in pouring rain, a ride Fuller described in her dispatch as a great lark. As she told Richard, while lost, she did everything to *avoid* dying. *FL*, IV, 10; Beatrice E. Borchardt, "Lady of Utopia: The Story of Rebecca Buffum Spring," n.p. Spring Papers, CSmH.

22. Thomas Delf to JN, Oct. 9, 1846, in ("a moment's repose"); JN to MF, Nov. 6, 1846, FMW, X, 113 ("congratulations" and "right cause").

23. Nov. 6, 1846, FMW, X, 113 ("my anxiety to be clearly understood"); to JN, [Apr. 15, 1845], *FL*, IV, 78 ("mutually exchange"); to JN, [May 15?, 1845], ibid., 100 ("leave my letters" and "let me burn them"); to JN, May 23, [1845], ibid., 104 ("destroy them"); quoted in JN to MF, Nov. 27, 1846, FMW, X, 115 ("*you have deceived me*"); JN to MF, Nov. 27, 1846, FMW, X, 115 ("philadelphia lawyer"); *OM*, II, 37 ("blindfold"). There is no evidence in the surviving papers that Nathan kept the letters in order to extort money from her or her family. Gotendorf was the name of a place in Holstein that had belonged to his father. *FLL*, 190.

24. "The Literati in New York City," in *The Complete Works of Edgar Allan Poe*, ed. James A. Harrison, 17 vols. (New York, 1902), XV, 74, 75, 79, 82, 82–83 ("except Miss Fuller").

25. To James T. Fields, Dec. 29, 1846, in Griswold, *Passages from the Correspondence*, 221 ("rabid"); *The Prose Writers of America* (Philadelphia, 1846), 538 ("generally excellent"); Edwin P. Whipple to Rufus W. Griswold, Apr. 26, 1847, in Griswold, *Passages from the Correspondence*, 228 ("sulky magnificence"); Griswold, *Prose Writers*, 537, 538 ("created female"); Edwin P. Whipple to Rufus W. Griswold, Apr. 26, 1847, in Griswold, *Passages from the Correspondence*, 228 ("shabby-genteel"); *Prose Writers*, 538 ("brown stout"); Mar. 7, 1847, in Griswold, *Passages from the Correspondence*, 224 ("Greeley is angry"); *Literary World*, 1 (Mar. 20, 1847), 150, 151 ("*degrade*"); ibid. (Mar. 27, 1847), 183 ("species of antagonist").

26. RFF to MF, Sept. 27, [1846], FMW, XVII, 22 ("thoughtless of consequences"); *Christian Examiner*, 42 (Jan. 1847), 140 ("few superiors"); review of *A Fable for Critics* by James Russell Lowell, *Southern Literary Messenger*, Mar. 1849, in *Complete Works of Poe*, 169 ("silly and conceited"); to George W Eveleth, Jan. 4, 1848, *PoLe*, 355 ("grossly dishonest"); to Fredrick W. Thomas, Feb. 14, 1849, ibid.., 427 ("detestable old maid"); *American Whig Review,* 4 (Nov. 1846), 515 ("eulogism"); *Graham's* Magazine, 29 (Oct. 1846), 262 ("spiteful"); United *States Magazine and Democratic Review*, 19 (Sept., 1846), 198–202, and ibid. (Oct. 1846), 316–20 (Sarah Helen Whitman's review).

27. *Godey's Lady's Book*, 33 (Nov. 1846), 288 ("dozen male writers"); *Brooklyn Daily Eagle*, Nov. 9, 1846, 2 ("why don't she print it"); *Columbian Lady's and Gentleman's Magazine*, 6 (Oct. 1846), 192 ("bad taste"); *American Whig Review* 4 (Nov. 1846), 515 ("gentler sex").

28. *New York Illustrated Magazine*, 2 (Nov. 1846), 432 ("admired by thousands"); *Blackwood's Edinburgh Magazine*, 62 (Nov. 1847), 576, 582 ("Mrs Margaret Fuller"); *Knickerbocker*, 31 (Jan. 1848), 68–71 (reprinted sarcasms); *Critic*, 4 (Oct. 3, 1846), 401 ("high position"); *Athenaeum*, no. 999 (Dec. 19, 1846), 1287 ("speculative"); quoted in Walter Graham, *English Literary Periodicals* (New York, 1930), 323 ("magisterial seriousness"); *Spectator*, no. 900 (Sept. 27, 1845), 931 (panned *Woman*); *Spectator*, no. 952 (Sept. 26, 1846), 930–31 ("We have seen enough"); *People's Journal*, 3 (Jan. 16, 1847), 89 ("congratulate America").

29. "TTE," Dec. 1846, *NYDT*, Feb. 2, 1847, 1 ("stock shows"); "TTE," [n.d.], ibid., Feb. 19, 1847, 1 ("atmosphere of Art"); "TTE," [n.d.], ibid., Mar. 31, 1847, 1 ("hieroglyphics of pictures"); Journal, FMW, box A (pamphlet); "TTE," [n.d.], *NYDT*, Mar. 3, 1847, 1 (cooking smells and "model-prison"); "TTE," Dec. 1846, ibid., Feb. 2, 1847, 1 ("peaceful revolution").

30. "TTE," Dec. 1846, *NYDT*, Feb. 2, 1847, 1 ("'*the* season'"); Oct. 2, [1846], *FL*, IV, 229 ("fifth best"); to EAD, Oct. 30, 1846, ibid., 234 ("prized by many"); to RFF, Oct. 2, [1846], ibid., 229 ("high-handed 'Spectator'"); to RWE, Oct. 30, 1846, ibid., 234 ("real misfortune").

31. To ?, [ca. mid-November 1846, *FL*, IV, 242 ("admirable"); "TTE," [n.d.], *NYDT*, Mar. 3, 1847, 1 ("new era in England"); to CS, [Nov. 16?, 1846], *FL*, IV, 240–41 ("highly valued by English women"); "TTE," Dec. 1846, *NYDT*, Feb. 2, 1847, 1 ("withered flowers").

32. "TTE," [n.d.}, *NYDT*, Feb. 19, 1847, 1 ("stupidly comfortable"); to Catharine Maria Sedgwick, [ca. July 8, 1847], Channing Family Papers, MHi ("prodigious"); *People's Journal*, 1 (Jan. 3, 1846), 1, 2 ("in the spirit of Thomas Carlyle"). For a sketch of the *People's Journal*, see Carl Ray Woodring, *Victorian Samplers: William and Mary Howitt* (Lawrence, Kans., 1952), chap. 6; but the best source is the journal itself. For useful details on this circle of radical Unitarians, see R. K. Webb, *Harriet Martineau: A Radical Victorian* (New York, 1960); and Kathryn Gleadle, *The Early Feminists: Radical Unitarians and the Emergence of the Women's Rights Movement* (New York, 1995).

33. William Hodgson to MF, Sept. 18, 1846, Spring Papers, CSt (Martineau's letter); to EAD, Oct. 30, 1846, *FL*, IV, 235 ("exceedingly"); to ?, [ca. mid-Nov. 1846], ibid., 243–44 ("unpoetical"); "TTE," 1846, *NYDT*, Jan. 5, 1847, 1 ("homely adaptation"); "TTE," Dec. 1846, ibid., Feb. 2, 1847, 1 ("your scissors"). Martineau's connections with the *People's Journal* crowd are highlighted in Webb, *Harriet Martineau*. Despite the differences in philosophy and style between the more spiritualistic American Transcendentalists and the utilitarian radical English Unitarians, Harriet Martineau's prominent Unitarian minister brother, James Martineau, detected then a "via media opened up between the

between the mere moralism of the English Unitarianism and the subjective transcendentalism of the American New School." Manuscript notes on a letter Martineau received from R. H. Hutton, Sept. 18, 1847, quoted in Gleadle, *Early Feminists*, 18.

34. Goodwyn Barmby to Moncure Conway, June 17, 1870, quoted in Conway, *Autobiography*, II, 395 ("talked to death"); *People's Journal*, 3 (Jan. 16, 1847), 88, 89 ("American school of Transcendentalism").

35. To Thomas Ballantyne, Dec. 31, 1841, *CCC*, XIII, 332 ("very ghostly"); Parke Godwin quoted in EAD to George L. Duyckinck, Jan. 28, 1848, Duyckinck Family Papers, NN-M ("accept the universe!"); *The Varieties of Religious Experience* (Cambridge, Mass., 1985), 41, in *Works of William James*, ed. Frederick H. Burkhardt et al. (Cambridge, Mass., 1975–); Perry Miller, ed., *Margaret Fuller: American Romantic* (Garden City, N.Y., 1963), ix ("honor").

36. Unpublished manuscript quoted in Fred Kaplan, *Thomas Carlyle: A Biography* (Ithaca, 1983), 333 ("Phallus"); July 31, 1846, *ECC*, 407 ("our citizen of the world"); July 15, 1846, ibid., 403–4 ("send you no other such"); to RWE, Nov. 16, 1846, *FL*, IV, 246 ("at once"); Oct. 8, 1846, *CCC*, XXI, 73 ("not nearly such a bore"); Nov. 16, 1846, *FL*, IV, 246 ("delighted with him"). The best modern biography of Carlyle is Kaplan's. For Jane Carlyle, see Lawrence and Elizabeth Hanson, *Necessary Evil: The Life of Jane Welsh Carlyle* (London, 1952); and Virginia Surtees, *Jane Welsh Carlyle* (Wilton, Salisbury, 1986).

37. To RWE, Nov. 16, 1846, *FL*, IV, 248 ("only *seen*"); Oct. 19, 1846, in *Selections from the Letters of Geraldine Endsor Jewsbury to Jane Welsh Carlyle*, ed. Mrs. Alexander Ireland (London, 1892), 215 ("I loathe her"); *CCC*, XVIII, 260 (admired *Summer*); *Letters of Charles Eliot Norton*, 2 vols., ed. Sarah Norton and M. A. DeWolfe Howe (Boston, 1913), I, 500 ("peremptorily"); to RWE, Nov. 16, 1846, *FL*, IV, 246, 248 ("unfit" and "perfect prisoner"); RBS, "Journal Abroad," NjHi, 14 ("nice bright answers"); George Jacob Holyoake, *Sixty Years of an Agitator's Life* (London, 1893), 244 ("all silenced"). The only surviving negative remark of Jane about Fuller likewise came from the unreliable Amalie Bölte, who claimed that when Jane, who was interested in women's rights, had given Bölte a copy of Fuller's *Woman in the Nineteenth Century*, she had told her "it was hateful; we were both glad we had not written it." *Amely Böltes Briefe aus England an Varnhagen von Ense (1844–1858)* (Düsseldorf, 1955), 65, quoted in *CCC*, XXIIII, 94 n2.

38. JWC to MF, Oct. 1846, FMW, XVI, 105 (proposed another meeting); Nov. 16, 1846, *FL*, IV, 249 ("All Carlyle's talk"); RBS, "Journal Abroad," NjHi, 14 ("glad to hear it!"); Nov. 16, 1846, *FL*, IV, 249 ("melodious"); "TTE," [n.d.], *NYDT*, Feb. 18, 1847, 1 ("shams and conventions").

39. Dec. 18, 1846, *CCC*, XXI, 113–14 ("high-soaring, clear, enthusiast soul"); "TTE," [n.d.], *NYDT*, Feb. 19, 1847, 1 ("as the hawk its prey"); to RWE, Mar. 2, 1847, *CCC*, XXI, 172 ("*en beau*"); Mar. 8, 1852, *CCC*, XXVII, 66 ("surprising she didn't"); Mar. 2, 1847, *CCC*, XXI, 172 ("true heroic mind"); Dec. 18, 1846, ibid., 114 ("*phosphorescence*")

40. Diary, Apr. [1847], Alcott Papers, MH ("diplomatic"); to MF, [ca. May 14, 1847], FMW, X, 38 ("seems whimsical").

41. The best modern biographies are Roland Sarti, *Mazzini: A Life for the Religion of Politics* (Westport, Conn., 1997); and Denis Mack Smith, *Mazzini* (New Haven, 1994), the former for Mazzini's ideas and the latter for his political career.

42. "Thoughts upon Democracy in Europe," *People's Journal*, 2 (Aug. 29, 1846), 116 ("*under the leading*"). Mazzini's series and supporting documents are conveniently collected in Mazzini, *Thoughts upon Democracy in Europe (1846–1847: Un "Manifesto" in inglese*, ed. Salvo Mastellone (Firenze, 2001). Mazzini's views of America are surveyed

in Joseph Rossi, *The Image of America in Mazzini's Writings* (Madison, 1954), which includes a chapter on Fuller. For English liberal support for the Italian political refugees and their cause, see Roderick Cavaliero, *Italia Romantica: English Romantics and Italian Freedom* (London, 2005).

43. GM to MF, [Oct. 14, 1846], FMW, XI, 79 (given him her writings); *MS*, LXXVII, 272 ("distrust"); [Oct. 27, 1846], *FL*, IV, 84 ("no cause for fearing"); "Thoughts upon Democracy in Europe," *People's Journal*, 2, Oct. 3, 1846, 188 ("a democrat"); Nov. 16, 1846, *FL*, IV, 248–49 ("became very sad"). GM to MF, [Oct. 14, 1846] is misdated in *MS, Appendice*, VI, 506–7.

44. W. J. Linton, "The Italian Gratuitous School," *People's Journal*, 2 (July 4, 1846), 147 ("Inquisition").

45. George Haven Putnam, *George Palmer Putnam: A Memoir* (New York, 1912), 399 ("remark"); quoted in C. S. H., "Italian School, Greville-Street," *People's Journal*, app., 4 (Jan. 16, 1847), 5 ("international moral exchange"); C. S. H., "Italian School" ("best book").

46. Nov. 13, 1846, *MS*, XXX, 269 ("very moving speech"); to GM, Mar. 3, 1849, *FL*, V, 196, and RBS, "Journal Abroad," 16, NjHi (plan); GM to MF, [Dec. 24, 1846], FMW, XI, 88 ("scheme"); "TTE," [n.d.], *NYDT*, Feb. 19, 1847, 1 ("Here these poor boys").

47. [Nov. 16?, 1846], *FL*, IV, 240 ("most beauteous"); "TTE," [n.d.], *NYDT*, Feb. 19, 1847, 1 ("too much to be done").

48. Nov. 16, 1846, *FL*, IV, 245 ("that mountain of shams"); to EAD, Oct. 30, 1846, ibid., 234 ("*very* much"); Feb. 8, 1847, FMW, X, 46 ("dazzled or awed"); to EAD, Oct. 30, 1846, *FL*, IV, 234 ("fine"); to [?], [ca. mid-Nov. 1846], ibid., 244, and CS to SGW, [ca. Apr. 1847], Ward Papers, MH (return to write); SC to MF, [ca. May 14, 1847], FMW, X, 38 (hoped she would).

49. *FL*, IV, 239–40, 240 ("wasted on obstructions"); Nov. 16, 1846, ibid., 245 ("fish in water"). Fuller's often-quoted lament has had a curious history. In *OM* it is inserted, presumably by Emerson, in a letter she wrote him from Italy a year later in a very different tone, an error followed in *FL*, IV, 315. Whether he did this accidentally or, perhaps to insert himself into the drama of Fuller's European years, intentionally, it effectively obscured the fact that she was developing an "expatriate" consciousness nearly four months before she arrived in Italy. More important, in changing "obstructions" to "abstractions," Emerson unwittingly provided spurious evidence to scholars eager to exaggerate Fuller's complete alienation in Europe from American "idealism." The most notable of these appropriations was that of Stanley Elkins, who in his account of the Transcendentalists in his influential *Slavery*, used the incorrect word to support his Burkean thesis about the dangerously "abstract" character of Transcendentalist and abolitionist reform thought. See *OM*, II, 224–25; *FL*, IV, 239–40, 314; and Stanley M. Elkins, *Slavery: A Problem in American Institutional and Intellectual Life*, 3rd ed. (1959; Chicago, 1976), 155.

50. "TTE," Dec. 1846, *NYDT*, Feb. 2, 1847, 1 ("different world"). French opinion of the United States is surveyed in René Rémond, *Les États-Unis devant l'opinion française, 1815–52*, 2 vols. (Paris, 1962); and Theodore Zeldin, *France, 1848–1945*, vol. II, *Intellect, Taste and Anxiety* (Oxford, England, 1977), 126–38. For "bourgeois" as a negative referent in French culture in the early nineteenth century, see Sarah Maza, *The Myth of the French Bourgeoisie: An Essay on the Social Imaginary, 1750–1850* (Cambridge, Mass., 2003).

51. "TTE," [n.d.], *NYDT*, Mar. 3, 1847, 1 ("fine shows"); "TTE," [n.d.], ibid., May 15, 1847, 1 ("passably pretty"); *FL*, IV, 241 ("*getting dressed*"); "TTE," [n.d.], *NYDT*, Mar. 3, 1847, 1 ("overcloud our public assemblies").

52. "TTE," [n.d.], *NYDT*, Mar. 31, 1847, 1 ("The American"). For American travelers in France, see Guillame de Bertier de Sauvigny, *La France et les Français vus par les voyageurs américains, 1814–1848*, 2 vols. (Paris, 1982–85); and Levenstein, *Seductive Journey*, chaps. 3–9.

53. "TTE," [n.d.], *NYDT*, Mar. 3, 1846, 1 ("execrable"); to George Palmer Putnam, Nov. 28, [1846], *FL*, IV, 252 (saw Rachel); Nov. 28, [1846], ibid., 250 ("severest culture"); to CS, Jan. 11–12, 1848, *FL*, V, 43–44 (hundred letters a day); Nov. 28, [1846], *FL*, IV, 250–52 ("really bad reputation").

54. To RWE, Jan. 18, 1847, *FL*, IV, 258 ("assiduous daily"); "TTE," [n.d.], *NYDT*, Mar. 3, 1847, 1 ("'You can go, Madame'").

55. "TTE," [n.d.], *NYDT*, Mar. 31, 1847, 1 ("Ether").

56. "TTE," [n.d.], *NYDT*, May 15, 1847, 1 ("School for Idiots").

57. "TTE," [n.d.], *NYDT*, May 15, 1847, 1 ("sharp-shooters"); "TTE," Jan. 27, ibid., Mar. 13, 1848, 1 ("shabbiness and falsehood").

58. "TTE," [n.d.], *NYDT*, May 15, 1847, 1 ("While Louis Philippe lives"); "TTE," [n.d.], ibid., May 15, 1847, 1 ("kept out of sight"); MF, journal, FMW, box A ("lively"); "TTE," [n.d.], *NYDT*, Mar. 3, 1847, 1 ("*Crèches*"); "TTE," [n.d.], ibid., May 29, 1847, 1 ("Fourier's observations").

59. Paul Bénichou, *Les Temps des prophètes: Doctrines de l'âge romantique* (Paris, 1977), and Sarane Alexandrian, *Le Socialisme romantique* (Paris, 1979), are comprehensive on French Romantic socialism, but for a penetrating short analysis and a fine biographical study, respectively, see George Lichtheim, *The Origins of Socialism* (New York, 1969), chaps. 1–5; and Jonathan Beecher, *Victor Considerant and the Rise and Fall of French Romantic Socialism* (Berkeley, 2001). For the influence of Romantic socialists on the political thinking of French artisans and peasants, see Edward Berenson, *Populist Religion and Left-Wing Politics in France, 1830–1852* (Princeton, 1984).

60. Dec. 24, 1846, OC, 101 ("their propaganda"); "TTE," [n.d.], *NYDT*, May 15, 1847, 1 ("precepts of Christ").

61. "TTE," [n.d.], *NYDT*, May 15, 1847, 1 ("The more I see").

62. To MCF, Dec. 26, 1846, *FL*, IV, 253 ("with Cupid, of course"); RBS, "Journal Abroad," [17], NjHi ("while we play"); Jan. 18, 1847, *FL*, IV, 258 ("touched only the glass").

63. MF, journal, Mar. 17, 1847, *OM*, II, 194 ("very bad French"); Jan. 18, 1847, *FL*, IV, 259 ("I find slippery"); Feb. 28, 1847, *EL*, III, 376 ("our queen of discourse"); to ES, Apr. 16, 1850, *FL*, VI, 78 ("master"); to RFF, Jan. 31, 1847, *FL*, IV, 259 ("hard"); to CS, Nov. 28, [1846], ibid., 250 (three hours); receipt, Jan. 1847, FMW, XI, 120 (twenty-five francs); to RWE, Jan. 18, 1847, *FL*, IV, 259 ("like an Italian").

64. To RWE, Jan. 18, 1847, *FL*, IV, 259 ("some friend"); to ES, Apr. 17, 1850, *FL*, VI, 78 ("entrée to almost any place" and "all the best people"); Feb. 22, 1847, FMW, XI, 125 ("union of opposite qualities").

65. "TTE," [n.d.], *NYDT*, May 15, 1847, 1 ("tribune"); Feb. 28, 1847, *EL*, III, 376 ("hardly any other"). The best short work in English on the social Romantics remains David Owen Evans, *Social Romanticism in France, 1830–1848* (New York, 1951). For an excellent discussion of the social and cultural position of the French literati in this period, see Jerrold Seigel, *Bohemian Paris: Culture, Politics, and the Boundaries of Bourgeois Life, 1830–1930* (New York, 1986), chaps. 1–5. D. G. Charlton, *Secular Religions in France, 1815–1870* (London, 1963), is helpful on French post-Christian religious thought. See also the works on Romantic socialism cited in note 59 above.

66. To Giuseppe Lamberti, Nov. 10, 1846, *MS*, XXX, 268, Giuseppe Lamberti to MF,

Nov. 18, 1846, FMW, XI, 78, Nov. 28, 1846, *PGI*, IV, 190, and GM to MF, Dec. 16, 1846, FMW, XI, 78 (articles and addresses); Dec. 1, [1849], *BML*, III, 285 ("lowest cafés"); Ferdinand François to MF, [ca. Dec. 1846], FMW, XI, 143 ("assistant editor for English literature"); to MCF, Dec. 26, 1846, *FL*, IV, 253 ("interesting woman"); "De la Littérature Américaine," *La Indépendante*, 6th yr., 2nd ser. (Dec. 10, 1846), 341–64 ("American Literature"); to MCF, Dec. 26, 1846, *FL*, IV, 253 ("manufacturing names"); Pauline Roland to MF, Dec. 16, 1846, FMW, XI, 132, Feb. 16, ibid., 122, [ca. Winter 1846–47], FMW, X, 34 (articles and Emerson).

67. "TTE," [n.d.], *NYDT*, Mar. 3, 1847, 1 ("I see well"); "TTE," [n.d.], *NYDT*, May 15, 1847, 1 (protest in *La Réforme*"); 1847, *FL*, IV, 254 ("affairs in our country").

68. *FL*, IV, 256 ("true in the outline"); CS to ABW, Apr. 8, [1847], Ward Papers, MH (circulated Hoar's report); to William Charles Macready, Jan. 1847, in George Sand, *Correspondance*, 26 vols. (Paris, 1964–95), VII, 601 ("quite involuntary"); Mar. 17, 1847, MH, and *OM*, II, 194, 195, 196 ("I never shall forget"). For Lamennais, Chopin, and other details of Sand's life at this time, see Curtis Cate, *George Sand: A Biography* (Boston, 1975), chaps. 27–32.

69. Mar. 17, 1847, *OM*, II, 197, 197–98 ("interior life").

70. J. W. Stirling to MF, [ca. early Feb. 1847], FMW, XI, 145, to RWE, Mar. 15, 1847, *FL*, IV, 262, and to Jane Stirling, Mar. 8, 1848, *FL*, V, 54 (Chopin lesson); "TTE," [n.d.], *NYDT*, May 29, 1847, 1 ("exquisitely organized"); Mar. 17, 1847, *OM*, II, 198, 198–99 ("Lying is ingrained"); Apr. 30, 1847, *EL*, III, 394 ("high time, dear friend").

71. Quoted in Czesław Miłosz, *History of Polish Literature* (1969; Berkeley, 1983), 217 ("objective lyricism"). The French originals of *MOW* are in FMW, XI. Mickiewicz's social and political thought is given contrasting treatment in Manfred Kridl, "Two Champions of a New Christianity: Lamennais and Mickiewicz," *Comparative Literature*, 4 (Summer 1952), 239–67; Wiktor Weintraub, "Adam Mickiewicz, the Mystic-Politician," in *Harvard Slavic Studies*, 1 (Cambridge, Mass., 1953), 137–78; and Andrzej Walicki, *Philosophy and Romantic Nationalism: The Case of Poland* (Oxford, England, 1982), 247–76. For Mickiewicz in the context of Europe's exile capital, see Lloyd S. Kramer, *Threshold of a New World: Intellectuals and the Exile Experience in Paris, 1830–1848* (Ithaca, 1988), chap. 4.

72. Mar. 15, 1847, *FL*, IV, 261 ("did not meet him anywhere"). For Emerson's appeal to Mickiewicz and his Parisian intellectual friends in the mid-1840s, see Ralph L. Rusk, *The Life of Ralph Waldo Emerson* (New York, 1949), 327–29; and Edmund Ordon, "Mickiewicz and Emerson," *University of Buffalo Studies* 23 (July 1956), 33–49. For Mickiewicz's Collège de France lectures, see Wiktor Weintraub, *Literature as Prophecy: Scholarship and Marinist Poetics in Mickiewicz's Parisian Lectures* (The Hague, 1959).

73. "Auld Acquaintance," 64 (came often); Władysław Mickiewicz, *Żywot Adama Mickiewicza*, 4 vols. (Poznan, 1890–95), III, 451, translated in *OMW*, 9 ("strong impression"); *OMW*, 8 (one scholar); quoted in Mickiewicz, *Żywot Adama Mickiewicza*, III, 451–52, translated in *OMW*, 9–10 ("authoress").

74. [Late February]* 1847, *OMW*, 12–13 ("innate right").

75. *FW*, v–vi ("angel or messenger").

76. Mar. 15, 1847, FL, IV, 261–62 ("only with Mickiewicz").

Chapter Nine

1. Jan. 18, 1847, *FL*, IV, 259 ("more at home").

2. Scholarship on the Risorgimento is formidable. Good starting points in English are the collections and commentary of Denis Mack Smith, *The Making of Italy, 1796–1870*

(New York, 1968); and Derek Beales and Eugenio F. Biagini, *The Risorgimento and the Unification of Italy*, 2nd ed. (1971; London, 2002). Bolton King, *A History of Italian Unity, Being a Political History of Italy from 1814 to 1871*, 2 vols. (London, 1899), is still useful, but essential is Giorgio Candeloro, *Storia dell'Italia moderna* (Milan, 1956–), vols. II–IV. Despite its bias against Risorgimento radicals, G. F.-H. and J. Berkeley, *Italy in the Making*, 3 vols. (London, 1932–40), is valuable for extracts from interviews with surviving participants. The two best analytical studies in English are, for social contexts, Stuart Woolf, *A History of Italy, 1700–1860: The Social Constraints of Political Change* (London, 1979), chaps. 9–15; and, for political developments, Harry Hearder, *Italy in the Risorgimento, 1790–1870* (London, 1983). For events leading to the Roman Republic of 1849, despite their various biases, three older works are helpful for their compendia of documents and firsthand recollections: Luigi Carlo Farini, *The Roman State, from 1815 to 1850*, 4 vols. (London, 1851–54); R. M. Johnston, *The Roman Theocracy and the Republic, 1846–1849* (London, 1901); and Luigi Rodelli, *La Repubblica Romana del 1849* (Pisa, 1955).

3. I follow the practice of participants and later historians in capitalizing the terms "Liberal," "Democrat," "Moderate," "Radical," "Republic," and "Republican" to denote a party, affiliation, or government. I have used lower case for these terms to indicate an ideological tendency or characterization.

4. For the influence of Italophilia on the Romantics and English culture, see C. P. Brand, *Italy and the English Romantics: The Italianate Fashion in Early Nineteenth-Century England* (Cambridge, England, 1957); and Roderick Cavaliero, *Italia Romantica: English Romantics and Italian Freedom* (London, 2005). Early nineteenth-century American travelers' attitudes toward Italy's past and present are discussed in Paul R. Baker, *The Fortunate Pilgrims: Americans in Italy, 1800–1860* (Cambridge, Mass., 1964). For a panoramic account of American writers and intellectuals' responses to Rome since the time of the early American Republic, see William L. Vance, *America's Rome*, 2 vols. (New Haven, 1989). For a sweeping interpretation of the American image of preunification Italy in which Fuller figures as the "shining exception" to her literary compatriots' evasion of the "reality" of contemporary Italian history, see A. William Salomone, "The Nineteenth-Century Discovery of Italy: An Essay in American Cultural History, Prolegomena to a Historiographical Problem," *American Historical Review*, 73 (June 1968), 1359–91. A similarly sympathic portrayal of Fuller's *Tribune* dispatches as juxtaposed with other American literary responses to nineteenth-century Italy may be found in Leonardo Buonomo, *Backward Glances: Exploring Italy, Reinterpreting America (1831–1866)* (Madison, N.J., 1996). In the sense that I describe it, Italophilia could be considered a form of eighteenth- and nineteenth-century "exoticism," in which a supposedly inferior or simply different (and usually non-Western) Other is made into an allegory of one's own (often Western) fashioning in varyingly negative and positive degrees. For two influential contrasting exegeses of this trope, see Edward W. Said, *Orientalism* (New York, 1978); and Tzvetan Todorov, *On Human Diversity: Nationalism, Racism, and Exoticism in French Thought* (Cambridge, Mass., 1993).

5. "Autobiographical Romance," *OM*, I, 18 ("indomitable will"); Nov. 2, 1830, *FL*, VI, 177 ("Father is reading aloud").

6. May 23, 1847, *FL*, IV, 273 ("cream of all the milk"); to CS, Aug. 22, 1847, ibid., 290 ("terrible regrets"); ibid., 291 ("wicked irritation"); to MS and RBS, Apr. 10, [1847], ibid., 263 (glum about Mickiewicz); "TTE," [n.d.], *NYDT*, May 29, 1847, 1 ("life in those days").

7. GM to MF, [Dec. 24, 1846], FMW, VI, 88 (scheme); Nov. 24, 1846, *MS*, XXX, 286 ("toward crisis"); Giuseppe Mazzini, *Thoughts upon Democracy in Europe (1846–*

1847): Un "Manifesto" in inglese, ed. Salvo Mastellone (Firenze, 2001), 11 (only eminent dissenters); [Dec. 24, 1846], FMW, VI, 88 ("Contemplation!").

8. [Dec. 24, 1846], FMW, VI, 88 ("esteem and love you"); to Giuseppe Lamberti, Dec.
17, 1846, ibid., 314, and to MF, [Dec. 1847], FMW, XI, 97 (mail drop); to Maria Mazzini,
May 31, 1847, *MS,* XXXII, 163, and Maria Mazzini to MF, July 5, 1847, FMW, XI, 94
(opened Fuller's letters); *MS, Appendix,* VI, 517 ("Peoples' International League"); GM
to MF, [Jan. 17, 1847], FMW, XI, 89 ("sterile benthamism"); to Mary Howitt, Apr. 18,
1847, *FL,* IV, 267–68 (dissemble); Feb. 10, 1847, FMW, XI, 91 ("confidence that you
show me").

9. [Dec. 24, 1846], FMW, XI, 88 ("wherever you will go"); to Enrico Mayer, Dec.
24, 1846, *MS,* XVI, 321 ("rarest of women"); "TTE," [n.d.], *NYDT,* May 29, 1847, 1 ("Very
attractive"); RBS, "Journal Abroad," [18], Spring Papers, NjHi, (Mazzini's room); to MF,
[Dec. 24, 1846], FMW, XI, 88 ("wherever you will go"); Mar. 27, 1847, *MS,* XXXII, 93
("affectionate way[s]"); Mar. 20, 1847, ibid., 76 ("very happy"); June [30?], 1847,
Mazzinian Institute of Genoa ("Benedetta"); Maria Mazzini to MF, July 5, 1847, FMW,
XI, 94 (Maria Mazzini obliged); Mar. 27, 1847, *MS,* XXXII, 93 ("Don't worry!"); RBS,
"Journal Abroad," [18], Spring Papers, NjHi ("unmarried and homeless").

10. Quoted in George Haven Putnam, *A Memoir of George Palmer Putnam,* 2 vols.
(New York, 1903), I, 143 ("throw you your things"); "TTE," [n.d.], *NYDT,* May 29, 1847,
1 ("hardly seemed worth while").

11. *OMW,* 19, 20 (Zaluska); "TTE," [n.d.], *NYDT,* May 29, 1847, 1 ("*my* Italy").

12. Apr. 15, 1847, *FL,* IV, 266 ("very happy here").

13. "TTE," Aug. 9, 1847, *NYDT,* Sept. 11, 1847 ("grave but dull"); "TTE," May 1847,
ibid., July 31, 1847, 1 ("cant of connoisseurship").

14. George Duyckinck to EAD, Easter Monday, 1847, Duyckinck Family Papers, NN-
M ("Democratic Pope"); May 15, 1848, FMW, X, 147 ("portrait of the Pope"); Feb. 8,
1847, ibid., 45 ("ask the Pope"); William Cullen Bryant to Charles Elbert Anderson, Oct.
1, 1845, in *Letters of William Cullen Bryant,* ed. William Cullen Bryant II and Thomas G.
Voss, 6 vols. (New York, 1975–92), II, 406 (banned newspapers). For the general enthusiasm in America toward the reforming pope, see Howard R. Marraro, *American Opinion
on the Unification of Italy, 1846–1861* (New York, 1932), chap. 2.

15. "TTE," May 1847, *NYDT,* July 31, 1847, 1 ("set his heart"); May 23, 1847, *FL,*
IV, 274 ("oftener frivolous"); "TTE," May 1847, *NYDT,* July 31, 1847, 1 ("Italians do
not feel it"). One exception at the time was the Young America Democrat Joel T. Headley,
who similarly noted the limits of the pope's reforms. See his *Letters from Italy* (New York,
1848), v–xii.

16. "TTE," May 1847, *NYDT,* July 31, 1847, 1 (narrative of the dinner); George L.
Duyckinck to EAD, May 4, 1847, Duyckinck Family Papers, NN-M, to Mr. Page, [May
1847]*, *FL,* V, 62–63, and to William Cullen Bryant, *FL,* May 22, 1847, VI, 371 (exchange newspapers); "TTE," May 1847, *NYDT,* July 31, 1847, 1 ("'law of *opportunity*'").

17. June 20, 1847, *FL,* IV, 276 ("seldom permitted"); to WHC, May 7, 1847, ibid.,
271 ("Art is not important").

18. To CS, Aug. 22, 1847, *FL,* IV, 290 ("terrible regrets"); May 23, 1847, ibid., 274
(feeling much better); to RWE, June 20, 1847, ibid., 276 (French fluently); Sept. 25, 1847,
ibid., 295 ("incorrect"); to RWE, June 20, 1847, ibid., 276 ("to know the common people");
to SC, Jan. 18, 1849, *FL,* V, 172 ("master"); to RWE, June 20, 1847, *FL,* VI, 276 ("all
night long"); quoted in RBS, "Journal Abroad," [19], NjHi ("Why").

19. To Maria Rotch, May 23, 1847, *FL,* IV, 275 ("herds"); to SC, Jan. 18, 1849, *FL,*
V, 171 ("*good* English society"); clipping of *Sharpe's Magazine,* [ca. 1852], ABA, [Au-

tobiographical Collections], IV–VI (1834–55), Alcott Papers, MH ("lifting up her upper lip"); to RWE, June 20, 1847, *FL*, IV, 276 ("little"); George Duyckinck to EAD, Easter Monday, 1847, Duyckinck Family Papers, NN-M (left a card); GWC to George Bradford, [ca. Apr.–May 1847]*, quoted in Gordon Milne, *George William Curtis and the Genteel Tradition* (Bloomington, Ind., 1956), 37 ("wise and witty accounts"); Apr. 15, 1847, *FL*, IV, 266 ("friendship of the mind").

20. Mar. 8, 1849, *FL*, V, 199 ("not intellectual enough"); to Thomas Hicks, Apr. 23, 1847, *FL*, IV, 269 ("Dear Youth"); May 4, [1847], FMW, XI, 115, 115–16 ("but little fire in the hut"); to CST, Mar. 8, 1849, *FL*, V, 199 (most intimate); "TTE," Mar. 20, 1849, *NYDT*, May 16, 1849, p. 1 ("man of ideas"); Oct. 25, 1847, *FL*, IV, 307 (his paintings); Thomas Hicks to MCF, Aug. 2, 1850, FMW, XVI, 65 ("sister").

21. Manuscript, OC, 178 ("further knowledge"); Putnam, *Memoir*, 100 ("quite bewildered"); Donald Yanella and Kathleen Malone Yannella, "Evart A. Duyckinck's 'Diary: May 29–November 8, 1847,'" in *SAR, 1978*, 225 ("singular suggestions"). Emelyn Story's account of Fuller's report is printed in *OM*, II, 281–93, but because it includes numerous alterations made by Channing, I have used the manuscript version in OC.

22. Quoted in *Letters and Journals of Thomas Wentworth Higginson, 1846–1906*, ed. Mary Thacher Higginson (Boston, 1921), 30 ("Spanish"); LMC to EGL, Mar. 24, 1850, *ChL*, 253 ("melancholy eyes"); ES to Maria Lowell, [ca. Dec. 1849–Jan. 1850]*, quoted in Maria Lowell to SC, [ca. Nov. 1849]*, *HO*, 244 ("much younger").

23. OC, 178 ("uncommon degree of character"). The best source for materials on Ossoli and his family is the Ossoli collection in the State Archive of Rome. See also AOA to EFC, May 9, 1851, FMW, 16, 139.

24. Dec. 11, 1849, *FL*, V, 292 ("I never dreamed"); Apr. 15, 1850, FMW, XI, 136 ("I saw"). For further supporting evidence on Ossoli's offer, see *OM*, II, 283, and Mary Peabody Mann to SPH, [ca. Aug. 1850], NN-B.

25. "Journal Abroad," [19–20], NjHi (return to Paris); "ON," 503 (marry Fuller); Mar. 1847, *OMW*, 18 ("seeing you again"); Apr. 10, [1847], *FL*, IV, 262, 263 ("walk by the inner light alone"); "Journal Abroad," [20], NjHi (almost plunged). There seems to have been nothing to the rumor, however, which Emerson probably got from Rebecca and later repeated in his journal, that Mickiewicz wanted to divorce his wife and marry Fuller. See "ON," 503.

26. Mar. 1847, *OMW*, 17, 18 ("Your organism").

27. Apr. 26, 1847, *OMW*, 20 ("that little Italian"); Aug. 3, 1847, ibid., 23, 24 ("Live and act, as you write").

28. To CS, Jan. 11, 1848, *FL*, V, 43 ("intoxicated"); to CS, Aug. 22, 1847, *FL*, IV, 290 ("peculiar life"); to RFF, July 1, 1847, ibid., 277 (Rome); Aug. 22, 1847, ibid., 290 ("last glorious nights"); May 23, 1847, ibid., 275 ("dream of my life"); to CS, Aug. 22, 1847, ibid., 290 (suffer[ing] from parting"); to RFF, July 1, 1847, ibid., 277 (reluctantly left Rome).

29. "TTE," Aug. 9, 1847, *NYDT*, Sept. 11, 1847, 1 ("Who can ever be alone").

30. "TTE," Aug. 9, 1847, *NYDT*, Sept. 11, 1847, 1 ("ironed out"); Aug. 22, 1847, *FL*, IV, 291 ("like Boston"); "TTE," Aug. 9, 1847, *NYDT*, Sept. 11, 1847, 1 ("glum as death"); quoted in Joel Myerson, "A Margaret Fuller Blurb for Hiram Powers," *Margaret Fuller Society Newsletter*, 5 (Winter 1997), 4 (pamphlet).

31. To RWE, Aug. 10, 1847, *FL*, IV, 287 ("two full, rich days"); "TTE," Aug. 9, 1847, *NYDT*, Sept. 11, 1847, 1 ("learned Bologna"); to RFF, [late July 1847], *FL*, IV, 284 ("glorious"); GWC to CPC, July 28, 1847, Cranch Family Papers, MHi (loved Venetian architecture); "TTE," Aug. 9, 1847, *NYDT*, Sept. 11, 1847, 1 ("scene of fairy land").

32. "Journal Abroad," [21], Spring Papers, NjHi (letters to and from cousin); May 7, 1847, Spring Papers, NjHi ("live with constantly"); to CS, Aug. 22, 1847, *FL*, IV, 291 ("wicked irritation"); Jan. 11, 1848, *FL*, V, 42 ("very weary"); "Journal Abroad," [21], NjHi, (letter from cousin). "Nowhere else but in Rome, and as an artist," the sculptor Kenyon remarked, speaking of the mystery surrounding the young artist Miriam's origins, "could she hold a place in society without giving some clue to her past life." *The Marble Faun*, in *Nathaniel Hawthorne: Novels*, Library of America (New York, 1983), 943.

33. Robert Wesselhoeft to Johan Peter Eckermann, n.d., FMW, XVI, 110 (glowing letters); to RFF, Apr. 15, 1847, *FL*, IV, 265, and to MR, May 23, 1847, ibid., 273 (another year); to RFF, July 1, 1847, ibid., 277 (fly through and "thinking of Rome").

34. To CS, Aug. 22, 1847, *FL*, IV, 291 ("high time"); to RFF, July 1, 1847, ibid., 277 (financial straights); Jan. 11, 1848, *FL*, V, 42 ("some bitterness"); "Journal Abroad," [22], NjHi, ("parting with Margaret"); July 10, 1847, *FL*, IV, 282 ("Natural tears"); to GAO, Sept. 10, 1848, *FL*, V, 113 (named their child).

35. To MS and RBS, July 10, 1847, *FL*, IV, 282 ("ladylike air"); GWC to CPC, July 28, 1847, Cranch Family Papers, MHi ("left yesterday morning"); [late July 1847], *FL*, IV, 284 ("in the gondola").

36. To MS, Aug. 9, 1847, *FL*, IV, 285 ("really well"); "TTE," Oct. 1847, *NYDT*, Dec. 25, 1847, 3; to MCF, Aug. 1, 1847, *FL*, IV, 284 ("sweet and pure").

37. Oct. 8, [1847], FMW, VIII, 222 ("no lady can guide herself"); Oct. 16, 1847, *FL*, IV, 300 ("die on the road"); statement of Domenico Albieri, Sept. 6, 1847, FMW, XI, 33 (fired him); quoted in RBS, "Journal Abroad," Spring Papers, [22], NjHi ("stab me").

38. To MS, Aug. 9, 1847, *FL*, IV, 285 ("very weak"); to MS, Feb. 1, 1848, *FL*, VI, 372 ("gastric troubles"); to RFF, Sept. 25, 1847, *FL*, IV, 295 ("really love").

39. To RWE, Aug. 10, 1847, *FL*, IV, 287 ("frank, expansive"); Oct. 1847, "TTE," *NYDT*, Dec. 25, 1847, 3 ("too much to suffer").

40. Julia Ward Howe, *Reminiscences, 1819–1899* (Boston, 1899), 119 (entertained Howe); CAV to MF, July 28, [1847], FMW, XI, 54 (letters of introductions); Sept. 1847, *FL*, IV, 294 ("really highbred lady").

41. ERF to MCF, Dec. 24, 1851, FMW, XVII, 46 ("deeply to adore"); CAV to MF, May 18, 1847, FMW, XI, 41 ("distinguished"); Sept. 2, 1847, ibid., 40 ("spectacle of moral beauty"); Sept. 25, [1847], ibid., 43 ("thrown a spell"); Sept. 1847, *FL*, IV, 294 ("seems to love me").

42. Aug. 22, 1847, *FL*, IV, 291 ("These ladies"); Nov. 22, [1847], FMW, XI, 42 ("You have penetrated"); to [?], Nov. 17, 1847, *FL*, IV, 311 (*"envies me"*).

43. Gaetano _____ to MF, Oct. 2, 1847, FMW, XI, 129 (entourage at Bellagio); to CS, Aug. 22, 1847, *FL*, IV, 290 ("fair and brilliant"); to CS, Jan. 11, 1848, *FL*, V, 42 ("'the American Countess'"); "TTE," Oct. 1847, *NYDT*, Dec. 25, 1847, 3 ("obtuse in organization"); Aug. 22, 1847, *FL*, IV, 291–92 ("life here on the lake"); to [?], Aug. [22?], 1847, ibid., 288 ("everywhere well received").

44. "TTE," Aug. 9, 1847, *NYDT*, Sept. 11, 1847, 1 ("some important change"); "TTE," Oct. 1847, ibid., Dec. 25, 1847, 3 (*"in the backs"*).

45. To RFF, July 1, 1847, *FL*, IV, 277, and to MCF, Oct. 16, 1847, ibid., 300 (Mozier); "TTE," Oct. 18, 1847, *NYDT*, Nov. 27, 1847 (*Alba* and *Patria*); Sept. 25, 1847, *FL*, IV, 295–96 ("most deeply interested"); Sept. 1847, ibid., 293 ("long lost child").

46. To MCF, Oct. 16, 1847, *FL*, IV, 299, 300, 301 ("untouched"); [ca. Oct. 1847], journal, FMW, box 4 ("weeds are beautiful"); to SC, Jan. 18, 1849, *FL*, V, 172 ("total abstinence"); Oct. 16, 1847, ibid., 299–300 ("Italians sympathize"); Oct. 25, 1847, ibid., 305–6 ("dream of my heart"); Oct. 16, 1847, *FL*, IV, 302 ("Oh! what joy!").

47. Sept. 16, 1847, *OMW*, 25 ("*harsh*").
48. Oct. 29, 1847, *FL*, IV, 310 ("not give a pin"); Oct. 16, 1847, ibid., 301 ("ignore all these circumstances"); to MCF, Dec. 16, 1847, ibid., 312 ("remain undisturbed").
49. To MS, Oct. 1847, *FL*, IV, 298 ("restless impertinence"); Oct. 28, 1847, ibid., 309 ("live alone"); to EFC, Mar. 13, 1849, *FL*, V, 207 ("frank love-songs"); to SSS, Oct. 25, 1847, *FL*, IV, 306 ("colours flying"); Oct. 28, 1847, ibid., 309 ("with half Rome"); Oct. 29, 1847, ibid., 309 ("getting better"); Oct. 29, 1847, ibid., 310 ("Yes I *am* happy).
50. HG to [Emma Whiting], Dec. 1, 1847, HG Papers, NN-M ("Castle Doleful"). For another account of all the literary Bostonians then in Rome, see GWC to CPC, Mar. 25, 1848, June 23, 1848, and July 17, 1848, Cranch Family Papers, MHi.
51. ES, journal, Mar. 24, [1849], quoted in Henry James, *William Wetmore Story and His Friends*, 2 vols. (London, 1903), I, 127 ("quiet little upper chamber"); Mar. 8, 1849, *FL*, V, 199, 200 ("It is odd").
52. To Henry Russell Cleveland, *LL*, II, 492 (beautiful); WWS to JRL, Apr. 28, 1848, quoted in James, *Story and His Friends*, I, 102 ("bondage of Boston"); to ES, [ca. Oct. 25, 1847], *FL*, IV, 305 ("one of the very best"); James, *Story and His Friends*, I, 122 (breakfasting with the Crawfords); OC, 178 ("To me she seemed"); JRL to WWS, Mar. 10, 1848, quoted in James, *Story and His Friends*, I, 103 ("S. M. F."). For other examples of this mild alienation from American culture that European travel provoked in friends of Fuller, see CPC, manuscript fragment, [ca. 1849], and GWC to CPC, Apr. 2, 1849, Cranch Family Papers, MHi.
53. OC, 178 ("She still refused"). For other accounts that Fuller later gave that largely jibe with Story's, see, for example, to EFC, Dec. 11, 1849, *FL*, V, 292; and Mary Peabody Mann to SPH, [ca. Aug. 1850], NN-B.
54. OC, 178 ("utterly false"); Dec. 11, 1849, Gale Family Papers, MWA ("no old maid need despair"); quoted in *OM*, I, 281 ("nothing extraordinary"); RBS, "Auld Acquaintance," 94, CSt ("men fell in love with her") .
55. ES to Maria Lowell quoted in Maria Lowell to SC, [ca. Nov. 1849]*, *HO*, 245 ("black sheep"); to MCF, [Dec. 15?], 1849, *FL*, V, 299 ("life-long want"); AOA to Matilde MacNamara, Mar. 15, 1850, FMW, XVI, 138 ("that Black heart"); to Giuseppe Ossoli, Sept. 18, 1850, OFC ("If you had guided him"); OC, 178 ("must marry").
56. To ?, [early 1840s]*, *FL*, VI, 150 ("obliged to live myself"); Mary Peabody Mann to SPH, [Aug? 1850?], NN-B ("burst into tears"); quoted in "ON," 500 ("wife & mother"); to SGW and ABW, Oct. 21, 1849, *FL*, V, 271 ("readin ritin and richmetic"); Notebook, Apr. 3, 1858, *HW*, XIV, 155 ("half an idiot"); OC, 178 (standard fare).
57. Quoted in Maria Lowell to SC [ca. Nov. 1849]*, *HO*, 244 ("ardent adherence to Mazzini's views"); to MF, Aug. 17, 1848, FMW, XVI, 120 ("odious brothers"); statement of Hurlbert in *OM*, II, 326 (reserved and curt); *Letters of Horatio Greenough to His Brother, Henry Greenough*, ed. Frances Boott Greenough (Boston, 1887), 217 ("grave and dignified"); quoted in *Letters and Journals of Thomas Wentworth Higginson, 1846–1906*, ed. Mary Thacher Higginson (Boston, 1921), 29 ("uninteresting Italian"); *OM*, II, 326 ("quick and vivid fancy"). In Emelyn Story's later account of their marriage, she attributed to Fuller more influence on Ossoli's politics than she did at the time in her letter to Maria Lowell. OC, 178.
58. Quoted in *Letters and Journals of Higginson*, 29–30 ("imagined possibility"); to CAV, Oct. 16, 1849, *FL*, V, 270 ("enthusiasm"); to WHC, [ca. late] July 1849, ibid., 248 ("domestic wants"); to WHC, Dec. 17, 1849, ibid., 300 (little children); to EFC, Dec. 11, 1849, ibid., 292 ("sacred love").
59. Nov. 17, 1847, *OMW*, 27 ("You will regret it"); Dec. 11, 1849, *FL*, V, 292 ("I acted out my character").

60. Dec. 16, 1847, *FL*, IV, 312 ("Rome is so dear"); Dec. 20, 1847, ibid., 315 ("glorious to me"); RBS, "Journal Abroad," [22], NjHi to RFF, July 1, 1847, *FL*, IV, 277, to MS, Aug. 9, 1847, ibid., 286, to RFF, Sept. 25, 1847, ibid., 294–95, to Richard H. and Mary Weeks Manning, Oct. 18, 1847, ibid., 302, to RFF, Jan. 12, [1848], *FL*, V, 48, and RFF to MF, Feb. 20, 1848, FMW, XV, 34 (loans and remittances); July 29, 1847, FMW, X, 46 ("How you imbibed"); HG to MF, Sept. 14, 1847, *FL*, IV, ibid., 47 ("at discretion"); ABF to EF, Apr. 11, 1847, FMW, XIII, 138, MCF-MF, Oct. 16, 1847, *FL*, IV, 300, to MR, [Oct. 25, 1847], ibid., 304, and *FL*, ibid., 278 n278 (Abraham's death and bequest); Dec. 16, 1847, ibid., 312 ("at most"); JRL to Sydney H. Gay, Apr. 20, 1851, *LoL*, I, 190 (about half); to MR, Oct. 22, 1847, *FL*, IV, 304 (prolong her stay); to Richard H. and Mary Weeks Manning, Dec. 16, 1847, ibid., 314 ("I trust heaven").

61. Dec. 16, 1847, *FL*, IV, 312 ("since I was a child"); FMW, box A ("I hail thee, Rome"); to CS, Jan. 11, 1848, *FL*, V, 43 ("childlike well-being").

62. Oct. 29, 1847, *FL*, IV, 310 ("really *in* Rome"); "TTE," Dec. 17, 1847, *NYDT*, Jan. 29, 1848, 1 ("ancient and modern Rome").

63. "TTE," Dec. 17, 1847, *NYDT*, Jan. 29, 1848, 1 ("artist-people").

64. To [?], Nov. 17, 1847, *FL*, IV, 310, 310–11 ("unnatural divorce"). "They are the least educated of all travellers one meets," Charles Sumner stigmatized the English to his brother George in Florence. "Always alter your journey in order to get rid of them." Sept. 6, 1839, in *Selected Letters of Charles Sumner*, ed. Beverly Wilson Palmer, 2 vols. (Boston, 1990), I, 68.

65. "TTE," May 1847, *NYDT*, July 31, 1847, 1 ("Vetturinoed"). For contrasting interpretations of the "antitourist" tradition in travel writing, see Paul Fussell, ed., *The Norton Book of Travel* (New York, 1987), esp. 13–17, 651–53; and James Buzard, *The Beaten Track: European Tourism, Literature, and the Ways to Culture, 1800–1918* (Oxford, England, 1993), chap. 2.

66. "TTE," [ca. late November 1847]*, *NYDT*, Jan. 1, 1848, 1 ("servile American").

67. "TTE," [ca. late November 1847]*, *NYDT*, Jan. 1, 1848, 1 ("genuine Democracy").

68. "TTE," [ca. late November 1847]*, *NYDT*, Jan. 1, 1848, 1 ("I have found many"); "TTE," Oct. 18, 1847, *NYDT*, Nov. 27, 1847, 1 ("AMERICA").

69. Quoted in [early Jan., 1848]*, *NYDT*, Feb. 19, 1848, 1 ("cause to rise around you"); quoted in Berkeley and Berkeley, *Italy in the Making*, II, 330 ("Greatly deceived"). For differing interpretations of Mazzini's intentions in writing his letter to the pope, see Denis Mack Smith, *Mazzini* (New Haven, 1994), 52; and Roland Sarti, *Mazzini: A Life for the Religion of Politics* (Westport, Conn., 1997), 122.

70. "TTE," [ca. early Jan.]*, *NYDT*, Feb. 19, 1848, 1 ("one of the milestones"); GM to MF, [Dec. 1847], XI, 97 (sent her); Jan. 12, [1848], FMW, XI, 49 ("presumptuous"); GM to Maria Mazzini, Dec. 13, 1847, *MS*, XXXIII, 142 (*Times* writer); [Dec. 1847], FMW, XI, 97 ("visibly raging"); *People's Journal* 4 (Oct. 9, 1847), 328 ("this epithet, sanguinary").

71. "TTE," Dec. 17, 1847, *NYDT*, Jan. 29, 1848, 1 ("requires much acquaintance").

72. "TTE," Dec. 17, 1847, *NYDT*, Jan. 29, 1848, 1 ("Affairs look well here").

73. [Dec. 1847], FMW, XI, 97 ("I admire him").

74. "TTE," [ca. early Jan. 1848]*, *NYDT*, Feb. 19, 1848, 1 ("windows thrown open").

75. Quoted in Marraro, *American Opinion*, 315 ("what Italy was"); HG to MF, Jan. 27, 1848, FMW, X, 49 (Greeley sent package); "TTE," Dec. 30, 1847, *NYDT*, Feb. 7, 1848 ("proud of my country"); "TTE," [ca. early Jan. 1848]*, ibid., Feb. 19, 1848, 1 ("only the Roman Press"); CAV to MF, Jan. 24, 1848, FMW, XI, 48 ("wounded" and "du haut en bas"); *FL*, IV, 315 ("*evviva*-ing them").

76. Dec. 20, 1847, *FL*, IV, 315 ("great heart"); "TTE," [ca. early Jan. 1848]*, *NYDT*, Feb. 19, 1848, 1 ("real cause for it too").

77. CAV to MF, Jan. 24, [1848], FMW, XI, 48 (Boston tea boycott).

Chapter Ten

1. To MS, Feb. 1, 1848, *FL*, VI, 373 ("very depressed"); Jan. 12, 1848, *FL*, V, 46 ("atmosphere is dreadful"); to MS, Feb. 1, 1848, *FL*, VI, 372 ("nervous headach" and "Greeley diet"); "Foreign Correspondence," Jan. 31, 1848, *Literary World*, 3 (Mar. 25, 1848), 147 (seriously ill); to MCF, Oct. 16, 1848, *FL*, IV, 301 ("fruit of my travels"); to MS, Feb. 1, 1848, *FL*, VI, 373 ("quite good enough" and "I don't know").

2. Oct. 22, 1847, *FL*, IV, 304 (Paris and Germany); Dec. 16, 1847, ibid., 312 (child in Rome); to EFC, Dec. 11, 1849, *FL*, V, 292 ("dread"); Dec. 20, 1847, *FL*, IV, 314, 315 ("incubus of the future"); *FL*, V, 41, ("tears"). Because of the obvious allusions as well as the many deletions presumably made by Fuller's *Memoirs* editors, it is possible that in this letter she specifically indicated that she was pregnant. In any case, whether or not she did, that clearly was what she was talking about. For later letters of Fuller to Tappan that either probably or definitely mention specifically her son, see to CST, Mar. 8, 1849, ibid., 198–99, and Mar. 16, 1849, ibid., 208.

3. *FL*, V, 41, 42, 43 ("cast your lot").

4. LC to EFC, May 10, 1851, FMW, XVI, 155, and OC, 178 (documents). For Catholic canon law on the question of mixed marriages, see John T. Noonan, Jr., *Power to Dissolve: Lawyers and Marriages in the Courts of the Roman Curia* (Cambridge, Mass., 1972), chap. 6. For statements shortly after Fuller's death that one or both of the couple had told the writers that they had married, see, OC, 178; LC to EFC, May 10, 1851, FMW, XVI, 155; and AOA to EFC, May 9, 1851, FMW, XVI, 139. For later explicit statements of Fuller and her friends while she and Ossoli were alive that they had married and were "husband" and "wife," see to MCF, [Aug. 31, 1849], *FL*, V, 260; to CAV, Oct., 16, 1849, ibid., 269; to SGW and ABW, Oct. 21, 1849, ibid., 271; to WWS, Dec. 2, 1849, ibid., 286; to EFC, Dec. 11, 1849, ibid., 292; to CST, [ca. Dec. 17, 1849], ibid., 304; GWC to WWS, Nov. 26, 1849, Story Family Papers, TxU; Horace Sumner to MF, [ca. Winter 1850], FMW, XI, 119; to AHC, Feb. 16, [1850], *FL*, VI, 64–65; Catherine F. M. Black to MF, Feb. 21, 1850, FMW, XI, 134; Louisa Gore Greenough to MF, [ca. Spring 1850], ibid., 146; to ES, Mar. 15, 1850, *FL*, VI, 71; GAO to Matilde [(Ossoli) MacNamara], Mar. 31, 1850, FMW, XVI, 138; and AOA to EFC, May 9, 1851, ibid., 139.

5. To GAO, Sept. 7, 1848, *FL*, V, 111 ("consorte"); GAO to MF, Sept. 8, 1848, FMW, XVI, 121 ("consorte"); to GAO, [June 1849], *FL*, V, 235 ("tua moglie"); quoted in Danato Tamblé, "Documents on Margaret Fuller in the State Archive of Rome," in Charles Capper and Cristina Giorcelli, eds., *Margaret Fuller: Transatlantic Crossings in a Revolutionary Age* (Madison, forthcoming) ("even that of the wife!"); "Baptismal Record of Birth of Angelo Eugenio Filippo Ossoli," Nov. 5, 1848, Archivio della Cattedrale di Rieti ("married Mr. Giovanni Angelo"), in Joan von Mehren, "Establishing the Facts on the Ossoli Family: An Experiment in E-Mail Research," *Margaret Fuller Society Newsletter*, 9 (Winter 2001), 2.

6. Giuseppe Ossoli to AOA, Sept. 14, 1850, quoted in Tamblé, "Documents on Margaret Fuller" (divine punishment); MCF to RFF, Oct. 1, 1850, FMW, VIII, 138 (hiring a lawyer); OC, 178 (position in the new government). My analysis here is largely consistent with Emelyn Story's speculations, which she probably at least partly got from Fuller herself, about the reasons for her secrecy. See OC, 178. On Fuller's fear of her childbirth causing her mother anxiety as one motive for her secrecy, see to MCF, Nov. 16, 1846, *FL*,

V, 145; to MCF, [Aug. 31, 1849], ibid., 260; to EFC, Dec. 11, 1849, ibid., 292–93; and CST to MCF, Jan. 1851, FMW, XVII, 62. On concern about Ossoli's inheritance, see especially to CAV, [Aug. 1849], *FL*, V, 250; and OC, 178.

7. GAO to Matilde MacNamara, Mar. 31, 1850, FMW, XVI, 138 ("for some time"); to GAO, Sept. 7, 1848, ibid., 111, and GAO to MF, Sept. 8, 1848, ibid., 121 ("consorte"); OC, 178 ("soon after"); GAO to MF, June 8, 1848, FMW, XVI., 111 ("Mrs. G. Ossoli"); to MF, Apr. 3, 1849, ibid., 134 ("our darling"); to GAO, Apr. 4, 1849, *FL*, V, 222–23 ("How very strange"). An additional reason for preferring the early April date for Fuller's marriage is that a month and a half later, she gave Hicks an account of her relationship with Ossoli to relay to her mother, which would have been easier for her to write if she had been married. See to MCF, Nov. 16, 1848, *FL*, V, 145; and to TH, May 17, 1848, ibid., 66.

8. SC to MF, Mar. 5, 1850, FMW, X, 41 (obstinate refusal); journal, [ca. Dec. 1852], MH to AH ("till near"); [Aug. 1849], *FL*, V, 250 ("only half the truth"); Dec. 11, 1849, ibid., 291 ("still a member"); *FL*, V, 41, 43 ("reap what I have sown"); Edward Shorter, *Women's Bodies: A Social History of Women's Encounter with Health, Ill-health, and Medicine* (1982; New Brunswick, 1991), 69 (historian's estimate). For higher estimates, of antebellum women's deaths in child birth, see Pamela S. Eakins, ed., *The American Way of Birth* (Philadelphia, 1986), chap. 2.

9. Journal, [ca. 1852], MH to AH ("only a *continuation*"); to WHC, [ca. late] July 1849, *FL*, V, 248 (suitability); Dec. 17, 1849, ibid., 300 ("pined too much"); Feb. 16, [1850], *FL*, VI, 65 ("But for the child"); Dec. 11, 1849, ibid., 292 ("strong impulse").

10. [Ca. Summer–Fall 1844]*, *OM*, II, 140, 141 ("one grand type"); "ON," 463 ("too vast to brave"); *FW*, 65 ("higher aim"); "Aglauron and Laurie. A Drive through the Country near Boston," FMW, box A (one tale); to RFF, Sept. 25, 1847, *FL*, IV, 296 (terrible marriages); [late July 1847], ibid., 283 ("present arrangements of society"); Jan. 1, 1848, ibid., 40 ("God knows"). In Fuller's *Memoirs,* Channing said not a word of his private speculation to Emerson about Fuller not marrying but, on the contrary, both said and implied just the opposite. In Channing's defense, one should note that in the *Memoirs* he at least took up the hot topic of Fuller's "marriage," which Emerson, though he wrote most of the rest of the chapter "Europe," probably with great relief, left to him. *OM*, II, 270.

11. To [?], *FL*, IV, 311 ("emancipated"); to WHC, [ca. late] July 1849, *FL*, V, 248 ("corrupt social contract"); to AHC, Feb. 16, [1850], *FL*, VI, 65 ("trifling business arrangements"). The two books that first publicly introduced Americans to Fourier's ideas about sex and marriage were Godwin's *Popular View of the Doctrines of Charles Fourier* (1844) and Victor Hennequin's *Love in the Phalanstery* (1848). While the former was critical of them, the latter included a sympathetic preface by Henry James, Sr., which he followed up with articles in the *Harbinger*. For fascinating revelations of Child's anguished musings over "free-love" and "tyrannical" marriage laws at this time, see *ChiL*, 226–29, 235. For a report on a curious debate among leading Transcendentalists about various alternative kinds of marriages and families, see F. B. Sanborn and William T. Harris, *A. Bronson Alcott: His Life and Philosophy*, 2 vols. (Boston, 1893), 412–13. Fuller probably did not know that Mazzini himself had fathered a child out of wedlock. See Sarti, *Mazzini*, 61–62. For the emergence of free-love ideas among some radical reformers at this time, see the sources cited in chap. 5, note 44.

12. Quoted in Julia Ward Howe, *Reminiscences, 1819–1899* (Boston, 1900), 301 ("much changed"); quoted in Caroline Healey Dall, journal, Feb. 1, 1865, in Joel Myerson, "Caroline Dall's Reminiscences of Margaret Fuller," *Harvard Library Bulletin*, 22 (Oct. 1974), 427 (hunchback and "pent-up secret"); Mar. 8, 1848, *FL*, V, 55 ("my tomb-stone"); to RFF, Jan. 12, [1848], ibid., 48 ("long silences"); Jan. 11, 1848, ibid., 41 ("heart's blood"); Feb. 24, 1848, enclosure to MCF to MF, Feb. 21, 1848, FMW, VIII, 216 ("You could not

have alluded"); RFF to MF, Feb. 20, 1848, FMW, XV, 34 (heavy postage charges); MCF to MF, [Oct.] 5, 1849, FMW, VIII, 221 ($1.25); *FL*, V, 57 ("tired of life").

13. ERF to MCF, FMW, XVII, 42 (cultural travel advice); Jan. 12, [1848], *FL*, V, 48 ("Never forget"); Mar. 17, 1848, ibid., 57 ("There are circumstances"); Feb. 20, 1848, FMW, XV, 34 ("due to you").

14. To RFF, Jan. 12, [1848], *FL*, V, 48 (exact amount); MCF to MF, May 27, 1847, FMW, VIII, 217 ("contract" and mother cut off); May 14, 1847, FMW, X, 38 ("unholy curiosity"); May 29, 1848, *FL*, V, 70–71 ("rather sore"); July 7, 1846, FMW, XV, 33 ("not of your views"); May, 29, 1848, *FL*, V, 71 ("If his ghost").

15. April 1848, *FL*, V, 59 ("The Gods themselves"); Apr. 1, 1848, "TTE," May 4, 1848, *NYDT*, 1 ("burnt my face"); Mar. 17, 1848, *FL*, V, 57, 57–58 ("forget my English"); April 1848, ibid., 59, 60 ("You would be amazed").

16. Feb. 28, 1848, *CCC*, XXII, 257 ("The righteous Gods"). The literature on the revolutions of 1848 is immense. William L. Langer, *Political and Social Upheaval, 1832–1852* (New York, 1969) provides an overview. Priscilla Robertson, *Revolutions of 1848: A Social History* (Princeton, 1952), is still useful for background, but Peter N. Stearns, *1848: The Revolutionary Tide in Europe* (New York, 1974), and Jonathan Sperber, *The European Revolutions, 1848–1851* (Cambridge, England, 1994), are more analytical. For sheer comprehensiveness, Dieter Dowe, Heinz-Gerhard Haupt, Dieter Langewiesche, and Jonathan Sperber, eds., *Europe in 1848: Revolution and Reform*, trans. David Higgins (New York, 2000), is essential. R. J. W. Evans and Hartmut Pogge von Strandmann, eds., *The Revolutions in Europe, 1848–1849: From Reform to Reaction* (Oxford, England, 2000), is a fine briefer recent collection. For opposing retrospectives by two important political figures whose works Fuller read, see Alexis de Tocqueville, *Recollections: The French Revolution of 1848* (1893; New Brunswick, 2003), and Louis Blanc, *1848: Historical Revelations* (1870; New York, 1971). Still worthy of serious attention are the brilliant interpretations in two books by another famous participant-observer: Karl Marx, *The Class Struggles in France* (1850), and *The Eighteenth Brumaire of Louis Bonaparte* (1852). For an updated version of Marx's analysis, see Eric Hobsbawm, *The Age of Capital, 1848–1875* (London, 1975), chap. 1.

17. Although tendentious and dated, J. L. Talmon, *Political Messianism: The Romantic Phase* (New York, 1960), is a still thought-provoking conservative liberal appraisal of the ideological spirit of the intellectual 1848ers. For the scholarship on theories of nationalism, see preface note 7.

18. For discussions of Risorgimento politics in 1848, see the works cited in chapter 9, note 2.

19. Denis Mack Smith, "Italy," in J. P. T. Bury, ed., *New Cambridge Modern History*, vol. X, *The Zenith of European Power, 1830–1870* (Cambridge, England, 1960), 562 ("Milan, like Sicily").

20. For Charles Albert's role in the sentencing of the Savoy conspirators, see Denis Mack Smith, *Mazzini* (New Haven, 1994), 8.

21. *FL*, V, 54 ("stirring times"); Apr. 26, 1848, FMW, XI, 131 (Colman); Apr. 7, 1848, *FL*, V, 60 ("hear so very little"); May 15, 1848, FMW, X, 147 ("not speak of the paintings"); Apr. 7, 1848, *FL*, V, 61 ("I am nailed here").

22. Mar. 29, 1848, *FL*, V, 58, 58–59 ("I always dreamed of"); to JFC, May 4, 1830, *FL*, I, 167 ("asking, aimless hearts"); Apr. 7, 1848, *FL*, V, 60–61 ("rub a dub").

23. Feb. 8, 1848, *FL*, V, 51 ("very celebrated"); Dec. 30, [1847], FMW, XI, 46 ("We don't get along"); [Feb. 7, 1848], ibid., 52 ("little value"); [ca. Jan. 1848], ibid., 81 ("very early habits"); Feb. 8, 1848, *FL*, V, 51 ("woman of gallantry"). The best modern biography of Belgioioso is Beth Archer Brombert, *Cristina Belgioioso* (New York, 1977).

24. To RFF, Jan. 12, [1848], *FL*, V, 48 (dying to go); Mar. 14, 1848, ibid., 55 ("he I wanted to see"); [ca. May 1848], ibid., 63 ("You will not see"); "TTE," Apr. 19, 1848, *NYDT*, June 15, 1848, 1 ("barbarian of the North"); Apr. 16, 1848, *OMW*, 33 ("choose among your acquaintances).

25. "TTE," Jan. 22, 1848, *NYDT*, Mar. 13, 1848, 1 ("murder"); "TTE," Jan. 27, 1848, ibid., Mar. 13, 1848, 1 ("keenest satire").

26. "TTE," Dec. 17, 1847, *NYDT*, Jan. 29, 1848, 1 ("mass of juggleries"); "TTE," Dec. 30, 1847, ibid., Feb. 7, 1848, 1 ("quite worldly"); "TTE," [ca. early Jan. 1848]*, ibid., Feb. 19, 1848, 1 ("sermon" and "Were I a European").

27. "TTE," [ca. Jan. 12, 1848], *NYDT*, Mar. 13, 1848, 1 ("orphan" and "Awake, indeed, Romans!").

28. May 15, 1848, FMW, X, 147 ("our puritan descendants"); *NYDT*, Feb. 24, 1848, 1 ("direct insult" and "ultra-Protestant").

29. "TTE," Mar. 29, 1848, *NYDT*, May 4, 1848, 1 ("This week indescribable rapture"); Raymond Grew, "The Paradoxes of Italy's Nineteenth-Century Political Culture," in Isser Woloch, ed., *Revolution and the Meanings of Freedom in the Nineteenth Century* (Stanford, 1996), 239 ("lived in the piazza"); "TTE," Mar. 29, 1848, *NYDT*, May 4, 1848, 1 ("transport of the people"). Of course, these political "festivals" and "politics of the street" were also to some degree a Europe-wide phenomenon created by the revolutionary political situation. See Dowe et al., *Europe in 1848*, chaps. 32–34.

30. "TTE," Mar. 29, 1848, *NYDT*, May 4, 1848, 1 ("illiberal, bristling English"). For the precipitous decline of the Italianate fashion and the growth of anti-Italian sentiment in England in the 1840s, see Brand, *Italy and the English Romantics*, esp. chaps. 13–15 and Conclusion. For accounts of American views, mostly based on the writings of American artists and writers in Italy, see Paul R. Baker, *The Fortunate Pilgrims: Americans in Italy, 1800–1860* (Cambridge, Mass., 1964), 188–89, 191–92; and William L. Vance, *America's Rome*, 2 vols. (New Haven, 1989), II, 101–38. A contemporary confirmation of Fuller's dim view of American travelers' judgments about Italians may be found in Joel T. Headley, *Letters from Italy* (New York, 1848), xi–xii, in which even this staunch Democrat expressed the thought that Italy's rich were too corrupt and its poor too compliant to assert their nation's liberty.

31. "TTE," Mar. 29, 1848, *NYDT*, May 4, 1848, 1 ("instructing the Americans abroad!").

32. "TTE," May 7, 1848, *NYDT*, June 15, 1848, 1 ("final dereliction"); May 29, 1848, *FL*, 72 ("priestly environment").

33. "TTE," May 7, 1848, *NYDT*, June 15, 1848, 1 ("momentary stupefaction"). For a succinct historical appraisal of the shift in Roman opinion against the pope after his Allocution, see G. M. Trevelyan, *Garibaldi's Defence of the Roman Republic 1848–9* (1907; London, 1988), 72–76.

34. CAV to MF, [Feb. 7, 1848], FMW, XI, 52 (send her money); Jan. 12, [1848], FMW, XI, 49 ("assassinate the Jesuits"); Jan. 14, 1848, *FL*, V, 49 ("What black and foolish calumnies"); Jan. 24 [1848], FMW, XI, 49 ("lowest of his party").

35. Apr. 26 [1848], FMW, XI, 50 ("no longer mere theory"); May 27, 1848, *FL*, V, 69 ("my Radicalism"); June 3, 1848, FMW, XI, 50 ("opposed to an Italian republic"); June 22, 1848, *FL*, V, 73 ("no bigoted Republican").

36. "TTE," Mar. 29, 1848, *NYDT*, May 4, 1848, 1 ("the political is being merged"); "TTE," Apr. 19, 1848, ibid., June 15, 1848, 1 ("Mazzini sees not all").

37. "TTE," Mar. 29, 1848, *NYDT*, May 4, 1848, 1 ("LABORING CLASSES").

38. *FL*, V, 71 ("as great an Associationist").

39. To Evert A. Duyckinck, Mar. 5, 1848, Duyckinck Family Papers, NN-M ("our country leads the world"); "TTE," May 7, 1848, *NYDT*, June 15, 1848, 1 ("My friends urge my return"). For a good discussion of the variety of American "exceptionalist" reactions to the European revolutions of 1848–49, see Timothy Mason Roberts, "The American Response to the European Revolutions of 1848" (Ph.D. diss., University of Oxford, 1998). An ideologically minded anti-American exceptionalist interpretation may be found in Paola Gemme, *Domesticating Foreign Struggles: The Italian Risorgimento and Antebellum American Identity* (Athens, Ga., 2005). For canonical American writers' responses, see Larry J. Reynolds, *European Revolutions and the American Literary Renaissance* (New Haven, 1988). American newspaper dispatches from Paris are conveniently collected in Bertier de Sauvigny, *La Révolution parisienne de 1848 vue par les Américains* (Paris, 1984).

40. Mar. 2, 1848, *EL*, IV, 28 ("come live with me"); Apr. 25, 1848, ibid., 61 ("You are imprudent"); May 19, 1848, *FL*, V, 66 ("I have much to do"); Dec. 20, 1847, *FL*, IV, 315 (interested in Italian politics); *FL*, V, 66 ("I cannot marvel"); May 29, 1848, ibid., 72 ("loves not Europe").

41. June 3, 1848, FMW, XI, 50 ("lover at Rome"); Apr. 4, 1848, FMW, X, 50 ("miserable health"); Apr. 8, 1848, *FL*, V, 51 ("troubled Europe"); June 27, 1848, FMW, X, 52 ("I regret the resolution"). For examples of the Fuller family's use of the term "confinement" to mean strict rest, see to GAO, Sept. 19, 1848, *FL*, V, 113, and MCF to RFF, Dec. 10, 1851, FMW, VIII, 152.

42. TH to MCF, Aug. 2, 1850, FMW, XVI, 65 ("very intimate"); to SGW, Oct. 31, [1849], *FL*, V, 279 ("very intimate"); TH to MCF, Aug. 2, 1850, FMW, XVI, 65, and to MCF, Nov. 16, 1848, *FL*, V, 145 (not survive); May 17, 1848, ibid., 66 ("nothing came right"); May 4, 1848, *OMW*, 34 ("I see little improvement"). In Fuller's later letter to her mother, she would say that when she had thought she would die, she had provided "a person, who has given me . . . the aid and sympathy of a brother"—obviously Hicks—with an account of the "strange and romantic chapters in the story of my sad life," presumably including her liaison with Ossoli. For Mickiewicz's knowledge of her pregnancy and childbirth, see also to GAO, Oct. 7, 1848, *FL*, V, 125.

43. GAO to MF, June 8, 1848, FMW, XVI, 111 (Ossoli and Fuller left Rome); to ES, June 22, 1848, *FL*, V, 75 ("sated"); to CST, Mar. 8, 1849, ibid., 199 ("intoxicating beauty"); to [?], [ca. Aug. 15, 1848], ibid., 101 ("a thousand landscapes"); to ES, June 22, 1848, ibid., 75 ("chose for the best" and "pure"); June 22, 1848, ibid., 73 ("It grows upon me").

44. To CAV, May 27, 1848, *FL*, V, 69 ("bad institutions"); June 22, 1848, ibid., 77 ("pacing up the hills"); July 11, 1848, ibid., 86 ("I am so *simpatica*");

45. June 22, 1848, *FL*, V, 77 ("lively Italian woman"); to GAO, July 8, [1848], ibid., 85 ("good heart"); to EFC, ca. Aug. 1848]*, ibid., 251 ("chats," "*un gran carbonaro!*" and "'*E sempre sola soletta*'"); June 22, 1848, ibid., 77–78 ("stricken deer").

46. GAO to MF, July 27, 1848, FMW, Works, II, 15 ("very indiscreet" and "much perturbed"); July 22, [1848], *FL*, V, 93 ("not too prudent"); to EFC, [ca. Aug. 1848]*, ibid., 251 ("great polish and culture").

47. *FL*, V, 79 ("I feel lonely, imprisoned"); June 29, [1848], ibid., 81 ("excellent cologne"); June 20, 1848, FMW, Works, II, 5 ("your arms"); *FL*, V, 85 ("more relaxed" and "really a martyrdom"); June 20, 1848, FMW, Works, II, 3 ("every post day"); July 8, [1848], *FL*, V, 85 ("Do not be 'very sad'").

48. *FL*, V, 85–86, 86 ("you were quite right").

49. To CAV, June 22, 1848, *FL*, V, 73 ("lonely mountain home"); to RFF, July 3,

1848, ibid., 82 ("Mountains of Central Italy"); to RFF, July 1, 1848, ibid., 81 ("several years"); [ca. Aug. 1848]*, ibid., 251 ("I will not tell you where"); June 22, 1848, ibid., 73 ("just written to each"); ibid., 87 ("They made me cry"); July 22, 1846, FMW, Works, II, 9 ("make you glad").

50. To [?], [early Aug. 1848]*, FL, V, 101 ("Full of enchantment"); July 30, 1848, ibid., 96 ("too bored there"); [June] 27, 1848, ibid., 79 ("troops of these infants"); ibid., 87 ("come to Rieti"); July 15, [1848], ibid., 89 ("Still more soldiers").

51. To MCF, Nov. 16, 1848, FL, V, 149 ("delicious"); to EFC, [ca. Aug. 1848]*, ibid., 252 ("rude"); Aug. 16, 1848, ibid., 104 ("white as snow" and "never in my life").

52. Aug. 16, 1848, FL, V, 104 ("'go mad writing.'"); Nov. 16, 1848, ibid., 149 ("wanted no present"); "TTE," Dec. 2, 1848, NYDT, Jan. 26, 1849, 1 ("cries of mothers").

53. To MCF, Jan. 19, 1849, FL, V, 177 (forged her signature); July 3, 1848, ibid., 82 (run out of money); Aug. 16, 1848, ibid., 103, 104 ("In an evil hour").

54. July 29, 1848, FMW, X, 53 ("I have to imagine"); MCF to MF, Oct. 3, 1848, FMW, VIII, 219 ("railing"); Nov. 19, 1848, FMW, X, 54 (*"you would write no more!"*).

55. July 30, 1848, FL, V, 97 ("What times").

56. FL, V, 99 ("going against us"); to GAO, Aug. 22, 1848, ibid., 109 (suffering of her Milanese friends); Aug. 16, 1848, ibid., 105 ("All goes wrong"); GAO to MF, Aug. 17, FMW, II, 21–23 ("odious"); Aug. 18, 1848, FL, V, 106 ("close"); ibid., 107 ("terrible night" and "very bad moment").

57. FL, V, 109 ("To wait!!"); Aug. 19, 1848, ibid., 110 ("your coffee"); to EFC, Dec. 11, 1849, ibid., 293 (midwife).

58. Sept. 29, 1848, FMW, Works, II, 47 ("How ignorant"), Oct. 24, 1848, ibid., 61, 65 ("sign of change"); [Oct.] 25, [1848], FL, V, 137 ("Jews and Romans"); Oct. 28, 1848, FMW, Works, II, 71, 73 ("Gregorian party!").

59. Sept. 7, 1848, FL, V, 111 ("cries a lot"); to CS, Mar. 16, 1849, ibid., 209 (attributed); to GAO, [Sept, 9, 1848], ibid., 112 ("nursing fever"); to GAO, Sept. 23, [1848], ibid., 121 ("perfidious"); to GAO, [Sept, 9, 1848], ibid., 112 ("cannot do anything"); Sept. 16, 1848, FMW, Works, II, 35–37 ("so sad"); Sept. 17, [1848], FL, V, 117 ("to be alone"); Sept. 22, 1848, FMW, Works, II, 43 ("usual way of babies"); Sept. 25, 1848, ibid., 45 ("makes me so happy").

60. Mar. 8, 1849, FL, V, 199 ("How many nights"); FL, V, 118 ("He is so dear"); Sept. 21, 1848, ibid., 120 (keep him while she lived); Sept. 22, 1848, FMW, II, 41 ("greatest imaginable caution"); Sept. 23, [1848], FL, V, 121 ("you can not see him"); Sept. 26, 1848, ibid., 123 ("impossible to leave him"); Sept. 28, 1848, ibid., 124 ("as a ballerina's).

61. Oct. 15, 1848, FL, V, 131 ("free to come back"); GAO to MF, Oct. 25, 1848, FMW, Works, II, 67 ("unwearied"); [Oct.] 13, [1848], FL, V, 130 ("die for him").

62. Sept. 11, 1848, FL, V, 113 ("not to look for you"); [ca. Oct. 1848, FMW, XI, 8 ("carry the baby"); Oct. 18, 1848, FL, V, 133 ("very unpleasant for me"); Sept. 10, 1848, ibid., 113 ("house where I live").

63. Mar. 16, 1849, FL, V, 208–9 ("most ferocious and mercenary"); Sept. 23, [1848], ibid., 121 ("detestable"); Oct. 11, 1848, ibid., 128 ("say goodbye"); [Oct.] 28, 1841, ibid., 141 (*"corrupt"*); Mar. 16, 1849, ibid., 207–8 ("so wicked"); [Oct.] 28, [1848], ibid., 141 ("spying"); WHCl to EFC, Sept. 1, [ca. 1850], FMW, XVII, 45 ("wept much").

64. FL, V, 135 ("dying of small pox"); [Oct.] 25, [1848], ibid., 137 ("You do not have to say"); Oct. 24, 1848, FMW, Works, 61 ("given him to us"); Oct. 27, 1848, ibid., 69 ("immediately").

65. FL, V, 125 ("He knows"); [Oct.] 13, [1848], ibid., 129 ("find a *godfather*"); Oct. 14,

1848, FMW, Works, II, 53 ("prudent"); Oct. 15, 1848, *FL*, V, 131 ("Do not think for a moment"); Oct. 7, 1848, ibid., 125 ("You must realize"); Oct. 27, 1848, FMW, II, 71 ("*procura*"); Proxy for Baptism, FMW, XI, 7 ("baptismal font"); Oct. 27, 1848, FMW, II, 71 ("fill it up").

66. Nov. 1, [1848], *FL*, V, 144 ("very heavy"); Mar. 16, 1849, ibid., 208 ("not sleep at all"); Oct. 8, 1848, ibid., 127 ("many good things of Chiara"); Oct. 25, 1848, FMW, Works, II, 65–67 ("so many kisses"); Oct. 8, 1848, ibid., 141 ("much fatter").

67. [Oct.] 27, [1848], *FL*, V, 138 ("the only Italian"); Sept. 26, [1848], ibid., 122 ("cursed small cart"); Oct. 29, 1848, ibid., 143 ("prepare the trunks"); Proxy for Baptism, Nov. 4, 1848, FMW, XI, 7 ("the H[oly] M[other] Church").

Chapter Eleven

1. Nov. 16, 1848, *FL*, V, 148–49 ("I enjoyed it highly").

2. *FL*, V, 103 ("Mountains"); November 14, 1848, FMW, VIII, 127 ("intense anxiety"); Nov. 25, [1848], FMW, XVII, 39 ("Where is she"); [to SSS]*, [Nov. 23], 1848, *FL*, V, 154 ("dark and tangled"); June 13, 1848, FMW, X, 39 ("always"); SC to MF, Sept. 10, [1848], ibid., X, 39 ("we shall forget you"); Jan. 29, 1849, ibid., 55 ("grow old yourself"); to Marianne Silsbee, Nov. 9, 1848, *ChiL*, 240 ("her last dollar"); *Literary World*, 3 (Dec. 2, 1848), 878 ("Miss Fuller's letters").

3. To Charles F. Briggs, Mar 26, 1848, *LoL*, I, 128 ("ill-natured turn" and "temptation"); *A Fable for Critics*, in *The Complete Works of James Russell Lowell*, 16 vols., vol. XII (Boston, 1904), 62, 63, 64 ("I-turn-the-crank-of-the-Universe air"). Poe certainly thought that Fuller's judgement of Lowell as a wretched poet had motivated his satire: "this set him off at a target and he has never been quite right since." To Fredrick W. Thomas, Feb. 14, 1849, *PoLe*, II, 427. Six weeks after Lowell had hesitated, he disingenuously (or self-deceptively) wrote to Briggs: "With her I have been perfectly good-humored, but I have a fancy that what I say will stick uncomfortably. It will make you laugh." May 12, 1848, *LoL*, I, 131. Lowell apparently did try to get Briggs, then editing the *Fable* for him, "if it is not too late," to remove these four quoted lines. Oct. 4, 1848, *LoL*, I, 142–43.

4. *Fable for Critics*, 1 ("series of jokes"); *Female Poets of America* (1849; New York, 1877), 251 ("change of opinion); *North American Review*, 61 (Jan. 1849), 199 ("Transcendental blue-stocking"); review of *A Fable for Critics* by James Russell Lowell, *Southern Literary Messenger*, Mar. 1849, in *The Complete Works of Edgar Allan Poe*, ed. James A. Harrison, 17 vols. (New York, 1902), XIII, 170–71 ("*such* a passion"); *Harbinger* 8 (Dec. 16, 1848), 55 ("upon a woman").

5. Nov. 10, 1848, quoted in John T. Morse, Jr., *Life and Letters of Oliver Wendell Holmes*, 2 vols. (Boston, 1897), II, 108 ("Miranda is too good"); EPP to Ednah Dow Cheney, May 24, 1870, quoted in Ednah Dow Cheney, "Margaret Fuller," *Evening Transcript*, June 10, 1885 ("personal resentment"); Edward Everett Hale, *James Russell Lowell and His Friends* (Boston, 1899), 58 ("too sharp"); to TWH, Mar. 28, 1868, FMW, box A ("better for his reputation"); Mar. 21, 1849, quoted in Henry James, *William Wetmore Story and His Friends*, 2 vols. (Boston, 1903), I, 170–71 ("one thing I regretted").

6. Sept. 9, 1849, quoted in James, *Story and His Friends*, 2 vols. (Boston, 1903), I, 180, 181 ("without any *malice*"); newspaper clipping, ca. 1870, ABA, [Autobiographical Collection], XIII (1868–71), Alcott Papers, MH (Longfellow's honor).

7. Dec. 9, 1848, *FL*, V, 161 ("*never* to make my hay"); ERF to MCF, Jan. 19, 1849, FMW, XVII, 42 ("too laborious"); Nov. 28, 1848, *FL*, V, 157, 157–58 ("*my* country"); Dec. 9, 1848, ibid., 161 ("I do not like it").

8. Nov. 28, 1848, *FL*, V, 159 ("Murray guide book mob"); to [?], [ca. Aug. 15, 1848],

ibid., 100, 101 ("dabbling and pretension"); Dec. 2, 1848, "TTE," *NYDT*, Jan. 26, 1849, 1 ("City of the Soul!").

9. To MCF, Nov. 16, 1848, *FL*, V, 146 ("pure air"); ERF to MCF, Jan. 19, 1849, FMW, XVII, 42 (food bill); Nov. 28, 1848, *FL*, V, 158 ("lowest possible peg"); to MCF, Nov. 16, 1848, ibid., 146 ("delightful old couple"); to ES, Nov. 28, 1848, ibid., 158 ("cunning"); to MCF, Nov. 16, 1848, ibid., 146 ("pays himself for his trouble").

10. Nov. 28, 1848, *FL*, V, 158 ("almost alone"); Joan von Mehren, "Establishing the Facts on the Ossoli Family: An Experiment in E-Mail Research," *Margaret Fuller Society Newsletter*, 9 (Winter 2001), 2 ("scapolo"); December 9, 1848, *FL*, V, 161 ("I always go with Ossoli").

11. Oct. 3, 1848, FMW, VIII, 219 ("actual poverty").

12. *FL*, V, 145 ("strange and romantic chapters").

13. Jan. 5, 1849, FMW, XIII, 48 ("Margaret's letter"); Jan. 7, 1849, FMW, VIII, 129 ("I cannot prevent"); *FL*, V, 160 ("it is still brown").

14. Nov. 16, 1848, *FL*, V, 149 ("Is it not cruel"); Nov. 23, 1848, ibid., 155 ("two terrible drawbacks").

15. Oct. 15, 1848, *FL*, V, 131 ("I cried so much"); Jan. 19, 1849, ibid., 177 ("no expectations"); May 29, 1848, ibid., 71 ("to put an end"); "ON," 500 ("sneering"); to MCF, Mar. 9, 1849, *FL*, V, 202 ("dreadful").

16. OC, 178 ("Margaret's charities"); [ca. 1850], FMW, X, 42 ("mild saint"); Aug. 3, 1851, Ward Papers, MH ("It was here with her").

17. ERF to MCF, Jan. 19, 1849, FMW, XVII, 42 ("some undertaking" and "devise some means"); ERF quoted in to MCF, Jan. 19, 1849, *FL*, V, 177 ("most loving friends"); ERF to MF, Mar. 20, 1849, FMW, XI, 133 ("comfort and relief"); to MCF, Jan. 19, 1849, *FL*, V, 177–78, 178 ("unspeakably grateful"); ERF to MF, Mar. 20, 1849, FMW, XI, 133 ("your Aunt Sarah is dead").

18. To CST, [ca. Dec. 17, 1849], *FL*, V, 303 ("frightfully unnatural"); to MS and RBS, Feb. 5, 1850, *FL*, VI, 53 ("pet name"); Dec. 7, 1848, *FL*, V, 160 ("straight and safe to Caroline"); to CST, Mar. 16, 1849, ibid., 209 (asked for money); to CST, Mar. 8, 1849, ibid., 198 ("lacerated affections").

19. Dec. [22], [1848], *FL*, V, 165 ("I am stingy"); to CST, Mar. 16, 1849, ibid., 209 ("plunder"); Dec. 24, [1848], ibid., 166 ("thousand things").

20. Jan. 19, 1849, *FL*, V, 181 ("Ah, what human companionship"); Jan. 7, 1849, ibid., 169, 170 ("in my corner"); to RWE, Jan. 21, 1849, ibid., 187 ("lonely").

21. To ES, Nov. 28, 1848, *FL*, V, 159 ("fast forgetting me"); Jan. 19, 1849, ibid., 179, 182 ("new prospects"); Jan. 20, 1849, ibid., 186 ("ran away"); ABF to RFF, Sept. 17, 1847, FMW, XIII, 31 (poisoning him). Jan. 20, 1849, *FL*, V, 185 ("some path may open").

22. Jan. 27, 1849, *FL*, V, 187 ("thieves and prostitutes"); Dec. 1848, *CL*, 146, 147 ("let the good Pio Nono"); Jan. 19, 1849, *FL*, V, 174 ("very inconsistent").

23. Jan. 19, 1849, *FL*, V, 175 ("I have written jestingly").

24. To MS, Nov. 23, 1848, *FL*, V, 153 ("old acquaintance").

25. Jan. 31, 1849, FMW, XI, 50 ("The folly"); Feb. 5, 1849, *FL*, V, 192 ("march straight onwards").

26. *FL*, V, 153, 154 ("always dreamed of"); Nov. 28, 1848, ibid., 158 ("a Rome without Pope or Cardinals").

27. "TTE," Dec. 2, 1848, *NYDT*, Jan. 19, 1849, 1 ("great dramatic interest"); "TTE," Dec. 2, 1848, ibid., Jan. 26, 1849, 1 ("what was most precious").

28. "TTE," Dec. 2, 1848, *NYDT*, Jan. 19, 1849, 1 ("No one should dare"). At the time,

Cattaneo succinctly formulated Fuller's argument: "While Charles Albert was collecting votes, Radetsky was collecting men." Quoted in D. Mack Smith, "Italy," chap. 21, in Bury, *New Cambridge Modern History*, X, 563. For a cogent presentation of the dominant modern historiographic view of Charles Albert's "war of lost opportunities" see Stuart Woolf, *A History of Italy, 1700–1860: The Social Constraints of Political Change* (London, 1979), 381–82. For a defense of the king's motives and actions in the war as an inevitable consequence of factors beyond his control, see G.F.-H and J.Berkeley, *Italy in the Making*, 3 vols. (London, 1932–40), chaps. 17, 19

29. "TTE," Dec. 2, 1848, *NYDT*, Jan. 19, 1849, 1 ("mental courage").

30. "TTE," Dec. 2, 1848, *NYDT*, Jan. 19, 1849, 1 ("All the Popes").

31. "TTE," Dec. 2, 1848, *NYDT*, Jan. 26, 1849, 1 ("His carriage approached").

32. "TTE," Dec. 2, 1848, *NYDT*, Jan. 26, 1849, 1 ("The sense of the people"); Nov. 16, 1848, *FL*, V, 147 ("terrible justice").

33. "TTE," Dec. 2, 1848, *NYDT*, Jan. 26, 1849, 1 ("Nothing could be gentler").

34. "TTE," Dec. 2, 1848, *NYDT*, Jan. 26, 1849, 1 ("To fly to Naples").

35. "TTE," Dec. 2, 1848, *NYDT*, Jan. 26, 1849, 1 ("cool and composed"); "TTE," Dec. 2, 1848, ibid., Jan. 19, 1849, 1 ("pure"); to MS, Nov. 23, 1848, *FL*, V, 153 ("little talent"). In an earlier letter to her mother, after quoting her landlady's response to seeing a wounded man in the street and the carriage of Prince Barberini racing with its frightened passengers through their courtyard gate—"'Thank Heaven, we are poor, we have nothing to fear!'"—Fuller had written: "This is the echo of a sentiment which will soon be universal in Europe." Nov. 16, 1848, *FL*, V, 147.

36. "TTE," Dec. 2, 1848, *NYDT*, Jan. 26, 1849, 1 ("Another century").

37. Journal, Jan. 1, 1849, FMW, box 4 ("This year").

38. Journal, Jan. 1 and Jan. 6, 1849, FMW, box 4 ("The power of the priests").

39. Journal, Jan. 14, Jan 20–21, and Feb. 5[–9], 1849, FMW, box 4 ("Things were said").

40. Journal, Jan. 19, 1849, FMW, box 4 ("Treachery"); Jan. 1849, *FL*, V, 168 ("My poor Italian brothers"); Mar. 13, 1849, ibid., 207 ("so very unintellectual"); Feb. 23, 1849, ibid., 194 ("I am ardently interested").

41. "TTE," Feb. 20, 1849, *NYDT*, Mar. 31, 1849, 1 ("variety of tones").

42. Journal, [Feb. 30], 1849, FMW, box 4 ("this coarse people"); "TTE," Mar. 20, 1849, *NYDT*, May 16, 1849, 1 ("wonderfully patient").

43. Quoted in G.M. Trevelyan, *Garibaldi's Defence of the Roman Republic 1848–9* (1907; London, 1968), 107 ("No war of classes"); 148 ("indigenous"). Even the anti-Democrat Farini concedes the relative absence of crime against lives and property in Republican Rome. Luigi Farini, *The Roman State, from 1815 to 1850*, 4 vols. (London, 1851–54), III, 271–72.

44. "TTE," Mar. 20, 1849, *NYDT*, May 16, 1849, 1 ("'illlustrious Gioberti'"); Feb. 23, 1849, *FL*, V, 194 ("I expect to write the history").

45. *Southern Literary Messenger*, reprinted in the *NYDT*, Sept. 11, 18[50?], FMW, box A ("Her recent political disquisitions"); "TTE," Feb. 20, 1849, *NYDT*, Apr. 4, 1849, 1 (dispatch appeared); Lucy Genry to John Bigelow, May 4, 1849, John Bigelow Papers, NN-M ("most heinous articles"). Both Moderates and Democrats alike were shocked by the ignorance and prejudices even professedly liberal northern Europeans displayed toward the Italian scene and Italians' political and intellectual capacities. "A fictional image of Italy exists in the minds of foreigners," Cattaneo wrote in September 1848 from Paris, of a country of a tiny fraction of "white people" who had gotten some cosmopolitan education through their travels and an ignorant "brown race" who were aching to plunder and

kill the rich and noble. Quoted in Simonetta Soldani, "Approaching Europe in the Name of the Nation: The Italian Revolution, 1846–1849," in Dieter Dowe, Heinz-Gerhard Haupt, Dieter Langewiesche, and Jonathan Sperber, eds., *Europe in 1848: Revolution and Reform*, trans. David Higgins (New York, 2000), 72.

46. Quoted in *NYDT*, May 23, 1848 ("How happens it"); Lewis Cass, Jr., to John M. Clayton, Apr. 21, 1849, in Leo Francis Stock, ed., *United States Ministers to the Papal States: Instructions and Despatches, 1848–1868* (Washington, D.C., 1933), 27 ("ultrademocratic faction"). For an account of American newspaper views of the Risorgimento and the Roman Republic, see Howard R. Marraro, *American Opinion on the Unification of Italy, 1846–1861* (New York, 1932).

Chapter Twelve

1. "TTE," Mar. 20, 1849, *NYDT*, May 16, 1849, 1 ("left alone!"); "TTE," Feb. 20, 1849, *NYDT*, Apr. 4, 1849, 1 ("that crowning disgrace"); "TTE," Mar. 20, 1849, ibid., May 16, 1849, 1 ("bloody, angry, well-armed" and "tottering").

2. "TTE," Mar. 20, 1849, *NYDT*, May 16, 1849, 1 ("natural ally"); Luigi Carlo Farini, *The Roman State, from 1815 to 1850*, 4 vols. (London, 1851–54), IV, 88 ("bewitched"); Jan. 26, 1849, FMW, box 4 ("as if nothing were pending"); "Declaration of the Roman Government," Dec. 8, 1848, quoted in Farini, *Roman State*, III, 63 ("protect"); Mar. 17, 1849, FMW, box 4 ("French government"); "TTE," Feb. 20, 1849, *NYDT*, Apr. 4, 1849, 1 ("hoodwinked and enslaved?"); "TTE," Mar. 20, 1849, ibid., May 16, 1849, 1 ("dereliction from principle").

3. For a standard criticism of Mazzini for lingering in Milan, see Bolton King, *A History of Italian Unity, Being a Political History of Italy from 1814 to 1871*, 2 vols. (London, 1899), I, 120–21.

4. Nov. 23, 1848, *FL*, V, 152 ("far above"); "TTE," Mar. 20, 1849, *NYDT*, May 16, 1849, 1 ("*Dio e Popolo*"); journal, Mar. 6, 1849, FMW, box 4 ("Now he is here"); "TTE," Mar. 20, 1849, *NYDT*, May 16, 1849, 1 ("simple conversational tone").

5. Mar. 3, 1849, *FL*, V, 196, 197–98 ("man of ideas").

6. Mar. 9, 1849, *FL*, V, 201 ("I heard a ring"); Mar. 16, 1849, *FL*, V, 210 ("Mazzini is a great man").

7. Mar. 9, 1849, *FL*, V, 202 ("entrance into Jerusalem"); "Ode, Inscribed to W. H. Channing," in *Ralph Waldo Emerson: Essays and Poems* (New York, 1996), 1111 ("sole patriot"); Mar. 10, 1849, *FL*, V, 205, 206 ("chastened libertine").

8. "TTE," Mar. 20, 1849, *NYDT*, May 16, 1849, 1 ("coarse, flashy things").

9. "TTE," Feb. 20, 1849, *NYDT*, Apr. 4, 1849, 1 ("no great idea").

10. "TTE," Feb. 20, 1849, *NYDT*, Apr. 4, 1849, 1 ("If there were a circle").

11. Mar. 9, 1849, *FL*, V, 203 ("no time for an artist"); "TTE," Mar. 20, 1849, *NYDT*, May 16, 1849, 1 ("Forgive")

12. Mar. 13, 1849, *FL*, V, 206, 207 ("only three thousand"); to ES, Nov. 28, 1849, ibid., 159 ("fast forgetting me"); Mar. 13, 1849, ibid., 206 ("I am now so neglected"); Mar. 18, 1849, ibid., 216 ("You must not be indifferent").

13. Feb. 9, 1849, FMW, XV, 36 ("refrain from all expressions"); Mar. 17, 1849, *FL*, V, 212, 213, 214 ("singularly guarded").

14. *FL*, V, 198, 199 ("learned more fortitude").

15. Mar. 16, 1849, *FL*, V, 207, 208, 209, 210, 211 ("Your letter received yesterday").

16. Mar. 27, [1849], *FL*, V, 218 ("very fat"); Apr. 13, [1849], ibid., 225 ("into his mouth").

17. Statement of W. H. Hurlbert in *OM*, II, 322 ("hot-bed of homicide"); to GAO, Oct. 8, 1848, *FL*, V, 127 ("good"); Mar. 30, 1849, ibid., 220 ("I spoke to Niccola"); statement of W. H. Hurlbert in *OM*, II, 324 ("reverent enthusiasm"); Mar. 30, 1849, *FL*, V, 220 ("tell our secret"); Mar. 31, 1849, FMW, Works, II, 79 ("very much disquieted").

18. Apr. 4, 1849, *FL*, V, 223 ("Garibaldi has no control"); quoted in OC, 178 ("kill us"). Even Farini, who never missed an opportunity to lambaste Democrats, conceded that Garibaldi's recruits "committed no serious excesses." *Roman State*, III, 269.

19. "TTE," Mar. 20, 1849, *NYDT*, May 16, 1849, 1 ("dereliction from principle").

20. FMW, box 4 (*"towards* Italians"); WWS, journal, Apr. 25, 1849 and Apr. 28, 1849, Story Family Papers, TxU (speeches); FMW, box 4 ("tragedy so begun"). For the Storys' even greater skepticism, provoked by watching the young Italians' supposed laziness in building barricades, see WWS, journal, Apr. 25, 1849, Apr. 28, 1849, and Apr. 29, 1849, Story Family Papers, TxU.

21. WWS, journal, May 3, 1849, Story Family Papers, TxU ("timid at first").

22. Apr. 30, 1849, FMW, XI, 29 ("Go there at twelve"); to LC, May 2, 1850, *FL*, VI, 83 (stayed through the night); LC to EFC, May 10, 1851, FMW, XVI, 155 ("high rank"); Dr. Gionanni Negri et al. to Dr. Andrea Pasqauli, June 12, 1849, quoted in Danato Tamblé, "Documents on Margaret Fuller in the State Archive of Rome," in Charles Capper and Cristina Giorcelli, eds., *Margaret Fuller: Transatlantic Crossings in a Revolutionary Age* (Madison, forthcoming) ("superiority and tyranny"); Priscilla Robertson, *Revolutions of 1848: A Social History* (Princeton, 1952), 375 (six thousand women).

23. OC, 178 ("Night & day"); WWS, journal, Apr. 30, 1849, Story Family Papers, TxU (very severely); to LC, May 2, 1850, *FL*, VI, 83 (groaning); OC, 178 ("walked through the wards"). For another vivid report on Fuller's work as a hospital administrator and nurse, see LC to EFC, May 10, 1851, FMW, XVI, 155.

24. LC to EFC, May 10, 1849, FMW, XVI, 155 ("insecure abode"); to GWC, Oct. 25, 1849, *FL*, V, 275 (Casa Dies).

25. To EFC, Dec. 11, 1849, *FL*, V, 293, and MF, "Recollections of the Vatican," *United States Magazine and Democratic Review*, 27 (July 1850), 65 (blood on the wall); OC, 178 ("haggard"); May 4, 1849, *FL*, V, 227 ("do not fail to see me"); to EFC, Dec. 11, 1849, ibid., 293 ("Mater Dolorosa"); OC, 178 ("I well remember").

26. "TTE," May 6, 1849, *NYDT*, June 5, 1849, 2 ("barricaded Rome").

27. "TTE," May 6, 1849, *NYDT*, June 5, 1849, 2 ("We all feel very sad"); Joseph Rossi, *The Image of America in Mazzini's Writings* (Madison, 1954), 67–68 (Cass's instructions); "TTE," May 6, 1849, *NYDT*, June 5, 1849, 2 ("Who knows"). For the controversy over American recognition of the 1848 and 1849 revolutionary governments, see Timothy Mason Roberts, "The American Response to the European Revolutions of 1848" (Ph.D. diss., University of Oxford, 1998), chap. 5. Marking the difference between American actions toward France and Italy, secretary of state James Buchanan recalled Nicholas Brown, the United States consul in Rome, for displaying excessive public sympathy for the Roman Republic and rebuked John Marston, the consul in Sicily, for unilaterally extending formal recognition to its revolutionary government.

28. To RFF, May 22, 1849, *FL*, V, and to ES, May 29, 1849, ibid., 233 (money and Heath).

29. Aug. 28, 1849, *FL*, V, 258 ("calling me"); Dec. 11, 1849, ibid., 292, 293 ("In the burning sun"); Luigi Bassini to MF, May 8, 1849, FMW, XI, 22, and OC, 178 (Chiara's

threat); May 18, 1849, FMW, XI, 23; June 19, 1849, ibid., 28 ("coughing fits"); May 18, 1849, ibid., 23 ("proclivity for nourishment"); June 28, 1849, ibid., FMW, XI, 28 ("To cheer you up").

30. ES to Maria Lowell, [ca. Nov. 1849]*, quoted in Maria White to SC, [ca. Dec. 1849–Jan.1850]*, *HO*, 244 (told her that May); OC, 178 ("If I live"); ES to Maria Lowell, [ca. Nov. 1849]*, quoted in Maria White to SC, [ca. Dec. 1849– Jan. 1850]*, *HO*, 244 ("pledge of secrecy"); June 6, 1849, *FL*, V, 238 (helped a lot).

31. May 22, 1849, *FL*, V, 229 ("I remain alone"); James E. Freeman, *Gatherings from an Artist's Portfolio in Rome* (Boston, 1883), 130–31 ("molestation"); Arthur Hugh Clough, *Amours de Voyage*, ed. Patrick Scott (St. Lucia, Queensland, 1974 (epistolary poem); to WWS, Dec. 2, 1849, *FL*, V, 287 ("much pleased"); Nov. 30, 1849, ibid., 285 ("advanced in thought"); Mar. 25, 1852, in *The Correspondence of Arthur Hugh Clough*, ed. Frederick L. Mulhauser, 2 vols. (Oxford, 1957), I, 262 n2 (description to Blanch Smith). It is possible that Clough included with his poems parts of his *Amours de Voyage*, which he finished around that fall. See Clough, *Amours de Voyage*, 9.

32. WHCl to MF, April 1, 1849, FMW, X, 59 ("dissipated"); to LC, May 2, 1850, *FL*, VI, 83 (first met Cass); LC to MF, [ca. Apr. 1, 1849], FMW, XVI, 159 ("do anything"); [ca. July 1849], ibid., 157 ("I liked you"); Jan. 30, 1850, ibid., 152 ("never before felt for any woman"); [ca. July 1849], ibid., 157 ("matter of romancing"); Leo Francis Stock, ed., *United States Ministers to the Papal States: Instructions and Despatches, 1848–1868* (Washington, D.C., 1933), 17–44 (State Department instructions and Cass's reports). For Brown and Cass in Rome, see also Howard R. Marraro, *American Opinion on the Unification of Italy, 1846–1861* (New York, 1932), 69–73,78–79; and Rossi, *Image of America*, 62–74.

33. "TTE," July 6, 1849, *NYDT*, Aug. 11, 1849, 2 ("inland city").

34. "TTE," May 27, 1849, *NYDT*, June 23, 1849, 1 ("decisive event"); to William Short, Jan. 3, 1793, *Jefferson: Writings*, Library of America, ed. Merrill D. Peterson (New York, 1984), 1004 (sauguinary future).

35. "TTE," May 27, 1849, *NYDT*, June 23, 1849, 1 ("When I first arrived in Italy").

36. "TTE," May 27, 1849, *NYDT*, June 23, 1849, 1 ("Protestant she already is").

37. "TTE," May 27, 1849, *NYDT*, June 23, 1849, 1 ("War near at hand").

38. John M. Clayton to Lewis Cass, Jr., June 25, 1849, in Stock, *United States Ministers to the Papal States*, 44–45 (changed instructions); "TTE," May 27, 1849, *NYDT*, June 23, 1849, 1 (*"do without us"*). For accounts of changing American opinion of the Roman Republic, see Marraro, *American Opinion*, chap. 4; Rossi, *Image of America*, chap. 5; and Roberts, "American Response," chaps. 4–5.

39. June 23, 1849, FMW, X, 56 ("deprived me"); "Letter from Bishop Hughes," quoted in *NYDT*, June 27, 1849, 2 ("the stiletto").

40. *Boston Daily Evening Transcript*, June 27, 1849, 1 ("blow with a broomstick"); "Letter from Bishop Hughes," quoted in *NYDT*, June 27, 1849, 2 ("Where is the evidence?"); *National Anti-Slavery Standard*, 10 (July 12, 1849), 26 ("Miss Fuller").

41. "TTE," May 27, 1849, *NYDT*, June 23, 1849, 1 ("thirsts for money"); Farini, *Roman State*, IV, 53–58 (murders). Fuller did not mention that another possible reason why a French newspaper might have taken alarm at red flags in Rome was that red had become associated with the "*démoc-socs*" or "red France" of the reorganized Left.

42. "TTE," May 27, 1849, *NYDT*, June 23, 1849, 1 ("trust that people").

43. "TTE," June 10, 1849, *NYDT*, July 24, 1849, 1 (second act); FMW, XVI, 143 (remained deadlocked); "TTE," May 27, 1849, *NYDT*, June 23, 1849, 1 ("pitfalls and traps!").

44. "TTE," June 10, 1849, *NYDT*, July 24, 1849, 1 ("to force back Pius IX").

45. Quoted in Farini, *Roman State*, IV, 175 (*"attack of the place"*).

46. May 29, 1849, *FL*, V, 232 ("I miss you"); June 6, 1849, ibid., 238 ("real battle"); June 9, [1849], FMW, XI, 101, 102 ("be *woman*").

47. June 10, 1849, *FL*, V, 239, 240 ("cannonade and mustketry").

48. "TTE," June 10, 1849, *NYDT*, July 24, 1849, 1 ("sad but glorious days"). She does not seem to have walked alone at night, however, at least during the siege. See to Caroline Clements Brown, [ca. May–June]*, 1849, *FL*, VI, 94.

49. Certainly, some among the Radicals fantasized about a violent overthrow of the government, but both the actions and even the rhetoric of the vast majority showed no such clear intent. See the persuasive testimony of Bryant reporting from Paris in William Cullen Bryant, *New-York Evening Post*, Paris, Sept. [17], 1849, *Letters of William Cullen Bryant*, ed. William Cullen Bryant II and Thomas G. Voss, 6 vols. (New York, 1975–92), III, 103–5. My analysis of the failed uprising generally follows, albeit without the brilliant vitriol, Marx's in his *Class Struggles in France* and *Eighteenth Brumaire of Louis Bonaparte*. For an excellent recent account, see Jonathan Beecher, *Victor Considerant and the Rise and Fall of French Romantic Socialism* (Berkeley, 2001), chap. 11.

50. [Ca. June 17, 1849], *FL*, V, 242 ("My journal"); [ca. late] July 1849, ibid., 247 ("prayed him to capitulate").

51. Carlo Fabiani to GAO, June 16, 1849, FMW, XI, 4 (commissioned captain); Carlo Fabiani to GAO, n.d., ibid., 36 ("cowardice").

52. *FL*, V, 241 ("state of siege"); June 20, FMW, XI, 103, 104 ("you too!"). The rumor about blowing up the Vatican and St. Peter's if the French entered Rome even reached Fuller's old friend Charles King Newcomb, who despite his Brook Farm proto-Catholic rituals, responded in a remarkably anticlerical fashion. "Would you not be willing this should be," he asked her in a letter he wrote just before the start of the siege, "if Superstition should lose by the destruction of its ancient seats? The loss would have been cosmopolitan, but let it be if needs be. I hoped I might have seen them first, however!" May 28, 1849, FMW, X, 150.

53. June 19, 1849, *FL*, V, 242 ("so strangely wrong!").

54. "TTE," June 21, 1849, *NYDT*, July 23, 1849, 1 ("boyish and foolish"); "TTE," June 23, 1849, ibid., 1 ("such barefaced liars?").

55. June 10, 1849, *FL*, V, 240 ("too true"); [ca. late June 1849]*, ibid., 236 ("It does me good"); "TTE," June 21, 1849, *NYDT*, July 23, 1849, 1 ("Wounds and assaults"). Cass estimated that there were thirteen thousand refugees in Rome. LC to EFC, May 10, 1851, FMW, XVI, 155.

56. "TTE," June 21, 1849, *NYDT*, July 23, 1849, 1 ("these young men").

57. "TTE," July 6, 1849, *NYDT*, Aug. 11, 1849, 2 ("tremendous cannonade").

58. FMW, XI, 112 ("we *shall* resist to the last"); "TTE," June 10, 1849, *NYDT*, July 24, 1849, 1 ("firm as a rock"); June 17, [1849], *FL*, V, 241 ("perpetual murder"); "TTE," July 6, 1849, *NYDT*, Aug. 11, 1849, 2 ("further resistance was idle").

59. To EFC, May 10, 1851, FMW, XVI, 155 ("very heavy").

60. To LC, May 2, 1850, *FL*, VI, 83 ("heartsick, weary"); LC to EFC, May 10, 1851, FMW, XVI, 155 ("I . . . found her"); OC, 178 (gave them back); [ca. late June 1849]*, *FL*, V, 235–36, 236 ("How hard"); to EFC, May 10, 1851, FMW, XVI, 155 ("I saw them walking"); to EFC, Dec. 11, 1849, *FL*, V, 293 (bomb).

61. [Ca. late] July 1849, *FL*, V, 247 (*"never* to yield"); Farini, *Roman State*, IV, 214 ("God and the People"); July 3, 1849, FMW, XI, 108 ("It is all over").

Chapter Thirteen

1. *FL*, V, 244 ("Private hopes); RFF to MF, May 18, 1849, FMW, XV, 38 (probably assuming); Jan. 30, 1850, FMW, XVI, 152 ("frightful state"); Feb. 14, 1850, ibid. ("hunting out").

2. Sept. 9, 1849, *OMW*, 38 ("Roman catastrophe"); LC to MF, Aug. 10, 1849, FMW, XVI, 148 ("by sleuth"); LC to MF, Jan. 30, 1850, FMW, XVI, 152 (close to Fuller); June 23, 1849, FMW, X, 56 ("stranger"); July 3, 1849, FMW, XI, 108 (Mazzini asked Fuller); GM to MF, [July] 7, [1849], ibid., 109, 110, JRL to RWE, Nov. 17, 1852, *LoNL*, 40–41, and *Joseph Mazzini: His Life, Writings, and Political Principles* (New York, 1872), 334 (persuaded by Fuller); [ca. late] July 1849, *FL*, V, 247 ("not of that mould").

3. "TTE," July 10, 1849, *NYDT*, Aug. 11, 1849, 2 ("sick of breathing"); [ca. July 8, 1849], *FL*, V, 243 ("shut up here"); "TTE," July 10, 1849, *NYDT*, Aug. 11, 1849, 2 (Oudinot's order); July 8, 1849, *FL*, V, 243 ("But for my child"); [ca. Fall 1849], ViU ("sold my hair").

4. "TTE," July 6, 1849, *NYDT*, Aug. 11, 1849, 2 ("Never have I seen");

5. "TTE," July 10, 1849, *NYDT*, Aug. 11, 1849, 2 ("The men of Rome").

6. Lewis Cass, Jr. to John M. Clayton, July 6, 1849, in Leo Francis Stock, ed., *United States Ministers to the Papal States: Instructions and Despatches, 1848–1868* (Washington, D.C., 1933), 45–49 (Brown incident); "TTE," July 8, 1849, *NYDT*, Aug. 11, 1849, 2 ("Will America"); [ca. early July 1849], FMW, XVI, 157 ("satisfaction for this insult"); "TTE," July 10, 1849, *NYDT*, Aug. 11, 1849, 2 (*"do something"*).

7. To EFC, Dec. 11, 1849, *FL*, V, 293 (near death); July 19, 1849, ibid., 246 ("worn to a skeleton"); ES to Maria Lowell, [ca. Nov. 1849]*, in Maria Lowell to SC, [ca. Winter 1849–1850]*, in *HO*, 246 (milk failing); July 30, 1849, ibid., 249 ("a few scudi"); GWC to WWS, Nov. 26, 1849, Story Family Papers, TxU, and ES to Maria Lowell, [ca. Nov. 1849]*, in Maria Lowell to SC, [ca. Winter 1849–1850]*, in *HO*, 246 (bread and wine); July 19, 1849, *FL*, V, 246 ("If he dies"); to CST, Aug. 28, 1849, ibid., 259 ("incessant"); Aug. 13, 1849, ibid., 254 ("again peaceful"); July 30, 1849, ibid., 249 ("fine healthy girl"); to CST, Aug. 28, 1849, ibid., 258 ("the tomb").

8. LC to MF, [ca. July 9, 1849], FMW, XVI, 160, to LC, July 10, [1849], *FL*, V, 244–45, LC to MF, [ca. July 10], 1849, FMW, XVI, 145, to LC, Oct. 8, 1849, *FL*, V, 268 (passports); July 19, 1849, *FL*, V, 245, 246 ("different world"); to LC, Aug. 13, 1849, ibid., 254 ("never dreams").

9. Statement of W. H. Hurlbert in *OM*, II, 324 ("undoubtedly"); Aug. 9, 1849, *FL*, V, 253 ("You can imagine"); statement of Hurlbert in *OM*, 327–28 (recognized his name); August 13, 1849, *FL*, V, 254–55 ("one beautiful provincial town").

10. *FL*, V, 258 ("I forget the great ideas").

11. *Souvenirs*, 195, quoted in Jonathan Beecher, *Victor Considerant and the Rise and Fall of French Romantic Socialism* (Berkeley, 2001), 248 ("flagrant disobedience"); quoted in Denis Mack Smith, *Mazzini* (New Haven, 1994), 73 ("tyranny of Mazzini"); "TTE," Aug. 31, 1849, *NYWT*, Oct. 6, 1849, 2 ("now enslaved and hireling"). For Tocqueville's lame attempt to disassociate himself from the French invasion, see Charles Sumner's amazed letter to Frances A. Longfellow: "My brother George writes me that he has recd a letter from Madame de Tocqueville, 'in which she abjures for her husband all connection or sympathy with the Roman expedition.' And yet de Tocqueville is minister of Foreign affairs! They all begin to be ashamed of themselves!" Monday, [July 1849], in *Selected Letters of Charles Sumner*, ed. Beverly Wilson Palmer, 2 vols. (Boston, 1990), I, 268.

12. "TTE," Aug. 31, 1849, *NYWT*, Oct. 6, 1849, 2 ("That intervention"). Among mod-

erate observers and historians, Farini presents perhaps the worst picture of disorder in Republican Rome, but he, too, emphasizes its gross exaggeration by the regime's enemies. See *Roman State*, IV, 55–58, 152–59. For Cass's picture of the city before and after the Roman surrender, which largely jibes with Fuller's account, see Stock, *United States Ministers*, 39–80.

13. "TTE," Aug. 31, 1849, *NYWT*, Oct. 6, 1849, 2 ("the Italian sun").

14. To LC, Oct. 4, 1849, *FL*, V, 267 (left alone); to LC, Sept. 30, 1849, ibid., 265 ("perfect elixir" and "generous and consoling").

15. To Edgar T. Welby, Aug. 31, 1849, *FL*, V, 263 (in gold); to ES, Aug. 31, 1849, ibid., 262 ("ready money"); to MCF, [Aug. 31, 1849], ibid., 260, and to SGW and ABW, Oct. 21, 1849, ibid., 271 (expectation of a little money); to ES, Aug. 31, 1849, ibid., 262–63 ("It is odd"); "TTE," [ca. late] Jan. 1848*, *NYDT*, Mar. 13, 1848, 1 ("orphan").

16. June 19, 1849, *FL*, V, 242 ("If they had triumphed").

17. To WHC, [ca. late] July 1849, *FL*, V, 247 ("come home humbler"). To varying degrees, the "true womanhood" narrative, usually mixed with invocations of Fuller's altruism in Italy, was embraced by an astonishing range of commentators in the nineteenth century from right to left and friend to foe. For just a few examples, see *Sharpe's Magazine* (London), [1852]; Caroline Healey Dall, in Joel Myerson, "Caroline Dall's Reminiscences of Margaret Fuller," *Harvard Library Bulletin*, 22 (Oct. 1974), 426; Higginson, "Margaret Fuller Ossoli," in James Parton et al., *Eminent Women of the Age* (Hartford, 1868), 196; *Harriet Martineau's Autobiography*, 3 vols. (London, 1877), I, 383; Lindsay Swift, *Brook Farm: Its Members, Scholars, and Visitors* (New York, 1900), 216–17.

18. [Aug. 1849], *FL*, V, 250 ("Will you have patience"); Oct. 16, 1849, ibid., 269 ("offensively strange"); Oct. 5, [1849], FMW, XI, 50 ("give wings to my assurance"); Oct. 16, 1849, *FL*, V, 269, 270 ("offensively strange").

19. [Ca. late] July 1849, *FL*, V, 248 ("What shall I say"); Dec. 17, 1849, ibid., 300 ("My love for Ossoli"); "ON," 463 (Channing had told Emerson).

20. Feb. 16, [1850], *FL*, VI, 64–65 ("living with my husband").

21. MCF to MF, May 21, 1849, FMW, VIII, 220 ("I have not been present"); to CST, [ca. Dec. 17, 1849], *FL*, V, 304 ("great pang of remorse"); July 23, 1849, FMW, X, 57 ("Pickie is dead!"); to MCF, [Aug. 31 1849], *FL*, V, 259 ("rivers of tears"); to HG, Aug. 25, [1849], ibid., 257 ("Aunty Margaret"); [ca. Dec. 17, 1849], ibid., 304 ("half-killed me"); [Aug. 31, 1849], ibid., 260, 261 ("The first moment"). Fuller would later become greatly distraught when she heard that news was circulating that she had earlier disclosed the facts of her marriage and child to Caroline Tappan.

22. [Oct.] 5, 1849, FMW, VIII, 221 ("move the depths of my spirit").

23. [Dec. 15?], 1849, *FL*, V, 298, 299 ("who has a mother like mine?").

24. To CST, [ca. Dec. 17, 1849], *FL*, V, 304 (made her worry); Oct. 2, 1849, FMW, XIII, 56 ("Particulars"); ABF to MF, enclosure to MCF-MF, [Oct.] 5, 1849, ibid., 221 ("I know not your husband"); Dec. 4, 1849, FMW, XV, 40 ("all greatly surprised"); to LGL, Mar. 16, [1853], *ChiL*, [ca. 267–68] (priggish Christian piety); Dec. 4, 1849, FMW, XV, 40 ("*your act*"); Jan. 8, 1850, *FL*, VI, 45 ("The way you speak"); Jan. 7, 1850, FMW, XIII, 141 ("*mere* personal beauty").

25. Weston Papers, MB ("married to an Italian"); *Literary World*, 5 (Nov. 10, 1849), 406 ("Miss Margaret Fuller"); [to SSS]*, Nov. 29, 1849, *FL*, V, 283 (why she married Ossoli); Oct. 21, 1849, ibid., 271 ("commonly called culture" and "domestic place").

26. Nov. 30, 1849, *FL*, V, 284 ("Thus far my friends"); to Elizabeth Buffum Chace, quoted in Lillie Buffum Chace Wyman and Arthur Crawford Wyman, *Elizabeth Buffum, 1806–1899: Her Life and Its Environment*, 2 vols. (Boston, 1914), I, 115 ("isn't it queer");

to MS and RBS, Dec. 12, 1849, *FL*, V, 295 ("sleeping"); Nov. 25, 1849, Story Family Papers, TxU ("somewhat surprized me"); to CST, [ca. Dec. 17, 1849], *FL*, V, 304] ("a little hurt"); Dec. 2, 1849, ibid., 286 ("painful burden of secret").

27. Mar. 5, 1850, FMW, X, 41 ("You say your friends"); *FL*, V, 284–85 ("She was annoyed").

28. [Ca. Fall 1849], ViU ("Never blame him"); *FL*, V, 291, 291–92 ("Mr Emerson for one").

29. Dec. 11, 1849, *FL*, V, 293 ("she and Mr Emerson"); Dec. 12, 1849, ibid., 295 ("sadly disappointed"); William Emerson to RWE, Oct. 15, 1849, Emerson Papers, MH ("suitable match?"); to William Emerson, Oct. 17, 1849, *LE*, IV, 168 (evaded the question); Aug. 14, 1849, FMW, X, 58 ("Aunty Margaret").

30. Oct. 21, 1849, *ChiL*, 250 ("I approve"); Mar. 5, 1850, FMW, X, 41 ("ever loyal"); quoted in *OM*, I, 300 ("she can defend").

31. To LC, Sept. 30, 1849, *FL*, V, 265 ("delightful" and "cheerful and busy"); Oct. 25, 1849, ibid., 274, 275 ("home-sick" and "*my* Country!"); GWC to CPC, Mar. 3, 1848, Cranch Family Papers, MHi ("Revolutionists"); Oct. 21, 1849, *FL*, V, 273–74 ("a kind of Boston").

32. To LC, Oct. 4, 1849, *FL*, V, 267 (police); Oct. 8, 1849, ibid., 267 ("malevolen[t]"); ibid., 268 (may have hurt him); to SGW and ABW, Oct. 21, 1849, ibid., 273, to SC, Nov. 18, 1849, ibid., 281, to MCF, [Dec. 15?], 1849, ibid., 299, to CST, [ca. Dec. 17, 1849], ibid., 303, and Pauline Roland to MF, Oct. 2, [1849], FMW, X, 34 (permission); Dec. 2, 1849, *FL*, V, 287 ("through the post"); statement of W. H. Hurlbert in *OM*, II, 328 (under surveillance). Cass denied to Secretary Clayton that he gave passports to Italians in which he represented them as Americans, which was apparently true, although the passports he issued Mazzini, Sterbini, and Giuseppe Avezzana, the Republic's minister of war, did say they were under American protection. For Cass's somewhat contradictory denials, see LC to John Clayton, Sept. 20, 1849, in Stock, *United States Ministers*, 59; LC to MF, Oct. 5 [1849], FMW, XVI, 158; and to LC, Oct. 8, 1849, *FL*, 268. Cf. Cass's actions reported in to LC, July 10, [1849], *FL*, V, 244; LC to MF, [ca. July 10, 1849], FMW, XVI, 145; to LC, Aug. 8, 1849, *FL*, V, 252; and LC to MF, Aug. 25, 1849, FMW, XVI, 149.

33. Feb. 15, 1850, *FL*, VI, 61 ("balm to me"); *Letters of Horatio Greenough to His Brother, Henry Greenough*, ed. Frances Boott Greenough (Boston, 1887), 217 (sixth-floor apartment); statement of W. H. Hurlbert in *OM*, II, 322 ("decisive power"); to LC, Oct. 8, 1849, *FL*, V, 268 ("heavy depressing"); to LC, Sept. 30, 1849, ibid., 265 ("grow better"); [Dec.] 29, [1849], ibid., 305 ("No one was there"); Feb. 24, 1850, *FL*, VI, 68 ("I feel works of art"); statement of Hurlbert in *OM*, II, 328 (depressed her); Mar. 5, 1850, *FL*, VI, 69–70, 70 ("the People hiss" and "ten million Florences").

34. Mar. 5, 1850, *FL*, VI, 70 ("Tis but little"); to MS and RBS, Dec. 12, 1849, *FL*, V, 297 (postage bill); Dec. 2, 1849, ibid., 287 ("do call on Mr. C"); LC to MF, July 25, 1849, FMW, XVI, 147 ("flirtations"); to LC, July 30, 1849, *FL*, V, 249 ("married ladies"); to GWC, Oct. 25, 1849, ibid., 277 ("They might be worth knowing").

35. CAV to MF, [ca. Dec. 1849], FMW, XI, 66 (Belgioioso); CAV to MF, Apr. 18, 1850, ibid., 71 (Charles Albert); [ca. Dec. 1849, ibid., 67 (children's illnesses); to SGW, Oct. 31, [1849], *FL*, V, 279 ("transgress"); to ES, Feb. 15, 1850, ibid., 62 ("German"); Oct. 25, 1849, ibid., 275, 277 ("coming past the Duomo").

36. Nov. 29, 1849, Story Family Papers, TxU ("vein of intense enthusiasm"); to Anna D. Gale, Dec. 15, 1849, in Edward D. Hoyt and Loriman S. Brigham, "Glimpses of Margaret Fuller: Green Street School and Florence, "*New England Quarterly*, 29 (Mar. 1956), 98 ("old woman"); Dec. 29, 1849, ibid. ("*whisky punch*").

37. To MCF, Feb. 6, 1850, *FL*, VI, 59 ("fat round-eyed old lady"); MF to George Henry Calvert, May 10, 1850, ibid., 84 (Elizabeth Calvert's recommendation); Nov. 28, 1848, *FL*, V, 159 ("woman of the world"); Apr. 16, 1850, *FL*, VI, 77 ("Boston part"); Nov. 30, 1849, *FL*, V, 285 ("I like her loyalty").

38. Oct. 16, 1849, *FL*, V, 269 ("a little surprized"); to CST, [ca. Dec. 17, 1849], ibid., 303 ("adopted"); statement of W. H. Hurlbert in *OM*, II, 329 (sympathy and counsel); [ca. Nov. 1849], *FL*, V, 280 ("taste for books"); Feb. 5, 1850, *FL*, VI, 54 ("All true people").

39. Nov. 29, 1849, Story Family Papers, TxU ("clings to Margaret"); [ca. Nov. 1849], quoted in *HO*, 245 ("devoted lover"); *OC*, 178 ("He cared not how trivial"); May 2, 1853, *OC*, 25 (*con amore*); statement of W. H. Hurlbert in *OM*, II, 326 ("the Marchese").

40. TC to John Kenyon, Apr. 13, 1847, quoted in *BC*, XIV, 370 (Carlyle's recommendation); [Aug. 15, 1846], *BC*, XIII, 253 ("I almost *must* see her"); EBB to MF, Mar. 3, 1848, FMW, XVI, 59 (missed connections), to ES, Jan. 27, 1849, *FL*, V, 189 (Storys had met the Brownings); [to SSS]*, Nov. 29, 1849, ibid., 282 (across the Arno); Dec. 1 [1849], *BML*, III, 285 ("taken us by surprise").

41. SC to ABW, Feb. 1, 1854, Ward Papers, MH ("vivacious"); to ES, [ca. Nov. 1849], *FL*, V, 280 ("singularly external"); Barbara Channing to MCF, Apr. 15, [1851?], FMW, XV, 120 ("intense"); Dec, 6, [1849], *FL*, V, 289 ("a curtain fell down" and "exchange a few looks"); Feb. 15, 1850, *FL*, VI, 62 ("Genuine Saxon!" and "drawn out"); Apr. 17, 1850, ibid., 77 ("I love and admire them both"); [Apr. 15–16, 1850], *BAL*, I, 309 ("I like her much").

42. [Jan. 4, 1846], *BC*, XI, 281 ("How I hate"); Dec. 1 [1849], *BML*, III, 285 ("out & out Reds"); [Jan. 4, 1846], *BC*, and June [14–]16, [1850], *BAL*, I, 321–22 (so venerating).

43. Apr. 30, [1850], *BML*, III, 297 (*"exalteè* in her opinions"); to ABW, Feb. 1, 1854, Ward Papers, MH ("did not suspect"); June [14–]16, [1850], *BAL*, I, 321, 322 ("she *drew* me"). For Elizabeth Browning's views of spiritualism, Louis Napoleon, and socialism, see, for example, [Jan. 15–17, 1853], ibid., I, 531–33; *Postmark*: Mar. 2, 1853, ibid., 543–44; and Apr. 12, [1853], ibid., 561–566.

44. To MF, Feb. 21, 1850, FMW, XI, 135 (*"so happy"*); Feb. 16, [1850], *FL*, VI, 64 ("unalloyed quiet joy"); to MCF, [Aug. 31, 1849], *FL*, V, 261 (fair-skinned); to WWS, Nov. 26, 1849, Story Family Papers, TxU ("heavy and not handsome"); quoted in to EGL, Mar. 24, 1850, *ChiL*, 253 ("image of his mother"); EH to CST, July 27, 1850, MB ("very beautiful"); EH to CST, Sept. 3, 1850, MB (*"whitest* child"); Jan. 8, 1850, *FL*, VI, 47 ("anything but an Italian").

45. Feb. 15, 1850, *FL*, VI, 62 ("Just when our little one"); Oct. 21, 1849, *FL*, V, 271 ("with my own"); to SGW and ABW, Oct. 21, 1849, ibid., 273 (cholera); to SGW, Feb. 24, 1850, *FL*, VI, 68 ("great stout Roman mother"); Apr. 16, 1850, ibid., 77 ("great fun"); Dec. 30, 1849, *FL*, V, 306 ("great bully").

46. June 19, 1849, *FL*, V, 242 ("will conquer more ill"); Nov. 29, 1849, ibid., 283 ("no special visions"); Oct. 16, 1849, ibid., 269–70 ("nothing particular about him"); Dec. 4, 1849, FMW, XV, 40 ("second birth"); Jan. 8, 1850, *FL*, VI, 46 ("a thousand masters"); Apr. 16, 1850, ibid., 77 ("intelligent little one"); Dec. 29, 1849, *FL*, V, 305–6 ("I was just up").

47. [Ca. Nov. 1849], *FL*, V, 280 ("What a difference"); Mar. 5, 1850, *FL*, VI, 69 ("I feel the tie"); [ca. Dec. 17, 1849], *FL*, V, 303 ("no more separated").

48. Statement of Hurlbert in *OM*, II, 320 ("surrounded by her books"); to MS and RBS, Dec. 12, 1849, *FL*, V, 294 ("better to give the world"); Feb, 5, 1850, *FL*, VI, 55 ("If I cannot make").

49. RWE notation on TC to MF, Aug. 17, 1849, FMW, XI, 132 ("partly finished

work"); Aug. 17, 1849, FMW, XI, 132 ("voice of the Craft"); Aug. 9, 1849, *CCC*, XXIV, 183 ("Miss Margaret Fuller"); Aug. 13, 1849, ibid., 193 ("the heroic Margaret"); Aug. 17, 1849, FMW, XI, 132 ("if the *Ms.* were actually *ready*"); [Sept. 1849], *FL*, V, 264 ("I had foreseen"). Carlyle's letter to Fuller does not appear in *CCC*. Chapman's namesake was John Chapman, Emerson's and the *Dial*'s English publisher, whom scholars have mistakenly identified as the bookman at Chapman and Hall to whom Carlyle conveyed Fuller's proposal.

50. Quoted in to RWE, Aug. 13, 1849, *CCC*, XXIV, 193 ("History of the late Italian Revolutions"); Sept. 24, [1850], *BML*, III, 309 ("raw material"); to CST, [ca. Dec. 17, 1849], *FL*, V, 303 ("two volumes"); to RFF, Mar. 17, 1849, ibid., 213 (work on it through the spring); to ?, [ca. Feb. 1?, 1850], *FL*, VI, 51 (too cold); *Home Journal*, Feb. 2, 1850, 3 ("nearly completed").

51. Mar. 17, 1849, *FL*, V, 213 ("This work"); Dec. 17, 1849, ibid., 301 (""do not expect any thing very good"); Sept. 24, [1850], *BML*, III, 309 ("the only production"); *Home Journal*, Feb. 2, 1850, 3 ("condition of the country"). For letters that either say or strongly imply she had finished a good part of her history, see to CST, [ca. Dec. 17, 1849], *FL*, V, 303; to?, [ca. Feb.? 1850?], *FL*, VI, 51; to MS and RBS, Feb. 5, 1850, ibid., 55; to MCF, Feb. 6, 1850, ibid., 60; and to AHC, Feb. 16, [1850], ibid., 64.

52. To WWS, Dec. 2, 1849, *FL*, V, 287 ("He says James II"); to ?, [ca. Feb. 1?, 1850], *FL*, VI, 51 (Lamartine and Blanc); Theodore Dwight, *The Roman Republic of 1849 with Accounts of the Inquisition and the Siege of Rome* (New York, 1851) (polemic); A. William Salomone, "The Nineteenth-Century Discovery of Italy: An Essay in American Cultural History, Prolegomena to a Historiographical Problem," *American Historical Review*, 73 (June 1968), 1376–77 (one historian).

53. Sept. 24, [1850], *BML*, III, 309 ("those blood-colours"); "TTE," Aug. 31, 1849, *NYWT*, Oct. 6, 1849, 2 ("tracked in blood"); to MS and RBS, Dec. 12, 1849, *FL*, V, 295–96 ("the peace way"). The *Memoirs* editors deleted these passages from their printed version of Fuller's letter. See *OM*, I, 302–3.

54. To MS and RBS, Dec. 12, 1849, *FL*, V, 295 ("enthusiastic Socialist").

55. "Italy," Aug. 31, 1849, *NYWT*, Oct. 6, 1849, 2 ("Radical Reform"); "TTE," Nov. 15, 1849, *NYDT*, Jan. 9, 1850, 1 ("Here lie my hopes").

56. "TTE," Nov. 15, 1849, *NYDT*, Jan. 9, 1850, 1 ("it is refreshing").

57. "TTE," Jan. 6, 1850, *NYDT*, Feb. 13, 1850, supp., 1 ("Joy to those"). For American socialists and other radicals' turn away from association with European revolutionaries after their defeats, see Carl Guarneri, *The Utopian Alternative: Fourierism in Nineteenth-Century America* (Ithaca, 1991), chap. 13; and Timothy Mason Roberts, "American Response to the European Revolutions of 1848" (Ph.D. diss., University of Oxford, 1998), chaps. 6, 7. Although Roberts shows that the revolutions of 1848 continued to echo in American politics even into the 1850s, he also demonstrates that most of those echoes were negative.

58. Aug. 16, 1843, *FL*, III, 142 ("where is that home?"); Dec. 17, 1849, *FL*, V, 300–1 ("taking away the child"); Nov. 29, 1849, ibid., 283 ("more full and true way"); Nov. 26, 1849, Story Family Papers, TxU ("too much rooted in Rome").

59. To ?, [ca. Feb.? 1850], *FL*, VI, to AHC, Feb. 16, [1850], ibid., 64, and James J. Barnes, *Authors, Publishers, and Politicians* (Columbus, Ohio, 1974), 153, 167 (English copyrights); to SGW and ABW, Oct. 21, 1849, *FL*, V, 271 (Delf's offer); MS and RBS, Feb. 5, 1850, *FL*, VI, 54 ("great disappointment"); to MCF, Feb. 6, 1850, ibid., 60 (Mozier was eager); to SGW, Oct. 31, [1849], *FL*, V, 278 ("Letters from Florence"); Dec. 12, 1849, ibid., 296–97 (interest Wiley and Putnam); Feb. 5, 1850, *FL*, VI, 55 (shocking and unacceptable); to ?, [ca. Feb.? 1850], ibid., 51 ("on the spot"). It is possible Delf did not an-

swer Fuller's letter because he had become something of a pariah in publishing circles for selling volumes in Putnam's revised version of Washington Irving's works, which violated John Murray's English copyright. See George Haven Putnam, *George Palmer Putnam: A Memoir* (New York, 1912, 198–99); and Ezra Greenspan, *George Palmer Putnam: Representative American Publisher* (University Park, Pa., 2000), 275–76.

60. To RFF, Mar. 17, 1849, *FL*, V, 213 (classes); to Henry Colman, Apr. 7, 1848, ibid., 61 (expanded edition of *Woman*); Dec. 2, 1849, ibid., 286–87 ("strange and lonely there"); [Dec. 15?], 1849, ibid., 299 ("All this is dark"); Dec. 17, 1849, ibid., 301 ("I trust we shall find means"); [ca. Dec. 17, 1849], ibid., 303 ("If we cannot place ourselves"); GAO to Matilde [MacNamara], Mar. 31, 1850, FMW, XVI, 138 ("My wife"); to RFF, Jan. 8, 1850, *FL*, V, 45 (May or June).

61. To MCF, Feb. 6, 1850, *FL*, VI, 60, and to ES, Apr. 16, 1850, ibid., 76 (Eugene); ABF to EF, May 21, 1850, FMW, XIII, 144 (Arthur's wedding); Jan. 8, 1850, *FL*, VI, 46 ("difficult to other than like him"); GAO to Matilde [MacNamara], Mar. 31, 1850, FMW, XVI, 138 (Ossoli confirmed).

62. [Oct.] 5, 1849, FMW, VIII, 221 ("my income"); Jan. 8, 1850, *FL*, VI, 45, 46 ("feel less exiled").

63. Feb. 15, 1850, *FL*, VI, 62 ("I shrink"); Jan. 8, 1850, ibid., 48 ("women in Europe"); Alexis de Tocqueville, *Democracy in America*, 2 vols. (1945; New York, 1972), II, 211–16 ("superiority" of American women); Feb. 16, [1850], *FL*, VI, 64 ("like to go back"); Jan. 8, 1850, ibid., 48 ("easy chair"); Feb. 6, 1850, ibid., 60 ("three or four years"). For European critics' agreement on the "superiority" of American women, see Theodore Zeldin, *France, 1848–1945*, vol. II, *Intellect, Taste and Anxiety* (Oxford, 1977), 128–30.

64. [Dec. 15?], 1849, *FL*, V, 299 ("all this is dark"); "Trans-national America," *Atlantic Monthly*, 118 (July 1916), 86–97 ("dual citizen").

65. Feb. 5, 1850, *FL*, VI, 52 ("toward *America*"); [ca. Nov. 1840]*, *HO*, 245 ("the better part"); Jan. 1, [1850], FMW, X, 60 ("heartily ashamed"); Mar. 5, ibid., 41 ("Lowell regretted"); Mar. 24, 1850, *ChiL*, 253 ("I suppose you saw").

66. Quoted in to LGL, Oct. 21, 1849, *ChiL*, 250 ("She *bought* the boy"); to JFC, Jan. 9, 1845, *FL*, VI, 357 ("exceedingly disagreeable"); *FL*, V, 303 ("meddling curiosity"); Feb. 5, 1850, *FL*, VI, 53 ("not care for him"); ibid., 76–77 ("good deal of contempt").

67. July 19, 1850, "ON," 257 (de Staël); to SGW, Feb. 24, 1850, *EL*, VIII, 237 ("Margarita Marchesa"); Apr. 17, 1850, FMW, XI, 136 ("business & politics"); *Love Marriage, and Divorce and the Sovereignty of the Individual: A Debate between Henry James, Horace Greeley, and Stephen Pearl Andrews*, ed. Stephen Pearl Andrews (New York, 1853), 178 ("indissoluble"); EPP to Ellen D. Conway, June 28, 1880, *PL*, 402 ("a virgin still"); Feb. 6, 1850, *FL*, VI, 57 ("cloud of false rumors"). For the Duyckinck-Jones quarrel, see EAD to William A. Jones, William A. Jones to EAD, and Mrs. William A. Jones to EAD, August and September 1848, Duyckinck Family Papers, NN-M.

68. July 19, 1850, "ON," 256 ("What shall we do?"); MS to RWE, Apr. 7, 1850, Spring Papers, NjHi ("*Marchioness Ossoli*" and contacted Emerson); Apr. 25, 1848, *EL*, IV, 61 ("take the first steamer"); Apr. 11, 1850, ibid., 199 ("proposed book").

69. SC to MF, Mar. 5, 1850, FMW, X, 41 ("much interested"); Apr. 14, 1850, FMW, XI, 136 ("we say stay!"); MS to RWE, Apr. 7, 1850, Spring Papers, NjHi (Caroline Kirkland confirmed); Apr. 17, 1850, FMW, XI, 136 ("how much your residence in Italy").

70. Apr. 17, 1850, FMW, XI, 136 ("other things); Apr. 14, 1850, ibid. ("lose"); *FL*, VI, 87 ("Your packet").

71. *FL*, VI, 76 ("necessary to go to the U.S."); ibid., 87 ("Let us hope"); Mary Peabody

Mann to SPH, [ca. Aug. 1850], NN-B (Channing also advised her); *FL*, VI, 87–88, 88 ("a phantom").

Chapter Fourteen

1. Dec. 12, 1849, *FL*, V, 296 ("I want nothing of thee"); Feb. 5, 1850, *FL*, VI, 53 ("I cannot bear to spend"); Aug. 7, 1849, FMW, XV, 39 ("wealth or power"). Feb. 24, 1850, *FL*, VI, 66 ("*worldliness* of your sister"); EFC to RFF, [ca. 1852], FMW, XVII, 11 (two hundred dollars).

2. To RFF, Feb. 24, 1850, *FL*, VI, 66 (did not have); to [SSS], Nov. 29, 1849, *FL*, V, 283 (Ossoli's family property); Nov. 29, 1849, ibid., 283 ("poverty a great evil"); enclosure to MCF to MF, [Oct.] 5, 1849, FMW, VIII, 221 ("left us naught"); Oct. 8, 1849, ibid., 222 ("your resources").

3. To CAV, Apr. 6, 1850, *FL*, VI, 74 ("constant headache"); to CAV, Apr. 12, 1850, ibid., 75 ("uncommonly good vessel" and "I cannot have an idea"); *Letters of Horatio Greenough to His Brother, Henry Greenough*, ed. Frances Boott Greenough (Boston, 1887), 217 (talked to her); *FL*, VI, 75 ("horrors of indecision"); to MF, Apr. 18, 1850, FMW, XI, 71 ("I don't feel competent"); SC to EH, Jan. 12, 1851, OC, 5, and Catherine F. Hasty to MCF, Sept. 2, 1850, FMW, XVII, 66 (came up to Florence and "frank & gentlemanly"); to MS, June 3, 1850, *FL*, VI, 89 ("excellent" and "most highminded"); ibid., 76 ("very likely"); Catherine F. Hasty to MCF, Sept. 2, 1850, FMW, XVII, 66 (Mozier wrote to Hasty).

4. Journal "Mythology," [ca. 1842], FMW, box 1 ("According to a calculation"); [Spring 1850], *FL*, VI, 70 ("miserable coward"); *OM*, I, 219 ("a little pagan"); Journal, [ca. 1842], FMW, box A ("Fate is law"); Feb. 6, 1850, *FL*, VI, 57 ("fates of a Greek tragedy"); ibid., 70 ("shuffle the cards").

5. *FL*, VI, 74 ("*last thoughts*"); to ES, Apr. 16, 1850, ibid., 79 ("strange coincidence"); [Apr. 21, 1850], ibid., 81 ("odd combination").

6. May [14], 1850, *FL*, VI, 88 ("Should I arrive"); ibid., 83, 83–84 ("profound regret"); May, 10, 1850, ibid., 85 ("head full of boxes"); MCF to RFF, June 28, 1850, FMW, XVI, 164 ("very sad"); May 14, 1850, *FL*, VI, 86, 86–87 ("I will believe I shall be welcome").

7. *Letters of Greenough*, 217–18 (carried Elizabeth Browning); Sept. 24, [1850], *BML*, III, 309 ("sad presentiment"); [Aug. 15, 1850], *BAL*, I, 336 ("jestingly they told us"); Catherine F. Hasty to MCF, Sept. 2, 1850, FMW, XVII, 66 ("in fine spirits").

8. "TTE," Aug. 9, 1847, *NYDT*, Sept. 11, 1847, 1 (admired Powers's Calhoun).

9. Catherine F. Hasty to MCF, Sept. 2, 1850, FMW, XVII, 66 ("sweet"); "H Thoreau's Notes," MB ("used such expressions"); Catherine Hasty quoted in EH to CST, Sept. 3, 1850, MB ("as long as my finger"); to MCF, Sept. 2, 1850, FMW, 66 ("We studied in the morning"); to MS, June 3, 1850, *FL*, VI, 89 ("I thought during the voyage").

10. To MS, June 3, 1850, *FL*, VI, 89, 89–90 ("enemy" and "how beautiful").

11. EH to CST, Sept. 3, 1850, MB ("would have died"); EBB, quoted in *Autobiography, Memories and Experiences of Moncure Daniel Conway*, 2 vols. (Boston, 1904), II, 21 ("so foul"); Aug. 15, 1850, *BAL*, I, 336 (burned it); June 3, 1850, *FL*, VI, 90 ("I submit"); quoted in EH to CST, Sept. 3, 1850, MB ("little hands," "don't understand," and "never saw").

12. Quoted in EH to CST, Sept. 3, 1850, MB ("holy"); to MCF, Sept. 2, 1850, FMW, XVII, 66 ("*so near home*"). Unless otherwise noted, my account of the *Elizabeth*'s wreck is based on New York and Long Island newspaper accounts, eyewitness reports collected afterward by Thoreau and Channing, and letters of Fuller's friends. Where a contradiction ap-

pears among sources—which is often—I have either noted it or tried to resolve it by applying the historian's usual tests of internal evidence and external corroboration, including the degree of firsthand information the accounts contain and my sense of the writer's reliability.

13. "H Thoreau's Notes," MB ("too difficult"); to Eliza Robbins, [ca. Aug. 1850], in *Letters of William Cullen Bryant*, ed. William Cullen Bryant II and Thomas G. Voss, 6 vols. (New York, 1975–92), III, 139 (scattering wrecks); quoted in "H Thoreau's Notes," MB ("ask what the weather was"). For a speculative case that Bangs's blunders were due to exhaustion rather than overconfidence, see John Rousmaniere, *After the Storm: True Stories of Disaster and Recovery at Sea* (Camden, Me., 2002), 55–58.

14. "H Thoreau's Notes," MB ("low public houses").

15. Quoted in WHC, manuscript, [ca. 1850]*, OC, 4 ("if we had known").

16. Quoted in *OM*, II, 343 ("We must die"); "H Thoreau's Notes," MB ("in her white night dress").

17. Quoted in *OM*, II, 344 ("your life is important"); quoted in EH to CST, Sept. 3, 1850, MB ("no more confusion"); "H Thoreau's Notes," MB (long prayer); quoted in EH to CST, Sept. 3, 1850, MB ("heretic"); quoted in WHC, "Papers," MB ("What is most valuable to me").

18. Journal, [ca. early 1840s], FMW, box A ("I can rarely think"); Apr. 16, 1850, *FL*, VI, 76 ("painful and difficult"). Although Higginson did not have available all the evidence and was unable to reconstruct important details, he presented a strong case, for which he was effusively praised by Fuller's friends, that Fuller's actions were rationally defensible under the circumstances. See *HO*, 275–80; Ednah Dow Cheney to TWH, May 26, 1884, OC, 196; and SC to TWH, May 26, 1884, OC, 202. Two formidable scholars, Perry Miller and Ann Douglas, have suggested or implied that Fuller deliberately refused to try for the shore for psychological or political reasons. Perry Miller, ed., *Margaret Fuller: American Romantic* (1963; Ithaca, 1970), xxviii; and Ann Douglas, *The Feminization of American Culture* (New York, 1977), 287.

19. Quoted in "H Thoreau's Notes," MB ("The men had not courage"); quoted in WHC, "Papers," MB ("cd hardly restrain"); "H Thoreau's Notes," MB ("do his duty?").

20. *OM*, I, 15–16, 35–36 ("Autobiographical Romance"); [Oct. 30], 1842, "FJ42–2," 290 (throw her in).

21. July 19, 1849, *FL*, V, 246 ("this last shipwreck"); Aug. 28, 1849, ibid., 259 ("separated from him"); Apr. 16, 1850, *FL*, VI, 77 ("the loss of *my* child"); Mar. 5, 1850, ibid., 69 ("death shall not part us").

22. Manuscript, [ca. 1850]*, OC, 4 ("*one* desperate effort"); quoted in "From the Wreck on Fire Island," *NYDT*, July 24, 1850, 4 ("I see nothing but death"); quoted in WHC, "Papers," MB ("plunged into the sea"); quoted in "H Thoreau's Notes," MB ("*very sure of this*"). In his letter to Emerson, Thoreau indicated that Ossoli and Angelino had drowned before Margaret, but that was before he and Channing had spoken to the cook and carpenter, who insisted that Margaret was swept off the ship first. See HDT to RWE, July 25, 1850, *TC*, 262–63.

23. *NYDT*, July 24, 1850, 4 ("FATAL WRECK"); ibid., July 27, 1850, 4 ("Our informant states").

24. Ca. July 20, 1850, Spring Papers, NjHi ("Poor dear Margaret"); ca. July 20, 1850, ibid. ("how can her poor mother"); ABF to EF, May 21, 1850, FMW, XIII, 144, ABF to EF, June 18, 1850, ibid., 145, and EFC to RFF, [ca. early July 1850], FMW, XIV, 39 (anxious); June 16, 1850, FMW, VIII, 223 ("look constantly"); *FC*, 101–2 (read a telegram); "Auld Acquaintance," 98–99, Spring Papers, CSt ("sat like a stone"); EPP to ABW and SGW, Sept. 13, 1850, Ward Papers, MH (Ellen's sanity); Sept. 29, [1850], FMW, XIV, 40 ("I can hardly live here")

25. To MS, July 23, 1850, *EL*, VIII, 254 (tapped Thoreau); "H Thoreau's Notes," MB ("Almost every chest"); to H. G. O. Blake, Aug. 9, 1850, *TC*, 265 ("Held up").

26. EFC to RFF, June 19, 1854, FMW, XIV, 57, and EF to RFF, June 13, 1854, FMW, XVI, 163 (briefly excited); EF to RFF enclosure to EFC to RFF, Aug. 6, 1854, FMW, XIV, 61 ("application"); Arthur Dominy to Anna Parker Pruyn, June 21, 1901, NIC, and "Margaret Fuller's Strange Fate," *Providence Journal*, Jan. 12, 1908 (Arthur Dominy's story). On one point, Felix's and Arthur's stories seem contradictory: the former apparently suggested to Richard that some remains had recently turned up, while the latter claimed the boatmen had buried the bodies at night in an unmarked grave, and so they could never again be found. Eugene indicated not knowing the "*spot*" where the bodies were buried or the person who buried them were two other reasons to disregard Felix Dominy's letter. See EF to RFF enclosure to EFC to RFF, Aug. 6, 1854, FMW, XIV, 61. Most important, without Felix's letter, it is not clear how he knew what he related, and Arthur never says in his recollections how he did either. At the top of a clipping of the newspaper article someone has written, "Miles Homan was the man who carried the body of Margaret Fuller to New York," but I have been unable to find a record of a person with that name living then in New York. In 1854, Angelino's remains, along with those of Margaret's father and her two infant siblings, were moved to the new family plot in Mount Auburn Cemetery.

27. "H Thoreau's Notes," MB ("late in the day"); WHC, "Papers," MB ("This proves"); *OM*, II, 350 ("pages"); to ?, Aug. 23, 1850, MB ("serious loss").

28. *Henry James: Autobiography*, ed. Frederick W. Dupee (Princeton, 1983), 37 (Irving told Henry Sr.); to EFC, May 10, 1851, FMW, XVI, 155 ("with a degree of sorrow"); "Death of Margaret Fuller," *NYDT*, July 23, 1850, 4 ("no woman").

29. *Southern Literary Messenger*, reprinted in the *NYDT*, Sept. 11, 18[50?], FMW, box A ("happy to notice").

30. *Transcendentalism in New England: A History* (New York, 1876), 300 ("'just as well so'"); William H. Prescott to Miss Lincoln, July 29, 1856 ("woman of showy parts"); "The Free Love System," *New-York Daily Times*, Sept. 8, 1855 ("Free Love System"); ABF to HG, Sept. 14, 1855, HG Papers, NN-M ("lightly").

31. Aug. 1, 1850, Dorthea L. Dix Collection, MH ("much injury"); Henry I. Bowditch, "Brief Memoranda of Our Martyr Soldiers who fell during the Great Rebellion," Feb. 22, 1875, MHi ("Martyr Soldiers").

32. To TWH, May 26, 1884, OC, 202 ("cruel charges"); [to EH], [ca. late July 1850], FMW, XVII, 59 (William Sturgis's opinion); Oct. 19, 1850, JFC Papers, MH ("When I look back"); [ca. July 19, 1850]*, "ON," 256, 258 ("Margaret dies").

33. Sept. 9, 1850, NN-B ("really glad she died"); ca. Aug. 1850, NN-B ("nothing here"); [ca. late July 1850], FMW, XVII, 59 ("sensitive to coldness"); [ca. July 19, 1850]*, "ON," 256–57 ("only to open her mouth").

34. To Joann Miller, July 24, 1850, Duyckinck Family Papers, NN-M ("happy release"); to Mary Moody Emerson, Aug. 11, 1850, *ESL*, 173 (Lidian); Aug. 5, 1850, *EL*, IV, 224 ("happy hour"); Diary, July 19, 1850, Ward Papers, MH (Anna Ward); EPP to ABW and SGW, Sept. 13, 1850, ibid. "till *all three* met"); [ca. July 19, 1850]*, "ON," 259 ("fit & good conclusion"); July 23, 1850, JFC Papers, MH ("Margaret's Euthenasia").

35. CST to RWE, Aug. 7, 1850, MNS (happy with Ossoli); to EH, [ca. late July 1850], FMW, XVII, 59 ("right to live"); WHC, "Papers," MB ("great friend of new life"); to ?, Aug. 23, 1850, MB ("life spilled"); Diary [1851], Feb. 3, 1851, Alcott Papers, MH ("a fate in her").

36. *HO* (Higginson's biography). For the success of Fuller's volumes and Greeley's and Arthur Fuller's efforts on their behalf, see HG to RFF and ABF, in FMW, X, 61–67, 69, 71; ABF to EF, June 9, 1855, Feb. 15, 1856, and May 13, 1856, FMW, XIII, 150, 153, 155; and RFF to HG, Dec. 14, 1853 and June 27, 1868, HG Papers, NN.

37. Mar. 28, 1968, FMW, box A ("Margaret's reputation"); SGW, *Ward Family Papers* (Boston, 1900), 102, (Ward); CPC, "Ode," 1870, clipping in ABA, [Autobiographical Collections], XIII (1868–71), and Alcott Papers, MH (much easier time).

Index

Cross-references preceded by a Roman numeral are to the subsections under the entry FULLER, MARGARET.